三訂版

和英
日本の文化・観光・歴史辞典

A Japanese-English Dictionary
of Culture, Tourism and History of Japan

山口百々男・Steven Bates

三修社

装幀──清岡秀哉

本書のねらいと特長

　本書は主に次の【1】～【4】を念頭において編纂しました。

【1】外国の人に「日本の文化と歴史」および「日本の観光名所」を正しく紹介したい人のために

　日本の「観光名所」や「神社仏閣」また「歌舞伎・文楽・茶道・相撲」などの名前は知っていても，いざ外国の人に説明しようとするとき，その英語表現がとっさに頭に浮かばないという経験をされた方も多いと思います。また，日本の「料亭」や「居酒屋」，「和式の宴会」などに外国の人を招待して，その場で用いる英単語がすぐに口から出てこなかったり，さらには現代社会において日常的に用いられている「オタク」や「ネットカフェ難民」，「振り込め詐欺」や「学校裏サイト」などをどのように英語で表現するか適切な単語がひらめかない，といったこともよく聞きます。本書は，そのようなシチュエーションで必要とされる日本文化を紹介するキーフレーズを，歴史的な事柄から現代の日常生活に関するものまで幅広く取り上げました。見出し語として，約5,500語を収録しています。

【2】海外に「留学・勤務」する人・外国に「旅」する人のために

　海外に留学するとき，また勤務するときなどには，必ずといってよいほど外国の人から「日本文化・日本事情」について尋ねられます。また短期に外国に旅行するときなどに想定外の機会に遭遇して，外国の人から「日本文化・日本事情」について聞かれるのも決して珍しくありません。海外において日本文化・日本事情を語ることによって多くの友人の輪が広がることは経験が教えています。和英辞典を持ってはいても内容によっては記載されていない，または単語はあるがその用例がないため，あまり役に立たない場合があります。

　本書では「日本文化・日本事情」に関する単語について訳語にあたる英単語だけでなく，用例を豊富に掲載しました。読者がアレンジして活用できるように，短く言い換える際の類語や例句，また比較的長い表現で説明する言い換えの用例をとくに充実させています。また，文化事情についての補足説明を随所に日本語で盛り込みましたので，自分があまり得意としない分野の文化事情についての基礎的な情報源として活用できます。

【3】英語「通訳案内士（通訳ガイド）試験」（国家試験）の合格をめざす人のために

　最近の「通訳ガイド試験」（正式名・通訳案内士試験）の英語部門における出題傾向を分析すると，出題される内容の大部分は「日本文化・日本事情」であり，その基盤になるのは英単語（キーワード）の知識です。とくに日本文化・日本事情を伝えるための「英単語」の出題は，通訳ガイド試験が実施されて以来完全に定着しており毎回出題されます。

　通訳ガイド試験（第一次筆記と第二次口述）で問われる「外国人が日本に関して聞きそうな身近な話題」と「通訳ガイドに求められる日本文化・日本事情の内容」を本書では十分にカバーするよう編纂されています。

　また，巻末付録に掲載した「日本の祭り」（日付順に134の祭りを掲載）と「日本の歴

史年表」，および本文の☆印に掲載したミニ補足解説などは，一次試験の日本語による『社会知識』（日本地理，日本歴史，一般常識）を問う出題の対策としても活用できます。

【4】「観光英語検定試験」の合格をめざす人のために

「観光英語検定試験」の最大の特色は，その出題内容が「海外観光事情」と「国内観光事情」であることです。とくに観光英検1級の出題内容は「海外観光」と「国内観光」とがほぼ同じ比重で出題されています。

英語を学習する上では，一般的な学習素材はどうしても海外に関する内容のものになりがちですが，「観光英検」では必ず「国内観光事情」が出題されるので，本書に収録された「日本の観光」に関する英語を習得することにより多大の効果を発揮するはずです。

海外・国内を問わず外国の人々と接する機会が多い現代の日本人にとって，日本を語るための「日本文化・日本事情」に関する英単語の知識はますます重要性を増しています。

日本文化に関する「知識」を持ち，それを「やさしい英語」で表現することにより，外国の人々に「日本の姿と心」を正しく紹介することは，日本人としての使命だといっても過言ではないでしょう。本書が，日本文化を英語で伝えようとする方々のよきパートナーとなることを願っています。

三訂版発行にあたり

今回の改訂にあたり，記述内容を全面的に見直し，さらに使いやすい表現へと細部にわたり調整を行なうとともに，日本におけるユネスコの世界遺産や無形文化遺産の最新情報を盛り込むなどの更新をいたしました。さらに，令和時代への改元に伴う情報の刷新と増補を行いました。

最新のユネスコ世界遺産の登録を巡る動向や，2021年に開催された東京オリンピック・パラリンピックなどで，世界からの注目が高まる中，日本文化を伝えるための一助として改訂した本書がより一層の役割を果たすことを期待してやみません。

山口百々男

目　次

●本書の記号等について●

① 【　】　　見出し語の代表的な漢字の表記である．内容によっては複数の書き方がある．
[例1] **あいくち**【合口・匕首】
[例2] **まいこ**【舞子・舞妓】

② ；　　　　見出し語に関して複数の表現が可能である場合に，表現と表現の区切りを表示する．
[例1] **アイヌ**〈一人〉an Ainu; 〈人々〉the Ainu people; the Ainu(s). 〈民族〉a member of an indigenous Caucasoid people of Japan.
[例2] **はちまき**【鉢巻き】❶〈頭部に巻く布〉a headband; a frontlet; a (hand) towel worn around the head; a kerchief of cotton cloth tied around the head.

③ （　）　　語句または説明文を省略することができる．
[例1] 単語の省略
いはい【位牌】a (Buddhist) mortuary tablet.
[例2] 語句の省略
いまりやき【伊万里焼】Imari porcelain ware (produced around Arita district of Saga Prefecture and once exported from the port of Imari).

④ [　]　　　直前の語句と書き換えができる．
本書では多様な用語（同意語）を列挙してあるので，使用するときは自分の使いやすい単語を選ぶこと．また本書に挙げられていない単語もあり得るので，自分で補足するのも一法である．
[例1] 単語の置き換え
あきのななくさ【秋の七草】the seven grasses[herbs] of autumn[fall].
[例2] 語句の置き換え
こんぺいとう【金平糖】a sugar candy; a Japanese-style confetto[sugar candy ball] made by crystallizing sugar around a poppy-seed core.

⑤ ❶ ❷　　見出し語の意味を区分する．
[例1] ＜意味内容が類似する＞
あい【藍】　❶〔植物〕an indigo (plant); a Chinese indigo plant. タデ科の1年草．栽培して茎・葉から染料を採る．
❷〈葉からとる青い染料〉indigo; indigo dye. ¶**藍染め物** indigo dyeing.
⇨ 紺絣

❸〈藍色〉indigo; indigo blue.¶**藍色に染めた着物** a *kimono* dyed indigo. ⇨ 隈取 / 友禅五彩
[例2] ＜意味内容が類似しない＞
あかちょうちん【赤提灯】 ❶〈提灯〉a red paper lantern (often used for the signs for cheap drinking and eating establishments). (安価な飲食店の標識に用いる) 赤い紙を張った提灯.
❷〈酒場〉a Japanese-style cheap pub[drinking tavern] (often hanging a red lantern at an outside entrance); a pothouse (安い一杯飲み屋). Workers drop in at a Japanese-style pub with a red paper lantern outside to eat food and drink *sake* with colleagues at reasonable prices.

⑥ ¶ 見出し語に関する<u>関連語</u>を示す.
[例] **あん【庵】** a hermitage (for monks to live in); a monastery (僧庵); a place of seclusion (人里離れた棲家).「いおり」ともいう.¶**庵室** a hermitage; a monastery; a hermit's cell. **庵主** a master of a Buddhist hermitage; an occupant of a monastery.

⑦ ☆ 見出し語または前文の英語を補足的に説明する.
[例] **あかちゃんポスト【赤ちゃんポスト】** a baby hatch facility; a foundling wheel. ☆ 2007 年熊本県のキリスト教系の医療法人がはじめた，新生児を匿名で預かる「コウノトリのゆりかご」(stork's cradle).

⑧ ⇔ <u>反意語・対義語を示す</u>.
[例] **くろぼし【黒星】** 〈黒くて丸い印〉a black mark [circle]; 〔相撲〕〈負け星〉a loss [defeat] mark; a loss [defeat] in a *sumo* bout (recorded with a black mark[circle]). 勝負での負け星のこと. ⇔白星.¶**黒星を取る** be beaten; be defeated.

⑨ ⇨ <u>参照</u>：相互に参照すべき見出し語．または見出し語を使用している関連語.
[例] **あえもの【和物】** *aemono*; dressed[marinated] food; Japanese-style mixed salad tossed with dressing. *Aemono* is a Japanese-style salad of chopped vegetables and seafoods dressed with various seasonings such as *shoyu*[soy sauce], *miso*[bean paste], sesame seeds and vinegar. 和風サラダのこと. 野菜や魚介類などを醤油，味噌，胡麻，酢などで混ぜ合わせた食品. ☆日本語で「～和え」という場合が多い. ⇨朝地和え / 梅和え / 卸し和え / 木の芽和え / 芥子和え / 酢和え / 味噌和え

⑩ 〔　〕　該当する語句・表現に関する項目の名称・表示.
　　　　　　〔例〕〔歌舞伎〕〔能楽〕〔文楽〕〔華道〕〔茶道〕〔相撲〕〔柔道〕など

⑪ 米　　米国式
　　英　　英国式

⑫ 複　　複数形

⑬ 形　　形容詞
　　動　　動詞

本文イラスト INDEX

あ

あい【藍】❶〔植物〕an indigo (plant); a Chinese indigo plant. タデ科の一年草. 栽培して茎・葉から染料を採る.
❷〈葉から採る青い染料〉indigo; indigo dye. ¶**藍染め物** indigo dyeing. ⇨紺絣
❸〈藍色〉indigo; indigo blue. ¶**藍色に染めた着物** a *kimono* dyed indigo. ⇨隈取り / 友禅五彩

アイウエオ the *a-i-u-e-o*; the Japanese (*kana*) syllabary. This is one of the two fixed orders of the Japanese syllabary system, which is officially used today. The other is the Japanese syllabary beginning with the "*iroha*". 日本語の音節文字表〔字音表〕. 日本語の音節組織の固定された2種類のうちのひとつであり, 現在正式に使用されている. もうひとつは「いろは」で始まるものである. ⇨いろは. ¶**アイウエオ順に** in (the) order of the Japanese syllabary.

あいがも【合鴨・間鴨】❶〔鳥〕an *aigamo* duck; a crossbreed between a wild and a domestic duck; the hybrid of domestic and wild ducks. ガンカモ科の鳥. アヒル (domestic duck)とマガモ (wild duck)との雑種.
❷〔鳥肉〕the meat of an *aigamo* duck. 焼き物, 鍋物, 煮物, 蕎麦の鴨南蛮などに用いる. ⇨鴨鍋 / 鴨南蛮うどん[そば]

あいきどう【合気道】 *aikido*; a Japanese martial art of weaponless self-defense derived from a type of *jujutsu*[*judo*]. The main technique employed is to grasp joints, resulting in throwing or holding down attackers by using their momentum to work against them. 武器を持たない自己防衛の日本の武芸で, 柔術[柔道]を起源とする. 主たる護身術は手首 (wrist)やひじ (elbow)など相手の関節の弱点 (weakness in the opponent's joints)を利用する「関節固め」と, 相手の攻撃の瞬時の力を利用する「投げ技」または「押さえ技」である. ☆開祖は植芝盛平(1883-1969年).

あいきょうげん【間狂言】〔能楽〕a comic interlude. It is performed by a kyogen player between the two acts of a Noh play while the main actor (*shite*) changes his costume. 2場面の能楽の中で, 狂言方が受けもつ滑稽な話を演ずる幕間の演芸 (interlude). その間にはシテ(主役)が衣装を着替える. ⇨狂言

あいくち【合口・匕首】 a dagger; a short sword without a hand guard. It is usually carried in one's breast in secret or concealed under one's clothes. 鍔(つば)のない短刀. 通常は懐(bosom)または衣服に隠し持つ.

あいさいべんとう【愛妻弁当】 a packed lunch made with loving care by one's wife; a box lunch prepared by one's beloved wife. 愛情のこもった妻の手作り弁当.

あいさつまわり【挨拶回り】 (make) a round of courtesy visits; (pay) a courtesy call. It is customary for the Japanese to make courtesy visits during the New Year season. 表敬訪問. 新年や盆暮 (the Bon Festival and the year-end season)などに行う. ⇨三が日

あいさつじょう【挨拶状】〔一般の挨拶〕⊛ a greeting card; ⊛ a greetings card; a letter of greeting;〈暑中[寒中]見舞いの〉a card with the season's greetings;〈引越しの〉a change of address card; a notice of one's new address.

アイスキャンディー(和製英語) ⊛ a Popsicle (商標名);⊛ an ice-lolly.

あいぜんみょうおう【愛染明王】 the God of Love (found at the side of the Deity [Goddess] of Mercy). He is portrayed with three pairs of arms and three eyes and painted red all over the body. 観音の近くに侍る愛の神である. 六本の腕と三つの目を

あ

あいづぬり【会津塗】 *Aizu* lacquer ware (produced around Aizuwakamatsu in Fukushima Prefecture). ⇨漆器

アイドル a teenage star[entertainer]; a (popular) pop star.

あいなめ【鮎並・鮎魚女】〔魚〕a rock trout; a greenling. 日本近海産. 身はやわらかく美味. 関西地方では「あぶらめ」という.

アイヌ 〈一人〉an Ainu;〈人々〉the Ainu people; the Ainu(s).〈民族〉a member of an indigenous Caucasoid people of Japan. The Ainus are aboriginal Caucasoid people on the Japanese archipelago, most of whom are living in Hokkaido. 日本列島に住むコーカサス原住民. 主として北海道に住む民族の名. ¶**アイヌ語** Ainu. **アイヌ族** the Ainu race. **アイヌ集落** the Ainu village. **アイヌ新法** the new Ainu law; the Ainu Cultural Promotion Law.

あいぼし【相星】〔相撲〕an equal number of wins (or defeats) with one's opponent; (have) even records. 対戦する相手と同じ勝ち(または負け)の星数.

あえごろも【和え衣】 a Japanese style dressing (made from *miso*[bean paste], sesame and vinegar). (味噌, 胡麻, 酢などでつくる)和風ドレッシング.

あえもの【和え物】 *aemono*; dressed [marinated] food. Japanese-style mixed salad tossed with dressing. *Aemono* is a Japanese-style salad of chopped vegetables and seafoods dressed with various seasonings such as *shoyu*[soy sauce], *miso*[bean paste], sesame seeds and vinegar. 和風サラダのこと. 野菜や魚介類などを醤油, 味噌, 胡麻酢などで混ぜ合わせた食品. ☆日本語で「〜和え」という場合が多い. ⇨朝地和え / 梅和え / 卸し和え / 木の芽和え / 辛子和え / 酢和え / 味噌和え

〔料理〕**胡麻の和え物** food dressed with ses-

ame. ☆ food は通常 vegetables または fish [shellfish] などを指す.

あお【青】 blue; green. ☆日本語の「あお」は英語で green をさす場合が多い. ⇨青信号 ¶**青菜** greens. **青草** green grass.

あおい【葵】❶〔植物〕a hollyhock; a mallow. 多くは観賞用に栽培される. ⇨葵祭 **❷**〈紋所の名〉the family crest of the Tokugawas[Tokugawa clan]. 徳川家の紋. **【葵祭】** the Hollyhock Festival of Shimogamo and Kamigamo shrines. (5月). ⇨付記(1)「日本の祭り」

あおいろしんこく【青色申告】 a blue tax return; a blue form income tax return.

あおうめ【青梅】〔植物〕a green *ume*[plum]; an unripe[immature] *ume*[plum]. 熟していない青い梅. ☆梅酒などを作るときに用いる. ⇨梅〈梅酒 / 梅干など〉 〔料理〕**青梅の甘露漬け** candied[sweetened] green *ume*[plum]. **青梅の塩漬け** green *ume*[plum] pickled in salt.

あおえんどう【青豌豆】〔植物〕green peas(複数形で). 別称「グリーンピース」. ⇨豌豆 / 青豆

あおがえる【青蛙】〔両〕a green frog; a tree frog; a hyla. ⇨あまがえる

あおかび【青黴】 blue[green] mold[英] mould]. パン・餅・みかんなどの食べ物に生える. ⇨かび

あおさ【石蓴】 a sea lettuce. 浅海の岩につく海草. 粉末にして青海苔 (green laver)の代用として焼きそばやたこ焼きに振りかける. ⇨青海苔

あおざかな【青魚】〔魚〕bluefish; fish with blue backs. 背の部分が青光りする魚. 大衆魚(⇨イワシ, サバ, サンマ, アジ, コハダなど). ☆すし屋では「光り物」という.

あおじそ【青紫蘇】〔植物〕green perilla;〈葉〉green beefsteak plant leaves. 薬味などに用いる. ⇨しそ

あおじる【青汁】 green vegetable juice;

green-leaf vegetable juice. 青菜を搾り取ったジュース.

あおしんごう【青信号】 a green light; a green (traffic) signal. ☆英語では blue ではなく green を用いる.

あおぞらいちば【青空市場】 an open-air market; an outdoor market.

あおぞらちゅうしゃ【青空駐車】 illegal parking outdoors; unauthorized parking; roadside parking.

あおだいしょう【青大将】〔爬〕 a blue-green snake; a rat snake. ネズミなどを食べる. 毒がない. ⇨へび

あおたがり【青田刈り】❶〈収穫前の米購入〉 buying rice before the harvest; purchasing rice while it is still unripe in the paddy field. ☆元来は「未成熟の稲を刈ること」（reap rice before it is ripe）❷〈学生の早期採用の内定〉 early scouting of college students; advance contract made with college students even before they graduate; company's picking-out[choosing] of promising college students for employment prior to the official due time[officially agreed date]. 「青田買い」ともいう.

あおたけふみ【青竹踏み】 a green bamboo foot-massaging board; (a piece of) green bamboo slit in a half lengthwise. It is used to keep one's health by treading on it barefoot to stimulate the arches (of the feet). 縦に半分切り開いた青い竹. 素足で踏み, 土踏まずを刺激する健康増進具.

あおだたみ【青畳】 a new *tatami* mat; a fresh and greenish straw mat. ⇨畳

あおづけ【青漬け】 greens pickled in salt. 青野菜の色を生かした塩漬け.

あおとうがらし【青唐辛子】 a green pepper. 緑色の唐辛子の総称. ⇨唐辛子 / 赤唐辛子

あおのどうもん【青の洞門】 the Rock Tunnel (cut by hand through a big rock beside the Yamakuni(gawa) River). ☆大分県. 禅海

和尚が30年かけて掘削した洞窟.

あおな【青菜】〔植物〕 green vegetables; greens（複数形で）. ホウレンソウ, 小松菜など緑色の葉菜類の総称.

あおねぎ【青葱】〔植物〕 a green onion; a scallion. ユリ科の多年草. ⇨ねぎ

あおのり【青海苔】〔海草〕 *nori* seaweed;〈食用〉green laver (dried in flakes). 浅海の岩につく細い管状の緑藻. 粉状の乾燥品として食用にする. 焼きそばやお好み焼き, またとろろ汁などの振りかけに用いる. ⇨あおさ

あおぶさ【青房】〔相撲〕 the green tassel. ⇨房

あおまめ【青豆】〔植物〕 green peas[beans]（複数形で）. ⇨青豌豆
〔料理〕青豆御飯 green peas rice; rice cooked with green peas. 青豆を炊き込んだご飯.

あおむし【青虫】〔虫〕 a green caterpillar; a grub(芋虫). 幼虫.

あおめ【青芽】〔植物〕 young buds of green perilla. 青紫蘇の芽. 赤身魚の刺身のツマに用いる. ⇨青紫蘇 / 赤紫蘇

あおもの【青物】❶〈野菜の総称〉greens（複数形で）; green vegetables. ¶青物市場 a fruit and vegetable market. ⇨青菜
❷〈青魚の総称〉 bluefish; fish with blue backs. ⇨青魚

あおもりねぶた【青森ねぶた】 the Aomori Nebuta[Dummy-Float Parade] Festival.（8月）. ⇨付記(1)「日本の祭り」

あおやぎ【青柳】 ❶〔植物〕a leafy green willow. 葉が茂った青々した柳. ⇨やなぎ
❷〔貝〕〈ばか貝〉a trough shell; a surf clam; a Japanese red clam; a round clam;〈ばか貝の身〉the meat of a trough[surf] clam. 刺身や酢物に用いる. ☆貝柱は「あられ」ともいう.「あられそば」に用いる. ⇨ばかがい

あおゆず【青柚子】〔植物〕 a green *yuzu* citrus. 吸口や薬味に用いる. ⇨ゆず. ¶青柚子の千切り strips of green *yuzu* citrus peel.

あおりいか【障泥烏賊】〔魚〕 a Japanese oval

あ

squid; a bigfin reel squid. 刺身は美味.

あかいか【赤烏賊】〔魚〕a flying squid. フライに調理する. 別名「ムラサキイカ」. ⇨いか

あかいはねきょうどうぼきんうんどう【赤い羽根共同募金運動】 the Red Feather campaign; the Community Chest drive. ㊎ the charity fund raising. ☆毎年11月1日から始まる.

あかえい【赤鱏】〔魚〕a stingray. ムニエルや煮つけに調理する. ⇨えい

あかえび【赤蝦】〔魚〕a whiskered velvet shrimp. クルマエビ科のエビ. 8cmほどの小型. かき揚げやから揚げなどに用いる.

あかおに【赤鬼】a red ogre. ⇨鬼

あかがい【赤貝】〔貝〕an ark shell; a reddish shell. 浅海にすむ二枚貝. 刺身, 酢の物, 鮨などに用いる. ⇨かい

あかかます【赤魳】〔魚〕a red barracuda. 干物や塩焼きに用いる. ⇨かます

あかがれい【赤鰈】〔魚〕a red halibut; a flathead flounder. 刺身や塩焼きに用いる. ⇨かれい

あかかぶ【赤蕪】〔植物〕a red turnip; ㊎ a red beet; ㊇ a beetroot. ☆ビートの食用根. ⇨かぶ

あかがみ【赤紙】 a draft[call-up] notice; a call-up card[paper]. 第二次世界大戦中における旧日本軍の召集令状.

あかさかごようち【赤坂御用地】 Akasaka Palace Site; Akasaka Imperial Premise.

あかざ【藜】〔植物〕wild spinach; goosefoot (㊇ goosefoots). 若葉は食用. ホウレンソウ (spinach)に代用する.

あかざとう【赤砂糖】brown sugar. 精製していない赤茶色の砂糖. サトウキビから作る. ⇨砂糖

あかじそ【赤紫蘇】〔植物〕a red perilla; red beefsteak plant leaves. 漬物を赤くするのに用いる. ⇨しそ

あかず【赤酢】dark-colored vinegar. 酒粕から造る酢. 色が濃く濃厚な味がある.

あかずのふみきり【開かずの踏切】a level[㊎ grade] crossing which often appears to be closed; a (railroad) crossing gate that rarely opens.

あかせん【赤線】 a red-light district. 売春婦の密集地帯.

あきたかんとうまつり【秋田竿灯まつり】the Akita Kanto Lantern Parade Festival. (8月). ⇨付記(1)「日本の祭り」

あかだし【赤出し】 dark-brown *miso*[bean paste] soup; reddish-brown *miso* soup; soup prepared from dark-brown *miso*. It usually contains *tofu*, vegetables, clams, etc. But it was originally cooked with steamed, ground fish in the Osaka-style specialty. 通常は豆腐, 野菜, 蛤などを入れた赤味噌汁をさす. 元来は「大阪風の料理」(魚の切り身を入れる味噌汁)のこと. ⇨赤味噌

あかちゃんポスト【赤ちゃんポスト】 a baby hatch facility; a foundling wheel. ☆2007年熊本県のキリスト教系の医療法人がはじめた, 新生児を匿名で預かる「コウノトリのゆりかご」(stork's cradle).

あかちょうちん【赤提灯】 ❶〈提灯〉a red paper lantern (often used for the signs for cheap drinking and eating establishments). (安価な飲食店の標識に用いる)赤い紙を張った提灯.
❷〈酒場〉a Japanese-style cheap pub [drinking tavern] (often hanging a red lantern at an outside entrance); ㊇ a pothouse. Workers drop in at a Japanese-style pub with a red paper lantern outside to eat food and drink *sake* with colleagues at reasonable prices. 赤い紙を張った提灯を下げた大衆向けの日本式酒場. 日本の労働者が赤提灯のある安価な酒場にちょっと立ち寄って手ごろな値段で仲間といっしょに飲食する.「安い一杯飲み屋」.

あかとうがらし【赤唐辛子】 a red (chili)

pepper. 赤色の唐辛子の総称. ⇨唐辛子 / 青唐辛子

あかとんぼ【赤蜻蛉】〔虫〕a red dragonfly. ⇨とんぼ

あかね【茜】〔植物〕a madder. 根から赤黄色の「染料」をとる. ¶茜色 madder red; dark red.

あかのたにん【赤の他人】a complete stranger; a total[an utter] stranger.

あかぶさ【赤房】〔相撲〕the red tassel. ⇨房

あかふだ【赤札】a red tag (indicating a price reduction). It also indicates that the article has been sold out. 商店で見切り品や売約済みなどを示す札.

あかべこ【赤べこ】a red papier-mâché cow[ox]; a traditional toy made from papier-mâché which is shaped and painted to look like a red ox[cow]. 張り子(パピエマシェ)の牛. 福島県会津地方の郷土玩具. ☆「べこ」は東北地方の方言で「牛」の意.

あかみ【赤身】❶〔肉〕red meat(牛肉); dark meat(鶏肉); lean meat(脂肪の少ない肉); red(-colored) flesh(魚肉). ⇔白身. ¶赤身の魚 a fish with red flesh.
❷〔木材〕heartwood(木材の中心の赤い部分).

あかみそ【赤味噌】dark-brown *miso* [bean paste] (made mainly from fermented [malted] soybeans). 原料は発酵大豆[大豆麹]である. ⇨白味噌

あかむつ【赤鯥】〔魚〕a black-throat sea perch. スズキ科の魚. 蒲鉾の原料にする.

あがり【上がり】❶green tea.「上がり花」(入れたてのお茶)の略.
❷〈すし屋の隠語〉green tea (to finish off the meal) in a *sushi* bar. ⇨符丁

あがりかまち【上がり框】a front portion of the floor placed at the entrance hall of a Japanese-style house. 家の上がり口の床の横木 (thick plank).

あがりゆ【上がり湯】clean hot water to rinse the bath water off (oneself); fresh hot water to splash (oneself) just as one steps out of the bath. 風呂上がりに身体を洗うきれいな湯.「おか湯」「かかり湯」ともいう.

あきさめぜんせん【秋雨前線】the autumn(al) rain front.

あきす【空き巣】〔行為〕sneak-thieving(空き巣狙い); 〈人〉a prowler; a sneak thief (複) thieves); a thief who steals from a house in the absence of the dwellers.

あきなす【秋茄子】an autumn eggplant; an eggplant harvested in autumn[fall]. 秋に収穫するナスで, 味がよい.

あきのななくさ【秋の七草】the seven autumn[fall] herbs; the seven grasses [herbs] of autumn[fall]. ⇨① 萩 (Japanese bush clover) ② 薄(または尾花) (Japanese pampas grass[flowering eulalia]) ③ 葛 (*kudzu* arrowroot; pueraria) ④ 撫子 (fringed[wild] pink) ⑤ 女郎花 (patrinia [maiden flower]) ⑥ 藤袴 (thoroughwort; eupatorium) ⑦ 桔梗(または朝顔) (Chinese [Japanese] bellflower; althea [morning glory]). ⇨春の七草

あきばけい【秋葉系】Akihabara geeks; geeks frequenting the Akihahabara *otaku* area in Tokyo. ⇨オタク

あきばしょ【秋場所】〔相撲〕the Autumn Grand Sumo Tournament. 別名「9月場所」. ⇨場所

あく【灰汁】❶〈肉汁・煮汁の不純物〉(broth) scum.「浮きかす」ともいう. ¶(おたまで煮え湯の上に浮いてくる)灰汁を引く skim off the scum (that rises to the surface of the cooking water with a ladle).
❷〈野菜・果物の不純物〉harshness; harsh taste; bitter taste. ¶(野菜の)灰汁を抜く remove[get rid of] harshness (from vegetables).

あくせいしゅよう【悪性腫瘍】a malignant tumor; a malignancy; a carcinoma.

あ

あくとくぎょうしゃ【悪徳業者】 an unscrupulous business operator[broker]; a fraudulent dealer.

あくとくしょうほう【悪徳商法】 an unscrupulous business practice[method]; fraudulent sales tactics; a vicious[dishonest] business practice.

あくま【悪魔】 a devil(キリスト教の)；a demon(ギリシア神話の)；Satan(特にキリスト教の). ☆日本の祭事(⇨玉垂宮 鬼夜)や寺社の神事(⇨福は内! 鬼は外!)などでよく用いる単語. ⇨鬼. ¶悪魔払い exorcism. ⇨清め

あぐら【胡坐】 cross-legged sitting. 座禅の姿勢の一種. ¶あぐらをかく sit cross-legged (on a *tatami*-mat floor); sit down with one's legs crossed (on a cushion).

あげ【上げ】 a tuck (for a *kimono*). 着物の縫い上げ. ¶上げをおろす undo[let out] a tuck. 上げをする put[make] a tuck in.

あげ【揚げ】 deep-fried *tofu*[bean curd]. ⇨揚げ豆腐

あげあぶら【揚げ油】oil for deep-frying (used for cooking *tempura*). 揚げ物に用いる油の総称.

あげく【挙句】 the closing verse;〈連歌〉the last 14 syllables[7-7 syllables] of a *renga*[linked verse];〈短歌〉the last 14 syllables[7-7 syllables] of a *tanka*[31-syllable poem]. 連歌・短歌で，最後の七・七の句. ⇔発句

あげしお【上げ潮】 the rising[flowing] tide; (a)high tide; (a) flood tide. ⇔引き潮

あげだしどうふ【揚げ出し豆腐】 lightly-fried *tofu*[bean curd]; *tofu* fried with light flour coating and served in a light savory sauce. 豆腐に小麦粉，片栗粉などをまぶして揚げ，つけ汁を添えた食品.

あげだま【揚げ玉】 deep-fried *tempura* batter balls; deep-fried batter balls left over from making *tempura*; pellets of deep-fried *tempura* batter; pieces[bits] of *tempura*-batter crusts; refuses remained after *tempura* batter is deep-fried. てんぷらを揚げるときに出る衣の玉.「天滓」「揚げかす」ともいう. タヌキそば[うどん] などに用いる.

あげどうふ【揚げ豆腐】 deep-fried *tofu*[bean curd] cutlet; *tofu* fried with batter-coating of *tempura*. 薄揚げ豆腐は「油揚げ」，厚揚げ豆腐は「厚揚げ・生揚げ」ともいう. ⇨油揚げ / 厚揚げ

あげに【揚げ煮】 simmering deep-fried food. 揚げてから，または油で通してから煮る料理.

あげばし【揚げ箸】 (a pair of) long chopsticks for cooking. 天ぷらなどを揚げるときに用いる. ☆箸の素材は竹製，木製，金属製などがある.

あげパン【揚げパン】 a deep-fried bun; a deep-fried ball of dough.

あげまき【揚巻・総角】 an ancient hairdo worn by children. The hair is parted in the middle and done up in a bun[in loops] over each ear. 昔の子供の髪の結い方. 髪を左右に分け耳の上で輪をつくったもの. ¶揚巻結び a style of decorative cord knot tied in trefoil shape. 三つ葉形に結わいた一種の飾り紐のまげ.

あげまく【揚げ幕】 ❶〔能楽〕 an entrance curtain hanging between the greenroom [mirror-room] and the passageway to the Noh stage. It is lifted up and pulled down by two bamboo poles when the actors enter and exit. 役者の支度部屋[鏡の間]と能舞台への通路[橋掛] に掛かる出入り口の幕. 役者が出入りするときに2本の竹棒で揚げ下ろしする.

❷〔文楽・歌舞伎〕a curtain hanging at the entrance and exit of actors to the bunraku [kabuki] stage. It is pulled open and closed for the appearance and disappearance of actors. 舞台へ通ずる役者の出入り口にある掛け幕. 役者の登退場のたびに開閉する.

あげもち【揚げ餅】 (slice of) deep-fried rice cake.

あげもの【揚げ物】 deep-fried foods(揚げた食品); deep-fried dishes(揚げた料理); seafoods or vegetables deep-fried in vegetable oil. 植物性油で揚げた魚介類・野菜. ☆「天麩羅」(衣 [batter] 有り)と「空揚げ」(衣 [batter] 無し)に大別される. ⇨天婦羅 / 空揚げ

あこうじけん【赤穂事件】 the incident of the Forty-Seven Loyal Retainers of the Ako domain. Under the leadership of Oishi Yoshio, they carried out a vendetta against Kira Yoshinaka, taking revenge for dishonorable death of their former master lord (Asano Takuminokami Naganori). 赤穂藩浪士と大石内蔵助良雄らが主君(浅野内匠頭長矩)の不名誉な死の仇討ちをするため吉良上野介義央を討つ. ☆1702年. 元禄15年12月. ⇨忠臣蔵 / 四十七士

あこうだい【赤魚鯛】〔魚〕 a red sea bream; a red rockfish; an ocean perch. 冬から春が旬. 塩焼きや煮つけ, かす漬などにする. ⇨鯛

あこうろうし【赤穂浪士】 ⇨四十七士

あこやがい【阿古屋貝】〔貝〕a pearl oyster. 別名「真珠貝」

あさ【麻】❶〔植物〕a hemp (plant); a flax (plant); 〈麻の実〉hemp seeds.
❷〔繊維〕hemp(麻・大麻の繊維); linen(麻製品). ¶麻織物 hemp fabrics. 麻糸 hemp yarn. 麻紐 hemp twine[tread]. 麻縄 hemp rope. 麻布 hemp cloth. 麻の葉模様 geometric hemp-leaf pattern. ⇨亜麻

あさいち【朝市】 a morning fair[market]; a fair[market] held during the morning. 囲石川県輪島の朝市

あさがお【朝顔】〔植物〕a (Japanese) morning glory. ¶朝顔市 a morning glory

fair[market]; open-air street stalls selling various morning glories.

あさくさのり【浅草海苔】 dried laver; dried purple laver (cultivated at Asakusa during the Edo period). 江戸時代, 浅草付近の隅田川で採れ, 浅草観音参りの土産物として売ったのが由来. 「干し〔乾〕海苔」また「甘海苔」(seasoned laver)ともいう. すしには不可欠の素材.

あさじあえ【朝地和え】 food dressed with chopped sesame seeds. 茹でたホウレンソウを切り, 白ゴマで和えた物. 「小町和え」ともいう. ⇨和え物

あさせ【浅瀬】 shallows (川・海などの); a shoal (砂などの); a ford (川など歩いて渡れる). ⇨潮干狩り. ¶浅瀬の海岸 a shoal beach (in Kisarazu City). 浅瀬の海水浴場 a shoal swimming beach (in Oarai(kaigan) Beach).

あさつき【浅葱・糸葱】〔植物〕 (flowering) chives(複数形); onion. ユリ科の球根植物. ネギの一種. 若い葉と茎は食用. 薬味(「刻みチャイブ」 chopped chives)として用いる

あさづけ【浅漬】 lightly pickled vegetables; vegetables lightly salted and pickled; vegetables lightly preserved in salted rice bran[in salt or rice bran] for a short time. 野菜を塩やぬかであっさりと漬けたもの. 「薄塩の漬物」ともいう. ⇨一夜漬け
〔料理〕**浅漬の胡瓜** lightly pickled cucumber; cucumber preserved in salted rice-bran for a short time. 別名「きゅうりの浅漬」. **浅漬の沢庵** lightly pickled *daikon*[Japanese radish]; *daikon* preserved in salted rice-bran for a short time.

あざみ【薊】〔植物〕a thistle; a plumed thistle.

あざらし【海豹】〔動物〕a seal; a hair[an earless] seal; a sea calf.

あさむし【浅蒸し】〔料理〕cooking by light steaming; 〈食べ物〉foods cooked by light

あ

steaming.

あさり【浅蜊】〔貝〕an *asari* clam; a littleneck clam; a short-neck[baby-neck] clam. マルスダレガイ科の二枚貝．冬から春が旬．☆ヨーロッパでは cockle ともいう．

〔料理〕浅蜊の酒蒸し *sake*-steamed short-neck clams; baby-neck clams steeped in *sake* and steamed. *Asari* clam steamed after steeping in *sake*. ⇨酒蒸し．**浅蜊の佃煮** an *asari* clam boiled down with *shoyu* and sugar. ⇨佃煮．**浅蜊飯** rice cooked with littleneck clams.「深川飯」ともいう．

あし【葦・蘆】〔植物〕a reed; a ditch reed. イネ科の多年草,「よし」ともいう．⇨よし¶**葦の茂った沼地** reed-grown[reedy] marshes. **葦笛** reed flute[pipe].

あじ【鯵】〔魚〕a horse mackerel(単複同形)；a jack mackerel; a saurel; a pompano.¶**鯵の干物** dried horse mackerel.

〔料理〕**鯵鮨** horse mackerel *sushi*; vinegared rice with horse mackerel.(鯵の酢じめをすし飯にのせたもの)．**鯵の塩焼き** salt-broiled[salt-grilled] horse mackerel; horse mackerel sprinkled with salt and broiled over a charcoal fire.（塩をふりかけ，炭火の上で焼いた鯵）．**鯵のたたき** minced[chopped] raw horse mackerel; minced raw horse mackerel topped[mixed] with ginger and leeks.(生姜とネギをのせた[混ぜた]ぶつ切りの鯵)．**鯵の開き** horse mackerel cut open and then dried.(腹を切り開いてから干した鯵)．**鯵のフライ** deep-fried horse mackerel.

あしいれこん【足入れ婚】a tentative marriage.

あしか【海驢】〔動物〕a sea lion; an eared seal.

あしがる【足軽】 a foot[common] soldier; *samurai*(warrior) of the lowest rank (serving as a foot[common] soldier). 戦いのとき歩兵となる最下位の武士．

あしきり【足切り】 pre-test screening system; the system of eliminating students

[candidates] in advance who are bad at the entrance examination. 入試の不合格者を排除する．

あじさい【紫陽花】〔植物〕 a hydrangea; a garden hydrangea. ⇨甘茶

あじしお【味塩】 salt mixed with a chemical seasonings[MSG]. 化学調味料をまぜ合わせた塩．

あしだ【足駄】(a pair of) wooden *geta*[clogs] with high supports (worn in wet weather). A pair of clogs[footwears] with high wooden supports is often used by *kimono*-clad people on rainy days. (悪天候の日に履く)歯の高い下駄．雨の日に着物を着た人がよく使用する．

あしだい【足代】 traveling expenses; car fare; taxi fare; train[bus] fare. 交通費．車代．

あしたば【明日葉】〔植物〕a Japanese parsley[angelica]. セリ科の多年草．若葉をてんぷら，浸し物，和え物などに使用する．健康野菜で有名．八丈島の産地で,別名「八丈草」(a Japanese herb that grows on Hachijo Island).

あしづかい【足遣い】〔文楽〕the leg manipulator (of the puppeteer trio in bunraku). He is a manipulator who moves the legs and feet of a single puppet. 文楽人形の足[脚]を操る人．人形遣いの三人組の中で第3番目の人 (the third man of the bunraku puppeteer trio)である．☆「主遣い」(the head manipulator)と「左遣い」(the left-arm manipulator)と共演する．⇨三人遣い / 主[面]遣い / 左遣い

あじつけ【味付け】 seasoning; flavoring.¶**味付けご飯** seasoned boiled rice. **天然塩の味付け** mineral salt seasoning. **味付け海苔** flavored *nori*[laver]; dried and seasoned *nori*[laver]. ⇨海苔 / 焼き海苔

あしながいくえいかい【足長育英会】 Ashinaga scholarships; a nonprofit organization that supports students in need of financial help by providing scholarships. 遺児への支援を行う非営利団体.「足長おじさん」an anonymous benefactor(匿名の恩人).☆1993年設立，2019年一般財団法人に移行.

あじのもと【味の素】　*Aji-no-moto*; a powdered seasoning used in cooking. 料理に用いる粉末調味料.☆日本では代表的な「化学調味料の商標」(the popular brand of monosodium glutamate[MSG]).

あしばらい【足払い】〔柔道〕　*ashibarai*; leg flicking; sweeping one's opponent's legs from under him/her.　⇨柔道

あしゆ【足湯】　(take[英] have]) a footbath; soaking feet in hot[warm] water.　⇨温泉

あしらい❶〔華道〕supplementary branches (or stems) added to the main branches (used in a flower arrangement of the Ikenobo school). 主枝にとり合わせる補助的な枝（または茎）の配合のこと．池坊流の華道で用いる.　⇨従枝(草月流) / 中間枝(小原流)❷〔能楽〕musical accompaniment in a Noh play. 能楽で用いる音楽の伴奏.❸〈食べ物の配合〉garnish; arrangement. 料理の取り合わせ.　⇨付け合わせ

あじろ【網代】❶〔編み物〕a wickerwork (made of split bamboo or wood[twig]). （割竹または小枝などの）編み細工.　¶網代笠 a wickerwork hat. 網代籠 a wickerwork palanquin. 網代車 a wickerwork (bullock) carriage. 網代天井 a wickerwork ceiling.❷〈捕魚の仕掛け〉a wickerwork fishnet [trap]. It is used for catching fish in the shallows of a river. 川の浅瀬で魚を捕獲するのに用いる.

あずき【小豆】　an *adzuki*[*azuki*] bean. マメ科の一年草.　¶小豆アイス *adzuki*-bean sherbet. 小豆餡 *adzuki*-bean paste[jam]. 〔料理〕小豆粥 *adzuki*-bean gruel; rice gruel cooked with *adzuki* beans and rice cake.

1月15日の小正月に食べる伝統食.　⇨粥. 小豆御飯 rice cooked[boiled] with *adzuki* beans.「小豆飯」ともいう.

あずまや【東屋・四阿】a small garden hut(庭の小屋)；a small arbor(日よけができる休憩所)；a gazebo(見晴台)；a bower(木陰の休憩所). It is usually open on all sides and sheltered by a low thatched roof. 草葺き屋根で四方にふきおろした小屋.　☆回遊式庭園 (a strolling garden) などの休憩所として設けられている.

あぜくらづくり(けんぞうぶつ)【校倉造り（建造物）】*azekura-zukuri*, a log storehouse on stilts; a storehouse built of squared logs. It is a high-floored log cabin construction with walls which are made of interlocked timbers triangular in shape. 木材で支えている倉庫．三角形の長い角材を組み合わせて壁面をつくった建築様式.　⇨正倉院宝物殿

あそじんじゃどろうちまつり【阿蘇神社泥打祭】the Mud-Throwing Festival (of Aso Shrine). (3月).　⇨付記(1)「日本の祭り」

あそん【朝臣】a courtier[court noble] (in the Nara period). 奈良時代の廷臣.　☆五位以上の貴族につける敬称.

あつあげ【厚揚げ】(a piece of) thick deep-fried *tofu*[bean curd] pouch[puff]; thick block of deep-fried *tofu*.⇨油揚げ.　⇨揚げ豆腐

あつかん【熱燗】hot *sake*; heated *sake*. ☆温度の目安は「ぬる燗」40-45度，「熱燗」55-60度，「適温」45-55度.　⇦冷や

あつぞこブーツ〔くつ〕【厚底ブーツ〔靴〕】(a pair of) platform boots[shoes; sandals].

あつもの【羹】〈濃い汁〉rich hot soup; 〈薄い汁〉hot broth (containing meat and vegetables). （肉と野菜を入れた）熱い汁料理.

あつやきたまご【厚焼き卵】a thick omelet [omelette] (containing ground fish paste). （魚のすり身に）卵をまぜて厚めに焼きあげ

あ

たもの. ⇨伊達巻(だてまき)

あてわざ【当て技】〔柔道〕*atewaza*; the art of the knockdown blow (including the kick(蹴り技), thrust(突き技) and hit(打ち技)). ⇨柔道

アド〈能狂言〉an *ado*; the supporting actor in a kyogen comic play; the actor supporting[the actor who supports] the protagonist in a kyogen play. An *ado* corresponds to the *waki*[the second(ary) actor] in a Noh play. 狂言で主役を支える相手役. 能で演じる「ワキ役」に相当する. ⇨主アド

あとざ【後座】〔能楽〕the rear stage portion (in the Noh theater); the back portion of the acting stage (in the Noh theater); the space for the orchestra behind the acting area. The instrumental musicians (*hayashikata*) sit in a row across the front of the *atoza*, facing the audience. 能舞台の後部. 実際に演じる舞台の後部にある座.「囃子方」が観衆に向かって後座の前で横1列に座っている. ⇨能「能舞台」/ 囃子方

アトピーせいひふえん【アトピー性皮膚炎】(have) atopic dermatitis. ☆「(卵)アレルギー症」be allergic to (eggs)

あなご【穴子・海鰻】〔魚〕a conger; a conger eel; a sea[salt water] eel. ⇨うみうなぎ〔料理〕**穴子鮨** *sushi* topped with cooked conger (eel). ⇨鮨. **穴子丼** conger (eel) bowl; (a bowl of) rice topped with cooked conger (eel). ⇨丼物. **穴子蒲焼き** broiled conger (eel) flavored with thick sweetened *shoyu*[soy sauce]. ⇨蒲焼き

アニメ *anime*; animation(動画); an animated cartoon(作品；映画)；a cartoon(漫画)；an animated[a cartoon] film(映画)；an animated cartoon character[figure](アニメ・キャラ). ☆ anime という言葉が英語として定着している.「鉄腕アトム」(手塚治虫)は "Astro Boy",「となりの

トトロ」(宮崎駿)は "My Neighbor Totoro" と紹介されている. ⇨まんが

あねったい【亜熱帯】the subtropical zone [region]; the semitropical region; the subtropics. ¶亜熱帯気候 a subtropical climate. 亜熱帯植物 a subtropical plant. 亜熱帯動物 a subtropical animal.

あばれまつり【あばれ祭】the Raging-Parade Festival. (7月). ⇨付記(1)「日本の祭り」

あひる【家鴨】〔鳥〕a (domestic) duck; a duckling(あひるの子); a drake (雄あひる). ⇨合鴨. ¶あひるの肉[肝臓] duck meat [liver]. あひるの卵 duck egg. あひるの丸焼き roast duck.

あぶ【虻】〔虫〕a gadfly; a horse-fly.

あぶらあげ【油揚げ】(a piece of) thin deep-fried *tofu*[bean curd] pouch[puff]. An oblong thinly-sliced pouch[puff] of deep-fried *tofu* is seasoned with *shoyu*[soy sauce] and *mirin*[sweetened *sake*]. It is used for making *inari-zushi*. 豆腐を薄めに切って食用油で揚げた長方形の袋状の食品. 醤油と味醂で味付ける. 稲荷鮨などをつくるのに用いる.「薄揚げ」「稲荷揚げ」ともいう. ⇨厚揚げ. ⇨稲荷鮨 /揚げ豆腐

あぶらいため【油炒め】pan-fried[stir-fried] food; food sautéed in oil. ¶野菜の油炒め pan-fried vegetables.

あぶらえ【油絵】an oil painting; a painting [picture] in oils. ¶油絵画家 an oil painter; a painter in oils.

あぶらぜみ【油蝉】〔虫〕a large brown cicada; a frying-pan cicada. ⇨せみ

あぶらな【油菜】〔植物〕(oil-seed) rape; (Chinese) colza; canola.「菜の花」(通称)の正式名称. 花は観賞用. 柔らかい若葉は食用(和え物や浸し物など). 種子からは「菜種油」(rape-seed oil)が採れる. ⇨なのはな / なたね

あぶらむし【油虫】〔虫〕a cockroach; an

Oriental cockroach; ㊇ a black beetle; ㊇ a plant louse (複 lice).

あべかわもち【安倍川餅】 *abekawa-mochi* sweet rice cake; a rice cake coated [covered] with sweetened yellow soybean flour. Slices of rice cake are dipped in boiling[hot] water and dredged in a blend of yellow soybean flour[powder] and sugar. 黄粉と砂糖をまぶした餅. ☆静岡県安倍川付近の名所から命名された.

あま【尼】 a nun; a (Buddhist) priestess. She is bound to celibacy and lives with other nuns in a nunnery[Buddhist convent]. 独身を守り, 尼寺で他の尼と共同生活する. ⇨尼寺

あま【海女】 a female[woman] diver. 女性潜水者. ¶真珠[アワビ]採りの海女 a female pearl[abalone] diver; a female diver who collects pearl oysters[abalones] from the sea without using diving gear[suit]. 潜水具[潜水服]を用いずに真珠貝[アワビ]を採集する.

あま【亜麻】〔植物〕 flax (plant); linen. ⇨あさ ¶亜麻糸 linen (yarn). 亜麻布 linen fabric

あまえ【甘え】 *amae*; desire for emotional dependence; reliance on somebody's favor.

あまえび【甘海老】 a raw shrimp[prawn]; a northern pink shrimp; a red shrimp. ☆刺身やすし種に用いる.

あまがえる【雨蛙】〔両〕 a tree frog; a tree toad; a hyla.

あまがき【甘柿】 a sweet persimmon. ⇨柿

あまくだり【天下り】❶ descending from the heavens to the humans. 天上界から人間界へ降りること.

❷〈天下り人事〉 government parachutists into private industry; the descent of high-ranking government official to private companies upon retirement; retired bureaucrats parachuting into private firms; the appointment of ex-government officials to high positions in private organizations. 退職した高級官僚が民間企業などに優遇された条件で再就職すること.

あまぐり【甘栗】 sweet roasted[broiled] chestnuts. ⇨くり

あまごい【雨乞い】 a ritual prayer for rainfall. They pray for sufficient rainfall for a good harvest during spells of dry weather. 降雨を願う儀式. 日照り続きのなか豊作に要する十分な降水を祈願する.「雨乞い祭り」ともいう. ¶雨乞いの踊り the dance praying for rain.

あまざけ【甘酒】 *amazake*; a sweet beverage [drink] made from fermented rice gruel (or *sake* lees); *sake*[slight alcoholic drink] brewed by blending malted rice with rice gruel. もち米の粥を米麹で発酵させて作る甘い飲み物. 最近は酒粕から作る. アルコール度数1%未満. ¶甘酒漬け vegetables[fish] pickled in *amazake*. 甘酒を使用した漬け物[野菜・魚]. ⇨べったら漬け

あまじおのさけ【甘塩の鮭】 lightly-salted salmon. ⇨さけ

あまず【甘酢】 sweetened[sugared] vinegar. 味醂または砂糖をまぜて甘くした酢. ¶甘酢生姜 sweet-vinegared ginger(口直しやあしらいに用いる). 甘酢漬け vegetables pickled in sweetened vinegar(らっきょう漬けなどがある). ⇨らっきょう

あまだい【甘鯛】 a tilefish; a kind of sea bream. 冬が旬で, 冬の食材によく用いる. ⇨たい

あまちゃ【甘茶】❶〔植物〕 hydrangea. ユキノシタ科アジサイ属. 茎・葉は紫陽花に似ている.

❷〔飲物〕 hydrangea tea; sweet tea made from the leaves of hydrangea. hydrangea の若葉を加工した甘味のある茶. 4月8日の「花祭り」(潅仏会)に天露になぞらえて釈迦の像にかける. ⇨あじさい/潅仏会

あ

あまでら【尼寺】 a nunnery; a Buddhist convent; a nunnery built as a hermitage of perfect seclusion for those seeking a religious life. 信仰生活を求める人の完全な隠遁所として建立された女性用の寺. 圏京都の寂光院. ⇨尼

あまてらすおおみかみ【天照大神】 Amaterasu Omikami; the Sun Goddess; Great Deity illuminating Heaven. She is enshrined, with the Sacred Mirror (as one of the three regalia[treasures] of the Japanese imperial throne), in the Inner Sanctuary of Ise Grand Shrine in Mie Prefecture. The Sacred Mirror is believed to represent the sacred body of Amaterasu Omikami, the original ancestress of the Imperial Family. She is regarded as the national goddess of Japan. 三重県伊勢神宮の内宮に「八咫の鏡」とともに祀られている. 鏡は皇室の初代祖先である天照大神の御身体を表すと信じられている. 日本の国民的神として仰がれている. ☆神話によると, イザナギとイザナミの女（むすめ）高天原（たかまがはら）(the High Plain of Heaven)の主神また皇室の祖先 (the supreme deity of Shintoism and the ancestral goddess of the Imperial Family). 「日の神」(英語で the Sun Goddess)と仰がれ, the female deity of Shinto mythology who is identified with the sun.（太陽と同一視される神道神話の女神）とも表現できる. ⇨天孫降臨（てんそんこうりん）/ 三種の神器

あまど【雨戸】 a wooden sliding shutter; a wooden sliding rain door set on the outside of the house. It is made of a thin wooden board protecting the house from rain or storm. 風雨・暴風などを防ぐために外に立てる戸. ⇨戸袋

あまなつ【甘夏】〔植物〕a sweet summer orange; a sweet Chinese[Watson] orange. 甘味(sweet flavor)が強く, 酸味(sour taste)が少ない.

あまなっとう【甘納豆】 sugared[sweetened] *adzuki* beans; sugar-glazed[candied] beans. It is a Japanese confection of beans boiled in molasses and rolled in sugar. 豆を糖蜜で煮詰めて砂糖をまぶした和菓子. ☆小豆 (*adzuki* beans), 隠元豆 (kidney beans), うずら豆 (mottled kidney beans)などがある.（すべて複数形）

あまに【甘煮】 food simmered and seasoned with sugar and *shoyu*[soy sauce] (or *mirin* [sweetened *sake*]). 砂糖・醤油（または味醂（みりん））で煮上げた食物. 金時豆などがある.

あまのいわや【天の岩屋】 the Heavenly Rock Cave. ☆日本神話によると天照大神がスサノオノミコト［弟］に侮辱され身を隠した岩屋. 入り口の扉を「天の岩(屋)戸」(the Door[Gate] of the Heavenly[Celestial] Rock Cave) という. ⇨天照大神

あまのがわ【天の川】 the Milky Way; the (Milky Way) Galaxy. ⇨七夕

あまのはしだて【天の橋立】 Amanohashi-date, a long pine-covered sandbar. It is a narrow peninsula which is located on the Japan Sea Coast to the north of Kyoto and juts out into Miyazu Bay. 松樹に覆われた砂州. 京都北部の日本海沿岸にあり, 宮津湾に突き出る細長い半島. ⇨日本三景

あまのり【甘海苔】〔植物〕laver.〔食品〕seasoned laver. ⇨浅草海苔

あまみそ【甘味噌】 mild *miso*[bean paste]; low-salt *miso*. 塩分含有量は6%前後. ⇨白味噌

あみがさ【編み笠】 a braided[woven] sedge [straw, rush] hat; a broad-brimmed hat made of braided[woven] sedge[straw, rush]. It is worn to protect the sun or to disguise one's identity. わら・すげなどで編んだ笠. 日よけまたは身分を偽装するために装う. ¶深編み笠 a Japanese-style broad-brimmed sedge hat for covering one's whole head. 頭全体にかぶる編み笠.

あみだ(にょらい)【阿弥陀(如来)】 Amitabha Tathagata; Amitabha; Amida (Nyorai) Buddha (the savior of mankind). Amida Nyorai is the supreme Buddha presiding over the Paradise of the Pure Land in the West (where believers may gain rebirth from death). Amida Buddha is usually depicted as sitting cross-legged on lotus-flower pedestal with both hands resting on his lap or with his left hand on his lap and right hand raised. 人類の救主. 西方の極楽浄土 (the Western Paradise of the Pure Land〈信じる者が死後に生き返る所〉)を統治する最高の仏陀. 阿弥陀は通常蓮の花の台座にあぐらをかきながら両手を膝にのせているか, 左手を膝におき右手を挙げた状態で表現されている. ☆大乗仏教の仏陀 (the Buddha in Mahayana Buddhism). 浄土宗・浄土真宗の本尊. 圀鎌倉の大仏(浄土宗高徳院の境内にある). ⇨南無阿弥陀仏

【阿弥陀三尊】 the Amitabha Triad (三人組); the Amida Buddha Trinity(三位一体); a set of three statues consisting of the Amida Buddha and his two attendants on either side; a set of three images comprising the Amida Buddha attended by two Bodhisattvas on either side. 「阿弥陀仏」(the Amida Buddha rested on a lotus-flower pedestal)と, その左右の「観世音菩薩」(the Bodhisattva Kannon attending on the left side)と「勢至菩薩」(the Bodhisattva Seishi attending on the right hand)の三体.

【阿弥陀堂】 an Amida Buddha[Amitabha] Hall. The hall is dedicated to the Amida Buddha enshrined as the main statue of Buddha. 阿弥陀を本尊として安置するお堂. 圀京都・平等院の鳳凰堂 (the Phoenix Hall of Byodoin Temple)

あみもと【網元】 a fishermen's boss. 漁師の親方. 網主.

あみやき【網焼き】 broiling[grilling] on a grid. ¶牛肉[魚]の網焼き beef[fish] broiled on a grid.

あめ【飴】 ㊍ (a piece of) candy; ㊎ (two pieces of) sweets. ¶飴細工 a candy work; figures made of soft candy. 飴細工の人形 a doll made of soft candy.

〔食品〕飴煮 candied[sweetened] food; food simmered with a spiced sweet syrup. ⇨甘露煮. 飴湯 drink[beverage] made of thick sweet malt syrup.

あめとむち(のせいさく)【飴と鞭(の政策)】 carrot-and-stick policy[approach]. ☆馬を調教するとき好物の「ニンジン」(carrot)を用いる. こどもを教育するときに御仕置(punishment)の「たたく棒」(stick for scolding: 欧米でよくみかける)を用いるたとえ.

アメリカンコーヒー (和製英語) mild coffee; weak coffee. ☆ American coffeeは「アメリカ製のコーヒー」の意.

あめんぼ【水馬】〔虫〕a pond skater; a water strider; a water skipper.

あや【綾】〈織り〉a twill weave;〈織り布〉a fabric (made) with a twill weave; cloth with a pattern diagonal stripes.

あやおり【綾織り】〈織り方〉a twill weave;〈人〉a twill weaver.

あやつり【操り】 manipulation. ¶操り芝居 a puppet show[play]; a marionette[string-puppet] drama. (糸で操る人形劇). 操り人形 a puppet; a string puppet; a marionette. 操り人形師 a puppeteer; a marionette man[woman].

あやとり【綾取り】 (play) cat's cradle. A long string is looped around the fingertips of both hands and manipulated to form various patterns. It is played by one person [girl] or two people[girls] by turns. 両手の指で長い紐を輪にして操り, いろいろな形をつくって, 1人[少女]または交代で2人[少女たち]が遊ぶ.

あやにしき【綾錦】〈生地〉damask and brocade;〈衣服〉elegant clothes.

あ

あやめ【菖蒲】〔植物〕an iris (複 irises, irides); a blue flag; (古語) a sweet flag. ⇨しょうぶ / 水郷. ¶菖蒲庭園 an iris garden (which is splendid with flowers in June in Meiji Shrine)

あゆ【鮎】〔魚〕an *ayu* (fish); a Japanese river trout; a sweetfish; a river smelt. 日本固有の川魚. ¶鮎簗 weir fishing for *ayu*[sweetfish]. ⇨潤香
〔料理〕鮎鮨 *sushi* topped with vinegared *ayu* (fish); fermented *sushi* with *ayu* (fish). 鮎の塩焼き grilled *ayu* (fish) with salt; broiled *ayu* (fish)with salt on a grid. 鮎の背越し raw slices of *ayu* (fish) with bone. 鮎の煮浸し simmered *ayu* (fish) grilled and dried over low heat. 鮎の味噌焼き grilled *ayu* (fish) with *miso*[bean paste] on a grid.

あゆやき【鮎焼き】 Japanese cake shaped like *ayu* (fish). 鮎の姿に似る和菓子.

あら【粗】 fish head and bones; head and bony parts of a fish. They are used to make stock for a one-pot dish. 魚を料理した後にまだ残った肉のついている骨や頭. 鍋料理などのだし汁に用いる.
〔料理〕粗煮 head and bony parts of a fish cooked in sweetened *shoyu*[soy sauce]; dish made by boiling the bony parts of a fish in *shoyu*.「粗炊き」ともいう. ⇨鯛の粗煮

あら【鯎】〔魚〕a saw-edged perch. スズキ科の魚. 鍋[チャンコ]料理や煮魚また刺身などに用いる.

あらい【洗い】 fresh *sashimi*[sliced raw fish] soaked[chilled] in icy water. 鯉・鯛などの魚肉を切って冷水でさらし縮ませたもの. ⇨活き造り. ¶鯉の洗い slices of raw carp rinsed in cold water; sliced raw carp washed in icy water.

あらかん【阿羅漢】a Buddhist monk who has attained spiritual enlightenment. 煩悩を断ち，悟りを開いた修行者.「羅漢」とも略す.

⇨修行(修行者)

あらぎょう【荒行】 asceticism; rigorous ascetic exercises; religious austerities. Buddhist monks and mountain ascetics perform religious austerities to gain enlightenment of the ultimate truth. They stand under the freezing water of waterfalls while chanting sutras to transform themselves onto a holy state. 僧侶や山伏などが悟りを開くために激しい苦業を行う (practice asceticism). 精神を変容させるために経を唱えながら滝に打たれたりなどする.

あらこ【粗粉】 rough-ground rice flour. 荒く粉にした米粉. 干菓子の材料.

あらごと【荒事】〔歌舞伎〕 a masculine style of kabuki acting. It features an expression of anger with exaggerated posture (*mie*), makeup (*kumadori*) and movements of an actor performing in a kabuki play. 歌舞伎で演じる勇猛なしぐさ (energetic style). その特長は誇張されたポーズ(見得)，化粧(隈取)，動作などで表す怒りの表情である.☆鬼神・勇士などを主役にした芝居に見られる. ⇨隈取り / 見得. ⇦和事. ¶荒事師 an actor who plays robust and brave roles.

あらじお【粗塩】 coarse[crude] salt; unrefined salt; bay salt; solar salt.

あらに【粗煮】 ⇨粗

あらひとがみ【現人神】 a living god[deity]; god[deity] in human form. An emperor was worshipped as a living god before World War II. The defeat of Japan in 1945 brought renunciation of divinity by the emperor. 現世に人の姿で現れる神 (a "living-god" emperor). 天皇は第二次世界大戦前神格化されていた. 1945年敗戦により(昭和)天皇の神格化が否定された.☆人間宣言:「人間天皇」(the emperor as a human being)を宣言する.

あらまき【荒巻・新巻】❶〈塩漬けの鮭〉a slightly salted salmon. 通常「新巻」と書く.

❷〈わら[いぐさ]で包まれた鮭〉a salted salmon wrapped in straw[rush].

あられ[ひょう]【霰[雹]】 hail(気象現象)；hailstone(霰の粒).

あられ【霰】 small[tiny] rice crackers; rice-cracker cubes[pellets]. *Arare* are bite-sized chips[bits] of dried pounded rice and flavored with *shoyu*[soy sauce] and sugar. 「霰餅」の略称．「おかき」「かき餅」ともいう. ⇨煎餅

あられそば【霰そば】 buckwheat noodles with deep-fried scallops. 貝柱のかき揚げをのせたそば．☆貝柱 (scallops)を「霰」に見立てる．⇨貝柱

あり【蟻】〔虫〕an ant. ¶白蟻 a white ant; a termite. 赤蟻 a red ant. 黒蟻 a black ant.

ありたやき【有田焼】 Arita porcelain ware (produced in Arita district of Saga Prefecture). ☆酒井田柿右衛門の色絵磁器は有名．欧州にも輸出される．別称「伊万里焼」.

ありのみ【有りの実】⇨なし(梨)

アルコールけんしゅつき【アルコール検出器】 an alcohol detector; a drunkometer; Breathalyzer(商標).

あわ【粟】〔植物〕(foxtail) millet.〈実〉millet grain；〈粒〉a grain of millet. イネ科の一年草. ⇨五穀

〔食品〕粟おこし millet cake; cake[confection] made of millet grain. ⇨岩おこし. 粟餅 steamed rice-millet cake; millet dough. It is eaten with red *adzuki*-bean paste or roasted soybean flour. (蒸してついた粟を餡子で包むか黄粉 (soybean powder[flour])をまぶすかして食べる).

あわおどり【阿波踊り】 the Awa Folk Dance. (8月). ⇨付記(1)「日本の祭り」

あわせ【袷】 a lined *kimono* (for winter wear); a *kimono* with a lining (worn in cold season). 裏布をつけた着物. ⇔単. ¶袷仕立 a lining；〔衣類〕a lined garment. 袷羽織 a lined *haori*[Japanese half-coat] (裏のある羽織)

あわせじょうゆ【合わせ醤油】 a mixture of *shoyu*[soy sauce] and *mirin*[sweetened *sake*]. 醤油にみりんを混ぜたもの (blend). ¶合わせ醤油の照り焼き *Teriyaki* cooked with a strong-flavored *awase-joyu*.

あわせみそ【合わせ味噌】 a mixture of several types of *miso*[soybean paste]; a blend of different kinds of *miso*. 混合した味噌，主として味噌汁に用いる.

あわび【鮑】〔貝〕an *awabi*; an abalone; a sea shell; an ear shell. ミガイ科の巻き貝. ¶干し鮑 a dried abalone. ⇨熨斗
〔料理〕鮑の酒蒸し *sake*-steamed abalone; abalone steeped in *sake* and steamed; abalone steamed after steeping in *sake*. (アワビに酒を振りかけて蒸す). ⇨酒蒸し

あわもり【泡盛】 *awamori*; rice liquor; millet liquor; Okinawan liquor distilled from indica-type rice. 米・粟からつくる酒. インディカ米からつくる沖縄特産の焼酎. ☆製造過程で滴り落ちる液が「泡」(froth)となってかめに「盛り」上がる (swell) ことからの呼称. ⇨焼酎 / 米

あん【庵】 a hermitage (for monks to live in); a monastery(僧庵)；a place of seclusion (人里離れた棲家).「いおり」ともいう. ¶庵室 a hermitage; a monastery; a hermit's cell. 庵主 a master of a Buddhist hermitage; an occupant of a monastery.

あん【餡】❶ sweet bean paste; paste made from *adzuki* beans and boiled with sugar. 小豆などの豆類を煮て潰し，砂糖を加え甘くしたもの.「餡子」ともいう.
〔食品〕鶯餡 sweetened green peas paste; sweet paste made from green peas. 小倉餡 mixture of whole and powdered sweet *adzuki* bean paste; sweet *adzuki*-bean paste made from both whole and mashed beans. 栗餡 sweetened chestnut paste; sweet paste

made from chestnuts. 漉し餡 strained sweet *adzuki* bean paste. 晒し餡 powdered sweet *adzuki* bean paste. 潰し餡［粒餡］ slightly crushed[smashed] sweetened *adzuki* bean paste; unstrained sweet *adzuki* bean paste. 生餡 *adzuki* bean paste before sweetening with sugar. 餡子玉 sweet *adzuki* bean-paste ball.

【餡ころ餅】 a rice cake coated[covered] with sweet bean paste.(餡をまぶした餅).

【餡パン】 a bean-paste bread[bun]; a bread[bun] stuffed[filled] with sweetened bean paste.

【餡饅】 a bean-paste bun; a bun stuffed [filled] with sweetened bean paste. ⇨饅頭

【餡蜜】 ***anmitsu***: (a bowl of) boiled peas mixed with sweet bean paste and topped with agar-agar jelly cubes in molasses[英] treacle] and some pieces of fruit. 餡を混ぜた煮豆と糖蜜(syrup)をかけたサイの目に切った寒天と果物の上にのせ合わせたもの. ☆ molasses (=英 treacle)「糖蜜」は砂糖の製造過程で生じる黒いシロップ. (サトウキビの)「糖液」の意味である. 元来ラテン語の「はち蜜」の意. ⇨蜜豆(餡がない)

❷〈葛餡〉 *kudzu*[arrowroot starch] thick sauce (for foods); a thick *kudzu* starch cake. 葛粉(または片栗粉)を水でとき, 沸騰したすまし汁の中へ流してとろりとさせたもの. ⇨葛餡／餡掛け

あんか【行火】 an *anka*; a bed warmer; a foot warmer (kept inside the bed under a quilt); an earthenware pot (containing a charcoal fire). 寝具を暖める器具. 布団の中に入れて手足を温める器具. 炭火などを入れた土製の容器. ☆現在では「電気行火［器］」(an electric foot warmer[device])がある.

あんかけ【餡掛け】 dish dressed with liquid *kudzu*[arrowroot starch]; food dressed with a thick starchy sauce. 葛餡をかけた料理.

⇨餡❷

〔料理〕**餡掛け豆腐** *tofu* covered with a thick starchy sauce. 葛餡を掛けた豆腐. ⇨餡❷

【餡掛けうどん［そば］】 (a bowl of) wheat noodles[buckwheat noodles] covered with a thick starchy soup. It is seasoned with *shoyu*[soy sauce] and fish flavor including fish-paste cake, fried bean curd, mushroom and vegetables in a thick starchy soup. 葛餡をかけたうどん［そば］. 餡掛け汁にかまぼこ, 油揚げまた野菜などを入れ醤油と魚の風味で味付ける. ⇨餡❷

あんぎゃそう【行脚僧】 an itinerant monk [Buddhist priest] who goes on a pilgrimage; a Buddhist priest traveling on a pilgrimage. He goes on a walking tour[pilgrimage] for ascetic self-discipline. 巡礼に出る巡回僧侶.

あんぐう【行宮】 ⇨行在所

あんこ【餡子】 ⇨餡

あんこう【鮟鱇】〔魚〕an angler; an anglerfish; a goosefish; a fishing frog.

〔料理〕**鮟鱇鍋** an anglerfish hot pot; a hot-pot dish of anglerfish with vegetables. It is a dish of anglerfish and vegetables boiled in a hot pot. 野菜などを入れたアンコウ魚の鍋料理.

あんざいしょ【行在所】 a temporary Imperial palace; a temporary palace for an Emperor (away from the capital). 旅先での天皇の仮の御所.「行宮」ともいう.

あんしょうばんごう【暗証番号】 a personal [secret] code number(キャッシュカードなど); a PIN number. ☆ PIN= personal identification number(個人識別番号).

あんしんりつめい【安心立命】 (attain) spiritual peace and enlightenment; (achieve) peace of mind.

あんず【杏】〔植物〕(実) an apricot; (木) an apricot tree. ¶杏のジャム apricot jam.

あんどん【行灯】 an *andon*; a paper-covered

lamp stand; a standing lamp[lantern] in a wooden box frame with a paper shade. It is a standing lamp made of a round[square] frame of wood covered with a strong rice paper. The top and bottom are open. It is lit with rapeseed oil on an oil plate inside. 丸い[四角い]木の枠に和紙をはった立ち照明具. 上下はあいている. 中に菜種油皿などをおいてともす.

あんらくし【安楽死】 mercy killing; easy [painless] death; euthanasia(専門用語).

い

い【亥】 the Boar, one[the last] of the 12 animals of the Chinese zodiac. 十二支の第十二. ⇨十二支. ¶**亥の方** the Direction of the Boar[north-northwest]. 方角の名. ほぼ北北西. **亥の刻** the Hour of the Boar[9-11 p.m.] 午後10時頃(およびその前後2時間). **亥年** the Year of the Boar. **亥年生まれ** (be) born in the Year of the Boar.

い【藺】 ⇨藺草

いあい(どう)【居合(道)】 *iai*(*do*); the martial art of quick drawing one's sword from a squat, slashing one's opponent all in one motion and sheathing the sword skillfully. うずくまり姿勢から刀を抜き, すばやく (in one stroke)相手に切りつけて (cutting down), 巧みに鞘に納める武芸. ¶**居合抜き** drawing one's sword while squatting and cutting down one's opponent in one motion. (居座りながら刀を抜き, すばやく相手を切り倒す)

いいだこ【飯蛸】〔魚〕a small[midget] octopus; an ocellated octopus. 煮付けやおでんの種に用いる. ⇨たこ

いえい【遺影】 a photograph or portrait of a deceased person. 故人の写真 (picture)または肖像画. ⇨葬儀

いえもと【家元】 the *iemoto*. ❶〈宗家〉the head family of a school; the representative family of a school. The *iemoto* is the main family associated with schools of the traditional performing arts, such as the tea ceremony, the flower arrangement, Noh and kyogen plays. 華道や茶道また能楽や狂言などの芸道の流派と深く関連する家系. ¶**華道の家元** the head family of a flower arrangement school. **茶道の家元** the head family of a tea ceremony school.
❷〈当主〉the hereditary headmaster of a school. He/She maintains his/ her particular traditional art of the school and passes it on to the next generations by transmitting the correct methods of that school. He/She grants licenses to his/her pupils who complete courses of instruction. 伝統的な特殊芸を固持し (consolidates), その流儀の正統技法を伝えながら, その流派を統率する. 伝授修了者には免許状を与える. ¶**華道[茶道]の家元** the hereditary headmaster of a school of the flower arrangement[tea ceremony]. **能[歌舞伎]の家元** the hereditary headmaster of a school of the Noh play[kabuki play].

【家元制度】 the *iemoto* system. It is a monopolized system of licensing teachers by a school that practices a traditional art. 芸道を実施する流派によって教員免許を授与する独占的制度.

いおり【庵】 ⇨庵

いか【烏賊】〔魚〕a squid(⊛ ~, ~s); a cuttlefish; a devilfish. ⇨ほたるいか. ¶**イカの足** squid arms[tentacles] (げそ: 下足). **イカの甲** a cuttlebone; a squid[cuttlefish] bone. **イカの墨** squid[cuttlefish] ink.
〔料理〕**イカ燻製** smoked cuttlefish[squid]. ☆酒のつまみとして食す. **イカの糸造り** raw squid[cuttlefish] sliced into thin strips. ☆「イカ素麺」ともいう. ⇨糸造り. **イカ刺し** *sashimi* of squid[cuttlefish]; slices

of raw squid; sliced raw squid. **イカ素麺** long and thin (noodle-shaped) strips of raw squid[cuttlefish]. They are eaten by dipping in *wasabi*[horseradish] and *shoyu*[soy sauce]. ☆「イカの糸造り」「イカの細造り」ともいう. **イカの沖漬け** raw squid[cuttlefish] seasoned in *shoyu*[soy sauce]. ⇨沖漬け. **イカの塩辛** salted and fermented squid[cuttlefish] guts; strips of squid preserved in salted entrails. **イカ飯** simmered squid[cuttlefish] stuffed with steamed rice. ☆北海道の郷土料理.

いがい【貽貝】〔貝〕a (sea) mussel. 食用の海産二枚貝.「ムールガイ」「ムラサキイガイ」ともいう.

いかどっくり【烏賊徳利】a *sake* bottle made from a dried squid[cuttlefish]. ⇨いか

いかなご【玉筋魚】〔魚〕a sand eel; a sand lance[launce]. ☆「チリメンジャコ」は関西ではイカナゴから, 関東ではイワシから作る. 幼魚は佃煮にする.

いカメラ【胃カメラ】a gastrocamera; a (gastro)fiberscope(内視鏡).

いがやき【伊賀焼き】Iga ceramic ware (produced in the Iga region of Mie Prefecture).

いかんそくたい【衣冠束帯】❶〈古代〉a formal dress of courtiers; a formal court costume and brimless headgear worn by nobles in the traditional fashion. 衣装と冠[烏帽子]をかぶる貴人・宮廷人の正装. ⇨束帯 / 烏帽子 ❷〈現在〉a traditional court dress[costume and brimless headgear] worn by the male members of the Imperial Family or by Shinto priests. 宮中祭事の際に男性の諸皇族, また神社界では神職が着用する. ⇨束帯

いきづくり【活き造り・生き作り】fresh slices of live raw fish arranged to look lifelike on a big platter; sliced raw fish arranged in the shape of the original fish on a large platter; sliced fish prepared while still alive and served in its natural form. Sliced fish is laid on a plate with its head and tail fin, looking as if it were[was] still alive. 生きたままの魚を薄く切って, 実物そっくりに[もとの姿に]大皿に盛り付ける. 皿の上に刻まれた魚の頭と尾ひれをそえ, あたかも生きているかのように盛り付ける (arrange(d) to make the fish appear alive).「活け造り」「活け盛り」ともいう. ⇨洗い / 伊勢海老の生き造り

いぐさ【藺草】〔植物〕a rush (often used to weave *tatami* covers). 畳の表を編むのに用いる. 単に「藺」ともいう.

イクラ ❶〈成熟卵〉salmon roe(サケの成熟卵); trout roe(マスの成熟卵). ☆ロシア語の魚卵 (ikra)から由来. ❷〔食品〕salted salmon roe. ⇨さけ. ¶**イクラ卸し** salmon roe with grated Japanese radish. 〔料理〕**イクラ丼** salmon rice bowl; a bowl of rice topped with salmon roe.

いけ【池】a pond; a pool(小さい池). ¶**猿沢池**(奈良県) Sarusawa Pond (that has the reflection of the five-story pagoda cast on its surface). ⇨湖 / 沼(地)

いけうお【活け魚・生け魚】fish and shellfish kept alive in a restaurant's tank[pool]. ⇨生け簀

いけす【生け簀・生洲】a fish preserve; a fish tank of the restaurant (used for keeping fish alive). レストランなどで魚介類を一時的に生かしておく所. ☆川にある箱型の「生け簀」は a live-box. 漁船にある「生け簀」は a well. 養魚池の「生け簀」は a fishpond.

いけばな【生け花・活け花】〔華道〕*ikebana*; (the Japanese art of) flower arrangement; (the traditional Japanese art of) arranging cut flowers and branches. Three types of natural stems[flowers and branches] are

arranged in a triangular open space called "ten-chi-jin"[heaven, earth and mankind]. 「天・地・人」という三角形の生け方がある．☆主として「盛花」(pile-up style arrangement)と「瓶花 / 投げ入れ」(free-style arrangement)がある．⇨盛花 / 瓶花 (小原流) / 投げ入れ(草月流 / 池坊流)．☆「生けた花」は arranged flowers; flowers arranged in a vase[bowl].

イケメン a good-looking[handsome] man; an attractive man;〈米俗〉a hunk.

いご【囲碁】 *igo*; (the game of) Japanese *go*. ⇨碁．¶**囲碁棋士** a professional *go* player. **囲碁名人戦** a battle to decide the grand champion in *go* game.

いこう【衣桁】 a *kimono* rack; a rack[stand] for hanging a *kimono*. 着物をかけるための和風家具．☆着物にしわをつけず，柄を美しく見せる役目．⇨衣紋掛け❷

いざかや【居酒屋】 an *izakaya*; a Japanese-style bar[pub]; a bar; a saloon;㋐ a tavern;㋑ a pub; a public house. An *izakaya* is a small counter-style drinking place where drinks[*sake* and *shochu*] and foods[*sashimi* and *yakitori*] are prepared in front of customers. 顧客の面前で飲食物を出す田舎風の飲み屋．日本では「赤提灯」「酒場」「一杯飲み屋」「縄のれん」などの呼称がある．⇨飲み屋

いさき【伊佐木】〔魚〕a grunt; a grunter. 夏が旬．淡白な味で，刺身・洗い・塩焼きなどに用いる．

いざよい【十六夜】 the sixteenth night of a lunar month(陰暦16日の夜)；the night of August 16 on the lunar calendar(陰暦8月16日の夜)．¶**十六夜の月** the moon on the night after the full moon; the moon on the night of August 16 on the lunar calendar.

いさりび【漁り火】a light on a fishing boat.

いしうす【石臼】 a stone mill(ひき臼)；a stone mortar(つき臼).

いしがきいちご【石垣いちご】 stone-wall-grown strawberries; strawberries grown along stone walls on sunny slopes. ⇨いちご

いしがめ【石亀】 a Japanese pond turtle. 日本産の淡水ガメ．⇨かめ

いしかりなべ【石狩鍋】 a one-pot dish of salmon and vegetables cooked with *miso*[bean paste]; a dish of salmon and vegetables cooked in a pot with *miso* broth. 鮭と野菜を味噌で煮た鍋料理．北海道バターを加える郷土料理．

いしがれい【石鰈】〔魚〕a stone flounder. 小型は塩焼きやから揚げ，大型は刺身などに用いる．⇨かれい

いしずりえ【石摺絵】 a stone rubbing-like print.

いしじぞう【石地蔵】 a stone statue[image] of *jizo*. *Jizo* usually holds a Buddhist priest's jingling staff in one hand and a gemstone in the other. *Jizo* is often found on the roadside, wearing red bibs around his neck. 片方の手には錫杖，もう片方の手には宝珠(jewel ball)を持つ．首まわりに赤いよだれ掛けをした姿で，路上でよくみかける．⇨地蔵 / 子安地蔵 /錫杖

いしだたみ【石畳】 a stone pavement; a stone floor[flooring]; cobble paving(丸石を敷いた)；flagstones(敷石)．¶**石畳の小道**[**道路**] a stone-paved path[road]; a path[road] paved with stones.

いしだん【石段】 (a flight of) stone steps (一続きの石段)．¶**山頂の神社までの石段** stone steps to reach the shrine on the mountaintop.

いしどうろう【石灯籠】 a stone lantern. It is often placed in the shrine or temple precincts and in Japanese-style landscape gardens. 通常神社の境内または日本式造景庭園などにある．⇨灯籠 / 春日大社節分万燈籠 / 春日大社中元万燈籠

い

い

いじめ【苛め】 bullying (the weak); tyrannizing (over the weak); tormenting; teasing; ⊛ hazing. ¶苛め自殺 bullying-related suicide. 苛めっ子 a bully; a tormentor. 苛められっ子 a bullied child; a child constantly harassed by a bully. 学校［学級］での苛め bullying at school[in the classroom]. 学校での苛め自殺 school bullies following students' suicide. 集団苛め group harassment.

いしやきいも【石焼(き)芋】 stone-baked sweet potatoes; sweet potatoes roasted on[in] hot pebbles fired from underneath. 下から加熱した小石で焼いた(baked)さつまいも. ⇨焼(き)芋

いしやきざかな【石焼(き)魚】 fish broiled on hot[heated] stones.

いしやきどうふ【石焼(き)豆腐】 tofu[bean curd] roasted on hot[heated] stones.

いしゃりょう【慰謝料】 consolation money; compensation; a solatium.

いしん【維新】 the (Meiji) Restoration; renovation(刷新). ⇨明治維新

いじんかん【異人館】 a Western-style residence (built for Westerners in the Meiji period).

いしんでんしん【以心伝心】 mental telepathy; tacit understanding; communication of thought without the medium of words; What the mind thinks, the heart transmits. 暗黙の了解.

いずし【飯鮨】 rice, vegetables and fish preserved until well fermented. ご飯・野菜・魚をよく発酵するまで漬け込んだすし.「秋田のハタハタずし」, 金沢の「カブラずし」, 北海道の「サケずし」などがある.

いずものかみ【出雲の神】 Izumo Shinto God[Deity] (enshrined in Izumo Grand Shrine in Shimane Prefecture). *Izumo no kami* is known as the god of marriage who presides over matchmaking of a young couple. 島根県の出雲大社に祀られている神(大国主命). 若いカップルの縁結びを主宰する. 通称「縁結びの神」. ⇨縁結びの神

いせえび【伊勢海老】〔魚〕 a lobster; a rock lobster; a spiny lobster; ⊛ a crayfish; ⊛ a crawfish. ☆元来三重県の伊勢湾で多く産するのが由来. 祝事(結婚・長寿・御節料理など)の高級食材. ⇨海老

〔料理〕**伊勢海老の活き造り** fresh slices of live spiny lobster arranged in the shell. ⇨活き造り

いせき【遺跡】 remains(過去から残された物); ruins(廃墟の意味が強い); archaeological sites.☆すべて複数形で用いる. ¶登呂遺跡(静岡県) the Toro remains; the prehistoric archaeological sites at Toro. 吉野ケ里遺跡(佐賀県) the Yoshinogari remains[ruins].

いせまいり【伊勢参り】 a pilgrimage to Ise Grand Shrine. Grand Shrine of Ise consists of the *Naiku*, the Inner Shrine, and the *Geku*, the Outer Shrine. The Inner Shrine is dedicated to Amaterasu Omikami and contains the Sacred Mirror, one of the Three Imperial Regalia as an object of worship. 伊勢神宮には内宮(皇大神宮)と外宮(豊受大神宮)がある. 内宮の祭神は天照大神で, ご神体は三種の神器の一つである「八咫鏡」. ⇨三種の神器/神体

いそぎんちゃく【磯巾着】〔魚〕 a sea anemone; an actinia.

いそしぎ【磯鴫】〔鳥〕 a sandpiper. ⇨しぎ

いそべやきもち【磯辺焼き餅】 a toasted rice cake seasoned with *shoyu*[soy sauce] and wrapped in a dried *nori*[laver] sheet. 醤油で味をつけてこんがり焼き (grilled), 海苔で包んだ餅.「磯辺巻き」ともいう.

いそりょうり【磯料理】 a seafood meal[dish]

いたこ an *itako*; a medium between the living and the dead. An *itako* medium summons the dead spirit and deliver messages in her voice (*kuchiyose*) in the Shimokita Peninsula. 生者と死者の仲介者 (mediator). 下北半島に見られる「口寄せ」（死者の霊を呼びその声を聞かせる）をする霊媒[巫女]. ⇨市子

いたずらでんわ【いたずら電話】 a prank [crank, nuisance] phone call; an obscene phone call（わいせつな電話）.「イタ電」ともいう. ⇨迷惑電話

いたち【鼬】〔動物〕 a weasel; a Japanese mink.

いたちごっこ【鼬ごっこ】 (play) a rat race; (play) a cat-and-mouse game.

いたど【板戸】 a wooden sliding door [shutter]; a wood paneled door[shutter].

いたどこ【板床】 a decorative alcove with a plank floor. 板張りの床の間.

いたどり【虎杖】〔植物〕a knotweed. タデ科の多年草. 若芽は食用. 若い茎は天ぷらや酢の物また煮物などに使う. 根は薬用.

いたのま【板の間】〈床〉 a wooden floor;〈部屋〉a room with a wooden floor.

いたのまかせぎ【板の間稼ぎ】 a bathhouse thief. 風呂屋での盗人.

いたば【板場】〈調理場〉 the kitchen (in a restaurant);〈料理人〉a cook; a chef. ⇨板前

いたぶき【板葺き】 a shingle roofing. ¶**板葺きの家** a shingle-roofed house. **板葺き屋根** a shingle roof.

いたまえ【板前】 a cook; a chef (in a traditional Japanese cuisine).

いために【炒め煮】 braised dish; food first dried and then simmered in broth. ¶**キャベツの炒め煮** braised cabbage.

いためもの【炒め物】 stir-fried[pan-fried] food; sauté(e)d food. ¶**肉と野菜の炒め物** stir-fried meat with vegetables.

いたわさ【板山葵】 slices of *kamaboko*[fish-paste cake] served with grated *wasabi* [horseradish] and *shoyu*[soy sauce]; sliced *kamaboko* served with *wasabi* and *shoyu*.

薄切りの板かまぼこに, おろしわさびと醤油を添えた料理. 酒の肴の一品.「いたわび」の略. ☆「いた」は板付きのかまぼこの意

いちい【一位・水松】〔植物〕 a yew; a Japanese yew (tree). 墓地に植える常緑樹. 実は食用. 材は「笏」を作る.

いちこ【市子・巫子】 a (spiritualist) medium (霊媒)(® mediums); a sorceress; a channeler. 神や死者などの霊の様子を語る巫女 (shrine maiden).「口寄せ」などともいう. ⇨いたこ（東北地方の巫女）

いちご【苺】〔植物〕 a strawberry. ⇨石垣いちご. ¶**野いちご** a wild strawberry. **いちごミルク** strawberries with milk; strawberry-flavored milk. **いちご大福** a soft round rice cake stuffed with strawberry. ⇨大福(餅)

いちごいちえ【一期一会】 unique meeting only once in a lifetime. Every single encounter never repeats in a lifetime. Every encounter is an once-in-a-lifetime opportunity. 生涯に一度だけ会うこと. 茶道では「出会い」(an encounter)また「心の交流」(a shared sense of communication[rapport] between the host and the guests)を大切にし, 主人は床の間の掛け軸や活け花また茶碗に心を込めてもてなす. 客はそれに謝意を表す. ☆『茶道の教訓』Treasure every meeting, for it will never recur.「どの出会いも大事にしなさい. また会うこともないでしょう」

いちげいにゅうし【一芸入試】 an entrance examination for a college[university] given to examinees[applicants] with non-academic abilities; a special admission for students who have outstanding merit or record achievements.

いちじく【無花果】〔植物〕〈実〉a fig;〈木〉a fig tree;〈葉〉a fig leaf. 果実の内部にある粒々が花である.

いちじゅういっさい【一汁一菜】 one dish

い

with one soup; a simple meal of rice, soup and a single dish. A simple meal comprises a bowl of soup and one dish in addition to rice. 菜も汁も各一種類の食事．ご飯に汁物と菜からなる簡素な食事．⇨会席料理

いちじゅうさんさい【一汁三菜】 three dishes with one soup; a simple meal of rice, soup and three dishes. A simple meal comprises a bowl of soup and three side dishes (sliced raw fish, broiled and boiled foods) in addition to rice. ご飯，汁物と三種の菜(刺身・焼物・煮物)からなる食事．⇨会席料理

いちぜん【一膳】❶〈一杯〉a bowl. ¶**飯一膳** a bowl of rice.

❷〈一対〉a pair. ¶**箸一膳** a pair of chopsticks.

【一膳飯】 a bowl of rice offered to the deceased. 故人に供する飯．⇨葬儀

【一膳飯屋】 a cheap restaurant; a hash house[establishment]; 米 an eatery. 大衆食堂．

いちにんまえ【一人前】 a single serving;〈一人分〉a portion for one person;〈食べ物の〉one helping (of salad). ¶**一人前のすし** one portion of *sushi*[vinegared rice]; a single serving of *sushi*. **一人前の刺身** one helping of *sashimi*[sliced raw fish]. **一人前の料理** a meal for one person.

いちのぜん【一の膳】 the main course of a traditional Japanase-style dinner. It is served at the beginning of a formal Japanese meal. 正式の日本料理の膳立てで，最初に出す膳．「本膳」ともいう．二の膳，三の膳が続く．⇨本膳料理

いちのとり【一の酉】❶〈日取〉the first Day of the Cock in November.

❷〈市場〉a market[fair] held on the first Day of Cock in November. ⇨酉の市

いちのみやけんかまつり【一宮けんか祭り】 the Rage Festival at Ichinomiya.（4月）．⇨付記(1)「日本の祭り」

いちばんせんじ【一番煎じ】 the first brew [infusion] of tea.

いちばんだし【一番出し】 the best stock; primary soup stock made from dried bonito and *kombu*[kelp]. 鰹節と昆布で最初に引いた出し汁．吸い物にする．

いちばんちゃ【一番茶】 the first pick of tea.

いちぼくぼり【一木彫】 a carving from one block; a sculpture carved out of a single block of wood.「一木造り」ともいう．

いちまつもよう【市松模様】 checks; a check(ed) pattern; a checkerboard[英 chessboard] pattern. It is a checked[米 checkered, 英 chequered] pattern arranged with black and white square forms alternately. 黒と白の四角形を交互に(by turns)並べた碁盤じま模様．☆江戸時代．歌舞伎役者の佐野川市松がこの模様の衣装を着たのが呼称の由来．

いちみとうがらし【一味唐辛子】 Chili powder; ground red Chili pepper; chilled red pepper powder (unmixed with other spices). 赤唐辛子を粉末にした香辛料．他のスパイスとは混合していない．

いちもん【一門】❶〈同じ一族〉a clan; a family; one's kinsfolk. ¶**平家一門** the Taira clan; the Tairas. **林家一門** the Hayashiya family.

❷〈同じ宗派・流派〉the whole sect; a school. **❸**〈相撲〉a (stable master's) faction.

いちやづけ【一夜漬け】❶〈漬物〉vegetables pickled overnight; greens salted overnight; pickles made overnight. 一夜漬けた野菜．「即席漬け」ともいう．⇨浅漬

❷〈勉強〉 overnight cramming; cramming (for an exam) overnight.

いちやぼし【一夜干し】 fish[vegetables] dried overnight. 一晩干した魚[野菜]．⇨日干し / 陰干し

いちょう【銀杏・公孫樹】〔植物〕a gingko [ginkgo]（複 ~s, ~es); a maidenhair tree. ⇨

銀杏

いちょうぎりにんじん【銀杏切り人参】 carrots cut into quarter-rounds (that look like the leaves of the gingko tree). (銀杏の葉形のように)四つ割にして切った人参.

いちょうまげ【銀杏髷】 men's hairdo in which the back hair is worn puffed and looped in half circles suggesting a gingko leaf. (江戸時代中期に見られる)男性髪型で，後部にたばねた髪をふくらませ，銀杏の葉形のように二つに分けて輪をつくる. ⇨大銀杏(相撲)

いちりんざし【一輪挿し】〔華道〕 a single-flower vase; a vase for one flower.

いっかんばり【一閑張り】 (a kind of) lacquered papier-mâché (figure); papier-mâché (figure) coated with lacquer. 物に紙を重ねてはり固め，漆を塗ったもの. ☆江戸時代の創始者飛来一閑にちなみ，この名がつく. 技法は，粘土で形を取った後，その上から和紙数百枚ほどを貼り重ね厚みを作り中の粘土を取り外す. その和紙の上から漆を塗り重ね，その上に金箔や銀箔で仕上げる. 例「唐津くんち」(11月). ⇨付記(1)「日本の祭り」

いっき【一揆】 a riot; a revolt; an uprising. 地侍や農民が団結して権力者に対して実力行使にでる. ☆「土一揆」(土民と呼ばれる農民による一揆. 1428年の「正長の土一揆」など)と「国一揆」(国人による一揆：1458年の「山城の国一揆」など)がある. ⇨一向一揆

いっきのみ【一気飲み】 emptying a large glass (of beer) without a pause; drinking down a mug (of beer) in one gulp; quaffing down alcohol in a single gulp. ㊥ chugalugging. ☆「乾杯!(一気に飲み干そう)」は Bottoms up!

いつくしま(じんじゃ)かんげんさい【厳島(神社)管弦祭】 the Music Festival of Itsukushima Shrine. (7月). ⇨付記(1)「日本の祭り」. ⇨宮島管弦祭/管弦

いっこういっき【一向一揆】 the *Ikko* uprising [revolt]; peasant farmers of Buddhist zealots rising against the government. Buddhist priests and adherents of the *Jodo-Sinshu* sect of Buddhism broke down the army of the governor (*shugo*) of Kaga Province and established autonomous rule there. 浄土真宗(一向宗)の僧侶や熱心な信徒である農民が国に対して実力行使をなし，加賀の守護勢を打破し，自治支配を確立する. ☆1488年の加賀一向一揆. ⇨一揆

いっこだて【一戸建】 a single house; a detached house; an independent housing.

いっこん【一献】 ❶〈一杯の酒〉(offer) a cup of *sake*.
❷〈小酒宴〉(hold) a small drinking party.

いっさいきょう【一切経】 a complete collection of Buddhist scriptures and all the sacred writings of Buddhism and their commentary. 仏教経典とすべての仏教聖典(経・律・論の三蔵を指す)とその注解書の叢書. ⇨大蔵経

いっしきおおちょうちんまつり【一色大提灯まつり】 the Big Lantern Festival at Isshiki Town. (8月). ⇨付記(1)「日本の祭り」

いっしゅうき【一周忌】 the first memorial anniversary of a person's death. ⇨法事

いっしんきょう【一神教】 monotheism; monotheistic religion. ⇔多神教

いっとうぼり【一刀彫り】〈彫ること〉carving with a single knife;〈技法〉technique of wood carving using a single knife;〈彫り物〉sculpture carved with a single knife;〈作品〉simple wood carving.

いっとうりゅう【一刀流】 Japanese fencing with a single[two-handed] sword. ¶北辰一刀流 the single-sword school of Hokushin.

いっぱ【一派】〈宗派〉 a sect; the denomination;〈集団〉a group;〈派閥〉a faction.

い

いっぱんさんが【一般参賀】 congratulatory greetings to the Imperial Family by the general public[crowds of well-wishers]. The Imperial Palace grounds are open to the public to offer their congratulations to the Imperial Family on New Year's Day (January 2) and on the Emperor's Birthday (February 23). ☆「新年一般参賀」(New Year Greeting by the general public) は皇居のバルコニーにて新年の挨拶を受ける. ⇨参賀

いっぽんづくり【一本造り (仏像の)】 carving (of Buddhist statue) made from a single tree trunk. ⇔寄木造り

いでんしくみかえしょくひん【遺伝子組換え食品】 genetically modified organism food(s).

いとあやつり【糸操り】〈操り人形〉 manipulation of string puppets[marionettes].

いとこんにゃく【糸蒟蒻】 thin-formed *konnyaku* [devil's tongue] noodles; noodle-like thin strips made from the starch of *konnyaku*. 糸のように細く切ったこんにゃく (*konnyaku* in shreds). ☆長さ15cmほどの糸状に加工する. さらに細く切ったものを「しらたき」という. ⇨しらたき

いとすぎ【糸杉】〔植物〕 a cypress(tree). ヒノキ科の高木. ⇨すぎ

いとづくり【糸造り】 thinly sliced *sashimi* [raw fish]; thin strips of *sashimi*; raw seafood sliced into thin strips. (イカや魚肉などの身を) 細長く切ってつくる刺身. 「細造り」ともいう. ¶イカの糸造り thin slices of raw squid.

いどばたかいぎ【井戸端会議】 lively and lengthy (housewives') gossip session.

いとやなぎ【糸柳】〔植物〕 a weeping willow. 別称「しだれ柳」. ⇨やなぎ

いな【鯔】〔魚〕 a gray mullet. ボラの幼魚. ⇨ぼら

いなおりごうとう【居直り強盗】 a potential-ly violent sneak-thief; a sneak-thief who threatens violence when detected. 見とがめられて(cornered)急に強盗に変わるこそどろ (robber).

いなかに【田舎煮】 country-style dishes of vegetables boiled in fish broth heavily laced with *shoyu*[soy sauce].

いなかりょうり【田舎料理】 country-style cooking; rural dishes.

いなご【蝗・稲子】〔虫〕 a locust; a rice grass-hopper. ⇨ばった. ¶蝗の佃煮 locusts roasted and boiled in sweetened *shoyu*[soy sauce].

いなだ【鰍】〔魚〕 a young yellowtail. ブリの幼魚(全長40cm前後). ☆関東での呼び名. 関西では「はまち」という. 近年では養殖物を「ハマチ」, 天然物を「イナダ」ともいう. ⇨ぶり

いなり【稲荷】 the *Inari* god; the god of grains[cereals]; a local guardian god. *Inari* was originally the god[deity] of good harvest, later worshipped as the guardian deity of an area as well as the deity of commerce. *Inari* is also commonly the fox deity. 穀物の神. その土地の守護神. 元来は五穀豊穣の神, 後年その土地[地域] また商業の守護神. 俗説では「狐の神」を指す.

【稲荷神社】 the *Inari* shrine; a tutelary shrine guarding the local people. The *Inari* shrine is guarded by a pair of white stone-carved statues of foxes, messengers of the *Inari* shrine. There are many vermilion-painted *torii* gates leading to the sanctuary in the shrine precincts. 地域人を守護する氏神神社. 稲荷神社の使者である1対の白い石造の狐に護衛されている. 神社の境内には本殿に通ずる朱塗り (魔除けの意)の鳥居が多数ある. 京都の伏見稲荷神社が有名. ⇨狛犬

いなりずし【稲荷鮨】 a *sushi*[vinegared rice] ball wrapped up in a pouch[bag] of *aburage*[deep-fried bean curd]. It is mixed with various ingredients such as shredded carrots, dried *shiitake* mushrooms, and white parched sesame in the rice. It is stuffed in a pouch of *aburage* seasoned with sugar, *mirin*[sweetened *sake*] and *shoyu*[soy sauce]. 袋状 (bag)の油揚げの中に酢飯を詰めたもの．ご飯に刻み人参・椎茸・白胡麻などの食材を混ぜ，砂糖・味醂・醤油で味付けした袋状の油揚げに詰める．☆「稲荷」は a fox deity(狐の神)．「油揚げ」は狐の大好物である(俗説)．⇨油揚げ

いぬ【犬】〔動物〕a dog；〈雌犬〉a bitch；〈猟犬〉a hound；〈子犬〉a puppy；a pup；a whelp．☆「小さい犬」は a small[little] dog．¶犬張り子 a papier-mâché dog (used as a toy)．

いぬ【戌】 the Dog, one[the eleventh] of the 12 animals of the Chinese zodiac. 十二支の第十一．⇨十二支

¶戌の方 the Direction of the Dog[west-northwest]. 方角の名．ほぼ西北西．戌の刻 the Hour of the Dog[7-9 p.m.] 午後8時頃(およびその前後約2時間)．戌年 the Year of the Dog. 戌年生まれ (be)born in the Year of the Dog.

いぬくぼう【犬公方】 the Dog Shogun. *Inukubo* is the nickname of the fifth Tokugawa Tsunayoshi shogun who enacted Animal Protection Law. ⇨生類憐みの令

いね【稲】〔植物〕a rice plant. ☆英語の rice は稲，米，御飯のすべてを指す．¶水稲 a paddy-rice plant. 陸稲 a dry-field rice plant. 稲穂 an ear of rice. 稲の苗[早苗] rice seedlings. 稲の栽培 rice cultivation.

いのしし【猪】〔動物〕a wild boar; a young wild boar(猪の子)．¶猪狩りの天城地域(静岡県) Amagi area noted for boar-hunting. ⇨亥

いのちのせんたく【命の洗濯】 recreation; refreshment; refreshing diversion.

いのちのでんわ【命の電話】 hotline for would-be suicides; crisis center.

いはい【位牌】 a (Buddhist) mortuary tablet. It is a wooden Buddhist memorial tablet [plaque] inscribed with the posthumous Buddhist name of the deceased and the date of his death. It is often kept in at the family Buddhist altar. 死者の銘板．故人の戒名と命日を記入した木製の平板[札]．家庭の仏壇に祀る．⇨戒名／葬儀．¶位牌堂 a Buddhist mortuary chapel. 先祖の位牌 an ancestral memorial tablet. 板位牌 a wooden mortuary tablet.

いはつ【衣鉢】 a Buddhist surplice and a begging bowl. (師僧から弟子に伝える) 袈裟と鉄鉢[托鉢用の鉢]．¶衣鉢を継ぐ assume the mantle of one's master; inherit[carry on] the tradition[secrets] of one's mentor.

いばら【茨・棘】〔植物〕a thorn(とげ)；a thorny shrub(とげのある潅木)；a bramble (いばら)．

いぼだい【疣鯛】〔魚〕a butterfish; a harvest fish. 別名「エボダイ」．秋が旬の白身魚.

いまがわやき【今川焼き】 a Japanese pancake containing sweetened *adzuki* bean paste; a Japanese-style muffin filled [stuffed] with sweetened *adzuki* bean paste. It is baked on an iron plate fired from underneath and usually served[eaten] hot. 小豆餡を詰めた和製パンケーキ[マフィン]．下から加熱した鉄板で焼き，通常熱いうちに出される[食べる]．☆今ではカスタードクリーム (pastry cream)なども入っている．元来江戸時代中期に神田の「今川橋」で売り出されたので商品名になった．⇨鯛焼き

いまりやき【伊万里焼】 Imari porcelain ware (produced around Arita district of Saga Prefecture and once exported from the port of Imari). 佐賀県有田地方で生産され，伊万里から輸出した．⇨有田焼

いみ【忌】 abstention（宗教的節制）；mourning（喪に服すこと）. ⇨清め

イメクラ costume-play parlor.

いも【芋・藷】a potato（ジャガ芋など）；a taro（里芋など）；a yam（山芋など）. ☆「芋（やぼったい人）」は an unrefined person；〈男〉a clod[bumpkin]. ¶薩摩芋 a sweet potato. 里芋 a Japanese taro. 長芋 a Chinese yam. 〔料理・食品〕芋飴 sweet-potato candy；candy made from sweet potatoes. 芋餡 sweet-potato paste；paste made from sweet potatoes. ⇨餡. 芋粥 rice-and-sweet-potato gruel[porridge]；rice gruel cooked with sweet potatoes. ⇨粥. 芋茎 dried stems of the taro. 芋焼酎 sweet potato *shochu*；liquor distilled from sweet potatoes and rice. ⇨焼酎. 芋田楽 taros (on bamboo skewers[spits]) broiled with *miso*[bean paste]. ⇨田楽. 芋羊羹 (a bar of) jellied sweet-potato paste；sweet potato jelly. ⇨羊羹

いもむし【芋虫】〔虫〕a green caterpillar. 幼虫.

いもり【井守】〔両〕a newt；a water lizard. イモリ科の両生類で日本固有の動物.

いやがらせでんわ【嫌がらせ電話】 a harassing telephone call；a crank call；an annoying call. ☆「いたずら電話」a prank call

いやくぶんぎょう【医薬分業】the separation of dispensary[pharmacological dispensary] from medical practice.

いやしけいおんがく【癒し系音楽】 soothing[healing] music.

いよかん【伊予柑】〔植物〕*Iyokan*；an *Iyo* orange[tangerine]. ☆「伊予」は旧国名で，現在の愛媛県. そこで栽培された柑橘（citrus *Iyo*）.

いらか【甍】 a tile(d) roof（瓦屋根）；a tile（瓦）

いらくさ【刺草】〔植物〕a nettle. 若芽は茹でるとやわらかくなるので山菜として用いる.

茎の繊維は糸・織物の原料.

いりえ【入り江】a bay（湾）；a cove（小湾）；an inlet（細長い湾）；an indentation（湾入部）. ¶狭い入り江で海と結ばれた湖 the lake connected with the sea by a narrow inlet. 99の入り江がある九十九湾（石川県）Tsukumo Bay with 99 indentations in the shoreline. ⇨浦

いりおもてやまねこ【西表山猫】〔動物〕 an Iriomote wildcat. ネコ科の哺乳動物. 沖縄県西表島に生存する. 特別天然記念物.

いりきなこ【煎り黄粉】 parched soybean flour[powder]. ⇨きなこ

いりこ【煎り子・炒り子】 small dried fish [sardines]. 雑魚を炒って干したもの. 小さい鰯などの煮干. 汁物の出し用にする. ⇨煮干し

いりこ【炒り粉】 parched rice flour. 炒った米の粉. 菓子の材料にする.

いりこ【海参・熬[煎]海鼠】 dried sea slug；dried sea cucumber；dried sea trepang. なまこの腸をとり除き，ゆでて干したもの. 「干しなまこ」ともいう. ⇨なまこ

いりごま【煎り胡麻】parched sesame. ⇨ごま

いりどり【炒り鶏】 ⇨筑前煮

いりにのさといも【煎り煮の里芋】 taro simmered in soy-flavored stock.

いりまめ【炒り豆】toasted soybeans（大豆）；roasted[parched] broad beans（そら豆）. 節分の豆まきに用いる.

いりもやづくり【入母屋造り】 a Japanese-style gabled house；a Japanese house with a gable roof. 破風の屋根がある家. ☆切妻として上部は二方へ傾斜させ，下部は四方へ傾斜させる.

いりもややね【入母屋根】a gambrel roof.

いりょうミス【医療ミス】 a medical malpractice；a medication error.

いるか【海豚】〔動物〕a dolphin；a porpoise（ネズミイルカ）. ☆動物学上の習慣として体長4m以上は「クジラ」，それ以下は「イルカ」

と呼んでいる. ⇨くじら

いれいさい【慰霊祭】a memorial service (for the war dead).

いれいひ［とう］【慰霊碑［塔］】 a war memorial; a cenotaph (built in memory of the war dead); a memorial (erected to war victims). 戦没者記念碑(遺骨を埋めた場所とは別に戦死した人を記念して建てた記念碑［塔］). ⇨原爆(原爆被爆者慰霊碑(と碑文)). ☆ cenotaphはギリシア語で「からの墓」の意.

いれずみ【刺青［入れ墨］】 a tattoo(複 tattoos); tattooing. ¶刺青師 a tattoo artist. ⇨彫物❷

いろがみ【色紙】 (a piece of) colored[fancy] paper (used in the Japanese art of folding paper). ⇨色紙

いろぐすり【色ぐすり】 color glaze. 陶磁器に用いる. ⇨上薬/釉薬

いろとめそで【色留袖】 a light[single]-colored formal silk *kimono* for women. *Iro-tomesode* has one, three or five family crests on a *kimono*, depending on the degree of formality. It is worn by both married and unmarried women on ceremonial occasions such as wedding receptions and formal parties. 女性盛装用の(黒以外の)単色の絹製着物. 正式の度合いにもよるが1つ, 3つ, または5つの家紋がほどこされている. 既婚者または未婚者が結婚披露宴や公式パーティーなどの儀式に着用する. ⇨留袖

いろなおし【色直し】⇨お色直し

いろは【伊呂波】 the *iroha*; the Japanese syllabary (in the traditional order); the *Iroha* syllable[Japanese alphabet] corresponding to the English ABCs. The *iroha* covers all 47 syllables of the Japanese phonetical system. The phrase *iroha* is used to refer to a first step, just as the English "ABC" is. 日本語の音節表[音節文字表]. 「いろは」には日本語音標組織の全47字がある. 「いろは」の句は, ちょうど英語の「ABC」のように最初の段階であることを言及するために用いる. ☆比喩的にthe Japanese version of the ABCともいえる. ⇨アイウエオ

【いろは歌留多】〈カード〉the *Iroha* cards: 〈遊ぶ〉 the *Iroha* game; a pack ([❋ deck] of) cards comprising 47 pairs of cards to be played as a card-matching game. One pack of cards consists of two decks, 47 Japanese proverb cards (each of which begins with a short Japanese phrase) to be read and 47 picture cards (which illustrates the proverb and the first *kana* of the phrase is written in the upper corner) to be picked up. The winner ends up with the most picture cards. 札合わせの遊びとして47枚一対の遊びカードから構成されている一組の札. 一揃いの札は2組から成り, 読み札「文字札」の「**日本の諺札**」(各札は短い日本語句で始まる)と取り札の「**絵札**」(諺を説明し, 上部の片隅に読み札の日本語句の最初のカナを記載)がある. 一番多くの絵札を取った者が勝つ (The player who collects[captures] the most pairs wins.)

【いろは歌】 the *Iroha* poem; the Japanese syllabary poem. Poems consists of all 47 syllables covering all the *kana* of the Japanese phonetic alphabet. 日本の音節文字表[字音表]の詩歌. 日本語音標組織にあるすべてのカナを含む全47字がある. ☆「いろはにほへと…」で始まる手習い歌 (the first learning).

いろはざか【いろは坂】 the Iroha(zaka) slope. The Iroha slope is a steep zigzagging road with numerous hairpin bends in Nikko. 日光にあるつづら折の険しいジグザグとした道路.

いろむじ【色無地】 an unpatterned *kimono*; a *kimono* fabric of a solid color without a

い

colored pattern.

いろり【囲炉裏】 an *irori*; a sunken hearth; an open hearth sunk in the floor; Japanese-style fireplace without a chimney. An *irori* is an open hearth cut[dug] square into the floor in the center of a room to make a fire. A pothook (*jizai-kagi*) suspending from the ceiling hangs down over the middle of the sunken hearth. くぼんだ炉床. 床上にくぼんだ炉. 煙突のない暖炉. 部屋の中央の床を四角に切り[掘り]抜いて, 火を燃やす所. 囲炉裏の中央(center)には自在鉤が吊るされている. ☆通常は90cm四方または180cm四方の大きさがある. ⇨自在鉤

いわいざけ【祝い酒】 a celebratory drink.

いわいばし【祝い箸】 (a pair of) special festive chopsticks; (a pair of) chopsticks used on festive occasions.

いわおこし【岩おこし】 cake made of pop rice. It is made of finely crushed rice, ginger and sesame hardened with starch syrup. 米を砕いて, 生姜. 胡麻. 水あめで固めた菓子. ☆江戸時代に大阪で縁起のよい食べ物 (auspicious food:「身[家・国]を起こす」)として広がる. 大阪の名物. ⇨粟おこし

いわし【鰯】〔魚〕a sardine(真鰯); a sprat(小鰯); a pilchard. ニシン科の魚. ⇨カタクチイワシ/畳いわし/ちりめんじゃこ/煮干し/目刺し

〔食品〕鰯のオイル漬け sardines in oil. 鰯の陰干し[日干し] sardines dried in the shade[in the sun]. 鰯の缶詰 canned[(英) tinned] sardines; a can[tin] of sardines.

〔料理〕鰯のつみれ汁 sardine dumplings soup; soup cooked with boiled dumplings of ground sardines. ⇨つみれ. 鰯の味醂干し dried *mirin*-seasoned sardines; dried sardines seasoned with *mirin*, *shoyu* and sugar. 鰯の梅干煮 simmered sardines with pickled plums

いわたおび【岩田帯】a maternity *obi*[supportive band of cloth]; an obstetrical binder. It is worn from the fifth month of pregnancy to protect the fetus[unborn baby]. 妊婦の帯. 胎児 (fetus)保護のため妊娠5か月頃から腹に巻く. ☆「戌の日」に巻く習慣がある. ⇨帯祝い

いわたけ【岩茸】〔植物〕 a rock tripe; (a kind of) lichen; mushrooms found deep in the mountains. 岩壁などに生えるキノコ (mushroom). 和え物や酢の物に調理する.

いわつばめ【岩燕】〔鳥〕 a (Japanese) house martin. ⇨つばめ

いわな【岩魚】〔魚〕a char; (英) a charr; a Japanese char; a mountain trout. 山間の清流にすむサケ科の淡水魚. 初夏が旬. 塩焼き・から揚げなどにする.

～いん【～院】 a temple; a monastery(男性用); a nunnery(女性用). ¶寂光院(京都府) Jakko(in) Temple. ⇨寺/堂

いん【院】❶〈上皇・法皇の尊称〉an ex-emperor; a retired emperor;〈皇太后〉the Empress Dowager. ¶後鳥羽院 the ex-Emperor Go-Toba; the former Emperor Go-Toba. ⇨院政

❷〈戒名に添える号〉the suffix (-*in*) used in posthumous names of the deceased. It is inscribed in the Buddhist memorial tablet. 死者の戒名に用いる接尾辞. 位牌に明記する. ⇨位牌

いんかん【印鑑】〈印章〉a personal seal;〈押した印鑑〉a personal seal mark. It has the engraving of one's family name in a circle or square. It is used to identify oneself legally or stamp on documents. 丸型または角型で姓名が刻んである. 法的な身分証明として, あるいは書類に押印するために使用する.「判子」ともいう. ☆「認印」(an ordinary seal for everyday use) と「公印[実印]」(an official seal registered seal in the local government) がある. ⇨判子/実印

/認印/三文判. ¶**印鑑入れ** an *inkan* case; a case for a personal seal. ⇨朱肉. **印鑑証明** a seal certification; a certified seal registration [impression]; a registration of one's seal impressed by local authorities. **印鑑証明書** a seal-registration certificate; a certificate verifying registration of one's seal impression. **印鑑登録[届け]** the legal registration of one's official seal[seal impression]. **印鑑登録証** a personal seal registration card.

いんげん(**まめ**)【隠元(豆)】〔植物〕㋐ kidney beans; ㋑ haricot beans; ㋻ navy beans; string beans(さやいんげん). マメ科の一年草. 甘納豆や餡, また煮豆などに用いる. ☆中国明の僧・隠元が日本に伝えたことから出た語. 英名は kidney(腎臓)の形状に似ていることからの呼称. ⇨まめ
〔料理〕隠元の胡麻和え kidney beans with sesame dressing.

いんご【隠語】 secret language; jargon(of a trade); (academic) cant; (robbers') argot. ⇨符丁(すし屋の隠語)

いんせい【院政】 *insei*; cloister government; rule by a retired[cloistered] emperor. *Insei* is the government administered by an ex-emperor after his abdication and surpassed the Imperial Court in real power in ancient Japan. 天皇に代わって, 上皇(または法皇)が退位後も統治し, その御所で実権を握った政治体制のこと. ☆1086年白河上皇が創始者. 1840年に廃止された. ⇨法皇/上皇

いんぜん【院宣】 orders from an ex-emperor. 上皇の命令.

いんぞう[**いんそう**]【印相】 ❶〈仏像〉 the symbolic finger gesture of Buddha's hands. The Buddha makes sacred signs with his hands and fingers. 仏・菩薩が手や指で結ぶ印(gestures)の形.
❷〈印章〉 one's fortune[good or bad luck]

as told in one's personal seal. Fortune is told on the form of the characters on the seal. 判子に現れる吉凶の相.

インターネットカフェ cyber-café. ⇨ネット/ネットカフェ難民

いんないかんせん【院内感染】 an in-hospital infection; a nosocomial infection.

いんにく【印肉】 an inkpad; a stamp pad; a personal seal (ink)pad[stamp pad]; ink paste in a small container used to stamp a personal seal. 印を押すときに使う肉.

いんぶん【韻文】 verse(散文に対して). ⇔散文 (prose); a poem(小説に対して); poetry(総称).

いんぺいこうさく【隠蔽工作】 a cover-up operation; concealment.

いんぽん【院本】 ⇨丸本

いんれき【陰暦】 the lunar calendar; the old calendar(旧暦). ☆月の満ち欠けを基準としてつくられたこよみ. 明治初期まで用いた. ⇨旧暦

いんろう【印籠】 an *inro*; a seal case(印箱); a pillbox[medicine box] (薬箱). An *inro* is a portable container hung from the waistband of a *samurai* in feudal Japan originally to carry a seal, and later a pillbox[medicine box]. It is often made of lacquered wood with elaborate designs and decorations. 当初は「印(器)」(a case for a seal; a case to keep seal), その後は「薬(器)」を入れて腰に下げて持ち運ぶ小さな容器[箱]. 精巧な模様や装飾入りの漆塗りの木材からつくられているものが多い. ☆元来は「印」(seal) を入れたのが呼称の由来.

う

う【卯】 the Rabbit[Hare], one[the fourth] of the 12 animals of the Chinese zodiac. 十二支の第四. ⇨十二支. ¶卯の方 the

う

Direction of the Rabbit[east]. 方角の名. 東. 卯の刻 the Hour of the Rabbit [5-7 a.m.] 午前6時（およびその前後約2時間）. 卯年 the Year of Rabbit. 卯年生まれ (be)born in the Year of the Rabbit.

う【鵜】〔鳥〕a cormorant.

【鵜匠】a cormorant fisherman; a cormorant-fishing master (wearing ancient costume and ceremonial headgear). 鵜を操る漁夫. 古風な衣装と被り物を装っている.

【鵜飼】〈漁法〉cormorant fishing; fishing with cormorants; using cormorants for fishing. *Ukai* is the ancient method of catching *ayu* (sweetfish, river smelt) by using well-trained cormorants. *Ukai* takes place on the river at night under the light of blazing torches. The cormorants capture *ayu* with their beaks, but have a cord tied at the base of their necks to prevent them from swallowing the catch. よく訓練された鵜をあやつりながら鮎を捕る古風な漁法. かがり火 (decoy fire burning in a basket)のもとで夜の川で行う. 鵜は嘴で鮎を捕るが，捕獲したものを飲み込まぬように首元にひもを結んでいる. ☆1300年 余の歴史を有する「長良川鵜飼漁法」(5月中旬から10月中旬まで行う)は岐阜県指定無形民俗文化財，「鵜飼用具一式(122点)」は国指定の重要有形民俗文化財である. ¶鵜飼船 a boat for cormorant fishing; a boat for fishing with cormorants.

ういろう【外郎】 *uiro*; sweet rice jelly; sweet jelly made[steamed] from rice flour with water and sugar. 米の粉に水・砂糖を加えて蒸した菓子.「ういろう餅」の略. 名古屋の名産.

うえき【植木】 a garden plant[tree, shrub]（庭木）; a potted plant（鉢植えの）. ¶植木鉢 a flowerpot. 植木鋏 (a pair of) garden shears. ⇨盆栽. 植木市 a plant fair (selling a variety of potted plants and garden plants).

うえすぎまつり【上杉まつり】 the Feudal Lord Parade of Uesugi Shrine at Yonezawa City. (4月). ⇨付記(1)「日本の祭り」

うおがし【魚河岸】 ❶ a fish market; a waterside area where a fish market is located. 魚市場のある河岸.

❷ the Tsukiji Wholesale Fish Market (in Tokyo).「築地の中央卸売り市場（水産卸売）」の通称. ☆2018年10月豊洲市場に移転.

うおそうめん【魚素麺】 fish noodles. 魚のすり身をそうめん状にしたもの.

うおすき【魚鋤】 seafood[fish] *sukiyaki*; food cooked in a pan with seafood[fish] (instead of beef). （牛肉の代わりに）魚介類を用いてのスキヤキ.

うおどうふ【魚豆腐】 steamed *tofu*-like fish paste. 魚のすり身を豆腐に似せて，蒸した料理.

うおふ【魚麩】 boiled food mixed with wheat gluten and whitefish. 麩と白身魚のすり身を混ぜて煮た食品.

うかし【浮かし】 ingredients floating on a soup. 軽い汁の実.「浮実」ともいう.

うき【雨季】 the rainy season; the wet season; the monsoon season. ⇨梅雨

うきくさ【浮草】〈水草〉a floating waterweed; a floating aquatic plant:〈アヒルの食用〉a duckweed.

うきこ【浮粉】 fine rice powder. 米の細かい粉. 菓子の材料に用いる.

うきばな【浮き花】〔華道〕the floating arrangement of flowers; the floating style of flower arrangement. 花を浮かせて生ける様式. ☆水花の生け方が最適.

うきぼり【浮き彫り】 a relief; a (carved [sculptured])relief; a relief carving[sculpture].「レリーフ」(浮き上げ彫り). ¶浮き彫り作品 a work in relief. 浅[高]浮き彫りの像 a sculpture in low[high] relief.

うきよえ【浮世絵】 an *ukiyo-e*; a woodblock print and painting[picture] (of the Edo period). An *ukiyo-e* is a genre of paintings and color woodblock prints depicting landscapes and everyday life of the commoners in the Edo period. It developed from the 17th through the 19th centuries. 江戸時代の木版画. 風景や庶民の風俗を描いた絵画(風俗画). 17世紀から19世紀にかけて発展した. ☆多くは「多色刷りの版画」(multicolored[varicolored] woodblock print and painting)をいう.
【関連語】「絵師」 an *ukiyo-e* painter. 「彫師」 an *ukiyo-e* carver. 「摺師」 an *ukiyo-e* printer. ☆17世紀後半に 菱川師宣[1618-1694]が浮世絵を創始. 挿絵 (illustrations of texts)に使われていた木版画を1枚の絵として独立させた. 菱川師宣の代表作「見返り美人」(Beauty looking back over her shoulder). 安藤広重[1797-1858]の代表作「東海道五十三次」(Fifty-Three Stages on[Fifty-Three Views of] the Tokaido Highway). 葛飾北斎[1760-1849]の代表作「富岳三十六景」(Thirty-Six Views of Mt. Fuji)などが有名.

うきよぞうし【浮世草子】 an *ukiyo* story-book; a realistic novel of everyday life in the Edo period. 江戸時代の風俗小説(popular story). ☆主な作者は井原西鶴[1642-1693].

うぐい【石斑魚】〔魚〕a dace (単複同形または daces); a white mullet; a minnow. コイ科の淡水魚. ☆関東では「ハヤ[鮠]」, 関西では「イダ」「ハエ」ともいう. 酢みそ和えに用いる. ⇨こい

うぐいす【鶯】〔鳥〕a (Japanese) bush warbler. The combination of Japanese bush warblers and plum trees has become subject matter of poetry and paintings in Japan. 鶯と梅の組み合わせは詩歌や絵画の題材になっている. ☆「鶯色」は brownish green; olive green.

うぐいすあん【鶯餡】 ⇨餡

うぐいすじょう【うぐいす嬢】 a female announcer (or female telephone operator) with her beautiful[sweet] voice. Japanese bush warblers are birds that announce springtime with their uniquely beautiful cry. 声の美しい女性アナウンサー[電話オペレーター]. 鶯は比類なく美しい鳴き声で春の訪れを告げる鳥. ☆「鶯の鳴き声」は the song of a bush warbler in flight.

うぐいすばり【鶯張り】 a squeaking floor-board; a squeaky floor.
【鶯張りの廊下】 a hallway floorboard that emits a bush-warbler-like chirp whenever trod on. The squeaky floor prevents enemies from intruding into the temple [castle]. 廊下の床板を踏むと鶯の鳴き声に似た音を出すしくみ. 寺院[城]への敵の侵入を防ぐための床. 圀 京都の知恩院は有名.

うぐいすまめ【鶯豆】 sweetened, boiled peas; green peas cooked and sweetened with sugar. 甘く煮た青エンドウ豆.

うぐいすもち【鶯餅】 rice cake stuffed with bean paste and coated with green peas powder; rice cake filled with bean paste and powdered with green peas flour. 中に餡を入れ青きな粉をまぶした餅. ☆形と色が「鶯」に似るのが呼称の由来.

うこん【鬱金】〔植物〕 a turmeric; a curcuma (植物の総称);〈香辛料〉turmeric. ショウガ科の多年草. 根茎は黄色染料また香辛料・カレー粉やたくあん漬けに用いる. 健胃剤としても使用. ☆「うこん色」は saffron (yellow).

うさぎ【兎】〔動物〕a rabbit (家兎); a hare(野兎).

うざく【鰻ざく】 vinegared cucumber with chopped broiled eel. うなぎの蒲焼を混ぜたキュウリの酢の物.

う

うし【丑】 the Ox, one[the second] of the 12 animals of the Chinese zodiac. 十二支の第二. ⇨十二支. ¶丑の方 the Direction of the Ox[north-northwest]. 方角の名. ほぼ北北東. 丑の刻 the Hour of the Ox [1-3 a.m.] 午前2時（およびその前後約2時間）. 丑年 the Year of the Ox. 丑年生まれ (be) born in the Year of the Ox.

うし【牛】〔動物〕〈雌〉a cow;〈雄〉a bull;〈去勢牛［食肉用］〉a bullock[steer];〈荷車用〉an ox (複 oxen). ⇨牛車;〈子牛〉a calf (複 calves). ☆食肉用の「子牛」は calf veal; 米 vealer; cattle（総称）. ☆食肉用の牛肉は beef calf. ⇨牛肉

うじ【蛆】〔虫〕a maggot（はえ・はちなどの幼虫）; a grub（地虫など）; a gentle（釣りの餌）.

うじ【氏】❶ a clan; a social group consisting of kindred families having the common ancestors. 共同の祖先をもつ諸家族で構成された社会的集団.「氏族」.
❷〈血統〉birth.
❸〈家柄〉family.
❹〈家名・家系〉a family name; lineage. ¶氏素性 one's family background.

うしお【潮】〈海水の干満〉 the tide.〈海水〉seawater;〈海流〉current.
〔料理〕潮汁 fish and shellfish broth; fish and shellfish soup seasoned simply with seawater; thin soup cooked from boiling fish and shellfish in seawater[salted water].（海水［塩水］で味をつけた，魚介類の吸い物［すまし汁］）. ☆ハマグリの潮汁 clam broth; clam soup seasoned only with salt. 潮煮 fish and shellfish boiled in salted water.（水で煮て塩味をつけた魚介類）

うしがえる【牛蛙】〔両〕a bullfrog. 別名「食用蛙」(edible frog). ⇨かえる

うじがみ【氏神】 ❶〈鎮守の神〉a guardian god[deity] of a local community (*chinju*); a local guardian god; a village tutelary

god. ⇨氏子. ☆キリスト教の「守護の聖人」(a patron saint) また「守護の天使」(a guardian angel) に類似する. ¶土地の氏神 a local Shinto god[deity]; a god protecting the local area (or shrine). 氏神の神社 the shrine of the local god[deity].
❷〈祖先として祭る神〉 an ancestral god[deity] of a clan (*uji*); a god worshipped as an ancestor's spirit. ¶源氏の氏神 an ancestral god of the Genji clan.

うじきんとき【宇治金時】 (a bowl of) shaved ice topped with powdered green tea syrup and sweet *adzuki* bean paste; shaved ice with powdered green tea syrup poured on the top and stuffed with sweet *adzuki* bean paste. 抹茶シロップを上にかけ，小豆餡を添えたかき氷. ☆「宇治」は有名な茶の産地（京都府）.「金時」は甘い餡を作るために用いる金時豆. ⇨金時豆

うじこ【氏子】〈家族〉 a family belonging to a specific shrine;〈人〉a parishioner of a Shinto shrine; a supporting member [supporter] of a specific shrine; people under the protection of the local guardian deity. Shinto parishioners venerate the same tutelary deity in a Shinto shrine. 特定の神社に所属する信徒. 同じ氏神鎮守を崇敬する地元民. ☆神社の氏子は寺の檀家に相当する. ⇨檀家 / 氏神. ☆ parishioner 「教区民」，欧米における教区[教会区]（教区教会 (parish church)と教区司祭 (parish priest)をもつ宗教上の区域）に所属する信徒.

うじごおり【宇治氷】 (a bowl of) shaved ice covered with powdered green tea syrup. 抹茶シロップをかけたかき氷. ⇨宇治金時

うしろみごろ【後ろ身頃】 the back part of a *kimono*; the (two) back sections[panels] of cloth of a *kimono*. 着物の背［胴の後］の部分. ⇔前身頃

うす【臼】 ❶〈木製の臼〉a wooden mortar.

穀物を杵 (pestle)でつく臼. ⇨杵. ¶臼で(もち米)をつく pound (glutinous rice) in a wooden mortar.

❷〈石のひき臼〉quern; hand mill. 穀物などを手で回して挽く臼. ¶臼の石 quern stone.

うすあじのすいもの【薄味の吸い物】 lightly seasoned clear soup; thin soup. 主として関西での食べ物. ☆「薄味のコーヒー」は weak[mild] coffee. 別名「アメリカン・コーヒー」(和製英語)

うすあじのかいせきりょうり【薄味の懐石料理】 lightly seasoned dish served before the tea ceremony. ⇨懐石料理

うすい【雨水】 rainwater; the season when snow turns to rain. 雪が雨に変わる季節. ⇨二十四節気

うすがき【薄書き】 writing in thin black [Indian] ink. ⇨ 香典[香典袋]

うすがたテレビ【薄型テレビ】 a flat-screen television[TV]; thin display television sets. ¶薄型大画面テレビ a large-screen flat-panel television.

うすかわまんじゅう【薄皮饅頭】 sweet bean-paste bun with a thin covering[coating]; sweet bean-paste bun with a thin envelope of dough.

うすき【薄器】〈茶〉a caddy for foamy tea powder. 薄茶用抹茶の茶器. 「棗」ともいう. ⇨棗

うすぎぬ【薄絹】 thin[light] silk; thin [lightweight] silk fabric.

うすぎりのきゅうり【薄切りの胡瓜】 thin slices of a cucumber; a cucumber cut into thin slices. 〈一切れ〉a thin slice of a cucumber; a thinly-sliced cucumber.

うすくちしょうゆ【薄口醤油】 lightly[thinly]-flavored *shoyu*[soy sauce]; light-colored and thin-tasted *shoyu; shoyu* of light color and taste. 煮物や吸い物などの素材の色を生かす加熱料理に用いる.⇔濃口醤油

うすじおのさけ【薄塩の鮭】 lightly[slightly] salted salmon.

うずしお【渦潮】 an eddying current; a swirling (ocean) current of the tide.（潮の流れ）; a whirlpool of the tide.（潮の渦巻き）. ¶鳴門海峡の渦潮 the whirlpool of the Naruto Strait.

うすちゃ【薄茶】❶〔茶道〕 thin powdered tea; foamy green tea (used in the formal tea ceremony). In the tea ceremony, *usucha* (prepared by the host) is served individually[in an individual bowl for each guest] while *koicha* is shared by several guests from the same tea bowl. *Usucha* is served at the later stage of the proceedings of the tea-serving manners in the tea ceremony. 抹茶の量を少なくしてたてた茶. 茶の湯では(主人が立てた)「薄茶」は各人に出されるが, 「濃茶」は同じ茶碗から回し飲みする. 薄茶は茶の湯のお手前上最後の段階で出される. ⇔濃茶. ¶薄茶点前 formal manners observed when serving thin powdered tea in the tea ceremony. 茶の湯で薄茶を出す作法 (etiquettes).

❷〈薄めに入れたお茶〉weak[mild] tea. ⇔濃茶

うすづくりのふぐ【薄造りの河豚】〈作り方〉thin slicing of raw globefish;〈薄く削ぎ切った河豚〉thin slices of raw globefish; a thinly sliced raw globefish. 刺身用で「フグ造り」ともいう. ⇨ふぐ(刺し)

うすばた【薄端】〔華道〕 a flat-topped bronze vase(used for semiformal style of the *seika* flower arrangement). 上部が水平な青銅花瓶. ⇨生け花

うすやきせんべい【薄焼き煎餅】 thinly-toasted rice crackers.

うずら【鶉】❶〔鳥〕 a (Japanese) quail. ¶鶉の卵 a quail egg.

〔料理〕鶉そば buckwheat noodles cooked with quail eggs.

❷〈客席〉 the lower seat box of the kabuki

う

theater (in the Edo period). 江戸時代の歌舞伎を演じる劇場の桟敷の下の客席.

うずらまめ【鶉豆】 a pinto bean; a mottled kidney bean. ⇨まめ

うそ【鷽】〔鳥〕a (Japanese) bullfinch. アトリ科の小鳥. 口笛のような鳴き方をする.

【鷽人形】 a bullfinch figure; a wooden carving doll in the shape of a bullfinch. A bullfinch is regarded as a symbol of a lucky bird. It is believed to turn bad into good for the coming year. 鷽は幸運を呼ぶ鳥の象徴. 来る年で悪運を幸運に変えると信じられている.

【鷽替神事】 the Bullfinch Exchanging Rite. (1月). ⇨付記(1)「日本の祭り」

うたあわせ【歌合わせ】 a *tanka* poetry contest[*waka* composition match] (held in the Heian and Kamakura periods). Two teams of poets compete with one another in the *tanka* poetry contest. 歌人を左右二組に分け, その詠んだ短歌[和歌]を相互に競って組み合わせる. 平安時代から鎌倉時代に盛んに行われた. ⇨短歌 / 和歌

うたい【謡】〔能楽〕(an) *utai*; a Noh chant [recitation]. *Utai* is a unique chanting [reciting] of a Noh drama text containing the narration and the lines. 能楽を吟ずること. 物語と台詞をのせた能楽を謡うこと.「謡曲」ともいう. ⇨謡曲. ¶謡い本 an *utai* libretto; a libretto of a Noh drama; a Noh drama text containing the narration and the lines. 謡の台本. 能楽の物語と台詞がある.

うたいもの【謡物】 ballad; song. ☆「小唄」little ballad.「地唄」ballad or folk song.「長唄」long epic song.「端唄」short love song.

うだいじん【右大臣】 the Minister of the Right (in ancient Japan); the Junior Minister of State; the chief officer of the Grand Council of State. He is inferior in rank to the Minister of the Left. 昔, 太政官の長官. 太政大臣・左大臣につぐ官. ⇨太政官 / 左大臣

うたいほうだいカラオケ【歌い放題カラオケ】all-you-can-sing *karaoke*.

うたかい【歌会】 a poetry-reading party; a *tanka*-reading competition. ⇨歌会. ¶歌会始め the New Year('s) Poetry Party; Poetry Reading Party held in celebration of the New Year. 歌会始の儀 New Year's Poetry Party at the Imperial Palace. 新年御歌会 the Imperial Poetry Party for the New Year (held at the Imperial Palace); the Imperial Poetry Reading held at the New Year. ⇨宮中歌会始め

うだつ【梲】 a short pillar set on a beam to support a ridgepole. 梁の上に立て, 棟木をのせる短い柱. ☆「うだつがあがらない」cannot[be unable to] succeed; cannot[be impossible to] get ahead in the world(成功[出世]しないこと)

うたひめ【歌姫】a diva; a famous female singer. ¶昭和の歌姫美空ひばり Misora Hibari dubbed the diva of the Showa era.

うたまくら【歌枕】❶〈著名な場所〉a place cited in famous poems; a place famed in classical Japanese poems; a famous place of poetical association. 古来多く詠まれた歌詞で有名な場所.

❷〈書物〉poet's handbook of place-names, words and phrases used when composing classical Japanese poetry. 和歌をつくる資料(名所や枕詞など)となる歌人の手引き書.

うたよみ【歌詠み】 a *waka* composer; a *tanka* poet. ⇨和歌 / 短歌

うちあわび【打ち鮑】 pressed and dried abalone strips. 細く切って乾燥させた鮑

うちいり【討ち入り】〈四十七士の〉the raid [attack] on Kira's residence made by the Forty-Seven Loyal Retainers (of the feudal lord Asano Takuminokami to avenge their lord's dishonorable death). （主君浅野内匠頭長矩(たくみのかみながのり)の不名誉な死の仇討ちをするための)四十七士による吉良邸 (mansion)への襲撃 (attack). ⇨赤穂事件

うちいわい【内祝い】 ❶〈祝い〉a family celebration; a private celebration. 身内の親しい者だけの祝い. ¶(父の)**病気回復の内祝い**(をする) (hold) a family celebration for (father's) recovery.

❷〈贈り物〉a small present[gift]. It is given on the occasion of a family[private] celebration. 家族の祝い事の記念として贈る物.

うちうみ【内海】an inland sea. ⇦外海(そとうみ)

うちかけ【打掛け・裲襠】 a long ceremonial overgarment. The silk cloth is richly embroidered with gold and silver thread. 長い式典用の上着. 絹の布地に金銀糸で刺繍が施されている.

❶ a formal gown worn over a woman's *kimono* in the Edo period. 江戸時代, 武家婦人の礼服 (attire).

❷ a formal gown worn over a bride's wedding *kimono*. 現在, 結婚式に着物の上に着る礼服 (attire).

うちくら【内蔵】 ❶〈古代朝廷の蔵〉an Imperial warehouse in ancient times.

❷〈家屋に接した蔵〉a warehouse attached to a dwelling.

うちこ【打粉】❶〈剣〉sword powder (used to sharpen a Japanese sword). 刀身を磨く砥の粉 (polishing powder).

❷〈調理〉 wheat flour (used for sprinkling over the board to stretch *soba*[*udon*]). そば・うどんなどを伸ばすときまわりにつかないように板にまぶす小麦粉. ☆餅などの打粉には「米粉」(rice flour)を用いる.

うちだし【打ち出し】 ❶〈興行の終わり〉the close; the end; the closing of public performance (in *sumo* wrestling or theater). （相撲や芝居で)その日の興行の終わり. ¶**打ち出しの太鼓の音** drumbeats announcing the end[close] (of a day's *sumo* matches).

❷〈細工〉 embossment; embossed work. 浮き出し模様. 浮き彫り模様. ¶**羽子板の打ち出し絵**[押し絵] an embossed picture cloth of a battledore. ⇨羽子板. **青銅の打ち出し細工** an embossed bronze.

うちづま【打づま】 shredded vegetables for garnishing *sashimi*. 刺身のつまに用いる細かく切った野菜(大根・キュウリなど).

うちでのこづち【打出の小槌】 a good-luck mallet; a mallet for good luck representing monetary wealth. It is a magic wand that produces one's heart's desire at a wave. It is often kept as a mascot[good-luck charm] for wealth and prosperity. 望みを唱えながら振れば思いのままに何でも得られる魔法の棒. 富と繁盛を願う縁起物［お守り］として保持されることが多い. ☆ Aladdin's lamp「アラディンのランプ」(何でも人の望みをかなえる魔法のランプ：「千夜一夜物語」)ともいえる.

うちのれん【内暖簾】a (split) curtain separating the domestic area from a work area. 居宅部分と仕事場を分ける(細く切った)カーテン.

うちべんけい【内弁慶】a lion at home[inside] and a mouse abroad[outside]. A man who behaves bossily at home, but timid outside. 家の中ではいばり (bossy), 外ではいくじがない (meek)こと.

うちぼり【内堀】 an inner moat; a moat within the castle walls. 城内の堀. ⇦外堀

うちみず【打ち水】 watering; sprinkling water (on the road[lane] to lay the dust); sprinkling (the road[lane]) with water. It is customary for the Japanese to sprinkle water in[on] the garden in order to keep it cool. （ほこりを静めるために)道路に水をまくこと. 日本では涼風をとるため

う

(to cool the air)庭 (yard)や道に水をまく
(spray)習慣がある. ☆ in the garden「庭の
一部に」. on the garden「庭一面に」

うちゆ【内湯】 an indoor bath of hot-spring
inn. 温泉場の旅館の中に作った浴場. ⇔外
湯

うちゅうじん【宇宙人】 ❶〈地球人に対する〉
an alien; an extraterrestrial[ET]; a creature
from outer space. 他の惑星から地球に来る
人間的生物.

❷〈奇人〉 a person from another planet; an
eccentric (person); a strange person; an
odd person.

うちろじ【内露地】 the inner part of a tea
garden. It includes the path leading to the
tearoom and its surrounding area. 茶庭の内
部. 茶室に通ずる小道とその周辺区域があ
る. ⇔外露地.

うちわ【団扇】 an *uchiwa*; a Japanese
round[flat] paper fan (with a bamboo handle). It is made by pasting Japanese paper
on a thin framework of finely split bamboo.
It is used to fan oneself and to kindle a fire
in place of a bellows. (竹の柄がついた)丸
い[平らな]紙製の扇. 細く割った竹を広げ
て骨組の上に和紙を張って作る. 身体を涼
しくしたり (keep oneself cool), またふい
ご[火吹き]の代用をする. ⇨扇子 / 扇

【団扇太鼓】a fan-shaped hand drum; a
small hand drum shaped like[in the shape
of] a round fan. It is often used by followers
of the Nichiren sect of Buddhism. 日蓮宗の
信徒が用いる団扇型の手打ち太鼓.

うちわえび【団扇海老】 a slipper lobster. 団
扇のように平らなエビ. 伊勢エビより肉は
少ないが味が濃い. ⇨いせえび

うつぼ【鱓】〔魚〕a moray (eel).「ナマズ」とも
いう. 蒲鉾や竹輪などに調理する.

うど【独活】〔植物〕an *udo*; a Japanese
celery; a spikenard; an aralia cordata. ウ
コギ科の多年草. 若い茎は食用 (edible

shoots[sprouts]). 和え物や酢の物また天ぷ
らなどに用いる. ☆「**独活の大木**」は a big
but useless person(大きいばかりで役に立
たない人).

うどん【饂飩】 *udon*; wheat noodles(通常
は複数形）; thin wheat-flour noodles; thin
white noodles made from wheat flour.
Udon noodles are made by kneading wheat
flour with salted water,rolling it out,and
cutting it into narrow strips. *Udon* noodles
are usually boiled and served in a hot seasoned soup[hot soy-based broth] (*tsuyu*)
mixed with pieces of vegetables[meat],
minced green onions and red pepper (*yakumi*). 小麦粉を塩水で練って伸ばし, そ
れを細長く切って作る. 通常はゆでて, 味
付けの汁(つゆ)に薬味を加えて出される.
⇨蕎麦. ☆「日本三銘うどん」は名古屋の「
きし麺」(愛知県),「稲庭うどん」(秋田県),
「讃岐うどん」(香川県).

〔食品〕**うどん粉** wheat flour. **生うどん** raw
wheat-flour noodles. **半生うどん** half-dried
wheat-flour noodles. **茹でうどん** boiled
wheat-flour noodles. **煮込みうどん** stewed
wheat-flour noodles. **手打ちうどん** hand-
made[home-made] wheat-flour noodles. **乾
しうどん【乾麺】** dried wheat-flour noodles.
〔料理〕**饂飩鋤** *udonsuki*; noodles *sukiyaki*
with seafood and vegetables; wheat-
flour noodles cooked with seafood and
vegetables in a pot. 魚介類と野菜を鍋に入
れて料理したうどんの鍋物. ☆ 大阪「美々
卯」の商標名.

うなぎ【鰻】〔魚〕 an eel; a Japanese eel; a
freshwater eel. ☆「**穴子**」は a conger eel[salt
water eel]. ¶**鰻串** a skewer for broiling eel.
⇨あなご / 鰻巻き
〔料理〕**鰻雑炊** gruel rice with broiled eel.
鰻の肝吸い clear eel's liver soup. **鰻の肝
焼き** broiled eel's liver with sweetened
shoyu[soy sauce]. **鰻の白焼き** a steamed

eel. 鰻の骨のから揚げ deep-fried eel's backbone. 鰻茶漬け hot boiled rice with eel, soaked in tea. ⇨茶漬け

【鰻の蒲焼き】〈串に差した鰻〉a charcoal-broiled eel (put on a bamboo skewer); 〈丼のご飯にのせた鰻〉a broiled eel (placed on top of steamed rice). A split eel[An eel split down the belly] is broiled over a charcoal fire and flavored with basting sauce (*tare*) (made of *shoyu*[soy sauce], *mirin*[sweetened *sake*] and sugar). Broiled eel is served on steamed rice in a bowl [lacquered meal box]. It is eaten with a basting sauce (*tare*) poured over it and powdered Japanese pepper (*sansho*) sprinkled on top. (腹を)割いた鰻を炭火で焼き (grilled), タレ(醤油, みりん, 砂糖で作る)で味つける. 焼いた鰻は丼[重箱]に入った温かいご飯の上にのせて出される. 食べるときにはタレをつけ, 山椒をその上にふりかける. ⇨蒲焼き

【鰻重】 a charcoal-broiled eel on steamed rice, served in a lacquered meal box with a lid. It is eaten with a basting sauce (*tare*) poured over it and powdered Japanese pepper(*sansho*) sprinkled on top. うなぎの蒲焼きを漆塗りの蓋付き重箱に入れたもの. 食べるときはタレをつけ, その上に山椒をふりかける. ☆関西では鰻をご飯の上と間にも分けてむすので「まむし」(または「まぶし」)ともいう.

【鰻丼】 an eel bowl; a bowl of steamed rice topped with charcoal-broiled eel; charcoal-broiled eel served on steamed rice in a bowl. It is eaten with a basting sauce (*tare*) poured over it and powdered Japanese pepper (*sansho*) sprinkled on top. 焼いた鰻を上にのせた丼飯. 食べるときにはタレをつけ, その上にふりかける.「うなぎ丼」の略. ⇨土用の丑の日

うなぎのねどこ【鰻の寝床】 a long and narrow house[room].

うなばら【海原】 a vast ocean. ¶大海原 a vast expanse of ocean.

うに【海胆・雲丹】❶〈動物:海胆〉a sea urchin; a sea chestnut; an echinus (榎 echini).

❷〈食品:雲丹〉 seasoned sea-urchin roe [eggs]. うにの卵巣を塩漬けにした食品.

〔料理・食品〕雲丹和え food dressed with sea-urchin roe[eggs]. 雲丹酢 vinegared sea-urchin roe[eggs]. 雲丹の塩辛 salted sea-urchin roe[eggs]. 雲丹焼き fish grilled with kneaded sea-urchin roe[eggs] (煉り雲丹に卵黄を混ぜ, 素焼きにした魚介類(白身魚・エビ・イカなど)に塗り焼いたもの. 御節料理として用いる)

うねめ【采女】 a lady-in-waiting at court in ancient Japan. 昔の後宮の女官. 天皇の食事に奉仕していた.

うのはな【卯の花】❶〈植物〉a Japanese sunflower; a deutzia(うつぎ).「うつぎ」の白い花.

❷〈食物〉 *tofu*[bean-curd] refuse; *tofu* waste; *tofu* lees. *U-no-hana*[*Tofu* lees] are pulpy remains of boiled soybean after the soybean milk has been extracted. 豆腐の搾りかす. 豆乳を搾った後に残る蒸した大豆の柔らかい肉状の残留物. 通称「おから」. ⇨おから

〔料理・食品〕卯の花和え dishes mixed with *tofu* lees. 卯の花汁 soup with *tofu* lees. 卯の花漬け fish[vegetables] preserved in *tofu* lees. 卯の花炒り *tofu* lees boiled with chopped vegetables seasoned with *shoyu*[soy sauce].

うばがい【姥貝】 ⇨北寄貝

うま【馬】〔動物〕a horse; a pony(小馬); a mare(雌馬): a stallion(雄馬); a foal(子馬); a colt(子馬(雄)); a filly(子馬(雌)). ⇨絵馬

【馬の脚】〔歌舞伎〕 (a couple of) horse-costumed players who serve as (the front and

う

hind) legs of a horse on stage. 舞台上で馬の(前・後)脚の役割を果たす馬の衣装をつけた演技者 (actors).

うま【午】 the Horse, one[the seventh] of the 12 animals of the Chinese zodiac. 十二支の第七. ⇨十二支. ¶午の方 the Direction of the Horse[south]. 方角の名, 南. 午の刻 the Hour of the Horse [11 a.m. -1 p.m.] 正午(およびその前後約2時間). 午年 the Year of the Horse. 午年生まれ (be) born in the Year of the Horse.

うまき【鰻巻き】 broiled eel's fillet wrapped [rolled] in thick omelet[omelette]. 卵焼きで包んだ[巻いた]鰻の蒲焼き.

うまだし【旨出汁】a mixture of bonito broth, *shoyu*[soy sauce] and *mirin*[sweetened *sake*]. 鰹のだし汁に醤油と味醂を加えただし. つゆ汁やかけ汁にする.

うまに【旨煮・甘煮】 *umani*; food[fish or meat] boiled down with vegetables in *shoyu*[soy sauce], *mirin*[sweetened *sake*] and sugar; vegetables (potato, bamboo root, lotus root, etc.) and fish (or meat) stewed in *shoyu*, *mirin* and sugar. 魚・肉・野菜(芋・筍・蓮根など)を醤油・味醂・砂糖で甘く煮しめた料理[煮しめ]. ☆正月の重詰めには不可欠. ⇨煮しめ

うみ【海】 the sea; the ocean(大洋). ¶海の幸 seafood; marine products. ⇨〜海

うみうなぎ【海鰻】〔魚〕 an conger eel; a sea eel. ⇨穴子

うみがめ【海亀】〔動物〕a sea turtle. ⇨亀

うみがらす【海烏】〔鳥〕a murre; a guillemot.

うみつばめ【海燕】〔鳥〕 a storm petrel; a storm finch.

うみねこ【海猫】〔動物〕 a black-tailed gull. ¶ウミネコの繁殖地(天然記念物)a nesting place of black-tailed gulls (natural monuments). ☆山形県飛島が有名.

うみのひ【海の日】 Marine Day (the 3rd Monday of July). This national holiday was established in 1995 (and first held in 1996) as a day to express gratitude for the blessings of the oceans and pray for the prosperity of Japan as a maritime nation. Originally held in July 20, it was changed to the third Monday of July in 2003. 1995年に海の恩恵に感謝し, 海洋国日本の繁栄を祈願する日として施行された. 元来7月20日に施行された祭日は2003年には7月第3月曜日に移行した.

うみびらき【海開き】 the formal start of the swimming season; the opening of an ocean beach (to swimmers).

うみへび【海蛇】〔魚〕a sea snake; a sea serpent. ⇨蛇

うみほたる【海蛍】〔甲〕 a sea firefly; a seed shrimp. ウミホタル科の発光動物で, 海水に触れると青色の光を放つ (a blue-fluorescing swimming crustacean). 秋頃日本の太平洋沿岸(the Pacific coast of Japan) に多く見られる. ☆ crustacean 「(カニ・エビなどの)甲殻類の動物」

うめ【梅】〔植物〕an *ume*; *mume*(学名の梅). 〈木〉a Japanese apricot[plum] tree;〈実〉a Japanese apricot[plum];〈花〉a Japanese apricot[plum] blossom; plum blossoms. バラ科の落葉高木. 中国原産の鑑賞植物・果樹. ¶白梅 white Japanese apricot[plum] blossoms. 赤梅 red Japanese apricot[plum] blossoms. ⇨青梅
〔料理・食品〕梅和え dishes dressed[flavored] with flesh of a pickled *ume*[plum]. (梅肉と和えたもの. ハモ, イカ, レンコンなど色白の食材と和える). ⇨和え物. 梅のお握り rice ball packed with a pickled *ume*[plum]. ⇨お握り. 梅昆布茶 *ume*-flavored kelp tea; kelp flavored with flesh of a pickled *ume*[plum]. 梅紫蘇巻き rolled *sushi* containing *umeboshi*[pickled and dried *ume*] paste and perilla leaves in the center; *sushi* rolled up in a sheet of dried laver

with *umeboshi* paste and perilla leaves in the center; *sushi* wrapped in a thin sheet of dried laver with *umeboshi* paste and perilla leaves in the center. ⇨細巻き鮨. **梅酒** *ume*[plum] liquor; *ume* liqueur; liquor made from *ume*; spirits[*shochu*] flavored with a green[an unripe] *ume* and sugar candy. (青梅を焼酎と氷砂糖で漬け込んだ果実アルコール). ⇨青梅 / 焼酎. **梅酢** the salted *ume*[plum] juice; the juice of salted *ume*; the sour liquid made from a salted *ume*. (梅の実を塩漬けにしたときに出る酸味の強い汁. 漬物用・料理用). **梅漬け** a pickled *ume*[plum] with salt.「梅の塩漬け」のこと.

【梅干】 ***umeboshi***; a pickled and dried *ume*[plum] (usually light brown or reddish in color). *Umeboshi* is a plum pickled in salt together with red beefsteak plant (*shiso*) leaves and exposed to the sun for drying. 赤いしそ葉(perilla leaves)といっしょに塩漬けにし, 日光にさらした梅. ☆戦国時代 (the Warring State period) に, 梅干は疲労回復 (fatigue relieving) また抗菌作用 (antibacterial effect) などの薬効 (medicinal effect) があるとして, 戦場での保存食用に携帯された.
〔料理・食品〕**梅干茶漬け** boiled rice with an *umeboshi*, soaked in tea. ⇨茶漬け. **梅干飴** an *ume*-like candy; a candy that resembles an *umeboshi* in both shape and size. (形と大きさが梅干に似た (looks like)あめ). **梅干粥** rice gruel with an *umeboshi*. **梅干煮** (bluefish)simmered with an *umeboshi*. (梅干を入れて煮る(青魚)). ⇨青魚

うめきざいく【埋め木細工】 marquetry; inlaid woodwork; mosaic.

うめたてち【埋め立て地】 reclaimed land[ground]; a land reclamation site.

うめまつり【梅祭り】 the Plum-Blossom-Viewing Festival. (2月). ⇨付記(1)「日本

の祭り」(北野天満宮梅花祭)

うら【浦】 a beach; a creek; an inlet; a lagoon; a lake.¶仏ヶ浦(青森県)Hotoke(gaura) Beach. 壇ノ浦(山口県)Dan-no-ura Beach. 霞ヶ浦(茨城県・千葉県)Lake Kasumigaura (the second largest lake in Japan). ⇨海岸 / 浜 / 砂丘

うらがねもんだい【裏金問題】 scandal involving shady fund[dirty money] deals; scandal involving off-the-books fund [money]; scandal involving a bribe[secret fund].

うらぐちにゅうがく【裏口入学】 backdoor admission[entry] to a school[college]; buying one's way into school[college].

うらけんきん【裏献金】 an illicit donation; a concealed contribution. ☆「偽装献金」a dubious donation

うらサイト【裏サイト】 an unofficial[illegal] Web site[website]; a fishy[dubious] Website. ⇨学校裏サイト

うらさく【裏作】 an offseason crop; a secondary crop (of the field).

うらじ【裏地】 a lining (in a *kimono*); lining material(生地). 衣服などの裏につける布. ¶ウールの裏地 a woolen lining (in a coat).

うらじろ【裏白】〔植物〕 an umbrella fern; a fern with white-backed leaves. 常緑性の大型シダ. 葉は正月の飾り物に使用する. ☆葉の裏が白いことからの呼称. ⇨注連飾り

うらせんけ【裏千家】 the Ura-Senke school of the tea ceremony.「三千家」の茶道流派の一つ. ⇨千家

うらない【占い】 fortune-telling; divination; augury. ⇨易. ¶占い師 a fortune-teller. ☆「手相見」a palmist

うらながや【裏長屋】 a row[terraced] house on a backstreet (in the Edo period). (江戸時代の)裏通りの庶民の家並み.

うらばんぐみ【裏番組】 a (competing) program (in the same time-slot) on a

う

different channel.

うらビデオ【裏ビデオ】 a hard-core porn(o) video; a black-market[an uncensored] pornographic video.

うらぼん（え）【盂蘭盆（会）】 the *Bon* Festival; the Feast of Lanterns; the Buddhist All Souls' Day; a festive time of reunion for living and departed members of the family. It is held from July 13 to 15[16] (or August 13-15[16] in some areas) in honor of the spirits of ancestors. 家族の生存者と死者の再会の祭事．7月13-15[16]日（地域により8月15[16]日）に祖先の霊を供養する行事．「盂蘭盆」・「お盆」ともいう．⇨（お）盆

うらみごろ【裏身頃】 the four lining panels of a *kimono*. ⇨ 表身頃

うらわざ【裏技】 a cheat code; a trick of the trade; a secret ploy; sharp practice

うり【瓜】〔植物〕a gourd; a cucurbit; a cucumber(キュウリ); a cucumber melon（マクワウリ）．「瓜の果実」は pepoという．☆「瓜二つ」be like[as alike as] two peas in a pod; be exactly alike.
〔料理〕**瓜揉み** thin slices of cucumber rubbed with salt and dressed in vinegar. 塩でもみ、酢で和えた細く切った瓜 (thinly sliced cucumber).

うるうどし【閏年】 a leap year; an intercalary year. ☆4年ごとにめぐる (come along every four years).

うるか【鮞鮞・潤香】 salted guts[entrails] and roe of *ayu*[sweetfish]. アユの腸や卵巣を塩漬けにした食品[塩辛]．

うるし【漆】❶〔植物〕a Japanese lacquer tree; a Japanese sumac (tree); a Japanese varnish tree.
❷〔塗料〕lacquer; varnish; japan. It is used as coating to add a lustrous finish to the surface of wooden articles. 木製品の表面に光沢のある仕上げを加えるために上塗りと

して用いる．⇨塗り(塗り盆／塗り椀など)

¶**漆絵** lacquer paintings; pictures done in colored lacquer. **漆工芸** lacquerwork art. **漆細工** lacquer ware; japan. **漆職人** a lacquer worker; a lacquerer. **漆塗りの箸**[盆] lacquered chopsticks[tray]. ⇨塗り. **漆塗りの飾り箪笥** a lacquered ornamental chest. ⇨塗り

うるち（まい）【粳（米）】 nonglutinous rice (eaten at meals). 粘り気の少ない普通の米．⇨米／もち米

うるめいわし【潤目鰯】〔魚〕a round herring. ニシン科の魚．干物やだしのウルメ節に加工される．

うわえ【上絵】 figures painted on cloth [pottery]; patterns[designs] dyed[printed] on cloth[pottery]. 白地[陶磁器] の上に描いた[染めた]絵または模様．

うわおび【上帯】 an outer sash; an outer belt.

うわぐすり【上薬・釉薬】 (a) glaze(陶磁器の)； enamel(金属の)．☆素焼きの陶磁器の表面に塗ってつやを出すガラス質の粉．⇨釉薬．¶**上薬をかける** apply a glaze; glaze (a piece of pottery); enamel (a brooch).

うわぬり【上塗り】〈塗り物の〉 a final[last] coat (of paint[plaster]); the last coating (of paint[plaster]); glazing(釉薬をかけること)．「仕上げ塗り」ともいう．¶**上塗りする** give the final coat[coating] (of paint)

うんが【運河】a canal; an artificial waterway. ¶**運河沿いの倉庫**（小樽市） warehouses lining the canals (in Otaru City)

うんかい【雲海】 a sea of cloud(s); a vast stretch of cloud(s).

うんざ【運座】a *haiku* contest; a meeting of *haiku* poets. 各人が俳句を読みあい，良い俳句を選び合う会．

うんしゅうあえ【温州和え】 dishes dressed with a satsuma mandarin orange.

うんしゅうみかん【温州蜜柑】〔植物〕a satsuma

mandarin orange; a satsuma tangerine orange. 日本で食べるミカンを指す. ☆英英辞典[OED] で使用されている. satsuma は九州の薩摩(現在の鹿児島県)のこと.

うんじょう【運上】 business taxes (levied in the Edo period). 江戸時代, 各種の業者に課した税. 運行金.

うんすい【雲水】〈行脚僧〉an itinerant[a mendicant] Zen Buddhist monk[priest];〈修行僧〉a Buddhist monk[priest] undergoing Zen ascetic training. 修行のため行脚してまわる禅僧. 禅寺で修行する禅僧. ☆ an itinerant monk「旅回りの僧」, a mendicant monk「托鉢する僧」

うんめいきょうどうたい【運命共同体】 groups[nations] sharing a common destiny; common fate shared with between workers and their company.

うんりゅうがた【雲竜型】〔相撲〕 the *Unryu* style of ring-entering ritual (performed by *yokozuna*, grand champion *sumo* wrestler). ⇨不知火型

え

えい【鱝】〔魚〕 a ray(鼻が短い); a manta ray; a skate(鼻が長い); a devilfish(大型). 海産の軟骨魚. ひし形で平たい. ☆主として肉は練り製品の原料となる. 身は煮魚と刺身にもなる.

えいたいくよう【永代供養】 eternal prayers for the repose of the deceased. Buddhist memorial service for the repose of the deceased is held by Buddhist priests eternally in exchange for money donated to their temple. 永年 (perpetual)にわたり行われる死者の冥福を祈る会式. 寺院に献金する引き換えに永劫に(permanently)行われる. ☆実際には「永代」は「永い代[長期]」(a long period of time) と解釈する場合が多い. 10[30/50] 回忌までといった内規が

ある. ⇨回忌

エーきゅうせんぱん【A級戦犯】 the class-A war criminal (in World War II). ⇨合祀

【A級戦犯分祀】 the separate enshrinement [enshrining] of the class-A war criminals at Yasukuni Shrine; the class-A criminals enshrined separately at Yasukuni Shrine. A級戦犯を分離して靖国神社に祀ること.

【A級戦犯靖国合祀】 the collective enshrinement[enshrining] of the class-A war criminals at Yasukuni Shrine; the class-A war criminals enshrined together[collectively] at Yasukuni Shrine. A級戦犯を靖国神社に合同で祀ること.

えき【易】 fortune-telling; divination (based on the Oriental zodiac). ⇨占い. ¶**易者** a fortune-teller.

えきコン【駅コン】 a concert held in a station (building).

えきしょう【液晶】liquid crystal. ¶**液晶カラーテレビ** a liquid crystal color television. **液晶表示** a liquid crystal display[LCD]. **液晶画面** a liquid crystal screen[picture]. **液晶テレビ** a LCD television

えきじょうかげんしょう【液状化現象】 (soil) liquefaction.¶**地震による地盤の液状化現象** a phenomenon that turns soil fluid in earthquakes; ground liquefaction accompanying the earthquakes.

えきでん【駅伝】❶ an *ekiden* (road relay); a long-distance relay foot race[road race].「駅伝競走」の略.

❷ a post horse (in the ancient Japan). 宿場間の連絡の馬.

えきナカ【駅ナカ】 an *ekinaka*; an in-station store; a retail shop found inside a railroad station (building).

えきビル【駅ビル】 an *ekibiru*; a railroad station building (containing[housing] a shopping complex[mall]); a commercial building constructed over a railroad station.

え

えきべん【駅弁】　an *ekiben*; a railroad box(ed) lunch;〈駅構内にて〉a packed [boxed] lunch sold at a railroad station (or on a train platform);〈車内にて〉a packed [boxed] lunch sold in (the aisle of) a long-distance train. An *ekiben* contains a variety of bits of cooked fish, meat and vegetables, often the local specialty together with boiled rice. 駅弁にはご飯といっしょに，多様な魚・肉・野菜，特にその地方の特産が少しずつ盛り付けられている.

えきべんだいがく【駅弁大学】　a minor local college[university];〈口語〉a Mickey Mouse college[university]

えこう【回向】〈供養〉a Buddhist prayer (said) for the repose of the deceased; a Buddhist memorial service (held) for the repose of a person's soul. 死者のために読経をする供養. ¶回向料 the fee for a Buddhist prayer[memorial service].

えことば【絵詞】　a story in pictures; an explanation of a scene in a picture scroll. 絵巻物の説明文.

エコノミークラスしょうこうぐん【エコノミークラス症候群】　economy-class syndrome; deep vein thrombosis[DVT]（旅行者血栓症）.

エコバッグ　an ecological[a reusable] shopping bag; an environmental friendly "eco-bag."

エコビジネス（和製英語）ecology-minded business. 地球環境の保全を図る企業活動. ☆「環境保全運動家」an ecologist

えしき【会式】a Buddhist memorial service. ⇨御会式（日蓮宗の法会）

えしゃく【会釈(15度)】　(make) a slight bow. ☆「うなずく」(give) a simple nod; (exchange) nods. ⇨お辞儀

えしゃじょうり【会者定離】Those who meet (in the world) must part. We meet only to part (in the world). 会う者は必ず別れる運命にあること.

えすごろく【絵双六】　picture *sugoroku*; Parcheesi played on a board with pictures telling a story. ⇨双六

えぞ【蝦夷】❶ Yezo, former name of Hokkaido. 北海道の古称.「蝦夷の地」. 蝦夷鹿〔動物〕a Yezo[Japanese] deer. 蝦夷松〔植物〕a Yezo[Japanese] spruce. ⇨まつ. 蝦夷雷鳥〔鳥〕a Yezo[Japanese] hazel grouse.
❷ Yezo, a native of Yezo; the Ainu. 古代, 北海道・奥羽地方に住んでいた種族. ⇨アイヌ

えぞうし【絵草紙・絵双紙】　an illustrated story book (published in the Edo period). 江戸時代, 事件などを絵入りで説明した紙に印刷したもの.「かわら版」ともいう. ⇨草双紙 / かわら版

えだまめ【枝豆】〔植物〕green soybeans in the pods; green soybeans (still attached to their stems). ¶(ビールの)つまみの枝豆 boiled green soybeans in the pods served as an appetizer (with beer).

エチケットぶくろ【エチケット袋】　an air sickness bag; a sick bag; a puke[barf] bag（嘔吐袋）.

えちごじし【越後獅子】　an acrobatic lion dance performed by a child wearing a carved lion's head. 子供が獅子頭をかぶりながら舞う曲芸. ☆越後（新潟県）にはじまった獅子舞. ⇨獅子舞

えちぜんやき【越前焼き】　Echizen ceramic ware (produced in present-day Fukui Prefecture).

えつ【斉魚】〔魚〕a (Japanese) tapertail anchovy. 有明海の特産.

えつけ【絵付け】　china-painting; (hand-) painting on china (in which pictures are drawn directly on the pot). 陶磁器に描いた絵.

えっちゅうふんどし【越中褌】　a string(ed)

え

loincloth for men. 男性用のひも付きの褌.
☆長さ約1m, 幅約35cmの布の端にひもを
つけたＴ字形の褌. 安土桃山時代の越中
守であった細川忠興 (1563-1646) が始めた
のが呼称の由来.

えと【干支】 ❶〈十二宮〉the twelve zodiac
signs;〈十二支〉the twelve animal signs
of the Chinese zodiac. *Eto* is the twelve
signs of the Chinese zodiac, each of which
is named after an animal. Each Chinese
zodiac sign covers[represents] one year.
十二宮. 各宮に動物の名があてられる. 1
年を表示する. ⇨十二支
❷〈六十干支〉the sexagenary cycle.(60
年の周期). ☆「十干十二支」(the ten
calendar signs and the twelve horary signs)

えど【江戸】 Edo; Yedo.「東京」の旧称. ¶江
戸小紋 a fine pattern on a formal *kimono*
[clothing] in the Edo period. 江戸時代 the
Edo period; the Tokugawa period. 江戸城
Edo Castle. 江戸幕府 the Edo shogunate
(government); the Tokugawa shogunate
(government). 江戸(町)奉行 a city commissioner in charge of keeping the peace
of Edo (in the Edo period). ⇨奉行 / 町
奉行. 江戸町年寄 a high-ranking city
official, who worked under the direction
commissioner. (江戸時代に町奉行の配下
にあった町村の長).

【江戸家老】 one of the highest ranking
vassals of a feudal lord during the Edo
period. He stayed in his lord's residence in
Edo and managed his lord's administration.
江戸時代に, 江戸の藩邸に勤務してい
た (took charge of)諸侯の家老 (highest
ranking retainers).⇨家老 ⇦国家老

【江戸っ子】《過去》a person born in Edo.
江戸で生まれた人 ;《現代》a Tokyoite; a
person who was born and bred in Tokyo;
a Tokyoite born and bred. 東京で生まれ
育った人. An *edokko* is a true native of

(backstreet) Tokyo whose family has lived
there for three generations or longer. 生粋
の東京生まれの人. 家族が東京に3代また
はそれ以上に渡って在住する.

【江戸文字】 Japanese calligraphy styles
with very wide brushstrokes which were
invented for advertising in the Edo period.
江戸時代に盛んに使用された書体文字の総
称. 特に「勘亭流」や「相撲字」は有名. ⇨
勘亭流 / 相撲[相撲字]

えどまえ【江戸前】 Edo[Tokyo] style(江戸
[東京]の流儀) : in the Edo[Tokyo] style(江
戸[東京]の流儀で). ☆東京湾でとれた魚
介類 (fish and shellfish from Tokyo Bay)な
どのネタを語るときに用いることが多い.
¶江戸前料理 Edo-style cuisine[cooking];
food cooked in the Edo style.

【江戸前鮨】 Edo-style[Tokyo-style] *sushi*;
sushi made in the Edo style; vinegared rice
balls topped with slices of raw fish and
shellfish. 江戸風 (in the Edo fashion)のす
しの総称. 広義では「握り鮨」のこと. ⇨大
阪鮨

えのきだけ【榎茸】〔植物〕an *enokidake*; an
enoki; an *enoki* mushroom. キシメジ科
の食用キノコ. 英米の料理書には velvet
shankあるいは velvet footとも呼ばれる.
鍋物には最適. 瓶詰めにもなっている.

えばはおり【絵羽羽織】 a figured *haori*[short
overgarment] worn with a stylish *kimono*
(for women). 縫い目にまたがって大柄の絵
模様のある羽織. 婦人用の外出着.「絵羽」
とも略す. ⇨羽織

えばもよう【絵羽模様】 figures[designs] on
a *haori*[short overgarment].

えび【海老・蝦】〔甲〕❶ a shrimp[小型] (小
エビ). ¶干し海老 a dried shrimp. 甘海老
a sweet shrimp. 桜海老 a small shrimp; a
stardust shrimp.
❷ a prawn[中型] (車エビ). ¶むき海老 a
shelled prawn. 芝海老 a small white prawn.

❸ a lobster［大型］. ¶**伊勢海老** a spiny lobster. アメリカでは chicken lobster（小）, jumbo lobster（大）ともいう.

〔料理・食品〕**海老煎餅**〈せんべい〉 rice crackers made with dried shrimps. **海老の躍り食い**〈おど〉 eating [swallowing] shrimps alive. ⇨躍り食い. **海老の掻き揚げ** fritters of vegetables deep-fried with small shrimps in batter. **海老の衣揚げ** soft batter-fried shrimps. **海老フライ** deep-fried breaded prawns. **海老ピラフ** shrimp pilaf[pilaff].

《象徴》 **Ebi(s)**[shrimps, prawns, lobsters] with their bent backs and long whiskers are symbols of longevity, because they resemble long-lived old people bent with long beards. They are served on festive occasions such as weddings and the New Year. 腰が曲がりほおひげの長い海老は, その形が長いあごひげをはやし腰の曲がった長生きの老人に似ている(look like)ので長寿の象徴である. 結婚式や新年などの祝事に出される.

えびす【恵比寿】 ⇨七福神

えびすこう【恵比寿講】 an **Ebisu** Festival. The festival is held by merchants in honor of **Ebisu**, the God of the Commerce, on October 20 of the lunar calendar, praying for business prosperity. Many merchants visit **Ebisu** shrine and buy decorated bamboo rakes, symbolic of prosperity[good business]. 陰暦の10月20日に商家で恵比寿を祭って繁盛を祈る行事. 商人が恵比寿神社に詣で, 商売繁盛の象徴である飾りたてられた竹製の熊手を買う. 別称「二十日恵比寿」. ⇨七福神(恵比寿)

えびら【箙】 a quiver (of arrows). 矢を入れて背負う道具.

えふみ【絵踏】〈絵を踏むこと〉 stepping [treading] on a copper tablet showing with a picture of Christ on the cross for testing one's belief in Christianity. The Tokugawa shogunate used a picture of Christ in order to identify [prove oneself as] a non-Christian in the Edo period. キリスト教の信仰を試すために十字架上のイエス・キリストを描いた銅板を踏ませること. 江戸時代, 徳川幕府は非キリスト教徒の身分を証明させるためにキリストの絵を利用した. ☆「踏絵」は, 「キリシタンではない」という証を見せるために絵踏をさせるときに使用された「聖画像」のこと. ⇨潜伏キリシタン

えほう【恵方・吉方】 a direction deemed to be lucky (according to the zodiac sign of the year); the auspicious direction of the year where the god of the year presides.(その年の干支により) 幸運が定められた方向 (compass bearing). 年神が統括するその年の縁起のよい方角. ⇨干支

【恵方参り】 the New Year's pilgrimage to a shrine or temple which lies in the *eho*[lucky] direction. Many pilgrims pray for happiness and good fortune during the year. 元旦(の朝)に恵方にあたる神社または寺院への参詣. その年の幸運を祈る参拝者の数は多い.

えぼし【烏帽子】 a brimless headgear; a formal hat lacquered black and without a brim. It was worn with court garments by court nobles in ancient times and *samurai* warriors during ceremonies in old Japan. Today it is worn by Shinto priests observing at rituals. 黒い漆塗りのつばなしの帽子. 昔の貴族・公家が宮廷衣装とともに着用した. 現在は神事をあげる神官が使用する.

えま【絵馬】 ❶〈絵画〉 an *ema*; a votive picture of a horse painted on a wooden tablet[plaque]. A horse is a mysterious animal on whose back the god comes down to this world. 木製の額に描かれた馬の絵画. 馬は神がその背に乗って現世に降臨する神秘的な動物(俗信). ☆現在は馬

以外の絵もある.

❷〈御札〉a votive horse tablet[plaque]; a wooden tablet painted with a votive picture of a horse on it. It is offered to a Shinto shrine or Buddhist temple when praying for divine protection (such as success in exams or business) or when giving thanks for an answered prayer. 神の加護を祈願(合格祈願・商売繁盛など)するとき (when one wishes a prayer to be answered), または願い事がかなったとき (when one's prayer has been answered) の感謝として寺社に奉納する絵の板. ☆昔の風習で神に献上していた「生き馬」(living horses) の代わりに, 「絵馬」を奉納したのが始まり.

えまき(もの)【絵巻(物)】〈絵画入りの巻物〉a picture[painting] scroll;〈巻物の絵画〉a scroll picture[painting]. It contains illustrations of historical and legendary subjects in chronological order. 年代順に描いた歴史的・伝説的な題目の挿絵[図解絵] がある巻物. ⇨巻物. ¶源氏物語絵巻 a picture scroll of the Tale of Genji (painted in the 12th century);〈書名〉the Tale of Genji Picture Scrolls. 王朝絵巻 a picture scroll of the imperial dynasty[the Heian period]. 歴史絵巻 a picture scroll depicting a sequence of scenes from a historical narrative.

えものがたり【絵物語】a picture story (物語を絵で表す);an illustrated story (絵入りの物語).

えもんかけ【衣紋掛け】❶ a *kimono* hanger; a hanger for a *kimono*. 着物を掛けてつるす短い棒.

❷ a (free-standing) rack for hanging a *kimono*. It is usually set up in the corner of a Japanese room. (支えなしで立つ)着物掛け. 通常は和室の隅にある. ⇨衣桁

えり【襟・衿】the neckband (of a *kimono*); a collar (of a suit). ¶襟当て the cloth used to cover the neckband (of a *kimono*).

えんか【演歌】an *enka* (song); a Japanese-style popular song. An *enka* is a type of balladic song featuring human frailty and love with a distinctively Japanese melody (which is often sung to *karaoke* (music)). 哀調を帯びた日本独自の歌謡曲. カラオケの定番.

えんがわ【縁側】❶〈板敷き〉a Japanese-style veranda floor; a narrow wooden deck outside. It is the narrow board floor under the eaves of the roof projecting from [adjoining] a Japanese-style *tatami*-mat room. 日本家屋で, 畳敷きの和室から突き出る[隣接する]屋根のひさしの下にある狭い板床[細長い板敷].

❷〈魚の肉〉the (tasty) flesh at the base of the (dorsal and ventral) fins of a flounder [flatfish]; the flesh running along the upper and lower sides next of the fins of a flounder[flatfish]. かれい・ひらめなどの魚のひれ[背[腹]びれ]のつけねにある肉. 刺身や酢の物などに用いる. ⇨かれい / ひらめ

えんがん【沿岸】the coast; the shore. ¶日本海の沿岸 the coast of the Japan Sea.

えんぎもの【縁起物】a good-luck charm [talisman]; a luck-bringer; a lucky amulet; something that brings good luck (such as an arrow with white feathers or *daruma* dolls); a mascot. It is usually sold at booths within the precincts of a shrine or temple. 縁起をかつぐ物(破魔矢・達磨など). 神社・寺院の境内で売られる. ⇨破魔矢 / 達磨. ¶ **縁起物売り場** booths[stalls] selling lucky amulets (at shrines or temples).

えんきょく(ひょうげん)【婉曲(表現)】euphemism(婉曲語法);an indirect expression; delicate hints; phrases in a roundabout way (to avoid hurting the other person's feelings).

えんきりでら【縁切り寺】a Buddhist nunnery

え

that gives refuge to runaway wives. 逃げて
くる妻を庇護する尼寺 (temples for nuns)
⇨駆け込み寺

えんこう【援交】　compensated[paid] dating
（報酬前提のデート）; juvenile prostitution
(for pocket money)（少女売春）; school-
girl prostitution (disguised as financial
support)（女子高生売春）; the act of selling
sexual favors to older men by teenage girls
（男性への十代少女の売春）.「援助交際」の
略

えんこさいよう【縁故採用】　company employment of applicants through personal
connections; nepotism: 英 jobs for the
boys.　⇨門閥制度

えんこにゅうがく【縁故入学】school admission of students through personal connections; nepotism.　⇨門閥制度

えんざい【冤罪】　a false charge; an unjust
accusation; a trumped-up charge.

えんすいがたかざん【円錐(コニーデ)型火
山】a conic(al) volcano.　⇨火山

えんすいけい【円錐形】a conic(al) shape (of
Mt. Fuji).

えんだいしょうぎ【縁台将棋】　a game of
shogi played on a bench outdoors.

えんだん【縁談】　a marriage proposal; an
offer of marriage; a proposal to introduce
prospective marriage partners; a matchmaking introductory offer. ¶縁談を受ける
［断る］accept[refuse] a marriage proposal.

えんとう【遠島】❶〈離れ島〉a remote[distant]
island.
❷〈島流し〉exile; banishment; being
exiled[banished] to a distant island.

えんどう【豌豆】〔植物〕a pea; a garden pea;
snow[sugar] pea. マメ科の一年草, 二年草.
☆「グリーンピース」green peas（複数形）.
⇨さやえんどう. ¶エンドウのすじ snow-
pea pods. さやをむいた乾しエンドウ split
pea.

えんにち【縁日】　a festival day; the day of
the fair; the fete day (for a deity). *Ennichi*
is the day connected to a certain Shinto or
Buddhist deity and set for worshipping the
deity of a particular shrine[temple]. 特定
の神仏に何かの縁があり, 神社仏閣に参詣
するとよいとされる日である. ☆祭りや供
養を行う. 露店・夜店が並ぶ. ¶縁日商人 a
booth keeper (at a fair); a stall keeper (at a
fair)

【縁日の露店】　a fair stall[booth]; an open-
air stall[booth]. It is set up along the
approach and in the compounds of a shrine
or temple. 神社仏閣の参道または境内に設
けられる.

【縁日の夜店】　an open-air stall erected on
festival days at night; an open-air stand set
up on the night fairs. 祭日の夜に設けられ
た露店.

えんばく【燕麦】〔植物〕oats(通常は複数形).
味噌・菓子などの原料. オートミールやクッ
キーにも用いる. ⇨むぎ

えんぶり the *Enburi* Dance Festival of
Hachinohe City.（2月）. ⇨付記(1)「日本の
祭り」

えんま【閻魔】　Enma; Yama（梵語名）;　the
King of Hell; the King of Hades. 地獄の王
［支配者］. ¶閻魔大王 the great Enma; the
great King Yama of the Buddhist Hades.

えんむすびのかみ【縁結びの神】　the god
of matchmaking; the god of matrimony
[marriage]; the god who presides over
marriage.「結びの神」ともいう. ⇨出雲の
神

えんめいちりょう[いりょう]【延命治療
［医療］】　life-sustaining[life-prolonging]
medical treatment. ¶延命治療の中止
suspension[cancellation] of life-prolonging
medical treatment.

お

おあいそ【お愛想】〈勘定〉㊅ a bill; ㊋ a check. ⇨符丁(すし屋の用語). ¶お愛想をする ①(店側) calculate the bill[check]. ②(客側) pay the bill[check]. ☆「お愛想！」(正しくは「お勘定！」) Can I have the check? / Check, please!

おい【笈】 a wicker suitcase (which a traveling monk carries on his back); a pannier (which a pilgrim carries on his /her back). 行脚僧(an itinerant priest) や巡礼者などが衣服・仏具などを入れて背に負う脚のついたかご[箱].
【笈摺】 a sleeveless *haori*[half-coat] worn by a Japanese pilgrim. A Japanese pilgrim wears a light coat without sleeves to prevent abrasion when he/she carries a wicker suitcase on his/her back. 巡礼者が着物の上から着る袖なしのひとえの羽織. 笈で着物の背がすれるのを防ぐために着る.「おいすり」のなまり.

おいえげい【お家芸】❶〈歌舞伎など〉 one's spcialty[㊅ speciality] (of the (Ichikawa) school of a kabuki play); a skill passed down in one's family. 代々伝わるその家[流派] の独特の芸のこと. 別称「十八番」⇨十八番
❷〈柔道など〉one's own forte[specialty]. 固有の得意技のこと. ⇨十八番

おいえそうどう【お家騒動】a family quarrel [feud](確執); a family trouble[problem](反目).

おいコン【追い(出し)コン(パ)】 a farewell [send-off] party for graduating seniors.

おいらん【花魁】 an *oiran* (of the Edo period); a high-ranking *geisha*; a high-class courtesan; a licensed prostitute of high class. 上位の遊女. 太夫. ⇨芸者 / 太夫. ¶花魁道中 a parade of an *oiran* in the pleasure district of Edo.

おいろなおし【お色直し】 changing one's clothes at one's wedding reception; a bride's[bridegroom's] change of the traditional wedding dress during a reception. A bride[bridegroom] often retires to change the formal *kimono*[dress] to the informal garment[clothes] at her/his wedding reception (or vice versa). 結婚披露宴で衣装を着替えること. 新婦[新郎] が衣装[正装から普段着(またはその逆)] を着替えること.

おうぎ【扇】 a fan; a folding fan (usually used for dance or decoration). 通常は舞踊または装飾に用いる. 別称「扇子」. ⇨扇子 / 団扇. ¶開いた扇 an open fan. 閉じた扇 a folded[closed] fan. 扇落とし a fan tossing game; a tossing game of a folding fan. 扇流し an elegant fan floating on the stream; the Fan-Floating Event held on a stream current.

おうし【雄牛・牡牛】[動物] an ox (㊵ oxen); a bull; a bullock. ⇨うし

おうじ【皇子】 a prince; an Imperial prince. ☆「皇女」 a princess; an Imperial princess.

おうせいふっこ【王政復古】 the Restoration of Imperial Rule.(1867年). They carry out a government with the Emperor at its center after putting an end to the shogunate. 武家政治を廃し, 天皇中心の政治に返ること. 明治維新の開花.

おうちょう【王朝】 a Japanese dynasty; an imperial dynasty; a government under direct imperial administration. 天皇が自ら政務を執ること. ¶王朝絵巻 a picture scroll of the ancient dynasty. 王朝時代 a dynastic age; the age of court rule (in the Herian period). 琉球王朝 the Kingdom of the Ryukyus.

おうみしょうにん【近江商人】 a merchant from Omi Province (well-known for his

お

acumen and diligence) (鋭い洞察力と勤勉で有名な)近江出身の商人.

おうみはちまんさぎちょうまつり【近江八幡左義長祭り】 the Fire Festival of Omi-hachiman Shrine. (3月). ⇨付記(1)「日本の祭り」

おうみはっけい【近江八景】 Eight Views of Omi Province; the eight scenic spots around Lake Biwa in Omi Province (the current Shiga Prefecture). ☆滋賀県の琵琶湖沿岸の景勝地.「近江八景」(江戸時代初期の選定)[比良の暮雪／堅田の落雁／唐崎の夜雨／三井の晩鐘／矢橋の帰帆／粟津の晴嵐／石山の秋月／瀬田の夕照]は湖南に限られているので1947年[昭和24年]には「琵琶湖八景」[彦根の古城／賤ヶ岳の大観／比叡の樹林／海津大崎の岩礁／竹生島の沈影／瀬田石山の清流／奥土八幡の水郷／雄松崎の白汀]が選定された.

おうむ【鸚鵡】 a parrot. ☆「おうむ返しに言う」repeat a person's words (like a parrot).

おうようかけい【応用型】 〔華道〕variation styles of flower arrangement; a free-style flower arrangement; the free version of a standard flower arrangement. 生け花の変形[応用した型].

おえしき【御会式】 a memorial service for Nichiren. 日蓮宗の法会. ☆10月13日に行う日蓮上人の忌日に行う法会. ⇨会式

おおいちょう【大銀杏】❶〔植物〕a big ginkgo tree. ⇨ぎんなん／いちょう

❷〔相撲〕a *sumo* wrestler's formal topknot [hairstyle] (that resembles a gingko leaf). Top-ranking *sumo* wrestlers (ranked in the *juryo* division) have their long, oiled hair combed into the elegant *oicho-mage* [ginkgo-leaf knot] during tournaments. 銀杏の葉に似る(looks like)正式な髷. 本場所中，上位(十両)力士は長い髪を油で固めた大銀杏髷を結う. ⇨丁髷／いちょう

おおいりまんいん【大入り満員】 full house.

☆〈掲示〉House Full.

おおおく【大奥】 an inner palace (for shogun's exclusive use); women's quarters of the shogun's palace (forbidden to men); quarters of the shogun's consort and concubines. It was the inner rooms of Edo Castle used exclusively for the wife of the shogun and the court ladies. 将軍専用の邸宅. 将軍邸に侍る女性(正室と側室)の居場所. 男子禁制であった.

おおかみ【狼】〔動物〕a wolf (複 wolves). ¶狼の群れ a pack of wolves.

おおごしょ【大御所】❶ a retired but still powerful shogun. 隠退しても有力な将軍. ¶大御所家康公 Shogun Ieyasu after his retirement. 大御所政治 a government by a retired shogun. ⇨将軍

❷ a leading figure in a specific world; a Mr. Big. その業界の第一人者 (powerful personage). ¶財団の大御所 an outstanding man in the business[financial] world.

おおさかずし【大阪鮨】 Osaka-style *sushi*; *sushi* made in the Osaka style[fashion]. 大阪風の押し鮨, 箱鮨, 太巻き鮨などの総称. ⇨江戸前鮨

おおさかなつのじん【大阪夏の陣】 Summer War in Osaka. Tokugawa Ieyasu ruined the Toyotomi family in 1615.

おおさかばんぱく【大阪万博】 Expo'70 opened in Osaka. (1970年開催)

おおさかふゆのじん【大阪冬の陣】 Winter War in Osaka. Tokugawa Ieyasu attacked Osaka Castle in 1614.

おおさんしょううお【大山椒魚】〔動物〕a giant [great] salamander. ⇨さんしょううお

おおじぬし【大地主】 a large landowner. ⇨小作農

おおしまつむぎ【大島紬】 Oshima (Island) pongee fabrics; a type of hand-spun raw [plain] silk fabrics (produced on Amami-Oshima Island in Kagoshima Prefecture).

大島の絹紬. 手でつむいだ生絹織物の一種. 鹿児島県奄美大島特産の 繊細で鮮やかな 絣 織り［模 様］のつむぎ. ☆ spun <spin, spun, spun>「つむいだ」, spun silk「紡績絹糸」. ⇨紬

おおしょうがつ【大正月】 New Year's Day on January 1; New Year's Holidays from January 1 to January 7. 1月1日の正月, または1月1日から7日までの正月. ⇦小正月

おおずもう【大相撲】❶〈興行〉Grand *Sumo* Tournament (held under sponsorship of the Japan Sumo Association). A professional *sumo* tournament is held six times a year, with each tournament lasting for a period of 15 days in every odd numbered month. 日本相撲協会が運営するプロの相撲. 各興行は年6場所, 各奇数月の15日間（2週間）にわたる. ⇨相撲. ¶**大相撲地方[海外]巡礼** a tour of the provinces [foreign countries] to show a Grand *Sumo* exhibition. **大相撲中継** a live TV broadcast of a grand *sumo* tournament.

【関連語】 January [Tokyo]: the New Year's Grand Sumo Tournament. 東京・初場所
March [Osaka]: the Spring Grand Sumo Tournament. 大阪・春場所
May [Tokyo]: the Summer Grand Sumo Tournament. 東京・夏場所
July [Nagoya]: the Nagoya Grand Sumo Tournament. 名古屋・名古屋場所
September [Tokyo]: the Autumn Grand Sumo Tournament. 東京・秋場所
November [Fukuoka]: the Kyushu Grand Sumo Tournament. 福岡・九州場所
❷〈熱戦〉an exciting bout (between evenly matched *sumo* wrestlers); a prolonged and hotly fought bout of *sumo* wrestling; an exciting long-drawn-out *sumo* bout. 長時間の, 力のはいった相撲取組.

おおぜき【大関】〔相撲〕 an *ozeki* champion; 〈位置〉the second-highest rank of *sumo* wrestlers; 〈力士〉a *sumo* wrestler of the second-highest rank; the second-ranking *sumo* champion in the *makuuchi* division. 「幕内」の2位. ⇨相撲の番付

おおだち【大太刀】 an extra-long Japanese sword.

おおつづみ【大鼓】a large hourglass-shaped drum; 〈歌舞伎・能楽〉a large hand drum (used in a traditional Japanese music and dance). The drum is struck with the tip of the middle finger of the right hand while it is placed on the left knee with the left hand holding the cords of the drum, 砂時計型 (sandglass-shaped)の大鼓. 手にとる太鼓. 左手で 調 緒（皮を張っている麻紐）をとり左ひざの上で横にしながら, 右手の中指の指先で打って演奏する. ☆歌舞伎・能楽の囃子では小鼓とならぶ重要な楽器. ⇦小鼓. ⇨ 鼓

おおはらえ【大祓】a Shinto purification rite. It has been performed twice a year[in June and December] since the Heian period. 罪・けがれをはらい清める神事. 平安時代以降年2回[6月と12月]に行う.

おおはらはだかまつり【大原裸まつり】 the Half-Naked Festival at Ohara Town.（9月）. ⇨付記(1)「日本の祭り」

おおばん【大判】 an *oban*; a large oval gold coin. An *oban* was issued and circulated from the Azuchi-Momoyama period to the late Edo period to use as gifts and for trade. 大型楕円形 (oblong-shaped)の金貨. 安土桃山時代から江戸時代末期まで贈答や貿易用として発行・使用された. ☆1枚は十両に相当する. ⇨小判

おおふりそで【大振り袖】〈袖〉large pendant sleeves (of a *kimono* worn by young women); 〈着物〉a silk *kimono* with full-length hanging[swinging] sleeves (worn by young unmarried women on very formal occasions). ⇨袋帯 / 丸帯

お

オープン戦〔和製英語〕an exhibition game [match]; a pre-season game.

おおまがりのつなひき【大曲の綱引き】 the Tug-of-War Festival. (2月). ⇨付記(1)「日本の祭り」

おおまんどころ【大政所】 the title of respect for Toyotomi Hideyoshi's mother. 摂政・関白の母の尊称. 特に, 豊臣秀吉の母. 「大北の政所」の略.

おおみえ【大見得】〔歌舞伎〕 (strike) a dramatic pose; a pose for a dramatic effect; a pose to attract a lot of attention. ⇨見得

おおみそか【大晦日】 New Year's Eve; the last day of the year. (December 31). ☆「晦日」は12月30日.

おおみやびと【大宮人】 a courtier (serving) at the Imperial Court; a court official [nobleman] of the Imperial Court. 宮中に仕える人.

おおむぎ【大麦】〔植物〕barley. イネ科の一年草. ビールの原料. 茎のわらは細工用. ☆「精白した料理用の大麦」は pearl barley. ⇨麦. ¶**大麦糖**〈飴〉barley sugar.

おおむこう【大向(こ)う】〔歌舞伎〕〈立ち見の席〉the gallery(劇場の最上段にある安い席); 〈見物の大衆〉the masses; the (general) public; the mass of the people (of the upper gallery)(天井桟敷の見物人[観客]).

おおもん【大門】 the main gate (of a castle or mansion). 城・屋敷などの表門. 「正門」ともいう.

おか【丘】a hill; heights(高台). ¶**羊ケ丘**(北海道)(the)Hitsuji-ga-Oka Hill. ⇨山 / 〜岳 / 峠 / 坂

おかえし【お返し】⇨返礼

おかか【おかか】 dried bonito shavings [flakes]; shavings[shaved flakes] of dried bonito. ⇨鰹節

〔料理〕**おかか入りの握り飯** a rice ball with a filling of dried bonito flakes seasoned with

shoyu[soy sauce].

おかき【おかき】 thinly-cut and dried rice cakes; thin slices of dried rice cakes. ⇨欠き餅

おかぐら【御神楽】⇨神楽

おかざり【御飾り】❶〈新年の〉a New Year's decoration. ⇨注連縄 / 松飾り / 鏡餅 ❷〈神社などの〉a divine ornament[decoration]; ornaments[offerings] prepared for gods. ⇨供え餅

おがさわらりゅう【小笠原流】the Ogasawara school[style] etiquette; the Ogasawara school[style] of ceremonial etiquette for a *samurai* class. 室町時代, 小笠原長秀が定めた礼儀作法・武家作法の一流派.

おかしらつきさかな[たい]【尾頭付魚[鯛]】 the whole fish[sea bream] with its head and tail; a fish[sea bream] served whole with its head and tail. 尾から頭までつけた姿焼きの魚[鯛]. ☆「尾頭付き鯛」はお祝い事また神事などに用いる. 頭は左, 腹は手前に盛る. ⇨鯛

おかず【御数】*okazu*; subsidary dishes (to go with the rice as a staple); accompaniments (often served in small individual portions in Japanese home cooking). 主食の米に適合する副食. 和食で各人に割り当てられた副食. ☆元来, 品を数々とりあわせることからの呼称. 京都では「おばんざい」(home cooking; homemade dishes of Kyoto)ともいう. 英語の side dish は別な皿に盛って主要料理に供する「添え料理」のこと. ⇨惣菜

おかっぱあたま【お河童頭】 (a girl with) bobbed hair; (a girl with) straight hair cut short.

おかっぴき【岡っ引き】 a detective in the Edo period; a low-ranking police official [constable] who arrested criminals in the Edo period. 江戸時代の賊の捕り手役人(hired thief-catcher). ⇨十手

おがのなまはげ【男鹿のなまはげ】 the Oga

Namahage Festival. (12月). ⇨付記(1)「日本の祭り」

おかばしょ【岡場所】 unlicensed red-light [brothel] districts in the Edo period. 江戸時代の赤線地区.

おかぼ【陸稲】 dryland[upland] rice; rice grown in a dry field. ⇔水稲 (lowland rice)

おかみ【女将】 an *okami*; the proprietress [hostess] (of a Japanese-style inn[restaurant]); a female innkeeper; a female proprietor; the landlady. 料亭や旅館の女主人. ¶若女将 the proprietress-to-be (of a Japanese-style inn[restaurant]).

おかみ【御上】 〈天皇〉the Emperor; His Majesty. 〈将軍〉the *shogun*; the shogunate; 〈主君〉one's lord[master]; 〈政府〉the Administration; ㊤ the Government; 〈権威者・役人〉the authorities.

おかみさん【お上[内儀]さん】 〈呼びかけ〉madam; ma'am. 〈主婦〉a housewife; a wife. 〈相撲部屋〉the wife of a *sumo* stable master. ⇨相撲部屋／親方

おかめ【阿亀】 an *okame*. ❶〈人〉a plump-faced woman; a round-faced woman with plump cheeks and a short, flat nose. ふっくらした顔の女性. 丸々した頬と鼻ぺちゃの丸顔をした女性.「お多福」ともいう. ⇔ひょっとこ

❷〈仮面〉a mask of a plump-faced woman; a Japanese clownish woman mask.

おかめうどん[そば]【お亀うどん[そば]】 (a bowl of) noodle soup with slices of *kamaboko*[fish-paste cakes]; (a bowl of) wheat noodles[buckwheat noodles] in fish broth seasoned with *shoyu*[soy sauce], topped with slices of *kamoboko*[fish-paste cakes], *shiitake* mushrooms and green vegetables. 蒲鉾, 椎茸, 野菜を上にのせた出し汁うどん[そば]. ☆具をおかめの面のように並べることからの呼称.

おかもち【岡持ち】 a wooden carrying pail[box]; a wooden pail[box] with a handle (and a lid) to carry foods. 料理を入れて運ぶ (a handle for carrying foods), (ふた付の)浅い木製の桶[箱] のこと. ☆飲食店の出前に使う.

おかゆ【お粥】 ⇨粥

おから【雪花菜】 *okara*; *tofu*[bean-curd] residue; *tofu* refuse; *tofu* waste (left remaining after *tofu* is made). *Okara* is the edible pulpy residue (of boiled soybeans which are) separated from soybean milk in the production of *tofu*. 豆腐を作った後の絞り[残り]かす. 豆乳から分離した(大豆の)どろどろ状態の食用残りかす.「卯の花」ともいう. ⇨卯の花
〔料理〕 **おからの炒り煮** simmered *tofu* residue[refuse]; *okara* cooked with carrot, onion, burdock, devil's tongue and dried *shiitake* mushrooms. 人参, 玉葱, 牛蒡, こんにゃく, 干ししいたけなどを入れて料理したおから.

おがわ【小川】 a stream; a streamlet; a brook; a brooklet; a creek; a rivulet.

おかわり【お代わり】 another helping. 〈食べ物〉another bowl[helping]. 〈飲み物〉another cup[glass]. ¶ご飯のお代わり another bowl of rice. お茶のお代わり another cup of tea.

おきあがりこぼし【起き上がり小法師】 a *daruma* tumbler; a self-righting *daruma* doll; a *daruma* doll made (in order) to right itself when knocked over. The *daruma* doll weighted on the bottom returns to an upright position when tipped over. 底におもりをつけ, 倒してもまっすぐに起き上がる玩具だるま.

おきいし【置き石】 ❶〈庭の石〉a decorative stone placed[set] in a garden[pond] (for scenic effect). (趣を添える)庭や池などに置く石.

❷〈碁石〉a handicap *go*-stone (given to

the weaker player); a *go* stone placed for handicap. 弱いほうの人に置く石. ☆あらかじめ2か所以上の星に碁石を置く.

おきごたつ【置き炬燵】 a portable[movable] foot warmer. 持ち運びのできる炬燵. 床に置いて使う. ⇨炬燵

おきづけ【沖漬け】 a pickled fish[squid] seasoned in *shoyu*[soy sauce]. イカ・小魚などを開き醤油で漬けたもの. ⇨イカの沖漬け

おきなのめん【翁の面】〔能楽〕 a Noh mask representing an old[elderly] man. 老人の能面.

おきなます【沖膾】 chopped raw fish meat (and vegetables) seasoned with vinegar (or *miso*[bean paste]). It is eaten aboard the boat on which the fish was caught. 捕ったばかりの魚を船上で膾(酢または味噌で味付け)にしたもの.「たたき膾」ともいう. ⇨膾

おきなわへんかんきょうてい【沖縄返還協定】 the Agreement on the Return of Okinawa; the Japan-US Agreement on the reversion of the Ryukyu Islands and the Daito Islands to Japan. ☆1971年調印, 翌72年に本土復帰する.

おきばな【置き花】 a flower arrangement placed in an alcove (or on a table).

おきびき【置き引き】〈盗人〉a baggage [luggage] thief; 〈犯罪〉baggage[luggage] stealing; walking off[away] with another person's baggage.

おきもの【置物】 an ornament(飾り物); a figure[figurine] (立像[小立像]). ¶床の間の置物 an ornament in[for] the alcove.

おきや【置屋】 *geisha* agency. *Geisha* entertainers are dispatched from *geisha* agency at the request of high-class Japanese-style restaurants and inns. 芸妓をかかえている特約店. 茶屋からの求めに応じて芸妓を差し向ける取次店. ☆芸者・舞妓は置屋に

籍(membership)を置き, 芸事(traditional accomplishments)や仕来たり(traditional [conventional] practice)を学ぶ. 現代の芸能所属事務所(entertainment agency). ⇨茶屋 / 芸者

おきゅう【お灸】 moxibustion. ⇨灸 / もぐさ

おきょう【お経】 a Buddhist sutra; the Buddhist scriptures. ⇨経典. ¶お経を読む chant[recite] a Buddhist sutra.

おくがた【奥方】 nobleman's wife; the lady of the house. ¶公家の奥方 feudal lord's lady.

おくざしき【奥座敷】 ❶〈奥の客間〉an inner guest room; a Japanese-style guest room towards the back of a house. ❷〈閑静な場所[温泉地]〉 a quiet place[spa resort] of retreat.

おくしゃ【奥社】 an inner sanctuary (of Shinto shrine). 神社にある本殿.

おくじょちゅう【奥女中】 a maidservant of a shogun or feudal lord; a waiting maid who manages household chores in the residence of a shogun or feudal lord during the Edo period. 江戸時代, 将軍や大名の住居 (domestic quarters)に仕え, 奥向きの用を務めた女性.「御殿女中」ともいう.

おくしょん【億ション】 a deluxe condominium; a hundred-million–yen condo[英] flat].

おくにわ【奥庭】an inner garden.

おくのいん【奥の院】 the inner[innermost] shrine[temple]; the innermost sanctum(聖所); the sanctuary(至聖所). The principal image of Buddha or the founder of the shrine[temple] is enshrined in the sanctuary. 神社・寺院の本堂[本殿]にあり, 本尊・開祖などの霊像を安置している堂.

おくのほそみち【奥の細道】 The Narrow Road to the Deep North (Matsuo Basho's travelogue). ☆1702年(元禄15年)刊.

おくみ【衽・袵】a gusset; a gore; a part of the front of a *kimono*. It is a long cloth sewed from the front neck to the bottom edge of a *kimono*. 和服の前襟から裾まで縫い付ける，細長い半幅の布.

おくやみ【お悔やみ】　condolence; sympathy. ⇨香典. ¶**お悔やみ状** a letter of condolence[sympathy]. **心からお悔やみ申し上げます**. Please accept my sincere condolence; I extend my heartfelt sympathy to you[your family].

オクラ〔植物〕(an) *okra*; ⊛ a gumbo. アオイ科の一年草. 若いさやは食用. ☆日本では「青納豆」，海外では lady's finger ともいう. ¶**オクラのさや** okra pods.（若い果実をさやごと食す）

おぐら【小倉】　confectionery and dishes using sweet *adzuki*-bean paste. 小豆を用いた菓子または料理.「小倉餡」の略. ⇨餡〔食品〕**小倉アイス** ice cream mixed with sweet *adzuki*-bean paste. **小倉餡** sweet *adzuki*-bean paste (containing both mashed and whole beans).

おぐらひゃくにんいっしゅ【小倉百人一首】 the Ogura Anthology of One Hundred Poems by One Hundred Poets. ⇨百人一首

おくりがな【送り仮名】　*kana* added to a Chinese character (*kanji*)(to show its reading[inflection] in Japanese); *kana* suffixed to a Chinese character (to express its reading[inflection] in Japanese).（日本語で漢字の読み方[語尾変化]を明示するために）漢字のあとにつける仮名. ⇨仮名 / 片仮名 / 平仮名

おくりび【送り火】 a send-off bonfire for the departing souls of the deceased; a bonfire for escorting the spirits of the deceased (on July 16 or August 16). *Okuri-bi* is the bonfire to send off[speed] the ancestral spirits safely back to the other world [heaven] after their brief annual visit to this world[their old homes]. A bonfire is lit to illuminate the way of the other world on the evening of the last day of the Bon Festival. 盂蘭盆の最後の日（7月16日または8月16日）の夜，祖先の霊[精霊](the spirits[souls] of the ancestors)を現世から冥土へ送るために門前でたく火. ⇨迎え火

おくりぼん【送り盆】 the last day of the Bon Festival when departed souls leave home; the last day of the Bon Festival when people send off their departing ancestral spirits back to the other world. 先祖の霊を見送るお盆の最後の日. ⇨迎え盆

おくるみ【御包み】　⊛ a bunting; a soft square cloth to swaddle a baby[an infant]; a padded garment to wrap up a baby (in order to protect from the cold). 赤子[幼児]を包む柔らかい四角い布. 赤子を抱くとき，防寒などのために衣服の上から包む詰め物入りの衣類.

おけ【桶】(手桶) a pail;〈たらい〉 a tub; a bucket. It is usually made of pieces of wood fastened with a metal (or bamboo) hoop. 金属(または竹)の箍で木片を締めて作られている.

おけらまいり【おけら詣り】 the Sacred Fire Rite of Yasaka Shrine（12月）. ⇨付記(1)「日本の祭り」

おこげ【お焦げ】　scorched rice (left at the bottom of the rice-cooker); crispy, slightly burned rice (left at the bottom of the pot for boiling rice). 釜の底にこげついた飯.

おこし【興・粔籹】　a millet-and-rice cake; a popped millet-and-rice candy. もち米やあわで作る干菓子.

おこし【御腰】　⇨腰巻き

おこぜ【鰧・虎魚】〔魚〕a stingfish; a scorpion fish; a stonefish. ⇨かじか

おこそずきん【御高祖頭巾】　a cowl worn by a woman (in the late Edo period); a hood-and-veil combination. It is a square cloth[headscarf] combined with hood and veil to cover the woman's face and head

お

except her eyes. 江戸末期の婦人用の被り物[頭巾], 目以外の顔や頭を全部かくす, 頭巾とベールが合体した四角な布. ☆御高祖(日蓮上人)の像の頭巾に似ていることからの呼称.

おこのみやき【お好み焼き】 *okonomiyaki*; a Japanese-style savory pancake fried with various ingredients. *Okonomiyaki* is made of batter of flour and water and eggs with bits of meat (or seafood) and chopped vegetables. It is spread with a thick spicy sauce and sprinkled with green *nori* laver flakes (*ao-nori*) and dried bonito shavings. It is usually cooked on a hot steel plate fitted into each table so that diners can fry their own pancakes in the restaurants. いろいろな食材で焼いた和式のパンケーキ. 卵と水溶きした小麦粉に肉(または魚介類)や野菜を加えて作り, 濃いからいソース(Worcestershire sauceウスターソース; pork cutlet sauceトンカツソース)をぬり青海苔 (green *nori* seaweed powder)とかつお節をまく. 通常はレストランで各人のテーブルに付いた鉄板で焼きながら食べる.

おこもり【御籠り】 confinement in a shrine or temple overnight in order to offer prayers to the gods. People confine themselves in a shrine or temple for an overnight retreat of prayer. 神仏に祈願するため, 一夜[一定期間]神社や寺院にこもること.「参籠」ともいう.

おこわ【御強】「御強飯」の略.「強飯」の丁寧語. ❶〈赤飯〉glutinous rice steamed with red *adzuki* beans (by a steaming basket). It is usually eaten on such an auspicious occasion as a birthday. もち米を(せいろで)蒸かした小豆入の飯. 誕生日などの祝日に食べる. ⇨赤飯

❷〈強飯〉glutinous rice steamed with chestnuts or edible wild plants[greens] instead of red *adzuki* beans. (赤飯と違い)小豆の代わりに栗や山菜などを用いてもち米を蒸かした飯. ⇨山菜

おさがり【お下がり】〈衣服〉 clothes handed down (from one's elder brother[sister]) ; a hand-me-down coat(お下がりの上着).

おざしき【御座敷】 a *geisha's* engagement to perform at a party. 芸者・芸人が客に呼ばれる宴席. ⇨芸者

おさと【お里】〈実家〉one's parents' home;〈素性〉 one's origin(s).

おさめだいし【納大師】 the last memorial rite for Kobo-Daishi. (December 21).

おさめばしょ【納め場所】〔相撲〕 the last [closing] grand *sumo* tournament of the year.

おしあゆ【押し鮎】 a salted and pressed *ayu* (fish). ⇨あゆ

おしいれ【押し入れ】 a sliding-door closet in a Japanese-style room. It is a Japanese-style closet with a thick papered sliding door serving as a room partition. It is used to store beddings during the daytime. 日本間に作りつけた物入れ (a built-in storeroom). 厚紙を張った襖 で部屋を仕切り, 昼間は夜具 (sleeping mattresses)などを入れる.

おしえ【押し絵】 a padded[wadded, raised] cloth picture; an embossed cloth picture. 綿を入れた布で包み板にはりつけた絵, ¶(歌舞伎役者の)押し絵羽子板 a battledoor bearing on one side a padded cloth picture (of a kabuki actor). ⇨羽子板

おじか【牡鹿】〔動物〕 a buck; a stag; a male deer. ⇨しか

おしき【折敷】 a square meal tray; a square tray with side dishes. 懐石料理などに用いる角盆のお膳.

おじぎ【お辞儀】 a bow.「座礼」(a sitting bow)と「立礼」(a standing bow)がある. ⇨会釈(15度) / 敬礼(30〜45度) / 最敬礼(45度以上) / 座礼 / 立礼. ☆発音に注意す

ること. bow/báu/ は「お辞儀」. bow/bóu/ は「弓」の意味. ¶**上品なお辞儀** a courtly bow. **愛想のよいお辞儀** a friendly bow. **堅苦しいお辞儀** a formal[rigid] bow. **丁寧なお辞儀(をする)** (make) a polite bow. ☆目線を合わせてあいさつ(例:「こんにちは」)をしてからお辞儀をする.

おしずし【押し鮨】 pressed *sushi*; *sushi* [vinegared rice] and marinated fish pressed in a square box-shaped utensil; pressed *sushi* topped with vinegared slices of fish in a square box-shaped utensil (in the Osaka style). Vinegared slices of fish[e. g., marinated mackerel] are pressed down on a bed of vinegared rice together in a rectangular box from the top to shut tightly and sliced into bite-sized pieces. 長方形の器に酢漬けの生魚[圖しめ鯖]を敷き, その上にすし飯をつめて押し, 一口サイズの大きさに切った鮨.「大阪鮨」(Osaka-style pressed *sushi*)また「箱鮨」(*sushi* pressed in box)ともいう. ⇨江戸前鮨

おしちや【御七夜】 the seventh night[day] after a baby's birth; 〈祝い〉celebration on the night[day] of the seventh day after a baby's birth. 子供が生まれて7日目の夜, またその日の祝い. ☆通常, このとき名前をつける.

おしどり【鴛鴦】〔鳥〕a mandarin duck. ガンカモ科の水鳥. ☆雌雄が常にともにいる鳥. ⇨おしどり夫婦

おしどり【おしどり】 a traditional hairstyle for *kimono*-clad dancing girls (such as young *geisha* and *maiko*). (芸者や舞妓のように)着物姿の踊り子のための髪型.

おしどりふうふ【おしどり夫婦】 a couple of lovebirds; a happy couple; a happily married couple (who are always together with each other). 仲のよい夫婦 (loving couple). ⇨ぼたんインコ /おしどり

おしぶた【押し蓋】 a pressure lid; a lid used for pressing down (the contents of a tub when making the pickled vegetables). (漬物などをつくるときに樽 (barrel)の中身を)押すために用いる蓋.

おしぼり【お絞り】 a wet towel (served either hot in winter or cold in summer); a small moistened[steamed] washcloth (served hot[cold]) to wipe the hands).

おじや ⇨雑炊(の女ことば)

おしゃく【お酌】❶〈酌〉pouring *sake* for each other; serving a person with *sake*. ⇨酌 ❷〈半玉・舞妓〉a young *geisha* girl; 〈酌婦〉a woman who pours *sake* for somebody.

おしょう【和尚】❶〈高僧〉a senior Buddhist priest. 修行を積んだ高僧の敬称.「お」は「和」の唐語. ☆「お尚さん」(呼びかけ語)は Your Reverence. または Masterあるいは Sir.
❷〈住職〉a Buddhist priest[monk] (in charge of a temple). 寺を担当する仏僧.

おしょうばん【お相伴】 (have) a share in a meal; sharing a meal; taking part[participating] in a meal.「相伴」とは客の相手となって, (食事などで)自分ももてなしを受けること. ¶**お相伴にあずかる** have a share in a meal; share[take part; participate] in a meal.

おしんこ【お新香】 (Japanese-style) pickles; (Japanese-style) pickled vegetables (in season); vegetables pickled in brine. 野菜の漬物. ⇨香の物 / 漬物
〔料理〕**お新香巻き** rolled *sushi* containing pickled *daikon*[radish] in the center; *sushi* rolled up in a sheet of dried laver with pickled *daikon* in the center; *sushi* wrapped in a thin sheet of dried laver with pickled *daikon* in the center. ⇨細巻き鮨

おすまし【お澄まし】 clear soup.「お清汁」とも書く.「澄まし汁」の女性語. ⇨澄まし汁

おせいぼ【お歳暮】 ⇨歳暮

おぜがはら【尾瀬ケ原】 Oze-ga-hara

お

Marshland[Marshy Moor] (noted for wild flowers and unspoiled nature). ☆福島・新潟・群馬の3県にまたがる.

おせちりょうり【御節料理】 (a variety of) special New Year's dishes; (a variety of) traditional dishes prepared for the New Year. *Osechi-ryori* are traditional Japanese dishes served on the New Year holidays[during the first three days of the New Year]. A variety of ingredients are artistically arranged in a set of 3-tiered[3-layered] lacquer(ed) boxes. 正月の3が日に食する料理. 多種多様な食材が3段重ねの漆塗りの重箱に芸術的に盛られている. ☆御節料理は主婦が3日間休めるように, また食材が3日間保存できるように作られている. (These dishes are made so that housewives can rest for three days and food can be preserved for three days.) 元来, 御節料理は「その季節のごちそう」(the delicacies of the season)である. 御節料理は「元旦」以外にその他季節の祝いである5つの「節句」(the five seasonal festivals)に

神に供えるごちそうであった. ⇨節句
【関連語】正式には5段であるが, 最近では『3段の重箱』(山の幸, 海の幸, 里の幸の3要素)に盛り付けられている.

① 『1の重』(on the first tier)《口取り[hors d'oeuvre]》:「数の子」(herring roe).「黒豆」(black beans).「田作り」(young, dried sardines).「紅白の蒲鉾」(boiled fish paste colored red and white).「紅白なます[刻み大根と人参]」(red and white pickles; pickles[grated radish and carrots] colored red and white).「昆布巻」(rolled *kombu* [kelp]). 「栗きんとん」(sweet potatoes mixed with chestnuts).「ごぼう」(burdocks).「いくら」(salmon roe).「酢の物」(vinegared food)など.

② 『2の重』(on the second tier)《焼き物[grilled fish and meat]》:「甘鯛」(broiled sea bream).「伊達巻」(rolled omelet[omelette]).「かち栗」(dried chestnuts).「鮭」(salmon).「伊勢エビ」(lobster, prawn).「鶏」(chicken). など.

③ 『3の重』(on the third tier)《煮物[boiled

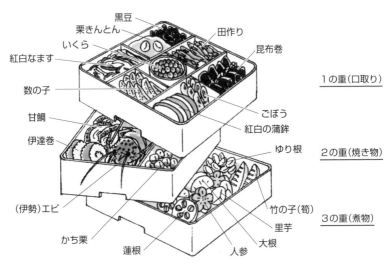

vegetables]》:「大根」(*daikon*, Japanese radish).「人参」(carrots).「蓮根」(lotus root).「里芋」(taro potatoes).「竹の子[筍]」bamboo shoots[sprouts].「ゆり根」(lily bulbs)など.

☆食材には縁起 (food bringing good lucks; food charged with good wishes)を担ぐものが多い.

『鯛・昆布』Sea bream (*tai*) is *auspicious* (mede*tai*) and rolled tangle[kelp] (*kobumaki*) means a wish for *happiness* (yoro*kobu*). 鯛は「めで<u>たい</u>」,<u>昆布</u>巻きは「よろ<u>こぶ</u>」.

『紅白かまぼこ・紅白なます』The red and white coloring reflects the festive [auspicious] occasion in Japan. 日本で紅白は<u>吉事</u>を示す.

『黒豆』Bean(*mame*) means to work hard [diligently]. The black beans represent a wish for a healthy year or work.「豆」は「<u>まめに</u>」働く. 年中「まめに(勤勉に)」働けるように健康を願う.

『数の子』Herring roe represents a wish for the blessing of many children and the prosperity of descendants. <u>子宝</u>と<u>子孫繁栄</u>を願う.

『田作り』Sardine, which once was scattered as fertilizer for the rice harvest, represents a wish for a good rice harvest. 昔稲作の肥料に撒いたイワシは<u>稲の豊作</u>を願う.

おせんまい【汚染米】 ⇨事故米

おそなえ(もの)【御供え(物)】 ❶〈神社・寺院での〉a shrine[temple] offering; an offering made at a shrine[temple]; 〈神棚・仏壇の〉a Shinto[Buddhist] altar offering; an offering placed on a household Shinto[Buddhist] altar. People eat and drink the same foods and drinks (offered to a god) to get closer relations to the god. 神をもてなした飲食物を食べることにより神

と人との関係を強める.「供え物」の丁寧語. ⇨神饌

❷〈鏡餅の〉a rice-cake offering; a rice cake offered to a god; a rice cake placed on [in front of] a household Shinto altar. 神[神棚]に供える餅.「御供え餅」の略. ⇨鏡餅

おそばごようにん【御側御用人】 ⇨側用人

おたいこ【お太鼓】「お太鼓結び」の略. ⇨太鼓結び

おたうえしんじ【御田植神事】 the Rice-Planting Rite of Sumiyoshi Shrine. (6月). ⇨付記(1)「日本の祭り」

おたく[オタク]〈熱狂的ファン〉*otaku*; a fanatic; a maniac(ファン, マニア); a geek[geekhead] (変人, 奇人); a nerd (変わり者); a freak; a buff; an addict. *Otaku* is a Japanese term used to refer to people with obsessive interests, particularly *anime* and *manga*. Common uses are *anime otaku* (an obsessive fan of *anime*) and *manga otaku* (an obsessive fan of *manga*[Japanese comic books]). 特に「アニメ」や「マンガ」などに対して熱狂的な関心をもつ人のことを言う場合に用いる.「アニメオタク」「マンガオタク」のように用いる. 特定の関心事に「ハマッタ人」(people being ruled by one interest from which they cannot be freed by reasoning)のこと. ¶**おたく族** freaks; junkies. **アニメおたく** an animation nerd[geek, freak]; an animaniac; an *anime* obsessive. **カメラおたく** a camera nerd[geek]. **コンピューターおたく** a computer nerd[geek]. **コンピューター・ゲームおたく** a computer game nerd[geek]. **テレビゲームおたく** a video-game freak[nerd]; a video-game addict. **マンガおたく** a comic-book fanatic.

おたちだい【お立ち台】❶〈皇居の〉the Balcony of Appearances (in the Imperial Palace). The Emperor and members of the Imperial Family appear on the balcony to offer their

お

congratulations to the public. ⇨一般参賀

❷〈競技場・野球場など〉 an interview platform for the game[match] heroes; a temporary platform for interviewing the game[match] winners[victors] (in a baseball park or stadium)

❸〈ディスコなど〉 a dancing platform [stage] for the dancers (in a discotheque).

おたびしょ【御旅所】 a temporary place to put a portable shrine (in the festival parade); a place where a portable shrine rests for a while (during the parade). 神社の祭礼のとき，（巡行中）神輿を本宮から移して一時的に安置する所. ⇨神輿

おたふく【お多福】 an *otafuku*; a round-faced woman with plump cheeks and a flat nose. ふっくらした頬と低い鼻の丸顔の女性. ⇨おかめ

おたふくまめ【お多福豆】❶ big broad beans (that look like the face of an *otafuku*). 大粒のそらまめ. ⇨そらまめ／お多福

❷〈甘く煮た豆〉 sweet boiled broad beans; sweetened broad beans.

おたま【お玉】 〈玉じゃくし〉a soup ladle; 〈柄杓〉 a dipper; 〈杓文字〉a rice scoop. ⇨お玉杓子

おだまきむし【小田巻き蒸し】 egg custard with *udon*[wheat noodles] added; egg custard dish added with a base of *udon*, chicken meat, fish paste and *shiitake* mushrooms. うどんの入った茶碗蒸し. 鶏肉，蒲鉾，椎茸なども加えて蒸す. ⇨茶碗蒸し

おたまじゃくし【お玉杓子】 ❶〔幼生〕a tadpole; ㊍ a polliwog.「かえるの子」

❷〈杓子〉 a soup ladle; a dipper. 汁をすくう柄杓. 単に「お玉」ともいう. ⇨お玉

❸〈音符〉a musical note.

おだわらちょうちん【小田原提灯】 a folding cylindrical paper lantern. 伸び縮みできる(collapsible)，筒のような細長い提灯. ⇨提灯

おち【落ち】 a (humorous) punch line (of a joke) (which makes the audience laugh at unexpected conclusion of comic storytelling); a humorous surprise ending (of comic storytelling). 落語などの話を結ぶ洒落 (wordplay)や冗談の要点. ⇨落語

おちあゆ【落ち鮎】 an *ayu*[a sweetfish] coming down the river to spawn in autumn; an *ayu* going downstream to spawn in fall. 秋に産卵のため川をくだる鮎.

おちうど[おちょうど]【落人】 a refugee; a fugitive; a defeated warrior[soldier] on the run from the enemy. 戦争に負けて逃げる侍[兵士].「おちびと」の音便. ¶平家の落人 defeated warriors of the Heike clan.

おちむしゃ【落ち武者】 a fleeing *samurai* (of a defeated army); a surviving *samurai* (of the Heike clan).

おちゃ【お茶】「茶」の丁寧語. ⇨茶

おちゃづけ【お茶漬け】 ⇨茶漬け

おちゃや【お茶屋】 ⇨茶屋❷

おちょこ【お猪口】 a small *sake* cup. ⇨猪口

おちゅうげん【お中元】 ⇨中元

おっかけ【追っかけ】 stalking(行為)；a stalker(人)；a groupie(人)

おつくり【お作り】 sliced raw fish. ⇨刺身 ¶マグロのお作り (a dish of) sliced raw tuna.

おつけ【お付け】 *miso*[bean paste] soup served at the formal dinner. 本膳の「おつゆ」(特に味噌汁).

おっとせい【膃肭獣】 〔動物〕a fur seal; a sea bear.

おつぼね【お局】 ⇨局

おてしょ【お手塩】 a small plate. 浅い小皿. ☆女性詞

おてだま【お手玉】❶〈袋〉 an *otedama*; a beanbag (used as a toy by girls).

❷〈遊戯〉 an *otedama* game; a game of tossing-up beanbags (played mostly by girls).

おてつき【御手付き】〈カルタ取り〉touching [picking up] the wrong card. ⇨歌留多

おてまえ【御手前・御点前】〔茶道〕tea-serving manners in the tea ceremony; procedures of the tea-serving etiquette in the tea cult. 茶の湯の作法. ⇨手前（薄茶手前・濃茶手前）☆『お手前拝見させていただきます』It is a great honor to watch you perform the tea ceremony.『結構なお手前でした』It was a well-performed tea ceremony.

おてもと【お手元・お手許】 (a pair of) chopsticks. 日本料亭などで用いる「箸」の丁寧語. ⇨箸

おでん【御田】 *oden*; Japanese hodgepodge [英 hotchpotch] of foods（寄せ集め料理）; Japanese stew-like dishes simmered long in flavored stock. (a dish of) *Oden* contains many kinds of vegetables and seafoods of *oden* ingredients which are simmered slowly and long in dried kelp stock (or fish broth) in a large earthenware pan[pot]. Hot mustard paste is often served as a condiment. おでんにはいろいろな野菜や魚介類などの具があり，大きな土鍋の中の昆布出し汁 (stock made from dried kelp) でゆっくりと長くぐつぐつと煮る．薬味としてねり芥子が出る．☆「煮込み田楽」の略称．「田楽」の女房詞．関西では「関東だき」ともいう．自動販売機の「おでん缶」は canned *oden*という．

〔料理〕味噌おでん Japanese hotchpotch of foods cooked in *miso*-flavored sauce.

【御田のネタ[具]】 *oden* ingredients stewed in dried kelp stock[fish broth] and served hot. ⇨厚揚げ/竹輪/大根/豆腐/がんもどき/はんぺん/いか/じゃがいも/昆布/こんにゃく/さつま揚げ/ゆで卵/つみれ/練り物/しらたき/きんちゃくなど．

おとうまつり【御灯祭】 the Fire Festival (of Kannokura Shrine). (2月). ⇨付記(1)「日本の祭り」

おとおし【お通し】 an appetizer; hors d'oeuvre; a relish. It is served with a drink or before the meal. 食前の軽いつまみ物また飲み物. ☆日本では「通し」「おつまみ」「突き出し」「先づけ」「箸づけ」などともいう. 日本の料理屋で顧客を通してすぐに出す「酒の肴」のこと. ⇨肴

おとしだま【お年玉】 New Year's monetary gift (presented to children); money given as a present at the New Year. *Otoshidama* is money given by parents or relatives to their children as a New Year's present. ☆元来，新年の祝いに目上の者(superiors)が目下の者(servants)に与える贈物であった．また正月の終り頃に年神に供えた「年魂[年玉]」という丸い餅 (round-shaped rice cakes offered the deity of the year) を子供や使用人に与える習慣があった．年神の力 (the power of Toshigami[the deity of the year]) が宿るという(俗信)餅を食して健康を祈願した．⇨餅

【お年玉付き年賀はがき】 a (prize-winning) New Year's lottery postcard. It is an official New Year's postcard with a lottery number printed at the bottom of the address side. 住所側の下に印刷されたくじ番号のある官製はがき. ⇨宝くじ

おとそ【お屠蘇】 ⇨屠蘇

おどりぐい【躍り食い】eating small fish (that are) still alive and moving. The Japanese swallow ice gobies or shrimps alive after dipping them in a cup of vinegar-and-*shoyu* sauce. 小さい素魚（またはエビ）を生きたまま酢醤油で飲み込むこと．☆福岡市室見川の名物．⇨エビの躍り食い/しろうお

おに【鬼】 a demon（悪魔）; a devil（悪鬼）; a fiend（悪霊）; an ogre（怪物）. *Oni* [Demons], imaginary symbols of evil, are generally depicted as humans with horns

お

and fangs, and as beings of superhuman strength with fearsome facial features. 鬼は想像上の悪の象徴. 角や牙のある人間の形をし, 恐ろしい顔形をした怪力のあるものとして描かれている. ⇨悪魔. ¶鬼面 a demon mask. **鬼打ち豆** roasted soybeans thrown at imaginary demons (on the Bean-Throwing Ceremony on February 3 or 4.). ⇨節分

おにおこぜ【鬼虎魚】〔魚〕a demon stinger; a scorpion fish; a stonefish. ちり鍋やから揚げに用いる.

おにがらやき【鬼殻焼】 a grilled[broiled] whole lobster[prawn] with its shell on. 殻のついたままの伊勢エビ[車エビ]などを焼く料理.

おにがわら【鬼瓦】 a ridge-end tile with a devil's head. It is an ornamental [decorative] tile placed at the ridge end of a tiled roof with a devil's head to ward off evil spirits. 屋根の棟の端にある鬼面の瓦. 屋根の棟の両端に置く, 鬼の面をかたどった装飾的な瓦. 魔除け(keep away evil)に使用する. ☆ headは neck(首)より上の部分をさし, face(顔)をも含む.

おにぎり【お握り】 a rice ball (rolled with both hands); a hand-rolled[hand-molded] boiled rice. It is made by molding rice into the shape of a round ball (or a triangle) in the palms of both hands. It is usually seasoned with a sprinkling of salt. It is often wrapped in[covered with] a thin sheet of dried laver on the outside and stuffed[filled] with a pickled plum (or salted salmon flakes) in the center[middle]. ご飯を丸形(または三角形)に両手で握ったもの. 薄い塩味がついている. 外側は海苔で巻き, 中部には梅干(または塩鮭)などを入れる場合が多い. 「握り飯」の丁寧語. 「おむすび」などともいう. ⇨梅のお握り / 鮭のお握り / 焼きお握り

おにご【鬼子】〈親に似ない子〉a child with features unlike its parents; a changeling; 〈歯肉に歯が生えて生まれた子〉a newborn baby with its teeth on its gums[its teeth coming through].

おにごっこ【鬼ごっこ】 (play a game of) tag; 英 tig; blindman's buff (目隠しの鬼).

おにのせんたくいわ【鬼の洗濯岩】 sea-eroded rock formations which look like the devil's washboard. These strangely shaped rocks are protruding from the sea between the waves (found in Nichinan Beach in Miyazaki Prefecture). 海の波間に突き出た(侵食)奇岩. 宮崎県の日南海岸にある.

おにゆり【鬼百合】〔植物〕a tiger lily; an ogre lily; a crumble lily. ⇨ゆり

おにわばん【お庭番】 a shogun's spy; a spy who served the shogun in the Edo period.

おはぎ【お萩】 *ohagi*; 〈餡子でまぶす〉a glutinous rice ball[dumpling] covered with sweetened red *adzuki* bean paste; 〈黄粉でまぶす〉a glutinous rice ball[dumpling] coated with yellowish soybean flour; 〈胡麻でまぶす〉a glutinous rice ball[dumpling] sprinkled with sesame seeds and salt. It is customarily offered at[in front of] the tablet of the deceased[offered to the spirits of the ancestors] in the vernal and autumnal equinoctial week. 小豆餡(または黄粉や胡麻)をまぶした丸型の(もち米)ご飯の団子. 慣例上お彼岸時 (in the spring and autumn equinoctial week)の仏前[先祖の霊]に供える. ☆秋は「お萩」(萩 (Japanese bush clover)の季節), 春は「牡丹餅」(牡丹 (peony)の季節). ⇨彼岸会 / 牡丹餅

おはこ【十八番】 one's favorite party trick; one's specialty[英 speciality]; one's forte. 得意の芸. ⇨お家芸

おはじき【お弾き】 ❶〈遊び〉(a game of) flicking-out marbles (played by girls). Girls flick the pieces of variously colored glass[pebble] discs back and forth with their fingers. 色とりどりのガラス[小石] を指で前後に「弾いて」遊ぶ. ☆「ビー玉遊び」は a game of marbles.

❷〈玉〉 marbles; variously colored glass (or pebble)discs used in the flicking-out marbles game.

オバタリアン a pushy[an obnoxious] middle-aged woman; an old hag.

おはち【お鉢】 a rice bowl[tub]; a container for boiled rice; a tub for steamed rice. ⇨おひつ

おはらい【お祓い】〈清めの儀式〉a (Shinto) purification rite; a (Shinto) rite of purification;〈悪魔祓い〉Shinto exorcism. It is performed by a Shinto priest to remove evil spirits. Impurity and calamity are exorcised by having a Shinto priest wave in a sweeping motion a sacred staff with cut paper at the Shinto shrine. 神主が悪霊をはらい清めるために行う儀式. 神社で神主に御幣を振ってもらい, 穢れや災難を取り払う. ⇨清め / 御幣. ¶厄払いのお祓いをしてもらう have oneself purified to drive out[away] evil spirits. ⇨厄払い

おばんざい〈京都の用語〉⇨おかず

おび【帯】 an *obi*. (優 *obi*; *obis*); a sash (worn with a *kimono*); a belt. ¶帯を締める tie[do up, put on] an *obi*. 帯を解く untie[undo] an *obi*.

❶〈男女共通〉an *obi*[a sash] for a *kimono* (for both men and women); a *kimono* sash [belt]. 着物用の帯. 着物の上にしめる帯(男女兼用).

❷〈男帯〉a narrow *obi* tied in a decorative bow at the back, worn with a *kimono* (for men). 背中で装飾的な結びでしめた狭い帯. 着物と着用する. 角帯 / 兵児帯

❸〈女帯〉 a broad *obi* tied in a decorative bow at the back, worn with a *kimono* (for women). It often uses extra cords. 背中で

装飾的な結びでしめた広い帯. 着物と着用する. 追加のひもを使用する場合が多い. ⇨名古屋帯 / 袋帯 / 丸帯 / 半幅帯

【帯揚げ】 an *obi* support[bustle]; a support[bustle] for an *obi*; a support[bustle] worn the *kimono obi*. It is a decorative piece of (silk) cloth used with the *obi*[sash] when wearing a *kimono*. It is passed through the bow and tied in front so that the knot does not sag. (It is tied to prevent a knot of a sash from sliding down. / It is tied to keep the main bow from slipping down.) 帯の支え[腰あて]. 着付けのとき帯といっしょに用いる上品な(絹)布. (女性の締めた)帯がくずれないように結び目の中を通し, 後ろから前に回して結ぶ.

【帯板】 an *obi* board. It is a flat piece of stiff material slipped between the front folds of an *obi* to give it shape when wearing a *kimono*. 着付け時に形を整えるため帯の折り目の間にそっと入れる平たい硬い生地.

【帯地】 an *obi* material[cloth]; a material [cloth] for the *kimono* belt. 帯にする布地.

【帯下】 a narrow belt worn under the *obi*. 帯の下に締める紐.

【帯芯】 *obi* padding.

【帯締め】 an *obi* cord[band, belt]; a cord for securing the whole *obi*; a belt for holding an *obi* in place. It is fastened over a tied sash (*obi*) so that the sash will not be undone when wearing a *kimono*. 帯のひも. 帯全体をしっかり締めるひも. 帯を適度に保持するひも. 着付けのとき帯が解けないように結んだ帯の上で締めて帯を押さえる細いひも.

【帯留め・帯止め】 ❶〈帯止めのひも〉a *kimono* sash cord[clip] (used to hold an *obi* in place). 着物の帯の上を適切に押さえて締めるひも[留め具]. ❷〈帯止めの飾り〉an ornamental clasp[decorative clip] attached to a *kimono* sash cord; an ornamental

お

fastener for a sash cord. It is a kind of *an obi-dome* brooch made of gems (or ivory) and fixed in the center of a sash. 着物の帯締めにつける装飾をほどこした留め金具[留め具]．珠玉石(または象牙)などで作られ，帯の中央につける一種のブローチ．

【帯紐】 an *obi* fastener (used when wearing a *kimono*); a webbing.

【帯枕】 a pillow-like oval pad[cushion] for an *obi* (used to keep the *obi* knot in place). It is a thick pad for holding up the bow of the *obi* at the back when wearing a *kimono*. It is used to keep the *obi* support in shape. (帯の結び目を適切に保つために用いる)帯用の枕型の丸い当て物．着付けのとき帯の結びを背後で持ち上げるための当て物で，帯の結び目の形を整えるために用いる．

おびいわい【帯祝い】 the maternity *obi*-binding[*obi*-wrapping] ceremony in the fifth month of pregnancy in pray for an easy childbirth; the ceremony of binding[wrapping] a supportive *obi* of cloth around a fifth-month pregnant woman's waist. 妊娠5か月目に，安産を祈って妊婦が岩田帯をするときの祝い．⇨岩田帯

おびときのぎょうじ【帯解きの行事】 ⇨七五三

おひがん【お彼岸】 ⇨彼岸

おひたし【お浸し】 ⇨浸し物

おひつ【お櫃】 boiled rice chest[tub]; wooden container for boiled rice (used to keep freshly rice in). ご飯を入れておく木製の器．「めしびつ」の丁寧語．「お鉢」ともいう．⇨お鉢

おびな【男雛】 the emperor doll (displayed as one of the *hina* dolls in the Girls' Festival). ⇨女雛

おひなさま【お雛様】 a set of dolls displayed on a tiered stand during[in] the season of the Girls' Festival. ⇨ひなまつり

おひねり【お捻り】 a monetary gift wrapped in paper; a tip[gratuity] wrapped in a twisted piece of paper. お金を包んでひねりたもの．☆人に祝儀として与えるとき，または賽銭箱に入れるときなどに用いる．

おひや【お冷】 (a glass of) cold water.

おひょう【大鮃】[魚] a (Pacific) halibut. カレイ科の魚．刺身に用いる．⇨かれい

おひらき【お開き】 a close; a conclusion,「終わり」の忌み詞．¶お開きにする bring to a close[conclusion]. 宴会[会合]をお開きにする close a banquet[meeting]; bring up.

おひろめ【お披露目】 an announcement; an introduction．¶襲名のお披露目 an announcement of one's succession to one's predecessor's name．芸者のお披露目 a round of calls to make an announcement of one's debut．結婚のお披露目の宴 a wedding reception.

オフかい【オフ会】 an off-line gathering; an off-line party;〈俗語〉face time. ☆「オフ会」オンライン (on-line)で知り合った仲間同士が集まること．

おふくろのあじ【おふくろの味】 the taste of one's mom's[mother's] cooking; the taste of home cooking; food like mother used to make; good old home cooking．⇨肉(肉じゃが)

おふせ【お布施】 ⇨布施

おふだ【お札】 a charm(お守り)；an amulet(護符)；a talisman(呪い札)．*Ofuda* is a thin strip[piece] of wood on which a special invocation or the name of a shrine[temple] is written. It can be obtained at a shrine[temple] and placed on the household Shinto[Buddhist] altar. 神社[お寺]で出す守り札．お札には特別な祈願または神社[お寺]の名前がある．神社[お寺]で入手し，神棚[仏壇]に納める．⇨お守り

おへんろさん【お遍路さん】 ⇨遍路

おぼろ【朧】 mashed and seasoned fish (or shellfish); seasoned fish-mince; minced (and) boiled fish. 魚肉(魚介類)を蒸し，細かくほぐして味つけした食品. ⇨そぼろ

〔食品〕朧昆布 thinly shaved[shredded] and steamed tangle[kelp]; tangle[kelp] shaved[shredded] into thin sheets. It is used in clear soup or vinegared food, sometimes over rice. 干し昆布を細く削った食品. 吸物や酢の物，時にご飯に使う. ⇨こぶ. 朧豆腐 soy-milk curd. 豆乳ににがりを加えて，固まりかけた豆腐.

おぼろづきよ【朧月夜】a (spring) night with a hazy moon.

おぼん【お盆】⇨盆

おまいり【お参り】a visit to a Shinto shrine [Buddhist temple]. ¶お参りする. visit a shrine[temple]; worship at a shrine [temple]. ⇨参詣

おまじり【お交じり・お混じり】thin rice gruel containing a small amount of solid rice; thin rice gruel with some soft grains. 重湯の中に，少量の米粒が混じっているもの. ☆病人などの食べ物. ⇨重湯

おまもり【お守り】an *omamori* (said to summon good fortune and expel misfortune); an amulet (厄除け) ; a talisman (魔除け); a good-luck charm (幸運をよぶ). It is a small portable handmade tablet covered with fine brocade cloth that ensures the safety of its holder, on which a special invocation is written. It is believed that a god resides in it. お守りは幸運を招き，邪悪を払うといわれる. 保持者の身の安全を保障する錦織の布で巻いた (wrapped in) 携帯用の手製の小札で，その上に特殊な祈願文が書いてある. 神が宿ると信じられている. 「お札」ともいう. ¶お守り袋 an amulet[a talisman] bag; a good-luck charm case. 家内安全のお守り a good-luck charm for the well-being of one's family. 安産祈願のお守り a good-luck charm for a healthy childbirth[for an easy delivery]. 災難除けのお守り a talisman against calamities; a talisman to ward off [drive off] misfortune. 交通安全のお守り an amulet for traffic safety. 合格祈願のお守り a good-luck charm for the passing of entrance examination. 商売繁盛のお守り an amulet for business prosperity. 無病息災のお守り an amulet for good health[for a perfect state of health].

おみおつけ【御御御付(御味御付)】*miso* soup. 本来は具が多数ある味噌汁の意. 「味噌汁」の丁寧語. ⇨味噌汁

おみき【お神酒】sacred *sake* offered to a Shinto god (in Shinto rites and festivals). It is used as a ritual libation offered to a Shinto god in the indigenous religion of Japan. 神前に供える儀式用の献酒. ☆libationは「神に供える酒」. ¶お神酒徳利 (a pair of) sacred *sake* bottles offered on[in front of] the Shinto altar.

おみくじ【お神籤】an *omikuji*; a written oracle[divination] (picked at a Shinto shrine or Buddhist temple); a fortune-telling paper[slip] (drawn at a Shinto shrine or Buddhist temple); a piece[strip] of paper on which a prediction of one's fortune[luck] is written[printed]. *Omikuji* paper tells a lottery message of a god with a short explanation added. After reading their oracle, people usually tie the fortune paper to a branch[twig] of a tree in hope that their prayer may come true. (社寺で引く)書面の神託[運勢を告げる紙]. 吉凶の運勢を占うために神仏の意が書かれた[印刷された]一枚の紙. お御籤には短い説明を加えた神のお告げが書いてある. 読んだあとは樹木の枝に結び付け，祈願の成就を祈る.

【関連語】The fortune-telling paper[slip] reads messages of the best luck[fate] (大吉), the better luck[fate] (吉), good luck[fate] (**中吉**). poor luck [fate] (**小吉**), bad luck[fate] (**末吉**), the worse luck[fate] (**凶**) and the worst luck [fate] (**大凶**).

おみこし【お神輿】 ⇨神輿

おみずとり【お水取り】 the Water-Drawing Ceremony (at Todai-ji Temple). (3月). ⇨付記(1)「日本の祭り」

おみなえし【女郎花】〔植物〕a maiden flower; a patrinia. ⇨「秋の七草」

おむすび【お結び】a rice ball. ⇨おにぎり

おめでたこん【おめでた婚】 the wedding of a pregnant bride and her groom. ⇨できちゃった婚

おもアド【主アド】 an ***omo-ado***; the main [principal] supporting actor in a kyogen comic play; the main[principal] supporting actor[an actor who supports] the protagonist in a kyogen comic play. 狂言で主役を支える主な相手役. ⇨アド

おもがし【主菓子】 ❶〔茶道〕fresh[moist] sweets (often served with thick powdered green tea in the tea ceremony). 茶道で「濃茶」といっしょに出される. ⇨茶菓子／干菓子(薄茶)

❷〔菓子〕 wet cake; moist confection [confectionery]. ***Omogashi*** is molded from sweet ***adzuki***-bean paste or soft pounded[glutinous] rice. Most are formed into dumplings in the shape of flowers or leaves expressive of a particular season. 餡子また柔らかく捏ねたもち米[糯米]で作り, それぞれの季節を表す花や葉などの形にする.「生菓子」ともいう. ☆羊羹, 大福餅などの和菓子. ⇨生菓子／羊羹／大福餅

おもづかい【主遣い・面遣い】〔文楽〕 the head manipulator (of the puppeteer trio in bunraku). He is the main manipulator who operates the head[face] as well as the right arm and hand of a single puppet. He appears with his face uncovered, while the

other two[*ashi-zukai* and *hidari-zukai*] wear hoods over their entire heads. 文楽人形を操る三人遣いの中で「主役」を演ずる. 人形の頭[顔]と右腕と右手を操る.「主遣い」は顔を覆うことはないが「足遣い」と「左遣い」は頭に頭巾を被る. ⇨足遣い／左遣い／三人遣い

おもてがき【表書き】 handwritten label, including the purpose for the gift and the full name of the presenter. 贈答のときに贈り物の目的(御入学祝など)と送り主(gift-giver)の名前を表面に書く. ⇨贈答

おもてせんけ【表千家】 the Omote-Senke school of the tea ceremony.「三千家」の茶道流派の一つ. ⇨千家

おもてみごろ【表身頃】 the four outer panels of a *kimono*. ⇨裏身頃

おもや【母屋・母家】the main house [building] (where the housemaster often lives). (家の中央に位置し, 家長が在住する)主な家[建物].

おもゆ【重湯】 thin rice gruel[porridge]; the liquid part of rice gruel. 水分を多くして米を煮た, のり状の薄い汁. ☆病人用や乳児用の流動食. ⇨粥／お交じり

おやかた【親方】〔相撲〕a stable master for the *sumo* wrestlers (who runs a *sumo* training gym). All stable masters were often former senior wrestlers (*sekitori*), and the only people entitled to train new *sumo* wrestlers. They are members of the Japan Sumo Association. 相撲部屋を管理・指導する. 日本相撲協会に属す. ⇨相撲部屋／お上さん／年寄

おやこでんわ【親子電話】a party line; a telephone with additional cordless handsets; a set of main and extension telephones.

おやこどんぶり【親子丼】 (a bowl of) steamed rice served with chicken and eggs on top; (a bowl of) steamed rice with a topping of boiled chicken and eggs.

Oyakodon is a bowl of steamed rice topped with pieces of boiled chicken meat and thinly-sliced green onions boiled in beaten eggs, seasoned with *shoyu*[soy sauce], *mirin*[sweetened *sake*] and sugar. 鶏肉と卵をのせた丼飯. 醤油・味醂・砂糖で味つけした卵とじで煮た鶏肉と細かく切ったタマネギをのせた丼飯. ☆ chicken and eggは「親(parent) 子 (child)」. ⇨丼物

おやこのだんぜつ【親子の断絶】 generation gap between parents and their children.

おやごろし【親殺し】 parricide; the murder of one's own parents. ☆父親殺し (patricide)/ 母親殺し (matricide). ⇨尊属殺人

オヤジがり【親父狩り】〈中年男性を襲う〉 attacking a middle-aged[elderly] man;〈金を奪う〉the mugging of a middle-aged man by (a group of) juveniles; preying on a middle-aged man beaten up by (a group of) youngsters.

オヤジギャル【親父ギャル】 a young woman with the brusque habits of a middle-aged man.

オヤジギャグ【親父ギャグ】 a worn-out joke; a corny[unfunny] joke; an older man's attempt at humor. 使い古した冗談.

おやつ【お八つ】 an afternoon snack; ㊧ afternoon tea; a light meal; refreshments. 昔の「八つ時」（現在の午後2時から4時）に食したことが由来. 現在の「3時のお茶の時間」. ¶**お八つの時間** snack time; ㊧ teatime. **お八つにする** take[have] a refreshment break.

おやばか【親ばか】 blind parental love; a doting[fond] parent[father, mother].

おやぶんこぶん【親分子分】 a boss-flunky relationship; a relationship between a boss and his henchmen.

おやま 【女形】*oyama*. ❶〔歌舞伎〕a kabuki female impersonator; a kabuki actor who plays female roles. 歌舞伎で女役をする男

性の役者. ⇨女形. ¶**立女形** the leading actor for female kabuki roles.

❷〈人形〉a doll female impersonator; a doll who plays female roles. あやつり人形で女装の人形.

おやゆびぞく【親指族】 a thumbster; a thumb tribe; a cell-phonist (who operates a cell-phone with one hand[thumb]). 携帯電話を親指で器用に操作する人.

おり【澱・滓】〈複数形で〉 the dregs; the lees; the grounds; (a) sediment. 液体の底に沈殿したかす. ¶**お茶の滓** the dregs of tea.

おりがみ【折り紙】 *origami*. ❶〈用紙〉 *origami* paper; the colored paper used for folding into various figures[shapes]; the colored paper used for making figures[shapes] by folding. いろいろな形状に折りあげるための色紙. ☆「**折りあげた紙**」は folded paper. ⇨千代紙

❷〈細工〉 the art of folding paper to form shaped figures. *Origami* is the traditional art of folding square, colored pieces of paper into various shapes[figures] of animals, flowers or various things without using scissors or paste. 造形物を折る技術. （四角の）紙を鋏や糊を用いずに動物や花などの形に折る日本古来の紙芸術. ⇨折り鶴

おりづめ【折詰】food packed in a thin[small] wooden box with a lid (*kyogi-bako*). It contains various kinds of food such as vegetables, fish and meat together with steamed rice. 蓋のある薄い木製の箱[経木箱] に詰めた食物. ご飯といっしょに野菜・魚・肉などが盛りつけられている. ⇨経木箱

〔料理〕**折詰鮨** *sushi* packed in a thin wooden box with a lid. **折詰弁当** a box lunch; a packed lunch; a lunch packed in a thin wooden box with a lid.

おりづる【折り鶴】 a folded-paper crane (made in pray for somebody's recovery).

⇨折り紙／千羽鶴

お

おりど【折り戸】　a folding door. It is often used as the doorway of the household Buddhist altar. 中央から折りたためるようにした戸. 仏壇などの入り口に用いられている.

おりべやき【織部焼】　Oribe ceramic ware (characterized by geometrical designs). It is made according to the designs of Oribe Furuta, one of the disciples of Sen no Rikyu. 茶人千利休(1521-91)の弟子である古田織部(1544-1615)の文様で作成する. 美濃地方の特産.

おりもの【織物】　(textile) fabrics; woven cloth(s); woven textiles; woven stuff. ☆ fabricは clothより堅い語. ¶毛織物 woolen fabrics. 絹織物 silk fabrics. 綿織物 cotton fabrics. 合成織物 synthetic fabrics. 織物製品 textile goods; woven goods. ⇨西陣織／大島紬

オリンピック　the Olympic Games; the Olympics; the Olympiad. ¶東京オリンピック Tokyo Olympic Games(1964年・2021年開催)

おれいまいり【お礼参り】　(pay) a visit of thanks to a shrine[temple]. ¶(入試合格の)お礼参りする visit[go to] a shrine[temple] to offer one's thanks (for the success of entrance examination)

オレオレさぎ【オレオレ[俺・俺]詐欺】　money-transfer fraud; a pretense of [pretending to be] a son (or grandson) in trouble who calls an elderly person to demand money; an "it's me" scam.「振り込め詐欺」ともいう. ⇨振り込め詐欺

おろし【卸し・下ろし】〈おろし器〉a grater. ☆ grated「卸した」
〔料理〕卸し和え dishes dressed with grated *daikon*[Japanese radish]; dishes in grated *daikon* seasoned with *shoyu*[soybean sauce] and vinegar. (醤油や酢で味付けした大根卸しで具を和える. ⇨白子の卸し和え／なめこの卸し和え／まぐろの卸し和え). 卸し生姜 grated ginger. 卸し生姜を添えた豆腐 *tofu*[bean curd] served with grated ginger. 卸しそば buckwheat noodles topped with a mound of grated *daikon*[Japanese radish]. 卸し大根 grated *daikon*[Japanese radish]. 卸し山葵 grated *wasabi*[Japanese horseradish].

おろしがね【卸金・下し金】　a grater. ¶大根卸金 a *daikon*[Japanese radish] grater.

おわらいばんぐみ【お笑い番組】　a comedy program[show].

おわらいタレント【お笑いタレント[芸人]】　a comedian; a comic.

おわらかぜのぼん【おわら風の盆】　the Bon Dance of the Wind. (9月). ⇨付記(1)「日本の祭り」

おわりつしまてんのうまつり【尾張津島天王祭】　the Lantern Festival (at Tsushima Shrine). (7月). ⇨付記(1)「日本の祭り」

おんがくはいしん【音楽配信】　an online music distribution. ¶無料音楽配信 a free music distribution. 違法音楽配信 an illegal music distribution. 電子音楽配信 an electronic music distribution[EMD].

おんきゅう【温灸】an indirect moxubustion; an indirect moxa treatment. ⇨灸

おんせん【温泉】　*Onsen*; a hot[thermal] spring; a spa. *Onsen* is used not only as treatment for rheumatism or neuralgia but also for relaxing in a hot bath. 温泉はリュウマチや神経痛などの治療だけでなく骨休みに利用する. ☆「掛け流し」は free-flowing hot-spring water,「湯中り」は feeling dizzy after taking a long bath; discomfort caused by prolonged bathing.
¶熱海温泉 Atami spa[hot spring]; the spa at Atami City. 温泉郷 a hot-spring village. 温泉客 a visitor to[at] a hot-spring facility. 温泉卵 a hot-spring egg; an egg boiled

in hot-spring waters; a boiled egg with a semi-solid white and a solid yellow[yolk] (白身が半熟 (soft-boiled white)、黄身が堅ゆで (hard-boiled yellow)の卵. **温泉保養地**[温泉場] a hot-spring resort; a spa. **温泉宿**[旅館] a hot-spring hotel[inn]; a hotel[an inn] with hot-spring bathing facilities. **温泉療法** hot-spring cure[therapy]. **温泉巡り** a tour of hot-spring resort. **日本三古湯** the Three Oldest Hot Springs in Japan(有馬温泉[兵庫県]・白浜温泉[和歌山県]・道後温泉[愛媛県])

【関連語】「**砂湯**(鹿児島県の指宿温泉)」 mineral sand bath. ⇨ 砂風呂.「**泥湯**(大分県の別府温泉)」 mineral mud [clay] bath. 「**温泉蒸気浴**(秋田県の後生掛温泉)」 steam hot bath.「**温泉熱気浴**」 hot air bath (秋田県の玉川温泉の岩盤浴).「**全身浴**」 full-body soak; soaking the whole body in hot-spring water.「**半身浴**」 half-body soak; soaking the lower half of the body in hot-spring water.「**腰湯**」 taking a lower-body bath; soaking the lower body in hot-spring water.「**足湯**」 taking a footbath; soaking feet in hot-spring water.「**かぶり湯**」 pouring hot-spring water on the body. 「**打たせ湯**」 cascading hot-spring water on the body.

おんたい【温帯】 the Temperate Zone. ⇨ 寒帯 / 熱帯

おんどり【雄鶏】〔鳥〕 ㊐ a cock; ㊗ a rooster. ⇨ にわとり

オンドル風呂 a Korean-style floor heater; a Korean system of underfloor heating ducts (found in Goshogake hot spring); a hypocaust. 秋田県の後生掛温泉のオンドル風呂は有名.

おんながた【女形】 a female impersonator; a female role[actor]. ☆演劇で女役を演じる男優のことを「**女形**」(an actor who plays female roles)という. 歌舞伎で女役をす

る男性の役者のことを「**女形**」(a kabuki female impersonator)という. ⇨ 女形

おんばしらさい【御柱祭】 the Tree-Pillar-Erecting Festival. (4月). ⇨ 付記(1)「日本の祭り」

おんみつ【隠密】 a spy[detective] in feudal times; a secret agent in the service of a *shogun* (or feudal lord) during the Edo period. 封建時代のスパイ[探偵]. ⇨ 忍者

おんよみ【音読み】 the Chinese-style reading of a character; reading a Chinese character phonetically.

か

か【蚊】〔虫〕 a mosquito(㊢ ~es, ~s). ⇨ ぼうふら / 蚊帳 / 蚊取り線香. ¶**藪蚊** a striped mosquito.

が【蛾】〔虫〕 a moth. ¶**衣蛾** a clothes moth. **蓑蛾** a bagworm moth. **刺蛾** an oriental moth.

が【賀】 celebration.¶**賀の祝い** the celebration of one's birthday; the celebration of one's longevity[long life]. 長寿を祝うこと. ⇨ 還暦(60歳) / 古希(70歳) / 喜寿(77歳) / 米寿(88歳) / 卒寿(90歳) / 白寿(99歳) / 上寿(100歳) =近年の慣習として[百寿]

かい【貝】〔貝〕 a shellfish. ⇨ 青柳 / 赤貝 / 浅蜊 / 蛤. ¶**貝殻** shell. **貝**[殻]**細工** shellwork. **貝合わせ** a game in which participants compete to find matching shells (played in the Heian period). ⇨ 歌合わせ

〔料理〕**貝の佃煮** shellfish boiled down in *shoyu*[soy sauce].

かい【～海】 the sea. ¶**日本海** the Japan Sea; the Sea of Japan. **内海** the Inland Sea. ⇨ 灘 / 海峡 / 湾 / 水道

かいうんのおまもり【開運のお守り】 a good-luck charm. ⇨ お守り

がいえん【外苑】 the outer garden. ⇔ 内苑. ¶**明治神宮外苑** the Outer Gardens of Meiji Shrine; Meiji Shrine Outer Gardens.

がいかい【外海】 the open sea; the ocean; the high seas(公海). 入り江・湾・岬などの外に広がる海.「そとうみ」. ⇔内海(ないかい・うちうみ).

かいかどん【開化丼】 ⇨牛丼

かいかよそう【開花予想】 the flower forecast; the expected time for flowering.

かいがん【海岸】 the (sea) coast(沿岸); the seashore(海辺); the beach(砂・小石のある海辺); the seaside(行楽地の海岸). ¶日南海岸(宮崎県)the Nichinan(kaigan) Coast. 海岸公園 the seaside park(横浜の山下公園など). 海岸砂丘 marine terrace. 海岸地方 coastal area[district]. 海岸保安林 coastal protection forest. ⇨浜／浦／砂丘

かいき【回忌】 an anniversary of a person's death. 毎年の命日.「年忌」「周忌」などともいう. ⇨周忌. ¶三回忌 the second anniversary of a person's death. ☆三回忌以降は死んだ年を含めて数えるので second となる. 七回忌 the sixth anniversary of a person's death; the sixth-year memorial service. ⇨法事

かいき【開基】 the foundation[founding] of a Buddhist temple[sect]. 寺院・宗派などを創立すること(開山). またその僧(開祖). ⇨開山／開祖

かいき【皆既】 an eclipse (of the sun[moon]). ¶皆既月食 a total eclipse of the moon; a total lunar eclipse. 皆既日食 a total eclipse of the sun; a total solar eclipse.

かいきょう【海峡】 a strait; a channel (strait より広い). ¶津軽海峡 the Tsugaru Straits. ⇨灘／湾／水道

かいけい【海景】 a seascape; a sea-view. ¶美しい海景に富む海岸線 the coastline with spectacular seascapes

かいけん【懐剣】 a dagger; a short sword. It is kept in the bosom of a Japanese *kimono* for self-defense. It was formally used by women to commit suicide in a moment of danger. 着物の懐におさめる護身用の短剣. 昔の婦人はいざという時に自害するのに用いた.

かいげん【改元】 the change of the name of an era. 国の年号を改めること.「改号」ともいう. ¶平成から令和に改元する change the name of the era to Reiwa from Heisei; move from the Heisei to the Reiwa Era.

かいげんくよう【開眼供養】 the consecrating ceremony of a newly-completed Buddhist statue[image]. It is held to call down the spirit of Buddha to it so that the statue[image] can become an object worthy of worship in a Buddhist temple. 仏像[仏画] の奉納式. 寺院で礼拝に値するよう新しくできた仏像に仏の霊(魂)を迎える儀式. ⇨大仏(開眼供養). ¶開眼供養する hold[observe] a consecrating ceremony of a newly-made Buddhist statue[image]. ☆consecration(カトリック用語)「聖変化, 聖別」ミサ聖祭のときパンとブドウ酒をキリストの体と血に変化させる (consecrate)こと.

かいこ【蚕】〔虫〕a silkworm. ☆繭 (cocoon)から生糸(silk)をつくる. ¶蚕の繭 a silkworm cocoon. 蚕棚 a silkworm growing-bed; a rack of shelves for 米 raising [英 rearing] silkworms. ⇨桑

かいご【介護】 nursing(看護); care(世話); nursing care; home-help assistance; looking after (the aged). ¶要介護度 the level of care needed[required]. 要介護認定 a care need assessment. 寝たきり老人の介護 (home) care for bedridden old people. ⇨寝たきり老人. 訪問介護 nursing care at home; nursing care services for the elderly living at home.

¶介護休業制度 family-care leave system. 介護認定 government authorization to receive nursing care. 介護保険制度 the nursing-care[home-care] insurance system;

the long-term care insurance system. 介護予防サービス services to prevent the necessity of full nursing care for the aged. 介護ロボット nursing robot. 介護福祉士 a licensed[qualified] nursing care worker[care giver]. 介護タクシー nursing taxi. 介護ビジネス nursing business.

かいこく【開国】 the opening of Japan to the world (in 1854). ⇔鎖国 (in 1639)

がいこくぶぎょう【外国奉行】 a (Japanese feudal) commissioner of foreign affairs.

かいざん[**かいさん**]【開山】❶〈寺の建立〉 the foundation[founding] of a Buddhist temple. ⇨開基. ¶**開山する** found a Buddhist temple.

❷〈寺の創始者〉 the founder of a Buddhist temple;〈開祖〉the founder of a Buddhist sect. ⇨開祖. ¶**開山堂** the building dedicated to the founder (of a Buddhist temple).

かいさんぶつ【海産物】 marine products; seafood(海産食品). ⇨農産物. ¶**海産物商** a seafood dealer; a dealer in seafood.

かいし【懐紙】 ❶〈茶道〉a pocket wiping paper; (a set of) sheets of folded white paper kept inside a *kimono*. It is used to place Japanese sweets on before drinking powdered green tea during the tea ceremony. It is also used to wipe the tea bowl dry after drinking tea at the tea ceremony. 着物などの懐中にたたんで入れておく和紙. 茶道で抹茶を飲む前に菓子をのせたり, また茶を飲んだ後に茶碗をふいたりするのに用いる.

❷〈詩歌・和歌用〉 (a set of) fine paper for writing a Japanese poem[*waka*, *tanka*] on. 和歌・連歌などを正式に書く上品な用紙.

かいしゃく【介錯】 assistance as a second; assisting a *samurai* in committing *seppuku* [ritual suicide by disembowelment] by cutting off his head to terminate his suffering. 介添人としての援助. 切腹する侍に

付き添って苦しむのを終わらせる (bring his agony to an end)ためにその首 (neckではない)をはねること. ⇨切腹. ¶**介錯人** a second assisted at ritual *seppuku*; a second appointed to assist in *seppuku*.

かいしょ【楷書】 the square[printed] style of letters or Chinese handwriting. 文字・漢字の書体の一つ. 字画をくずさない書き方. ⇨書体 / 草書 / 行書. ¶**名前は楷書で書く** print one's name; use block letters (in writing one's name). ☆英文の申請書などの "print" は「活字体で書く」の意.

かいしょく【海食・海蝕】 sea erosion; wave erosion; coastal erosion; erosion formed by the sea. ⇨浸食 / 風食. ¶**海食岩** a sea-eroded rock. **海食崖** a sea-eroded cliff. **海食台地**(千葉県・犬吠埼など) an abrasion platform; a tableland formed through erosion by the sea. **海食洞** a sea cave [grotto]; a cave formed by sea erosion. **海食で形成された奇岩怪石** fantastic-shaped rock formations created by sea erosion: sea-eroded strangely-shaped rocks.

かいじょけん【介助犬】 a service dog.

かいしん【改新】 reform(社会制度の改善)；reformation(改革)；renovation(刷新). ¶**大化改新** the Taika Reform.

がいじん[**げじん**]【外陣】 the outer shrine [temple]; the outer chamber[nave] of a Shinto shrine or Buddhist temple (where worshippers pay their respects). 神社・寺院の本殿や本堂の外にあり, 一般の参拝者が礼拝する所. ☆ nave「ネーブ, 身廊」教会堂の中央にある一般信者席のある部分. ⇔内陣

かいすいぎょ【海水魚】a sea fish; a saltwater fish. ⇨鹹水魚

かいせいじょ【開成所】 the Western school established by the Tokugawa shogunate. 江戸幕府の洋学校.

かいせきぜん【会席膳】 a Japanese dinner

tray (for each individual).「会席盆」ともいう.

かいせきりょうり【会席料理】 Japanese banquet-style full-course cuisine; Japanese party-style dishes served with *sake* when entertaining guests. It is a Japanese traditional meal served on each individual lacquered tray in a full course at a banquet. Diners eat several different courses in a relaxed atmosphere at a banquet while pouring *sake* for each other. 日本の宴会式フルコース料理. 接客するときに酒でもてなす会食. 宴会では伝統的な和食をフルコースで盛りつけた漆塗りの盆が各人に出される. 会食者は相互に酒を交わしながらいろいろな料理をくつろいだ雰囲気で食す. ☆「会席」とは元来連歌や俳諧を興行する歌会の席のことで, 宴席では酒を飲みながら食を楽しんだ. ⇨ 連歌 / 俳諧
☆「**本膳料理**」の略式化した料理.「**一汁三菜**」(one soup and three dishes <sliced raw fish, broiled and boiled foods>) が基調となる. 最初に「杯 (alcoholic beverages), 口取り (hors d'oeuvre), 刺身 (sliced raw fish)」, 次に「汁 (clear soup), 焼き物 (grilled seafoods), 煮物 (boiled foods of fish and vegetables), 蒸し物 (steamed foods of *chawanmushi*), 酢の物 (vinegared[pickled] foods)」, 最後に「飯」(steamed rice),「汁」(*miso* soup),「香の物」(pickles),「水菓子」(dessert)が出される. 現在は宴会・会食・結婚披露宴などの酒宴席の上品な料理 (a semiformal banquet cuisine served in delicate courses)をさす場合が多い.

かいせきりょうり【懐石料理】〔茶道〕tea-ceremony dishes; a simple meal served to entertain guests before a formal tea ceremony. It is prepared with the best and freshest foods and dishes expressive of the season. The meal enhances the flavor of the thick pasty tea (*koicha*) and thin foamy tea (*usucha*). 正式な茶の湯で, 茶を出す前に食べる簡単な食事. 季節感のある旬の新鮮な食材を使用する. 食事をすることによって濃茶・薄茶がおいしくいただける.
☆「懐石」は元来禅僧が座禅中寒さや飢えをしのぐ〔腹を温める〕ために着物の懐に入れた温石〔懐の石〕(a heated[warm] stone kept inside the *kimono* bosom that helps Zen monks forget cold and hunger during Zen practice)のこと. この料理も腹を温め空腹をしのぐ程度の軽い食事 (a light meal for warming the empty stomach and stave off the pangs of hunger)である. 通常, 茶道では「懐石」・「茶懐石」, 日本料亭では「懐石料理」という. ⇨茶懐石

かいそ【開祖】 ❶〈宗教界〉the founder of a Buddhist temple[sect]. 寺院・宗派の創始者. ⇨開基
❷〈芸術界〉the founder of an art school[a martial art]. 芸術・武芸などで, 一派・流派の創始者.

かいそう【海草・海藻】 seaweed(s); sea grass(es); marine plant(s). ☆緑藻・褐藻・紅藻の3種類がある.

かいぞえ【介添え】 ❶〈助手〉a helper[an assistant] (of the patient). (患者などの)そばについて世話する人.
❷〈花嫁の〉a bridesmaid;〈花婿の〉a best man 花嫁・花婿の世話役.

かいだん【戒壇】 the ordination platform [seat] in a big Buddhist temple. 僧に戒律を授ける儀式を行うために築いた壇. ¶**戒壇院** the Buddhist temple building that houses an ordination platform[seat].

かいちゅうこうえん【海中公園】 an undersea [underwater] park; a submarine park. ¶**展望台にある海中公園** a submarine park with an observation tower.

かいちゅうりん【海中林】 an undersea [underwater] forest of kelp.

かいちょう【開帳】 the exhibition[unveiling]

of a Buddhist statue or painting. 通常は未公開の仏像・仏画などを参詣者に拝ませること. ¶秘仏の開帳 the unveiling of a treasured Buddhist statue[image].

かいていかざん【海底火山】 a submarine[an undersea] volcano. ⇨活火山 / 休火山 / 死火山

かいていてつどうトンネル【海底鉄道トンネル】 a submarine[an undersea] railway tunnel. ¶青函トンネル the Seikan Tunnel, the world's second longest undersea railway tunnel (completed between Aomori and Hakodate in 1988). ☆全長53.85km.

かいてんずし【回転寿司】 (a plate of) *sushi* rested[set] on a circular conveyor belt at the *sushi* bar. 回転寿司店にある丸いコンベヤーベルトに盛られたすし.

【回転寿司店】 a revolving *sushi* bar; *sushi*-go-round restaurant; *sushi* bar[restaurant] with revolving counter carrying plates of *sushi*. Plates of *sushi* are rotated around the counter on a conveyor belt. Customers[Diners] choose whatever items they want as the plates of prepared *sushi* pass by on a circular conveyor belt in front of them. すし皿を運ぶ回転式カウンターがある寿司店. 顧客はコンベヤーベルトの上に準備された好きなすし皿をとる. ☆店によって皿は色分けされ (the color-coded plates), すしの値段 (the prices of *sushi*) を表す.

かいどう【街道】 a highway; a (high) road; a (main) route. ☆「裏街道」は a byway; a byroad; a backstreet. ¶甲州街道 the Koshu Highway. 青梅街道 the Ome Road. 街道筋(の町) a town on the main route (to Odawara).

かいばしら【貝柱】 the adductor muscle (of certain bivalve shellfish); the eyes of scallops. 二枚貝の貝殻を閉じる働きをする筋肉[肉柱] (主としてホタテ貝やバカ貝

など). 酢の物やすし種などに用いる. ☆「四珍」とはカイバシラ, アワビ, フカヒレ, イリコのこと. ⇨二枚貝 / 帆立貝 / あられそば. ¶ホタテ貝柱 scallops; scallop adductor muscle. 干し貝柱 dried scallops; dried shellfish adductor muscle.

かいまき【搔巻】 a sleeved quilt; a cotton-stuffed sleeping garment; a cotton-stuffed quilt with sleeves. 綿が薄く入った袖付きの夜着. 掛け布団の一種.

かいみょう【戒名】 ❶ a posthumous Buddhist name (given to a deceased person by a Buddhist priest). This name is written in several Chinese characters, which are engraved on his/ her memorial tablet to be placed in the family[household] Buddhist altar (or on the gravestone). 僧侶が死者[故人]に付ける名前. 数個の漢字で書かれ, 仏壇におく位牌(または墓石)に刻まれる. ☆浄土真宗では「法名」または「法号」という. ⇔俗名❶. ⇨位牌 / 仏壇. ¶戒名料 a fee (payable to a Buddhist priest[temple]) for a posthumous name.

❷ a Buddhist name given to a new Buddhist priest; a name given to a person who enters the Buddhist priesthood. 戒を受けて仏門に入った者に与える名. ⇔俗名❷. ⇨法名

かいものいぞんしょう【買物依存症】 manic[compulsive] shopping: (人) a shopaholic.

かいやき【貝焼き】 broiling in a shell; grilling in one's own shell. ❶ホタテ貝 (scallops)の殻に魚や野菜などを入れて直火で焼く. 秋田地方では「かやき」という. ❷牡蠣や蛤などの貝を殻ごと焼く. ⇨さざえの壺焼き

かいゆうしきていえん【回遊式庭園】 a stroll-type landscape garden; a going-around-type landscape garden; a landscape garden in a circular style. This garden is laid out to be viewed from various vantage points while strolling[going around] along the garden paths. A hill, a pond, a bridge, a small island and a tea hut[house] are found in this garden. 庭園の小道を散策しながら見晴らしのきく場所から観賞できるように設計された庭園．庭園内には丘，池，橋，小島また茶室などがある． 例 京都の「平安神宮」や「銀閣寺」．東京の「六義園」．岡山の「後楽園」． ⇨枯山水(庭園) / 日本庭園

かいらいせいふ【傀儡政府】 a puppet government; a puppet regime. 自分の意志を持たず他人にあやつられる政府．「傀儡政権」ともいう． 例 中国東北部の満州国． ☆「傀儡」は puppet(あやつり人形)のこと．

かいり【海里】 a nautical mile; a sea mile. 海上の距離の単位． ☆1海里は1852メートル． ¶20海里沖合漁業 a fishing ground 20 nautical miles (off the coast).

かいりつ【戒律】religious precepts[commandments] (that must be observed by Buddhist priests).

かいりゅう【海流】 an ocean current; a sea current. ¶日本海流 the Japan Current. 対馬海流 the Tsushima Current. ⇨寒流 / 暖流

がいりんざん【外輪山】 the outer rim of a crater. 複式火山で外側を輪状に囲む旧火山口壁． 例 阿蘇山(熊本県)． ⇨内輪山

かいろ【懐炉】 a portable body warmer. It is placed against the belly or in the *kimono*[dress] to keep oneself warm and comfortable during the cold season. Formerly it was a small metal box with a piece of a burning charcoal stick placed inside. 寒い季節に腹部にあてて，または衣服の内側に入れて身体を暖める携帯用道具．昔は内部には炭火を入れた金属製の小箱をさしていた． ¶懐炉灰 solid fuel for a body warmer (containing a burning charcoal stick).

かいわれ(だいこん)【貝割れ(大根)】 white *daikon*[radish] sprouts. 大根の貝割れ菜．和え物，すし種，即席漬けなどに用いる． ⇨大根

かいわれな【貝割れ菜】 leaf vegetable sprouts. 芽が出て双葉のときに食べる野菜．「つまみ菜」ともいう．

かえだまじゅけん【替え玉受験】 taking an examination under a false[an assumed] name; using a stand-in for one's examination.

かえだまとうひょう【替え玉投票】 voting illegally under a false[an assumed] name; using a stand-in to cast a person's name.

かえで【楓】〔植物〕a maple (tree);〈北米〉sugar maple. 通称「もみじ」(a Japanese maple). ⇨もみじ

かえりにゅうまく【帰り入幕】〔相撲〕coming back[returning] to the top[senior-grade] division of *sumo* wrestling. A *sumo* wrestler, who has once fallen to the *juryo*[the second division], comes back[returns] to the *makunouchi*[the top division]. 「十両」に一度陥落していた力士が「幕内」に再度戻ること．

かえる【蛙】〔両〕a frog; a toad. ¶雨蛙 a tree frog. 殿様蛙 a leopard frog. 食用蛙 an edible frog; a bullfrog(牛蛙)

かえんこうはい【火炎光背】a halo of flames adorning behind a Buddhist statue. 仏像の背後にある飾りで，燃えさかる炎の後光． ☆不動明王などにみられる． ⇨後光

かえんだいこ【火炎太鼓】〈雅楽〉 a large drum used in *gagaku* performances. 雅楽で用いる大太鼓． ☆周囲に炎をかたどった飾りがある．

かえんびん【火炎瓶】㊤ a petrol bomb; a Molotov cocktail.

かおきき【顔利き】 an influential person (with a lot of connections); a big wheel.「顔役」ともいう．

かおじゃしん【顔写真】 a picture[photograph] of one's face;〈犯罪者の〉a mug shot; a photograph of a suspect's face.

かおパス【顔パス】　a gate-crasher; the right to free entry; the strong name to enter free of charge; free admission for being well known.

かおみせ【顔見せ・顔見世】　❶〔歌舞伎〕 an all-star cast; a formal introduction of all the actors in a kabuki theatrical troupe; a play in which all the actors in a troupe appear on the stage. 一座の歌舞伎役者が総出であいさつし, 舞台上で顔ぶれを披露すること. ¶**顔見世興行** an all-star cast show; a once-a-year all-star run of kabuki performances; performances in which the entire troupe appears. 通常は毎年11月に行う.

❷ (make) a public appearance (before many onlookers[theatergoers]); (make) one's debut[first appearance on stage]. 見物人に初めて顔を見せること.

かおもじ【顔文字】　an emoticon(emotionとiconの合成語)；a smiley. ☆Eメールなどで用いる顔マーク.

かかあてんか【かかあ天下】　〈女性支配〉a petticoat government;〈女性上位の妻〉a henpecked husband(恐妻家)；a wife wearing the trousers[米 pants] in the house; a wife leading her husband around by the nose. ⇨亭主関白

かかい【歌会】　a *tanka* (reading) party; a gathering of *tanka* poets. ⇨歌会

ががく【雅楽】　*gagaku*; (ancient) court music and dance native to Japan (in the Heian period); ceremonial music and dance of the Imperial Court of Japan (today). *Gagaku* includes both an ancient court dance and music (called *bugaku*) and the orchestral music performed with percussion, wind and string instruments (called *kangen*). 平安時代からつづく日本古来の宮廷音楽舞踊で, 現在も宮中で儀式の際に行われる. 雅楽は宮廷で舞われた「舞楽」と, 打

楽器・管楽器・弦楽器の総称である「管弦」から成る. 特に「宮内庁雅楽部」(the Music Department of the Imperial Household Agency)が継承する. ☆雅楽は日本の五大芸能(歌舞伎・文楽・能・狂言・雅楽)の一つである. 2009年にユネスコ無形文化遺産に登録される. ¶**雅楽師** a *gagaku* musician. ⇨舞楽／管弦

かかし[かがし]【案山子】　a scarecrow; a doll[figure of a man] standing on one leg in the rice field. It is set[put] up to protect farm crops from birds and other animals. 田畑に1本足で立つ人形. 田畑の作物を荒らす鳥獣を防ぐために立てる. ¶**田んぼの案山子** a one-legged scarecrow set up in a rice field (to frighten birds away from growing crops).

かがぞめ【加賀染め】　Kaga dyeing; silk textile dyed plain or with patterns (produced in Kaga Province in Ishikawa Prefecture).

かがひゃくまんごくまつり【加賀百万石まつり】the Feudal Lords Parade Festival (6月). ⇨付記(1)「日本の祭り」

かがみ【鏡】　❶〈姿見道具〉a mirror; a full-length mirror; a looking glass; a pier glass. ❷〈酒樽の蓋〉(take out) a barrel head; (crack open) a lid on a barrel (of *sake*). ⇨鏡開き❷

かがみいた【鏡板】〔能楽〕a backdrop wall painted with a large pine tree. It is a scene panel of the backdrop of the Noh stage upon which a picture of an old stylized pine tree (symbolic of god) is painted. All Noh plays are performed in front of this kagamiita. 松の木が描かれた背景の壁. 能舞台の正面の背景となる羽目板のことで, 象徴的な老松(神の象徴)の絵が描かれている. この鏡板の前ですべての能楽が演じられる. ⇨能「能舞台」

かがみのま【鏡の間】〔能楽〕a greenroom (for

か

dressing-up and wearing the mask). It is a waiting room for Noh actors used until they are ready to appear on the stage. They make a final check on their costume and makeup in front of the mirror. (盛装や面を着用するための)楽屋. 能役者が舞台に登場するまで待機する部屋[控え室]. 鏡の前で衣装や化粧の最終検査を行う. ⇨能「能舞台」/ 楽屋

かがみびらき【鏡開き】 ❶《鏡割り》the cracking of the *kagami-mochi*[the New Year's round mirror-shaped rice cakes]; an annual event of cracking of the *kagami-mochi* (rice cakes) which have been used as offerings to Shinto gods at homes. This event is held on January 11 when the *kagami-mochi* (rice cakes) are cracked open by hand using a mallet[with a hammer], and then cooked[eaten] in sweet *adzuki*-bean paste soup. It is under (a) taboo to cut[break] the *kagami-mochi* with a (sharp) knife. 家で神に供えてあった鏡餅を開くこと. 正月の11日にお供えの鏡餅を手や木槌[金槌]で開いて (split open), お汁粉にして食べる行事. (鋭い)刃物では切らない. ☆「開き」(open)は「割る」(break)の忌み詞.「鏡割り」ともいう. ⇨鏡餅
❷《鏡抜き》the *sake*-cask-opening ceremony; the opening ceremony of the *sake* cask by breaking its lid. The lid on a cask of *sake* is cracked open using a wooden mallet in an auspicious occasion such as weddings and housewarmings. The *sake* is consumed by those at the gathering. 酒樽のふたを叩いて開ける行事. 結婚式や新築祝いなどのめでたい行事のとき木槌で酒樽 (barrel of *sake*) のふたを開ける. その後酒を振る舞う.
【関連語】「木槌」wooden mallet[hammer].「枡」square cypress *sake* cup.「柄杓」ladle.「菰」straw matting (used to wrap a *sake* cask[barrel]).

かがみもち【鏡餅】 a round mirror-shaped rice cake (offered to a deity[god] on New Year's Day). *Kagami-mochi* is a pair of two round, flat mirror-shaped rice cakes used as New Year's offerings. The two rice cakes are slightly different in size, and stacked[piled] a smaller one upon the other large one. They are decorated with sacred twisted straw, bitter citron orange, fern, dried persimmons, a sheet of kelp and other foods in honor of the deity[god] of the incoming new year(*toshi-gami*). They are placed on a small wooden offering stand with two pieces of cut white paper. A set of *kagami-mochi* is often placed in the alcove of the main room of the house with the hope that the new year will be brighter and happier than the last. 正月に神に供える丸くて平たい鏡型の餅. 大きさは若干異なる大小の二つを重ね, 歳神を称えて注連縄, ダイダイ, ウラジロ, 干柿, 昆布などで飾る. 紙垂[四手] とともに三方に置く. 新年は旧年以上に明るく幸せな年であることを願って床の間に置くことが多い. 略して「鏡」ともいう. ☆「鏡餅」の用語は, 古代に使用していた銅製の鏡に似た丸い形の餅 (round-shaped rice cakes which look like[resemble] the copper-made mirror used in ancient times) を指す. ⇨鏡開き / 垂[四手]. ¶(神棚に供えた)鏡餅一重[据]

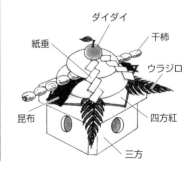

ダイダイ
干柿
紙垂
ウラジロ
昆布
四方紅
三方

a set of *kagami-mochi* (on a Shinto altar)

かがみわり【鏡割り】the cracking of the New Year's round mirror-shaped rice cakes. ⇨ 鏡開き❶

かがゆうぜん【加賀友禅】 Kaga painted silk fabrics; silk fabrics dyed in the colorful *Yuzen* fashion (produced in Kaga Province in Ishikawa Prefecture). The Kaga-yuzen uses much brighter colors with shadings than Kyoto-Yuzen. 加賀友禅のぼかしの色彩は京都友禅よりは明るい. ⇨友禅(友禅五彩)

かがりび【篝火】 (make) a bonfire (祝いなどの); a fishing fire(鵜飼いなどの); a beacon[watch] fire(警護の).

かき【花器】〔華道〕 a flower container. It includes a vase (花瓶), a basin[bowl] (水盤) and a basket(かご型容器). The Japanese make much of the harmonic combination of flowers with the container in the flower arrangement. 華道では花と花器の融合を重視する. ¶花器に生けた花 flowers arranged in a vase[bowl].

かき【柿】〔植物〕a *kaki*; 〈実〉a persimmon; 〈木〉a persimmon tree;〈種子〉a persimmon stone;〈へた〉a persimmon calyx. カキノキ科の落葉高木. ¶渋柿 an astringent persimmon; a bitter persimmon. 甘柿 a sweet persimmon. 干し柿 a dried persimmon. 柿渋 the astringent[bitter] juice of the persimmon; persimmon tannin[tannic acid]. ⇨柿の種(米菓).

かき【牡蠣】〔貝〕an oyster. ☆他国と区別して別名 a Japanese oyster; a Pacific oyster ともいう. 通称「海のミルク」. ¶前菜の牡蠣 an oyster on a half shell served as an appetizer. 生牡蠣 a raw oyster. 焼き牡蠣 a baked oyster. 牡蠣のむき身 a shucked [shelled] oyster. 養殖牡蠣 a cultivated oyster. 牡蠣の殻 an oyster shell. 殻付きの牡蠣 an oyster on the (half) shell. 牡蠣床 an oyster bed[bank]. 牡蠣の養殖場 an oyster farm. 牡蠣の養殖 oyster farming[culture]. 〔料理〕牡蠣鍋 an oyster hot-pot; an oyster stew cooked in a broth seasoned with *miso*[bean paste]; a one-pot cooking of oysters with vegetables in *miso* broth(牡蠣と野菜を味噌味で煮る鍋物). 牡蠣の煎煮 oysters stir-fried with onions (牡蠣をタマネギと炒め甘辛く煮る). 牡蠣の味噌汁 *miso*[bean paste] soup of oysters (牡蠣を入れた味噌汁). 牡蠣のみぞれ和え oysters with grated *daikon*[radish] (大根おろしとまぜた牡蠣). 牡蠣フライ deep-fried oysters; oyster fritters. 牡蠣飯 oyster rice; rice cooked[boiled] with oysters.

かきあげ【掻き揚げ】 *tempura* with mixed ingredients; a mixture of vegetables and seafood deep-fried in batter; a mixture of deep-fried food with chopped ingredients of vegetables and seafood coated with batter. 野菜や魚介類をてんぷら衣で混ぜ合わせ, 油で揚げる. ⇨海老の掻き揚げ

【掻き揚げうどん[そば]】 wheat noodles [buckwheat noodles] in fish broth mixed with *kakiage*[a mixture of vegetables and seafood deep-fried in batter]. 掻き揚げをのせたうどん[そば]

【掻き揚げ丼】 a bowl of rice topped with vegetables and seafood deep-fried in batter. ⇨天丼

かきごおり【欠(き)氷】❶ cracked ice. 冷や水やカクテルなどに入れる.

❷ (a portion of) shaved ice; chipped ice; chips of ice. 細かく削った氷, 「ぶっかき」「みぞれ」ともいう.

❸ (a bowl of) ice shavings flavored with sweet syrup poured over the top; (a bowl of)shaved ice doused with sweet syrup. シロップをかけた氷. ¶イチゴシロップをかけた欠き氷 (a bowl of) shaved ice flavored with strawberry syrup. ⇨宇治金時

かきぞめ【書き初め】 the New Year's calligraphy; the first calligraphy (written) with a brush for the New Year. *Kakizome* is the ceremony of calligraphic writing (drawn) with a brush and India ink for the first time in the New Year. It is usually done on January 2. 新年の２日に筆と墨で初めて書道による文字を書く行事. ☆元来日本の宮中で行われた儀式. 若水 (the first water drawn from a well in the New Year) で墨をすり、恵方 (the auspicious direction of the year) を向いて詩歌を書いた. この習慣は江戸時代に庶民の間に広がった. ⇨若水 / 恵方

かきたま(じる)【搔(き)玉(汁)】 egg soup; clear soup over which beaten eggs are poured. Clear soup is added with beaten eggs while it is hot. 煮たった澄まし汁に、溶き卵(scrambled eggs)を流し込んだもの.
【搔(き)玉うどん[そば]】 wheat noodles [buckwheat noodles] cooked in fish broth served with *shoyu*[soy sauce], topped with beaten eggs. 搔き玉をのせたうどん[そば]

かきのたね【柿の種】 (brown spicy) rice crackers shaped like persimmon stones; small rice cakes in the shape of persimmon stones seasoned with hot pepper. 柿の種の形をした米菓. ☆「柿ピー」は a snack-food mixture of spicy rice crackers and peanuts.

かぎっこ【鍵っ子】 a latchkey child[kid]; a door-key child[kid].

かきもち【欠き餅】 thin slices[chips] of dried rice cakes; thinly-sliced[thinly-cut] and dried rice cakes. 通称「おかき」. ⇨おかき / 煎餅. ¶搔き餅を焼く toast[grill] *kakimochi* (over an open fire).

かきん【家禽】 a domestic fowl; poultry(総称). 鶏、家鴨、七面鳥など. 卵・肉をとるために家で飼育する. ⇦野禽

かくあんどん【角行灯】 a square paper lantern. ⇨行灯

かくおび【角帯】 a stiff *obi*[sash] worn by men. It is a stiff, narrow (about 10-cm-wide) *obi* worn by men with a *kimono*. 二つ折りに仕立てた、かたくて幅の狭い(約10cm)男性用の帯. ⇨帯 / 浴衣

かくかい【角界】〔相撲〕 the *sumo* world; the world of *sumo; sumo* circles. 相撲業界. ☆「角」は角力の意.

かくかぞく【核家族】 a nuclear family; a social unit composed of father, mother and children. 両親と未婚の子供からなる家族.

かくしカメラ【隠しカメラ】 a hidden[concealed] camera; a candid camera; a spy camera.

かくしげい【隠し芸】 a parlor trick[stunt]; a secret[hidden] talent.

かくしご【隠し子】 a secret love child; an illegitimate child whose birth has been kept a secret.

がくじん【楽人】 a music player. ¶雅楽の楽人 a player of *gagaku*[ancient court music and dance]. ⇨雅楽

がくせい【学制】 the educational system; the Education Order (issued in 1872). All people six years of age and older were obliged to receive elementary education. 6歳以上の全男女は小学教育を受ける. (1872年に公布)

がくそう【楽箏】 *koto*[13-stringed musical instrument] used as the musical instrument of *gagaku*[ancient court music and dance]. 雅楽の楽器に用いる琴. ⇨雅楽 / 琴

かくそで【角袖】 ❶ square[bag] sleeves (of a *kimono* worn by men). 男物の和服の四角いそで.
❷ ⟨a⟩ *kimono*; ⟨b⟩ Japanese-style men's coat; Japanese-style clothes worn by men, 洋服に対して「和服」の異称. 特に男性の和装.

がくどうそかい【学童疎開】 evacuation of schoolchildren (from cities during World

War Ⅱ）

がくどうほいく【学童保育】 after-school children care; care of children after school hours; out-of-school children care.

がくとしゅつじん【学徒出陣】 mobilization of students to the war; departure of students for the front. Students (over 20-year-old boy) were drafted into military service and went off to the battlefield during World War II in 1943. 戦場への学徒動員. 1943年第二次世界大戦時, 学生(20歳以上の理科系を除く男子)は軍事に召集され戦場に行った. ☆翌年(1944年)には徴兵適齢は19歳に引き下げられた.

かくに【角煮】 simmered cube pieces of meat[fish]; stewed chunk of meat[fish]; diced meat[fish] boiled down in *shoyu*[soy sauce]. 肉[魚]を四角に切って[角切りにして]柔らかくゆで, 甘辛く煮込む. ⇨豚の角煮 / 鮪の角煮 / 鰹の角煮

がくばつ【学閥】 an academic clique [background]; alma mater clique.

がくや【楽屋】 a greenroom(出演者の控え室や休憩室); a dressing room(出演者の準備室). ⇨鏡の間. ¶**楽屋口** a stage door.

かぐら【神楽】 *kagura*; Shinto dance and music; (traditional Japanese) dance and music for the Shinto gods. *Kagura* is a form of dancing and singing performed at Shinto shrines by maidens celebrating Shinto gods for Shinto rituals[on sacred occasions]. It is accompanied by the music of drums, flutes, etc. 神道の祭事で神を祭るために巫女が神社で奏する(日本古来の)舞踊・音楽のこと. 太鼓や笛(大和笛)などの音楽の伴奏がある. ☆「**御神楽**」(*kagura* performed at the Imperial Court)と「**里神楽**」(*kagura* performed as the popular folk form at shrines in various regions)の2種がある.

¶**神楽歌** a *kagura* song[chant] (sung in *kagura* performances). **神楽師** a *kagura* performer[dancer]. **神楽堂**[殿] a *kagura* hall[stage] (built in the shrine precincts for *kagura* performances). **神楽囃子**〈伴奏〉a musical accompaniment to *kagura* dance; 〈人〉a *kagura* musician accompanied by *kagura* dance.

がくれき【学歴】 one's academic records; one's academic[educational] background.
【**学歴詐称**】 false statement about one's academic background; falsifying[faking] one's academic records.
【**学歴社会**】 an education-conscious society; a diploma-oriented society; an academic background-oriented society; a school-record society overemphasizing educational background.「何ができるか」よりも「どの学校を出たか」を評価する.
【**学歴偏重**】 overvaluation of educational background; overemphasis of educational qualifications; excessive emphasis placed on academic records. 学歴や学業成績を過剰に評価する.

かくれキリシタン【隠れキリシタン】Hidden Christians. ⇨潜伏キリシタン

かくれんぼ【隠れん坊】hide-and-seek (game) (usually played by children).

がけ【崖】a cliff(海に面している); a precipice (山などの絶壁). ¶**海岸に面した崖** an ocean cliff. **高くそびえる崖** a towering cliff. **垂直に切り立った崖** a perpendicular cliff. ⇨柱状節理(の岩石)

かけい【筧】⇨懸樋

かげうた【陰唄】〔歌舞伎〕a song sung behind the scenes in a kabuki play. 歌舞伎の演劇中, その背後で歌う唄. 下座唄ともいう.

かけうどん[そば]【掛けうどん[そば]】 plain wheat noodles[buckwheat noodles] covered with hot broth; (a bowl of) plain wheat noodles[buckwheat noodles] in a fish broth seasoned with *shoyu*[soy sauce], served hot without any special trimmings. 特別な添え合わせがなく熱い醤油味のかけ汁だけを入れて出す. ☆「うどんかけ」, 単に「かけ」, 関西では「素うどん」ともいう. ⇨掛け汁

かけえり【掛け衿[襟]】 (a piece of) collar-cloth sewed on a *kimono*. 和服の衿の部分にかける布.

かけおちけっこん【駆け落ち結婚】elopement marriage; marriage by eloping; runaway match with one's lover.

かけこみでら【駆け込み寺】a refuge temple; a Buddhist nunnery giving refuge to an abused wife from her husband; a Buddhist temple that offers refuge to women seeking (a) divorce in the Edo period. 江戸時代夫と離別するために逃げ込んだ尼寺.「縁切り寺」ともいう. ☆3年間そこに滞留すると夫が反対しても離婚は容認された. ⇨縁切り寺

かけじく【掛け軸】a *kakejiku*; a hanging scroll; a long vertical hanging scroll with a painting of natural objects or a scroll of calligraphy on paper[silk]. It is made of paper[silk] with a roller (*jiku*) at the top and at the bottom. It is usually hung (*kakeru*) on the wall of the alcove in a Japanese-style guest room. 花鳥風月の絵画または書画の長い垂直の巻物. 上下に「軸」(an axis)のある紙[絹布]で作られる. 通常は床の間の壁に「掛ける」(display).「掛け物」また「掛け字」ともいう. ⇨風鎮 / 床の間

かけじる【掛け汁】❶〈掛けうどん[そば]への〉basic soup broth[stock] (used for *kake-udon*[*soba*]).「かけづゆ」ともいう. ⇨掛けうどん[そば].
❷〈サラダへの〉dressing.
❸〈肉汁〉gravy; sauce.

かげぜん【陰膳】 a meal set for an absent person (with wishes for his/her safe return); a meal offered to a person far away

from home (to pray for his/her safe return). 長く家を離れている者のために, 留守の者が無事に帰れるように祈って供える食事.

かけそば【掛けそば】 ⇨掛けうどん

かけづつ【掛け筒】〔華道〕a cylindrical flower vase hung on the wall[post]. 壁[柱] などに掛ける円筒状の花瓶.

かけながし【掛け流し】 free-flowing hot-spring water. ⇨温泉

かけばな【掛け花】〔華道〕flowers arranged in a vase hooked onto the wall[post]. 壁[柱]などに鈎で掛ける花瓶に盛られた花. ⇨吊り花

かけひ【懸樋・筧】 a conduit(導水管); a bamboo water pipe[spout] (through which water flows and falls into a stone water basin (*tsukubai*)). 水が流れる管. 竹を管にして水を通す蹲に水を流す. ⇨蹲

かげふみ【影踏み】 a game of stepping on each other's shadows.

かげぼし【陰干し】 drying(fish[vegetables]) in the shade. (魚・野菜を)日陰で干すこと. ⇨風干し/日干し. ☆「一夜干し」(drying overnight)は一晩陰干しにすること. ¶魚[野菜]を陰干しにする dry fish[vegetables] in the shade[out of direct sunlight]; shade-dry fish [vegetables]. 陰干しにした魚[野菜] shade-dried fish[vegetables]; fish [vegetables] dried in the shade.

かけむしろ【掛け筵】 a mat curtain of straw [rushes].

かけもの【掛け物】 ⇨掛け軸

かご【駕籠】❶〈乗り物の〉a *kago*; a palanquin for carrying a person in feudal times. It was carried[shouldered] on a long pole by two bearers. 封建時代, 人を乗せるために使用された. 2人が長い棒を前後から肩に担いで運ぶ. ☆「庶民の駕籠」(a palanquin used by the general public),「公家の駕籠」(別称「乗物」)(a palanquin used by the feudal lord and nobility)などの種類がある.

西洋では sedan chairという．⇨輿．¶駕籠
かき a palanquin bearer.
❷〈ひな祭りの〉a palanquin for carrying *hina* dolls (displayed on the tiered stand).
⇨ひな壇

かこう【火口】 a (volcanic) crater; a caldera（直径1キロ以上のもの）．¶火口丘 a volcanic cone. 火口原 a crater basin. 火口壁 a crater wall. **死火山である男体山の火口**(栃木県) the crater of Mt. Nantai(san), an extinct volcano. ⇨溶岩．火口湖 a crater lake; a lake formed by the crater of a volcano. ☆日本最大の火口湖（十和田湖［青森県・秋田県］）the largest crater lake in Japan. ⇨カルデラ湖

かこうがん【花崗岩】 granite(みかげ石)．¶花崗岩の断崖と奇岩怪石の多い昇仙峡(山梨県)Shosen(kyo) Gorge with the high granite cliffs and rocks of fantastic shapes.

かさ【笠】a sedge hat(菅笠)；a woven hat (of bamboo or rushes). ⇨菅笠

かざぐるま【風車】〈玩具〉㊀ a windmill; ㊤ a pinwheel.

かさねもち【重ね餅】 two pieces of rice cake with one on top of the other; two rice cakes of decreasing size piled one on the other. ⇨鏡餅

かざぼし【風干し】〈風干しにすること〉half-drying fish[vegetables] in the wind. (魚・野菜を)風にさらして干すこと．⇨陰干し／日干し．¶魚[野菜]を風干しにする dry fish[vegetables] in the wind; wind-dry[half-dry] fish[vegetables]. **風干しにした魚[野菜]** wind-dried[half-dried] fish[vegetables]; fish[vegetables] dried in the wind.〈風干しにしたもの〉half-dried fish[vegetables].⇨陰干し／日干し

かざん【火山】a volcano.（㊤ volcano(e)s）．☆ volcanic 形「火山の」．¶火山ガス(二酸化硫黄) volcanic gas (sulfur dioxide). 火山活動 volcanic activity. 火山岩 a volcanic

rock[block]. 火山国 a volcanic country; a country with many volcanoes. 火山帯 a volcanic zone; a volcanic belt. 火山島 a volcanic island. 火山灰 volcanic ashes. 火山噴火[爆発] a volcanic eruption. 火山峰 a volcanic mountain; a volcanic peak. 火山脈 a volcanic chain[range].

種類 活火山 an active volcano. 休火山 a dormant volcano. 死火山 an extinct volcano. 海底火山 a submarine volcano. 成層火山 a stratovolcano. 複合火山 a compound[complex] volcano. 複式火山 a composite volcano.

かし【樫】〔植物〕an oak; an oak tree. ⇨椎茸 ¶樫の実(どんぐり) acorn. ⇨どんぐり

かしおり【菓子折り】❶〈折り箱〉a box of cakes (or sweets).
❷〈進物用〉a box of confectionery presented as an expression of thanks[appreciation];〈手土産用〉a box of cakes or sweets brought as a small gift when visiting someone's home.

かじか【鰍】〔魚〕a sculpin; a miller's-thumb.「オコゼ」「ゴリ」（金沢のゴリ料理）ともいう．甘露煮や，姿のままから揚げにする．⇨ごり

かじき(まぐろ)【旗魚(鮪)・梶木(鮪)】〔魚〕a marlin; a swordfish(メカジキ)；a spearfish(マカジキ)．すし種や刺身，また照り焼きや塩焼きなどに用いる．

かじきとう【加持祈祷】 incantations and prayers; Buddhist prayers to protect against misfortune. 災害・病気などの不幸を除くために神仏の守りと助けを祈ること．

かしこどころ【賢所】 the Imperial Sanctuary[Shrine]; the Sanctuary[Shrine] in the Imperial Palace. 宮中三殿の一つ．八咫鏡をまつる神殿．⇨三種の神器

かしばらしゅっさん【貸し腹出産】 offering a womb to bear another couple's child.

かしまだち【鹿島立ち】 departure on a

journey[trip]. 旅に出ること. ☆昔, 防人
が旅に出る前に鹿島神宮(茨城県)に無事を
祈ったことに由来. ⇨防人

がしょう【賀正】 (I wish you) a Happy New Year; Best Wishes for a Happy New Year. 「迎春」「謹賀新年」ともいう. ☆年賀状に書く場合「賀正」(正月おめでとう)は目上の人には用いない.

がじょう【賀状】 a New Year's greeting card. ⇨年賀状

かしょくしょう【過食症】 (have) bulimia; hyperphagia.

カシラ【頭】〈焼き肉屋の〉 head; brain-pork; temple-meat. ⇨焼肉

かしわ【柏】〔植物〕 an oak tree(木); an oak leaf(葉).
【柏餅】 a rice cake wrapped in an oak leaf; a rice cake stuffed with sweet *adzuki*-bean paste and wrapped in an oak leaf. It is usually made on the Boys' Festival[called Children's Day today] on May 5. 餡を入れ柏の葉で包んだ餅. 5月5日端午の節句[現在は「こどもの日」]の供え物.

かしわで【拍手・柏手】 handclapping (done in worship at a Shinto shrine[altar]). Worshippers clap their hands in front of the Shinto shrine[altar] to summon the gods and draw their attention to the prayer. 参詣者は神社[神棚]の前で神を拝むとき, 両手のひらを打ち合わせて鳴らし, 神を呼び求め(awaken), 祈りに専念する (concentrate). ⇨合掌(hand-joining)
☆明治神宮の場合は『二拝二拍手一拝』 First the worshipper bows politely twice at the main oratory. Then he/she claps his/ her hands twice. Lastly he/ she bows politely once again.

かしん【家臣】 a vassal[retainer] (of a feudal lord). ¶家臣明智光秀に襲われた織田信長. Oda Nobunaga attacked by his vassal Akechi. ⇨重臣／家来

かじん【歌人】 a (*tanka*) poet(男性); a (*tanka*) poetess(女性). ⇨短歌

かす【粕・糟】 *sake* lees (複数形で). 酒を漉したあとに残るもの. ☆「滓」(茶がらなどの) the dregs; grounds
〔料理・食品〕粕汁 *sake* lees soup[broth]; soup[broth] with *sake* lees; soup cooked with a *sake* lees base.《魚[野菜]の粕汁 fish[vegetables] soup with *sake* lees; *sake* lees soup with fish[vegetables]》. 粕酢 *sake* lees vinegar; vinegar made from *sake* lees. 粕漬け魚[野菜] fish[vegetables] pickled[preserved] in *sake* lees.《サケ[タラ]の粕漬け salmon[cod] preserved in *sake* lees. ナス[キュウリ]の粕漬け eggplants [cucumbers] pickled in *sake* lees》

かすがわかみやおんまつり【春日若宮おん祭り】 the Festival of Kasuga-Wakamiya Shrine. (12月). ⇨付記(1)「日本の祭り」

かすがたいしゃせつぶんまんとうろう【春日大社節分万燈籠】 the Lantern-Lighting Rite of Kasuga Grand Shrine. (2月). ⇨付記(1)「日本の祭り」

かすがたいしゃちゅうげんまんとうろう【春日大社中元万燈籠】 the Lantern-Lighting Rite of Kasuga Grand Shrine. (8月). ⇨付記(1)「日本の祭り」

カステラ a soft sponge cake. Eggs, wheat flour and sugar are mixed and baked to form a soft sponge cake. 卵, 小麦粉, 砂糖を混ぜて焼いた柔らかいスポンジ・ケーキ菓子. ☆ポルトガル語 (pāo de Castella)に由来.

かずのこ【数の子】❶〈卵巣〉 herring roe ニシンの卵巣. ⇨にしん
❷〔食品〕 herring roe soaked in *shoyu*[soy sauce]. ニシンの卵巣の加工食品. ☆子孫繁栄の縁起物 (a symbol of the prosperity of one's posterity). 正月や婚礼などの祝儀の膳に用いる. ⇨重箱. ¶塩数の子 salted herring roe. 干し数の子 dried herring roe.

かずら【葛】〔植物〕a vine; a creeper. つる草の総称. ¶**深い谷間のかずら橋** a vine-made suspension bridge in a deep valley（徳島県の祖谷渓）

かずらもの【鬘物】〔能楽〕Noh play with a female leading character wearing a wig in an exaggerated form. 女性を主人公とし, 鬘をつけて誇張した様子で演じる能楽.

かすり【絣・飛白】❶〈模様〉a splashed pattern. 小さくかすったような[飛び散らしたような]模様.
❷〈織物・布〉a Japanese fabric[cloth] with splashed patterns; a Japanese cotton fabric [cloth] designed with blurred patterns, mostly white patterns on an indigo background. ぼかし模様をところどころに置いた織物[布]. その大部分は藍色の生地に白い模様がある木綿の織物[布]. ⇨紺絣. ¶**絣の着物** a splash-pattern *kimono*; a *kimono* with splashed patterns (mostly white patterns on indigo). （絣模様（藍色に白色まじりが多い）の入った着物）. ⇨矢絣（の着物）

かせき【化石】a fossil; fossil remains. ¶**貝の化石** fossil shells.

かせん【河川】river(s). ¶**一級河川** an A-class river. **河川敷** a dry riverbed. **日本三大河川** the Three Longest Rivers in Japan（利根川[群馬県]・石狩川[北海道]・信濃川[新潟・長野・群馬の３県]）

かせん【歌仙】a great (*waka*) poet. 和歌の名人.

かそうぎょうれつ【仮装行列】a fancy-dress parade; a costume parade. ⇨博多どんたく

かそうば【火葬場】㊤ crematory; ㊧ crematorium (㊴ crematoriums; crematoria). ☆「棺」(coffin)を載せた「霊柩車」(hearse)が火葬場に着くと, 遺体は「荼毘に付される」(cremate the remains; reduce the body to ashes). その後遺族の「箸渡し」(a pair of chopstick-like tongs)で「骨揚げ / 骨拾い」

(gather the bones of the deceased)があり,「骨壺」(funerary[cinerary] urn)に収められる. 欧米では「土葬」(burial; interment)が多い.

かぞえどし【数え年】one's age using traditional Japanese reckoning[counting]. One year old is reckoned[counted] at birth, with one year added at every New Year. 生まれた年を1歳として数え (calculated), 元旦ごとに1歳ずつ加える年齢. ¶**数え年で40歳**（である）. (be) 40 years old according to traditional Japanese reckoning.

かぞく【華族】the nobility class; the family of the nobility; the title categorized in 1869 after the Meiji Restoration. 貴族階級. 明治維新後1869年に区分された貴族の名称. ¶**華族の位** the peerage; a peer（男性の華族の一員）; a peeress（女性の華族の一員）. 【関連語】「公爵」(duke). 「候爵」(marquis). 「伯爵」(count; earl). 「子爵」(viscount). 「男爵」(baron)の5爵位があった. 1947年に廃止された. ⇨士族

かぞくだんらん【家族団欒】the pleasure of a happy family.

かぞくぶろ【家族風呂】a bath for family use (at a hot-spring inn).

かた【潟】a lagoon（外海と分離してできた湖）; an inlet（浦）. ¶**八郎潟**（秋田県）Hachirogata Lagoon (Japan's largest area of reclaimed land). **宍道湖の潟**（鳥取県）lagoon(s) in Lake Shinji(ko). 能取湖（北海道）にある**サンゴ草**で覆われた円形の潟 round lagoon covered with coral grasses in Lake Notoro.

かたおやかぞく【片親家族】a single-parent family. ☆「母子家庭」a fatherless family; a single-mother family; a mother-child family.「父子家庭」a motherless family; a single-father family; a father-child family.

かたおやのこども【片親の子供】a motherless [fatherless] child; a child being raised [brought up] by a single parent.

かたがき【肩書】(formal) job title[description]; one's status[position]. ⇨学歴

かたかな【片仮名】 *katakana*; *katakana* syllabary writing; a square form of *kana* script in the Japanese syllabary writing. *Katakana* is one of the two kinds of Japanese *kana* scripts used for Japanese syllabary writing: *katakana* and *hiragana*. Today it is often used for writing foreign words, technical names of the flora and fauna. 日本語を表記するときに用いる角ばった形態 (an angular version) をなす表音文字.「平仮名」書体と並び仮名の一種. 外来語や動植物名の表記などに用いる場合が多い. ☆「個々の片仮名」は a *katakana* character[letter]. ⇨仮名／平仮名

かたぎぬ【肩衣】 ❶ a stiff-shouldered sleeveless robe; a broad-shouldered jacket. It is worn over the striped robe (*noshime*) by a samurai warrior as a formal vest in the Edo period. It is also worn with loose-fitting trousers (*hakama*), both made of the same color and cloth. 肩幅の角張った袖なしの衣服, 江戸時代に武士の礼服として熨斗目の上に着た. 肩衣は同色布の袴と合わせて着用する. 袴の上衣のこと. ⇨熨斗目／袴

❷〔能楽〕a wide-shouldered sleeveless ceremonial top robe. It is worn by a servant in a comic interlude in a Noh play. 肩幅の広い袖なしの上着. 能狂言で下僕が着る.

かたくちいわし【片口鰯】〔魚〕an anchovy; a half-mouthed sardine. 幼魚はチリメンジャコや煮干しの原料. ⇨いわし／ちりめんじゃこ／白子干し

かたくり【片栗】〔植物〕a dogtooth violet; an adder's tongue lily. ユリ科の球根性多年草.〔食品〕**片栗粉** potato starch（ジャガイモの澱粉）; starch made[obtained] from potatoes; 〓 cornstarch; 〓 cornflour. ☆元来は dogtooth violet starch（片栗の根から作った澱粉）であったが, 現在は potato starch（ジャガイモの澱粉）からとることが多い.

かたしろ【形代】❶ a white paper doll used to throw into the river for rubbing away all evils in a Shitno purification rite. 御祓いのときに川に流す白紙の人形. ⇨御祓い

❷ a paper doll representing a sacred object of worship. 御神体の代わりに置く人形. ⇨神体

かたたたき【肩叩き】 shoulder tapping;〈退職勧告〉suggestion for voluntary resignation; advice concerning resignation; persuasion of an employee to retire early before the compulsory retirement age.

かたつむり【蝸牛】〔動物〕a snail. ☆「エスカルゴ」(escargot)は食用種のカタツムリ. ¶ かたつむりの殻 a snail shell.

かたな【刀】a *katana*; a sword;〈日本刀〉a Japanese sword. Along with a long sword (called *daito*), a *samurai* warrior carried a short one (called *wakizashi*) in ancient times. 日本の刀. 昔の武士は「大刀」と「脇差し」を携帯していた. ⇨日本刀. ¶刀掛け a sword rack. 刀銘 a sword signature. 刀鍛冶 swordsmith（「刀工」ともいう）. 刀を抜く draw[unsheathe] a sword. 刀を納める put up[sheathe] a sword. 刀を差す carry a sword. 刀を差している wear a sword (in one's sash). 刀を構えて向かい合う face each other with drawn sword.

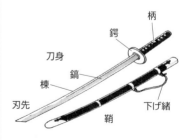

【関連語】『刀』には「刀身」(the (curved) blade of a sword), 「刃先」(the edge of a sword), 「鎬」(the flat of a blade), 「棟」(the back of a blade)がある. 『刀の付属物』には「鞘」(the scabbard[sheath] of a sword), 「柄」(the hilt of a sword). ☆「小刀の柄」は the shaft of a dagger.「長刀[槍]の柄」は the shaft of a long sword.「鍔」(a hand guard; the guard on a sword).「下げ緒」(swordknot; the knot of a sword)がある.

【刀狩令】 the order[edict] of the sword hunt. Toyotomi Hideyoshi gave orders [issued edicts] prohibiting possession of weapons by peasants in 1588. He confiscated farmers' swords and spears. 1588年(天文16年)豊臣秀吉が百姓(武士以外の者)の武器所有の禁止令を布告[発令]する. 刀と槍を押収した.

かたびら【帷子】 ❶〈着物〉a hemp[raw silk] *kimono* for summer wear. 麻・生糸でつくった夏向きの着物.
❷〈単物〉 an unlined *kimono* of light material; an unlined hemp[linen] garment for summer wear. 薄地の単物. ⇨単
❸〈布〉 a thin cloth used for hangings [hanging screens]. 几帳・帳に使った薄い布.

かためわざ【固め技】〔柔道〕 the art of stranglehold and joint lock. It is the art of grappling or getting a grip on one's opponent so that he/she cannot move on the mat. 押さえ技, しめ技, 関節技の総称. ⇨柔道

かたやきせんべい【堅焼煎餅】 hard-baked rice crackers. ⇨煎餅

かたり【語り】〔能楽〕〈語りの部分〉a narration; the narrative[narrated, recited] part of the story (in a Noh play);〈語り手の部分〉the narrator's[reciter's] part of the story (in a Noh play). ふしをつけず, ことばだけで一場の物語をすること. またその文句. ¶語り口 the way of narrating[reciting] a *joruri*. ⇨浄瑠璃. 語り手 the narrator [reciter] of *gidayu*. ⇨義太夫. 語り物 the narration[recitation] style of *gidayu*. (ふしをつけ楽器に合わせて語る). ⇨謡物.

かたりべ【語り部】 an ancient professional storyteller in the service of the Imperial Court in early Japan. 古代に, 朝廷に仕えて古い言い伝えや伝説を専門に語り伝えた人 (narrator; reciter).

かだん【歌壇】 the world of *tanka* poets; *tanka* composers' circles. 歌人の社会(society). ⇨短歌

かだん【華壇】 the world of floral artists; floral artists' circles. 華道の社会 (society).

がだん【画壇】 the painting world; painting circles; painters'[artists'] circles. 画家の社会 (society).

かちぐり【勝ち栗】 dried and peeled chestnut. 干して皮をとった栗のこと. ☆「勝ち」に通じるので出陣や祝勝また正月の祝いに用いる.

かちこし【勝ち越し】〔相撲〕 winning a majority of *sumo* wrestling bouts[matches]; *sumo* wrestler's net victory record; more wins than possible losses for a *sumo* wrestler in a tournament. Victory record generally results in promotion in the ranking. This is 8 wins for a *sekitori* with 15 bouts in a tournament, and 4 wins for lower-ranked wrestlers with 7 bouts in a tournament. 相撲の勝負で勝ちの回数が負けの回数より多いこと. 勝ち越せば番付の昇格に影響する. 関取は15試合中8勝すること. それ以外の下幕では7試合中4勝すること. ⇨負け越し

かちぼし【勝ち星】〔相撲〕 (get) a victory; (rack up) a win; the white mark indicating a victory[win]. ⇨負け星

ガチャガチャ[ガチャポン] a capsuled-toy vending machine.

か

かちゅう【家中】〈個人〉a retainer(家来); a vassal(家臣); a clansman(藩士);〈集合的に〉the retainers of a feudal lord 大名の家来. ¶薩摩藩の家中 the retainers of the Satsuma clan.

かちょう【家長】the head of a family;〈男性〉a patriarch;〈女性〉a matriarch. ¶家長制度 the patriarchal system.

がちょう【鵞鳥】〔鳥〕a goose (雌)(複 geese); a gander[male goose] (雄); a gosling[young goose] (子). ☆「フォアグラ」(foie [肝臓] gras[肥えた])は鵞鳥・家鴨の肥大した肝臓(脂肪肝)のこと.「トリュフ」「キャビア」と共に三大珍味のひとつ.

かちょうが【花鳥画】a bird-and-flower painting; a (Chinese and Japanese traditional) picture of birds and flowers.

かちょうふうげつ【花鳥風月】〈自然の美〉the beauty of nature; beautiful landscapes. ¶花鳥風月を描く paint beautiful landscapes. 花鳥風月を歌に詠む compose *tanka* poems on beautiful landscapes.

ガチンコしょうぶ[たいけつ]【ガチンコ勝負[対決]】a do-or-die contest; a hotly contested game.

カツa deep-fried cutlet. ☆英語の cutlet(肉の切り身)のなまったもの.「カツレツ」(a breaded and deep-fried cutlet)の略. 牛・豚・鶏の肉に小麦粉・卵をつけ, パン粉でまぶして油で揚げた料理.
〔料理〕豚カツ[ポークカツレツ] a(breaded and) deep-fried pork cutlet. 一口カツ a bite-sized deep-fried pork cutlet. 味噌カツ a deep-fried pork cutlet covered with *miso*[bean paste]. カツカレー curried rice covered with a deep-fried pork cutlet. カツサンド sandwich with a deep-fried pork cutlet.
【カツ丼】(a bowl of) rice topped with a pork cutlet, eggs and vegetables; (a bowl of) rice served with a topping of a pork cutlet, eggs and vegetables. *Kastudon* is a bowl of rice topped with slices of deep-fried pork cutlet covered[dressed] with beaten eggs and vegetables[sliced onions and mushrooms] that have been simmered in *shoyu*[soy sauce], sugar and *sake*. 豚カツ(油で揚げたカツレツ), 卵(かき混ぜた卵), 野菜(刻んだタマネギとキノコ)を盛りつけた丼物. 具材はすでに醤油・砂糖・酒で煮つめてある. ⇨丼物

かつお【鰹】〔魚〕a bonito (複 ~s, ~es); an oceanic bonito. サバ科の海産硬骨魚. 回遊魚で, 日本近海には黒潮にのって初夏にやってくる. ¶戻り鰹 a bonito going down south in autumn[early winter](秋[初冬]に南下する鰹). ☆脂がのった味になり, 鰹の叩きや刺身に最適. カツオ漁船 a skipjack fishing vessel. ☆ skipjack(s)「(カツオのように)水中から水面に飛び上がる魚」
〔食品〕鰹の塩辛 salted and fermented bonito guts. ⇨酒盗. 〔料理〕鰹の角煮 stewed cubes of bonito; simmered bonito cubes; cubes of bonito simmered in sweetened *shoyu*[soy sauce] with ginger. ショウガを入れた甘醤油で煮た角切りの鰹. ⇨角煮
【鰹の叩き】lightly roasted and sliced bonito; lightly grilled and chopped bonito. It is served in slices and eaten by dipping it in soy sauce with grated ginger, minced green onions, and grated radish. 軽く焼き厚めに切った鰹. 卸しショウガ, 刻みネギまた大根卸しなどを入れた醤油に浸して食べる.
【鰹節】①〈干したもの〉(a piece of) dried bonito; (a piece of) dried fillet of bonito flesh. It looks like a piece of driftwood. 鰹の身を背割りにし, 煮て干したもの. 流木に見える. ¶粉鰹 powder of dried bonito.
②〈削った物〉dried bonito shavings[flakes]; shaved bonito flakes; shavings[shaved

flakes] of dried bonito. They are used as the base for Japanese soup stock. 干した鰹を削ったもの. 日本料理の「だし」の下味材料. ☆関東の「鰹出し」(bonito stock) に対して関西の「昆布出し」(kelp stock) といわれる. ⇨ 出汁[出し汁]. ☆「勝男武士」(祝儀の贈答品用の当て字). ⇨おかか

【鰹節削り(器)】 a dried-bonito plane; a plane for shaving dried bonito. (a piece of) Dried bonito is shaved over the blade of a shredder placed on the top of an oblong box (into which the flakes fall). 干した鰹節を削るかんな. 長方形の箱の上にある寸断器の刃で干し鰹節を削る(箱の中に薄片が落ちる).

かつおぎ【鰹木】 ornamental logs placed crosswise on the ridge of a shrine roof; short logs in a row between the two crossbeams(*chigi*). These logs look like the shape of dried bonito. 神社・宮殿の棟木[千木]の上に横に並べて飾りとする丸太状の木.「鰹節」に似ていることからの呼称. ⇨ 千木

かっかざん【活火山】 an active volcano; a live volcano. ⇨火山. ¶阿蘇活火山(熊本県) Mt. Aso, an active volcano.

がっきゅうほうかい【学級崩壊】 classroom chaos[collapse]; chaos[collapse] in the classroom. ☆「崩壊した学級」は chaotic classroom.

かつぎょ【活魚】 live fish(before cooking). 料理するまで生きている魚. ¶活魚料理 fresh-fish cuisine.

かっこう【郭公】〔鳥〕 a Japanese cuckoo. ホトトギス科の鳥. ¶かっこう時計 a cuckoo clock.

がっこううらサイト【学校裏サイト】 unofficial school Web sites[websites] (where kids can e-mail whatever they want); a dubious Web site[website] set up by junior and senior high school students to exchange information about school life. Anyone can fall victim to brutal verbal mob violence lynching by their peers. 学校が認めていない非公式サイト(子供が自由にメールを送れる). 中高生が情報交換のために使う非公式サイト. 残忍なことばの集団暴力によって誰かが犠牲になる場合がある.

がっこうぎらい【学校嫌い】 school phobia.

がっしょう【合掌】 hand-joining (done in worship at a Buddhist temple). Worshippers put their hands and fingers flat together in prayer in front of the Buddhist temple to summon the gods and draw their attention to the prayer. 両手と指をそろえ合わせて(join their hands and fingers flat)拝み, 神を呼び求め祈りに集中する. ⇨拍手(神社: handclapping)

がっしょうづくり【合掌造り】〈建造物〉a traditional Japanese-style domestic architecture built in the shape of a triangle, similar to hands joined[folded] in prayer. 合掌する両手のように, 三角形に建てた伝統的な日本の家屋建築.

【合掌造り家屋】 a thatched house with a steep roof. The steep slope of the roof allows the heavy snow to slide off more easily. 険しく勾配する屋根の茅葺家屋. 屋根の険しい傾斜は積雪を落としやすくするために用いる.

かつだんそう【活断層】 an active fault. ¶活断層地帯 a zone[region] of active faulting.

かっちゅう【甲冑】 armor; ㊩ armour. ⇨よろい

ガッツポーズ(和製英語) holding up [raising] one's fist(s) in triumph.

かってぐち【勝手口】 the kitchen door; the back door; the service entrance.

かっぱ【合羽】 a raincoat; a waterproof coat; a raincape(袖なし); ㊩ a mackintosh. ☆ポルトガル語 (capa)から由来.

かっぱ【河童】 ❶〈架空の生物〉a *kappa*; a

water[river] sprite; an imaginary creature with a plate on its head living in the river. 川で生き, 頭上に皿のある想像上の生き物. ☆「泳ぎ上手な人」は a good swimmer. ❷〈鮨屋での隠語〉 a cucumber. Cucumber is said to be a favorite food of *kappa*. 「キュウリ」は河童の大好物. ⇨カッパ巻き

カッパまき【カッパ巻き】 cucumber rolled *sushi*[vinegared rice]; *sushi* containing thin strips[sticks] of cucumber rolled in a sheet of *nori*[dried laver]; *sushi* wrapped in a sheet of *nori* with pieces of cucumber rolled in the middle[center]. キュウリを芯にした細い海苔巻き. ⇨河童❷

カップめん【カップ麺】 instant[precooked] noodles in a cup. ☆1971年から市販された. ¶1〔2〕個のカップ麺 a cup[two cups] of instant noodles.

かつべん【活弁】 a silent movie interpreter; an interpreter of silent movies. The plot of a silent movie[film] was explained by a narrator while it was being shown on the screen. 無声映画で, 上映中説明したり, せりふを言ったりする役の人. 「活動写真の弁士」の意.

かっぽう【割烹】 ❶〈日本料理〉 Japanese-style cooking（和食の料理）; traditional Japanese cuisine（和食の料理法）. ☆「割」は包丁で食材をさく, 「烹」は食材を煮るの意. ¶割烹料理 Japanese-style cooking[cuisine]; meal served at a Japanese-style restaurant. ❷〈日本料理の店〉 a Japanese-style restaurant. ¶割烹着 a Japanese-style cooking apron (with sleeves). 割烹料理屋 a Japanese-style restaurant. 単に「割烹」ともいう. 割烹旅館 a Japanese-style inn[hotel] that prides itself on its cuisine[cooking].

かっぽれ a *kappore* dance; a Japanese traditional comic dance in the late Edo period.（江戸時代末期の）日本古来の滑稽な舞踊.

かつら［かずら］【鬘】 a wig; a hairpiece. ☆はげた部分を隠す男性用の「かつら［入れ毛］」は toupee という. ¶日本髪の鬘 a Japanese female hairdo wig. 鬘師 a wig maker.

かつらりきゅう【桂離宮】 the Katsura Detached Palace.（京都府）

かつらむき【桂剥き】 peeling[shaving] thinly all the way around vegetables; paring vegetables into a long, thin stripe. 巻紙のように細くむく野菜の切り方. ¶人参［大根］の桂剥き peeling[shaving] thinly all the way around carrots[radishes].

かていないさつじん【家庭内殺人】 homicide; killing members in one's family. ☆「家庭崩壊」はfamily breakdown. ¶未成年者による家庭内殺人 homicide committed by minors.

かていないべっきょ【家庭内別居】〈状態〉 living separate lives under the same roof; 〈人〉 strangers living apart in the same house; couples living separately under the same roof.

かていないりこん【家庭内離婚】 in-home separation; quasi-divorce; separate life under the same roof.

かていないぼうりょく【家庭内暴力】domestic violence[DV]; violence in the home; violence toward one's family. ☆「妻への虐待」wife battering, 「児童虐待」child abuse.

かどう【華道・花道】 floral art; the Japanese art of flower arrangement; the Japanese traditional floral art of expressing harmony between man and nature. The flowers are arranged to create a form symbolic of the harmony between man and nature. 草木の花や枝を整えて花瓶にさすこと（またその芸術）. 人間と自然の調和をシンボルとした形態を創造する. ☆室町時代, 仏前に飾る「供花」に始まり, 「生け花」には神仏の心があり, あるいは宇宙の調和があるという

観念が生まれた.「花を生ける」という「技術」(technique)とその「精神性」(spirituality)を重視する. ⇨「生け花」「天地人」. その主要な様式は ⇨「立華」「投げ入れ」「盛花」

【華道の流派】 a school of flower arrangement. ☆日本三大流派は「池坊」「小原流」「草月流」. 近年, 花以外の素材を用いる造形芸術も現れる.

かどう【歌道】 the art of (composing) *tanka*[*waka*] poetry; the art of Japanese versification. ⇨短歌

かどばん【角番】 ❶〔相撲〕 a do-or-die *sumo* tournament. A *sumo* wrestler's promotion or demotion in rank depends on the outcome of the relevant tournament. 死活の相撲試合. 相撲の番付における昇進・降格はその試合の結果次第である.

❷〔将棋・囲碁〕 a do-or-die game. The title is at stake in the game of *shogi*[*go*]. 次の一戦で連続した対局の勝敗が決まる局番.

かどまつ【門松】 *kadomatsu*. ❶〈飾り松〉 the New Year's decorative pine trees[branches]; the decorative pine trees[branches] set up at the gate of a house for the New Year. 新年を祝って, 門前に立てて (put up) 飾る松. ❷〈松飾り〉 traditional New Year's decorations; traditional decorations for the New Year. *Kadomatsu* is made up of pine branches, bamboo stalks and plum-tree twigs, which symbolize longevity, constancy and purity respectively. It is set up in pairs at (both sides of) the gate of a house to serve as a dwelling place for the god of the incoming new year (*toshi-gami*) who brings good luck. それぞれ長寿・堅実・潔癖を表す松の枝 (pine boughs), 竹の茎 (bamboo grass), 梅の木の小枝で構成され, 一対で玄関に飾る. 幸運をもたらす年神の依代 (an abode for the *Shinto* deity of the incoming new year)である. ⇨年神

かとりせんこう【蚊取り線香】 a mosquito-repellent incense coil; mosquito coil of the incense.

かな【仮名】 *kana*; the Japanese syllabary (consisting of 47 letters). There are two kinds of *kana* syllabaries: *katakana* and *hiragana*. *Kana* are commonly used in combination with Chinese characters to write the Japanese language. 47文字から成る表音文字. 片仮名と平仮名があり, 仮名は漢字と併用して日本語の表記に用いる. ⇨片仮名 / 平仮名. ¶仮名遣(い) the use of *kana*; *kana* orthography. 漢字に仮名をふる give[show] the reading of a Chinese character in *kana*. かな漢字変換 conversion from *kana* to *kanji*[Chinese character].

かなえ【鼎】 a tripod[three-legged] bronze vessel (in ancient China). (古代中国の)三本足の青銅製の器.

かなぐし【金串】 an iron skewer; a metal spit. ¶金串に刺した肉[魚] meat[fish] on an iron skewer.

かなぞうし【仮名草子】 short stories written in the *kana* script in the early Edo period. 江戸初期に仮名で書かれた通俗小説の総称.

かなでほんちゅうしんぐら【仮名手本忠臣蔵】 *Chushingura*; The Treasury of Loyal Retainers. It is a beloved play of the bunraku and kabuki theaters. 赤穂浪士の仇討ちを脚色した文楽や歌舞伎の戯曲. ⇨忠臣蔵

カーナビ global positioning system[GPS]; satellite navigation system.

かに【蟹】〔甲〕 a crab. ¶鱈場蟹 a king crab. 沢蟹 a river crab. 高足[高脚]蟹 a giant spider crab. 磯蟹 a beach[sand] crab. 兜蟹 a helmet crab; a king crab; a horseshoe crab. 毛蟹 a hairy crab. ズワイ蟹 a snow crab; a queen crab; a king crab. 山陰地方では「松葉がに」, 北陸地方では「たらばがに」という.《カニの体》カニの甲羅 the shell of a crab; a carapace. カニのはさみ the

か

か

claws[pincers] of a crab; nippers. **カニの足** the legs of a crab. **カニの肉** crab meat; meat of a crab. **カニ味噌** crab butter; edible brown crab meat; edible crab organs.
〔料理・食品〕 **カニ釜飯** rice cooked with crab meat in a small pot. **カニ缶**㊍ canned crab meat; ㊌ tinned crab meat. **カニ子** salted crab roe(カニの卵を塩漬けにしたもの). **カニ御飯** rice cooked with crab meat.「カニめし」ともいう. **カニ玉** large omelet(te) with crab meat and vegetables in it(カニ肉と野菜入りの玉子). **カニと胡瓜膾**(きゅうりなます) crab meat and cucumber salad dressed with sweet vinegar(甘酢で和(あ)えたカニ肉ときゅうり). **カニのスープ** crab meat soup.
【カニ蒲鉾(かまぼこ)】 imitation crab sticks (made of steamed[boiled] fish paste); steamed fish paste shaped and colored to resemble crab meat. かに肉に似せた蒲鉾.「**カニかま**」ともいう. ☆英語で surimi(擂り身[魚肉をたたいてつぶしたもの])ということもある. 販売名は seafood sticks[legs]; artificial crab などがある.

かにく【果肉】 sarcocarp (専門用語); the flesh[pulp] of fruit. ¶**メロンの果肉** the flesh of a melon. 果肉入りの[抜きの]ジュース juice with[without] pulp of fruit.

かね【鉦】 a gong; a small bell (used in a Buddhist service[rite]); a handbell.(手で振って鳴らす). ¶**撞木(しゅもく)で鉦を鳴らす** strike[sound] a gong with a wooden bell hammer. ⇨撞木

かね【鐘】 a bell. ¶**寺の鐘の音** the peal[sound] of the temple bell. ⇨除夜の鐘. **鐘撞き堂** a belfry; a bell tower. (鐘撞き堂で)**鐘を鳴らす** strike[toll; sound] a bell (in the belfry)

かのうは【狩野派】 the Kano school of Japanese painting.

かのこ【鹿の子】 ❶〔動物〕 a fawn. 鹿の子. ☆鹿の子の毛は茶色で白い斑点(はんてん)が散らばっている.「か」は「鹿」の古語.
❷「鹿の子絞り」「鹿の子斑」の略. ☆「鹿の子斑(まだら)の(模様)」 形 dappled (pattern); white-spotted (pattern). ¶**鹿の子模様** a dappled pattern; a pattern of dapples; a white-spotted pattern; a pattern with white spots on it.
【鹿の子絞り】 a dapple-dyed cloth; a tie-dyed cloth with a pattern of minute white rings; a cloth dyed in a white spotted pattern with small dapples. 絞り染めの一種. 布を小さく絞って染色し, 小さな白い斑点模様を染め出した織物.「鹿の子染め」(a cloth made by tie-dying)ともいう.

かのこもち【鹿の子餅】 rice cake with sweet-boiled beans mixed into it. 甘く煮た(インゲン)豆をつけた餅.

かば【河馬】〔動物〕 a hippo(㊐ ~s). hippopotamus (㊐ ~es, hippopotami) の略 ; a river horse.

かば(のき)【樺(の木)】〔植物〕 a birch. ⇨白樺 ¶**樺色** reddish yellow.

かばやき【蒲焼き】 barbecued fish[eel]; broiled[grilled] fish[eel]; fish[eel] split and broiled over a charcoal fire after being dipped in thick sweetened barbecue soy sauce; fish[eel] grilled over a charcoal fire after being mixed with *shoyu*[soy sauce], *mirin*[sweetened *sake*] and sugar. 濃厚なタレ(醤油・味醂(みりん)・砂糖の混合)をつけてから炭火で焼いた魚[鰻]. ⇨鰻の蒲焼き

かひ【歌碑】 a (stone) monument inscribed with a (*tanka*[*waka*]) poem. 短歌[和歌]を刻み付けた(石製)記念碑.

かび【黴】 mold; ㊌ mould. ¶**青黴** green mold. **白黴** mold(食物の) ; mildew(葉などの). **黴の生えたパン[チーズ]** moldy bread[cheese]; mold formed on the bread [cheese]. **黴の生えた米** moldy rice. ⇨事故米[汚染米]

かびん【花瓶】〔華道〕 a (flower) vase (especially used for the throw-in style arrangement of flowers). ¶花瓶にさしたユリの花 a lily put in the vase. ⇨投げ入れ(型) / 花器

かぶ(ら)【蕪】〔植物〕a turnip. アブラナ科の越年草. 別名「すずな」(春の七草の一つ). ¶蕪の葉 turnip greens.
〔食品〕**蕪寿司** pickled turnip *sushi*. **蕪漬け** pickled turnip. **蕪の酢漬け** turnips pickled in the mixture of vinegar *shoyu*[soy sauce] and sugar.

かぶき【冠木】 a crossbeam[lintel] of the *torii* gate. 鳥居の横木. ⇨鳥居

かぶき【歌舞伎】 (the) ***kabuki***; (the) *kabuki* drama[play]. *Kabuki* is a highly-stylized traditional drama[play] with singing and dancing. Kabuki was originally started by a woman dancer (Izumo no Okuni) in the 17th century. Since the Tokugawa shogunate prohibited women from performing in public, the kabuki drama has been performed exclusively by actors, including female impersonators. 歌謡と舞踊を伴う日本古来の伝統的な劇. 起源は出雲の阿国(出雲大社の巫女)の「念仏踊り」に始まる(1603年頃). 徳川幕府の女性演技の禁止令以来, 女形を含む男優のみが演じるようになった. ☆江戸時代の元禄期(1688-1729)に発達・完成する. ⇨女形
☆Kabuki Theater was registered as a UNESCO Intangible Cultural Heritage in 2008.『歌舞伎』は2008年(平成 20年)ユネスコ無形文化遺産に登録された.

【歌舞伎音楽】 *kabuki* music. ☆『下座音楽』background music performed from enclosed seats in a *kuromisu* (black bamboo blind). ⇨下座音楽.『所作音楽』background music preformed on the stage. ⇨所作音楽. Most *kabuki* dances use the lyrical *nagauta* (a form of singing accompanied by *shamisen*[three-stringed musical instrument]). ⇨長唄

【歌舞伎座】 the ***Kabuki-za*** Theater in Tokyo (東京・銀座にある劇場). ☆歌舞伎を上演する劇場には他に the National Theater in Tokyo(東京の国立劇場)と the Minami-za in Kyoto(京都の南座), また regional *kabuki* theater(地方の歌舞伎座)や rural *kabuki* theater(農村歌舞伎座)などがある.

【歌舞伎十八番】 the eighteen best repertoires of a kabuki drama[play]; a repertoire comprising the eighteen best classical plays[pieces] of the Ichikawa family of kabuki actors. 市川(団十郎[1660-1704])家に伝わる当たり歌舞伎の十八番上演種目. ☆特に7種の上演種目は有名 :「勧進帳」(The Faithful Retainers),「助六」(The Love of Sukeroku),「鳴神」(Thunder God),「矢の根」(The Arrowhead),「毛抜」(Hair Tweezers),「鎌髭」(Shaving with a Large Sickle),「暫」(Wait a Minute).

【歌舞伎舞台】 a kabuki stage. ☆歌舞伎舞台では『上手』the right (side of the) stage

下手　　　回り舞台　　　上手

チョボ床

黒御簾

定式幕

スッポン

花道　　　セリ　　　揚幕

seen from the audience(観衆から見て舞台の右側)と『下手』the left (side of the) stage seen from the audience(観衆から見て舞台の左側)という。 ☆英語の the right stage は観客の方を見て立つ役者の「右側」, the left stage は観客の方を見て立つ役者の「左側」をいう. ⇨上手/下手

① 『花道』an elevated passageway through which kabuki actors enter and exit. ⇨花道/仮花道

② 『スッポン』a trapdoor and lift which allows actors to raise from beneath the stage. ⇨スッポン

③ 『回り舞台』a revolving stage which allows for rapid change of scenes. ⇨回り舞台

④ 『セリ』a movable platform through which allows actors to enter and exit the center stage. ⇨迫り出し

⑤ 『黒御簾』a black bamboo blind in which background music is performed. ⇨黒御簾/下座音楽

⑥ 『チョボ床』the *gidayu* accompaniment placed on the *chobo* platform. ⇨チョボ

⑦ 『揚げ幕』a curtain (hanging at the entrance and exit). ⇨揚げ幕

⑧ 『定式幕』a vertically-striped stage draw curtain. ⇨定式幕

【歌舞伎役者】 a kabuki actor. There are several characters, such as male roles, female roles, villain's role and so on. 「立役」(the male protagonist), 「女方[女形]」(female parts). ⇨女形.「敵役[仇役]」(the antagonist)などがある.

カプセルホテル a capsule hotel; cheap[low-budget] accommodations with sleeping modules. ☆日本では1979年大阪ではじめて開業する. 最近はインターネットカフェ (cyber-café) などの利用に移行する. おしゃれな女性専用カプセルホテルも利用されている.

かぶと【兜】 a (battle) helmet; a warrior's helmet[protective headpiece] (used in feudal times). ¶兜と鞭〈五月人形〉a helmet and a whip. ⇨五月人形

【兜飾り】 a display of a *samurai* warrior's helmet. Families with young boys will display *samurai* warrior's helmet and armor, together with sword, bow and arrows in front of a folding screen on the stand. 男児のいる家庭では段上にある屏風の前に刀や弓矢といっしょに兜や鎧を飾る.

かぶと【兜】 the head of a fish. 魚の頭. ☆調理した形が兜に似ていることに由来.
〔料理〕兜焼き〈鯛〉 broiled[grilled] fish[sea bream] head; broiled head of a fish[sea bream]. 兜煮〈鯛〉 boiled fish[sea bream] head; simmered head of a fish[sea bream]. 兜蒸し〈鯛〉 steamed fish[sea bream] head; steamed head of a fish[sea bream].

かぶとがに【兜蟹】〔甲〕a horseshoe[helmet] crab. ⇨かに

かぶとむし【兜虫】〔虫〕a beetle; a horned beetle; a Japanese rhinoceros beetle. コガネムシ科の昆虫. ⇨くわがた

かぶら【蕪】 ⇨かぶ(ら)

かぶりつき【囓り付き】 a front-row seat; the first row of seats in a theater; ⊛ the orchestra; ⊛ the stalls. 劇場1階の最前列の座席.

かぶりもの【被り物】 headgear(総称); a head covering; a hat; a cap. ☆「仮装用の被り物」は a headpiece.「ミッキーマウスの被り物」は a Mickey Mouse headpiece; a Mickey-Mouse-head stage prop.

かふんしょう【花粉症】 hay fever (caused by cedar pollen); pollen allergy; allergy to pollen; pollinosis(医療用語). ¶スギ花粉症 an allergy to cedar pollen. 花粉症患者 a hay fever sufferer.

かべかけテレビ【壁掛けテレビ】 a wall-mounted television (set); a wall-hanging TV (set).

かほう【家宝】 a family treasure; a heirloom (handed down in a family for generations).

カボス〔植〕*kabosu* lime; a citrus fruit; a Chinese lemon. 柚子の雑種. 焼き魚やちり鍋などに(しぼりながら振りかけて)用いる. ⇨柚子

かぼちゃ【南瓜】〔植物〕a pumpkin(丸形)；㊍ a squash(ひょうたん形)；㊑ a vegetable marrow. ウリ科カボチャ属の一年生草木. 種(seeds)も食用.

〔料理〕南瓜の煮物 a simmered[boiled] pumpkin; a pumpkin simmered[boiled] in seasoned liquid.

かま【釜】❶〔茶道〕a teakettle; an iron pot (used for boiling water). ⇨炉. ¶茶の湯の釜 a teakettle for the tea ceremony. 釜据え wooden stand for a teakettle. 釜日 the day when pupils gather together under their master to practice a tea ceremony. (弟子らが茶道を習うために師匠のもとに集う日)
❷〈炊飯器〉a rice cooking pot; a rice-cooker; an iron pot (used for boiling rice); an electric rice cooker(電気がま). ¶釜敷き a pot stand; a trivet.

かま【窯】 a furnace(かまど)；a kiln(陶器などを焼く)；an oven(パンなどを焼く). ¶陶器を焼く窯 a kiln used to fire ceramics. 窯印 kiln mark. 窯出し removing[taking out] fired pottery from a kiln. 窯元〔場所〕a pottery；〈人〉a potter; a ceramist.

がま【蒲・香蒲】 a cattail; a reed mace. ガマ科の多年草. 花粉は薬用. 葉は干してむしろなどをつくる.

がま(がえる)【蝦蟇(蛙)】〔両〕a toad. ⇨かえる
【蝦蟇の脂・膏】❶〈油〉toad oil；〈英米〉snake oil.
❷〈薬〉 toad-oil treatment; toad's grease used as a medicine. It is believed to cure

cuts, burns and skin diseases. It is often packed in clam shells. きり傷，やけど，皮膚病などに効く. はまぐりの貝殻に詰められている場合が多い.

かまあげうどん【釜揚げうどん】 wheat noodles boiled in a heavy iron pot. Noodles are served and eaten with hot seasoned sauce on the side by dipping them directly from the iron pot. 鉄釜で茹でたうどんを釜からそのまま掬いあげ，温かいつゆ汁につけて食べる.

かまきり【蟷螂】〔虫〕a (praying) mantis (㊼ ~es; mantes)

かまくら ❶〈雪の室〉a (an igloo-like) snow hut (setting up a Shinto altar for the god of water inside).
❷〈祭り〉The annual event of snow huts held in February in northern Japan. Children spend chatting and eating around a warm brazier in the snow huts. (2月). ⇨付記(1)「日本の祭り」

かまくらござん【鎌倉五山】 the Five Great Zen Temples of Kamakura. ☆建長寺，円覚寺，寿福寺，浄智寺，浄妙寺.

かまくらばくふ【鎌倉幕府】 the Kamakura shogunate; the shogunate (government) at Kamakura. The system of the Kamakura shogunate consists of *Samurai-dokoro* (a board of *samurai*[retainer]), *Man-dokoro* (a board of administration) and *Monchu-jo* (a board of inquiry). 鎌倉幕府［1183-1333］は「侍所」「政所」「問注所」から成る. ⇨幕府

かまくらぶっきょう【鎌倉仏教】 Buddhism of the Kamakura period; the sects of Buddhism flourishing in the Kamakura period.

かまくらぼり【鎌倉彫】 the Kamakura lacquer ware; the Kamakura style of carving and lacquering (in black and vermilion). Rough designs are first carved on hard wood in bold relief. Then the work is finished with elaborate chiseling and layers of lacquer in black and vermilion. The *kamakura-bori* carvings range from small articles of a handy size to high quality goods of an heirloom. 鎌倉の漆器．鎌倉様式の彫刻と漆塗り技法．まず大ざっぱなデザインを堅い木にくっきりと浮き彫りにして彫刻する．次に精巧にのみで削り，黒と朱の漆塗りを何度も重ねて作品を完成させる．鎌倉彫には手頃な小物から家宝にできそうな高級品まである．

かまくらまつり【鎌倉まつり】 the Kamakura Festival of Tsurugaoka Hachiman-gu Shrine. (4月)．⇨付記(1)「日本の祭り」

かます【梭魚・魳】〔魚〕a barracuda. 秋から冬が旬．干物，塩焼き，煮付け，刺身などにする．

かまち【框】 a frame（建物）; a doorframe（戸の）; window frame（窓の）．戸・障子などの総称．⇨上がり框

かまど【竈】 a traditional cooking stove; ⊛ a kitchen stove; a (kitchen) range.

かまぼこ【蒲鉾】 *kamaboko*; fish sausage; boiled fish-paste cake on a piece of wooden plank; steamed fish-paste cake in the shape of a half-cylinder. After white fish meat is made into a seasoned paste and steamed, it is formed into a half-cyclindrical shape over a board. It is usually cut into slices when served. 木製の板にのせて蒸した魚のすり身．魚のすり身を調味料で練り上げて蒸し，それから板の上で半円筒形にして作る．通常は細かく切って出される．⇨竹輪/いたわさ

〔食品〕笹かまぼこ *kamaboko* shaped like a bamboo leaf. 板付きかまぼこ *kamaboko* molded onto a board. 半円筒形のかまぼこ *kamaboko* made in the shape of a half-cylinder. 紅白のかまぼこ *kamaboko* colored red and white（祝い事に用いる）．

かまめし【釜飯】 rice boiled with meat and vegetables in a small pot. Rice is boiled in stock[fish broth] with a variety of meat (or seafood) and vegetables and served in an individual small earthenware pot with a wooden lid. 一人前用の小釜に入れて，肉や野菜などを味付けにして炊き込む(cooked)ご飯．⇨カニ釜飯/鶏釜飯

かみ【神】 deity;〈一神教〉God（大文字で）;〈多神教〉god[gods];〈女神〉goddess. ☆deityはラテン語の Deus（神）に由来する．「デウス様」（神）は江戸時代の潜伏キリシタンが用いていた単語．¶縁結びの神 the deity[god] of matrimony[marriage] ; the deity[god] of matchmaking; the deity[god] who presides over marriage. 商売の神 the deity[god] of commerce. 守り神【守護神】 a guardian god. ⇨天照大神 (the Sun Goddess)

かみおきのぎょうじ【髪置きの行事】 ⇨七五三

かみおむつ【紙おむつ】 a disposable diaper [nappy].

かみがき【神垣】 a fence around a Shinto shrine.

かみかぜタクシー【神風タクシー】 a *kamikaze* [recklessly-driven] taxi.

かみかぜとっこうたい【神風特攻隊】❶〈部隊〉the *kamikaze* air attack corps[suicide squad]. The Japanese air attack corps in World War II were assigned to make a suicidal crash on a target at an enemy ship. 敵船めがけて死を覚悟の体当たり攻撃を命じられた第二次世界大戦時の航空特攻隊．⇨人間魚雷

❷〈隊員〉the *kamikaze* air attack pilots [suicide pilots]. They flew suicide mission by crashing their planes into American [enemy] ships toward the end of World War II. 第二次世界大戦末期ころ米船[敵船]に体当たりして決死の任務を果たした特別攻撃隊員．☆片道だけのガソリンを積

んだ戦闘機零戦に20歳前後の青年たちが乗り込み，尊い命が海上に散った．

かみがた【上方】 *kamigata*; the Kyoto-Osaka area[district]; Kyoto and its vicinity [environs]. 明治時代以前，皇居は京都にあったので「京都・大阪・その近郊」の総称．関西地方や京阪地方をさす．¶**上方歌舞伎** the *kamigata* kabuki drama; a kabuki drama originating in the Kyoto-Osaka region. **上方芸能** the *Kamigata* performing arts. **上方語** the *kamigata* dialect; the Kansai dialect(関西弁). 「上方言葉」ともいう．**上方訛り** a *kamigata* accent. **上方文学** *kamigata* literature originating in the Kyoto-0saka area. **上方落語** the comic storytelling in the Osaka tradition. **上方歌.** ⇨地唄

かみこ【紙子】 a plain[sober] paper robe. 紙製の質素な衣服 (garment).

かみざ【上座】 (sit at) a place[seat] of honor; (sit at) the top[highest] seat; (sit at) the head of the table; (take) the seat honor; (take) the best seat. It is the highest-ranking position for the main guest in the traditional Japanese guest room nearest to the alcove. 上位の人が座る席．和室では床の間に最も近い場所が最上位席． ⇔下座

かみしばい【紙芝居】❶〈紙絵〉a picture card story show; a paper picture show. It consists of a series of colored picture cards illustrating adventure stories or representing popular scenes for children. 子供向けの冒険物語や人気の場面を描写した一連の絵. **❷**〈語り〉 storytelling[story told] with picture cards. A series of colored picture cards are removed one by one from a set of pictures in a wooden-frame stage while the storyteller narrates changing scenes of a story dramatically. 話し手が物語の変化する場面を劇的に語りながら，木枠の舞台にある一続きの芝居絵を順にめくって見せ

る．

かみしも【裃】 a *kamishimo*; the formal dress of a *samurai*; the formal dress worn by a *samurai*; the ceremonial costume for the *samurai* class in the Edo period. A *kamishimo* consists of a broad-shouldered sleeveless jacket (*kataginu*) and pleated loose-legged trousers (*hakama*) worn over a *kimono*, both made of the same color and cloth. The *kataginu* has a family crest on the back and two on the front. 江戸時代の武士の礼服．同色布の「肩衣」と「袴」からなり，着物の上に着る．肩衣には家紋が背中には1つ，前には2つある． ⇨肩衣／袴

かみだな【神棚】 a family[household] Shinto altar. It is a miniature Shinto altar made of plain cypress wood with roofs and steps. It is placed on a high shelf over a lintel[near the ceiling] to worship family guardian gods. Sacred objects, such as an amulet from the Ise Grand Shrine and a charm tablet from the local tutelary shrine, are enshrined in the center of the Shinto altar. 神道の家庭祭壇．屋根と階段がある白木の檜造りの小型祭壇で，家族の守護神を礼拝するために鴨居の上［天井近く］の棚に置かれる．神棚の中央には伊勢神宮のお札(大麻)や氏神神社のお札 (an amulet; a talisman)などの神符が祀られている． ⇨仏壇(仏教)／お札

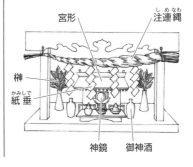

宮形　注連縄
榊
紙垂
神鏡　御神酒

【関連語】「宮形」small-scale shrine.「神鏡（神の御霊代）」divine mirror (venerated as deity spirit and object). ⇨神体.「御神酒」sacred *sake* (offered to gods before the Shinto altar).「榊」*sakaki* twig. ⇨榊.「注連縄と紙垂」sacred twisted rope tied with zigzag strips of paper. ⇨垂

かみつつみやき【紙包み焼き】foods wrapped in Japanese paper and grilled. 和紙などで材料を包み、蒸し焼き (baked)にする食物. 白身魚やキノコなどがある.

かみて【上手】〈歌舞伎などの舞台〉the right (side of the) stage seen from the audience. 客席から見て舞台の右側 ; the left (side of the) stage facing the audience. 客席に向かって左側の舞台. ⇨下手/歌舞伎(舞台)

かみなりおこし【雷おこし】 a crisp millet-and-rice cake. It was originally sold at the *Kaminari-mon* gate of Senso(ji) Temple (in Tokyo). ⇨おこし

カミナリ族 reckless motorcycle riders; motorcycle gangs; hot rodders; ㊨ motor-bike hooligans[tearaways].

かみなりもん【雷門】 the Thunder Gate[the Gate of Thunder] (of Senso(ji) Temple), a huge red lantern hanging under its eaves. At both sides of the gate stand a pair of Deva King statues[guards], *Fujin*, the God of the Wind (the Wind God), and *Raijin*, the God of Thunder (the Thunder God). 浅草寺(東京都内最古の寺)の雷門 の 両 側 に「風神」と「雷神」の仁王像が配されている. ☆幅3.3m, 高さ3.9mの「赤い提灯」(3.3-m-wide and 3.9-m-tall red lantern)が下がる.

かみのく【上の句】 the first three lines of a *tanka* (poem); the first[former] half of *tanka* (poem); the first 17 syllables of a *tanka* (poem). 短歌で最初の五・七・五の三句[17音節]. ⇨下の句

かみやしき【上屋敷】 the city residence of a high-ranking *samurai*[feudal lord or direct retainer of a shogun] during the Edo period. 地位の高い武士が市中に在住した屋敷. 江戸時代の大名・旗本などの屋敷. ⇦下屋敷

かめ【瓶・甕】 an earthenware pot; a jar（広い）; a jug(注ぎ口と取っ手がある). 瓶子.

かめ【亀】〔爬〕a tortoise (陸生); a turtle (海亀). A turtle, together with a crane, is a symbol of longevity [long life]. 亀は鶴と同様に長寿の象徴である. ⇨すっぽん / 鶴. ¶亀の甲〈甲羅〉the shell of a tortoise [turtle]; carapace;〈べっこう細工の材料〉tortoiseshell.

かめのこだわし【亀の子束子】 a tortise-shaped scrub brush.

かめんふうふ【仮面夫婦】the couple who go through the motions of being husband and wife.

かも【鴨】〔鳥〕a duck (家畜); a wild duck (野生); a drake (雄); a hen (雌); a duckling (子鴨); a teal (小鴨). ☆「だまされやすい人」は a sucker; an easy mark. という. ¶鴨肉 duck meat. 鴨すき *sukiyaki* with duck meat. ⇨すきやき. 鴨鍋 hot-pot dish cooked with duck meat and vegetables.

【鴨南蛮うどん[そば]】 wheat noodles [buckwheat noodles] topped with duck meat and scallions[Welson onions] in soup; wheat noodles[buckwheat noodles] cooked in fish broth with duck meat and scallions[Welson onions] atop. 合鴨(または鶏)のささ身とネギを上にのせた掛けうどん(またはそば). ☆「なんばん」は大阪のねぎの産地だった「難波」の変化したもので「ネギ」の意といわれる.

かもい【鴨居】 a lintel; a slotted upper beam fitted for a door[*shoji* or *fusuma*] to slide in. 戸[障子・襖]をはめ込む上の横木. ⇦敷居

かもしか【羚羊】〔動物〕a Japanese serow; an antelope. 日本特産. 特別天然記念物.

かもめ【鷗】〔鳥〕a gull; a seagull(海鷗).

かもん【家紋】 a family crest; a family emblem; a crest fixed for each family; a coat of arms. It is dyed onto the *kimono* used for the formal occasions. It is usually put on not only the formal *kimono* but also on lanterns, etc. Popular motif of the family crest is generally a plant and an animal such as the *aoi* (hollyhock: the crest of the Tokugawa shogun family) and the *kiku* (the chrysanthemum crest of the Imperial Family). 家紋(家々に定められた紋)は公式行事などで使用する着物に染め付けられ，正装着だけでなく提灯などにも見られる．家紋のモチーフには動植物が多く，「葵」(徳川将軍家の「葵の紋」)や「菊」(皇室の「菊の紋」)などがある．¶**家紋の付いた着物** a *kimono* bearing the family crest.

かや【蚊帳】 a mosquito net. It is put up indoors for keeping out mosquitoes on summer nights. It is suspended from the ceiling at the four corners of a room. 夏の夜に蚊を中に入れないように室内に吊るす(set up). 部屋の四隅に天井から吊るす.

¶**蚊帳をはずす** take down a mosquito net.

かや【茅・萱】〔植物〕thatch (plants); plants used for thatching; miscanthus reed. ☆「茅葺の」 thatched. ¶**茅葺き** roofing with thatched grass; roofing of thatched grass, **茅葺小屋** a thatch-roofed cottage[house]; a cottage with a thatched roof. **茅葺き屋根** a thatched roof; a thatch-covered roof.

かやく【加薬・加役】 ingredients of fish and vegetables (used for mixing with rice to make *kayaku-gohan*). (加薬飯などをつくるためご飯と混ぜる)魚や野菜の具. ¶**加薬御飯**. ⇨五目飯

【加薬うどん[そば]】 wheat noodles [buckwheat noodles] in fish broth cooked with fish, vegetables and various ingredients. 魚・野菜などの具を入れた出し汁のうどん[そば].

かゆ【粥】 rice porridge (濃い粥); rice gruel[thin rice porridge] (薄い粥；重湯). Rice is boiled in a lot of water until it is sticky. It is usually plain with salt added and mixed with various vegetables. 米に水分を多く入れて柔らかくなるまで炊いたもの．通常は塩を加えて野菜を混ぜる．通称「おかゆ」. ¶**粥をする** eat rice gruel[porridge]. ⇨小豆がゆ / 芋がゆ / 白かゆ(白がゆ) / 茶がゆ / 七草がゆ / 重湯

かよいぼん【通い盆】a serving tray.

からあげ【空揚げ・唐揚げ】 deep-fried food without the use of batter. Fish, meat and vegetables are deep-fried without any coating at all to retain natural colors and shapes. Foods cooked in this way are usually deep-fried after lightly dredging[covering] with flour. 魚・肉・野菜などの自然の色や形を保つために衣をつけずに揚げる，通常は小麦粉を薄くまぶして揚げる．☆「ジャガイモの空揚げ」は French-fried potatoes; (French)fries; 米 chips.

〔料理〕**鶏の空揚げ** deep-fried chicken without the use of batter.

からえ【唐絵】 a *kara-e* painting (dealing with Chinese themes); a Chinese-style painting. (大和絵に対して)中国風の絵画. ⇨大和絵

からおり【唐織】❶〈織物〉a Chinese brocade; a heavy brocade for garments (originally from China); a silk cloth of Chinese weave (with heavy elaborate patterns). 中国から渡来した織物．精巧な模様をほどこした絹織物.

❷〔能楽〕a rich brocade used for Noh costumes. It is used for making garments worn

か

by actors playing the main female roles in a Noh darma. 能装束用の豪華な織物. 能楽で女性役を演じる役者が着る衣装をつくる.

からかさ【唐傘】 a Japanese waterproofed-paper umbrella; a bamboo-and-oiled-paper umbrella. It is made of oiled paper pasted on a thin bamboo frame, bamboo ribs and bamboo handle. 細い割竹の骨組みの上に油紙を張り，それを支える竹製の骨と柄でつくる. ☆「番傘」(男子用)と「蛇の目傘」(女性用)に大別される. ⇨番傘 / 蛇の目傘

からかみ【唐紙】 ❶〈中国の紙〉colored paper introduced from China; thick printed paper used to cover sliding doors. 中国から渡来した色模様の紙. また，それをまねて色模様を摺り出した装飾用の紙. ☆ふすまなどに用いる.

❷〈襖〉a (paper-covered) sliding screen; a sliding door. 唐紙を張った引き戸.「唐紙障子」の略.

がらがらへび【ガラガラ蛇】〔爬〕a rattlesnake. 毒蛇. 尾の先でガラガラと音を鳴らす.

からくりにんぎょう【からくり人形】 a mechanical puppet[doll]; a movable marionette (controlled with rods and wires). ⇨付記(1)「日本の祭り」〈春の高山祭り[4月]〉

からし【芥子・辛子】 mustard; chili pepper; powdered seeds of mustard. 芥子菜の種子を粉にしたもの. 調味料に用いる.

〔料理・食品〕辛子和え (vegetables) dressed with mustard. ☆蓮根の辛子和え lotus root dressed with *shoyu*[soy sauce] and mustard. ⇨和え物. 辛子醤油 *shoyu*[soy sauce] mixed with mustard. 辛子酢 vinegared mixed with mustard. 辛子酢味噌 white *miso*[soybean paste] flavored mustard and vinegar. 芥子漬け (vegetables) pickled in mustard. ☆きゅうりの芥子漬け cucumber pickled in mustard. 芥子菜

漬け pickled[salted] leaf mustard; Indian [Chinese] mustard. 辛子明太子 spicy cod roe; salted cod roe flavored with chili pepper; cod roe seasoned with[pickled in] salt, red pepper and hot mustard. ⇨明太子 辛子蓮根 deep-fried mustard-stuffed lotus root; deep-fried lotus root stuffed with mustard and *miso*[bean paste]. (蓮根に芥子と味噌を詰め，油で揚げる. 熊本名産).

からしな【芥子菜】〔植物〕leaf mustard. アブラナ科の一年草または二年草. 葉は辛味があり，種子を粉末にして「芥子」をつくる. ⇨芥子

からしゅっちょう【空出張】 a fictitious [phony] business trip.

からす【烏・鴉】〔鳥〕a crow; a raven(渡烏). ¶烏城 Crow Castle.「松本城」の別称.

からすがい【烏貝】〔貝〕a freshwater mussel. ⇨むらさきいがい

からすのぎょうずい【烏の行水】 (have) a quick dip in the bath; (take) a hurried bath. 早くすませる入浴. ⇨行水

からすみ【唐墨】 salted and dried mullet roe; botargo. ボラの卵巣を塩漬けにして干した食品. ☆中国製の墨である書道用の「唐墨」に形が似ていることに由来. ⇨ぼら

からすむぎ【燕麦】〔植物〕an oat (plant);〈穀物〉oats(複数形). ⇨麦 / 燕麦

からたち【枳殻】〔植物〕a trifoliate orange. ミカン科の落葉低木.

からっかぜ【空っ風】 a dry wind (in cold season).

からつくんち【唐津くんち】 the Karatsu Kunchi Autumn Festival. (11月). ⇨付記(1)「日本の祭り」

からつやき【唐津焼】 Karatsu ceramic ware (produced in the Karatsu region of Saga Prefecture).

からつゆ【空梅雨】 a dry[rainless] rainy season.

からて【空手】 *karate*; the Japanese martial

art of unarmed self-defense (using only the bare hands, elbows, knees and feet as weapons). The basic techniques include the kicks (*keri*), the thrusts with the fist (*tsuki*) and arm[elbow] strikes[the chop with the open hand] (*uchi*). 武器を持たずに身を守る武術（素手・肘・膝・足などを武器とする）. 主たる技術は「蹴り」「突き」「打ち」である. ☆有段者は「黒帯」(black belt), 初心者は「白帯」(white belt)を締める.

【空手道】 the way of *karate*; the Ryukyuan art of weaponless self-defense developed on the islands of Okinawa. 沖縄で発達した武器を用いない護身術.

【空手試合】 *karate* competition. There are two sections in *karate* competitions [matches] : form competition (*kata*) and sparring match (*kumite*). Form competitions are demonstrations of various combinations of techniques by a person or a group, which are judged by the techniques' accuracy and posture displayed. Sparring matches against an opponent are scored by launching effective thrusts and kicks, but blows must stop short of hitting the opponent's body. 「型試合」では1人または団体による多様な組み合わせ技の正確さや姿勢などを判定する.「組手試合」では1対1の対戦で有効な突きや蹴りの技を判定する. しかし相手の身体を打つ手前で打撃は止める.

からふと【樺太】Sakhalin. ¶**樺太犬** a Sakhalin dog.

からふとます【樺太鱒】〔魚〕 a pink salmon. 肉は薄紅色で柔らかい. ムニエルとして食す. サケ缶の原料.

ガラポン a lottery wheel. 回転式の抽選器.

からまつ【唐松】〔植物〕a (Japanese) larch (tree). マツ科の落葉高木. 木材は建築用. ⇨松

からみもち【辛み餅】 a rice cake served with grated *daikon*[radish] and *shoyu*[soy sauce]. 大根卸しと醤油でまぶした餅.

からもん【唐門】 a Chinese-style gate (with Chinese-style gables). ☆日光の陽明門をくぐると見られる国宝の唐門は有名.

がらん【伽藍】 a Buddhist temple (with several buildings in the precincts). 寺院の建築物（境内に建造物が複数ある）. ☆「キリスト教の伽藍」は cathedralという. ⇨七堂伽藍(7つの主要寺院建造物). ¶**大伽藍** a grand temple complex; a cathedral.

かり【雁】〔鳥〕a wild goose (⊛ geese). ⇨がん

ガリ slices of vinegared ginger; red ginger pickled in sweetened vinegar. It is eaten to refresh one's mouth. 甘酢漬けのショウガ. 口の中をさっぱりさせるために食べる.「紅生姜」の符丁. ☆鮨に添えて食べる時ガリガリと音がすることに由来. ⇨符丁

かりぎぬ【狩衣】 a hunting costume; a formal dress for hunting. It was worn by men over their *kimono* when hunting in ancient times. It was used as casual dress for court nobles and *samurai* warriors in the Heian period, and later as a formal dress in the Edo period. 昔, 狩りのときに男性が着用した衣装. 平安時代には公家・武家の平服, 江戸時代には礼服に用いた. ⇨狩袴

かりしゅうげん【仮祝言】 (hold) a private wedding.

カリスマびようし【カリスマ美容師】 a charismatic hairstylist; a hairstylist with charisma; a hairstylist with flair and personality.

かりばかま【狩袴】 a long *hakama* for hunting. It is a long pleated skirt worn by men over their *kimono* when going out for hunting. 狩猟に出かけるときに衣装の上に着用する男子用の長い袴. ⇨狩衣

かりはなみち【仮花道】〔歌舞伎〕. ⇨花道

かりばら【借り腹】 surrogate mother (代理母). ¶**借り腹で子をもうける** have a baby by a surrogate mother

カリフラワー〔植物〕a cauliflower. 別名「花野菜」. 野生キャベツ(wild cabbage)が改良されたもの.

かりゅう【下流(川の)】 the lower reaches [course] (of a river[stream]). ⇔上流

かりん【花梨】〔植物〕a Chinese quince (tree). バラ科の落葉高木. 果実酒などに加工される. マメ科のカリンは高級材として床柱や三味線の胴などに用いる.

かりんとう【花林糖】 Japanese-style sweet pretzels; Japanese fried-dough cookies[biscuits]; small sugar-coated cookies[sticks] made from fried dough. 小麦粉に砂糖を加えてねり, 油で揚げる.

かるかん【軽羹】 a steamed sweet bun (made from grated yam and rice flour). (芋卸しと米粉を蒸して作る)甘い菓子パン.

カルスト Karst.(ドイツ語)石灰岩が雨水に溶食された地形. ¶**カルスト地形の美観で有名な秋芳台**(山口県) Akiyoshidai Limestone Tableland[Plateau] noted for the beauty of the Karst topography.

かるた【歌留多】 *karuta*; 〈札〉traditional Japanese playing cards; 〈遊戯〉a Japanese game of *karuta*; an indoor game played with two decks[(英) packs] of cards at a *karuata* party. *Karuta* are rectangular playing cards, with pictures or Japanese writing(s) drawn on them. When playing, one player reads out a reading card[a card to be read up] (*yomi-fuda*) and the other players compete to take a picture card (*e-fuda*) or a card to be picked up (*tori-fuda*) that matches the one read out. The winner is the player who takes the most cards. 絵や文字が描かれた長方形の遊戯札. 1人が「読み札」を読み, 遊戯者がそれに適合する「絵札」(または「取り札」)を競って取り合う. 最も多く札を取った者が勝ち. ☆ポルトガル語の (carta)に由来. ⇨いろは

歌留多 / 百人一首

カルデラ a caldera; a large crater. Caldera is a deep, caldronlike cavity on the summit of a volcano. 火山の噴火作用によって生じた円形に近い大型のくぼ地. ¶**世界最大のカルデラを有する阿蘇山**(熊本県) Mt. Aso with the largest caldera in the world. **カルデラ湖** a caldera[crater] lake. カルデラの中に水がたまってできた湖(十和田湖[青森県・秋田県], 田沢湖[秋田県]など).

かれい【鰈】〔魚〕a flatfish; a (right-eyed) flounder; a halibut; a sole. カレイ科の海産硬骨魚. ☆「左ヒラメの右カレイ」(正面から見て両目が左側にあれば「ヒラメ」, 右にあれば「カレイ」). ⇨ひらめ. ¶**石鰈** a stone flounder. **沼鰈** a starry flounder. **真鰈** a right-eyed flounder; a brown sole. **子持ち鰈** a flounder (filled) with roes.

〔料理・食品〕**鰈の空揚げ** deep-fried flounder [sole] without the use of batter. ⇨空揚げ. **鰈の生干し** half-dried flatfish.

かれいしゅう【加齢臭】 aging odor[(英) odour]; odor of aging; age-induced body smell[odor]; body smell[odor] that comes with aging; the smell of an aged[elderly] person.

カレー curry. ¶**カツカレー** curry with a (pork) cutlet. ⇨カツ. **カレー粉** curry powder. **カレー料理** a curry; curried dish[food]. **カレールー** a curry roux. **激辛カレー** an extremely[a very] hot curry.

〔料理〕**カレーうどん** curry *udon*; wheat noodles cooked with curry sauce. **カレー南蛮** curry and wheat noodles cooked with green onions; wheat noodles cooked in fish broth seasoned with soy sauce and curry. **カレーライス** curry and rice; curried rice; rice cooked with curry sauce. ☆明治中期頃イギリス料理として伝わり, 戦後カレールーが商品化され, 日常食となった. 別称「ライスカレー」.

かれさんすい（ていえん）【枯山水（庭園）】　a dry landscape garden. The garden consists of rocks and sand representing mountains and rivers without water. The rocks are placed in a sea of gravel to create a miniature cosmos for contemplation. This garden is found at Zen Buddhist temples, such as the rock garden of Ryoanji Temple in Kyoto. 水を用いず，石組みや砂によって山水を表現する庭園．石組みは砂利の海に配置され，瞑想するための小宇宙を造り出している．このような庭園は禅寺にある．例「龍安寺の石庭（京都府）」．⇨回遊式庭園/日本庭園

かれすすき【枯れ薄】　dead Japanese silver grass; (a clump of) withered pampas grass. ⇨薄

かろう【家老】a chief counselor of a shogun [shogunate]; a chief retainer[vassal] of a feudal lord (as the highest-ranking official [minister] in the government of *samurai*). He was in charge of general management of the governmental or household affairs. 幕府の相談役．大名の重臣（家中の武士を統率した最高位の職にある者）．政治・家事を統括した.

かろうし【過労死】　death from overwork [overfatigue]; death from excessive work; working oneself to death.

かろうじさつ【過労自殺】　overwork-related suicide.

かわ【皮】❶〈生物の皮〉the skin; a hide; a fur. ¶チキンの皮 a chicken skin. 魚の皮 a fish skin.
❷〈果物・野菜の皮〉a rind; a peel. ¶レモンの皮 a lemon rind. リンゴの皮 an apple peel.
❸〈パン・パイなどの皮〉crust. ¶パイの皮 a pie crust. パンの皮 a bread crust.

かわ【川・河】　a river（大きな川）→ a stream [creek]（小さな川）→ a brook（小川）→ a

rivulet（細い川）→ a streamlet[rill]（細い川）．⇨渓流．☆「淀川」（米国式）the Yodo River.（英国式）the River Yodo．書く場合 the Yodoとすることもある．地図では the を略して Yodo Riverとする．☆日本三清流(the Three Clearest Rivers in Japan). 四万十川(高知県)，長良川(岐阜県)，柿田川(静岡県).

かわうお［かわざかな］【川魚】〔魚〕a river [stream] fish; a freshwater fish. ¶川魚料理 a freshwater fish cuisine.

かわうそ【川獺】〔鳥〕a (river) otter.

かわかます【川梭魚・川鮖】〔魚〕a pike; a lice. 大型の淡水魚．⇨かます

かわごえまつり【川越まつり】the Kawagoe Festival.（10月）⇨付記(1)「日本の祭り」

かわせみ【川蝉・翡翠】〔鳥〕a kingfisher; an Indian kingfisher.

かわどこ【川床】　the riverbed; the stream bed. 川底・河床ともいう．

かわのじ【川の字】　sleeping one's child between husband and wife[mother and father]. 夫婦［父母］の間に子供が眠ること．

かわます【河鱒・川鱒】〔魚〕a brook trout; a speckled trout. サケ科イワナ属の魚．秋から冬が旬．塩焼きにする．⇨ます

かわや【厠】　water closet[WC]．☆古風な言い方．今風の「手洗い」（米 comfort station; 英 convenience)

かわゆか【川床】　a platform built out over a river for enjoying the cool. 涼を得るために川の上に突き出て設けられた桟敷．☆京都四条の川床が有名．

かわら【瓦】　a tile (made of fired clay). 焼き粘土からつくる．¶屋根瓦 a roofing tile. 平瓦 a plain tile. 棟瓦 a ridged tile. 鬼瓦 a tile with[bearing] the figure of a devil. ⇨鬼瓦．瓦葺き roof tiling. 瓦塀 roof-tile and mortar fence. 瓦葺きの家 a tile-roofed house; a house roofed with tiles; a house

か

laid tiles on the roof. 瓦葺き屋根 a tile(d) roof; a tile-covered slanting roof (of a traditional house).

かわらけ【土器】 unglazed earthenware; earthen cup（杯）; earthen vessel（器）. 素焼きの土器・陶器.

かわらせんべい【瓦煎餅】 a tile-shaped semisweet rice cracker.

かわらばん【瓦版】 *kawaraban*; a commercial block-printed newssheet of the Edo period. *Kawaraban* was a single-page block-printed newspaper as the forerunner of the newspaper[an extra] in Japan. 江戸時代における読み売り用の木版印刷の新聞. 日本における新聞［号外］の先駆けとしての1枚刷りの木版印刷物. ☆粘土に文字や絵などを彫り, 瓦のように焼いたものを原版として印刷したことからの呼称.

かわりもの【変わり者】an eccentric (person); a queer; a freak; Ⓜ a screwball. ⇨おたく／宇宙人

かん【貫】 a *kan*. a unit of weight. One *kan* equals 3.75 kilograms. 重さの単位. 3.75 kg.

がん【龕】cabinet-sized shrine for a Buddhist icon. 仏像を安置する厨子.

がん【雁［鴈］】〔鳥〕a wild goose. ¶雁の群れ a flock of wild geese. ⇨かり

かんい【官位】 office and rank（官職と官位）; official rank（官職の等位）; office[government] post and rank.

かんい【冠位】 the rank of a nobleman at the ancient Japanese imperial court. 朝廷での貴族の官位.

【冠位十二階】 the system of twelve cap ranks of the noblemen at the ancient Japanese imperial court (indicated by the twelve colors of their caps). It was established by Prince Shotoku in 603 and abolished in 701. 宮中における貴族の12の冠位は色分けされていた. 603年聖徳太子により制定され, 701年に廃止. ☆役職は家柄ではなく才能や業績がある人物から選ぶ.

かんえん【肝炎】 hepatitis. ¶B型肝炎 hepatitis B ¶C型肝炎ウイルス hepatitis C virus[HCV] ☆肝硬変 hepatic cirrhosis

かんおうかい【観桜会】 a cherry-blossom-viewing party. 別称「花見」

かんかんせったい【官官接待】wining and dining of central government officials by local government bureaucrats (using money from public funds[coffers]). 地方役所が中央役人を（公費で）飲食接待する.

かんぎくかい【観菊会】 a chrysanthemum-viewing party.

かんきだん【寒気団】cold air mass. ⇨暖気団

かんきつるい【柑橘類】citrus fruits. ミカン, レモン, ライム, オレンジなどの総称.

かんきょうホルモン【環境ホルモン】 a hormone[an endocrine] disrupter; a hormone-disrupting chemical. ☆内分泌攪乱化学物質.

ガングろ【顔黒】❶〈日焼け顔〉a deeply[thoroughly] sun-tanned face[skin]. ❷〈化粧の流行〉a cosmetic vogue for a deeply tanned face, white eyeliner, and false eyelashes;〈少女〉a deeply-tanned gal; a gal with blackface makeup who flatters herself to look black.

かんぐん【官軍】 the Imperial army[troops]（朝廷方の軍）; the government army[forces]（政府軍）. ⇨白虎隊

かんげつかい【観月会】 a moon-viewing party (on the night of the full moon).「観月の宴」ともいう.

かんけつせん【間欠泉】 a geyser; an intermittent spring; natural hot spring which at intervals shoots water up into the air. 一定の間隔をおいて噴出する温泉. 圏別府温泉

かんげん【管弦・管絃】〈雅楽〉*kangen*; the orchestral music of gagaku. Kangen consists of wind instruments (*kan*) , stringed instruments (*gen*) and percussion instruments. It is performed by playing the flute, drums and Japanese stringed instruments used in Japanese court music (*gagaku*). 雅楽の管弦楽. 管弦は「管楽器」,「弦楽器」そして「打楽器」から成る. 雅楽で用いる笛・太鼓・弦楽器などで演奏される. ⇨雅楽 / 舞楽 ☆「管弦」には下記3種の楽器がある.

①『打楽器』(percussion instruments)には「羯鼓」(side drum).「鉦鼓」(standing drum).「楽太鼓」(suspended drum) がある.

②『管楽器』(wind instruments)には「篳篥」(double-reed oboe instrument with a strong nasal sound).「竜笛」(flute).「笙」(mouth-organ-like wind instrument with a standing circle of 17 bamboo pipes)がある.

③『弦楽器』(stringed instruments)には「琵琶」(*biwa* lute).「楽箏」(*koto* zither)がある.

かんげんさい【管弦祭】 the Music Festival of Itsukushima Shrine in Miayajima Island. (7月). ⇨付記(1)「日本の祭り 」

かんこうちょう【観光庁】 Japan Tourism Agency[JTA] (established with the aim of attracting more foreign tourists to Japan).

かんこうりっこく【観光立国】 tourism-oriented nation.

かんごうぼうえき【勘合貿易】 a tally trade (between Japan and the Ming Dynasty). It was an official trade with the Ming-Dynasty Government by cracking down on pirate ships (*wako*) in the Muromachi period. 室町時代に海賊船(倭寇)を取り締まりながら実施された明朝(中国)との正式な貿易. ☆1404年足利義満が開始. ⇨倭寇

かんごうふ【勘合符】 a tally stick. It was used to tell official trade vessels from pirate ships (*wako*) in the Muromachi period. 室町時代, 正式な貿易船と海賊船(倭寇)を区別するために使用した割り符.

☆日本からの貿易船に対して, 明朝(中国)の政府が正式な貿易船であるしるしに出した割り符. 日本の貿易船は左側の合札. 中国は右側の合札.

かんこくへいごう【韓国併合】 the Japan-Korea Annexation; the annexation of Korea by Japan. ☆1910年日本は韓国を併合し, 朝鮮総督府を置く. 1945年まで続く.

かんこんそうさい【冠婚葬祭】 ceremonial functions[occasions]; ceremonies of Coming-of-Age, marriage, funeral and ancestor worship. 元服, 婚礼, 葬儀, 祖先崇拝の四大礼.

かんさいりょうり【関西料理】 Kansai-style dishes; Kyoto-Osaka area dishes. ☆薄味の料理. 野菜・乾物などの素材を生かした料理. ⇔関東料理(濃味の料理)

かんざけ【燗酒】 a warmed *sake*; a heated *sake*. ¶熱燗 a hot *sake*. ⇨冷

かんざし【簪】 an ornamental hairpin (with some elaborate handiwork). It gives a woman's hair a gorgeous look. (装飾的な手細工をほどこした束髪用の)飾り留め金. 女性の髪を華やかにする髪飾り.

かんざらし【寒晒し】 the exposure to cold air in midwinter. *Mochi*[rice cakes] and *tofu*[bean curd] are bleached through exposure to cold weather in winter in order to preserve them. 餅または豆腐などを保存用に寒中の戸外の冷たい空気にさらす (exposed to the cold) こと. ⇨寒餅 / 凍み大根. ¶寒晒し粉 glutinous rice flour bleached through exposure to the cold air in midwinter. 寒中に冷たい空気にさらしてから製粉した餅米の粉.「白玉粉」「餅粉」ともいう. ⇨白玉粉

かんし【干支】 the sexagenary cycle (of the Chinese zodiac). 60年の周期. ☆十干と十二支を組み合わせ年月・時刻・方位を表す. ⇨えと

かんじ【漢字】 a *kanji*; a Chinese character

(used in Japanese writing). A *kanji* is an ideograph that represents an idea or object. 漢字は思考または対象物を表す(stands for)表意文字である. ⇨仮名(漢字と併用する). ☆characterは「(それ自体が意味をもつ)表意文字」. letterは「(仮名やアルファベットのようにそれ自体意味をもたない)字」〈capital letter「大文字」(A, B, Cなど)〉. ⇨当用漢字 / 常用漢字

かんじき【樏】 (a pair of) snowshoes made of vines. 蔓で作る雪靴. ☆深い雪に足が埋まらないように, また滑らないように履物の下につける.

がんじつ【元日】 New Year's Day (January 1). This national holiday was established in 1948 as a day to celebrate the beginning of the new year as the most important day in Japan. People visit shrines or temples on the morning of New Year's Day to pray for happiness and prosperity for the coming year. ☆一年の最初の日, 1月1日. ⇨元旦/門松 / 御節料理 / 初詣

かんしつぞう【乾漆像】 a dry-lacquered image[figure] (of the Buddha); a lacquered wooden (Buddhist) statue. 乾湿(漆の液の乾いたかたまり)で作った(仏)像. 単に「乾湿」ともいう. ☆奈良時代に唐(中国)から伝来した漆工技術.

かんじゅ【貫主・貫首・管主】 the chief abbot of a Buddhist temple[sect]. 寺院[宗派]の貫長. 天台宗で最高の僧職. ¶輪王寺[栃木県・ユネスコ世界文化遺産]の貫主 the chief abbot of Rinnoji Temple.

かんじょ(かんにょ)【官女】〈宮中に仕える女性〉a court lady; a lady-in-waiting. (⊛ ladies-in-waiting);〈未婚の女官〉a maid-in-waiting; a maid of honor.

かんしょうしきていえん【観賞式庭園】 a viewing-style landscape garden; a Japanese landscape garden to be seen and appreciated from the building.

かんしょう【環礁】an atoll. ☆環状さんご島

かんじょうせん【環状線】〈鉄道〉a loop line; a belt line;〈道路〉⊛ a belt highway; ⊛ a ring[loop] road. ¶山の手環状線 the Yamanote Loop Line (in Tokyo).

かんじょうぶぎょう【勘定奉行】⇨奉行

かんじん【勧進】❶ Buddhist missionary work and enlightenment. 仏の教えを説き入信させること.

❷ funds for the construction or restoration of a Buddhist temple or Buddhist statue. 寺院・仏像の建立や修理のための寄付 (contributions). ¶勧進元 a promoter[an organizer] of fund-raising held in aid of a temple or shrine. 勧進の興行主.

【勧進相撲】 a fund-raising *sumo* show; *Sumo* show is held to raise funds for pious purposes such as constructions and repairs of a temple or a statue of Buddha. 勧進用の募金集めを行う相撲興行.

かんじんちょう【勧進帳】 ❶ a fund-raising prospectus for a temple or shrine; prospectus for funds solicited by a temple or shrine. 勧進の理由を記して寄付を集める帳面.

❷〔歌舞伎〕 one of the eighteen best pieces of a kabuki play. 歌舞伎十八番の一つ. ⇨歌舞伎十八番

かんす【鑵子】〔茶道〕a teakettle; a kettle.「茶釜」のこと.

かんすいぎょ【鹹水魚】a saltwater fish; a sea fish. ⇨淡水魚

かんぜおん【観世音】*Kanzeon*; the Bodhisattva of Compassion; the Buddhist Deity of Mercy.「観世音菩薩」(*kanzeon-Bosatsu*)の略. 慈悲の権化とされる菩薩. ⇨観音(菩薩)

かんたい【寒帯】 the Frigid Zone. ⇨温帯 /熱帯

かんたいへいようかざんたい【環太平洋火山帯】 the Pacific Rim volcanic belt; circum-Pacific volcanic zone.

かんたくち【干拓地】 reclaimed land (from

かんだまつり【神田まつり】 the Kanda Festival of Kanda Myojin Shrine. (5月). ⇨付記(1)「日本の祭り」

がんたん【元旦】❶〈1月1日の朝〉 the (first) morning[dawn] of January.
❷〈1月1日〉 the first day of *shogatsu*[the first month of the year]. ☆「元」は「最初の」(the first),「旦」は「夜明け」(morning; dawn) の意. ⇨元日

かんチューハイ【缶チューハイ】 canned *shochu* cocktail; a can of *shochu* mixed with soda water or soda pop. ⇨焼酎

かんちゅうみまい【寒中見舞い】 midwinter greetings; an inquiry after the health of a person at the height of winter[in the cold season]. 暦のうえでは小寒から大寒が終わるまでの間の見舞い. ⇔暑中見舞
【寒中見舞状】 a letter of midwinter greetings; a midwinter greeting postcard (in place of a New Year greeting card). It is a letter [postcard] sent to inquire after a superior's [good customer's] health in the cold season in appreciation of their daily favor. 1月7日以降の挨拶.「寒中伺い」ともいう. ⇔暑中見舞状

かんちょう【干潮(引き潮)】 low tide; ebb tide; low water. ⇔満潮

かんつばき【寒椿】〔植物〕 a winter camellia; a camellia blooming in the middle of winter. ⇨つばき

かんていりゅう【勘亭流】 the *kantei* style of calligraphy. The style of writing is characterized by round, bold and thick strokes. It is used typically in kabuki posters and in bills showing the ranking lists of *sumo* wrestlers. 書体の一種. 丸みを帯びた筆太の字体. 歌舞伎の看板や相撲の番付［相撲字］などを書く書体. ☆「江戸文字」の一種. 江戸中村座の手代で書道家である岡崎屋勘六(号, 勘亭[1746-1805])

が始めた.

かんてん【寒天】〔食品〕 *kanten*; agar (weed); agar-agar; Japanese vegetable gelatin (made from *tengusa* seaweed). てんぐさ (agar seaweed)を煮て凝固させ, さらに凍結させて乾かしたもの. ⇨てんぐさ. ¶寒天1本 one stick of agar(-agar).

かんとう【竿灯】 *kanto*; a long bamboo pole hung with many lighted paper lanterns. *Kanto* is a long bamboo pole with nine horizontal bars attached to it. It has about 50 lighted lanterns hung in the form of abundant crops of rice on the both sides of swinging bars. 竿灯とは照明のある紙提灯が多数つるされた長い竹竿のこと. 最大では9本の水平棒をとりつけた長い竿があり, その揺れる棒の両側には豊作の米穀の形をした約50本ほどの明が点された提灯がつるされている.
【竿灯まつり】 the Akita Kanto Lantern Parade Festival at Akita City. 秋田竿灯まつり(8月). ⇨付記(1)「日本の祭り」

がんどう【龕灯】 a votive light[candle] on a Buddhist altar. 仏壇の灯明.

がんどうちょうちん【龕灯提灯】 a cylindrical lantern. It is made of copper (or tin) with a reflector at one end behind a candle-stand enabling one to cast a beam of light. 円筒状の提灯. ろうそく立ての背後に前方を照らす反射鏡のある銅(ブリキ)製の照明具.「強盗提灯」とも書く.

がんどうがえし【龕灯返し・強盗返し】〔歌舞伎〕 a complete reversal of large stage sets. Large three-dimensional stage sets tip over to reveal an entirely new scene without the use of the revolving stage. 大舞台のセットを完全に逆転させること. 回り舞台を用いないで, 立体的に飾られた舞台道具を後ろに回し［倒れ］, 底になっていた面を垂直に立ててまったく別の新しい背景に変える装置.「がんとうがえし」とも. 通称「どんでん

返し」

かんとうしょう【敢闘賞】〔相撲〕 the Fighting Spirit Prize[Award] (in *sumo* wrestling). The prize is given to a top division *sumo* wrestler (except *yokozuna* or *ozeki*) who demonstrates the most fighting spirit during a given tournament. 相撲の場所中最も闘志を燃やした（横綱または大関以外の）上位力士に授与される賞. ⇨三賞

かんとうだいしんさい【関東大震災】 the Great Kanto Earthquake (in 1923). ☆1923年9月1日東京・横浜を中心に関東地方を襲った地震（マグニチュード7.9を記録）. それに伴う火災などの災害多数. 死者10万人以上.

かんとうだき【関東炊き】 a Kanto-style *oden*. 「関東煮」ともいう. ⇨おでん

かんとうふうぞうに【関東風雑煮】 a Kanto-style rice cake soup. It is the traditional New Year's dishes cooked with various ingredients such as chicken thighs, *naruto* fish paste roll, *komatsuna* mustard spinach, carrots, *yuzu* rind, etc. 鶏のもも肉, 鳴門巻き, 小松菜, 人参, 柚子の外皮などの具材で料理した関東風の雑煮. ⇨雑煮

かんとうりょうり【関東料理】 Kanto-style dishes; Tokyo area dishes. ☆濃味の料理. 江戸前で捕れた魚介類を中心にしたすし, てんぷら, おでんなどの料理. ⇔関西料理（薄味の料理）

かんどくり【燗徳利】 a *sake* bottle (to heat[warm] *sake* in); a small bottle to heat[warm] *sake*; a small bottle for heating[warming] *sake*. 酒を温める小さな徳利. ⇨燗酒

かんなべ【燗鍋】 a *sake* pan (to heat[warm] a *sake* bottle in); a pan with a lid and spout for warming *sake*. 酒を温める蓋と口のある鍋.

かんなめさい【神嘗祭】 the *Kanname-sai* rite; the Thanksgiving Ritual in the Ise Grand Shrine. At the ritual, the Emperor makes offerings of the newly harvested crops[rice] of the year to the Imperial ancestor (Amaterasu Omikami[the Sun Goddess]) as a token of his gratitude. 伊勢神宮での祭事. 天皇がその年の新穀[米]を感謝しながら皇族の先祖[天照大神]に奉る祭礼.（10月15日から17日）. ☆現在は天皇による皇族だけの祭事 (It is observed by the Emperor to thank the god for a good harvest year at the Imperial Palace.)

かんぬし【神主】 a Shinto priest (who ministers at a Shinto shrine). A Shinto priest wears an old brimless headgear (*eboshi*) and holds a wooden ritual scepter (*shaku*) when he is formally dressed in a Shinto robe (*kariginu*). He serves the gods by making offerings and saying[reciting] a Shinto prayer, and also performs the purification rite for worshipers. 神主が狩衣で正装するときには「烏帽子」を被り, 「笏」を持つ. 神への供え物や祝詞をあげる. また参詣者には御祓いをする. ⇨社司 / 神職 / 笏 ❷

がんねん【元年】 the first year (of an era). ¶令和元年 the first year of the Reiwa (era).

かんのあけ【寒の明け】 the end of midwinter [the coldest season (of the year)]; the arrival of spring in earnest. ⇨寒の入り

かんのいり【寒の入り】 the beginning of midwinter[the coldest season (of the year)]; the arrival of winter in earnest. ⇨寒の明け

かんのん【観音】 *Kannon*; *Kwannon*; the (Buddhist) Deity of Mercy; the (Buddhist) Merciful Deity; Avalokiteshvara(梵語). ☆「観世音菩薩」. 単に「観世音」ともいう. 「観音」は中国語の発音 [Kwan-Yin] から用いられている. 英語で the Goddess of Mercy(慈悲の女神)と訳される場合がある. しかし観音は男女の性別を超越した中

性の存在 (neutral super-sex being)である. したがってgoddess「女神」またはgod(男神)よりはdeity「神」(ラテン語の deus(神)に由来)の単語を用いる方がよい. *Kannon is the Deity of Mercy who is believed to deliver people from suffering.* 人間を苦悩から救い出す無限に慈悲溢れる神. ⇨ 神. ¶**十一面観音** (the statue of) the eleven-faced *Kannon*. **馬頭観音** (the statue of) *Kannon* with a horse head in the crown and a human body. **観音菩薩** the *Kannon* Bodhisattva. **観音経** the *Kannon* sutra (観世音菩薩の功徳を説く). **観音堂** a Buddhist temple dedicated to *Kannon*.

かんのんびらき(のさかな)【観音開き(の魚)】〈2枚の切り方〉a butterfly cut (of fish); 〈2枚に切り開いた魚〉 a butterflied fish. ☆butterfly動「(魚・肉などをチョウの翅のように)2枚に切り開く」. ⇨ 背開き(魚)

かんのんびらきのとびら【観音開きの扉】hinged double doors (of a *Kannon* altar cabinet); (a set of) two wooden folding double doors that open outwards on hinges. (観音壇の箱に付いた) 蝶番 のある二重の扉. 左右外側に引いて開ける2枚の木製開き戸. ☆観世音菩薩の像をおさめた厨子の造りから由来した語. ⇨ 厨子

かんぱく【関白】 a *kampaku*; the Imperial adviser; the chief adviser to the Emperor; an imperial regent(摂政:代理で政務を統括する者). A *Kampaku* advises to the Emperor and the supervisor of all court officials, and administered all the governmental affairs of the Emperor. It was abolished with the Restoration of Imperial Rule in 1867. 天皇や宮廷官吏に助言し, 天皇の政務をつかさどる. 明治維新の王政復古(1867年)のとき廃止された. ☆887年藤原基経(836-91)が始めて就任. その後豊臣秀吉(1536-98)・秀次(1568-95)が就任.

かんぱち【間八】〔魚〕an amberjack; an allied kingfish. アジ科のブリ属の魚. 刺身・すし種には不可欠. 長崎県では小型を「ねりご」, 大型を「あかばな」という. 関西では「あかはな」ともいう. ☆頭を上から見ると「八の字形」のまだらな模様があるのが呼称の由来.

かんばつ【旱魃】 a drought; a long period [spell] of dry weather; want of rain.

かんぴょう【干瓢・乾瓢】 *kanpyo*; dried gourd shavings[strips]; long shavings [strips] of dried gourd. Bottle gourd pulp is shaved into long strips and dried in the sun. 夕顔の果実を帯状にむき, 太陽で乾燥させたもの. 巻きずしや五目ずしには不可欠. ⇨夕顔 / ひょうたん
〔食品〕**干瓢巻き** rolled *sushi* containing *kanpyo* in the center; vinegared rice rolled [wrapped] in a sheet of dried laver with pickled gourd shavings in the center.

かんぶきんさぎ【還付金詐欺】a refund fraud. ☆役所から税金(taxes)や保険料(insurance premiums)を返すといって金をだましとる振り込め詐欺の手口.

かんぶつえ【灌仏会】 the (Gautama Shakya-muni) Buddha's Birthday Festival (April 8); the celebration commemorating the anniversary of Buddha's birth. 釈迦の誕生日. 4月8日の法会.「花祭り」ともいう. ⇨付記(1)「日本の祭り」

がんぺき【岸壁】❶〈断崖〉a rock wall[cliff]; sheer walls of the cliff. ❷〈船着場〉a wharf; a quay.

かんぽう【漢方】 traditional Chinese medicine.¶**漢方医** a doctor of a Chinese medicine. **漢方処方** a prescription for traditional medicine. **漢方薬** 輿 a[輿 an] herbal medicine.

かんまん【干満】 the ebb and flow (of the tide). 潮の満ち干. ⇨潮 / 干潮 / 満潮

かんみどころ【甘味処】 a sweet parlor; a

き

shop serving *kanmi*[traditional sweets peculiar to Japan] containing red *adzuki*-bean paste. 小豆餡が入っている甘い食品を出す店. ⇨あんみつ / しるこ / ぜんざい

かんみりょう【甘味料】 a sweetener; sweetening ingredients[agents]; sweetening agents. 食品に甘みをつける調味料. ¶人工甘味料 an artificial sweetener.

かんめん【乾麺】 dried thick noodles. そうめん, 冷麦など干した麺類.

かんもち【寒餅】 a midwinter rice cake; a rice cake made in midwinter; a rice cake preserved in water during the winter. 寒中に搗いた餅. かびがはえない. ⇨寒晒し

がんもどき【雁擬き】 a mashed deep-fried *tofu*[bean curd] burger mixed with bits of vegetables (shredded carrots, burdock roots and ginkgo nuts) and other ingredients (*hijiki* seaweed). くずした豆腐に野菜(ニンジン・ゴボウ・ギンナンなど)や他の具(ヒジキ)を混ぜて油で揚げた食品. 関西では「ひりょうず」という.

かんゆ【肝油】 cod-liver oil; shark-liver oil. タラ・サメ[フカ]などの魚類の肝臓からとった油脂.

かんようしょくぶつ【観葉植物】 a foliage plant; a leafy plant; a plant with attractive foliage.

かんりゅう【寒流】 a cold current. ⇔暖流

かんれい[かんりょう]【管領】 a shogun's assistant of the Muromachi shogunate; a deputy to the shogun in the Muromachi period. 室町時代において将軍を補佐し, 幕政を統括する役(人).

かんれいぜんせん【寒冷前線】 a cold front.

かんれき【還暦】 (celebrate) one's sixtieth birthday.

【還暦祝い】 the celebration of one's sixtieth birthday. The Japanese celebrate their 60th birthday. It is the 60th anniversary of their birth, one of the special ages to celebrate their longevity. There is a complete life cycle spanning 60 years according to the ancient Japanese calendar system. On their 60th birthday, their full cycle is completed. At this age they are said to enter a new life or to be born again as a child. On this day they wear a red sleeveless *kimono* and red hood, symbolic of childhood, to celebrate this second life. 満60歳の祝い. 日本古来の暦体系によると, 60年に及ぶ全人生周期がある. 60歳の誕生日にはひとつの周期が完結する. この年になると新しい人生に入る. または再度幼児に戻るといわれる. この日には第二の人生を祝って幼児の象徴である赤いちゃんちゃんこと赤い被り物を着用する. ☆数え年では61歳である. ⇨賀 / ちゃんちゃんこ

かんろ【寒露】 (drops of) cold dew; the season when the foliage turns red[yellow]. 紅葉も盛りで, 晩秋から初冬にかけて露がおりる季節. ⇨二十四節気

かんろづけ【甘露漬け】 candied[sweetened] preserves. ⇨青梅の甘露漬け

かんろに【甘露煮】 candied[sweetened] food; sweet food stewed[simmered] slowly in *mirin*[sweetened *sake*], *shoyu*[soy sauce] and syrup. とろ火で味醂, 醤油, 蜜で煮る食品. 「あめ煮」(caramelized food)ともいう. ⇨栗の甘露煮 / ふなの甘露煮

き

きいちご【木苺】 〔植物〕a raspberry; a blackberry. バラ科の落葉低木. 熟した実は食用.

きいっぽん【生一本】 a pure *sake*; an undiluted *sake*. 純粋で (genuine)混じりけのない酒. ⇨生酒. ¶灘の生一本 a pure[an undiluted] Nada *sake*.

きいと【生糸】 raw silk. 繭からとったままの絹糸.

きおりもの【生織物】 a fabric woven of raw

silk. 生糸からおった織物.

ぎおんだいこ【祇園太鼓】large drum beating during the Gion Festival. ⇨付記(1)「日本の祭り」(7月:小倉祇園太鼓祭)

ぎおんばやし【祇園囃子】 a refined and elegant music of the Gion Festival. It is played by musicians on elaborate festival floats decorated with colorful cloths which parade through the city streets. 祇園祭りの上品で雅やかな音楽. 市中を行列する多彩な布で飾った豪華な山車の上に座る囃子方が演奏する.

ぎおんまつり【祇園祭り】the Gion Festival. (7月). ⇨付記(1)「日本の祭り」

ぎがく【伎楽】 *gigaku*; an ancient masked drama (in pantomime). *Gigaku* is a comical dance and ballad drama performed without words, wearing ancient masks. 仮面をかぶり, 音楽に合わせ無言で踊る劇.

きがんかいせき【奇岩怪石】 fantastically [strangely] shaped rocks; weird-looking rocks.

きかんこう【期間工】 seasonal factory worker. ¶期間工や派遣労働者を切る move to slash jobs for seasonal factory and dispatch workers.

きき【記紀】the Records of Ancient Matters and the Chronicles of Japan. 古事記(712年)と日本書紀(720年)

ききざけ【利き酒】 *sake* tasting; *sake* sampling; testing the quality of *sake* by tasting. 酒を口に含んで, その品質のよしあしを判断すること, また, その酒. ¶利き酒師 *sake* taster; a person who tastes *sake* to judge the quality.

ききょう【桔梗】〔植物〕a balloonflower; a (Chinese) bellflower. キキョウ科の多年草. 「秋の七草」の一つ.

きく【菊】〔植物〕a chrysanthemum. キク科の多年草. ¶野菊 a wild chrysanthemum. 寒菊 a winter chrysanthemum. 春菊 a

garland chrysanthemum. 菊酒 *sake* steeped in chry-santhemum blossoms.(菊の花で浸した酒). 菊の紋 a chrysanthemum crest. 菊の節句 the Chrysanthemum Festival; the Feast of the Chrysanthemum. ☆「重陽の節句」ともいう. 観菊会 a chrysanthemum-viewing party.

【菊人形】a chrysanthemum figure; a figure formed from live chrysanthemum flowers. Traditional life-sized figures are decorated with chrysanthemum flowers and leaves attached to a wire frame. Figures of historical heroes and heroines are often displayed at the chrysanthemum figure exhibition. 針金の骨組に取り付けた菊の花と葉で飾られた伝統的な等身大の人形. 菊人形展では歴史上の英雄・女傑の人形などが展示される. ¶菊人形展 a chrysanthemum figure exhibition (held throughout the country). 等身大の菊人形 a life-size figure rendered with different-colored chrysanthemums.

【菊の御紋】 the Imperial chrysanthemum crest (in a conventionalized form with 16 open petals); the Imperial crest of the chrysanthemum (in a conventionalized form with 16 complete rays). It is used as the heraldic emblem of the Japanese Imperial Family. 皇室の紋章(開花した16花弁の様式化された形状)として用いられている.「菊花の御紋章」ともいう.

きくか[きっか]【菊花】 ⇨菊(の花). ¶菊花展 chrysanthemum show.

きくな【菊菜】〔植物〕a crown daisy; an edible leaf chrysanthemum. 別名「春菊」. ⇨春菊

きくらげ【木耳】〔植物〕 a Jew's-ear; Judas's ear; a wood ear; a cloud ear. 干して食用にする. けんちん汁や豆腐の和え物などに用いる.

きぐるみ【着ぐるみ】 a stuffed-animal suit[costume]. ☆「縫いぐるみ」は a stuffed animal[doll].

き

きげんぎれしょうひん【期限切れ商品】 food and confectionery past their expiration and best-before dates.

きかんげんていひん【期間限定品】 a product [an item] on sale for limited period only.

きげんせつ【紀元節】 the anniversary of the accession of Japan's legendary first Emperor Jinmu; the formal National Foundation Day. 日本の伝説上の初代神武天皇が即位したとされる記念日. ☆1948年に廃止. ⇨建国記念の日

きご【季語】 a season word[phrase] (used in composing a *haiku*[17-sylallable poem]); a code phrase that denotes the season (used in composing a *haiku*); a word[phrase] expressing one of the four seasons (used in making up a *haiku*). 俳句・連歌で, 句に読みこむように定められた季節を表す語. ⇨俳句

きざけ【生酒】 pure[undiluted] *sake*; unprocessed *sake*. 混ぜもののない純粋の酒. 別称「生一本」. ⇨生一本

きざみこんぶ【刻み昆布】 shredded kelp; kelp cut into thin strips. ⇨こぶ

きし【棋士】 a (professional) *shogi*[*go*] player. ⇨将棋 / 囲碁

きじ【雉】〈鳥〉 a (Japanese) pheasant. ☆日本の「国鳥」(the national bird). ⇨雉焼き

きじ【生地】❶〈織物の地質〉(plain) cloth(布地); fabric(生地); texture(織物地); material(服地). ❷〈パン・パイなどの〉dough. 粉などを本仕上げする前の材料. ¶パン**生地** bread dough. ピサの**生地** pizza dough.

きじ【素地】 bisque; biscuit; earthenware [porcelain] ready for glazing. 陶磁器で, 釉薬を塗っていないもの.

ぎし【義士】 a loyalist; a loyal retainer. 忠義の臣. 【義士祭】 the Forty-Seven Loyal Retainers Festival of Sengakuji Temple. (4月1-7).

(東京都：泉岳寺). ⇨四十七士

ぎしき【儀式】❶(宗教上：宗教的な荘厳な祭式) a rite; a ritual; a service. ☆「おけら参り」Sacred Fire Rite (held from New Year's Eve to New Year's morning at Yasaka Shrine in Kyoto)(12月). ⇨付記(1)「日本の祭り」 ❷ (式典上：宗教上または社会的・国家的な公式行事) a ceremony. ☆「結婚式」a wedding ceremony.

きしめん【碁子麺】 *kishimen*; long, flat wheat noodles; wheat noodles made in long, flat strips. *Kishimen* noodles are cooked in fish broth (seasoned with *shoyu* [soy sauce]), topped with sliced fish-paste cakes, deep-fried *tofu*[bean curd] and vegetables. 平たくて細長いうどん. (醤油で味つけした)出し汁で調理し, 細切り蒲鉾や油揚げまた野菜などを上にのせる. ☆名古屋の名産. 関東では「紐皮うどん」という. 「碁子麺」とも書く. ⇨紐皮うどん

きしもじん[**きしぼじん**]【鬼子母神】 the Buddhist goddess of women's easy childbirth and childrearing. 安産と幼児保護の女神.

きじやき【雉焼き】 fish[chicken] grilled after marinating in *shoyu*[soy sauce] and *mirin*[sweetened *sake*]. キジ肉に似せた料理. みりん醤油に漬けて焼く魚[鶏肉]料理. キジ焼き丼やキジ弁当などがある.

きじゅ【喜寿】 (celebrate) one's seventy-seventh birthday. 【喜寿の祝い】 the celebration of one's seventy-seventh birthday. The Japanese celebrate their 77th birthday. It is the 77th anniversary of one's life, one of the special ages to celebrate one's longevity. 77歳の祝い. ⇨賀

きじょうゆ【生醤油】 raw[unboiled] *shoyu* [soy sauce] (熱処理していない); undiluted *shoyu* (水割りのない); pure[unmixed]

shoyu(混合物がない)；*shoyu* that contains no additives and has not been boiled(添加物を含まず熱処理していない).

きしわだだんじりまつり【岸和田だんじり祭り】 the Kishiwada Danjiri Festival [Wheeled-Float-Rushing Parade Festival]. (9月). ⇨付記(1)「日本の祭り」

きす【鱚】〔魚〕a sillaginoid (fish); a sillago; a Japanese whiting. キス科の海産硬骨魚. 内湾の砂底にすむ. 夏が旬. すし種や天ぷらに用いる.

きせい【棋聖】 a *shogi*[*go*] master; a great master of *shogi*[*go*]. 将棋または碁の名人.

ぎせいどうふ【擬製豆腐】 a *tofu*[bean curd] mélange; a dish made of fried[steamed] *tofu* mixed with scrambled eggs and vegetables (chopped carrots, burdocks, etc.). 水気を切った豆腐に炒り卵と野菜(ニンジン・ゴボウなど)を加えて焼いた[蒸した]もの. 精進料理に用いる. ☆ mélange(メイランジュ)はフランス語で「混ぜ合わせたもの」の意.

きせいラッシュ【帰省ラッシュ】 annual homecoming rush of holiday-makers; annual year-end[mid-year] homecoming rush during the holiday seasons (on the trains[buses] or at airport terminals). ☆「省」は「安否を伺う」の意.

きせいれっしゃ[**バス**]【帰省列車[バス]】 a train[bus] for homebound passengers during the holiday seasons[during the Bon season or during the New Year season]; a train[bus] for city dwellers going home [back to the country] for the holidays.

きせかえにんぎょう【着せ替え人形】a dress-up doll.

きせつりょうり【季節料理】 seasonal dishes; dishes of the season. 旬の材料を用いて季節感を出した料理.

キセル【煙管】 a (long, slender) tobacco pipe. *Kiseru* has a pipe head with a round piece at the end (*gankubi*), a small metal bowl for packing a few of pinches of tobacco(*hizara*), a metal mouthpiece (*suikuchi*) and a long bamboo stem[tube] (*rau*). It is smoked by refilling it with shredded tobacco. キセルには雁首(キセルの頭), 火皿(キセルの煙草をつめる器), 吸い口(キセルを口にくわえる所), 羅宇(キセルの竹のくだ)がある. 刻みタバコを入れて吸う道具.

キセルじょうしゃ【キセル乗車】〈不正乗車〉a train fare cheating. ¶キセル乗車客 a train ticket cheater; a train fare cheater. キセル乗車する cheat on the train fare; get a free ride[steal a ride] (without paying the middle parts of a trip); dodge one's train fare.

ぎぞうカード【偽造カード】 a forged cash card; a counterfeit credit card. The credit card is produced by stealing ID numbers from a depositor. 預金者の暗証番号を盗んで造られる.

ぎそうかんりしょく【偽装管理職】 false pretenses of managerial posts in name only. 名ばかりの見せかけ管理職.

ぎそうけっこん【偽装結婚】 camouflaged marriage.

ぎぞうしへい【偽造紙幣】 a fake note[bill]; a counterfeit note[bill]; a forged[bogus] banknote.

ぎそうひょうじ【偽装表示】 a fake label (of foods); a false labeling practice (of foods).

きそぶし【木曾節】a Kiso folk song (sung in Gifu Prefecture).

きだい【季題】 a seasonal topic[theme] (used in composing a *haiku*[17-syllable poem]). ⇨季語

きたくきょひしょう【帰宅拒否症】refuseniks to return home; home-phobia, a type of depression that stops people from going home after work;〈人〉a home-phobe.

き

きたまちぶぎょう【北町奉行】 a Kitamachi Commissioner[Magistrate] (who has his office in the northern part of Edo). ⇨奉行. ¶北町奉行所 the Kitamachi Commissioner's Office. ⇨南町奉行所

ぎだゆう【義太夫】〔文楽〕*gidayu*; the narrative style of musical vocalization (in bunraku); the narrative ballad recitation of vocal music (in bunraku). (文楽における)音楽的な語り口調の語り.「義太夫節」(国の重要無形文化財)の略. ☆(三味線の名手である)竹本義太夫(1651-1714)によって始められた浄瑠璃を代表する流派. ⇨文楽 / 浄瑠璃

【義太夫語り】 a *gidayu* reciter. He[She] gives life to each doll on the stage by expressing each character vocally and by reciting the story to the accompaniment of the *shamisen* music. 義太夫の吟唱者. 三味線の伴奏に合わせながら登場人物を声に出して表現したり，また物語を語りながら舞台上の各人形に生気を与える.

【義太夫本】 a *gidayu* recitation text. It is written about story-recitation sung for bunraku puppet drama show. 義太夫の吟唱本. 文楽で歌う物語の語り内容が書かれた本.

きち【吉】 good luck[fate]; good fortune(幸運). ⇨おみくじ

きちゅう【忌中】 the mourning period. ☆ In Mourning. (表示)

きちんやど【木賃宿】 a cheap lodging house; a cheap hotel; a flophouse. 下級の安宿.

きっきょう【吉凶】 fortune and/or misfortune; good and/or bad luck. 縁起の良いことと悪いこと.

ぎっくりごし【ぎっくり腰】 (have) a slipped disk; (have) a strained back; (have) a sharp lower-back pain.

ぎっしゃ【牛車】 a *gissha*; an ox-drawn carriage[cart] with two wheels; a two-wheeled one-ox carriage[cart]; a carriage [cart] with two wooden wheels drawn by an ox. It was used to transport upper class nobles in the Heian period. 平安時代の牛にひかせた貴人(aristocrats)の乗る屋形車.

きっちょう【吉兆】 a good[lucky] omen; a happy augury. 縁起の良いことか悪いことが起こる前兆.

きつつき【啄木鳥】〔鳥〕a woodpecker, 鋭いくちばしで樹皮を破り，虫を捕食する.

きつね【狐】〔動物〕a fox; a vixen(雌)；a cub(子). イヌ科の哺乳類. ¶狐像 a fox statue; a statue of the fox. ☆「稲荷神社の神の使いである青銅の狐像」 the bronze statues of foxes,messengers of deity[god] of Inari shrine. ⇨稲荷(神社)

きつねいろ【狐色】 light brown; golden brown. ¶こんがり狐色に焼いたパン bread toasted light brown.

きつねうどん[そば]【狐うどん[そば]】 noodles in soy soup with deep-fried *tofu* [bean curd] (*abura-age*); (a bowl of) wheat noodles[buckwheat noodles] in fish broth (seasoned with *shoyu*[soy sauce]), topped with a few thin pieces of deep-fried *tofu* cut into triangles. (醤油で味付けした)出し汁に入れ，(三角形に切った)油揚げをのせたかけうどん[そば]. ☆「油揚げ」は狐の大好物 (favorite food). ⇨狐 /油揚げ

きつねのよめいり【狐の嫁入り】 a sunshine shower; a shower[rainfall] when the sun is shining. 天気雨.

きど【木戸】〈出入り口〉a gate; a door.〈小門〉a wicket (door); a garden wicket; a fence gate. ☆相撲・芝居などの見物人の出入り口. または庭・通路などの出入り口にある屋根のない開き戸の門. ¶木戸口 entrance(入り口); gateway(木戸のついた出入り口). 木戸御免 free admission; a free pass; privilege of free entrance(入場無料の特典). 木戸銭なしで出入りできること. ☆ Admission Free「入場無料」(掲示). 木

戸銭 admission[entrance] fee; door money (for paying at the theater). 興行の木戸口で払う見物料金.

きなこ【黄粉】 yellowish soybean flour [powder]. It is made by grinding roasted [parched] soybeans into flour[powder]. With sugar and salt added, it is often sprinkled over rice cakes or dumplings. 大豆を炒って粉末にした食品. 砂糖と塩をまぜてから，餅や団子に振りかける. ⇨安倍川餅 / 葛餅

〔料理〕**黄粉餅** rice cake powdered with sweetened *kinako*.

きぬおりもの【絹織物】 silk weavings; silk fabrics;〈絹地〉 silk cloth;〈絹製品〉silk goods; silks. ⇨織物. ¶**絹織物の中心地** major center for silk weaving. ☆山形県・米沢市が有名. **絹織物業** silk weaving[textile] industry; manufacturing of silk fabrics. ☆埼玉県・秩父銘仙が有名.

きぬごしどうふ【絹漉し豆腐】 soft[silken] *tofu*[bean curd]; fine-grained[fine-textured] *tofu*. It is so called because its texture is as fine as silk. It has a high water content and appears smooth. 絹のようにきめ細かで滑らかなことが名前の由来である. 水分が多く，見た目が滑らかである. ⇨豆腐 / 木綿豆腐

きぬた【砧】 a wooden[stone] block for beating cloth. 布を打つための木[石]の台. ☆木づちで布を打ってつやを出したり，また柔らかくしたりする.

きね【杵】 a pestle; a pounder; a mallet. ¶**杵でもち米をつく** pound glutinous rice with a pestle (in a wooden mortar). **杵で胡麻をする** crush sesame with a pounder.

きねんさい【祈年祭】 a Shinto service to pray for a bumper harvest and the peaceful security of the nation. 五穀豊穣と国家安泰を祈る神事.「祈年祭り」ともいう. ☆明治以降は賢所・皇霊殿・神殿の宮中三か所

と全国の神社で行う.

ぎのうしょう【技能賞】〔相撲〕 the Outstanding Technique Prize[Award] (in *sumo* wrestling). The prize is given to a top division *sumo* wrestler (except *yokozuna* or *ozeki*) who demonstrates the most outstanding technique during a given tournament. 相撲場所中最も優れた技能を見せた(横綱・大関以外の)上位力士に授与される賞. ⇨三賞

きのこ【茸】〔植物〕 a mushroom; a toadstool [poisonous mushroom](有毒); champignon (食用茸); edible fungus (㊶ fungi). ¶**椎茸** a *shiitake* mushroom. **松茸** a pine mushroom. **原茸** a common mushroom.

きのめ【木の芽】 ❶〈木の新芽〉a (leaf) bud. 春先に萌え出る芽.
❷〈山椒の芽〉a young leaf[leaf bud] of Japanese pepper. Japanese pepper leaves [leaf-buds] are used for flavor and decoration in cooking. 料理で風味づけや飾り物に用いる. 山椒の若葉[芽]を指す場合が多い.「このめ」ともいう. ⇨さんしょう

〔料理〕**木の芽和え** pepper leaf bud salad with *miso*[bean paste]; dishes[vegetables or fish] dressed with *miso* and leaf buds of Japanese pepper. (山椒の芽を味噌で和えた物. 野菜[タケノコなど]や魚介類[イカ・タコなど]に和える.「このめあえ」ともいう). **木の芽田楽** *tofu*[bean curd] roasted[baked] and spread with *miso* and leaf buds of Japanese pepper; grilled *tofu* dressed with a mixture of *miso* and leaf buds of Japanese pepper. (山椒の芽を味噌にすり混ぜて豆腐にぬり，火であぶったもの).

きはちじょう【黄八丈】 yellow Hachijo weave; checkered (or vertically striped) yellow silk cloth[fabric]. *Kihachijo* is yellow silk cloth woven in checkers or vertical stripes produced in Hachijojima Island. Black or brown checkers (or

き

vertical stripes) are woven into the yellow background. 格子縞または縦縞を表した黄色の絹織物. 東京南部・八丈島の特産. 黄色の生地に黒色または茶色の格子縞(または縦縞)が織りこまれている.

きび【黍】〔植物〕 millet. イネ科の一年草. 餅米と混ぜて団子などを作る. 五穀の一つ. ⇨五穀. ¶黍団子 a millet and rice dumpling. ☆岡山県の名産.

ぎふぢょうちん【岐阜提灯】 a Gifu lantern; an elegant oval paper lantern made in Gifu Prefecture. 優雅な卵形(egg-shaped)の和紙の照明器具. 岐阜県特産の提灯. ☆細い骨に白や水色の薄い和紙(美濃紙)を張ってつくる. 秋草などが描かれ, 下に絹ぶさの飾りがある.

きぶつ【木仏】 a wooden Buddhist statue[image]; a wooden statue[image] of a Buddha. 木彫りの仏像.

きぼうたいしょく【希望退職】 voluntary early retirement.

きぼり【木彫】〈木製〉wood carving;〈木版〉wood engraving;〈作品〉a wooden carving[engraving]. ¶木彫りの仏像 a carved wooden Buddhist figure[image]; a Buddhist figure[image] carved in[out of] wood. 木彫りの人形 a carved wooden doll; a doll carved in[out of] wood. 木彫り師〈像・人形などの〉a wood carver;〈木版の〉a wood engraver.

きほんかけい【基本花型】〔華道〕 the basic styles of flower arrangement. 花を生ける基本的な型. ☆ⓐ『池坊流派』(3基本花型): ①「直態」an upright style. ②「斜態」a slanting style. ③「垂態」a hanging style. ⓑ『草月流派』(4基本花型): ①「傾真型」a slanting style. ②「立真型」an upright style. ③「垂真型」a hanging style. ④「平真型」a horizontal style.

きまりて【決まり手】〔相撲〕winning techniques [tricks] in a *sumo* bout; the maneuver that decides a *sumo* match. ⇨相撲の決まり手

きみがよ【君が代】*kimigayo*. ❶〈天皇の治世〉His Majesty's Reign; the Imperial Reign. ❷〈国歌〉the Japanese national anthem; the national anthem of Japan. ☆「和漢朗詠集」から抜粋した31音節の短歌. 作曲は林広守. 1893年宮内庁 (the Imperial Household Agency)より認証される.

きめこみにんぎょう【木目込み人形】 a wooden doll clothed[dressed] in a *kimono*; a wooden doll fitted with Japanese costumes wedged into narrow grooves. 着物を装った木製の人形. (金襴・ちりめんなどの)日本の衣装を狭い溝にはりこんだ[木目込んだ]木彫りの人形. 京都の「加茂川人形」(江戸中期に始まる)が有名.

きもすい【肝吸い】 eel liver soup; clear soup cooked with eel liver. 鰻の肝が入った澄まし汁. ⇨うなぎ

きもの【着物】 a *kimono*; the national costume of Japan. A *kimono* is a Japanese traditional costume[robe] with wide sleeves, which is kept in place by a sash(*obi*). The left side of the *kimono* is lapped over the right side in front. The two sides are fastened in back at the waistline with a long sash. 着物は広い袖のある衣装で, 帯でしっかりと巻きつける. 前方では着物の左側は右側の上に重ねる. 後部では胴のまわりに帯で締める. ☆「女性」の和服には「振袖」(未婚者)と「留袖」(既婚者・未婚者)そして訪問着.「男性」の和服には「羽織袴」,「男女共通」和服には「浴衣」がある. ⇨ 振袖 / 留袖 / 羽織袴 / 浴衣. ¶着物を着る put on a *kimono*. 着物を脱ぐ take off a *kimono*. 着物を着ている wear[be dressed in] a *kimono*. 着物をたたむ fold a *kimono*. 着物姿の少女 a *kimono*-clad girl; a girl (dressed) in a *kimono*.

【関連語】「袖」sleeve.「袖口」sleeve opening.「裄」sleeve length. 「襟」collar.「共襟」

き

浴衣　　留袖　　羽織袴

振袖　　　　　　　襟
　　　　　　　　帯揚げ
　　　　　　　　袖口
　　　　　　　　帯締
　　　　　　　　帯
　　　　　　　　袖
　　　　　　　　裾

over-collar.「衽」front panel below collar.「裾」bottom; bottom neck.「帯」*obi*; sash.「帯締」*obi* belt.「帯揚げ」support for an *obi*.「後ろ身頃」back main section.「前身頃」front main section.「下前［上前］」one half of the front[back] of the *kimono* lapped under the other.（着物を合わせたとき，下（内側）「上（外側）」になる部分）.

ぎゃくぎれ【逆切れ】 a counterblast; a counteroffensive; a backlash.

ぎゃくたまのこし【逆玉の輿】 a man marrying into wealth; a man's marriage to a wealthy[rich] woman. ⇨玉の輿

キャッチバー a "pick-up" bar.

キャッチホン（和製英語）〈電話機〉a telephone with a call waiting feature;〈機能〉a call-waiting feature.

キャベツ【甘藍】 a cabbage; (a head of) cabbage. アブラナ科の二年草. 18世紀にオランダから長崎に伝わる. ¶ロールキャベツ a cabbage roll. キャベツの葉 a cabbage leaf; ㊤ spring greens.

キャラクターグッズ cartoon character merchandise[goods]; goods featuring popular characters.

きやり（おんど）【木遣り（音頭）】 a log-carriers' chant[song]; a lumber-carriers' chant[song]; a firemen's chant[song] in a procession. 音頭をとりながら材木・大木などを運ぶ人たちのかけ声［歌］.「木遣り歌」.「木遣り節」などともいう.

きゅう【灸】 moxibustion; moxa treatment; moxa cautery. "Moxa" (made from dried mugwort leaves) comes from the Japanese word *mogusa*（艾）. A tiny pinch of moxa (rolled into a tiny cone) is put on the body[skin] and burned[cauterized] for improvement of the health. The heat stimulates certain healing points to cure the illness. 漢方療法の一つ. 小さなもぐさ（小型の円錐形にまるめたもの）を身体にのせて焼き，健康改善をはかる. 体のツボに熱の刺激を与えて病気を治す. ⇨艾

きゅうかざん【休火山】 a dormant volcano; an inactive volcano ; a quiescent volcano. ⇨火山. ¶休火山の岩木山（青森県の最高峰）Mt. Iwaki(san), a dormant volcano.

きゅうきゅういりょうようヘリコプター【救急医療用ヘリコプター】 helicopter[air] ambulance; EMS copter. ☆ EMS は emergency medical service の略. copter は helicopter の短縮形（日本では「ヘリ」(heli ［和製語])という).「ドクターヘリ」.

きゅうきゅうきゅうめいし【救急救命士】 a paramedic.

きゅうこん【球根】 a bulb. ¶チューリップの

き

球根 tulip bulbs. **球根植物** a bulbous plant.

ぎゅうさし【牛刺し】 sliced[slices of] raw beef. 牛肉の刺身.

きゅうじつしゅっきん【休日出勤】 working on one's day off; working on non-working days.

きゅうじゅつ【弓術】 *kyujutsu*; an archery; a traditional Japanese martial art of archery. ⇨弓道

きゅうじょう【宮城】 (the) Imperial Palace. 「皇居」の旧称.

きゅうしょうがつ【旧正月】 the lunar New Year. 旧暦の正月.

きゅうす【急須】 a small teapot (for making green tea); a small teapot (made of ceramic[earthenware]). 陶器[土器]の茶瓶. 「茶出し」ともいう. ⇨土瓶. ¶**急須の口** a spout of a teapot. **急須の支え** a holder of a teapot.

きゅうせき【旧跡】 a historic spot[site]; a place of historic interest; ruins(遺跡). ⇨名所旧跡

きゅうせっきじだい【旧石器時代】 the Old Stone Age; the Paleolithic Age[Era].

きゅうちゅう【宮中】 the Imperial Court; the Imperial Palace. 天皇の住む御所. ¶**宮中に**(仕える) (serve)at Court. **宮中行事** seasonal observances of the Imperial Palace[Court].

【**宮中歌会始め**】 the New Year('s) Imperial Poetry Party; the Imperial Poetry Reading held at the New Year. The Poetry[The 31-syllable poem(*tanka*)] Recitation Party is held annually in the Imperial Palace at the beginning of the year. The poems composed by members of the Imperial Family and by the public participants are recited in a time-honored, ceremonial tone by experts. 年始にあたり短歌吟唱の会合が毎年皇居にて行われる. 皇室各位また一般参加者の詠む短歌は名手によって古式豊か

な口調で吟唱される. ⇨歌会

きゅうてい【宮廷】 the Court. ¶**宮廷生活** life at Court.

きゅうどう【弓道】 *Kyudo*; Japanese-style archery as martial art. *Kyudo* (also known as *kyujutsu*) is a traditional martial art of archery. *Kyudo* values good manners or courtesy rather than victory or defeat. 武芸としての日本式弓術. 弓で矢を射る術 (art of shooting arrows at a target).「弓術」ともいう. 弓道では勝敗よりは礼節を重んじる. ☆鎌倉時代に発達し, 武士の本道として「弓と馬」(*samurai*'s duty to master both bow and horse)を修めた. 鉄砲の伝来で衰退するが明治時代に精神修養 (spiritual training)としての弓道が普及した. ⇨流鏑馬

【関連語】「**的**」target (「星的」star target.「霞的」mist target). ☆的の射程距離位置は「近距離」(short range) で28m (室内競技用. 的の直径36cm).「遠距離」(long range) で60m以上(屋外競技用. 的の直径100cm). 「**弓**」bow (made of laminated wood and bamboo). 木と竹を張り合わせたもの, 長さは約2m. ⇨弓矢.「**矢**」arrow (made of bamboo).「**矢筒**」quiver.「**弓懸**」leather glove (on one hand). 片手にはめる革手袋.

弓懸 弓 矢筒 矢 的

ぎゅうどん【牛丼】 beef bowl (米国にある「吉野屋牛丼」の看板名); beef-topped rice in a bowl; (a bowl of) steamed rice topped with thin slices of stewed beef and vegetables. *Gyudon* is a bowl of rice served with a topping of thinly-sliced stewed beef and various ingredients such as green onions, mushrooms and *shirataki* vermicelli. Red pickled gingers are often sprinkled over *gyudon*. 薄く切った煮込みの牛肉と野菜をのせた丼物. 紅生姜をかける場合が多い.「開化丼」ともいう. ☆「つゆだく」は plenty of broth (in a beef bowl)という. ⇨丼物

ぎゅうなべ【牛鍋】 ❶〈食物〉. ⇨すきやき ❷〈鍋〉a *sukiyaki* pot.

ぎゅうにく【牛肉】 beef; veal(食肉用子牛肉. 日本では10か月未満).¶**和牛肉** Japanese cattle beef. ⇨和牛. **霜降り牛肉** marbled beef. **牛肉のたたき** quick-seared beef.

きゅうぼん【旧盆】 the Bon Festival according to the lunar calendar; Buddhist All Souls' Day by the lunar calendar. ⇨盆

きゅうり【胡瓜】〔植物〕 a cucumber; a gherkin.(ピクルス用の小型).ウリ科の一年草.¶**胡瓜の蛇の目切り** rings of cucumber. **胡瓜の末広切り** fan cuts of cucumber. 〔食品〕**胡瓜揉み** thinly-sliced cucumbers kneaded with salt and dressed with vinegar; thin slices of cucumbers hashed with salt and seasoned with vinegar, *shoyu* [soy sauce] and *mirin*[sweetened *sake*].

きゅうりゅう【急流】 rapids (複数形で: 激流);〈早い流れ〉a rapid stream; a fast-flowing stream;〈奔流〉a fast[swift] river; a torrent.¶**木曾川の急流下り**(長野・岐阜・愛知・三重の4県) shooting the rapids of the River Kiso(gawa) by boat. **遊覧船で急流の舟下りを楽しめる天竜川**(長野・愛知・静岡の3県) the River Tenryu(gawa) which offers excursion boats shooting the rapids. **日本三急流** the Three Fastest Rivers in Japan(最上川[山形県]・富士川[静岡県・山梨県]・球磨川[熊本県])

きゅうりょう【丘陵】 a hill; a hillock(hill より小さい).¶**丘陵地帯** the hills; hilly regions; hill[hilly] country.

きゅうれき【旧暦】 the old calendar(旧暦); the lunar calendar(太陰暦). ☆月の満ちかけをもとにした暦. 明治6年に現在のグレゴリオ暦(Gregorian Calendar:太陽暦[新暦])になる以前の暦のことで, 現在の暦とは約1か月ずれている. 旧暦の正月は現在の2月である.「陰暦」ともいう. ⇨陰暦 ¶**旧暦の正月** New Year's Day according to the old calendar; the lunar New Year's Day. ⇦新暦

きょう【京】 capital (首都・みやこ); Kyoto (京都). ⇨京懐石 / 京人形.¶**藤原京** the Fujiwara Capital. **京へ上る** go up to Kyoto [the Capital].

きょう【凶】 the worse luck[fate]; the worse misfortune. ⇨おみくじ

きょう【経】 (chant) a Buddhist sutra(個々の経); the Buddhist scriptures(集合的な経). ⇨お経 / 経典

きょう【～峡】 a gorge; a ravine; a glen.¶**鳴子峡**(宮城県) (the) Naruko(kyo) Gorge. ⇨渓 / 渓谷 / 峡谷 / 谷

きょういくちょくご【教育勅語】the Imperial Rescript on Education. It was distributed to all schools in 1890. 1890年にすべての学校に配布. ⇨勅語

きょういくママ【教育ママ】 education-obsessed mother; mother obsessed with education; education-minded[education-oriented] mother; mother overly concerned with education; pushy mother when it comes to education.

きょういんさいようおしょく【教員採用汚職】 scandals involving the rigged recruitment of schoolteacher.

きょうか【狂歌】 a comic *tanka* poem; a satirical poem. 洒落や風刺のおかしみをよんだ短歌. ⇨短歌

き

きょうかい【境界】a border(山・川などの); a boundary(領土などの). ¶県境 the border of the prefecture; the border between two prefectures.

きょうかいせき【京懐石】 Kyoto *Kaiseki* cuisine; a light meal that used to be served before a tea ceremony. 茶会の前にいただく軽食であった.

【関連語】〈各項目を参照〉⇨「先付け」「八寸」「向付け」「蓋物」「焼物」「強肴」「ご飯・香の物・止椀」「水物」

蓋物　水物　ご飯　止椀　焼き物　香の物　向付け　強肴　吸い物　八寸　先付け

きょうかしょけんてい【教科書検定】 the textbook authorization; the screening [examination] of school textbooks by the Ministry of Education, Culture, Sports, Science and Technology. ¶教科書検定制度 the textbook screening system. 教科書検定会議 the Textbook Authorization Research Council.

きょうかたびら【経帷子】 a (burial) shroud; a winding sheet. It is a white garment of the dead body dressed by family members in a Buddhist burial. 仏式で埋葬するとき死者に着せる白い着物. ⇨帷子

きょうかん【経巻】Buddhist sutra scrolls. 経文の書いてある巻物. ⇨経典

きょうぎ【経木】 wood shavings[chips]; a paper-thin sheet[slice] of wood. 節のない材木を紙のように薄く削ったもの. ¶

経木に包んだ団子 dumplings wrapped in a paper-thin sheet of wood. 経木箱 a box made from a paper-thin sheet of wood. It is used to wrap up fish or *tsukudani*[salt-sweet preserves]. ⇨折詰

きょうく【狂句】 a comic *haiku* poem. 滑稽な俳句. ⇨俳句

きょうげん【狂言】❶〔能楽〕a *kyogen*; a Noh farce (making use of mime and comical situations); a Noh farcical play (based on comic dialogue). (物真似と滑稽仕草を用いる)笑劇. (滑稽な対話形式の)喜劇. ¶狂言師 a Noh comedian.

《本狂言》kyogen performed independently. 単独で演じる狂言. 《間狂言》kyogen performed as supplementary entertainment during a Noh program. It features a comical story written from the commoners's viewpoint. 能楽の間に補足的に演じられる軽い滑稽な劇. 普通一般の視点から書かれているのが特色の滑稽な語り物である. ⇨間狂言

❷〔歌舞伎〕a kabuki play[drama]; a kabuki performance[piece]. 歌舞伎の劇[芝居]. 歌舞伎劇の演目. ¶前[幕開き]狂言 the first play in a kabuki program; a curtain raiser. 切り狂言 the last[final] play in a kabuki program; a curtain closer. 狂言回し a major supporting role[subsidiary character] (in a kabuki play) important to the development of the plot. (場面の展開の上で重要な補助役[ワキ役])

きょうげんごうとう【狂言強盗】〔行為〕a fake robbery[theft]; a feigned robbery; 〈人〉a fake robber[thief].

きょうげんじさつ【狂言自殺】a sham[mock] suicide; a phony suicide.

きょうこく【峡谷】 a valley; a gorge; a ravine; a canyon. ☆ valley 両側を山に囲まれたなだらかで広い平地で，その中を川が流れる谷間: Akikawa Valley(秋川渓谷[東

京都]). gorge; ravine両側が絶壁となって
いる谷間：Kurobe Gorge[Ravine](黒部峡
谷[富山県]). canyon深く切り立った絶壁
の谷間：Grand Canyon(グランドキャニオ
ン). ⇨渓谷 / 谷

きょうさく【凶作】　a lean[bad] crop (of
rice); a lean[poor] harvest. ⇔豊作

きょうさく[**けいさく**]【警策】　a *Zen* stick
(for patting[tapping] a *zazen* meditator
on the shoulder). It is a sheet stick used to
chastise a dozing *zazen* meditator[punish
a sleeping *zazen* contemplator] by tapping
him/ her on the shoulder during the *Zen*
meditation. 禅堂で座禅をするとき，眠気
をさますために肩を打つ板状の棒. ⇨座禅

ぎょうじ【行司】〔相撲〕　a *sumo* referee [um-
pire]. He is dressed in a traditional costume of brocade with a black ceremonial
headgear and carries a ritual fan in his right
hand. He is ranked according to the color
of his breast cords and the tassels attached
to his ritual fan. He first announces the
names of the two wrestlers prior to a bout.
Then he urges them into starting position
at the time of their initial charge (*tachiai*).
Finally he points his ritual fan toward the
winner's side of the ring at the moment the
match is decided. 黒い烏帽子装束(伝統的
な錦織の衣装)を着用し，右手に軍配団扇
を持つ. 胸の紐と団扇に付く房の色彩に
よって格付けされている. 取組前には2人
の力士の四股名を告げる. 立合い時には始
動を促す. 取組の決定時には勝者に軍配団
扇を差し向ける. ⇨軍配団扇. ☆懸賞金の
ある場合は軍配団扇にのせて勝ち力士に
手渡す. 力士が「手刀を切る」. ⇨懸賞金
/ 手刀. ¶**立行司** the top[highest-ranking]
sumo referee; a chief[senior] *sumo* referee.
行司溜り a seat[place] (near a ring) for a
waiting *sumo* referee.

ぎょうじゃ【行者】　an ascetic; a person who

leads an ascetic life. 仏道・修験道の修行を
する人. ⇨修験者

ぎょうしょ【行書】〈書道〉*gyosho*; the semicursive[semiformal] style of writing letters
or Chinese characters; the intermediate
style in calligraphy, neither as stiff as *kai-
sho* nor as flowing as *sosho*. 文字・漢字の書
体の一つ. 書道では楷書のように硬くなく，
草書のように流麗でなく，その中庸の書体.
☆楷書の画を少しくずし，まるみの線のあ
るもの. ⇨書体 / 楷書 / 草書

ぎょうずい【行水】(have) a quick bath; (take)
a quick scrub in a shallow wooden bathtub
in the summertime. 夏季に浅い木製の浴槽
で早くこすり洗うこと. ⇨烏の行水

きょうせいれんこう【強制連行】the strategy
of bringing many people against their will
from Korea and China to Japan (to secure
manpower). (労働力確保のため)本人の意
志に反しながらも韓国・中国から多数の人
を日本へ連れてくる戦略. ☆第二次世界大
戦中に実施された.

きょうそ【教祖】〈開祖〉　the founder of a
religion; the head of a religious sect; 〈創
始者〉the originator of a religion[religious
sect].

きょうぞう【経蔵】　a Buddhist sutra
repository of a Buddhist temple; a storehouse holding sutras and other Buddhist
texts in a Buddhist temple. 寺で，経文を納
めておく蔵. ⇨七堂伽藍

きょうそく【脇息】　an armrest; an elbow
rest; a freestanding armrest(支えなしの脇
息). 座ったとき，肘をかけ身体をもたせ
かけるための道具. ¶**脇息にもたれる** lean
on an armrest.

きょうだいごろし【兄弟殺し】fratricide.「姉
妹殺し」ともいう.

きょうてん【経典・教典】　a Buddhist sutra
(containing the teachings of Sakyamuni
Buddha). 釈迦牟尼仏陀の聖典. ☆経典は

き

元来サンスクリット語 (Sanskrit)で書かれ, 中国語に翻訳された. 中国から日本へ伝わり, 日本語の発音で唱えられている. ⇨写経. ☆「けいてん」と読めばキリスト教の「聖書」(the Bible)やイスラム教の「コーラン」(the Koran)のこと. キリスト教とイスラム教以外の教典は scriptureという.

きょうと【教徒】 a believer (in)(信者)；a follower (of)(支持者)；an adherent (of)(信奉者). ☆通常は a Buddhist(仏教徒), a Christian(キリスト教徒)などという.

きょうと【京都】 Kyoto. ⇨京. ¶**京都人** kyotoite. ⇨江戸っ子. **京都五山** the five principal temples of the Rinzai sect of Zen Buddhism, located in Kyoto. ☆京都の禅宗(臨済宗)の寺格. 天竜寺, 相国寺, 建仁寺, 東福寺, 万寿寺. すべて南禅寺(最高位)の下位にある. **京都御所** the Kyoto Imperial Palace. **京都守護職** a military commissioner for the Kyoto area. **京都所司代** a Kyoto police deputy. (江戸幕府の職名. 京都の警備, 朝廷・公家の監察と連絡などを行う)

きょうとぎていしょ【京都議定書】 the Kyoto Protocol.「地球温暖化防止条約」(the Global Warming Convention)のこと. 1997年12月に開かれた京都会議で採決された. ☆「気候変動枠組み条約」(Kyoto Protocol to the United Nations Framework Convention on Climate Change).

きょうど【郷土】 one's hometown(故郷の市町村)；one's home(郷里)；one's birthplace(出生地)；one's native place [province] (生育した地). ¶**郷土の誇り** the pride of one's town. **郷土愛** love of[for] one's hometown. **郷土史** local history. **郷土芸能** a local performing art; a performing art peculiar to a locality; a folk entertainment unique to a certain district with much local color. **郷土色** local color. ☆郷土色豊かな祭り［踊り］a festival

[dance] full of local color. **郷土玩具** a local toy; a folk toy (often sold to tourists as a souvenir). **郷土人形** a local folk doll; a doll peculiar to a certain district (often sold to tourists as a souvenir). **郷土料理** local dishes[specialities]; regional dishes [specialities]; dishes peculiar to a certain locality.

きょうどう【経堂】 a library of Buddhist sutras. 経文をおさめておく建物.

きょうにんぎょう【京人形】 a Kyoto doll. It is a doll of a girl with bobbed hair and is dressed in traditional specially-woven *kimono*. おかっぱ頭の少女人形で, 伝統的な織物の着物を装っている.

きょうねん【享年】 one's age at death. ¶彼女は享年70歳だった She died at (the age of) seventy.

きょうは【教派】 a (religious) sect; a denomination. ⇨宗派. ¶**教派神道** a Sect Shinto. ⇨国家神道

きょうはくでんわ【脅迫電話】 a threatening telephone call.

きょうまい【京舞】 Kyoto dancing; a traditional Kyoto dance performed to the accompaniment of *shamisen*.

きょうもん【経文】 ❶ a Buddhist sutra; Buddhist scriptures. 仏教の経典. ⇨経典 ❷ the text of a sutra. 経典の文章

きょうやき【京焼】 Kyoto pottery (陶器)；Kyoto ceramics (陶磁器全体).

ぎょえい【御詠】 an Imperial poem; a *tanka* (poem) composed by a member of the Japanese Imperial Family. 天皇・貴人の詩歌の尊称.

ぎょえん【御苑】 an Imperial garden. 皇室所有の庭園. ¶**新宿御苑** Shinjuku Gyoen National Garden.

ぎょかいるい【魚介類】 seafood(海産食品)；fish(es) and shellfish(es)(魚類と貝類)；marine products(海産物).

ぎょくおんほうそう【玉音放送】the Emperor's speech on the radio; the Showa Emperor's speech on the radio broadcast the termination of World War II. 第二次世界大戦の終焉を告げる昭和天皇によるラジオ放送のスピーチ．☆「玉音」とは「天皇の声」(Emperor's speech; the voice of Japan's Emperor)の尊称.

ぎょくざ【玉座】 the Emperor's seat; the throne. 天皇の座るところの尊称.

ぎょくさいこうげき【玉砕攻撃】 a suicidal attack; a *kamikaze*[*banzai*] charge. ⇨神風特攻隊

きょくすいのえん【曲水の宴】a poetry feast held at the stream in the palace garden (in the Heian period). 平安時代，宮廷の庭に流れる水辺で催された詩歌作りの宴会．☆上流から流した杯が自分の前から流れ過ぎないうちに詩歌を作る.

ぎょくだい【玉代】⇨花代❷/半玉

きょくとうこくさいぐんじさいばん【極東国際軍事裁判】 the International Military Tribunal for the Far East (1946-48). ☆1946年から1948年にかけて東京で行われた日本の主要な戦争犯罪人に対する連合軍による軍事裁判．通称「東京裁判」(the Tokyo Trial; the Tokyo War Criminals Trial).

ぎょくろ【玉露】 high-quality[top-quality] green tea; green tea of the finest[best] quality; the highest-graded aromatic green tea. It is made from the freshest leaves of heavily shaded tea bushes[shrubs]. The tea leaves are steeped in lukewarm water at a temperature of about 60 degrees so that the flavor can be mild and fragrant. (甘みと香りのある)上等の煎茶．濃く茂った茶の潅木の最も新鮮な葉から作る．甘みと香をだすために茶葉は約60度の温度のぬるま湯で煎じる．⇨緑茶

きょしょくしょう【拒食症】anorexia (nervo-sa); 〈患者〉an anorexic.

ぎょせい【御製】an emperor's poem[*tanka*]; a poem of imperial composition. 天皇・貴人の作った詩歌の尊称.

ぎょたく【魚拓】a fish rubbing[print]; an ink rubbing[print] of a fish; a fish impression. 魚の拓本.

ぎょでん【魚田】 a broiled[grilled] fish coated with *miso*[bean paste]. 田楽みそをつけて焼いた魚.

ぎょにくだんご【魚肉団子】 a fish meatball; a fish cake. 魚のすり身を団子状に丸めたもの.

きよみずやき【清水焼】 Kiyomizu ware [ceramics] (produced in the area around Kiyomizu Temple in Kyoto Prefecture).

きよめ【清め・浄め】 (an act of) purification (清めの行為). ⇨手水舎 ; a Shinto rite of purification(清めの神事). ☆神道の「清め」では通常「禊」(ablution)，「祓い」(exorcism),「濯ぎ」(rinse; cleansing)の3種が重視される．⇨禊 / お祓い /濯ぎ

【清めの会場】 the purification room. Mourners gather to eat food and drink together in the purification room after a wake or funeral service. 会葬者は通夜または葬儀が終わると清めの会場に集まり，飲食を共にする.

【清めの塩】❶〈通夜・告別式〉cleansing salt; purification salt; salt sprinkled to purify things, areas or persons. Mourners are provided with a sachet of salt as a purifier after a wake or funeral service. They cleanse themselves with a sprinkling of salt before entering their own home again. 通夜と告別式の参列者には塩の袋が渡される．参列者は自宅に入る前にその塩で身を清める．

❷〔相撲〕(a handful of) salt thrown by *sumo* wrestlers on the ring (to purify noxious vapors in the clay[dirt]).（地中の邪気を追

い払うために)力士が土俵にまく一握りの塩.

きよもと【清元】〔文楽〕the ***Kiyomoto*** style of *joruri* chanting[reciting]. *Kiyomoto* is a traditional chanting[singing] style of ballad dramas in falsetto to *shamisen* accompaniment. The vocalization has the pitch higher than that of other styles of *joruri*. It is a school of Bungo *joruri* developed by Kiyomoto Enjudayu in the late Edo period. 三味線の伴奏に合わせて謡う. 裏声[作り声]による伝統的な謡い方. 発声には通常の浄瑠璃よりは高度な声の高低がある. 江戸時代末期(1814年), 清元延寿太夫(1777-1825)の創始した豊後浄瑠璃の一派.「清元節」の略. ☆歌舞伎・舞踊に用いられる三味線歌曲[伴奏音楽]のひとつ.

ぎょらん【魚卵】 roe; fish egg. まだ卵巣内にある魚の卵. ⇨イクラ / 数の子 / 明太子 / からすみ / たらこ. ¶シシャモの卵 capelin roe

きらず【雪花菜】 ⇨おから

きり【霧】 fog(濃い); mist(薄い); haze(もや). ¶霧の摩周湖(北海道) the fog enveloping Lake Mashu(ko). 霧雨 a misty rain; a drizzle.

きり【桐】〔植物〕a paulownia. ゴマノハグサ科の落葉高木. 材は家具用. ☆500円玉の模様になっている. ⇨五三の桐. ¶桐材 paulownia wood. ⇨琴. 桐の下駄 paulownia-wood *geta*[clogs]; clogs made of paulownia wood. 桐箱 paulownia-wood box; a box made of paulownia wood. 桐の紋 the imperial crest of the leaf and flower of paulownia. 桐の箪笥 a paulownia-wood chest of drawers; a chest of drawers made of paulownia wood.

ぎり【義理】 moral obligation; morality(道義); courtesy(礼儀)

【義理人情】 (sense of) obligation and hu-manity; duty and love; mutual obligation (what one's mind tells him to do) and human feeling (what one's heart tells him to do).

【義理チョコ】 social courtesy chocolates; social obligatory chocolates; chocolates given out of moral obligation; chocolates presented as a matter of courtesy; 〈口語〉just-to-be-nice chocolates.

きりがみ【切り紙】 the paper-cutting art. It is a traditional Japanese art of making ornamental designs by folding and cutting paper in various shapes. 紙を折りそして切りながら, 装飾的な物の形を表す細工. ☆「切り絵[画]」は a cutout.

きりぎりす【蟋蟀】〔虫〕a katydid; a (long-horned) grasshopper.

きりごたつ【切り炬燵】 ⇨堀り炬燵

キリシタン【切支丹】 ❶〈キリスト教〉Christianity (in feudal Japan). ☆「キリスト教布教」a Christian mission, フランシスコ・ザビエル(Francisco de Xavier; 1506-1552: スペイン宣教師)が1549年鹿児島に来日し, 始めてキリスト教を伝えた.「キリスト教弾圧」a persecution of Christians(迫害); an inquisition of Christians(尋問). ❷〈信者〉a (Catholic) Christian (in feudal Japan). A (Catholic) Christian kept his/ her faith from the Muromachi and Sengoku periods through the early Meiji era. 室町・戦国時代から明治初期まで信仰を遵守した(カトリック)信者. ⇨潜伏キリシタン.

【キリシタン伴天連(神父)】 Christian missionary [priest]; Father(「神父」の呼称)

【キリシタン禁(教)令】 the ban on Christianity. The Tokugawa shogunate enacted to restrict Christianity and forced Christians to renounce their faith in 1612. 徳川幕府は1612年にキリスト教の制限と信者の棄教の強要を発令した.

【キリシタン宣教師追放令】 an edict expelling Christian missionaries from Japan. 日本からの国外追放令.

【キリシタン大名】 a Christian feudal lord (who protected Christianity to trade with Europeans). Otomo Sorin was one of the devoted Christian feudal lords in Kyushu. キリシタン大名(ヨーロッパ人との貿易を奨励するためキリスト教を保護した). 大友宗麟(1530-1587)は九州(大分県)出身の熱心なキリシタン大名の一人でもあった.

【キリシタン禁制】 the ban on Christianity (禁止令); a prohibition of Christianity(禁止).

きりたんぽ【切りたんぽ】 *kiritampo*; (a piece of) mashed rice paste on a skewer [stick]. Mashed rice paste is formed into cylinders around a cedar skewer[stick] and toasted near an open hearth[fire]. Pieces of *kiritampo* are also cooked as dumplings in soups. ご飯をつぶし, 串[棒]の周りに円筒状にぬりつけて, 囲炉裏火のそばで焼いたもの. 汁鍋で団子のように煮ても食べる. 秋田県の郷土料理.

きりづま【切妻】 a gable. ☆「切妻」とは本を伏せたような三角形のこと. 茅葺きの「切妻造り」は風通しがよい. ¶**切妻壁** a gable(d) wall. **切妻屋根** a gable(d) roof. **切妻造りの家** a gabled house; a house with a gable(d) roof.

きりのうもの【切能物】〔能楽〕an ending[last] piece in a program of Noh plays. The main character (*shite*) performs the role of a demon. 一日の最後に演じる能楽. シテは悪魔役を演じる. ⇨シテ

きりど【切戸】 ❶〔能楽〕a side entrance door (upstage left on the main stage). This door allows entrance from the back of the stage. It is a high sliding door used by stage assistants and the members of the chorus. 能舞台の奥の出入り口(舞台に立って左手にある). 舞台と舞台裏をつなぐ出入り口.

後見(舞台の世話役)と地謡(合唱者)が使用する.

❷ a wicket[gate]; an entrance in a small wicket[door] set within a large gate. 大きな扉につけてある小さな戸の出入り口. ⇨潜り戸

きりぼし【切干し】 steamed and dried slices[strips] (of vegetables). 切ったり蒸したりして日に干した(野菜).

〔食品〕**切干し芋** (steamed and) dried sweet potato shavings; dried slices[strips] of sweet potato. **切干し大根** dried *daikon* [radish] shavings; dried slices[strips] of *daikon*[radish]

きりもち【切り餅】 cut rice cake. ⇨鏡餅

きりん【麒麟】〔動物〕**❶** a giraffe. キリン科の哺乳動物.

❷ an imaginary[a legendary] Chinese animal with a deer-like body, a bull[an ox]-like tail, a wolf-like brow and the horse-like hooves[hoofs]. It is often painted on ceramic ware. 中国の想像[伝説]上の動物. 体は鹿, 尾は牛, 額は狼, ひづめは馬. 陶器などに描かれていることが多い.

キレる losing one's patience[cool]; blowing one's top; exploding in anger; snapping.

きんいっぷう【金一封】 a gift of money (in an envelope); a gift of money (as a contribution); a monetary gift (in appreciation of one's services[favors]); a special[an extra] (cash) bonus. 一包みのお金. ☆謝礼, 寄付金, 賞金などを贈るときに用いる語.

きんがしんねん【謹賀新年】 ⇨賀正/迎春

きんかん【金柑】〔植物〕a kumquat; a cumquat; a kumquat[cumquat] tree(木); a Chinese orange. ミカン科の常緑低木. ¶**金柑の砂糖漬け** a candied[preserved] kumquat in sugar.

きんぎょ【金魚】〔魚〕a goldfish. ☆「出目金」は a popeyed[telescope-eyed] goldfish.

き

¶**金魚鉢** a goldfish basin; a goldfish bowl. **金魚売り** goldfish sellers[vendors] (who carry around gold-fish-filled buckets suspended from a shoulder on a pole). （金魚を入れた水桶を天秤棒でかついでいる）. **金魚掬い** the goldfish scooping; the scooping of goldfish with a fragile water-thin dipper[net]. （もろくて水に弱い紙の網で金魚を掬う遊び）

きんきょく【琴曲】 (a piece of) *koto* music. 琴で演奏する曲.「箏曲」ともいう. ⇨琴/箏曲

きんこう【金工】〈工芸〉metalworking;〈工芸品〉metalwork; goldwork;〈職人〉a metal-worker; a craftsman in metal; a goldsmith. 金属に細工を施す工芸, またその職人.

きんこんしき【金婚式】 a golden wedding anniversary. 結婚50周年記念. ⇨結婚式

ぎんこんしき【銀婚式】 a silver wedding anniversary. 結婚25周年記念. ⇨結婚式

ぎんじょうしゅ【吟醸酒】 high-quality [deluxe-class] *sake*; the best-quality *sake*; carefully brewing *sake*. It is brewed at low temperatures from rice grains milled to 60 percent or less of their original weight. 原料米を精選して仕込み, 低温処理した酒. （1975年以降は）玄米を6割以下になるまで精白する. ☆精米歩合5割以下のものを「大吟醸酒」(top-quality *sake* brewed at low temperatures from rice grains milled to 50 percent of their weight or less)という.

きんたろう【金太郎】 *kintaro*, a plump, ruddy-faced boy (doll); a legendary strong boy (doll) with a plump and ruddy face. ふっくらと健康そうな顔つきをした伝説上の少年(人形).

【金太郎飴】 *Kintaro* candy bar; *Kintaro* wheat gluten. It is a stick of hard candy with a picture of the face of *Kintaro*. His face appears wherever the candy bar is cut. （断面が）金太郎の顔の絵の棒状の飴. ど

こを切っても金太郎の顔が出てくる.

きんちゃく【巾着】 a purse; a money pouch (hung at one's side[waist]). （腰に下げた）金を入れる小袋. ☆「腰巾着」は a hanger-on.「巾着切り」は a pickpocket(すり)という.

きんちゃく deep-fried bean curd with rice cake (used in eating *oden*). 餅を入れた油揚げ. ⇨おでん

きんつば【金鍔】 ❶〈金の鍔〉a golden guard on a sword. 金色[黄金]で作った刀の鍔.

❷〈和菓子〉a pancake stuffed with sweetened bean paste; a confection of sweetened bean paste wrapped in a thin wheat-flour dough. It is baked in the flat, round shape of a sword guard on an oiled griddle. 小麦粉で餡を薄く包んだ和菓子. 油を塗った鉄板上で刀の鍔の平らな形のように焼く.

きんときまめ【金時豆】 ❶〈豆〉large *adzuki* beans(アズキ豆); reddish kidney beans (いんげん豆).

❷〈煮豆〉red *adzuki* (or kidney) beans cooked with sugar. 砂糖で甘く煮た豆. 別称「金時あずき」単に「金時」.

きんとん【金団】 *kinton*; (dishes of) mashed [strained] sweet potatoes containing sweetened chestnuts; (food of) strained sweet potatoes mixed with sweetened chestnuts. さつまいもを裏ごしして甘く煮た栗を混ぜた料理[食品].「栗金団」ともいう. ☆正月の御節料理に出す. ⇨栗金団

ぎんなん【銀杏】 a ginkgo[gingko] nut(実).「いちょう」の実. 茶碗蒸しや土瓶蒸しに用いる. ⇨いちょう

きんのう【勤王・勤皇】 loyalty to the Emperor. 天皇に忠義・忠勤を尽くすこと. ¶**勤王攘夷**. ⇨尊王攘夷

【勤王の志士】 a loyalist to the Emperor; an Imperial loyalist; an Imperialist[a patriot supporting the Emperor]; a loyal supporter of the Emperor around the end of the Edo period (or early in the Meiji Restoration period). 天皇に忠誠を尽くす人. 江戸末期頃(明治時代初期頃)に幕府を倒して朝廷中心の政権をたてようとする一派. ⇔幕末の志士

きんぱく【金箔】 (a piece of) gold leaf (薄手の); (a piece of) gold foil (厚手の); gilt (金メッキ). 金をたたいて紙のように薄くのばしたもの. ¶金箔の屏風 a folding screen covered with gold leaf. ⇨金屏風

ぎんぱく【銀箔】 (a piece of) silver leaf (薄手の); (a piece of) silver foil (厚手の). 銀をたたいて紙のように薄くのばしたもの. ¶銀箔の屏風 a folding screen covered with silver leaf; a sliver-leaf-covered folding screen.

きんびょうぶ【金屏風】 a gilded[gilt] folding screen; a gold-leaf-covered folding screen. 下地の紙全体に金箔を貼った屏風.

きんぴら(ごぼう)【金平(牛蒡)】 flavored burdock roots; thin slices[strips] of chopped burdock roots and carrots. They are cooked[stir-fried and boiled] in sesame-seed oil with *shoyu*[soy sauce], sugar, chili pepper and *mirin*[sweetened *sake*]. 牛蒡と人参を細くきざんでごま油でいため, 醤油・砂糖・唐辛子・味醂で調理したもの.

ぎんぷら【銀麩羅】 deep-fried food covered with a batter made from buckwheat flour and egg white. そば粉に卵白(白身)を加えた衣で揚げたてんぷら. 卵黄(egg yolk)を使うと「金麩羅」になる.

ぎんぶら【銀ブラ】 a stroll on[down] the streets of Ginza; strolling along the streets of Ginza.

きんぼし【金星】〔相撲〕 (score) an outstanding victory over a *yokozuna*[grand champion]. It is a big win against a *yokozuna* by a *maegashira sumo* wrestler during the *sumo* tournament. 平幕力士が横綱に勝ったときの勝ち星.

ぎんぼし【銀星】〔相撲〕 (score) an outstanding victory over an *ozeki*[senior champion]. it is a big win made against an *ozeki* by a *maegashira sumo* wrestler during the *sumo* tournament. 平幕力士が大関に勝ったときの勝ち星.

きんみずひき【金水引】 golden paper strings [cords] (used for decorative tying of a gift package[envelope]). 金色の紙ひも. 贈物の包み[封筒]を飾りたてて結ぶのに用いる. ⇨水引

きんめだい【金目鯛】〔魚〕 a red snapper; an alfonsino. キンメダイ科の魚, 全身鮮紅色で, 目は大きく黄金色. タイとは別種. 冬が旬. 刺身, 塩焼き, 煮つけ, ちり鍋などにして食用.

きんもくせい【金木犀】〔植物〕 a fragrant-olive; a sweet-scented olive. ⇨木犀

きんらん【金襴】 gold brocade; brocade with patterns in gold thread. 錦地に金糸で模様を織ったきらびやかな織物. ¶金襴の袈裟 a surplice of gold brocade. ⇨袈裟

【金襴緞子】 gold brocade and satin damask. They are often made into an *obi*[sash] worn with a *kimono*. 金襴と緞子(ダマスク織). 高価な織物で, 飾り帯に使われる. ⇨緞子. ¶金襴緞子の帯 a gold-brocade(d) *obi* [sash]; a dask *obi*[sash] with gold brocade; an *obi*[sash] made of gold-brocade satin damask.

きんろうかんしゃのひ【勤労感謝の日】 Labor Thanksgiving Day (November 23). This national holiday was established in 1948 as a day to express gratitude to each other for their labors throughout the year and for the fruits of those labors. They honor working people and recognize the importance of labor on this day. Prior to the establishment of this holiday, November 23 was celebrated as an Imperial rice harvest festival called *Niiname-sai*. 勤労を尊

き

び，生産を祝って国民が相互に感謝する．この日には勤労者に敬意を払い，勤労の大切さを自覚する．古来「新嘗祭」として祝った．⇨新嘗祭

く

く【区】 ❶〈市の〉a ward. ¶**目黒区** Meguro Ward. **区役所** a ward office.
❷〈区域の〉a district; a section. ¶（バス）**1区150円** 150 yen for a section.

く【句】❶〈語句〉a phrase;〈文句〉an expression.
❷〈詩歌の1行〉a line;〈詩歌の1節〉a verse;〈詩歌の1連〉a stanza;〈詩〉a poem.
❸〈俳句・俳諧〉(compose) a *haiku*; a Japanese 17-syllable poem. ⇨俳句

ぐ【具】〈料理の材料〉ingredients (used for cooking)(複数形で). 刻んで料理に入れる「ねた[種]」のこと．別称「具材」．ご飯の場合は「かやく」という．⇨かやく．¶**味噌汁の具** the ingredients of *miso*[bean paste] soup.

ぐう【〜宮】 a shrine. ¶**東照宮** Tosho(gu) Shrine(栃木県・ユネスコ世界文化遺産).⇨神社

ぐうじ【宮司】 the chief Shinto priest; the chief priest of a Shinto shrine. 神社の最高位の神官.

くうしゅう【空襲】 an air raid[attack]. ¶**空襲警報** an air-raid alarm[warning].

くかい【句会】 a *haiku* gathering[meeting]. ⇨俳句

くぐりど【潜り戸】 a wicket (gate); a small, low side door fixed in a gate. くぐって出入りする小さな戸口. ⇨切り戸❷

くげ【公家・公卿】 a court noble; a court-related noble (in feudal times). They served as courtiers with the Imperial Family. (封建時代，武家に対して)朝廷に仕える人[貴族]．皇族とともに朝臣として仕えた．☆

奈良・平安時代は「皇族とその直系子孫」(the Imperial Family and its direct descendants)をさした．⇨武家．⇨朝臣．¶**公家諸法度** the Laws for the Court in the Edo period (1615). 公家(また天皇家や高官僧侶)が厳守すべき法令(全17条).

くげ【供花・供華】 the Buddhist ritual flower offerings; the flowers placed on the Buddhist altar. 仏前に花を供えること．またその花.

ぐざい【具材】 ⇨具

くさいち【草市】 a fair selling flowers and other Buddhist offerings for ancestral spirits during the Bon Festival. 盂蘭盆会に用いる草花や仏具などを売る市 (market).「盆市」ともいう．☆陰暦7月12日の夜から翌朝にかけて立つ.

くさく【句作】 a *haiku* (poem) composition; composition of a *haiku* (poem). ⇨俳句

くさずもう【草相撲】〔相撲〕an amateur *sumo* wrestling; a local *sumo* tournament;〈人〉an amateur[a local] *sumo* wrestler.

くさぞうし【草双紙】 an illustrated storybook with narrative and dialogue (published from the mid Edo period to the early Meiji era). (庶民の間に流行した)物語や会話のある絵入りの読み物 (picture book). 江戸時代中期から明治初期にかけて出版された．⇨絵双紙

くさなぎのつるぎ【草薙の剣】 ⇨三種の神器

くさだんご【草団子】 a mugwort-flavor sticky rice-flour dumpling; a rice-flour dumpling mixed and flavored with mugwort leaves[shoots]. 蓬の若葉を混ぜてつくる団子. ⇨蓬団子

くさぶきやね【草葺き屋根】 a thatched roof; the roof of thatch. ☆「茅葺の家」a thatched house[cottage].

くさもち【草餅】 a mugwort-flavor sticky rice cake; a rice cake mixed and flavored with mugwort leaves[shoots]. It is eaten on the Girls' Festival on March 3. 蓬（よもぎ）の若葉を混ぜてつくる餅．3月3日の雛祭りに食す．⇨蓬餅

くさやきゅう【草野球】 a sandlot baseball. 都会などの空き地で遊ぶ野球．¶草野球選手 a sandlotter.

くし【串】 ❶ a skewer（小さな串）; a spin（丸焼き用の串）．¶竹串 a bamboo skewer. 串で焼いた魚 fish grilled on a skewer. ❷ a spit（大きな串．丸焼き用）; a brochette（金属の串）．¶串で焼いたラム a lamb roasted[broiled] on a spit (over a open flame).

〔料理・食品〕串揚げ deep-fried kebab[kebob]; deep-fried foods[meat, fish or vegetables] affixed on a bamboo skewer.（竹串に刺して揚げたもの）．☆kebab[kebob]（アラビア語で「あぶり肉」の意）は「カバブ（肉と野菜の串焼き料理）」．串カツ pieces of pork and vegetables[onions or leeks] deep-fried on a skewer; pork cutlet and vegetables[onions or leeks], coated with batter, and deep-fried on a skewer.（豚肉と野菜［タマネギ・ネギ］を串に刺して衣をまぶして油で揚げたもの）．串団子 sweet rice dumplings affixed on a skewer.（串に刺した団子）．串焼き fish[meat] roasted[broiled]on a skewer.（串に刺して焼いた魚［肉］）．

くし【櫛】 (wear) a comb. ¶櫛の歯 the teeth of a comb.

くじ【籤】 a lot; a lottery (ticket). ¶くじ引き a lottery; a drawing. 宝くじ a public lottery (ticket). ⇨宝くじ

くじゃく【孔雀】〔鳥〕a peacock（雄）; a peahen（雌）; a peafowl（雌雄共）; a peachick（雛）．キジ科の大形の鳥．¶扇のように尾を広げた一面の孔雀 a peacock with its tail feathers spread out in[like] a gorgeous fan. ☆孔雀は「1面」であって1羽とはいわない．扇の数え方に由来する．

ぐじょうおどり【郡上おどり】 the Gujo Bon-Folk-Dance Parade.（8月）．⇨付記(1)「日本の祭り」

くじら【鯨】〔動物〕a whale（体長 4m 以上）; a bull[male] whale（雄鯨）; a cow[female] whale（雌鯨）; a whale calf（子鯨）．☆霜降り状の尾肉は刺身やステーキ，赤肉は鍋物，照り焼き，から揚げにする．⇨いるか（体長4m以下）．¶背美鯨 an arctic whale; a black right whale. 抹香鯨 a sperm whale. 長須鯨 a fin whale; a finback. 鰯鯨（いわし）a sei whale. 座頭鯨 a humpback whale.

くじらじゃく【鯨尺】 a cloth measure (used in Japanese dressmaking). 和式洋裁で布の長さを測るのに用いるものさし．☆昔，鯨のひげでつくられたことに由来．

くじらまく【鯨幕】 black and white striped curtain[bunting]. 黒白の布を一枚おきに縫い合わせた幕[まん幕]．葬式などに使う凶事用の黒白幕．☆鯨の皮と脂の部分が黒と白になっていることに由来．

くず【葛】〔植〕a *kudzu*（日本語から英語になった）; an arrowroot; a pueraria. マメ科のつる性多年草．「秋の七草」の一つ．¶葛蔓 a *kudzu* vine. 葛粉（葛の根のでんぷん）*kudzu* starch; *kudzu* arrowroot starch. 葛衣 *kudzu* sheet. 葛餡 *kudzu*-starch (thick) sauce. ⇨餡❷

〔料理・食品〕葛掛け dishes dressed with *kudzu*-starch sauce.（葛餡を入れてつくる料理）．⇨餡掛け．葛切り (strips of) jellied *kudzu* starch; short noodles made from *kudzu* flour and sugar (eaten with syrup).（葛粉と砂糖でつくる紐状に切ったもの．冷やして糖蜜で食べる）．葛桜 a steamed *kudzu*-starch bun stuffed with sweet bean paste and wrapped in a pickled cherry leaf.（餡を入れ，桜の葉で巻いた葛粉の蒸し饅頭）．葛団子 a *kudzu*-starch dumpling.（葛粉でつくる団子）．葛練り a sweetened paste of *kudzu* starch; a confection made with sweetened *kudzu*-starch dough.（葛粉を甘くして煮た菓子）．☆「葛餅」ともいう．

葛饅頭 a steamed *kudzu*-starch bun stuffed with sweet bean paste; a steamed bun with a sweet bean-paste filling covered with *kudzu* starch.（練った葛粉で餡を包んだ饅頭）．☆桜の葉 (a cherry leaf)で包んだものもある．**葛餅** a pudding-like *kudzu* cake; a pudding-like cake made from *kudzu*-starch dressed with sweetened soybean flour; a *kudzu*-starch cake coated with sweetened soybean flour.（葛練りに黄粉をまぶした菓子）．**葛湯** a *kudzu*-starch gruel; a gruel[porridge] made from *kudzu* flour and sugar.（葛粉と砂糖でつくる飲み物［薄いかゆ］）．**葛羊羹** jellylike sweets[cakes] made with *kudzu*-starch and red *adzuki* bean paste.（葛粉と小豆餡でつくる羊羹）．

くすだま【薬玉】❶〈袋〉an ornamental scent bag. 香料を袋に入れ，飾り付けたもの．❷〈玉〉a hanging paper[cloth] ball (with long tassels of five-different colors). It is used for festive occasions such as a launching ceremony.（五色の長い房をたらしている)紙［布］製の飾り玉．進水式など祝賀用である．☆垂れ下がった糸［飾り房］を引くとふたつに割れ，紙吹雪 (confetti; ticker tape)が降ってくる．

くすのき【楠・樟】〔植物〕a camphor tree. クスノキ科の常緑高木．材は堅く，家具・細工物用．☆「樟脳の玉」は camphor ball; mothball. 別称「虫除け玉」．⇨樟脳

くすりだんす【薬箪笥】a many-drawer medicine chest.

ぐそくに【具足煮】a dish of lobster boiled with its shells on. 伊勢エビを殻のついたまま輪切りにして煮ること．☆伊勢エビの殻を甲冑 (armor[armour])の具足にたとえる．

くたにやき【九谷焼】Kutani ceramic and porcelain ware (produced in Ishikawa Pre-

fecture). ☆派手な色彩が多い．

くちとり【口取り】an hors d'oeuvre (of assorted fish served first in a Japanese meal); a dish of assorted delicacies (arranged beautifully on a lacquered plate). 和食で最初に出される前菜．魚, かまぼこ, きんとんなどを盛り合わせたもの．漆塗りの皿に見栄えよく盛りつけた珍味．「口取り肴」の略．

くちとりがし【口取り菓子】〔茶道〕a tea cake (served first in the tea ceremony). 茶道で茶を出す前に器に盛って出す菓子．

くちなおし【口直し】refreshing the mouth; removing the aftertaste. A diner takes the unpleasant taste out of his/ her mouth by cleansing[clearing] his/ her palate. 前に飲食したものの不快な味を除くこと (taking away). またその飲食物．通称「お口直し」

くちなし【梔子】〔植物〕a gardenia(木・花)；a Cape jasmine. アカネ科の常緑低木．完熟の実は黄赤色となり「栗きんとん」の着色料に用いる．薬用でもある．

くちよせ【口寄せ】⇨いたこ

くないちょう【宮内庁】the Imperial Household Agency; the Imperial Household Office. ¶宮内庁御用達 purveyors to the Imperial Household Agency.

くにがろう【国家老】one of the highest ranking vassals[retainers] of a feudal lord during the Edo period. He stayed in his lord's domain all the time and managed his lord's administration while his lord stayed in Edo. 江戸時代，諸侯が(参勤交代制などで)江戸にいる間，領土の留守をあずかって勤務した重臣．⇔江戸家老．⇨家老

くぬぎ【櫟】〔植物〕a Japanese oak (tree). ブナ科の落葉高木．果実は「どんぐり」，材は薪炭用．樹皮からは染料をとる．

くひ【句碑】a stone tablet[monument] inscribed with a *haiku*; a stone slab with a *haiku* engraved on it. 俳句を彫りつけた石

碑.

くぼう【公方】 ❶ a shogun(将軍)；the shogunate(将軍職). 鎌倉時代以降の将軍. 将軍職. 幕府. 通称「公方様」
❷ the Emperor(天皇)；the Imperial Court (朝廷).

くま【熊】〔動物〕 a bear; a bear cub(熊の子). ¶北極熊 a polar bear. 熊の皮 a bearskin. 熊のぬいぐるみ a teddy bear; a stuffed bear
【熊祭り】〈アイヌの祭儀〉a bear-sacrifice festival; the ritual killing of a bear.

くまで【熊手】❶〈用具〉a rake；〈竹製用具〉 a bamboo rake; a rake made of bamboo(used to scrape[rake] up fallen[dead] leaves and grains). 落ち葉[枯れ葉]や穀物をかき集める道具. ☆熊の手のような爪 (bear claws) が広がっていることからの呼称.
❷〈縁起物〉a decorative[ornamental] bamboo rake (used as a charm for raking in good luck during the coming year). 来る年に幸運 (good fortune)をかき集める (gathering)縁起物として飾り立てた竹製の熊手.
【熊手市】 a rake fair; a fair selling decorative[ornamental] rakes. A variety of rakes decorated with trinkets and masks of lucky gods are sold at open-air stalls set up in shrine compounds. 小さな飾り物(小判や枡)や好運をよぶ神の面で飾った熊手が神社の境内にたつ屋台で売られる. ☆毎年11月の酉の市 (the Rooster Festival)で売られる. ⇨酉の市

くまどり【隈取り】 ❶〔歌舞伎〕*kumadori*; kabuki stage makeup[make-up]; exaggerated facial makeup used in a kabuki play (to emphasize passionate feeling of an actor). *Kumadori* is an established set of mask-like makeup style shading the muscles in the face. Heavy[violent] makeup of various colors is applied on the face of a kabuki actor to represent the nature of the character and emotions. (役者の情熱的な表情を強調するために用いる)誇張した歌舞伎の顔化粧. 隈取は仮面を思わせる定型化した化粧模様で, 顔の筋肉の陰影を表す. 歌舞伎役者の性格や感情を表現するために多彩な色の厚化粧(紅隈・藍隈)を役者の顔に塗りつける. ⇨荒事. ☆「紅隈」red-on-white lines (of makeup designated as strength and righteousness). 力と正義を表す.「藍隈」indigo[blue]-on-white lines (of makeup designated as an evil character and a demon). 邪悪と鬼を表す.
❷〈日本画のぼかし〉shading; gradation (of a Japanese painting).

くも【蜘蛛】〔虫〕a spider. ¶クモの巣 a spider('s) web; a cobweb. クモの糸 a spider's thread.

くもすけ【雲助】❶ a palanquin[sedan-chair] bearer (in the Edo period). (江戸時代に宿場や街道で)駕籠かきをする人.
❷ a ruffian; a hoodlum; a tough (ゆすり・たかりをする)ごろつき, ならず者. ☆「雲助タクシー」は a taxi driven by a dishonest (cab) driver. その「運転手」は a bad taxi driver (who demands an unreasonable fare)

くようとう【供養搭】 a memorial (column); a tower for the consolation of the dead person's soul; a tower for the memorial service to console the dead person's soul. 死者の冥福を祈るための塔. ☆「供養(する)」(hold) a memorial service.

くら【蔵・倉】〈貯蔵用の蔵〉a storehouse (貯蔵庫)；a warehouse(商品倉庫)；a granary(穀物倉庫)；a thick-walled fire-proof earthen building (black and white in designs). It is used for stowing away important or precious goods. 厚い壁におおわれた防火用になっている土蔵(白黒の模様がある). 貴重品を人目につかないように貯蔵しておく建物. ¶蔵主 the owner[proprietor] of a warehouse. 蔵

入れ warehousing; storing goods. 蔵出し delivery of goods from a warehouse; taking goods out of a warehouse. 蔵開き the opening of a warehouse for the first time in the new year. 蔵出し酒［味噌・醤油］ *sake*[*miso, shoyu*] fresh from the brewery. ⇨蔵元❶. 蔵造りの家屋 a traditional warehouse-style house (built in the Edo period). (江戸時代に建てられた)伝統的な蔵屋敷. ☆小江戸と呼ばれる埼玉県・川越市の「蔵屋敷」は有名.

くらげ【水母・海月】〔動物〕 a jellyfish; a sea jelly; a medusa (複) ~sae, ~s). 和食では酢の物に用いる. ¶くらげの傘 the bell[umbrella] of a jellyfish. 干しくらげ a dried jellyfish. 塩くらげ a salted jellyfish.

くらまのひまつり【鞍馬の火まつり】 the Fire Festival of Yuki Shrine in Kurama. (10月). ⇨付記(1)「日本の祭り」

くらもと【蔵元】❶〈酒・味噌・醤油などの貯蔵所〔蔵〕〉a *sake*[*miso, shoyu*] warehouse;〈酒・味噌・醤油などの醸造所〉a *sake*[*miso, shoyu*] brewery;〈酒・味噌・醤油などの醸造者〉a *sake*[*miso; shoyu*] brewer.
❷〈穀倉〉a granary; a garner. 穀物を納める建物. ¶米倉 a rice granary
❸〈幕府・大名の倉庫の役人〉a supervisor in a business office set up in warehouse by a shogun (or feudal lord).

クランベリー〔植物〕 cranberry. ¶クランベリーソース cranberry sauce. 七面鳥料理用.

くり【栗】〔植物〕a (Japanese) chestnut(実); a chestnut tree(木). ブナ科クリ属の植物の総称. ¶栗の皮 a chestnut shell. 栗のいが a chestnut bur. 甘栗 sweet roasted chestnuts. 勝栗 a dried chestnut.
〔料理・食品〕栗餡 sweetened chestnuts paste; sweet paste made from chestnuts. ⇨餡. 栗甘露煮 candied[sweetened] chestnuts; chestnuts stewed[boiled] slowly in *mirin*, *shoyu* and syrup. ⇨甘露煮. 栗金団 mashed sweet potatoes[sweet potato paste] containing sugared[sweetened] chestnuts. ⇨金団. 栗汁粉 sweet red bean soup with chestnuts. ⇨汁粉. 栗饅頭 chestnut-paste bun; brown oven-baked bun stuffed with sweetened chestnut paste. ⇨饅頭. 栗飯 rice cooked[boiled] with chestnuts. 栗羊羹 sweet bean-paste jelly containing chestnuts; sweet bean-jelly mixed with chestnuts. ⇨羊羹

グリーンしゃ【グリーン車】 first-class car; (英) first-class carriage; special reserved-seat coach.

くるまいど【車井戸】 a draw well. It is a well from which water is drawn[taken] in a bucket hoisted by using a rope and a pulley. 汲み上げ井戸. 綱と滑車を使ってバケツで引き上げて水をくむ井戸.

くるまえび【車海老】〔甲〕 a prawn;(英) a shrimp. ☆ lobsterよりは小さく, shrimpよりは大きい. ⇨えび
〔料理〕車海老の塩焼き prawns sprinkled with salt broiled over a charcoal fire.

くるみ【胡桃】〔植物〕a walnut(実); a walnut tree(木). クルミ科の落葉高木. 種子は食用と油用. 材は器具用. ¶クルミの殻 a walnut shell. 胡桃割り (a pair of) nutcrackers.

ぐれんたい【愚連隊】 (a gang of) hooligans; (米) hoodlums.

くろおび【黒帯】❶〈着物〉a black *obi*[sash]. ❷〈柔道・空手〉*kuro-obi*; a black belt. ⇨柔道帯

くろかわのう【黒川能】 the Kurokawa Noh Play Presentation[Performance]. (2月). ⇨付記(1)「日本の祭り」

くろこ［くろご］【黒子・黒衣】〔歌舞伎〕〔文楽〕❶〈人〉a *kuroko*[*kurogo*]; a stage assistant attired[dressed] in black; a stagehand dressed in black. A *kuroko* is a black-attired assistant of an actor who helps on the stage in kabuki and bunraku plays. He wears a black robe that covers his head and face. He helps kabuki and bunraku actors onstage in various ways during a performance. 黒い衣を着た，歌舞伎・文楽舞台上における役者の後見役．頭と顔を覆う黒い布を被る．①〔歌舞伎〕On the kabuki stage, a *kuroko* serves to help the actors change[take off] clothes.〈歌舞伎舞台上では〉役者が衣服を着替える［脱ぐ］のを手伝う．②〔文楽〕On the bunraku stage, the puppeteers of a leg manipulation and a left-arm[hand] manipulation are attired in black.〈文楽舞台上では〉足遣いと左遣いの人形遣いは黒の衣を着用する．⇨三人遣い ❷〈黒い衣服・被り物〉black costumes and hoods that cover all the heads and faces of kabuki stage assistants or bunraku puppeteers. 歌舞伎役者の後見役また文楽人形遣いの頭と顔を覆う黒い衣装と被り物．

くろざとう【黒砂糖】 raw sugar; unrefined sugar. 精製する前の黒茶色 (brown)の砂糖．サトウキビから作る含蜜糖．「黒糖」「大島糖」ともいう．羊羹や花林糖などに用いる．

くろしお【黒潮】 the Kuroshio Current; the Japan Current. ☆「日本海流」ともいう．⇔親潮 (the Okhotsk current)

くろしょうぞく【黒装束】 black clothes; a black costume. ⇔白装束．¶黒装束の武士 a *samurai*[warrior] dressed in black.

クールたっきゅうびん【クール宅急便】 a refrigerated delivery service; a refrigerated delivery of food parcels; a refrigerated parcel of delivery. ⇨宅配便

くろず【黒酢】 dark vinegar; vinegar flavored with toasted and grated kelp.

くろとめそで【黒留袖】 a black ceremonial silk *kimono* for women. **Kuro-tomesode** is worn by married women[female relatives of the bride and bridegroom] on such auspicious occasions as weddings. It has five family crests on it: one on each sleeve, one on each side of the chest and one on the back. 正式な黒色の留袖．既婚者〔新郎新婦の母親や親戚〕が結婚式などの祭典に着用する．袖に2つ，胸に2つ，背中に1つの合計5つの家紋がほどこされている．⇨留袖

くろぶさ【黒房】〔相撲〕the black tassel. ⇨房

くろふね【黒船】 the black ship[steamship]. American vessels reached Japan around the end of the Edo period. The ship reached Uraga Bay in 1846 and Shimoda in 1856. 江戸時代末期に来日したアメリカ船．1846年には浦賀湾，1856年には下田港に到着する．

くろぼし【黒星】 ❶〈黒くて丸い印〉a black mark[circle]. ❷〔相撲〕〈負け星〉a loss[defeat] mark; a loss[defeat] in a *sumo* bout (recorded with a black mark[circle]). 勝負での負け星のこと．⇔白星．¶黒星を取る be beaten; be defeated.

くろまめ【黒豆】 a black soybean (boiled in *shoyu*[soy sauce] and sugar). ☆御節料理には欠かせない．⇨御節料理

くろみす【黒御簾】〔歌舞伎〕a black bamboo blind[screen] (located on the downstage (*shimote*)). Behind the black blind[screen] is an ensemble of singers, *shamisen* players and percussionists providing background music for sound effects (*geza-ongaku*). 黒御簾〔格子〕の中では歌や，三味線や打楽器 (太鼓・笛)などの演奏や，背景の効果音などの「下座音楽」が演奏される．⇨下手 / 下座音楽

くろみずひき【黒水引】 a black and white paper string. It is used for wrapping package[envelope] containing a condolence gift. It is often used on sad occasions such as funeral[condolence] offerings. 白黒の紙製のひも (cord). お悔やみ物の包み

け

［封筒］を結ぶのに用いる．葬儀のような弔事に用いる． ¶**香典袋を黒水引で包む** tie the envelope containing an obituary money gift with a black and white string. ⇨水引 / 香典袋

くろみつ【黒蜜】 a brown sugar syrup; a syrup made from brown sugar and water. 黒砂糖と水でつくるシロップ.

くろもじ【黒文字】❶〔植物〕a spicebush; a spicewood. クスノキ科の樹木．香りがよいので爪楊枝や箸の用材にする．

❷〔茶道〕a toothpick with the bark of the tree on one side. It is often used to pick up sweets during the tea ceremony. 片面には樹皮がある．茶会での和菓子用. ⇨爪楊枝 / 楊枝

くわ【桑】〔植物〕 a mulberry tree（木）; a mulberry（実）. クワ科の落葉高木．葉は蚕の飼料．実は果実酒・ジャムなどの原料．繊維は織物の原料．材は家具に用いる. ⇨蚕

くわい【慈姑】〔植物〕an arrowhead; an arrowhead bulb（球根）. オモダカ科の多年草.「クワイモ」の短縮形．地下茎は「芽が出る」（めでたい）ので正月料理の煮物に用いる.

くわいれしき【鍬入れ式】 (hold) a ground-breaking ceremony. 着工の行事.

くわがた【鍬形】❶ a hoe-shaped helmet crest. 鍬 (hoe) の形をした甲 (helmet) の前立ての一つ.

❷〔虫〕a stag beetle.「鍬形虫」の略. ⇨かぶとむし

ぐん【郡】㊗ a county; ㊤ a district. ¶**伊賀郡** Iga county.

ぐんかんまき【軍艦巻き】 a battleship-like[gunboat-like] *sushi*; a bite-sized lump of *sushi* bound with a strip of dried laver (*nori*) and topped with sea-urchins (or salmon roes). It looks like a battleship, viewed from the side. すし飯を海苔で巻き

(wrapped in), その上にウニ(またはイクラ)などをのせる．横からみると軍艦に似ていることからの呼称.

ぐんこくしゅぎ【軍国主義】 militarism. ¶**軍国主義の廃絶と民主主義の定着** the abolition of militarism and the establishment of democracy.

くんせい【燻製】 smoked food. ¶**鮭の燻製** smoked salmon. 燻製の鮭 salmon smoked in the smokehouse[smokeroom].

ぐんせん【軍扇】 a war fan; the military leader's fan. It was used to communicate commands to their soldiers in the battlefield of the ancient times. 昔，大将が軍隊を指揮するために用いた扇.

ぐんて【軍手】(a pair of) cotton work gloves.

ぐんとう【群島】 an archipelago; a group of islands. ⇨諸島 / 列島

くんどく【訓読】⇨訓読み

ぐんばい【軍配】〔相撲〕❶ judgment[judgement] of a winner in *sumo* wrestling. 相撲で勝ちの判定をくだすこと.

❷「軍配団扇」の略.

ぐんばいうちわ【軍配団扇】❶〔相撲〕a *sumo* referee's fan. A ritual fan is used by a *sumo* referee to signal his judgment and final decision of the winner during a *sumo* bout. 相撲の取組で勝利者(victor)を判断・決定する行司の団扇. ⇨行司

❷〈武将の軍扇〉a military leader's fan (used in the battlefield). ⇨軍扇

❸〈五月人形〉a military leader's iron fan (displayed with warrior dolls). ⇨五月人形

くんよみ【訓読み】 the reading of a Chinese character in the Japanese pronunciation.「訓読」ともいう.

け

けい【渓】 a gorge; a valley; a ravine; a canyon. ¶**厳美渓**（岩手県）(the) Genbi(kei)

Gorge. ⇨渓谷／谷／～峡／峡谷

けいかん【景観】 the landscape; the scenery. ¶景観法 Landscape Law（2005年施行）. 景観条例 landscape ordinance. 景観サイト preservation ordinance（景観保護の条例）.

けいかんび【景観美】 scenic beauty; beautiful landscape[scenery]. ¶景観美に富む山々 the mountains blessed with scenic beauty.

げいぎ【芸妓】 ⇨芸者

けいこ【稽古】〈華道・茶道〉 practice（技能取得）; lesson（授業での習得）; training（運動・技術取得）; exercise（体力訓練）. ¶稽古着 training wear; practice suit. 稽古場〈柔道・空手〉 dojo; a practice hall; a training room. 稽古始め the first practice[lesson] of a new year. お花の稽古 practice[lesson] in the flower arrangement. お茶の稽古 practice[lesson] in the tea ceremony. 琴[三味線]の稽古 koto[shamisen] lesson; lesson in koto[shamisen]. 柔道の稽古 training in judo. 稽古事 accomplishments; lessons（複数形で）. ⇨芸事

【稽古総見】〔相撲〕 attendance at a final sumo training session before a tournament (by all directors of Japan Sumo Association [the Yokozuna Promotion Council]). All the council members see practice matches of sumo wrestlers in a large group. In particular they attend a special practice session to inspect the top sumo wrestlers in the makunouchi division. 日本相撲協会の諮問機関である横綱審議委員会が東京場所前に相撲練習の総仕上げ状態を視察すること. 特に幕の内の上位力士を監視する.

けいご【敬語】 an honorific; an honorific word[expression].

【関連語】尊敬語（相手に対して）respectful language[word, expression] (used for others). 謙譲語（自分に関して）modest [humble] language[word, expression] (used for oneself). 丁寧語（品格ある）

polite language[word, expression]. 丁重語 courteous language[word, expression]. 美化語 elegant language[word, expression].

げいこ【芸子】 ⇨芸者

けいこく【渓谷】 a gorge; a glen; a ravine; a canyon; a valley. ¶秋川渓谷（東京都）(the) Akikawa Valley. ⇨渓／～峡／峡谷／谷

げいごと【芸事】 accomplishments (of shamisen, koto and odori[dance])（複数形で）. 三味線・琴・舞踊などの遊芸に関すること.

けいさく【警策】 ⇨きょうさく

げいしゃ【芸者】 a geisha（複）geishas); a geisha girl; a professional female entertainer, well-trained in traditional dance and music. A geisha is invited to a traditional Japanese-style banquet to wait on guests[a group of men] with sake and entertain with classical Japanese dance and music accompanied by shamisen. They wear beautiful kimonos with their Japanese coiffure upswept. 三味線の伴奏に合わせ日本舞踊や音楽で日本式酒宴の席に興をそえることを職業とする女性. 彼女らは結い上げた日本髪の, 美しい着物姿である.「芸子」「芸妓」ともいう. ⇨半玉. ¶芸者をあげる call in a geisha[geishas]

げいじゅつひん【芸術品】 a work of art; an art object.

げいしゅん【迎春】 (I wish you) a Happy New Year. ⇨賀正／謹賀新年

けいしょう【継承】 succession; inheritance. ¶昭和天皇の崩御, 明仁親王の継承 Death of Emperor Showa and Succession of Crown Prince Akihito. 継承者 a successor; an heir.

けいしょう【景勝】 picturesque scenery; beautiful scenery. ⇨景色. ¶景勝地 a scenic spot[area]; a spot[place] of scenic beauty.

けいしんけい【傾真型】〔華道〕 a slanting style

け

け

of flower arrangement (one of the three basic styles in the Sogetsu school). 傾けて花を生ける型(草月流). ⇨基本花型 / 斜態型(池坊流).

けいだい【境内】（複数形で）the precincts; the grounds; the compounds. ¶神社[仏閣]の境内 the shrine[temple] precincts[grounds]. 社寺の境内で in the precincts[on the grounds] of a shrine[temple].

けいちつ【啓蟄】 the season when hibernating insects come out[emerge] from underground. 冬眠していた虫が地下から出る季節. ⇨二十四節気

けいちょうひ【慶弔費】 expenses for gifts of celebration or condolence; the expenditure of gift money[money on gifts] for happy and unhappy events[occasions]. 慶事と凶事に要する費用.

けいてん【経典】 ⇨きょうてん(経典)

げいのう【芸能】 public entertainment(演芸); the performing arts(公演芸術). ¶伝統芸能 the traditional performing arts. 郷土芸能 the local performing arts. 民族芸能 the folk entertainment. 芸人 an entertainer; a performer; vaudevillian（寄席芸人）. 芸能人 an entertainment[a TV] celebrity. 芸能界の人々 people in show business[show biz].

けいはくたんしょう【軽薄短小】 compactification; miniaturization; light-thin-short-small articles.

けいひ【桂皮】 cinnamon; cassia (bark). クスノキ科の常緑高木. 桂の樹皮を乾燥させたもの. 芳香がある. ⇨八橋煎餅

けいひん【景品】 a giveaway; a free gift; a freebie. ¶景品券 a gift coupon; 㕗 a voucher. 景品交換所 the gift-coupon exchange counter. ⇨パチンコ

けいやくしゃいん【契約社員】 a contract(ed) worker[employee]; a temporary worker [employee]（臨時社員）. ☆「正社員」a full-fledged employee.「派遣社員」a temp.「出向社員」a loaned worker.

けいりゅう【渓流】 a mountain stream; a mountain torrent. ¶奥入瀬渓流（青森県）the Oirase Stream. ⇨川

けいれい【敬礼（30〜45度）】 (give) a salute; (make) a full bow. ⇨お辞儀

けいろうのひ【敬老の日】 Respect-for-the-Aged Day (the 3rd Monday of September). This national holiday was established in 1966 as a day to honor the aged[the elderly citizens], thank them for their past contributions to society and wish for their longevity and happiness. This day was also established to commemorate the enactment of the Law concerning Welfare for the Aged in 1966. Originally held on September 15, in 2003 it was changed to the 3rd Monday of September. 老人を敬愛し，過去の社会貢献に敬意を払い，長寿と幸福を祈願する. この祝日は1966年の老人福祉法の制定を記念して定められた. 元来9月15日に祝ったが2003年には9月の第3月曜日に変更された. ☆外国の人にはElderly People's Dayまたは Seniors' Day, Senior Citizens' Day のほうが理解しやすい.

ケーキバイキング an all-you-can-eat cake buffet

ゲーターまつり【ゲーター祭り】 the *Geta*[big wheel]-Tossing-Up Festival.（1月）. ⇨付記(1)「日本の祭り」

けおりもの【毛織物】 wool; woolen goods; woolen fabrics[textiles]; woolen cloth. ¶毛織物業 the woolen textile industry. 毛織物製造業者 a woolen manufacturer.

げくう【外宮】 the Outer Sanctuary of Ise Grand Shrine (dedicated to the God of a Rich Harvest). 伊勢神宮の外陣. 五穀豊穣の神を祀る. ☆「豊受大神宮」. ⇨内宮

げこ【下戸】 a non-drinker. 酒がほとんど飲

めない人. ⇔上戸

げこくじょう【下克上】 inferiors overthrowing[defeating] their superiors; the forcible displacement of a superior by his inferior. Lower rank people require high rank people to do something. 身分の下の者が上の者をおしのけ, しのぐこと.

けさ【袈裟】 a *kesa*; a Buddhist priest's surplice; a Buddhist priest's stole. A *kesa* is a rectangular cloth garment worn aslant over the robe of a Buddhist priest from the right shoulder down to the left armpit. 仏僧の上衣. 右肩から左脇下にかけて仏僧の衣服の上に斜めにまとう長方形 (oblong) の布製衣服. ☆ surplice「サープリス」(カトリック用語)儀式にて司祭・聖歌隊員などが着る短い白衣[上衣]. stole「ストラ」(カトリック用語)司祭が肩にかけてひざ下までたらす帯状の布.

げざ【下座】〔歌舞伎〕the musicians' box located on the left side of the stage (*shimote*)(seen from the audience). The music (called *geza-ongaku*) is played from the musicians' stall behind a black bamboo blind[grille] (*kuro-misu*) in the offstage room (in a kabuki play).「下手」(観客から見て舞台の左側)にある囃子方の席. 下座音楽は(歌舞伎の)舞台下手にある「黒御簾」の背後に座す囃子方が演奏する. ⇨黒御簾/下手

【下座音楽】〔歌舞伎〕the offstage background music for sound effects in a kabuki play. It is an ensemble of singers, *shamisen* players and percussionists of drums and gongs. 歌舞伎で音響効果を出すための舞台裏音楽. 囃子方, 三味線演奏者それに太鼓や鉦の打楽器演奏者などの合奏である.

けし【芥子】〔植物〕a poppy; an opium poppy. ケシ科の一年[二年]草. 薬草・麻薬などの原料. ¶芥子の種子 a poppy seed. (菓子類に用いる). ⇨金平糖. 雛芥子 a field[corn] poppy. 花芥子 a garden poppy.

げし【夏至】 the summer solstice; the season [day] marking midsummer. ⇨二十四節気

けしき【景色】 scenery (全体の); a view (個々の); a landscape (陸の); a seascape (海の). ⇨景勝地

けしょう【化粧】 makeup[make-up]. ¶化粧台 a dressing table; ⊛ vanity. 化粧鏡 a toilet mirror. 化粧室 a dressing room. ☆「手洗い」は bathroom; restroomなどという.

けしょうがみ【化粧紙】❶〔相撲〕a purifying paper. It is used by a *sumo* wrestler to remove perspiration or wipe over his body before a bout. 清めの紙. 力士が取組前に身体の汗をふき清めるために使う. ⇨力紙

❷ a cleansing tissue[paper] for the face; a facial tissue. 化粧直し用.

けしょうじお【化粧塩】〈料理〉salt sprinkled over fish before cooking; sprinkling salt on the fins when grilling fish. 調理「塩焼き」前に魚(アユ・アジ・タイなど)に塩をまくこと.「飾り塩」ともいう. ☆焼き上げを美しくするために用いる.

けしょうだち【化粧立ち】〔相撲〕false start (in a *sumo* wrestling bout). 力士が立ち上がる気がないのに形だけ立つこと.

けしょうまわし【化粧回し】〔相撲〕a *sumo* wrestler's ornamental[ceremonial] loincloth. It is worn by *sekitori sumo* wrestlers during the *sumo*-ring-entering ceremony that precedes each day of bouts. It is elaborately embroidered with individual elegant designs unique to each *sumo* wrestler. 力士の飾りたてた前垂れ型の回し. 関取が取組前の土俵入りの儀式に着用する. 各力士固有の優雅なデザインで華麗な刺繍入りの装飾が施されている. ⇨回し

けしょうみず【化粧水】〔相撲〕*sumo* wrestlers' drinking water (placed at the ringside).

け

The *sumo* wrestlers rinse their mouths with a dipper of this water which is usually offered by the winner of the preceding bout[match]. 土俵際にある飲み水. 柄杓1杯の水で口をゆすぐ. 通常は前の取組での勝者 (victor)から受ける. ⇨力水

げじん【外陣】 ⇨外陣

けずりぶし【削り節】 dried bonito flakes; shavings of dried bonito. 乾燥したカツオ節・イワシ節・サバ節などを薄く削ったもの. ⇨花鰹 / 鰹(鰹節)

げた【下駄】 (a pair of) *geta(s)*; (a pair of) Japanese wooden clogs[footgears]. *Geta* are rectangular wooden footgears with two wooden supports on the bottom[two raised wooden platforms under the sole], and V-shaped thongs between the big toe and the other toes on the top. *Geta* are often worn with a *kimono*. 長方形の木製の履物で，下面には2枚の木製歯[足底の2枚の木台]，上面には親指と他の足指との間にあるV字型の鼻緒 (straps) がすげてある. 下駄は着物といっしょに履くことが多い. ⇨鼻緒

げたばきじゅうたく【下駄履き住宅】 a house over a shop; a home with stores and offices on the lower floors. 店舗・事務所などの上にある家屋.

げたばきマンション【下駄履きマンション】 an apartment with shops and offices on the first[㊍ the ground] floor. 一階に店舗・事務所があるマンション［アパート］.

けっかふざ【結跏趺坐】 the sitting manner of Zen meditation. 座禅(またはヨーガ [the Yoga posture])をするときの座り方. ☆「趺」とは足の甲のこと，「結」とは趺を交差させること，「跏」とは反対の足の太ももの上に乗せること. したがって左足を右ももの上に乗せ，右足を左ももの上に乗せること. 「蓮華坐」(悟りを開いた者の坐法)ともいい，英語で the lotus position; a cross-legged sitting posture(in which the feet are placed on the opposite thighs) という. ⇨座禅

げっけいかん【月桂冠】 (win) a laurel crown [wreath]; (gain) a crown of laurel[honors]; (wear) the laurels.

げっけいじゅ【月桂樹】〔植物〕 a laurel (tree); a bay tree; a sweet bay. クスノキ科の常緑高木. 乾燥した葉「ベイリーフ」(a bay leaf) は料理の香料用.

けっこん【結婚】 wedding; marriage; matrimony. ¶結婚祝い a wedding gift[present]. 結婚参列者 guests[participants] at a wedding. 結婚式 a wedding[marriage] ceremony. 結婚資金 marriage fund; money saved up for marriage. 結婚適齢期 a marriageable age. 結婚届 a registration of one's marriage; a marriage registration form. 結婚年齢 the legal age for marriage. 結婚披露宴 a wedding banquet[reception] (held after the wedding ceremony). 結婚指輪 a marriage ring. できちゃった結婚 a shotgun marriage[wedding]. 事実上の結婚 de facto marriage; common-law wedding. 結婚詐欺 false[fake] marriage; marriage fraud[scam].
【関連語】『結婚記念日』(a wedding anniversary):

紙婚式 paper wedding (1周年).

綿婚式 cotton wedding (2周年).

革婚式 leather wedding (3周年).

花婚式 flower wedding (4周年).

木婚式 wooden wedding (5周年).

鉄婚式 iron[steel] wedding (6周年).

銅婚式 bronze wedding (7周年).

錫婚式 tin wedding (10周年).

水晶婚式 crystal wedding (15周年).

磁器婚式 china wedding (20周年).

銀婚式 silver wedding (25周年).

真珠婚式 pearl wedding (30周年).

珊瑚婚式 coral wedding (35周年).

ルビー婚式 ruby wedding（40周年）.

サファイア婚式 sapphire wedding（45周年）.

金婚式 golden wedding（50周年）.

エメラルド婚式 emerald wedding（55周年）.

ダイアモンド婚式 diamond wedding（英 60周年 [米 75周年]）.

げっしゃ【月謝】〔華道〕a monthly tuition fee (paid for flower arrangement).

げっしょく【月食・月蝕】 a lunar eclipse（正式用語）; an eclipse of the moon. ¶皆既月食 a total lunar eclipse; a total eclipse of the moon. 部分月食 a partial lunar eclipse; a partial eclipse of the moen. ⇨日食

けっとうち【血糖値】 (test) the blood-sugar level; (check) the level of sugar in the blood.

けまり【蹴鞠】*kemari*. ❶〈まり〉a kick-ball (usually made of deer skin). 通常は鹿の皮で作る.
❷〈遊戯〉 an ancient Japanese imperial kick-ball game played by court nobles in the Heian period. A leather ball is kicked back and forth into the air by several players forming a circle. They kick a ball by turns to keep it from touching the ground. 平安時代, 宮廷で貴人 (courtiers) が数人で輪になって交代しながらまりを蹴り続ける遊戯.

けむし【毛虫】〔植物〕a (hairy) caterpillar.

けやき【欅】〔植物〕a *keyaki* (tree); (a Japanese) zelkova (tree). ニレ科の落葉高木. 日本特産. 材は硬く良質のため建築・器具用. ☆清水寺の舞台は139本の欅作りの支柱で構成されている. また東京・表参道の「ケヤキ並木」(Omote-sando Avenue lined with the zelkova trees)は有名.

けやり【毛槍】 a long spear with bunches of feathery ornaments attached to the tip. It is carried upright by spear-bearers at the feudal lord's procession. 束にした鳥の毛の飾りを鞘の先 (spearhead) につけた長い槍. 大名行列で, 先頭を行く槍持ちが持つ.

けらい【家来】⇨家臣

けん【県】a prefecture. ¶宮崎県 Miyazaki Prefecture. ⇨府. 県庁 a prefectural government[office]. ⇨県庁. 県花 a prefectural flower. 県政 a prefectural administration. 県人 a native of prefecture; a person who comes from (Miyazaki) Prefecture. 県制度 the prefectural system. (1871年確立). ⇨廃藩置県. 県庁［府庁・道庁］所在地 a prefectural capital; the capital of the prefecture; the seat of a prefectural government. ☆宮崎の県庁所在地 the capital of Miyazaki Prefecture. 県境 the prefectural boundary; the boundary[border] between the two prefectures. ☆群馬と新潟の県境 (be located on) the border between Gunma and Niigata prefectures.

けん【剣】 a sword. ¶剣客 a master swordsman; an expert in *kendo*. ⇨剣道. 剣劇 a sowrd-fighting play. 剣の達人 a master of swordplay. 剣豪 a great swordsman.

けん【間】 a *ken*. A *ken* is equivalent to 1.82 meters. (1.82m). A *ken* is equal to six *shaku* or about six feet. (6尺. 約6フィート). 長さの単位. ¶(部屋の)間数 the length[width, breadth] (of the room) in *ken*. 一間の床の間 an one-*ken*-wide alcove. ⇨床の間

げんえん【減塩】 the reduction of salt. ☆「減塩の」low-salt; reduced-salt. ¶減塩醤油 low-salt *shoyu*[soy sauce]; reduced-salt *shoyu*. 減塩食 low-salt diet[food]. 減塩食品 reduced-salt food; food with a low-salt content.

けんえんけん【嫌煙権】the right to a smoke-free environment; the right to live free from others's tabacco smoke.

けんがい【懸崖】a precipice; an overhanging

cliff. ¶懸崖作りの菊 cascaded chrsysan-
themums in a pot.

けんぎゅう(せい)【牽牛(星)】〔アルタイル
星〕 the Cowherd Star; (天体) Altair. ⇨
七夕

けんけん(あそび)【けんけん(遊び)】 a hop-
scotch played by hopping on one foot in a
square map drawn on the ground. 地面に描
いた四角の地図の上を片足でぴょんぴょん
跳んで遊ぶ石蹴り遊び.

げんこう【元寇】 the Mongolian Invasions;
Mongolian attacks on Japan. Khubilai
Khan, the first Mongol Emperor of China,
sent the naval expeditions to Japan twice
in 1274 and 1281. 日本に対する元(世祖フ
ビライハンの時代)の国の侵略. 1274年(文
永11年:文永の役)と1281年(弘安4年:弘
安の役)に襲来. ☆北条時宗時代の事件.

げんごう【元号】 an (imperial) era name; the
(official) name of an era. The traditional
Japanese era name[era-naming] system
is based on the reigning emperor. At the
accession of an emperor, an ideal phrase is
chosen from the Chinese classics. 元号は天
皇の即位に基づいている. 天皇が即位する
ときに古典から理想的なことばを選ぶ.
【関連語】(7世紀から使用. 主な年号名)「大
化」(645~650).「天平」(729~749).「延喜」
(901~923).「保元」(1156~1159).「平治」
(1159~1160).「文永」(1264~1274).「天正」
(1573~1592).「慶長」(1596~1615).「元和」
(1615~1624).「寛永」(1624~1644).「元禄」
(1688~1704).「享保」(1716~1736).「寛政」
(1789~1801).「天保」(1830~1844).「安政」
(1854~1860).「慶応」(1865~1868).「明治」
(1868~1912).「大正」(1912~1926).「昭和」
(1926~1989).「平成」(1989~2019).「令和」
(2019~)

けんこくきねんのひ【建国記念の日】 Na-
tional Foundation Day (February 11).
This national holiday was established in
1966 and first held in 1967 as a day to
celebrate the establishment of the nation
and to foster a love for the country. From
1872 to 1948, February 11 was known as
Kigensetsu, a holiday commemorating the
legendary enthronement of Japan's first
Emperor Jinmu who founded the imperial
line in 660 BC (according to the *Nihonshoki*). 1966年(昭和41年)に国民の祝日に
加えられ, 翌1967年2月11日から適用さ
れた. 日本の建国を記念し, また愛国心を
養うために祝う. 1872年から1948年まで
は「紀元節」として, 伝説上の初代天皇(紀
元前660年に皇族家系を築いた神武天皇)
即位を記念する祝日であった. ⇨紀元節

げんごろう【源五郎】〔虫〕a (Japanese) diving
beetle. ゲンゴロウ科の昆虫.

けんさやく【検査役】〔相撲〕a ringside judge;
a referee adviser; an adviser to a *sumo*
referee. 土俵の下にいる相撲の勝負審判.
現在は「審判委員」と改称. ⇨審判委員

けんざん【剣山】〔華道〕 a *kenzan*; a frog; a
pinholder; a metal plate with many needles
for holding flowers[plants]. *A kenzan* is a
needle-point holder used to fix branches
or stems in arranging flowers in a shallow
container[bowl]. 花[植物]を生けるために
太い針を植えつけた(鉄製)板. 浅い水盤
で生け花の枝[茎]を固定するために用い
る. ⇨七宝. ¶剣山おこし a needle-point
straightener (used in flower arranging)

げんさんち【原産地】 the place[country] of
origin; the original home; home. ¶茶の原
産地 the (original) home of tea. 原産地表
示 the indication of the place of origin.

げんしばくだん【原子爆弾】 an atom(ic)
bomb; an A-bomb[atom bomb] dropped on
Hiroshima and Nagasaki in 1945. ☆第二
次世界大戦の時, 広島には1945年8月6日,
長崎には1945年8月9日に投下された. ⇨
ポツダム宣言

けんしゅ【原酒】 unprocessed[unblended] *sake*(日本酒). ⇨生酒

けんじゅつ【剣術】 swordsmanship; a Japanese fencing. ☆「剣術」(刀剣で戦う術)は12世紀頃武家階級の間で発展し, 室町時代(15世紀)には剣術の流派が生まれる. 江戸時代には竹刀を使った練習が主流になる. 明治時代には精神訓練の一環として「剣道」(竹刀で勝敗を決める武道)が発展した. ⇨剣道

けんじょ【見所】〔能楽〕the seating area for the audience (in the Noh theater). 能楽堂における観客席.

けんしょうきん【懸賞金】〔相撲〕cash prize (for a *sumo* winner); prize money (based on sponsorship of the bout). The banners of the sponsors are paraded around the *sumo* ring prior to the bout. Prize money is awarded to the winner upon the referee's ritual fan. 勝利者に与えられる賞金. スポンサーの旗が試合前に土俵周辺を廻る. 行司の軍配があがった勝者に与えられる.

けんじょうご【謙譲語】 a modest term [expression]; an honorific word expressing the speaker's humility. ⇨敬語

けんじょうのびとく【謙譲の美徳】the virtue of modesty.

けんすい【建水】〔茶道〕a waste-water container[㊤ slop basin] used in the tea ceremony; a vessel used to dispose of the water after rinsing a tea bowl in the tea ceremony. 茶の湯で茶碗のすすぎ水を捨てる器.「水こぼし」ともいう.

けんずいし【遣隋使】 (dispatch of) a Japanese envoy to Sui Dynasty China[to Sui Court in China]. 中国の隋に派遣した使節. ☆中国の文物輸入のため最初に小野妹子を派遣する. 計4回.

げんせいかえん【原生花園】the Wild Flower Garden (サロベツ原生花園・北海道)

げんせいりん【原生林】 a virgin forest(処女林); a primeval forest(古代以来の森林). ¶屋久杉の原生林(鹿児島県)virgin forests of Yakusugi, Japanese cedars[crytomerias] in Yakushima Island. ☆ユネスコ世界自然遺産(1993年登録). ⇨杉

げんせんちょうしゅう【源泉徴収】 income tax withholding at the source; deduction of tax from income at the source; tax collected[withheld] at the source; collection of taxes through withholding.

けんだい【見台】〔歌舞伎〕〔文楽〕a bookrest; a bookstand; a small decorative wooden desk used for placing a book (about 50 centimeters high). A narrator places his script[A musician places his score] on a bookstand in kabuki and bunraku dramas. 書見台. 装飾をほどこした小さな木机. 歌舞伎・文楽で語り手が台本[楽士が楽譜]を置く台.

けんだま【剣玉】❶〈玉〉a cup and ball. ❷〈遊び〉(play at) a cup-and-ball game.

けんちょう【県庁】 the prefectural governments(自治体の行政府); the prefectural offices(事務所); the prefectural officials [authorities](役人). ⇨県. ¶県庁舎 prefectural office building.

けんちんじる【巻繊汁】 Japanese vegetable chowder[stew]; *kenchin*-style soup cooked with shredded vegetables (such as carrots, white radish, burdock roots) and fried *tofu*[bean curd]. 細切りにした野菜類(人参・大根・牛蒡など)を油で炒め, その中に焼き豆腐を加えた汁物.

けんていきょうかしょ【検定教科書】 a textbook approved by the Ministry of Education, Culture, Sports, Science and Technology. ☆「教科書検定」は textbook authorization; textbook screening.

けんていしけん【検定試験】licensing examination(免許授与試験); proficiency test (資格試験). ¶観光英語検定試験 Tourism

English Proficiency Test.

けんとう【献灯】 a votive lantern (lit in honor of a Shinto god or Buddha). 社寺の神仏に奉納する灯明.

けんどう【剣道】 *kendo*; traditional martial art of swordsmanship; Japanese-style fencing (based on the techniques of the two-handed sword of *samurai*). *Kendo* is a Japanese martial art with a bamboo sword (*shinai*). The contestants[*kendo* fencers] wear protective outfits[equipments] including a protective face mask (*men*) with a throat protector, arm guards (*kote*), waist protector (*tare*) and chest protector (*do*). (武士の諸手遣いの操刀術を基本とする)日本古来の武道. 剣道は竹刀を使った武術競技である. 競技者は突き垂れのある「面」(head protector; headgear[helmet] to protect the face),「籠手[小手]」(arm and hand protectors; gloves[gauntlets] to protect the arm and hand),「垂」(thigh[waist] protector),「胴」(chest[body] armor protector)の防具を着用する. ☆「面」には〈面金〉headgear grill.〈面紐〉headgear cord.〈面ぶとん〉cloth part of headgear. 喉を守る「垂」は「突き垂れ」(throat protector). ⇨剣術 / 竹刀

【剣道家】 a *kendo* fighter[swordsman].「剣士」ともいう.

面
小手
竹刀
胴
垂
剣道着

【剣道達人】 a *kendo* fencing master [swordsman].「剣豪」「剣客」ともいう.

【剣道審判】 a referee. Matches are monitored by a chief referee and two sub referees. 1人の主審と2人の副審で審判する.

【剣道着】 a *kendo* protective padded clothing. Fencers wear *kendo* clothing[jacket] and a *hakama*[pleated skirt-like trousers] under the body armor. The cotton towel is wrapped around the head, under the helmet(*men*). 防具の下には剣道着と袴を着用する. 面の下には手ぬぐいを巻く.

【剣道試合】 a *kendo* (Japanese fencing) match. *Kendo* matches last five minutes and total three points. The winner is the first competitor to score two points out of three full points. A point is scored by a successful strike or thrust to certain parts of an opponent's armor. 試合は5分間で3本勝負. 先に2本をとれば勝者. 相手の防具の特定の部位を上手に打突すれば得点になる. ☆『打突部位』は「面」(head),「胴」(body[trunk]),「籠手」(glove[forearm]).「突き」(thrust to the throat). 公式大会の決勝戦での試合時間は10分である.

けんとうし【遣唐使】 (dispatch of) a Japanese envoy sent to Tang Dynasty China (from the 7th through the 9th century); Japanese diplomatic delegation to China during the Tang Dynasty. (7-9世紀)日本から中国の唐朝 (to the Tang Court in China)へ制度・文物の輸入のため派遣された使節. ☆630年初派遣. 894年菅原道真(845-903)により廃止.

けんとうろう【献灯籠】 a dedicatory lantern in a shrine or temple. ⇨灯籠

けんぱい【献杯・献盃】❶ offering a person a cup of *sake* (in honor of a person). (敬意を表して)相手に杯を差し出すこと.

❷ drinking to a dead person's memory (at funeral). (葬儀などのとき)死者の霊に対し

て杯を差し出すこと.

げんばく【原爆】 A-bomb; atom(ic) bomb. ¶原爆犠牲者 an A-bomb victim. 原爆記念館 the Atomic Bomb Memorial Museum. 原爆記念日 Atomic Bomb Memorial Day. 原爆死没者慰霊碑(と碑文) Memorial Cenotaph for the Atomic Bomb Victims (and its Epitaph). 原爆症 Atomic-bomb illness; radiation sickness; illness caused by atomic-bomb radiation. 原爆ドーム the A-bomb Dome; the Atomic Bomb Memorial Dome (testifying to its tragic history). (ユネスコ世界文化遺産)

けんばん【検番・見番】 an assignation office for *geisha(s)*. 芸者を割り当てる事務所. ☆芸者への取次ぎや送迎, 玉代の清算などをする. ⇨玉代

けんぱくしょ【建白書】 (submit) a (written) petition (to a superior). 上役などに自分の意見を陳情する書.

けんぶ【剣舞】 (perform) a sword dance (to the accompaniment of a recitation of a Chinese poem). (詩吟に合わせて)剣を抜いて舞うこと.

げんぶがん【玄武岩】 basalt; an extrusive volcanic rock. 柱状をなす岩. ☆火山岩の一種. 兵庫県の玄武洞の名に因んで命名された. ¶玄武岩台地 a basaltic plateau.

げんぷく【元服】 a ceremony to celebrate a young man's coming of age (in olden times); an ancient ritual to mark a young man's attainment of manhood. 昔, 男子の成人を祝った儀式. ☆髪を結い, 衣服を改め, 冠をかぶせる儀. 奈良・平安時代には12歳から16歳までの男子は前髪を剃った (shave off one's forelock). 封建時代には刀を与え, 衣装と髪型を変えた. ⇨成人の日 /裳着(女性)

けんぽうかいせい【憲法改正(憲法第9条)】 a constitutional amendment[revision] (article 9 of the Constitution). ☆「改憲派」advocates of the constitutional amendment. 「護憲派」supporters of the current constitution.

けんぽうかいせいろんぎ【憲法改正論議】 the debate over the revision of the Constitution.

けんぽうきねんび【憲法記念日】 Constitution Memorial Day. (May 3). This national holiday was established in 1948 as a day to commemorate the new constitution of Japan, which was promulgated in 1946 and came into effect in 1947. 1946年に公布, 1947年に施行された日本国新憲法を記念して祝う日.

けんぼうしょう【健忘症】 amnesia(記憶喪失; 病名); forgetfulness. 〈人〉amnesiac; a person who has a poor memory.

げんまい【玄米】 brown rice; unpolished rice; unmilled[uncleaned] rice. もみがらをとっただけでまだ精米していない米. ⇨白米
〔食品〕玄米食 meal cooked with unpolished[brown] rice; diet of unpolished[brown] rice (玄米で炊いたご飯). 玄米茶 brown rice tea; coarse green tea mixed with roasted brown[popped] rice (炒ってはじかせた米と混ぜた茶). ⇨茶. 玄米パン a whole-rice bread[bun]; a bread[bun] made with brown rice(玄米で作ったパン)

けんむのしんせい【建武の新政】 the *Kenmu* Restoration; the political innovation introduced by Emperor Go-Daigo. The new government power of direct imperial rule restored to Emperor Go-Daigo at its center after the defeat of the Kamakura shogunate. 鎌倉幕府滅亡後, 後醍醐天皇による天皇親政の復古政治. ☆1333-1336年に展開.「建武の中興」ともいう.

げんや【原野】 〈平野〉a plain; 〈荒野〉wasteland; a wilderness; the wilds. ¶サロベツ原野(北海道)(the) Sarobetsu (genya)

Plain. ⇨平野／湿原

げんろくそで【元禄袖】 a short *kimono* sleeve (worn by women). 女性用の和服の短い袖. 短めのたもとに丸みをつけたもの.

こ

こ［みずうみ］【湖】 a lake. ¶琵琶湖 Lake Biwa. 地底湖 an underground lake(龍泉洞・岩手県). 海水湖 a salt-water lake(網走湖). 淡水湖 a freshwater lake (猪苗代湖). 凍結湖 an ice-covered lake(網走湖・ワカサギ釣りが有名). 人造湖 a man-made lake; the lake used as man-made water reservoirs (黒部湖・多摩湖・狭山湖など). 淡水と海水混合の湖 the part-fresh and part-salt water lake (サロマ湖). 日本三大湖 the Three Largest Lakes in Japan (琵琶湖［滋賀県］・霞ヶ浦［茨城県・千葉県］・サロマ湖［北海道］). ⇨沼／池

ご【碁】 (the game of) Japanese *go*. *Go* is also commonly called *igo*. Two players take turns[alternate] placing round black and white stones on the intersection of the grids[lines] on a *go* wooden board. They try to take each other's stones or occupy their field on the board. The player with more territory than one's opponents is the winner. 2人の対局者が碁盤上に交互に黒と白の石を打つ. 碁盤上で相手の石と空間を相互に取り合う. 自石で囲い取った碁盤目の数によって勝敗を争う. 通称「囲碁」. ⇨囲碁

【関連語】「碁石」a *go* stone[piece] (black and white).「碁会所」a *go* players'club; a *go* parlor. ☆「対局者」は a *go* player.「碁笥」a bowl to hold *go* stones.「碁笥の蓋」the lid of a *go* bowl (used to place captured stones so that the other player can see them).「碁盤」a (square wooden) *go* board. It has 361 lattice points formed by

19 vertical and 19 horizontal lines. (碁を打つ正方形で木製の台. 縦横19本ずつの線, 合計361の目がある)

こい【鯉】〔魚〕 a carp. (復 carp, carps). コイ科の淡水魚. ¶緋鯉 a red carp. 真鯉 a black carp. 錦鯉 a varicolored carp.

〔料理・食品〕鯉の洗い sliced raw carp[slices of raw carp] chilled in icy water(冷水で冷やした鯉の刺身). ⇨洗い. 鯉こく carp soup; (thin round slices of) carp cooked in thick *miso*[bean paste] soup(鯉を(輪切りにして)煮込んだ味噌汁)

【鯉の滝登り】 a carp swimming up a waterfall. The carp is a symbol of strength and courage because it can climb upstream against rapid currents and overcome all obstacles. 鯉は激流をさかのぼり障害を克服するので強さと勇気の象徴である. ⇨鯉 幟. ☆〔中国の伝説〕黄河 (the Yellow River)の三門峡(Three Gate Narrows)にある滝を鯉が飛び越えて「竜」(dragon)になったという伝説.

こいぐち【鯉口】 the mouth of a sword scabbard[sheath]. 刀の鞘口. ☆鯉が口をあけた形に似ていることに由来. ¶鯉口を切る loose one's sword slightly in the scabbard[sheath] for swift [immediate] use. 刀をすぐに抜けるように (so that it can be swiftly[immediately] drawn)鯉口をゆるめる.

こいくちしょうゆ【濃口醤油】 strong[dark]-flavored *shoyu*[soy sauce]; rich-colored and strong-tasted *shoyu*; *shoyu* of rich color and taste. つけ醤油やかけ醤油などに用いる. ⇦薄口醤油

こいちゃ【濃茶】❶〔茶道〕thick powdered tea; pasty green tea (used in the tea ceremony). In the tea ceremony, *koicha* (prepared by the host) is sometimes passed among several guests in a single[the same] tea bowl while *usucha* is served individually.

Koicha is served in the earlier stage of the procedures of the tea-serving manners in the tea ceremony. 抹茶の量を多くしてたてた茶. 茶の湯では主人がたてた濃茶は通常は同一の茶碗から数人で回し飲みするが, 薄茶は各人に出される. 濃茶は茶の湯のお手前上最初の段階で出される. ⇨薄茶. ⇨主菓子. ¶濃茶手前 formal manners observed when serving thick powdered tea in the tea ceremony. 茶の湯で濃茶を出す作法.

❷〈濃く入れた茶〉strong tea. ⇨薄茶

こいのぼり【鯉幟】 carp-shaped streamers; streamers in the shape of the carps (made of paper or cloth). A set of carp-shaped streamers[a black male carp and a red female carp] are traditionally hoisted on the top of a tall[long] pole erected in the yard for the Boys' Festival with the hope that boys can be as strong and courageous as carp. The carp is a symbol of strength and courage in Japan because it swims up a torrent and ascends a waterfall. 紙または布で鯉の形につくった[真鯉と緋鯉の]吹き流し. 男児が鯉のように強くまた勇敢になるようにとの願いをこめて端午の節句(Boys' Festival)には中庭に鯉幟一組が高い竿に揚げられる. 鯉は急流をさかのぼって泳ぎ, また滝を上るため日本では強さと勇気の象徴である. ⇨鯉(「鯉の滝登り」)

こいも【小芋】〈里芋〉a taro;〈芋の子〉a taro tuber bud; daughter tuber[corn] of a taro.

-こう[みなと]〔～港〕the port; the harbor [英 harbour]. ¶神戸港 Kobe Port; the port of Kobe. 横浜港 Yokohama Harbor [Harbour]; the harbor of Yokohama. ⇨港

こう【香】〔茶道〕(an) incense (used to enjoy various fragrances). It is burned by tea devotees before guests enter the tearoom (in the tea ceremony). 多種の香を楽しむお香. 客が茶室に入る前に茶人は香をたく,

通称「お香」. ⇨香道

ごう【合】 a *go*. ❶ A *go* equals 0.18 liters.(0.18リットル).〈量目の単位〉1升の10分の1;〈面積の単位〉0.33㎡. ¶1合徳利 a ceramic *sake* bottle with a capacity of one *go*. 酒1合 a *go*[cup] of *sake*. 1合枡 a measuring box of one *go*. 米1合 one *go*[cup] of rice.

❷ a stage; a station. 登山路の10分の1. 頂上までの道のりを10区分にしたその1つ. ¶富士山の5合目 the 5th station[stage] of Mt. Fuji; the 5th station[stage] (of 10) on the path to Mt. Fuji's summit.

こうあん【公案】 a *koan*; a catechetical [paradoxical] question for Zen meditation; a conundrum for Zen meditation. A *koan* is asked in Zen Buddhism to attain spiritual enlightenment. An intuitive dialogue is opened between the master and his disciples as an exercise for the mind [mental] training. 禅の瞑想時に行う教理質問[問答]. 禅宗で参禅者が悟りを開く(to obtain a direct realization of truth)ように考えさせる教理問答が行われる. 心を磨くために師弟間で直接的な[瞬時にものの本質を感じとる]対話が交わされる. ☆ catechetical 圏「教理問答の」. catechism 图(カトリック用語)「教理問答書；公教要理」(宗教的教理の質疑応答式の教科書)

こういけいしょう【皇位継承】 the Imperial succession; the accession to the Imperial Throne. ¶皇位継承第一位 first in line to the Imperial Throne. 皇位継承順位 the order of the succession to the Imperial Throne.

こういしょう【後遺症】 an aftereffect; a sequela (徳 sequelae). ¶交通事故の後遺症 the aftereffect of a traffic accident.

こううりょう【降雨量】〈降水量〉 (the amount of) rainfall; precipitation(専門用語)

こうえいとばく【公営賭博】 publicly-controlled[-managed] gambling; munici-

こ

pally-operated gambling(市町村の).

こうえん【公園】 a park; a public garden. ☆固有名詞の場合は冠詞をつけない. ¶日比谷公園 Hobiya Park. 日光国立公園 Nikko National Park. 国立公園 a national park. 国定公園 a quasi-national park. 県立公園 a prefectural park, 州立公園 a provincial park. 市立公園 a municipal park. 記念公園 a memorial park.

こうがい【笄】 an ornamental hairpin (worn on a Japanese-style coiffure). 日本髪にさす飾り. ☆通常，金・銀・べっこうなどでできている.

こうかがくスモッグ【光化学スモッグ】 photochemical smog.

こうかくるい【甲殻類】shellfish. カニやエビなどの甲羅 (shell)をもつ生物. ⇨かい

こうぎ【公儀】 the imperial court (朝廷)；the shogunate (幕府). 「御公儀」ともいう.

こうきょ【皇居】 the Imperial Palace. It is situated on the site of the former Edo Castle, the home of Tokugawa Ieyasu. It has been the official residence of the Imperial Family since the Meiji Restoration of 1868. 旧江戸城の跡地にある. 1868年の明治維新後皇居の正式の居城であった. 「御所」ともいう. ☆天皇を中心とした一族のことを「皇室」(the Imperial Household) または「皇族」(the Imperial Family)という. ¶皇居前広場 the Palace Plaza[Square]. 皇居御殿 the official residence of the Imperial Family. 皇居一般参賀 a congratulatory visit to the Imperial Family at the Imperial Palace. 【関連語】1968年に現在の皇居が竣工される. 「表御座所」(公務を行う) the emperor's office for official duties. 「正殿」(公式儀式を行う) the hall for official ceremonies. 「豊明殿」(国賓の晩餐を行う) the hall for banquets entertaining state guests. 「長和殿」(接客を行う) the hall for receptions.

こうげい【工芸】 (artistic)handicraft(s); industrial art. ¶伝統工芸 traditional handicrafts; a traditional industrial art. 美術工芸 arts and crafts. 工芸品 an art work; a craft object[item]; craft products. 工芸美術 applied fine arts. 工芸家 an artisan; a craftsman(男性)；a craftswoman (女性)；industrial artists.

こうけん【後見】〔歌舞伎〕〔能楽〕a *Koken*; an on-stage assistant to an actor (in kabuki and Noh plays). A *koken* is a black-attired assistant who helps an actor (especially the main character) on the stage. 役者(主に主役)の舞台公演中，その背後で黒衣装を着て演技の世話をする人 (prompter). 「後見役」ともいう. 黒子よりは威厳がある. ⇨黒子. ☆「未成年者の後見人」は (a) guardian.

こうげん[**こうち**]【高原[高地]】 the highlands(山岳地帯) (⇔ lowlands); the heights (高地・高台)；a plateau (複 plateaus, plateaux) (山の台地)；a tableland. ¶那須高原(栃木県) Nasu Highlands; the highlands of Nasu. 志賀高原(長野県) Shiga Heights. ⇨平野 / 原野 / 平 / 湿原

こうごう【皇后】 an empress. ¶皇后陛下 Her Majesty[H. M.] the Empress. ⇔天皇陛下

こうごう【香合】 an incense holder[burner]. An incense container with a perforated lid is made of porcelain or lacquer with artistic designs. In the tearoom, incense is burned in a container using a charcoal fire. 香の入れ物. 穴のあいた蓋付きの容器は芸術的なデザインをほどこした磁器または漆器でつくられている. 茶室では炭火を使って風炉で香がたかれる. ☆香合には香を3つ入れておき，2つは炭火に入れて，残りは順に鑑賞する. ⇨香道

こうこく【皇国】 the Empire. 天皇の治める国. ☆「日本」の旧称.

【皇国史観】 the historical view of Japan

based on the reigns of the "living-god" emperors.「現人神」の天皇による統治に基づいた日本国の歴史観. ⇨現人神

こうこつのひと【恍惚の人】 a senile person; a person suffering from senility[senile dementia]; a person in one's second childhood.

ごうこん【合コン】❶ a student get-together（親睦会）; a mixer（懇談会）; a joint party (sponsored) by two or more students from several colleges. 学生の社交の会.
❷ a matchmaking party (held) in groups; （英）a speed-dating. 男女の出会いの場

こうさつ【高札】 an official notice board (in the Edo period). The board was used to make official announcements by authorities of the Edo period. 江戸時代の掲示版. 江戸時代の為政者が公示するために路上に立てた掲示板.

こうざんしょくぶつ【高山植物】 an alpine wild plant; the alpine flora.

こうざんどうぶつ【高山動物】 an alpine wild animal; the alpine fauna.

こうし【子牛】〔動物〕a calf. (復 calves). ⇨牛 ☆「子牛の肉」は veal. 日本では10か月未満.「食肉用の子牛」は veal calf; （米）vealer. ¶子牛の皮 calf leather; calfskin（高級品）

こうし【格子】a lattice（戸・窓などの）; a grid（鉄の）. ☆「格子戸」(a lattice(d) door)の略. ¶格子細工 latticework; trellis-work. 格子縞 checkered pattern; checkers; cross stripes. 格子模様 a latticework. 格子窓（外から見えにくい）a lattice(d) window (hard to see from the outside)

こうじ【麹】 *koji*; malt. ☆米・麦・大豆などを蒸して, これに麹かびを繁殖させたもの. 酒・醤油・味噌などをつくるのに用いる. ¶米麹 malted rice. 大麦麹 malted barley. 大豆麹 malted soybean. 麹漬け food preserved in malted rice and salt（米麹と塩で漬けた食品）

ごうし【合祀】 collective enshrinement (of two or more gods or human spirits at a single shrine). （多くの神や人間の霊を一か所の神社に）合わせ祀ること. ¶合祀する（靖国神社に戦争被害者［戦死者］の霊を祀る）enshrine together[collectively](the spirits of the war victims[the war dead at Yasukuni Shrine]). ⇨エー級［A級］戦犯靖国合祀

こうしつ【皇室】 the Imperial Household（皇室）; the Imperial Family（皇族）; the family headed by the Emperor. The Imperial Household has no surname but uses appellation prince or princess (called *miya*) granted by the Emperor. 皇室には名字がないので天皇から与えられる「宮」の称号を用いる.「皇族」（天皇を中心とした一族）ともいう. ⇨皇族. ¶皇室会議 the Imperial household council[Imperial conference] (presided over by the prime minister). 皇室の紋章 the Imperial crests; the crests of the Imperial family. ⇨菊の御紋. 皇室典範 the Imperial Household Law. 皇室の男系［女系］the male [female] line of the Imperial Family.
【関連語】「上皇陛下」His Majesty the Emperor Emeritus.「上皇后陛下」Her Majesty the Empress Emerita.「天皇陛下」His Majesty the Emperor.「皇后陛下」Her Majesty the Empress.「天皇皇后両陛下」Their Majesties the Emperor and Empress.「大行天皇」the Late Emperor.「皇太后陛下」Her Majesty the Empress Dowager.「皇太子殿下」His Imperial Highness the Crown Prince.「皇太子妃」the Imperial Highness the Crown Princess.「〇〇宮様［宮殿下］」His Imperial Highness Prince 〇〇.「〇〇宮妃［宮妃殿下］」Her Imperial Highness Princess 〇〇.「〇〇宮ご夫妻」Their Imperial Highness Prince and Princess 〇〇.

こうじょう【口上】 an address (on the stage); a verbal massage (from the stage); a prologue（芝居の）. 舞台に出て述べるあいさつ. ¶口上を述べる deliver an address[a (verbal) message] (from the stage). ⇨襲名披露

こうしんりょう【香辛料】 (cooking) spice. ☆和食の香辛料には山葵，生姜，柚子，木の芽などがある. ¶香辛料で調味した料理 food seasoned with spice.

こうせき【皇籍】 membership in the Imperial Family. ¶皇籍を離脱する leave the Imperial Family; renounce one's membership in the Imperial Family.

ごうせつちたい【豪雪地帯】 a heavy snowfall area[district]; an area of heavy snowfall.

こうそ【皇祖】 the ancestor[founder] of the Imperial Family of Japan; Emperor Jinmu, the founder of the Imperial Family. 天皇家の先祖. 特に神武天皇のこと. ¶皇祖神 god-ancestors of the Imperial Family. 天皇家の代々の神々.

こうぞく【皇族】〈全体〉the Imperial Family; royalty;〈個人〉a member of the Imperial Family; an Imperial prince[princess]. ⇨皇室. ¶皇族会議 a convocation of the male members of the Imperial Family.

こうた【小唄】a *kouta*; a traditional Japanese short song with *shamisen* accompaniment; a short popular song of humor and irony sung to the accompaniment of *shamisen*. A thin-shafted *shamisen* is used for a *kouta* by plucking with the fingers instead of a plectrum. This short popular song may accompany traditional dances by *geisha* and amateur performers. 三味線の伴奏に合わせて歌う日本古来の洒落や風刺の歌謡. 細棹の三味線を用い，撥の代わりに爪弾きをする. 短い大衆歌曲で，芸者や素人芸人の舞いを伴うことがある. ⇨端唄 / 長唄 / 地唄

こうたいごう【皇太后】 the Empress Dowager（天皇に対して）.

こうたいし【皇太子】 the Crown Prince. ¶皇太子殿下 His Imperial Highness the Crown Prince.

こうたいしひ【皇太子妃】 the Crown Princess. ¶皇太子妃殿下 Her Imperial Highness the Crown Princess.

こうだん【講談】 a *kodan*; a historical storytelling[narrative]; a rhythmical and humorous storytelling of historical events. A professional storyteller (*kodan-shi*) narrates historical episodes in a unique tone before an audience[on the stage], while tapping a low desk[small table] (*shakudai*) with a paper-covered folded fan (*harisen*) for beating out rhythm. 軍記などの話に調子をつけておもしろく語り聞かせる寄席演芸. 「講談師」は調子をあげるために「張り扇」で低い「釈台」を打ちながら，聴衆の前で[舞台上で]軍記などを独特の調子で語る. 例「水戸黄門漫遊談」

こうち【高地】 the highlands（高地地方）; the heights（高台）; a plateau（山の台地）. ⇔低地.

こうちよさこいまつり 【高知よさこいまつり】 the Yosakoi-Folk-Song Parade Festival at Kochi City. (8月). ⇨付記(1)「日本の祭り」

こうちゃ【紅茶】 (a cup of) tea; (a pot of) tea; black tea. ☆日常生活では単にteaを用いる. ¶紅茶茶碗 a teacup.

こうでん【香典・香奠】an obituary[a funeral] monetary offering; an obituary[a funeral] gift of money (given in place of an incense or flowers). *Koden* is a condolence monetary gift (offered) to the departed soul, which is usually given to the bereaved family of the deceased by those attending a funeral. (香代・花代として)死者の霊前に供

える金品．通常は会葬者から遺族に贈られる．「香料」(incense money)ともいう．神道では「榊料」または「玉串料」という．☆金額は故人との付き合い(relationship)によって異なる．また事前に用意しておいた旨を避けるため「新札」(new bills)は使用しない．⇨香料．¶**香典帳** a recording book of money donations made by mourners at a funeral (or wake). 葬儀（または通夜）で会葬者からの贈与金を記録する帳面．

【**香典返し**】 a return gift for an obituary money received; a gift in return for a funeral monetary offering received. The bereaved family of the deceased makes a return for obituary monetary offerings to people who have made a funeral monetary offering. 香典をくれた人に香典返礼として品物をおくること (gives a present in return for a funeral offering). またその品物．⇨半返し / お悔やみ

【**香典袋**】 an envelope for a monetary gift at a funeral; an envelope for a funeral offering; an envelope containing an obituary monetary gift. Mourners wrap a sum of money in an envelope which is embossed with a lotus design and tied with black and white cords[strings] in a formal manner. The label for a condolence envelope is usually written in thin black ink in the front. 香典用の封筒．香典を入れた封筒．会葬者は正式様式で蓮の花を浮き彫りにし白黒の紐(黒水引)で結んだ封筒に一定額の金銭を包む．表書きは通常薄墨で書く．「不祝儀袋」ともいう．⇨祝儀袋

こうどう【香道】 the Japanese art of appreciating incense; the traditional art of incense burning and smelling. It is the traditional aesthetic pastime of incense burning and smelling to appreciate a refined sense of fragrance from burning fragrant[aromatic] wood. 香木をたいてそ

の香りを鑑賞して楽しむ芸道．☆「わび・さび」の美 (the aesthetic value of subtle taste and elegant simplicity)を追求する．⇨香(茶道) / わび / さび

こうどう【講堂】 a lecture hall of a Buddhist temple. 禅宗では「法堂」(doctrine hall) という．僧侶が仏教を講義する読経や公案を行いながら研鑽する場所．⇨七堂伽藍．☆金堂と仏舎利塔に次いで重要な建造物である．⇨読経 / 公案 / 禅寺

こうねんきしょうがい【更年期障害】〈男女両方の〉climacteric suffering[distress];〈女性の〉the menopause; a menopausal disorder; the changing of life.

こうのとり【鸛】〔鳥〕a white stork.「こうづる」ともいう．☆日本では特別天然記念物．

こうのみやはだかまつり【国府宮裸まつり】the Half-Naked Festival.（2月）．⇨付記(1)「日本の祭り」

こうのもの【香の物】 pickles; pickled vegetables (such as radish, eggplant , cucumber and cabbage). (大根・茄子・胡瓜・キャベツなどを)漬けた物．別名「漬物」「おしんこ」「こうこ」など．☆懐石料理では季節の野菜の盛り合わせが出る．⇨漬物

こうはい【後背】⇨後光

こうばい【紅梅】〔植物〕〈木〉 an apricot tree with deep-pink blossoms; a plum with red blossoms;〈実〉an apricot with deep-pink blossoms; a plum with red blossoms. 濃いもも色の花が咲く梅．¶**紅梅煮** fish boiled in *shoyu*[soy sauce] and added *umeboshi* [pickled plum](醤油に梅干を加えて煮た魚（鰯，鯖，秋刀魚など))

こうはく【紅白】 red and white.¶**紅白試合** a game[contest] between two (opposing) teams of reds and whites. 紅白の餅 red and white rice cakes. 紅白饅頭 red and white bean-paste buns.

【(NHK)紅白歌合戦】the Red-versus-White Singing Competition (televised annually by NHK (Nippon Hoso Kyokai) on New Year's Eve); An NHK music program broadcast on New Year's Eve in which the annual competition is held between white male and red female popular singers. 男女の人気歌手の間で行われる紅白対抗歌合戦．例年大晦日に NHK がテレビ放送する．☆1951年以降の年中行事．

【紅白の幔幕】 a red-and-white-striped curtain; a curtain with vertical red and white stripes. It is often used on auspicious occasions such as a school opening ceremony or commencement. 縦の紅白ストライプ模様のある幕．入学式または卒業式などのめでたい行事で使用する．

こうぶがったい【公武合体】 the reconciliation between the Imperial Court and the Shogunate; the unification[union] of the Imperial Court and the Shogunate. The Imperial Court was united with the Shogunate to check *Sonno-joi* movement. 公家と武家の合体．江戸幕府は尊王攘夷運動を抑えるために朝廷と強い関係を築こうとした．囫徳川家茂（14代将軍）は孝明天皇の妹（和宮）を妻にして，徳川家と天皇家を親戚関係にした．⇨尊王攘夷

こうふくじたきぎのう【興福寺薪能】 the Torchlight Noh Play Performance at Kofukuji Temple.（5月）．⇨付記(1)「日本の祭り」

こうもり【蝙蝠】〔動物〕 a bat. ¶大蝙蝠 a flying bat. 雛蝙蝠 an evening bat.

こうやどうふ【高野豆腐】 freeze-dried *tofu* [bean curd]; frozen and dried *tofu*. A fine sponge-like *tofu* is made by freezing it outside in winter and then drying it. It was invented[made] by Buddhist priests [monks] who lived in the temple on Mt. Koya. 豆腐を寒中に凍らせて乾燥させたもの．僧侶が高野山の宿坊で作りはじめた．煮物や巻きずしの具などにする．「凍り豆腐」ともいう．⇨豆腐

こうよう【紅葉】 autumnal colors of leaves; tinted autumn leaves.

こうり【行李】 a wicker basket[suitcase]. It is woven from[made of] strips of bamboo or willow twigs. It is used for storing or carrying clothing. 枝編みのかご．衣類などを収納・携帯する竹・柳などを編んでつくった物入れ．「衣類箱」．⇨柳行李

こうりょう【香料】 ❶〈香典〉 incense money; an obituary[a funeral] monetary offering given in place of an incense. It is offered as a consolation gift to the relatives to pay for incense to be burned for the deceased. 線香の代わりにおくる香典．死者の霊に対する焼香用に親族にお悔やみとしておくる金銭．⇨香典 / お悔やみ
❷〈薬味〉 spice(s).
❸〈芳香物〉 (a) perfume.

こうれいかしゃかい【高齢化社会】 an aging [ageing] society; a graying society; (the graying of) an aging population. ¶超高齢化 a rapidly graying population.

こうれいしゃかいご【高齢者介護】 a nursing care for the elderly people[senior citizens].

こうれいしゃいりょうせいど【高齢者医療制度】 the system of medical care for the elderly people.

こうろ【香炉】 an incense burner. 香をたくための器具．⇨香道 / 葬儀. ¶香炉の灰に線香を立てる stand incense sticks in the ashes in the incense burner.

ごえいか【御詠歌】 a pilgrim's Buddhist hymn. 巡礼者が仏や霊場をたたえる歌．

こえだ【小枝】 a twig（細枝）; a sprig (of holly)（柊のように花や葉がついた枝）; a spray (of cherry blossoms)（桜のように花・葉・果実がついた枝）. 華道でよく用いる．☆「枝」は branch，「大枝」は bough.

こえび【小海老】〔甲〕 a shrimp. ⇨えび / しゃこ (mantis shrimp).

ごえもんぶろ【五右衛門風呂】 a Goemon bath. A bath (tub) is heated directly on a fire from below. It has a floating wooden lid[board] (*sugeita*) to be pressed[pushed] under the hot water with bather's feet. It is so named because a notorious robber in the feudal times named Ishikawa Goemon who was boiled to death in a boiling bath[cauldron]. 浴槽の下から直火で熱する．菅板が浮いていて，入浴者が乗ってお湯の底に沈めて入る．昔，釜ゆでの死刑になった悪名高い盗人の石川五右衛門にちなんで名づけられた．

ゴーヤー〔植物〕 a *goya*; a bitter gourd [melon]; a balsam pear[apple]. ⇨にがうり 〔料理〕**ゴーヤーチャンプル** *goya* fried with pork, *tofu* and other vegetables. 豚肉と豆腐そして野菜といっしょに炒めたゴーヤー．沖縄の郷土料理．

こおり【氷】 ice. ¶**氷枕** an ice pillow[bag]. **氷削り器** ice slider[crusher]. **氷菓子**. ⇨アイスキャンディー. **氷砂糖**. ⇨砂糖 〔食品〕**かき氷** (a bowl of) shaved ice with sugar syrup. **氷小豆** (a bowl of) shaved ice with boiled sweet *adzuki* bean paste. **氷いちご** (a bowl of)shaved ice covered with strawberry syrup. **氷レモン** (a bowl of) shaved ice covered with lemon syrup.

こおりどうふ【凍り豆腐】 a frozen and dried *tofu*[bean curd]. 「高野豆腐」ともいう．巻きずしや煮物の具にする．⇨高野豆腐

ゴールデン・アワー（和製英語）**番組** (the) prime-time (TV) program; (the) prime-hour (TV) show;(the) peak (TV) viewing time.

ゴールデン・ウイーク the holiday-studded week (between the end of April and the beginning of May); the week with a string of holidays[vacations](from the end of April to the beginning of May). ☆「昭和の日」(4/29)，「憲法記念日」(5/3)，「みどりの日」(5/4)，「こどもの日」(5/5)の国民の祝日がある．「黄金週間」(the Golden Week (from April 29 through May 5, a period stranding four national holidays)) や「大型連休」，「飛石連休」などともいう．名称の由来は大映が松竹と競作して1951年(昭和26年)に上映した「自由学校」(獅子文六原作)が大映創設以来最高の売上げを記録した週間に関する宣伝用語として使用したことによる．⇨国民の祝日

こおろぎ【蟋蟀】〔虫〕a cricket. ☆雄が秋の夜に鳴く．¶**こおろぎの鳴き声** the chirping of a crocket.

ごかじょうのせいもん【五箇条の誓文】 the Five Imperial Oaths; the Charter Oath of Five Articles; the Meiji Doctrine of Five Articles. The five articles declared in 1868 in the name of Emperor Meiji as the fundamental principles in carrying out the reforms of the new Meiji regime. 1868年に明治天皇の名義で公布した誓文(誓いのことばを記した文書)．明治時代の新政府の改革を遂行する基本原理を宣言した．

こかた【子方】〔歌舞伎〕〔能楽〕a child actor [role]; an actor cast for child's role (in kabuki and Noh plays). 子供が演じる役．

ごがつにんぎょう【五月人形】 martial dolls for the Boys' Festival; a display of *samurai* warrior dolls set on three-tiered stands celebrating for the Boys' Festival [Children's Festival]. These dolls are displayed in the hope that boys can grow up to be as strong as *samurai* warriors. 端午の節句［こどもの日］を祝って三段の飾り台に展示する一式の武者人形．男児が武士のようにたくましく成長することを願って人形を飾る．⇨端午の節句 / 兜飾り ① 『**最上段**』(the top row): A *samurai* warrior doll dressed in a suit of armor and a helmet is standing in front of a folding screen and military banners. There are a

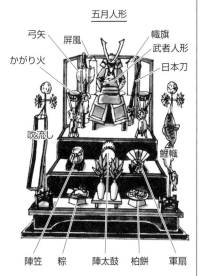

五月人形

弓矢 屏風 幟旗 武者人形 かがり火 日本刀 吹流し 鯉幟 陣笠 粽 陣太鼓 柏餅 軍扇

bow and arrow on the right and a sword with a hilt and scabbard on the left. Bonfire stands are set on the far right and left.「鎧・兜」を装った「武者人形」が「屏風・幟旗」の前に立つ. 右側に「弓矢」があり，左側に「日本刀」がある. それぞれ左右には「かがり火」がある.

② 『2段目』(the second row): A military iron fan and a war drum (used by ancient warlords to direct battles) are displayed. A thin steel warrior's helmet and whip (used by generals to convey commands in battles) are lined up on the same level, in addition to carp-shaped streamers or a *kintaro* doll.「軍扇・陣太鼓(戦場で指揮する将軍用)」が配列されている.「陣笠・鞭(戦場で命令する将軍用)」，それに加え「鯉幟」または「金太郎人形」が整列する.⇨鯉幟/金太郎

③ 『3段目』(the bottom row): Steamed rice cakes stuffed with sweet bean paste and wrapped in oak leaves, fermented rice

dumplings wrapped in bamboo leaves and a bottle of iris-flavored *sake* on a small stand are lined up.「柏餅」・「粽」・「菖蒲酒」.

ごがつびょう【五月病】 May depression syndrome; a feeling of depression that afflicts newcomers[freshmen] early in May. 5月に襲う憂鬱なノイローゼ的症候. 5月初旬頃新入社員［新入生］が陥る無気力感.

こがねむし【黄金虫】〔虫〕 a gold beetle; a gold bug; a scarab (beetle). コガネムシ科の昆虫の総称.

こがらし【木枯らし】 a cold[biting] winter wind (blowing late in autumn). 秋の終わり頃から冬にかけて強く吹く冷たい風.

こき【古稀】 (celebrate) one's seventieth birthday.

【古希の祝い】 the celebration of one's seventieth birthday. The Japanese celebrate their 70th birthday. It is the 70th anniversary of one's life, one of the special ages to celebrate one's longevity. 70歳の祝い. ⇨賀

こき【子機】 a cordless telephone; an extension phone.

ごきぶり【ごきぶり】〔虫〕a cockroach; a black beetle. ⇨あぶらむし. ¶ごきぶり捕獲器 a cockroach trap.

こギャル an obsessively trendy-conscious teenage[junior or senior high-school] girl (who reflects the latest teenage styles in personal appearance, clothing and speech). 妄想的に流行を追う十代［女子中高生］の少女.

ごぎょう【御形】〔植物〕 a cudweed; a cottonweed; an everlasting flower (花).「母子草」の異名.「春の七草」の一つ. ⇨春の七草

こきんわかしゅう【古今和歌集】 the Anthology of Ancient and Modern Poems [Verses]. 紀貫之などの撰による平安初期の

勅撰和歌集. 905年頃成立. ⇨付記 (2)「日本の歴史年表」(905年)

こく【石】 a *koku*; a Japanese unit of measurement of volume[capacity]. 容量を測定する日本の単位.

❶ One *koku* is equivalent to 180 liters. (180リットル). 穀物の容積の単位. 一升の10倍. ¶**米10石** ten *koku* of rice.

❷ bales (*koku*) of rice received as the annual stipend[revenue] of feudal lords and officials. 大名・役人が年俸［歳入］として受領した米の石. 昔, 大名の知行高を表したもの. ⇨知行. ¶**大名の領する1万石** the fief of 10,000 *koku* of rice held by a feudal lord. **加賀百万石** the fief of one million *koku* of rice yielded by the Kaga clan; the fief of the Kaga clan, which yields one million *koku* of rice. **三万石の大名** a feudal lord with a thirty thousand *koku* stipend.

こくう【穀雨】 grain rains; the season when grains grow in spring rains. 春雨が降って百穀をうるおす季節. ⇨二十四節気

こくがいついほう【国外追放】 deportation[expulsion] from Japan. ¶**キリシタン宣教師の国外追放(令)** deportation[expulsion] of all Christian missionaries from Japan; (edict) expelling all Christian missionaries from Japan (in 1587).

こくぎ【国技】 a national sport[game]. ¶**国技館** the Kokugikan Arena.

こくさいれんめいだったい【国際連盟脱退】 the withdrawal from the League of Nations.

こくし【国司】 the provincial officer sent from the Imperial Court (in the Nara period). (奈良時代, 律令制のもとで)朝廷から諸国に派遣された地方官. 「くにのつかさ」

こくし【国師】 the master of the nation; the governor of the province appointed directly by the Imperial Court. The honorific title is given to the virtuous Buddhist priest from the Imperial Court. 国家の師. 朝廷から直接任命され, 諸国の寺院・僧侶を監督する. 国家の師としてふさわしい高徳の僧に朝廷から贈られた称号.

こくそうちたい【穀倉地帯】 a granary; the breadbasket; the farm belt.

こくぞうむし【穀象虫】〔虫〕a rice weevil; a grain weevil. 「こめくいむし」ともいう.

こくたん【黒檀】〔植物〕an ebony; a blackwood. 材(ebony)は黒くて硬い. 家具用. ☆「黒檀の箸」(a pair of an ebony chopsticks)は有名.

こくちょう【国鳥】 the national bird. ☆日本の国鳥は「雉」(pheasant).

こくていこうえん【国定公園】 a quasi-national park. ⇨公園. ¶**津軽国定公園** Tsugaru Quasi-National Park.

こくぶんじ【国分寺】 (official) provincial temple. Emperor Shomu (701-756) ordered to build Buddhist temples in each province of Japan in the late Nara period[in 741](praying for the welfare of the country and a good harvest). 奈良時代末期[741年, 一説には738年]に聖武天皇の命により(国家安泰と五穀豊穣を祈願して)諸国に寺(国分寺と国分尼寺)を建立した. ☆**僧寺**[国分寺] (provincial temple for monks; provincial monastery)と**尼寺**[国分尼寺] (provincial temples for nuns; provincial nunnery[convent])がある. ☆monastery(男子修道院), nunnery [convent](女子修道院)は欧米のキリスト教での用語.

こくべつしき【告別式】 a funeral service; the farewell service for the deceased. The Buddhist rite of bidding farewell to a deceased person is observed before cremation (*kaso*). People attending a farewell service bring monetary gift (*koden*). They burn pinches of incense (*shoko*)at the altar while the Buddhist priest recites sutras. 告別式は「火葬」の前に行われる. 会

葬者は「香典」を持参する．僧侶が読経をあげる間，祭壇に向かって「焼香」する．⇨火葬場 / 香典 / 焼香

こくほう【国宝】 a national treasure[heirloom]. ⇨人間国宝. ¶国宝指定の建造物［寺院］the building[temple] designated as a national treasure. 国宝級の絵画 the painting of a national treasure class. 国宝保存法 the National Treasure Preservation Law.

こくみんせばんごうせい【国民背番号制】 a system giving every citizen an ID number.

こくみんのしゅくじつ【国民の祝日】 National Holiday(s); legal holiday(s)（法律で定められた）. ☆ミニ解説は各項目を参照.
・元日 New Year's Day（January 1）
・成人の日 Coming-of-Age Day（2nd Monday of January）. ★ / ☆
・建国記念の日 National Foundation Day（February 11）
・天皇誕生日 Emperor's Birthday（February 23）
・春分の日 Vernal Equinox Day（around March 21）
・昭和の日 Showa Day（April 29）
・憲法記念日 Constitution Memorial Day（May 3）
・みどりの日 Greenery Day（May 4）
・こどもの日 Children's Day（May 5）
・海の日 Marine Day（3rd Monday of July）. ☆
・山の日 Mountain Day（August 11）
・敬老の日 Respect-for-the-Aged Day（3rd Monday of September）. ★★ / ☆
・秋分の日 Autumnal Equinox Day（around September 23）
・スポーツの日 Health and Sports Day（2nd Monday of October）. ☆
・文化の日 Culture Day（November 3）
・勤労感謝の日 Labor Thanksgiving Day（November 23）

㊟外国人には ★ Day celebrating the legal age for adulthood または Adult's Day, ★★ Seniors' Day または Senior Citizens' Day が理解しやすい. ☆印は「ハッピーマンデー制度」を参照.

こくみんえいよしょう【国民栄誉賞】 the People's Honor Award; the National Medal of Honor.

こくもつ【穀物】 (food) grain; cereal crop; cereals; corn（米国では「とうもろこし」，英国では「小麦」）. 米・麦・豆・粟など人が常食とする作物.「穀類」ともいう.

ごくらく【極楽】 (the Buddhist) paradise; heaven. ⇦ hell（地獄）. ¶極楽往生 a peaceful death.

ごくらくじょうど【極楽浄土】 the Paradise of Pure Land; the Land of Perfect Bliss. ¶西方の極楽浄土 the Paradise of Pure Land in the West. 極楽浄土は阿弥陀如来仏の居所である安楽の世界. ☆西方十万億土を経た所にあり，苦悩のない世界で，念仏行者は死後ここに生まれ変わるという.

ごくらくちょう【極楽鳥】 a bird of paradise; a paradise bird.「風鳥」ともいう.

こくらたいこぎおん【小倉太鼓祇園】 the Kokura Drum-Beating Gion Festival.（7月）. ⇨付記(1)「日本の祭り」

こくりつこうえん【国立公園】 a national park. ⇨公園. ¶日光国立公園 Nikko National Park.

こけ【苔】〔植物〕 (a) moss; a moss plant; liverwort（銭苔）; lichen（地衣）. ¶岩苔 rock moss. 苔寺（京都府）Moss Temple (famous for its moss-covered garden). 正式名称「西芳寺」.

こげ【焦げ】 scorched rice. ⇨お焦げ

こけし【小芥子】 a *kokeshi* doll. A *kokeshi* is a wooden folk doll with a limbless cylindrically-shaped body[torso] and a round ball-shaped[spherical] head. 手足のない円筒形の胴に球形の丸顔をつける木製人形.

¶**一本木から作るこけし** a *kokeshi* made from a single piece of wood. **頭が分離できるこけし** a *kokeshi* having a detachable head.

ごけにん【御家人】 a retainer serving the shogun; the title applied to a retainer in the service of the shogun. 将軍に仕える家臣(に適用された呼称). ❶ an immediate (hereditary) retainer serving the shogun in Kamakura and Muromachi periods. 鎌倉・室町時代, 将軍直属の(世襲)家臣(vassal). ❷ a low-ranking retainer serving the Tokugawa shogun (ranking below the *hatamoto*). 江戸時代, 将軍に仕える下層の家臣(vassal). 旗本以下の者. ⇨旗本

こけもも【苔桃】〔植物〕a blueberry; a cowberry; a mountain cranberry; a lingonberry;〈欧州〉a whortleberry. ツツジ科の常緑低木. 果実酒やジャムなどに用いる.

こけらおとし【柿落とし】 the formal[inaugural] opening of a new[rebuilt] theater. 新築[改築]の劇場で初めて演じること. ¶**柿落とし公演** the opening[inaugural] performance of a new[rebuilt] theater. 新築[改築]の劇場での初めての公演.

ごけんうんどう【護憲運動】 a movement for the defense of the Constitution; a movement opposing revision of the Constitution. 憲法を擁護し, 立憲政治を守る運動.「憲政擁護運動」ともいう. ☆犬養毅・尾崎行雄等が擁護した.

ごこう【後光】 a halo (⑰ halos, haloes) (around the body[head] of a saint or the Buddhist image); an aureole; a nimbus. 聖者・仏の身体[頭]の周りから発する光.「光背」ともいう. ⇨火炎光背

ごこく【五穀】 the five (staple) grains; the five cereals.「五種の穀物」. ☆米 (rice)・麦 (wheat)・豆 (bean)・粟 (foxtail millet)・稗または黍 (Japanese millet). ¶**五穀豊穣** (pray for) a good[rich] harvest; (pray for) an abundant[a bumper] crop. 穀物が豊かに実ること.

ござ【茣蓙・蓙】 (spread) a straw mat;〈総称〉matting.「ござむしろ」ともいう.

ごさい【五彩】 ceramic piece with red, blue, yellow, white, black glaze.「赤・青・黄・白・黒」の5色. ☆陶磁器に色の釉薬で文様を表現したもの. ⇨友禅五彩

ございしょ【御座所】 the Imperial chamber; the Emperor's apartments; the nobles' apartments. 天皇のいる部屋. 貴人の部屋.

こさつ【古刹】 an old[ancient] temple (with a long history). 由緒ある寺. ⇨古寺

ごさんけ【御三家】❶〈徳川御三家〉the three branch families of the Tokugawa clan; the three major Tokugawa branch families descended from three sons of Tokugawa Ieyasu. They descended directly from Tokugawa Ieyasu, the first shogun of the Tokugawa government. They were appointed as lineage feudal lords of Owari (Nagoya), Kii (Wakayama) and Hitachi (Mito), who ranked above all the other feudal lords in the Edo period. 徳川家の尾張・紀伊・水戸の三家柄の総称. 徳川家康の直系で,「尾張藩」(現在の名古屋:9男義直),「紀伊藩」(現在の和歌山:10男頼宣),「水戸藩」(現在の茨城:11男頼房)の親藩大名として任命され, 江戸時代の他の大名の上位にあった. ❷〈業界の有力三者〉the top three; the big three. ¶**茶道の御三家** the big three leading schools of the tea ceremony.

ごさんのきり【五三の桐】 the family crest with paulownia flowers superimposed on three paulownia leaves. 3枚の桐の葉を重ねた桐花のある家紋.

こし【輿】 a palanquin; a palankeen; a litter. It is carried by two poles on the shoulders of two or several bearers. It was used as a means of transportation for women of

こ

nobility and the *samurai* military class in ancient times. (日本・中国・インドなど東洋諸国に見られた) 1人乗り用の駕籠. 2名または数名の担ぎ手の肩にのせて2本の棒で運ぶ乗り物. 昔は貴族や武士階級の女性用の乗り物として使用していた. ⇨駕籠

こじ【古寺】 an old Buddhist temple; an ancient Buddhist temple with a long history. ⇨古刹

こしあん【漉し餡】 strained sweet *adzuki* bean paste; pureed sweet bean paste; puree of sweetened bean paste. 汁粉や和菓子の材料. ⇨餡. ☆ puree ⒡「ピューレ; 裏ごし(したもの)」. 囲「裏ごしする」

こしいれ【輿入れ】 a wedding; a marriage. (女性の)婚礼. 嫁入り.

こじき【古事記】 ***Kojiki***; the Record of Ancient Matters; the Ancient Chronicle; the Legendary Stories of Old Japan. *Kojiki* is Japan's oldest historical account and oldest remaining[extant] chronicle in Japanese. (three volumes). 現存する日本最古の年代記(3巻). ☆元明天皇の勅により, 稗田阿礼に誦習 (oral recitation) させていたものを太安万侶が撰上した. 712年(和銅5年)に成立. 神代の神武天皇から推古天皇までの天皇家を中心とする皇室の系図(imperial genealogy)とその歴史的伝承 (historical events and oral accounts) の記録.「上巻」(天地創造の神話),「中巻」(神武天皇から応神天皇まで),「下巻」(仁徳天皇から推古天皇まで)

こしだかしょうじ【腰高障子】 a low sliding door; a paper-covered sliding door with waist-high paneling. (1メートルほどの)低い腰板を張った障子.「腰高」ともいう. ⇨障子

こしつビデオてん【個室ビデオ店】a private-room video shop; an all-night video parlor (offering private viewing booths[separate viewing rooms]); a building with multiple video rooms (often used for a night's lodging).

こしひも【腰紐】 a waist cord[string]; a cord [string] tied around the waist. It is used under the *obi*[sash] for securing a *kimono*. 着物を固定する(fixing a *kimono* in place)ために帯の下に結ぶ細い布ひも.

こしびょうぶ【腰屏風】a low folding screen; a folding screen with waist-high paneling. 腰の高さほどの低い屏風. ⇨屏風

こじま【小島】 an islet; a small island. ¶松島(宮城県) Matsushima, pine-clad islets. ⇨島

こしまき【腰巻き】 a woman's waistcloth; a Japanese underskirt worn by women with[beneath] a *kimono*. 女性が着物を着るときの下着で, 下半身にまとう布.「御腰」ともいう.

ごしゅいんじょう【御朱印状】 ⇨朱印状

ごしゅいんせん【御朱印船】 ⇨朱印船

ごじゅうのとう【五重塔】 a five-story[five-storied] pagoda (usually found in the precincts of a Buddhist temple). The pagoda is built to enshrine ashes (or relics) of Buddha (or Buddhist saints) as sacred objects in an altar, and Buddhist scriptures and Buddhist statues. 五層になった仏塔. 祭壇には聖遺物として仏舎利, また経典や仏像が安置されている. ☆仏教の教えによると,「5層」は《地 [earth]・水 [water]・火 [fire]・風 [wind]・空 [heaven]》の五大をかたどり, 現世はこの5要素 (the five elements of the universe) から成る. 人が死去すれば, この5元素に還元される. 囲奈良・法隆寺の五重塔(607年建立. 現存する最古) / 京都・東寺の五重塔(796年建立. 現存する最大). ☆ pagoda「仏塔」アジア諸国における仏教やヒンズー教などに見られる多層の仏塔. ⇨仏舎利

ごしょ【御所】 the Imperial Palace; the Imperial Court. 天皇の住まい. 皇居.

【御所車】 an ox-drawn court carriage[cart] (used by the nobles of the Heian period); an elegant court carriage[cart] drawn by an ox[a bullock]. 宮中で使われる牛車. 平安時代の貴族が用いた.

【御所人形】 *Gosho* dolls modeled on plump naked infants; a naked clay doll portraying an infant with a chubby round face, a big head and white skin (produced in Kyoto). It was originally used as a toy for children in the Imperial Court in Kyoto in the Edo period. ふっくらした丸顔と大きな頭そして白い肌をした幼児の裸人形. 江戸時代, 京都御所における子供の玩具として使用された.

こしょう【胡椒】 ❶〔植物〕 pepper. コショウ科のつる性常緑低木. 「葉」はサラダ, 「種子」は香辛料に用いる. ¶**胡椒の果実** peppercorn. **黒胡椒** black peppercorn. **白胡椒** white peppercorn.
❷〈香辛料〉 pepper; peppercorns(粒胡椒). ¶**挽き胡椒** ground pepper. **胡椒入れ** a pepperbox; ㊇ a pepper shaker; ㊇ a pepper pot. **胡椒挽き** a pepper grinder; a pepper mill.

こしょうがつ【小正月】 Little[Lesser] New Year's Day on January 15; New Year's holidays from January 14 to 16 (by the lunar calendar). 1月15日の正月. また陰暦で1月14日の夜から16日までの正月. ⇨**大正月**

ごしんぶつ【護身仏】 one's guardian [tutelary] Buddha. 危険から身を守るための仏.

ごしんえい【御真影】 a picture of the Emperor and Empress (before World War II). (第二次世界大戦前の)天皇・皇后の写真.

ごしんたい【御神体】 ⇨神体(内部・外部)

ごしんとう【御神灯】 〈神社の〉 a sacred light [lantern] (placed in front of the shrine sanctuary); 〈神棚の〉 a sacred light[lantern] (placed in a household[family] Shinto altar). 神に供える灯火[提灯]. ⇨**神灯**

コスプレショー a costume party; a fancy dress party; a costume fetish gathering.

コスプレきっさ【コスプレ喫茶】 a cosplay [costume play] café. ⇨**メイドカフェ**

ごせいばいしきもく【御成敗式目】 the codification of warrior house law; the legal code for *samurai*. 武家社会の習慣をまとめて制定した武士の最初の法律. ☆御家人の権利や義務, 領地の相続などがある. 1232年北条泰時が制定.

こせき【戸籍】 a family register. ¶**戸籍原本** the initial entry of a family register. **戸籍抄本** an extra[a partial] copy of one's family register; an abstract of one's family register. **戸籍謄本** a full copy of one's family register.

ごぜん【御前】 an honorary title added to the name of ladies of a certain rank (as opposed to the court noble). 身分のある婦人を敬って用いる尊称. ¶**巴御前** an honorary title given to the wife of a feudal lord.

ごぜんかいぎ【御前会議】 an Imperial Council; a conference in the presence of the Emperor. 天皇が出席して開催される会議.

ごぜんじあい【御前試合】 a game[match] in the presence of the Emperor [Shogun]. 天皇[将軍]の前で行う試合.

こせんじょう【古戦場】 a historic site of the battle; an old battlefield; an ancient battleground. ¶**八島にある源平の古戦場**(香川県)the historic site of the Battle of the Yashima Peninsula between the Minamoto and Taira clans.

ごぜんじるこ【御膳汁粉】 a sweet soup containing strained *adzuki* bean paste with *mochi*[rice cake]. 餅入りのこし餡の汁粉.

こそで【小袖】❶ a *kimono*[garment] with

こ

short[tight] sleeves (worn by both men and women). (男女共用)狭い筒袖の着物[衣服].

❷ a *kimono*[garment] with short sleeves worn as underclothing. (昔, 礼服の大袖の)下着として着る狭い袖の着物[衣服].

❸ a silk-quilted *kimono*[garment]; a wadded silk garment. 絹の綿入れ着物[衣服].

こそどろ【こそ泥】a sneak[petty] thief; a cat burglar; a pilferer; Ⓜ snitch.

ごたいろう【五大老】 the five most powerful feudal lords[elder councilors] appointed in 1597 by Toyotomi Hideyoshi to support Toyotomi rule[to rule Japan in the place of his son, Hideyori]. 1597年に豊臣秀吉が豊臣支配を支援するため[豊臣秀頼の後見として全国を統治するために]設けた有力五大名. ☆徳川家康(関東地方), 前田利家(北陸地方), 毛利輝元(中国地方), 宇喜多秀家(中国地方), 小早川隆景(北九州)の没後には上杉景勝(東北地方).

こだち【小太刀】 ❶〈剣道〉a short bamboo sword. ⇨竹刀.
❷〈脇差〉a short sword on one's side. ⇨刀

こたつ【炬燵】a ***kotatsu***; a foot warmer (with wooden frame and quilt[coverlet] over it); a quilt-covered frame with a heating device inside. A *kotatsu* is a Japanese traditional heating device made of a low table which has a square latticed wooden frame covered with a coverlet (*futon*). A ceramic container with a burning charcoal filled with ashes (today with an electric foot warmer) is placed under the table[attached to the bottom of the table]. (木わくに布団をかぶせ)足を入れて暖める器具. 布団をのせた四角い格子になった木わくのある低いテーブル状の日本古来の暖房器具である. テーブルの下には灰につつまれた炭火 (charcoal fire)が入った陶器[fireproof clay

pot](現在では電気暖房装置)が備わっている. ☆炭火には「練炭」(coal briquette)や「豆炭」(charcoal briquette) などがある. ⇨炭(炭火)

¶ **置き炬燵** a portable[movable] *kotatsu*[foot warmer] placed directly on the *tatami* mat or on the floor (畳または床の上に置いて使用する可動式炬燵). **掘り炬燵** a sunken *kotatsu*[foot warmer] set in a recess in the floor; a *kotatsu* with legroom sunk in the floor；a *kotatsu* with foot space built into the floor. They sit with their legs outstretched in a *kotatsu*. (床板の奥まった所に掘りさげ, 脚が伸ばせる炬燵). ☆「据(え)炬燵」ともいう. 明治時代に始まる.

電気炬燵 an electric *kotatsu*[foot warmer] (often used today instead of *kotatsu* with a charcoal burner); a low table with a built-in electric heater, covered with a quilt. **炬燵布団** a quilt[coverlet] for a *kotatsu*[foot warmer]. **炬燵櫓** a (latticed) wooden frame over a *kotatsu*[foot warmer] supporting a quilt and tabletop.

こつあげ【骨揚げ】 gathering the pieces of the bones of the deceased into an urn. It is a cremation rite of placing[putting] the bones[ashes] of the deceased into a cinerary urn at the crematorium. 火葬後の遺骨を拾って骨つぼに納める儀式. 「骨拾い」ともいう. ⇨納骨 / 火葬場

こっか【国歌】a national anthem. ⇨君が代
¶ **国家斉唱** singing the national anthem in unison.

こっか【国花】［桜］a national flower. 日本では「桜」(cherry blossom)

こづか【小柄】 a small dagger attached to the sheath[scabbard] of a Japanese sword (worn at one's side). 脇差の鞘の外側にさし添える小刀.

こっかしんとう【国家神道】 State Shinto. It was administered by the government from the Meiji era to World War II. 明治時代から第二次世界大戦終焉まで政府が管轄した. ⇨教派神道

こっきょう【国教】 a national religion; a state religion. After the Meiji Restoration (1868), the government tried to establish Shinto as the national religion. 明治維新後, 政府は神道を国教に制定しようとした. ⇨廃仏毀釈
<small>はいぶつきしゃく</small>

こつずいバンク【骨髄バンク】 a bone marrow bank. ¶日本骨髄バンク Japan Marrow Donor Program[JMDP].

ごったに【ごった煮】 ⊛ a hotchpotch; ⊛ a hodgepodge; ⊛ mulligan stew. すき焼きやおでんなどの料理. ⇨すき焼き/おでん

こつつぼ【骨壺】 a cremation urn; a cinerary urn; an urn for cremated bones[ashes]. At the crematory family members put the bones of a deceased person into a cinerary urn using a pair of chopsticks. 火葬した遺骨[遺灰]用の(骨)壷. 火葬場で家族は箸を使って死者の遺骨を骨壷に入れる. ⇨納骨

こづち【小槌】 a small mallet. ⇨打ち出の小槌

こつづみ【小鼓】 a small hourglass-shaped drum. 〔歌舞伎・能楽〕a small shoulder drum (used in the traditional Japanese music and dance). The drum is struck with the fingertips of the middle and ring fingers of the right hand while it is held on the right shoulder with the left hand holding the cords of the drum. 砂時計型の小型の打楽器. 肩にのせる小さな鼓. 左手で太鼓の調緒をとり右肩にのせながら, 右手の中指と薬指で打って演奏する. ☆歌舞伎・能楽の囃子では大鼓とならぶ重要な楽器. ⇨大鼓. ⇨鼓
<small>おおつづみ / つづみ</small>

こて【小手・籠手】❶〈剣道〉ⓐ(防具) an arm guard (used in *kendo*); a gauntlet to protect the arm and hand. ⇨剣道. ⓑ(技:決まり手) a *kote*; a hit[blow] to[on] the forearm (in

kendo); a stroke to the wrist.
❷〈弓道〉a bracer (腕甲); a bracelet (鎧の籠手). 弓を射るときに, 左の手首から肘のあたりにつける皮製の用具.

こてんらくご【古典落語】 a classic comic storytelling (traditionally inherited[passed down] by masters of the art). ⇨落語

こと【琴】 a *koto*; a Japanese 13-stringed harp-style musical instrument; a Japanese zither-style horizontal musical instrument with thirteen strings, each stretching over bridges. A *koto* is laid on the floor and plucked with picks attached to the thumb and two fingers[index and middle fingers] of the right hand. Thirteen strings are stretched over bridges and the pitch is determined by the position of the bridges. The musical instrument is often made of paulownia wood (about 180cm long[in length] and 30-40cm wide[in width]). 琴柱の上に13本の琴弦を張ったツィター[ハープ]型の水平の弦楽器. 床の上に置き, 右手の親指と2本指[人差指と中指]に付けた琴爪(plectrums)を用いて弾き鳴らす. 13本の弦が柱の上に張ってあり, 音の高低は柱の位置で決まる. この楽器(長さ約180センチ, 幅約30-40センチ)は通常は桐製である.「箏」ともいう. ¶琴弦 a *koto* movable string[cord]; the movable strings[cords] of the *koto*. 琴爪 a *koto* pick; the pick of a *koto*; a *koto* plectrum; the plectrum of the *koto*. 琴の曲 (a piece of) *koto* music.

【琴柱】 a *koto* bridge; the movable bridge of a *koto*; a stop on a *koto*. A *kotoji* is used to support the *koto* strings on dragon's head (*ryuto*) on the right side and dragon's tail (*ryubi*) on the left side. The pitch of the sound is determined by their positions. 琴の琴弦を支えるための用具. 琴本体の右端の「竜頭」, 左端の「竜尾」の間に琴柱を立てる位置で音の高低を調節する. ☆琴が「竜」

(dragon)に似ていることからの呼称.

ごとく【五徳】〔茶道〕a trivet; a tripod teakettle holder; an iron ring-shaped teakettle holder with a short tripod stand. It is placed over a charcoal fire in the brazier (made of iron or pottery) to boil water in the tea ceremony. It is also set in a sunken hearth in the tearoom. 三脚台のある鉄輪型の釜をのせるもの. 茶の湯で湯を沸かすために[鉄製・陶製]火鉢の炭火の上にのせる. 茶室の埋め込み炉床にも使用する. ⇨風炉 / 火鉢

こどくし【孤独死】solitary[lonely] death; be dead alone at home.

ことぶきたいしゃ【寿退社】resignation from a company on marriage; quitting a job in order to get married; to get married and quit working.

こどものひ【こどもの日】Children's Day. (May 5). This national holiday was established in 1948 as a day to celebrate to wish for the health and happiness of Japan's children. Traditionally this day was celebrated as *Tango no Sekku* [the Boys' Festival] among families with young boys. On this day carp-shaped streamers are hoisted outside the home and *samurai* dolls are decorated[displayed] inside. 子供の健康と幸福を祈願して祝う. 古来男子のある家庭では「端午の節句」として祝った. この日, 外には鯉のぼりを揚げ, 内では武者人形を飾る. ☆祝日法では「母に感謝する日」(a day to express gratitude to mothers)でもある. ⇨端午の節句 / 五月人形 / 菖蒲湯

こな【粉】powder (粉末); flour (小麦などの穀類). ☆ powder 動「粉にする」. ¶粉山椒 powdered horseradish. ⇨山椒. 粉茶 powdered green tea.

コニーデ(型火山)a conical volcano; a strato-volcano(成層火山); a composite volcano (円錐型火山). ☆ドイツ語の Konide (火

山成層)に由来.

ごにんばやし【五人囃子】〈ひな祭り〉(a set of) five dolls representing ancient Japanese court musicians (who perform a chorus, a flute and three drums). They are displayed on the third row from the top tier of the doll stand during the Doll Festival[at the Girls' Festival]. 五人囃子は「地謡, 笛, 太鼓, 大太鼓, 小鼓」で行う演奏. この形を模した5体の人形. ひな祭りの時, ひな壇の上から3段目に置かれている. ⇨雛壇

こねばち【捏鉢】a bowl[receptacle] used to knead dough for buckwheat noodles. そば粉を捏ねるために用いる鉢[容器].

このしろ【鮗・鰶】〔魚〕a gizzard shad(約15〜25cm); a spotted sardine. ニシン科の海魚. ニシンに似た出世魚. 冬が旬. 幼魚を「ジャコ」または「シンコ」(6cm), 若魚を「コハダ」(10cm前後)という. すし種や酢の物に合う. ⇨こはだ

このめ【木の芽】⇨きのめ

このわた【海鼠腸】salted and fermented entrails of sea cucumber[trepang]. なまこのはらわたの塩辛. 酒の肴として最適. ☆江戸三大珍味とは「三河のこのわた」「越前のうに」「長崎のからすみ」.「こ」は「なまこ」の意. ⇨なまこ

こはぜ【小鉤・鞐】a clasp; a tiny metal clasp with a *tabi*. 足袋の合わせ目を留める金具. ⇨足袋. ¶(足袋の)鞐をかける[はずす] fasten[unfasten] the claps (of one's *tabi*)

こはだ【小鰭】〔魚〕a medium-sized[young] gizzard shad (10cm前後); a spotted sardine.「このしろ」の若魚. すしの種や御節料理の薬漬けにする. ⇨このしろ(出世魚)

こばち【小鉢】❶〈料理の〉a small ceramic bowl (used for serving individual portions of foods at meals). 1人分に盛る小さな器. ☆献立では「和え物」「酢の物」などを指す用語でもある.

②〈植木の〉a small plant-pot; a small flower-pot. 植木・花などを入れる小さな容器.

こはるびより【小春日和】 warm[balmy] autumn weather; ⊛ (an) Indian summer; ⊛ St. Luke's summer.

こばん【小判】 a *koban*; a small-sized oval[oblong-shaped] gold coin. A *koban* was issued and circulated as currency from the Tensho period to the late Edo period. 小型楕円形の金貨. 天正時代(1573-1593)から江戸時代(1603-1868)末期まで通貨として発行された. ⇨大判

ごはん【御飯】〈米を炊いたもの〉 boiled [cooked] rice; steamed rice(蒸しご飯). ☆「生米」(uncooked rice)をさす場合以外は rice の1語で用いることが多い.〈食事〉a meal. ¶ご飯粒 a grain of rice. 芯のあるご飯 half-boiled rice; half-cooked rice. 白米の飯一膳 a bowl of plain rice. ご飯のお代わり(をする) (have) another serving of rice.

ごはん・こうのもの・とめわん【ご飯・香の物・止椀】 boiled rice, pickles and soup. This set of three dishes comes at the end of the traditional meal.「飯物」「漬物」「汁物」は日本料理を閉める三点セット.

ごばん【碁盤】 a go board; a board used in the game of go. ¶碁盤の目 the squares of a go board.

こぶ【昆布】〔植物〕*kobu*; kelp(大型の海草); tangle (weed); (sea) tangle.「こんぶ」(*kombu*)ともいう. 広く英語化されている. 煮物・吸い物などの和食に不可欠. ⇨子持昆布 / 出し昆布 / とろろ昆布 / 刻み昆布 〔料理・食品〕昆布締め〈料理法〉seasoning with *kobu*;〈魚〉vinegared fish rolled with *kobu*; vinegared fish pressed between sheets of *kobu*(昆布で押し, 昆布の味と香をしみこませた酢魚). 昆布茶 *kobu*-flavored tea[beverage]; salty tea[beverage] made from powdered and seasoned *kobu*

(粉末状の味付け昆布にお湯を注いだお茶). ⇨梅昆布茶. 昆布巻 rolled *kobu*; a roll of *kobu* containing a broiled dried fish and some vegetables; fish rolled in *kobu* and simmered till soft 焼いた干魚(鰊や鯊など)を昆布で巻いた煮物. ☆「こんぶ巻」ともいう. 正月の御節料理(よろこぶ)には不可欠. ⇨御節料理 / にしんの昆布巻

ごふ【護符】 a protective amulet[charm]; a talisman as a good-luck charm. ⇨お守り / 魔除け

ごふく【呉服】〈着物の生地〉 cloth for kimonos; kimono fabric; traditional Japanese clothes and fabric;〈反物・織物類〉⊛ dry goods; ⊛ drapery. ¶呉服店[屋] a kimono shop; a dry goods store.

こぶつき【瘤付き】 a divorced guy with a kid. ⇨バツイチ. ¶瘤付き女性 a woman with a child[children] by her ex-husband[former husband]. ⇨バツイチ(子持ちのバツイチ)

ごぶつぜん【御仏前】 **❶**〈仏[みたま]の前〉(flowers offered) before the tablet of the deceased[departed]. 位牌前(に捧げる花). **❷**〈仏への供物〉an offering made before the tablet of the deceased[departed](after the funeral service). 仏にそなえる供物. 葬儀の後に用いる. ☆49日の法要以降に捧げる. 死者の霊は49日が過ぎると成仏する. ⇨御霊前(葬儀の前)

こふん【古墳】 a tumulus (⊛ tumuli, tumuluses); an ancient burial mound; an ancient tomb. The tumulus [tomb covered with large mounds of earth] was made for powerful rulers in the *Kofun* [Tumulus] period (presumably from the 3rd to the 7th centuries). 土を盛り上げて築いた古代の墳墓のこと.「古墳時代」(推定3-7世紀間)に有力者のために作られた. ☆ mound は「(古代の墓の)塚」(小高い丘のような形をした墓). tomb[tu:m]「墓」(=grave). 通常は広い内部を有する装飾された墓所. ⇨

こ

埴輪．**古墳群** tomb cluster．**高松塚古墳**（奈良県） the Takamatsuzuka Tumulus Mound[Tomb]．**大仙古墳**（大阪府） the Daisen Tumulus; the keyhole-shaped Mausoleum of Emperor Nintoku (the largest of its kind in the world, measuring 486 m in length, 305 m in width and 35 m in height)．仁徳天皇陵（墓域面積は世界最大．墳長486m，前方部は幅305m，高さ約35m）．☆ユネスコ世界文化遺産（2019年登録）

ごへい【御幣】 a wand tipped with pendant strips of white paper; a sacred staff strung with white paper streamers. It is a sacred rod with a bundle of cut and plaited pieces of white paper dangling at intervals from it. It is used in purification and other Shinto rites to invite the descent of gods and ward off evils. 細く段々に切った白い紙を串［棒・杖］にはさんだもの．神が降り悪を除くための清めの式 (exorcism) や他の神事(Shinto rituals)などに用いる．「幣束」の敬称．⇨幣｜垂

ごぼう【牛蒡】〔植物〕 a burdock root(根)；(an edible) burdock(食材)．キク科の二年草．⇨金平牛蒡．¶**牛蒡胡麻和え** a crushed burdock with sesame dressing.

こま【駒】 a shogi piece; a piece used in playing shogi; a chessman (⑳ chessmen). ⇨将棋

こま【独楽】 a spinning top (used as a plaything for a child). A top is usually made of wood and pieced through the middle with a rod that is the stem for rotating. 通常は木製で，回転させる心棒が貫いている．☆「京独楽」は色彩豊かな布を巻いて作る．⇨貝独楽．¶**独楽を回す** spin a top.

【独楽回し】〈回すこと〉top-spinning;〈遊び〉a top-spinning game. The top is spun by winding around the stem with a long slender cord, or by simply using the hands.

軸に細長い紐 (string) を巻きつけて，また は手だけで回す．⇨博多独楽

ごま【護摩】 fire ritual observed in Esoteric Buddhism (by making a holy fire for invocation). Small pieces of holy cedarwood (called *goma-gi*) are burned on the altar in the ceremony to invoke a god's help, accompanied by prayers and bell-ringing. 密教で，護摩木を焚いて不動明王，愛染明王の加護を祈る火の儀式．⇨付記(1)「日本の祭り」（高尾山の火渡り祭．3月）．

¶**護摩木** a holy cedarwood[cedar branches] (for burning in the fire rituals). （火の儀式で燃やす聖なる木[小枝]）．**護摩壇** a sacred altar for burning a holy cedarwood; a fire offering altar. **護摩符** a talisman[amulet] of Esoteric Buddhism.

ごま【胡麻】 a sesame; (実) sesame seed. ゴマ科の一年草．

〔食品〕**洗い胡麻** washed and dried sesame seeds. **擂り[ひき]胡麻** ground[pounded] sesame seeds. ☆ ground (grind「擂り砕く」の過去分詞)．**炒り胡麻** parched[roasted] sesame seeds. **煎じ胡麻** toasted sesame seeds. **切り胡麻** cut-up sesame seeds. **練り胡麻** sesame paste. **白[黒]胡麻** white[black] sesame. **胡麻油** sesame (-seed) oil. **胡麻酢** sesame vinegar. **胡麻醤油** sesame-flavored *shoyu*[soy sauce]. **胡麻塩** parched[roasted] sesame seeds mixed with salt (often sprinkled over boiled rice in a lunch box). （塩を混ぜた炒り胡麻（弁当のご飯の上にかける））．**胡麻垂れ** sesame sauce; sauce made with ground sesame.（擂り胡麻で作るソース）．**胡麻味噌** sesame *miso*[bean paste]; *miso* made with ground sesame seeds and *mirin* [sweetened *sake*].（擂り胡麻と味醂で作る味噌）

〔料理〕**胡麻和え** vegetables[spinach] dressed with ground sesame seeds and other seasonings (such as *shoyu* and sugar) （すり胡

麻と他の調味料(醤油・砂糖など)で味つけした野菜[ホウレンソウ]). ⇨和え物. **胡麻酢和え** vegetables dressed[mixed] with ground (roasted) sesame seeds and vinegar (擂り胡麻と酢で味つけした野菜). **胡麻豆腐** sesame *tofu*[bean curd]; *tofu* made with ground white sesame seeds (白い擂り胡麻で作る豆腐)

こまい【古米】 old rice; long-stored rice; rice stored[preserved] from a previous year's harvest. 収穫して1年以上長く貯蔵した古い米. ⇨新米. ¶**古古米** rice stored for two years.

こまいぬ【狛犬】 *komainu*; (a pair of)stone-carved guardian dogs; (a pair of) lion-shaped stone statues of guardian dogs (placed to protect the shrine from evil spirits). A pair of *komainu* dogs squat facing each other, one with its mouth open and the other with it closed. They squat in pairs at the left and right sides of the entrance gate or in front of a Shinto shrine. They guard the sanctity of the shrine by warding off devils. (魔除けのために置かれた)一対の獅子に似た犬の石像. 狛犬は互いに向かい合い, 1匹は口を開き, もう1匹は閉じている. 神社の入り口または社殿の前に左右に坐っている. 悪霊を払い除けながら神社の聖域を守護する. ☆稲荷神社には「狐の石像」がある. ⇨神社 /稲荷神社

こまげた【駒下駄】 (a pair of) low wooden clogs; (a pair of) low clogs made of a single wood. (1つの木材からつくる)低い下駄. ☆ 形は駒 (a horse)のひづめに似ている.

ごますり【胡麻擂り】 an apple-polisher; a flatterer. 他人にへつらう人.

こまちむすめ【小町娘】 a girl of exceeding loveliness; a very beautiful girl; a beauty. 美人の評判が高い娘.

こまつな【小松菜】〔植物〕*komatsuna* (a kind of Chinese) cabbage; an edible species of (oil-seed) rape; a vegetable similar to spinach. アブラナ科の一年草.「油菜」の一変種. ホウレンソウに似た野菜. 和え物や浸し物などに用いる. ☆東京都江戸川区の小松川付近で多数産(特産)したことからの呼称.

こまどり【駒鳥】〔鳥〕a (Japanese) robin. ヒタキ科の小鳥.

ごまめ【鱓】 small dried sardines; dried young anchovies; sardines laid out to dry in the sun. カタクチイワシの幼魚を干した物.「田作り」ともいう. ☆「達者」(元気)という意味があり, 祝儀・正月の御節料理には欠かせない. ⇨田作り

こみ【木密】〔華道〕a forked plant holder (used in a cylindrical vase in flower arranging). (花を生けるとき円筒状の花器の中で動かないように)留める二股の木.「花留め」「留め」ともいう. ⇨花留め / 留め

ゴミしょり【ゴミ処理】 waste[garbage] disposal; waste collection and processing. ¶**可燃ゴミ** burnable waste. **不燃ゴミ** unburnable waste. **資源ゴミ** recyclable waste. ☆「3Rキャンペーン」"3Rs" campaign. Reduce(ゴミ減少), Reuse(再使用), Recycle(再生利用).

ごみごしょくごほうのりょうり【五味五色五法の料理】 five flavors, five colors and five basic methods of preparation (in a Japanese-style cooking). 【関連語】『**五味**』(five flavors) : sweet(甘い), sour(酸っぱい), hot(辛い), bitter(苦い) and salty(塩気の).『**五色**』(five colors): white(白い), yellow(黄色い), red(赤い), green(緑の) and black(黒い).『**五法**』(five preparations) : raw(生の), boiled(煮た), grilled(焼いた), deep-fried(油で揚げた) and steamed(蒸した).

こむぎ【小麦】〔植物〕wheat; 米 corn (米国では「とうもろこし」の意). イネ科の一年[二

年]草. 種から味噌・醤油を作る. 粉はうどん・パンの原料(「メリケン粉」). ⇨むぎ. ¶**小麦胚芽** wheat germ. **小麦フスマ** wheat bran. **小麦粉** wheat flour.

こむすび【小結】〔相撲〕 a ***komusubi***; a *sumo* wrestler of the fourth highest rank and the lowest *sanyaku* rank; the fourth-ranking *sumo* champion in the *makuuchi* division. 「三役」の下位,「幕内」の4位. ⇨相撲の番付

こむそう【虚無僧】 a mendicant Zen Buddhist priest. He is a mendicant priest of the Fuke sect, a branch of Zen Buddhism. He goes on a pilgrimage wearing a large braided basket-like sedge hood[hat] covering the entire head (*tengai*), and a surplice (*kesa*) around the neck. He strolls from door to door asking for alms by playing a vertical bamboo flute with five finger holes (*shakuhachi*). 禅宗の一派・普化宗の托鉢僧. 頭全体を隠す天蓋 (sedge visor)をかぶり, 首に袈裟をつけて諸国を行脚する. 尺八を吹きながら家々に布施を求め巡業する. 「普化僧」ともいう. ☆ head「(顔を含めた)頭部」(首から上の頭部全体). ⇨尺八 / 天蓋

こめ【米】〔植物〕 rice. イネ科の一年草. 「ジャポニカ米」(Japonica[short-grain] rice［炊くと粘りの多い短粒米］)と「インディカ米」(Indica[long-grain] rice［炊くと粘りが少ない長粒米］. 泡盛の原料)がある. ☆主として「うるち米」(nonglutinous rice eaten at meals)と「もち米」(glutinous rice used for rice cakes)がある. 米は日本人の主食(staple food)であり, 米と関連するものが多数ある. 「酒」(rice wine), 「煎餅」(rice crackers), 「赤飯」(rice boiled with red *adzuki* beans), 「おにぎり」(rice balls), 「すし」(vinegared rice topped with slices of raw fish)など. ⇨五穀. ¶**米糠** rice bran. **米粒** a grain of rice(もみがついている); **米の飯** boiled[steamed] rice. **米櫃** a rice chest[bin]. **米俵** a straw rice-bag. ⇨白米(精白した米) / 玄米(精白していない米) / 胚芽米

こも【菰・薦】❶〈菰〉 a rush mat. 荒く織った(マコモ草葉の)むしろ.

❷〈薦〉 straw mat; straw matting (used to wrap a *sake* cask). (酒樽を包む)ワラのむしろ. ⇨酒樽. ¶**薦包み** a package wrapped in straw matting. **薦被り** a straw[rush]-covered cask of *sake*; a *sake* cask wrapped in a rush[straw] mat. こもで包んだ酒樽.

ごもくずし【五目鮨】 mixed *sushi*; *sushi* [vinegared rice] mixed with various vegetables (such as carrots and *shiitake* mushrooms) and topped with pieces of fish [shellfish]. 野菜を混ぜ魚介類をのせた鮨. 「ばら鮨」「混ぜ鮨」. 関西では「ちらし鮨」ともいう. ⇨ちらし鮨

ごもくならべ【五目並べ】 simplified version of a *go* game (played on a *go* board). The players try to be the first to arrange five stones in a consecutive row. 碁の簡素版. 先に連続した(縦横斜めのいずれかの)列に5個の碁石を並べるように競う.

ごもくめし【五目飯】 rice cooked in seasoned stock with various ingredients (of vegetables and meat or fish). Rice is boiled in seasoned stock with small pieces of chicken (or seafoods), a variety of seasonal vegetables (chestnuts, ginkgo nuts, bamboo shoots, etc.) and *aburage*[deep-fried *tofu* puff]. いろいろな具を味つけした汁で調理した飯. 鶏肉(または魚介類), 季節の野菜(栗・銀杏・筍など)また油揚げなどを炊きこんだ飯. 「加薬ご飯」(大阪), 「炊き込みご飯」「混ぜご飯」などともいう.

ごもくやきそば【五目焼きそば】 fried [boiled] buckwheat noodles cooked[mixed] with various vegetables and seafood (or meat). 野菜と魚介類(または肉類)を混ぜて焼いた[煮た]麺.

こもちこんぶ【子持昆布】 (salted) *kombu* [kelp] filled with herring roes. 昆布にニシンの卵(数の子)が産み付けられているもの. 通常は塩漬けにされている.

こもりうた【子守歌】 a lullaby; a cradle-song; a nursery song.

こもん【小紋】 a fine pattern on *kimono* fabric[material] (made by the repetition of small motifs). 細かい模様を着物の布地一面に染め出したもの. ¶**小紋染** cloth dyed with a fine pattern.

こやすじぞう【子安地蔵】 a Jizo, the patron deity of pregnant women; a Jizo statue [image] worshipped for an easy childbirth [easy delivery]. 妊婦の守護者. 安産にご利益がある地蔵. ⇨地蔵 / 石地蔵

ごようおさめ【御用納め】 the last business day of the year (prior to the New Year holidays); the final workday of the year [year-end closing] of government offices and large companies. (December 28). ⇔御用始め

ごようたし【御用達】 the purveying of goods to the government. ¶**宮内庁御用達の品物** goods purveyed to the Imperial Household Agency.

ごようてい【御用邸】 an Imperial villa. 皇室の別邸. ¶**那須御用邸**(栃木県)the Imperial Villa in the Nasu Highlands.

ごようはじめ【御用始め】 the first business day of the year (after the New Year holidays); the first workday of the year [early-year reopening] of government offices and large companies. (January 4). ⇔御用納め

ごらいこう【御来光】 the beautiful view of the sunrise from a mountaintop; the first sunrise seen from the top[summit] of a high mountain. 高山から拝む日の出. またその美しい景観. ¶**富士山の御来光を拝む** pray to the (first) rising sun from the summit of Mt. Fuji.

ごらいごう【御来迎】 ⇨来迎

ごり【鮴】〔魚〕a freshwater goby; a bullhead; a (Japanese) sculpin.「鰍」の異名.「金沢のゴリ料理」は有名. ⇨かじか

ごりやく【御利益】 an answer to a prayer; a receipt of divine grace[god's help]. 祈祷への返答. 神の恵みを拝受すること.

ごりょう【御陵】 an Imperial mausoleum. 天皇・皇后などの墓所.「陵」ともいう. ☆mausoleum (複 ~s, ~lea)「霊廟, みたまや」. ¶**多摩御陵** the Tama Mausoleum (enshrining the remains of Emperor Taisho).

ごりょうかく【五稜郭】Pentagonal Fortress; Japan's first Western-style Five-Pointed-Star-Fort. It was built in Hokkaido in 1864 by the Tokugawa. 五角形の要塞. 日本最初の五角形の洋式城郭. 1864年徳川幕府によって築かれた. ☆1868年, 榎本武揚が中心になって明治維新新政府に反抗し, ここに立てこもって戦った. ⇨戊辰戦争

こりょうり【小料理】 a Japanese simple à la carte dish[meal](一品料理); a Japanese plain fare. 手軽なちょっとした料理. 主に和風料理のこと. ¶**小料理屋** a small Japanese-style restaurant (serving liquor and simple à la carte dishes).

ごりん(のみち)【五倫(の道)】 the Five Norms of Ethics; the five principles of morality in Confucianism. 儒教の五条の道徳律. ☆『五箇条の人間関係の絆』(the bond of five human relationships)を規制する. ①「君臣の義」(justice between lord [ruler] and vassal[subordinate]). ②「父子の親」(benevolence between parent and child). ③「夫婦の別」(propriety between husband and wife). ④「長幼の序」(order between elder and younger). ⑤「朋友の信」(sincerity between[among] friends).

ごれいぜん【御霊前】 ❶〈仏の前〉(flowers offered) before the spirit of the deceased [departed]. 故人の霊の前(に捧げる花).

こ

❷〈仏への供物〉an offering made to the spirit of the deceased[departed] (before the funeral service). 霊前にささげる供物. 葬儀の前に用いる. ☆通夜または葬儀の時に渡す「香典袋」に書く. ⇨御仏前(葬儀の後)

ころも【衣】❶〈衣服〉clothes; a garment. ¶**衣替え** seasonal changes in[of] clothes; changing (one's) dress for the season.
❷〈僧衣・法衣〉a (Buddhist priest's) robe; a gown. ¶**法衣を着けた和尚** a bonze[Buddhist priest] worn in a robe.
❸〈天麩羅の〉*tempura* batter (made of egg, water and wheat flour); a coating of batter (used for making *tempura*). It is coated on fish or vegetables to make *tempura*. 卵・水・小麦粉を混ぜて作る. てんぷらを作るには魚または野菜に衣をまぶす. ⇨てんぷら

こわめし【強飯】⇨お強

こんがすり【紺絣】 dark-blue cloth with white splash patterns; tie-dying textile with white patterns on an indigo-blue ground. 紺地に白いかすり模様のある, 絞り染めをした織物. ⇨絣. ¶**紺絣の着物** an indigo-blue *kimono* with a fine pattern of white splashes on it.

ごんげん【権現】❶ incarnation of Buddha (appearing in the guise of a god to save all people). 仏の化身. 仏・菩薩が仮に姿を変え, 人類救済の神としてこの世に出現したもの.
❷ (the name applied to) Tokugawa Ieyasu, the founder of the Tokugawa shogunate. 「権現さま」(通称)の形で, 徳川家康(徳川幕府の創始者)の尊称. ☆また徳川家康を祀った「東照宮」を指す.

ごんげんづくり【権現造り】 a style of architecture in which outer and inner shrines are joined by a paved room. 神社建築の一様式. 本殿と拝殿の間に中殿があって, それぞれの屋根の続いているもの. ☆祀られた「東照大権現」による呼称.

こんごうりきし【金剛力士】⇨仁王

こんじきどう【金色堂】 Golden Hall. ¶**中尊寺の金色堂** the Golden Hall of Chuson(ji) Temple. ☆1124年建立. 阿弥陀三尊の下には藤原三代(清衡, 基衡, 秀衡)の遺体が埋葬されている.

こんどう【金堂】 the main hall[sanctuary] of a Buddhist temple (where the principal Buddhist image is enshrined); the worship hall (enshrining the principal Buddhist image of the temple). 本尊を安置する仏堂. ⇨七堂伽藍. ☆本堂の内部は通常「金塗り」であるため金堂と呼ばれる. ¶**法隆寺の金堂** the main hall of Horyuji Temple. ☆「阿弥陀三尊」, 「吉祥天」, 「毘沙門天」, 「四天王像」が安置されている. ⇨阿弥陀三尊/四天王

こんにゃく【蒟蒻】❶〈植物〉a *konnyaku*; a konjak; devil's tongue; devil's tongue yam (root)(蒟蒻イモ). サトイモ科の多年草. 地下茎は「こんにゃく玉」(tuberous root 食用)という.
❷〈食品〉(a piece of [1枚/1丁]) *konnyaku* [devil's tongue] paste[jelly]; paste[jelly] made from *konnyaku* flour. *Konnyaku* is a jelly-like[gelatin-like] food made from the starch of devil's tongue yam. 蒟蒻イモの粉末から作ったゼラチン状の食品. おでん・すき焼・精進料理などには不可欠. ¶**こんにゃく玉** a konjak bulb[ball]; a bulb[ball] of *konnyaku*. **ねじりコンニャク** twist knots of *konnyaku*. **長方形の蒟蒻** rectangular *konnyaku*. **うどん状の蒟蒻** noodle-like *konnyaku*. ⇨糸こんにゃく/しらたき

コンパニオン a party hostess(宴会); a convention guide(展示会); a trade show hostess(見本市); booth attendant(展示コーナー)

コンピューターおたく a computer geek [nerd]. ⇨おたく

こんぺいとう【金平糖】 a sugar candy; a

Japanese-style confetto[sugar candy ball] made by crystallizing sugar around a poppy-seed core. It is a tiny hard candy with various colors, which is pointed all-round like a star. 芥子の実を芯にして砂糖をまぶし固めて作る．星型の突起状をし，多彩な色を有する小粒の飴菓子．☆ポルトガル語の confeito のなまり．confetto[⽶ confetti] は「イタリアの砂糖菓子」．ポルトガル宣教師(ルイス・フロイス)が織田信長へ献上した贈物として知られる．⇨芥子

こんよく【混浴】 mixed bathing (of men and women at hot-spring resorts). People of both sexes bathe together at spa resorts.

こんりゅう【建立】 construction; erection. ¶法隆寺の建立(奈良県) construction of Horyuji Temple (in 607).

こんろ【焜炉】 a portable cooking stove; a portable clay cookstove. ⇨七輪

さ

サービスタイム(飲食店や酒場の) ⽶ happy hour. ☆英語の service には日本語での「値引き」(discount),「おまけ，景品」(giveaway),「(飲食)店のおごり」(on the house) という意味はない．

さいき【祭器】 a ritual utensil (used in Shinto rites). 神道儀式に用いる道具．「祭具」ともいう．

さいきょう【西京】 Kyoto (and neighboring districts); the Western Capital. 京都(東京に対して西の方にある都)，西の都．

〔料理・食品〕**西京味噌** saikyo-style sweet white[light-brown] *miso*[bean paste] produced in Kyoto（京都産の米を原料とした甘味の濃い白[薄茶色] 味噌）．⇨白味噌．**西京漬け** foods[fish or vegetables] preserved[pickled] in saikyo-style *miso*（西京味噌に漬けこんだ食品[魚または野菜]）．**西京焼き魚** (slice of) fish marinated in saikyo-style *miso* and broiled（西京味噌に漬け焼きあげた魚）．

ざいけ【在家】 a layman; a laywoman; a lay person; lay people. 在俗の人．⇔出家

さいけいれい【最敬礼(45度以上)】 (make) a deep bow. ⇨お辞儀

さいし【祭祀】 a religious service (of Shinto rites); an official cult (of the Shinto religion). 神を祭る神道儀式.

さいし【祭司】 an officiating priest. 宗教儀式を行う人.

さいじき【歳時記】 a glossary of seasonal words[terms] in *haiku* (classified by the four seasons), with illustrative verses; a compendium of seasonal words[terms] for *haiku* composers[poets], with example verses. ☆俳句の季語(season words)を四季順に配列し，解説して例句を載せた本．⇨季語

さいしきが【彩色画】 a colored picture; a picture in colors.

さいじょうあきまつり【西条秋まつり】 the Saijo Autumn Festival. (10月). ⇨付記(1)「日本の祭り」

ざいす【座椅子】 a legless chair[chair without legs] (used to sit on in a *tatami*-mat room).

さいせん【賽銭】 an offertory; a money [monetary] offering. Worshippers toss [throw] money into the wooden offertory box before praying (for their wishes to come true) at a shrine or temple. Coins are usually tossed into the offertory box, but notes[bills] are offered on New Year's days. 賽銭は社寺で礼拝する(願い事を祈る)前に参詣者が木製の賽銭箱に投げ入れる献金のこと．通常は硬貨だが元旦などでは紙幣も見受ける．☆賽銭は自分の罪業を金銭に託し身を清める (purify oneself by leaving[atoning for] one's sins with the money) との説もある.

【賽銭箱】 an offertory box[chest]; a square [rectangular] wooden box with slats across the top. It is placed in front of the oratory (*haiden*) at a shrine or temple to receive money offerings. 上部に薄板を差し渡した四角い(長方形の)木箱. 賽銭が受けられるよう神社や寺の拝殿前に置かれる.

さ

サイダー(日本での「清涼飲料水」) Ⓐ soda pop; Ⓑ lemonade. ☆ ciderは米国では「リンゴジュース」(=sweet cider). 英国では「リンゴ酒」(アルコールを含む. 米国では hard ciderに該当)の意. ¶**サイダー瓶** a pop bottle.

さいだいじえよう(はだかまつり)【西大寺会陽(裸祭り)】 the Half-Naked Men's Competition of Saidai-ji Temple. (2月). ⇨付記(1)「日本の祭り」

ざいたくきんむ【在宅勤務】 telecommuting; 〈人〉 telecommuter. ☆コンピューター通信を利用した自宅勤務(者).

ざいたくかいご(りょうよう)【在宅介護[療養]】 home care; home nursing (for one's parents suffering from terminal illness). ⇨介護

ざいたくケア【在宅ケア】 in-home care; in-home nursing care.

ざいテク【財テク】 speculative money management; financial engineering.

さいとうさい【祭頭祭】 the Stick-Clacking Parade Festival. (3月). ⇨付記(1)「日本の祭り」

さいばし【菜箸】❶〈料理を作るとき〉(a pair of) cooking chopsticks; (a pair of) long chopsticks used in cooking.

❷〈料理を個々に盛りつけるとき〉(a pair of) serving chopsticks; (a pair of) long chopsticks used in serving food to an individual dish.

ざいばつ【財閥】 a ***zaibatsu***; a financial clique; a financial combination[combine]. A *zaibatsu* is a great financial conglom-erate which ruled the Japanese economy after the Japanese-Russo War. 日露戦争後, 日本経済に勢力を振るった大企業の一族[一団]. ¶**三井財閥** the Mitsui *zaibatsu*; the Mistui financial combine.

さいばんいん【裁判員】 a lay judge; a citizen judge. ¶**裁判員裁判** a lay judge trial. **裁判員制度** the citizen judge system.

さお【竿・棹】❶ a pole; a rod. ¶**竿竹** a bamboo pole. **釣竿** a fishing rod.

❷〈三味線の〉the neck (of a *shamisen*). ⇨三味線. ❸**太棹** a wide neck of a *shamisen*; a wide-necked *shamisen*. **中棹** a medium-sized neck of a *shamisen*; a medium-necked *shamisen*. **細棹** a narrow neck of a *shamisen*; a narrow-necked *shamisen*.

さおとめ【早乙女】 a rice-planting girl [maiden]. At the rice-planting rite, girls dressed in rice-planting costumes plant rice seedlings while they chant a ritual rice-planting song. 田植えする娘[乙女]. 田植え神事のとき, 田植え姿の少女が儀式の田植え歌を歌いながら苗を植える. 「さ」は接頭語.

さおもの【棹物】 traditional bar-like sweets: stick-like confectioneries (such as *yokan* or *uiro*). Sweets are often cut in bite-sized pieces from long blocks when eating. 羊羹や外郎など棒状の和菓子. 食べるときには長い固まりを一口サイズに切る.

さか【茶菓】 refreshments; tea and cakes. ¶**茶菓を出す** serve refreshments. ⇨茶[茶菓子]

-さか[-ざか]【〜坂】 a slope; a hill. ¶**いろは坂**(栃木県) the Iroha(zaka) Slope (a steep zigzagging road with numerous[a total of 48 continuous] hairpin bends). **上り坂** an upward[uphill] slope; an ascent. **下り坂** a downward[downhill] slope; a descent. ⇨山/岳/峠/丘

さかき【榊】〔植物〕a *sakaki* tree; a *sakaki*

branch[twig]; a kind of camellia (*tsubaki*) with thick, dark-green leaves. *Sakaki* twigs are offered to the gods in Shinto rituals. ツバキ科の常緑高木. 枝葉は神前に供える. ⇨玉串

さかきりょう【榊料】 ⇨香典

さかさふじ【逆さ富士】 an inverted image of Mt. Fuji (reflected on the water); an inverted reflection of Mt. Fuji (seen on the surface of the water). ☆箱根の「芦ノ湖」また富士五湖の「河口湖」などは特に有名である.

さかずき【盃・杯】 a *sake* cup (usually made of lacquer ware or ceramic ware); a *sake* goblet(足付き). ⇨一献. ¶杯をさす offer a *sake* cup. ⇨献杯❶. 杯を受ける accept a *sake* cup. 杯をくみ交わす exchange cups of *sake* (with). 返杯する offer a *sake* cup in return.

さかだる【酒樽】 a *sake* barrel; a *sake* cask. ☆「薦」 straw matting used to wrap a *sake* cask. ⇨鏡開き❷/薦❷

さかな【魚】❶ a fish. ☆複数形も fishだが「種類」を指す場合はfishesという. ¶海の魚 saltwater fish. 淡水の魚 freshwater fish. 水族館の種々の珍しい魚 various rare fishes in the aquarium. 鯉や鱒などの淡水魚 freshwater fishes like carp and trout. ❷《料理用》fish. ¶食用魚 edible fish. 切り身の魚 fish fillet; filleted fish. 塩漬けの魚 salted fish. 燻製の魚 smoked fish. フライの魚 deep-fried fish. 蒸し焼きの魚 casseroled fish. 生の魚 raw fish. 赤[白]身魚 fish with red[white] flesh.

さかな【肴】〈酒の〉a relish (eaten with *sake*); a relish (eaten as an accompaniment to *sake*); a side dish (to go with *sake*)*;* an hors d'oeuvre[appetizer] (taken with *sake*). ☆「さか」は酒, 「な」は菜でおかず. 酒をのむときに添える食品(枝豆・そら豆・塩辛など)または料理(酢の物・和え物など). ⇨お通

し/摘み

さがにんぎょう【嵯峨人形】 a richly-decorated wooden doll (with a rotating head). 華やかに飾りたてた木製の人形(頭が回る).

さかまんじゅう【酒饅頭】 a bean-paste bun flavored with *sake*. 酒で味つけした餡入りの饅頭

さかむし【酒蒸し】❶〈料理法〉steaming after steeping in *sake*. 酒に浸した後で蒸すこと. ❷〈酒蒸しの魚介類〉*sake*-steamed fish [shellfish]; fish[shellfish] steamed after steeping in *sake*; fish[shellfish] steeped in *sake* and steamed. 魚介類を酒に浸した後で蒸してつくる料理. ⇨あさりの酒蒸し/あわびの酒蒸し

さかや【酒屋】❶〈店〉a *sake* store[shop]; liquor store;〈人〉a *sake* dealer[merchant]. ❷〈醸造所〉a *sake* brewery; *sake* producer [maker].

さかやき【月代】 the shaved forepart[front and top part] of an adult man's head. (武家時代)男子の額から頭の中央にかけて頭髪を剃った部分. ⇨ちょんまげ

さがり【下がり】*sagari*:〔相撲〕the decorative cords[ornamental strings] (hanging from a *sumo* wrestler's belt[loincloth]). *Sagari* cords are worn tucked into the front folds of a *sumo* wrestler's belt[loincloth] (*mawashi*) during competition. まわしの前から垂らす飾りひも (stiff braids). 相撲力士が競技用としてまわし[褌]の前のくぼみに挟み込んで (inserted)着ける. ⇨まわし

-さき[-ざき]【〜崎】a cape. ¶犬吠埼(千葉県)Cape Inubo(saki); 竜飛崎(青森県)Cape Tappi(zaki). ⇨ 岬

さぎ【鷺】〔鳥〕an egret; a heron;〈白鷺〉a white egret; a snowy heron. ¶鷺舞 Heron dance (performed at Yasaka Shrine in Shimane Prefecture). 通称白鷺城の姫路城 Himeji Castle nicknamed "Hakuro-jo",

White Egret[Heron] Castle. ☆「しらさぎ じょう」は訓読.

さぎちょう【左義長】 ⇨どんど焼き

さきづけ【先付け】 an appetizer that goes well with *sake;* an appetizer made with seasonal ingredients in the traditional Japanese meal. 酒に合うお通し. 和食で旬の食材を用いた前菜. ☆最初に出される「お通し」で, 小鉢で酢の物や和え物を盛り付ける. ⇨酢の物 / 和え物

さきもり【防人】 soldiers stationed[garrisoned] at strategic posts in Kyushu (after the Taika Reform). (大化の改新後)九州に置かれた守護兵. ⇨鹿島立ち / 大化の改新

さきゅう【砂丘】 a sand dune; a sand hill. ¶ 鳥取砂丘(鳥取県)(the)Tottori Sand Dune. ⇨海岸 / 浜

さくら【桜】〔植物〕a cherry tree(木); cherry blossoms(花); a cherry leaf(葉). バラ科の落葉高木. ☆日本の国花 (the national flower). ¶彼岸桜 spring-equinox cherry tree[blossoms]. 一重桜 single-petaled cherry tree[blossoms]. 八重桜 multi-petaled cherry tree[blossoms]. 枝垂桜 dropping cherry tree[blossoms]. 山桜 mountain cherry tree[blossoms]. 桜並木 a row of cherry trees lining the street. 桜吹雪 a flurry[blizzard] of falling cherry blossom petals. 桜開花予想 cherry blossom forecast; the expected date for blooming of cherry blossoms (予想日).

【桜前線】 the cherry-blossom front. The cherry blossoms begin to bloom, moving from South (Kyushu) to North (Hokkaido) through Japan (like a rain front). 国内を南から北へと時期を追って開花していく.

【桜餅】 cherry-leaf rice cake; rice cake stuffed with sweet bean paste and wrapped in a salted cherry leaf. It is a pinkish ball of glutinous rice filled with sweet bean paste and wrapped in a pickled cherry leaf. 粒餡

を入れ, 塩漬けにした桜の葉で巻いた餅.

【桜湯】〈湯の中の桜花〉a cherry-blossom hot drink[tea]; a hot drink[tea] seasoned with salty pickled cherry blossoms; a salt-preserved cherry blossoms in hot water. It is often served on such an auspicious occasion as a wedding ceremony[reception]. 桜漬けに熱湯を注いだ飲み物. 花が開くことから結婚式や披露宴などでの祝儀に出される.

さくらえび【桜蝦】 ❶〔魚〕a small pink shrimp; a spotted shrimp. ⇨えび ❷〔食品〕small dried shrimps. 干しえび.

さくらそう【桜草】〔植物〕a primrose. 観賞用.

さくらだい【桜鯛】〔魚〕a red sea bream;〈ハタ科の魚〉a cherry bass.

さくらにく【桜肉】 horsemeat; horseflesh. 「馬肉」の別称. ☆肉が桜色をしていることからの呼称. ⇨馬刺し

さくらんぼ【桜ん坊・桜桃】 a cherry (fruit). ⇨さくら. ¶桜ん坊の種 a cherrystone; a cherry pit.

ざくろ【石榴】〔植物〕a pomegranate (木・実). 鑑賞用・食用.

さけ【鮭】〔魚〕a salmon(単複同形). ☆卵は「イクラ」(salmon roe)または「スジコ」(salted salmon roe)として食用. ⇨新巻. ¶鮭の幼魚 a parr. 紅鮭 a red salmon. 銀鮭 a silver salmon. 塩鮭 salted salmon. 鮭のフレーク salmon flakes. 鮭の切り身 a salmon steak. 鮭の燻製 smoked salmon. 〔料理〕鮭のお握り rice ball stuffed with salmon flakes. ⇨お握り. 鮭の親子蒸し steamed salmon and roe. 鮭のちり蒸し steamed salmon casserole. 鮭茶漬け boiled [steamed] rice topped with slices of roast salmon in hot tea.

さけ【酒】❶〈飲物〉*sake*; Japanese rice wine; alcoholic beverage brewed with rice and water. *Sake* is a clear alcoholic beverage made with fermented rice and water. It has an alcoholic content of about 15 percent. 米と水で作る醸造酒. 蒸した米を発酵させて作り，アルコール分は 15%前後である. ⇨地酒

【関連語】 「ちょこ」a small *sake* cup. 「とっくり」a small ceramic *sake* bottle. 「杯」a flat lacquered *sake* cup. 「酒樽」*sake* cask. 種類 「特級酒」top-class[special-grade] *sake*. 「一級酒」first-grade *sake*. 「二級酒」second-grade *sake*. 燗酒 hot *sake*; warmed *sake*. 冷酒 cold *sake*; chilled *sake*. 生酒 raw *sake*. 煮切り酒 heated *sake*. 枡酒 *sake* served in a small square wooden cup. 辛口酒 dry *sake*. 甘口酒 sweet *sake*. 純米酒 pure *sake* brewed from only rice. 吟醸酒 quality *sake* brewed from refined rice. 料理酒 cooking *sake* used for seasoning.

❷〈雛祭り〉sweet white *sake* (used as a celebratory drink at the Doll Festival). ⇨白酒

さけかす【酒糟】 *sake* lees; rice-wine lees. *Sake-kasu* is the residue left after *sake* is made from unrefined *sake*. It is used for preserving fish or pickling vegetables. もろみから清酒を搾った残りかす. 魚の保存や漬け物（粕漬け）に使用する. ⇨もろみ / 粕漬け

ざこ【雑魚】〈小さい魚〉 small fish[fry]; coarse fish; 〈多種（大物）に混じった小物魚〉mixed small fish.

さこく（せいさく）【鎖国（政策）】 national seclusion (policy); national isolation (policy); a closed door policy (from the outside world). The Tokugawa shogunate prohibited all Westerners from entering Japan to unify the nation and traded only with Holland[the Dutch] and Qing（清）in 1639. 1639年江戸幕府は国家統一を名目として，オランダと中国以外の外国人の渡来と貿易を禁じた（第5次鎖国令）. ☆「鎖国」体制は徳川秀忠の時代から始まりペ

リー来航まで続いた. 「開国」はハリスとの日米修好通商条約で事実上完成する（1858年）. ⇨付記(2)「日本の歴史年表」

ささ【笹】〔植物〕bamboo grass. 「笹竹」の略. 「笹」は国字. ¶笹の葉 a bamboo leaf [blade]. 笹薮 a thicket of low bamboo; a striped bamboo grass. 笹舟 a bamboo-leaf boat. 笹笛 bamboo-leaf whistle

〔料理・食品〕笹飴 candy wrapped in a bamboo leaf. 笹蒲鉾 boiled fish paste shaped like a bamboo leaf. ⇨蒲鉾. 笹巻 food (or *sushi*) wrapped up in a bamboo leaf. 笹団子 a dumpling wrapped in a bamboo leaf. The dumpling is made by steaming glutinous rice with minced moxa (mugwort) leaves mixed in, and has a filling of sweet red-bean paste.

さざえ【栄螺】〔貝〕a turbo (複 turbos); a horned turban; a turban[wreath] shell. 春から夏が旬. 刺身や壺焼きにする.

【さざえの壺焼き】 a turbo broilcd[grilled] in its own shell; a turbo baked with its own shell. The minced meat of a turban shell is usually seasoned with a little *shoyu*[soy sauce] and *sake* in its own shell. 貝殻に入れて焼いたさざえ. 刻んださざえの身は貝殻に入れたまま小量の醤油と酒で味をつける.

ささみ【笹身】 chicken breast meat[fillet]; white meat[tenderloin] of chicken. 鶏の胸につく柔らかい上質肉. ☆笹の葉の形をしていることからの呼称.

さざんか【山茶花】〔植物〕a sasanqua; Chinese hawthorn; a kind of camellia that blooms in late autumn. ツバキ科の常緑小高木. 晩秋から冬に咲く. 種子から採油する.

さし【砂嘴】 a sandbar; a spit. ☆湾[岸]の一方から細長く突き出た砂堤状の地形. ⇨砂州. ¶野付半島の砂嘴（北海道）（the largest) spit in the Notsuke Peninsula. ☆野付崎ともいう. 日本最大の分岐砂嘴.

ざしき【座敷】 a Japanese-style *tatami*-matted room. *Zashiki* is a Japanese-style room covered with *tatami* mats on the floor, which is often used for entertaining guests formally. It has an decorative alcove and staggered shelves in the corner. 畳を敷きつめた和室，特に接客用の日本間．飾りのある床の間や違い棚などがある．⇨床の間 / 違い棚

さしこ【刺し子】〈縫い〉quilting;〈衣服〉quilted clothes[coat] (often used on *judo* outfits). Indigo cotton clothes[coat] with repeated patterns are made by stitching white thread. 綿布を重ね合わせ，面に細かい刺し縫いをしたもの．柔道着などに用いる．

さしちがえ【差し違え】〔相撲〕a misjudgment [wrong decision] by a *sumo* referee.

さしみ【刺身】 *sashimi*; thinly-sliced raw fish (and shellfish); thin slices of raw fish (and shellfish); fresh raw fish (and shellfish) cut in thin sizes. *Sashimi* is served with *wasabi*[grated horseradish] and *tsuma*[decorative raw vegetables]. It is eaten after being dipped[by dipping it] in a small dish of *shoyu*[soy sauce]. 「おつくり」「お刺身」などともいう．¶刺身の妻[具] garnishings served with *sashimi*; trimmings for *sashimi*. 刺身包丁 a (raw) fish-slicing kitchen knife; a kitchen knife for slicing (raw) fish.
〔料理〕マグロの刺身 (a dish of) sliced raw tuna; slices of raw tuna. タイの刺身 (a dish of) sliced raw sea bream; slices of raw sea bream.

さす【砂州・砂洲】 a sandbar; a sandbank. ☆砂嘴がさらに長く伸びて，その先が対岸の陸地につながったもの．⇨砂嘴．圀京都府の天橋立．¶天橋立 pine-covered sandbar (located on the Japan Sea Coast to the north and juts out into Miyazu Bay).

ざす【座主】 the head[chief] priest of a Buddhist temple; a Buddhist abbot. 寺をとりしきる最高位の僧．

さずかりこん【授かり婚】 a wedding[marriage] when the bride is pregnant.

ざぜん【座禅】 *Zazen*; Zen meditation; Zen contemplation (in the lotus position); meditation in Zen Buddhism. *Zazen* is a religious meditation practiced in Zen Buddhism while sitting in a cross-legged posture with the back straight to attain the ideal state of supreme enlightenment. 座禅とは雑念を払い悟りの境地を得るために両足を組んで座りながら[あぐらを組んで]瞑想する修行．
《座禅の作法》⇨結跏趺坐 / 警策
① Sit on the floor with your legs crossed and your hands lightly clasped on your thighs. 床の上であぐらを組み，両手を腿の上で軽く組む．
② Straighten your back, tuck on your chin and breathe gently. 背中を伸ばし，あごを引き，緩やかに呼吸する．
③ Open your eyes slightly and look faintly in front of you. 目をわずかに開き，前方をかすかに見る．
④ Concentrate mentally and spiritually, dismissing worldly thoughts from your mind. 雑念を払い，全身全霊で集中する．
⑤ Try to attain the ideal state of supreme enlightenment. 悟りの境地に入るように努力する．

ざぞう【坐像・座像】〈仏像〉a seated statue [image] of Buddha;〈像〉a statue[an image] of a seated figure. ⇨立像

さそり【蠍】〔動物〕a scorpion. クモ綱サソリ目の有毒な動物．

さだいじん【左大臣】 the Minister of the Left (in ancient Japan); the Senior Minister of State; the chief officer of the Grand Council of State. He is superior in rank to the Minister of the Right. 昔の太政官の長官. 太政大臣の下位・右大臣の上位にある. 太政官の政務をすべて統制する. ⇨太政官 / 右大臣

さっちょうどうめい【薩長同盟】the Satsuma-Choshu Alliance[the Alliance of Satsuma and Choshu] (formed against the Tokugawa shogunate in 1866).「薩長連合」ともいう.

さつまあげ【薩摩揚げ】deep-fried fish-paste patty containing various vegetables; deep-fried cake[ball] of ground fish with a variety of ingredients of vegetables (such as carrots and burdocks). 魚肉をすり, 細切りの野菜の具(ごぼう・にんじんなど)を入れて油で揚げた食品. ☆鹿児島では「つけ揚げ」という. ☆ patty「パティー」ひき肉などを小さな平たい丸形につくった食品.

さつまいも【薩摩芋】〔植物〕a sweet potato. ¶丸焼きの薩摩芋 a sweet potato baked whole. ⇨いも / 焼(き)芋 / 石焼(き)芋

さつまやき【薩摩焼】Satsuma ceramic ware (produced in Kagoshima Prefecture).

さといも【里芋】〔植物〕a taro (potato). サトイモ科の多年草. ☆「芋茎」は stalk of a taro. ⇨いも / タロ芋
〔料理〕里芋の煮物 simmered taro; boiled taro.

さとう【砂糖】sugar.
種類 赤砂糖 brown sugar. 白砂糖 refined sugar (＝精製砂糖). 黒砂糖 unrefined [raw, crude] sugar (＝粗製砂糖). 粉砂糖 powdered sugar; (英) castor sugar. 角砂糖 cube[cut, block] sugar. 氷砂糖 crystal sugar; (米) rock candy; (英) sugar candy. 三温糖 less refined sugar (with brown color). ざらめ糖 granulated sugar. ⇨粗目
〔食品〕砂糖漬け food preserved in sugar. 野菜(芋・蓮根など)や果物(梅・柚子など)などの砂糖を用いる保存漬け. 口取りや茶菓子にも用いる.

さどう【茶道】(the) tea ceremony; the art of ceremonial tea-making. *Sado* is the ritualized way[the traditional etiquette] of preparing, serving and drinking tea when the host has the guests.

《**tea ceremony procedures**》The tea is made by adding hot water to powdered green tea (*matcha*) which is put into a teacup, and whipping[stirring] it with a bamboo whisk till it foams[gets foamy].
《**rapport**》Another important element is a shared sense of communication between the host and the guests throughout the tea ceremony.
茶道は来客の際, 作法に従って茶をたてて味わうことである. 《点前》茶は茶碗に入れた抹茶にお湯を注いでから, 泡立つまで茶せんでかき混ぜる. ⇨手前. 《心の交流》次に大事な点は茶会における主人と客人との心の交流である. ⇨一期一会
☆「茶道」(さどう；ちゃどう)は「茶の湯」ともいい,「茶をたてる作法を通じて礼儀作法を修め精神修養を究める道」のこと. 茶道は禅寺においてお茶を楽しむ儀礼 (a ceremony to enjoy tea in[at] Zen temples) として始まる. 室町時代の僧, 村田珠光 (1422-1502)によって創始され, 千利休 (1522-1591)が禅の精神を取り入れて大成した. 現在は主として表千家・裏千家・武者小路千家の御三家がある. ⇨茶の湯

さとうきび【砂糖黍】〔植物〕sugar cane; Japanese cane. イネ科の熱帯性の多年草. 砂糖の原料. ¶サトウキビ畑 sugar cane fields.

さとうだいこん【砂糖大根】〔植物〕sugar beet. アカザ科の越年草. 根のしぼり汁から砂糖をつくる. 酒の原料でもある.

さどおけさ【佐渡おけさ】the Sado *Okesa* folk song and dance (originating in Sado Island). ⇨佐渡島のまつり

さとおやせいど【里親制度】a foster-parent system; a foster-home system.

さとがえり【里帰り】a visit to one's old

family (for the first time) after (one's) marriage; a return to one's hometown after (one's) marriage. 結婚後，嫁が実家に帰ること. ¶新婦の里帰り a bride's first call at[visit to] her parents' home.

さどがしまのまつり【佐渡島のまつり】 the Sado Island Festival. (4月). ⇨付記(1)「日本の祭り」

さとり【悟り】 spiritual enlightenment [awakening] (in Zen Buddhism);〈仏教〉Buddhahood. 迷いを去り，真理を会得すること. ¶悟りを開く attain spiritual enlightenment[awakening]; be spiritually enlightened[awakened].

さなえ【早苗】〔植物〕rice sprouts; rice seedlings. ⇨いね

さなぎ【蛹】〔虫〕a chrysalis (特に蝶の ⑱~es; chrysalides)；a pupa(昆虫の: ⑱ pupas; pupae). 幼虫と成虫(adult)の間にある昆虫. ⇨ちょうちょう

さぬきうどん【讃岐饂飩】 Sanuki *udon* [noodles] (made at Kagawa Prefecture). ⇨饂飩

さば【鯖[鯖]】〔魚〕a mackerel (単複同形. または mackerels). サバ科の海産硬骨魚.
〔料理・食品〕鯖の塩漬け mackerel fillet preserved in[with] salt. 鯖の生干し half-dried mackerel. 鯖の煮物 simmered mackerel fillets. 鯖節 dried mackerel. しめ鯖 vinegared[seasoned] mackerel.
【鯖鮨】 mackerel *sushi;* pressed *sushi* cut into a rectangular shape, topped with vinegared mackerel slices. 長方形の形に切った押し鮨で，鯖の切り身を上にのせてある，大阪では「バッテラ」という. ⇨バッテラ
【鯖の味噌煮】 stewed fillet mackerel with *miso*[soybean paste]; simmered fillet mackerel in *miso* (cooked with onion and ginger). 味噌で煮込んだ料理.

さばく【砂漠】a desert.

さばく【佐幕】 adherence to the Tokugawa shogunate; the support of political groups for the Tokugawa shogunate, and against the overthrow of the shogunate at the end of the Edo period. 徳川幕府への忠誠. 幕末時代，倒幕の動きに対抗して幕府を支持し協力すること. ☆「佐」は助ける. ¶佐幕派 the supporters of the Tokugawa shogun; the shogunate party.

さび【寂】 *sabi*; elegant[quiet] simplicity; serenity; tranquility. 枯れて渋味があること. ⇨わび

サビ *sabi*[wasabi]; horseradish.「山葵」の符丁. ⇨符丁
〔料理〕サビの利いた鮨 *sushi* with *wasabi; sushi* included[used] plenty of horseradish. サビ抜きの鮨 *sushi* without *wasabi; sushi* excluded *wasabi*. ⇨山葵

ざふ【坐蒲】 a round[rectangular] cushion used for sitting cross-legged in a *Zen* meditation. 坐禅のときに使用する円形状(曹洞宗)また長方形状(臨済宗)の小さな座布団.

ざぶとん【座布団】 a *zabuton*; a floor cushion (for sitting on). It is made by stuffing cotton in cloth bags. It is used when sitting on one's knees on the *tatami*-matted floor of a Japanese room. 布袋に綿を入れてつくる. 正座をするとき和室の畳の間で使用する.

サボテン【仙人掌】〔植物〕a cactus (⑱ cactuses, cacti). サボテン科の常緑多年草. ¶サボテン公園 Cactus Park(静岡県・伊東温泉).

ザボン【朱欒】〔植物〕a shaddock; ⑱ a pomelo. ミカン科の常緑高木. 砂糖漬け，ゼリーやジャムなどに用いる. ☆ポルトガル語の zambca に由来.

さみせん【三味線】⇨しゃみせん

さみだれ【五月雨】 early summer rain; the long rains of early summer.

さむらい【侍】 a *samurai* (⑭ ~(s)); a (*samurai*) warrior. 身分の高い人のそば近くに使えた者. ⇨武士. ☆「地侍」a local *samurai* (who comes from some powerful peasants)(地主的な侍)と**国人** a powerful local *samurai*(その地に住む有力な侍)がいた.

【侍所】 a government agency which controlled the activities of *samurai*'s vassals[retainers] in the Kamakura and Muromachi periods. 鎌倉・室町時代の御家人(武士の家来)の活動を統括した幕府機関. ⇨御家人

さめ【鮫】〔魚〕a shark; a dogfish(小さい鮫). 関西では「フカ」、山陰では「わに」ともいう. 蒲鉾やはんぺんなどの原料. ヒレは中華料理の高級食材. ⇨ふか. ¶**鮫肝油** shark liver oil. **鮫皮** sharkskin; shagreen(研磨用).

さや【鞘】〈刀の〉 a scabbard (of a Japanese sword); 〈刃物の〉a sheath. ¶**刀の鞘を払う**[抜く] pull one's sword out of its scabbard; draw[unsheathe] one's sword. **刀を鞘に納める** sheathe one's sword.

さや【莢】 a pod; a shell; a hull. マメ科の植物の種子が入っている殻. ¶**さや入りの豆** peas in the pod.

さやいんげん【莢隠元】〔植物〕 kidney beans; green beans; string beans ⑭ French beans. さやのまま食べるいんげん豆.「菜豆」ともいう. ⇨いんげん豆

さやえんどう【莢豌豆】〔植物〕field peas; garden peas; sugar[snow] peas. さやのまま食べるえんどう豆.

さゆ【白湯】 (plain) hot water; (plain) boiled water. 何も混ぜない飲用の湯. ⇦冷や

さより【針魚・細魚】〔魚〕a halfbeak. サヨリ科の海産硬骨魚. 内湾に群れをなしてすむ. 刺身やてんぷら、また酢の物や焼き物などに用いる.

サラきん【サラ金】 consumer loans; consumer financing. ¶**サラ金業者** a loan shark; a consumer financing firm. ☆高利貸し (high-interest consumer credit firm), 金融会社 (consumer credit firm)のこと. **サラ金地獄** loan-shark hell; the plight of people in debt to loan sharks. 高利貸しに追われる地獄.

さらしあん【晒し餡】 powdered bean paste. こし餡をさらして粉にしたもの.「干し餡」ともいう. ⇨餡

さらしこ【晒し粉】 bleaching powder. 水にさらして白くした米の粉.

さらしねぎ【晒し葱】 minced[sliced] green onion[leek]. It is blanched[soaked] in water and then lightly squeezed. It is usually used as a condiment for noodles, a hot-pot dish, etc. せん切りにしたねぎ. 水にさらして水分を切ったもの. うどん・鍋物などの薬味に用いる.

さらしもめん【晒し木綿】 bleached cotton cloth.

ざらめ【粗目】 granulated sugar (細かい粒子の白ざらめ); brown sugar (赤ざらめ). 結晶の荒い, ざらざらした砂糖.「ざらめ糖」ともいう. 綿菓子に用いる. ⇨綿菓子

ざりがに【蝲蛄】〔甲〕⑧ a crawfish; a crayfish. ザリガニ科のエビの一種.

さる【申】 the Monkey, one[the ninth] of the 12 animals of the Chinese zodiac. 十二支の第九. ⇨十二支. ¶**申の方** the direction of the Monkey[west-southwest]. 方角の名. ほぼ 西南西. **申の刻** the Hour of Monkey [3-5 p.m.] 午後4時頃(および前後約2時間). **申年** the Year of Monkey. **申年生まれ** (be) born in the Year of the Monkey.

さる【猿】〔動物〕a monkey(尾のある猿); an ape(尾のない猿；類人猿); a male[female] monkey(雄[雌]猿); a baby monkey(小猿); a boss monkey(ボス猿).

【猿回し】❶〈余興〉a monkey show (performed on the street[stage]); a variety of street [stage] performance using monkeys. 「猿芝居」ともいう. ❷〈人〉a monkey showman; a trainer of performing monkeys.

ざる【笊】 a bamboo colander; colander made of bamboo. 竹で編んだ目の細かい容器. 水を切るために用いる.

【笊そば】 *zaru-soba*; cool buckwheat noodles topped <u>with</u> slices of seasoned laver. *Zaru-soba* are buckwheat noodles cooled in cold water and served[piled up] on a flat bamboo colander[slatted bamboo tray] placed on a lacquered wooden frame. Buckwheat noodles are sprinkled with pieces of seasoned laver on top. Buckwheat noodles are eaten after[by] dipping into a soy-based sauce (*soba-tsuyu*) mixed with *wasabi* [Japanese horseradish] and sliced green onions. 海苔を振りかけた冷えたそば. 茹でたそばを冷水にさらした後, 漆塗りの木枠にのせたせいろ[竹簾を敷いた盆「容器」(split-bamboo ware)]に盛りつける. 刻んだ焼き海苔を振りかける, 山葵と晒しネギを混ぜた汁につけて食べる. ⇨**盛りそば**(<u>海苔の振りかけがない</u>そば).
¶**笊そば二枚** two bamboo platters[plates] of *zaru-soba*; two bamboo platters[plates] piled up with *zaru-soba*.

さるがく【猿楽・申楽】〈能〉*sarugaku*; a mixture of song and dance combined with a humorous mimicry and acrobatics (till the Muromachi period). (室町時代までは)滑稽な物まねや軽業・曲芸などを伴う歌謡や舞踊を融合したもの. ☆能楽・狂言の原型 (a prototype of the Noh play and the Kyogen farce) である. その起源は奈良時代に中国から伝来した「散楽」(物まねや軽業・曲芸の総称 (a general term of acrobatics, magic, and song-and-dance))に見られる.

さるすべり【百日紅】〔植物〕a crepe[crape] myrtle; an Indian lilac. ミソハギ科の落葉

高木.

さるのこしかけ【猿の腰掛け】〔植物〕a bracket [shelf] fungus; a polypore. ⇨きのこ

サルビア〔植物〕a salvia; a (scarlet) sage. 葉は薬用・香料に用いる.

さるまた【猿股】(a pair of) underpants (worn by men). 男性用下着(ズボン下・パンツなど)

ざれい【座礼】 a sitting bow; a bow of respect made when seated on the *tatami* mat. The bow is made by putting three fingers of each hand flat on the *tatami*-mat floor, and bending forward from the waist. 畳上に座って行う礼. 畳の上に手の3本指を平たく置き, 腰から前方にかがめてお辞儀をする. ⇨立礼. ⇨お辞儀

さわ【沢】a swamp (湿地); a marsh (沼地); a gorge (山間の渓谷); a mountain stream (谷川). ¶**沢を登る** climb up along the mountain stream.

さわがに【沢蟹】〔甲〕a (Japanese) river crab; a (Japanese) freshwater crab. 谷川に生息するカニ. 生きたサワガニを姿のままから揚げ・甘辛煮に調理する. ⇨かに

さわら【鰆】〔魚〕 a (Japanese) Spanish mackerel. サバ科の海産硬骨魚. 「西京焼き」に調理する. ☆「さごし」(関西での呼び名)は young Spanish mackerel.
〔料理〕**さわらの西京焼き** grilled Spanish mackerel wrapped with aromatic Kyoto-style sweet white *miso*[soybean paste]. ⇨西京(西京焼き魚)

さわり【触り】❶〔文楽〕the most moving [exciting] passage; the impassioned punch-line; the climax. 義太夫のいちばんの聞かせどころ.
❷〈接触・要点〉touch; the high point (of a story or music). 話し・音楽などの聞かせどころ.

さん[ざん]【〜山】 Mount 〜; Mt.〜 (mountと読む). ¶**富士山** Mount Fuji; Mt. Fuji. ⇨山

さんエル・ディー・ケー【3LDK】 a house [an apartment] with three rooms plus a combination of a living room, and a dine-in-kitchen room.

さんえん【三猿】 the simian trinity; the trinity of monkeys; three monkeys:one holding over its eyes, one over its ears and the other over its mouth. ☆人間の一生の理想が順に描かれている「三匹の猿」の彫刻 (three carvings of monkeys).「悪を見ざる，悪を聞かざる，悪を言わざる」(See no evil, hear no evil, speak no evil). ☆ simian 图形「猿(の)」(=monkey). trinity「3つの組み」. 大文字の Trinity 图 (ラテン語のTrinitas から)は「三位一体」(父なる神・その御子キリスト・聖霊の三位を一体と見る)というキリスト教の用語.

さんが【参賀】 congratulatory greetings to the Imperial Family. It is a visit to the Imperial Palace to congratulate the Imperial Family on the New Year. 新年に皇居へ行って祝賀のことばを述べること. ⇨一般参賀

さんかいき【三回忌】 ⇨回忌

さんがく【散楽】 ⇨猿楽

さんがく【山岳】 mountain(s). ¶山岳信仰 mountain worship. 山岳地帯 mountain district. 山岳仏教 mountain Buddhism. 山岳避暑地 mountain resort area. 山岳修験者 (Japanese) Buddhist hermit; mountaineering[mountain] ascetic. ☆山岳修験者の霊山 sacred site of worship for mountaineering ascetics. 例「出羽三山(山形県)」(羽黒山・月山・湯殿山)

さんがにち【三が日】 the first three days of the new year (observed as holidays for the New Year celebration); the period between January 1st and 3rd; the period from January 1st through 3rd. During this period, people visit shrines or temples to pray for good luck for the new year and also pay visits to relatives and friends to exchange greetings. 正月の1日から3日間. 新年の祝賀としての休日. この期間中，その年の幸運を祈願して神社仏閣に参詣，親戚・友人への挨拶回りをする. ⇨松の内

さんかんぶ【山間部】 mountain areas; a mountainous region. ¶山間部の僻地 a remote[an isolated] district in the mountains.

さんかんしおん【三寒四温】 (a cycle in winter of) three cold days followed by four warm days; (a cycle in winter of) three cold days and four warm days. 三日間ほど寒く，四日間ほど暖かい冬期の気候循環.

さんきょそうこ【山居倉庫】 rice warehouse (having a row of 12 storehouses for rice). 12棟が連なる米の倉庫(山形県)

さんきょく【三曲】 a trio of Japanese musical instruments. *Sankyoku* is a trio of ensemble performed by three Japanese musical instruments: *koto*, *shamisen* and *shakuhachi* (or *Chinese fiddle*). 琴・三味線・尺八(または胡弓)の合奏. また，その楽器. ⇨琴 / 三味線 / 尺八

さんきんこうたい【参勤交代】 (the system of an obligatory) alternate-year residence of feudal lords in Edo; (the feudal system of a mandatory) alternating attendance of feudal lords at the shogun's court in Edo. All feudal lords were forced to spend alternate years in residence in Edo and at their fiefs[domains]. This feudal system was enacted in 1635 by the Tokugawa shogunate to show their loyalty to the shogunate. 江戸時代，諸国の大名が1年おきに(every two years)江戸へ出て江戸屋敷で過ごした. 1635年幕府が大名に忠誠を誓わせるために制定した(1862年まで). ⇨大名行列

さんケー【3K】 the three Ds: difficult [demanding], dirty and dangerous works. 「きつい」「きたない」「きけんな」仕事.

さ

さんけい【参詣】 a visit to a Shinto shrine [Buddhist temple]; a pilgrimage. ¶**参詣人** a visitor to a shrine(or temple); a pilgrim. **神社[寺院]に参詣する** visit[pay a visit to] a shrine[temple]; make a pilgrimage to a shrine[temple]; go to pray[worship] at a shrine[temple].

さんけい【三景】 the three most scenic spots. ¶**日本三景** the scenic trio of Japan; the three most famous beautiful spots[views] in Japan. ☆松島[宮城県]・宮島[広島県]・天橋立[京都府]

さんげん【三弦・三絃】❶〈三味線の別名〉a three-stringed musical instrument used among professionals. It is also called *shamisen*[*samisen*]. 専門家の間で用いられる三味線. ⇨三味線
❷〈雅楽〉a trio of ensemble of musical instrument used in *gagaku*: *biwa*, *sou* and *wagon*. 雅楽で用いる三種の弦楽器〈琵琶・箏・和琴〉の合奏. ⇨琵琶/箏/和琴

さんご【珊瑚】 coral. ¶**珊瑚礁** a coral reef; an atoll(環礁). **珊瑚樹** a coral formation. **珊瑚島** a coral island. **珊瑚珠** a coral bead.

さんさい【山菜】 edible wild plants; edible wild grasses. 山野に自生する食用植物(わらび, ふき, ぜんまいなど).
〔料理〕**山菜料理** a meal[dish] cooked with edible wild plants. **山菜うどん[そば]** wheat noodles[buckwheat noodles] in fish broth cooked with edible wild plants.

さんざし【山査子】〔植物〕〈木〉a hawthorn; a blackthorn; a may tree;〈花〉a may flower;〈実〉thorn apple. バラ科の落葉低木. 果実は薬用.

さんさんくど【三三九度】 an exchange of nuptial *sake* cups. At a Shinto wedding ceremony, the bride and groom take three sips each of *sake* from a set of three separate cups graduating from small to large size, totaling nine sips. They drink sacred *sake* from the same cups as the nuptial pledge [oath] between the two to live a happy life together. 婚礼酒の杯を交わすこと. 神道の結婚式で新郎新婦が大小異なる三つが組になった杯を用い, 三杯ずつ総計九度, 杯の酒を交わす. 幸福な生活を共にするという夫婦間の結婚の誓いとして同じ杯から酒を交わす.

さんしきすみれ【三色菫】 ⇨さんしょくすみれ

さんじゃくおび【三尺帯】 a (about 1-m-long) *kimono* girdle; a (3-*shaku*-long) *kimono* waistband (made of silk crepe). It is worn by men (or children) with an ordinary *kimono*. (三尺(約 1m)の長さの)着物の腰帯(絹ちりめん製). 男性(または子供)が普段着の着物といっしょに締める. ⇨兵児帯/尺

さんじゃまつり【三社祭】 the Sanja Festival of Asakusa Shrine. (5月). ⇨付記(1)「日本の祭り」

さんじゅうのとう【三重搭】 a three-story[three-storied] pagoda. ⇨五重搭

さんしゅのじんぎ【三種の神器】 the Three Imperial Regalia(皇室における三種の王位の象徴); the Three Sacred Treasures of the Japanese Imperial Family(日本の皇室における三種の神聖な宝物); the Three Divine Symbols of the Japanese Imperial Throne[legitimacy and authority of the Emperor] (日本の王位継承[天皇の正統性と権威]における三種の神聖な象徴). ☆日本神話によると, 天孫降臨の時に天照大神(the Sun Goddess)は地上に天下ったニニギノミコト(孫)に日本列島を統治する使命の印に「三種の神器」(天照大神の依代)を授与した. 初代天皇(神武天皇)から現天皇まで始祖代々に継承されてきた. ☆regalia は「(王冠(crown)・笏(scepter) などの)王位・王権の象徴」(王であることを認めさせる象徴)の意味.

☆「三種の神器」は本来「君主制における三種の聖なる標章」(the three sacred emblems of sovereign rule)である．比喩的な意味では「日本社会における地位の象徴」(the three status symbols in Japanese society)を指す．戦後高度成長期には「３Ｃ三種の神器」と呼ばれる「クーラー」(air conditioner)，「カラーテレビ」(color television)，「自動車」(car)，平成時代に入り「デジタル三種の神器」と呼ばれる「デジタルカメラ」，「DVD レコーダー」，「薄型テレビ」が登場する．

① 『八咫の鏡』the Sacred Mirror (enshrined at the Inner Sanctuary of the Ise Grand Shrine). This mirror is said to represent the sacred body of Amaterasu Omikami[the Sun Goddess], the original ancestress of the Imperial Family. According to Japanese mythology, the mirror was cast by the gods to induce Amaterasu Omikami to come out from a cave where she was hiding. 伊勢神宮の内宮に安置されている．鏡は皇室の初代先祖である天照大神のご神体といわれる．日本の神話によれば，天照大神が天の岩戸(the Gate of the Celestial Cave)に隠れていたときに外に出るように神々が誘引して差し出した鏡．☆「八咫」とは「巨大なこと」の意

② 『草薙の剣』 the Grass-Mowing [Grass-Cutting] Sword (enshrined at Atsuta Shrine in Nagoya). According to Japanese legend, Susano no Mikoto killed a big eight-headed snake and found a sword in its stomach. With this sword, Yamato Takeru no Mikoto (one of the ancestors of the Imperial Family) mowed[cut] burning grass set afire by an enemy and managed to get out of danger. 名古屋の熱田神宮に安置されている．スサノオノミコト(皇室の祖先の一人)は八岐大蛇を殺し，その腹から剣を見つけた．ヤマトタケルノミコト

はこの剣で敵がつけた燃える草を刈り[切り]取り，首尾よく難を逃れた．

③ 『八尺瓊の勾玉』the Comma-Shaped Jewel [Curved Gemstone] (enshrined in the Imperial Palace in Tokyo). Jewels were used to make necklaces[accessories] in the earliest period of Japanese history. Beads made of polished stones, jade, crystal or agate were worn as accessories by Japanese sovereigns and nobles in the ancient Japan. 東京の皇居の御所に安置されている．湾曲した珠玉．古代日本史の初期には首飾り[装身具]を作るのに用いていた．光沢のある石，翡翠，水晶または瑪瑙などで作られ，古代日本の君主や貴族が装身具として着用していた．

ざんしょ【残暑】 the lingering summer heat; the heat of late summer. 夏の暑さの名残．夏の終わりの炎暑．¶残暑見舞い autumn greetings during[in] the lingering summer heat. ⇨暑中見舞い．**残暑見舞状** a greeting postcard[letter] sent to inquire after superior's[good customer's] health during[in] the lingering summer heat. 立秋(8月8日)を過ぎて送る挨拶状．⇨暑中見舞状

さんしょう【三賞】〔相撲〕 the three prizes (given to top division *sumo* wrestlers except *yokozuna* or *ozeki*). A top division *sumo* wrestler who finishes the tournament with net victory record (*kachikoshi*) is eligible for one of the three prizes awarded for outstanding technique (*gino-sho*), fighting spirit (*kanto-sho*) and outstanding performance (*shukun-sho*). 横綱または大関を除く勝ち越しで終えた上位力士に授与される三種の賞．⇨技能賞/敢闘賞/殊勲賞

さんしょう【山椒】 ❶〔植物〕 a Japanese pepper tree; a Japanese prickly ash. ミカン科の落葉低木．若葉は食用．果実は香辛料用また薬用．

❷〈香辛料〉Japanese pepper; powdered pepper (used to garnish barbecued eels, etc.)粉末山椒は鰻の蒲焼などに用いる. ⇨七味唐辛子. ¶**山椒味噌** *miso*[bean paste] flavored with Japanese pepper.

さんしょううお【山椒魚】〔両〕 a salamander. 「イモリ」に似た両生類で, 谷川に生息する.

さんしょくすみれ【三色菫】〔植物〕a pansy. スミレ科の一年・二年草. 春に「紫・黄・白」からなる花が咲く.「パンジー」「さんしきすみれ」ともいう. ⇨すみれ

さんしょくひるねつき【三食昼寝つき】three free meals plus a nap; a leisurely life with three meals and a nap.

さんすい【山水】 ❶〈山と水〉hills and water. ❷〈自然の風景〉landscape; scenery. ¶**山水画**〈画法〉a (Chinese-style) landscape painting;〈画〉a (Chinese-style) monochromatic painting of landscape(自然風景を描いた中国風の絵画). **山水画家** a landscape painter. **山水庭園** a hill-and-lake landscape garden; landscape garden arranged with hills and ponds.(築山と池のある庭園)

さんすけ【三助】 a bathhouse attendant; a male worker at a public bath. He is in charge of boiling water and scrubbing the bather's back. 銭湯で湯をわかしたり, 客の背中を洗ったりする男性の使用人.

さんずのかわ【三途の川】 (cross) the River Styx. ☆人が死んであの世へ行く途中, 初七日に渡る川.「三途」とは亡者の行く三つの道(地獄道・餓鬼道・畜生道). the Styx「スティクス, 三途の川」ギリシャ神話で死者の国 (hades)を7巻きして流れる川.

さんそう【山荘】 a mountain villa(別荘); a mountain retreat(休養所); lodge(山小屋); summer house(夏の別宅).

さんだんめ【三段目】〔相撲〕 the *sandanme*: the third division in the *sumo* wrestling, above *jonidan* and below *makushita*. ⇨相撲の番付

さんち【山地】 a mountain district[range]; a mountainous terrain; highlands(高地). ¶**白神山地**(青森県・秋田県: ユネスコ世界自然遺産) Shirakami Mountain Range

さんち【産地】 ⓐgrowing district; ⓑ producing area; ⓒ breeding center; the center for the production of (apple, rice). ¶**リンゴの産地** apple-growing district. **米の産地** rice-producing area. **馬の産地** horse-breeding center. **産地直送の野菜** vegetables direct from the farm; farm-fresh vegetables. **産地直送の梨** pears fresh direct from the orchard; farm-fresh pears.

さんチャンのうぎょう【三チャン農業】mom-grandpa-grandma farming; farming engaged in by mother, grandparent and grandmother (while father works at other jobs). 母・祖父・祖母の営む農業 (agriculture). 父は別仕事.

さんどう【参道】 the approach to a Shinto shrine; an entrance path through the *torii* gate to the oratory of the Shinto shrine; an entrance pathway connecting worshippers with a Shinto deity. 神社へ参詣するための道. 鳥居を経て拝殿に続く道. 神と人を結ぶ道である.

さんにんかんじょ【三人官女】 the three ladies-in-waiting (of the Doll Festival). ⇨ひな祭り

さんにんづかい【三人遣い】〔文楽〕❶〈三人組〉a trio of puppeteers (performed as a team in manipulating a single bunraku puppet). 文楽人形の一体をチームとして操る三人組の人形遣い. ⇨主[面]遣い (a head and right-hand manipulator)/ 足遣い (a leg manipulator)/ 左遣い (a left-arm manipulator). ⇨文楽人形 ❷〈巧妙な合同操作〉the manipulation of a single bunraku puppet jointly by three operators.

ざんねんかい【残念会】 consolation party;

booby-prize party

さんのうまつり【山王祭】 the Sanno Festival of Hie Shrine.（6月）. ⇨付記(1)「日本の祭り」

さんぱい【参拝】 a visit to a shrine[temple]; worshipping at a shrine[temple]. ¶**参拝者** a visitor to a shrine[temple]; a worshipper.

さんばいず【三杯酢】 three-flavor vinegar; a dressing made from equal parts of vinegar, *shoyu*[soy sauce] and *mirin*[sweetened *sake*] (or sugar); a mixture[combination] of equal parts of vinegar, *shoyu* and *mirin*; seasonings mixed[combined] with vinegar, *shoyu* and *mirin* in equal quantities. 酢・醤油・味醂(または砂糖)を同量混ぜあわせた甘みのある合わせ酢. ☆キュウリの酢の物などの調味料. ⇨二杯酢(酢と醤油)

さんばし【桟橋】 a pier（船の発着所）; a wharf（埠頭）; a quay（小規模な岸壁）.

サンフランシスコこうわじょうやく【サンフランシスコ講和条約】 the San Francisco Peace Treaty（1951年調印）. ⇨日米安全保障条約

さんぶん【散文】 prose; prose writing. ⇦韻文（verse）. ¶**散文詩** a prose poem; prose poetry（全体）.

さんぼう【三方】 a small square wooden tray stand (used for placing offerings to gods before the Shinto or Buddhist altar). The stand is made of unpainted Japanese cypress wood with four supporting panels under the tray. Formerly such a tray stand was used to place gifts offered to superiors. 神仏への供物をのせる小さな四角の木製台[神具]. 檜の白木で作られ, 盆の下に4枚の板で囲んだ形の台がある(盆を折敷といい, 台の3枚の板に剞り穴が開けられていることから三方という). 昔, 身分の高い人に捧げる贈物を載せていた. ⇨蓬莱

さんま【秋刀魚】〔魚〕a (Pacific) saury; a saury pike; a mackerel pike. サンマ科の海水硬骨魚.

〔料理〕**秋刀魚の蒲焼き** broiled saury seasoned [flavored] with thick sweetened barbecue soy sauce. ⇨蒲焼き. **秋刀魚の塩焼き** saury sprinkled with salt and broiled over a charcoal fire. ⇨塩焼きの魚. **秋刀魚の開き** saury cut open and dried.

さんみゃく【山脈】 a mountain; a mountain range[chain]. ¶**日高山脈**（北海道）the Hidaka mountains; the Hidaka mountain range.

さんもん【山門】 a Buddhist temple gate; the main gate of a Buddhist temple (marking the entrance to the temple). 寺の門. 特に禅宗の寺. 寺への入り口を表示する. ☆「鳥居」は神社への入り口を表示する. ⇨鳥居

さんもんばん【三文判】a cheap[inexpensive] standard seal (used for routine chores); ready-made seal. ⇨実印 / 認印

さんやく（**りきし**）【三役（力士）】〔相撲〕the three top-ranking *sumo* wrestlers. They are the top *sumo* wrestlers of the three highest ranks below *yokozuna* and above the *maegashira*. There are actually 4 ranks in *sanyaku*: in ascending order, *komusubi*, *sekiwake*, *ozeki*, and, at the pinnacle of the ranking system, *yokozuna*. 大関, 関脇, 小結の総称, 通常は横綱を頂点に含む4階級. ⇨相撲（の番付）

【**三役揃い踏み**】 a ritual foot-stomping performance preceding the final three bouts of a *sumo* tournament day. The three top-ranking *sumo* wrestlers each from the East and West divisions in turn perform the alternate foot-stomping ceremony in the ring (*shiko*) in unison. 千秋楽の最後の三番に先立って行う儀式. 東方と西方から三役力士が交互に登場し, 四股を揃い踏みする. ⇨四股

さんろう【参籠】 ⇨御籠り

し

し【市】 a city; a town; a municipality (行政区画). ¶**金沢市** Kanazawa City; the city of Kanazawa.

し【詩】 poetry (文学の詩); a poem (一篇の詩); a (line of) verse (一編の韻文〈散文に対して〉). ¶詩を作る compose[write] a poem.

しい【椎】〔植物〕a chinquapin(tree); a kind of oak.(ドングリの木). ブナ科の常緑高木. 材は建築用, 薪炭用. 樹皮は染料. ¶**椎の実** a chinquapin; a sweet acorn.(ドングリの実)

じいん【寺院】 ⇨寺

しいざかな【強肴】 side dish (to get a *person* ready for *sake*). 酒を勧めるための料理. ☆日本[懐石]料理で「一汁三菜」の後, 酒を勧めるためにもう一品を加える. 酢の物や浸し物などがある. ⇨一汁三菜

しいたけ【椎茸】〔植物〕a *shiitake* mushroom (cultivated on oak logs). キシメジ[マツタケ]科のきのこ. しい, なら, くぬぎなど広葉樹の枯れかかった樹木に生える. 春と秋が旬.「干し椎茸」は煮物や出汁,「生椎茸」は天ぷら, 炒め物, 直火焼きなどに用いる. 海外では Oriental black mushroom ともいう. ¶**椎茸の笠** caps of *shiitake* mushrooms. **椎茸の柄** stems of *shiitake* mushrooms. ⇨生椎茸 / きのこ

じうた【地唄】 *jiuta*; a traditional form of singing accompanied by the *shamisen*. *Jiuta* is chanted to the accompaniment of the *shamisen* music that developed in Kyoto and Osaka (*kamigata*) (in the Edo period). (江戸時代)京都・大阪(上方)で行われた三味線歌謡曲の総称.「上方歌」ともいう. ⇨長唄 / 端唄

じうたい【地謡】〔能楽〕*jiutai*; a Noh chorus; a chorus in the Noh drama. *Jiutai* is a chorus chanting Noh drama texts to the accompaniment of the Noh orchestra (*hayashi*). 能楽の合唱. 能舞台の一隅(地謡座)に並んだ者が能囃子の伴奏に合わせて能台本(地の文の部分)を謡うこと.

【地謡座】 the Noh chorus seating area; a group of (four to eight) chanters[singers] seated on the right of the Noh stage (as seen from the audience). (観客から見て)能舞台の右側に座す(4-8人の)囃子方. ⇨能「能舞台」

【地謡方】 singers[intoners] of the Noh chant (*yokyoku*) (on the right of the Noh stage). 謡曲を謡う人. ⇨能「能舞台」

しお【潮】 the tide(海潮); a current(潮流). ¶満潮 flood (tide). 干潮 ebb (tide).

しお【塩】 salt. ☆古来, 塩は「清め」に用いる. ⇨塩まき / 塩払い / 清めの塩. ¶**海水塩** sea salt. **精製塩** fine[refined] salt. **藻塩** salt made by burning seaweed. **原塩** raw salt. **粗製塩**(あら塩) crude salt. **食卓塩** table salt. ☆ salt▣「塩で味をつける, 塩漬けにする」

〔料理・食品〕**塩締めの鯖** a mackerel fillet coated with salt. **塩煎餅** a salted rice cracker; a rice cracker coated with salt. **塩豆** salted beans [peas]; parched beans[peas] coated with salt. **塩揉みの胡瓜** sliced cucumbers rubbed [squeezed] with salt. **塩茹での人参** carrots boiled in salt water. **塩漬け(物)** salted food; food pickled with salt. **塩(漬けの)鱈** salted cod. **塩(漬けの)鮭** salted salmon. **塩漬けの魚**[野菜] salted fish[vegetables]; fish[vegetables] preserved in salt; fish [vegetables] pickled with salt (and pressed with a heavy stone). ⇨鯖の塩漬け / ナスの塩漬け / 白菜の塩漬け. **塩焼きの魚** fish grilled[broiled] with salt; fish sprinkled with salt and broiled[grilled] over a charcoal fire. ⇨鯛の塩焼き / 秋刀魚の塩焼き

しおがまみなとまつり【塩竈みなと祭】 the Shiogama Port Festival. (7月). ⇨付記(1) 「日本の祭り」

しおから【塩辛】 salted (and fermented) fish guts; salted (and fermented) internal organs[entrails] of fish; fish guts pickled in salt. 魚，貝，烏賊などの内臓，卵，肉片などを塩漬けにし(発酵熟成させ)た食品.「酒の肴」に好適. ⇨イカの塩辛／カツオの塩辛

しおからい【塩辛い】 salty. ¶塩辛いスープ salty soup. 塩辛い食物 salty food; food with too much salt.

しおばな【塩花】❶ salt cast[scattered] about for purification. 清めのためにまく塩.
❷ a small mound[heap] of salt placed at the door of a restaurant[bar] (to bring good luck[to keep out bad luck]). 縁起をかついで[不運を塞いで]料理屋[居酒屋]などの出入り口に小さくつまんで並べて置く塩.「盛(り)塩」ともいう.

しおばらい【塩払い】〈葬儀から帰宅するとき〉 sprinkling[scattering] (a pinch of) salt on a person who has just returned home from a funeral to drive away bad luck;〈不快な訪問者が去ったとき〉scattering salt on an unpleasant visitor to purify one's doorway; purifying one's doorway by throwing salt out of it.

しおひがた【潮干潟】a tidal flat.

しおひがり【潮干狩り】 shellfish gathering [hunting]; gathering[hunting] for shellfish (at low tide); clams digging; digging for clams (at low ebb); gathering shells and catching fish in the shoal beach on the tide's ebb. 干潮時に海水の引いたところで貝をとる.

しおまき【塩まき】〔相撲〕 salt-tossing; salt-scattering; salt-throwing. This is an act of purification rite before each *sumo* bout. Each *sumo* wrestler picks up a handful of salt and tosses onto the ring to purify it. 相撲の取組の前に行う清めの儀式で，各力士は一握りの塩を掴み土俵にまく.

しか【鹿】〔動物〕 a deer (単複同形); a stag [buck, hart](雄鹿); a hind[doe] (雌鹿); a fawn(子鹿). シカ科の哺乳動物. ¶鹿の角 an antler; a pair of antlers. 鹿皮 deerskin; buckskin. 鹿の頭 a staghead(壁飾用). 鹿肉 venison. ☆日本語で「もみじ」ともいう.

しがいせん【紫外線】 ultraviolet rays[UV rays]. ¶紫外線カットグラス(自動車などの) UV-blocking glass; UV-filtering glass.

しかく【刺客】 a killer(殺人者); an assassin (暗殺者).「しきゃく」ともいう.

しかざん【死火山】 an extinct volcano; a dead volcano. ⇨火山. ¶九住山死火山(大分県) Mt. Kuju, an extinct volcano.

じかたび【地下足袋】 (a pair of) split-toed and rubber-soled socks; (a pair of) rubber-soled canvas boots[shoes] with the separate big toe. Rubber-soled footwears are separating the big toe from the other four in the same shape as socks (*tabi*). Tough cloth is used for the uppers and rubber for the sole. They are chiefly worn by construction workers[carpenters]. 足のつま先が分かれたゴム底の足袋. 足袋同様に親指と他の指とが分かれている. 上部には厚地の布，そして足の裏[底]にはゴムが使用されている. 主として建築業者[大工職人]用である. ⇨足袋

しがらきやき【信楽焼】 Shigaraki ceramic and porcelain ware (produced in Shiga Prefecture). It is characterized by ceramic figurines of raccoon dogs holding *sake* jugs. 酒壺を背負った陶製の狸像が有名である. ☆「たぬき」は「他を抜く」の意味から店先などによく見かける. また「茶器」の逸品が多い.

しぎ【鴫】〔鳥〕a sandpiper; a snipe. シギ科の鳥の総称. 春秋には日本に渡来する.

じき【磁器】 (a piece of) porcelain (ware);

china(ware). It is made with white translucent glazed body. 上薬［釉薬］をかけ焼いた，白色・半透明の焼き物．☆白い粘土 (white clay)，陶石を砕いた粉 (ceramic stone powder) と石英(crystal)を混ぜ，約1300 度で焼く．「伊万里焼［有田焼］」(佐賀県)，「九谷焼」(石川県)，「瀬戸焼」(愛知県)，「清水焼」(京都府)などがある．⇨陶磁器

しきい【敷居】 ❶〈障子の〉a groove for a removable paper-covered sliding door; a lower beam grooved for a *shoji* screen or a door to slide in. 障子・戸などをはめ込む下の溝［横木］．⇦鴨居．

❷〈玄関の〉a threshold ; 〈戸の〉a doorsill; 〈窓の〉a windowsill.

しきいし【敷石】〈茶庭の〉stones paved at the path to the teahouse;〈板石〉a flag(stone); 〈平石〉a paving stone.

じきさん【直参】 *jikisan*. ❶ a direct retainer of a feudal lord; a direct vassal serving a feudal lord. 主君に直接仕える者．

❷ a direct retainer[vassal] of the shogun; a *samurai* warrior (having a revenue of 10,000 *koku*) serving the shogun directly in the Edo period. 江戸時代，将軍家に直属した(所得1万石未満の)武士．☆旗本・御家人の総称．⇦陪臣．⇨旗本 / 御家人．¶直参旗本 a high-ranking direct retainer[vassal] of the shogun.

しきし【色紙】 a square card; (a square piece of) thick[heavy] decorated paper board. It is used for writing a poem or calligraphy with brush on, or for painting a Japanese–style picture on. 綺麗な正方形の厚紙．筆で和歌・俳句を書いたり，絵画を描いたりするために用いる．⇨色紙

じきどう【食堂】 the dining hall of a Buddhist temple. ⇨七堂伽藍

しきのう【式能】〔能楽〕a ceremonial performance of a Noh play; a formal Noh pro-gram. 儀式として行われる能楽．

しきねんせんぐう【式年遷宮】 a periodical transfer of god[goddess] to a new shrine building. 神社で，一定の年に新しい神殿を建て，祭神を移すこと．☆「伊勢神宮」の神殿は20年ごとに建て替えられる．

しきぶとん【敷布団】 a sleeping mattress (laid either directly on the *tatami* floor or on a mattress).

しぎやき【鴫焼き】 grilled[fried] eggplant[㊤ aubergine] served with *miso*[bean paste]. ナスに油をぬって焼き，味噌をぬった料理．「茄子田楽」ともいう．⇨茄子田楽

しきゃく【刺客】 ⇨しかく

じぎょうしわけにん【事業仕分け人】 budget-cutting committee[cost-cutting team] (identifying wasteful spending). 無駄遣いを明かす予算削減委員［コスト削減チーム］．

しきり【仕切り】〔相撲〕 *shikiri*; crouching to charge; the rituals of *sumo* wrestlers before crouching to an initial charge. It is a preparation period of a ritual performed by *sumo* wrestlers before a bout starts from a squatting position. They squat on their heels while facing each other, clap their hands (*chirichozu*), spread them wide (traditionally to show they have no weapons). The salt tossing ritual is performed during the intervals. 立合いの身構えをする儀式．しゃがみ姿勢から取組が始まる前に力士が儀式として行う準備時限である．力士は相互に睨み合いながら (staring at)かかとでしゃがみ，両手を打ち(塵手水)，広く伸ばす(武器を所持しない証)．その合間には塩まきの儀式を行う．⇨塵手水 / 四股 / 塩まき

【仕切り直し】 crouching to charge once again[once more]. 仕切りをやり直すこと．

【仕切り時間】 the time limit for the *shikiri*; the allotted time for the warm-up ritual before *sumo* wrestlers start to grapple. 力士

が取組前に行う軽い準備運動のために配分された［割り当てられた］時間．☆「幕内」は4分，「十両」は3分，「幕下」は2分である．

【仕切り線】 two white parallel starting lines placed at the center of the *sumo* ring. These two lines serve as markers where the *sumo* wrestlers place their fists on the ring. 土俵上の２本の白い平行線．力士が線上に握りこぶしを置く目印として使用する．

しぎん【詩吟】 recitation[chanting] of a Chinese poem. It is a Japanese form of recitation[chanting] in which a Chinese poem is chanting in singing voice[tone]. 漢詩に節をつけて吟詠すること．

しぐれ【時雨】❶〈季節〉late-autumn[early-winter] drizzling rain; drizzling rain in November; rain shower[drizzle] falling from late autumn[fall] to early winter.
❷〈料理〉. ⇨時雨煮

しぐれに【時雨煮】 stewed seafood; seafood [fish and shellfish] boiled down in soy-flavored sauce with ginger and *mirin* [sweetened *sake*]. 生姜と味醂を加えた魚介類などの佃煮．「生姜煮」（ショウガを入れるので）ともいう．また単に「時雨」ともいう．食材はカツオ，マグロ，ハマグリ，アサリなど．⇨時雨蛤

しぐれはまぐり【時雨蛤】 boiled clams; clams boiled down in soy-based sauce with ginger and *mirin*.

しこ【四股】〔相撲〕 *shiko*; the alternate leg-stomping[foot-stamping] in the *sumo* ring. A *sumo* wrestler stomps his leg alternately in the *sumo* ring with his right and then his left foot. He lifts each leg as high as possible and then brings down to stomp on the ground with force. This act is ritually done before each bout to drive off evil spirits that may be hidden in the ring. 力士が片足ずつ高く上げて力強く地を踏むこと．土俵に潜む悪霊を払う儀式である．☆

stomp one's leg「足を踏みつける」. stamp one's foot[feet]「足を踏み鳴らす」

しせん【子午線】 (pass) the meridian.

じこチュー【自己チュー】〈人〉a self-centered person; an egoist; an egotist. 〈自己本位〉self-centeredness; selfishness; egoism; egotism.

しごとおさめ【仕事納め】 the last business day of the year; the last day of business in the year; the closing of work. ⇨御用納め

しごとはじめ【仕事始め】 the first business day of the new year; the first day of business in the new year; the commencement of work. ⇨御用始め

しこな【醜名・四股名】〔相撲〕 the *sumo* wrestler's professional name; the fighting [professional] name of a *sumo* wrestler. 相撲力士の呼び名．

じこまい【事故米】 contaminated[tainted] rice（汚染米）; inedible tainted rice（非食用米）; rice contaminated with mold or pesticide（黴または駆除剤で汚染された米）; moldy and pesticide-tainted rice（黴臭い有害汚染米）. ⇨黴

しこみ【仕込み】❶〈料理〉preparation of the dishes on the menu. 料理を下ごしらえすること．
❷〈醸造〉preparation of ingredients for *sake*; preparation of the raw materials for making *sake*. 醸造で，酒の原料を調合すること．⇨酒

しこみづえ【仕込み杖】 a sword stick; a stick for keeping a sword inside. 内部に刀などを仕込んだ杖．

じざいかぎ【自在鉤】 a pothook; an adjustable pothook[pot hanger] suspending from the ceiling. It is an adjustable hook with a chain for hanging an iron pot[pan] or kettle over the fire of a sunken hearth in the floor. S字型の鉤．天井から吊るされている調整可能な鉤［鍋をかける道具］．囲炉裏の火の

上に鉄鍋・鉄びんを鎖のついた鉤で吊るし，自由自在に上下できるようにした装置．⇨囲炉裏

じざけ【地酒】 a locally brewed *sake*; (the) *sake* brewed in the district. *Jizake is a local sake* brewery in every region across the country, which makes its respective characteristic taste based on the quality of rice and water and difference in brewing process. その土地でできる酒．その土地の米と水の質，あるいはその醸造法の違いによって独自の味を作る．⇨酒

じさしゅっきん【時差出勤】 staggered working hours (to avoid overcrowded commuter trains).

じさつサイト【自殺サイト】 suicide website; suicide-related website; cell phone website offering suicide tips; cell phone accessible suicide assistance website.

じざむらい【地侍】 *samurai*[warriors] who have local military power but do not serve the shogunate (in the feudal times). （封建時代）軍事力はあるが将軍には仕えない土着の武士．⇨侍（地侍と国人）

しし【志士】 a noble-minded patriot[loyalist] (who is ready to lay down one's life for one's country); a loyal supporter of a noble cause. 高貴な志をもつ愛国者（その国のために生命を投げうつ覚悟がある者）．⇨勤王の志士／幕末の志士

しし【獅子】〔動物〕a lion; a lioness(雌)．⇨獅子舞

ししおどし【鹿威し】 a water-powered [hydraulic]bamboo clapper; a set of stone basin and bamboo water pipe. After the bamboo pipe[cylinder] is filled with water falling from a stream, water spills out. The bamboo water pipe rebounds, striking a stone basin with a loud sound. 石製の「鉢」(石だけの場合もある)と「筧」「水を通す竹筒の樋」の装置．竹筒に流れる水

が溜まると，水はこぼれ落ちる．その反動で竹筒がはね返って下の石を打ち音を出す (Water pipe makes a sound by water falling down.). 「添水」ともいう．☆客人が音を楽しむために日本庭園などに設けられている．

じじつこん【事実婚】 de facto marriage; common law marriage. Some couples do not file a marriage registration certificate at the public office, but rather live together. 役所に結婚届けを提出しないで，共同生活をする．☆ de facto「事実上(の)」副形ラテン語で "from the fact" の意．

ししとう（がらし）【獅子唐(辛子)】〔植物〕a *shishito* pepper; a small green pepper; a sweet chili pepper; a pimento. ピーマンの品種の一種．略して「ししとう」．焼き物や天ぷらなどの日本料理の付け合せに用いる．⇨ピーマン

ししなべ【猪鍋】a wild-boar stew.

ししまい【獅子舞】 a lion dance; a ritual dance with a (wooden) lion's head[mask]. A lion dance is supposed to have the power to expel evils and to ensure plentiful crops. It is performed at a shrine festival or at the New Year's by a performer wearing a lion's head[mask]. 獅子頭［面］を被って演じる舞踊．悪魔祓い (protect against evil spirits)や豊年 (bountiful harvests)の祈りとして神社の祭りまたは新年に舞う．¶二人獅子舞 a lion dance performed by a couple wearing a baggy splotched cloth. One tosses the head and front legs of the lion while the other becomes the hind legs. （だぶだぶの斑点模様の布をまとう二人組(two people)の舞踊．一人は獅子の頭と前足を上下に揺すり，もう一人は後足を演ずる）．**一人獅子舞** a lion dance performed by a single person while playing a drum at his/her waist(腰にある太鼓を鳴らしながら単独で舞う)．

しじみ【蜆】〔貝〕a corbicula (複 ~lae)(clam); a freshwater clam. ヤマトシジミ科の淡水二枚貝. だしの素材としての食用. ¶蜆の味噌汁 *miso*[bean paste] soup cooked with corbiculae[freshwater clams]; *miso* soup based on corbicula broth.

じしゃぶぎょう【寺社奉行】⇨奉行

ししゃも【柳葉魚】〔魚〕a (*shishamo*) smelt; a longfin smelt; a capelin[caplin](カラフトシシャモ; 現在流通している魚). キュウリウオ科の海水魚. 日本固有の魚で, 北海道の太平洋沿岸に分布する. ¶子持シシャモ a capelin[smelt] with roe. シシャモの卵 capelin[smelt] roe.

しじゅうくにち【四十九日】the forty-ninth day after a person's death (counting the day of death as well). Buddhist services are held by family members for the repose of the deceased on the forty-ninth day after a person's death. 人の死後四十九日の忌日. 死者の冥福を祈って法事を行う. 死んだ日を入れて数える. ⇨法事

しじゅうしちし【四十七士】the Forty-Seven Loyal Retainers of the Ako domain. They took revenge for dishonorable death of their former master[lord] in 1702. 赤穂藩の47人の忠誠を誓う家臣が1702年に亡き主君の不名誉な死の仇を討つ (avenged). ⇨赤穂事件 / 忠臣蔵

しじゅく【私塾】a private school[academy] (of the Edo period). 江戸時代の私設の塾・蘭学塾(現在の慶応大学)など. ⇨藩校

ししょう【師匠】a master[an expert] of the art; a teacher; an instructor. ¶日本舞踊の師匠 a master of the traditional Japanese dance. 踊りの師匠 a dancing master[instructor]

しじん【詩人】a poet (男女); a poetess [woman poet] (女性).

じしん【地震】an earthquake; an earth tremor. ¶東日本大震災(2011年) Great East Japan Earthquake. 関東大震災(1923年) Great Kanto Earthquake. 阪神淡路大震災(1995年) Great Han-Shin Awaji Earthquake. 地震予報 earthquake prediction. 本震 principal earthquake. 震源地 earthquake center; seismic center.

ししんでん【紫宸殿】the Hall for State Ceremonies. 賀賀, 節会, 即位などの公事や儀式を行う御殿.

じしんばん【自身番】an Edo-period police box[station]; a guardhouse in the Edo period; a civil patrol unit of the Edo period. 江戸時代, 江戸などの市中の警備のため, 各町内に設けられた番所.

じせいのく【辞世の句】a farewell *haiku* [*tanka*]; a *haiku*[*tanka*] composed on the bed of one's death[on one's deathbed]. 死に際に残す歌や詩.

しせき【史跡】a historic spot (歴史上の名所); a historical site(史実の場所); a place of historical interest(歴史的に興味深い場所); historic remains(遺構のある場所). ☆日本三大史跡 the Three Famous Historical Sites in Japan. 平城京(奈良県)・大宰府(福岡県)・多賀城(宮城県). ¶アイヌ民族と住居に関連する史跡 a historical site associated with the Ainu people and their dwellings. 史跡公園 a park with historic remains. 史跡名勝天然記念物保存法 Law for the Preservation of Historical Sites, Places of Scenic Beauty and Natural Monuments. ⇨天然記念物

しぜんいさん【自然遺産】Natural Heritage Site. ⇨ユネスコ世界遺産

しそ【紫蘇】〔植物〕(a) perilla; a beefsteak plant. シソ科の一年草. 花と葉は食用・香味料. ¶紫蘇の実 perilla seeds; seeds of a perilla. 紫蘇の葉 (a) perilla leaf; beefsteak plant leaves. 赤紫蘇 (a) red perilla; red beefsteak plant leaves (梅干・柴漬けなどに用いる). 青紫蘇 (a) green perilla; green beefsteak plant leaves.(刺身 ・薬味などに用いる)

〔食品〕紫蘇巻き *sushi*[vinegared rice] rolled up in a sheet of dried laver and placed perilla leaf and pickled *ume*[plum] in the center. 紫蘇の葉と梅干を中に入れて，海苔で巻いた鮨。「梅紫蘇巻き」ともいう.

じぞう【地蔵】 *Jizo*; (the) guardian god[deity] of children, travelers and pregnant women. A stone statue of *Jizo* is represented as a monk with a shaved head, holding a staff in one hand and a gemstone in the other. He is erected as travelers' guardian deity on the roadside and crossroads. *Jizo* is also believed to rescue the spirits of children when they die. 子供，旅人，妊婦の守護神。地蔵の像は石で作られ，頭を剃った僧侶姿で表し，手には錫 杖 と珠玉を持っている。石地蔵は道祖神として道端や辻に建てられている。地蔵は子供の死後に魂を救済するといわれる。「地蔵菩薩」(jizo-Bosatsu)の略。⇨石地蔵 / 道祖神. ¶**地蔵堂** a small shrine[hall] where *Jizo* is housed. ⇨石地蔵 / 子安地蔵

しぞく【士族】 ❶〈武士の家柄〉the *samurai* class; the family of *samurai* origin. This title[social class] was granted to former *samurai* and their families with descendants after the Meiji Restoration. This class ranked between the nobility and the commoners. 武士階級。武士出身の家族。明治維新後，武士とその子孫をもつ家族に与えた名称[社会階級]。「華族」(士族の上位)と「平民」(士族の下位)の中間に位置する。☆1879年に設定されたが1947年に廃止された。⇨華族

❷〈人〉 a descendant of a *samurai*; a member of the *samurai* class. 武士の子孫.

しぞく【氏族】 a clan; a family. ¶**氏族社会** a clan society; a clan community. **氏族制度** the clan system.

しだ【羊歯】 ❶ a fern; a fern leaf(葉); fernery (集合的). ぜんまい，わらび等の植物の総称. ⇨ぜんまい / わらび
❷「裏白」の別名. ⇨裏白

じだい【時代】 a period; an age; an era; an epoch. ¶**石器時代** the Stone Age. **徳川時代に** in the Edo period; in the days of the Tokugawa shogunate. **明治[平成；令和]時代に** in the Meiji[Heisei; Reiwa] era.

じだいまつり【時代まつり】 the Festival of the Ages[Eras]. (10月). ⇨付記(1)「日本の祭り」

じだいもの【時代物】〔歌舞伎〕〔文楽〕 historical plays of kabuki and bunraku dealing with the events set in the remote past in the feudal times. Most events are depicted from the world of the *samurai* class with stories of succession dispute or military commanders of the strife period. 封建時代における歴史的な事柄を扱うもの。お家騒動や戦国武将など武家社会の話が多い。囫「仮名手本忠臣蔵」(the 47 Faithful Retainers).「菅原伝授手習 鑑 」(the Sugawara School of Penmanship)などがある。⇨世話物 / 心中物

したくべや【支度部屋】 ❶〔相撲〕 the dressing room (for *sumo* wrestlers). There are two communal dressing rooms (east and west) where *sumo* wrestlers put on their loincloths and warm up for their bouts. 東西の支度部屋があり，力士が回しを締め，取組に向けての準備運動を行う所.
❷〈楽屋〉the dressing room (for actors [actresses]). 役者が身なりを整える所.

しだし【仕出し】❶〈料理の調達〉catering; supplying food[dishes] to order; delivery of food[dishes] catered[supplied] upon order. 注文に応じて料理を作って配達すること。☆「出前」と区別すること。⇨出前

¶**仕出し弁当** catered box lunch; a box[英] packed] lunch prepared by a caterer. 仕

出し料理 catered food; food prepared by a caterer. **仕出し屋** caterer. **宴会**[パーティー]**の料理を仕出しする** cater (for) a banquet[party].

❷〈芝居の端役〉a minor[small] role[part] (in the play); a walk-on role[part](in the drama). ⇨端役

したじき【下敷き】 ❶〈書道〉a felt underlay (laid under the Japanese paper).

❷〈学用品〉a plastic sheet[board] (laid under writing paper).

したびらめ[**したがれい**]【舌平目・下鰈】〔魚〕 a sole. ☆tongue fish, tongue soleともいう. 〔料理〕**舌ビラメのムニエル** sole meunière. **舌ビラメの網焼き** grilled sole.

したまち【下町】 the old commercial and industrial districts (of Osaka); the traditional shopping, entertainment and residential districts (of Tokyo). 主として都会の商工業地区. 伝統的な商店や娯楽地域. ☆downtownは「市の中心部・繁華街・商業地区」の意. ⇨山の手. ¶**下町情緒** the cordial atmosphere of the old commercial and residential districts (of Tokyo). **下町人情** the warm fellow feeling[warm-heartedness; neighborliness] found in the backstreet areas of the old cities (of Tokyo).

しだれざくら【枝垂れ桜】 a weeping[drooping] cherry tree[blossoms]. ⇨さくら

しだれやなぎ【枝垂れ柳】 a weeping[drooping] willow. ⇨やなぎ

じだん【示談】 out-of-court settlement; settlement out of court(法廷外の解決); a private[amicable] settlement(友好的な解決). ¶**示談金** settlement money; money paid to settle out of court.

しちごさん【七五三】 *shichi-go-san* celebration; the celebration for children of seven, five and three years of age; the festival day for children of three-year-old boys and girls, five-year-old boys, and seven-year-old girls

observed on November 15. *Shichi-go-san* is a traditional Japanese custom of taking children (of seven, five and three years of age) to a Shinto shrine to offer gratitude for the healthy growth of the children and pray for their happy future. Many children are dressed up in their best clothes[*kimono*]. They receive a *chitose-ame*[a long thin candy stick colored in red and white, which is believed to bring children happiness] after a rite of blessing at the shrine. 3歳の男児・女児, 5歳の男児, 7歳の女児の祭事. 11月15日には神社に子供と参詣し, 子供の健やかな成長に感謝し, さらなる明るい未来を祈願する. 子供は晴れ着[着物]を着用する者が多い. 神社での祝福の儀式が終了すれば「千歳飴」を受ける. ⇨千歳飴

1️⃣『髪置きの行事』the ceremony for three-year-old children to change their hairstyle. 3歳児が髪型を変える儀式.

2️⃣『袴着の行事』the ceremony for five-year-old boys to wear the formal *hakama* [the pleated skirt-like trousers] for the first time and wish for a good health. 5歳男児がはじめて正装の袴を着て, 健康を祈る儀式

3️⃣『帯解きの行事』the ceremony for seven-year-old girls to wind the broader[wider] *kimono* sash (instead of a single cord). She is no longer a baby girl but has become a young lady. 7歳児の少女が(紐に代わり)広い帯を締める儀式. 少女から淑女へ変身する. ☆「紐落しの行事」とも言う.

しちごちょうのし【七五調の詩】 a poem [verse] in the seven-five-syllabic meter (characteristic of Japanese poetry). 七音・五音の二句連合の調子を繰り返す和歌の詩.

しちどうがらん【七堂伽藍】 the main seven-hall buildings of a Buddhist temple. 寺院内にある7つの主要建造物. ⇨①仏舎利塔, ②金堂, ③鐘楼, ④経蔵, ⑤僧坊, ⑥

講堂，⑦食堂

しちふくじん【七福神】 the Seven Lucky Deities[Gods]; the Seven Deities of Good Luck; the Seven Gods that bring good luck including Japanese Shintoism, Chinese Taoism, Chinese Buddhism and Hinduism. On New Year's Eve, a treasure boat[ship] bearing the Seven Lucky Gods is believed to come to Japan and bring good luck for the coming year. 福徳(good fortune)の神として信仰される七神．神道(恵比寿)，道教(福禄寿・寿老人)，中国の仏教(布袋)そしてヒンドゥー教(大黒天・毘沙門天・弁財天)などの神や聖人からなる(神仏習合)．大晦日には七福神と宝物を載せた船が来て，来る年の幸運をもたらすといわれる．

¶七福神巡り[詣] a pilgrimage to the Seven Deities of Good Luck. There is a Japanese custom to make a pilgrimage[pay a visit] to the seven temples and shrines dedicated to the Seven Deities to pray for good luck and good heath as well as prosperity and longevity during the New Year season [from January 1st through 7th]. 正月期間[1月1日から7日］に幸運と健康，繁栄と長寿を祈願して七福神を祀る寺社を参詣する習慣がある．

① **『弁財天』** the Goddess of Eloquence, Music and Wisdom. She is a talented beauty and plays a *biwa* lute[four[five]-stringed musical instrument]. 弁舌・音楽・知恵の女神．琵琶を弾く才媛美女．「弁天」ともいう．☆インド・ヒンドゥー教の女神 (female deity of India).

② **『毘沙門天』** the God of War and Warriors. He is fierce looking with glaring eyes. He is clad in armor, holding a spear in his left hand and a small pagoda in his right hand. He subjugates evildoers and protects people from evils by the power of his spear and pagoda. 戦争と軍人の神．怒りの形相で，甲冑をまとい，左手には槍，右手には小宝塔を持つ．剣と宝塔の威力で悪人を制覇し，人を悪から守護する．☆元来，インドのヒンドゥー教の「クヴァーラ神」で，後に仏教の「多聞天」になり，現在の「毘沙門天」となる．

③ **『大黒天』** the God of Wealth and Harvest. He is a smiling old man wearing a hood. He is usually seated on two bales of rice as he brings good luck to farmers. He carries a huge sack full of treasures on his left shoulder and holds a magical gavel that brings good luck in his right hand. He is popularly known as Okuninushi no Mikoto of Japanese myth. 財福と豊作の神．頭巾をかぶり微笑む老人．豊作をもたらす神でもあるので通常は2つの米俵の上に座っている．左肩に大きな袋(bag)を担ぎ，右手に打ち出の小槌 (lucky mallet symbolic of good luck)を持つ，通称日本神話に登場する「大国主命」．別称「大黒」「大黒さま」．☆インドのヒンドゥー教のシヴァ神と日本古来の大国主命の習合．

④ **『恵比須』** the God of Fishery and Commerce. He carries a fishing rod on his right shoulder and holds a red sea bream under his left arm. He is represented as a big, portly, smiling figure with pointed hat and long robe. 漁業と商業の神．右肩には釣竿 (fishing pole)，左腕の下には鯛を抱えている．風折烏帽子をかぶり，長衣をまとい，小太りで微笑む姿をしている．☆「商売繁盛」と「五穀豊穣」の神として日本の土着信仰の対象である．

⑤ **『福禄寿』** the God of Wealth and Longevity. He is an old man with a long bald head and a long full beard. He has a crooked cane with a rolled-up scroll tied to it on his left hand. He is usually accompanied by a crane, symbolic of longevity. 財福と長寿の神．頭は禿げ，ひげが長い老人．

左手には巻物を付けた曲がった杖(staff)を持つ. 通常は長寿の象徴である鶴を伴う. ☆中国・道教の三徳, 幸福[福徳]・俸禄[扶持]・長寿から名付けられた.

⑥『布袋』 the God of Happiness and Contentment. He has a fat potbelly and a smiling face with puffed-out cheeks. He carries a bug sack filled with treasures on his back. He has a flat fan in his hand. 幸福と満悦の神. 太った太鼓腹とふっくらとした頬をして笑顔を浮かべる. 大きな宝袋(treasure bag)を背負い, 手に扇を持っている. ☆中国・唐の末期に実在した禅宗の僧.

⑦『寿老人』the God of Longevity. He is an old man with a long head and a white beard. He holds a flat fan in one hand and carries a holy cane with a rolled scroll attached to the top. He is usually accompanied by a stag, symbolic of longevity. 長寿の神. 頭が長く白いひげをたらし, 手にはうちわと卜に巻物をつけた杖(staff)を持つ. 通常は長寿の象徴である鹿を連れている. ☆中国・道教の神である南極星の化身の老子.

しちみとうがらし【七味唐辛子】 seven-flavored[㊤ seven-flavoured] spice(s); a mixture of hot red pepper and six other spices. *Shichimi-togarashi* is used as a flavoring to sprinkle over *udon*[*soba*], and as a condiment for pot dishes. It is also used as a seasoning for broiled fish and meat. 七つの素材からなる混合調味料. うどんやそばに振りかける. 薬味また焼き魚や焼き肉の調味料としても使用する. 「七色唐辛子」ともいう.
《7種のスパイス》①「唐辛子」ground red pepper. ②「山椒の粉」powdered Japanese pepper seeds. ③「陳皮(蜜柑の皮をほしたもの)」dried orange[mandarin] peel. ④「胡麻」sesame seeds. ⑤「麻の実」hemp-seeds. ⑥「芥子の実」white poppy seeds. ⑦

「青海苔(または紫蘇の実)」green laver (or perilla seeds).

しちめんちょう【七面鳥】〔鳥〕 a turkey; a turkey cock(雄)；a turkey hen(雌)；a turkey poult(雛). 〔肉〕turkey. ☆欧米では七面鳥の肉は感謝祭やクリスマスには欠かせない伝統料理に使用する.

しちょうそん【市町村】 cities, towns and villages; municipalities(地方自治体). ¶**市町村合併** consolidation of two (or more) municipalities; mergers between two (or more) municipalities.

しちょうりつ【視聴率】an audience rating; a viewer rating.

しちりん【七輪】a charcoal cooking stove; a portable clay cooking stove with charcoal fire. It is used to broil fish or meat over a burning charcoal fire. 土製のこんろ. 炭火の上で魚や肉を焼く. ⇨焜炉

じちんさい【地鎮祭】 the Shinto ceremony of land purification; the ground-breaking ceremony. *Jichinsai* is the Shinto ritual of purifying a construction site to pacify the local guardian spirits. 土地を清める神道の式典. 建築・工事などの着工前に, 土地の神を祭って工事の安全・無事を祈る式典.

じついん【実印】 *jitsu-in*[true seal]; a registered personal seal; a legal[an official] personal seal. It is officially registered at one's regional government, and a registration certificate is delivered. It is used exclusively for legal and official documents such as contracts. 法的[公式]に登録された印章. 地方自治体(local public office)で公式に登録されれば, 印鑑登録証(certificate of authenticity)が交付される. 実印は法律上公式の書類[契約書など]のみに用いる. ⇦認印. ⇨印鑑

しっき【漆器】 lacquer ware; lacquered ware; japan(ware)(欧米での用語)；〈工芸品〉lacquered craft; craftwork coated with lacquer. It is made using the concentrated sap of the *urushi*[a Japanese lacquer tree]. Famous types of artificially crafted article with a lacquer finish include Aizu lacquer ware, Wajima lacquer ware and Shunkei lacquer ware. 漆塗りの器物. 漆の木 (a Japanese sumac tree)の濃縮した樹脂を用いて作る. 漆塗りの工芸品には輪島塗り, 会津塗りそして春慶塗りなどがある. ⇨漆 ¶漆器の吸い物椀 lacquer(ed) soup bowl; soup bowl coated with lacquer. ⇨蒔絵／螺鈿

しっくい【漆喰】 plaster(壁や天井に使う); mortar(煉瓦・石などに使う); stucco(化粧用に使う). ☆「石灰」の唐音. 石灰に粘土・ふのりなどを加えて練った壁や天井塗りの材料. 姫路城の白壁などに見られる. ¶(壁に)漆喰を塗る cover (the wall) with plaster; plaster (over the wall).

しっけん【執権】〈人〉a regent(for a shogun);〈職: 執権政治〉a (shogunal) regency (held by the Hojo family in the Kamakura period). 将軍を代理・補佐し政務を統括する職（鎌倉時代に北条家が行った）. ⇨管領 ¶執権政治 government ruled by a regent (for a shogun).

しつげん【湿原】 a marsh(land); a marshy ground; a swamp; a wetland. ¶釧路湿原（北海道）(the) Kushiro Marsh. 湿原植物 marsh plants. ⇨平野／原野／〜平／沼沢地

じって【十手】 a short metal truncheon [㊇nightstick] with a hook. It was carried [used] by a low-ranking police official[㊇constable] (*okappiki*) who arrested criminals in feudal Japan. It was also used as a means of protecting oneself against a sword attack. 手もとに鉤がある短い鉄棒［警官の警棒］. 封建時代に犯罪人の捕り手［岡っ引き］が使った(捕り物道具). また刀の攻撃からの護身具としても用いた. ⇨

岡っ引き

しっぽう【七宝】〔華道〕a frog; a metal plant holder with no needles. It is used to arrange flowers in a shallow container[bowl]. 生け花の剣山. 金具の花留め. 浅い水盤に花を生けるときに用いる. ⇨剣山

しっぽう(やき)【七宝(焼き)】 cloisonné (ware). *Shippo* is the fine art of enameling[glazing] on a metal base of copper or silver, with colorful designs of things such as flowers and birds. 銅や銀などの素地［下地］に釉薬をかけて彩色模様(花鳥風月)を表した美術品. ☆「七宝」(seven gems)は金 (gold)・銀 (silver)・珊瑚 (coral)・水晶 (crystal)・真珠 (pearl)・瑪瑙 (agate)・翠玉 (emerald). ¶七宝焼きの花瓶 a cloisonné vase.

しっぽくりょうり【卓袱料理】 *shippoku* dishes; Japanized Chinese-style dishes in Nagasaki Prefecture. Noodles cooked with vegetables, mushrooms and slices of fish paste are served on big plates from which diners help themselves[eat freely]. 中国系の日本化した(長崎特有の)料理. 麺類[そばやうどん]に野菜・しいたけ・かまぼこなどを大皿に盛った食べ物を食卓の中央に置き, 各人が自由に取り分けて食べる. ☆「卓袱」は中国風の食卓を覆う布のこと. 転じて中国風の食卓の意味.

じつめいけいひ【実名敬避】 respect through avoidance of real name.

シテ【仕手】〔能楽〕a *shite*; the principal actor in a Noh play; a protagonist in a Noh play. The *shite* plays the leading role in a Noh play. He always wears a Noh mask and portrays various characters (including an old man, a woman or a god). He is accompanied by *tsure*, *tomo* or *ko-kata*. 能楽・狂言の主役(the main character)をつとめる人. 常に能面をかぶり, 多様な役柄を演じる. 「連」や「供」または「子方」を伴う. ⇨

ワキ(脇). ☆ protagonist「(演劇の)主役；(物語の)主人公；(能楽の)シテ役」(=the principal[main] actor in a Noh play). ギリシア語の first actorの意.「ワキ役」は deuteragonist (=the second actor[an associate] in a Noh play).「ツレ役」はtritagonist (=the third actor[a companion] in a Noh play).

【シテ子方】 a principal actor's juvenile actor (accompanying the *shite* in a Noh play).

【シテ連】 a principal actor's assistant (accompanying the *shite* in a Noh play).

【シテ供】 a principal actor's attendant (accompanying the *shite* in a Noh play).

【シテ柱】 the *shite* pillar; the rear pillar on the left side of the Noh stage. The *shite*[main actor] takes position at the pillar when he appears on stage. ⇨能楽「能舞台」

しで【垂・四手】 ***Shide***; white paper strips; pieces of cut white paper. *Shide* are dangling strips of white paper suspended[zigzag-shaped white paper streamers hung] from the twisted straw rope or the twig of the sacred *sakaki* tree. ジグザグに細長く切った白い紙片. 注連縄や玉串などにつけて垂らす白い紙片.「紙垂」とも書く. ☆神社 (Shinto shrine) や神棚 (Shinto household altar) などに見られる. ⇨注連縄/玉串

してんのう【四天王】〈仏教〉the Four Devas; the four Guardian Kings; a group of the Four Deities guarding the Buddhist world in four directions. They are enshrined in the Golden Hall of Horyu-ji Temple. 四方を守る神. 法隆寺の金堂に安置されている. ☆『四柱の神』:「持国天王」the god guarding the east. 東の守護神.「広目天王」the god guarding the west. 西の守護神.「増長天王」the god guarding the south. 南の守護神.「多聞天王」the god guarding the north. 北の守護神.

してんのうじどやどや【四天王寺どやどや】 the Half-Naked Festival of Shitennoji Temple. (1月). ⇨付記(1)「日本の祭り」

じとう【地頭】 an estate steward; the head of estate; a local land administrator. He is in charge of a lord's manor under the Kamakura shogunate government. 鎌倉幕府下で, 荘園・公領を管理した役人.

じどうぎゃくたい【児童虐待】 child abuse; child-battering.

しとふめいきん【使途不明金】 (an) unspecified expenditure; (an) unaccounted-for expenditure.

じどり【地鶏】 a free-range chicken; a local [locally produced] chicken[poultry]; native Japanese breeds of chicken[poultry]. その土地産のニワトリ. ☆食用のニワトリの在来種.

しない【竹刀】〈剣道〉 a *shinai*; a bamboo sword (used for practicing a *kendo*). It is made of four strips[shafts] of split bamboo attached together. The length varies for different age groups.（剣道用の)竹製の刀. 割り竹4本をたばね合わせて作る. 長さは年齢によって異なる. ☆「上段の構え」(raising the bamboo sword over the head)や「下段の構え」(holding the bamboo sword low)などがある. ⇨剣道

しなんやく【指南役】 a master[mentor] (of Japanese fencing); a coach[an instructor] (of the martial art). 幕府・大名などに仕えて武芸を教える人.「指南番」ともいう. ¶鎌倉幕府の指南役 a fencing master[mentor] of the Kamakura shogunate.

しにせ【老舗】 a long-standing store; a store with a tradition of a long-established business; a highly reputed store established a long time ago. 先祖代々の業を守り続けた由緒ある店 (shop).

しのうこうしょう【士農工商】the four feudal classes[divisions] of people in Japanese society during the Edo period: *Shi* [*samurai* and warrior], *No* [farmer and peasant], *Ko* [craftsman and artisan], and *Sho* [merchant and tradesman[shopkeeper]]. 江戸時代に身分を武士・農民・工人[職人]・商人の四階級に順序づけた.

しのぎ【鎬】 the ridges on the sides of a sword[spear] blade. 刀・槍などの刃と背の中間の, もりあがっている部分.

しのやき【志野焼】 Shino ceramic ware (produced in the Mino region, now Gifu Prefecture). 岐阜の美濃産の陶器.

しば【芝】〔植物〕turf; Japanese lawn grass. イネ科の多年草. 庭園などに芝生をつくる.

しば【柴】〔植物〕 brushwood (雑木・小枝); firewood (薪にする). ¶柴垣 a (woven) brushwood fence.

じばさんぎょう【地場産業】 a traditional local industry (to produce a regional specialty). 地域の特産品を生産する地元の伝統産業.

しばづけ【柴漬け】 eggplants pickled in salt with red *shiso*[beefsteak plant leaf]. 赤しそで塩漬けした茄子. ☆京都の伝統的な漬物.

しはん【師範】〈武芸・技芸の教師〉a master; an instructor; a coach. ¶剣道の師範 a Japanese fencing master. 師範代 a substitute master[coach]; an acting master[coach].

しふく【仕覆・仕服】〔茶道〕 a silk bag for a ceramic tea caddy; a silk bag[pouch] for keeping a tea caddy used in the tea ceremony. 茶道で用いる陶器の茶入れ用の絹袋. 濃茶用. ⇨茶入れ／㠶(薄茶用)

じぶくろ【地袋】 a storage space[cabinet] on the floor under staggered shelves. 違い棚の下部にあり, 床上に接する小さな袋戸棚. ⇨天袋

しぶん【士分】 the status of *samurai*; the *samurai* class. 武士の身分.

シベリアしゅっぺい【シベリア出兵】 the Siberian intervention. (1918年~1922年)

シベリアよくりゅう【シベリア抑留】 detainment in Siberia.

しほうはい【四方拝】 the ceremony of worshipping the deities in the four directions. This rite is performed by the Emperor in the Imperial Palace early on the morning of New Year's Day. He pays homage to various shrines and imperial tombs in the four directions[in all quarters] and offers prayers for the health and happiness of the nation. 元日の早朝, 天皇は四方[東西南北の方位]の諸神と皇室の陵墓を拝し, 天下泰平を祈願する.

しほうべに【四方紅】 a white square sheet of paper with red edges (used for stacking[setting] a pair of New Year's rice cakes). It is believed to ward off fires in[for] the coming year. (鏡餅をのせる)赤く縁取った白い正方形の紙. 来る年の火災を払うとされる. ☆無い場合は「半紙」(plain paper)を用いる. ⇨半紙

しぼりぞめ【絞り染め】〈業〉tie-dyeing;〈布〉tie-dyed fabrics;〈技〉 a method of dyeing with parti-colored dapple spots. After cloth tied up in places with a thread is dyed and untied, white spots come out parti-colored dapples. ところどころ糸でくくった布地を染めてときほどくと, まだらな白い斑点模様が出る. ¶絞り染めの浴衣 a tie-dyed light cotton *kimono*.

しま【~とう】【島】an island; an islet; an isle (小島). ¶淡路島(兵庫県) Awaji(shima) Island; the Island of Awaji; 礼文島(北海道) Rebun(to) Island. 伊豆七島(東京都) the Seven Islands of Izu. 島巡り (make) a tour of the island. ⇨諸島／半島／列島／小島

しま【縞】a stripe. ¶縦縞 vertical stripes. 横縞 horizontal stripes 赤と白の縞模様 a pattern of red and white stripes. ☆「縞の」縞 striped (=with a pattern of stripes). ¶縞模様[縞柄] a striped pattern. ピンクと白の縞

の**着物** a striped pink-and-white *kimono*.

しまあじ【縞鰺】〔魚〕a striped jack; a yellow jack. 夏が旬の高級魚.

しまい【仕舞】〔能楽〕an abbreviated performance of a Noh dance in plain clothes [costumes]; a Noh dance performed out of costumes and accompanied only by a stage chorus without using any musical instrument. 能楽の略式演技. 装束・囃子なしで舞台合唱(謡)のみの略式の舞. ☆シテ(the principal actor)だけが能楽の一部を抜粋して舞う. ⇨シテ

しまいごろし【姉妹殺し】fratricide.「兄弟殺し」ともいう.

しまうま【縞馬】〔動物〕a zebra. ウマ科の哺乳動物. ⇨うま

しまぐにこんじょう【島国根性】insularism; insularity; an island-nation[islander] mentality.

しまだ【島田】the ***shimada*** coiffure. It was a traditional Japanese hairstyle worn by an unmarried woman in the Edo period. Today an elaborate variation of this hairstyle (called the *takashimada*) is worn by a bride in a Japanese-style wedding.「島田髷」の略. 日本髪の一種. 江戸時代には未婚の女性(young single women of marriageable age)が結う伝統的な髪型であった. 現在ではこの髪型の念入りな変形「高島田」は花嫁が和式結婚で結う. ⇨高島田

しまつしょ【始末書】a written apology; a formal letter of apology[explanation].

しまながし【島流し】an exile[a banishment]; being exiled[banished] to a distant island. ⇨遠島❷

しまばらのらん【島原の乱】the Shimabara Uprising[Rebellion]; a rebellion by Christians and peasants against the Tokugawa shogunate along the Shimabara Peninsula. 島原半島で起きた徳川幕府に対するキリシタン信徒を中心とした農民の一揆. ☆3万7千人の農民一揆(日本史上最大規模)で, その首領は天草四郎時貞. 一揆軍は12万6千人の幕府軍に抗戦して島原の原城に90日間籠城して敗戦する(1637年～1638年).

ジミこん【地味婚】a quiet, simple wedding [marriage]; the paring of expenses for one's wedding ceremony and reception.

しみだいこん【凍み大根】boiled *daikon* [radish] dried and frozen outside (for a preserved food). ゆでた大根を野外で凍らせて干した保存食. ⇨寒晒し

しみんびょうどう【四民平等】(abolition [abrogation] of the class system of the Edo period and) establishment of the equality of all people in the early Meiji period. (江戸時代の階級制の廃止にともなう)明治初期における人民平等制の樹立. ☆『四民』(the four social classes in the feudal Japan)とは封建時代の四階級. 特に江戸時代には「士農工商」〈武士 (*samurai*)・農民 (peasant)・工人[職人] (craftsman)・商人 (merchant)〉を順序づけた. 明治維新後は「平民」(commoner; common people)と呼ばれ,「苗字」(family name)を名乗れるようになった. ⇨士農工商

じむしょ【寺務所】a temple office; an office of a temple administration. 寺院の庶務を統括する事務所. ⇨社務所

しめかざり【注連飾り】sacred straw ropes with festoons;〈正月用〉a New Year's decoration of a twisted straw festoon (stuck with strips of white paper (*shide*) hanging from it). It is hung above the entrance of a house to indicate a purified place for receiving New Year deities[gods] (*toshi-gami*) on New Year's Day. It is decorated by attaching good-luck charms like a bitter orange (*daidai*), a lobster (*ebi*), fern leaves (*shida*), etc. to the sacred twisted rope (*shime-nawa*). These decorations are

し

symbolic of prosperity from generation to generation (*daidai*), longevity (*choju*) and good fortune (*koun*) respectively. (垂[四手]を差し込んだ)注連縄を張って飾る新年の飾り物．年神を迎える清浄な場所を示すために玄関に張る．注連縄にはダイダイ(代々), エビ(長寿), シダの葉[裏白](幸運)などの縁起物が象徴的に飾られる．「注連縄飾り」ともいう．⇨注連縄

しめこみ【締(め)込み】⇨回し

しめさば【締鯖】　salted and vinegared raw mackerel; salted raw mackerel pickled in vinegar. Raw mackerel is firmed up with salt and soaked in vinegar, served in slices. 塩をふり，酢をしみこませた鯖の刺身．関西では「生ずし」という．

しめじ【占地・湿地】〔植物〕 a ***shimeji*** mushroom; a champignon. シメジ科のきのこ．ブナなどの倒木に発生する．現代では人工栽培する．

しめだいこ【締太鼓】 a small Japanese drum covered with animal skins over both ends and tied together with cords. It is played with a pair of wooden drumsticks. 両側に皮を張り紐で締めた和太鼓．2本の木製桴で叩く．

しめなわ【注連縄】　***shimenawa***; a sacred twisted[plaited] straw rope[festoon]; a sacred rope[festoon] made of twisted [plaited] rice straw. *Shimenawa* is festooned with dangling narrow strips of white paper[cloth] (*shide*) and some pieces of straw bunches. It is used in Shintoism to distinguish between secular and holy areas and to prevent evil spirits from entering the holy places. It is hung on the *torii* gate before a Shinto shrine or household Shinto altar at home. It is also hung on the front door of the house to demonstrate the temporary abode of the *toshi-gami*[god of the incoming new year] who brings good

luck on New Year's Day. ねじった[編んだ]神聖なわら縄[飾り縄]．注連縄には「垂」と呼ばれる白い紙[布]片と藁の房(tufts)を下げる．神前などに掛け渡して神聖な場所と不浄な外界との境界を示し (to indicate sacredness that separates sacred Shinto grounds from the unclean outer world), 汚れの入るのを禁じるため (for warding off evil spirits)の縄．神社の鳥居や家庭の神棚に張る．また新年に「年神」の依代として玄関先にかける．⇨垂・四手 / 注連飾り / 年神

しも【霜】 frost.　¶霜柱 frost columns [crystals].

しもざ【下座】　(take) a lower seat; (sit at) the foot of the table. It is the lower-ranking position in the traditional Japanese guest room nearest to the entrance. 下位の人のすわる座．和室では入り口に近い場所．⇦上座

しもて【下手】〈歌舞伎などの舞台〉 the left (side of the) stage seen from the audience. 客席から見て舞台の左側 ; the right (side of the) stage facing the audience. 観客席に向かって右側の舞台．⇦上手．⇨歌舞伎(舞台)

しものく【下の句】　the final two lines of a *tanka*[poem]; the second[latter] half of a *tanka* (poem); the last 14 syllables of a *tanka* (poem). 短歌で最後の七・七の二句[14音節]．⇦上の句

しものせきせんていさい【下関先帝祭】　the Courtesan Festival of Akama Shrine. (5月). ⇨付記(1)「日本の祭り」

しもふりにく【霜降り肉】 marbled beef; beef streaked with fine veins of fat. The thinly slices of this beef is best used in *sukiyaki*. 脂肪が白くまだらに入っている高級牛肉．⇨牛肉．☆ marbled (beef)「サシ(肉)」牛肉にある霜降りの網目状の脂肪．「**サシの入った赤肉**」a lean slice of meat marbling.

しもやしき【下屋敷】　a suburban residence

[villa] of a high-ranking *samurai*[feudal lord or direct retainer of a shogun] during the Edo period; a secondary dwelling[villa] of a rich merchant during the Edo period. 江戸時代，大名・旗本など地位の高い武士が郊外に設けた別荘．江戸時代の裕福な商人の別宅．⇨上屋敷

しもんさいしゅとかおじゃしんさつえい【指紋採取と顔写真撮影】 fingerprints and facial recognition photographs (at Immigration). ☆biometrics information (生体認証)の一種である．

しゃか【釈迦】 [S(h)akyamuni] Buddha. ☆サンスクリット語形ではSiddhārtha Gautama（シッダルタ〈名〉・ガウタマ［ゴータマ］〈姓〉）．Gautamaは英語でS(h)akyamuniという．「釈迦」は「釈迦牟尼」の略である．「釈迦」は「名」(部族名または国名)，「牟尼」は聖者・修行者の意味．つまり「釈迦牟尼」は「釈迦族の聖者」(sage of the Shaka clan)の意味の尊称である．称号を加え「釈迦牟尼仏」「釈迦牟尼陀」，「釈迦牟尼如来」などともいう．略して「釈迦仏」「釈迦如来」．称号だけを残して「ブッダ」「仏陀」「如来」．通常は「お釈迦様」，「仏様」(「死者」の意味もある)などと呼ぶ．古代インドの宗教家．仏教の開祖 (the founder of Buddhism). 29歳で出家 (He left his royal family at the age of 29.). 35歳で菩提樹の下に座して悟りを開いた (He experienced ultimate realization of the supreme truth under the sacred bo tree when he was 35 years old.). その後各地で「すべての生きものに慈悲の心を向ける」という仏法を説く．80歳で入滅する (He died at the age of 80.).

じゃがいも【ジャガ芋】 〔植物〕a potato; ㊍ an Irish[a white] potato(サツマイモと区別する用語)．ナス科の多年草．南米の原産．別名「馬鈴薯」．「ジャガタラいも」の略．⇨いも

しゃきょう【写経】 (make) a sutra-copying;

(make) a handwritten copy[hand-copying] of a (Buddhist) sutra; transcription of a sutra. The practice of sutra-copying is quite popular because it gives one[a person] peace of mind. 経文を書き写すこと．☆「**写した経文**」は hand-copied sutra.

しゃく【笏】 ❶〈貴人の〉a (thin, oblong) wooden court scepter[mace]. It was kept by nobles in the right hand when they performed court affairs in full court costume during the rituals. 宮廷で用いる薄い長方形の木製板 (tablet). 貴人が衣冠束帯の姿のとき，右手に持っていた板．⇨衣冠束帯．☆約36cmの長さ．1尺にちなんで「シャク」と呼称．scepter [=㊍ sceptre] は「王位・王権の象徴として手にもつ棒」の意．❷〈神主の〉a (thin, oblong) wooden ritual scepter[tablet]. It is kept by Shinto priests in the right hand when they hold Shinto religious services in formal dress during the rituals. 神道で用いる薄い長方形の木製板．神主が正装して神事を行うとき，右手に持つ．

しゃく【尺】 ❶〈長さの単位〉a *shaku*. 一寸の十倍．30.3cm．❷〈尺度〉a measure; a ruler; a scale.

しゃく【酌】 serving[pouring] of *sake*. ⇨お酌．¶酌をする serve a person with *sake*; fill a person's *sake* cup.

しゃくし【杓子】 〈スプーン状〉a (wooden) ladle (used to dip soup into a bowl); 〈カップ状〉a dipper[scoop] (used to scoop liquid from a container). ⇨しゃもじ

しゃくじょう【錫杖】 a (jingling) Buddhist priest's staff[stick]; a staff[stick] used by Buddhist priests or ascetics undergoing religious journeys. 僧侶または修行者が持ち歩く杖．頭部の円環に数個の鉄の小さな環をつける杖．⇨石地蔵

しゃくなげ【石楠花】 〔植物〕a rhododendron; ㊍ a rosebay. ツツジ科の常緑低木．花は観

賞用.

しゃくはち【尺八】　a *shakuhachi*; a five-holed vertical bamboo flute (as a traditional Japanese wind instrument). A *shakuhachi* is a vertical flute with five holes (four in the front and one in the back) which is made by hollowing out the base of a bamboo stem near the root. It is traditionally used as an accompaniment to Japanese folk song. 竹製の管楽器で，竹の根元の部分の節を抜いて作った縦笛（前面に四つ，背面に一つの穴がある）．日本民謡の伴奏楽器として古くから使用されている．☆長さの標準が「1尺八寸」（約55cm/約1.8フィート）であることから「尺八」という．⇨三曲（尺八・三味線・琴）/ 虚無僧

しゃくやく【芍薬】〔植物〕a peony. ボタン科の多年草．花は観賞用．根は薬用．⇨ぼたん

しゃこ【蝦蛄】〔魚〕a squilla（複 squillas, squillae）; a mantis shrimp[crab]. シャコ科の甲殻類．てんぷらやから揚げに調理する．

しゃし【社司】　a Shinto priest; the chief priest of a Shinto shrine. 神主．神社の祭司．⇨神主

しゃしんマニア【写真マニア】　a camera maniac[buff]; a shutterbug. ⇨おたく

しゃたい【斜態】〔華道〕a slanting style of flower arrangement (one of the three basic styles in the Ikenobo school). 花を傾けて生ける型．（池坊流）．⇨基本花型 / 傾真型（草月流）

しゃち【鯱】〔動物〕a killer whale; a grampus. イルカ科の海獣．「海のギャング」と呼ばれる．☆「鯱」は国字.

しゃちほこ【鯱】　*shachihoko* ornament; (a pair of) fabulous dolphinelike fish; (a pair of) bronze image of a legendary sea creature similar to a dolphin. *Shachihoko* has a mythical lionlike head, dragonlike scales along the back, and an arched tail pointing skyward. イルカに似た架空[伝説上]の魚．頭が虎のようで，背に竜のようなとげがあり，尾は空に向かう想像上の海獣．「しゃち」ともいう．☆しゃちほこの飾り瓦は「魔除け」(a talisman to ward off evil spirits) または「防火」(a talisman against fire) 用である．　¶名古屋城の屋根にある鯱 a pair of golden *shachihoko*[sea creatures, male and female] attached to[mounted on] both ends of the ridgepole of Nagoya Castle.

しゃっく【赤口】六曜の一つ，「しゃっこう」⇨六曜

しゃっけい【借景】　a view-borrowed natural landscape; a natural landscape utilizing [borrowing] the outside background scenery. In some Japanese gardens, the beautiful surroundings of natural scenery (such as trees, hills and mountains in the distance) are served as a backdrop in landscaping to form an integral part of the garden. 外部の背景にある自然の風景を利用[借用]する景色．日本庭園の中には（遠くの山水や樹林などの）自然景観の環境が景色の背景として庭園の全構成の一部に見立てられているものがある．　囲金閣寺（京都・北山鹿苑寺）(通称 Golden Pavilion). 桂離宮（京都）(Katsura Detached Palace[Imperial Villa])

しゃでん【社殿】the sanctuary[sacred place] of a Shinto shrine; the main building of a Shinto shrine (in which an object of worship venerated as a deity is enshrined). 神社のご神体が祀ってある聖所[本殿]．「社」ともいう．⇨神体

じゃのめがさ【蛇の目傘】　an oiled paper umbrella with a bull's-eye design. It is usually used by women when wearing a *kimono*. 蛇の目に塗った油紙の傘．通常は女性が着物を着るときに用いる．☆「蛇の目」とは幾重かになった太い輪の形（中心を白く，周辺を紺または赤で塗る）の模様．

し

英語では a bull's eyeまたは a double ring
という. ⇨番傘(男子用)

じゃびせん【蛇皮線】 a *jabisen*; a snakeskin
samisen; a three-stringed musical instrument with a snakeskin-covered sound box.
胴の表裏に蛇の皮がはってある三弦の楽
器. ☆中国(元代)から琉球を経て日本本土
に入った. 三味線の原型. ⇨三味線

しゃふ【車夫】 a ricksha(w) puller; a
rickshaw man. 人力車を引く人. ⇨人力車

しゃぶしゃぶ *shabushabu*; a hot-pot dish of
thinly-sliced beef and various vegetables
(cooked[parboiled] in lightly flavored
broth). The diners dip thinly-sliced beef
(or pork)and vegetables into a pot of
simmering stock[boiling broth] at the table.
Then they help themselves to thin slices of
beef and vegetables by dipping either in a
sesame-flavored sauce or a citrus-flavored
sauce. Lastly noodles are often added to
the leftover soup. コンブだし汁の鍋に薄切
りの牛肉(または豚肉)と野菜を入れ, 自由
に取ってごまダレまたはポン酢に浸して食
べる (eat freely) 鍋料理. 最後に残り汁に
うどんを入れる. ⇨ingredients[具] : 肉
/ 白菜 / ねぎ / 椎茸 / 春菊 / 豆腐 / うどんな
ど.

しゃみせん【三味線】 a *shamisen*; a *samisen*;
a three-stringed musical instrument with
a long neck and a cat skin-covered sound
box. A *shamisen* is a traditional Japanese
banjo-like musical instrument with three
strings. The body[sound box] is covered
with catskin. It is played with a triangular
ivory plectrum by plucking the three
strings. The heavier the string, the deeper
the tone given. 長い棹と猫の皮で覆われた
共鳴箱を有する三弦楽器. 三味線は日本古
来のバンジョーに似た三弦楽器で, 本体(胴
の部分の共鳴箱)は猫の皮で覆われている.
三角形の象牙のばちを用いて三弦をはじい
て演奏する. 弦が太いほど, 低音になる.
☆プロの間では「三弦(さんげん)」ともいう. ⇨蛇皮線
/ 三弦 / 棹(太棹・中棹・細棹)

【三味線奏者】〔文楽〕 a *shamisen* player
[accompanist] (who is seated on the elevated
platform (called *yuka*)). In a bunraku
play, the puppets' movements must be
synchronized with the *tayu*'s chanting and
the *shamisen* accompaniments. 「床」に座す
三味線奏者[伴奏者]. 文楽での人形の動き
は, 太夫の語りと三味線の伴奏に合わせる.
⇨床 / 太夫

しゃむしょ【社務所】 a shrine office; an
administrative office of a shrine; an office
of a shrine administration. 神社の庶務を統
括する事務所. 「社務殿」ともいう. ⇨寺務
所

しゃも【軍鶏】〔鳥〕 a (brown-red) gamecock;
a fighting cock. 鶏の一種. 闘鶏用・食用.
⇨にわとり

しゃもじ【杓文字】 a serving spoon (used for
dishing out soup or rice). ❶〈汁の〉 a soup
ladle; a wooden spoon (used to dip the
soup into a bowl). ⇨しゃくし
❷〈飯の〉 a rice scoop; a wooden paddle
(used to take rice into a bowl); a wooden
spoon for serving rice. ⇨おたま

しゃようぞく【社用族】 expense-account
businesspeople; company employees who
live off expense accounts.

しゃメール【写メール】 (a) photo-e-mail.

シャリ【舎利】 *shari*;〈米粒〉white rice
grains; boiled white rice;〈すし飯〉vine-
gared rice(used for *sushi*). *Shari* is made
by adding vinegar, sugar, salt and *mirin*
[sweetened *sake*] to steamed rice in a
shallow wooden container[tub]. It is
cooled very quickly with a hand fan. 半切
に炊きたての飯を入れ, 酢・砂糖・塩・味醂
を加えて作り, うちわで素早く冷ます.「銀
舎利」(polished rice)ともいう. ☆仏教の

し

仏舎利が語源. ⇨隠語(鮨屋) / 符丁

しゃり【舎利】 ❶〈仏陀の遺骨〉Sakyamuni's bones[ashes]; Buddha's bones[ashes]; the holy relics of Buddha.「聖者の遺骨」と区別するため「仏舎利」ともいう. ⇨仏舎利. ¶舎利殿 a reliquary hall (especially installed to enshrine the holy relics of Buddha). 仏舎利を奉安する堂宇. ⇨仏舎利. 舎利塔 a Buddhist reliquary; a miniature pagoda (for enshrining the holy relics of Buddha).
❷〈聖者の遺骨〉holy person's ashes; the holy relics of saints.

じゃり【砂利】 gravel; (small) pebbles(複数形). ☆石(stone)よりも小さく, 砂(sand)よりも大きいもの.「神社の参道」(a gravel path leading to the shrine)などによく見られる.

じゃんけん the "rock-scissors-paper" game to decide the winner or loser. When two (or several) people play the *janken* game, they hold out a hand: making a fist[the rock], outstretching the index and middle finger[scissors], or extending a palm[paper]. The rock (a fist) cannot cut with scissors[wins over the scissors]. The scissors (two fingers: index and middle fingers) can cut the paper[wins over the paper]. The paper (five fingers; palm) can wrap up the stone[wins over the stone].「ぐう」(拳:石),「ちょき」(人差し指と中指:鋏),「ぱあ」(掌:紙)を選んで勝負を決める遊び. ☆英米では順番などを決めるとき, 硬貨を投げ上げて, その表裏(heads or tails: 表は勝ち, 裏は負け)で決める (toss-up; tossing a coin). "Let's toss (up) for it." (じゃんけんで決めよう)などという.

しゅ(いろ)【朱(色)】 vermilion (color); cinnabar (red). ¶(神社の)朱塗りの柱 vermilion-painted column (of the shrine hall). ☆朱色は魔除 (ward off evil spirits)の意.

しゅいん【朱印】 ❶ a seal affixed with vermilion inkpad. 朱肉で押した印.
❷ a vermilion official seal of a shogun; a shogun's vermilion-sealed license. 将軍の公式朱印, またはその書類.

しゅいんじょう【朱印状】 a vermilion-sealed permit[license] of a shogun; a vermilion official seal used to identify the authorized merchants. Documents sealed in vermilion were given by the Tokugawa shogunate government to the feudal lords and merchants when traveling abroad or trading with foreign countries early in the 17th century. 将軍の朱印を押した許可書. 公認商人である身元保証に用いた正式な朱色の捺印. 17世紀初頭, 徳川幕府は海外渡航や海外貿易をするときに朱印を押した公文書を大名や商人に与えた.

しゅいんせん【朱印船】 a trade ship[vessel] licensed by the shogunate; a Japanese foreign trading ship having a vermilion-sealed permit of a shogun; a Japanese foreign trading ship authorized with an official sealed license by the shogunate government (early in the 17th century). 朱印状を受けて幕府から海外貿易を許可された船 (a trade vessel authorized by the shogunate).

しゅいんせんぼうえき【朱印船貿易】 a trade done by *shuin-sen* with shogunal charter for foreign trade. 朱印船で海外貿易を行うこと. ☆特に東南アジアとの貿易を行い, 米・漆器・七宝などを輸出し, 絹・綿・皮などを輸入した.

しゅう【〜宗】〈宗派〉a sect (of Buddhism). ⇨宗派. ¶真言宗 the Shingon sect of Buddhism (founded by Kukai in 805:空海). 浄土宗 the Jodo sect of Buddhism (founded by Honen in 1175: 法然). 臨済宗 the Rinzai sect of Buddhism (founded by Eisai in 1191: 栄西). 浄土真宗 the Jodo-Shin(shu) sect of Buddhism (founded by Shinran in 1224: 親鸞). 曹洞宗 the Soto sect of Buddhism (founded by Dogen in 1227: 道元). **日蓮宗** the Nichiren sect of Buddhism (founded by Nichiren in 1253: 日蓮)

じゅういちめんかんのん【十一面観音】 the eleven-faced Kannon Bodhisattva; the Deity of Mercy crowned with eleven faces. ⇨観音

じゆうかけい【自由花型】〔華道〕a free-style flower arrangement.

しゅうき【周忌】 the anniversary of a person's death. 人の死後に年ごとに回ってくる忌日. ⇨回忌. ¶**母の三周忌** the second anniversary of mother's death. ☆三周忌以降は死んだ年を含めて数えるので second となる.

しゅうぎ【祝儀】 ❶〈祝賀〉celebration; festivity; a wedding[marriage] (ceremony). 祝いの儀式. 祝典, 特に婚礼.
❷〈祝い物〉a congratulatory gift[present]; congratulatory money and gift. 祝いの儀式のときに贈る金品. 引き出物.
❸〈チップ〉a gratuity; a tip. 心付け.
【祝儀袋】〈金品用〉a gift envelope;〈心付け用〉an envelope for giving a tip[gratuity];〈祝儀用〉an envelope for a congratulatory monetary gift (given on celebrating occasions);〈婚礼用〉an envelope for presenting a gift of money (given) at a wedding. The envelope has a congratulatory emblem (*noshi*) and gift-binding cord (*mizuhiki*) attached to it. A gift envelope with a gold-and-silver cord is used for a wedding. It is customary to write one's name and the purpose of the gift on the front. 封筒には熨斗と水引が付いている. 婚礼用には金銀の水引が付いている. 慣例上表には名前と贈物用途を表書きする. ☆「結婚式の祝儀袋」に入れる金額は通常奇数(1, 3, 5)である. ⇨熨斗紙 / 水引. ⇦香典袋[不祝儀袋]

じゅうきネット【住基ネット】 *Juki* Net; the Nationwide Resident Registry[Registration] Network.「住民基本台帳ネットワークシステム」(the Basic Residential Register[Registry] of Network System)の略.

じゅうぐんいあんふ【従軍慰安婦】 a wartime comfort woman; a forced prostitute for the soldiers during World War II; a prostitute licensed by the military in World War II. 第二次世界大戦中の慰安婦.

しゅうげん【祝言】〈婚礼(式)〉a wedding (ceremony). ¶**仮祝言** a private wedding. **祝言を挙げる** hold a wedding ceremony.

じゅうごや【十五夜】 ❶ the night of the full moon; the night when there is a full moon of the 15th day in the lunar calendar. 満月の夜. 陰暦15日の夜.
❷ the 15th night of the eighth month in the lunar calendar. 陰暦8月15日の夜. 満月は, この夜に最も明るく美しく輝く. 月見の宴 (moon-viewing party) を催す慣習がある. ⇨ 月見の宴. ¶**十五夜の月** a full moon on the 15th day; the harvest moon(秋分の頃). ⇨中秋(中秋の名月)

しゅうじ【習字】 calligraphy; penmanship. ¶**習字帳** a writing book; a copybook. **習字が上手[下手]** a good[poor] calligrapher.

じゅうし【従枝】〔華道〕the subordinate [supplementary] branches[stems] added to the principal[main] branches[stems] (used in a flower arrangement of the the Sogetsu school). 主枝にとり合わせる補助的な枝(または茎)のこと. 草月流の華道にて用いる. ⇨中間枝(小原流) / あしらい(池坊流) / 主枝

じゅうしちじょうのけんぽう【十七条の憲法】 A Seventeen-Article Constitution. The Constitution of the 17 Articles, Japan's first written code of laws, was promulgated by Prince Shotoku in 604. 聖徳太子が日本初の成文法[成文律]を604年に公布した.

じゅうじゅつ【柔術】 *jujutsu*; the weaponless art of self-defence, one of the traditional martial arts; the original form of *Judo* (developed in the Edo period). 柔道の前身. ⇨柔道

じゅうしょく【住職】 the chief priest[head abbot] of a Buddhist temple; the superior of a Buddhist temple. 寺の長である僧侶.

じゅうしん【重臣】 a chief vassal (of a feudal lord); a senior retainer (of a feudal lord). 重要な役職にある家来.

しゅうせんきねんび【終戦記念日】 War-End Memorial Day (August 15); the anniversary of the end of World War II; the day commemorating the end of the Pacific War.

じゅうたくローン【住宅ローン】 a home[housing] loan; a home[housing] mortgage.

しゅうだんけっこん【集団結婚】 a group[mass] wedding; a wed-in. ⇨集団見合い

しゅうだんそかい【集団疎開】 a group evacuation; an evacuation in a group. Many children were evacuated in a group [en masse] to rural regions during World War II (to prevent them from an air raid[attack]). (空襲を避けるために)第二次世界大戦中子供は地方に集団で疎開をした. ⇨疎開

しゅうだんみあい【集団見合い】 a group meeting with a view of marriage; a collective interview for marriage. ⇨集団結婚

じゅうづめ【重詰め】 foods packed in tiered lacquer boxes. ⇨重箱. ¶**重詰めにした御節料理** New Year's foods packed in tiered lacquer boxes; foods arranged in a tier of lacquer boxes for New Year celebrations. (正月用の重箱に詰めた料理)

じゅうどう【柔道】 *judo*; a traditional martial art of unarmed[weaponless] self-defense (even though *Judo* is no longer practiced as a martial art today). *Judo* takes the form of fighting without any weapons between two contestants. It takes advantage of an opponent's strength and weight to get him/ her off balance[to defeat him/ her]. 素手で相手(combatants)と戦う武道(今や武道として実施されていない場合もある). 相手の腕力と重量を利用して相手に攻撃する.

【柔道の段位と級位】 *judo* ranks[grades] and classes

① 『**段位**』 There are ranks[grades] 1 to 10, with 10 the highest. Those in ranks 1 to 5 wear a black belt. Those in ranks 6 to 8 wear a red[scarlet] and white striped belt. Those in ranks 9 to 10 wear a red[scarlet] belt. 初段から10段までであり, 10段が最高位. 初段から5段までは「黒帯」(black belt for the first to the fifth grade), 6段から8段までは「紅白帯」(red[scarlet] and white belt for the sixth up to eighth grade), 9段と10段は「紅帯」(red[scarlet] belt for the ninth and tenth grade)を締める.

② 『**級位**』 The classes are below the ranks and ranges from the fifth class to the first and highest class. Adults in the first to the third class wear a brown belt. Children in the first to the third class wear a purple belt. Those in the fourth and fifth class wear a white belt. 級は段の下位にあり, 5級から最高位の1級まである. 成人の1級から3級は「茶帯」(brown belt of adults for the third to the first class), 子供の1級から3級は「紫帯」(purple belt of children for the first to the third class), 4級と5級は「白帯」(white belt for the fifth (beginner) and fourth classes)を締める.

【柔道技】 *judo* techniques; techniques used in *judo*.

① 『**投げ技**』 «throwing techniques»「手技」hand techniques. (圏「一本背負い投げ」one-arm shoulder throw).「腰技」hip techniques.（例「払い腰」sweeping hip throw).「足技」leg techniques.（例「内股」inner thigh reaping throw).「真捨て身技」rear[back] sacrifice techniques.（例「巴投げ」circle[stomach] throw).「横捨て身技」side sacrifice techniques.（例「横車」side wheel throw)など.

②『固め技』«grappling[holding down] techniques»「抑え込み技」holding technique.（例「肩固め」shoulder hold).「絞め技」choking[strangle] techniques.（例「並十字絞め」normal cross choke[strangle]).「関節技」armbarring[armlock] techniques.（例「腕がらみ」entangle armlcok)など.

③『禁止技』«prohibited techniques»「足がらみ」entangled leg lockなど.

【柔道判定】judgement.

『一本』[I: Ippon] full point victory.『技あり』[W: Waza-ari] half point.「指導」warning.「反則負け」disqualification.☆「一本勝ち」は winner by Ippon などと表示されている.

【柔道着】 a judo suit[uniform]; a suit for doing[practicing] judo; a special uniform for judo practice.☆「帯」belt.「奥襟[後襟]」back lapel.「前襟」front lapel.「横襟」side lapel.「奥袖」upper sleeve; armpit.「中袖」

奥襟
横襟
奥袖
中袖
前襟
袖口
帯
裾
裾口
柔道着

sleeve.「袖口」sleeve cuff.「裾」hem.「裾口」hem of the pants; pants hem.

【柔道帯】 a belt worn by a participant in a judo match. It is a judo belt tied at the waist of a happi-style jacket to keep it closed. In judo there are ten grades (dan) and five classes (kyu) that indicate degree of proficiency. The degree of mastery is indicated by the color of the belt.　⇨柔道の段位と級位

【柔道家】a judoka; a judoist; a judo expert; a judo wrestler; a judo competitor; a judo practitioner.　☆「女性柔道家」a female judoist.

【柔道師範】a judo instructor.

【柔道場】a dojo; a judo hall.

【柔道有段者】a rank-holding judo competitor.

【柔道試合】a judo match (presided over by one chief referee and two judges). ☆「主審」referee.「副審」judge.

じゅうにし【十二支】 Twelve Signs of the Chinese[Oriental] Zodiac. The cycle of 12 signs [animals] consists of nine beasts, two reptiles and one fowl. Formerly the Chinese zodiac was used for denoting directions and the hours of the day. Today it is used in referring to a particular year. 12匹の動物は獣9匹, 爬虫類2匹そして鳥1羽からなる. 昔は方位やその日の時間 (time)を表示するのに用いていた. 現在では特定の年を言及するときに用いる.

☆各項目を参照すること. ⇨「子」（ね） the Rat[Mouse].「丑」（うし） the Ox.「寅」（とら） the Tiger.「卯」（う） the Rabbit[Hare].「辰」（たつ） the Dragon.「巳」（み） the Snake[Serpent].「午」（うま） the Horse.「未」（ひつじ） the Sheep.「申」（さる） the Monkey.「酉」（とり） the Cock[Rooster].「戌」（いぬ） the Dog.「亥」（い） the Boar[(中国では) Pig].

じゅうにひとえ【十二単】 (a suit of) twelve-layered *kimonos*[robes](worn on ceremonial occasions by women of the upper classes); a Japanese ceremonial costume for court ladies and noblewomen in the Heian period. *Juni-hitoe* consists of twelve brightly-colored unlined *kimonos*[robes] worn one over the other. Today it is still worn by Imperial princesses (or the members of the Imperial Families) at their weddings. 平安時代の女官や貴族の正装. 12枚の裏地のない優雅な着物を重ねて着る. 今日では皇女の婚礼時に着用する. ☆まず白小袖に緋の袴をはき, 次に単・五衣・打ち衣・表着と着て, さらに唐衣を着用し, 裳をつける. 上になるほど裄が短く, 袖が重なって見えるのでこのように呼ばれる. 十二単を着るときは後ろに「垂髪」, 手には「檜扇」を持つ. ⇨垂髪 / 檜扇

しゅうは【宗派】 a (religious) sect; a (religious) denomination. ⇨「〜宗」/ 教派 / 宗門

じゅうばこ【重箱】 tiered lacquer boxes; a tier of wooden lacquer boxes with a lid on top; a set of layered lacquer boxes. A tier of wooden lacquer boxes is used to pack[arrange] many kinds of foods for New Year celebrations. 積み重ね式の箱型のふた付き容器. 御節料理を詰めるのに用いる.
【重箱料理】 foods packed[arranged] in tiered lacquer boxes. ☆最近は『三段重』(a tier of three lacquer boxes; a three-tiered serving lacquer boxes)が多い. ⇨御節料理

しゅうぶん【秋分】 the autumnal equinox; the autumn[fall] equinox. ⇨二十四節気

しゅうぶんのひ【秋分の日】 Autumnal Equinox Day (September around 23). This national holiday was established in 1948 as a day to honor one's ancestors and remember the dead. *Shubun-no-hi* occurs on the central day of a seven-day Buddhist memorial service (*higan-e*). The Buddhist belief says that the dead can cross the river leading to the other world from this world. On this day, the Japanese visit their family graves and observe Buddhist memorial services at homes or at temples. 1948年に制定. 祖先を敬い死者を想起する日. 秋の彼岸の中日にあたる. 仏教では死者が現世からあの世に通ずる川を渡ると信じられている. この日には家族は先祖の墓参りをし, 家庭内または寺院内で法要をあげる. ⇨彼岸 [彼岸会](秋の彼岸)

しゅうまつきぎょう(か)【週末企業(家)】 weekend business (person); a business operated by a salaried worker on weekends.

しゅうまつこん【週末婚】 a weekend marriage; weekend wedlock.

じゅうみんきほんだいちょうネットワーク【住民基本台帳ネットワーク】 the Basic Resident Registration Network; the Nationwide Resident Registry Network. ⇨住基ネット

じゆうみんけんうんどう【自由民権運動】 the Democracy Movement; the Movement for Civic Rights and Freedom (for establishing the Diet by the people in 1874). ☆板垣退助や大隈重信などが憲法の制定 (drawing-up of a constitution)や政党政治 (party politics)を求めた民主主義的政治運動 (political movement for the democracy[democratic government]). 明治前期に藩閥政府に対抗して起こった.

じゅうみんひょう【住民票】 a certificate of residence; a resident card. ¶住民票コード a resident registration code number; eleven-digit individual identification number assigned to a resident for the national registry system.

しゅうめい【襲名】 succession to a hereditary [stage] name (in the pursuit of an art).

師匠の芸名などを受け継ぐこと.

【襲名披露】 *shumei* ceremony to celebrate an actor's succession to a hereditary[stage] name. After an actor's succession to the stage name, he delivers from the stage an address in which he requests the continued patronage of the audience. 襲名した役者は舞台上から観客に向かって変わらぬ引き立てを望む口上を述べる. ⇨口上

しゅうもん【宗門】 a religious sect; a (religious) denomination. ⇨宗派. ¶**宗門改め** a religious inquisition for suppressing Christianity (under the Tokugawa shogunate). キリシタン禁教のための宗教調査.

しゅうもんあらためしょ【宗門改所】 the Inquiry Office. It was set up by the Tokugawa shogunate in 1640 to register every man's own religion[religious sect] in an attempt to eliminate Christianity after the Shimabara Uprising of Christians and farmers. キリシタンや農民による島原の乱以降にキリシタン撲滅をたくらみ各自の宗派 (denominations)を登録するように1640年徳川幕府が制定する. ⇨島原の乱

じゅうよう(な)【重要(な)】 important; essential. ⇨文化財

【重要文化財】 an important cultural property[asset]. ☆1950年に発布された「文化財保護法」(the Cultural Property Protection Law)で正式に保護されたもの. 建造物, 絵画, 彫刻, 考古学上の発掘物などがある. 中には「国宝」(national treasure)級のものもある.

【重要無形文化財】 an important intangible cultural property[asset].

【重要無形文化財保持者】 a living national treasure. ⇨人間国宝

【重要無形民俗文化財】 an important intangible folk cultural property[asset].

【重要伝統的建造物群保存地区】 (National) Important Preservation Districts for Groups of Historic Buildings. 囫「白川郷と五箇山」の合掌造集落(ユネスコ世界遺産).

じゅうりょう【十両】〔相撲〕 the *juryo*; the second-highest division of *sumo* wrestlers, below *makuuchi* and above *makushita*, and the lowest division where the wrestlers receive a salary and full privileges. *Sumo* wrestlers ranking above the *juryo* division are collectively called *sekitori*. 幕内の下で, 幕下の上の位. 十両以上は「関取」の総称. ⇨相撲の番付

じゅかい【樹海】 a sea[an ocean] of trees; woodland(森林地帯); forest(森林). ¶**青木ヶ原樹海**(山梨県) the Sea of Trees of Aokigahara Virgin Forest (that lies at the base of Mt. Fuji). (富士山の裾野に広がる広大な原生林).

しゅぎょう【修行】 an ascetic practice [training]; a religious practice[self-disciple]. ¶**修行の道場** a training hall for ascetic[religious] practice. **修行者** an ascetic; a Buddhist monk engaged in ascetic practices.

じゅきょうのしそう【儒教の思想】 Confucian idea; Confucianism; the teachings of Confucius. *Jukyo* is traditional ethical teachings developed by Confucius (551-479 B.C.) in China and followed by his disciples to maintain social order. 儒教とは「孔子の教え」を中心とする中国の伝統的道徳思想. 社会秩序の維持のため, その弟子によって遵守されてきた. ☆「五倫の道」(君臣の義, 父子の親, 夫婦の別, 長幼の序, 朋友の信)は有名. 日本人の社会生活や人間関係に多大の影響を与える. ⇨五倫の道

じゅく【塾】 a private school; a cram(ming) school. It is a private tutoring supplemental school where children cram after regular school hours. 子供に正規の授業終了後に私的授業の補習をする学校.

しゅくじ【祝辞】 (deliver) a congratulatory

address[speech] (at a ceremony); (offer) congratulations (to a person).

しゅくじつ【祝日】 a national[public] holiday（国定の）；a legal holiday（法律の）；a festival day（祭日）．⇨国民の祝日

じゅくねんりこん【熟年離婚】 middle-aged divorce; divorce of a middle-aged couple; divorce in the later years; vintage year divorce; late divorce.

しゅくば【宿場】 a post station (during the Edo period); a stage（街道の）．「宿駅」ともいう．

【宿場町】 a post town; a post-station town; a town developed as a relay station along major roads. 昔は街道の要所にあって，旅行者が宿泊・休憩したり，馬の乗り継ぎをしたりする中継地として発達した町．

しゅくぼう【宿坊】 temple accommodations [lodges] designed for pilgrims; a guest-house established for pilgrims at a temple. Pilgrims are lodged for the night in the temple abode within the precincts of the temple. 参詣者・巡礼者が泊まるために，寺の境内につくられた宿泊所．

しゅくん【主君】 one's lord; one's master. ⇨四十七士

しゅくんしょう【殊勲賞】〔相撲〕the Outstanding Performance Prize[Award] (in *sumo* wrestling). The price is given to a top division *sumo* wrestler who defeats *yokozuna* during a given tournament. 相撲場所中に横綱を負かした上位力士に授与される賞．⇨三賞

しゅげい【手芸】 handicrafts; handicraft manual arts; craftwork. ¶**手芸品** a handicraft item; handicrafts（手工芸品の）；fancywork（刺繡などの）．

じゅけん【受験】 taking[㊟ sitting for] an entrance examination. ¶**受験地獄** the entrance examination ordeal; the ordeal of the entrance examination. **受験戦争** a fiercely competitive entrance examination.

しゅげんじゃ【修験者】〈修験僧〉an ascetic Buddhist monk[priest]; a Buddhist monk [priest] who leads an ascetic life in the mountains.〈修験者〉a mountain ascetic; a Buddhist hermit. 修験道 (mountain asceticism) を修行する者.「山伏」ともいう．⇨山伏

しゅご【守護】 ❶ protection; (safe)guard; defense. ¶**守護神** a guardian deity[god]; a tutelary deity[god].

❷ a military[provincial] governor [commissioner, constable]. *Shugo* is an administrative official, the head of provinces, who is in charge of security in the provinces under the Muromachi and Kamakura shogunate governments. 鎌倉・室町時代に国ごとにおかれ，御家人の統率と治安警備をつかさどる．¶**守護大名** a feudal lord[ruler] of military governorship.

しゅこう【酒肴】〈酒と料理〉food and drink; wine and food;〈酒と酒の肴〉*sake* and something to go with a drink[alcohol]; an accompaniment to *sake*[alcohol].

しゅこうぎょう【手工業】 handicrafts; handicraft industry[manufacturing]. 西陣の絹織物や瀬戸の陶器などを製作する．¶**手工業者** handicraftsman（㊵ ~men）．

しゅこうげい【手工芸】 handicrafts (and manual arts). ¶**手工芸品** a piece of handicraft work.

しゅごしん【守護神】 ⇨守護❶

しゅし【主枝】〔華道〕the principal[main] branches; the three principal[main] stems in a flower arrangement. The principal stems are the longest, the second longest and the shortest, each referred to differently according to schools. Subordinate stems are added to the three principal stems in arranging flowers. 生け花における主要な枝[茎]のこと.「最長」,「準最長」,「最短」が

あり，各流派によってその呼称が異なる．
花を生けるときに従枝は主枝に加えられる．⇨従枝

《主枝の流派》 ① 『池坊』:「真」(the longest stem)・「副」(the second longest stem)・「体」(the shortest stem). ② 『小原流』:「主」(the longest stem)・「副」(the second longest stem)・「客」(the shortest stem). ③ 『草月流』:「真」(the longest stem)・「添」(the second longest stem)・「控」(the shortest stem)

しゅしょく【主食】　the staple food; the principal food; a (diet) staple．☆「主菜」は the main dish(主食以外の主な料理)．⇨副食．¶米を主食とする live on rice; eat rice as a staple.

じゅしんりょうふばらい【(NHK)受信料不払い】　refusal to pay (NHK) TV reception[listening]fee; refusal to pay subscription[英 license] fee for (NHK) TV.

じゅず【数珠】　a *Juzu*; a Buddhist rosary (used as a way of praying); (a string of) prayer beads. A *juzu* has a string of 108 Buddhist prayer beads, one standing for each of the 108 worldly desires of human beings. Buddhists count off a bead with fingers for each prayer. They usually hold the Buddhist rosary over their joined hands as they pray. 仏を拝むときに用いるロザリオ[輪]．108の玉が輪になっており，各玉は人間の108の煩悩を表している．念仏を唱えながら数珠を指で繰り，その回数を数える．通常は祈りのとき合掌した手の上に持つ．「念珠」ともいう．現在では a short Buddhist rosary with 54 beads (or 27 beads)などがある．☆ rosary「ロザリオ」(カトリック信者が祈りの回数を数えるときに用いる数珠)．¶**数珠玉** the beads of a Buddhist rosary.

しゅっけ【出家】〈仏門に入ること〉becom-ing a Buddhist priest[monk]. A layman renounces the world and leads a hermit life;〈仏門に入った人〉a Buddhist priest; a Buddhist monk[bonze]. 俗人が世俗を捨て隠遁生活に入る．⇨在家

しゅっけつサービス【出血サービス】　a give-away price.

しゅっけつセール【出血セール[投げ売り]】　a sacrifice sale; a below-cost sale; a dis-tress selling.

しゅっこう【出向】　temporary transfer; loan (of an employee); 英 secondment. ¶出向社員 a loaned worker; a worker on loan; a seconded staff.

しゅっせうお【出世魚】　fish with changing names; fish that acquires[is called by] dif-ferent names as it grows larger. 成長に伴い名前が変わる魚．⇨ぶり / ぼら / すずき

しゅっせりきし【出世力士】〔相撲〕a newly-advanced *sumo* wrestler. 相撲の番付にはじめて名が出る力士.

しゅとう【酒盗】　salted (and fermented) bo-nito guts; bonito guts pickled in salt. 鰹の内臓を塩漬けにして発酵させた塩辛．酒の肴に最適．高知県・土佐の名物．⇨鰹 / 塩辛

しゅとけん【首都圏】　a metropolitan area; Tokyo and seven neighboring prefectures.

しゅにく【朱肉】　a vermilion inkpad[stamp pad] (used for a Japanese seal); cinnabar seal ink．⇨印鑑

じゅばん【襦袢】　underwear for use with a *kimono*; an undergarment worn with a *kimono*. 和服用の肌着．☆ポルトガル語(gibão)から由来する．別称「ジバン」

じゅひょう【樹氷】〈氷点以下に冷却した濃霧〉snow and frosty rime crystals;〈樹氷の木〉a rime-covered[hoarfrost-silvered] tree; a tree covered[silvered] with rime[hoarfrost]; an ice-covered tree; a tree covered with ice. ¶樹氷で有名な蔵王山(山形県・宮城県)　Mt. Zao(zan) noted for trees coated with snow and frosty rime [hoarfrost] crystals in winter.

しゅみだん【須弥壇】 a dais[pedestal] for a statue[image] of Buddha (enshrined in a Buddhist hall). 仏堂内の仏像を安置する壇.

しゅもく【撞木】 a wooden bell hammer (used to strike a Buddhist gong). (仏教での)鉦をつき鳴らすための木製の棒. ⇨鉦

しゅりけん【手裏剣】 a small throwing-knife[throwing-dagger]; a small circular (or straight) pointed weapon. It is hidden in the palm of hand and then thrown at an opponent. It was used by *ninja* and *samurai* warriors. 手のひらに隠し, 敵に投げつける円形(または直型)の先のとがった小型剣. 忍者や侍が使用していた. ⇨忍者

しゅれいもん【守礼門】 the Gate of Courtesy (known as a fine example of traditional Ryukyuan Architecture). 伝統的な琉球建築の最高傑作. ☆重層の楼閣(2層造りの門)としては16世紀の代表的な装飾建造物. 正式名は「待賢門」, また「首里」の扁額が常掲されていたことから「首里門」と称するようになった. しかし後年「守禮之邦」の額が常時掲げられたので「守礼門」と呼ばれるようになった.

しゅろ【棕櫚】〔植物〕 a hemp palm (tree); a windmill palm (tree). ヤシ科の常緑高木. 葉柄は長く葉は手のひら (the palm of hand)に似る. 葉鞘の繊維は縄 (hemp-palm rope)・箒(hemp-palm broom)などに用いる.

じゅろうじん【寿老人】 ⇨七福神

しゅん【旬】 seasonality; the height of good season; the height of the season. ¶旬のカキ[野菜] oysters[vegetables] in season; in-season oyster[vegetables]. 旬でないカキ[野菜] oysters[vegetables] out of season.

しゅんが【春画】 an erotic[obscene] picture; a pornographic painting.

しゅんぎく【春菊】〔植物〕 a crown daisy; an edible leaf chrysanthemum; a garland chrysanthemum; a chrysanthemum coronarium. キク科の一年草. 関西では「菊菜」ともいう. すき焼きや鍋物などに用いる. 和え物や浸し物にも使う. ⇨菊 / 菊菜

じゅんきょう【殉教】 martyrdom. ¶殉教者 a martyr. 日本二十六聖人殉教者 the Twenty-six Martyrs of Japan (who were crucified in 1597 in Nagasaki). (1957年長崎にて十字架に架けられた)日本の二十六聖人の殉教者.

じゅんぎょう【巡業】〔相撲〕 provincial tour held between grand *sumo* tournaments.

しゅんけいぬり【春慶塗】 Shunkei fine-grained lacquer ware. 木目の美を生かした漆器. ☆春慶塗の名称は, 応永年間(1394-1428)に大阪近郊の漆工(lacquerer)春慶が考案した漆塗り技法による. 日本三大春慶塗には「飛騨春慶塗」(岐阜県),「能代春慶塗」(秋田県),「粟野春慶塗」(茨城県)がある. ⇨漆器

じゅんさい【蓴菜】 a water shield. スイレン科の多年生水草. 若芽と花の蕾は汁物や和え物などの食用にする.

しゅんぶん【春分】 the vernal equinox; the spring equinox. ⇨二十四節気

しゅんぶんのひ【春分の日】 Vernal Equinox Day (March 20 or 21). This national holiday was established in 1948 as a day to admire nature and love living things. *Shunbun-no-hi* occurs on the central day of a seven-day Buddhist memorial service (*higan-e*). The Buddhist belief says that the dead can cross the river leading to the other world from this world. On this day, the Japanese visit their family graves and observe Buddhist memorial services at homes or at temples. 1948年に制定. 自然を賛美し, 生き物を慈しむ日. 春の彼岸の中日にあたる, 仏教では死者は現世からあ

の世に通ずる川を渡ると信じられている．この日には家族は先祖の墓参りをし，家庭内または寺院内で法要をあげる．⇨彼岸[彼岸会](春の彼岸)

じゅんまいしゅ【純米酒】 pure nice *sake*; pure *sake* brewed from only rice and yeast; *sake* in which the only ingredients are rice and yeast. 米と麹からのみで醸造した酒．¶純米吟醸酒 good-quality *sake* brewed from refined rice. ⇨吟醸酒. **純米大吟醸酒** best-quality *sake* brewed from polished rice. ⇨吟醸酒

じゅんれい【巡礼】 a pilgrimage (of holy places for salvation). The pilgrim walks to holy places for salvation while ringing a small handbell and chanting[singing] a hymn. (救済のため聖地に)参拝して歩くこと．巡礼者は金剛杖を持ち，御詠歌を唱えながら救済を求めて聖地に向かう．⇨遍路．¶(四国)八十八箇所の巡礼(に出る) (make[go on]) a pilgrimage to the eighty-eight temples[sacred places] closely related to Kobo-Daishi, a Buddhist priest. **巡礼者** a pilgrim. **巡礼地** a pilgrimage site; a destination[goal] of a pilgrimage; holy places visited by pilgrims. **巡礼寺** a

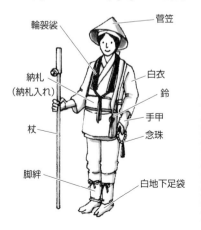

輪袈裟　菅笠
納札(納札入れ)　白衣
杖　鈴
　手甲
　念珠
脚絆　白地下足袋

pilgrimage temple. 囫善光寺. **巡礼宿** an inn that caters to pilgrims.

【巡礼衣装】 a pilgrimage dress (all white). ☆「白衣」white robe[*kimono*]. 「菅笠」wide-brimmed sedge hat. 「(金剛)杖」(diamond)staff[stick]. 「脚絆」leggings. 「輪袈裟」neck surplice. 「白地下足袋」white rubber-soled socks (with the big toe separated). 「草鞋」straw sandals. 「手甲」wrist glove. 「念珠」Buddhist rosary. 「納札」pilgrimage sticker. 「鈴」small bell. 「御詠歌」chanting hymn (仏を称えて歌う賛美歌)

しょいん【書院】 ❶〈書斎・客間〉a study (room); a drawing room; a living room. ❷〈書院造りの座敷〉a drawing room floored with *tatami* mats (in the *shoin* style of traditional Japanese architecture).

【書院造り】 a Japanese-style drawing[guest] room; a drawing room in the traditional Japanese residential architecture. The *shoin* style of residential architecture provides for a *tatami*-mat room with an alcove, a decorative sliding door and an ornamental sliding screen. Some houses are built in this style with dry landscape garden and the style of the Zen temple. (日本の伝統的な住宅建築の)座敷．書院造り様式では，床の間や飾りのある障子・襖のある畳部屋が設けられている．枯山水庭園や禅宗寺院の様式が設けられた家屋もある．囫京都の二条城(二の丸御殿)．☆室町時代に始まり桃山時代・江戸時代初期に完成する．⇨寝殿造り

しょう【升】 a *sho*. A *sho* is equal to about 1.8 liters. (1.8リットル)．容積の単位．10合．¶醤油1升びん a *sho*[1.8-liter bottle] of *shoyu*[soy sauce].

しょう【笙】〈雅楽〉a *sho*(-*no-fue*); a traditional Japanese wind instrument with 17 bamboo pipes (resembling panpipes). It is made up of a standing circle of 17 slender bamboo pipes of various sizes and a lacquered box. It is played by a performer continuously while blowing[inhaling and exhaling], providing a cloud of sound. It was introduced from China in the Nara period and is now used in gagaku (court music and dance). 17本の竹管をもつ管楽器(アシ笛に似る). 笙は漆器塗りの碗型の箱のまわりに大小17本の細い竹の管(17 long and short slender bamboo pipes)を環状に立て並べて作られる. 吹きながら[吸ったり吐いたりしながら]音色を出して間断なく演奏する. 奈良時代(7世紀)に中国から伝来する. 現在「雅楽」に用いる. ⇨雅楽

じょうい【攘夷】 antiforeign sentiment; exclusion of foreigners (in the late Edo period); exclusionism. (幕末における)外国人排斥運動. ⇨尊王攘夷. ¶攘夷論者 an exclusionist.

じょうい【上意】 the shogun's will[order]; the lord's will[order]; the command of the shogun[lord]. 将軍[主君]の意思・命令

¶上意下達 communications from the top down; the transmission of the orders[wishes] of those in authority to their subordinates. (上位者の命令を下位者に通じさせること)

しょういだん【焼夷弾】 a fire bomb; an incendiary bomb. 人や建物などを高熱の放火で殺傷・破壊する爆弾[弾丸]. ¶無差別攻撃の焼夷弾 fire bombs of a random attack.

じょうえいしきもく【貞永式目】 ⇨御成敗式目

しょうえん【荘園】 a manor (in medieval Japan). It is the private land of the powerful nobles and temples expanded from the Nara period to the Muromachi period. 中世の領地. 奈良時代から室町時代にかけて普及した貴族や寺院の私有地. ¶荘園領主 the lord of the manor. 荘園領主の邸宅 a manor

house[mansion](館). 荘園制度 the manorial system; manorialism.

しょうが【生姜】〔植物〕a ginger plant;〈香辛料〉 ginger. ショウガ科の多年草. 食用・薬用. ¶おろし生姜 grated ginger. 甘酢生姜 sweet-vinegared ginger. ⇨豚(肉の生姜焼き) / 時雨煮(生姜煮)

しょうがいきょういく[がくしゅう]【生涯教育[学習]】 lifelong education[learning].

じょうかく【城郭】〈城壁〉castle walls;〈城〉a castle; a citadel. 城のまわりの構え.

しょうがつ【正月】〈新年〉the new year[New Year];〈三が日〉new year[New Year];〈元旦〉New Year's Day (January 1) ; Ⓐ New Year's; Ⓑ New Year. ¶正月休み the New Year Holidays[Ⓐ Vacations]. 正月料理 New Year's dishes; traditional dishes for the New Year. ⇨御節料理

しょうかどうべんとう【松花堂弁当】 a *shokado* lunch box. A lunch box is divided by four square compartments[crisscross partitions] containing boiled rice, *sashimi* [raw fish], assorted simmered foods and appetizers. 中が四角に[十文字に]仕切られ4つに分けられた弁当箱で, ご飯, 刺身, 炊き合わせや前菜などが盛り込まれている. ⇨弁当(箱と昼食との区別)

じょうかまち【城下町】 a castle town; a town centering around the castle of a feudal lord; the town of a feudal lord's fief. In the ancient times, powerful merchants lived near their castle town which was the center of politics, economy and culture. 諸侯が住む町. 武家時代, 有力な商人は政治・経済・文化の中心地である諸侯の居城周辺に生活を営んでいた. 圀江戸・水戸・金沢・仙台などの城下町. ¶伊達正宗の旧城下町(仙台市) the former castle town of Date Masamune.

しょうかん【小寒】 the lesser cold; the season when the colder weather comes near[approaches]. 寒い時期が近づく季節. ⇨二十四節気

しょうぎ【将棋】*shogi*; the Japanese (version of) chess. *Shogi* is a board game for two players with the aim of checkmating the opponent's "King". They take turns moving pieces on a checkered board with 81 squares (nine by nine). Each player starts with 20 pieces which have eight different ranks. 2人の対局者が相手の「王将」を取るために競うゲーム. 81ますに区切られた盤上で交互に駒を動かす. 各遊戯者は違った8階級の駒20個をもって開始する. ¶**将棋盤** a *shogi* (square wooden) board; a chess-board. **将棋の駒** a *shogi* piece. **将棋の駒台** a table for captured *shogi* pieces

【将棋の駒】「**王将**」King.「**金将**」Gold General.「**飛車**」Castle[Rook](「竜王」Promoted Castle[Rook]).「**角行**」Bishop(「竜馬」Promoted Bishop).「**銀将**」Silver General.(「成銀」Promoted Silver Generals).「**桂馬**」Knight(「成桂」Promoted Knight).「**香車**」Lance (「成香」Promoted Lance).「**歩兵**」Pawn. (「と金」Promoted Pawn).

しょうきち【小吉】 the poor luck[fate]. ⇨おみくじ

しょうきゃく【正客】 ❶〔茶道〕〈主客〉the principal[main] guest (of all the participants in the tea ceremony). 茶会での最上位の客. ☆茶道の進行中重要な役割を演じ, 参加者各位は主客の作法に従う.
❷〈主賓〉the guest of honor. 招かれた客の第一の客.

しょうきん【賞金】〔相撲〕 cash reward; prize money (awarded to the winners of *sumo* wrestlers). ⇨敢闘賞 / 技能賞 / 殊勲賞

しょうぐん【将軍】 ❶〈幕府の〉a shogun; generalissimo; the highest authority[the head] of the shogunate government. A *shogun* was used as a formal title for a shogunate general. 最高司令官. 幕府の最高権威の武官[首長].「征夷大将軍」の略. ☆1868年に明治維新によって廃止される. ⇨征夷大将軍. ¶**5代将軍綱吉** Tsunayoshi, the fifth Tokugawa *shogun*. **将軍家** the shogunate; the family of *shogun*. ⇨幕府. **将軍職** the shogunate; the office of *shogun*.
❷〈軍隊の〉a general; an army commander; the highest military leader[commander-in-chief]. 軍隊の最高司令官. ¶**乃木将軍** General Nogi. **マッカーサー将軍** General MacArthur.

しょうこ【小鼓】 a small hand-drum. ⇨鼓

しょうこ【鉦鼓】 ❶〈雅楽〉a small bronze gong. It is a bell-shaped metal percussion instrument used in the court music and dance (*gagaku*). 青銅製の鉦. 雅楽で用いる鐘型の金属製打楽器. ⇨雅楽
❷〈仏具〉a round bronze gong. It is beaten by a Buddhist priest when chanting the Buddhist invocation. 円盤状で青銅製の鉦. 僧侶が念仏を唱える時にたたく.

じょうご【上戸】 a drinker; a tippler. 酒のみ. ⇔下戸. ¶**怒り上戸** a vicious[quarrelsome] drinker. **泣き上戸** a sentimental[crying] drinker. **笑い上戸** a cheerful[merry] drinker.

しょうこう【焼香】 incense-burning (at a Buddhist funeral service); incense-offering (to the spirit of the deceased). The chief mourner and all mourners in attendance burn[offer] incense before the coffin of a dead person while a Buddhist priest chants a sutra. (葬儀で)香をたいて仏にたむけること. 僧侶が読経する間, 喪主から会葬者まで棺の前で焼香する. ¶**焼香台** an incense-burner stand.

【焼香の仕方】 the way of offering incense at the Buddhist funeral service.

1 Mourners bow to the chief mourner and bereaved family. 会葬者は喪主・遺族に一礼

し

する.

② Mourners face the Buddhist altar holding their Buddhist rosary. Then they press both palms together in pray and bow to the picture[portrait] of the deceased. 仏壇の前で手に数珠をかけ, 合掌して遺影に一礼する. ⇨数珠

③ Mourners burn pinches of powdered incense three times for the repose of the deceased. 死者の冥福を祈って三回焼香する. ☆「三回焼香」(仏法僧の三界に差し上げること)を行うが, 回数は宗派によって異なる.

④ Once again, they press both palms together in prayer and bow to the picture of the deceased. 再度合掌して遺影に一礼する.

じょうこう【上皇】〈引退した天皇〉 an Emperor Emeritus; an ex-emperor; a retired emperor; a cloistered emperor;〈前の天皇〉 the former emperor. 天皇の位を譲ったのちの尊称. ⇨法皇. ¶亀山上皇の山荘であった南禅寺(京都府) Nanzen(ji) Temple built as a villa for the retired Emperor Kameyama.

【上皇陛下】 His Majesty the Emperor Emeritus. ☆emeritus(ラテン語で「退職した」の意)は多大な功績のあった者に対する経験と敬意を示す称号. ちなみにに「名誉教授」は an emeritus professor ; a professor emeritus.

じょうこうごう【上皇后】 an Empress Emerita.

【上皇后陛下】 Her Majesty the Empress Emerita. Emperor Akihito is called "Emperor Emeritus" and Empress Michiko "Empress Emerita" following his abdication in April, 2019. 2019年4月の退位後, 明仁天皇は「上皇」そして美智子皇后は「上皇后」と呼ばれる.

しょうじ【障子】 a *shoji*; a paper(-covered)

sliding door. A *shoji* is a sliding screen covered with a single layer of white Japanese paper which is pasted over wooden latticeworks built into a thin wooden framework. It is used to separate a Japanese room[the inside] from the corridor[the outside]. It is also used not only as a room divider in a Japanese-style house but also as a substitute for windows. 木製の細い枠に組み込んだ木の格子 (laths)の上に一重の和紙を貼った引き戸[すべり戸]. 部屋[内部]と廊下[外部]を区分したり, 和室の部屋と部屋の仕切り (a partition between rooms)に立てたり, 窓に代用したりする建具. ¶障子紙 a *shoji* paper; a paper used for *shoji*; a sliding-door paper. 明かり障子 a translucent sliding screen.

じょうし【城址】 the ruins of an old castle; the site of a former castle. ⇨城跡

しょうしか【少子化】 a declining[decreasing] birthrate; a continued drop in the birthrate. ¶少子化社会 a society with a declining birthrate; a society with fewer children. 超少子化 a sharply declining birthrate. 少子化対策 measures to reverse the declining [falling] birthrate.

じょうしきまく【定式幕】〔歌舞伎〕〔文楽〕 a vertically-striped curtain (used for the kabuki and bunraku theaters). The stage curtain is made up of vertical strips in black, dark-green and orange-brown[persimmon] colors. It is drawn open from left to right to the sound of wooden clappers. (歌舞伎・文楽に用いる)正式の縦縞の引き幕. 舞台幕は三色(黒色・緑色・柿色)の色を縦につぎ合わせた布で作られている. 拍子木の音に合わせて左から右へ引いて開ける. ⇨引き幕

しょうしこうれいか【少子高齢化】 a declining birthrate combined with an aging population; increase in aging population due to a declining birthrate.　¶**少子高齢化社会** an aging[graying] society with a declining birthrate; a society with an aging population due to a low birthrate.

じょうじゅ【上寿】 ⇨百寿

しょうしゅうれいじょう【召集令状】 ⇨赤紙

しょうしょ【小暑】 the lesser heat; the season when the hot summer begins. 暑い夏が始まる季節. ⇨二十四節気

しょうじょうぶっきょう【小乗仏教】 Hinayana Buddhism. ☆小乗は「狭い乗り物 (the Lesser Vehicle)」の意味. 「多数の人を忘れて，自己だけを救う」という立場. 出家仏教 (俗世間を捨て，寺にこもり修業して自分の悟りを得る [attain(ing) emancipation or self-enlightenment by becoming a Buddhist priest and undergoing ascetic practices in a temple]). 仏門に入る人のための仏教. 僧侶が尊敬される. 東南アジア (タイやスリランカなど) に普及する. ⇨大乗仏教

しょうじんあげ【精進揚げ】 deep-fried vegetables; vegetable *tempura*. 野菜類のてんぷら. ⇨てんぷら

しょうじんりょうり【精進料理】 a vegetarian dish[meal] (prepared for religious discipline); dishes[meals] served without meat and fish. The food consists of only vegetables, seaweeds and grains. It is eaten by Zen Buddhist monks as a part of the Buddhist asceticism. (修行を目的とした) 菜食主義者の食事. 肉や魚の食品を使用しない食事 (abstinence from eating meat and fish). 野菜類，海藻類，穀類だけ調理した料理. 禅宗の僧侶が修行の一環とする食事. ☆「精進」は仏教用語で「一心に仏道を修行する」(in a Buddhist term, "Shojin" means "practicing the Buddhist austerities with one's whole heart")という意味.

じょうせき【城跡】 the ruins of the old castle. ⇨城址. ¶**小諸城跡の懐古園**（長野県）

Kaiko Garden situated in the ruins of the old Komoro Castle.

しょうせつ【小雪】 the lesser snow; the season when the first snow begins to fall. 初冠雪の季節. ⇨二十四節気

しょうそういん(ほうもつでん)【正倉院(宝物殿)】 the *Shosoin* Treasure House (in Nara Prefecture). *Shosoin* is a treasure repository, built in the Azekura log-cabin style, with a raised floor. It contains some 3,000 historic articles and many works of art of the late Nara period and a collection of fine art objects from abroad, showing Chinese, Korean and Persian influences. 宝物殿(高床式丸太家屋)には奈良時代末期の約3千件の歴史的資料や美術工芸品，それにまた中国・韓国・ペルシアの影響を受けている外国の芸術品を収蔵している. ☆奈良東大寺大仏殿の一部として西北に位置する. ⇨校倉造り

じょうぞうしゅ【醸造酒】 *sake*[liquor] made by fermentation. 発酵させてつくった酒. 清酒など.

じょうだい【城代】 ❶ a keeper of a castle; a castle warden; a deputy representing a governor of a castle in his lord's absence. 城主の留守中，その代理として城を守る人. ❷ a deputy governor of the shogunate castle[a keeper of the shogunal castle] at Osaka or Sumpu. 徳川幕府の職名. 大阪城・駿府城などを守る職.

【城代家老】 a feudal lord's chief councilor in charge of the castle in his lord's absence (in the Edo period). He kept guards over a feudal lord's castle and domain in his lord's name, and administered the government affairs while his lord was absent on military business or alternate-year attendance at Edo. 江戸時代，藩主が軍事または参勤交代などで不在のとき，君主の名において城を守り政務をとった家老. ⇨家老

/ 参勤交代

しょうたくち【沼沢地】 a marsh; a swamp; a swampy area. ¶沼沢地の植物 marsh plants.

しょうちくばい【松竹梅】 ❶〔植物〕 pine, bamboo and plum[apricot] branches. ❷〈祝い事〉 (a piece of) pine, bamboo and plum branches used as symbols of felicity; (a set of) pine, bamboo and plum twigs symbolic of good luck. The combination of the three plants used as New Year's decorations (*kadomatsu*) has auspicious significance, each symbolizing longevity, constancy and purity. 幸運を招く祝い事の象徴として使用する. 正月の飾り物として用いるこの三種の植物にはめでたい意味合いがあり, 各々が長寿・貞節・清浄を象徴する. ⇨門松 ❸〈料理・酒類など3種の等級〉 pine, bamboo and plum used as a three-stage classification (of quality or price). ☆「松」(pine)〈最上級〉 the top[upper, deluxe] grade; the first class. 「竹」(bamboo)〈中級〉 the middle[medium, special] grade; the second class. 「梅」(plum)〈並級〉 the lower[lesser, standard] grade; the third class.

しょうちゅう【焼酎】 *shochu*; a low-class distilled liquor[spirits]. *Shochu* is a traditional Japanese alcoholic beverage distilled from grain such as rice, sweet potatoes, wheat or other materials. 焼酎は日本古来の蒸留酒(醸造酒). 米・(薩摩)芋・麦などからつくるアルコール分の強い飲み物. ☆アルコール分 (alcohol concentration)は20%から45%まであるが, 通常は25%. 鹿児島・宮崎の「芋焼酎」(yam *shochu*), 熊本の「米焼酎」(rice *shochu*). 壱岐の「麦焼酎」(wheat *shochu*). 長野の「蕎麦焼酎」(buckwheat *shochu*)などが有名. ¶焼酎のお湯割り *shochu* mixed with hot water. ⇨泡盛(沖縄) / 酎ハイ

しょうつき【祥月】 the same month when[in which] a person died; the month of a person's death. (一周忌以降において)故人の死んだ月と同じ月. ⇨命日. ¶父の祥月命日 the same month and day when[in which] one's father died; the anniversary of one's father's death. (父の死んだ同じ月の命日).

じょうど【浄土】〈仏教〉 the Pure Land; Paradise. ¶浄土教 the Jodo[Pure Land] dogma[doctrine, teaching]. 浄土宗 the Jodo sect (of Buddhism). 浄土真宗 the Jodo-Shinshu sect (of Buddhism). 浄土思想 Pure Land thought[Buddhism]. 極楽浄土 paradise. 西方浄土 the Pure Land in the West; the Western Paradise of the Pure Land.

しょうとう【小刀】 a short(er) sword; the shorter of two swords worn by a *samurai*. ⇦大刀

しょうどうがい【衝動買い】〈買い物〉impulse buying; buying on impulse; 〈人〉impulse buyer.

しょうどうさつじん【衝動殺人】 a murder on impulse; a murder on the spur of the moment.

じょうとうしき【上棟式】 a house frame-work-raising[roof-raising] ceremony. It is a ceremony celebrating the raising[putting up] of the ridge beam for the roof when completing the framework of a new house. 新家屋の骨組が完成し, その上に屋根用の棟木をあげたことを祝う儀式. 「棟上式」ともいう.

しょうにゅうせき【鍾乳石】 a stalactite (in the Akiyoshi(do) Limestone Cave). ⇨石筍

しょうにゅうせきちゅう【鍾乳石柱】 a limestone pillar. ¶龍河洞の鍾乳石柱(高知県) limestone pillars in Ryuga(do) Limestone Cave.

しょうにゅうどう【鍾乳洞】 a limestone

cave[cavern]; a stalactite cave[grotto]. ☆石灰岩(limestone)が多い地方にある洞穴(cave; grotto)のこと. ¶**日本三大鍾乳洞** the Three Largest Limestone Caves in Japan. ☆秋芳洞[山口県]・龍河洞[高知県]・龍泉洞[岩手県]

しょうにん【上人・聖人】a high-ranked priest; a holy priest; a saint; the Venerable ~. 日蓮・法然・親鸞など「高徳者」の尊称. ¶**日蓮聖人** the Venerable Nichiren.

しょうのう【樟脳】camphor. 楠(camphor tree)の細片を蒸留してつくる. 防虫剤の原料. ⇨楠. ¶**樟脳の玉** camphor ball; mothball. 別称「虫除け玉」.

しょうばん【相伴】⇨お相伴(通称)

しょうひきげん【消費期限】a consume-by date; a use-by date; a label of expiration date; a label to know when a product has expired. ⇨賞味期限

しょうひんけん【商品券】a gift certificate; ㉇ a gift voucher; a merchandise coupon [voucher].

しょうぶ【菖蒲】❶〈花菖蒲〉an iris. ❷〈菖蒲〉a sweet flag; a sweet sedge. サトイモ科の多年草.「アヤメ」. ⇨あやめ

【菖蒲湯】 a sweet-flag bath; a bath with sweet flag leaves floating on the hot water. The Japanese think of a sweet flag leaf (in the shape of a sword) as a weapon to fight against epidemics. They take a *shobu-yu* to prevent disease and drive[ward] off evil spirits on the Boys' Festival (May 5). 日本では(葉が刀型の)菖蒲は疫病と戦う武器と考えている. 端午の節句に, 病気予防や邪気払いとして菖蒲の根・葉の浮かぶ風呂に入る (take a bath with iris leaves; have an iris leaf bath). ☆「菖蒲」(アヤメ)は「勝負」(victory or defeat)の同音異義語(homonym)である. そのため「勝負強い子供」になることを願って端午の節句には「菖蒲」が用いられる.

しょうぶ【勝負】victory or defeat(勝敗); a match; a game; a bout(試合). ¶**13勝2敗** a record of 13 wins[victories] and two defeats[loses].

しょうぶけんさやく【勝負検査役】〔相撲〕committee of *sumo* judges. They decide *sumo* ranking lists according to the win-loss of *sumo* wrestlers. 力士の勝敗に準じて相撲の取組表を決める. ☆勝負審判委員の旧称.

しょうぶしんぱん【勝負審判】〔相撲〕*sumo* judges; referee advisors (who are all retired *sumo* wrestlers). Five *sumo* judges are seated around the *sumo* ring during the *sumo* matches and have the final say on the issue of a *sumo* bout. 5人の審判が相撲の取組中に土俵周辺に座し, 物言いのときに最終決着をつける (make the final decision). ⇨物言い. ¶**勝負審判長** the chief judge of a *sumo* bout.

しょうへいが【障屏画】paintings (drawn) on sliding doors or folding screens (of traditional Japanese-style rooms). Some decorative paintings are colorfully sprinkled with gold dust or covered with silver leaf. (和室の)襖や屏風などにかかれた絵画. 金銀箔の色鮮やかなものもある. ☆「障壁画」(屏風画 (a sliding-door painting)と壁画(a wall painting))は桃山時代から江戸時代初期に完成した書院造りなどに見られる大がかりな室内装飾画をさす.

しょうまん【小満】lesser ripening; the season when all things grow well. 万物の成長が良い季節. ⇨二十四節気

しょうみきげん【賞味期限】the best-before date; eat-by freshness date; the expiration date; ㊂ pull date, ㉇ sell-by date. ☆包装紙などには Best if used by (August 5, 2022). または Best if consumed before (May 5, 2022). などのように用いられる. ¶**食品賞味期限** the expiration date for food. **賞味**

期限切れ食品 food and confectionery past their expiration and best-before dates. (肉の) 賞味期限が過ぎている (This meat is) past its sell-by date. ⇨消費期限

しょうみょう【唱名・称名】 the chanting of the holy invocation (by Buddhist priests at the ceremony[rite]). (仏式で僧侶が)仏の名号を唱えること.

しょうみょう【声明】 the chanting of Buddhist hymns (by Buddhist priests in front of the Buddhist statue). (仏前で僧侶が)ふしをつけて仏徳を称える声楽. ☆平安前期の仏教音楽.

じょうもんすぎ【縄文杉】 *Jomon sugi,* Japanese cedar[cryptomeria]. It is the oldest huge cedar growing high in Yakushima Island, Kagoshima Prefecture. ⇨杉

じょうもんどき【縄文土器】 *Jomon* ware (made in the Japanese Neolithic period); straw-rope pattern pottery; the earthenware with patterns of rope on the surface. (日本の新石器時代に製作された)土器. 表面に縄目模様がある.

しょうや【庄屋】 a village headman (in the Edo period). He was in charge of administration under a local magistrate in the Edo period. 村の頭[首長]. 江戸時代, 代官の下で村の行政事務を扱った首長. ☆主として関西で用いられた称. 関東では「名主」といった.

しょうゆ【醤油】 *shoyu*; (dark brown) soy sauce; soybean sauce; soya sauce. *Shoyu* is made from fermented soybeans and wheat, mixed with a special yeast in brine for six months to a year. *Shoyu* is often used not only as a dipping sauce for *sashimi* or *sushi* and grilled fish, but also as an ingredient in boiled and fried foods. 大豆・小麦・食塩水に麹を混ぜて半年から1年ほど発酵させて作る. 刺身や寿司, 焼き魚の浸し用の味付け, また煮物や炒め物の調味料として使用する場合が多い. ☆ brine「(食品保存用の)濃い塩水」. saltwater「(普通の)塩水」. 単に soy. 英国では soya ともいう. 元来英語の soy sauce の soy は日本語の「しょうゆ」に由来する. 主な種類は「溜り(濃厚な醤油)」(a thick *shoyu*, which is used as a dip for raw fish[*sashimi*]).「濃口」(a dark *shoyu*),「薄口」(a light *shoyu*)などがある. 主要な産地は千葉の「野田・銚子」や兵庫の「龍野」などがある. ⇨薄口醤油 / 濃口醤油 / 減塩醤油. ¶醤油入れ *shoyu* container. 醤油樽 *shoyu* keg. 醤油差し *shoyu* cruet[pot]. 醤油かす *shoyu* lees. 醤油だれ soy-based sauce (used for dipping *shabu-shabu* food into).

じょうようかんじ【常用漢字】 Chinese characters for daily[common] use in Japan. 1,945 Chinese characters were officially designated by the government for everyday use in 1981. 1981年に日常生活に使用する目安として1945字の漢字が指定された. 2010年には改定され2136字になった. ⇨当用漢字

じょうりゅう【上流(川の)】 the upper reaches (of a river). ¶荒川の上流(東京都) the upper reaches of the River Arakawa. ⇔下流

しょうりょう【精霊】〈死者の魂〉the spirit of a dead person; the spirits of the dead; the spirits of one's ancestors; one's ancestral spirits. ¶精霊送り sending off the spirits of the dead; sending off one's ancestral spirits. 精霊迎え welcoming back the spirits of the dead; welcoming back one's ancestral spirits.

【精霊棚】 a stand for food set up in front of the Buddhist family altar (*butsudan*). It is used to welcome back one's ancestral spirits by offering food and beverages during the period of the Bon Festival. 仏壇

の前に置かれた供物用の棚. 盂蘭盆の間飲食物をそなえ, 精霊をまつるために用いる. 「盆棚」ともいう.

【精霊流し】 an event of floating lanterns for the spirits of one's ancestors on the last day[at the end] of the Bon Festival. An event of launching a straw boat loaded [laden] with a paper lantern (or votive offerings) on the water is observed to see off the spirits of one's ancestors on the last day[at the end] of the Bon Festival. 盂蘭盆の最終日に精霊を冥界に送り返すため川などに灯籠や供物をわら舟にのせて流す行事.

【精霊舟】 a straw boat for the spirits of one's ancestors to sail in (on the day[at the end] of the Bon Festival). 精霊をのせるためのわら舟.

しょうるいあわれみのれい【生類憐みの令】 the Animal Protection Law[Act]. Tokugawa Tsunayoshi, the 5th shogun, enacted an edict to prohibit the killing of animals[an edict to forbid cruelty to living creature] in 1685. 動物保護法. 1685年, 第5代将軍, 徳川綱吉が発令した動物殺傷の禁令. ☆1709年に廃止.

じょうるり【浄瑠璃】〔文楽〕 (a) *joruri*; a narrative ballad recited[chanted] to *shamisen* accompaniment[to the accompaniment of *shamisen*[a three-stringed musical instrument]]; a dramatic narrative chant accompanied by *shamisen*. The term *Joruri* refers mainly to the vocal music (g*idaiyu-bushi*) of bunraku[Japanese puppet theater]. 三味線伴奏に合わせて語る[詠唱する]語り物の叙事的歌謡. 特に文楽での「義太夫節」をさす. ⇨義太夫 / 文楽. ☆ ballad(バラッド)は, 素朴な語と短い連で書かれた民間の伝承的な物語詩, またはその曲. ¶**浄瑠璃芝居** *joruri* play[drama]; puppet play[drama] associ-ated with narrative ballad (物語的な歌謡と関連する人形劇[文楽])

しょうろう【鐘楼】 a belfry; a bell tower; a tower hanging the temple bell. The temple bell is hung together with a wooden hammer in the tower structure. 寺の鐘つき堂. ⇨七堂伽藍. ¶**鐘楼守** a belfry keeper.

しょうわのひ【昭和の日】 Showa Day; Day of Showa. (April 29). This national holiday was established in 2007 as a day to reflect on the events of the Showa era. The Japanese celebrate the birthday of Showa Emperor who reigned before, during and after World War II. This day is celebrated to think back on Japan's Showa era when recovery was made after turbulent days, and to think of the country's bright future. 2007年に制定. 昭和時代を回顧する日. 戦前・戦中・戦後にわたって在位(1926(昭和元年)-1989(昭和64年))された昭和天皇 [裕仁天皇](1901-1989, 第124代天皇)の誕生日を祝う日. 激動の日々を経て, 復興を遂げた昭和の時代を顧み, 国の明るい将来に思いをいたすために祝う.

しょきばらい【暑気払い】 forgetting the hot heat; beating the summer heat; getting out of the heat. 夏の暑さを追い払うこと.

しょぎょうむじょう【諸行無常】 All things flow[are in flux] and nothing is permanent; All things of this world are transient and impermanent. 万物は常に移り変わり, やむことなく生滅する. ☆仏教の根本思想.

しょくざい【食材】 foodstuffs; ingredients (for cooking). ☆ materialは使わない. ¶**旬の食材** ingredients in season; foodstuffs [foods] of the season.

しょくじょ(せい)【織女(星)[ベガ星]】 Vega; the Weaver Star; woman weaver. ⇨七夕

しょくひん【食品】 food(s); foodstuff(s). ⇨生鮮食品. ¶**食品期限表示** best before indication for food. ⇨賞味期限/ 消費期限.

食品添加物 food additive. **食品保存料** food preservative（食品保存添加物）. **食品衛生** food hygiene.

しょくもつせんい【食物繊維】 dietary fiber; roughage. ¶**食物繊維飲料** a fiber drink.

しょくようがえる【食用蛙】 a bullfrog; an edible frog. 別名「牛蛙」. ⇨かえる

じょけいてんのう【女系天皇】 a female-line Emperor (of Japan). ☆母方の皇統（天皇の血統）に属する天皇を指す呼称.（徳仁天皇の子供）愛子内親王の子供が天皇になった場合「女系天皇」である. ⇨女性天皇

しょこう【諸侯】 feudal lords in the feudal times. 封建時代の大名たち.

しょさおんがく【所作音楽】〈歌舞伎〉background music performed on the stage to accompany the actions and dances of the *kabuki* actors. 舞台上で演奏される歌舞伎役者の舞踊の伴奏をする音楽. ⇨歌舞伎「歌舞伎の音楽」

しょさごと【所作事】〔歌舞伎〕 kabuki dance play; kabuki dance accompanied by chanted song and pantomime. 歌舞伎で，長唄を伴奏とする舞踊と無言劇. ⇨出し物

しょしだい【所司代】 the chief administrator of the imperial capital and of the imperial lands (in Kyoto) during the Edo period. He was appointed by the shogun from among his vassals[retainers].「京都所司代」(a Kyoto police deputy; an administrator of justice in Kyoto) の略. 江戸時代（京都の）市政・検察をつかさどる長官. 将軍が家臣から任命した.

しょしょ【処暑】 manageable[bearable] heat; the season when autumn winds begin to blow. 暑さも和らぎ秋風が吹きはじめる季節. ⇨二十四節気

じょせいてんのう【女性天皇】 a female emperor (of Japan). ☆天皇個人の性別に関する用語. 過去8人在位された.（徳仁天皇の子供）愛子内親王が天皇になった場合は「女性天皇」である. ⇨女系天皇

しょたい【書体】 ❶〈文字の書き方〉(a style of) handwriting; calligraphic modes. ❷〈漢字の書き方〉a script style; the print style of writing Chinese characters in calligraphy. There are mainly the three calligraphic modes: *kai-sho* (noncursive [square] style; block or printed style), *gyo-sho* (semicursive style) and *so-sho* (cursive style; swift-brushed style). 三種の書体「楷書」「行書」「草書」がある. ⇨楷書 / 行書 / 草書

しょちゅうみまい【暑中見舞い】 midsummer greetings; an inquiry after health of a person at the height of summer. ☆（暦のうえでは）夏の土用の18日の間（7月20日ごろから立秋8月8日の前日ごろ）に行う.「暑中伺い」ともいう. 立秋を過ぎると「残暑見舞い」という. ⇨寒中見舞い

【暑中見舞状】 a summer greeting card; a midsummer greeting postcard[letter] (offering best wishes for the hot season). It is a letter[postcard] sent to inquiry after superior's[good customer's] health in the hot season in appreciation of their daily favors. 日ごろのお世話に感謝して夏季中に上司や得意先の健康を伺うために送る挨拶状. ⇨寒中見舞状 / 残暑見舞状

しょっきり【初っ切り】〔相撲〕 comic *sumo* performance. It is demonstrated during the course of a *hana-zumo* exhibition matches by lower rank *sumo* wrestlers. 花相撲で下位相撲力士によって行われるこっけいな余興相撲. ⇨花相撲

しょっつる【塩汁】 sandfish-based fish sauce; sauce made from salted and fermented sandfish meat. *Shottsuru* is a sauce formed when sandfish are pickled in salt. It is used to season fish and vegetable stews. ハタハタを塩漬けにし，しみ出た上澄みを濾してつくる魚醤. 塩汁鍋のだしに

使う. ☆秋田地方の特産. ⇨はたはた

〔料理〕**塩汁鍋** a hot-pot dish of fish and vegetables prepared with sandfish-based fish sauce. 塩汁で魚や野菜を煮る鍋料理. ☆代表的な秋田料理.

しょとう〔諸島〕(a group[chain] of) islands; an archipelago. ¶**小笠原諸島**(東京都) the Ogasawara Islands. (1968年日本へ返還). **沖縄諸島** the Okinawa Islands.(1972年日本へ返還). ⇨島 / 半島 / 群島

しょどう〔書道〕(the art of) Japanese calligraphy; penmanship. *Shodo* is a traditional formative art of writing Chinese characters and *kana*[Hiragana and Katakana] syllabary with a Japanese brush and dark India ink. 毛筆と墨で漢字や文字を書く一種の造形芸術. ¶仮名[平仮名・片仮名]. ¶**書道の大家** a great calligrapher; a calligraphy master.

【書道用具】 calligraphy implements [instruments]. 「筆」brush. 「筆置き」brush rest. 「文鎮」paperweight. 「硯」inkstone. 「硯箱」inkstone case.「墨」dark Indian ink. 「水滴」water drop. 「和紙」Japanese paper. 「半紙」calligraphy paper. 「巻紙」rolled calligraphy paper. 「手本」calligraphy samples; example book.「下敷」desk pad. ⇨書体(楷書・行書・草書)

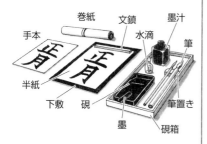

しょなぬか[**しょなのか**]〔初七日〕 the seventh day after a person's death (counting the day of death as well). A Buddhist memorial service for the deceased is observed[held] on the sixth day after a person's death. 人の死後 7 日目の忌日(死んだ日を入れて数える). 死後 6 日目に行われる法事. ☆通常の換算方式は, 死去した日を 1 日として数える. 囲16日死亡の場合初七日は22日となる. ⇨法事

じょにだん【序二段】〔相撲〕 the *jonidan* division; the second-lowest division in the *sumo* wrestling, below *sandanme* and above *jonokuchi*.「三段目」の下位,「序の口」の上位. ⇨相撲の番付

しょにち【初日】〔相撲〕 the first[opening] day of a *sumo* tournament.

じょのくち【序の口】〔相撲〕 the *jonokuchi* division; the lowest-ranking division in the *sumo* wrestling; the lowest division[rank] of *sumo* wrestlers. 相撲番付の最下位. ⇨相撲の番付

じょのまい【序の舞】❶〔能楽〕a slow graceful dance of a Noh play. 能楽での静かで優雅な舞.

❷〔歌舞伎〕a soft music of a kabuki play. 歌舞伎での, 静かで落ち着いた囃子.

じょやのかね【除夜の鐘】 New Year's Eve bells; the Buddhist bells tolling[ringing] on the eve of the New Year. *Joya-no-kane* is the 108 peals of the Buddhist temple bells which are rung out at midnight on New Year's Eve to announce the passing of the old year and to herald the New Year. It is believed that the 108 peals of the temple bell represent the 108 worldly passions [earthly desires] of human beings. With each toll of the temple bell, one earthly desire is dispelled. When the last stroke of the temple bell reverberates, all the evils of the past year are expelled and people greet the New Year with a pure state of mind. 大晦日に寺院でつく108の鐘で, 旧年が去り新年を迎えることを告げる. 鐘をつくこ

とにより人間のもつ108の煩悩をぬぐい去る.

しらあえ【白和え】 a salad with *tofu*[bean curd] dressing; a salad of vegetables and fish flesh dressed with *tofu*, white *miso* and white sesame. 豆腐と白味噌また白ごまをすり混ぜて，野菜や魚肉を和えた料理.

しらうお【白魚】〔魚〕an icefish; a whitebait（単複同形）. 近海にすむシラウオ科の硬骨魚. フライにして塩とレモンを添えて食べると美味. ☆しろうお（「おどり食い」の魚）とは別種. ⇨しろうお

しらうめ【白梅】〔植物〕a plum tree with white blossoms（木）; white plum blossoms（花）. ⇨うめ

しらおいポロトコタン【白老ポロトコタン】 Shiraoi Poroto Kotan. ☆「白老」は北海道の登別と苫小牧にはさまれた太平洋に面した町.「ポロト（湖畔）」は湖の呼称.「コタン」はアイヌ語で集落のこと.「白老ポロトコタン」ではかつてのアイヌの暮らしや歴史を伝える伝統文化が見学できる.

しらかば【白樺】〔植物〕a white birch; a silver birch. カバノキ科の落葉高木. 材は細工用. ¶白樺の原始林で覆われた黒姫山（長野県）Mt. Kurohime(yama) covered by virgin forests of birch trees. ⇨かば(のき)

しらき【白木】 plain wood; unpainted wood; unvarnished wood. 塗料をぬらない木地のままの材. ¶白木造りの神社 a Shinto shrine built of plain wood.

しらこ【白子】 milt (of fish)(魚精); soft roe(魚の精巣). フグ(blowfish)やタラ(codfish)の白子は美味. ¶白子をもつ魚 soft-roed fish.

しらさぎ【白鷺】〔鳥〕a white heron; a white egret; a silver egret. ⇨さぎ

しらす【白子】〔魚〕a whitebait; a tiny young sardine(イワシの幼魚); the young of the sardine.「カタクチイワシ」などの稚魚. ¶白子干し dried and seasoned young sardines[anchovies]; dried sardine fry. ⇨縮緬雑魚

〔料理〕白子の卸し和え dried young sardines dressed with grated *daikon*[radish].

しらす【白州・白洲】❶〈川の〉a white sandbar; a bar of white sand. 白い砂の州. ❷〈庭の〉an area of white sand[gravel] laid in a dry landscape garden. 枯山水庭園などの白い砂[砂利]を敷きつめた所. ❸〈奉行所の〉a law court (in the Edo period); an area of white sand laid in a law court[a court of justice] where criminals were judged by a magistrate. 江戸時代，奉行所などで砂の上に座す罪人を裁く所. ❹〔能楽〕a pure area of white gravels [pebbles] which divide the Noh stage from the audience. 能舞台と観客とを区分する(separate) 白い石のある箇所. ¶白洲梯子 stairs to white gravels.

しらすだいち【白砂台地】a volcanic ash and sand plateau.

しらたき【白滝】 *konnyaku*[devil's tongue] noodles; thinly stripped *konnyaku*; thin noodles made from *konnyaku* starches (often used in *sukiyaki* and *nabemono*). 関西では「糸こんにゃく」(*konnyaku* strings)ともいう. ⇨こんにゃく / 糸こんにゃく

しらたま【白玉】 rice-flour dumplings; dumplings made from glutinous rice flour. 白玉粉でつくった団子. 〔食品〕白玉粉 refined glutinous rice flour (for dumplings or sweets). もち米を水でさらしてからひいた粉. 団子や菓子の材料.「寒晒し粉」ともいう. ⇨寒晒し粉

しらに【白煮】 simmering of foods[lotus roots or taros] with salt only (or without *shoyu*[soy sauce]). (蓮根や里芋などの白い)食材を塩だけで(醤油を使わずに)煮ること.

しらぬいがた【不知火型】 the *Shiranui* style of ring-entering ritual (performed by *yokozuna*, grand champion *sumo* wrestler). ⇨雲竜型

じりきほんがん【自力本願】salvation[justification] by ascetic training. 厳しい修業をすることで救済される. ☆禅宗における座禅による瞑想を通して悟りを開く. ⇔他力本願

しりとり【尻取り】 *shiritori*; a Japanese word-chain game; a word game played by making a chain of words. A player must give a word starting with the last syllable of the word given by the previous player. 物の名の終わりの音を次の物の名のはじめに置いて, 順番で物の名をいい合うことば遊び.

しる【汁】〈吸い物〉soup;〈煮出し汁〉soup stock; broth; sauce;〈肉汁〉gravy;〈果実・野菜〉juice;〈草木〉sap. 別称「つゆ」. ⇨つゆ. ¶汁の実 ingredients in soup. 汁椀 a soup bowl. 汁物 soup; broth. *Soup* in a Japanese dish can be roughly divided into two types; *sumashi-jiru* (clear soup) and *miso-shiru* (*miso* soup). ⇨澄まし汁 / みそ汁

しるこ【汁粉】 sweet *adzuki*-bean paste soup; a thin, sweet crushed *adzuki*–bean paste soup with a piece of rice cake (or a few rice-flour dumplings); a sweet creamy soup made from crushed *adzuki*–bean paste containing a piece of rice cake (or a few rice-flour dumplings). 小豆餡を溶かして砂糖を加えて煮た薄い汁に, 餅(または白玉)を入れた食べ物. ⇨善哉

シルバーシート priority seat; seat reserved for senior citizens; seats reserved for the aged and the disabled on trains or buses.

しろ【城】 a castle. The castle was designed not only for a military function but also for a regional political and economic center. 城は軍事的な要塞(中世)また地方の政治的・経済的な中心地(近世)として築かれた. ☆日本の城は三種に大別される. 「山城」castle built on a mountaintop (圀岐阜城),「平山城」castle built on a hill (圀松山城),「平城」castle built on a plain (圀松本城). ⇨城下町. ¶姫路城 Himeji Castle (通称「白鷺城」)(訓読：しらさぎ). White Heron[Egret] Castle). 城跡 the ruins of a castle. 城主 the lord of a castle. 日本三大名城 the Three Famous Castles in Japan. ☆姫路城[兵庫県]. 名古屋城[愛知県]. 熊本城[熊本県].

【関連語】「天守閣(戦闘の指令塔)」a donjon; a keep; a castle tower; the tallest, most massive donjon. ⇨天守閣.「本丸(城の中核)」the castle keep; the main enclosure[central portion] (of a castle); main citadel.「二の丸(家臣の住居)」the second[secondary] enclosure (of a

天守閣

鉄砲狭間
石垣
城壁

櫓門

物見櫓
堀

隅櫓

castle); second citadel. 「三の丸」the third[tertiary] enclosure. 「櫓」a turret; a watchtower; a guard tower. ⇨櫓「隅櫓」corner tower. 「櫓門［橋櫓］」barbican gatehouse. 「渡り櫓」connecting tower. 「堀」moat. 「石垣」stone wall. 「鉄砲狭間」loophole for matchlock[muskets]. 「物見櫓」a watchtower; a lookout tower. 「城門」a castle gate, 「城壁」a castle wall; a rampart.

しろあり【白蟻】〔虫〕a white ant; a termite. ¶**白蟻の駆除** eradication of termites. ⇨あり

しろあん【白餡】sweet white bean paste. ⇨餡

しろうお【素魚】〔魚〕an ice goby; a white goby. ハゼ科の小形の海魚. 透明な体は細長くうろこがない. 春先に産卵のため河にのぼる. 「踊り食い」で知られる. シラウオ(icefish)とは別種. ⇨躍り食い

しろかゆ【白粥】plain rice gruel[porridge]. ⇨かゆ

しろくのくしにんぎょうしばい【白久の串人形芝居】the Puppet Show at Shiroku area. (4月). ⇨付記(1)「日本の祭り」

しろくま【白熊】〔動物〕a polar bear; a white bear. ⇨くま

しろくろえいが【白黒映画】a black-and-white movie(日米語の語順に注意); a monochrome film.

しろざけ【白酒】sweet white *sake*. It is made by fermenting a blend of *shochu*[low-class distilled liquor] and *mirin*[sweetened sake] with steamed glutinous rice and rice malt. As it is not a regular alcoholic beverage, it is served as a celebratory drink on the Doll Festival. 蒸したもち米と米麹に焼酎またはみりんを混ぜ, すりつぶして作る. 通常のアルコールではないのでひな祭りに祝い酒として用いる. ⇨ひな祭り

しろしょうぞく【白装束】white clothing [dress] (worn by a *samurai* when commit-ting *seppuku*). (武士が切腹するときなどに着用する)白ずくめの服装. ☆神事にも用いる. ⇔黒装束／切腹. ¶**白装束の武士** a *samurai* (dressed) in white.

しろタク【白タク】an unlicensed taxi (不法タクシー); a car (with a white license plate) illegally operated as a taxi.

しろナンバー【白ナンバー】a private car(自家用車); a privately-owned car (with a white license plate) legally used as a non-commercial vehicle.

しろバイ【白バイ】〈車〉a police motorcycle (painted white); 〈人〉a motorcycle police-man[policewoman].

しろぶさ【白房】〔相撲〕the white tassel. ⇨房

しろぼし【白星】❶〈白い印〉a white mark [circle];
❷〔相撲〕〈勝ち星〉a victory[win] mark; a victory[win] in a *sumo* bout (recorded with a white mark[circle]). 勝負での勝ち星のこと. ⇔黒星. ¶**白星を上げる** win a victory (over); be the victor.

しろみ【白身】❶〈魚の〉white flesh; 〈鶏の〉white meat. ¶**白身の魚** a white-flesh fish; a fish with white flesh; ㊤ a whitefish. **白身のさしみ** a white-flesh *sashimi*[sliced raw fish].
❷〈卵の〉the white (of an egg); egg white(s); albumen. ¶**卵の黄身と白身** the egg yolk and the egg white; the yolk of an egg and the white of an egg.

しろみそ【白味噌】white[light-brown] *miso* (made mainly from fermented[malted] rice). 原料に発酵米[米麹]を使った甘みの強い白色の味噌. その代表が「西京味噌」. ⇨西京味噌／甘味噌

しろむく【白無垢】a pure-white *kimono* [dress]; an all-white *kimono*[dress]. 上着から下着まで白づくめの着物. ¶**白無垢の花嫁** a bride dressed in white; a bride wearing a pure-white *kimono*.

しんうち【真打ち】 the headliner[topliner] of storytelling performance; a full-fledged master of storytelling; a top-ranked comic storyteller. (落語・講談などの寄席で)最後に出演する，最も芸のすぐれた人の称．目玉になる立役者．最高の資格．☆「主演者」を指す場合 the main[principal] entertainer, the star performerともいう．

しんえん【神苑】 the precincts[grounds] of a Shinto shrine; the sacred garden of a Shinto shrine; the garden attached to a Shinto shrine. 神社の境内，またはそこにある庭園．¶平安神宮の神苑 a sacred garden of Heian Shrine.

しんか【臣下】 a vassal; a retainer; a subject. ⇨重臣

じんがさ【陣笠】 a warrior's camp hat; a camp metal[wooden] hat in the battle; a hat made of metal or strong wood worn in the camp. In feudal times it was worn by foot soldiers[rank-and-file soldiers] in the camp instead of a battle helmet. 昔，足軽［雑兵・下級兵士］などが陣中で兜の代わりにかぶった鉄製［木製］の笠．☆「陣笠(政党の幹部をとりまく平議員)」は the rank and file (of a political party); 〈個人〉㊧ a backbencher.

しんがたインフルエンザ【新型インフルエンザ】 the new swine flu; the new strain of swine flu virus.

しんかん【神官】 a Shinto priest observing rituals; a Shinto ritualist. 神社で神事にたずさわる祭司．「神主」ともいう．

じんぎ【仁義】 humanity and justice; benevolence and righteousness; moral code; duty (義理)．¶仁義立て doing one's duty.

じんぎ【神器】 the sacred treasures (of a Shinto shrine); the Imperial Regalia; the emblems of the Japanese Imperial Throne. 「三種の神器」の略．⇨三種の神器

じんぎ【神祇】 the deities[gods] of heaven and earth. 天地の神々．天の神と地の神．

じんぎかん【神祇官】 a commissioner of the Shinto religion; an official in charge of matters relating to Shintoism. 神事をつかさどり，諸国の社を統括する長官[管理官]．⇨太政官

ジンギスカンなべ【ジンギスカン鍋】[料理] a Mongolian-style mutton barbecue; a dish of thinly sliced mutton and vegetables barbecued on an iron griddle. 鉄鍋で羊肉や野菜を焼きながら食べる料理．

しんきゅう【鍼灸・針灸】 acupuncture and moxibustion. ¶鍼灸師 a practitioner of acupuncture and moxibustion.

しんきろう【蜃気楼】 a mirage (appearing on the horizon of Toyama Bay). 富山湾の水平線に(4〜5月頃)見られる蜃気楼は有名．

しんぐう【新宮】 subordinate shrines[subshrines] (which were branched off from the original Shinto shrine). 本宮から神霊を分けてもらって建てた神社．⇨本宮

じんぐう【神宮】 a Shinto shrine. ¶明治神宮 Meiji-jingu Shrine. 伊勢大神宮 Ise Grand Shrine; Grand Shrine of Ise. ⇨神社

しんげんこうまつり【信玄公祭り】 the Memorial Festival for Takeda Shingen. (4月).⇨付記(1)「日本の祭り」

しんけんしょうぶ【真剣勝負】 (have) a fight with real swords. 本物の刀で勝負すること．

しんこ【新香】 Japanese pickles; pickled vegetables; vegetables pickled in brine. ⇨お新香

しんこ【糝粉】〈粉〉rice flour; 〈餅〉rice-flour dough. ¶糝粉細工 figures made of rice-flour dough. 糝粉餅 rice-flour dumplings.

じんこうちゃくしょくりょう【人工着色料】 an artificial coloring agent. ⇨着色料

しんさくらくご【新作落語】 a new creative comic storytelling (composed to describe current[modern] phenomena); a new work

by a comedic storyteller. ⇨落語

しんしき【神式】 Shinto rites; Shinto rituals.
¶**神式結婚(式)** a wedding ceremony held with Shinto rites; a wedding ceremony performed according to Shinto rites; a Shinto-style wedding ceremony. ⇨神前結婚. **神式葬儀** a funeral conducted according to Shinto rites; a Shinto-style funeral service.

じんじゃ【神社】 the *Jinja*; a Shinto shrine; a building for the worship of Shinto gods. The *jinja* is dedicated to one or more gods, god-ancestors of the Imperial Family or historical figures. 神道の神を礼拝する所. 神社には神々, 皇祖神あるいは歴史上の人物を祀る. ¶**神社仏閣** (Shinto) shrines and (Buddhist) temples. **神社建築** shrine building; Shinto architecture. **神社本庁** the Association of Shinto Shrines. ⇨神道(神社神道 / 教派神道)
☆『神社の呼称』
① 『神社』 Inari-jinja Shrine「稲荷神社」/ Yasaka-jinja Shrine「八坂神社」
② 『神宮』 Ise-jingu Shrine「伊勢神宮」/ Meiji-jingu Shrine「明治神宮」. ⇨神宮
③ 『宮』 Tosho-gu Shrine「東照宮」/ Tenman-gu Shrine「天満宮」. ⇨〜宮
④ 『大社』 Izumo-taisha Grand Shrine;

Grand Shrine of Izumo「出雲大社」. ⇨大社
☆『神社の主な構成』
① 『参道』 the approach[an entrance path of worship] to a Shinto shrine. ⇨参道
② 『鳥居』 the *torii* gate (erected on the approach to a Shinto shrine). ⇨鳥居
③ 『手水舎』 the roofed purification pavilion. ⇨手水舎(ちょうずや / てみずや)
④ 『狛犬』 a pair of stone-carved guardian dogs (placed to protect the shrine from evils). ⇨狛犬
⑤ 『賽銭箱』 the offertory box. ⇨賽銭箱
⑥ 『注連縄』 sacred twisted rope (which divides the holy area from the outer world). ⇨注連縄
⑦ 『拝殿』 a Shinto oratory (where worshippers make offerings to gods). ⇨拝殿 / 拝礼
⑧ 『本殿』 a Shinto sanctuary (where an object of worship regarded as a deity is enshrined). ⇨本殿
⑨ 『神楽殿』 Kagura Hall[Stage] (where a kagura (Shinto music and dance) is offered to gods. ⇨神楽殿
⑩ 『社務所』 shrine office. ⇨社務所

しんじゅ【真珠】 a pearl. ¶**真珠貝** a pearl oyster[shell]. ⇨あこやがい. **真珠貝の筏** rafts of pearl oyster. **真珠層** a mother-of-

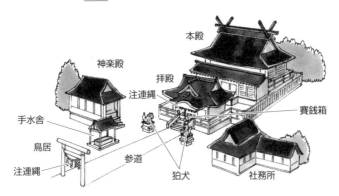

pearl; a nacreous layer. 真珠の養殖 pearl culture; pearl cultivation; cultivation of pearls. 真珠養殖場 a pearl farm[bed]; beds of cultivated pearls. 真珠採りの海女 a female pearl diver; female divers who pick up the oyster shells containing pearls from the seafloor. ミキモト真珠島 Mikimoto Pearl Island. 養殖真珠 a cultured pearl.

しんじゅう【心中】 a double suicide (committed by an unhappy couple[by a man and a woman]); a lovers' suicide. 二人以上の者がともに自殺すること.「情死」. ¶一家心中 a family suicide. 親子心中 a parent-child suicide. 無理心中 a forced double suicide; a murder-suicide. 心中未遂 an attempted double suicide.

【心中物】〔歌舞伎〕〔文楽〕a lovers' suicide drama (in kabuki or bunraku plays); a double suicide play of kabuki or bunraku plays dealing with a lovers' suicide[an unmarried couple of different social classes] in the feudal times. 封建時代に相愛する男女の情死をあつかった歌舞伎または浄瑠璃. 囫「曽根崎心中」(a Double Suicide at Sonezaki).「心中天網島」(a Double Suicide at Amijima). ⇨時代物 / 世話物

しんじゅわんのきしゅうこうげき【真珠湾の奇襲攻撃】 the Japanese attack on Pearl Harbor (in 1941). 日本軍によるハワイ州オアフ(Oahu)島への攻撃(1941年).

しんしゅんうたかいはじめ【新春歌会始め】 the New Year's Imperial Poetry Reading (Party). ⇨新年歌会始め

しんしょく【神職】〈人〉a Shinto priest;〈職務〉the Shinto priesthood. ⇨神主

しんしょく【浸食】 erosion. ¶海蝕 sea erosion. 風浸 wind erosion. 波の浸食 erosion caused by the waves. 氷河の浸食 glacial erosion. 浸食作用 erosion; erosive action. 浸食台地 an eroded plateau.

しんじんるい【新人類】new breed of humans; new human race; new humans.

しんせん【神饌】 foods and drinks offered to a god[deity]. 神前に供える酒食.「供物」「お供え物」などともいう.

しんせんぐみ【新選組】 Shinsengumi; (a group of) special police force at the end of the Edo period to guard Kyoto. 江戸時代末期の京都にて警察活動に従事した軍事組織. ☆徳川幕府を守った武士集団 (a group of *samurai* warriors defending the Tokugawa shogunate). 反幕府勢力を弾圧する.

しんぜんけっこん【神前結婚】 a Shinto-style wedding (ceremony); a wedding (ceremony) performed according to Shinto rites. Wedding rites are attended by close relatives of the couple only, who are invited to the reception that follows. ⇨神式結婚

☆『結婚式次第』(Shinto Wedding Procedures)

① 『手水の儀』purifying washing of hands and mouthと「入場」entry[entrance].

② 『修祓の儀』purification rites.「祓串」Shinto wand used by a Shinto priest for ritual purification.

③ 『献饌の儀』ceremony for making offerings to the deities[gods].

④ 『祝詞奏上』recitation of a Shinto ritual prayer.

⑤ 『三献の儀』(三三九度の儀) the sharing of three cups of *sake*. The bride and groom make their vows with an exchange of cups of ceremonial *sake* brought by a shrine maiden. They drink ceremonial *sake* three times each from three stacked *sake* cups. ⇨三三九度

⑥ 『豊栄の舞』(奉納) sacred dance performed by shrine maidens.

⑦ 『誓詞奏上』recitation of marriage vows. The bride and groom go before the Shinto altar and read their marriage oath.

⑧『新郎新婦玉串奉奠』the offering of a branch of the sacred *sasaki* tree to the deities[gods] by the bride and groom.

⑨『指輪交換』exchange of wedding rings.

⑩『媒酌人夫婦，親族代表による玉串奉奠』the offering of a branch of a sacred *sasaki* tree to the deities[gods] by the go-between and his wife, and representatives of the families.

⑪『豊栄の舞』(奉納) sacred dance performed by shrine maidens.

⑫『親族 杯 の儀』the sharing of *sake* by the gathered relatives. Relatives on both sides take sacred *sake* as a way of signifying the formation of a strong relationship.

⑬『退場』departure[exit].

じんぜんけっこん【人前結婚】 secular wedding; non-religious wedding; wedding ceremony without religious rites; civil marriage. 宗教儀式を行わない結婚.

しんそうさい【神葬祭】 Shinto funerals. 神式で行う葬式.

しんたい【神体】 a *shintai*; an object of worship venerated as a deity; a sacred object or place of worship where the spirit of a deity is believed to reside. 神社などで神霊の宿るものとして祭られる礼拝の対象になる物体.「御神体」(敬称)・「御霊代」ともいう.
❶〈神社内に安置〉 an object of worship venerated as a deity (which is) enshrined in the main sanctuary of a Shinto shrine. 神社(本殿)内にある. 圀 伊勢神宮の内宮に安置する「八咫の鏡」など.
❷〈神社外に配置〉 an object of worship venerated as a deity (which is) placed near a Shinto shrine. 神社近辺にある. 圀「那智の滝」，また神社境内の「神木」などがある. ⇨神木

じんだいこ【陣太鼓】 a war drum; a military drum; a large drum used to control troop movements on the battlefield. 陣中[戦場]で軍勢の進退を統制する太鼓.

じんだいじだるまいち【深大寺だるま市】 the Daruma-Doll Fair of Jindaiji Temple. (3月). ⇨付記 (1)「日本の祭り」

じんたん【仁丹】 oral deodorant pills. They are carried in a small container with a hole on the top for dispensing them. 経口防臭丸薬. 服用のため上に穴のあいた小さな容器に入れて携帯する.

しんちゃ【新茶】 the new tea; the newly picked tea; the first tea of the season; tea produced from new spring leaves.

じんちょうげ【沈丁花】〔植物〕a daphne. ジンチョウゲ科の常緑低木. 鑑賞用.「ちんちょうげ」ともいう.

しんてきがいしょうごストレスしょうがい【心的外傷後ストレス障害】 post-traumatic stress disorder[PTSD]

しんでん【寝殿】 an aristocratic mansion estate; a palace centered around the chief dwelling[residence] of the Emperor and nobles(in the Heian period). 貴族風の住居, 御殿. (平安時代)天皇・貴族が日常寝起きした宮殿.

【寝殿造り】 *Shinden*-style[palace-style] architecture. It is a style of palatial architecture used in aristocratic residence in the Heian period. Narrow corridors extend southward from the annexes, forming a U-shape around the court. 平安時代の貴族の住居(aristocratic mansion)として使用された宮廷の建築様式. コの字形に寝殿を挟む廊下でつないでいた. 板張り床(wooden floor)，置き畳(portable *tatami*)，可動式の襖・障子(removable *fusuma* and *shoji*)が見られる. ⇨畳 / 襖 / 障子. ☆平安時代の「寝殿造り」に始まり，鎌倉時代の「武家造り」，室町時代の「書院造り」，桃山・江戸時代の「数奇屋造り」へと変貌する. ⇨武家屋敷(武家造り) / 書院造り / 数奇屋造り

しんでん【神殿】a shrine; a sanctuary; 〈神社〉 a Shinto shrine. ⇨本殿

しんとう【神灯】 ❶〈神前の灯火〉 a sacred lantern[light] (placed in front of a shrine sanctuary).
❷〈神棚の灯火〉 a sacred lantern[light] (offered in a household shrine).
❸〈家の門前の灯火〉 a festive lantern[light] (hung at the house door).
❹〈祭礼の灯火〉 a festival lantern[light] (offered for special auspicious events).

しんとう[しんどう]【神道】 Shinto; Shintoism; Shinto, Japan's indigenous religion; Shinto, the religion indigenous to Japan; Shinto, the indigenous religion of Japan. *Shinto* is based on the worship of myriad deified nature spirits[800 myriad gods], mythological ancestors and historical heroes. 神格化した大自然の神々[八百万(やおよろず)の神々]を敬い，神話的な祖先や歴史上の人物を崇めることを基本とする日本固有の宗教. ¶**皇室神道** Imperial Shinto. **神社神道** Shrine Shinto. **教派[宗派]神道** sect [sectarian] Shinto. **国家神道** State Shinto (based on the religious observance of the deified Emperor). ☆明治維新後の1882年に国の祭祀とされ，1889年には天皇を神格化する. しかし第二次世界大戦の敗戦後(1945年)に廃止. **神道信者** a Shintoist.

しんない【新内】 the Shinnai narrative-style of *joruri* chanting (sung to *shamisen* accompaniment). 「新内節」の略. 浄瑠璃の一派. 三味線の伴奏に合わせて歌う浄瑠璃の語り様式. ☆鶴賀若狭掾(わかさのじょう)(1717-86)が創始し鶴賀(つるが)新内(?-1810)の艶麗(えんれい)で哀愁(あいしゅう)をおびた語り (plaintive and sentimental chanting[song])で人気を博した.

しんにゅうまくのりきし【新入幕の力士】〔相撲〕 a newly promoted *makuuchi*[top division] *sumo* wrestler. ⇨相撲の番付

しんねんいっぱんさんが【新年一般参賀】 a visit to the Imperial Palace for New Year('s) Greeting. ⇨一般参賀

しんねんかい【新年会】a New Year('s) Party (to celebrate the New Year). ⇨忘年会

しんねんしゅくがのぎ【新年祝賀の儀】 Their Majesties'New Year Reception.

しんねんうたかいはじめ【新年歌会始め】the New Year's *Waka* Poetry Recital; 〈宮中の〉 the New Year's Imperial Poetry Reading Party. ⇨新春歌会始め

しんのう【親王】 an Imperial prince; the honorific title for a prince of the Imperial Family. 皇室男子(または皇孫の男子)に対する尊称. ☆昔，天皇の兄弟・皇子の称号. ¶**親王殿下** His Imperial Highness Prince. ⇔内親王

じんばおり【陣羽織】a battle surcoat; a half-length military surcoat worn over armor. It is a vestlike sleeveless coat worn by warriors over their armor (*yoroi*) in camp in feudal times. 戦場での(鉄帷子(かたびら)の上に着る)上半身の軍用羽織. 封建時代，陣中で武士が鎧の上に着た袖なしのベストに似た羽織. ⇨羽織

しんぱんいいん【審判委員】〔相撲〕ringside judges (as a group). There are five judges for each bout who wear traditional formal *kimono*. 土俵下にいる勝負審判. 各取組には伝統的な正装を着用した5名の審判がいる. ⇨検査役

しんぱんだいみょう【親藩大名】 ⇨大名

しんぷ【神符】 charm tablets and amulets from Shinto shrines. 神社のお札・お守り. ⇨神棚

しんぶつこんこう【神仏混淆[混交]】 the mixture of Buddhism and Shinto(ism); the syncretism[syncretistic fusion] of Buddhism and Shintoism. The Japanese have funerals with Buddhist rituals and visit the family grave in the Buddhist temples while they hold weddings with Shinto rituals (or in Christian churches). Both Buddhist family altars and Shinto family altars are commonly set up in the same house. 仏教と神道の共存. 葬式は仏式で, 墓参も寺院にて行う. 他方神社 (またはキリスト教教会) で結婚式を挙げる. 仏壇と神棚が同じ家庭内にあるのもめずらしくない.「神仏習合」ともいう.

【神仏混淆の建築】 the mixture[union] of Buddhist and Shinto architecture (as seen in its Buddhist five-story pagoda and Shinto *torii* gate in Tosho-gu Shrine). ☆「東照宮」「二荒山神社」「輪王寺」〈二社一寺〉(ユネスコ世界文化遺産)

しんぶつぶんりれい【神仏分離令】 the Edict for Separation of Shintoism and Buddhism. ⇨廃仏毀釈

じんべい【甚平】 men's short-sleeved casual wear worn in the summertime; a men's casual summer wear[outfit] of knee-length shorts[pants] and short-sleeved jacket. It is often worn by men in the summertime festivals. 夏に着る膝までのショーツと短い袖のジャケットの男性用普段着. 夏祭によく着用する.「甚兵衛」「じんべ」などともいう.

しんぼく【神木】 a sacred tree (in the shrine). It may be the object of worship venerated as the symbol of the sanctuary in a Shinto shrine. 神木は神域の象徴として「ご神体」になることもある. ⇨神体

じんや【陣屋】 a camp(陣営); a manor house (代官の役所); a station[post] (役人の詰め所).

じんりきしゃ【人力車】 a *jinrikisha*; a *rikisha*; a rickshaw; a man-pulled cart with a folding hood. It is a small two-wheeled passenger vehicle with a folding hood, pulled by one man. 一人の車夫がひっぱる折りたたみ式幌(collapsible top)のある二輪車 (two-wheeled conveyance). ¶**人力車夫** a rickshaw puller[man]. ☆車夫は「挽き子」ともいう.

しんりゃく【侵略】 invasion; aggression. ¶**朝鮮侵略** (the first) invasion of Korea. (1592年)

しんりん【森林】 a forest; deep woods. ¶**自然林** a natural forest. **原生林** a virgin [primeval] forest. **森林浴** a stroll in [through] the woods.

しんれき【新暦】 the solar calendar(太陽暦); the Gregorian Calendar(グレゴリオ暦:1582年グレゴリオ教皇13世がユリウス暦 (Julian Calendar) を改正した現行の太陽暦). ⇨旧暦

しんろうしんぷ【新郎新婦】 the bride and (bride)groom(日英語の語順に注意); bridal pair; contracting parties.

しんわ【神話】 myth(個々の); mythology(集合的に).

す

す【酢】 vinegar. ¶**米酢** rice vinegar. **玄米酢** brown-rice vinegar. **穀物酢** grain vinegar. **リンゴ酢** cider vinegar. ⇨サイダー

〔料理・食品〕**酢和え** food[dishes] dressed with vinegar. ☆野菜の酢和え vegetables dressed with vinegar. **酢牡蠣** vinegared oysters; oysters marinated in vinegar. **酢締魚** fish marinated in vinegar. ⇨締鯖. **酢醤油** *shoyu* [soy sauce] mixed with vinegar; (a mixture of) vinegar and *shoyu*. **酢漬け** vinegared pickles. ☆キュウリの酢漬け cucumbers pickled in vinegar. **酢蛸** vinegared octopus; boiled octopus marinated in vinegar. ⇨たこ. **酢の物** a vinegared dish; vinegared food; food[sliced vegetables and seafood] dressed with vinegar and some other seasonings (such as salt, sugar, sesame seeds, etc.). **酢蓮** lotus root preserved in sweetened vinegar(蓮根

の甘酢漬け．「酢蓮根」ともいう．**酢味噌** vinegared *miso* [bean paste]．☆酢味噌和え food dressed with vinegared *miso* [bean paste]．**酢飯** vinegared rice; *sushi* rice（炊きたてのご飯に三杯酢をかけてつくるすし飯）．

【酢肴】 vinegared food; sliced seafood (or vegetables) dressed with vinegar (in the traditional Japanese meal)．（日本料理で）「焼物」と「強肴」の間に出る「口直しの料理」(food[dish] used to clear[cleanse] one's palate)で，酢の物が多い．⇨口直し

すあげ【素揚げ】 deep-frying without (the use of) batter．衣をつけないで油で揚げること．⇨空揚げ

〔料理〕**素揚げ物** deep-fried food without batter．**素揚げ青唐辛子** deep-fried green pepper without batter．

すあま【素甘】 a soft, sweet rice cake; (red and white) rice-cake sweets made of (nonglutinous) rice flour．米粉でつくった甘い餅菓子．粳の粉を水でこねて蒸し，砂糖で甘くした紅白の餅菓子．☆紅白一対の「鳥の子餅」(「鶴の子餅」ともいう)は祝儀の引き出物に用いられる．⇨鳥の子餅

すいか【西瓜】 〔植物〕a watermelon plant;〈果実〉a watermelon．ウリ科のつる性一年草．¶**西瓜の種** a watermelon seed．**西瓜の皮** a watermelon rind．**西瓜割り** a watermelon bust．

ずいき【芋茎】 the stem of a taro (plant)．里芋の茎．いもがら．⇨さといも

すいぎゅう【水牛】 〔動物〕a water buffalo．単に buffalo (⑧ buffalo(e)s)ともいう．ウシ科の哺乳動物．

すいくち【吸い口】 a fragrant garnish added to soup．吸い物・汁物に入れる香味を添えるもの(ショウガまたはユズの皮など)．¶**吸い口に使うユズ** (a piece of) citron peel floated in soup to give it an extra fragrance．

すいごう【水郷】 a water district; a riverside district(川地域); a canal district(運河地帯); a lake district(湖水地域)．¶**アヤメの花で有名な水郷**(茨城県) the water district noted for the iris blossoms (in Ibaraki Prefecture)．**船での水郷巡り** (enjoy) a boat excursion in the canal district．

すいさいが【水彩画】 a watercolor painting; a picture in watercolors．水彩絵の具で描いた絵．¶**水彩画家** a watercolor painter; a watercolorist．

ずいしん[ずいじん]【随身】 ❶〈宮廷の護衛者〉ancient court guards (to protect the superiors such as nobles and princes)． ❷〈神社の守護像〉statues[images] of two shrine guards (to protect the shrine from evils)．¶**随身門** the gate protected by the *Zuijin* guards at a Shinto shrine．

すいしんけい【垂身型】 〔華道〕the hanging [drooping] style of flower arrangement (of the Sogetsu school)．花をぶら下げて[垂らして]生ける型(草月流)．⇨垂態(池坊流)

すいせいしょくぶつ【水生植物】 an aquatic plant; a water plant．

すいせいどうぶつ【水生動物】 an aquatic animal．

すいせん【水仙】 〔植物〕a narcissus (⑧ narcissuses; narcissi); a daffodil (ラッパ水仙); a jonquil(キズイセン)．ヒガンバナ科の多年草．観賞用．¶**水仙の群生で知られる越前岬海岸**(福井県) Echizen(kaigan) Coast noted for fields of daffodils．

すいたい【垂態】 〔華道〕the hanging[drooping] style of flower arrangement (of the Ikenobo school)．花をぶら下げて[垂らして]生ける型(池坊流)．⇨垂真型(草月流)

すいでん【水田】 a paddy field; a rice field; a rice paddy．¶**水田地帯** paddy regions [areas]．

すいとう【水稲】 lowland rice; paddy rice; wet-field rice．⇦陸稲 (dryland[upland] rice)．⇨いね

すいどう【水道】〈海峡〉a channel (strait より大きい). ⇨水路. ¶**紀伊水道**(和歌山・徳島・兵庫の3県によって囲まれた海域) the Kii Channel. ⇨海／内海／灘／海峡／湾

すいとん【水団】〈汁〉vegetable soup containing wheat flour dumplings;〈団子〉wheat flour dumplings boiled in vegetable soup. 小麦粉で作った団子を野菜と煮た汁.

すいばん【水盤】〔華道〕a (shallow) flower vase[basin] with a flat bottom; a traylike container[bowl] used to arrange piled-up flowers. 盛り花を生ける盆型の器. ⇨剣山／七宝

すいぼくが【水墨画】 an India-ink painting; a black-and-white painting; a painting (drawn) in India ink. *Suiboku-ga* is a monochrome style of painting drawn with a brush only in India ink. The use of color contrast is created[made] by shades of India ink[black and white] and the strokes of the brush. 筆を用い墨だけで描く単色画[白黒画]. 色の明暗は墨[白黒]の濃淡や筆致の描線で表現される.「墨絵」ともいう. ☆室町時代の禅宗の画僧雪舟(1420-1506)が日本の水墨画を完成させた. ⇨墨絵

すいもの【吸い物】a clear soup(澄まし汁); Japanese broth(煮汁). It is made from dried bonito (or kelp stock) and seasoned with salt, *shoyu*[soy sauce] and *mirin*[sweetened *sake*]. 鰹節(または昆布)を用いて作り, 塩・醤油・味醂などで調味した汁. ¶**タイの吸い物** sea bream soup; clear soup with sea bream. **ハマグリの吸い物** clam soup; clear soup with clam. **吸い物椀** a soup bowl. **吸い物を吸う** eat clear soup.

すいれん【睡蓮】〔植物〕 a water lily; a pond lily. スイレン科の多年草. ハス (lotus)に似た水生植物. 観賞用. ¶**睡蓮の葉** a lily pad.

すいろ【水路】 a waterway(船が通れる); a watercourse(水が流れる); a channel(水道); a canal(運河); a passage. ⇨水道. ¶**今治と大島の間にある狭い水路**(愛媛県・来島海峡 (Kurushima Strait)にある) a narrow passage[channel] between Imabari and Oshima Island.

すうたい【素謡】〔能楽〕 chanting a Noh text without musical accompaniment and dance. 囃子や舞をともなわない謡.

すうどん【素うどん】 (a bowl of) plain wheat-flour noodles without any special ingredients; white-flour noodles served in a hot broth with chopped green onions and red pepper seasoning sprinkled on top. 特別な具のないさっぱりしたうどん. ただ熱いつゆ(汁)に刻んだねぎと七味をふりかけたシンプルなうどん.

すえき【須恵器】〈陶器〉an ash-glazed ceramic ware; a gray colored hard pottery;〈土器〉an earthenware in the ancient Japan. 素焼きの陶器. 古代日本の素焼きの土器.

すえきち【末吉】the bad luck[fate]. ⇨おみくじ

すえごたつ【据(え)炬燵】 ⇨堀(り)炬燵

すえぜん【据(え)膳】a meal set before one[a person]; a table set before one[a person] for a meal. すぐに食事ができるように人の前に整える食膳.

すえひろ(せんす)【末広(扇子)】 a pair of white folding fans used for betrothal gifts. 結納などに用いる扇[扇子]. 繁栄の象徴 (symbol of rising prosperity)として贈られる. ⇨結納／扇子. ☆「末広」〈先が広くなる〉widen[broaden] toward the end;〈徐々に栄える〉get[grow] more and more prosperous (as time passes).

すえぶろ【据(え)風呂】a bathtub with a side oven. ☆大きな桶にかまどを据えつけた風呂.

すがたずし【姿鮨】 *sushi* arranged in a fish[an *ayu*] stuffed with vinegared rice and served in its original shape. (内臓と中

骨をとった)魚(アユなど)に酢飯を詰めて
元の姿につくる鮨.

すがたづくり【姿造り】 *sashimi* served in
the original shape of fish; a whole raw fish
(cut as *sashimi*) arranged to preserve its
original appearance.

すがたに【姿煮】 a whole fish boiled in its
original shape. ¶蝦の**姿煮** a whole prawn
boiled in its shell.

すがたむし【姿蒸し】 a whole fish steamed
in its original shape. ¶鯛の**姿蒸し** a whole
sea bream steamed in its original shape.

すがたやき【姿焼き】 a whole fish grilled
[broiled] in its original shape. ¶蝦の**姿焼き**
a whole prawn grilled in its shell.

すぎ【杉】〔植物〕*sugi*; a (Japanese) cedar; a
crytomeria. スギ科の常緑高木. 建材用・
器具用. ¶**杉皮** cedar bark. **杉板** a cedar
board[plank]. **杉戸** cedar-board door. **杉
板葺き**(屋根) a roof covered with cedar
boards. 屋久杉の原生林 primeval[virgin]
forests of large cedars called Yaku-sugi
(growing on Yakushima Island, Kagoshima
Prefecture). **杉林に覆われた天城峠**(静岡
県) Amagi Pass covered with cedar groves.
杉の集散地(秋田県・大館市) marketing
center for Japanese cedar wood.

すぎかふん【杉花粉】 cedar pollen. ¶**杉花
粉症** cedar pollen allergy; allergy to cedar
pollen; hay fever caused by cedar pollen.
杉花粉アレルギー体質 be allergic to cedar
pollen.

すぎな【杉菜】〔植物〕a field horsetail. トクサ
科の多年草しだ植物. 早春に胞子茎として
つくし(食用)を生む. ⇨つくし

すきや【数寄屋】〔茶道〕❶〈茶室の建物〉a detached tea-ceremony house; a small arbor
[rustic cottage] with a thatched roof used
for the tea ceremony. 茶の湯のための茶室
の整った離れの建物. 藁葺き屋根の侘びた
小屋.

❷〈茶室〉a tea-ceremony room[hut]. ⇨茶
室

【数寄屋造り】 the style of residential architecture with features of a detached tea-
ceremony house. 離れの茶室風に作った住
居建築. ☆桃山・江戸時代に始まる.

すきやぶくろ【数寄屋袋】 a bag for carrying
small belongings. 小物を入れて携帯する
袋. ☆袱紗や扇子など茶の湯に必要な道具
を入れる袋でもある.

すきやき【鋤焼き】 *sukiyaki*; a hot pot dish
of beef and vegetables in soy-flavored
sauce. *Sukiyaki* is a dish made of thinly-
sliced beef cooked in a shallow[flat] iron
pan with various vegetables and ingredients
(such as *shiitake* mushroom, green onions,
tofu[soybean curd], etc.). These ingredients
are seasoned with *shoyu*[soy sauce],
mirin[sweetened *sake*] and sugar. *Sukiyaki*
is eaten by[after] dipping the hot foods
picked directly from the pan into a small
bowl of beaten raw eggs. 薄切り牛肉とい
ろいろな野菜食材(しいたけ, ねぎ, 豆腐
など)を浅い鉄製の鍋に入れて醤油・味醂・
砂糖で味付けして煮る料理. 鍋から直接に
取った熱い食べ物を生の溶き卵を入れた小
鉢につけて食べる. ☆㊀ hot pot「肉や野菜
などを鍋で蒸し焼きにしたもの」. ¶**鋤焼き
鍋** a *sukiyaki* pan; a shallow[flat] iron pan
(used for cooking *sukiyaki*).

すぐき【酢茎・酸茎】 a pickled turnip.「すぐ
き菜」の根と葉をとらずにすっぱく漬けた
物. 京都特産(Kyoto specialty)の漬物. ☆
「すぐき菜」(*brassica rapa*)は蕪 (turnip)の
一種. rapaはラテン語で「蕪」の意. ここで
は turnipを用いる.

スクラッチたからくじ【スクラッチ宝くじ】
⇨宝くじ

すげ【菅】〔植物〕(a) sedge. カヤツリグサ科の
多年草の総称. 葉は笠や蓑などの材料. ⇨
蓑

【菅笠】 a sedge hat (made of dry sedge grass with a bamboo frame). A sedge hat worn during the 88-site pilgrimage of Shikoku bears the Chinese characters of "*dogyo-ninin*" (the two persons who walk together). It means that one is the pilgrim and the other Kobo Daishi. (竹製の骨組がある)菅の葉で編んだ笠. 四国八十八箇所巡りで着ける菅笠には「同行二人」の漢字がある. その意味は「一人は巡礼者, もう一人は弘法大師」. ⇨巡礼

すげいた【菅板】 a floating wooden lid[board] for the *goemon-bath*. 五右衛門風呂に浮かぶ木製の蓋[板]. ⇨五右衛門風呂

すけそうだら【助惣鱈】 ⇨介党鱈

すけだち【助太刀】 〈援助〉help; assistance; 〈助っ人〉a helper; an assistant; a supporter; a backer.

すけとうだら【介党鱈】〔魚〕an Alaska pollack [pollock]; a walleye pollack. タラ科の海産硬骨魚. 練り製品の原料. 卵巣の塩蔵品は「タラコ」. タラコをトウガラシでつけこむと「辛子明太子」(博多名物)になる. ⇨たら/たらこ/辛子明太子

すけろくずし【助六鮨】 a *sushi* set comprised of *maki-zushi* (rolled *sushi*) and *inari-zushi* (fried bean-curd stuffed with boiled rice). 巻き鮨と稲荷鮨のセットずし. ⇨巻き鮨/稲荷鮨

すごろく【双六】 *sugoroku*; a Japanese backgammon; a Japanese parcheesi. *Sugoroku* is a race-type indoor board game played on a large piece of paper containing a series of sections and pictures drawn on it. Pieces are advanced after throwing a die[㊤ dice]. The player tries to advance to the final picture quicker than one's opponent. 一連の区切られた絵柄がある紙上で早い上がりを競う室内遊戯. さいころを振って, そこに出た目の数で進む. 相手より早く最後の絵柄に着くように競う. ☆ backgammon「バッ

クギャモン, 西洋すごろく」(2人が各15のこまをさいころをふって進めるゲーム). parcheesi「インドすごろく」. a die「さいころ」(㊤ dice). 通常は2個1組 (a pair of dice)で用いる.

すし【鮨・寿司】 *sushi*(日本語から国際英語化); vinegared rice topped with slices of raw fish[shellfish] or vegetables. *Sushi* is a unique Japanese dish of rice flavored with vinegar, salt, sugar and *mirin*[sweetened *sake*]. Fish[shellfish] or vegetables are placed on small balls of vinegared rice. *Sushi* is usually served by smearing with a dab of *wasabi*[grated horseradish] between vinegared rice and fish[shellfish] or vegetables. *Sushi* is eaten after dipping in *shoyu*[soy sauce]. 酢飯と魚介類または野菜を取り合わせた食品. 酢・塩・砂糖・味醂で味つけした酢飯に魚介類または野菜を添える. 通常は酢飯と魚介類[野菜]の間に少量の山葵をつけて出される. 醤油に浸してから食す. ☆英語で sushi といえば「握り鮨」を指す. ⇨握り鮨. ¶**鮨種** (seafood used for) *sushi* toppings; *sushi* prepared ingredients. 鮨屋 a *sushi* restaurant[shop; bar]. ⇨回転寿司. **鮨カウンター** a *sushi* bar. 鮨桶 a *sushi* tray[tub]; a tray[tub] for serving *sushi*. 鮨職人 a *sushi* chef.

ずし【厨子】 a miniature shrine; a miniature cabinet with a double-hinged door with the appearance of a small shrine. It houses the image of Buddha, the holy relics of Buddha and the canonical book of Buddhism. 観音開きの扉がついた小型の神社のような小さな箱. 仏像・舎利・経巻[経典]などを安置する.

すじこ【筋子】 ❶〈鮭の卵〉salmon roe. ⇨鮭 ❷〔食品〕salted salmon roe; salted trout roe. サケ・マスの卵を卵巣ごと塩漬けにした食品.

すすき【薄・芒】〔植物〕(Japanese) pampas

grass; silver grass; zebra grass; reed. イネ科の多年草.「秋の七草」の一つ.「尾花」ともいう. ⇨秋の七草 / 月見の宴. ¶**枯れすすき** withered pampas grass. **すすきの原** a field of pampas grass.

すすぎ【濯ぎ】   a ritual rinse. The pilgrims ritually rinse their hands and mouth before they worship at a Shinto shrine. 参詣者が神社で参拝する前に水で手や口を清める. ⇨清め / 手水舎

すずき【鱸】〔魚〕a (Japanese) sea bass; a sea perch; a striped bass. スズキ科の海産硬骨魚. 出世魚で稚魚は「セイゴ」(約25cmの1年魚). さらに成長した魚は「フッコ」(約30cmの2～3年魚),「スズキ」(60cm以上の4年魚)という.

〔料理〕**鱸の塩焼き** a sea bass grilled with salt.

すずしろ【蘿蔔・清白】〔植物〕Japanese *daikon* [radish]; a (garden) radish.「大根」の古名.「春の七草」の一つ. ⇨春の七草

すずな【鈴菜・菘】〔植物〕a turnip.「蕪」の古名.「春の七草」の一つ. ⇨春の七草

すすはらい【煤払い】〈煤の除去〉soothsweeping-off[away];〈家屋の掃除〉housecleaning (at the end of the year). The entire house, especially the household Shinto (or Buddhist) altar, is cleaned in preparation for the New Year. 新年を迎える準備の一環としての全家屋, 特に神棚・仏壇の掃除.

すずむし【鈴虫】〔虫〕a bell-ringing cricket; a bell-ringing insect. コオロギ科の昆虫. 鳴くのは雄(虫).

すずめ【雀】〔鳥〕a sparrow. ハタオリドリ科の小鳥. 害虫を食う.「寒スズメ」は食用で美味. ⇨雀焼❶

すずめばち【雀蜂】〔虫〕a wasp; a yellow hornet(大型); a yellow jacket. 黒い体に黄色の模様がある. ⇨はち

すずめやき【雀焼】❶〈雀の照り焼き〉a sparrow marinated in *mirin*[sweetened *sake*] and grilled over a charcoal fire.

❷〈鮒のつけ焼き〉a crucian carp (opened by cutting along its spine) broiled with *shoyu*[soy sauce]. ☆背開きにした鮒の形が雀に似るところから. ⇨背開き

すずらん【鈴蘭】〔植物〕a lily of the valley; a may lily; a lily bell[cup](花). ユリ科の多年草.

すずり【硯】〔書道〕an inkstone; an ink slab. It has a smooth surface to rub an India-ink stick and depression on one end to hold a small amount of water. 墨をする滑らかな表面と上部には水を少量入れる凹みがある. ⇨墨

【硯箱】   an inkstone case; a Japanese writing box. It contains a set of calligraphy utensils, such as an inkstone, an ink stick and a few writing brushes. 書道用具の一式(硯, 墨, 数本の筆)が入っている.

すそ【裾】the hem (of a *kimono*); the hemline (of a *kimono*)(裾の線); the bottom (of a *kimono*)(着物の下のふち). ¶**裾捌き** the way (that) he/she controls the flapping of his/ her *kimono* hems when walking. **裾回し** the lower lining at the hem of a *kimono*: the hemline at the bottom of a *kimono*. **裾上げ** raising a *kimono* hem; raising a hem of a *kimono*. **裾綿** cotton padding inserted at the hem of the main panels of a *kimono*.

すだち【酢橘・酸橘】〔植物〕a *sudachi* citrus (lemon); (a kind of) a small sour citrus fruit. ミカン科の常緑低木. ユズに似た植物. 果実の酢汁は風味があり調味料に用いる. 鍋物のポン酢として用いる. またマツタケ料理や焼き物に最適. 徳島県の特産. ⇨ポン酢

すだれ【簾】a bamboo blind(竹製); a rattan blind(藤製); a reed screen[curtain](葦製). It is made of slender split bamboo slats (or reeds) fastened[bound] together with strings[threads]. It is often hung up at the entrance to a home or at open windows[doors] to keep out the sun and admit cool breezes into the room in summer. 細い割り竹(または葦)を並べて紐[糸] で編んだブラインド. 家屋の出入り口または開いた窓[戸] などに吊るし, 夏の日除けとして, また室内に微風を入れるために使用する.「御簾」ともいう.

すっぽん【鼈】 a softshell turtle; a snapping turtle. スッポン科の爬虫類. 肉または血は食用. ⇨かめ. ¶鼈雑炊 porridge of rice and vegetables cooked with a softshell turtle.

スッポン〔歌舞伎〕 the ***suppon***; the special trapdoor and lift[movable platform] in the *hanamichi*[extension stage running through the audience that leads to the left side of the stage]. The *suppon* (meaning a softshell turtle) enables an actor to appear from beneath the stage and disappear into beneath the stage like the head of a softshell turtle. 花道にある迫り上がる穴のことで, 役者がスッポン(亀)の頭のように上下に出入りする.「迫り穴」ともいう. ⇨花道 / 迫り出し(本舞台にある)

すててこ (a type of) men's long summer underwear; a long garment worn by men under trousers and over underpants in the summer. 男性用の長い夏用下着. スボンの下・パンツの上に着用する.

すなかぶり【砂被り】〔相撲〕 a *sumo* ringside seat; a seat nearest to the *sumo* ringside. Sand kicked up by the the *sumo* wrestlers may be sprinkled onto the spectators. 土俵際に最も近い観客席. 力士が蹴り上げる砂が観衆にかかるほど近い場所. ☆「溜席」または「維持費席」(the sponsors' *sumo* ringside seat)ともいう.

すなぎも【砂肝】 a gizzard. 鳥[鶏] の胃袋. ⇨焼き鳥

すなば【砂場】 (米) a sandbox; (英) a sandpit.

すなはま【砂浜】 a sandy beach; the sands.

¶白い砂浜で有名な今井浜温泉(静岡県) Imaihama Onsen noted for its white sandy beach.

すなぶろ【砂風呂】 a sand bath; a steaming sand bath on the coast. Bathers in *kimono* are covered up to their neck by being half-buried in steaming hot sand. 海岸にある砂の蒸し風呂. ☆鹿児島県の指宿は有名.

すなゆ【砂湯】 ⇨温泉

すのこ【簀の子】 ❶〈台所の〉a slatted drain-board; (英) a draining board. (台所の流し台の横にある)水切り台[板].
❷〈風呂場の〉duckboards; draining floor boards for a bathroom. 敷き板. 浴室用の水切り床板.

すのもの【酢の物】 ⇨酢

すべらかし【垂髪】 a woman's loose hair-style. It is a woman's hair gathered at the nape of the neck and tied at the back of the head to hang down the back. It is a traditional coiffeur worn by a *samurai*'s wife (or an upper-class woman) and Shinto maiden[priestess]. 婦人の髪型の一種. うなじに集めて後部で結び[髻の末], そこから長く垂れ下げる婦人の髪. 武士の妻(上流階級の女性)や神道の巫女などが結ぶ伝統的な髪型.「御垂髪」ともいう. ⇨巫女

すべりどめじゅけん【滑り止め受験】 an application of a second-choice university for entrance examination; an entrance examination taken as a backup safety measure (against failure to be admitted at other colleges). ☆「滑り止め学校[大学]」a fallback school [college].

スポーツのひ【スポーツの日】 Health and Sports Day (the 2nd Monday of October). This national holiday was established in 1966 as a day to promote good mental and physical health through physical activities. This day was originally established to commemorate the opening day of the

Tokyo Olympics held in 1964. On this day a lot of annual sporting events are held all over Japan. Many schools hold sports [athletic] meetings every year during the period around the Health and Sports Day. The Health and Sports Day used to be October 10. Due to the Happy Monday system, it was changed to the Second Monday of October from the year 2000 so that people can have a long weekend. この祝日は運動に親しみながら心身の健康を促進するための日として1966年(昭和41年)に制定された. この日は元来1964年(昭和39年)に開催された東京オリンピック大会の開会を記念して制定された. この日には国内で多数のスポーツ行事が毎年開催される. 多くの学校ではこの期間中に毎年の運動会が行われる.「スポーツの日」(旧称「体育の日」)はもともと10月10日であったが, 2000年(平成12年)からはハッピーマンデー制度により連休が取れるように10月第2月曜日に変更された.

すぼし【素干し】 a plain dried fish. 味付けせずにそのまま乾燥させる魚介類. ⇨陰干し /たたみ鰯

すましじる【澄まし汁】 clear soup. The stock (*dashi*) is thinly flavored with salt and *shoyu*[soy sauce]. 出しに塩と醤油で薄めに味付けした透明な汁. ⇨吸い物

すみ【炭】 charcoal. It is used to boil water for the tea ceremony. It is also burned to grill[broil] an eel or a chicken. 炭は茶の湯で湯を沸かすための必需品. 鰻や鳥を焼くためにも利用する. ¶炭火 (a) charcoal fire. ☆炭火には「練炭」(coal briquette) や「豆炭」(charcoal briquette) などがある. ⇨炬燵. 炭俵 a charcoal sack. 炭焼窯 a charcoal(-burner's) kiln. 炭焼きの鰻 a charbroiled eel; an eel broiled[grilled] over a charcoal fire.

すみ【墨】 ❶〈書道〉①〈固形の墨〉 an India(n) ink stick; an ink-cake. It is made by mixing soot with glue to solidify it, then molded and dried. 煤に膠を混ぜて煉り固め, 型で抜き乾燥させて作る. ☆「煤」は soot (made from burning the branches and roots of pine trees. 松の枝や根を燃やして出るもの). ¶墨をする rub down[grind] an India ink stick.
②〈液体の墨[墨汁]〉 India(n) ink; Chinese [China] ink; Japan ink. It is made by rubbing a solid India ink stick on the surface of an inkstone after pouring water on the stone. 硯に水を入れてから, その表面を固形の墨でこすりながら作る. ⇨墨汁. ¶墨をつける dip (a brush) in Indian ink. 墨字 an inked letter. ⇨点字.
墨壺 ①〈墨汁入れ〉 an inkpot; an ink bottle. ②〈大工の〉 an[a carpenter's] ink pad. It consists of a long string wound at one end and a shallow bowl for holding a pad of cotton soaked in ink. 片方に巻いた長いひも[糸]とインクで浸した綿の詰め物を入れる浅い器がある. 墨縄〈ひも〉 a black inking string (attached to a carpenter's ink pad);〈線〉 a carpenter's inking snap-line. It is used by the carpenter to draw straight lines in black on boards. (大工の墨壺についた)インクをつけるひも (cord). 大工が板に黒で直線を引くのに用いる. ⇨墨壺②(筆に)
❷〈イカ・タコの吐き出す墨〉 ink; sepia. ¶(イカが)墨を吹く spurt ink

すみえ【墨絵】 (a) *sumie*; an India(n)-ink painting[drawing]; a monochrome[black-and-white] painting; a painting drawn with India ink only. 墨だけで描いた絵.「水墨画」ともいう. ⇨水墨画

すみぞめのころも【墨染めの衣】 a (Buddhist priest's) black robe. 黒い僧服.

すみよしたいしゃおたうえしんじ【住吉大社御田植神事】 the Rice-Planting Rite at

Sumiyoshi Shrine.(6月)． ⇨付記(1)「日本の祭り」

すみぬりまつり【墨塗りまつり】 the Ink-Smearing Festival. (1月)． ⇨付記(1)「日本の祭り」

すみれ【菫】〔植物〕 a violet. スミレ科の多年草． ☆「三色すみれ」は a pansy.

すもう【相撲】 *sumo* (wrestling)〔国際英語化した日本語〕; the traditional national sport of Japan. Two *sumo* wrestlers try to force each other to step out of a circular ring (*dohyo*) or to touch the ground[the surface of *dohyo*] with any part of the body other than the soles of the feet. 相撲の勝負は相手を土俵から突き出すこと，または足の裏以外の身体の部分を地面につけることで決まる． ⇨大相撲 / 福祉相撲 / 奉納相撲 / 勧進相撲 / 台覧相撲． ¶**相撲絵** a *sumo* wrestler print. **相撲字** a calligraphy style with very wide brushstrokes (used to write the *banzuke*).「相撲文字」ともいう． ⇨江戸文字

【相撲の取組】 pre-bout rituals(試合前の儀式)． ☆「蹲踞」squatting.→「塵手水」ritual hand clapping. →「力水」power water. →「塩まき」salt-tossing[salt-throwing]. →「四股」feet stomping[stamping]→「仕切り」toeing the mark. →「立合い」initial charge. ⇨四股

【相撲部屋】 a *sumo* stable; a training gymnasium[quarters] for the *sumo* wrestlers. A stable is managed under the absolute control of a single *sumo* master [boss] (*oyakata*). The *sumo* wrestlers must live together in the training stable while they are in the lower divisions. 親方の絶対的な統率のもとで運営される． 番付の幕下在籍中は相撲部屋で寝食を共にする． ¶**相撲部屋制度** a *sumo* stable system.

【相撲の決まり手】 winning techniques in a *sumo* bout (announced by the referee on declaring the winner). Here are the some examples out of many winning techniques[maneuvers] that decide a *sumo* match.

《**基本技**》 Basic techniques.

【浴びせ倒し】 backward force-down; to force down the opponent on his back by leaning forward while being in a grabbing position.

【押し倒し】 frontal push-down; to push down the opponent.

【押し出し】 frontal push-out; to push the opponent out of the ring without holding his belt, or to push the opponent off the ring from behind.

【突き倒し】 frontal thrush-down; to topple the opponent out of the ring onto his back with hard shove[thrust].

【突き出し】 frontal thrust-out; to push the opponent out of the ring by pushing his body hard with the palms open.

【寄り切り】 frontal force-out; to push the opponent out of the ring while lifting his body[belt] up.

《**投げ技**》 Throwing techniques.

【上手投げ】 overarm throw; to throw the opponent off his feet by grasping his belt firmly.

【上手出し投げ】 pulling overarm throw; to pull the opponent forwards to the ground by grabbing his belt.

【首投げ】 headlock throw; to throw the opponent down by wrapping his head [neck].

【小手投げ】 armlock throw; to throw the opponent down by grasping his arm below the elbow and pivoting.

【下手投げ】 underarm throw; to throw the opponent off his legs by grasping his belt under his arm.

【掬い投げ】 beltless arm throw; to throw the opponent off his legs without grasping his belt.

《掛け技》 Tripping techniques.

【足取り】 leg pick; to hold the opponent's leg in both hands and throw him down.

【内掛け】 inside leg trip; to trip the opponent by hooking the inside of his leg while holding his body[by putting his leg between his legs and leaning on him].

【外掛け】 outside leg trip; to trip the opponent by hitching the outside of his leg, while holding his body.

【裾払い】 leg trip; to trip up the opponent by the leg.

【蹴たぐり】 kick-down; to kick the opponent's inner legs to the outside and slap him down.

《捻り技》 Twisting techniques.

【とったり】 arm bar throw; to grab the opponent's arm and spinning him around several times until he is thrown out of the ring[until he is knocked down flat on the ground].

《特殊技》 Special techniques.

【送り出し】 rear push-out; to drive the opponent out of the ring from behind.

【うっちゃり】 backward pivot throw; to throw the opponent backwards out of the ring rim after being forced to the rim.

【吊り出し】 lift-out; to lift[carry] the opponent out of the ring, grabbing his sash with both hands.

【相撲の番付】 a *sumo* ranking list[chart]; an official list ranking professional *sumo* wrestlers. It reflects changes in rank due to the results of the previous tournament. It is written out in a particular calligraphy and released two weeks prior to the tournament. 前回の取組結果で階級に反映する. 独特な「相撲文字」で書かれ，大相撲の2週間前に発表される.

① 『幕内』 *Makuuchi*: the highest[top]

division on the *banzuke*.

(1)「横綱」 *Yokozuna*: the highest rank on the *banzuke*, Grand Champion.

「三役」 *Sanyaku*: the three highest ranks below *Yokozuna*.

(2)「大関」 *Ozeki*: the second-highest rank on the *banzuke*.

(3)「関脇」 *Sekiwake*: the third-highest rank on the *banzuke*.

(4)「小結」 *Komusubi*: the fourth-highest rank on the *banzuke*.

(5)「前頭」 *Maegashira*: the fifth-highest rank on the *banzuke*.

② 『十両』 *Juryo*: the lowest rank of salaried *sumo* wrestler on the *banzuke*.

③ 『幕下』 *Makushita*: the fourth and last lowest non-salaried division on the *banzuke*.

④ 『三段目』 *Sandanme*: the third lowest non-salaried division on the *banzuke*.

⑤ 『序二段』 *Jonidan*: the second lowest non-salaried division on the *banzuke*.

⑥ 『序の口』 *Jonokuchi*: the first lowest non-salaried division on the *banzuke*.

すもも【李】〔植物〕 a (Japanese) plum tree (木)；a (Japanese) plum (実). バラ科の落葉小高木. ¶干李 a prune.

すやき【素焼き】❶〈焼き物〉unglazed pottery [earthenware]; bisque (ware). 釉薬をつけないで低い温度で焼く陶器. ⇨釉薬 ❷〈焼き魚〉a fish broiled plain[without sauce]. タレをつけずに焼いた魚.

すりあし【摺り足】〔能楽〕 a shuffle; shuffling one's steps; sliding one's feet. Players shuffle quietly[without lifting the feet off the ground] on the Noh stage. 能舞台上で，足の裏を立っている面から離さず，するように静かに歩くこと.

すりこぎ【擂粉木】 a wooden (grinding) pestle. ⇨擂鉢. ¶ゴマを擂粉木で細かくつぶす grind[pound] sesame seeds with a wooden pestle to crush in pieces.

すりばち【擂鉢】 a mortar; an earthenware mortar; a grinding bowl. ⇨擂粉木. ¶**擂鉢でゴマをすりつぶす** grind[pound] sesame seeds in a mortar.

すりみ【擂身】 ground fish flesh(魚肉); minced chicken meat(鶏肉); raw fish [meat] paste minced in grinding bowl. 擂鉢で魚肉・鶏肉などをたたいてすりつぶしたもの.

するめ【鯣】 (a) dried squid; (a) dried cuttlefish.

スロットマシン slot machine with liquid crystal displays. ⇨パチンコ

ずわいがに【ずわい蟹】〔甲〕 a snow crab; a queen crab. 別名「松葉ガニ」(山陰地方),「越前ガニ」(北陸地方). ⇨かに

すわりかた【座り方】 the way of sitting on the *tatami*-mat; the way *one*[a person] sits. ⇨正座/胡坐

すん【寸】 a *sun*. 長さの単位. 一尺の10分の1. 約3.03cm.

すんし【寸志】 a small present[gift]; a small[little] token of one's gratitude [appreciation]. わずかな志. こころばかりの贈物. ☆封筒などの上書きの「寸志」は With compliments.

せ

せいいたいしょうぐん【征夷大将軍】❶〈平安時代〉Generalissimo; Great General; the barbarian-suppressing general; the barbarian-subduing [-subjugating] general. It was the title given to a great general to suppress barbarians[the Ezo race] in the north in the Heian period. 平安時代, 北方の異民族(蝦夷)征伐のために任ぜられた軍事最高指揮官に授与された呼称. ☆794年大伴弟麻呂が初代の征夷大将軍. ⇨将軍 ❷〈鎌倉時代以降〉(the title given as a)

shogun; (the title given to) the head of military government. 武家政権の長(に授与された呼称). ☆1192年に源頼朝(1147-99)が後鳥羽天皇より征夷大将軍に任命される. それ以降, 武家政権の首長として幕府を開き, 政権をとった者の職名になった. 略して「将軍」. 源家・足利家. 徳川家は明治維新までこの称号の下で実権を握った. ⇨幕府

せいうち【海象】〔動物〕a walrus.(複) ~(es)) セイウチ科の食肉哺乳動物.

せいか【生花】❶〈華道・生け花〉the art of flower arrangement; the style of using flowers and branches as they appear in real life. 自然のありのままの花や枝を生ける芸事. ⇨生け花[活け花] ❷〈生きた花〉a fresh flower; a natural flower. ☆造花(an artificial flower)に対して「自然花」. ¶**生花1対** a pair of vases with arranged natural flowers.

せいかつしゅうかんびょう【生活習慣病】a lifestyle-related illness; diseases associated with lifestyle habits; chronic lifestyle diseases. ☆「成人病」(adult disease)の新呼称. ⇨糖尿病予備軍

せいかつほご【生活保護】livelihood protection; welfare benefits. ¶**生活保護家族**[世帯] a family[household] on welfare; a family[household] on the dole. **生活保護法** the Livelihood Protection Law. **生活保護を受ける** get[receive] livelihood protection[英 income support];米 be on welfare; 米 be on the dole.

せいかんせんしょう【性感染症】 a sexually transmitted disease[STD].

せいかんろん【征韓論】 the policy of conquering Korea. Japan wanted to open Korea using military power and to have a great influence on Korea. 韓国征服の政策.

せいぎょ【生魚】〈生きている魚〉a live fish;〈鮮魚〉a fresh fish. ⇨生魚

せいぎょ【成魚】 a full-grown fish; an adult fish. 成長した魚. ⇔稚魚

せいきょういっち【政教一致】 the unity of religion and politics; the union of church and state.

せいきょうぶんり【政教分離】 the separation of religion and politics; the schism between church and state.

せいこうほうしゅう【成功報酬】 a contingency[contingent] fee; a fee contingent on success.

せいざ【正座・正坐】 the formal way of sitting on the *tatami* mats. One sits in the proper posture of sitting down the buttocks resting on top of the ankles[sitting on one's heels with one's back straight by kneeling] at such formal gatherings as the tea ceremony and the flower arrangement. 畳の上に座るときの正式な座り方. 茶道や華道のような正式な集会では, 尻を足首の先の上において座る[ひざまずいて背中をまっすぐにしながらかかとの上に座る] ⇨座り方

せいざ【静座・静坐】 the formal way of sitting quietly on the *tatami* mats in Zen Buddhism; the proper practice of abdominal respiration in a sitting position of Zen meditation. 禅宗で呼吸を整え, 心を落ち着けて静かに座ること.

せいさんち【生産地】 the place of production; (fruit/grain-)producing area[region, district]. ¶ぶどうの生産地(山梨県)(甲府盆地) the grape-producing area (in the Kofu Basin). 米の生産地 the rice-producing region.

せいし【整枝】〔華道〕 restoration.

せいじ【青磁】 celadon porcelain[ware]; green ceramics with a glassy glaze. 淡緑色[灰青色](celadon green)の磁器. 透明な青緑色の釉薬をかけて焼いた高級磁器. ☆起源は中国の唐朝 (the T'ang Dynasty: 618-

907)・宋朝 (the Sung Dynasty: 960-1279) の時代に遡る.

せいしつ【正室】 the legitimate wife of a nobleman (in ancient Japan). 身分の高い人 (an aristocrat)の正妻, 本妻. ⇔側室

せいしゅ【清酒】 *seishu*; refined *sake*; a typical Japanese *sake*[rice wine]. *Seishu* (15-16% alcohol) is brewed by adding water and malt to rice. 清酒(アルコール分15-16%)は米に水と麹を加えて発酵させたもの.

せいじんのひ【成人の日】 Coming-of-Age Day (the 2nd Monday of January). This national holiday was established in 1948 as a day to congratulate and encourage youths who have reached the age of 20 years during the year. They gain the right to vote and are treated as adults with responsibilities in society. Originally held on January15, in 2000 it was changed to the second Monday of January. 1948年に制定. 20歳に達した青年を祝い鼓舞する日. 成人者は投票権を持ち, 社会で責任ある大人として対処される. 元来, 1月15日であったが, 2000年に1月の第2月曜日に変更された. ⇨ハッピーマンデー制度

せいせんしょくひん【生鮮食品】 fresh foods (新鮮な食品); perishable foods(腐りやすい食品); perishables.

せいそうかざん【成層火山】 a stratovolcano. 圆富士山. ⇨火山

せいぞうねんがっぴ【製造年月日】 the date of manufacture(製造の日付); the date of packing(梱包の日付).

せいそくち【生息地】 a habitat; the home of plants and animals. ☆動植物〈日本語の語順に注意〉. ¶鯛の生息地 the habitat of sea bream.

ぜいちく【筮竹】 divination sticks; divining sticks used for fortune-telling. Fortune-tellers use 50 divining sticks made of

せ

bamboo when they practice fortune-telling. 占いに使う50本の細い竹の棒 (rods).

せいちゅう【成虫】an adult (insect); an imago (㊤ imago(e)s; imagines). ⇨蝶々

せいてんかんしゅじゅつ【性転換手術】 a sex-change operation; a sexual reassignment surgery. ☆「性転換者」a transsexual.

せいとう【製陶】 pottery (manufacture).¶製陶術 the ceramic arts; ceramics.

せいどう【青銅】 bronze.¶青銅器 bronze ware; bronze tools.青銅貨 bronze coin. ⇨銅鐸 / 銅剣 / 銅鏡

せいどういつせいしょうがい【性同一性障害】gender identity disorders[GID].

せいはくさい【青柏祭】 the Huge-Float-Parade Festival.(5月). ⇨付記(1)「日本の祭り」

せいはくまい【精白米】 polished rice; cleaned rice.米をついて皮を取り除き白くした米.「精米」ともいう.⇔玄米(未精白米)

せいぼ【歳暮】 ❶〈歳末・年末〉the year-end; the end of the year.¶歳暮売り出し a year-end sale.

❷〈年末の進物〉a year-end gift[present]; a year-end present given to express appreciation for special favors received during the year. It is customary for the Japanese to send a year-end gift to any person to whom they feel indebted. その年に受けた恩義に謝意 (gratitude)を表すために送る歳暮の贈物. お世話になった人への歳暮の進物を送る日本人の習慣. ⇨中元❷

せいまい【精米】 ⇨精白米

せいめい【清明】 pure and clean; season when pleasant weather comes near. 快適な天候の訪れが近い(approaches). 春分後の15日目にあたる. ⇨二十四節気

せいりょうじのおたいまつしき【清涼寺のお松明式】 the Torches-Lighting Ceremony at Seiryoji Temple.(3月). ⇨付記(1)「日本の祭り」

せいろ(う)【蒸籠】 a steaming basket; a basket steamer; a bamboo basket[wooden receptacle] used for steaming. 食物(だんご・まんじゅうなど)を蒸す竹製[木製]の容器. ☆釜の上にのせて湯気を通す.

せかいいさん【世界遺産】the World Heritage Site.⇨ユネスコ世界遺産

せかいたいせん【世界大戦】 a world war.¶第二次世界大戦 World War II; the Second World War. ⇨太平洋戦争

せきじゅん【石筍】 a stalagmite (in the Akiyoshi(do) Limestone Cave).⇨鍾乳石

せきしょ【関所】 (pass) a barrier (station); (pass through) a checkpoint[checking station](検問所); (go through) an inspection point(検査所). Travelers were inspected by the officials at a barrier[checking station] before being allowed to continue traveling in feudal Japan. 封建時代, 役人が交通の要所に設けて通行人・貨物を審査した場所.¶箱根関所 the Hakone Barrier. 関所手形 a travel permit[pass]; a permit to pass a barrier[checking station].

せきてい【石庭】 a rock garden. It is made of rocks and sand, symbolizing mountains and rivers in a natural landscape (without trees or ponds). 石や砂を敷きつめた庭園で, 自然風景を模し, 山や川を象徴する(樹木や池はない). ⇨枯山水. 囲「龍安寺の石庭」(京都府) The rock garden consists of 15 rocks arranged in a sea of white gravel. It is so contrived that viewed from any vantage point one rock remains hidden from view. (一面の白い砂利に配した15個の石から成る. この庭はどの視点からも1個だけ石が見えない)

せきどう(せん)【赤道(線)】 the equator (line).¶赤道地帯 the equatorial region

せきとり【関取】〔相撲〕a *sumo* wrestler in the top-ranking division ranking above the *juryo*[junior-grade] division. 「十両」以上の

力士の総称. ⇨相撲の番付

せきはん【赤飯】 glutinous rice steamed with red *adzuki* beans (by a steaming basket). It is usually sprinkled with sesame-salt and eaten on auspicious occasions such as birthdays and wedding receptions. あずきを混ぜたもち米の蒸しご飯（ごま塩が振ってある）. 誕生日や結婚披露宴などの祝儀の時に食す.「お強」「あずき飯」ともいう. ☆「赤色」は邪気を払い (drive away evil spirits), めでたい色 (the color of joy) であると考えられている. ⇨お強

せきぶつ【石仏】 a stone statue[image] of Buddha.

せきもりいし【関守石】 a barrier stone; a stone placed on a stepping stone in a tea garden. It is a small stone tied with straw rope in the shape of a cross at the crossroads of a garden. It is used to indicate that the area beyond it is out of bounds. 茶庭の飛び石におかれた石. 庭の岐路に十字形の縄を結んで据えた石である.「それから先へは行けない」という意味を明示するのに用いる.

せきれい【鶺鴒】〔鳥〕a (water) wagtail. セキレイ科の小鳥.

せきわけ【関脇】〔相撲〕a *sekiwake*; the third-highest rank of *sumo* wrestlers; the third-ranking *sumo* champion in the *makuuchi* division.「幕内」の３位. ⇨相撲の番付

セクハラ sexual harassment. ¶セクハラ加害者 a sexual harasser. セクハラ被害者 a victim of sexual harassment. セクハラ訴訟 a sexual-harassment suit.

せしゅうくんしゅせい【世襲君主制】hereditary monarchy. ¶世界最古の世襲君主制である日本の天皇制 Japan's imperial institution, the oldest hereditary monarchy in the world.

せっかいがん【石灰岩】 limestone; (a) limestone rock. ¶石灰岩の奇岩怪石で有

名な秋川渓谷（東京都）Akikawa(keikoku) Valley featuring unusual limestone formations. 石灰岩台地 limestone tableland. 例秋吉台（山口県）. 石灰洞 limestone cave.

せっかん【摂関】 regents and Imperial advisers. 摂政と関白のこと. ⇨摂政 / 関白 【摂関政治】 regency government; government by regents and Imperial advisers. ☆10世紀半ばから11世紀にかけて藤原一族が摂政と関白を独占し, 天皇の代理者または天皇の補佐者として政治の実権を独占した政治形態.

せっき【炻器】 ⇨陶器

せっく【節句・節供】 a seasonal festival. *Sekku* was one of the five festival days marking seasonal changes. Today the Girls' Festival and the Boys' Festival are still observed. 季節の変わり目に行われる年5度の祝い日. 今日では特に「桃の節句」（3月3日）と「端午の節句」（5月5日）が残る. ☆5節句 (five festive days)の式日.

① 『若菜の節句』the Day of the Seven Herbs. (January 7).「人日」ともいう. ⇨春の七草

② 『桃の節句』the Girls' Festival; the Doll Festival.（March 3）. 現在では「ひな祭り」.「上巳」ともいう.

③ 『端午の節句』the Boys' Festival; Children's Day. (May 5). 現在では「こどもの日」.

④ 『七夕祭り』the Star Festival. (July 7). ⇨七夕（祭り）

⑤ 『菊の節句』the Chrysanthemum Festival. (September 9).「重陽の節句」ともいう.

せっしょう【摂政】〈地位・職務〉regency;〈人〉a regent (for an emperor who is still a minor or for a female sovereign). 天皇が幼少または女性の場合, 天皇に代わって政治を行う. ☆臣下では866年の藤原良房が初例. ¶聖徳太子の摂政 regency served by Prince Shotoku Taishi; Prince Shotoku

せ

Taishi acted as regent. 摂政殿下 the Prince Regent.

せった【雪駄】　(a pair of) leather-soled *zori* [sandals]; (a pair of) Japanese *zori*[sandals] with leather[animal-hide] soles and metal wedges attached to the heels (to reduce wear). 足底に牛革[獣皮]をはり，（消耗減少用として）かかとに金物を打った草履. ⇨草履

せっちん【雪隠】　a toilet in a garden. 茶庭の便所.「かわや」ともいう.

せっぷく【切腹】　*seppuku*; *hara-kiri*: ritual suicide by self-disembowelment; ceremonial suicide by cutting the belly. *Seppuku* is a ceremonial[ritual] suicide committed by Japanese *samurai* in feudal times. It was considered as an honorable way of dying when a high-ranking *samurai* was condemned to death. He cuts open the belly by inserting a dagger[short sword] into the left side and drawing it across the right side. 自分で腹 (abdomen) を切って死ぬ儀式. 封建時代，武士に科せられた刑罰の一種で，死刑が宣告されたときには栄誉あるもの (an honorable manner of suicide) とみなされた. 腹を開け，小刀を左に差し込み (plunge into)，右に横切って引きながら切る (rip open). ☆死刑としての切腹は明治時代に廃止された. ⇨介錯

せつぶん【節分】　❶〈季節の移り変わり目〉the day before the season changes; the day before the calendrical beginning of each season (occurring four times a year). 季節の変わる日の前日. 立春・立夏・立秋・立冬の前日で年に4回ある.

❷〈立春の前日〉the day before the calendrical beginning of spring; the day preceding *setsubun* that is the first day of spring according to the old Japanese calendar; the last day of winter in the traditional lunar calendar. *Setsubun* falls on February 2 or 3 by the present calendar. On this day, the bean-scattering ceremony[the practice of scattering roasted soybeans] is held in homes and at shrines or temples to drive away demons and bring in good luck. 立春の前日. 2月2日または3日に家庭内または寺社で鬼を払い，福を呼ぶ「豆まき行事」を行う. ⇨立春／豆まき

ぜっぺき【絶壁】　a cliff (海岸の)；a precipice (急な絶壁)；precipitous walls of cliffs; perpendicular cliffs. 屏風のような垂直な形をする. ⇨断崖

せつり【節理】　a joint. 岩石の割れ目. ⇨柱状節理 (a columnar joint)

せと【瀬戸】　a (narrow) strait(狭い海峡)；a (large) channel(広い海峡). ¶音戸の瀬戸(広島県) the Ondo-no-Seto Straits[the Straits of Ondo]; a strait in the Seto Inland Sea. ⇨海峡

せとうち【瀬戸内】　the districts along the ocean of the Seto Inland Sea. 瀬戸内海の沿岸地域.

せとないかい【瀬戸内海】　the Seto Inland Sea. ☆「瀬戸内」ともいう.

せともの【瀬戸物】❶〈瀬戸物類・陶磁器〉porcelain; a chinaware[earthenware]; (a piece of) china; a pottery; ceramics. ⇨瀬戸焼. ¶瀬戸物屋〈店〉a china shop[store].；〈人〉a dealer in china

❷〈陶器類〉pottery and porcelain (produced in any region). ⇨瀬戸焼／有田焼／信楽焼／常滑焼／九谷焼

せとやき【瀬戸焼】　Seto ceramic and porcelain ware (produced in Seto City of Aichi Prefecture). 日本最古・最大の製陶地. ☆「瀬戸物」という場合もある. しかし「瀬戸物」は陶器を代表する用語. ⇨瀬戸物

せびらき（さかな）【背開き（魚）】　opening a fish by cutting along its spine[backbone]; butterflied fish. 背(骨)を切って開いた魚. ¶鮒を背開きにする open a crucian carp by cutting along its spine[backbone]; cut a crucian carp and open along its spine [backbone]; butterfly a crucian carp. ⇨観音開き(魚)

せみ【蝉】〔虫〕a cicada (⊛ cicadas, cicadae). セミ科の昆虫類の総称. ¶油蝉 a brown cicada. 蜩 a twilight cicada. みんみん蝉 a robust cicada. つくつく法師 a fall cicada. 蝉の抜け殻 the cast-off skin[shell] of the cicada.

せみしぐれ【蝉時雨】 a loud (high-pitched) chorus of cicadas; the chirring[singing] of cicadas in chorus. 多くのセミが一斉に鳴きたてる声. ☆「時雨」(drizzling rain in late autumn)の音に由来. ⇨時雨

せり【芹】〔植物〕a Japanese parsley; ㊇ a (water)dropwort. セリ科の多年草. 漬け物や浸し物に使う. 「春の七草」の一つ. ⇨春の七草

せりあな【迫り穴】〔歌舞伎〕. ⇨スッポン

せりだし【迫り出し】〔歌舞伎〕❶〈道具〉a trapdoor（跳ね［押し］上げ戸）; a stage elevator（迫り出し用装置）; a movable platform (on a kabuki stage)(可動式壇). A movable platform enables an actor to appear from beneath the stage and disappear into beneath the stage. 舞台下から舞台上へ役者を押し上げること. またその装置. 舞台や花道の床の一部を切ってその部分を上下させる. 「迫り(セリ)」「迫り上げ」ともいう. ⇨スッポン(花道の迫り) ❷〈役者の登場〉The actor's appearance on the main stage from a trapdoor[movable platform] in a kabuki theater. An actor comes up to the stage through a trapdoor from beneath the stage. 役者が舞台下から跳ね上げ戸を通って舞台上に登場する.

せわもの【世話物】〔歌舞伎〕〔文楽〕kabuki and bunraku plays dealing with the lives of commoners[ordinary people] especially in the feudal times. Many plays dealing with affairs of the common people of the Edo period have tragic love as their theme. 封建時代の町人 (townspeople)社会に見られる風俗・人情などを取材した出しもの. 中でも江戸時代の庶民を扱うものに男女の悲恋が多い. 囲心中天網島(a Double Suicide at Amijima). ⇨時代物 / 心中物

ぜん【膳】❶〈食べ物台・食卓〉a small dining table; a table set for a diner. *Zen*[*O-zen*] is a small (tray-like) table with legs used individually for meals. The bowls, dishes of foods and chopsticks are placed on this small meal table. 各人用に飲食物や箸・碗などをのせて出す(お盆のような)小型の脚付き食台. 「御膳」ともいう. ❷〈食べ物〉a meal set on a table; food served at a table. お膳にのせて出される食べ物または料理. ⇨本膳料理 ❸〈一対・一杯〉a pair of chopsticks. 箸1膳(箸の数え方). a bowl(ful) of rice. 飯1膳(飯の杯数の数え方).

ぜん【禅】 *Zen* (Buddhism). *Zen* is the term referring to the religious attitude toward ascetic practice which seeks to attain spiritual enlightenment through *zazen* meditation[sitting in meditation] rather than through scriptures. 教典よりは座禅を通して精神を統一し, 悟りを開くために修行する宗教的姿勢を指す用語. ⇨座禅 ¶禅画 a Zen painting; a Zen experience painting; a simple monochromatic painting suggesting the essence of Zen concept. 禅学 the doctrine[dogmatics] of Zen Buddhism. 禅師 a Zen master. ⇨達磨〈達磨大師〉. 禅杖 a stick used to chastise dozing *zazen* meditators. ⇨警策. 禅定印 a hand position of Zen meditation. 禅僧 a Zen priest; a monk who practices Zen meditation. 禅庭 a Zen garden. 囲京都の龍安寺. 禅堂 a Zen meditation hall; a meditation [contemplation] room of a Zen monastery (where Zen meditation is practiced). ⇨僧堂. **禅問答** a Zen dialogue. A catechetical dialogue is practiced between a Zen monk [priest] and his disciple in Zen Buddhism. ⇨公案

【禅宗】 Zen Buddhism; the Zen sect of Buddhism. ⇨禅. ☆座禅を主とする仏教の宗派. インドで始まり, 中国で広まり, 日本へは平安・鎌倉時代, 栄西・道元によって伝わる.「臨済宗」(the Rinzai sect: 座禅と公案を用いて悟りを開く),「曹洞宗」(the Soto sect: 只管打坐[ひたすら座禅すること] を通して悟りを開く),「黄檗宗」(the Obaku sect: 念仏を通して悟りを開く)の三派がある. ⇨座禅 / 公案 / 念仏

【禅寺】 a Zen temple; a temple of Zen Buddhism. The Zen Temple has three component structures; "*Hojo*" (the place where the chief priest abides[lives]), "*Hatto*" (the place where the chief priest teaches and trains ascetics) and "*Sodo*"(the place where *zazen* is practiced every day). 三構成の建造物,「**方丈**」(座主の居住所),「**法堂**」(座主が修行者を教練する所),「**僧堂**」(日々座禅を行う所)がある. ⇨座主 / 座禅

せんいせいひん【繊維製品】 textile goods; textiles.

ぜんえいいけばな【前衛生け花】〔華道〕avant-garde art[school] of flower arrangement. Materials of metal, plastic, stone, paper and things like that are used instead of the flowers. 金属・プラスチック・石・紙などが花に代用される.

せんかくしょとうのりょうどもんだい【尖閣諸島の領土問題】the territorial dispute over the sovereignty of the Senkaku Islands.

ぜんがくれん【全学連】 the National Federation of Students' Self-Government Association.

せんぎり【千切り】 julienne; shreds. ¶**大根の千切り** julienne of *daikon*[radish]; shredded *daikon*; *daikon* cut into thin shreds[strips].

せんぐう【遷宮】❶ the temporary removal of the object of worship venerated as a deity from the shrine during its rebuilding or repairing. 神社の改築・修理の前後にご神体［神霊］を仮殿または本殿に移すこと. ⇨神体

❷ the installation of the object of worship venerated as a deity in the new shrine. ご神体［神霊］を新神社に安置すること.

【遷宮式】 the dedication of a new shrine; the ceremony of installing the sacred symbol of a deity in the new shrine. 新神社の献堂式.

せんけ【千家】〔茶道〕the Senke school of the tea ceremony[cult]. The Senke school was originated by the great master Sen-no-Rikyu (1521-1591). There are the three Senke schools[called San-Senke]—the Omote Senke, Ura Senke and Mushanokoji Senke schools. 千家(茶道流派の家柄)は千利休によって始まる.「三千家」は表千家・裏千家・武者小路千家.

せんこう【線香】 a (thin) incense stick; a joss stick. One or more incense sticks are offered[burned] at funeral services and at most Buddhist ceremonies. It is customary for Buddhists to offer[burn] one joss stick a day in front of the family Buddhist altar. 葬儀また仏式で線香をあげる［たく］. 仏教徒は1日1回仏壇に線香をあげる習慣がある. ⇨焼香. ¶**線香立て** an incense holder[burner]. ⇨香炉. **線香代** incense money. 仏壇の線香 incense sticks offering[burning] at the Buddhist altar.

せんこうはなび【線香花火】 small sparklers; small fireworks which look like[resemble] incense sticks.

せんごくじだい【戦国時代】 the Civil War Age; the Warring States period. The Age of Civil[Provincial] Wars lasted from the Onin Revolt (1467) to the security of the country by Oda Nobunaga (1573). 応仁の乱から織田信長による国家安泰までの間続いた.

せんごくだいみょう【戦国大名】feudal lords in the Civil War Age. They had power to rule local *samurai*[vassals] and peasants in their territory. 領地内で家来や農民に対する支配力を保持していた権力者.

せんごほしょう【戦後補償】 (the issue of) postwar compensation; (the problem of) post-World War II reparations.

せんざ【遷座】❶〈神社の座の移動〉the transfer[removal] of a Shinto shrine[the object of worship or an image of Buddha] to a new site. 神社のご神体・寺の仏像などの座を他所へ移すこと. ¶遷座祭 ceremony for the transfer[removal] of a Shinto shrine to a new site.
❷〈天皇の座の移動〉 the transfer[removal] of the emperor('s seat) to a new site.

ぜんざい【善哉】〈関西地方〉a thick, sweet crushed *adzuki*-bean paste soup with a piece of rice cake in the Kansai district[Western Japan];〈関東地方〉sweet strained *adzuki*-bean paste coated[covered] with rice cakes in the Kanto district[Eastern Japan]. 関西では餅を入れた潰し餡の濃い汁粉. 関東では餅に漉し餡をかけたもの. ☆餅の代わりに「白玉だんご」(rice-flour dumplings)を用いることもある. ⇨汁粉 / 餡

せんじゃふだ【千社札】 colorful slips of paper[votive cards] left by pilgrims at Shinto shrines. Pilgrims (who have vowed to visit a thousand[many] shrines) write their names and home addresses on the small slips of paper[votive cards] and pasted them on[attached them to] the buildings [walls, pillars or ceilings] of Shinto shrines

as a token of a pilgrimage. 社殿に残す巡礼者の紙札.（千社詣での）巡礼者が自分の名前・住所などを小形の紙札に記し, 参詣のしるしに神社内の建物(壁・柱・天井など)に貼りつける.

せんじゃもうで【千社詣で】 a pilgrimage made to a large number of shrines in local districts. 地方にある多くの神社に巡礼すること.「千社参り」ともいう.

せんしゅうがっこう【専修学校】a vocational school; a business-technical school. ⇨専門学校

せんしゅうらく【千秋楽】〔相撲〕 the closing [last] day of a *sumo* tournament. ⇨相撲;〈演劇〉the closing day[night] of a show; the closing performance.

せんじゅかんのん【千手観音】the thousand-handed Kannon Bodhisattva[Goddess of Mercy]. A statue[an image] of *Kannon* has one thousand hands with an eye on the palm of each hand, which symbolize her immeasurable mercy to save human beings. 手のひらに目をもつ千本の手を備え, 衆生を救う測り知れぬ慈悲深い観音. ☆千は「広大無限」(boundless infinity)の意味で, 通常は42本のものが多い. ⇨観音

せんしょう【先勝】⇨六曜

ぜんしょう【全勝】〔相撲〕 (have) a perfect [clean undefeated] record; (win) a complete victory. ¶全戦全勝 the *sumo* tournament with a perfect record; the *sumo* tournament without losing once[losing a single match].

せんじょうがはら【戦場ヶ原】 the Senjoga-hara Plateau.（栃木県). ⇨高原

せんす【扇子】 a *sensu*; a fan; a folding fan. A *sensu* is made by pasting Japanese paper on a thin framework of finely split bamboo ribs on which is drawn an artistic picture or calligraphy. It functions as a tool to keep oneself cool in summer and as a decorative object in a traditional Japanese room. It is an indispensable hand prop for comic storytelling and Japanese dance as well as the tea ceremony and the Noh play. 折りたたみ式 (collapsible) の扇. 割り竹の骨の枠組みに和紙を張って作り，芸術的な絵または能筆がえがかれている. 夏季に涼をとる道具で，和室の装飾物などの機能も持つ. 茶道や能楽をはじめ落語や日本舞踊などにも不可欠の小道具である. ☆「扇子」は平安時代に発明される.「団扇」は中国伝来物. 扇子を広げた形は「末広がり」(末にゆくにしたがって次第に栄えることの象徴:future happiness) であるため，祝い事 (celebration) や結納品 (engagement gift) などに用いる. また正式の茶会にも茶道専用の扇子 (a folding fan used exclusively in the tea ceremony)を持参する. 別称「扇」. ⇨末広(扇子). ¶扇子の骨 the ribs of a fan. 扇子の要 the pivot of a fan. 扇子を開く open[unfold] a fan. 扇子をたたむ close[fold] a fan. 扇子をぴしゃっと閉じる snap a fan shut. 扇子を使う use a fan; fan oneself.

ぜんせん【前線】 a front. ¶寒冷前線 a cold front. 温暖前線 a warm front. 梅雨前線 a seasonal rain front. 停滞前線 a stationary front.

せんそう【戦争】 (a) war; warfare; battle. ¶戦争賠償 wartime reparations. 戊辰戦争 the Boshin War. 日露戦争 the Russo-Japanese War (1904-1905).

せんだいたなばたまつり【仙台七夕まつり】 the Star Festival at Sendai City. (8月). ⇨付記(1)「日本の祭り」

せんだいだんす【仙台箪笥】 a richly iron ornamental chest (produced in Sendai City).

せんだん【栴檀】〔植物〕 a Japanese bead tree; a chinaberry tree; a sandalwood tree. センダン科の落葉高木. 果実は薬用.

せんちゃ【煎茶】 *sencha*; a common[an

ordinary] green tea; a green tea of medium [middle] grade[quality] (between *gyokuro* and *bancha*). *Sencha* is a green tea made from the first and second picking of regular bushes. 「玉露」と「番茶」の間にある中級の品質の茶. 通常の潅木から1番または2番目に摘みとった緑茶. ⇨緑茶

せんてい【剪定】 trimming(形を整える); pruning(成長を促す). ☆庭木を整えるために枝の一部を切りとること. ¶剪定鋏 (a pair of) pruning shears; (英) secateurs.

せんていさい【先帝祭】 the Courtesan Festival of Akama Shrine at Shimonoseki City. 下関先帝祭(5月). ⇨付記(1)「日本の祭り」

せんと【遷都】 the capital relocation; the relocation[movement] of the capital; the transfer of the capital. 都[首都]を他所へ移すこと. ¶京都への遷都 the transfer of the Imperial Capital to Kyoto (in 794).

せんとう【銭湯】 a public bath. *Sento* is a bathhouse divided into two separate areas[sections] of men and women. It is customary for bathers to clean the body by washing outside the bathtub before soaking in the hot water. 公衆浴場は男女別になっている. 浴槽につかる前に浴槽の外で身体を洗う.

せんにちもうで【千日詣で】 a pilgrimage [visit] to pray at a shrine or temple for one thousand days in succession. 千日間続けて神社や寺院を参拝すること.「千日参り」ともいう.

せんにん【仙人】 mountain hermit; a legendary wizard living in the mountains.

せんにんむしゃぎょうれつ【千人武者行列】 the One-Thousand-Warriors-Parade of Tosho-gu Shrine in Nikko City (as part of the Grand Spring[Autumn] Festival). (May 17-18[Oct. 17]). ⇨付記(1)「日本の祭り」

せんばづる【千羽鶴】 (a string of) 1,000 folded paper cranes (linked together by a thread); a thousand or so cranes put on a string. It is often given as a present in the hope of someone's quick recovery from sickness. It is also given to pray for a long life because the crane is a symbol of longevity. (糸でつないだ)折り紙の鶴. 病気の早期全快の願かけとしての贈り物に用いる. また鶴は長寿の象徴であるため長生きを願って贈られる. ⇨折り紙 / 鶴

せんぶ【先負】 ⇨六曜

せんぷくキリシタン【潜伏キリシタン】 Hidden Christians. They adhered to the Christian faith in secret during the period of the edict of the ban on Christianity from the early Edo period to the early Meiji era. They held religious services, remaining true to their faith, in hidden places in western Japan (Nagasaki Region) until they gained freedom of religion in 1873. 潜伏キリシタンは江戸時代初期から明治時代初期までのキリシタン禁令の間キリスト教の信仰を守り抜いた. 1873年(明治6年)の宗教の解禁まで信仰を守りながら西日本(特に長崎地方)の隠れ場所で宗教儀式を行っていた. ⇨絵踏 / キリシタン

せんべい【煎餅】 a rice cracker; a thin, crisp rice cracker. It is made from rice-flour dough (or wheat flour) and flavored with *shoyu*[soy sauce] and sugar. 米粉(または小麦粉)に醤油と砂糖を加えて作る焼き菓子. ⇨あられ

〔食品〕**揚げ煎餅** a deep-fried rice cracker. **海苔巻き煎餅** a laver-wrapped rice cracker; a rice cracker wrapped in dried laver (*nori*). **甘辛煎餅** a salty-sweet rice cracker. **手焼き煎餅** a hand-made rice cracker. ⇨かき餅

せんべつ【餞別】 a going-away[send-off, good-bye] gift[present]; a farewell gift; a parting gift. It is given to friends or relatives who study abroad or go out for a long trip. 留学や長旅をする友人または親族に贈られる. ☆日本では通常金銭を伴うので a farewell money gift[present]; a farewell cash giftともいう.

せんまい【饌米】 washed rice offered to a deity[god]. 神に供える洗米.

せんまい【薇】〔植物〕a royal fern; a flowering fern; an osmund (leaf-bud). ゼンマイ科の多年草. 煮物や浸し物に調理する.

せんまいづけ【千枚漬け】〈薄切りカブラの漬け物〉pickles of sliced Japanese turnip; pickled slices of Japanese turnip〈京都特産〉thin slices of turnip pickled in vinegared, *kombu* seaweed and chili pepper. 聖護院カブラに昆布と唐辛子を利かせた薄切り酢漬け.

せんもんがっこう【専門学校】 business & technical college (authorized by the Minister of Education, Culture, Sports, Science and Technology). ⇨専修学校

せんりゅう【川柳】 a *senryu*; a 17-syllable humorous poem (composed in plain language); a witty poem[verse] arranged in a 5-7-5 pattern[format]. A *senryu* expresses satirically the foibles of society and people regardless of any seasonal word. (5-7-5の)17音節の滑稽[風刺・機知]な短詩[詩句](わかりやすいことばで作詩されている). 季語の制約なく世相や人々の弱点を風刺的に表現する. ☆川柳の起案者は江戸中期の柄井川柳(1718-1790). ⇨俳句(季語の制約がある)

せんりょうばこ【千両箱】 a-thousand-*ryo* box; a wooden chest for storing golden coins; a wooden box for containing a thousand pieces of golden coins. 小判金[千両]を入れた木箱. ⇨小判

せんりょうやくしゃ【千両役者】 a great actor[actress]; a star. 優秀な役者[男優・女優].

そ

そう【箏】 a *koto* musical instrument. ⇨琴
【箏曲】(a piece of) *koto* music; a music for
koto. 箏の曲. 箏をひいて演奏する楽曲.

ぞう【象】〔動物〕 an elephant; a bull elephant
(雄); a cow elephant(雌). ¶象の牙 an
elephant's tusk. 象の鼻 an elephant's trunk.

そうあん【草庵】 a thatch(ed) hut; a
thatch(ed) cottage. 草葺の小さな家.

そういん【僧院】 a Buddhist temple; a mon-
astery(男子の); a convent[nunnery](女子
の).

そうぎ【葬儀】 a funeral (service). The wake
and funeral service take place after the
body of the deceased has been placed in
a coffin. 故人の遺体を納める納棺のあと,
通夜と告別式がある. ¶葬儀場 a funeral
hall. 葬儀屋 an undertaker; ⊛ a funeral
home[parlor]; a mortician.
【関連語】仏式葬儀 (Buddhist funerals)にお
ける主な関連用語. 『祭壇』Buddhist altar.
『位牌』wooden Buddhist mortuary tablet.
⇨位牌/戒名. 『遺影』photograph[picture]
and portrait of the deceased. ⇨遺影.
『一膳飯』a bowl of rice offered to the
deceased. ⇨飯. 『香炉』incense burner (used
to stand incense sticks in the ashes). ⇨香
炉. 『経机』Buddhist sutra desk. 『献花』
floral tributes offered to the deceased. 『骨

壺』cinerary urn. 『棺』coffin. 『大鈴』large
Buddhist bell. 『燭台』candle holder.

ぞうき【臓器】 an (internal) organ; viscera.
¶臓器移植 an organ transplant. 臓器提
供カード an organ donor card. 臓器提供
者 an organ donor. 臓器移植者 an organ
recipient.

そうけ【宗家】 the head family[repre-
sentative] (of a school that practices a
traditional[classical] art). 一派の正統を伝
える中心の家[代表]. 「家元」(the head of
a school)ともいう. ⇨家元. ¶茶道の宗家
the head family of the tea ceremony.

ぞうげ【象牙】 an elephant tusk; ivory(工芸
の材質). ¶象牙細工 ivory work. 象牙彫り
〈事〉ivory carving; 〈物〉an ivory carving; a
carving in ivory.

ぞうけいていえん【造景庭園】 a landscape
garden. ⇨枯山水庭園

そうけん【総見】 seeing[inspecting](a special
practice) in a large group. 団体が総員で見
物すること. ⇨稽古総見(相撲).

そうげん【草原】 grasslands(大草原); a
grass-covered plain(平野); the prairie(s)
(牧草地).

そうこう【霜降】 first frost; the season when
frost begins to form the chilly morning. 秋
も終わり, 肌寒い朝には霜が降りる季節.
⇨二十四節気

そうざい【惣菜】 subsidiary dishes (to go
with a staple food); a daily[an everyday]
dish (served as a meal complement to rice).
毎日の食事の副食物. 日本の家庭でつくる
日常的な米食のおかず. ⇨おかず
¶夕食の惣菜 an everyday dish for dinner.
惣菜販売店 delicatessen; the prepared food
counter. ⇨デパ地下(惣菜売り場)

そうしょ【草書】〈書道〉*sosho*; the running
style of writing letters or Chinese characters; the highly cursive style written with
swift strokes in calligraphy. 文字・漢字の書

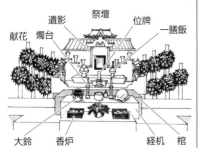

遺影　祭壇　位牌
献花　燭台　　　　　　一膳飯

大鈴　香炉　　　　　経机　棺

体の一つ．書道では滑らかな筆使いで続けて書く書体．☆行書をさらにくずした書体．⇨書体／楷書／行書

そうず【添水】⇨鹿威し

ぞうすい【雑炊】 a porridge of rice and vegetables; a *miso*-flavored (or *shoyu*-seasoned) rice gruel cooked with minced vegetables (or seafoods). Rice is boiled in plenty of soup flavored[seasoned] with *miso*[bean paste] or *shoyu*[soy sauce]. 米飯に野菜（または魚介類）を入れ，味噌（または醤油）で味をつけたかゆ．「おじや」ともいう．⇨おじや

ぞうとう【贈答】 an exchange of gifts [presents]. ⇨表書き／熨斗／水引. ¶贈答品売り場 the gift counter.

そうどう【僧堂】 a meditation hall (at a Zen temple); the hall for sitting in contemplation (of Zen Buddhism). 禅宗で僧が座禅し，起居する建物．⇨禅堂

ぞうに【雑煮】 *zoni*; rice cake soup; soup boiled with rice cakes, vegetables and various ingredients (for eating on New Year's Day). *Zoni* is a special rice-cake soup served to celebrate during the New Year holidays. (Generally speaking) A clear soup with some square rice cakes is served in eastern Japan[the Kanto district], while (light-brown) *miso*[bean paste] soup with some round rice cakes is prepared in western Japan[the Kansai district]. (元旦に食べる) 餅・野菜などを入れた汁物．新年を祝って出される．(一般的には) 東日本[関東地方] では四角い餅を入れた澄まし汁が出され，西日本[関西地方] では丸い餅を入れた (白) 味噌汁で仕立てる．☆味つけや具材 (野菜の種類，また魚や肉など) は各家庭や各地方の特産物によって異なる．¶雑煮餅 rice cakes boiled with vegetables (for eating on New Year's Day). (正月に食する) 野菜といっしょに煮た餅．☆この習慣

は平安時代に遡り，正月に人間界に天下る「年神」(the deity of the year) に餅を供えた．餅には神の力 (divine[deity's] power) が宿ると信じ，新年の幸福を願って食した．⇨直会

そうびょう【宗廟】❶ an ancestral mausoleum of the family. 祖先の霊をまつる所．「みたまや」ともいう．⇨霊廟

❷ an ancestral mausoleum of the Imperial Family. 皇室の祖先の霊をまつる所．

そうへい【僧兵】 armed monk soldiers; fighting monk warriors. They protect temple property from intruders by using the Japanese-style halberd. 武器をもち戦闘に従事する僧侶．槍を使い寺院の財産を侵入者から守る．

そうぼう【僧坊・僧房】 the living quarters for Buddhist priests; the priests' living quarters in a Buddhist temple. 寺院に付属し，僧侶が生活する建物．⇨七堂伽藍

そうほんけ【総本家】〈分家に対して〉 the head[main] family (of a school that practices a traditional art). 「宗家」ともいう．⇨宗家．⇦分家 ;〈元祖〉the original master; the originator.

そうほんざん【総本山】 the head temple (of a Buddhist sect). 一宗の中心となり，大本山・本山を総括する．¶天台宗の東北総本山 (中尊寺) the head temple of the Tendai sect of Buddhism in the Tohoku region. ⇨大本山／本山

そうまとう【走馬灯】 a revolving lantern. 「回り灯籠」「影灯籠」などともいう．

そうまのまおい【相馬野馬追】 the Horse-Chasing Festival. (7月). ⇨付記(1)「日本の祭り」

そうめん【素麺】 thin[fine] wheat noodles; Japanese vermicelli. *Somen* noodles are made of wheat flour and dried in a long and narrow strip of vermicelli. *Somen* noodles are usually served cold in a bowl

そ

containing water and ice cubes in summer. 小麦粉をこね，糸状にのばして乾燥した食品．夏には通常冷水を中に入れた器で供される．☆「太さ」の面で「素麺」（「丸い」切り口）は1.3mm未満.「冷麦」（「四角」切り口）は1.3～1.7mm未満.「日本二銘素麺」は兵庫県の揖保乃糸素麺と奈良県の三輪素麺. ⇨冷やし素麺／流し素麺／煮麺

ぞうり【草履】 (a pair of) *zori*; (a pair of) Japanese-style thonged sandals[slippers]. *Zori* sandals have a flat sole with a V-shaped thong passing between the big and the second toe. *Zori* sandals are often worn with split-toed socks (*tabi*). 底が平たく，親指と人差し指の間を通す鼻緒のある履物．通常は足袋といっしょに履く．⇨雪駄．¶わら草履 flat straw sandals; sandals made of straw.

そうりょ【僧侶】 a Buddhist priest; a monk; a bonze. He wears a surplice (*kesa*) over his robe. He holds a folding fan (*chukei*) in his hand and a long Buddhist rosary (*nenju*) on his arm. 衣の上に「袈裟」(monk's vestment)を着用する．手には「扇子(中啓)」そして腕には「念珠」を持つ．☆「法師」「和尚」「お坊さん」「坊主」(英語のbonzeが語源)などともいう．⇨袈裟

そかい【疎開】 (an) evacuation; removal for safety. ¶疎開児 evacuated children. 疎開者 an evacuee. 強制疎開 forced[compulsory] evacuation[removal]. 集団疎開 a group evacuation; an evacuation in a group. ⇨集団疎開

そくい【即位】 enthronement; imperial accession; accession to the throne (皇位の継承). ⇔abdication (退位). ¶即位の礼 the Enthronement of Emperor. 昭和天皇の崩御と明仁天皇の即位 the death of Emperor Showa and the enthronement of Emperor Akihito. (1989年). 明仁上皇の生前退位と徳仁天皇の即位 the

living abdication of Emperor Emeritus Akihito and the enthronement of Emperor Naruhito. (2019年). ⇨付記(2)日本の歴史年表「令和時代」

そくしつ【側室】 a mistress[concubine] of a nobleman (in ancient Japan). 身分の高い人(an aristocrat)のめかけ．そばめ．⇔正室

そくしんじょうぶつ【即身成仏】 attaining [attainment of] Buddhahood in this life; becoming a Buddha while still in the flesh [alive]. 現在の身体のまま仏になる(思想)．☆主として真言宗の教え．

そくせい【促成】 forcing. ¶促成栽培 forcing culture. 促成栽培の野菜 forced vegetables.

そくたい【束帯】 a nobleman's ceremonial court dress. It was a formal court costume worn by a male aristocrat during the rituals[ceremonies] or the court affairs from the Heian period onwards. 平安時代以降貴人が朝廷の儀式・公事などのときに着用する正式の服装．⇨衣冠束帯

ぞくみょう【俗名】 ❶ a person's secular name. 一般人の生存中の名前．⇔戒名❶ ❷ a person's name as a layman. 僧の出家前の名前．⇔法名／戒名❷

そしどう【祖師堂】 the temple where the founder of a sect of Buddhism is enshrined. 宗祖を祭る寺院.

そしな【粗品】 a small gift; a little present. It is usually given in return for a service. 奉仕のお返しなどによく用いる．☆「粗品ですが，どうぞ」(英語にはない). This is a small present for you. I hope you'll like it. ／ I know it's not much, but please accept it. ¶粗品謹呈 Gift presented to all customers; A free gift for every customer.

そせん【祖先】 an ancestor; a forefather; a progenitor. ¶祖先崇拝 ancestor worship. 祖先伝来の宝物 an ancestral treasure; a hereditary treasure; a family heirloom.

そぞう【塑像】 a clay statue[figure]; a statue

made of clay; a plaster image; a plastic figure. 粘土・石膏などでつくった像.

そだいゴミ【粗大ゴミ】 bulky garbage [refuse]; over-sized[large-sized] trash.

そちゃ【粗茶】 tea. ☆「粗茶ですが, どうぞ」（英語にはない）. Take a cup of tea, please. / Please have a cup of tea. または How about a cup of tea?

ぞっきょく【俗曲】 a folk song sung to *shamisen* accompaniment; a song sung to the accompaniment of *shamisen* at the banquet. 三味線などに合わせて酒の席で歌うような伝統的な歌謡. ⇨端唄

そっくりさん(の人) a look-alike; a double; 〈米口語〉clone. ☆「彼は佐藤にそっくりだ」He is Sato's look-like[a Sato clone].

そっくりしょうひん【そっくり商品】 mock food.

そつじゅ【卒寿】 (celebrate) one's ninetieth birthday.

【卒寿祝い】 the celebration of one's ninetieth birthday. The Japanese celebrate their 90th birthday. It is the 90th anniversary of one's life, one of the special ages to celebrate one's longevity. 90歳の祝い. ⇨賀

そで【袖】 ❶〈衣服の〉a sleeve; an arm. ¶袖裏 the lining of a sleeve. 袖幅 the sleeve width; the width of a sleeve. ☆ the length from armhole to the cuff of a *kimono*（着物の「袖ぐり」(sleeve-hole)から「袖口」(waistband)までの長さ). 袖丈 the sleeve length; the length of a sleeve. 袖山 the creased upper part of a sleeve. 袖下 the lower part of a sleeve. 袖の短い着物 a short-sleeved *kimono*. 袖なしの羽織 a sleeveless *haori*. ⇨羽織. 袖畳み an informal way of folding up a *kimono* 着物の略式の畳み方（着物の背を内にして, 両袖を合わせて折り畳むこと）.

❷〈舞台の〉a wing. ¶舞台の袖 the wings of a stage（舞台の両[左右の]わき）.

そてつ【蘇鉄】〔植物〕a Japan[Japanese] fern palm; a cycad. ソテツ科の常緑低木. 観賞用. 種子は薬用・食用. ¶野生馬の放牧と自生するソテツ(宮崎県・都井岬) wild horses grazing freely and the fern palms growing wildly (in Cape Toi).

そとうみ【外海】 the open sea; the ocean. ⇔内海

そとば【卒塔婆】 ❶〈仏舎利塔〉a stupa; a pagoda; a Buddhist grave monument (in the shape of a tower). 仏舎利[仏骨]を安置する塔. 塔形にした仏教の墓碑.

❷〈供養のための木製板〉a stupa-shaped wooden grave tablet[slat]. It is made from a long flat wooden board[narrow plank of wood] standing by[around] gravestone. It has the posthumous name of the deceased and a phrase from Buddhist sutra. 墓の後ろ周辺に立てる塔形の細長い木製板[狭い厚板]. 戒名や経文の一節を書く. ⇨仏舎利塔. ☆stupa「ストゥーパ, 仏舎利塔」(サンスクリット語)神聖な遺物を納めた円形の供養塔.「仏舎利」は「仏骨」の意. 日本の「卒塔婆」はstupaの音写でその頂部がこの塔の形に擬してある.「そとうば」ともいう.

そとぼう【外房】 the southern areas on the Pacific Ocean in the Boso Peninsula (in Chiba Prefecture).

そとぼり【外堀】 an outer moat; a moat outside the castle walls. 城外の堀. ⇔内堀

そとろじ【外露地】 the outer part of a tea garden. It includes the area close to the garden entrance with a waiting room. 茶庭の外部. 待合室のある庭口に近い区域がある. ⇔内露地. ⇨露地

そとゆ【外湯】 an outdoor bath at a hot-spring inn[resort]. 温泉場の旅館の外に設けてある浴湯.「外風呂」(detached bath; public bath)ともいう. ⇔内湯

そなえもの【供え物】 ⇨お供え(物)❶

そなえもち【供え餅】 a rice cake offering; an offering of rice cakes; rice cakes offered to a god; rice cakes placed in front of a family[household] Shinto altar. 神前［神棚］に供える餅. ⇨お供え❷／鏡餅

そば【蕎麦】 ❶〔植物〕buckwheat. タデ科の一年草. 種子からそば粉をとる.

❷〔食品〕*soba*; buckwheat noodles. *Soba* are thin long brownish noodles made of buckwheat flour kneaded with wheat flour, egg whites and yam starch added. *Soba* noodles(symbolic of longevity) are traditionally eaten on New Yea's Eve with prayer for a long life. そば粉に小麦・卵白・山芋等を混ぜて打ち延ばし, 細長くつくった茶色い麺. 大晦日には長寿を願ってそばを食べる伝統がある. ☆ビタミンB1を多く含むそばは, 白米の多食による脚気予防(beriberi prevention)の効用がある. 日本三大そばには「戸隠そば」(長野県), 「出雲そば」(島根県), 「わんこそば」(岩手県). ⇨年越しそば／笊そば／盛りそば

¶そば掻き *soba* mash; *soba* dough. そば殻 *soba* chaff. そば粉 *soba* flour. そば猪口 a *soba* cup; dipping sauce cup for *soba*; a (porcelain) cup for soy-based sauce to dip *soba* noodles in.(「ちょこ」は「ちょく」の転).

〔料理・食品〕そば焼酎 spirits distilled from *soba*. そば鮨 *sushi* made with *soba* (instead of vinegared rice), rolled in dried seaweed. (酢飯の代わりにそばを巻いたのり巻き). そば汁 *soba* soup[broth]; a soy-based dipping sauce[broth] for buckwheat noodles. *Soba* broth is made with *shoyu* [soy sauce], *mirin*[sweetened *sake*], salt and dried bonito.(醤油, みりん, 塩そして鰹節で作る). ☆関西では「そばだし」という. そば饅頭 *soba* bun stuffed with sweet bean paste. そば蒸し steamed *soba* rolled in fish cut open. (観音開きにした魚でそ

ばを蒸した食品). そば湯 ① *soba* starch gruel(そば粉を熱湯でとかしたもの). ② hot water in which *soba* noodles have been boiled(そばをゆでたあとの湯).

そばようにん【側用人】 a grand chamberlain of the Tokugawa shogunate. He relays messages between the shogun and his highest councilors (called *roju*). 徳川将軍の側に仕え, その命を老中に伝え, 老中の上申を取り次ぐ. ⇨老中

そぼろ seasoned ground[minced] fish [chicken meat]; powdered fish[chicken meat] seasoned with *shoyu*[soy sauce] and sugar. 魚肉［鳥肉］を蒸し, 細かくほぐして醤油や砂糖で味づけした食品. ⇨おぼろ

〔料理・食品〕そぼろご飯 steamed rice topped with minced seasoned ground fish[chicken meat]. 鳥そぼろ弁当 box lunch with seasoned ground[minced] chicken meat on top of steamed rice. そぼろ丼 (a bowl of) steamed rice topped with minced seasoned chicken meat. ⇨丼物

そめつけ【染め付け】 ❶〈染めること〉dyeing. ☆ dye(染める)の動名詞. ⇨染物❶

❷〈布〉 a cloth with indigo designs; a cloth dyed with a design in indigo blue. 藍色模様で染めた布. ⇨藍

❸〈磁器〉 a blue-and-white porcelain ware; a white porcelain ware with a design in indigo blue under the glaze. 藍色の模様を釉薬で焼きつけた焼き物. 「染め付け焼き」ともいう. ⇨藍

そめもの【染物】 ❶〈染めること〉dyeing. ☆ dying (die[死ぬ]の現在分詞・動名詞)と混同しないこと. ¶染物屋〈店〉a dye house;〈人〉a dyer. 染物業 a textile dyeing industry.染物工場 dye-works

❷〈染めた物〉dyed goods[textiles]. ¶染め模様 a dyed pattern[design]; a printed pattern.

❸〈染める物〉goods[textiles] to be dyed.

⇨紅型

そらまめ【空豆・蚕豆】〔植物〕broad beans（大粒種）；horsebeans（中粒種）；pigeon beans（小粒種）；⊛ lima beans; fava beans. マメ科の二年草.「おたふく豆」ともいう. ⇨まめ／お多福豆

そり【反り】a curve; a bend; an arch（橋の）. ¶刀の反り a slight curve of a Japanese sword. 反り橋 an arch(ed) bridge（太鼓橋）

そろばん【算盤】abacus（⊛ abacuses, abaci）. *Soroban* is a traditional calculating instrument[device] made of a wooden frame with parallel rows of sliding beads strung on fixed sticks[wires]. 伝統的な計算器（calculator）で，固定した棒［針金］に算盤玉を差し込んだ木製の枠から作られている. ☆約500年前に中国から伝来する. ¶算盤玉 a bead (on an abacus); a counter.

そんげんし【尊厳死】death with dignity.

そんぞくさつじん【尊属殺人】〈父親〉patricide;〈母親〉matricide;〈近親者〉parricide. ⇨親殺し

そんのう【尊王】reverence for the Emperor; royalism. 天皇を尊ぶこと. ¶尊王論 the doctrine of reverence for the Emperor 【尊王家】an imperialist; a royalist; an advocate of the restoration of Imperial rule. 天皇を国体の中心とする考えの持ち主.

【尊王攘夷】"Revere the Emperor and expel the barbarians" (slogan); absolute royalty to the Emperor and the expulsion of foreigners. 天皇を尊ぶ尊王論と外国人の排撃を主張する攘夷論. ⇨攘夷

【尊王攘夷思想】the imperialist's antiforeigner movement; the principle of revering the Emperor and eliminating foreigners. They opposed opening the country and insisted that Japan use military power to expel foreigners.「天皇を尊び外国人を追放する」という江戸幕末の思想. 長州藩が活

発に動く.

た

たい【鯛】〔魚〕(a) sea bream; (a) red snapper; (a) porgy. A sea bream is regarded as a celebratory fish, because the word "tai" with "medatai" means "happy[auspicious]" as a pun. タイ科の硬骨魚.「たい」は「めでたい」の語呂合わせがあるので縁起のよい「祝宴の魚」(fish used as an emblem of happy occasions)の表象として用いる. ⇨御節料理. ¶甘鯛 a tilefish. 黒鯛 a black porgy. 真鯛 a red sea bream.
〔料理・食品〕鯛茶漬け boiled rice poured with tea, and served with slices of sea bream on it. 鯛そうめん fine noodles served with sea bream. 鯛の粗煮 head and bony portions of sea bream stewed in *shoyu*, *mirin* and sugar. 鯛の活き作り fresh slices of live sea bream arranged to look lifelike. 鯛の塩焼き sea bream broiled with salt; sea bream sprinkled with salt and grilled over a charcoal fire. 鯛の塩煮 sea bream boiled in salt water. 鯛の浜焼き sea bream grilled[broiled] whole with salt. ⇨浜焼き. 鯛味噌 *miso*[bean paste] mixed with sea bream meat[flakes]. 鯛飯 boiled rice cooked with minced sea bream meat[flakes].

たいあん【大安】⇨六曜

たいい【退位】abdication. ⇔ enthronement（即位）. ¶生前退位 living abdication; abdicating while he is still well and capable. 健在中の退位. ⇨付記(2)日本の歴史年表「2016年」／「令和時代」

たいいくのひ【体育の日】⇨スポーツの日

ダイエットしょくひん【ダイエット食品】diet food; slimming food[product]; low-calorie food.

たいがいじゅせい【体外受精】a test-tube

fertilization; in-vitro fertilization[IVF]. ☆ in-vitro 囲「試験管内の(で)」. ¶体外受精児 a test-tube baby; a baby conceived out of the mother's body.

だいがくぜんにゅうじだい【大学全入時代】 an era where universities have space for everyone; an era where all applicants can secure university entrance; an era where everyone[all candidates] can enroll at colleges.

だいかぐら【太神楽】❶ a dedicatory *kagura* [sacred music and dancing] performed at Ise Grand Shrine. 伊勢大神宮で行われる神楽.「太太神楽」ともいう. ❷ a street performance of a lion dance and jugglery (in the Edo period). (江戸時代の芸能で)獅子舞や曲芸などの大道芸.「代神楽」ともいう.

たいかのかいしん【大化の改新】 the Taika Reform; the Reformation of Taika. A centralized government by the Emperor began to reform in 645. ☆中大兄皇子[後の天智天皇]と中臣鎌足[後の藤原鎌足]が蘇我氏を滅ぼし，645年天皇による中央集権国家が樹立する.

だいかん【大寒】 the coldest season. ⇨二十四節気

だいかん【代官】 a chief magistrate; a local magistrate. He executed government orders for the feudal lord in the Edo period. 地位の高い職にいる高官[行政長官]．江戸時代，大名の行政指令を代行した. ☆地方住民の領地(domains)，年貢 (land tax)，民事 (civil affairs)などを統治した. ¶代官所 a magistrate's office.

だいきち【大吉】 the best luck[fate]; the most excellent luck; the best of luck. ⇨おみくじ

だいきょう【大凶】 the worst luck[fate]; the worst of ill fortune. ⇨おみくじ

たいきょく【対局】 (play) a game of

shogi[*go*] (with a person). 相対して将棋をさす[碁をうつ]こと.

だいぎんじょうしゅ【大吟醸酒】 top-quality [superb] *sake* brewed from the finest rice. ⇨吟醸酒

だいぐうじ【大宮司】 the high[chief] priest of a major Shinto shrine. 神社の最高位の神官. ⇨宮司

たいけん【帯剣】 a Japanese sword worn at one's side[waist]. 腰に下げた剣.「帯刀」ともいう.

たいこ【太鼓】 a stick drum; a drum struck [beaten] with thick wooden sticks (*bachi*). ⇨和太鼓. ¶太鼓の皮 the head of a drum; a drumhead. 太鼓の音 the sound of the drum.

たいこう【太閤】 ❶ *taiko*; the father of *kampaku*[the Imperial adviser; the chief adviser to the Emperor]. 関白職をその子に譲った人の尊称. ⇨関白 ❷ Toyotomi Hideyoshi. 豊臣秀吉の別称. ¶太閤記 The Life of Toyotomi Hideyoshi. 【太閤検地】 Toyotomi Hideyoshi's land surveys; a national survey of lands and their productive capacity (made by Toyotomi Hideyoshi in 1582). (1582年豊臣秀吉による)全国的な土地とその生産力の調査.

だいこうビジネス(ぎょう)【代行ビジネス(業)】 a surrogate business[company]; a proxy service business.

たいこうぼう【太公望】 an angler. 魚を釣る人. ¶太公望連 a group of anglers.

だいこく(てん)【大黒(天)】 ⇨七福神

だいごくでん【大極殿】 the Daigokuden Hall; the Great Hall of State(in the ancient Imperial Palace); the former Audience Hall. The Emperor holds political activities and state rituals[ceremonies] in this hall. 謁見の間．天皇が政務を執り，(即位などの)大礼をおこなう所.

だいこくばしら【大黒柱】 ❶〈家の柱〉the

central pillar of a house.
❷〈家族の援助者〉the family breadwinner; the chief support of a family; the mainstay.

たいこばし【太鼓橋】an arched bridge. ⇨反り橋

たいこむすび【太鼓結び】 the drum knot fastening of an *obi*[sash] for women; the puffed-out bow of an *obi*[sash]. It is fixed at the back of a *kimono* in such a way that looks like the frame of the drum. 女性の帯の結び方の一種. 丸くふくらませて帯を結ぶこと. 太鼓の胴のように着物の背後で結ぶ. ¶**太鼓結びの帯** an *obi*[sash] of a drum knot.「太鼓帯」ともいう.

だいこん【大根】〔植物〕a *daikon*; a *daikon* radish; a Japanese[Chinese] radish; a giant white radish. アブラナ科の一年草または二年草. 別称「**すずしろ**」. ⇨かいわれ大根 / 切干し大根 / たくあん / 風呂吹き大根 / 凍み大根
〔料理〕**大根卸し** ❶〔食品〕grated Japanese *daikon*[radish]. It is usually served as a condiment for *tempura* and *nabemono*. ❷〈器具〉a *daikon* grater. **大根膾** sliced[shredded] *daikons* and carrots seasoned with vinegar; pickled salad of *daikons* and carrots(酢で味つけた大根と人参). ⇨膾.
大根煮 *daikon*[radish] simmered in broth.

だいこんやくしゃ【大根役者】 a poor[bad] actor[actress]; a ham.

だいざ【台座】 a pedestal (used to seat a Buddhist statue). 仏像を安置する台.

たいし【太子】 the Crown Prince. 皇位を継承する皇子. ¶**聖徳太子** Prince Shotoku.

だいし【大師】 ❶ Daishi(称号); Buddha (仏). 仏・菩薩の尊称.
❷ the great teacher; an eminent Buddhist priest. 高僧・名僧の称号. ¶**弘法大師** Kobo Daishi, the Reverent Kobo, an eminent Buddhist priest.

たいしぼう【体脂肪】body fat. ¶**体脂肪計**

body fat scale(s)[gauze(s)]. **体脂肪率** body fat ratio.

たいしゃ【大社】 a grand shrine; a large-scale and highly venerated[venerable] Shinto shrine. ¶**出雲大社** Izumo Grand Shrine; Grand Shrine of Izumo.
【**大社造り**】〈様式〉the oldest style[*Izumo-Taisha* style] of architecture in Shinto shrines;〈神社〉a shrine built with square gabled roof. 神社建築で最古の様式[出雲大社造り]. 正方形で, 切妻造り. ⇨神社

たいしょ【大暑】 greater heat; the season when the hottest summer begins. 厳しい暑さの季節. ⇨二十四節気

だいじょ【大序】〔歌舞伎〕〔文楽〕the prologue [opening act] in kabuki drama or joruri puppet theater. 歌舞伎の最初に演じる第一段(狂言). また浄瑠璃で第一段の部分(時代物).

だいじょうかん[**だじょうかん**]【太政官】 the Grand Council of State; the central administrative organs of Japanese government in ancient times. ❶[だいじょうかん]律令制における行政の中央最高機関. ❷[だじょうかん]1868年に設置された明治新政府の最高官庁. 1885年に廃止. 現在の内閣制度にかわる. ⇨大納言

だいじょうきょう【大乗経】 Buddhist sutras (containing the doctrines of Mahayana Buddhism). 大乗仏教の教義典を含む仏教の経典. ⇨大乗仏教

たいしょうごと【大正琴】 a *taisho-koto*; a Japanese-style zither[lyre] with keys (invented in the Taisho era). A *taisho-koto* is a (12×60cm) two-metal-stringed musical instrument played by pressing keys with one hand and strumming with the other. 大正初期に発明された和製のチター(指と爪で演奏する弦楽器). 片方の手で鍵盤を押え, 他方の手で弾く二本の金属弦の楽器(12×60cm). ☆ zither「チター［ツィター]」

た

約30-40本の弦を持ち，水平にして指と爪で弾く弦楽器． lyre「リラ」(古代ギリシアの)竪琴．

だいじょうだいじん[だじょうだいじん]【太政大臣】 the Grand Minister of State; the chancellor of realm; the highest-ranking commissioner of the state administration (who was at the helm of the government). 政治の実権を握る人． ❶[だいじょうだいじん]律令制で太政官の長官． ❷[だじょうだいじん]明治初期の太政官制の最高官職．

だいじょうぶっきょう【大乗仏教】 Mahayana Buddhism. ☆大乗は「大きな乗り物」(the Great Vehicle)の意味．多数の人が乗れる車のことで，「多数の人を慈悲の心をもって救う」という立場．在家仏教(出家しない在俗の人のための仏教．人はだれもが仏陀への信仰によって救われる[Everyone can be saved by faith in Buddha.]). 日本や中国で普及する．535年(一説には552年)に中国・韓国を経て日本に伝来する． ⇨小乗仏教

だいじん【大臣】 a minister(of a state). ¶右大臣 the Minister of the Right. ⇨右大臣. 左大臣 the Minister of the Left. ⇨左大臣.

たいしんきょうどぎそう【耐震強度偽装】 falsified earthquake-proofing of buildings.

だいじんぐう【大神宮】 a Grand Shinto Shrine (dedicated to Amaterasu Omikami). 天照大神を祀った宮． ¶伊勢の大神宮(＝内宮) Grand Shrine of Ise; Ise Grand Shrine. ⇨内宮

だいす【台子】〔茶道〕 a tea stand; the shelf-like stand for tea ceremonial utensils. It is used when the formal tea ceremony takes place in the large room. 茶道具をのせる棚のような台．大部屋で正式の茶道が行われるときに用いる． ☆風炉，茶碗，茶入れ，建水などをのせる4本柱の棚．四畳半の間などでは使用しない． ⇨茶道具

だいず【大豆】〔植物〕 a soybean; a soya bean; 〈実〉 soybeans; soya beans. マメ科の一年草．豆腐・味噌・醤油などの原料．「畑の肉」といわれ良質のタンパク質に富む． ⇨納豆／豆腐／味噌／醤油． ¶**大豆粕** soybean cake. **大豆もやし** soy sprouts. **大豆油** soybean oil. **大豆粉** soybean flour. ⇨黄粉. **大豆タンパク質** soy protein. **大豆タンパク質飲料**[食品] soy protein beverages[foods] (複数形で).

たいせいほうかん【大政奉還】the Restoration of the Imperial Rule; the return of political power[authority] to the Emperor. The 15th (last) Shogun, Tokugawa Yoshinobu, returned the political administration to the Imperial Court in 1867. 1867年に第15代将軍徳川慶喜は政権を朝廷に返上する．

たいせつ【大雪】 Greater Snow; the season when a lot of snow begin to fall. 大雪の降る季節． ⇨二十四節気

だいぞうきょう【大蔵経】 the complete collection of Buddhist Sutras, Laws and Treatises. すべての仏教経典(経・律・論)の叢書． ⇨一切経

だいそうじょう【大僧正】 a Buddhist priest of the highest rank; the chief abbot in the highest position of honor in the Buddhist hierarchy. 僧侶階級の最高位者．

だいだい【橙】〔植物〕a bitter orange; a sour orange. ミカン科の常緑小高木．果汁はポン酢として用いる．果皮は薬用． ⇨ポン酢. 果実は正月の飾り物に用いる．「だいだい」は「代々」(for generations; from generation to generation)に通じる縁起物． ¶だいだい酢 bitter orange vinegar.

だいち【台地】a plateau (複 plateaus, plateaux); a tableland; a height; a grassland. ¶石灰岩台地 limestone plateau. シラス台地 white sand plateau. 秋吉台(山口県) the Akiyoshidai Plateau. (日本最大のカルスト台地．特別天然記念物).

たいとう【帯刀】 ⇨帯剣

だいとう【大刀】 a long sword; the longer of

two swords (worn by a *samurai*). ⇨小刀

だいとうあきょうえいけん【大東亜共栄圏】
the Greater East Asia Co-Prosperity Sphere.
太平洋戦争中，日本がアジア支配のために
掲げた標語.

だいとうあせんそう【大東亜戦争】the Greater East Asia War. ⇨太平洋戦争

だいどうげい【大道芸】a street performance.
¶大道芸人 a street performer[entertainer,
comedian].

だいなごん【大納言】 a chief councilor of
state[the Imperial Court] (ranking below
the *daijo-kan* and above the *chunagon*) 政
務[朝廷]の重要参事官. 太政官の次官・
中納言の上位. ⇨太政官／中納言

だいにじせかいたいせん【第二次世界大戦】
World War II（World War two と読む）;
the Second World War. ☆1941年12月から
1945年8月まで続いた日本史上最大の世界
戦争. ⇨付記 (2)「日本の歴史年表」

だいにしんそつ【第2新卒】graduates seeking
jobs within a few years after leaving college.

だいにちにょらい【大日如来】 Dainichi
Nyorai Buddha; ［梵語］Mahavairocana
(Buddha); the principal Buddha wor-
shipped in esoteric Buddhism; the principal
Buddha in the Shingon sect of Buddhism
in Japan. 密教の本尊.日本の真言宗の本尊.

だいにっぽんていこくけんぽう【大日本帝
国憲法】 the Constitution of the Empire of
Japan (promulgated in 1889). It stipulated
that sovereignty rested with the Emperor
and gave strong power to Him. 主権は天皇
にあると規定.（1889年発布）

たいのうら【鯛の浦】 Tainoura Sea; the sea
bream habitat. Many sea breams can be
seen from the sightseeing boat in Chiba
Prefecture. 鯛の生息地で遊覧船から多数の
鯛が見物できる.（千葉県）

だいはちぐるま【大八車・代八車】 a large

hand-drawn cart[wagon]; a large two-
wheeled wooden cart[wagon] pulled by
several people. 大きな手押し車. 数人で引
く二輪の大きな木製の荷車. ☆「八人の代
わりをする車」の意.

たいびょう【大廟】❶〈天皇家の霊を祭る所〉
an Imperial Mausoleum.「霊廟」ともいう.
❷〈伊勢神宮の尊称〉 the Ise Grand Shrine.
「神廟」ともいう.

だいふく(もち)【大福(餅)】a soft round rice
cake stuffed[filled] with sweetened *adzuki*-
bean paste. It is made of *adzuki*-bean paste
enclosed in a thin pounded-rice skin. 小豆
餡を包んだ柔らかくて丸い餅. 薄い餅皮で
餡を包んだもの. ☆江戸時代に始まり，東
京の日本橋で完成する.

だいふくちょう【大福帳】an (old-fashioned)
account book[daybook] (used by merchants). 昔，商人が(収入・支出を)記した
台帳・元帳.

だいぶつ【大仏】 a great statue[image] of
Buddha; a giant Buddhist statue(usually
made of bronze); a monumental statue of
Buddha. ☆通常は「一丈六尺」(約4.85m)
以上の像をさす. ⇨仏像. ¶奈良の大
仏 the Great Statue of Buddha at Todai-
ji Temple in Nara (with its seated height
of 16.2 m and erected in 746). 鎌倉の大
仏 the Great Statue of Buddha at Kotokuin
Temple in Kamakura (with its seated
height of 11.4 m and built in 1252). 大
仏殿 the Great Buddhist Statue Hall; the
Hall of the Great Buddhist Statue; the Hall
housing the Great Statue of Buddha. 圀奈
良の東大寺の大仏殿(758年に建立. 世界
最大の木造建築. ユネスコ世界文化遺産)
【大仏開眼供養】 (observe) a consecration
ceremony of a new Buddhist statue; (hold)
a ceremony consecrating the newly-made
Great Buddhist statue. 新しくできた大仏に
仏の魂を迎える儀式. ⇨開眼供養

た

たいへいようせんそう（ぼっぱつ）【太平洋戦争（勃発）】 (the outbreak of) the Pacific War (1941-1945). ☆第二次世界大戦時の日本では「大東亜戦争」といった. ⇨大東亜戦争

だいほんえい【大本営】 the Imperial Headquarters of the army and navy (established under the direct control of the Emperor in times of war). 戦争時，天皇の直下におかれた陸海軍を指揮する最高機関.（1893-1945）

だいほんざん【大本山】 the main temple of a Buddhist sect; the headquarters of a religious sect. 総本山の下に，本山の上に位する大寺. 圏「大本山永平寺」(福井県). ⇨総本山／本山

たいま【大麻】 a paper amulet issued by Ise Grand Shrine[Shinto shrines]. 伊勢神宮[諸神社]が授けるお札.

たいま【大麻】〔植物〕 hemp; cannabis; marijuana. 麻から製した麻薬. ¶**大麻取締法** the Cannabis Control Law.

たいまつ【松明】 a (pine-tar) torch.「焚松」の音便. ¶**松明行列** (hold) a torchlight parade[procession].

だいみょう【大名】 a *daimyo*; a feudal lord; a land holder in feudal times; a great feudatory. *Daimyos* were the lords of fiefs who possessed great domains and administered a wide range of territory, but were supervised by the shogunate and were subject to the Code of the *Samurai* Warriors (*buke-shohatto*). They had revenues above 10,000 *koku* of rice annually. 封建時代の領主 (regional ruler). 多くの私有の田地や広い領地を支配した武士. 幕府に統括され，武家諸法度に服した. 大名は年間1万石以上の領地を保有した (received an annual stipend of above 10,000 *koku* as salaries). ⇨封建領主／武家諸法度. ¶**大名屋敷** a feudal lord's

residence[mansion] (in Edo).

【関連語】江戸幕府が1615年に将軍秀忠（1579-1632）の時，諸大名の武力を制限し，秩序をはかるために「武家諸法度」を下した. この頃の「大名」は3種に大別される.

① 『親藩大名』 lineage feudal lords; feudal lords who were from Tokugawa-lineage families. They were Tokugawa-related feudal lords who had high status in administrating shogunate governmental affairs. Three sons of Tokugawa Ieyasu, the first shogun, governed Owari, Kii and Mito provinces respectively. They were called the three honorable Tokugawa families.
徳川一門の大名. 徳川幕府の政治を動かす高い地位にいた. 徳川家康の3人の息子が尾張・紀伊・水戸を統治した.「徳川御三家」と呼ぶ. ⇨御三家

② 『譜代大名』 hereditary feudal lords; feudal lords who were hereditary vassals[retainers] of the Tokugawa shogunate. They pledged loyalty to the Tokugawa shogunate prior to and during the Battle of Sekigahara (in 1600). They had great domains in an important territory and took part in Tokugawa governmental affairs.
徳川幕府に仕えた世襲家臣から取り立てた大名. 関ヶ原の合戦以前また戦中に徳川幕府に忠誠を誓約した. 代々重要な地点に領地をもち，徳川幕府の要職についた.

③ 『外様大名』 outside feudal lords; feudal lords who were not hereditary vassals[retainers] of the Tokugawa shogunate. They submitted to the Tokugawa shogunate after the Battle of Sekigahara (in 1600). They were not allowed to participate in governmental affairs. Later, they devoted themselves to the collapse of the Tokugawa shogunate and contributed to the Meiji Restoration.
関ヶ原の合戦以後に徳川家に臣従した大

名．幕府への参与は通常許されなかった．その後幕府の崩壊と明治維新の際に頭角を現す．

だいみょうぎょうれつ【大名行列】 ❶〈行列〉 a procession of a feudal lord and his retainers[vassals] (when they went up[traveled] to and from Edo for the alternate-year attendance of feudal lords on the Tokugawa shogunate). In the Edo period, feudal lords were required to reside alternately[periodically (usually a year or two)] in Edo and serve the shogunate. 江戸時代，大名が参勤交代などで江戸への往復旅行をする時の家来を伴った大規模な行列．江戸時代には大名は隔年に[定期的に(通常1，2年)]江戸に在住し，徳川幕府に奉仕する必要があった．⇨参勤交代 ❷〈祭り〉 the Daimyo's Procession in Hakone.(11月，神奈川県・箱根町)．The procession features a faithful reproduction of the ceremonious journey made by a feudal lord and his retainers and vassals to demonstrate their power, when they went up to Edo for alternate-year attendance of feudal lords on the Tokugawa shogunate. 大名とその家来たちが徳川幕府に参勤交代で江戸に上る時に，その権勢を誇示するために行われた厳かな旅路の行列を再現している．⇨付記(1)「日本の祭り」(箱根大名行列)

だいみょうじん【大明神】 a Great Deity [God]; a gracious deity[god]; a great miracle-working deity[god]. ☆「明神」をさらに尊ぶことば．熱心に信仰する神の尊称．⇨明神．¶稲荷**大明神** the Great God Inari. ⇨稲荷

だいもく【題目】 a prayer of holy invocation of the Nichiren sect of Buddhism. It consists of the seven Chinese characters, "na-mu-myo-ho-ren-ge-kyo" (all Glory to the Lotus Sutra of the Supreme Law). 日蓮宗で唱える七文字の祈祷．通称「御題目」．⇨「南無妙法蓮華経」．¶**題目堂** the Prayer Hall (of Nichiren sect of Buddhist temple). **題目講** a fraternity of Nichiren Buddhist adherents(日蓮宗信徒の宗教団体)

だいもん【大門】 the great outer[main front] gate of a Buddhist temple. 寺院の外構えの大きな正門．

だいもんじござんのおくりび【大文字五山の送り火】 the Great Bonfire Event on Five Mountains in Kyoto. (8月)．⇨付記(1)「日本の祭り」

たいやき【鯛焼き】 a sea-bream-shaped pancake containing sweet *adzuki*-bean paste; a pancake in the shape of a sea bream filled with sweet *adzuki*-bean paste. It is baked on an iron plate with shallow depressions[hollows] shaped like a sea bream fired from underneath and served [eaten] hot. 小豆餡を詰めた(stuffed with)鯛型のパンケーキ．下から加熱する鯛型の浅い窪みのある鉄板で焼き，熱いうちに出す[食べる]．⇨今川焼き

ダイヤルイン(和製英語) a direct dialing; a direct line. ☆名刺の電話番号の後にDIRECT(LINE)と記してある．03-1234-5748 DIRECT(LINE)

だいら[たい]【〜平】 a highland(高地)；a plateau(高原)；a plain(山中の平地)．¶**八幡平**(岩手県・秋田県) (the) Hachiman(tai) Plateau. **室堂平**(富山県) (the) Muro-do(daira) Plateau. ⇨平野 / 原野 / 湿原

たいらぎ【玉珧】〔貝〕 pen shell; fan shell. 別名「平貝」．ハボウキガイ科の二枚貝の一種．ホタテ貝より上等である．冬が旬．貝柱は美味．刺身や酢の物に用いる．

たいらんずもう【台覧相撲】〔相撲〕 *sumo* wrestling matches held in the presence of the Emperor and/or Imperial Prince. ⇨相撲

だいり【内裏】 ❶〈皇居〉the Imperial Palace precincts；〈宮中〉the Imperial Court

た

precincts. 天皇の住む御殿を中心とする建物．皇居・宮中のこと．

❷〈内裏雛〉(a pair of)emperor and empress dolls.「内裏雛」の略．⇨内裏雛

【内裏雛】〈雛祭り〉emperor and empress dolls; (a pair of) dolls representing [portraying] the emperor and empress (displayed on the Doll Festival). These dolls are colorfully dressed in brilliant ancient court costumes for ceremonial occasions.（雛祭りに展示する）天皇・皇后の姿をまねて形作られた男女一対の雛人形．式典用の豪華な宮中衣装を優雅に装う．⇨雛壇(最上段)

だいりしゅっさん【代理出産】 a surrogate birth[parenthood]. ☆「**代理母**」は a surrogate mother.

たいりょうばた【大漁旗】 a big-catch flag; a good-catch banner. It is a banner used by fishermen to signal a large haul of fish to those on the shore. 大漁のとき漁師が岸辺にいる人々に知らせる旗．

たいりょうぶし【大漁節】 a song sung in celebration of[prayer for] a good-catch fish. 大漁を祝う[願う]歌．

たいろう【大老】 a *tairo*; the chief[senior] minister of the Tokugawa shogunate; the highest-ranked political advisor and assistant to the Tokugawa shogunate. He ranked above council members of elders [State] (*roju*). He was chosen from among hereditary feudal lords. 江戸幕府の最高の役職名．将軍に助言し，補佐した．老中の上に置かれ，譜代大名から選ばれた．⇨大名(譜代大名) / 老中

たうえ【田植え】 rice-planting; rice-trans-planting; transplantation of rice seedlings (from the nursery beds to the rice fields [wet paddy-field]). This rice-planting is done during the raining season in June [from mid-June to mid-July]. 苗床から田んぼ[水田]に苗木を植える．6月[6月中旬から7月中旬]の梅雨時期に行う．¶田植え歌 a rice-planting song. 田植え祭り a rice-planting festival. 田植え機 a mechanical rice-planter; a rice-planting tractor. 田植え時 the rice-planting season. ⇨案山子 / 苗 / 苗床 / 早乙女 / 田んぼ / 田の神

たか【鷹】〔鳥〕a hawk; a vulture(禿鷹)；a falcon(鷹狩りの). タカ目の鳥．⇨はやぶさ．¶鷹狩 falconry. 鷹匠 a falconer(鷹を飼いならし，将軍・大名の鷹狩に従った人)

たかおさんひわたりさい【高尾山火渡り祭】 the Fire-Crossing Rite at Mt. Takao.（3月）．⇨付記(1)「日本の祭り」

たかげた【高下駄】 (a pair of) high wooden *geta*[clogs]; (a pair of) wooden clogs with high supports[lifts]. 歯の高い下駄．☆舞妓さんが履く高下駄は「おこぼ」という．⇨下駄

たかさご【高砂】 a Noh chant[song] for a wedding ceremony; a Noh song of twin pine trees at Takasago — symbolic of a happy devoted old couple — chanted at a wedding. 相思相愛の幸せな夫婦[老翁と老婦]をとり合わせた能楽の歌．婚礼で歌う．☆兵庫県の高砂の浦には相互にしがみつくツインの老木(twin pine trees clinging to each other) がある．古来高砂の「尾上の松」(名木)として知られる．世阿弥(1363-1443)が能楽『高砂』を作った．

だがし【駄菓子】popular cheap sweets [cakes, confectioneries]. ¶駄菓子屋 a cheap candy store; an old-fashioned penny candy store (selling popular cheap sweets).

たかしまだ【高島田】 the *takashimada* hair-style for unmarried women. It features an elevated hair knot with the chignon worn up and arched back. The side locks are rounded out with ornaments added. This coiffure developed during the Edo period and was popular in the Meiji period. Today it is worn by a bride wearing a *kimono* in full dress in a traditional Japanese wedding. 未婚女性用の日本式髪型. 髷の根を高くもちあげ, 背後に曲げて結った束髪. 側面の髪の束は丸味を帯び, 装飾品をつけている. この髪型は江戸時代に進展し, 明治時代に流行った. 現代では伝統的な和式結婚時に正装した着物姿の花嫁が結っている. ⇨島田(髷) / 角隠し

たかな【高菜】〔植物〕 leaf mustard; Chinese mustard. アブラナ科の二年草. からし菜の一種. 葉・茎には辛味と風味がある. 漬物に調理する.

たかのつめ【鷹の爪】〔植物〕 a red pepper; a cayenne pepper(トウガラシの実). ナス科トウガラシ属. トウガラシの一品種. 実を干してからつくる粉末は辛みの強い香辛料. ⇨とうがらし

たかはりちょうちん【高張提灯】 a big paper lantern hung high on a long pole. 長い竿の先に高くとりつけた提灯. ⇨提灯

たかまがはら【高天原】 the High Plain of Heaven; the heavenly home of the gods in Japanese Shinto mythology. 古代の日本伝承で, 天照大神が支配し, 神々が住む天上界 (celestial dwelling place).

たかまきえ【高蒔絵】 an embossed gilt lacquer; a raised lacquerwork. 漆でもり上げ, その上に金蒔仕上げを施す. ⇨蒔絵

たかまくら【高枕】 a high pillow. It is used by women wearing a Japanese traditional hairdo. 高く作った枕. 日本髪の型くずれがないように女性が用いる.

たかまつづかこふん【高松塚古墳】 Takamatsuzuka Burial Mound[Tomb] (located in Asuka, Nara Prefecture). 白鳳時代〔7世紀〕の装飾古墳. 1972年, 奈良県明日香村にて発見. ⇨古墳

たかやままつり【高山祭り】 Takayama Spring Festival of Hie Shrine in Takamaya. (April 14-15)(岐阜県: 日枝神社); Ta-kayama Autumn Festival of Hachimangu Shrine in Takayama. (October 9-10) (岐阜県:八幡宮). ⇨付記(1)「日本の祭り」

たかゆか【高床】 an elevated floor; a floor elevated[raised] above the ground level. ¶**高床式神殿** a shrine on stilts; an elevated floor shrine; a shrine built on the floor elevated above the ground level. **高床式建築** a house on stilts; an elevated-floor structure[construction]; a structure built on the floor elevated above the ground level.

たからくじ【宝くじ】 a good-luck lottery; ⊛ a lottery; a public lottery with winning tickets redeemable for cash. 当せん金付証票のあるくじ. ¶**宝くじ運のよい**[悪い]**人** a lucky[unlucky] person in a public lottery. **1等の宝くじに当たる** win the first prize on a public lottery. 宝くじの当たり券 a winning lottery ticket. 前後賞を合わせて3億円が当たる Combined with the prizes for numbers before and after the first prize, the purchasers[buyers] can win up 300 million yen.

【宝くじ番号】 lottery numbers.「1[2, 3]等」1st[2nd, 3rd] prize.「1等の組違い賞」1st prize number in different groups.「1等の1字違い賞」missed-by-a-digit in 1st prize.「05組」group 05.「下3ケタ901」last three digits of 901.「下1ケタ2」last one digit 2.「前後賞」secondary prizes awarded to those whose tickets come within one digit of the winning number.

【関連語】『全国自治宝くじ』All-Japan Lottery.『5種・ブロック宝くじ』Five Block Lotteries:「東京都宝くじ」the Tokyo Metropolitan District Lottery.「地域医療等振興自治宝くじ(栃木県発売)」the Local Medical Care Promotion Lottery (issued by Tochigi Prefecture).「近畿宝くじ」the Kinki Lottery.「関東・中部・東北自治宝くじ」the Kanto-Chubu-Hokuriku Region

Lottery.「西日本宝くじ」the West Japan Lottery.

『スクラッチ宝くじ』"Scratch" Lottery; a scratch-off lottery ticket; an instant lottery (in which purchasers learn on the spot whether they have won or not at Takarakuji booths). 当たりくじの可否が宝くじ売り場で即座に判明する.

『ロト6宝くじ』Lottery Ticket with "Loto 6" Number in which purchasers can select [specify] their own numbers. 異なる6つの数字を自分で選ぶ宝くじ.

『ナンバーズ宝くじ』"Numbers" Lottery Ticket (in which purchasers can select [specify] their own numbers).

たからぶね【宝船】❶〈宝を積む船〉a treasure ship; a ship loaded with treasure.
❷〈七福神を乗せる船〉a picture of a treasure ship loaded with the Seven Deities of Good Luck (called *shichifukujin*). It is believed that a picture of a treasure ship placed under the pillow on January 1st (or 2nd) will ensure the first dream of the new year to be happy one. 七福神を乗せた帆かけ船の絵. 元日(または正月2日)の夜, この絵を枕の下に敷いてみる初夢は幸福を呼ぶと信じられた. ⇨七福神 / 初夢

宝船〈七福神〉

たき【滝】 falls; a waterfall; a cascade(別れ小滝); a cataract(大滝). ¶那智滝(和歌山

県) the Nachi Falls. 滝が見られる高千穂峡(宮崎県) Takachiho Gorge with beautiful cascades. 滝壺 the basin of a waterfall; the plunge pool of falls. ⇨瀑布

たきあわせ【炊き合わせ】assorted simmered foods; (a dish of) fish and vegetables each cooked separately, and then mixed together in a bowl. 魚や野菜などを別々に煮て, その後一つの器に盛り合せた煮物. 関東では「煮物」ともいう. ⇨煮物

たきぎのう【薪能】〔能楽〕an open-air torchlight[firelight] Noh performance; a Noh play performed by torchlight[firelight] on an outdoor stage. The Noh drama is performed outdoors at night by the light of bonfires[by firelight] at temples and shrines such as Kofukuji Temple in Nara and Heian Shrine in Kyoto. 夜間に松明の明かり近くで行う野外能. 奈良の興福寺や京都の平安神宮などの寺社で行う.

たきこみごはん【炊き込み御飯】 Japanese-style pilaf; rice seasoned with *shoyu*[soy sauce] and boiled with vegetables, and seafood or meat. Rice is cooked with various ingredients such as chicken thighs, burdocks, *shiitake* mushrooms, devil's tongues, depending on the season. 野菜(ゴボウやシイタケなど)や肉(鶏肉)または魚介類など季節に合わせた具を入れて醤油で味つけして炊いたご飯. ⇨筍御飯 / 鶏飯 / 松茸御飯

たくあん【沢庵】 *takuan*; yellow pickled *daikon*[Japanese radish]; *daikon* pickled yellow in salt and rice bran. *Takuan* is a dried *daikon*[radish] made yellow by putting into a barrel and sprinkling with salt and rice bran. Heavy weights (usually stones) are put on top of a wooden tub. It is so named after Takuan, a Buddhist priest, who invented it in the 17th century. 干し大根をたるに入れ, 食塩と米糠をまいて漬け

込み，たるの上に重しを置いて黄色くつくるもの．17世紀に発明した沢庵和尚の名に因んだ名称．「沢庵漬け」の略．「たくわん」「おしんこ」ともいう．¶**沢庵巻き** pickled *daikon*[radish] and rice rolled in dried laver.「おしんこ巻き」ともいう．

たくはいびん【宅配便】〈荷物を配達すること〉a door-to-door parcel delivery service; a home parcel delivery service：〈配達した荷物〉a home-delivered parcel; a parcel sent through a home delivery service. ☆「翌日配達[配送]」は next-day delivery; overnight delivery. ⇨クール宅急便

たくはつ【托鉢】 religious mendicancy(物乞い)．Buddhist monks go around houses asking[begging] for alms. 僧が鉢を持って家々を回り，経を唱えながら施し物を受ける．¶**托鉢僧** a mendicant monk; a begging bonze.

たけ【竹】〔植物〕(a) bamboo. イネ科の常緑多年草．若芽の 筍 は春の食用．⇨たけのこ ¶**竹の葉** a bamboo stem. **竹の節** a bamboo joint. **竹籠** a bamboo basket. **竹ぼうき** a bamboo broom. **竹楊枝** a bamboo toothpick. **竹竿** a bamboo pole[rod]. **竹筒** a hollow bamboo tube[container]. **竹箸** (a pair of) bamboo chopsticks. **竹笛** a bamboo whistle[flute]. **竹槍** a bamboo spear. **竹ひご** a thin bamboo stick. **竹藪** a bamboo grove[thicket]. **竹細工** a bamboo craft; bamboo work. **竹枕** a bamboo pillow [headrest]. **竹簾** a bamboo blind. ⇨簾． **竹製蒸し器** a wood and bamboo steamer; steamer made of wood and bamboo.

【竹串】 a bamboo skewer. It is used for barbecuing chopped chicken and vegetables, or broiling eel. 鶏肉や野菜を焼いたり，あるいは鰻を焼いたりするのに用いる．

【竹の皮】 a bamboo sheath; a dried sheath of bamboo stripped from a young bamboo culm. A thin strip of this bamboo sheath is used for wrapping[packing] foods (such as rice balls, minced meat, etc.). 竹のクルム［茎］からはいだ竹の鞘を干したもの．食物（握り飯や刻み肉など）を包むのに用いる．☆ culm「クルム；節のある中空の茎」．¶**竹の皮で包んだ握り飯** rice balls wrapped[packed] in a bamboo sheath.

【竹蜻蛉】 a bamboo-copter; a dragonfly-shaped[helicopter-like] bamboo flying toy; a toy helicopter made of bamboo rotor blades[with a rotary wing]. トンボ型[ヘリ型]の竹製の飛ばして遊ぶ玩具．

【竹馬】(a pair of) Japanese walking stilts; (a pair of) narrow wooden boards attached to two bamboo poles. People[Children] stand on the boards and walk on stilts, holding the upper ends of the bamboo poles in each hand. 一対の狭い木製の板を2本の竹竿につけてつくる．両手のそれぞれで竹竿の上端を握って板に乗って歩く．¶**竹馬に乗る** walk on stilts.

たけ[～だけ]【～岳】 Mountain; Mount; Mt. ☆ mountainは山名の後につける．Mount と Mt. は山名の前につける．¶**谷川岳**(群馬県) Mt. Tanigawa; Mount Tanigawa(dake); Tanigawa(dake) Mountain. ⇨山 / 峠 / 丘 / 坂

たけきりえ【竹伐会】 the Bamboo-Cutting Ceremony of Kurama Temple. (6月)．⇨付記(1)「日本の祭り」

たけしまりょうゆうけんもんだい【竹島領有権問題】the issue of territorial claim to the Takeshima Islands; the territorial dispute over the Takeshima Islands. ☆「竹島周辺海域」the waters around the Takeshima Islands.

たけとりものがたり【竹取物語】 the Bamboo Cutter's Tale; the Tale of Bamboo Cutter, the oldest Japanese folktale of an old bamboo-cutter and his Moon Princess.

平安時代の伝奇作品. 竹取の翁と美女かぐや姫に関する日本最古の物語. 作者・成立年未詳.

たけのこ【筍・竹の子】 a bamboo shoot; a bamboo sprout. ⇨若竹煮. ¶干し筍 dried bamboo shoots[sprouts].

〔料理〕筍煮 bamboo shoots cooked with *wakame* seaweed. 筍御飯 rice boiled with sliced bamboo shoots and *shoyu*[soy sauce].

たこ【蛸】〔動物〕an octopus(複 octopi, octopuses); a devilfish. タコ目の軟体動物の総称. 刺身, すし種, 酢の物などに用いる. ☆octopus はギリシア語で「8 本足を持つもの」の意. ¶蛸壺 an octopus trap[pot]. ゆで蛸 a boiled octopus. 酢蛸 a boiled octopus marinated in vinegar.

【蛸焼き】 *takoyaki*; griddle-cooked octopus dumplings[small balls] (wrapped in dough).*Takoyaki*, spherical dumplings, are made up of wheat-flour batter cooked on a griddle with bits[pieces] of octopus, green onion and ginger. *Takoyaki* dumplings are often eaten with a spicy sauce and dried bonito shavings. 小麦粉の衣でつくる球状団子に, 小片 (small pieces) の蛸, ネギまたはショウガなどを入れて鉄板で丸く焼いたもの. スパイスのきいたソースをつけて鰹節をふりかけて食べる場合が多い.

たこ【凧】 a kite (with a long stabilizing tail of paper). Japanese kites are made with Japanese paper glued on a bamboo framework. These kites are often painted with pictures of animals or human figures, or with designs indicating good fortune drawn on the surface with Japanese writing. These kites can be displayed in the home as decorations as well. (安定させる長い尾のついた)凧. 竹の骨組みに和紙をはり, 表面には動物や人物の図柄または日本語の文字入りで縁起のよい図柄が描かれ

ている. 屋内に飾り物としても置かれる. ¶凧糸 a kite string; a string[twine] for a kite. 凧の尾 a kite tail. 凧合戦 a kite-flying battle[contest]. 民芸凧 a folkcraft kite. 凧をあげる fly a kite; drive a kite skyward by the power of the wind. 凧をおろす bring down a kite; draw[reel] in a kite. 凧の糸をゆるめる let out a kite.

【凧揚げ】 (an outdoor game of) kite-flying. Kite-flying is enjoyed at almost any time of the year, but especially during the New Year season. It was formerly done to pray for children's happiness in the future. 年中いつでも楽しめるが特に正月期間中に凧揚げをする. 昔(江戸時代)は子供たちの明日の幸福を願って行われた.

【凧市】 a kite fair. The kites with many shapes and sizes are sold at the fair. ☆角形 (rectangular), 六角形 (hexagonal), 菱形 (diamond-shaped; lozenge-shaped)などの凧がある.

だし【出し】 *dashi*; stock (used in making soup); fish broth (used as cooking base). (スープを作る)出し汁 (soup stock). (料理の下味に用いる)魚の煮出し汁. 「出し汁」の略. ¶煮干の出し dried small fish[sardine] stock; stock made with small fish[sardine]. 鶏がらの出し chicken stock; stock made from chicken bones. 鰹節の出し汁 dried bonito stock; stock made from dried bonito(通称, 日本料理での「出し」「煮出し汁」をさす). 一番[二番]出し the primary[secondary] stock. 出しを取る make[prepare] stock (for soup). 出しの素 powdered instant stock[broth] (available on the market). (市場で販売されている). 出し汁の材料 ingredients of basic stock[broth]. (鰹節や昆布などの素材)

〔料理〕出し汁 stock[fish broth] (made of [flavored with] dried bonito and kelp)(鰹節と昆布からとる「煮出し汁」). 出し雑

魚 boiled and dried small sardines(used in making *miso* soup stock). 出し巻き卵 omelet(te) roll; rolled omelet(te) mixed with stock, *mirin*[sweetened *sake*], sugar and salt.

【出し昆布】 dried kelp[tangle] for making (soup) stock; dried kelp used to make (soup) stock. 煮出し汁を作るための昆布. ☆「昆布出し」(昆布で作った出し汁)は kelp stock; stock made with kelp.

だし【山車】 a festival float; a festival wheeled float (drawn during the festival parade). A festival float with a variety of colorful decorations is drawn around by people dressed in gay costumes during the festival parade. 多彩に装飾された祭事の車. 祭りの行列があるとき着飾った人々によってひき回される. ☆日本三大山車祭 the Three Biggest Festival Floats in Japan. 祇園祭[京都府]・秩父夜祭[埼玉県]・飛騨高山祭[岐阜県]. ¶巡行用の山車 a parade festival floats.

だしがら【出し殻】 〈茶の〉used tea leaves; 〈コーヒーの〉(coffee) grounds.

だしもの【出し物】〔歌舞伎〕a program[英 programme] of a kabuki drama; a kabuki performance. ¶国立劇場での主な出し物 the highlight[principal feature] of the program at the National Theater. ⇨時代物／世話物／所作事[舞踊劇]

だじょうかん【太政官】⇨だいじょうかん

だじょうだいじん【太政大臣】⇨だいじょうだいじん

たしんきょう【多神教】polytheism; polytheistic religion. ⇨一神教

たすき【襷】a cord for tucking up the sleeves of a *kimono*; a cord used for holding up tucked *kimono* sleeves. It is passed over the shoulders and under the armpits while crossing at the back to tuck up the sleeves of a *kimono*. たくしあげた着物の袖をとめ

るために結ぶひも. 着物の袖をたくしあげるために背中で交差しながら肩から脇の下へ通す. ¶襷をかける tuck up the sleeves of a *kimono* with a cord.

だだいこ【大太鼓】〈雅楽〉 (a pair of) big ceremonial drums (used on the gagaku stage). 雅楽で用いる儀式用の太鼓. ☆公式の雅楽では一対の大太鼓(「太陽」〈the sun〉と「月」〈the moon〉を表象する)が使用される. ⇨雅楽／和太鼓

たたき【叩き・敲き】 ❶〈料理法〉mincing; chopping. 包丁などで細かく刻むこと：〔魚〕minced[chopped] fish[meat]. 魚・肉などを細かくたたいた料理.
〔料理〕牛肉のたたき minced[chopped] raw beef. アジのたたき minced[chopped] raw horse mackerel.
❷〈料理物〉 lightly roasted and sliced raw fish; lightly grilled on the outer surface and chopped slices of raw fish. (カツオなど)表面を軽くあぶった刺身(の料理).
〔料理〕カツオのたたき lightly roasted and sliced bonito (served with onions or other pungent herbs).

たたみ【畳】 a *tatami* (複 *tatami*(s))；a *tatami* mat (used as floor covering of a Japanese-style room). A *tatami* is made of hard-packed, sewn straw. The mat surface is covered with tightly woven rushes, with the borders hemmed with decorative black or green cloth. One *tatami* mat measures about 90×180cm. (和室の床中に敷くために用いる)マット. 乾燥したわらを重ねて固めながら縫った敷物. その上にはイグサ (rush grasses)でかたく編んだ畳表をかぶせ, 装飾を兼ねた黒や緑の布で縁取ったへりがある. 畳1枚は約90cm×180cm (90 ×180 centimeters in size).
¶畳敷きの部屋 a *tatami*-floored room. 四畳半の部屋 a four-and-a-half mat room. 6畳[8畳]の部屋 a six-mat[an eight-

mat] room. 畳表(おもて) the *tatami* mat facing; the surface of a *tatami* mat; *tatami* facing made of wooden rushes. 畳べり[畳の縁(へり)] the border of a *tatami* mat. 畳糸 the *tatami* thread; the thread to stitch *tatami* mat facing or borders. 畳針 a *tatami* needle. 畳目(畳表の編み目) the mesh of a *tatami* mat. 畳屋〈人〉a *tatami* dealer; a *tatami* maker[weaver];〈店〉*tatami* store[shop]. 畳を敷く lay a *tatami* mat (in the room); cover (a room) with a *tatami* mat. 畳を替える recover[renew] a *tatami* mat; install[put in] new *tatami*s.

たたみいわし【畳鰯】young sardines packed in a (paper-like) sheet; sardine[anchovy] fry dried together in a (paper-like) sheet. 小イワシ[カタクチイワシ]の稚魚を薄板状に干した食品. ☆適度にあぶると酒のツマミに最適.

たち【太刀】〈刀〉a **katana**; a sword(used by a *samurai*). ☆刃渡りの長さは60cm以上. ¶太刀懸け Japanese sword rack (for holding a long one over a short one). 太刀先 the tip of a sword. 太刀銘 sword signature. 太刀捌(さば)き swordplay; swordsmanship. ⇨刀

たちあい【立ち合い】 the *tachiai*;〔相撲〕the initial charge (at the beginning of a bout to fight); the precise moment of starting up to fight (from the center *shikiri* line). Both *sumo* wrestlers jump up from a crouching position with their fists touching the center *shikiri* line simultaneously at the start of the bout. 二人の力士が試合開始と同時に仕切り線から立ち上がること, またその瞬間.

たちうお【太刀魚】〔魚〕㊺ a cutlass fish; ㊧ a hairtail; a scabbard fish. タチウオ科の硬骨魚. 夏が旬. 淡白な白身魚なので刺身や酢の物またから揚げなどに調理する.

たちぐい【立ち食い】 a stand-up meal(立食). ¶立ち食いをする take a stand-up meal; eat (food) standing. 立ち食い寿司 a stand-up *sushi* bar[counter]. ☆「すしを立ち食いする」eat *sushi* standing (at the bar [counter]). 立ち食い蕎麦 a stand-up *soba* noodle stall[counter]. ☆「そばを立ち食いする」eat *soba* noodles standing (at the stall[counter]).

たちとり【太刀取り】 ❶〈介錯(かいしゃく)〉an assistant at *harakiri*; a second at *seppuku*. 切腹のとき介錯する人. ⇨切腹 / 介錯.
❷〈刑場にて〉an executioner (in the ancient times). 昔, 刑場で死刑囚の首を切る人.
❸〔相撲〕⇨太刀持ち❶

たちのみ【立ち飲み】 stand-up drinking (at a stall[counter]). ⇨立ち食い. ¶立ち飲み酒場 a stand-up bar serving *sake* or alcoholic beverages. ☆「立ち飲みする」drink *sake* standing (at the bar[counter]).

たちばな【橘】〔植物〕a citrus (tree); a mandarin orange (tree). ミカン科の常緑小高木. 果皮は薬用また香料用.「みかん」「柑子(こうじ)」の古名. ⇨みかん

たちまわり【立ち回り】〔歌舞伎〕a mock fighting (in a kabuki play); a fight scene (played in a very stylized fashion, similar to dancing). 舞台上で乱闘や斬り合いをする擬闘.

たちもち【太刀持ち】❶〔相撲〕a sword-bearer; a sword carrier. He bears[carries] a sword and accompanies a *yokozuna* who enters to perform the formal ring-entering ceremony preceding *makuuchi*-division bouts. 幕内の取組に先立って行う横綱の土俵入りのとき, 太刀を持って同件する力士. ⇨土俵入り
❷〈小姓〉a page who carries his lord's sword at a *samurai* house. 武家で主君の刀を持って付きそった少年.

たちやく【立ち役】〔歌舞伎〕❶〈女役・子役に対する男役〉the male roles (in a kabuki play);〈女形に対する男優〉actors playing male roles (in a kabuki play) (as opposed to actors playing female roles); 〈男役［男優］の主演者〉the male protagonist (in a kabuki play); the principal male role (in a kabuki play).

❷〈善人になる男役〉the role of a good [virtuous] man (in a kabuki play); 〈敵役に対する善人の男優〉an actor playing the role of a good man (in a kabuki play) (as opposed to an actor playing an enemy role).

だちょう【駝鳥】〔鳥〕an ostrich. ¶駝鳥の卵 an ostrich egg.

だちん【駄賃】 a reward; a tip. 労力に対する報酬.

たつ【竜・辰】〔動物〕a dragon. ⇨竜

たつ【辰】 the Dragon, one[the fifth] of the 12 animals of the Chinese zodiac. 十二支の第五. ⇨十二支. ¶辰の方 the Direction of the Dragon[east-southeast]. 方角の名. ほぼ東南東. 辰の刻 the Hour of the Dragon [7-9 a.m.] 午前8時頃（およびその前後約1時間）. 辰年 the Year of the Dragon. 辰年生まれ (be) born in the Year of the Dragon.

だつあにゅうおう【脱亜入欧】 Out of Asia and Into Europe.（標語）

だつあろん【脱亜論】 the Leaving Asia Theory; the theory of de-Asianization.

たづくり【田作り】〔料理〕small dried sardines[anchovies] (simmered in *shoyu* [soy sauce] and sugar). Dried small sardines are often served as one of the New Year's dishes because sardines are used as a fertilizer which brings a good harvest. カタクチイワシの幼魚を乾燥させた加工品で，醤油と砂糖で煮つめた食品. イワシは耕地の肥料に適し豊作に効果があることから穀物の豊作を願って御節料理の一品として用いる. 関西では「たつくり」ともいう. 通称「ごまめ」. ⇨ごまめ / 御節料理

だつサラ【脱サラ】 a corporate dropout[refugee]; a self-employed person who starts business after a salaried position. ¶脱サラ志向 the desire to set oneself free from being an office worker; the wish to quit the life of a white-collar worker.

たつたあげ【竜田揚げ】 fish (or chicken) marinated in *shoyu*[soy sauce] and deep-fried; deep-fried fish(or chicken) coated in potato starch[seasoned flour] and marinated in *shoyu* and *mirin*[sweetened *sake*]. 魚または鶏肉を醤油と味醂で下味をつけてから片栗粉［味つけした粉］でまぶし，油で揚げたもの.

〔料理〕鶏肉の竜田揚げ deep-fried chicken coated in potato starch and marinated in *shoyu* and *mirin*.

たつのおとしご【竜の落とし子】〔魚〕a sea horse. ヨウジウオ科の硬骨魚. 「うみうま」「かいば」ともいう.

たで【蓼】〔植物〕a knotweed; a smartweed; a water pepper. タデ科の一年草(ヤナギタデ). 葉に辛味があり，薬味や刺身のツマに用いる. ¶蓼酢 vinegar mixed with mashed knotweed leaves; vinegar mixed with ground water pepper leaves. ☆アユなどの川魚の塩焼きに添える.

たてあな(しき)じゅうきょ(あと)【竪穴(式)住居(跡)】(the site of a) pit dwelling [house] in the Jomon period. 縄文時代の一般住居. ☆「竪穴式石室」a pit-style stone burial chamber.

たてうりじゅうたく【建売住宅】 ready-made houses; houses built for sale; houses in the housing development; ㊍ speculative-built houses.

たてがき【縦書き】 vertical writing; the system to write vertically[in columns] (from right to left). ⇦横書き

たてぎょうじ【立行司】 the top[senior] *sumo* referee; the highest-ranking *sumo* referee who administers[officiates] the *yokozuna*'s bouts. 相撲の行司の中で最高位の人で，横綱試合を行司する. ⇨行司

たてまえとほんね【建前と本音】 official stand and actual aim; facade intention and real intention; facade truth and real truth.

だてまき【伊達巻】 ❶〈帯〉an under-sash; a narrow sash (worn by women around the waist under an *obi*). 女性が帯の下にしめる，幅のせまい帯. ❷〔料理〕a rolled fish-paste omelet(te); a sweet rolled omelette mixed with fish paste; a fish-paste omelet rolled up and cut into slices. It is traditionally served as one of New Year's dishes. 魚肉のすり身をまぜた卵の厚焼きを巻いたもの. 御節料理の一品として用いる. 「伊達巻たまご」の略. ⇨厚焼卵

たてみつ【縦褌】 the crotch[vertical part] of a *sumo* wrestler's loincloth[belt]. まわしの股(の部分). ⇨前褌

だとつぶ【打突部】〈剣道〉predesignated parts of hitting. ⇨剣道
【関連語】「胴」(chest). 「小手」(forearm). 「面」(face). 「突」(throat).

たどん【炭団】 a small round charcoal briquette(te)[ball]. 炭の粉を球状に練り固めた燃料.

たなだ【棚田】terraced (slope of) paddy [rice] fields (extending down a mountainside like a staircase). ¶水田の棚田 terraced rice fields. 例石川県の千枚田

たなばた【七夕】 the Tanabata Festival; the Star Festival (observed on July 7, or in some areas on August 7). The Star Festival is based on a Chinese legend of two stars in love: Vega (or the Weaver Star) and Altair (or the Cowherd Star). Two stars resided on opposite sides of the Milky Way, but were allowed to meet just once a year on the evening of July 7th. Praying for this happy reunion in the Milky Way on this evening, people celebrate this romantic festival. 七夕祭りは相愛するベガ星(織女星)とアルタイ星(牽牛星)に関する中国伝来のもの. 2星は天の川の反対に住んでいるのだが，年に一度だけ7月7日には会うことが許された. 天の川での幸せな再会を祈願して，当日の晩に人々はこのロマンチックな祭りを祝う. 「七夕祭り」の略. ⇨天の川 / 牽牛 / 織女 / 色紙 / 吹流し / 短冊. ¶七夕送り the casting[floating] of the Tanabata bamboo decorations into the river or the sea.

【七夕祭り】 the Star Festival (held on July 7 all over Japan, except on August 6-8 in Sendai City). This Star Festival features a large number of huge colorful, gorgeous streamers that decorate the main street of the city. People display decorative bamboo branches with long, narrow strips of colored paper inscribing their wishes.

たに[～だに]【谷・渓】 a valley (盆地状の谷); a gorge(峡谷); a ravine(渓谷). ⇨峡谷. ¶大涌谷(神奈川県) (the) Owaku-dani Boiling Valley. ⇨渓 / 渓谷 / 峡谷 / 峡

たにくみおどり【谷汲踊り】 the Drum-Beating-Dance Festival. (2月). ⇨付記(1)「日本の祭り」

たにし【田螺】〔貝〕a mud snail; a river snail; a pond snail; a paddy shell. タニシ科の淡水産巻き貝の総称. 多くは水田にすむ. 下煮をしてから和え物や味噌汁などの食用にする.

たにまち【谷町】〔相撲〕the patrons[backers] of a *sumo* wrestler. 力士の後援者[支援者]たち.

たにんどん【他人丼】(a bowl of) rice topped with pork and eggs; (a bowl of) rice cooked with meat other than chicken and eggs on top. 豚肉[鶏肉以外の肉]と卵をのせたご飯

（の丼物）. ☆ chicken と egg は「親子（丼）」だが pork と egg は「他人（丼）」である.

たぬき【狸】〔動物〕a *tanuki*; a raccoon dog. イヌ科の哺乳動物. 剛毛は毛筆用. 毛皮は防寒用. 信楽焼

〔料理〕**狸汁** raccoon dog's meat *miso* soup; *miso* soup cooked with raccoon dog meat and vegetables. 狸肉と野菜で料理したみそ汁. ☆狸肉の代わりにコンニャクを用いる場合もある. *miso* soup cooked with vegetables and *konnyaku*[devil's-tongue jelly].

たぬきそば[うどん]【狸そば[うどん]】 (a bowl of) buckwheat noodles[wheat noodles] in hot fish broth topped with crispy crumbs[crusts] of deep-fried *tempura* batter and some greens. (関東)掛けそば[うどん]に揚げ玉（天かす）と青物を加えたそば[うどん]. ☆関西では「油揚げ」(deep-fried *tofu*[bean curd]) を加える. ⇨掛けうどん[そば] / 揚げ玉 / きつねうどん[そば]

たね【種】 a seed（植物・果実の）; a stone[㊍ pit]（梅・桃・サクランボなど果実の堅核の）; a pip（林檎・蜜柑などの）. ¶種芋 a seed potato. 種油 rape (seed) oil.

たのかみ【田の神】 the god of the field; the god that protects rice field and brings bumper rice crops. 田を守り, 米の豊作をもたらす神.

たび【足袋】 (a pair of) *tabi*; (a pair of) Japanese-style split-toed socks; Japanese-style socks with the toes split into two parts. *Tabi* are made with a split[cleft] between the big toe and the others[the other four toes]. They are fastened on the inner ankle with (three or four) tiny metal clasps (*kohaze*). They are made of cotton or silk, and often worn with *geta*[wooden clogs] and a *kimono*. 足の指が二つに分かれた靴下, 親指と他の指との間には割れ目が付いている. 足首の開き[合わせ目]を（3個または4個の）小さな金具の「小鉤」

(hooks: 爪形の留め具)で留める. 足袋は綿製か絹製で, 和装して下駄を履くときに着用することが多い. ⇨下駄 /小鉤

ダフや【ダフ屋】 ㊍ a (ticket) scalper; ㊎ a ticket tout; a ticket sold on the black market. ☆「だふ」は札の隠語.

ダブルスクール族 students attending two schools at the same time; daytime students who attend technical school[another college] at night to prepare themselves for their jobs after graduation.

たべほうだいのレストラン【食べ放題のレストラン】 an all-you-can-eat restaurant. ☆「千円, 食べ放題」（掲示） All you can eat for ¥1000.「温室[果樹園]内のイチゴ[ブドウ]は食べ放題である」You can eat as many strawberries[grapes] in the greenhouse[orchard] as you like. ⇨飲み放題の酒場

たまがき【玉垣】 the fence around a Shinto shrine (enclosing the oratory and the shrine hall).

たまぐし【玉串】 a sprig[twig, branch] of the sacred *sakaki*[cleyera] tree draped with white strips of paper[cloth]. The sprigs of the sacred *sasaki* tree dedicated to the Shinto gods are used by Shinto priests in Shinto rites. 紙[布]を垂らしている榊の枝. 神前にそなえる玉串は神主が神事に用いる. ⇨榊. ¶玉串奉納 offering a sprig of the sacred *sakaki* tree to a Shinto god in front of a shrine altar. 玉串料 monetary offering dedicated to the Shinto gods; money offering made for Shinto rites[ceremonies].

たまご【卵】 an egg; a roe（魚の体内の卵; はらご）; a spat（貝, 特にカキの）; a seed（イセエビ, 蚕など）; spawn（鮭が産んだ卵）. ¶ゆで卵 hard-boiled egg. 半熟卵 soft-boiled egg. いり卵 scrambled egg. 落とし卵 poached egg. 溶き卵 beaten egg.

生卵 raw egg. 地卵 locally produced egg; eggs of local production. 卵殻 egg shell. ゆで卵立て eggcup.

たまご【玉子】(卵を調理した料理名)〈寿司〉sweet egg custard; sweet omelet[英] omelette].

〔料理〕 **玉子豆腐** steamed egg custard; steamed pudding-like egg; egg cooked in the form of *tofu*[bean curd]. **玉子綴じ** egg soup; hot dish cooked with beaten eggs and vegetables. **玉子綴じうどん[そば]** wheat noodles[buckwheat noodles] cooked in fish broth with *shoyu*[soy sauce], served with egg soup.

【玉子丼】 an egg bowl; (a bowl of) rice topped with eggs and onions, simmered in *shoyu*[soy sauce]. It is usually served with pickles. 醤油で煮た, 卵と玉ねぎをのせたご飯(の丼). 通常漬物を添える. 「玉丼」ともいう.

【玉子巻き】 vinegared rice rolled up in a thick slice of sweetened omelet with various ingredients (mushrooms, dried gourd, greens, etc.) in the center. いろいろな具材(椎茸・干瓢・青物野菜など)を入れて厚焼き卵で巻いたすし.

【玉子焼き】 a sweetened and soy-flavored omelet; an egg fried in layers mixed[seasoned] with *shoyu*[soy sauce], sugar and *mirin*[sweetened *sake*]. 甘醤油で風味をつけたオムレツ. 醤油・砂糖・味醂を混ぜて層にして焼いた卵.

たまござけ【卵酒】 a *sake* eggnog[flip]; hot *sake* containing beaten egg and sugar. ☆風邪に効くといわれる.

たまごっち *Tamagotchi*; a palm-size electronic game; a high-technique-raising toy.

たますだれ【玉簾】 a bead blind[curtain]; a blind decorated with beads. 玉で飾った簾. 「すだれ」の美称.

たませせり【玉せせり】 the Ball-Catching

Festival. (1月) ⇨付記(1)「日本の祭り」

たまたれぐうおによ【玉垂宮鬼夜】 the Demon-Chasing Rite. (1月). ⇨付記(1)「日本の祭り」

たまねぎ【玉葱】〔植物〕an onion; a common onion. ユリ科の二年草. 多様な料理に適した食材. ¶玉葱の皮 peels[coats] of an onion; an onion skin

たまのこし【玉の輿】❶〈乗り物〉a bejeweled palanquin; a palanquin for the nobility. 玉で飾った輿. 貴人用.

❷〈結婚〉a woman marrying into wealth; a woman's marriage to a wealthy[rich] man[man of high status]; a Cinderella story. 裕福な[地位のある]男と結ばれる女性の結婚. ⇨逆玉の輿

たまむし【玉虫】〔虫〕a (two-striped green) buprestid; a jewel beetle. タマムシ科の甲虫.

たまり(じょうゆ)【溜り(醤油)】 ⇨醤油

たもと【袂】 a (*kimono*) sleeve; a (*kimono*) sleeve-pocket.

たゆう【太夫・大夫】 ❶〔文楽〕a narrator [reciter; chanter] of a *Joruri* performance. He narrates[recites; chants]the story-line and the lines for each character in the play to the accompaniment of *shamisen*. A single *tayu* speaks on behalf of all puppets on the stage – men, women, and children. 浄瑠璃の語り手. 三味線の伴奏に合わせ物語の筋また上演する各役割の台詞を語る. 太夫は1人で舞台上の人形全員に代わって男子・女子・子供の台詞を語る.

❷〔能楽〕an actor qualified to play the protagonist in a Noh play; the headmaster of a school of Noh performance; the headmaster of a school of Noh play. 主役になり得る有資格者. 能楽の家元.

❸〔歌舞伎〕a (the highest-ranking) female-role actor in a kabuki play. 女形役者の最上位者.

た

❹〈最上位の遊女〉a courtesan of the highest rank（花魁）.

たら【鱈[国字]】〔魚〕 a cod（⊛ cod(s)）; a codfish; a haddock; a whiting（小型）. タラ科の硬骨魚. ちり鍋や寄せ鍋には最適. ¶塩ダラ salted cod. 干ダラ dried cod. ⇨棒鱈

〔料理〕鱈ちり codfish stew; a hot-pot meal of codfish and vegetables; a codfish and vegetables boiled in a hot pot and served with seasoned vinegar. タラと野菜で料理したちり鍋. ⇨ちり（鍋）

たらこ【鱈子】❶〈鱈の卵〉cod roe. ❷〈食用〉salted pollack roe. 鱈の腹子. 特にスケトウダラの卵を塩漬けにした食品. ⇨すけとうだら／明太子

たらばがに【鱈場蟹】〔甲〕 a king crab. ☆北洋の海にすむ大型のかに（an Alaskan king crab）で, 鱈[タラ]の漁場でとれるのでこの名がある. 刺身やカニちりなどには最適. ⇨かに

たりきほんがん【他力本願】 salvation[justification] by faith (in the benevolence of Amida Buddha).（阿弥陀の寛容に対する）信仰による救済. ⇔自力本願

たる【樽】 a cask（酒樽）; a barrel（大型）; a keg（小型）. 【関連語】「樽板」a stave.「栓」a bung.「たが」a hoop. ¶樽酒 casked [barreled] *sake*; *sake* in a cask[barrel]. 樽柿 persimmon mellowed in a *sake* cask（酒樽で熟した柿）. 樽神輿 a portable shrine made of a *sake* cask[barrel].

だるま【達磨】❶〈達磨大師〉Bodhidharma (Daruma Daishi). He is a Zen Buddhist priest from India who went to China in the 6th century. He sat cross-legged for nine years in meditation to attain enlightenment, but afterwards he is said to have lost the use of his legs. インドの仏僧で, 6世紀に中国に渡り, 中国禅宗を開山する.（晩年少林寺にて）9年間座禅姿で瞑想の末悟りを開く (He continued meditating in a sitting position for nine years to awaken to the truth.) が, その後足が使えなくなったといわれる. ☆現在, 禅宗は臨済宗, 曹洞宗, 黄檗宗が存続. ⇨禅宗

❷〈縁起物の達磨人形〉a limbless *daruma* doll; a self-righting *daruma* doll without limbs[without arms or legs] in the shape of Daruma Daishi. *Daruma* is a tumbling red papier-mâché figure of a *daruma* doll with a weighted bottom. It is considered a good-luck charm for achievement because it always returns to an upright position whenever it is tipped over[pushed over]. 達磨大師の姿にかたどった手足のない自動復元する人形. 底に錘を入れてあり (a *daruma* doll that is weighted at[on] the bottom), 転がる赤い張り子の人形. 傾けて[倒して]も必ず起き上がるので目的の成就祈願の縁起物とされている. ☆江戸時代, 中国から伝来する.「赤い衣装」(a red robe) は邪気を払うという俗信がある. ☆『七転び八起き』the ups and downs of life. Life is full of ups and downs. People try to get this daruma doll in the hope that they can rise[get up] again eight times even if they may fall down seven times. ¶開運出世の縁起物としての達磨人形 the *daruma* doll used as a good-luck charm for promoting better fortune. People paint in only one (left) eye of a daruma effigy first, and then paint[brush] in the other (right) eye when their wishes have come true. 最初に片目（左目）だけに描き入れ, 開運成就後にもう片目（右目）に描き込む.

【達磨市】 an annual *daruma* doll fair [market]. *Daruma* dolls of all sizes and good-luck decorations are sold at open-air street stalls. Many people buy *daruma* dolls during the New Year season in the hope of a new year of happiness and prosperity. 大小様々な達磨人形や飾物が露店で売られる．新しい年に幸福と繁栄をもたらすよう正月期に達磨を買う人が多い．☆「日本三大だるま市」は全国最大の「毘沙門天祭だるま市」(静岡県・2月上旬)，「深大寺だるま市」(東京都調布市・3月3・4日)，「高崎だるま市」(群馬県・1月6・7日)．

だるまストーブ【達磨ストーブ】a potbellied stove.

たれ【垂れ】❶〈調味料〉sauce; basting sauce [soy-tasted sauce] (蒲焼などにつける調味料)；gravy(肉汁を用いたソース). *Tare* (sauce) is made of *shoyu*[soy sauce], *mirin* [sweetened *sake*], sugar, salt and other seasonings. It is often used for grilled meat [chicken] or boiled fish[eel]. 醤油，味醂，砂糖，塩などで味つけたもの．鶏肉や魚[鰻]を焼くのに用いる調味料．¶鰻の垂れ a sauce for broiled eels.

❷〈剣道〉 waist-groin[thigh] protectors; a shirt of padded cloth to protect the groin. ⇨剣道

タロいも【タロ芋】〔植物〕a taro. (⓿ taros). サトイモ科の多年草．☆taroはポリネシア語. ⇨さといも

たわし【束子】〈床の〉a scrub(bing) brush;〈台所の〉a kitchen brush; a pot cleaner. ⇨へちま

たわら【俵】❶ a straw bag. ¶米俵 a straw ricebag. 俵枕 a handy pillow shaped like a straw ricebag. 米俵型の枕.

❷〔相撲〕bales of rice straw (half-buried in the clay of the *sumo* ring (*dohyō*)). ⇨土俵

たん【反】❶〈反物〉a *tan*; a roll of cloth. 反物の長さの単位．約10.6m.

❷〈土地〉a *tan*; an acreage. 土地の面積．約992㎡；300坪.

だん【段】❶〈階層；重なりの一つ〉a tier; a layer's deck. ☆tiered「段々に積んだ」. ¶4段式の滝(袋田の滝・茨城県) a waterfall

falling from four cascading tiers; a four-tiered cascading waterfall. ⇨瀑布. **5段重ね重箱** a five-tiered set of lacquered boxes for cooked food.

❷〈階段〉a step (of the stairs). ¶本殿まで50の石段 (go up) 50 stone steps to the main shrine.

❸〈武道・剣道・碁・将棋などの等級〉a *dan*; a grade. ¶剣道5段 the fifth *dan* in[at] *kendo*;〈人〉a *kendo*-player of the fifth grade. 柔道5段 the fifth *dan* in[at] *judo*;〈人〉a judoist of the fifth grade. ⇨柔道

たんか【短歌】a *tanka* (poem); a 31-syllable Japanese poem; a Japanese poem of 31 syllables. A short poem consists of 31 syllables arranged in five lines with the 5-7-5-7-7 pattern syllables. A *tanka* is structured in a two-part form with the first part in 5-7-5 and the second part in 7 and 7. 31音節から成る和歌の一形式．5音・7音・5音・7音・7音の5句からなる和歌．前半部の5-7-5と後半部の7-7の2部で構成される．☆7世紀初頭に完成する．その原型は「万葉集」にある．俳句のような「季語」(season word) はなく自由に詠む (compose a *tanka*). ⇨万葉集 / 古今和歌集 / 季語

だんか【檀家】 a *danka*. 〈家族〉family belonging to a specific temple;〈人〉a Buddhist parishioner; an adherent of a Buddhist temple; a supporting member[a supporter] of a specific Buddhist temple. Buddhist parishioners belong to a specific temple and give financial support to it. Funerals and Buddhist memorial services are held by Buddhist priests of the *danka* family. 特定の寺に所属し，布施などをする家族または信徒．葬儀や法要などは檀那寺の僧侶が行う．☆徳川幕府はキリスト教の禁止令を出したとき，各家族は仏教に帰依し特定の寺に帰属するとする「檀家制度」を設けた．寺の檀家は「神社の氏子」

に相当する. ⇨氏子. ☆ parishioner「教区民」, 欧米における教区[教区民]（教区教会 (parish church)と教区司祭 (parish priest)をもつ宗教上の区域）に所属する信徒.

だんがい【断崖】 a precipice; a cliff; a bluff. ⇨絶壁. ¶**断崖絶壁** a sheer cliff[precipice]; a precipitous (walls of) cliff.

だんかいのせだい【団塊の世代】 the baby-boom generation; the boomer generation. ¶**団塊の世代の人** the baby-boomers. **団塊の世代の高齢化** the graying of the baby-boomers. **団塊世代退職** the retirement of the baby-boomer generation.

だんきだん【暖気団】 a warm air mass. ⇨寒気団

だんきゅう【段丘】 a terrace. ¶**河岸段丘** a river terrace. **海岸段丘** a marine terrace.

たんけん【短剣】 a short sword; a dagger(合口); a stiletto(小剣).

だんご【団子】❶ dumplings; rice-flour round dumplings. Rice-flour round dumplings are small balls steamed[boiled] with rice flour and water. Dumplings can be glazed with sweet bean paste (*anko*) or soy sauce (*shoyu*), and are sometimes rolled in yellow soybean flour (*kinako*). 「米粉」を水でこね, 蒸して[茹でて]つくる食品[菓子]. 餡子または醤油, 時には黄粉でまぶす. ☆「米粒」からつくるのは「餅」(rice cake). ⇨ 月見団子 / みたらし団子 / 焼き団子
❷〈団子状のもの〉 a ball; a ball-shaped object; a small round object. 団子に似た形. ¶**肉団子** a meatball.
❸〔貝〕 a scallop. ホタテ貝をさす. すし屋の隠語. ⇨帆立貝

だんごう（**にゅうさつ**）【談合（入札）】 (make) a rigged bid (for the contract); (make) an illegal price-fixing agreement (for the contract).

たんごのせっく【端午の節句】〈こどもの日〉 the Boys' Festival; the Iris Festival; the Feast of Irises; the Sweet Flag Festival. ☆「端」は「初め」,「午」は「旧暦の5月」で, 奈良・平安時代に中国から伝来した. ⇨節句 / こどもの日 / 五月人形

たんざく【短冊】「冊」は文字を書く紙の意.
❶〈七夕・風鈴〉 (a long narrow rectangular piece of) thin fancy paper used for writing letters[Chinese characters] on. It is hung by a thread from bamboo branches during the Star Festival or suspended by a string from the clapper in a wind-bell. 文字[漢字]を書く薄紙(細長い長方形の紙). 七夕祭りで竹の枝から紐で吊るす. または風鈴の舌から紐でぶら下げる.
❷〈短歌〉 (a long narrow oblong multicolored strip of) thick fancy paper used for writing a Japanese poem[a *tanka* or *haiku*] on. It is usually hung on a pole[pillar] in the Japanese-style room. 日本の詩[短歌・俳句]を書くのに用いる極上の厚紙(細長い長方形の多彩な紙). 和室の柱などにかける. ⇨短歌 / 俳句

たんさくちたい【単作地帯】 a single-crop area; a one-crop area. ⇦二毛作地帯

だんじょこようきかいきんとうほう【男女雇用機会均等法】 (enactment of) the Equal Employment Opportunity Law For Men and Women. (1985年成立)

たんしんふにん【単身赴任】 a job transfer [work] away from home; a single posting transfer[leaving for one's new post alone] without one's family; going to a distant post[a foreign country] unaccompanied by one's family. ¶**単身赴任者** a business bachelor.

たんす【箪笥】〈整理だんす〉a chest; a chest of drawers;〈洋服だんす〉a dresser; a wardrobe. Some traditional chest for storing *kimono* are made of paulownia wood to protect[keep] the *kimono* from humidity. 着物収納用の箪笥は湿気から守

た

ために桐の木材で作られる. ¶**重ね箪笥** a double chest of drawers. **桐箪笥** a chest of drawers made of paulownia wood; a paulownia-wood chest of drawers. ⇨茶箪笥 / 薬箪笥 / 仙台箪笥 / 和箪笥

たんすいぎょ【淡水魚】〔魚〕a freshwater fish. ⇔鹹水魚

たんぜん【丹前】a padded large-size *kimono*; a cotton-quilted *kimono*[robe]; a thick padded *kimono*-shaped gown. It is worn for warmth and relaxation in midwinter at home. It is often worn over a simple cotton *kimono* by overnight guests after taking a bath at Japanese inns in winter. 綿入れの広袖の着物. 冬の室内防寒用. 冬季には旅館の宿泊客が風呂上がりに着物の上に着ることが多い.「どてら」ともいう. ⇨どてら

だんそんじょひ【男尊女卑】(the) predominance [domination] of men over women. 女性に対する男性の優越主義. ☆(the) male chauvinism (男尊); (the) subjection of women (女卑). ¶**男尊女卑の社会** male-dominated society

だんだんばたけ【段々畑】terraced fields [farms]; farming terraces. ⇨棚田

だんちぞく【団地族】dwellers in a housing development; dwellers in modern apartments; residents of the Housing Corporation apartments (in the late 1950s and the early 1960s).

たんちょうづる【丹頂鶴】a Japanese crane; a (Japanese) red-crested white crane. ツル科の大形の鳥. 全身が純白で, 頭頂は赤い. ¶**特別天然記念物に指定された丹頂鶴の生息地**(北海道・釧路湿原) the habitat of red-crested white cranes designated as a special natural monument[a special protected species] (in Kushiro-Shitsugen, the largest marshland in Japan). ⇨つる

たんでん【炭田】a coalfield. ¶**石狩炭田**(北海道) Ishikari coalfield.

たんとう【短刀】a short sword (without a hand guard); a dagger(合口). 鍔のない短い刀.「短剣」ともいう.

だんぱつしき【断髪式】the ceremonial shearing of a *sumo* wrestler's topknot upon retirement; the *sumo* wrestler's retirement ceremony highlighted by the shearing [cutting-off] of his topknot. 力士の引退にともなう髷を切る儀式.

たんぼ【田圃】a rice field; a paddy field (水田). ¶**田圃道** a path[lane] through rice fields.

たんぽぽ【蒲公英】〔植物〕a dandelion. キク科の多年草. 花と葉は食用. ゆがいて水にさらしてから浸し物や和え物に用いる. 花はワインやビールの原料.

だんまり【黙り】「だまり」の転. ❶〈無言劇〉a dumb show.
❷〔歌舞伎〕a pantomime in a kabuki play. Kabuki players search blindly or fight in the dark without saying a word. 歌舞伎で二人以上の登場人物が暗闇の中で無言でさぐり合う, またからみ合う動作, あるいはその場面.

たんもの【反物】〈呉服・着物の織物〉cloth for a *kimono*; (textile) fabrics for a *kimono*; ⑱ dry[soft] goods; ⑲ drapery.

だんりゅう【暖流】a warm current. ⇨寒流

ち

ちいき【地域】an area (地方); a district (行政上の区画); a region (地理・社会・文化の地方); a zone(地帯). ⇨地方. ¶**農業地域** an agricultural district. **地域格差** regional differences[disparities].

ちがいだな【違い棚】staggered shelves (built in the side-alcove of a Japanese-style living room). Art objects are often displayed on decorative shelves of different levels. 和室

にある床の間の脇にある（上下・左右）段違いの飾りの棚．芸術品(works of art)などが展示されることが多い．⇨座敷 / 床脇棚

ちかてつサリンじけん【地下鉄サリン事件】the Tokyo Subway Sarin Gas Attack; the Sarin Gas Attack on the Tokyo Subway System.　⇨付記 (2)「日本の歴史年表」（1995年）

ちからうどん【力饂飩】　(a bowl of) wheat-noodle soup containing a piece of rice cake; (a bowl of) wheat-noodle soup with a piece of rice cake on it; (a bowl of) wheat noodles cooked in fish broth seasoned with *shoyu*[soy sauce] and topped with a piece of rice cake. 餅入りのうどん．醤油で味つけした魚の煮出し汁で調理し，その上に一切れの餅をのせたうどん．

ちからがみ【力紙】〔相撲〕　power paper; (a sheet of) paper used by a *sumo* wrestler to wipe his lip (after rinsing out his mouth before a bout). （力士が口をゆすいだ後に）唇を拭く紙．⇨化粧紙

ちからみず【力水】〔相撲〕　power water; (a ladle of) purifying water used by a *sumo* wrestler to rinse his mouth before a bout. A *sumo* wrestler ceremonially rinses out his mouth with purifying water prior to a bout and raises his fighting spirit in the arena. This is an act of ritual purification. Stepping out of the ring into their corners, each wrestler (who has just entered the ring) receives a ladle of water from a *sumo* wrestler (who won the previous bout or will fight in the bout following). 力士が取組前に力をつけるために口にふくむ水．一種の清めの儀式．土俵を出てその隅で，（土俵に上がった）力士が（前の取組の勝者または次の取組で戦う）力士から柄杓で水を受けとる．☆負けた力士は力水をつけることはできない．⇨化粧水

ちかん【痴漢】　a (sexual) molester （性的に淫らな行為をする者）; a groper （人混みで身体に触る人）; a masher （女性の尻を追う人）; a rapist （暴行魔）; a flasher （露出狂）. ¶痴漢の疑い suspicion of grouping a lady[girl] on a train[bus].

ちぎ【千木】　two crossbeams on the gable of a Shinto shrine; two ornamental crossed boards extending above the gabled roof of a Shinto shrine. 神社にある切妻屋根の棟（むね）の両端に交差して組み合わせた長い二本の飾り木．

ちぎょ【稚魚】　fry; the young fish; fingerling （さけ・ますなどの）. 卵からかえった魚．¶サケの稚魚 salmon fingerling[fry]. ⇦成魚

ちぎょう【知行】　the lordship over land; the right to govern an area of land and to enjoy the wealth coming as an advantageous result (in the feudal times). 土地の統治権．（封建時代）土地を支配し，そこから利益となる財産を享受する権利．☆「ちこう」と読めば「知識と行い；道理に従って行うこと」の意．

ちくぜんに【筑前煮】　*chikuzen*-style stew of chicken and vegetables; chopped chicken meat (or fish) and vegetables braised[fried and boiled down] in broth. 鶏肉と野菜の炒め煮（油で炒めてからとろ火で煮る）.「炒り鶏」ともいう．☆鶏肉の代わりに魚（鯉など）を用いることもある．

ちくわ【竹輪】　a hollow cylindrical fish sausage; a hollow bamboo-shaped fish-paste cake (of cod or shark). It is steamed and then broiled over a fire in the shape of a bamboo. It is usually sliced into rings when served. 円筒状に［中が空洞な竹筒形に］魚肉（鱈または鮫）をすりつぶした食品．竹の輪に似せて蒸してから火で焼く(roasted). 通常は輪型に切って出される．⇨蒲鉾

ちくわぶ【竹輪麩】　a hollow cylindrical [bamboo-shaped] roll of steamed wheat-

ち

ち

flour dough; a tubular roll of boiled wheat-flour dough. 小麦粉を水と練り合わせ竹輪型に入れて蒸しあげた食品. ☆おでんの種に用いる.

ちご【稚児】❶〈子供・乳児〉a child; an infant; boys or girls.

❷〈祭事の子供〉a child attendant in a traditional festival procession (who masquerades as a heavenly being at festivals of shrines and temples). 神社や寺院の催しの行列に着飾って加わる子供.

【稚児髷】❶〈昔の子供の髪型〉a traditional hairstyle[coiffure] worn by children in feudal times.

❷〈祭事の子供の髪型〉a hairstyle[coiffure] worn by children[girls] in traditional festival procession.

【稚児行列】 a festival parade of children [boys or girls] dressed in celestial costumes. 天童の衣服をまとった子供たちの祭事行列.

ちしま(れっとう)【千島(列島)】 the Kuril(e) Islands; the Kuril(e)s. ¶**千島海峡** the Kuril(e) Strait. **千島海流** the Kuril(e) Current. **千島火山帯** the Kuril(e) Volcanic Zone.

ちしゃ[ちさ]【萵苣】〔植物〕(a) lettuce. キク科の一年草・二年草. 別名「サラダ菜」

ちそかいせい【地租改正】 a land-tax reform. This reform was enforced to secure tax revenue in 1873. It imposed a three-percent tax on land price and forced the owners to pay cash. 財政収入を安定させるための租税制度改革. 税率を地価の3%として所有者に現金で納めさせる.(1873年公布)

ちちおやごろし【父親殺し】 patricide. ⇨母親殺し

ちちぶよまつり【秩父夜祭】 the Chichibu Night Festival. (12月). ⇨付記(1)「日本の祭り」

ちデジ(ほうそう)【地デジ(放送)】 digital terrestrial TV broadcasting airwaves; terrestrial digital TV broadcasting airwaves. ☆「地上波デジタル放送」の略.

ちとせあめ【千歳飴】 a longevity candy; (a pack of) a slender stick-shaped[long cane-shaped] candy colored in red and white. The candy with red and white swirls is wrapped in a richly-decorated long bag. It is distributed[given] to children of 7, 5, and 3 years of age on the *Shichigosan* Festival. The candy (having the blessings of gods) is said to bring children a long and happy life for many years. 紅白に染めた長い棒状の飴. 赤と白の渦巻きのある飴は長い飾り袋に包んである. 飴は七五三祝いの時に3歳・5歳・7歳の子供に配られる. 千歳飴(天恵を有する)は長年にわたり子供の幸福な人生を招くといわれる. ⇨七五三

ちはや【千早】 ⇨巫女

ちほう【地方】 a region(大地方); a district (中地方); an area(小地方). ⇨地域. ¶**関西地方** the Kansai region[district]. **京都地方** the Kyoto area.

ちまき【粽】 a steamed rice cake[dumpling] wrapped in bamboo leaves. It is traditionally made[eaten] as a good-luck bringer on Boys' Festival (May 5). 笹の葉で包んで蒸した餅. 端午の節句(こどものChildren's Day)に縁起物としてつくる[食べる].

ちゃ【茶】❶〔植物〕a tea plant[bush]; a tea tree(茶の木); a tea leaf(茶の葉). ツバキ科の常緑低木. ¶**茶畑** a tea plantation; tea bushes. **茶摘み** tea-picking; picking the new leaves of tea bushes. **茶所**(ちゃどころ) a tea-growing district.

❷〔飲料〕 (a cup of) tea. ¶**緑茶** green tea. ⇨緑茶. **濃茶** strong tea. **薄茶** weak tea. **粉茶** dust tea. **茶殻** used tea leaves. ⇨抹茶 / 緑茶(玉露・煎茶・番茶) / 玄米茶 / 昆布茶 / 焙茶 / 麦茶

❸〈茶の湯〉a tea ceremony; a tea cult. ⇨
茶道

【茶入れ】a ceremonial tea caddy[canister]. It is a ceramic receptacle[container] with a lid for (keeping) the thick powdered green tea (*koi-cha*) used in the tea ceremony. It is often kept in a silk bag[pouch] (*shifuku*). 抹茶を入れる蓋付きの茶器. 仕覆に保管することが多い. ☆「薄茶」用の茶器は「棗」などという. ⇨仕覆 / 棗

【茶会】 a tea party; a tea ceremony party; (hold) a simple gathering for the service of tea; (preside over)a simple party serving ceremonial tea to guests invited for the occasions. 客を招いて茶を供するだけの簡素な集まり. ⇨茶事 / 点前

【茶懐石】 a simple tea meal served before [during] a tea ceremony. Light tea meal consists of fresh, seasonal and carefully prepared foods. 茶道の前[間]に出る簡素な食事. 献立は新鮮な季節物を丁寧に料理した軽食. ⇨懐石料理

【茶掛け】a hanging scroll in the tea ceremony room; a hanging scroll of paintings and calligraphic works displayed in the alcove of a tea ceremony room. 茶室の床の間にかける書画の掛け物, 掛軸.

【茶菓子】❶〈茶道での菓子〉Japanese sweets served with foamy green tea in the tea ceremony. 「茶菓」ともいう. ⇨干菓子(薄茶)/ 主菓子[生菓子](濃茶). ❷〈茶にそえる菓子〉cakes served with tea.

【茶釜】 a ceremonial teakettle; a kettle used for boiling water in the tea ceremony.

【茶気】 knowledge of the tea ceremony. 茶道の心得のこと. ☆「袱紗」「懐紙」「扇子」「楊枝」の4点は必携品. 茶菓子が出される場合は持参する「懐紙」と「楊枝」を用いる.

【茶器】 a tea set[service] (一組の茶器) ; tea-things (茶道具一般の総称).

【茶巾】 a ceremonial tea cloth[napkin];

a small piece of white linen[cotton] used for wiping wet bowls[utensils] in the tea ceremony. 茶の湯で, 茶碗などを拭く麻布[木綿]巾.

【茶漉し】 a tea strainer (used in the tea ceremony). 茶がらをこす道具.

【茶事】 a full tea presentation with a meal; a formal tea party serving ceremonial tea with a meal to guests. 食事を伴う正式の茶の湯の会. ⇨茶会 / 点前

【茶室】〈小屋〉a tea arbor[hut]; 〈家屋〉a tea house; 〈部屋〉a tea-ceremony room. *Chashitsu* is a small building[room] designed for serving the ceremonial tea. There is a sunken square hearth fitted into the *tatami*-mat floor where an iron teakettle is placed. 茶の湯を出すための小さな建物[部屋]. 畳敷きの床に固定した正方形の掘り炉床があり, 鉄製の茶釜が置かれている. ⇨数奇屋 / 茶室

☆『茶室における主な設備』「四畳半の部屋」 four-and-a-half mat room. ⇨四畳半の茶室. 「点前畳」host's *tatami* mat. 「客畳」 guests' *tatami* mat.「踏み込み畳」entrance *tatami* mat. 「床前畳」*tatami* mat for viewing the alcove. 「炉畳」*tatami* mat for placing the fire-pit. 「炉」fire-pit; a sunken hearth. 「釜」kettle; teakettle. 「床の間」alcove. 「茶花」flower arrangement suitable for the season.「掛け軸」hanging scroll suitable for the season. 「茶道口」 host's entrance. 「躙口」crawling-through entrance for guests. ⇨にじり口. 「風炉先屏風」folding screen used to fence the tea ceremony place.

【茶渋】tea stains (in the tea cup); tea incrustations (in the tea bowl). 茶碗などにつく, 茶の煎じ汁のあか. ☆「茶渋のついた茶碗」は a tea-stained cup.

【茶杓】 ❶〈茶匙〉a (bamboo) tea scoop [spoon]; a spoon-like utensil for scooping

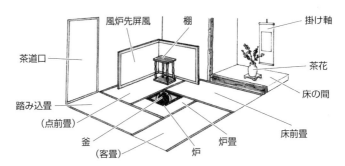

風炉先屏風　棚　掛け軸

茶道口

茶花

踏み込畳
（点前畳）

床の間

釜
（客畳）

炉畳

床前畳

炉

out powdered tea from a tea caddy to a tea bowl in the tea ceremony. 茶入れ［棗］から茶碗へ抹茶をすくい出す小さなさじ.
❷〈茶柄杓〉a tea ladle[dipper]; a dipper for ladling out hot water from a teakettle to a tea bowl in the tea ceremony. 茶釜から茶碗へお湯をくみ出すひしゃく.
【茶人】❶〈茶道の達人〉a tea master; an expert in the tea ceremony.
❷〈風流人〉a tea-cult devotee; a devotee of the tea cult; a person of refined taste.
【茶席】a tearoom proper（茶室）; the place where a tea ceremony is being performed. 茶会の座席. ⇨茶室
【茶筅】 a bamboo tea whisk; a tea whisk [stirrer] made of split bamboo (used to mix and whip ceremonial tea into froth). *Chasen* is a split bamboo utensil used for whisking[stirring] a mixture of ceremonial powdered green tea and hot water into froth. 茶道用の抹茶に湯を注ぎ, かき回して泡をたてる竹製の茶道具.
【茶筅通し】 the cleaning of a tea whisk in a tea bowl. 茶碗の中で茶筅を洗うこと.
【茶棚】a tea shelf; a shelf for tea things.
【茶箪笥】 a tea utensils cupboard; a tea cabinet; a cupboard[cabinet] used for storing tea utensils.
【茶筒】 a tea jar[canister, caddy]; a container for preserving tea leaves.

【茶壷】a tea urn; a tea jar.
【茶庭】 a tea (house) garden; a small landscape garden adjacent to a tea-ceremony room. The participants pass through the garden to enter a tea-ceremony room[hut]. There are usually stone lanterns, stepping stones and a stone washbasin as well as slightly-high stone for stepping up to the tea-ceremony room[hut]. 茶室に隣接した小さな造景庭園. 参加者は茶室に入るために茶庭を通る. そこには踏石［茶室に踏み入るための少々高めの石］だけでなく石灯籠, 飛び石, 蹲などがある.「露地」ともいう. ⇨露地
【茶道具】 (a set of) ceremonial tea utensils; (a set of) utensils used for the tea ceremony. ☆『茶室にある設備品』「抹茶」powdered green tea.「懐紙」paper napkin.「袱紗」silk cloth.「茶釜」teakettle.「釜の蓋」teakettle lid.「柄杓」ladle[dipper].「棗［薄茶器］」lacquered tea caddy.「水指」cold water container.「棚」utensil stand.「蓋置」lid rest.「風炉」portable hearth.「茶碗」tea bowl.「茶杓」tea scoop.「茶筅」(tea)whisk.「茶巾」tea cloth.「水こぼし」waste-water bowl.
【茶庭】 ⇨茶庭
【茶の湯】 the tea ceremony; the traditional Japanese way[art] of serving tea. ⇨茶道
【茶花】 a simple flower arrangement for

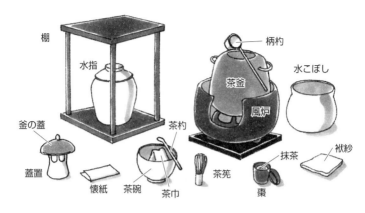

棚 / 水指 / 柄杓 / 水こぼし / 茶釜 / 風炉 / 釜の蓋 / 茶杓 / 袱紗 / 蓋置 / 抹茶 / 茶筅 / 懐紙 / 茶碗 / 茶巾 / 棗

ち

the tearoom. A simple flower is often only a bud. 茶室用の簡素な活け花. つぼみの花を用いる場合が多い.

ちゃがゆ【茶粥】　tea gruel; rice gruel [porridge] boiled with tea.　⇨かゆ

ちゃきんずし【茶巾鮨】　egg-wrapped *sushi*[vinegared rice]; *sushi* mixed with seafood and vegetables and wrapped in a thin omelet crepe, tied with a ribbon of *kanpyo*[dried gourd]. 魚介類や野菜を混ぜた鮨(五目鮨)を薄焼き卵 (a thin layer of omelet)で(茶巾のように)包み, 干瓢で結んだもの.「袱紗鮨」ともいう.　⇨五目ずし

ちゃくしょくりょう【着色料】　a colorant; a coloring agent. ¶人工着色料含有〈食品表示〉Contains artificial colorants.

ちゃくしんおん【着信音】　an incoming cell-phone tone[ring tone]; a sound of an incoming call (on the mobile phone).

チャグチャグうまコ【チャグチャグ馬コ】　the Horse-Parade Festival. (6月).　⇨付記(1)「日本の祭り」

ちゃくふく【着服】embezzlement; embezzling money (from one's company).

ちゃくメロ【着メロ】　a phone[ring tone] melody; a melody[tune] signaling a ringing melody[tune] for incoming calls;

an incoming cell-phone call[ring melody]; a musical ringing tune on the mobile phone.

ちゃそば【茶そば】　buckwheat noodles flavored with green tea. Noodles are served on a bamboo rack in a square lacquered frame. 乾燥した挽き茶の粉を混ぜ, 風味をつけて打ったそば. 漆塗りの正方形の枠のある竹の簀(敷物)に盛られる.

ちゃたく【茶托】　a teacup saucer; a saucer for a teacup (usually made of lacquered wood). 湯飲み茶碗をのせる受け皿. 通常は漆塗りの木製である.

ちゃどう【茶道】　⇨茶道

ちゃづけ【茶漬け】　(a bowl of) boiled rice with hot green tea poured over it. *Chazuke* [*O-chazuke*] is a simple meal made by pouring hot green tea over rice in a bowl and adding a garnish of salted salmon or pickled plum, together with a dab of *wasabi*[Japanese horseradish]. ご飯に熱い緑茶をかけた簡素な食事で, 少しのわさびといっしょに鮭または梅などの添え物を加える.「お茶漬け」ともいう.　⇨梅干茶漬け/鮭茶漬け/うな茶漬け/のり茶漬け

ちゃのま【茶の間】　a living room[㊑ sitting room] of a Japanese-style house.

ちゃばこ【茶箱】 a tea chest[wooden box] (used for keeping tea leaves).

ちゃばしら【茶柱】 a tea stalk (floating vertically in one's tea)

ちゃぱつ【茶髪】 brown-dyed hair; hair dyed brown[blond]; butterscotch hair.

ちゃぶだい【卓袱台】 a low collapsible dining table; a low folding tea table. 折りたたみ式の食卓[茶卓].

ちゃほうじ【茶焙じ】 a tea heater; a tea firer. 葉茶を火にかけてあぶる道具.

ちゃみせ【茶店】〈掛け茶屋〉 a teahouse (where tea and refreshments are served); a tea shop. ⇨茶屋❶

ちゃめし【茶飯】 ❶ rice cooked[boiled] in tea with salt. 茶の汁に塩気を加えて炊いた飯.

❷ rice cooked with *shoyu*[soy sauce] and *sake*. 醤油と酒を加えて炊いた飯.

ちゃや【茶屋】 ❶〈茶を売る店〉a tea store[shop];〈人〉a tea dealer. ⇨茶店

❷〔茶道〕 a tea-ceremony room[house]. 茶室の部屋.

❸〈待合い〉a high-class Japanese-style restaurant where guests[customers] are entertained by *geishas* with refreshments and amusements. 芸者を呼んで顧客に飲食・遊興させる店. 通称「お茶屋」. ☆「御座敷」と呼ばれる部屋を数箇所設けてある. ⇨置屋 /御座敷 /待合い❷

ちゃりば【茶利場】〔歌舞伎〕〔文楽〕a comical scene (in a kabuki play or in a bunraku puppet show). （歌舞伎や文楽などでの）こっけいな場面、またはこっけいな演技. 「茶利」ともいう.

チャルメラ〈ポルトガル語 charamela〉; a small trumpet-like wooden flute; a street-vendor's flute; a noodle vendor's flute. It is a small flute made of wood with two reeds at the top and seven finger holes in the middle and a brass ring at the bottom. ラッパ[トランペット]に似た木製笛. 夜鳴きそば屋が吹いて歩く笛. 上部に2枚のリード, 中部には7個の指穴, そして下部には真ちゅうの輪がある木管の笛. shawm(ショーム)ともいう.

ちゃわん【茶碗】❶〔茶道〕a ceramic tea bowl (used in the tea ceremony). It is sometimes appreciated for its elegant art object (during the tea cult). 陶器製の湯飲み茶碗. （茶の湯では）時として優雅な芸術品として鑑賞されることがある.

❷〈ご飯用〉a rice bowl; a small bowl used for serving[eating] boiled rice.

❸〈湯飲み用〉a teacup; a small cup used for drinking hot tea.

ちゃわんむし【茶碗蒸し】 *chawanmushi*; steamed egg custard; egg custard with various ingredients steamed in a teacup [bowl]. *Chawanmushi* is a hotchpotch [hodgepodge] dish of egg custard containing various[assorted] ingredients such as chickens, seafoods, sliced fish-paste cakes, *shiitake* mushrooms, ginkgo nuts steamed in a teacup[bowl]. Trefoil leaves are usually put on top as a garnish. 茶碗に多種の具材を入れ, 卵のとき汁といっしょに蒸した料理. 鶏肉, 魚介類, 蒲鉾, 椎茸, 銀杏などを盛り合わせた具にだし汁で溶いた卵を混ぜ入れ, 茶碗ごと蒸した料理. 上には付け合わせ[飾り]に三つ葉を添えることがある.

¶茶碗蒸し碗 a *chawanmushi*[egg custard hotchpotch] teacup[bowl]; a teacup[bowl] used for *chawanmushi* cooking.

ちゃんこ(なべ)【ちゃんこ(鍋)】〔相撲〕*chanko-nabe*; a *sumo* wrestler's hotch-potch dish; a traditional simmering stew meal for *sumo* wrestlers. A variety of foods[seafoods and vegetables, or some-times chicken and beef] are cooked at the table together in soup in a large pan for

professional *sumo* wrestlers. 相撲部屋の
ごった煮料理. 伝統的な煮込みのシチュー
料理. 魚介類や野菜, 時には鶏肉や牛肉の
食材を汁といっしょに大きな鍋に入れなが
ら食卓で料理する.「ちゃんこ料理」ともい
う.

ちゃんちゃんこ a padded sleeveless *kimono*
jacket[vest] (worn in cold season). A red
chanchanko and a red hood are worn by
a sixty-year-old person who reaches his/
her 60th birthday in celebration of his/ her
second life. 綿の入った袖なし羽織. 通常
は寒い頃着用する. 還暦祝いを迎える老人
は赤いちゃんちゃんこと赤い被り物を着用
する. ⇨還暦

ちゃんばら a sword fight[battle] (seen in
samurai movies or theaters).「ちゃんちゃ
んばらばら」の略. ¶**ちゃんばらごっこ** a
sword-fighting game (usually played by
children [mostly boys]). **ちゃんばら映
画** *samurai* movies (with plenty of sword
fights).

ちゃんぽん *champon*; a Chinese-style
hotchpotch dish (of boiled noodles with
various ingredients). A hotchpotch[hodge-
podge] dish containing meat (such as
a fried pork), seafood (such as a squid)
and stir-fried vegetables in a thick sauce
on top of Chinese noodles (originated in
Nagasaki). (雑多な具を入れた麺の)中国式
ごった煮料理. 肉(焼き豚肉など), 魚介類
(イカなど), 炒めた野菜などを濃厚な汁で
煮込み, 中華麺を炒めて混ぜてつくる長崎
の郷土料理.「長崎ちゃんぽん」ともいう.

ちゅうかんし【中間枝】〔華道〕 the supplementary branches (or stems) added to the main
branches (used in a flower arrangement of
the Ohara school). 主枝にとり合わせる補
助的な枝(または茎). 小原流の華道にて用
いる. ⇨あしらい(池坊流) / 従枝(草月流)

ちゅうきち【中吉】 good luck[fate]. ⇨おみ
くじ

ちゅうぐう【中宮】❶〈昔, 皇后の称号〉the
empress;〈昔, 皇后と同格の后〉the second
consort of an emperor.

❷〈昔, 皇后の宮殿〉the palace[residence]
of the empress.

ちゅうげん【中元】❶〈陰暦〉the 15th day of
the seventh month of the lunar calendar.
It falls on the Bon Festival in Japan. It is
the time to offer something to the dead
in appreciation for protection in the Bon
season. 陰暦7月15日. 日本では「盂蘭盆」
の日に当たる. この日は加護に謝意を表し
死者に供え物をする「お盆」の時期である.
☆古代中国では1月15日を「上元」, 7月
15日を「中元」, 10月15日を「下元」と呼び,
道教の祭事 (Taoism ritual) が行われた. 日
本では「中元」が紹介され日本の「盆」と結び
ついた. ⇨盂蘭盆

❷〈中元の進物〉a midsummer gift; a gift-
sending at midyear. *Chugen* is a midyear
present given to express appreciation for
special favors received during the year.
It is customary for the Japanese to send a
midsummer gift to any person to whom
they feel indebted. その年に受けた恩義に
謝意(gratitude)を表すために贈る進物. お
世話になった人へ中元の時期に進物を送る
日本人の習慣. ☆7月初旬から中旬にかけ
て贈る. ⇨歳暮❷

ちゅうこういっかんきょういく【中高一
貫教育】 an educational system integrat-
ing junior and senior high schools; a
comprehensive[combined] junior and
senior high school education.

ちゅうしゅう【中秋】 midautumn; the middle
of autumn[fall]; (the night of) August 15 of
the lunar calendar. 陰暦8月15日の別称. ¶
中秋の名月 the full moon in the middle of
autumn[fall]; the harvest moon. (収穫時の
月). ⇨ 十五夜の月

ち

ちゅうしゅん【仲春】 midspring; the middle of spring; the second month of the lunar calendar. 陰暦2月の別称.

ちゅうじょうせつり【柱状節理】 a columnar joint; a columnar joining; an interlocking column. 柱のような形をした岩石中の割れ目. ¶**柱状節理の岩石** huge rocks formed of columnar joints; a rock formation shaped like large columns. 大きな柱のような形をした岩石. **柱状節理の奇岩怪石の断崖のある渓谷で有名な高千穂峡**（宮崎県）Takachiho Gorge noted for sheer cliffs of columnar joints[rock formations shaped like large columns].

ちゅうしん【忠臣】 a loyal retainer[vassal]; a faithful subject.

ちゅうしんぐら【忠臣蔵】 *Chushingura*; the Treasury of (the Forty-Seven) Loyal Retainers. *Chushingura* (or *Kanadehon Chushingura*), the dramatized story of forty-seven *ronins*[masterless *samurais*], is the general title of kabuki and bunraku plays based on the historical *Ako* Incident of 1703. ⇨赤穂事件 / 四十七士

ちゅうせいしん【忠誠心】 ❶〈主君への〉loyalty[fidelity] to one's lord[master]. ❷〈会社への〉loyalty to one's company; Japanese strong devotion[identification] with one's company.

ちゅうなごん【中納言】 a vice-councillor [vice-minister] of state[the Imperial Court] (ranking below the *daijokan* and after the *dai-nagon*). 国〔朝廷〕の政務次官. 太政官の次官. 大納言の下位. ⇨大納言

ちゅうねんぶとり【中年太り】 a middle-aged spread.

ちゅうハイ【酎ハイ】 *shochu* liquor and soda water. (an alcoholic drink of) *shochu*[distilled liquor] mixed with soda [carbonated] water (or soda pop) with a squeeze of lemon[lime]. 焼酎を炭酸水で割った飲み物. ☆「ハイ」は「ハイボール」(whiskey and soda; ⊛ highball)の略. ⇨焼酎

ちゅうもん【中門】❶〔茶道〕a middle gate; a small gate located between the inner garden (where the tearoom stands) and the outer garden in a tea garden. 茶庭にある内露地（茶室がある）と外露地の間にある出入り口の門.「中くぐり」ともいう. ❷〈寺社の門〉a middle gate; an inner gate of a temple; the gate located between the front gate and the central building in the precincts of a Buddhist temple or Shinto shrine. 寺社の境内にある前門（楼門）と中央建造物（拝殿）の間にある門. ☆寺では通常は仁王像 (statues of the two Deva kings) がある. ⇨仁王（仁王門）

ちょう【蝶】 a butterfly. ⇨蝶々. ¶**蝶ネクタイ** a bow tie.

ちょう【〜朝】〈時代〉a period; an era; an age;〈治世〉a reign;〈王朝〉a dynasty. ¶**平安朝** the Heian period[era]. **明朝** the Ming Dynasty.

ちょうこう【朝貢】 (present) a tribute to the Imperial Court.（外国または諸侯が来朝して）朝廷への貢ぎ物（をたてまつること）. ¶**朝貢国** a tributary (nation).

ちょうこく【彫刻】〈事〉sculpture; engraving;〈物〉a sculpture; an engraving. ¶**彫刻家** a sculptor; an engraver. **彫刻刀** a chisel; an engraving knife.

ちょうざめ【蝶鮫】〔魚〕a sturgeon. チョウザメ科の海水魚で硬骨魚. ⇨さめ. ¶**蝶鮫の腹子** caviar; ⊛ caviare. ☆「キャビア」は蝶鮫の卵巣の塩漬け.

ちょうし【銚子】❶ a *sake* bottle; a *sake* holder; a *sake* decanter. 酒を温めて注ぐための容器.「徳利」ともいう. ⇨徳利. ❷ a *sake* receptacle with a handle and a spout. 柄と注ぎ口のある酒の器. ¶**お銚子（お燗）をつける** warm a *sake* bottle; warm *sake* in a bottle.

ちょうじ【弔辞】 (read) a message of condolence; (write) a letter of sympathy; 〈葬儀の席上で〉(make[give]) a funeral [memorial] address. くやみのことば.「弔詞」「弔文」などともいう.

ちょうしつ【彫漆】 lacquer ware coated in layers with different-colored lacquer. 多彩に厚く漆を塗って彫刻をほどこした漆器.

ちょうじゃばんづけ【長者番付】 a list of the richest[wealthiest] people; a ranked list of the largest income earners[millionaires] (in the past fiscal year).

ちょうじゅいりょうせいど【長寿医療制度】 longevity health care program (for people aged 75 or older).「後期高齢者医療制度」のこと.

ちょうじゅばんづけ【長寿番付】 a ranked list of long-lived people.

ちょうしん【朝臣】 a courtier; (集合的に) the court. (昔の)朝廷に仕える人.「廷臣」ともいう. ⇨公家

ちょうず【手水】「てみず」の音便. ❶ washing face and hands. 手や顔を洗い清めること. ❷ an act of spiritual purification using water before worshipping at a Shinto shrine. 神社で礼拝する前に水を使って心身を清めること. ⇨手水舎

ちょうずばち【手水鉢】㊇ a washbasin; ㊇ a washbowl; a basin[bowl] near a tearoom [privy] for washing hands. (茶室[便所]近くにある)手洗い用の水を入れておく器. ⇨蹲 (茶庭用)

ちょうずや【手水舎】 ⇨手水舎

ちょうせん【朝鮮】 Korea; ① 「南朝鮮」 South Korea[the Republic of Korea] (大韓民国). ② 「北朝鮮」 North Korea[the Democratic People's Republic of Korea [DPRK]]. (朝鮮民主主義人民共和国). ¶ **朝鮮人強制連行** transportation of Koreans for forced labor in Japan during World War

II. **朝鮮進出** the Invasion of Korea. **朝鮮通信使** the Korean Mission to Japan; the Korean goodwill mission to the shogunate.

ちょうそ【彫塑】 carvings and sculptures(彫刻と塑像); the plastic arts (造形美術).

ちょうちょう【蝶々】〔虫〕 a butterfly. 昆虫の一種. ☆ egg (卵) → lava (幼虫) → pupa (さなぎ) → adult (成虫).

【蝶々髷】 a butterfly-shaped hairdo. It is worn by young unmarried lady in feudal times. 封建時代の未婚女性が結った蝶々形の髪型.

ちょうちん【提灯・提燈】a Japanese paper (or silk) lantern (with a candle inside to give light). It is made with a Japanese paper (or silk) covering a bamboo frame. A candle is placed inside for illumination. Various lanterns are used outdoors as indispensable decorations for fairs and festivals as well as for festival floats. 割り竹の輪を骨にして和紙(または絹)の覆いを張って作る (made of a frame of finely split bamboo hoops covered with paper or cloth). 中にはローソクの明かりがある. 多様な提灯は縁日や祭事また山車の飾りには欠かせない. ⇨高張提灯 / 小田原提灯. ¶提灯行列 (hold) a lantern parade[procession]. 提灯持ち a lantern carrier[bearer].

ちょうてい【朝廷】the Imperial Court (where the Emperor administers the government). 天子[君主・天皇]が国の政治をとる場所.

ちょうてき【朝敵】 the emperor's enemy; rebel against the imperial government. 朝廷の敵. 天子に反逆する賊.

ちょうへいれい【徴兵令】 the conscription [㊇ draft] ordinance[law] (issued in 1873). All males 20 years of age and older were forced to serve three years conscription. 満20歳以上の男子は3年間の兵役 (military service)の義務(1873年布告).

ちょうみりょう【調味料】a seasoning; a condiment. ¶化学調味料 a synthetic seasoning (agent); monosodium glutamate [MSG] (グルタミン酸ナトリウム). 調味料を混ぜた食品 food mixed with the seasonings.

ちょうもん【弔問】 a condolence call[visit]; a call[visit] of condolence. ¶弔問客 a caller [visitor] for condolence. 弔問者芳名録 a condolence book. ⇨香典(香典帳)

ちょうようのせっく【重陽の節句】 the Chrysanthemum Festival. 陰暦9月9日の菊の節句. ⇨菊の節句

ちよがみ【千代紙】 Japanese paper with colored figures[patterns] (printed on it). It is used for decorating boxes, wrapping gifts and making dolls or animals. 多彩な模様を色ずりにした和紙. 箱の上張り，贈物の包み，また人形や動物などの折り紙に使う. ⇨折り紙

ちょく【猪口】 ⇨ちょこ /おちょこ

ちょくご【勅語】 Imperial Rescript. ☆皇室や国家の事務に関して口頭で発せられたみことのり. ⇨教育勅語

ちょくし【勅使】 an Imperial messenger [envoy]. 天皇の使者.

ちょくせん【勅宣】 a message[an official letter] from the emperor. 天皇の宣旨[公式書簡].

ちょくせんわかしゅう【勅撰和歌集】 an anthology of Japanese poetry collected [compiled] by Imperial command. 勅令によって編纂した和歌集.

ちょくたい【直態】〔華道〕 the upright style of a flower arrangement (used in the Ikenobo school). 華道で花を直立させた基本花型. ⇨立真型

ちょくれい【勅令】 an Imperial ordinance [decree, command, edict]. 天皇によって発せられた命令. ☆現憲法にはない.

ちょこ【猪口】 a small *sake* cup; a small ceramic cup for pouring[drinking] *sake*. ⇨杯 / 徳利. ¶猪口を干す empty one's

sake cup. 猪口で2杯飲む drink two cups of *sake*. 酒を猪口に注ぐ fill a cup with *sake*.

ちょぼ【チョボ・点】〔歌舞伎〕 *chobo*; the *gidayu* accompaniment in a kabuki play. *Gidayu* narrators and *shamisen* players are seated on an elevated platform at the rear of a kabuki stage. They describe the scene and emotions of the characters of a kabuki play. 歌舞伎で義太夫が語る伴奏. 義太夫の語りと三味線演奏者が歌舞伎舞台の後部に座し，歌舞伎の場面や役者の感情を解説する. ☆チョボの居る場所の床を「チョボ床」(*chobo* platform) という. 「チョボ」の語源は義太夫が目印のため自分の語る部分の詞章に「点」(dots) を打ったのでチョボという.

ちょんまげ【丁髷】〔相撲〕 a Japanese-style topknot (of a Japanese *samurai*). *Chonmage* was a hairstyle worn by men in feudal times according to social rank and occupation. *Samurai* warriors shaved the front and top part of their heads (*sakayaki*) and gathered the rest up in a topknot. Nowadays it is still tied up in a topknot worn by *sumo* wrestlers and actors in *samurai* drama. 封建時代に社会的な地位を表す男子の髪型. 月代(額から頭の中央にかけて(from the forehead to the top)頭髪を剃った部分)をそり，残りの髪で髷を結った. (1871年に廃止). 現在では相撲力士や時代劇の男優が結う髷がある. ⇨髷 / 大銀杏 / 月代. ¶丁髷を結う wear (one's hair in) a topknot.

ちらしずし【散らし鮨】 garnished *sushi* [vinegared rice] (具[つま]を添えたすし); *sushi* dressed with various ingredients〈関東〉topped [〈関西〉mixed] with seafood and omelet-like fried eggs. It is usually served in a shallow wooden bowl[lacquer ware box]. いろいろな具を魚介類や錦糸卵

など〈関東〉を上にのせて [〈関西〉と混ぜ合せて]仕上げるすし. 浅い木製の器[漆器の箱]に盛りつける.

☆《関東》A bowl of sliced fish[seafood], vegetables and omelet-like fried eggs arranged with various ingredients on beds of vinegared rice. 関東では酢飯の上にすし種(魚介・野菜・卵焼きなど)を並べる. 《関西》A bowl of fish[seafood], vegetables and omelet-like fried eggs mixed with vinegared rice. 関西ではすし種を酢飯に混ぜ合わせる.

☆《具材》は酢飯 (vinegared rice)にシイタケ (*shiitake* mushrooms), ごぼう (burdocks), かんぴょう (dried gourd strips), 千切りのニンジン(carrots cut into julienne strips), それに生魚の切り身(sliced raw fish)や錦糸卵(omelet-like fried eggs), 田麩(sweetened mashed fish meat), 海苔 (seaweed laver)などがある.「五目鮨」を指し,「ばら鮨」「混ぜ鮨」などともいう. ⇨五目鮨

ちり(なべ)【ちり(鍋)】a hot-pot meal[stew] of fish and vegetables; a dish of fish boiled with various vegetables in a pot. Fish (mainly codfish or blowfish) are cooked at the table with *tofu*[bean curd] and such vegetables as mushrooms, green onions, Chinese cabbages and others. It is eaten with seasoned citrous sauce and a few condiments (such as grated *daikon*[radish], minced green onions, red pepper, etc.). 魚肉(主にタラまたはフグ)・豆腐・野菜などを鍋で湯通しして, ポン酢や薬味(大根卸し・さらしねぎ, 赤唐辛子など)を入れて食べる鍋料理. ⇨たら(ちり) / ふぐ(ちり)

ちりちょうず【塵手水】〔相撲〕ritual hand clapping (on[in] the *sumo* ring). This act is done to get the attention of gods. This is also a ritual of swearing to fight openly and fairly performed by *sumo* wrestlers before each bout. When the *sumo* wrestlers

enter the ring, they squat on their heels while staring at each other. Then they stomp their feet and clasp their hands twice after rubbing their hands together. They extend their arms and rotate the palms of their hands up towards heaven and down towards earth. 土俵で手を打つ儀式. 神を呼びだす行為. また各取組の前に力士が正々堂々と戦うことを誓う行為 (an act of pledging). 力士は土俵に上がると, 相互に睨みあいながらしゃがむ. それから四股を踏み, 手をこすってから二回柏手を打つ. 腕を広げて両手の手のひらを上下に回転させる. ⇨仕切り / 四股

ちりめん【縮緬】 silk crepe; finely wrinkled fabric of silk. It is used to make *kimono*, *obi*, *furoshiki*, etc. 絹織物の一種. 生糸を用いて平織りに縮ませた織物. 着物, 帯, 風呂敷などを作るのに用いる.

ちりめんじゃこ【縮緬雑魚】boiled and dried small sardines; dried and seasoned young sardines[anchovies]. カタクチイワシの雑魚を煮て干した食品. ⇨白子干し

ちんきん(ぼり)【沈金(彫)】 gold (-inlaid) lacquer work; lacquer ware with gilt engravings. The lacquered surface (of the painting) is carved by a needle and filled with gold leaf. 金粉の彫り物がある漆器. (絵などの)漆面を針で彫り, 金粉をうめこむ. ☆蒔絵細工の一種. ⇨蒔絵

ちんごこっかしそう【鎮護国家思想】 the thought that brings peace to the nation by reciting Buddhist prayers. 仏教祈願を唱えて天下泰平をもたらす思想.

ちんこんさい【鎮魂祭】 a memorial service for the repose of the deceased; a ceremony for the pacification of spirits. 死者の魂をしずめる祭儀.

ちんじゅ【鎮守】❶〈神〉tutelary deity[god]; deity protecting[guarding] the local village and people living there. 鎮守の神, その土

地・住民を守る神.

❷〈神社〉a tutelary shrine; a shrine protecting[guarding] the local village and people living there. 鎮守神社, 鎮守の神を祀る神社. ¶**鎮守の森** the grove of the village shrine (served to protect from the farms from disasters). **鎮守の社**(やしろ) a village tutelary shrine.

チンドン屋 (a group of) ding-dong musical band for publicity. A group of fancy-dressed musicians[musical men and women] play musical instruments in front of the store or parade throughout the city streets to advertise the opening of new stores and other events. 宣伝広告用の音楽隊. 人目につく派手な服装をした音楽隊が, 開店や諸行事を宣伝するために, 店先で楽器を鳴らし, 市中を練り歩く.

ちんみ【珍味】〔食品〕a delicacy; dainties; 〈味〉a delicate flavor[taste]. ¶**山海の珍味** the delicacies of the sea and the land; many kinds of delicacies. **季節の珍味** the delicacies of the seasons.

つ

ついたて【衝立】 a single-leaf wooden screen (decorated with a picture). It is used to partition off space in a room (or an entrance). (絵画で飾った)1枚の木製の仕切り家具. 部屋[玄関]を仕切るのに用いる. 「衝立障子」の略.

つうきんでんしゃ【通勤電車】a jam-packed [crowded] commuter train.

つか【柄】 the haft (of a dagger); the hilt (of a sword). (刀剣などの)手で握る部分.

つか【塚】〈土の山〉an earth mound; 〈古墳〉a tumulus (複 tumuli); 〈墓〉a grave mound; a burial mound. 土を高く盛った墓. ⇨古墳

つかいすてカメラ【使い捨てカメラ】 a disposable[throwaway] camera; a single-use camera.

つかいまわしりょうり【使い回し料理】reusing[reserving] untouched leftovers; sales of expired and leftover food. 食べ残しを再利用する. ☆賞味期限の切れたもの, また食べ残しのものを販売する.

つきだし【突き出し】 a relish; a Japanese-style appetizer[hors d'oeuvre]; the first dish served with a drink. 料理屋などで日本料理の最初に出す, 軽い料理. 前菜. ⇨とおし

つきびと[**つけびと**]【付き[け]人・附き[け]人】❶〔相撲〕 an attendant on[to] a ranking *sumo* wrestler. 相撲力士(十両以上)の身の回りの世話をする人[付き添い人].

❷〈演劇〉 an attendant on[to] a performing actor[artist]. 役者[芸人]の身の回りの世話をする人[世話役].

つきみ【月見】a moon viewing (on the night of the full moon).

【月見の宴】 (have)a moon-viewing party (on August 15[September 13] on the lunar calendar). It is a traditional custom of enjoying the full moon in midautumn. People offer rice-flour dumplings to the full moon together with seasonal fruits, vegetables and grasses such as pampas grass (*susuki*) and bush clover (*hagi*), praying to the moon for a good harvest of rice to come or expressing gratitudes for the year's harvest. 陰暦8月15日(15夜), 9月13日(13夜)の観月. 仲秋の名月をめでる伝統的な習慣で. 季節の果物, 野菜, 薄[芒]や萩のような草木とともに月見団子を供え, 月に向かいながら豊作を祈願し, 感謝する. 「お月見」ともいう. ☆平安時代に中国から日本の宮廷に伝来する. ⇨中秋の名月 / 十五夜 / 観月会

【月見酒】 moon-viewing *sake*; *sake* enjoyed while viewing the moon. 月見をし

ながら飲む酒.

【月見団子】 (rice-flour) dumplings offered to the moon. People pile rice-flour dumplings on a small square wooden stand (*sanpo*) arranged on the edge of veranda floor. 縁先に配した小さな三方台に団子を積み上げる. ⇨団子 / 三方

つきみうどん[そば]【月見うどん[そば]】 (a bowl of) *udon*[*soba*] in broth topped with a raw egg; (a bowl of) wheat noodles[buckwheat noodles] in fish broth topped with a raw sunny-side up egg[placed with a raw sunny-side up egg on top]. *Tsukimi* (moon-viewing) noodles are so called because the egg yolk resembles[looks like] the full moon. 生卵を落としたうどん. 卵の黄身が満月に似ていることに由来.

つきみそう【月見草】〔植物〕 an evening primrose. アカバナ科の二年草.「宵待ち草」ともいう.

つきやま【築山】 an artificial miniature hill[small mountain] (in a Japanese landscape garden). (日本庭園に)小さな丘[山]をかたどって, 土砂を小高く盛り上げた所.

つきやまていえん【築山庭園】 a hilly landscape garden. It is arranged to show nature with artificial hills, ponds and streams. 丘陵の多い風景庭園. 人工的な丘, 池, 小川などを自然に見せるために配した庭園. 例「水前寺庭園」(熊本県).「六義園」(東京都). ⇨平庭(庭園)

つくし【土筆】 a field-horsetail sprout; a spore[fertile] shoot[stalk] of field horsetail. トクサ科の多年草. 杉菜 (field horsetail)に生じる胞子茎. 和え物や煮物などに調理する. ⇨すぎな

つくだに【佃煮】 *tsukudani*; preserved foods boiled down in sweetened *shoyu*[bean sauce]. *Tsukudani* is preserved foods[small dried fish, seaweed, kelp, shellfish, etc.] boiled down in a mixture of *shoyu* and sugar, *mirin*[sweetened *sake*] and other flavorings. 醤油・砂糖・味醂などで味を濃くして煮詰めた保存食品[小魚・海藻・昆布・貝類など]. ☆江戸の佃島で製造されたのが命名の由来. 漁民が幕府・大名に納めた残りの魚を醤油で煮詰め (fish boiled in *shoyu*)ておかずにしていた. ⇨あさりの佃煮 / のりの佃煮

つくつくぼうし【つくつく法師】〔虫〕 a fall cicada. セミ科の昆虫.「法師ぜみ」ともいう. ⇨せみ

つくね【捏ね】 a minced meatball; minced and kneaded meat[fish] formed into bite-sized balls. 団子状の肉[魚]. 一口サイズの団子状に丸めた挽き肉[すり身魚]. 鍋物や焼き物に用いる. ☆「捏ねる」は手でこねて丸くするという意からの呼称が由来.
〔料理〕捏ね揚げ a deep-fried meatball. 捏ね焼き a baked meatball. 鶏[鰯]つくね a minced chicken[sardine] meatball; a minced and kneaded chicken[sardine] meat formed into bite-sized balls.

つくばい【蹲踞】 ❶ (stone) washbasin; the basin for placing water to wash one's hands. 手を洗うために水を入れておく鉢. ☆「蹲う」(手を洗うためにうずくまる[しゃがむ]) crouch[squat] down (to wash one's hands); sit down one's heels (to wash one's hands).

❷〔茶道〕 a stone washbasin[⊛ washbowl] set in a Japanese garden; a water bowl (usually made of stone) set near the tearoom in a tea-ceremony garden. The guests participating in a tea ceremony crouch[squat] (*tsukubau*) and wash their hands with the water of the basin using a ladle before entering the tearoom. 日本庭園にある石の手水鉢. 茶室の庭先にある (石製の)手水鉢. 茶道に参加する人は茶室に入る前に 蹲 って柄杓を使って水盤の水(筧から流れる水)で手を洗う. ⇨手水鉢

❸ a stone washbowl (into which water pours[flows] through a bamboo pipe). (水が竹の管(筧)を通して流れ落ちる)石鉢. ⇨筧

つぐみ【鶫】〔鳥〕 a thrush; a dusky thrust. ヒタキ科の小鳥.「鶫」は国字.

つくり【造り・作り】 *sashimi*; sliced raw fish; slices of raw fish. 関東では「刺身」という.

つくりごえ【作り声】〔歌舞伎〕 a disguised voice; a feigned voice (in a kabuki play).

つくりざかや【造り酒屋】〈人〉a *sake* brewer; 〈醸造元〉a *sake* brewery; 〈仕事〉*sake* brewing business.

つげ【柘植・黄楊】〔植物〕 a (Japanese little-leaf) box; a box tree(柘植の木); boxwood (柘植材). ツゲ科の常緑小高木. 材質は緻密で加工性がよく(highly processible), 櫛, 印材, 将棋の駒, ソロバンの玉などに用いる. ¶(将棋の)**柘植の駒** a set of boxwood *shogi* pieces. **柘植の櫛** a boxwood comb; a comb of boxwood. It is used for combing the hair without damaging it. (髪の毛を傷めずにとかせる)

つけあわせ【付け合わせ】a garnish; a relish; trimmings; fixings. 主料理(main dish)に添えあしらう食品.「料理のつま」のこと. ⇨つま. ¶付け合わせのパセリ parsley used [added] as a garnish[relish]. 肉の付け合わせの野菜 vegetables used as trimmings for the meat; vegetables added fixings to the meat.

つけめん【付け麺】〈付けた麺〉noodles dipped in sauce (before eating). (食前に)つけ汁に付けた麺 ;〈付ける麺〉noodles served with a separate sauce to dip them in (before eating). (食前に)麺とつけ汁とが別な器に盛られている.

つけもの【漬物】 *tsukemono*; pickles; pickled vegetables[radish, eggplant, etc.]. Vegetables are pickled either by mixing with salt or by dipping in salted rice-bran paste, *sake* lees, etc. 塩を混ぜるか, または糠味噌, 酒かすなどに漬け込んで保存する野菜(大根・茄子など).「おしんこ」「こうこ」「香の物」などともいう. ⇨粕漬け (*sake*-lees pickles)/ 糠漬け (rice-bran pickles)/ 塩漬け (salt pickles)/ 味噌漬け (bean-paste pickles). ¶漬物石 a pickle stone; a stone weight used for pickles. 漬物桶 a pickling tub; a pickle barrel; a tub[barrel] used for pickles. 漬物器 a pickle press. 漬物屋〈店〉a pickle store[shop].〈人〉a dealer in pickles.〈製造元〉a pickle manufacturer.

つけやき【付け焼き】 (fish[meat]) broiled with *shoyu*[soy sauce]. (魚・肉などに)醤油のたれを付けて焼くこと. ⇨照り焼き. ¶ブリ[イカ]の付け焼き a yellowfish[squid] broiled with *shoyu*.

つじぎり【辻斬り】 a street attacker with a sword (at night); a *samurai* who attacks a passerby on the street to test a new sword (at night). 刀の切れ味を試すために(夜間)道ばたで通行人を襲う(人)

つじげい【辻芸】 street[sidewalk] performance. ¶辻芸人 a street (corner) performer; a sidewalk performer.

つじせっぽう【辻説法】 street preaching; preaching dogma[creed, teachings] to people going and coming at the crossroads [at the street corner]. 道ばたで往来の人に仏法を説くこと. ☆「キリスト教の辻説法」は street ministry.

つた【蔦】〔植物〕ivy; Japanese ivy. ブドウ科のつる性植物. ¶壁に蔦をはりつめた家屋 ivy-walled house; house covered with ivy. 蔦に覆われた壁 ivy-covered walls; walls covered with ivy.

つつじ【躑躅】〔植物〕an azalea; a rhododendron. ツツジ科の常緑[落葉]低木. 観賞用.

つづみ【鼓】 a small hand drum (used in

traditional Japanese dance and music). *Tsuzumi* has a skin stretched over both ends of a waisted body in the center. There are two kinds of Japanese-style small drums; *ko-tsuzumi* (a tabor; a small shoulder drum for tapping with the fingertips) and *o-tsuzumi* (a large knee drum for beating with the fingertips). 和楽器の一種.（日本の伝統舞踊音楽で用いる）手に持つ太鼓. 中央がくびれた胴の両面に革が張ってある.「小鼓」（肩に担ぎ, 指先で打つ太鼓）と「大鼓」（膝に置き, 指先で打つ太鼓）の二種がある. ⇨小鼓 / 大鼓. ¶（指先で）鼓を打つ tap a hand drum (with the fingertips).

つづら【葛籠】 *tsuzura* vine clothes box; a wicker basket[trunk] for storing and carrying clothes[merchandise] in. It was formerly made from strips of the *tsuzura* vine, but today it is usually made of bamboo or cypress. 葛藤（ツヅラフジ科の落葉つる植物）のつるで編んだ着物［商品］を収納・携帯する箱型の物入れ. 昔は葛藤のつるで作られていたが, 今は竹または檜で作られる場合がある.

つづれこじんじゃだいたいこ【綴子神社大太鼓】 the Drum-Beating Parade of Tsuzureko Shrine. (7月). ⇨付記(1)「日本の祭り」

つな【綱】〔相撲〕 the heavy rope worn by a *yokozuna*, *sumo* grand champion（from which that rank takes its name）. 横綱が締める太い綱. 相撲の「横綱」をさす. ¶綱取り a chance for the *ozeki sumo* wrestler to attain the rank of[gain promotion to] a *yokozuna*, *sumo* grand champion.

つなぎ【繋ぎ】 a thickener; thickening; liaison〈仏：リエゾン〉.（料理で）混ぜて粘り気を増すための材料. ☆卵・小麦粉・ヤマイモなど. ¶そば粉のつなぎに使う卵 eggs used as a thickener for buckwheat flour.

つなひき【綱引き】(have) a tug of war; (hold) a rope pulling contest.

つなみ【津波】 *tsunami* (wave); a tidal wave. ¶津波地震 *tsunami* earthquake; seismic sea wave. 津波警報 a *tsunami* warning. 津波予報 a *tsunami* forecast. 津波注意報 a *tsunami* advisory.

つのかくし【角隠し】 the bride's white hood (worn with a *kimono* in a traditional Japanese wedding). *Tsunokakushi* (literally "horn-hiding") is the white hood[cotton or silk head covering] worn on the head [coiffure] by a bride at the traditional wedding ceremony. It is believed to suppress and hide the feminine "horns of jealousy" by wearing this white hood fitted on bride's wig. It symbolizes humility in the nuptial pledge before gods. 和式婚礼で花嫁が頭［髪結い］にかぶる飾りの白い被り物［綿布または絹布の被り物］. 花嫁のかつらにまとった白い被り物をつけることによって女性の「嫉妬心の角」を抑え, 隠すことができると信じられている. 神前にて行う婚礼の誓約における謙虚さを象徴する.

つのだる【角樽】 a horned *sake* cask; a two-handled[horned] *sake* vermilion keg[barrel] (used for ceremonial occasions). 角のついた酒樽. 角のように二本の長い柄のついた朱塗りの樽（結納などの祝儀の酒用）. ⇨酒樽

つば【鍔】 a hand guard; the guard on a sword; a sword guard held between the blade and the hilt. 刀身と刀の柄の間にはさむ平たい金具. ⇨刀

つばき【椿】〔植物〕 a camellia; a japonica. ツバキ科の常緑高木. 種子から椿油をとる. ¶寒椿 a winter camellia. 白玉椿 a white-flowered camellia. 椿油 camellia oil. It protects the beauty of the hair and skin with natural moisture.（自然のうるおいで美しい髪と肌を保つ）

つばめ【燕】〔鳥〕a swallow; ㊍a barn swallow; ㊀ a chimney swallow; a swift(雨燕). ¶燕

の巣 a swallow's nest. ☆中国の高級料理 (an edible bird's nest)

つぶしあん【潰し餡】「粒餡」ともいう. ⇨餡

つぼ【坪】a *tsubo*; a unit for measuring (floor space and) area. One *tsubo* is about 6 by 6 *shaku* (=about 3.3 square meters). 面積を測る尺貫法の単位の一つ. 六尺平方(=約3.3㎡). ¶**20坪の家** a house with floor space of twenty *tsubo*.

つぼね【局】❶〈部屋〉a chamber[apartment] of a court lady. 宮廷[宮殿]に仕える女官の私室.
❷〈女官〉a court lady; a lady-in-waiting (occupying rooms at court[in the shogun's castle]). 宮廷・将軍邸の部屋に住む女官. ¶**春日局** the Lady Kasuga.

つぼやき【壺焼き】 shellfish broiled in the shell; shellfish baked with the shell[with its own shell]. 巻貝(サザエなど)を殻ごと焼く料理. ⇨さざえの壺焼き

つま【妻】〈刺身の〉 *tsuma*; a garnish for raw fish; trimmings served with *sashimi*[sliced raw fish]. *Tsuma* trimmings are ornamental vegetables (such as thinly shredded Japanese *daikon*[radish], cucumber, carrots, beefsteak plant leaves, etc.) or seaweeds[marine plants] served with sliced raw fish to look nice. They are eaten together with *sashimi* to help digestion as well. 刺身に添える付け合わせのもの. (刻み大根, 胡瓜, 人参, 紫蘇などの)装飾的な野菜または海藻類のことで, 見栄えをよくしたりするために刺身に添える. 消化を助けるために刺身といっしょに食べる. 「付け合わせ」ともいう. ⇨肴 / 付け合わせ

つま【褄】a hem (of a *kimono*). 着物のすそ

つまみ【摘み】〈酒の〉 (a) hors d'oeuvre(前菜); snacks served with drinks; something to eat[nibble] with drinks. ⊛ drink tidbits[⊛ titbits]; relishes that go well with alcoholic beverage. *Tsumami* snacks are

nuts, salted rice crackers, dried shredded cuttlefish, etc. 酒の肴に出す簡単な食べ物 (ナッツ, 塩煎餅, スルメ焼きなど). 「摘み物」の略. 通称「お摘み」. ⇨肴

つまもの【妻物】 a leaf[leaves] used for decorative purposes to put food on the dish (in a Japanese-style restaurant). 食べ物に添える飾りの木の葉. 和食に用いる.

つまようじ【爪楊枝】 a toothpick; a toothpicker; a pick. ⇨楊枝

つみれ【摘入】 a fish-paste dumpling[ball]; a boiled dumpling[croquette] of ground fish; a boiled dumpling made from ground and spiced fish meat. 魚肉のすり身につなぎをいれて蒸した食品. ⇨イワシのつみれ汁
〔料理〕摘入鍋 hot-pot food cooked with boiled dumplings of ground sardine(鰯の摘入を入れた鍋物). 摘入汁 fish-paste dumpling soup; soup cooked with boiled dumplings of ground fish meat.

つむぎ【紬】 (Japanese) pongee; fabric[cloth] woven from hand-spun threads of raw silk. 手でつむいだ絹生糸 (raw silk threads)で織った織物. 紬糸で織った絹布. 「大島紬」(鹿児島県)や「結城紬」(茨城県)などが有名. ⇨大島紬. ¶**紬糸** silk thread from inferior cocoons, woven into durable fabric(屑繭をつむいでよりをかけた絹糸)

つめ【詰め】〔茶道〕 the last guest in a tea ceremony. He/she takes the last seat in a tearoom to assist the host in many ways. 茶室で亭主を助けるために末席に座る客.「お詰め」ともいう.

つや【通夜】 a wake; an all-night wake. Family members mourn beside the dead body dressed in white robes in the coffin at the wake. The Buddhist priest confers a posthumous name (*kaimyo*) to a deceased person. 棺の経帷子の遺体のそばで喪に服す. 死者には戒名がつけられる. 葬儀の前日の宵に行う法要. ☆「**半通夜**」は a briefer "half wake" ⇨戒名 / 経帷子. ¶**通夜振る舞い** refreshments[*sake* and food] served at a wake.

つやもの【艶物】〔文楽〕 a chanted narration of a love story in the *gidayu* school of *joruri* puppet play. 情事を題材にした浄瑠璃.

つゆ[ばいう]【梅雨】 the rainy season. ¶**から梅雨** dry rainy season. **梅雨入り**[**入梅**] the start of the rainy season. **梅雨明け** the end of the rainy season.

つゆ【汁】〈吸い物〉soup;〈澄まし汁〉clear soup;〈麺汁〉noodle broth; seasoned sauce to dip noodles. ⇨麺(麺汁). *Tsuyu* is usually prepared with *shoyu*[soy sauce], *mirin* [sweetened *sake*], salt and dried bonito shavings. つゆは通常醤油, 味醂, 塩, 鰹節で調理される. 別称「しる」. ☆「**汁だく**」 plenty of sauce. ⇨しる

つゆはらい【露払い】 ❶〔相撲〕a *sumo* wrestler walking ahead of a *yokozuna* who performs the formal *sumo*-ring-entering ceremony before *makuuchi*-division bouts. He serves the usher of a *yokozuna* during the *sumo*-entering ceremony. 幕内の取組前に正式の土俵入りを行う横綱を先導する力士. ⇨土俵入り ❷〈行列の先導者〉 an outrider (for a procession); a forerunner. 行列などで人の先に立って導く人.

つらら【氷柱】 an icicle. ¶**つららの下がった軒** an icicle-hung eaves. **軒下のつらら** icicles hung[formed] on the edge of the eaves.

つりがき【釣(り)書き】 ❶〈身上書〉brief resume[personal history] and family background for marriage proposal. 縁談のときなどに取り交わす, 自分の履歴や家族の身上書. ❷〈系図〉family tree. 家系.

つりがね【釣鐘】 (strike) a Buddhist temple bell; (toll) a hanging bell of a Buddhist temple. It is a bell hanging in a belfry in the precincts of a Buddhist temple. It is believed that the peals of a Buddhist temple bell ward off evil. 寺院の境内にある鐘楼につるしてある鐘. 寺院の鐘の響きは悪を取り除くといわれる. ⇨除夜の鐘. ¶**釣鐘堂** a belfry.

つりがねそう【釣鐘草】〔植物〕a campanula; a (dotted) bellflower. キキョウ科の植物.

つりどうろう【釣灯籠】 a hanging lantern (made of iron or bronze); a lantern hanging[hung] by a chain from a corner of the eaves of the shrines or temples[a traditional Japanese house]. (石製または銅製の)吊り下げる灯籠. 神社仏閣[日本家屋]の軒から鎖で吊るされている[吊るされた]灯籠. ⇨灯籠

つりばし【吊り橋】 a suspension bridge; a rope bridge.

つりばな【吊り(釣)花】〔華道〕the flowers arranged in a pendant vase hanging from the ceiling. 天井から吊るされている垂れさがった花瓶にいける生け花. ⇨掛け花

つりやね【吊り屋根】〔相撲〕a suspended roof (on the *sumo* ring)

つる【鶴】〔鳥〕a crane. ツル科の鳥. 吉祥 (a good omen)の鳥としてめでたいものとされる. ☆「**鶴は千年, 亀は万年**」(the crane is a symbol of longevity filled with happiness as there is a proverb in Japan "A crane lives for 1,000 years, and turtles 10,000.") という諺にあるように, 長寿 (a long life)の象徴である. ⇨千羽鶴. ¶**丹頂鶴** a Japanese crane. **真名鶴** a white napped crane. ⇨亀. **鶴の子餅** ⇨鳥の子餅

つるがおかはちまんぐうれいさい【鶴岡八幡宮例祭】 the Annual Festival of Tsurugaoka Hachiman-gu Shrine. (9月). ⇨付記(1)「日本の祭り」

つるがにしまちのつなひき【敦賀西町の綱引き】 the Tug-of-War Festival of Tsuruga

City. (1月). ⇨付記(1)「日本の祭り」

つるぎ【剣】 a (double-edged) sword. ⇨刀

つるべ(おけ)【釣瓶(桶)】 a (well) bucket. ¶つるべで井戸から水をくむ〈縄紐・竿で〉 draw water from a well in a bucket (by using a rope[pole] attached to the bucket).

ツレ【連れ】〔能楽〕 a *tsure*; the second actor supporting in a Noh play. He acts as an assistant[a third supporting] performer for the *shite* (the main actor) and the *waki* (the second actor) in a Noh play. 能楽でシテ・ワキに伴って助演する人. ⇨シテ(仕手)／ワキ(脇)

つわののさぎまい【津和野鷺舞】 the Heron Dance at Tsuwano Town. (7月). ⇨付記(1)「日本の祭り」

て

であいけいきっさ【出会い系喫茶】 a dating café (where men pay to meet women).

であいけいサイト【出会い系サイト】 a dating website; an on-line dating site; an Internet dating site; the dating-service [matchmaking] website (where one person can meet another).

であいけいしょうじょばいしゅん【出会い系少女売春】 girls' prostitution through dating websites.

ていえん【庭園】 a (Japanese) garden; a landscape garden. ¶**日本三名園** the Three Famous Gardens in Japan. 兼六園(石川県)・後楽園(岡山県)・偕楽園(茨城県)

ていしゅ【亭主】 ❶〔茶道〕the host[hostess] in the tea ceremony (who provides hospitality for guests in the tea cult). 茶席で客に茶の接待をする主人[女主人]. ❷〈夫〉a husband; the head of the family. 家族の主. ❸〈店主〉㊍ a shopkeeper; ㊎ a storekeeper; the owner of a store.

ていしゅかんぱく【亭主関白】 a male chauvinist; an overbearing husband; a domineering husband; a husband leading his wife by the nose. 家庭内で夫が権力を振るって威張ること. ⇔かかあ天下

ていしょく【定食】 a set meal; a *table d'hôte* meal; a meal from the set[fixed] menu. ¶**和定食** a Japanese-style set meal (at a Japanese restaurant). It includes a bowl of rice, *miso* soup, pickles and the main dish of the day (fish or meat). ご飯・味噌汁・漬物それに日替わり食品(魚か肉). **B定食** set meal "B"; meal "B" from the set menu.

ていち【低地】 a low land[ground]; a lowland area (低地帯). ⇔高地

ていねいご【丁寧語】 respect language; polite language[expression]. ⇨敬語

ていねんせい【定年制】 a retirement age policy; an age-limit system; an age for mandatory retirement.

ていねんりこん【定年離婚】 divorce after retirement; divorce when one reaches retirement age.

てうち【手打】 handclapping in unison; the custom of clapping hands. People clap their hands (generally repeat three times) at the conclusion of a contract made between two parties. This is also done at the closing of a special party. 契約などが成立したとき両者が唱和して手を打ち鳴らすこと. 通常は3回. 特別会合のお開きの時にも行う. ☆「手締め」ともいう. ⇨手締め

てうちそば[うどん]【手打ちそば[うどん]】〈手製の〉 handmade buckwheat noodles [wheat noodles] ;〈自家製の〉homemade buckwheat noodles[wheat noodles]. The noodle maker kneads the dough, rolls it out with a rolling pin and slices it to make the noodles. うどんを作るには, こね粉をこねる, 麺棒で延ばす, そして切る.

でかせぎ【出稼ぎ】 seasonal working in a

big city away from home. ¶**出稼ぎ労働者** a migrant worker; a seasonal worker away from home.

てがた【手形】〔相撲〕a *sumo* wrestler's handprint. It is a *sumo* wrestler's handprint in red or black ink and his professional name (*shikona*) written by the *sumo* wrestler in calligraphy on a square paperboard. 四角の板紙に赤または黒インクで押した力士の手の形と能筆で書かれた醜名がある.

てがたな【手刀】〔相撲〕a victorious *sumo* wrestler's chopping motion with his right hand to the center, right and left. It is a traditional[conventional] chopping motion with a winning *sumo* wrestler's right hand over the prize to express his thanks to the three Shinto gods of victory before accepting it. 勝者力士の右手を中央から右側・左側へと切る手振り. 勝ち力士が懸賞金を受ける前に右手のひらの側面で物を切るようにする伝統的な所作. 勝利を与えてくれた神への感謝を表す.

でがたり【出語り】〔歌舞伎〕the recitation on the kabuki stage; the narrative ballad recitation performed by joruri narrators and *shamisen* players on the kabuki stage. 歌舞伎で, 浄瑠璃語りと三味線ひきが舞台に出て物語ること.

てがら【手絡】a decorative piece of silk cloth for women's hair-dressing[hairstyles]. It is a colored chignon ribbon rolled up in the *maru-mage* hair-do. 女性の日本髪に飾る(ちりめんなど)色染めの絹布. 丸髷を結う(tied)ときにくるくると巻き上げた多彩な髷リボン. ⇨丸髷

でがらしのちゃ【出がらしの茶】weak tea (made from used leaves)

できちゃったこん【出来ちゃった婚】a shotgun marriage[wedding]; a marriage [wedding] that results from an unexpected pregnancy; a marriage[wedding] prompted by the bride's pregnancy. ☆英語では父親が(婚前に妊娠した)娘の相手に shotgun(散弾銃)を突きつけて結婚させたことが由来. 「出来婚」ともいう.

てぎれきん【手切れ金】consolation money.

てさげぶくろ【手提げ袋】an ornamental handbag[hand-carried bag] (to go with a woman's *kimono*). (着物と調和する[似合う])飾り模様のある手にさげてもつ袋 (a bag with a handle).

でし【弟子】〈華道など〉a pupil; a disciple; an apprentice(徒弟). ¶**弟子入りする** become an apprentice (to).

デジタルまんびき【デジタル万引き】digital shoplifting; taking photographs of publications in bookstores.

てじめ【手締(め)】a ceremonial hand-clapping in unison (to celebrate its successful conclusion). It is customary for the Japanese to clap hands in union at the end of general meeting[banquet] or at the year-end party. (成功を祝って)唱和して手を打ち鳴らすこと. 総会の終わりや忘年会などで行う. ⇨手打

てすり(ぶたい)【手摺(舞台)】〔文楽〕a stage with a board[screen] to hide the lower bodies of puppeteers[puppet manipulators] during the bunraku play. *Tesuri* is a board [screen] which hides the performers' legs and makes it look as the puppets are walking on the ground. 人形遣いの腰から下が隠れるようにする板のある舞台. 演技者の足を隠し, 人形が地上を歩いているように見せる板のこと. ⇨文楽(文楽舞台)

でぞめしき【出初め式】the New Year's Demonstration by fire brigades. (1月). ⇨付記(1)「日本の祭り」

でづかい【出遣い】〔文楽〕the appearance of puppeteers in a bunraku play. The main puppeteer (*Omozukai*) dressed in cer-

て

emonial costume appears with his face uncovered during the performance. 文楽における人形遣いの登場．正装した主[面]遣いが顔を見せて登場し，人形をつかう．⇨三人遣い

てっかどん(ぶり)【鉄火丼】(a bowl of) vinegared rice topped with raw tuna; (a bowl of) vinegared rice served with slices of raw tuna on top; (a bowl of) vinegared rice topped with a few slices of raw tuna and some dried laver and a bit of grated horseradish. 生マグロの薄い切り身を焼きのりとおろしわさびを添えて上にのせたすし飯(の丼物)．⇨丼物

てっかまき【鉄火巻き】rolled *sushi*[vinegared rice] with raw tuna filling in the center; *sushi* rolled up in a sheet of dried laver with a slice of red raw tuna and grated horseradish in the center. 生マグロの赤身の薄切りとおろしわさびを芯にしたのり巻きずし.

てっちり【鉄ちり】 blowfish stew; a hot-pot meal of globefish cooked with vegetables. 野菜と調理したフグの鍋料理．☆「てつ」は「ふぐ」の異称．「ふぐのちり鍋」のこと．⇨ふぐ(ふぐちり)

てっぱんやき【鉄板焼き】 *teppanyaki*; (a dish of) sliced meat (or seafoods) and vegetables roasted on a hot iron plate. A variety of thinly chopped meat (often beef or chicken) or seafoods (usually shrimps or clams) are cooked on a hot iron plate[an electric griddle] with a few kinds of vegetables at the table. The foods are eaten by dipping them in a soy-based sauce and mixing with condiments (such as grated *daikon*[radish], minced green onions, etc). 熱い鉄板[電気鉄板]の上に肉(牛肉または鶏肉)または魚介類(エビまたはハマグリ)と野菜類をのせて焼く料理．料理した物は垂れにつけ，薬味(大根卸し・さらしネギな

ど)を混ぜて食べる.

てつびん【鉄瓶】an iron kettle. ⇨南部鉄瓶

てっぽうまき【鉄砲巻き】 thin rolled *sushi* [vinegared rice] with gourd strips in the center. かんぴょうをはさんだ細いのり巻き.

てっぽうやき【鉄砲焼き】 grilled chicken [fish meat] with *miso*[bean paste] and hot red pepper spread on it. 味噌と唐辛子で焼いた鶏肉[魚肉].

てば【手羽】a chicken wing. 鳥の胸から羽のつけ根にかけての骨付き肉.「手羽肉」の略. ⇨焼き鳥．¶**手羽先** a chicken wing tip; the wing tip of a chicken; the tip section of a chicken wing. **手羽元** a chicken wing stick; a wing stick of a chicken. 〔料理〕**手羽先と里芋の煮物** simmered chicken wing tips and taros.

デパちか【デパ地下】 the food department in the basement of the department store. ¶**デパ地下の惣菜売り場** delicatessen[the prepared foods] counter in a department store basement.

でばやし【出囃子】❶〔歌舞伎〕〈人〉the on-stage musicians in a kabuki play; 〈音楽〉music performance given by a group of on-stage musicians in a kabuki play. Musicians seated on the platform on the kabuki stage perform music, especially when there is a dance in a kabuki play. 歌舞伎の舞台上にいる一団の楽士による音楽演奏．特に歌舞伎を舞うときに演奏する音楽. **❷**〈寄席〉〈人〉the on-stage *shamisen* player in a *yose* drama; 〈音楽〉*shamisen* musical accompaniment played when introducing a comic storyteller on the stage. 寄席で噺家を壇上で紹介するときに演奏する三味線の伴奏. ⇨寄席

てほん【手本】〈書道〉model handwriting (in a calligraphy); handwriting as a good model

[example] (in a calligraphy). （書道におけ
る）模範となる手書.

てまえ【手前・（お）点前】〔茶道〕 *temae[o-temae]*; the tea ceremony procedures and manners; procedures and manners for making and serving tea in the tea ceremony; one's mastery of the etiquette of the tea ceremony. *Temae[O-temae]* is a ceremony procedure[etiquette] of preparing and serving tea ritually in front of guests: how to put powdered green tea [foamy green tea or pasty green tea] into a tea bowl, how to pour hot water into a tea bowl from the kettle, and how to whip the tea into froth and serve it in the tea ceremony. 茶の湯の作法・様式. 客の前で正式に茶を立てて差し出す礼儀作法[手順]. 茶碗への抹茶[薄茶・濃茶]の入れ方, 茶釜から茶碗へのお湯の注ぎ方, 茶の泡の立て方や差し出し方などがある. ⇨茶事 / 茶会.
¶**薄茶手前** the tea ceremony procedures for serving foamy green tea. **濃茶手前** the tea ceremony procedures for serving pasty green tea.
☆『**茶の立て方**』
①『**茶道具の清め**』The host[hostess] purifies the tea utensils.
②『**抹茶入れ**』He[She] puts a scoop of powdered green tea into a tea bowl.
③『**茶の湯入れ**』He[She] adds hot water from the kettle to the tea bowl with a ladle.
④『**茶筅回し**』Tea is made using a tea whisk to whip the mixture into a foam.

でまえ【出前】 ❶〈食物〉delivering food to customers' house. 注文先まで配達する料理.
❷〈配達〉meal delivery service; home-delivery service; delivery of meals to order; outside catering service; delivery service of prepared dishes (usually made by bicycle or motorcycle). 料理を注文先

まで配達すること（通常は自転車やバイクで配達する）. ☆「仕出し」と区別すること. ⇨仕出し. ¶**出前持ち** a delivery man[boy]

てまきずし【手巻き鮨】 hand-rolled *sushi* [vinegared rice]; *sushi* rolled by hand in a cone of dried laver; *sushi* rolled by hand in a sheet of dried laver with vegetables and other ingredients in the center. 焼きのりに酢飯, 野菜・魚などの具をのせて巻いた鮨. ⇨納豆巻き / ねぎトロ巻き

てまり【手鞠】 a small handball. It is traditionally made of tightly-wound multicolorful threads. 堅固に編んだ多彩な糸で作った小さなまり.
【**手鞠つき**】 a traditional Japanese game of bouncing handball (usually played for girls). Girls usually sing a ball-playing-song (*temari-uta*) while bouncing a ball on the ground outdoors. 少女たちが野外でまりつきをするあいだ「手まり歌」を歌うことがある.

てまりずし【手鞠鮨】 a bite-sized *sushi* ball (packed in a small wooden box with a lid). 一口大の丸い形の鮨. 折詰などに入れる. ⇨折詰

てみず【手水】 ❶〈手洗い用〉hand-washing water; water for washing hands. 手を洗う水. ⇨ちょうず
❷〈握り飯・餅つき用〉hand-wetting water; water for wetting hands. Water is used to wet the palm (of the hand) when making *mochi*[rice cake] by pounding glutinous rice or when making *onigiri*[rice ball]. 餅米を搗くとき, またはおにぎりなどをつくるときに手のひらを濡らせておく水.

てみずや【手水舎】 a small roofed building [pavilion] for washing hands and rinsing mouth. It has a stone washbasin filled with water which is prepared to purify hands and mouth by using the ladle before worshipping at a Shinto shrine. Lastly the

て

handle is rinsed with water by tipping the ladle. It is located on the approach to the main building of a shrine. （心身を清めるため）手を洗い，口をすすぐための屋根付き建物［施設］．神社には参詣者が柄杓を使って手（まず右手，次に左手）と口（左手の水で口をすすぐ）を清めるための水盤がある．最後に柄杓を立てて柄を洗う．神社の本殿に通ずる参道にある．☆キリスト教国の欧米人に対しては the font for ablution という方が理解しやすい．font はカトリック教会で洗礼に用いる水の入った「聖水盤」または「洗礼盤」のこと．ablutions は宗教儀式（清めの式）で手や足などを「洗い清める」こと．

てみやげ【手土産】 a caller's (small) present; visitor's (small) gift. ⇨菓子折り．¶**手土産**をもって訪問する visit (a person) with a gift; bring a present when a person calls on others.

てやきせんべい【手焼き煎餅】 hand-grilled rice crackers; rice crackers in manual production.

てら【寺】 a Buddhist temple (where the statue[image] of Buddha is enshrined and worshipped). The Buddhist priests and nuns reside to practice ascetic exercises and Buddhist ceremonies in the temple. 仏像を安置・礼拝する建物．寺では僧尼が居住して修行や仏事などを行う．「寺院」ともいう．⇨伽藍

☆『寺の呼称』

① 『寺（～でら）』Kiyomizu-<u>dera</u> Temple「清水寺」/ Hase-<u>dera</u> Temple「長谷寺」

② 『寺（～じ）』Todai-ji Temple「東大寺」/Kinkaku-ji Temple[the Golden Pavilion]「金閣寺」（正式名称「鹿苑寺」）

③ 『院』Byodo-<u>in</u> Temple「平等院」/Jakko-in Temple「寂光院」．⇨～院

④ 『堂』Sanjusangen-<u>do</u> Temple「三十三間堂」（正式名称「蓮華王院」）．⇨堂

⑤ 『庵』Shuon-<u>an</u> Temple「酬恩庵」（通称「一休寺」）

¶**寺町** the temple quarter (of an old castle town). **寺巡り** (go on) a pilgrimage to Buddhist temples. **寺参り** (pay) a visit to Buddhist temples.

【寺請(状)】 a certificate of conversion to Buddhism. People submitted the certificate to the shogunate magistrate's office as proof of their being non-Christian (in the Edo period). 仏教に帰依した証明書．（江戸時代には）非キリシタンである証明として奉行所に提出した．

【寺請制度】 the system of certifying people's affiliation with Buddhist temples. The Tokugawa shogunate forced people to belong to temples after being listed as Buddhists (in the Edo period). （江戸時代）キリシタン禁教令が出た頃，人民を仏教徒として宗門改帳に記し，いずれかの寺に信徒として所属させた．

【寺子屋】 a temple school of the Edo period. *Terako-ya* was a private elementary school for children of the common people which was operated at Buddhist temples in the Edo period. The curriculum consists of the three Rs: reading, writing and arithmetic (how to use the abacus). 江戸時代に寺院が経営する庶民の子供（寺子）のための初等教育機関．カリキュラム内容は「読み・書き・そろばん」．☆明治維新後1872年の「学制」(Education Order) の公布によって姿を消す．

てらせん【寺銭】〈博打の〉 the charge for a gambling house; the fee paid to a gambling house. 博打屋に払う金銭．場所の借り賃として貸し元［席主］に払う．

てりやき【照り焼き】 *teriyaki*; fish (or meat) broiled with *mirin*[sweetened *sake*] and *shoyu*[soy sauce]. Fish (often yellowtail) or meat (usually chicken) is broiled over a charcoal fire after being marinated in a mixture of *mirin* and *shoyu*. 照りをつけて焼いた魚[肉]. 味醂醤油をつけ炭火の上で焼いた魚(ブリ)または肉(鶏). ⇨ブリの照り焼き

てるてるぼうず【照る照る坊主】 a small paper doll with only a head and face. It is often hung by children outside under the eaves to pray for fine weather the next day. 紙でつくった頭と顔だけの人形. 子供が翌日の好天を願って [in the hope of bringing good weather] 外の軒下につるす.

テレクラ a telephone dating club; a telephone club date.

テレビかいぎ【テレビ会議】a teleconference; a videoconference.

テレビゲーム(和製英語) a video[computer] game. ¶家庭内テレビゲーム機 home video game machine.

てろたいさくとくべつそちほう【テロ対策特別措置法】 the Anti-Terrorism Special Measures Law.

てん【天】〈神〉Heavenly Gods[Deities]; Deva(s). 天の神々.「天部」ともいう. 仏教界を守る神. ☆主として『天』には「四天王」,「梵天」,「帝釈天」,「毘沙門天」,「持国天」,「仁王」, 女性では「弁財天」,「吉祥天」,「鬼子母神」などがいる.

てん【貂】〔動物〕a marten; a sable(黒); an ermine(白). イタチ科の哺乳動物. 毛皮(marten; sable; ermine)は珍重される.

でんか【殿下】 a prince; His Highness. ⇔妃殿下. ¶皇太子殿下 His Imperial Highness the Crown Prince. ☆呼びかけの場合は "Your (Imperial) Highness."

でんか【伝花】〔華道〕inherited forms of flower arrangements. 華道の各流派に伝承された形態.

てんがい【天蓋】 ❶〈絹傘〉a canopy; a ciborium; a baldaquin. 仏像・棺などの上にかざす絹笠.

❷〈編み笠〉a huge sedge-basket hat covering the entire head and face. It is a basket-like hood made of woven sedge [rush] worn by mendicant Zen monks. 頭全部を隠す虚無僧のかぶる深編み笠. ⇨虚無僧

でんがく【田楽】 ❶〈舞楽〉*dengaku*; ritual field music and dance (at shrines or temples); field music and dance performed ritually at shrines or temples for the festivities of rice-planting and harvesting. 神社仏閣で儀礼的に行われる田植え祭や収穫祭の舞楽. ☆平安時代から行われ, 鎌倉・室町時代には田楽の能に発展し, その後能楽に影響を与える.

❷〈料理〉 morsels of food spread with *miso*[soybean paste] and grilled on skewers. 味噌をぬり, 串に刺して焼いた一口大の食物. ¶田楽味噌 *miso* topping spread on *dengaku*.

【田楽豆腐】 strips of *tofu*[bean curd] spread with *miso*[bean paste] and grilled on bamboo skewers. (Rectangular) slices of *tofu* on bamboo skewers are spread with lightly scorched *miso* and grilled[broiled] over a charcoal fire. 竹串に刺して味噌をぬって (coated), 火であぶった(長方形の)豆腐.「豆腐田楽」ともいう.

【田楽(焼き)】〈料理〉grilled food[fish or vegetables] on skewers coated with a *miso* glaze. Morsels of food[fish or vegetables] are spread with *miso*[bean paste] and grilled on skewers. 野菜・魚介類などを串に刺して, 味噌をぬって焼いた料理. ⇨茄子田楽

てんかす【天滓】 ⇨揚げ玉

てんかとういつ【天下統一】 unification of the whole country; unification[pacification] of Japan. Toyotomi Hideyoshi pacified all of Japan in 1590 after he destroyed the later Hojo family (the Odawara Campaign). 豊

臣秀吉は北条氏を滅ぼし（小田原攻め），ほ
ぼ全国を統一する.

でんかのほうとう【伝家の宝刀】 a sword
treasured in one's family; a sword kept as
a family heirloom.

でんきごたつ【電気炬燵】 ⇨炬燵

てんぐ【天狗】 (an imaginary figure of) a
long-nosed goblin. *Tengu* is portrayed as
a human-like figure with a long nose and
a red face. He lives deep in the mountains
and forests. He has two wings on his back,
flying freely in the air with a feather fan in
his hand. 鼻の長い（想像上の）怪物. 天狗
の姿は人に似て，鼻は長く顔は赤い. 山奥
に住む. 背中には2枚の翼を持ち，手に持
つ羽団扇で自由に空中を飛ぶ.

てんぐさ【天草】〔植物〕 a Japanese agar; an
agar-agar; an agar weed; a Ceylon moss.
テングサ科の紅藻類. 寒天・ところてん（日
光にさらし白くなったものを乾燥させる）
の原料. ⇨寒天 / ところてん

でんごんダイヤル【伝言ダイヤル】 a telephone voice-mail service.

てんざる（そば）【天ざる（そば）】 cool buckwheat noodles piled up on a slatted bamboo
tray, served nearby with a plate[bamboo tray]
of assorted *tempura* [deep-fried prawns and
vegetables]. 竹簾を敷いた盆 (tray)にのせた
冷たいそばで，天ぷらが添えてある. ⇨笊
そば

てんじ【点字】a punched Braille letter. ⇨墨
字

でんし(の)【電子(の)】 electronic; compu-
terized. ¶電子マネー electronic money
[cash]; e-money; digital cash. 電子ペット
an electronic pet. 電子辞書 an electronic[a
computerized] dictionary. 電子書籍 a cy-
berbook; an e-book; an electronic book.

てんじゃ【点者】 a critic of *haiku* and/or
renga. 和歌・連歌などの評点をつけ優劣を
決める人.「判者」ともいう. ⇨俳句 / 連歌

てんしゅかく【天守閣】 a donjon; a keep; a
castle tower; the main tower of the castle
(devised as the biggest watch turret[guard
tower]). 城の本丸に築かれた最大・最高の
物見櫓. ☆戦時には司令塔 (headquarters),
平時には城主の権威の象徴 (symbolic
power of the castle lord) である. ⇨城. ¶
白亜の5層の天守閣 a white castle with the
five-story donjon.

てんしゅきょう【天主教】 Roman Cathol-
licism. ☆「天主」. ラテン語のDeus〈デウス〉
はカトリック用語で「神」(God)の意. 潜伏
キリシタンは神のことを「デウス様」と呼ん
でいた. ⇨潜伏キリシタン

てんしゅどう【天主堂】(Roman Catholic)
church; cathedral(大聖堂).

てんしん[てんじん]【点心】 ❶〔茶道〕 ①
〈茶会での軽食〉an informal light meal
(served at a tea gathering). ②〈茶うけの菓
子〉sweets[refreshments] (served at the tea
gathering).
❷〈禅寺での軽食〉a Buddhist monk's
simple meal[snack] (eaten during a Zen
Buddhist service). 禅家での僧侶用の軽食
（禅の修業時に食す）. ☆仏教では「昼食」
(lunch)または「昼食前の少量の食事」(light
meal before lunch)の意味もある.
❸〈中華料理〉dim sum; Chinese snacks. 菓
子・軽食のこと. 肉まん・シューマイなど.

てんじん【天神】 ❶〈神〉the gods of heaven;
the heavenly gods. 天井の神. 天の神々.
❷〈人〉the deified spirit of Sugawara no
Michizane. He was a famous scholar in the
Heian period. He is now worshipped as
the guardian deity of studies, in particular
calligraphy. *Tenmangu* shrines (consecrated
on his honor) are visited by many students
wishing for success in their entrance
examinations. 菅原道真(845-903)のこと.
平安時代の学者. 学問特に書道の守護神.
（彼を称えて奉献された）「天満宮」は，合

格を祈願する受験生たちの参拝が絶えない. 通称「天神さま」. 圀京都の北野天満宮. ⇨天満宮

てんじんまつり【天神祭】 the Tenjin Festival of Tenman-gu Shrine. (7月). ⇨付記(1)「日本の祭り」

てんすいおけ【天水桶】 a rainwater bucket; a rainwater cistern[tank]; a tub used to store rainwater for fire prevention. The rainwater buckets were formerly placed on roofs and at street corners on each block. The pyramids of rainwater buckets were stacked up under the eaves of the house. 防火用に雨水をためておく桶 (barrel). 屋根の上や各街路角に置かれたり, 家の軒下に積み上げられていた. ⇨防火用水

てんそんこうりん【天孫降臨】the descent of Ninigi-no-Mikoto from heaven to Mount Takachiho(-no-mine)(located on the border between Miyazaki and Kagoshima prefectures) to rule Japan (according to the Japanese mythology). 日本を統治するためにニニギノミコトが高千穂(宮崎と鹿児島の県境)に天降ったこと. ☆古事記・日本書紀が伝える神話. ニニギノミコトは天照大神の孫 (grandson) なので「天孫」. 天照大神の命を受けて高天原から日向の高千穂に天降る. そのとき「三種の神器」を授かる. 初代の神武天皇はニニギノミコトの曾孫. ⇨天照大神 / 三種の神器

てんちじん【天地人】圀華道〉the three elements [orders] of "heaven, earth and mankind" in the universe (applied to the basic rules of flower arrangement). The three natural stems[flowers and branches] are arranged to form a harmonious triangle at the base of flower arrangement, exemplified in the main stems – heaven (the longest stem), earth (the shortest stem) and mankind (the reconciling stem). 宇宙の万物には「天地人」の3つの要素[順位]があるとして, 華道

の基本的なルールに応用させたもの. 主要な3本の自然の枝花を華道における「天(最上位の花)・地(最下位の花)・人(中間位の花)」に見たてて三角形の調和を配して盛り込む. ⇨生け花 / 盛花 / 瓶花 / 投げ入れ

てんちゃ【点茶】 the (formal) preparation of powdered green tea. 抹茶をたてること.

でんちゅう【殿中】 within the shogun's living quarters (in the Edo period). (江戸時代)将軍の居所内.

てんちょうせつ【天長節】 ⇨天皇誕生日(の旧称)

てんつゆ【天汁】 *tempura* soy-based dipping sauce; soy-based dipping sauce for *tempura*; a light sauce for dipping *tempura* into. Sauce is made from *shoyu*[soy sauce], *mirin*[sweetened *sake*] and fish broth. It is used as a dip when eating *tempura*, mixed with grated *daikon*[radish]. てんぷら用のつけ汁. 醤油, 味醂, 出し汁を煮立てたもの. 天ぷらを食べるとき, 大根卸しを加えてつけて食べる. ⇨天ぷら

でんでんだいこ【でんでん太鼓】 a small toy drum. It has a handle with two small bells attached by strings on both sides as beaters. It is usually used by a baby-sitter to entertain a baby. 小型の玩具太鼓. 太鼓には柄があり, 左右に紐がついた2個の鈴がついている. 子守が赤子をあやすのに用いる.

てんどう【天童】 ❶〈仏教〉gods disguised as children. 子供に扮する神.
❷〈稚児〉children disguised as heavenly beings in a festival procession. 祭事の行列で天人に扮する子供.

でんとう【伝統】 (a) tradition. ¶**伝統芸術** a traditional art. **伝統芸能** a traditional performing arts. **伝統工芸** a traditional craft. **伝統料理** a traditional Japanese-style dishes.

でんどう【殿堂】 ❶〈聖なる場所〉a temple

（仏教の）；a shrine（神道の）；a sanctuary [hall] (enshrining the gods in a shrine or temple). 神仏を祀ってある至聖所[聖なる場所].

❷〈御殿・広壮な建物〉 a palace; a splendid hall[edifice]. ¶白亜の殿堂 a white palace. 野球の殿堂 the Baseball Hall of Fame.

てんとうむし【天道虫】〔虫〕🇺🇸 a ladybug; 🇬🇧 a ladybird; a lady beetle. テントウムシ科の昆虫.

てんとじ【天綴じ】(a bowl of) wheat noodles [buckwheat noodles] topped with a piece of deep-fried prawn covered with eggs. 卵をまぶしたエビの天ぷらを上にのせたうどん[そば]. ⇨天ぷらうどん[そば]

てんどん【天丼】 (a bowl of) steamed rice topped with a few pieces of *tempura*[deep-fried seafood and vegetables]; (a bowl of) steamed rice served with a topping of one or two pieces of *tempura*[deep-fried seafood and vegetables]. Ingredients are various deep-fried dishes such as prawns[shrimps], eggplants, etc. *Tempura* dipping sauce (*tare*) is poured over steamed rice topped with deep-fried seafood and vegetables in a bowl. どんぶりに盛った飯の上にエビ, ナスなどの魚介類や野菜類の天ぷらの具をのせ, その上に垂れをかけた飯.「天ぷらどんぶり」の略. ⇨丼物 / 垂れ

てんねんきねんぶつ【天然記念物】 a natural monument[treasure]; a natural preserve; a protected species. ⇨特別天然記念物. ¶天然記念物保存法 Law for the Preservation of Natural Monuments. ⇨史跡名勝天然記念物保存法

てんのう【天皇】 an emperor; the Emperor of Japan. ¶明治天皇 (the) Emperor Meiji. 天皇家 the Imperial Family. ⇨皇室. 天皇賞 the Emperor's Cup. 天皇杯 the Emperor's Trophy[Prize]. 天皇旗 the Imperial Stan-

dard.

☆ emperorは, 本来ローマ帝国の後継者にのみ与えられた称号である. 日本では明治以降, 一代の天皇には1つの「元号」(era system)を用いることが定められた. ちなみに日本の「日本書紀」「古事記」によると, 日本の初代天皇は神武天皇から始まり, 現在の天皇は126代目である. しかし実在した可能性のある天皇は第10代の崇神天皇からといわれる. 記録に残っている天皇は第33代の推古天皇からで, 592年から628年まで在位した. この時代に聖徳太子が登場する.

【天皇制】 the Emperor system; the Imperial system of Japan; Imperial Order. "the Emperor shall be the symbol of the state and of the unity of the people." (stipulated in the Constitution of Japan)「日本および日本国民統合の象徴である」(日本国憲法にて規定)

【天皇機関説】 the theory of the Emperor as an organ of government; the emperor-as-an-organ-of-the-state theory. 国家の主権は法人としての国家にあり, 天皇はその最高機関である.

【天皇陛下】 His Imperial Majesty; His Majesty[H.M.] the Emperor. ☆天皇に対する敬称である. 男性には His, 女性には Her, 両者にはTheir,そして直接の呼びかけに "Your Majesty."を用いる.「皇后陛下」Her Imperial Majesty,「天皇皇后両陛下」Their Majesties the Emperor and Empress.

てんのうたんじょうび【天皇誕生日】 (the) Emperor's Birthday. (February 23). This national holiday has been established as a day to celebrate the birthday of Japan's present reigning Emperor since 1868. Originally known as *Tencho-setsu*, it was renamed *Tenno Tanjobi* in 1948. 1868年(明治元年)以降, 天皇の誕生日を国民の祝日として祝う. 1873年[明治6年, 太陽暦

採用の年］に「天長節」として国家の休日とした ことに始まり，戦後1948年に「天皇誕生日」に改称された． ⇨「昭和の日」（昭和天皇の誕生日）

【天皇誕生日一般参賀】 well-wishers' visit to the Imperial Palace for the Emperor's Birthday. ⇨一般参賀

てんぶ【天部】 ⇨天

でんぶ【田麩】 sweetened mashed fish meat; mashed and seasoned fish meat. Fish meat is shredded[crumbled] and seasoned with *shoyu*[soy sauce] and sugar, then roasted. It is often used as an ingredient for *chirashi-zushi*. 細かくほぐして甘くした［味つけした］魚肉．魚肉を醤油と砂糖で味つけて炒った食品．散らし鮨の具に用いる． ⇨散らし鮨

てんぶくろ【天袋】 a storage space[cabinet] above staggered shelves, adjacent to the ceiling. 天井に接し，違い棚の上部にある小さな袋戸棚． ⇨地袋

てんぷら【天婦羅】 *tempura*（日本語から国際英語化）；Japanese *tempura* batter-fried foods; deep-fried seafood or vegetables; fritters of batter-fried seafoods and vegetables; seafoods and vegetable dipped in batter and fried in deep fat. The ingredients are dipped into a batter of wheat flour and water mixed egg, and deep-fried in vegetable oil until the batter turns a light brown (at 170-180℃). *Tempura* foods are eaten hot after being dipped[by dipping them] in a soy-based sauce (*tentsuyu*) containing grated *daikon*[radish]. 魚介類や野菜類に卵を混ぜ水でといた小麦粉の衣をつけて油で揚げた食品．衣が少し色づくまで熱した油（170-180度）で揚げる．大根卸しを入れた天汁につけて食べる． ☆ポルトガル語tempero（調理）に由来する語といわれる． ⇨天汁／天滓．¶天ぷら衣 *tempura* batter; batter used to cook *tempura*. 天ぷら

の盛り合わせ assorted *tempura*. エビの天ぷら prawns[shrimps] *tempura*; deep-fried prawns[shrimps] in batter.

【天ぷらうどん［そば］】 (a bowl of) wheat-noodles[buckwheat noodles] topped with *tempura*; (a bowl of) hot noodles served with *tempura* toppings; (a bowl of) wheat noodles[buckwheat noodles] in fish broth topped with a few pieces of deep-fried prawns and bits of greens; (a bowl of) wheat noodles[buckwheat noodles] in fish broth placed with two or three pieces of deep-fried prawns and bits of greens on the top. エビのてんぷらと青物をのせたうどん［そば］.

でんぷん【澱粉】 starch. ☆芋類や穀類に含まれる炭水化物の一種．無味無臭の白色粉末．¶澱粉糖 starch sugar.

てんぽうせん【天保銭】 an oval-shaped copper coin. It was issued by the Tokugawa shogunate after the Tempo era 6 and used as official currency until the Meiji era. 楕円形［卵型］の銅貨．徳川幕府が天保6年（1835）以降に造った銅銭．明治時代まで公認貨幣として使用された．「天保通宝銭」の略．

てんまんぐう【天満宮】 a shrine dedicated to Sugawara no Michizane, the patron saint of scholarship. ⇨天神

てんむすび【天むすび】 a rice ball topped with deep-fried shrimp; a rice ball made with a topping of deep-fried shrimp. 小エビの天ぷらをのせた握り飯．

てんもく【天目】 a tea bowl (for putting into powdered green tea used in the tea ceremony). 茶の湯に用いる抹茶を入れる茶椀（の一種）．「天目茶碗」(a Tenmoku teabowl; a dark conical tea bowl of Chinese origin)の略．☆浅く開いた，すりばち形をしている．中国の天目山(Mount Tenmoku)に因んで名づけられた．この

山中で修行をしていた禅僧(Zen Buddhist priest)が，この種の茶碗を日本へ持ち帰った.

てんもり【天盛り】 toppings of Japanese dishes. 日本料理の上に飾って添える物(ミツバ・ユズなど).

てんもりそば【天盛りそば】 buckwheat noodles with *tempura* served on a slatted bamboo tray. 竹簀の皿に盛りつけた天ぷら付きのそば. ☆盛りそばに別皿の天ぷらが付く場合が多い. 単に「天盛り」ともいう.

てんやもの【店屋物】 food ordered[delivered] from a restaurant[caterer] (or from a *soba* shop); sent-in food (from a caterer). 飲食店[そば屋]からとりよせる食べ物.

てんらんずもう【天覧相撲】〔相撲〕 *sumo* matches (held) in the presence of the Emperor. 天皇陛下の御前[御出席]で行う相撲.

と

と【都】 the Metropolis (of Tokyo). ¶都庁 the (Tokyo) Metropolitan Government

といや【問屋】 a carrier and warehouse (in the Muromachi period). 室町時代の運送業・倉庫業. ⇨とんや

とう【塔】 a tower; a pagoda(仏寺の)；a steeple(尖塔). ⇨五重塔 / 天守閣

とう【籐】 rattan; cane. ヤシ科のつる性植物. 茎は籐細工用. ¶籐椅子 a rattan[cane] chair; a chair with a cane seat. 籐家具 a rattan[cane] furniture. 籐細工 (a piece of) wickerwork; canework; rattan work. ⇨簾

どう【胴】〈剣道〉❶〈防具〉a body armor [protector]; a breast guard (used to cover the chest in *kendo*).
❷〈決まり手〉a blow[stroke] to the chest [torso] (in *kendo*). 相手のわきばらに打ち込むわざ. ⇨剣道

どう【堂】 a temple; a shrine; a hall; a chapel

(小聖堂). ¶三十三間堂 Sanjusangen(do) Temple(京都). 金色堂 Konjiki(do) Hall(岩手県・中尊寺). 五大堂 Godai(-do) chapel(宮城県・仙台松島). ⇨寺

どう【洞】 a grotto; a cave; a cavern. ¶秋芳洞(山口県) Akiyoshido, a limestone cave[grotto]. ⇨洞窟

とうか【刀架】 ⇨太刀懸け

とうがらし【唐辛子】〔植物〕ナス科の一年草. a pepper; a capsicum.〈香辛料〉red[chili] pepepr; chili (powder).〈香辛料の粉〉chili pepper powder; cayenne pepper.〈果実〉a red pepper; a chili (㊂ chilies). ⇨鷹の爪. ¶赤唐辛子 red pepper. 青唐辛子 green pepper. ⇨一味唐辛子 / 獅子唐辛子 / 七味唐辛子

とうがん【冬瓜】〔植物〕a wax gourd; a white gourd (melon); a Chinese watermelon. ウリ科の一年生つる草. 果実は食用.

とうき【陶器】 ceramics; ceramic ware. (陶器製品)；pottery.(陶磁器製品)；earthenware.(土器)；china; chinaware. (皿・茶碗などの陶器類)；The ceramic ware with a glazed opaque body is often used as a flower vase in the flower arrangement or a tea bowl in the tea ceremony. 上薬[釉薬]をつけて焼いた無光沢[不透明]な陶器製品は華道の花器や茶道の茶碗などとしてよく用いる. ☆「陶器」は吸水[浸透]性のある粘土 (porous clay) で作られ，約1100度で焼く.「唐津焼」(佐賀県),「萩焼」(山口県).「益子焼」(栃木県)などがある.「陶磁器」(「炻器」(stoneware))は吸水性のない粘土 (non-porous clay) で作られ，上薬をかけない素焼き (unglazed body) で，約1200度で焼く.「信楽焼」(滋賀県),「備前焼」(岡山県),「常滑焼」(愛知県)などがある. ⇨陶磁器

¶陶器製作者 a potter. 陶器製作所 a pottery. 陶器製造所 ceramic industry. 陶器商〈人〉a dealer in china;〈店〉a china shop[store]. 民

芸の陶器 (a piece of) folk pottery. ⇨陶芸.
古い陶磁器 (a set of) antique china (ware).

どうぎ【胴着】❶〈胴着〉a padded vest; a padded, sleeveless undergarment. It is worn between inner and outer clothes[*kimonos*] to keep the chest and back warm in cold seasons. 下着と上着の間に着る，胸部と背中の防寒用下着.
❷〈剣道〉an undergarment (worn for protecting body). 身体の防具用下着. ⇨胴❶

どうきょう【銅鏡】a bronze mirror; a mirror made of bronze. ☆神社の御神体として祀られる. ⇨神体

とうきょうオリンピックたいかい【東京オリンピック大会】 Tokyo Olympic Games; Tokyo Olympics. The 18th Summer Olympic Games in Tokyo (in 1964). The Games of the XXXII Olympiad (in 2021).

とうきょうさいばん【東京裁判】 ⇨極東国際軍事裁判

とうきょうとちょうビル【東京都庁ビル】 Tokyo Metropolitan Government Building. ⇨都

とうぐう【東宮】 the Crown Prince. 皇太子. ¶東宮御所 the Crown Prince's Palace.

どうくつ【洞窟】 a cave; a cavern; a grotto. ¶洞窟遺跡 cave artifacts; a cave bearing traces of use as dwelling by (stone-age) humans. ⇨洞

どうぐはいけん【道具拝見】〔茶道〕 the courtesy of observing and appreciating the aroma of tea and the tea utensils. 茶の香や茶道具を観察・鑑賞する儀礼.

とうげ【峠】a (mountain) pass (山頂)；a peak (頂上). ¶堀切峠 (宮崎県) the Horikiri Pass. ⇨山 / 岳 / 丘 / 坂

とうげい【陶芸】 ceramic art; the art of pottery; ceramics. ⇨陶器. ¶陶芸家 a potter; a ceramist; a ceramic artist. ⇨陶工. 陶芸品 works of pottery[ceramic art].

とうけん【刀剣】a sword; swords (刀の総称). ⇨刀. ¶刀剣商 a dealer in sword.

どうけん【銅剣】 a bronze sword; a sword made of bronze.

とうこう【刀工】 a swordmaker; a swordsmith. ⇨刀 (刀かじ)

とうこう【陶工】 a potter; a ceramist; a porcelain maker. ⇨陶芸 (陶芸家)

とうこうきょひ【登校拒否】 truancy (無断欠席)；school phobia (学校嫌い)；refusal to attend school[classes]. ¶登校拒否児童 a truant; a school refuser; a student who refuses to go to[attend] school.

とうさつしゃしん【盗撮写真】a sneak photo; a candid camera shot.

とうじ【湯治】a hot-spring cure. It is believed that the mineral content in the hot-spring water is good for ailments. 鉱物性の含有物が病気に良い. ¶湯治客 a visitor to the hot spring(s); a visitor staying at a spa to cure a disease. 湯治場 a spa; a health resort[spa]; hot spring. 湯治療法［治療］a hot-spring cure; spa treatment.

とうじ【冬至】the winter solstice. ⇨二十四節気

どうし【導師】 the presiding[officiating] priest at a Buddhist ceremony. 法会や葬式のとき中心となる仏僧. ⇨伴僧

とうじき【陶磁器】 ceramics; pottery and porcelain; china; chinaware. *Tojiki* refers to both ceramics (*toki*) and porcelain (*jiki*).「陶磁器」には「陶器」〈工芸品〉(ceramics; ceramic ware; pottery)と「磁器」〈実用品〉(porcelain; porcelain ware; chinaware)がある. ☆陶磁器のことを「瀬戸物」(china; chinaware)と呼ぶこともあるが，これは有名な陶磁器の産地である愛知県瀬戸市の名前からの呼称. ⇨陶器 / 磁器

とうしょうぐうしゅんきれいたいさい【東照宮春季例大祭】 the Grand Spring Festival of Toshogu Shrine. (5月). ⇨付記(1)「日本の祭り」

と

どうじょう【道場】❶〈修行場〉a training hall for Buddhist ascetic practices (to attain spiritual enlightenment). 〔悟りを開くため〕仏法を修行し，また仏道を説く所. **❷**〈柔道・合気道・空手〉 a *dojo*; a *judo*[an *aikido*, a *karate*] training[exercise] hall (used for practicing Japanese martial art). The training hall has *tatami*-matted floor. 武道を修練する所. 合気道・柔道・空手の道場には畳敷きの床がある. **❸**〈剣道〉a *dojo*; a *kendo* training[exercise] hall (used for practicing Japanese martial art). The *kendo* training hall has wooden floor only. 剣道の道場には木製の床のみがある.

どうしょくぶつ【動植物】 plants and animals. ¶**動植物相** the flora and fauna.

とうしん【刀身】a sword blade; the (curved) blade of a sword. 刀のさやに入っている部分. ⇨刀

どうせいあいて【同棲相手】a live-in partner; a cohabitant(同棲者).

どうそじん【道祖神】 a travelers'guardian deity[god]; guardian deity[god] of roads and village boundaries. Travelers' guardian gods are enshrined on roads or at village boundaries to prevent evil spirits from entering and protect travelers safely on trips. 旅人の安全を守る神. 路傍または村境にあって悪霊が入りこむのを防ぎ，旅人の安全を守る. ⇨地蔵

とうだい【灯台】❶ a lighthouse(船舶用の). ¶**灯台守** a lighthouse keeper. **❷** a light stand (made of wood); a wooden stand used to strike a light on top. 昔の照明器具.「灯明台」(上に灯火をつける木製の台)ともいう.

どうたく【銅鐸】a bronze bell-shaped article of the Yayoi period; a Yayoi-period bronze ceremonial implement shaped like the bell. 弥生時代の青銅器[鐘]. 鐘状に作られた銅

製の祭器.

とうちょう【盗聴】〈電話〉(wire)tapping; electronic eavesdropping. ¶**盗聴器** a wiretap; a bug; a laser listening device.

とうなんほうちき【盗難報知器】 a burglar alarm.

とうにゅう【豆乳】 soybean milk; soymilk; soya milk. ☆豆腐をつくるとき，つぶした大豆に水を加え，煮てこした白い乳状の液. 牛乳の代用として飲料また料理に用いる. ⇨豆腐

とうにょうびょうよびぐん【糖尿病予備軍】 incipient diabetics.

とうば【塔婆】 ⇨卒塔婆

とうばく【倒幕】 the overthrow of the (Tokugawa) shogunate. 幕府を倒すこと. ☆倒幕運動の中心は薩摩(鹿児島県)，長州(山口県)，土佐(高知県)，肥前(佐賀県)の4藩出身の下級武士であった.

とうふ【豆腐】 *tofu*; soybean curd; bean curd made from soybean milk coagulated with bittern. にがりで凝固させた豆乳から作る豆の凝乳. ☆水にひたした大豆をくだいた煮汁をしぼり，かすをとったものに，にがりを加えて固めた豆乳から作る. 主として「木綿豆腐」「絹漉し豆腐」がある. ⇨木綿豆腐 / 絹漉し豆腐 / 高野豆腐 / 冷奴 / 湯豆腐 / 焼き豆腐 / 揚げ出し豆腐 / 肉豆腐. ¶**豆腐1丁** a block[cake] of *tofu*; a *tofu* cake. **豆腐田楽** ⇨田楽豆腐

どうまき【胴巻き】❶〈腹巻〉a belt wound around the stomach. ☆woundは wind「巻く」の過去分詞. **❷**〈金銭入れの帯〉 a money belt; a waistband for carrying money[valuables] while traveling.

とうみょう【豆苗】 pea sprouts. エンドウ豆の新芽と葉を摘んだもの. 和え物や浸し物など食材として用いる.

とうみょう【灯明】 a votive light[lighted candle] (offered to a god on the Shinto

[Buddhist] altar). 神棚[仏壇]の上に座す神に供えるともしび.

どうみょうじこ【道明寺粉】 glutinous rice flour; flour made from steamed glutinous rice and dried in the sun. 蒸したもち米を陽に乾燥させて挽いた粉. 和菓子を作るのに用いる. ☆最初に道明寺(大阪の藤井寺市にある尼寺)で作られたのが呼称の由来.

とうもろこし【玉蜀黍】〔植物〕㋐ corn(英国では「小麦」の意); Indian corn; ㋑ maize. イネ科の一年草.「トウキビ」ともいう. ¶穂軸についたトウモロコシ corn on the cob. 皮つきトウモロコシ corn on the ear. トウモロコシのさや corn husk. トウモロコシの穀粒 corn kernel. トウモロコシの皮 cornhusk. トウモロコシの毛 corn silk[floss]. トウモロコシの穂軸 a corncob; a cob.

とうようかんじ【当用漢字】 Chinese characters for daily use in Japan. 1850 Chinese characters were officially specified[designated] by the government for everyday use in 1946. 1946年に制定された1850字の漢字. ☆1981年[昭和56年]に「常用漢字」に変わった. ⇨常用漢字

とうろう【灯籠】 a lantern (used for illumination or decoration)中に明かりをともす灯火用具または装飾用具; dedicatory lantern(祭事の献灯); garden lantern(庭の灯籠). ¶奉献[奉納]灯籠 a votive lantern hung in a shrine or temple. 盆灯籠 a dedicatory lantern hung for the Bon Festival. 石灯籠 a stone lantern (found in the precincts of a shrine or temple or in the Japanese garden); a lantern made of stone (with a candle placed in the hollowed-out center); 献灯籠 a dedicatory lantern hung in a shrine or temple. 流し灯籠 a floating lantern; a lantern floating on water. 釣灯籠〈家屋〉a lantern hung from the eaves of the house; 〈寺社〉a hanging lantern found in a shrine or temple; a lantern hung under the edge of the eaves of a shrine or temple. 立て灯籠〈家屋〉a standing lantern placed in front of the house; 〈寺社〉a standing lantern lined along the approach to the shrine or temple.

【灯籠流し】〈盆行事〉the lantern-floating (event); the floating of lighted lanterns on water (held as a Buddhist ceremony). At the close of the Bon Festival (on August 15 or 16), lighted lanterns are floated on the waters of the river or the sea to send off the spirits of ancestors who had returned to their family. 〈広島県〉Some lantern-floating events are held on August 6 as a memorial service for people who died in the war (in Hiroshima Prefecture). 盂蘭盆の最終日(8月15日の夜または16日の朝)に精霊 (the ancestral spirits)を冥界に送り返すために川の上または海上に明かりのついた灯籠 (lanterns lighted with candles)を流す行事. 原爆被災地の広島では8月6日に行う. ⇨精霊流し

【灯籠舟】 a miniature straw boat with a lighted lantern. It is used for floating the ancestral spirits away at the close of the Bon Festival. 明かりをともす灯籠をのせた小型のわら船. 盂蘭盆の最終日に精霊を送り流すのに用いる. ⇨精霊舟

とおあさ【遠浅】 a long shoal beach; a shallow water's edge for some distance from the shore. ⇨浅瀬

とおかえびす【十日戎】 the Ebisu Festival of Imamiya Ebisu Shrine. (1月). ⇨付記(1)「日本の祭り」

とおし【通し】⇨お通し

とおしきょうげん【通し狂言】〔能楽〕(presentation of) a whole *kyogen* play. 一つの狂言をすべて続けて上演すること. また, その狂言.

とおりま【通り魔】 a random killer(手当たり次第の殺人者); a phantom attacker[robber]

（妄想的な加害者）；a maniac who attacks a passerby[passersby] at random. (無差別に通行人〔達〕を襲う狂人). ¶**通り魔事件** a phantom assault.

とかげ【蜥蜴】〔爬〕 a lizard; a shink; a monitor（大型）. トカゲ科の爬虫類. ⇨やもり

とき【朱鷺・鴇(国字)】〔鳥〕a Japanese crested ibis. (⊛ ibis, ibises)トキ科の鳥. 国際保護鳥. ¶**特別天然記念物のトキ** the Japanese crested ibis designated as a special natural monument. ⇨特別天然記念物

どき【土器】 earthenware; an earthen vessel. ¶**土器片** a (pot)sherd; a shard(遺跡土器の).

どきょう【読経】 sutra recitation[chanting]. 声を出してお経を読むこと. ¶**読経をする** recite[chant] a Buddhist sutra aloud.

どぐう【土偶】 a clay figure; a clay figurine of the Jomon period. It was used to keep off evil spirits and to pray for the rich supply of food. 土で作った人形 (earthen doll). 縄文時代の素焼きの土製の小型人形. 悪霊を払い，豊作を祈願するために使用していた.

とくがわごさんけ【徳川御三家】 the three branch families of the Tokugawa clan. ⇨御三家

とくがわばくふ【徳川幕府】 the Tokugawa shogunate (founded in 1603). ☆17世紀初めに徳川家康が政治の実権を握り，江戸(東京)に徳川幕府(=将軍の住居・陣営)を開いて260年余の間全国を支配した. ☆shogunate「幕府；(日本幕府の)将軍職」, shogun「(日本幕府の)将軍」. ⇨幕府

どくきのこ【毒茸】 a toadstool; a poisonous mushroom.

どくしんきぞく【独身貴族】an aristrocratic[a swinging] bachelor; a rich unmarried person.(金持ちの未婚者)；a well-off unattached[single] young man[woman]. (裕福な若い未婚者)

どくだみ【蕺草】 (a) *docudami*; heartleaf; Chinese lizard tail. ドクダミ科の異臭のある多年草. 漢方薬としての用途が多い.

とくべつしせき【特別史跡】a special historic spot. ⇨史跡

とくべつてんねんきねんぶつ【特別天然記念物】 a special natural monument[treasure]. ⇨例〔動物〕とき／ニホンカモシカ／コウノトリ／〔植物〕マリモ／〔土地〕秋芳洞. ¶**トキは特別天然記念物に指定されている**. A Japanese crested ibis is designated as a special natural monument[is designated as a rare species and protected by law].

とくめいのでんわ【匿名の電話】 an anonymous (phone)call. ☆「**匿名の手紙**」は an anonymous letter.

とくり【徳利】 ⇨とっくり

とけいかかりけんさやく【時計係検査役】〔相撲〕 a time-keeper.

どげざ【土下座】 kneeling (down) on the ground. People were forced to kneel on the ground and bow low during the procession of a feudal lord and his vassals in feudal times. 封建時代の大名行列の時に，庶民は地にひれ伏し(prostrate themselves)頭を低くさげた. ☆現在は「(無分別な行為に対し)土下座して詫びる」(bow down on one's hands and knees to beg forgiveness one's indiscretion)のように使う.

とこかざり【床飾り】 ⇨床の間(の飾り物)

とこがまち【床框】 a front edge-beam of the alcove dais. 床の間の前につけた化粧横木.

とこだな【床棚】 a side-alcove shelves(複数形で).

とこなめやき【常滑焼】 Tokoname ceramic and porcelain ware (produced in Aichi Prefecture). ☆釉薬 (glaze)を用いず，高温で固く焼き締める.

とこのま【床の間】 a *tokonoma*; an alcove (in a Japanese-style room); a built-in [recessive] alcove (with a slightly raised

floor). *Tokonoma* is often raised up one step the floor and decorated with a hanging scroll of a painting or calligraphy on the back wall. A vase of arranged flowers and a decorative object are usually displayed on the wooden floor as well. (座敷の上座の一部を少し高くした床に設けられた)造り付けた[奥まった]くぼみの小部屋. 通常床の間は床を一段高く上げ、奥まった壁には絵画または書道の掛け軸が飾られている. 木製の床板には生け花または芸術的な置物などもある. ¶床の間の飾り物[床飾り] an alcove ornament; an artistic ornament for an alcove. 床の間付きの部屋 a room with an alcove.

とこばしら【床柱】 an alcove post[pillar] (in a Japanese-style guest room). 座敷の床の間の手前にある角の化粧柱.

とこぶし【常節】〔貝〕 a small abalone; an ear shell; an ormer. 小型の鮑. 前菜や刺身に用いる.

とこやま【床山】❶〔歌舞伎〕 a wigmaker (or hairdresser) for actors. (歌舞伎などの)役者の髪を結い、鬘の手入れをする職人. また場所 (dressing room)をさす.
❷〔相撲〕 a hairdresser for *sumo* wrestlers. 力士の髪を結う職人.

ところてん【心太】 *tokoroten* seaweed gelatin jelly strips; thin noodle-like strips of gelatin jelly made from agar-agar seaweed. It is eaten with vinegar and *shoyu* [soy sauce] using mustard[grated ginger] as a condiment. 天草の煮汁をこして型に入れ、麺のようなゼリー状に固めた食品. 酢醤油とからし[卸し生姜]の薬味で味つけて食べる. ⇨天草

とこわきだな【床脇棚】 a boarded shelf adjacent to the main alcove (in a Japanese-style guest room). (座敷にある)床の間のかたわらにある板張りの棚. ⇨違い棚

とさじょうゆ【土佐醤油】 *shoyu*[soy sauce] seasoned with dried bonito flavor[flakes of dried bonito] (used for dipping *sashimi*[raw fish]). かつお節(高知県の特産)で味付けした醤油. 刺身に用いる.

とさず【土佐酢】 vinegar seasoned with dried bonito flavor. かつお節で味付けた酢.

とさに【土佐煮】 fish (or vegetables like bamboo shoots and burdocks) simmered in *shoyu*[soy sauce] broth seasoned with dried bonito flavor. 土佐醤油とかつお節 (flakes of dried bonito)で煮た魚(またはタケノコやゴボウなどの野菜).

とさぶし【土佐節】❶ fine-quality dried bonito; fine flakes of dried bonito. 土佐の良質のカツオ節. ☆「カツオ」は土佐の名物.
❷ the Tosa style of *joruri* chanting[singing]. ☆江戸浄瑠璃の一派. 土佐少掾 橘 正勝が始めた. ⇨浄瑠璃

とざまだいみょう【外様大名】 ⇨大名

どさんこ【道産子】❶〈人〉 a native of Hokkaido; a person born in Hokkaido. 北海道生まれの人.
❷〈馬〉 a horse native of Hokkaido; a horse foaled in Hokkaido. 北海道産の馬.

としおとこ[おんな]【年男[女]】 a man [woman] (who was) born under the same sign of the Chinese zodiac as the current year. He[She] is qualified to scatter lucky beans at the bean-throwing ceremony. その年の干支に生まれた男[女]. (a man [woman] born under the zodiac sign for that year). 節分の豆まきをする有資格者. ⇨節分

としがみ【年神・歳神】 the Shinto deity[god] of the incoming new year (who brings good luck); the Shinto deity who protects the family. *Toshigami* is believed to visit each house between the end and the beginning of the year in Japan. 年神が旧年と新年の境に家々を訪れるという古い信仰がある.

と

① 「**注連縄**」 *Shimenawa*[sacred rope of straw] is hung over the front door of the house to demonstrate the temporary abode of the *toshigami*. 注連縄は一時的な年神の依代として玄関につるされる。 ⇨注連縄

② 「**門松**」 *Kadomatsu*[New Year's decoration] is placed beside the entrance gate of the house to serve as a dwelling place for the *toshigami*. 門松は年神の依代として玄関に立てられる。 ⇨門松

③ 「**鏡餅**」 A pair of *kagami-mochi*[mirror-shaped rice cakes] has a smaller round rice cake placed on a larger one on a stand (*sanpo*). People worship the *toshigami* with an offering of mirror-shaped rice cakes. 鏡餅は年神を拝礼するために供えられる。 ⇨鏡餅

としこし【年越し】❶ seeing the old year out (and the New Year in). 旧年を送ること（新年を迎えること）。

❷ New Year's Eve. 大晦日の夜。 ☆陰暦では節分の夜。

【年越しそば】 buckwheat noodles eaten on New Year's Eve. The Japanese customarily eat these long noodles on New Year's Eve in the hope that they can lead a long life like the long noodles and their family fortune will extend like the long noodles. そばのように長生きができ，一家の幸運も長く続くように祈願する習慣。

としだな【年棚】 a special altar piled high with New Year's offerings. *Kagamimochi*[a pair of mirror-shaped rice cakes], *sake*, persimmons and other foods are placed on the altar (*toshidana*) to welcome the god of the incoming year (*toshigami*). 新年の捧げ物をのせてある棚［祭壇］。年神を迎えるために鏡餅，酒，柿その他の食べ物をこの祭壇［年棚］にのせる。 ⇨鏡餅／年神

としだま【年玉】 ⇨お年玉

どじょう【泥鰌】〔魚〕a loach. ドジョウ科の

硬骨魚。口に10本のひげ (thin mustache) がある。 ☆産卵期（6月・9月）頃の骨がやわらかくて旬。 ¶どじょう掬い〈捕獲〉scooping[catching] loaches (with a basket); 〈踊り〉a loach-scooping[-catching] dance (with a basket).

〔料理〕**どじょう汁** loach soup; loaches cooked in *miso*[bean paste] soup. **どじょう鍋** loach chowder; loaches boiled in broth at the table. ⇨柳川鍋

としより【年寄】❶〈相撲〉 the retired *sumo* wrestlers who remain as councilors [trustees] of the Japan Sumo Association. 引退後に務める日本相撲協会の評議員。別称「親方」。 ⇨親方

❷〈幕府の重臣〉 a senior councilor under the Tokugawa shogunate.

❸〈江戸時代の町役人〉a town[village] official under the Tokugawa shogunate.

とそ【屠蘇】❶〈薬草を浸した酒〉spiced *sake*. It is made by putting a silk bag containing a mixture of spices[herbs] (*tososan*) into refined *sake* (or *mirin*[sweetened *sake*]). 屠蘇散を混ぜ合わせて絹袋に入れたものを清酒（または味醂）に浸してつくる薬酒。 ⇨屠蘇散

❷〈正月に飲む祝い酒〉New Year's spiced *sake*; spiced *sake* for the celebration of the New Year. It is served on the morning of New Year's Day and sipped to celebrate the New Year. It is said to have the power to expel evil influences and to invite good health for the coming year. 邪気を払い長寿の効果があるといわれるので新年に飲む。平安時代からの伝統で中国から日本の宮廷に伝来した。 ☆「屠蘇」とは「蘇」という悪魔を「屠る」という意味である。

【屠蘇散】 spices for *toso*; spicy herbs [spices]for making spiced *sake*; spicy herbs [spices]for flavoring New Year's *sake*. 屠蘇をつくる薬草［薬味］。 ☆「肉桂」(cassia bark), 「山椒」(Japanese pepper), 「桔梗」(Chinese bellflower[balloonflower])など数種の生薬がある. 胃腸薬や風邪の予防に効く.

どそう【土倉】 a pawnshop[moneylender] of the Muromachi period. 室町時代の質屋[高利貸し].

どぞう【土蔵】 a traditional Japanese store-house [warehouse]. It is made of walls plastered with mud and mortar. 泥やモルタルで塗った土壁でつくった蔵. ¶土蔵造りの家 a storehouse-style house.

とっくり【徳利】 a *sake* bottle; a ceramic[an earthenware] *sake* bottle[flask] (used when serving Japanese *sake*). It is set in hot water to heat up the *sake*. (陶磁器製の)酒を入れるびん. お燗するときにはお湯につける. 「銚子」「お猪口」などともいう. ⇨銚子 / 猪口. ¶徳利立て a *sake* bottle holder[stand]. 「はかま」ともいう. ⇨はかま

とていせいど【徒弟制度】 an apprenticeship; an apprentice system. 職工・職人の見習い(制度).

どてなべ【土手鍋】 one-pot dish of seafoods and vegetables cooked with *miso*[bean paste] spread around the lip of the pot. 味噌を鍋の縁に(土手のように)ぬりつけて, 魚介類[カキ・貝など]や野菜を入れて煮る料理.

どてら【褞袍】 a wide-sleeved, padded *kimono*; a padded *kimono* with wide sleeves. It is usually worn over a gown to keep the chest and back warm in cold seasons. 広袖の, 綿入れの着物. 胸部と背中の冬季防寒用で, 部屋着の上に着る. 「丹前」ともいう. ⇨丹前

どどいつ【都々逸】 a *dodoitsu* song; a love verse of the 26-syllable lines. It is a Japanese popular love song of the Edo period in the 7-7-7-5 syllable pattern and sung to the accompaniment of *shamisen*. 江戸時代の俗曲の一つ. 26音節の愛情の詩歌. 七・七・七・五の四句からなる男女の愛情をうたったもので, 三味線の伴奏に合わせて歌う.

とどうふけん【都道府県】 the Metropolitan and Prefectural Governments; the 47 prefectures of Japan. The largest administrative units[divisions] of Japanese local government: *To*[Tokyo], *Do*[Hokkaido], 2 *Fu*[Osaka and Kyoto] and *Ken*[43 prefectures]. 1都(東京都), 1道(北海道), 2府(大阪府・京都府), 43県. ¶都道府県知事 Metropolitan and Prefectural governors. ⇨都 / 府 / 県

とない【都内】 in the Tokyo Metropolitan area. ¶都内23区 the 23 Wards in the Tokyo Metropolitan area.

どなべ【土鍋】 an earthen (ware) pot.

とのさま【殿様】 a lord; a feudal lord. 大名・旗本の敬称. ¶殿様暮らし the life of a lord; living like a lord.

とのさまがえる【殿様蛙】〔両〕 a leopard frog. アカガエル科の蛙の一種. ⇨かえる

とばたぎおんおおやまがさ【戸畑祇園大山笠】 the Tobata Gion Float-Parade Festival. (7月). ⇨付記(1)「日本の祭り」

とび【鳶】❶〔鳥〕 a kite; a black-eared kite. ワシタカ科の大形の鳥.
❷〈鳶職〉a fireman (of the Edo period; 火消し職人); a high-rise construction worker (工事の人夫); a scaffold constructor(建築の足場を作る人) [英 spiderman]. ⇨鳶口

とびいし【飛石】 stepping-stones (laid out on a path in a Japanese landscape garden as well as in a tea house garden). 日本の造景庭園や茶庭などの小さな通路の上に並べた敷石.

とびいしれんきゅう【飛び石連休】 a series of holidays with one or two intervening workdays; a series of vacations separated by one or two workdays (in between). 1日・2日の出勤日があり，間が飛んでいる一連の休日．

とびいり【飛び入り】　an unofficial participant（非公式の参加者）；an unexpected [unscheduled] participant（想定外の参加者）；a volunteer（有志）．

とびうお【飛(び)魚】〔魚〕a flying fish. トビウオ科の硬骨魚．脂肪質が少ないので揚げ物や焼き物に調理する．「アゴ」ともいう．¶**飛魚子** flying-fish roe（飛魚の卵）

とびおりじさつ【飛び降り自殺】　death-leap; leaping[jumping] to one's death (from a high-rise building). ¶**飛び降り自殺をする** leap[jump, plunge] to one's death; kill oneself[commit suicide] by leaping (from a high-rise building).

とびきゅう【飛び級】　grade skipping; skipping ahead in school. ⇨飛び入学．¶**1年から3年に飛び級する** skip the first grade and enter the third.

とびぐち【鳶口】　a fire hook (used by firemen to stabilize a fire ladder). 火消し［消防士］がはしごを固定させるために用いた鉤．☆棒の先に鳶のくちばしのような鉄の鉤をつけた道具．⇨鳶❷

とびこみじさつ【飛び込み自殺】　death-leap; leaping[jumping] to one's death (in front of an on-rushing train); killing oneself[committing suicide] by leaping [jumping] (in front of a train).

とびにゅうがく【飛び入学】　early college admission[entrance]; entrance into an institution of higher education by skipping a grade; an entering into a college without graduating from high school. ⇨飛び級

とびはぜ【跳び鯊】〔魚〕a mudskipper.

どひょう【土俵】〔相撲〕a *sumo* (wrestling) ring; the elevated round clay ring in[on] which a *sumo* bout is held. The area is formed[piled up] by burying straw bags filled with earth and hardening them into an earthen mound, which provides a smooth surface of the *sumo* ring. It forms a circle 4.5 meters in diameter on a 5.5-m-square mound of hardened clay. 土を盛り上げた堅い円形の競技場．土入りの俵を埋め込み，土俵の表面が平らな土のマウンドになるように固めて作る．5.5mの正方形のマウンド上で直径約4.5m（15尺）の円形をなしている．　¶**土俵に上がる** step up into[enter] the *sumo* ring. **土俵を下がる** step down[retire] from the *sumo* ring. **土俵を割る** go out of the *sumo* ring; be pushed out of the *sumo* ring. **土俵際で踏んばる** make a stand at the edge of the *sumo* ring. **土俵際に追い詰める** be driven to the edge of the *sumo* ring.

☆『土俵』に関連する主な用語．

①『仕切線』two white parallel lines. ⇨仕切り(線)

②『行司』a *sumo* referee (dressed in the court costume and a black ceremonial cap). ⇨行司

③『呼び出し』a ring announcer[caller] of

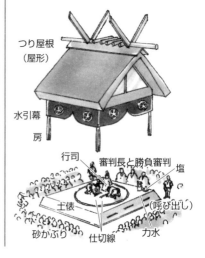

つり屋根（屋形）

水引幕

房

行司　審判長と勝負審判　塩

土俵

(呼び出し)

砂かぶり　仕切線　力水

sumo wrestlers. ⇨呼び出し

④『審判長』と『勝負審判』chief judge and five judges(sitting around the *sumo* ring at floor level).

⑤『砂かぶり』*sumo* ringside seats (where spectators may be hit by flying sand). ⇨砂かぶり

⑥『塩』salt (for tossing in the air to purify the *sumo* ring).

⑦『力水』power water(to rinse the mouth and purify the body). ⇨力水

⑧『つり屋根(屋形)』a suspended Shinto-style roof (hung above the *sumo* ring).

⑨『房』four tassels hanging each from the four corners of the suspended roof. ⇨房

⑩『水引幕』a purple curtain hanging from the edges of the suspended roof above the *sumo* ring.

【土俵入り】　a formal *sumo*-ring-entering ceremony. The ceremony of entering the *sumo* ring is symbolic of prayer which is performed according to the traditions of *sumo* wrestling. This ceremony is held to pledge to the gods of the ring that two *sumo* wrestlers will fight fairly. 土俵入りは相撲の古式に則って行う祈祷を象徴している．二人の力士が土俵の神に正々堂々と戦うことを誓うために行う.

☆ There are two types of *sumo*-ring-entering ceremony performed by all *sekitori sumo* wrestlers.

1. One ceremony is performed in a circle by all *makuuchi* and *juryo sumo* wrestlers wearing elaborately designed *kesho-mawashi*[ceremonial aprons]. The east and west sides perform their *dohyo-iri* together. During the ceremony the *sumo* wrestlers are introduced to the crowd one by one in ascending rank order and form a circle around the ring facing outwards. (In succession.)

2. The other ceremony is performed solely by *yokozuna* wearing a white rope[belt] over the ornamental *kesho-mawashi*[elaborately-embroidered ritual apron]. He is led by the highest-ranking referee (*tategyoji*) and accompanied by two attendants, a sword-bearer (*tachimochi*) and another herald, *makuuchi sumo* wrestler (*tsuyubarai*).

「関取」全員による土俵入りには、「幕内・十両の土俵入り」と「横綱の土俵入り」の 二種がある．①「幕内・十両の土俵入り」では豪華な化粧回しを着けた力士全員が東西に分かれて土俵入りをする．各人がランク順に紹介され，土俵の周りに環をなす．続いて ②「横綱の土俵入り」があり，化粧回しの上に白い綱を着けた横綱のみが単独で行う．横綱は最高位の「立行司」に先導され，「太刀持ち」(sword-carrier)と「露払い」(dew sweeper) を伴う．⇨太刀持ち / 露払い

【土俵溜まり】　the area around the *sumo* ring occupied by the referee, judges, and *sumo* wrestlers. 土俵近辺にある行司・審判員・力士の居場所.

どびん【土瓶】　an earthen[earthenware] teapot (for making green tea). お茶を沸かす土製容器．⇨急須．¶**土瓶敷き** a teapot rest[mat].

どびんむし【土瓶蒸し】　foods[seafoods and vegetables] steamed in an earthen teapot. 土瓶に入れて蒸した食物[魚介類や野菜]．☆「具」(ingredients)には松茸 / 白身魚 / エビ / 三葉 / 銀杏 / スダチなどが入る.

とぶくろ【戸袋】　rain doors[shutters] closet; a flat box-like closet to stow away rain doors; a flat box–like recess for stowing away shutters (attached to the wall). 雨戸を収納しておく所．⇨雨戸

どぶろく【濁酒】　raw *sake*; unrefined *sake*. It is made from rice without straining the lees. 白濁した酒．かすを漉し取らないで

米からつくる.「濁り酒」ともいう. 蒸した米に麹と水を加えて醸造したもの. ☆「自家製の醸造酒」(home-brewed *sake*)もあるが, 現在は禁止されている.

どま【土間】①〈家の中の〉an earth floor; ⊛ a dirt floor. It is an unfloored part of the rural house (where cooking is also done). 田舎の家に見られる床板のない地面のままの所. 台所としても使用する.

②〈劇場の〉the pit. 舞台正面の1階にあるます形の見物席.

とめ【留め】〔華道〕a plant holder. It is used for arranging the flower stalks and branches in a proper position in a vase. 植物を支えるもの. 花の茎や枝を花瓶に正しく生けるために用いる. ⇨花留め / 木密

とめそで【留袖】①〈袖〉a short sleeve (of a *kimono*). (和服の)短い袖丈. ⇔振袖

②〈着物〉a short-sleeved *kimono*. Tome-sode is a short-sleeved black or colored formal silk *kimono* decorated with auspicious patterns in gold and silver around the lower bottom[hem] and family crests on each sleeve. It is worn by both married and unmarried women on such ceremonial[auspicious] occasions as weddings, wedding receptions and formal parties. 短い袖丈の和服. 留袖は黒地(黒留袖)または単色(色留袖)の正装絹和服で, 前部には吉兆の金銀の裾模様そして両袖には家紋がある. 既婚または未婚女性の祝いの礼服で結婚式や結婚披露宴また公式パーティーなどに着用する. ⇨振袖(若い女性用). ☆主として「色留袖」と「黒留袖」がある. ⇨色留袖 / 黒留袖

とめわん【止椀】 a closing bowl (of *miso* soup); the final course of an elegant Japanese meal. ⇨「ご飯・香の物・止椀」

とも【供】〔能楽〕an attendant[a companion] to the main actor (*shite*) in a Noh play. He plays such a minor role as a sword-bearer. 能楽におけるシテの従者. 太刀持ちのような小役を演じる.

ともえり【共襟】 a (*kimono*) collar made of the same cloth as the *kimono*. 着物の表地と同じ布でかけたえり.

ともかせぎふうふ【共稼ぎ夫婦】a working couple; a dual-career couple[household]; a double-income[two-income] couple [family]; a two-paycheck couple[family]. 「共働き夫婦」ともいう. ☆「子供不在の共稼ぎ夫婦」は DINKS[Double Income No Kidsの略]という.

ともしび【灯し火】a light(明かり) ; a torch (松明).

ともしらが【共白髪】 a bundle of hemp string used for a betrothal gift. 結納で用いる麻ひもの束. ⇨結納

ともチョコ【友チョコ】 chocolates exchanged by girls on Valentine's Day.

ともびき【友引】 ⇨六曜

とや【鳥屋】〔歌舞伎〕actors' waiting room behind the curtain at the entrance of the *hanamichi*[passageway used for entry and exit of actors]. An actor usually takes a break before appearing on the kabuki stage. 役者が花道から舞台へ出る前に小憩する部屋. 揚幕の後部にある.

ドヤがい【ドヤ街】 ⊛ a flophouse district [quarter]; ⊛ doss-house district[quarter]; slums; skid row. There are usually drinking houses, cheap inns and snack bars where laborers drop in after a hard day's work. 簡易旅館が多数ある区域[地域]. 労働者が重労働を終えて立ち寄る安価な飲食店が散在する.

どやどや the Half-Naked Festival of Shitennoji Temple. (1月). ⇨付記(1)「日本の祭り」

どよう【土用】 (the) dog days; the hottest season in midsummer; the hottest period of summer in late June. (July 20[21] 〜

August 6[7]). 真夏日．立秋前の夏の土用．
¶**土用干し** summer airing (of clothes). **土用鰻** broiled eel eaten to beat the midsummer heat in the dog days[the hottest season]. **土用波** high waves during the dog days[in the hottest summer].

【土用の丑の日】 the hottest day of the midsummer. There is a custom to eat eel on the Midsummer Day of the Ox, known as the hottest day of the month of July so that people can overcome the fatigue of summer. 土用の丑の日には夏バテ予防のためにウナギを食べる習慣がある．

とら【虎】〔動物〕 a tiger(雄); a tigress(雌). ネコ科の哺乳動物．

とら【寅】 the Tiger, one[the third] of the 12 animals of the Chinese zodiac. 十二支の第三．⇨十二支
¶**寅の方** the Direction of the Tiger[east-northeast]. 方角の名．東北東．**寅の刻** the Hour of the Tiger[3-5 a.m.] 午前4時頃(およびその前後約2時間)．**寅年** the Year of the Tiger. **寅年生まれ** (be) born in the Year of the Tiger.

どら【銅鑼】 ❶〈船の〉a gong (of the ship when departing from the pier); a gong (announced sailing time). 出航の合図を知らせる船の鐘．
❷〔茶道〕a gong (used to signal the guests [participants] to reenter the tearoom during the tea ceremony). 茶道のとき茶室に再入場する旨を客[参加者]に合図する鐘．

トラピスト〈カトリック教会の〉the Trappists; (一修道士) a Trappist; (一修道女) a Trappistine. ¶**トラピスチヌ修道院** a Trappistne Abbey [Convent]. ☆1898年北海道・函館に日本で最初のカトリック女子修道院 (the first nunnery in Japan) が創立された．バター，クッキー，キャンディなどが名物．**トラピスト男子修道院** a Trappist Monastery.

どらやき【銅鑼焼】 sweet-bean pancake; a pair of round pancakes stuffed with sweet *adzuki*-bean paste in between. The confection is made by sandwiching *adzuki*-bean paste between two gong-shaped round pancakes (made from white flour, sugar and eggs). Pancakes are baked thin and flat on a hot iron plate with shallow round molds. (小麦粉，砂糖，卵を原料にした)銅鑼形に焼いた丸い皮(patties)2枚の間に，餡をはさんだ和菓子．皮は浅くて丸い流し型のある鉄板で薄く平らに焼く．

とり【鳥・鶏】〔鳥〕 a bird; a hen; a cock; a chicken; a fowl(食用). ⇨にわとり. ¶**鶏肉** chicken (meat); fowl. 別名「黄鶏」．**鶏殻** chicken bones (肉を取ったあとの鶏の骨). ⇨出し(鶏殻出し)
〔料理〕**鶏釜飯** rice, boiled chicken and vegetables in a small pot. ⇨釜飯．**鶏刺し** chicken *sashimi*; fresh slices of uncooked chicken. **鶏鍋** chicken and vegetables cooked in a cooking pot at the table. **鶏の空揚げ** deep-fried chicken without the use of batter. (衣を用いずに揚げた鶏肉). ⇨空揚げ．**鶏飯** boiled rice cooked with pieces of chicken and seasonal vegetables. (鶏肉と季節の野菜で炊いた飯).

とり【酉】 the Cock[⊛ Rooster], one[the tenth] of the 12 animals of the Chinese zodiac. 十二支の第十．⇨十二支. ¶**一の酉[二の酉／三の酉]** the first[second/ third] Days of the Cock in November. ¶**酉の方** the Direction of the Cock[west]. 方角の名．西．**酉の刻** the Hour of the Cock [5-7 p.m.] 午後6時頃(または5-7時の間)．**酉年** the Year of the Cock. **酉年生まれ** (be) born in the Year of the Cock.

【酉の市】 Cock[⊛ Rooster] Fairs; annual fairs held at the shrine on the days of the cock in[during] November. People sell ornamental bamboo rakes as good-luck

と

charms decorated with oval Japanese gold coins, cranes and tortoises as well as figures of the Seven Gods of Good Fortune in the shrine precincts. The bamboo rakes are believed to rake[gather] in good luck. It is held to wish for good business and prosperity. 11月の酉の日に神社で毎年行う恒例の市．神社の境内では大判・小判, 鶴・亀そして七福神の像で飾った縁起物の熊手が売られている．熊手は幸運をかき集めるといわれる．商売繁昌［繁盛］を祈願する. 圏東京の浅草また大阪の堺の西の市は有名．⇨熊手市 / 小判 / 大判 / 七福神

とりい【鳥居】 a *torii*, a Shinto shrine archway; a *torii* gateway at the entrance to a Shinto shrine. A *torii* is the archway erected on the approach to a Shinto shrine to mark the boundary between the holy precincts and the earthly world. It consists of two upright[standing] pillars connected by two horizontal crossbeams[lintels], one a little above the other. 神社の参道の入り口の門で, 聖域を示す．神域と俗世の間にある境界線を示す神社の入り口 (It symbolically separates the holy world inside from the secular world outside.). 大小2本の水平な冠木［笠木］(1本はもう1本の少し上にある)で連結させた2本の垂直の柱で構成される．☆「山門」は寺への入り口を示す．⇨山門 /冠木

とりがい【鳥貝】〔貝〕a cockle; an egg cockle; an edible cockle. ザルガイ科の二枚貝．すし種に用いる．

とりかぶと【鳥兜】〔植物〕(an) aconite; (a) wolfsbane. キンポウゲ科の有毒多年草．根は毒草, しかし乾燥すれば薬草.

とりくち【取(り)口】〔相撲〕*sumo* wrestling tactics; the style of *sumo* wrestling. It is *sumo* wrestling techniques for forcing the opponent out of the *sumo* ring or forcing the opponent touch the ground with any part of the body except the soles of the feet. 相手と取り組む方法・技巧．または勝負がつくまでの経過.

とりくみ【取組】〔相撲〕 a bout; a match; the bouts[matches] during a *sumo* tournament; the pairings for the *sumo* tournament. 相撲の組み合わせ．⇨相撲《相撲の取組》. ¶好取組 good matches; feature bouts; exciting matches. 取組表 a list[program] of bouts[matches]. 横綱同士の取組 a bout[match] between *yokozuna*(s). ☆相撲用語に限って送り仮名をつけずに「取組」と書く.

とりこえじんじゃどんとやき【鳥越神社どんと焼き】 the Fire Festival of Torikoe Shrine. (1月). ⇨付記(1)「日本の祭り」

とりこえじんじゃのよまつり【鳥越神社の夜祭】 the Night Festival of Torikoe Shrine. (6月). ⇨付記(1)「日本の祭り」

とりこぼし【取り零し】〔相撲〕an unexpected defeat through carelessness. 通常では負けるはずのない相手に負けること．「不覚の負け」.

とりなおし【取り直し】〔相撲〕 a rematch[second match] of a *sumo* wrestling round. When the result of a bout is too close to call even after the five judges' conference, they call for the bout to be refought from the initial charge (*tachiai*). 5人の審判員の合議の後も勝負が不明な(doubtful)場合, 立合いから再度勝負(restart)を決する.

とりのこもち【鳥の子餅】 (a pair of) red and white oval rice cake sweets (shaped like chicken eggs). 平たい鶏卵形の紅白(一対)の餅菓子．祝儀用．単に「鳥の子」また「鶴の子餅」ともいう．☆「鳥の子」は an egg(卵・鶏卵); a chick(ひな・鶴のひな). ⇨素甘

とりばし【取り箸】 (a pair of) serving chopsticks. 各人の皿に盛るときに用いる箸.

とりふだ【取り札】 cards to be picked out[up] in the game of *Hyakunin-isshu*; cards containing the final couplets[lines] of a *tanka* poem (which is) read out to players. The second half of a *tanka* poem is printed on a card. 遊戯者に読みあげられた短歌の後半の対句[七七の連句]が記された札. 歌カルタでは取るほうの札. ⇔読み札. ⇨百人一首

トリュフ truffle. 地下生の食用キノコ. 和名は「西洋松露」. フランス料理の高級食材.

トロ〈まぐろの〉fatty flesh[meat] of a tuna (often used for *sushi*); fatty belly of a tuna; an oily[fatty] tuna meat. マグロ肉のあぶらの多い部分. ¶**中トロ** medium-fatty flesh of a tuna; a moderately marbled fatty tuna; a belly of a tuna with a medium fat content. **大トロ** a top-quality-fatty[very fatty] flesh of a tuna; a heavily marbled fatty tuna; a belly of a tuna with a high fat content. ⇨まぐろ

とろいせき【登呂遺跡】 the Toro ruins [remains]; the Yayoi archeological site at Toro. 弥生時代の考古学跡地. ☆静岡県にある弥生時代の集落・水田遺跡. 国指定特別史跡.

とろみ thickener; thickness (made from dogtooth-violet starch or *kudzu* powder). (片栗粉や葛粉などで)濃厚にしたもの. ⇨片栗粉 / 葛(粉). ☆「澱粉でスープにとろみをつける」thicken the hot soup with starch.

とろろ【薯蕷】 grated yam (paste). It is a thick white paste made from the root of Japanese yam (*yamaimo*). 山芋卸し. 山芋の根から作るどろどろした白い練り物. 〔料理〕**とろろ汁** grated yam soup; soup mixed[cooked] with grated yam paste. **とろろそば** (a bowl of) buckwheat noodles topped with grated yam paste. **とろろ飯** (a bowl of) hot rice topped with grated yam paste.

とろろいも【薯蕷芋】〔植物〕a yam. ⇨山芋

とろろこんぶ【とろろ昆布】 thin *kombu* [tangle] flakes; thin shavings of *kombu*; *kombu* flakes thinly scraped with a blade. It is often eaten in clear soup. 刃物で薄く削った小片の昆布. 澄まし汁などに用いる.

とんカツ【豚カツ】 a deep-fried breaded pork cutlet. Pork is deep-fried after being coated with a batter of flour, beaten eggs and breadcrumbs. 豚肉に小麦粉, 溶き卵そしてパン粉の衣をつけてたっぷりの油で揚げる. ¶**とんかつソース** sauce for a pork cutlet.

どんぐり【団栗】 an acorn. くぬぎの実. 楢の実. ☆「団栗の木」は an oak tree. ⇨くぬぎ / なら

とんこつ【豚骨】 pig[pork] bones. ¶**豚骨スープ** pig[pork] bone soup; soup cooked with pig[pork] bones. **豚骨(煮)** boiled[simmered] pork with bones and root vegetables. **豚骨ラーメン** *Ramen*[Chinese brand noodles] cooked in pig[pork]-bone broth.

とんじる【豚汁】 (a bowl of) pork *miso*[bean paste] soup; *miso* soup with pork and vegetables; pork and vegetables soup flavored with *miso*. 豚肉と野菜を入れた味噌仕立ての汁.「ぶたじる」.

どんす【緞子】 damask (silk); satin damask. ダマスク織. 練り糸で織った地の厚い, 光沢のある絹織物. ⇨金襴緞子

どんちょう【緞帳】〈厚地の幕〉a thick curtain (hung in the theater); 〈垂れ幕〉a drop curtain (hung in the theater). 劇場などで巻いて上げ下ろしする幕.

どんでんがえし【どんでん返し】 ⇨がんどう返し

とんでんへい【屯田兵】 a farmer-soldier. Soldiers were recruited to colonize and defend Hokkaido after the Meiji Restoration. 明治維新後, 北海道の開拓や警備にあたった農場兵士.

どんど(ん)やき【どんど(ん)焼き】 *Dondo Bonfire*; the Burning Event of New Year's Decorations. (1月). ⇨付記(1)「日本の祭り」

トンネルがいしゃ【トンネル会社】 a dummy company(ダミー会社).

とんび【鳶】〈鳥〉 a kite. ⇨とび

どんぶり【丼】 ❶〈鉢〉 a bowl; a porcelain [ceramic] bowl; a china bowl. 深くて厚い磁器[陶器]の碗.「丼鉢」(medium-sized bowl) の略.
❷〈飯〉 rice served in a bowl.「丼飯」の略. ¶どんぶり一杯のご飯 a bowl of rice.
【丼物】 a bowl of rice topped with food; a bowl of rice with various cooked foods on top; rice served in a bowl with a topping of food; food-topped rice in a bowl. *Donburi-mono* is a bowl of rice topped with various kinds of ingredients[deep-fried seafood and vegetables]. 丼に入れたご飯にいろいろな食材 [魚介類や野菜などの具] を盛りつけた料理. ☆ food[seafood] は具 (ingredients) によって異なる. ⇨牛丼 / 天丼 / 親子丼 / カツ丼 / 掻き揚げ丼 / 鉄火丼 / 葱とろ丼 / そぼろ丼など.

どんぶりかんじょう【どんぶり勘定】 rough estimate(概算); sloppy accounting(いい加減な計算); hit-or-miss accounting practices(でたらめな計算事); Ⓜ ballpark figure (概数).

とんぼ【蜻蛉】〔虫〕 a dragonfly. ¶赤蜻蛉 a red dragonfly.

とんや【問屋】〈人〉 a wholesaler; a wholesale dealer[merchant];〈店〉 a wholesale store [house]; a wholesaling business. ¶問屋街 wholesale district.

な

な【菜】〈青物〉greens; (green) vegetables. 葉・茎を食用とする野菜の総称.「なっぱ」ともいう.

ないえん【内苑】 the inner garden. 宮中・神社の敷地内の庭. ⇔外苑. ¶皇居内苑 the Imperial Palace Inner Garden; the Inner Garden of the Imperial Palace. 明治神宮内苑 the Meiji Shrine Inner Garden; the Inner Garden of the Meiji Shrine.

ないかい【内海】 an inland sea. 陸地によってかこまれた海.「うちうみ」. ⇔外海. ¶瀬戸内海 the Inland Sea of Seto. ⇨～海 / 灘 / 海峡 / 湾 / 水道

ないかくしじりつ【内閣支持率】 the cabinet's public approval rating.

ないくう【内宮】 the Inner Sanctuary of Ise Grand Shrine (dedicated to Amaterasu Omikami, the Sun Goddess, the original ancestress of the Imperial Family). The Sacred Mirror, one of the three Divine Symbols of the Imperial Throne, is preserved there. 伊勢神宮の内陣. 皇祖神・天照大神を祀る. 三種の神器の一つである「八咫の鏡」が安置されている.「皇大神宮」. ⇨外宮 / 三種の神器

ないじん【内陣】〈神社仏閣〉 the inner shrine [temple]; the sanctuary of a Shinto shrine or Buddhist temple (where the object of worship or the principal statue of Buddha is enshrined). 御神体または御本尊のある神社・寺院の奥まった内部の本殿. ⇔外陣.

ないしんのう【内親王】 an Imperial princess; the honorific title for a princess of the Imperial Family. 皇室の皇女(または皇孫の子女)に対する尊称. ⇨親王. ¶内親王殿下 Her Imperial Highness Princess.

ないぞうしぼうがたひまん【内蔵脂肪型肥満】 visceral obesity. ☆「内臓脂肪」visceral fat

ないていとりけし【内定取り消し】 reneging on an acceptance of an informal job offer; renouncing unofficial acceptance for employment; cancellation of a promise[contract] of employment. ¶**内定取り消しの学生** students who have had would-be employers renege on[renounce] their informal job offers.

ないでん【内殿】〈神社仏閣の〉the innermost shrine; the sanctuary of a Shinto shrine or Buddhist temple. ⇨内陣；〈宮中の〉 the inner chamber[hall] of the Imperial Palace.

ないらん【内乱】a civil war（市民戦争）; a domestic warfare（国内戦闘）; a national conflict（国家紛争）; an internal rebellion [a disturbance]（内部反乱[紛糾]）.

ないりくけん【内陸県】a landlocked prefecture; a prefecture without a coastline; a prefecture without access to the sea. 海岸線がない県，海から遠く離れた県.

ないりくちほう【内陸地方】an inland district [province].

ないりんざん【内輪山】 the outer rim of a crater（火口のふち）; the volcanic cone within a crater（中央火口丘）. カルデラや旧噴火口の中に新たに発生した火山群. 圏阿蘇山（熊本県）や三原山（伊豆大島の最高峰）. ⇔外輪山

なえ【苗】〔植物〕a seedling（種から育てた苗）; a young plant. ¶**稲の苗** a young rice plant. **苗木** a nursery (tree); a young plant; a sapling. **苗木畑** a nursery garden. **杉の苗木** a cedar sapling. **苗床** a nursery (bed)（苗代）; a seed bed. **サツマイモの苗床** a nursery bed for sweet potatoes.

なおらい【直会】 a feast after a Shinto ritual in which participants eat and drink what was offered to the deity; a feast after a Shinto ceremony where people partake of the foods and drinks offered to the god. 神聖な祭りの儀式が終わったあとで，神に供えた酒や食物を下げて飲食する宴会. ⇨雑煮

なかい【仲居】〈旅館〉 a waitress at the Japanese-style inn (who is in charge of the guest room)；〈料亭〉a waitress at the Japanese-style restaurant (who serves Japanese dishes in *tatami*-matted rooms). 「旅館」での客室係で配膳 (set the table) や布団を敷く (spread out the *futon*).「料亭」での接客担当係で和室に料理を運び接待する.

ながいも【長芋】〔植物〕 a Chinese yam; a cinnamon vine. ヤマノイモ科のつる性多年草. 根をすりおろして「とろろ（汁）」として食用. ⇨やまいも

なかいり【中入り】 ❶〔相撲〕a break; ㋶ an intermission[㋗ interval] between two bouts in a *sumo* wrestling. 相撲の興行中に少し休憩する. ¶**中入り後の取組** the professional *sumo* makunouchi division bouts between top-ranked *sumo* wrestlers. In the meantime five judges change. 上位の相撲力士の間で行う幕内力士の試合. その間審判員が交代する.
❷〈能楽〉〈小休憩〉an intermission[interval] between two acts in a Noh play:〈シテの退場〉 a temporary exit from the Noh stage by the principal actor (*shite*) between two acts in a Noh play. 能楽の2場の幕間で少し休憩すること. 幕間時に主役（シテ）が舞台から一時的に退場すること.
❸〈演劇・寄席〉 an intermission[interval] between two acts in a (kabuki) drama or (vaudeville) theater. 演劇・寄席などの興業中に少し休憩すること.

ながうた【長唄】〔歌舞伎〕*nagauta*; (a piece of) a long epic ballad[lyrical song] chanted to *shamisen* accompaniment. *Nagauta* is chanted to the accompaniment of *shamisen* music for dances performed in a kabuki play, often with drums and flutes added. 歌舞伎の舞踊を演じるときに三味線の伴奏に合わせて歌う長編の俗謡で，通常太鼓や笛の音が加わる. ⇨地唄／端唄

ながえ【長柄】a long shaft[handle]. ¶**長柄の**

槍 a spear with a long shaft.

なかおび【中帯】 an *obi*[sash] tied over a tight-sleeved *kimono*. 小袖の上にしめる帯.

ながさきくんち【長崎くんち】 the Nagasaki Kunchi Autumn Festival. (10月). ⇨付記(1)「日本の祭り」

ながしそうめん【流し素麺】 fine wheat noodles eaten from running water; boiled thin wheat noodles carried in water down through the half-splitted bamboo tube, then eaten after being caught with chopsticks from running water. 竹管の流れ水から箸ですくい上げて食べる素麺. ⇨素麺

ながしびな【流し雛】 ❶〈人形〉 floating *hina*-dolls; *Hina*-dolls (made of straw or paper) floated away on the river (or out to the sea). 川[海]に流す(藁または紙で作った)雛人形.
❷〈行事〉the Doll-Floating Event. *Hina*-dolls are placed in small boats (or straw raft[basket]) together with offerings of foods or flowers and floated away on the river (or out to the sea) on the night of March 3rd. This event was originally observed to purify people by transferring evils to *hina*-dolls, but now to pray for girls' growth and good health. 3月3日の夜, 雛人形を食べ物または花などの供え物といっしょに積み, 小船(または藁製のいかだ[かご])にのせて川[海]に浮かべて流す(set afloat)行事. 元来人形に悪霊を移して(ward off evils)人を清める行事であったが, 今では子女の成長と健康を祈願する.

ながじゅばん[**ながじばん**]【長襦袢】 a long undergarment for a *kimono* (worn by both men and women). 着物用の長い下着. 男女兼用.

なかす【中洲】a river sandbar; a sandbank; a shoal. ☆川の中ほどで島のようになっている所.

なかせんどう【中山道・中仙道】 the Naka-sendo Highway; one of the five main highways in the Edo period that started at Nihonbashi and ended at Kyoto. 江戸時代における五街道の一つ. 日本橋を起点に(信濃路・美濃路を経て草津で東海道と合流し)京都を終点とする.「木曾街道」ともいう.

なかだち【中立ち】〔茶道〕the interval[recess] between the *kaiseki* meal and the tea-ceremony proper. 懐石料理と茶道儀礼の合間にとる中休み[休憩]. ☆この休憩中に閑談したり喫煙をする.

ながねぎ【長葱】〔植物〕a green onion; a leek; a scallion. ⇨ねぎ

なかのじょうとりおいまつり【中之条鳥追い祭】 the Bird-Chasing-Away Festival at Nakano-jo Town. (1月). ⇨付記(1)「日本の祭り」

ながばおり【長羽織】a long *haori* coat. ⇨羽織

ながばかま【長袴】 a long trailing *hakama* [skirt-like trousers]. It was worn with the *kataginu* and the *noshime* by *samurai* warrior as a formal wear in the Edo period. 後ろに裾を長く引いたはかま. 江戸時代, 武士の礼服に用い, 肩衣と熨斗目とともに着用した. ⇨袴 / 肩衣 / 熨斗目

ながはまひきやままつり【長浜曳山まつり】the Float-Parade Festival at Nagahama City. (4月). ⇨付記(1)「日本の祭り」

ながひばち【長火鉢】 an oblong box-shaped brazier; a rectangular wooden brazier with drawers used to warm one's hands. 箱型の火鉢. 引き出しなどがついている長方形の火鉢. 両手を暖めるのに用いる. ⇨火箸

なかまく【中幕】〔歌舞伎〕a short *kyogen* drama played between the two performances of a *kabuki* program. 一番目狂言と二番目狂言の間に客の目先を変えるために演じる短い一幕物の狂言.

なかみせ【仲見世・仲店】 shopping arcade; shops lining along the approach to the main hall of a Buddhist temple or Shinto shrine in the precincts. 神社仏閣の境内で, 参道に沿って立ち並ぶ商店(街).

ながもち【長持】 a big oblong wooden chest for clothing or bedclothes. 衣類・布団など を入れておく長方形の木箱.

ながや【長屋】㊋ a row house; ㊎ a terrace(d) house; 〈2軒続き〉㊋ a duplex (house); ㊎ a semidetached house; 〈3軒続き〉a row [terrace] house divided into three units. *Nagaya* is a small tenement house used by common people, all connected in a line under one roof, long and narrow in structure. One row-house was partitioned into many apartments. 一般庶民が使う小さな借家で, 一つ屋根の下で一列に結ばれている. その 構造には大小がある. 一軒長屋には多数の 住居区画がある. ¶**裏長屋** a row of houses on a narrow back street; row houses on back streets (built behind residents lining the main streets). **長屋の住民** a row house tenent.

なかよしクラブ【仲良しクラブ】 (a group of) good pals; a pally[chummy] groups.

なぎなた【長刀・薙刀】 a ***naginata***; a Japanese halberd; a Japanese sword with a long wooden-shaft[handle]. A *naginata* is a traditional weapon made of a curved single-edged blade attached to the tip of a long wooden shaft. 長い木製の<u>柄</u>(handle)の先 に幅の広いそった刃物(short sword)をつ けた武器. ☆「<u>日本刀の柄</u>」は the <u>hilt</u> of a sword.

❶〈真剣の長刀〉a real Japanese blade[short sword] with a long shaft.

❷〈競技の長刀〉a wooden pole blade[short sword] with a long shaft.

【長刀道】 the Japanese martial art of wielding[using] a Japanese halberd with a substitute blade of bamboo (practiced exclusively by women). 竹製の代用刃を つけた長刀を振り回す[使用する]武道(女 性のみが行う). ☆平安末期から戦場で使 用されていた. 特に僧兵 (warrior-monks; monk soldiers)は寺院守護のため使用した. 江戸時代には武家の女性の護身術 (self-protective martial art for women)となった. 明治時代には女性の精神の鍛錬 (spiritual training)として「長刀道」が発展した.

【長刀競技】 a *naginata* match (using the same protective clothing as *kendo*). Victory in a match is determined by a successful hit[lunge] of the opponent's protective gear by using a *naginata* [wooden pole halberd]. 剣道と同じ防具を着用する. 試合 競技では長刀を用いて相手防具への「打突」 (stabbing[striking] a part)が決まると勝 つ. ☆競技用の「長刀」の長さは約2m.「柄」 (shaft)は樫の木(oak tree)で作られ, 「先端 の刀」は竹を2枚張り合わせたもの (the tip of two layers of laminated bamboo). ⇨剣 道

【長刀防具】 *naginata* protective armor. ☆ 「面」face mask.「胴」chest protector.「垂れ」 waist protector.「籠手[小手]」arm guards. 「向うずね具」shin guards.

なげいれ【投げ入れ】〔華道〕the thrown-in style[free-style] flower arrangement. Flowers are freely arranged in a cylindrical vase without needle-point holders[pin frog] in the natural looking way. The simplest form of this style is often used in the tea ceremony. 投げ込み型の生け花で, 剣山を 用いずに自然な形で円筒形の花器に生け る. この簡素な形式は茶道に利用されるこ とが多い. (草月流・池坊流). ⇨盛り花 / 天 地人

なげわざ【投げ技】〈相撲・柔道〉 a throwing technique; an art of throwing or hurling one's opponent to the ground.

なこうど【仲人】 a go-between（仲立ちをする人）; a matchmaker（結婚の世話人）; a man[woman] who acts as (a) matchmaker [go-between]. He/She goes between a single man and woman, and formally arranges their marriage. ⇨媒酌人 / 見合い

なごやおび【名古屋帯】 *Nagoya obi*[sash] worn casually by women with a *kimono*. Nagoya *obi* is made from silk or cotton cloth with woven or dyed designs. One part of about 30 centimeters is tied in the back with a square-shaped drum bow. The other part folded in half is wrapped around the waist. 女性用のカジュアルな着物帯. 織物や染物にデザインした絹または木綿の布から作られる. 後部で四角い太鼓形に結ぶ幅約30cmの並幅と胴回りの部分を締める半幅に仕立ててある. ⇨帯

なし【梨】〔植物〕a pear tree（木）; a pear（実）. バラ科の落葉高木. ☆日本では梨は「無し」(nothing)に通ずるのを忌みさけて〈忌み詞［言葉］<a taboo word>〉, 梨の実を「有りの実」という.

なしじまきえ【梨子地蒔絵】 gold-sprinkled lacquerwork; pearskin-like gold finish lacquerwork.（梨の実の表面のように）金粉をまきちらし, 透明な漆を塗った蒔絵.

なす【茄子】〔植物〕㋐ an eggplant; ㋑ an aubergine. ナス科の一年草.「なすび」ともいう. ¶長茄子 a slim eggplant. 丸茄子 a round eggplant.
〔料理〕茄子田楽 grilled eggplants on skewers coated with *miso*[bean paste] glaze. ⇨田楽. 茄子の塩漬け eggplants preserved with salt; eggplants pickled in salt.

なずな【薺】〔植物〕 a shovelweed（ペンペン草）; a shepherd's purse. アブラナ科の二年草. 若菜は食用.「春の七草」の一つ. ⇨春の七草

なだ【灘】 an open sea; an ocean having strong and high wave. 波の荒い海. ¶玄界灘 the Genkai(nada) Sea; the Sea of Genkai ⇨海 / 内海 / 海峡 / 湾 / 水道

なたね【菜種】〔植物〕rape seed;（種子）a rape seed; rape（あぶら菜）; colza.「あぶら菜」の一種. ⇨なのはな / あぶらな. ¶菜種油 rape(-seed) oil; colza oil; canola oil. ☆rape（強姦）は犯罪を連想させることから, 宣伝文や商品名として canola[colza] oil が用いられている.

なたねづゆ【菜種梅雨】 a long spell of rainy weather in early spring. 早春の長雨.

なだのきいっぽん【灘の生一本】 pure Nada *sake*; finely-quality *sake* produced in Nada (in Hyogo Prefecture).

なだのけんかまつり【灘のけんかまつり】the Nada Fighting Festival.（10月）. ⇨付記(1)「日本の祭り」

なたまめ【鉈豆・刀豆】〔植物〕a sword bean. マメ科のつる性一年草. 種子は食用. 豆のサヤの塩漬けは「福神漬け」の材料.

なちのひまつり【那智の火まつり】 the Fire Festival at Kumano-Nachi Shrine.（7月）. ⇨付記(1)「日本の祭り」

なづけ【菜漬け】pickled greens[vegetables]; pickles made of leafy greens[vegetables]; greens pickled in salt. 野菜類の葉の塩漬け.

なっとう【納豆】 *natto*; fermented soybeans (with a slimy consistency or stickiness). *Natto* is made from fermented soybeans and *natto* fungus[bacillus]. *Natto* is eaten on top of cooked rice after being mixed with *shoyu*[soy sauce], hot mustard and minced onions.（ぬるぬるした粘りのある）納豆は大豆を納豆菌で発酵させて作る. 醤油, からし, さらしネギを混ぜ, ご飯の上にのせて食べる. ☆「納豆菌」は *natto* fungus; *natto* bacillus. ㉖ fungi[bacilli]. ⇨甘納豆
〔料理〕納豆汁 *miso*[bean paste] soup containing minced[chopped] *natto*[fermented

soybeans]. **納豆巻き** *sushi* rolled by hand in a sheet of dried laver with *natto*[fermented soybeans] in the center; *sushi* containing *natto* and rolled in dried laver. ⇨巻き鮨

なつみかん【夏蜜柑】〔植物〕a Japanese summer orange; a Chinese citron; a Watson pomelo. ミカン科の常緑低木.「ナツダイダイ」ともいう.

なつめ【棗】❶〔植物〕a jujube(実); a jujube tree(木); a Chinese date. クロウメモドキ科の落葉高木. 果実は食用・薬用. 特に乾果は菓子や料理の材料にする.
❷〔茶道〕a (lacquered) tea caddy[canister]. It is a (lacquered) tea container[receptacle] with a lid for keeping thin powdered[foamy] green tea[*usu-cha*] used in the tea ceremony. 点茶に用いる茶入れ. 抹茶[薄茶]を入れるのに用いる蓋付きの漆器の茶入れ. ☆形が「なつめ」に似ていることからの呼称.「濃茶」を入れる茶器は「茶入れ」という. ⇨茶(茶入れ)

なつめやし【棗椰子】〔植物〕a date palm tree (木); a date(実). ヤシ科の常緑高木. ジャムやジェリーなどを作る.

なでしこ【撫子】〔植物〕 a (fringed) pink; a (clustered head) pink. ナデシコ科の多年草.「秋の七草」の一つ. ⇨秋の七草 / 大和(やまと)なでしこ)

ななかいき【七回忌】 ⇨回忌

ななくさ【七草】 ❶〈春〉the seven spring herbs; the seven herbs of the spring. ⇨春の七草
❷〈秋〉the seven autumn flowers; the seven flowers of the autumn. ⇨秋の七草

ななくさがゆ【七草粥】❶〈七草を入れた粥〉 seven-herb rice gruel[porridge]; rice gruel[porridge] cooked with some kinds of the seven herbs[grasses].
❷〈1月7日に食べる七草粥〉spring-herb rice gruel; rice gruel[porridge] cooked with the seven kinds of spring herbs. There is a

Japanese custom to eat *nanakusa-gayu* on January 7 to ward off all kinds of diseases and prevent sickness in the coming year. 1月7日に来る年の万病を遠ざけ, 無病息災を願って (have good health throughout the coming year)「春の七草」を入れた粥を食す日本の習慣. ☆平安時代に宮中で儀式として始まり, 江戸時代には大衆に普及する. ⇨春の七草

なにわぶし【浪花節】*naniwa-bushi*; a Japanese ballad[storytelling about duty and humanity] recited by a solo chanter with *shamisen* accompaniment. *Naniwa-bushi* is a solo recitation partly chanted in a special sober intonation to the accompaniment of *shamisen* and partly narrated in the form of a dialogue. The ballad[epic song] is based on accounts of historical events, traditional stories, etc. 三味線の伴奏で(義理人情 (moral obligations and human feelings)を主題に)節をつけて一人で語る大衆的な物語風の日本バラッド[叙事詩]. 三味線の伴奏で節をつけて「唄う」(弾)部分と対話形式で「語る」(啖呵)部分がある. バラッド[叙事詩]は歴史的な事件や伝統的な物語の顛末に基づいている.「浪曲」ともいう. ☆江戸時代末期に大阪の芸人・浪花伊助が起こし, 明治以降に普及した.「落語」・「講談」と並ぶ三大大衆芸能の一つ. ⇨落語 / 講談

なのはな【菜の花】〔植物〕rape blossoms; colza[canola] blossoms. 正式名称は油菜. 柔らかい若葉は和え物や浸し物に用いる. ⇨油菜 / なたね. ¶菜の花畑 a rape field; a field of rape blossoms.

なはおおつなひき【那覇大綱挽】 the Tug-of-War Match Festival. (10月). ⇨付記(1)「日本の祭り」

なべ【鍋】a pot(深い); a pan(浅い). ¶土鍋 an earthenware pot. 鉄鍋 an iron pot. 鍋敷き a pot stand. 鍋蓋 a pot lid. 鍋釜 pots and kettles; kitchen utensils.

【鍋物】 a hot-pot[one-pot] dish (cooked at the table). Seafoods and vegetables are cooked in a communal pot at the table and are helped oneself from the pot while cooking. ひとつの鍋で料理する食べ物. 魚介類や野菜を共用鍋に入れて食卓で煮ながら各人鍋から自由にとって食べる.「鍋料理」(casserole; food[meal] served in a pot at the table)ともいう. ⇨石狩鍋 / 寄せ鍋 / 水炊き

【鍋焼きうどん】 pot-boiled noodles; wheat noodles boiled together with seafoods (or meat) and vegetables in an individual small earthenware pot. 魚介類[肉]や野菜を一人前用の小さな土鍋で煮て食べるうどん.

なまあん【生餡】 ⇨餡

なまがし【生菓子】 ❶〈和菓子〉 Japanese unbaked sweets. Most are made mainly from sweet *adzuki*-bean paste or soft pounded[glutinous] rice. 主として餡子または柔らかく捏ねた米[もち米]で作る. ☆大福餅・羊羹などの和菓子. ⇨主菓子(茶道用). ⇦干菓子

❷〈洋菓子〉 Western-style unbaked cake (made with fruits). 果物などを用いた西洋風菓子.

なまこ【海鼠】〔動物〕 a sea cucumber; a sea slug; a trepang. 腸の塩辛は「このわた」, 腸をとって乾燥させたものは「いりこ」. 卵巣を干したものは「このこ」. ⇨このわた(海鼠腸) / いりこ(海参・煎海鼠). ¶干しなまこ dried sea slug; dried sea cucumber. ☆「いりこ」ともいう. ⇨いりこ

なまこもち【海鼠餅】 a rice cake in sea cucumber shape; a rice cake prepared in the shape of a sea cucumber[flat semi-cylinder]. It is cut crosswise into thin slices and roasted when eaten. 海鼠の形[平らな半円筒]にした餅. 食べるときは賽の目に切り「欠き餅」(おかき)にする. ☆大寒の頃

つくるので「寒餅」ともいう. ⇨欠き餅

なまざかな【生魚】〈火を通していない〉 (a) raw fish; an uncooked fish. ⇨生魚

なましいたけ【生椎茸】 fresh *shiitake* mushroom. ⇨椎茸

なます【膾(野菜の場合)・鱠(魚介類の場合)】 a Japanese fish[vegetables] salad;〈酢で味つけしたもの〉(a dish of) sliced[chopped] raw fish[shellfish] and/ or vegetables seasoned with vinegar;〈酢で漬けたもの〉(a dish of) raw fish[shellfish] and/ or vegetables cut into thin pieces and marinated[soaked] in vinegar. 生の魚と[または]野菜を細かくきざみ, 酢で和えた食品. ⇨沖膾 / 大根膾

なまず【鯰(国字)】〔魚〕 a catfish. ナマズ科の硬骨魚. 焼物・煮物・てんぷらなどに調理する.

なまはげ(祭事) the Devil Festival in the Oga Peninsula. (12月). ⇨付記(1)「日本の祭り」

なまぼし【生干し・生乾し】 half-dried (fish). 充分に干さない生乾きのもの. ¶生干しのサバ half-dried mackerel. 生干しのイワシ half-dried sardine.

なまりぶし【生節】 boiled and half-dried bonito. 蒸した(steamed)カツオの身を生干しにしたもの. 別称「なま節」. 和え物や酢の物にする.

なみのはな【波の花】 ❶〈波頭〉 the crest of a wave; the foam from the waves blowing in the air during the winter. 波の峰. 冬季になると空中に吹き上げる波が白く砕けて泡だつ状態. 圏曽々木海岸(石川県).

❷〈塩〉 salt.「塩」の別称.

なむあみだぶつ【南無阿弥陀仏】 "I worship Amitabha[Amida Buddha] and follow his doctrine."〈阿弥陀仏を敬い, その教えに従います〉. ☆**南無**は I worship[pray to] and obey one's doctrine[teachings]. (敬い, その教えに従う),「**阿弥陀**」は Amida,「**仏**」は Buddhaである. 浄土教で阿弥陀仏に帰

依し (believe in Amitabha)，絶大な信頼を寄せる (depend on Amitabha)こと．これを唱えることを「念仏」という．⇨阿弥陀/念仏

なむみょうほうれんげきょう【南無妙法蓮華経】 All Glory to the Lotus Sutra of the Supreme Law. "I obey sutra [*myoho renge kyo*] and observe its doctrine[teachings]." 〈妙法連華経に従い，その教えを守ります〉. Repeated chanting of this prayer can lead believers to salvation. この祈りの言葉を何度も繰り返して唱えると救われる．☆「南無」は I pray.「妙法」は the Supreme Law.「蓮華経」は the Lotus Sutra. 日蓮宗で，法華経への帰依 (believe in the teaching of the Lotus Sutra)を表し唱える祈祷．「題目」「お題目」ともいう．⇨題目

なめくじ【蛞蝓】〔動物〕a slug. ナメクジ科の軟体動物．野菜や果物にとって有害．塩をかけると縮む．

なめこ【滑子】 a *nameko* mushroom; a champignon. モエギタケ科の食用キノコ．ブナの倒木などに群生する．別名「なめたけ」・「なめすぎたけ」．みそ汁や卸し和えなどに用いる．
〔料理〕**滑子の卸し和え** *nameko* mushrooms dressed with grated *daikon*[radish].

なめし【菜飯】〈炊き込み飯〉rice cooked with minced vegetables; rice boiled with finely-chopped vegetable greens. 刻み青菜を炊きこんだ飯．〈混ぜご飯〉hot rice mixed with salted *daikon*[radish] leaves. （刻み大根葉と混ぜたご飯）

なら【楢】〔植物〕a Japanese oak (tree). ブナ科の落葉高木．実はドングリ (acorn). 材は家具用(オーク材)．¶楢林 an oakwood.

ならづけ【奈良漬け】 *sake*-flavored pickles: vegetables pickled in *sake* lees[dregs]; pickles seasoned in *sake* lees[dregs]. 野菜の酒かす漬け．☆主としてウリ (cucumber melon)だが，ナス(eggplant)やダイコン (*daikon*[Japanese radish])なども用いる．

奈良県の特産 (specialty).

なりたりこん【成田離婚】 a Narita divorce; divorce on returning from one's honeymoon; getting divorced soon after the honeymoon.

なると(まき)【鳴門(巻き)】 (a roll of) steamed fish-paste cake with a whirlpool pattern; (a loaf of) steamed fish-cake shaped like a long cylinder. It contains a red design in the form of a whirlpool in the center. It is often used to decorate the top of noodles in a bowl. (鳴門の)渦巻き模様のある[長い円筒形の]巻き蒲鉾．中央には渦巻き形の薄紅色の模様がある．器に盛ったうどんの上にのせる飾りとして用いることが多い．

なれずし【熟鮨】 fermented *sushi*; *sushi* [food] made by acid fermentation of fish pickled in salt and preserved in rice. （酢を用いず）魚を塩漬けし，ご飯で熟成させた酸味発酵のある鮨[食品]．☆魚の発酵食品 (fermented fish) の一種である．「馴れ鮓」「腐れずし」とも書く．滋賀県琵琶湖近辺の特産である近江の「フナずし」，和歌山県の「サンマずし」，岐阜県の「アユずし」などが有名．

なわのれん【縄暖簾】 ❶〈暖簾〉a straw-rope curtain. It is hung at the entrance to a Japanese bar[㊇pub] for laborers. 縄を結んだ暖簾．勤労者が利用する居酒屋 (drinking establishments)につるしてある．⇨暖簾
❷〈酒場・飲み屋〉a bar; a tavern; ㊇ a pub.

なんが【南画】「南宗画」の略．❶〈流派〉the Southern school of Chinese paintings. It originated in China and was introduced to Japan in the mid-Edo period. 日本画の流派のひとつ．中国から始まり，江戸中期に伝わった．⇨北画
❷〈絵画〉a Nanga-style painting; a painting in the Nanga style. A landscape is depicted in black India ink or in thin coloring. 南画

形式の絵画．水墨または淡彩で，多くの山水を描く．「文人画」ともいう．

なんきんだいぎゃくさつ【南京大虐殺】　the Nanjing Massacre.

なんきんまめ【南京豆】〔植物〕a peanut; a groundnut. ⇨らっかせい

なんきんむし【南京虫】〔虫〕a bedbug. トコジラミ科の昆虫．人畜の血を吸う．

なんてん【南天】〔植物〕a nandin; a mandina; a sacred[heavenly] bamboo. メギ科の常緑低木．☆「難を転じ，福を招く」という意味合いの縁起物 (a good-luck bringer). 正月の飾り物として欠かせない．岐阜県・郡上八幡は日本最大の出荷量を誇る．

なんど【納戸】　a closet; ⊛ a storage room; ⊕ a box room.

ナンバーズたからくじ【ナンバーズ宝くじ】⇨宝くじ

なんばん【南蛮】❶①〈国〉Southeast Asian countries (called in Japan between the late-Muromachi and early-Edo periods). 東南アジア諸国．室町時代末期から江戸時代初期までの呼称．②〈人〉⇨南蛮人 ❷〈南方の蛮人〉southern barbarians. 南方の異民族． ❸〈唐辛子〉red[green] pepper; chili pepper. ⇨とうがらし

【南蛮画】　Western painting brought to Japan in the early 17th century. 17世紀日本の洋画．

【南蛮渡来品】　articles imported from Southeast Asian countries to Japan between the 14th and the early 17th century. 14世紀から17世紀間に東南アジアから日本へ輸入された物品．

【南蛮美術】　European-style fine arts brought to Japan in the 16th century. 16世紀に導入された欧州風の芸術品．

【南蛮屏風】　a painted (folding) screen depicting scenes of European visitors [Europeans visiting Japan] in the 16th to the 17th century. 16世紀と17世紀に来日した欧米人の風景を描いた屏風．

【南蛮文化】　Western and Christian culture introduced into Japan by Europeans [Spanish or Portuguese missionaries and merchants] in the 16th to the 17th century. 16世紀・17世紀に欧米人[スペインまたはポルトガルの宣教師や商人]によって日本へ紹介された西洋文化またキリスト教文化．

【南蛮貿易】　European trade with Japan; Japanese trade with Spain and Portugal between the 14th and the early 17th century. 日本とのヨーロッパ貿易．14世紀から17世紀初頭に行ったポルトガルとスペインとの貿易．☆鉄砲・火薬・生糸などを輸入する．

【南蛮焼】　ceramic ware imported to Japan from the West, especially in the 16th century. 16世紀に西洋から輸入された陶器(製品)．

【南蛮船】　European ships[a Spanish or Portuguese ship] in East Asian waters (in the 14th to the early 17th century); an early European ship from Spain or Portugal (arriving from the south). 14世紀から17世紀初頭にかけて東アジア海に見られたヨーロッパ[スペインまたはポルトガル]船．

【南蛮寺】　Christian churches built to propagate Christianity in the latter half of the 16th century. 16世紀後半，キリスト教布教のために建立された教会．

【南蛮人】　Europeans who came to Japan between the late Muromachi and early Edo periods[between the 14th and the early 17th century]. They are Spanish or Portuguese who reached Japan by way of the Southeast Asian countries. 室町時代から江戸時代[14世紀から17世紀初頭]にかけて来日したヨーロッパ人，特に南方地方を経て渡来したスペイン人やポルトガル人．

なんばんづけ【南蛮漬け】 deep-fried fish (or meat) marinated in seasoned vinegar with red peppers and leeks. 唐辛子やねぎなどを加え合わせた酢に揚げた魚[肉](アジ・エビ・イカまたは鶏肉など)を漬けたもの.

なんばんに【南蛮煮】 (a dish of) vegetables and fish (or meat) boiled with red peppers and leeks. 唐辛子やねぎを加えた野菜と魚[肉]を煮たもの.

なんぶてつびん【南部鉄瓶】 a Nanbu iron kettle; an iron kettle exclusively produced in the Nanbu region, Iwate and Aomori prefectures. 岩手県と青森県の特産.

なんぶまがりや【南部曲り屋】 Nanbu L-shaped farm houses (with an annexed stable). People living in the Nambu region dwell in the L-shaped farm houses with thatched roofs, where farm folk and their horses live together under one roof. The stables are attached at right angles to the family house. 南部地方のL字型の農家(馬小屋と続きになっている). 南部地方の住民はひとつ屋根の下で農民と馬が同居する. 馬小屋は家族の家屋と直角についている. 岩手県(特に遠野)と青森県の特色ある農家.

なんぼくちょうのじだい【南北朝の時代】 the periods of the Northern and Southern Courts[Dynasties]. 後醍醐天皇が吉野に朝廷(南朝 the Southern Court)を開いてから, 1392年後亀山天皇が京都に帰るまで朝廷が南北に分かれて対立した時代. ⇨付記(2)「日本史年表」室町時代(494頁)

に

ニートたいさく【ニート対策】 measures relating to NEET[Not in Education, Employment or Training].

にいなめさい【新嘗祭】 the ancient rice harvest festival. During the Niinamesai ceremony, the Emperor gives thanks to the gods for the rice harvest of the year and taste the rice dedicated to them for the first time. 天皇が新穀を神々に供え自らも食する行事. ☆1872年(明治5年)までは陰暦11月の卯の日に行われた. ⇨勤労感謝の日

に・エル・ディー・ケー【2LDK】 a house[an apartment] with two rooms plus a living room and a dine-in-kitchen room.

においぶくろ【匂袋】 a (fragrance) sachet (衣服たんすなどの保存用); a scent[sweet-smelling] bag (携帯用); a small cloth pouch containing fragrant materials; a perfume bag carried in *kimono* sleeves to enjoy fragrances. 香料を入れた小さな布袋. 香りを楽しむために着物の袂に入れて携帯する.

におう【仁王】 the two Deva Kings: *Kongo* and *Rikishi*; the guardian gods of a Buddhist temple gate (to keep out intruders). A pair of statues of the Deva Kings stand at both sides of a Buddhist temple gate (or a Buddhist statue) to protect the temple (or Buddha). They are fierce looking with glaring eyes to ward off evil spirits. 二体の天神: 金剛・力士. (外敵の侵入を防ぐために)山門を守る神. 伽藍と仏を守るために山門(または仏像)の両側におかれる一対の金剛力士の像. 悪霊を追放するためにらみつける目で獰猛な様相をしている. ☆右側の仁王は口を開け[阿形](*Kongo* with his mouth open as if saying "ah"[beginning]), 左側の仁王は口を閉じて[吽形](*Rikishi* with his mouth closed as if saying "hum[n]"[end])いる. "Ah-hum"(阿形・吽形)は仏教経典では「始めと終り」(alpha and omega)の意味である. ☆ Deva は「(インド神話の)天神. 提婆」

【仁王門】 a Deva (temple) gate. A Buddhist temple gate is guarded by *Nio*[the two Deva Kings] at both sides[each side] of the entryway[⊛ entranceway]. The structure has usually huge vermilion pillars. 入り口の左右に仁王像を安置した山門. 建造物には通常大きな朱塗りの柱がある.

にがい【煮貝】 abalone simmered in *shoyu*[soy sauce]. 醤油で煮しめたアワビ. ☆山梨県甲府の名産.

にがうり【苦瓜】〔植物〕a bitter gourd[melon]; a balsam pear[apple]. ウリ科のつる性一年草. 別名「ゴーヤー」. 皮は苦いが果肉は甘く食用. 炒め物・酢の物・和え物などに調理する. ☆「ゴーヤーチャンプル」は沖縄の郷土料理. ⇨ゴーヤー

にがよもぎ【苦蓬・苦艾】〔植物〕(a) wormwood. キク科ヨモギ属の多年草. 薬用またリキュールの香料に用いる. 臭みのある羊肉や野鳥などの調理に添える. ⇨艾

にがり【苦汁】 bittern (used to firm *tofu*); calcium salt; curdling agent; coagulant. 塩水から食塩をとったあとに残る溶液. 豆腐の凝固剤として用いる. ⇨豆腐

にきさく【二期作】 double-cropping; a semiannual crop. ⇨二毛作地帯

にぎりずし【握り鮨】 hand-rolled[hand-shaped] *sushi*[vinegared rice]; *sushi* rolled[shaped] by hand. ⓐ a palm-packed vinegared rice ball topped with a slice of raw fish or other delicacy (*neta*). ⓑ a bite-sized rectangular[oblong] vinegared rice with sliced fillet of fresh seafoods[fish and shellfish] or other ingredients (*neta*) placed on top. A bit of *wasabi*[horseradish] paste is often added[sandwiched] as a condiment between vinegared rice and sliced raw fish. *Nigiri-zushi* is eaten after[by] dipping it in *shoyu*[soy sauce] in the dish. Sliced ginger is usually served as a condiment.

酢めしを手で握った鮨. ⓐ生魚の切り身や他のネタを上にのせて手のひらで握った鮨. ⓑ生魚や他のネタをのせた一口サイズの長方形[楕円形]の握り鮨. 少量の練りワサビが薬味として酢めしと生魚の切り身の間につけられる. 皿にある醤油につけて食べる. 通常薬味として刻み生姜が添えられる. 「江戸前鮨」ともいう. ☆欧米では通常 "SUSHI"といえば「握り鮨」のことをいう. ☆三段階の品質がある. 『梅[並]』standard; regular. 『竹[上]』special; excellent. 『松[特上]』extra special; special excellent. ¶握り鮨一貫 a piece of hand-rolled *sushi*.

にぎりめし【握り飯】 ⇨ お握り

にく【肉】 meat; beef (牛肉); pork (豚肉); mutton (羊肉); chicken (鶏肉). ¶極上肉 prime meat. 上肉 choice meat. 中肉 good meat. 並肉 standard meat. 細切れ肉 minced meat.

〔料理〕肉団子 a meatball; a meat dumpling. 肉豆腐 simmered beef and *tofu* (cooked with shredded devil's tongue and onion). 肉饅頭 a steamed meat bun; a steamed bun containing ground meat mixed with vegetables. (野菜を混ぜたひき肉を入れた蒸し饅頭). 肉南蛮そば[うどん] (a bowl of) buckwheat[wheat] noodles cooked in broth seasoned with *shoyu*[soy sauce], topped with meat and leeks[Welsh onions]. (肉とネギを上にのせ, 醤油で味付けした汁で料理したそば[うどん]).

【肉じゃが】 braised beef and potatoes (stew); sliced beef simmered[boiled] with potatoes and onions in stock flavored with *shoyu*[soy sauce], *mirin*[sweetened *sake*] and sugar. 牛肉とジャガイモやたまねぎを煮合せ, 醤油, 味醂, 砂糖で味付けした煮物. ☆和食では「おふくろの味」(the taste of Mom's[home] cooking)で知られる. ⇨おふくろの味

にこごり【煮凝り】jellied food; jellied fish or meat broth. 煮汁が冷えてゼリーのように固まった食物[魚・肉].

にこみうどん【煮込みうどん】 stewed wheat

noodles; noodles simmered in broth with various ingredients.

にごりざけ【濁り酒】 unrefined *sake*. かすをこさない酒. ⇨どぶろく

にざかな【煮魚】 fish boiled[simmered] in *shoyu*[soy sauce] and sugar. 醤油と砂糖で煮た魚.

にじかい【二次会】 another[second] drinking party held at another place after the main dinner.

にしかた【西方】〔相撲〕the West Camp[Team]. ⇦東方. ¶西(方)の横綱 the (top-ranked) West *Yokozuna*; *yokozuna* in the west side of the ranking list[rank chart]. 西(方)の両大関 the two *ozeki*s on the west side of the ranking list[rank chart].

にしき【錦】〈絹織物〉(Japanese gold) brocade;〈着物〉fine dress. ¶錦絵〈木版〉a color print; a colored woodblock print;〈絵画〉a (brocade-like) picture reproduced in colored woodblock print(木版による多色ずりの美しい浮世絵)
【錦の御旗】❶〈金糸銀糸で刺繍した旗〉the banner made of gold brocade.
❷〈官軍の旗〉the Imperial standard made of gold brocade. ☆日と月を金銀で刺繍した赤い錦の旗.

にしきごい【錦鯉】〔魚〕a multi-colored[vari-colored] carp; a dappled carp; an ornamental carp. 鯉の一変種. 色彩や斑紋の美しい鯉. 鑑賞用. ⇨こい

にしきへび【錦蛇】〔爬〕a python; rock snake. ⇨へび

にじぐち【二字口】〔相撲〕the entrances, east and west, to the *sumo* ring. 力士が土俵へ上がる東西の出入り口.

にしじんおり【西陣織】 Nishijin brocade. The *Nishijin-ori* is generally a high-quality silk fabric produced in the Nishijin weaving district of Kyoto. It is used as the material for *obi* (a sash for a *kimono*), ties

and many other products. 西陣織は通常京都の西陣織地域で生産される高級な絹織物のこと. 着物用の帯, ネクタイといったような素材に用いられる. ☆祇園祭りの山車に使用する「綴織」は最高の傑作.

にじます【虹鱒】〔魚〕a rainbow trout. サケ科の淡水魚. 食用. ⇨ます

にしめ【煮染(め)】vegetables and meat[fish] boiled hard with *shoyu*[soy sauce] and *mirin*[sweetened *sake*]. Vegetables and meat[fish] are cooked with *shoyu* and *mirin* to dryness in broth[are stewed slowly with *shoyu* and *mirin* in a small amount of liquid] so that they retain their shape. 形をくずさぬように野菜(人参・牛蒡・里芋・椎茸など)や肉[魚]などを醤油と味醂で煮しめた[少量の液体でとろ火で煮た]料理. 御節料理には不可欠. ⇨煮付け(形がくずれることがある)

にしもないぼんおどり【西馬音内盆踊り】the Bon Folk Dance at Nishimonai. (8月). ⇨付記(1)「日本の祭り」

にじゅうしせっき【二十四節気】 the 24 seasonal divisions of a year in the solar year. 太陽年を太陽の黄道上の位置に従って, 24等分して季節を示す基準とした用語.
『春』(Spring)
[初春]立春[2月4日/5日]〜雨水[2月19日/20日]
[Early Spring]: Beginning of Spring 〜 Rainwater (Snow turns to rain.)
[仲春]啓蟄[3月5日/6日]〜春分[3月21日/22日]
[Mid-Spring]: End of Insects Hibernation 〜 Vernal Equinox
[晩春]清明[4月4日/5日]〜穀雨[4月20日/21日]
[Late Spring]: Pure and Clean (Pleasant Weather) 〜 Grain Rains (Grains grow in spring rains.)

『夏』(Summer)
〔初夏〕立夏[5月5日／6日]〜小満[5月21日／22日]

[Early Summer]: Beginning of Summer 〜 Lesser Ripening (All things grow well.)

〔仲夏〕芒種[6月6日／7日]〜夏至[6月21日／22日]

[Mid-Summer]: Grains[Rice] Transplanting 〜 Summer Solstice

〔晩夏〕小暑[7月7日／8日]〜大暑[7月23日／24日]

[Late Summer]: Lesser Heat (Hot Summer Weather) 〜 Greater Heat (Hottest Summer Weather)

『秋』(Autumn; Ⓐ Fall)
〔初秋〕立秋[8月7日／8日]〜処暑[8月23日／24日]

[Early Autumn]: Beginning of Autumn 〜 Manageable Heat (Autumn winds blow.)

〔仲秋〕白露[9月8日／9日]〜秋分[9月23日／24日]

[Mid-Autumn]: White Dew (Autumn Weather) 〜 Autumnal Equinox

〔晩秋〕寒露[10月8日／9日]〜霜降[10月23日／24日]

[Late Autumn]: Cold Dew (Colored Foliage) 〜 First Frost (End of Autumn)

『冬』(Winter)
〔初冬〕立冬[11月7日／8日]〜小雪[11月22日／23日]

[Early Winter]: Beginning of Winter 〜 Lesser Snow (Light Snowfall)

〔仲冬〕大雪[12月7日／8日]〜冬至[12月21日／22日]

[Mid-Winter]: Greater Snow (Winter Weather) 〜 Winter Solstice

〔晩冬〕小寒[1月5日／6日]〜大寒[1月20日／21日]

[Late Winter]: Lesser Cold (Colder Winter Weather) 〜 Greater Cold (Coldest Winter Weather)

にじゅうばし【二重橋】the Nijubashi bridge. *Nijubashi* is the double-arched bridge with a turret of the old Edo Castle in the background, forming the main entrance to the Imperial Palace. 江戸城の櫓が背後に見える2つのアーチがある橋で，皇居への表玄関になっている.

にじりぐち【躙り口】〔茶道〕a small low entrance to a teahouse (with a sliding door). The guests participating in a tea ceremony enter the tearoom by crawling through a small door while bending their heads[stooping] down low. 茶室特有の小さな低い出入り口(障子付き). 茶道に参加する客は頭を下げて[低く身をかがめながら]小さな戸を這うようにして茶室に入る. ☆通常高さ 66cm. 幅約 63cm. ⇨茶室

にじる【煮汁】broth (魚・肉などの); stock (野菜などを入れたスープのもととなる); juice(肉などからたれる). ものを煮た汁. または，ものを煮るために調味した汁. 「煮出し汁」(simmering sauce)ともいう. ¶魚の煮汁 fish broth[stock].

にしん【鰊・鯡】〔魚〕a herring(Ⓐ herring(s)). ニシン科の硬骨魚. 食用，油用，肥料用. 卵は「数の子」(herring roe). 「カド」(俳句の季語)ともいう. ¶鰊の小魚 a sprat. 身欠き鰊 a herring cut open and dried. 燻製鰊 a smoked herring; a herring cured in smoke; 〈開きの〉a kippered herring. 酢漬け鰊 pickled herring.
〔料理〕鰊漬け a herring preserved with vegetables. 鰊そば buckwheat noodles topped with a cooked herring. (京都の名物料理). 鰊の昆布巻 a herring rolled in *kombu*[kelp]. ⇨こぶまき

にせさつ【偽札】a counterfeit bill[Ⓐ note]; a bogus bill[note]; a fake[forged] bill[note]. ☆「偽金」counterfeit[fake] money. 「偽硬貨」a counterfeit[falk] coin.

にせたいじゅうたく【二世帯住宅】a two-family house; a house for a two-generation family; a house for two generations; a duplex house; ㊧ a semidetached house.

にちえいどうめい【日英同盟】 Anglo-Japanese Alliance.（1902年調印）.

にちどくいさんごくどうめい【日独伊三国同盟】 the Tripartite Pact signed by Japan, Germany and Italy.

にちべい【日米】 Japan and America. ☆「日米の」Japanese-American; Japan-U. S.; U.S.-Japanese. ¶日米安全保障条約 the U.S.-Japan Security Treaty;〈正式名〉the Treaty of Mutual Cooperation and Security between Japan and the United States of America.（1951年調印）. ⇨サンフランシスコ講和条約. 日米共同声明 the Japan-U.S. Joint Communique. 日米修好通商条約 the U.S.-Japan Treaty of Amity and Commerce; Treaty of Friendship and Commerce signed by Japan and U.S. 通称 the Harris Treaty.（1858年調印）. 日米防衛協力指針 the Guidelines for U.S.-Japan Defense Cooperation. 日米和親条約 Treaty of Peace and Amity between the United States of America and the Empire of Japan.（1854年調印）

にちようだいく【日曜大工】〈事〉home carpentry;〈仕事〉do-it-yourself ㊧ [D.I.Y.];〈人〉do-it-yourselfer; Sunday[weekend] carpenter. ¶日曜大工一式 do-it-yourself kit.

にちろ【日露】 Japan and Russia. ¶日露戦争 the Russo-Japanese War.（1904年～1905年）. 日露修好通商条約 Treaty of Friendship and Commerce between Russia and Japan.（1858年調印）. 日露和親条約 Treaty of Peace and Amity between Russia and Japan.（1855年調印）

にっかじへん【日華事変】 ⇨日中戦争

にっかん【日韓】 Japan and (the Republic of) Korea. ¶韓基本条約 the Treaty on Basic Relations between Japan and the Republic

of Korea.（1965年調印）. 日韓協定書 the Korean-Japanese Protocol. 日韓国交回復 the Restoration of diplomatic relations between Japan and the Republic of Korea.（1965年）. 日韓平和条約［日韓和約］the Japan-Korea Peace Treaty. 日韓併合条約 the Treaty regarding the Annexation of Korea to the Empire of Japan. ☆ Korea was made a colony of Japan in 1910.（1910年韓国は日本の植民地となる）.

につけ【煮付け】 fish (or vegetables) cooked and seasoned with *shoyu*[soy sauce], *mirin*[sweetened *sake*] and sugar; fish (or vegetables) poached briefly in a thick mixture of *shoyu*, *mirin* and sugar. 醤油, 味醂, 砂糖をまぜて煮付けた魚(または野菜). ☆具材の形がくずれることがある. ⇨煮染め(具材の形をくずさない)

にっけい【肉桂】〔植物〕a cinnamon tree（木）; cinnamon（香料）. クスノキ科の常緑高木. 香料用. 樹皮と根は健胃剤.「ニッキ」「シナモン」などともいう.

にっしょうき【日章旗】〈日の丸の旗〉 the Rising-Sun flag; the flag of the Rising Sun;〈国旗〉the national flag of Japan.

にっしょく【日食】 a solar eclipse(正式用語); an eclipse of the sun. ¶皆既日食 a total solar eclipse; a total eclipse of the sun. 部分日食 a partial sun eclipse; a partial eclipse of the sun. ⇨月食

にっしんせんそう【日清戦争】 the Sino-Japanese War.（1894~1895）. ⇨日中戦争

にっソ【日ソ】 Japan and the Soviet Union. ¶日ソ中立条約 the Soviet-Japanese Neutrality Pact.（1941年調印）. 日ソ共同宣言 the Japan-Soviet Joint Declaration.（1956年国交回復）. 日ソ基本条約 the Soviet-Japanese Basic Convention.（1925年調印）

にっちゅう【日中】 Japan and China. ¶日中共同声明 the China-Japan Joint

Communique.（1972年）. **日中国交回復** the Establishment of diplomatic relations between Japan and the People's Republic of China.（1972年）. **日中国交正常化** Restoration of diplomatic ties between Japan and China; Normalization of Sino-Japanese diplomatic relations.（1972年）. **日中戦争** the Sino-Japanese War.（1937年～1945年）.「日華事変」ともいう. ⇨日清戦争. **日中平和友好条約** the Japan-China Peace and Amity Treaty; the Japan-China Treaty of Peace and Friendship.（1978年）

にっちょう【日朝】 Japan and North Korea. ¶**日朝修好条規** the Korea-Japanese Treaty of Amity. **日朝平壌宣言** Japan-DPRK Pyongyang Declaration. **日朝貿易** the Japan-Korean trade.

に・ディー・ケー【2DK】 a house with two rooms and a combined dine-in-kitchen room.

にないだいこ【担い太鼓】 a portable drum. It is carried on a pole by a couple of men and beaten while the bearers are walking. 携帯用の太鼓. 2人が棒［竿］の上に載せ, 歩きながら打ち鳴らす.

にはいず【二杯酢】 two-flavor vinegar; seasonings mixed[combined] with vinegar and *shoyu*[soy sauce]（or salt）in equal quantities; a mixture[combination] of equal parts of vinegar and *shoyu*（or salt）. 酢と醤油（または塩）を同量に配合した酢. ☆魚介類の刺身また焼き物などに用いる調味料. ⇨三杯酢（二杯酢に味醂または砂糖を加えた酢）

にひゃくとうか【二百十日】 the 210th day after the setting-in[beginning] of spring（according to the lunar calendar）; the peak of the typhoon season. 立春（2月4日頃）から数えて210日目. 台風のピークの季節.

にべ【鮸】 a (Nibe) croaker. ニベ科の海産魚. 刺身や塩焼きにする. 肉は高級かまぼこの

原料.

にぼし【煮干し】 dried small sardines; anchovies[small sardines] boiled and dried. They are used to add flavor to boiled vegetables and to make a fish stock (*dashi*). いわしなどの雑魚を煮て干した食品. 煮た野菜の味つけ, 煮出しの具材に用いる.「いりこ」「出しじゃこ」などともいう. ⇨いりこ

にほんが【日本画】 a traditional Japanese-style painting[picture]; a painting[picture] drawn in Japanese style; a painting[picture] of Japan. ⇨水墨画[墨絵] / 浮世絵

にほんかい【日本海】 the Japan Sea; the Sea of Japan. ⇨海

にほんがみ【日本髪】 a Japanese coiffure [hairdo]; a coiffure done up in traditional Japanese style for special occasions (such as a wedding ceremony or the New Year holidays). Single[unmarried] women usually arrange their hair in the shimada coiffure when they wear a *kimono*. 未婚女性が着物を着用するときは島田髷に結う. ☆「島田髷」（日本の代表的な髪型）,「丸髷」（既婚女性の髪型）,「桃割れ」（少女の髪型）など日本女性の髪型. ⇨島田髷 / 丸髷 / 桃割れ

ニホンカモシカ the Japanese serow. ⇨特別天然記念物

にほんご【日本語】 Japanese; the Japanese language. Modern Japanese consists of three kinds of characters used for writing Japanese: the ideographic Chinese characters known as *kanji* and the phonetic characters known as *hiragana* and *katakana*. 現在日本語を書き表すのに用いられる文字には, 表意文字としての「漢字」と表音文字としての「平仮名」と「片仮名」がある. ⇨平仮名 / 片仮名

にほんこくけんぽう【日本国憲法】 The Constitution of Japan.（1946年成立）. It states three broad principles: Sovereignty with the people, Respect of fundamental human rights and Pacifism. 三大原則: 国民主権，基本的人権の尊重，平和主義.

にほんさんけい【日本三景】 the scenic trio of Japan; the three famous views[sights] of Japan; the most famous scenic spots [places] in Japan. ☆「松島」（宮城県），「宮島」（広島県），「天橋立」（京都府）

にほんしゅ【日本酒】 *sake*; Japanese rice wine; a Japanese alcoholic beverage made from fermented rice and water. 発酵させた米と水からつくった醸造酒.（「洋酒」に対して）「清酒」「和酒」ともいう. ☆「甘口」mild[light] (*sake*).「辛口」dry (*sake*). ⇨吟醸酒 / 純米酒

にほんしょき【日本書紀】 the Chronicles of Japan. *Nihonshoki* is Japan's second oldest remaining historical work compiled under Imperial supervision in 720 after the *Kojiki*.（30 volumes）. 古事記に次ぐ日本最古の勅撰歴史書（30巻）. 720年に成立. ☆別名「日本紀」. 天武天皇の勅により，舎人親王・太安万侶らが撰録 (compilation). 神代の神武天皇から持統天皇(645-703)までの事跡を皇室中心に年代順に (in chronological order)記述. 文体は漢文 (written in Chinese). ⇨古事記

にほんじんらちぎわく【日本人拉致疑惑】 alleged abduction of Japanese civilians.

にほんじんらちひがいしゃ【日本人拉致被害者】 abducted Japanese victims.

にほんじんらちもんだい【日本人拉致問題】 the issue of abducted Japanese; abduction issue of Japanese citizens. ☆「北朝鮮に拉致された日本人」Japanese citizens abducted by North Korea.

にほんすもうきょうかい【日本相撲協会】 the Japan Sumo Association. ☆1925年に設立された財団法人.

にほんていえん【日本庭園】 a traditional Japanese landscape garden. There are mainly three categories: the dry landscape garden (*karesansui*) with an influence from Zen Buddhism, the strolling garden (*kaiyushiki-teien*) attached to the residences of nobles or feudal lords and the tea garden (*chatei*) surrounding a tea hut. 禅宗の影響を受ける「枯山水庭園」，貴族や大名の邸宅に付随する「回遊式庭園」，そして茶室を囲む「茶庭」がある. ⇨枯山水庭園 / 回遊式庭園 / 茶庭［露地］

にほんとう【日本刀】 a *katana*; a Japanese sword (with decorated hilt and scabbard). ⇨刀

にほんにんぎょう【日本人形】 a Japanese doll. ⇨博多人形 / 京人形 / こけし

にほんのせかいいさん【日本の世界遺産】 ⇨ユネスコ世界遺産

にほんぶよう【日本舞踊】 classical Japanese dance[dancing] (usually accompanied by *shamisen* music). The main elements have a dance (*mai*) that involves circling movements and poses[postures](*furi*) giving a strong dramatic impression. 主要な要素に旋回運動の「舞」と演劇的表現の強い「振り」がある. ☆狭義では「歌舞伎舞踊」(kabuki dance; dance based in a kabuki play)また上方舞をさす. 現在「五大流派」（花柳流，藤間流，若柳流，西川流，坂東流）がある.

にほんほんど【日本本土】 Japan proper.

にほんまつちょうちんまつり【二本松提灯祭り】 the Lantern-Float Parade at Nihon-matsu City.（10月）. ⇨付記(1)「日本の祭り」

にほんれっとう【日本列島】 the Japanese Archipelago[islands]. ☆北から北海道・本州・四国・九州を主島とし，南は琉球列島に至る. ⇨列島

にまいがい【二枚貝】〔貝〕a bivalve. 二枚の貝殻をもつ（帆立貝，蛤，浅蜊，牡蠣など）. ⇔巻貝

にまいびょうぶ【二枚屛風】　a double-fold screen; a folding screen with two connected panels[with two leaves]. ⇨屛風

にまめ【煮豆】　boiled and seasoned beans; beans cooked sweet with *shoyu*[soy sauce] and sugar. 乾燥豆を甘醤油で煮たもの.

にもうさくちたい【二毛作地帯】　a double cropping area; a two-crop area. ⇔単作地帯

にもの【煮物】　simmered[boiled] foods: foods[vegetables or fish] simmered[boiled] in *dashi*[stock] with *shoyu*[soy sauce] and other seasonings[*mirin* and sugar]. 醤油や他の調味料を入れた出し汁で煮た食物. ⇨煮付け

にゅうめん【煮麺・入麺】　boiled thin[fine] wheat noodles cooked[served] in a hot soup (with *shoyu* or *miso*). ゆでた素麺を（醤油や味噌で）温かくさっと煮込んだもの. ⇨素麺

にょらい【如来】　*Nyorai*; a Buddha; a Tathagata(梵語); an enlightened one; a person who attained enlightenment and perceived ultimate truth[Buddhahood]. 悟りを開いた，真理の体現者としての仏.「仏」の美称 (an honorific title of Buddha). ☆主な如来には釈迦・阿弥陀・薬師・大日などがある.「菩薩」は悟りを開く前の仏.

にら【韮】〔植物〕　a leek; a Chinese[garlic] chive. ユリ科の多年草. 鍋物や玉子とじなどに用いる.

にらめっこ【睨めっこ】　a staring game (played by two people). A game of outstaring one another until one person bursts into laughter. 一人が笑うまで相互ににらみ合うゲーム.

にれ【楡】〔植物〕　an elm (tree). ニレ科の落葉高木. 材は建築・器具用.

にわとり【鶏】〔鳥〕　a chicken; a hen(雌); a cock(雄); a rooster(雄); a chick(ひな). キジ科の家禽. ¶矮鶏 a Japanese bantam. 尾長鳥 a long-tailed cock. ⇨「とり」(「鶏飯」

「鶏刺し」「鶏鍋」「鶏の空揚げ」)

ニワトリしょうこうぐん【ニワトリ症候群】　chicken syndrome. This syndrome means "eating alone"(孤食), "skipping breakfast"(欠食), "all family members eating different things"(個食) and "eating only what one likes"(固食). ☆「頭」(孤・欠・個・固)を取り上げれば「コケッコ」となる.

にんぎょうじょうるり【人形浄瑠璃】〔文楽〕　the *joruri* puppet ballad drama; the *joruri* puppet theater (in which a traditional narrative ballad and dialog are recited to the accompaniment of *shamisen*)人形をあやつる演技(浄瑠璃の語り（バラッド）と対話が三味線の伴奏に合わせて朗唱される). ⇨浄瑠璃 / 文楽. ☆ ballad「バラッド. 叙事的歌謡，物語詩」素朴な語と短い連で書かれた民間の伝承的な物語詩またはその曲. narrative ballad「物語的な詩または歌謡」

にんぎょうつかい【人形遣い】〔文楽〕　(a trio of) puppeteers; puppet manipulators. One puppet is manipulated by three puppeteers: *Omo-zukai*, *Ashi-zukai* and *Hidari-zukai*. The assistants of the *Ashi-zukai* and the *Hidari-zukai* wear black hoods over their entire heads, while the *Omo-zukai* appears with his face uncovered. 1体の人形は「主遣い」「足遣い」「左遣い」の三人で操作される.「足遣い」と「左遣い」の補佐役は黒い頭巾を頭に被るが,「主遣い」は観客に顔を見せている. ⇨三人遣い[主[面]遣い / 足遣い / 左遣い]

主遣い　足遣い　左遣い　人形

にんげんぎょらい【人間魚雷】 a human torpedo; suicide submarine. Small submarines equipped with two torpedoes and operated by two crewmen in World War II were assigned to make a suicidal crash on a target at an enemy ship. 2台の魚雷を搭載し2名の乗組員が操作し，敵船めがけて体当たりをする死を覚悟の任務を命じられていた第二次大戦時の小型潜水艦. ⇨神風特攻隊

にんげんこくほう【人間国宝】 a living national treasure. ☆文化財保護法によって文化庁が指定した重要無形文化財保持者. ⇨国宝／文化財

にんげんせんげん【人間宣言】 Humanity Declaration; renunciation of divinity. 神性を放棄すること. ¶昭和天皇の人間宣言 renunciation of divinity by Emperor Showa. (1946年). ☆第二次世界大戦終結まで天皇は「現人神」として崇められていた. ⇨現人神

にんげんドック【人間ドック】 a complete medical check-up; a thorough physical examination.

にんじゃ【忍者】 a ninja; a professional spy[secret agent] (highly trained in espionage activities in feudal Japan). 封建時代にスパイ活動を専門に訓練されていた忍びの者. ☆「伊賀」(三重県)や「甲賀」(滋賀県)の忍者は有名. ⇨隠密

にんじゅつ【忍術】 *ninjutsu*; the art of spycraft; the skills of stealth and secrecy practiced by the *ninja*. It was the art of making oneself invisible. It was developed in early feudal days as a system for obtaining information about the secret plans and intentions of one's rivals. 忍法. 忍者が使った，身をかくして巧妙に忍んで行動する術. 封建時代の初期頃に進展し，相手の秘密の計画や意図に関する情報をさぐる一法として利用された. ⇨忍者

にんじょうざた【刃傷沙汰】 a bloody affair [quarrel] (caused by a knife[sword]); the affair[quarrel] developed into bloodshed. 刃物で人を傷つける流血惨事[闘争].

にんじょうみ【人情味】 a human warmth [touch]; warm heartedness.

にんじん【人参】〔植物〕a carrot. セリ科の二年草または一年草. ¶朝鮮人参 ginseng. 毒人参 hemlock. 人参エキス ginseng extract.

にんちしょうこうれいしゃ【認知症高齢者】 senile elderly people; elderly people suffering from senile dementia.

にんちしょうろうじん【認知症老人】 a demented elderly person; an elderly person suffering from senile dementia. 老人性認知症に苦悩する老人.

にんにく【大蒜・葫】〔植物〕 a garlic;〈香辛料〉 (a clove of) garlic. ユリ科の多年草. 「ガーリック」. ¶微塵切りの大蒜 minced garlic. たっぷりと大蒜の利いた料理a dish strongly flavored with garlic.

ぬ

ぬか【糠】 bran; rice bran(米糠)；wheat bran(小麦糠). Bran is the finely ground husk and germ produced when rice[wheat] is polished[refined]. 玄米・玄麦を精白するときに出る外皮[果皮]と胚芽の細かい粉. 〔食品〕糠漬け rice-bran pickles. (野菜などを)糠味噌に漬けたもの. 「糠味噌漬け」ともいう. 糠(味噌)漬けの野菜 vegetables pickled (by dipping) in salted rice-bran paste. 糠味噌 salted rice-bran paste for pickling; fermented rice-bran paste mixed with salt(used for pickling vegetables). 糠に塩を混ぜて発酵させたもの. 野菜などを漬ける.

ぬさ【幣】❶〈榊にある〉a strip of white paper hanging from the twig of a *sakaki*-tree. It is used when the Shinto priest offers a prayer or conducts the purification

ぬ

ceremony. 榊の枝から吊してある細長い白紙. 神主が神に祈るとき，または清めの式を行うときに用いる.
❷〈神社にある〉 pendant paper strips (found) in a Shinto shrine. 神社に垂れ下がる細長い紙. ⇨御幣

ぬた【饅】 seafood and vegetables dressed with vinegar and *miso*[bean paste]; fish [vegetables] salad dressed with vinegared *miso*. 魚介類(マグロ・貝類など)や野菜(ネギなど)を酢味噌で和えた食べ物.「ぬた和え」ともいう.

ぬま(ち)【沼(地)】a pond(池); a swamp(湿地); a marsh(湿地帯). marshland(沼地). ¶五色沼(福島・新潟・栃木・群馬の4県) (the) Goshiki(numa) Pond. 尾瀬沼(群馬県) (the) Oze(numa) Swamp[Marshland].

ぬり【塗り】 ①〈漆〉lacquer;〈漆の〉lacquering; ☆ lacquered「漆を塗った」. ②〈漆喰の〉plastering. ③〈ニスの〉varnishing ⇨漆 / 輪島塗り. ¶塗り下駄 (a pair of) lacquered *geta(s)*[clogs]. 塗り箸 (a pair of) lacquered chopsticks. 塗り盆 a lacquered tray. 塗り物 a lacquer(ed) ware. 別称「漆器(類)」(articles made of wood coated with lacquer). 塗り椀 a lacquer(ed) bowl.

ぬりえ【塗り絵】 a color-in line drawing; a line drawing to be colored in. 色を塗るように描いた絵.

ぬれぼとけ【濡れ仏】 a Buddhist statue [image] exposed in the open air.

ね

ね【子】 the Rat, one[the first] of the 12 animals of the Chinese zodiac. 十二支の第一. ⇨十二支. ¶子の方 the Direction of the Rat[north]. 方角の名. 北. 子の刻 the Hour of the Rat [11 p.m. – 1 a.m.] 夜12時頃(およびその前後約2時間). 子年 the Year of the Rat. 子年生まれ (be) born in the Year of the Rat.

ネアカ【根明】 innate cheerfulness (生得の明朗性);〈人〉an innately cheerful person (明るい人); a natural optimist (楽天家); an extrovert (外向型の人); a happy-go-lucky person. ⇔ネクラ

ねぎ【葱】〔植物〕a scallion (ワケギ); a leek (ニラネギ); a green onion; a Welsh onion; 英 a spring onion. ユリ科の多年草.「白ネギ」(白い根の部分を食べる).「青ネギ」(緑の葉の部分を食べる).
〔料理〕葱トロ fatty flesh of pasted tuna mixed with chopped leeks. 葱トロ巻き *sushi* rolled in a sheet of *nori*[dried laver] with fatty flesh of pasted tuna and chopped green onions in the center. ⇨すし. 葱トロ丼 a bowl of steamed rice topped with fatty flesh of pasted tuna and chopped leeks. ⇨ 丼物. 葱南蛮 noodles served with parboiled leeks and fried *tofu*[bean curd] in soup(汁物に湯がいたネギと油揚を入れたうどん). 葱鮪 dish cooked hot with tuna and leeks in a pot (at the table) ネギとマグロで煮た鍋料理. 葱間 (an alternate piece of) chicken and leeks on a skewer (broiled on a charcoal fire). (炭火で焼いた)串刺しの鶏肉とネギ. ⇨焼き鳥

ネクラ【根暗】 congenital gloominess (先天的な陰気性);〈人〉an innately gloomy person (暗い人); a natural pessimist (悲観論者); an introvert (内向型の人). ⇔ネアカ

ねこ【猫】〔動物〕a cat; a kitten(小猫); a male cat(雄猫); a female cat(雌猫). ネコ科の哺乳動物. 皮は三味線の胴張りに用いる. ⇨招き猫. ¶山猫 a wild cat; a lynx. 虎猫 a tiger cat; a tabby cat. 三毛猫 a tortoise-shell cat. ペルシア猫 (a) Persian cat.

ねこやなぎ【猫柳】〔植物〕a pussy willow. ヤナギ科の落葉低木. ⇨やなぎ. ☆ pussy「猫ちゃん」(小児語)

ねずみ【鼠】〔動物〕 a rat; a mouse (複 mice). ネズミ科の哺乳動物. ¶二十日鼠 a mouse. 溝鼠 a brown rat. 野鼠 a field mouse. 家鼠 a house rat. 山鼠 a dormouse. 畑鼠 a field vole. ネズミ捕り a rattrap; a mousetrap.

ねずみこう【ねずみ講】 a pyramid sales [investment] scheme; a pyramid finance.

ねた, ネタ〈鮨の素材〉 seafood for *sushi*; *sushi* ingredients; a topping of *nigiri-zushi*. 「たね」の倒語. 料理などの材料. 「すしのネタ」.

ねたきりろうじん【寝たきり老人】 bedridden elderly people; bedfast aged[old] persons; old people confined to bed. ⇨介護

ねつけ【根付け】 a *netsuke*; a toggle for attaching things to a sash; a small pendant of ornamental ivory[wooden] carving (of people or animals). A *netsuke* was fitted with a *kimono* cord for fastening a seal (or purse, medicine case, etc.) to the sash. It was originally worn by men to suspend a tobacco pouch. 物を帯につけるための留め具. 象牙[木製]の飾りの彫刻物(人物または動物). 印籠[財布, 薬入れなど]を着物の帯につけるための紐(a string)で結ばれていた. 元来男性がたばこ入れを吊るすために携帯していた.

ねったい【熱帯】 the Torrid Zone; the tropics; the torrid zone. ⇨寒帯 / 温帯. ¶熱帯魚 a tropical fish. 熱帯植物 a tropical plant. 熱帯夜 a tropical night. ☆ The temperature at night does not fall below 25℃.

ねっちゅうしょう【熱中症】 heat stroke [heatstroke]. ¶熱中症にかかる suffer from heat stroke 熱中症で死亡する die of heat stroke.

ネット〈コンピューター〉 the Net; the Internet; network; the Website. ¶ネットアイドル an Internet idol; an online star. ネットいじめ cyberbullying; Net bullying; bullying on the Net. ネット依存症 Internet Addiction Disorder[IAD]. ネットオークション[競売] an on-line auction site; an Internet auction site. ネット株取引 Internet trading[business] of stocks. ネット書店 Internet Bookstore[bookshop]; online bookstore[bookshop]. ネット詐欺 Internet fraud[scam]. ネット商品 a product for sale on the Internet. ネット心中[集団自殺] Internet suicide pact; Internet group suicides. ネット選挙運動 election campaign over the Internet. ネット犯罪 Internet[network] crimes.

【ネットカフェ難民】 an Internet café refugee; a cyber-café refugee; a net café refugee; With no fixed[permanent] address, people regularly spend their nights at[in] 24-hour Internet cafés or the *manga* cafés. 定住所もなく24時間営業のネットカフェまたはマンガ喫茶で夜間をしのぐ.

ねはん【涅槃】 ❶〈悟りの境地〉 Nirvana; Buddhahood; supreme enlightenment; a spiritual awakening state of complete freedom from worldly passions. すべての煩悩を滅却した悟りの境地. ¶涅槃に入る enter[pass into] Nirvana; attain Buddhahood[enlightenment](by renouncing worldly desires).
❷〈釈迦の入滅[死]〉 the death of Buddha. ¶涅槃図 the picture depicting the scene of Buddha's death(釈迦の死の様子を描いた絵画); the picture of the dying Buddha surrounded by his disciples. 弟子に囲まれている臨終の仏の絵図. 涅槃像①〈釈迦の入滅〉the image of the dying Buddha. ②〈寝釈迦〉the recumbent image of Buddha immediately after his death. 涅槃会 the anniversary of the death of Buddha. A Buddhist service is held on February 15 when Gautama Buddha passed into Nirvana. (釈迦が入滅した日に行う法会).

(2月15日).

ねぶたまつり【ねぶた祭り】 the Nebuta [Dummy-Float Parade] Festival at Aomori City (August 2-7). ⇨付記(1)「日本の祭り」青森ねぶた祭り

ねぷたまつり【ねぷた祭り】 the Neputa [Dummy-Float Parade] Festival at Hirosaki City (August 1-7). ⇨付記(1)「日本の祭り」弘前ねぷた祭り

ねまき【寝巻き】a *kimono* worn as a sleeping garment.

ねまわし【根回し】 ❶〈樹木の移植〉 preparation for transplanting; trimming the roots of a tree to foster root growth before transplanting. 移植の準備. 移植する前に主根の育成を改良するために木の根の周りを掘ること (digging around).
❷〈計画の下工作〉 behind-the-scene negotiation[maneuver]（舞台裏での交渉）; behind-the-scene efforts for securing a consensus.（同意を確保するための裏工作）; laying groundwork behind the scenes (to obtain one's objective).（目的達成のために舞台裏で基礎調査を固める）.

ねむのき【合歓の木】〔植物〕 a silk tree. マメ科の落葉高木. 材が器具用. 樹皮は薬用.

ねむりねこ【眠り猫】 the Sleeping Cat (carving in Shinkyusha[Sacred Stable] in Toshogu Shrine in Nikko). 日光東照宮にある. ☆左甚五郎作の彫物.

ねりあん【練餡】 sweetened *adzuki* bean paste. ⇨餡

ねりうに【練り海胆・雲丹】paste of seasoned sea-urchin eggs (mixed with salt and flavorings). うにの卵巣をねり固めた食品（塩や調味料を入れる）.

ねりきり【練り切】 bean paste confection. It is made by adding sugar to white bean paste and then kneading the mix into various artistic shapes. 白餡に砂糖を加えてよく練って様々な芸術的な形に作られた

菓子. ☆季節に合わせて細工や着色を施す.

ねりもの【練り物】〈魚の〉boiled fish paste (used in eating *oden*). ⇨おでん ;〈菓子の〉kneaded sweet(s)

ねりようかん【練羊羹】 kneaded and jellied sweet bean paste. 餡と寒天を混ぜて練り固めたようかん. ⇨羊羹

ねんが【年賀】〈挨拶〉 (exchange) New Year('s) greetings ;〈訪問〉(pay a) New Year('s) visit[call]. ☆「年始回り」ともいう. 日本の伝統的な菓子などの手土産 (caller's gift; visitor's present)を持って挨拶する.『旧年中はたいへんにお世話になりました. 今年もよろしくお願い申し上げます』(Thank you for the favor you gave me last year. I hope I will keep a good relationship for this coming year, too.) ⇨年始回り

【年賀状】 a New Year's greeting card (sent for wishing a Happy New Year); a card sent as a greeting with happiness for the new year. The greetings may be often written with a few personal notes[lines] added in the card. 年賀状には個人的な挨拶を一筆添える場合が多い. ☆明治初期の「郵便制度の開始」(1871年)にともなって普及する. 親族・知人・上司を直接訪問する代わりに年賀状が送られた. 最近では写真つきのEメール挨拶カード (E-mail greeting cards) を送る人も多い.

【年賀はがき】 a New Year's postcard; a postcard bearing New Year's greetings. It often has a picture of an animal corresponding with the twelve animal signs of the Chinese zodiac (*eto*) of that year. It is usually sent at the middle[end] of December so that it can arrive on the early morning of New Year's Day. はがきにはその年の干支にあたる動物の絵 (design) を添えることが多い. 元旦の早朝に届く (deliver)ように12月中旬[下旬]には送る. ☆出していない人から届くと7日までに返

事を書く(send return cards)のが礼儀である. ⇨お年玉付き年賀はがき / 干支

ねんき【年忌】 ⇨回忌

ねんきん(せいど)【年金(制度)】 the pension [annuity] system. ¶**国民年金** the national pension[annuity]（20歳以上の男女で学生・主婦・自営業者また無職の人や外国人などが対象）. **厚生年金** the employee's pension insurance; the welfare annuity（民間企業(private companies)勤務者が対象）. **共済年金** the mutual aid pension; the mutual benefit annuity（国家公務員<national public servants>と地方公務員<local public servants> が対象）.
【年金受給者】 a pensioner; an annuitant; a recipient of pension; a person who lives on a pension[annuity].「年金生活者」ともいう. ☆「年金給付金」benefit(s)
【年金制度改革法案】 reform bill of the pension system.
【年金スライド制】 pension indexation

ねんぐ【年貢】 tribute; a tenant farmer's rent（小作料）; tax levied on farmers in past times. 昔農民に課された税金. ¶**年貢の徴収** collection of tributes. **年貢米** tribute rice.

ねんこうじょれつ(せいど)【年功序列(制度)】 the seniority system; promotion by seniority. ¶**年功序列型賃金** a seniority-based wage. **年功序列型賃金制度** a seniority-oriented wage system.

ねんしまわり【年始回り】 (pay) a New Year's courtesy visit (to relatives, superiors and customers to wish for continued favor for the new year). People visit one another[make a round of New Year's calls] to extend[exchange] greetings on the second and third days of the New Year holidays. Children receive *otoshidama* [New Year's monetary gift] from their relatives during these visits.（新しい年にも変わらぬ愛顧を願って親戚・上司・顧客に対して)年賀を述べる訪問. 新年の2日と3日[または2日から7日の期間 (visit between January 2nd and 7th)] に年始回りをする. 子供は親戚からお年玉をもらう. ☆元旦(1月1日)は年神 (the deity of the year) を迎える日なので外出を控えることが多い. ⇨年賀

ねんじゅうぎょうじ【年中行事】 an annual event[function]; a yearly event[function].

ねんど【粘土】 clay. ¶**粘土細工** handiwork in clay; (a piece of) terra-cotta.

ねんねこ a *kimono*-style short coat worn to protect the baby on one's back; a padded[lined] short, loose coat. It is worn in winter by a woman[nursemaid] who carries[protects] a baby on her back. 綿入りの[裏地のついた]袢纏. 背負った子供をおおう[守る]ために冬季に女性[子守(baby-sitter)]が着用する.「ねんねこ袢纏」ともいう. ⇨袢纏

ねんぶつ【念仏】 (chant) a Buddhist invocation of Amitabha[Amida Buddha]; (say) a prayer to Amitabha[Amida Buddha]. 阿弥陀仏への祈願. ☆「念仏」とは「仏, 特に阿弥陀仏の名号を唱えること」(the sincere repetition of the sacred name of Amitabha while chanting a prayer – "Namu Amida Butsu"[I sincerely believe in Amitabha]). 浄土宗・浄土真宗・時宗などの念仏宗での祈祷. ⇨「南無阿弥陀仏」. ¶**念仏踊り** the religious dance praying to Amitabha. **念仏行者** a person worshipping Amitabha.

ねんぽうせい【年俸制】 an annual salary system; a yearly pay[wage] scheme.

ねんまつきせい【年末帰省】 a year-end homecoming; a year-end mass exodus to hometowns; returning[going back] to one's hometown at the end of the year. ☆ exodus「出国; 外出; 多くの人が出ていくこと」. Exodus(大文字)は旧約聖書の「出エジプト

記」(モーゼに率いられたイスラエル人がエジプトを脱出した記録)のこと.

ねんまつジャンボたからくじ【年末ジャンボ宝くじ】 a year-end jumbo lottery ticket. ⇨宝くじ

ねんまつちょうせい【年末調整】 a year-end income tax adjustment.

の

のう【能】〔能楽〕Noh; a Noh drama[play]; the Noh theater. Noh is a highly-stylized traditional Japanese play performed with unique classical costumes and masks. A Noh play has three performances blended into one with harmony–*mai* (refined dance), *utai* (dramatic chant) and *hayashi* (drums and flutes). 古典的な能衣装や能面をまとって演じる日本古来の演劇.「舞い」「謡」「囃子」の見事な三位一体をなす. ☆起源は室町時代の「猿楽」に見られる歌舞に由来する. 観阿弥と世阿弥の父子が能の理論を確立する. 現在は観世, 宝生, 金春, 金剛, 喜多の5流派がある. ⇨猿楽

☆ Nogaku Theater was registered as a UNESCO Intangible Cultural Heritage in 2008.『能楽』は2008年(平成20年)ユネスコ無形文化遺産に登録された.

【能楽師】 a Noh player; a Noh performer. Noh players consist of *yakusha* (actors, dancers), *utai* (singers, chanters) and *hayashi* (instrumentalists). 能楽師は「役者・謡・囃子」から構成される. ⇨能役者／シテ (the main actor)／ワキ (the secondary actor)

【能楽】 Noh plays and kyogen interludes.「能」(solemn performances centered around singing and dancing)と「狂言」(comic entertainment unfolded through dialog)の両者を合わせた総称.

【能楽堂】 a Noh theater[英 theatre]; a Noh hall. A Noh hall has the stage made of plain cypress wood and the seats for the audiences under the same building. 総檜造りの舞台と観客席が同じ建物にある. ☆元来, 能楽は野外舞台(an outdoor stage)で公演された(薪能).

【能管】 a Noh flute; a horizontal flute with seven finger holes (used in a Noh music).

【能狂言】 ❶〈能と間狂言〉a Noh play and an interlude. ❷〈能と能の間に演ずる狂言〉(a) Noh farce (performed between the two Noh plays). ⇨狂言

【能装束】 (a) Noh costume. Noh costumes

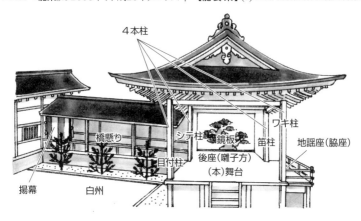

are worn in layers–generally a soft under-*kimono* covered by a stiff colorful brocade *kimono*. 能束帯は重ね着をし, 通常は柔らかい衣類を下に着て, その上に堅い豪華な錦織りの着物［唐織］を身に着ける. 「能衣装」ともいう.

【能舞台】 a Noh stage. A Noh stage, built of plain Japanese cypress, consists of a roofed platform with four pillars and a picture of pine trees painted on the back wall[panel] (*kagamiita*). 総檜造りの舞台には「4本柱」と「鏡板」の老松の絵画がある. ⇨「鏡板」(background for the stage). 「鏡の間」(greenroom). 「揚幕」(lifted curtain). 「切り戸」(small side entrance door). 「白州」(white gravel). ☆能舞台は下記の4部門から成る.

① 『(本)舞台』 a six-meter-square wooden stage floor for acting. 6mの正方形の板張り舞台.

② 『後座(囃子方)』 the rear stage position for the instrumentalists[orchestra]. ⇨後座(囃子方)

③ 『橋懸り』 the bridge-shaped raised passageway[corridor]. ⇨橋懸り

④ 『地謡座(脇座)』 the sitting area for the Noh chorus[chanters]. ⇨地謡座(脇座)

【能舞台の柱】 the four pillars on a Noh stage. ☆「4本柱」が設けられている.

① 『シテ柱』 the *shite* pillar; the left-side pillar used by the *shite* to position himself when he appears on stage. シテが舞台に登場するとき最初に所在の位置を決める左側の柱. ☆舞台に向かって左側の後方にある. ⇨シテ柱

② 『ワキ柱』 the *waki* pillar; the right-side pillar used by the *waki* to take his position near the pillar. ワキがそばに座る柱. ☆舞台に向かって右側の前方にある. ⇨ワキ柱

③ 『目付柱』 the eye-fixing pillar; the left-side pillar used by the *shite* to find his position on stage. シテが舞台上の所在地を確認するための目印用の柱. ☆舞台に向かって左側の前方にある. シテは能面のため視野が狭くなる. ⇨目付柱

④ 『笛柱』 the flute pillar; the right-side pillar used by the flute player. 笛方の後部の柱. ☆舞台に向かって右側の後方にある. ⇨笛柱

【能面】 a Noh mask; a lacquer-coated mask made of Japanese cypress wood and painted in layers (used in a Noh play). 檜製で胡粉とニカワの多層塗りの面. ☆「小面」(young woman). 「翁」(old man). 「般若」(jealous female spirit). 「邯鄲男」(young male god)など.

【能役者】 a Noh player; a Noh actor. Like kabuki, the actors are all men. Roles are roughly divided into *shite* and *waki*. 歌舞伎同様, 全役者は男性. 役割にはシテとワキがある. ⇨能楽師 / シテ / ワキ

のうかい【納会】 the last meeting of the year[term]; the closing session of the month.

のうかんし【納棺師】 undertaker (whose job is to clean the deceased body and place it in a coffin). ☆映画「おくりびと」(第81回アカデミー賞外国語映画賞)の英語版のタイトルは Departures (旅立ち).

のうかんしき【納棺式】 rites of placing the deceased body in a coffin. 遺体を棺に入れる儀式.

のうこつ【納骨】❶ keeping cremated bones in a cinerary urn. 火葬した遺骨を拾い骨壷に入れること. ⇨骨揚げ. ¶骨壷 a cinerary urn.

❷ interment; burying a cinerary urn into a grave (or charnel house). 骨つぼを墓(または納骨堂)に納めること. ☆地方によって異なるが, 墓がある場合「四十九日」または「一周忌」の法事に合わせて行う. ⇨法事. ¶納骨堂 a cinerarium; a charnel house (where cinerary urns are kept).

のうさぎ【野兎】〔動物〕a hare. ウサギ科の哺乳動物. ⇨うさぎ

のうさくぶつ【農作物】agricultural products; farm products. ⇔海産物. ¶農産物市場 market center for farm products.

のうさつ【納札】a votive tablet[pilgrimage card] (offered by a pilgrim to[at] a temple or shrine). (社寺に参詣する者が祈願のために)納める札.

のうし【脳死】brain death; cerebral death.

のうむ【濃霧】(a) dense[heavy, thick] fog. ¶濃霧警報 dense fog warning. ⇨霧

のうりょうせん【納涼船】a pleasure boat to enjoy the evening cool of the river[ocean].

のうりょうはなびたいかい【納涼花火大会】a fireworks display in the cool of a summer evening.

のうりょくきゅう【能力給】merit-based salary[wages]; performance-based pay; wages based on merit[performance]. ¶能力給制度 merit-pay system.

のき【軒】the eaves (made wide to protect from rain). ¶軒板 eaves board. 軒瓦 eaves tile.

のざわな【野沢菜】a *nozawa-na* turnip; brassica rapa. アブラナ科の一年草・二年草. 蕪(turnip)の改良種である. 「カブ菜」ともいう. ☆rapaはラテン語で「蕪」の意. ¶野沢菜漬け pickled *nozawa-na* turnip leaves and stalks (野沢菜の葉と茎を漬物にする. 長野の名産).

のざわのひまつり【野沢の火まつり】the Fire Festival at Nozawa Spa. (1月). ⇨付記(1)「日本の祭り」

のし【熨・熨斗】*noshi* (decoration); a thin strip of dried abalone (folded[wrapped] in red-and-white paper); a ceremonial paper-folding attached to a gift. A *noshi* is attached to a gift as an auspicious symbol or a courtesy emblem, expressing the respect of the sender. A *noshi* is attached on the upper right-hand corner of the wrapping paper, while a *mizuhiki*[gift-binding cord] around the middle. Today an informal *noshi* is occasionally printed on a gift-wrapping paper. 薄く伸ばして乾燥させたアワビ(紅白の紙に包んである). 慶事の象徴または儀礼の印として贈物につけ, 贈る者の敬意を表する.「熨斗」は包装紙の右上の端につけ,「水引」は真ん中にかける. 現代では包装紙にプリントされている非公式の熨斗もある. ⇨水引. ¶熨斗鮑 (a thin strip of) pressed and dried abalone(薄くはいで伸ばして干したアワビの肉).

【熨斗紙】a gift-wrapping paper (with a decorative *noshi* attached[printed] on it); a traditional paper for wrapping[covering] a gift. (装飾の熨斗がつけて[印刷されて]ある)贈答品用の包装紙. 贈答品を包んである[覆ってある]紙.

【熨斗袋】a gift-wrapping envelope (with a decorative *noshi* attached[printed] on it); a traditional envelope for wrapping[keeping] gift money. (装飾の熨斗がつけて[印刷されて]ある)贈呈用の紙袋. 贈呈金を納める袋. ⇨祝儀袋

のしめ【熨斗目】a ceremonial striped robe. It was worn under the sleeveless robe (*kataginu*) as formal wear for a *samurai* warrior in the Edo period. 無地で, 腰のあたりに縞を織り出した衣類. 江戸時代の武士の礼服用として肩衣の下に着る. ⇨肩衣

のしもち【伸し餅】a flat[flattened] rice cake. 長方形に, 平にのばした餅.

のだて【野点】〔茶道〕an open-air tea ceremony (held in the natural landscape garden); a garden tea ceremony (held in the open air). A straw mat or a red carpet is spread out on the ground where the tea ceremony is to be performed outdoors. 野外で行う茶の湯のこと. 茶の湯が行われる

の

野外にはむしろまたはじゅうたんが敷かれる. ☆16世紀戦国時代 (the Age of Civil War) の武将たちが遠征の途中で茶会を楽しんだのが起源. ⇨御園棚

のちじて【後仕手】〔能楽〕the main[principal] actor reappearing in the form of a deity (or ghost) in a second part of a Noh play. 能楽第2部で神［亡霊］の姿で再登場する主役［シテ］. ⇨前仕手 / 仕手

のびる【野蒜】〔植物〕a wild rocambole; a red garlic. ユリ科ネギ属の多年草. ゆでた若葉は浸し物や和え物に用いる. 焼いて（あるいは生で）味噌をつけて食べることがある.

のぼり【幟】❶〈旗〉a banner; a flag.〈劇場・相撲〉long narrow vertical banners (presented to actors (or *sumo* wrestlers) by their fans or patrons). A variety of banners are often displayed[raised] in front of the traditional theater where the actors perform (or the *sumo* stadium where the *sumo* wrestlers perform). 細長い縦型の旗(支援者や後援者から役者・力士に贈られる). 多種多様な幟が劇場または相撲会場の前に掲げられる.
❷〈吹流し〉a carp-shaped streamer[banner] hoisted[displayed] on Boys' Festival in May. 5月の子供の日に揚げる鯉型の吹き流し.「鯉幟」の略. ⇨鯉幟
❸〈戦場での幟〉a war banner carried into the battlefield. 戦場での戦旗.

のみ【蚤】〔虫〕a flea. ノミ科の昆虫.¶**蚤の市** a flea market.

のみこうい【呑み行為】 bookmaking(競馬で); bucketing(証券取引で).

のみともだち【飲み友達】 a drinking pal[buddy]; a drinking partner[companion].

のみほうだいのさかば【飲み放題の酒場】 all-you-can-drink bar. ☆「千円でビール飲み放題」(掲示) All the beer you can drink for ¥1,000.「当店では酒は飲み放題です」You can drink as much you like in our bar. ⇨食べ放題のレストラン

のみや【飲み屋】 a bar; ㊧ a pub; a tavern; ㊂ a saloon; a cheap pub[bar] (where a lot of inexpensive drinks are found on the menu). ⇨居酒屋

のり【海苔】❶〔海草〕(seaweed) laver; (an edible) seaweed.¶**青海苔** green laver. **岩海苔** spontaneous purple laver; laver adhered to rocks in a mossy form. ⇨浅草海苔
❷〔食品〕*nori*; dried (and pressed) laver; dried laver sheet. *Nori* is often used in cooking after first drying it in the sun. It is usually eaten after lightly parching [toasting] it over a charcoal fire [gas flame]. It is indispensable for making *onigiri*[rice balls] and *nigiri-zushi*[hand-rolled *sushi*]. 太陽に干してから料理に用いる. 通常は軽く火であぶってから食べる.「お握り」や「握り鮨」をつくるには欠かせない.
〔食品〕**干し海苔** dried (and seasoned) laver. ⇨味付け海苔 / 焼き海苔. **海苔の佃煮** *nori*[dried laver] boiled down in *shoyu*[soy sauce] and sugar. ⇨佃煮
【海苔茶漬け】 (a bowl of) boiled rice with hot (green) tea poured over it, topped [sprinkled] with crushed *nori*[dried laver]. お茶をご飯にそそぎ, その上に海苔をふりかける.
【海苔巻き】 laver-rolled *sushi*; vinegared rice and ingredients rolled in a sheet of *nori*[dried laver]. *Norimaki* is vinegared rice wrapped in a sheet of *nori* on a bamboo rolling mat (*makisu*) with various ingredients (such as egg, mushroom, dried gourd, greens, etc) in the center. 海苔で酢飯と具を巻いたすし. 竹製の巻き簀の上にいろいろな具を並べ1枚の海苔で巻いたすし.「海苔巻き鮨」「巻き鮨」「太巻き」などともいう. ⇨巻き簀

のりと【祝詞】 (recite) a ritual Shinto prayer. It is a prayer offered by a Shinto priest to gods participating in a Shinto ritual. 神主が神事で神に祈り (invocation)を捧げるときに唱える言葉. ☆「宣命書き」の表記で書かれる古体の文章.

のれん【暖簾】 ❶ *noren*;〈店先の〉a shop [store] split-curtain;〈食堂の〉a Japanese restaurant split-curtain. *Noren* is a short cloth curtain hung outside over the entrance of a traditional store[restaurant]. It indicates that a store or restaurant is open [started] for business. 店[和食堂]に掲げる分割したカーテン. 伝統的な店[和食堂]の入り口の外にかかる短い布製のカーテン. ☆営業中の表示.

❷〈室内の〉a partitioning curtain; a split-curtain used to divide rooms within a Japanese-style house[kitchen]. 部屋[台所]の間仕切り用カーテン.

のれんわけ【暖簾分け】 allowing a person to open a new establishment[set up a branch] bearing the same name as the store owner; taking over independent business with the same name from the previous owner. *Noren* often serves as a symbol to reflect the long-standing tradition and reputation of the store. 店主と同じ名前をもつ新しい施設[支店]を開設する許可を与えること. 営業権を得て支店を出すこと. 暖簾は店舗が保つ老舗の伝統と評判を反映する象徴である.

ノンポリがくせい【ノンポリ学生】 an apolitical student; a non-political-minded student who has no interest in political activities.

は

は【葉】〔植物〕a leaf (⑧ leaves); foliage (集合的). ¶**大根の葉** the leaves of *daikon* [radish].

ばい【棓】 a stick (used to beat a fish-shaped wooden gong). 木魚を打つ棒. ⇨木魚

ばいう〔つゆ〕【梅雨】 the rainy season. ¶**梅雨前線** a seasonal rain front.

はいが【胚芽】〔植物〕a germ; an embryo bud. 種子の内部にありまだ外に出ない芽. ¶**麦芽** wheat germs.

【胚芽米】 unpolished rice; rice with the germ[embryo buds]; polished rice with the germ unremoved; whole rice. 完全に白米にしないで, 胚芽を残してある米. ☆ビタミンBを多く含む. ⇨米

はいかい【俳諧】 *haikai*; a witty 17-syllable verse; a playful rhymed[linked] 17-syllable verse; a short form of poetry consisting of 17 syllables arranged in a 5-7-5 line. 韻を踏んだ17音節(発句, 第二句目は7+7音節)の滑稽な詩歌.「俳諧連歌(滑稽趣味の連歌)」また「俳諧歌(和歌の一体. 滑稽な歌)」の略. ☆室町末期, 山崎宗鑑(1465-1554)と荒木田守武(1473-1549)らが始めた. 江戸時代に松永貞徳(1571-1654)が確立し, 松尾芭蕉の「俳句」の先駆をなす. ¶**俳諧師** a *haikai* poet.

ばいかさい【梅花祭】 the Plum Blossom Festival. It is held in commemoration of the death of Sugawara no Michizane, well-known by his posthumous name, *Tenjin sama*, at Kitano Tenmangu Shrine in Kyoto. 天神さまの神号で有名な菅原道真の命日を記念して, 京都の北野天満宮で行われる.

バイキング〔料理〕smorgasbord dishes; an all-you-can-eat buffet.

はいく【俳句】 a *haiku* (poem); a 17-syllable poem (arranged in a 5-7-5 pattern). A *haiku* is a set form of classical Japanese poem that consists of three metrical units of 5-7-5 syllables. Each *haiku* in this form contains a seasonal term[a word or phrase expressive of the season]. 5音・7音・5音の3つの句からなる17音節を並べた定型詩. どの俳句にも「季語」(a season word[phrase])

がある。☆俳句は俳諧の発句(5・7・5)から派生した短詩。⇨短歌 / 発句 / 季語。¶**俳人** a *haiku* poet; an expert in the art of the 17-syllable poem. **俳壇** *haiku* circles; the world of *haiku*. **俳文** a *haiku* prose; (a piece of) poetical prose written by a *haiku* poet. **俳名** a pen name as a *haiku* poet.

バイクびん【バイク便】 a delivery service by motorcycle; a motorbike courier[messenger] service. ☆英語の bike は通常 bicycle（自転車）の略である。

ばいしゃくけっこん【媒酌結婚】 an arranged marriage; a marriage arranged by a matchmaker who introduces the prospective bride and groom. 結婚の縁を取りもつ媒酌人 (go-between)の仲立ちによる結婚。

ばいしゃくにん【媒酌人】 a go-between; a matchmaker. The term of *baishakunin* is more commonly referred to at the wedding ceremony and the reception party. 媒酌人の用語は通常，結婚式と披露宴の際に使われる。⇨仲人

ばいしん【陪臣】 *baishin*. ❶ a lower retainer [vassal] under the direct control of the retainer[vassal] of his master. 臣下の家来。「又家来」。

❷ a direct retainer[vassal] of the feudal lord in the Edo period; the rear retainer of the shogun. 江戸時代，諸大名の家臣。⇔直参

ハイテクおんち【ハイテク音痴】 techno-illiterate.

はいでん【拝殿】 an oratory (of a Shinto shrine); the worshippers' hall[place] (in front of a Shinto shrine). *Haiden* is the hall[place] of worship directly in front of the Shinto sanctuary (*honden*) where the object of worship venerated as a god(*go-shintai*) is enshrined. The Shinto priests conduct their rituals and worshipers make their offerings at the oratory of the shrine.

御神体が安置されている本殿のすぐ前にある礼拝堂のこと。神社の拝殿で神主は儀式を行い，拝礼者は捧げ物をする。⇨本殿。☆ oratory はキリスト教の大聖堂 (cathedral)にある小礼拝堂のこと。⇨神体

ばいにく【梅肉】 plum pulp; the soft flesh [fleshy part] of *umeboshi*[pickled plum]. ¶**梅肉エキス** plum extract.

はいはんちけん【廃藩置県】 the abolition of clans[feudal domains] (*han*) and establishment of prefectures (*ken*). Prefectures replaced domains in 1871. After putting an end to the *han* system, the new Meiji government placed prefectures and appointed prefectural governor in each country. 1871年(明治4年)，新明治政府は藩体制を廃止し，全国に県を置き，県知事が任命される。☆中央集権体制が確立する。⇨版籍奉還

ハイビジョン・テレビ high-definition TV [HDTV]. 高品位テレビ。

はいぶつきしゃく【廃仏[排仏]毀釈】 the separation of Shintoism from Buddhism; the anti-Buddhist policy[movement] early in the Meiji period that led to the destruction[removal] of Buddhist temples. After the Meiji Restoration (1868), many Buddhist temples were disestablished while Shinto was established as the national religion. 明治維新の初期「神仏分離令」によって起こった仏教排斥運動(仏教を廃止して，捨て去ること)。一方では国家神道が確立する。⇨神仏分離令

はいれい【拝礼】 worship; bowing one's head in worship. At the oratory of the shrine, the worshipper bows his/ her head politely twice, then claps his/ her hands twice (and makes a wish), and finally bows politely once again. 頭をさげておがむこと。明治神宮では「二拝二拍手一拝」。☆出雲大社では「二礼四拍手一礼」。⇨礼拝(れいはい；らいはい)。¶**拝礼者** a worshipper.

は

はうた【端唄】　*hauta*; a short Edo-period song [ballad] sung to the accompaniment of *shamisen*. *Hauta* and *Kouta* are short popular forms of singing accompanied by *shamisen* that flourished late in the Edo period. 三味線の伴奏で歌う小唄曲．江戸末期頃，町人の間で流行した短い俗謡の一種．⇨長唄／地唄／小唄

はえ【蝿】〔虫〕 a fly. 幼虫は「蛆」(a maggot; a grub). ¶家蝿 a house fly. 金蝿 a green-bottle fly. 黒蝿 a blowfly. 蝿取り紙 flypaper. 蝿取り器 a flytrap.

はえ【鮠】　⇨はや

はおり【羽織】　a *haori*; a short half-length coat[overgarment]. A *haori* is a short outer half-coat worn over a formal *kimono*. It reaches between the thigh and the knee, and is tied by short braided cords at the front. The formal *haori* has three or five family crests of the wearer on the back and sleeves. 正装和服の上に着用する丈の短い衣服．丈は腰下から膝上ぐらいで (extends to the knee or above the thigh)，前は短い編んだ紐で結ぶ．正装の羽織の背中と袖には着用者の三つないし五つの家紋がある．¶羽織袴 *haori* and *hakama* (worn by men in full dress)(羽織と袴を着用した男性の正装)；formal half-coat (*haori*) with pleated skirt-like trousers (*hakama*). ⇨袴. 羽織ひも short braided cords around the front of the half-coat. 羽織袴で身支度する wear formal coat and trousers; be dressed in formal Japanese *kimono*[attire].

はか【墓】　a grave; a tomb(大きな墓)．¶墓石 a gravestone; a tombstone. 墓場［墓地］ a graveyard; a cemetery. 墓参り (pay) a visiting to one's grave; (pay) a visit to an ancestor's grave for prayer. 墓誌 burial inscription; a record of deceased ancestors buried in the burial grounds.

ばかがい【馬鹿貝】〔貝〕a mussel; a surf clam; a trough shell. バカガイ科の海産二枚貝. 刺身や酢の物にする．むき身は「あおやぎ」といわれる．貝柱は「あられ」という．⇨あおやぎ／あられそば

はかたおり【博多織】　a *Hakata* textile; glossy textiles woven in the Hakata area in Kyushu.

はかたぎおんやまかさ【博多祇園山笠】　the Hakata Gion Yamakasa Festival. (7月)．⇨付記(1)「日本の祭り」

はかたこま【博多独楽】　a top with a long shaft spun with both hands. 両手で回す長い芯棒つきの独楽．⇨独楽

はかたどんたく【博多どんたく】　the Fancy-Dress Parade Festival in Hakata City. (5月)．⇨付記(1)「日本の祭り」

はかたにんぎょう【博多人形】　a *Hakata* earthenware[clay] doll; a doll made of clay with beautiful[colorful] baked finish produced in Hakata City. 博多産の粘土人形．精密な色彩をほどこして焼き上げた粘土人形．

はかま【袴】a *hakama*. ❶〈着物〉a pleated skirt-like ceremonial garment; long loose-legged pleated trousers. A *hakama* is worn over a *kimono* and tied around the waist. Originally a *hakama* was worn by men on formal occasions. A long trailing *hakama* was reserved for high-ranking *samurai*. ひだのあるゆるいスカート風の正式衣服 (formal wear)．足元がだぶだぶの長い衣服［ズボン］．着物の上にはいて，腰あたりで結ぶ．袴は元来男子が着用する正装．長く尾を引いた袴は上位の侍が着用した．⇨袴／長袴／羽織
❷〈徳利立て〉a *sake* (bottle) stand[holder]. 酒の徳利をおくための浅い器．⇨徳利立て

はかまぎのぎょうじ【袴着の行事】⇨七五三

はぎ【萩】〔植物〕bush clover; lespedeza. マメ科の多年性落葉低木.「秋の七草 」の一種．⇨秋の七草／月見の宴

はぎやき【萩焼】 Hagi ceramic and porcelain ware (produced in the Hagi region of Yamaguchi Prefecture).

ばくが【麦芽】 malt. 通称「モルト」. 大麦を発芽させ乾燥したもの. ビールや水あめなどの原料. ¶**麦芽エキス** malt extract(病人の栄養食). **麦芽酒** malt liquor (ale, beer, stoutなど). **麦芽汁** wort(ビール・蒸留もろみのの原料). **麦芽乳** malted milk(麦芽入りの粉ミルク). **麦芽糖** malt sugar; maltose(水あめの原料).

はくさい【白菜】〔植物〕(a) Chinese cabbage; (a) Chinese lettuce. アブラナ科の一年草または二年草. 日本では漬物や鍋物, 韓国ではキムチ(kimchi)の原料として使う. ¶**白菜2[3]個** two[three] heads of Chinese cabbage.
〔料理〕**白菜の一夜漬け** Chinese cabbage pickled[salted down] overnight; salted pickles of Chinese cabbage. **白菜の塩漬け** Chinese cabbage pickled in salt; Chinese cabbage sprinkled with salt.

はくじ【白磁】 white porcelain(developed in the Orient, especially in Korea). It features its smooth glaze and flawless surface. 文様のない純白の磁器製品. 東洋, 特に韓国で発達した. その特色は滑らかな釉薬と無傷な表面である.

はくじゅ【白寿】 (celebrate) one's ninety-nineth birthday. ⇨賀
【白寿祝い】 the celebration of one's ninety-nineth birthday. The Japanese celebrate their 99th birthday. It is the 99th anniversary of one's life, one of the special ages to celebrate one's longevity. 99歳の祝い. ☆漢字の百の一画目を除いた字.

ばくしん【幕臣】 a vassal[retainer] of the shogunate; a shogun's vassal[retainer]. 幕府の臣下. ☆御家人や旗本などをさす. ⇨幕府

ばくせい【幕政】 the shogunate government [administration]. ¶**鎌倉幕政** the Kamakura shogunate. ⇨幕府

はくぞう【白象】〈花祭り〉 a papier-mâché white elephant. 張り子の白象.

はくちょう【白鳥】 a swan. ガンカモ科の水鳥. ¶**渡来する白鳥**［北海道・風蓮湖］migratory white swans; white swans migrating from Siberia to the lake[Lake Furen(ko)].

ばくはんたいせい【幕藩体制】 the shogunate and *han*[domain] system; the feudal political system consisting of the shogunate and the feudal lords' domains. The Tokugawa shogunate directly controlled Edo and heartland of the country while the feudal lords governed the *han*[domain]. 幕府と大名の藩からなる政治体制. 徳川幕府は江戸とその要地を直轄支配下におき, 藩を大名に支配させた. ⇨藩

ばくふ【幕府】 the shogunate; the military shogunate government[regime] (as opposed to the imperial government); the feudal political system of the military government. The shogunate controls the feudal lords nationwide by assigning them fiefs and requiring loyalty to the shogun in return. 武家による政治を行うための権力機構[中央政治機関](朝廷による政治に対して). 幕府は領地を割り与えて大名を統治し, 見返りに幕府に忠誠を求めた. ☆鎌倉・室町・徳川の三代に及ぶ. ⇨将軍
[1]『鎌倉幕府』the Kamakura shogunate (established by the shogun Minamoto Yoritomo at Kamakura in 1192). 1192年に源頼朝(1147-99: 鎌倉幕府初代将軍)が開いた幕府. ☆直属の家臣を全国に配置して支配し, その勢力を伸ばす. 初めて武家が実権を握る. 1333年に滅亡.
[2]『室町幕府』the Muromachi shogunate (established by the shogun Ashikaga Takauji in Kyoto in 1338). 1338年足利

尊氏（1305-1358: 室町幕府初代将軍）が開いた幕府．☆朝廷・公家の政権が弱体化し，完全に武士の政権に統治される．1573年に滅亡．

③『**徳川幕府**』the Tokugawa shogunate (established by the shogun Tokugawa Ieyasu in Edo in 1603)．1603年徳川家康（1542-1616: 徳川幕府初代将軍）が開いた幕府．☆関が原の合戦を経て，大阪冬・夏の陣で豊臣氏を滅ぼし，強固な幕藩体制 (centralized feudal system)を敷き，安定した時代を築く．1867年最後の将軍・徳川慶喜による大政奉還で幕府は終焉した．

ばくふ【瀑布】 waterfall; falls. ¶**日本三瀑布** the Three Famous Waterfalls in Japan. ☆華厳滝（栃木県）・那智滝（和歌山県）・袋田滝（茨城県）．⇨滝

はくまい【白米】 polished white rice; cleaned white rice; polished rice with the germ part removed. ☆玄米をついて，糠と胚を除いて白くした米．別称「精米」．⇔玄米．¶**白米のご飯** cooked white rice.

ばくまつ【幕末】the last[closing] days of the Tokugawa shogunate[regime]. 徳川幕府・江戸時代の末期．

【幕末の志士】 a loyalist[loyal subject] in the closing days of the Tokugawa shogunate; a loyal supporter of the Tokugawa shogunate around the end of the Edo period. 徳川幕府末期の忠臣．江戸時代末期頃に将軍に忠誠を尽くした幕府支持者．⇔勤皇の志士

はくらいひん【舶来品】〈総称の〉foreign-made[imported] goods; 〈個々の〉a foreign-made[an imported] article.

ばくり【幕吏】a shogunate official. 幕府の役人．

はくろ【白露】 (drops of) white dew; the season when the autumn[fall] weather begins. 秋の気配が立ちそめる季節．⇨二十四節気

はげたか【禿鷹】〔鳥〕a vulture（禿鷲）; a condor. 別名「コンドル」．⇨たか / わし

はけん【覇権】〈支配力〉hegemony; supremacy. Tokugawa Ieyasu established hegemony over Japan after winning the Battle of Sekigahara. 覇者（武力的な征服者）としての権力．徳川家康は関が原の合戦後日本中に覇権を確立した．

はけんしゃいん【派遣社員】a temp; a temporary employee[worker](from a temp agency).

はけんむら【派遣村】a tent village set up for dispatch workers who lost their jobs and homes (in central Tokyo during the year-end and New Year holidays).

はけんろうどうしゃ【派遣労働者】 a dispatch[temporary] worker; a laborer dispatched for temporary work. ¶**日雇い派遣労働者** a dispatch day laborer; a day laborer who is registered with a temp agency as a dispatch worker. ⇨日雇い派遣制

はごいた【羽子板】 a battledore; a square wooden racket with an embossed picture made of cloth on one side. A battledore is used to hit a shuttlecock (*hane*) when playng a traditional badminton-like game called *hanetsuki*[a battledore-and-shuttlecock game] (during the New Year holidays). The battledores are artistically decorated on one side with raised cloth pictures of a kabuki actor or a famous personality. The other side is used to hit the shuttlecock (*hane*) back and forth[bat the *hane* to and fro high]. The battledore is also displayed as a good-luck charm during the New Year season. 片面に押し絵がある四角形の木製ラケット (wooden paddle). 羽子板は（新年に）「羽根突き」と呼ばれる（バドミントンのような）伝統的な遊技をする時に羽子 (a feathered shuttle weighted

は

with tiny balls[beans])を打つために使う. 羽子板の片面は歌舞伎や有名人の押し絵で芸術的に装飾されている. 他面は前や後ろに高く羽根を突くのに用いる. 羽子板は正月には縁起物として飾られることもある. ⇨羽根突き / 押し絵. ¶**羽子板(遊び)** a game of battledore and shuttlecock (played during the New Year holidays).

【**羽子板市**】 a battledore fair. Various types of decorative battledores are sold annually at open-air stalls in the precincts of shrines and temples in December. 12月には神社仏閣の境内にある露店では飾りたてられた多種多様な羽子板が売られる. 圀浅草寺. ☆「邪気を「ハネ」除け」来る年の幸を祈る. 羽根先の玉は邪気払いといわれる.

はこずし【箱鮨】 ⇨押し鮨

はこにわ【箱庭】 a box garden; a miniature landscape garden arranged in a box[box-like container] (with natural materials combined with man-made materials). 箱に配した小型の山水庭園(人工素材と自然素材を融合させている). 別称「盆景」. ⇨盆❷

はこねせきしょあと【箱根関所跡】 the site of the old Hakone Barrier. It was an important checkpoint set up at the Hakone Pass between Edo and Kyoto in 1618 by the Tokugawa shogunate to screen people traveling to Edo. 江戸へ入る旅人を審査するために, 1618年徳川幕府によって江戸と京都間にある箱根峠に置かれた重要な施設.

はこねだいみょうぎょうれつ【箱根大名行列】 the Feudal Lord Procession in Hakone. (11月). ⇨付記(1)「日本の祭り」

はこねだいもんじやき【箱根大文字焼】 the Great Bonfire Event at Hakone. (8月). ⇨付記(1)「日本の祭り」

はこべ[はこべら]【繁縷】〔植物〕 a chickweed; a starwort. ナデシコ科の二年草.「春の七草」の一種. ⇨春の七草

はこまくら【箱枕】 a box-supported pillow; a box-shaped wooden pillow; a pillow with an oblong wooden box. It is used by women done their hair up in the Japanese old-fashioned style (such as *takashimada*). 箱で支えた枕. 長方形の木製箱にのせた枕. (高島田のような) 昔の髪型を結った女性が使用した. ☆中にそば殻 (buckwheat chaff)などをつめ, 両側をくくってある枕を箱形の台の上にのせてある. ⇨高島田 / そば殻

はこやなぎ【箱柳】〔植物〕 an aspen; a (white) poplar(ポプラ). ヤナギ科の落葉高木. 街路樹・防風林用. 材はマッチの軸・製紙・器具用.「白楊」ともいう. ⇨ポプラ

はごろも【羽衣】a robe of feathers; a legendary robe[raiment] of feathers worn by an angel[a celestial nymph]. 天人[天使・天の妖精]が着て空を飛ぶという鳥の羽で作った薄くて軽い伝説上の衣[衣服]. ¶**天の羽衣** the celestial robe of an angel.

ばさし【馬刺し】 sliced raw horsemeat; a slice of raw horsemeat. 桜肉の刺身. ⇨桜肉

はさみしょうぎ【挟み将棋】 a checker-like game played with *shogi* pieces on the *shogi* board. The game is won by taking away all of the opponent's pieces by capturing the opponent's pieces between player's pieces. 将棋盤の上で将棋の駒で遊ぶチェッカー遊戯に類似した遊び. 駒と駒の間に相手の駒をはさんで取りながら, 相手の駒を全部取った者が勝つ.

はし【箸】 (a pair of) chopsticks. ¶塗り箸 lacquered chopsticks. 木製箸 wooden chopsticks. 竹箸 bamboo chopsticks. 象牙箸 ivory chopsticks. 割り箸 splittable unpainted wooden[bamboo] chopsticks; half-split (disposable) wooden[bamboo] chopsticks. ⇨柳(柳箸). 箸置き a chopstick rest; a rest for chopsticks. 箸紙 a

paper sheath for chopsticks. 箸供養 a memorial service for old chopsticks. 箸立て a chopstick holder[stand]. 箸箱 a chopstick case; an individual container for a pair of chopsticks. 箸袋 a chopstick wrapper; a paper envelope for chopsticks.
☆『嫌い箸』(improper chopsticks etiquette): 「刺し箸」using chopsticks to skewer food. 「渡し箸」resting chopsticks sideways across the top of a bowl[dish].「ねぶり箸」licking one's chopsticks.「探り箸」using chopsticks to rummage food in a dish.「迷い箸」wavering chopsticks back and forth over various dishes.「寄せ箸」using chopsticks to draw a dish nearer to oneself.「指し箸」using chopsticks to point at people.

はし[-ばし]【橋】 a bridge. ¶大鳴門橋 the O-Naruto Bridge (completed between Shikoku and Awaji(shima) Island in 1985). 日本三奇橋 the Three Famous Bridges in Japan. ☆ 神橋(栃木県)またはかずら橋(徳島県)・猿橋(山梨県)・錦帯橋(山口県)

はしあらい【箸洗い】〔茶道〕 simple soup served in a small cup (at a formal tea ceremony dishes). (懐石料理のとき)小さな茶碗で出る簡素な汁物.

はしがかり【橋懸り】〔能楽〕a raised passageway[walkway] leading from the actors'greenroom[dressing room] to the main stage.It is used as a bridge-shaped extension with a roof and a parapet in the Noh theater. 役者の楽屋[支度部屋]から本舞台へ斜めにかけ渡した通路. 屋根・欄干などがある橋型の延長部分として用いる. ⇨能「能舞台」

はしござけ【梯子酒】 ㊞barhopping; ㊞pub-crawling. ¶はしご(酒)をする人 ㊞barhopper; ㊞ pub-crawler. はしごをする go barhopping; go on a pub-crawl (はしごをして回る); go drinking at many bars in succession.

ばしゃく【馬借】 a carrier on land (in the Muromachi period). 室町時代の陸上の運送業者.

はしやすめ【箸休め】 a light[side] dish served between the main courses. 主な料理の途中に味を変化させるため口直しに出す添え料理(酢の物・和え物など). ⇨酢の物 /和え物

ばじゅつ【馬術】 an equestrian art; horse-manship; horseback riding. ⇨流鏑馬

ばしょ【場所】〔相撲〕a (*sumo*) grand tournament. 相撲の興行を行う所, またその期間. ¶5月[夏]場所 the May[Summer] grand *sumo* tournament. ⇨相撲

ばしょう【芭蕉】〔植物〕a Japanese banana plant; a plantain. バショウ科の大形多年草. ¶芭蕉布 plantain cloth; cloth woven by the fibers of plantain leaves. 芭蕉の葉の繊維で織った布. 夏の着物, 蚊帳, 座布団などに用いる. 沖縄の名産.

はしらえ【柱絵】 a tall, narrow print for pillar hanging.

はしり【走り】 the first fish[vegetables] of the season. その季節の先に出る魚・野菜など.「初物」ともいう. ⇨旬 / 初物. ¶カツオの走り the first bonito of the season. ⇨初鰹. マツタケ[タケノコ]の走り the first *matsutake* mushroom[bamboo shoots] of the season.

はす【蓮】〔植物〕a lotus. (㊟ lotuses) スイレン科の多年生水草. 仏教では, この花を「蓮華」(a lotus flower)といい, 極楽浄土の象徴とする. 根茎は「蓮根」(lotus root). ⇨蓮華. ¶蓮の花 a lotus flower. 蓮の葉 a lotus leaf. 蓮の実 a lotus pip. 蓮池 a lotus pond.

はすのうてな【蓮の台】 a lotus calyx. 仏・菩薩が座るという「蓮の花」の座席. ☆ calyxは「萼」(うてな:花びらの外側でつぼみを含むもの). ⇨蓮華座

はぜ【沙魚・鯊】〔魚〕 a goby; a mudfish; a mudskipper(トビハゼ). ハゼ科の硬骨魚. 甘露煮や天ぷら・刺身・から揚げなどに調理する. 小さいハゼは佃煮にする.
〔料理〕ハゼの甘露煮 sweet-boiled goby; simmered goby with *shoyu*[soy sauce] and sugar.

はたき【叩き】 a duster. It is made of strips of cloth tied to the tip of a long (bamboo) stick handle. (竹)棒の先につけた布切れでつくるほこり払い用具.「ちりばらい」.

はたはた【鰰・鱩(国字)】〔魚〕 a sandfish. ハタハタ科の海産硬骨魚. 食用として正月料理の「はたはたずし」, 秋田名物の「塩汁」がある. 初冬に雷(はたはたがみ)が鳴る頃, 産卵のために日本海沿岸に押し寄せることから「雷魚」ともいう. ☆「はたはたがみ」は「雷」の方言. ⇨塩汁(秋田料理)

はたもと【旗本】 a direct retainer of the shogun. He ranks below a feudal lord and serves the shogun with immediate vassals (*gokenin*) under the Tokugawa shogunate government. 徳川幕府の将軍家直属の家臣. 大名の下位にあり, 徳川幕府の下で御家人とともに将軍に仕えた. ☆武士のうち禄高が1万石(a revenue of 10,000 *koku*)未満で将軍に謁見できる者. ⇨御家人

はち【蜂】〔虫〕a bee(蜜蜂); a wasp(雀蜂); a hornet(熊蜂・地蜂など). ¶女王蜂 a queen bee. 足長蜂 a long-legged hornet. 樹蜂 a wood wasp. 働き蜂 a worker bee. 蜂蜜 honey. 蜂の巣 beehive; honeycomb. 蜂の子 a wasp larva.

はち【鉢】❶〈食器〉a bowl; a container. ¶鉢物 food served in a bowl.
❷〔華道〕 a ceramic basin (used for the flower arrangement)(水盤); a (flower) pot(植木鉢). ¶鉢植え a potted plant(植木鉢に植えた花木); a house plant (室内用に植えた花木). 鉢生け a plant[flower] arranged in a basin(鉢で生ける花木)

ばち【撥】a plectrum(複 plectra, plectrums); a hand-held pick (used for plucking the strings of a musical instrument such as *shamisen* or *biwa*)(三味線や琵琶などの弦をかき鳴らす)手に持ってつまびく道具. ¶撥さばき the handling of one's plectrum. 三味線[琵琶]の撥 a *shamisen*[*biwa*] plectrum.

ばち【桴・枹】 a drumstick; (a pair of) sticks used for beating drums. It is used not only in the kabuki and Noh theaters but also in traditional folk music. (太鼓などを)打つ棒. 歌舞伎や能楽また日本の伝統音楽に用いる. ¶枹さばき the handling of one's (drum) sticks.

はちじゅうはちや【八十八夜】 the eighty-eighth day from the setting-in[beginning] of spring. It falls on[around] May 2 according to the solar calendar. This is the best time[season] for sowing rice seeds and picking tea leaves. 立春から数えて八十八日目. 太陽暦で5月2日頃. 稲の種まきや茶摘みの季節. ☆この日に摘んだ新茶は上質(fine quality)で, 飲むと1年間健康が保てる(remain good health for the year)といわれる.

はちじゅうはっかしょれいじょうめぐり【(四国)八十八箇所霊場巡り】 (make) a pilgrimage to the eighty-eight Holy Temples (of Shikoku). ⇨遍路

はちのへえんぶり【八戸えんぶり】 the Hachinohe *Enburi* Dance Festival. (2月). ⇨付記(1)「日本の祭り」

はちまき【鉢巻き】❶〈頭部に巻く布〉 a headband; a frontlet; a (hand) towel worn around the head; a kerchief of cotton cloth tied around the head. ¶ねじり鉢巻 a twisted headband (worn by carpenters and workmen). 向こう鉢巻 a towel tied on the forehead and at the back.
❷〈集中力の象徴〉a kerchief[towel] tied

[worn] around the head, symbolic of concentration to carry out one's aim. ☆運動会・神輿担ぎ・集中学習などの時に使用する.

はちまん【八幡】the God of War. ¶八幡様 Hachiman shrine (dedicated to the God of War)

パチンコ pachinko; a Japanese-style pinball game (played in a *pachinko* parlor). In the *pachinko* machine, players manipulate a handle and try to steer[shoot] small steel balls into a winning hole along a vertical[upright] board to get as many balls as possible. パチンコ屋での日本式ピンボール遊戯. パチンコ台ではできるだけ多くの球を取るために垂直に立てた盤に沿ってハンドルを操作しながら小さな鉄球を入賞口に入れようとする. ☆「**スロットマシン**」(slot machine with liquid crystal displays)も導入されている. ¶**パチンコ依存症** the *pachinko* dependence syndrome. **手動式パチンコ機** the *pachinko* machine with the manually-operated systems of striking balls. **電動式パチンコ機** the *pachinko* machine with electronically-powered systems of striking balls. **パチンコで大当たりする** hit the jackpot in the *pachinko* machine.

【パチンコ景品交換】 prize exchange. Players exchange the *pachinko* balls for money and various prizes such as food and leisure goods according to the number of balls won. They can exchange the winning prize gold tokens for cash outside at the price exchange center. パチンコをする人は勝ち取ったパチンコ玉 (balls acquired)の数に応じて現金化できる特殊景品や食べ物, 嗜好品と交換する. 店外の景品交換所では特殊景品を現金化できる.

ばつ【閥】 a clique (徒党); a faction (派閥); a nepotism (縁者贔屓); a group of exclusive-minded colleagues who are closely bound together with the same background[purpose]. 同じ経歴[目的]で強く結ばれ排他的な同志の集団. ¶**学閥** an academic clique. **派閥** a political faction. **藩閥** a clan clique. **財閥** a financial clique.

バツイチ a once-divorced person. ⇨瘤付き. ¶**子持ちのバツイチ** a once-divorced man (or woman) with a child[children].

はっか【薄荷】〔植〕 mint; peppermint; spearmint. シソ科の多年草. 香料に用いる. ¶**ハッカ入りのガム** spearmint[peppermint] gum.

はつかだいこん【二十日大根】a radish; a red turnip(赤蕪). アブラナ科の一, 二年草. 種をまいて20〜30日で食用となる. 主にサラダ用に使う. ⇨かぶ／だいこん

はつがつお【初鰹】 the first bonito of the season; the first catch of bonito in early summer. ⇨走り

はつかねずみ【二十日鼠】〔動物〕a mouse(複 mice); a house mouse. ネズミ科の小形哺乳動物. ⇨ねずみ

はつがま【初釜】〔茶道〕the first tea ceremony of the year. その年の最初の茶会.

はつガンぶっしつ【発ガン物質】 cancer-causing substance[agent]; carcinogenic substance[agent] (医学用語).

はっけい【八景】the eight scenic spots. ⇨近江八景

はっこう【発酵】 fermentation; ferment. ☆ferment 動「発酵する；発酵させる」. ⇨納豆 (fermented soybeans). ¶**自然発酵** natural fermentation. **発酵食品** fermented food. **発酵乳** fermented milk; cultured milk. **発酵菌** ferment bacillus[複 bacilli] (発酵作用がある微生物など)；ferment fungus[複 fungi] (キノコ・カビなど).

はっさく【八朔】〔植物〕 a *hassaku* orange; a thick-skinned orange; a thick-skinned grapefruit-like fruit. ミカンの一種. 広島県の原産.

はっすん【八寸】 a simple meal [collection of appetizers] served on a wooden square tray called *hassun* (8-inch). It is a dish of several small portions served as a relish at a tea ceremony. 八寸四方の器に盛り付ける前菜の盛り合わせ．少量の配分を盛り付けた懐石料理の「酒の肴」のこと．☆一口サイズの海の幸・山の幸 (morsels from the mountains and the sea) を少しずつ食する．酒の肴を盛り合わせた白木の「八寸膳」の略．⇨肴

はつぜっく【初節句】 (celebration of) the first Boys'[Girls'] Festival for a newborn baby. 赤子の生後はじめて行う男子(女子)の節句(の祝い)．⇨節句(端午の節句 / 桃の節句)

ばった【飛蝗】〔虫〕 a grasshopper; a locust(飛ぶ飛蝗)．バッタ科の昆虫．

はつだいし【初大師】 the year's first memorial rite for Kobo-Daishi. (January 21)

バッテラ (Osaka-style) pressed mackerel *sushi*; pressed *sushi* topped with slices of vinegared mackerel. 関西風のサバの押鮨［棒鮨］．☆ポルトガル語の bateira「小舟」(boat)にみたてることからの名称．⇨さば鮨

はっとう【法堂】 ⇨講堂

はつどひょう【初土俵】 a debut of a *sumo* wrestler; one's first appearance on the *sumo* ring.

はつに【初荷】 the first cargo[delivery] of merchandise during the New Year season. ☆昔は1月2日, 今は1月4日の出荷.

はっぴ【法被・半被】 a *happi*(coat); a type of Japanese jacket. A *happi*-coat with a wide sleeve reaches the hip and is fastened with an *obi*[sash] tied around the waist. It often bears the family crest (or the name of a store) on its back or collar. 袖口の広がった法被着は腰まで届き，腹部に帯を巻いて締める．法被の背中やえりには家紋(または

屋号)などがある.

❶〈武家の上着〉a *kimono*-style short coat (worn by *samurai* warriors). 武士が着る着物型の短い上着．

❷〈職人の上着〉a livery outer short jacket (worn by workers[craftsmen] including carpenters and gardeners). 大工や庭師などの職人が着る揃いの短い上着．⇨半纏

❸〈祭事の上着〉a festive short coat (worn by youths bearing[carrying] a portable shrine on their shoulders or pulling the festival floats during the festivals). 祭りのとき，肩に神輿を担いだり，山車を引っ張る若者が着る短い上着．

ハッピーマンデーせいど【ハッピーマンデー制度】 the Happy Monday System.This system was decided by the government of Japan to move several national holidays to Monday, creating a three-day weekend for those who normally have a five-day work week. Coming-of-Age Day (2nd Monday of January), Marine Day (3rd Monday of July), Respect-of-the-Aged Day (3rd Monday of September) and Health and Sports Day (2nd Monday of October). 国民の祝日の一部を従来の日付から特定の月曜日に移動させる制度．5日制(週休2日制)が一般化したことから月曜日を休日として3連休を創出(ゆとりある暮らしの実現の一環として)．⇨「成人の日」「海の日」「敬老の日」「スポーツの日」．⇨国民の祝日

はつひので【初日の出】 (the) sunrise on the New Year's Day.

はつもうで【初詣】 (pay) the first visit of the year to a shrine or temple (at New Year's). Worshippers often visit noted shrines or temples on New Year's Eve or the first of January to pray for happiness and prosperity in the new year. Some people visit shrines or temples on one of the first three days of the New Year or later during

は

the first week. They buy good-luck charms such as *hamaya* and *daruma* at the stalls on their way back home. 参拝者は大晦日 (at midnight of the old year) または元旦 (early in the morning of the New Year)に新年の幸福と繁栄を祈願して名の知れた神社や寺院を参詣する. 人によっては新年の三が日または最初の一週間中に参拝する. その帰路には破魔矢や達磨などの縁起物を買う.「初参り」ともいう. ⇨破魔矢 / 達磨

はつもの【初物】 〔農産物〕the first product of the season;〔魚介類〕the first catch of the season. その年の季節に初めてとれた農産物また魚介類. ☆日本では初物を食すると75日寿命がのびる(俗信)といわれている. ¶初物の梨 the first pear of the season. 初物のまぐろ the first tuna of the season. ⇨走り

はつゆめ【初夢】 one's first dream in the New Year. The dream occurs on the first night of the New Year's Day to the morning of the second (or on January 2) to foretell one's fate for the coming new year. 来る年の運勢を占うために元旦の夜から2日の朝にかけて(または2日に)みる夢. ☆七福神を乗せた宝船の絵を枕の下におく習慣があった. ⇨七福神

バテレンついほうれい【伴天連追放令】 the edict to expel Christian missionaries from Japan in the Edo period. ☆「伴天連」はポルトガル語のpadre(パードレ【神父】;室町時代末期に伝道のため渡来したキリスト教の司祭)からの呼称.「神父」は「カトリックの司祭」Catholic priest; Father[Fr.]~. 加藤神父 Padre Kato; Father Kato; Fr. Kato.

はと【鳩】 〔鳥〕a dove(野鳩. 小型); a pigeon (doveよりも大型の飼い鳩). 平和の象徴 (a symbol of peace). ¶伝書鳩 a carrier pigeon. 野生鳩 a wild pigeon. (食用の)ヒナ鳩 a squab.
〔料理〕ヒナ鳩の照り焼きロースト glazed squab roast.

ばとうかんのん【馬頭観音】 the Horse-Headed *Kannon* (the Deity of Mercy); Image of *Kannon* with a human body and horse's head (worshipped as the guardian deity of horses or other animals). 頭上に馬頭を置く観音. 人身馬頭の観音. 馬など動物の病気を防ぎ安全を守護する観世音菩薩.

はとば【波止場】 a landing stage; a wharf (船の発着場); a pier (突堤); a quay (岸壁).

はとむぎ【鳩麦】〔植物〕adlay; adlai. イネ科の一年草. 種は食用・薬用. ¶はと麦茶 adlay tea(硬い皮を除いて煎じた茶).

はなお【鼻緒】 a *geta* thong[strap]; (a pair of) thongs[straps] of a *geta*[wooden footgear]; the V-shaped thong[strap] fitted onto the face of a *geta*[*zori*] (to secure foot). (足をしっかりつなぐために)下駄[草履]の表面にすげるV型のひも. ⇨下駄 / 草履

はながさ【花笠】 a flower-sedge hat; a low, round sedge hat brightly decorated with colorful artificial[natural] flowers. 美しく造花[生花]でかざった低くて丸いすげ笠. ⇨すげ

はながさまつり【花笠まつり】 the *Hanagasa* Festival in Yamagata City.(8月). ⇨付記(1)「日本の祭り」

はながつお【花鰹】 shaved dried bonito; dried bonito shavings[flakes]; shavings [flakes] of dried bonito. 薄く細かくけずったかつお節. ⇨けずり節 / かつお節

はながるた【花加留多】 ⇨花札

はなくばり【花配】〔華道〕a way of arranging flowers or branches in the vase (in the flower arrangement). 花器にさす花や枝の生け方. ☆生花を花器に固定するための枝や茎で工夫した花留のこと. 二重, 竪柱, 半月, 一文字, 十文字など. 盛り花では剣山を使う. ⇨剣山 / 花留め

はなしか【噺家・咄家】 a professional comic

storyteller. A single storyteller develops a story in the form of a dialog, using puns and word-play. (落語などの)滑稽な話を聞かせる職業の人. 一人の語り手が語呂合わせやシャレを用いながら話を展開する.「落語家」ともいう. ⇨落語(落語家)

はなしょうぶ【花菖蒲】〔植物〕 an iris; a Japanese iris. アヤメ科の多年草. ⇨菖蒲

はなずもう【花相撲】〔相撲〕 the *sumo* performance held outside the regular tournaments. It is a special professional *sumo* exhibition including a variety of activities and actual bouts. 本場所以外に行う臨時の相撲. 余興や実際の取組などの相撲実演も行われる. ⇨初っ切り

はなだい【花代】 ❶〈花の代金〉 the price of some flowers; the price of a bouquet. ❷〈玉代〉 a *geisha*'s charge; the charge for a *geisha*'s services; the entertainment fee paid for *geisha*'s services at parties. お座敷で芸者をあげて遊興する料金. ☆関西では「花代」, 関東では「玉代」「線香代」と呼ぶ.

はなどめ【花留め】〔華道〕 a flower-arranging holder; a holder used for arranging flower (such as a needle-point holder (*kenzan*) or an open-type metal holder (*shippo*)). 生ける花を支える[立てる]物, 剣山や七宝など. ⇨剣山 / 木密 / 留め

バナナ banana. バショウ科の多年草. ¶一房のバナナ a bunch of bananas. バナナの皮 a banana peel[skin]. 青いバナナ a green banana (熟していない : blueではない).

はなばいまつり【花奪祭】 the Flower-Scrambling Festival. (1月). ⇨付記(1)「日本の祭り」

はなばさみ【花鋏】〔華道〕 (a pair of) flower scissors or clippers (used in arranging flowers).

はなび【花火】 fireworks; firecracker(音のでる花火). ¶打ち上げ花火 skyrockets. 回転花火 spinning[rotating] fireworks;

pinwheel. 仕掛け花火 set-piece fireworks; a piece of fireworks(1個). 線香花火 sparklers. ねずみ花火 pinwheels. 花火師 a pyrotechnist; a pyrotechnician. 花火大会 a fireworks display; a display of fireworks; an exhibition of fireworks.

はなふだ【花札】 ❶〈札〉 a deck of Japanese playing cards with flower designs. There are twelve kinds of flowers representing the twelve months of the year. 花模様合わせに用いる遊びかるた. 1年12か月を表す12種類の花がある.「花加留多」ともいう. ❷〈遊び〉 a game using cards with flower designs with the object of matching the various kinds of flower pictures. いろいろな種類の花絵を組み合わせるために花模様の札を使用する遊び.

はなまつり【花祭り】 ⇨灌仏会

はなみ【花見】〈季節の花〉 flower viewing; 〈桜の花〉 cherry-blossom viewing. ¶花見会 cherry-blossom viewing party (held when cherry blossoms are in full bloom). 花見客 (a group of) cherry blossom viewers; visitors to see the cherry blossoms. 花見酒〈花見の酒〉 *sake* drunk when viewing the cherry blossoms; 〈花見の宴〉 *sake*-drinking party under a cherry tree[the cherry blossoms].

はなみずき【花水木】 a (flowering) dogwood. ミズキ科の落葉高木.

はなみち【花道】 an aisle stage (in the theater or stadium)(座席間の通路)

❶〈歌舞伎〉 a raised walkway[an elevated passageway] extending from the stage to the rear of the theater through the audience in the kabuki theater. *Hanamichi* serves not only as a means of entrance and exit of the actors but also as a means to perform in closer contact with the audience. This extension stage is situated on the left side of the theater, while temporary *hanamichi* (*kari-hanamichi*) on the right side of the

は

theater (as seen from the audience).「花道」は舞台から続いて客席を貫いて劇場後部にまで設けられた通路である. 俳優が出入りする通路としてだけでなく, 観客との共感交流の場ともなる. この花道は(観客から見て)舞台の左側にあり, 他方「仮花道」は舞台の右側にある. ☆「出入り」entrance and exit(日本語と英語の語順の違いに注意). ⇨スッポン

❷〔相撲〕 (one of two) flat walkways [corridors] in the *sumo* stadium. The two East and West walkways lead from the dressing room[entrance and exit] to the *sumo* ring through the audience. 相撲競技場にある平らな通路. 東西の二大通路は観客席を貫いて力士の支度部屋[出入り口]から土俵に通じている.

はなみどう【花御堂】〈花祭り〉 a small chapel decorated with a variety of flowers (in which the small Buddhist statue is placed). (中に釈迦の誕生像を安置する)花で飾った小さな堂. ⇨花祭り(4月)付記(1)「日本の祭り」

はなむすび【花結び】 a square knot [㊤ reef knot] tied loosely in a bow (used for celebration such as childbirth). It is not used for weddings and funerals. (出産のような祝い事に用いる)緩く締めた飾り結び. 結婚や仏事には使用しない. ☆「蝶結び」ともいう. 紐の端をほどいて何度でも結べる. 出産は何度繰り返してもよい(One had better often have a baby.). ⇨結び切り / 水引

はなもち【花餅】 flower-shaped rice cakes; flowers made of rice cakes. The flattened, thin rice cakes are cut into small round pieces to form red and white flower-like shapes. They are decorated on twigs of the trees praying for the family's health in the new year. 餅で作った花. 紅白の花模様の形になるように, 平らにした薄い餅を小さな丸型断片に切り込む. 花型の餅はその年の家族の健康を祈願して木の枝に飾る. ☆東北地方や飛騨地方に見られる.

はなれんこん【花蓮根】 a flower-shaped lotus; lotus cut in the shape of a flower. ⇨蓮根

はなわ【花環・花輪】 a (floral) wreath [garland]. A wreath of natural or artificial flowers is entwined in a circle and supported by a pole covered with striped paper or cloth. The black-and-white floral wreath is used in condolence for the spirit of the deceased at funerals or wakes. 生花・造花を輪のようにつくり, 縞模様の紙または布を巻いた竿で支える. 白黒の花輪は死者の霊を哀悼して弔事(葬儀・通夜)に用いる. ☆「首にかける花輪」は a lei.

はにわ【埴輪】 a *haniwa*: a clay figure [figurine]; an (ancient Japanese) unglazed earthenware figure[figurine]. *Haniwas*, bisque-fried clay figures[images] representing humans or animals, are found[lined] around the exterior of some ancient burial mounds[tumuli] (*kofun*) as funerary objects. 釉薬をかけない粘土の彫像[小型の立像]. 古墳外部の周囲に副葬品として埋め[並べ]られた人間や動物などを表す素焼きの粘土でつくられた彫像. ☆「円筒型埴輪」(cylindrical *haniwa* in the shape of a receptacle)と「形象型埴輪」(figurative *haniwa* in the shape of humans or animals)に大別される. ⇨古墳

はねつき【羽根突き】 a battledore-and-shuttlecock game; a game of battledore and shuttlecock. *Hanetsuki* is a traditional Japanese-style badminton-like game with shuttlecock (*hane*) and battledore (*hagoita*) played outdoors during the New Year holidays. A shuttledore is used to hit a shuttlecock[hard tiny ball[bean] with colored cock feathers attached] back and forth. It is customary for a loser to get a daub of India ink on the face as a penalty. The tiny ball[bean] attached to the tip of the shuttlecock is believed to ward off evil spirits. 正月に野外で遊ぶバドミントンに似た遊戯. 羽根[多彩な羽を付けた小さな玉[豆]]を打ち合うために羽子板[木製ラケット]を使う. 負ければ罰として顔に墨をぬる (smear one's face with India ink)習慣がある. 羽根の先についている玉[豆]は邪鬼を払うといわれている. ⇨羽子板

ははおやごろし【母親殺し】 matricide. ⇨父親殺し

はぶ【波布】〔爬〕a *habu*; a poisonous snake [venomous pit viper] native to the *Ryukyu* Islands[common in the Okinawa Islands]. クサリヘビ科の毒蛇. ☆人畜を襲う. 沖縄諸島や奄美諸島などに生息する. ⇨へび

はぶたえ【羽二重】 *habutae*; a soft silk cloth[fabric] with a fine weave; a smooth, glossy silk cloth[fabric] in plain weave. It is often used for making a *kimono*. 薄く滑らかでつやのある絹織物. 着物などを作る. ☆北陸地方産が多い

はぶたえもち【羽二重餅】 creamy smooth rice-cake dough (made from refined rice flour). (もち米粉から作る)クリームのようにの滑らかな餅菓子.

はぼうき【羽箒】〔茶道〕a feather brush (often made of eagle feathers). It is used to dust the edge of a brazier[hearth] in a tearoom. 鷲の羽を束ねたほうき. 茶室にある風炉[炉床]の端のほこりを払うために用いる. 「はねぼうき」ともいう.

はぼたん【葉牡丹】〔植物〕(a) kale; a flowering [an ornamental] cabbage. アブラナ科の二年草. キャベツの変種.

はま【浜】 the beach(水泳用の浜: 川・湖にも用いる); the (sea)shore(海岸); the sands (砂浜). ¶浄土ヶ浜(岩手県) (the) Jodoga-hama Beach. ⇨海岸／浦／砂丘

はまぐり【蛤】〔貝〕a clam; a littleneck; a clamshell(ハマグリの殻). マルスダレガイ科の二枚貝. 早春が旬. ⇨焼き蛤
〔料理〕**蛤の潮汁** clam broth; soup cooked with clams. **蛤の吸い物** clear soup cooked with clams. ☆結婚披露宴の定番 (wedded bliss). **蛤のバター焼き** butter-fried clams.

はまち【鰤】〔魚〕a young yellowtail. ブリの1年魚[幼魚]. 関東では天然物は「イナダ」, 養殖物を「ハマチ」と区別することがある. 刺身・すし種の定番. 照り焼き・塩焼きにも用いる. ⇨ぶり

はままつまつり【浜松まつり】 the Hama-matsu Festival. (5月). ⇨付記(1)「日本の祭り」

はまや【破魔矢】 a ceremonial arrow with white feathers. It is a symbolic weapon against evil and calamity as well as a swift and sure carrier of good luck. 白羽のついた矢. 悪事・災害に対する象徴的な武具であり, 同時に迅速・確実に幸運を招く縁起物.
❶〈正月の飾り矢〉 a lucky white-feathered arrow with a good amulet. It is decorated on the New Year to ensure good luck for the coming year. It is sold at shrines[temples] at New Year's as a charm to bring good luck. 縁起物としての白羽つきの矢. 来る年の幸運を呼び込むため正月に飾る. 幸福を呼ぶ守り札として新年に神社[寺院]で売られる.
❷〈魔除けの矢〉 an exorcizing[exorcising] arrow with white feathers. It is sold at shrines[temples] at New Year's as a talisman to exorcize[ward off] evil spirits. 白羽つきの魔除けの矢. 悪霊を払う守り札として新年に神社[寺院]で売られる.

はまやき【浜焼き】 a fish broiled[poached] whole with salt. 取った魚を浜ですぐ塩焼き(grilled)にする[熱湯で煮る]. ⇨鯛の浜焼き

はも【鱧】〔魚〕a pike conger[eel]; a (sharp-

は

toothed) sea eel. ハモ科の海産硬骨魚. 京都・大阪では夏の祭りに出る代表的な料理. 東北地方ではハモは「アナゴ」(a conger eel)を指す.

はや【鮠】〔魚〕a minnow; a dace. コイ科の硬骨魚. 淡水小魚.「はえ」ともいう.

はやく【端役】 a small role[minor part] (in the play); a walk-on role[part] (in the drama).(演劇などでの)あまり重要でない役(またその役の人).「仕出し」ともいう. ⇨主役 (a principal role)

はやし【囃子】〔歌舞伎〕〔能楽〕a musical accompaniment[band ensemble] (of drums and flutes for traditional Japanese stage and folk performances of the kabuki and Noh plays). Drums (*tsuzumi* and *taiko*) and the flutes (*fue*) are played in a Noh play. The *shamisen* is added to the drums (*taiko*) and flutes (*fue*) in a kabuki play. 歌舞伎や能楽などで太鼓・笛などを用いて拍子をとるために行う「伴奏音楽」(musical accompaniment in Japanese folk or classical music).「能楽」では鼓と笛が演奏され,「歌舞伎」では太鼓や笛に加えて三味線が演奏される.

【囃子方】〔歌舞伎〕〔能楽〕 (a band of) instrumental musicians (of the kabuki and Noh plays); (a band of) the instrumental accompanists[musicians] of flutes and drums for traditional stage and folk performances of the kabuki and Noh plays. 歌舞伎や能楽で太鼓や笛などの囃子の伴奏[演奏]にあたる人. ☆「能の囃子方」は能舞台で楽器を演奏する人たち (instrumental musicians for Noh stage performances).「伴奏楽器」は鼓と太鼓それに笛 (musical accompaniments of hand drums, stick drums and the Noh flutes)である.「囃子方」は後座の前で横1列に座っている.

【囃子詞】① a refrain. (詩歌の節の終わりのない)繰り返し語句[文句].「リフレイン」.

② a meaningless[nonsense] word[phrase] added to a song for rhythmical effect. 歌の中に調子をとるために入れることば.

【囃子物】 musical background instruments used as accompaniments (in the kabuki and Noh plays); music accompanied by small and big hand drums, flutes and *shamisen*. (歌舞伎や能楽での)囃子に用いる楽器. 太鼓, 鼓, 笛, 三味線などの伴奏音楽.

ハヤシライス rice with hashed meat[beef] and onions. 肉・玉葱などを炒めたものをご飯に添える料理. ☆日本で考案された洋風料理.

はやせ【早瀬】 rapids (急流); a torrent (激流); a swift current. ¶保津川下り(京都府) shooting the Hozu(gawa) Rapids.

はやぶさ【隼】〔鳥〕a peregrine (falcon); a falcon. 雄は鷹狩りに使う. ⇨たか

ばら【薔薇】〔植〕 a rose. バラ科の落葉低木. 観賞用. ¶野バラのとげ a rose thorn. バラのつぼみ a rose bud. バラの木 a rose bush[tree].

はらい【祓い】 ⇨御祓い

はらきり【腹切り】 ⇨切腹

はらげい【腹芸】 ❶〈腹の芸〉a dance by drawing a face on one's stomach and animating it by flexing one's abdominal muscles. 腹に人の顔を書き, 腹の筋肉を伸び縮みさせて活気づける踊り[芸当]. ❷〈暗黙の相互了解〉 an implicit mutual understanding; Japanese problem-solving technique by getting goals without outspoken assertion of one's desire. 本人の希望をことばで主張することなく目的を成就させる問題解決の技法.

はらこ【腹子】 fish eggs; (hard) fish roe. 魚の卵.

パラサイトシングル living off one's parents; sponging off one's parents. 自立できず両親に頼って暮らすこと. ¶パラサイトシングルな人 an unmarried person [男性(a bachelor）；女性(a single woman)〕who lives with and is supported by his/her parents because he/she cannot stand on his/her own feet.

ばらずし【散鮨】⇨五目鮨

はらまき【腹巻き】❶〈腹帯〉a woolen[cotton] waistband; an abdomen band[a belly supporter] made of wool or cotton. It is worn to keep the abdomen[belly] warm or to keep people from catching a chill at night. 腹を暖めたり，寝冷えしないように腹に巻くウール［綿］製の布．「腹帯」ともいう．

❷〈財布の代用〉a wallet belt. It is used by men to carry money when traveling. 旅行中に金銭を携帯する財布としての帯．

はり【梁】a beam; a crossbeam（横木，横桁）．

はり【鍼・針】〈治療〉acupuncture;〈針〉a needle (inserted at the vital points (*tsubo*) of the body for acupuncture treatment).（鍼治療のため身体のツボ (acupoint) に打つ）針．¶鍼治療［ギックリ腰/肩こり］acupuncture treatment (for strained back[stiff shoulders]). 鍼灸 acupuncture and moxibustion. 鍼医(師) an acupuncturist.

はりおうぎ【張り扇】a paper-covered folding fan (for beating out rhythm). The fan is used by a professional storyteller to raise the pitch of his narration by beating the desk. 外側を紙で張った扇．講談師が釈台を打って調子をとる．⇨講談

はりくよう【針供養】a needle memorial service; a memorial[requiem] service observed for old used[broken] needles and dull pins. The needle memorial service is held at Shinto Shrines on February 8 and December 8 by sticking[piercing] the old used[broken] needles and dull pins into a soft bean curd (*tofu*). It is customary for tailors[dressmakers] and ordinary people to express thanks to the needles and pray for greater skill in sewing. 針供養は2月8日（関東地方）と12月8日（関西・九州地方）に寺院で行われ，折れた針や鈍ったピンなどを豆腐に刺す．仕立屋また一般人が針に感謝し，さらなる裁縫技能を祈願する．「針納め」ともいう．☆淡島神社または淡島の神を祀っている寺堂［淡島堂］(small shrines enshrining the Shinto god of Awashima Shrine［圀浅草寺境内にある淡島社］)で行われる．「淡島の神」（裁縫・安産の神）は人の指ほどの大きさであるため日本民話における「一寸法師」(a Tom Thumb in the Japanese folk story) のモデルともいわれる．

はりこのとら【張子の虎】a papier-mâché tiger.

はりだしおおぜき【張り出し大関】〔相撲〕an additional *ozeki* (if there are more than two *sumo* wrestlers at *ozeki* rank). (2人以上の大関力士がいる場合の）追加大関．番付の欄外に記される．

はりだしぶたい【張り出し舞台】an apron stage.

はりねずみ【針鼠】〔動物〕a hedgehog. ハリネズミ科の哺乳動物．夜行性で雑食．

はるいちばん【春一番】the first spring gale [storm]; the first gale[storm] in the spring; the first strong south wind of the year (signaling the arrival of spring). その年の春の初めに吹く強い南風（春の訪れの兆候）．☆立春2月4日頃から春分3月21日頃の間に初めて吹く南風

はるさめ【春雨】❶〔食品〕bean-starch vermicelli（豆そうめん）；potato-starch vermicelli（芋そうめん）．緑豆また芋（ジャガイモまたはサツマイモ）のでんぷんからつくる透明な糸状の食品．

❷〈春の雨〉(a) spring rain[drizzle]; (a) spring shower. ⇨時雨

はるのななくさ【春の七草】〔植物〕the seven spring herbs; the seven herbs of spring.

Rice gruel is cooked with the seven spring herbs on January 7 to prevent sickness in the coming year. 正月7日にはその年の無病息災を願って (have good health throughout the coming year) 粥にして食べる. ⇨七草粥. ⇨ ① 芹 (dropwort[Japanese parsley]) ② 薺 (shepherd's purse) ③御形 (cotton weed; cudweed) ④繁縷 (chickweed) ⑤ 仏 の座 (henbit) ⑥菘 (turnip) ⑦蘿蔔 (Japanese white radish).

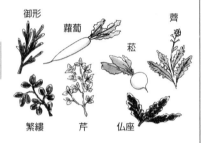

御形　薺　菘　繁縷　芹　仏座　蘿蔔

はるまき【春巻き】⊛ an egg roll; ㊇ a spring roll; deep-fried pork and vegetables wrapped with wheat crust. 豚肉と野菜を小麦粉の皮で包んで揚げた料理.

はれぎ【晴れ着】 a colorful *kimono* (worn on Coming-of-Age Day or commencement); one's best clothes (worn for auspicious occasions such as a wedding); ⊛ one's Sunday best (成人式や卒業式で着る)色鮮やかな着物. (結婚式のような慶事に着る)最良の衣装. ⇦普段着 (one's everyday clothes[*kimono*]).

はん【藩】 a feudal clan(一門); a feudal domain[fief] (領地). *Han* was a fief and its people, and a governmental organization ruled by a feudal lord under the control of the Tokugawa shogunate in the Edo period. The members of the clan had firm vertical ties of loyalty and protection. 江戸時代の大名が幕府統括の下で統治した領地 (a territory)とその民衆. またはその政治機構.

藩同士には忠誠と加護の堅固な結束があった. ☆明治維新後(1871年)「藩」は「県」(prefecture)に改称された. ⇨廃藩置県

¶加賀藩 the Kaga clan; the domain[fief] of Kaga. 藩士 a vassal[retainer] of a feudal lord(大名の家来); a clansman(藩に属する武士). 藩主 a feudal lord; a lord of a domain; a domainal lord(藩の領主. 大名. 別称「藩侯」). ☆藩主伊達政宗 the feudal lord Date Masamune. 藩閥 *han* clique; a faction of *samurai* from a particular *han* [feudal clan].

【藩校】 a domain school; a public school established and administered by a feudal clan during the Edo period. 江戸時代, 各藩で開校・経営した学校. 別称「藩学」. ☆当初は武士の教育機関で, やがて庶民の入学が許可された. 儒教(Confucianism)の学習を中心に書道・剣道などの訓練があった. 明治維新後「学制の公布」(Education Order issued in 1872)で改革された.

【藩札】 paper money[⊛ bill; ㊇ note] issued by the feudal clans in the Edo period. Circulation of this local paper currency was limited to use within the boundaries of the respective fiefs. 江戸時代, 各藩で発行し, 藩内のみで通用した紙幣.

はんえり【半襟】 a collar on a *kimono*; a replaceable neckband sewed on an undergarment; a replaceable fancy cloth worn over the collar of woman's *kimono* undergarment. 着物の襟. 下着に縫った取替え可能な襟. 婦人の, 襦袢の襟にかける交換可能な飾り布.

はんが【版画】〈木版画〉 a woodblock print; a woodcut. ⇨版木;〈銅版画〉 a copperplate engraving;〈石版画〉 a lithograph. ¶版画家 a printmaker;〈木版の〉 a woodblock artist;〈銅版の〉 a copperplate engraver;〈石版の〉 a lithographer.

はんがえし【半返し】 returning half the gift;

a half return of the gifts received. 受けた贈物の半分を返すこと. ⇨返礼. ¶(香典・結婚の)**半返しをする** make a half return of the (obituary or wedding) gift received; send a return gift of about half the amount of a monetary gift received at a wedding or funeral.

ばんがさ【番傘】 an oiled-paper umbrella; an umbrella made of bamboo frame and oiled paper (usually used by men). 竹の骨組みと油紙で作った傘(通常は男性用). ⇨蛇の目傘(女性用)

はんがん【判官】「ほうがん」ともいう. **❶**〈裁判官〉a judge.
❷〈源義経のこと〉Minamoto Yoshitsune.

はんがんびいき【判官贔屓】 sympathy for the weak[a tragic hero]; an inclination to support for the underdog; a tendency to cheer for[side with] the team that's behind. 弱者[不遇の英雄]に対する同情. 負け犬を支援する傾向. 勝ち目のない方を応援する傾向.「ほうがんびいき」ともいう. ☆兄の源頼朝に滅ぼされた不運な英雄の九郎判官源義経に同情したことから.

はんぎ【版木】 a woodblock; a woodcut; a (printing) block. 木版画を刷るための木. ⇨版画

ばんぎ【板木】〔茶道〕a resonant wooden board[gong](音が反響する木製の板[どら]); a thwacking board(たたいて打つ合図する板). It is struck to inform all the participants[guests] that the host has made preparations for the tea ceremony. 亭主が茶の湯の準備が完了したことを参加者[客]に知らせるために鳴らして合図する(板). 寺院でも使われる.

はんぎょく【半玉】 an apprentice *geisha*. 見習い芸者. ☆一人前でない若い芸者.「玉代」(a *geisha* charge[fee])が半分であることからの呼称. 一人前の芸者は「一本」(a professional *geisha*)という. ⇨芸者 /玉代

はんぎり【半切り】 a wooden *sushi*-making [*sushi*-cooling] bowl. It is a round, shallow wooden container[tub] used when making [cooling] *sushi* rice by mixing boiled rice with vinegar. 酢飯を混ぜて鮨飯をつくる[冷ます]盤台[丸くて浅い桶]. ⇨舎利

はんこ【判子】 a personal seal (with the engraving of the family or personal name). It is used as the legal method[means] of identification. (姓名を刻んである)個人用の印鑑. 法的な身分証明として用いる.「印鑑」ともいう. ☆素材は木材 (wood), 象牙 (ivory), 角 (horn), 水晶 (crystal) などがある. ⇨印鑑 /実印 /認印 /三文判

ばんこんか【晩婚化】 a tendency to marry later; an inclination to put off marriage; a tendency to delay the age of marriage.

ばんざい【万歳】 **❶**〈歓声〉*banzai*; a cheer [short shout of joy] (uttered to express felicitation on happy occasions). *Banzai* is often addressed to the Emperor in wishing Him a long life three times, "Long Live the Emperor!". めでたいこと, 祝うべきことに関する祝福のことば. 天皇陛下の長寿を祈願して「天皇陛下万歳」(May you live a long life.) を三唱する.
❷〈三唱〉 *banzai, banzai, banzai*!!; (give) three cheers; (raise) three shouts of celebration; (give) three cries of triumph. *Banzai* is customarily repeated three times while both hands are raised in the air. 祝福の歓声, 勝利の歓喜. 両手を上げて三唱する.

はんし【範士】〈剣道〉 a Japanese-fencing master of the top rank (in the martial art of *kendo*). 武道家に与えられる階級中で最高の称号. ⇨剣道

はんし【半紙】〈書道〉(a sheet of) plain paper (mainly used for calligraphy). (主として書道用の)薄手の和紙. ☆半紙の大きさは,

縦は約25cm, 横は約35cm. ☆元来, 延紙(のべがみ)を半分に切って使用したことに由来する. 欧米人は rice paperという人も多い. ⇨和紙

はんし【藩士】 ⇨藩

ばんしゃく【晩酌】 a supper-time alcoholic drink; a dinner-time[an evening] drink. ¶晩酌する have a drink[*sake*] with one's dinner.

はんしゅ【藩主】 the lord of a domain; a domanial lord.

ばんしょ【番所】 a guardhouse[guard station] in the Edo period. 江戸時代の番人の詰める所. 見張り所.

はんしょう【半鐘】 a (hanging) fire bell. It is installed[settled] in a fire tower to inform people of[sound the alarm in case of] a fire. 火事を知らせる釣り鐘. 火事の警報用に火の見やぐらにとりつけられた.

ばんしょう【晩鐘】 the evening bell; a curfew (bell); a vesper bell. 夕方に鳴らす寺院の鐘. ☆vesper「晩課, 晩課の時刻」(カトリック用語) 聖務日課 (canonical hours) のひとつで, 日没前後に行う夕べの祈祷. vesperはラテン語で「夕方, 夕暮れ」(evening)の意. ¶東大寺の晩鐘 the evening bell of Todai-ji Temple.

はんしんあわじだいしんさい【阪神淡路大震災】 the Great Hanshin-Awaji Earthquake. (1995年1月17日)

はんせきほうかん【版籍奉還】 the return of the *han*[domain] registers to Emperor Meiji (in 1869); the feudal lords' return of their *han* domains[lands] and the people living in them to the Imperial Court (in 1869). 1869年(明治2年)各藩主が藩の領有権[大名の土地〈版図〉と人民〈戸籍〉]を朝廷[明治天皇]に返還すること. ⇨廃藩置県(はいはんちけん)

ばんそう【伴僧】 an assistant priest in a Buddhist temple (who accompanies[goes with] the presiding priest at the Buddhist ceremony). 寺院での副僧侶. 法会や葬式などで導師に同伴する. ⇨導師

ばんだい【番台】 a watch stand[counter] at a public bathhouse (or show tent); a casher's stand[seat] in a public bathhouse (or show tent) to collect the fees. It is an elevated seat for sitting at the entrance to a public bathhouse (or show tent) in order to collect fees. 公衆浴場(または見世物小屋)で見張り番をする者[集金者]の座席台. 料金を徴収するために入り口に設けられた高い座席台.

ばんちゃ【番茶】 *Bancha*; a coarse tea. *Bancha* leaves picked along with stems are made from tough tea leaves. *Bancha* leaves are the cheapest grade of Japanese tea as the third picking of the leaves of tea bushes. 茶茎をつけたまま摘みとる堅い茶葉. 二番摘み以降の葉で作った品質の劣る茶. ⇨緑茶. ¶番茶も出花 fresh-drawn coarse tea(番茶でも入れたてはおいしい). ⇨茶 / 焙茶

ばんちょう【番長】 the leader of a group of juvenile delinquents; a school gang leader. 非行仲間の長.

ばんづけ【番付】〔相撲〕 a *sumo* ranking list; a rank chart of *sumo* wrestlers (for each tournament); an official list of *sumo* wrestlers according to the rank for a grand *sumo* tournament. *Sumo-banzuke* is announced two weeks prior to the tournament. 相撲場所の順位に応じて力士の名前を記したもの. 場所前の2週間には発表される. ⇨相撲の番付. ☆演芸などの番付は a program という. ¶1月場所の番付 the ranking list of *sumo* wrestlers for the January tournament.

【番付外力士】〔相撲〕 an outside *sumo* wrestler to the list. He is not yet ranked in *banzuke* due to injury or non-participation for other reasons. 負傷または他の不参加の

理由があって番付に記載されない力士.

【番付編成会議】 a *sumo* ranking compilation conference. Conference members discuss changes in rank due to the results of the previous tournament. 会議の全委員が前回の取組の結果によって順位の変更を協議する.

はんてん【袢纏・半纏】〈男女用〉 a (*kimono*-style) short coat. ⇨ねんねこ. 〈職人用〉 a workman's *happi* coat. It is a livery *kimono*-style short coat worn by a traditional workman. It has the crest of the employers or the name of the store on the back. (着物型の)短い上着. そろい[仕着せ]の職人の法被. 通常背中には雇い主の家紋・店の屋号がついている.「しるし袢纏」「法被」ともいう. ⇨法被❷

はんとう【半島】 a peninsula. ¶知床半島(北海道) the Shiretoko Peninsula (ユネスコ世界自然遺産). ⇨島 / 諸島 / 列島

ばんとう【番頭】〈店の〉 a head clerk; a chief clerk; the general manager of a merchant business.

はんドン【半ドン】 a half-holiday. 半日勤務のこと. ☆「ドン」はオランダ語 zondag(ドンタク:休日)からの呼称.

ばんぱく【万博】 an international exposition; World Exposition[EXPO]; universal and international exhibition.「万国博覧会」の略. ¶大阪万博 Expo'70 Osaka. 沖縄海洋博 Ocean Expo'75 Okinawa. 筑波博 Expo'85 Tsukuba. 愛知万博 Expo 2005 Aichi; the 2005 World Exposition, Aichi.

はんはばおび【半幅帯】 a half-width *obi* [sash]; a narrow *obi* worn by women with a casual *kimono*[*yukata*]. 平素な着物[浴衣]に着用する帯(幅約15cm). ⇨浴衣

はんぺん【半平】 a soft[fluffy] steamed fish-paste cake; a light, puffy cake made of ground fish. It is a soft steamed fish cake made of fish by mixing yam and rice flour

with seasonings. やわらかい[ふわふわした]蒸した魚肉のすり身. 魚肉のすり身を平たく固めたもの. 山芋や米粉を調味料と混ぜて蒸し固めた魚肉のすり身食品. ☆かまぼこに類似した食品. おでんに用いる.

ばんめん【盤面】❶〈将棋〉 a face[surface] of checkered *shogi* board (with 81 squares). ⇨将棋

❷〈囲碁〉 a face[surface] of checkered *go*[*igo*] board (with 361 points of intersection). ⇨碁

ひ

ピーマン〔植物〕 a green pepper; a sweet pepper; a bell pepper; a paprika. ナス科の一年草. とうがらしの変種. 西洋とうがらし. ☆フランス語は piment. 英語で a pim(i)ento.
〔料理〕ピーマンの肉詰め meat-stuffed green pepper[paprika].

ひいらぎ【柊】〔植物〕 holly; a holly (tree); holly osmanthus. In the evening before the calendrical beginning of spring, a twig of Japanese holly may be seen hung together with the head of sardine at the entrances[doors] of some houses to shut out evil spirits. モクセイ科の常緑小高木, 盆栽用. 材は細工用. 節分の夕方には魔除けのため, ヒイラギの小枝に塩イワシの頭を家の門戸にかける習慣がみられる. ☆欧米ではクリスマスの装飾に用いる. ⇨節分❷

ひえ【稗】〔植物〕 Japanese millet; barnyard millet[grass]. イネ科の一年草. 五穀の一つ. 現在, 健康食品として愛用されている. ⇨五穀

ひえしょう【冷え性】 excessive[abnormal] sensitivity to (the) cold; a tendency to feel the cold; poor circulation.

ひおうぎ【桧扇・檜扇】❶〈扇〉a cypress fan; a

fan made of Japanese cypress slats. 檜の薄板をとじて作った扇. 十二単を着るときにもつ. ⇨十二単

❷〔植物〕 a blackberry lily. アヤメ科の多年草. 葉は平らな剣状で扇形につく.

ひがえりおんせん【日帰り温泉】a hot spring (bath) for day trippers[visitors].

ひかえりきし【控え力士】〔相撲〕a *sumo* wrestler waiting at ringside for the following match[next bout]. 自分の出番を土俵下で待つ力士.

ひがし【干菓子・乾菓子】❶〔茶道〕dry Japanese sweets[confections] (served with thin powdered tea in the tea ceremony). 茶道で「薄茶」といっしょに出される. ⇨茶菓子 / 主菓子(濃茶)

❷〈菓子〉dry Japanese sweets[confections; confectioneries]. These sweets are molded from rice flour[wheat flour] mixed with sugar and little water. Sweets are artistically formed into the shape of flowers or leaves expressive of the season. 砂糖と少しの水分を混ぜた米粉[小麦粉]で作り, 季節を表す花状や葉状にする. ☆落雁や煎餅などの菓子. ⇦生菓子. ⇨落雁 / 煎餅

ひがしかた【東方】〔相撲〕the East Camp [Team]. ⇦西方. ¶東(方)の横綱 the (top-ranked) East *Yokozuna*; *yokozuna* in the east side of the ranking list[rank chart]. 東(方)の両大関 the two *ozeki*s on the east side of the rank chart[ranking list].

ひがしにほんだいしんさい【東日本大震災】Great East Japan Earthquake.(2011年3月11日)

ひがた【干潟】㊟ tideland; tidal[tide] land; tidal[mud] flats; beach at ebb tide(引き潮の海辺). ☆有明海 (the Sea of Ariake) は日本最大の干潟 (Japan's largest tideland). ⇨鯥五郎

ひがん【彼岸】❶〈彼岸の季節〉the equinoctial week(s); the seven-day period centering on the vernal or autumnal equinox. The sun reaches the vernal or autumnal equinox, and the length of day and night is equal. The coming of the equinoctial week signifies the advent of spring or autumn. 春分 (the spring equinox)・秋分 (the autumn equinox)の日を中日とする前後7日間. 太陽が春分点・秋分点に達するので昼と夜の長さが等しい. 彼岸の訪れは春または秋の到来を意味している. ⇨春分 / 秋分

❷〈彼岸の行事〉 the week of Buddhist memorial services (observed twice a year, in spring and autumn). According to Buddhist belief, the deceased can cross the river from the shore of this world (*shigan*) to the other shore (*higan* meaning eternal paradise[nirvana]). People visit their ancestral graves and hold Buddhist memorial services for the deceased at homes or temples during the weeks of the spring and autumn equinoxes. (春秋の年2回に行われる)仏事の週間. 仏教の教えでは, 死者が「この世」(生者の世界)の此岸から「あの世」(死者の世界)の彼岸へと川を渡ることが出来る.「彼岸」は極楽浄土[涅槃]の意. 彼岸の時期には家族の墓参りをし, 家庭または寺院で死者の霊をしのぶ.「彼岸会」の略. 通称「お彼岸」.

¶ 彼岸の明け the final day of the equinoctial week[the week of the equinox]. 彼岸の入り the first day of the equinoctial week[the week of the equinox]. 彼岸の中日 the fourth day of a week-long Buddhist observances, centered on the spring or autumn equinox, during which prayers are said[read] for the deceased. (春[秋]の彼岸を中心に行われる法事の4日間. その間に死者への祈祷を唱える)

【彼岸参り】 (pay) a visit to the Buddhist temple or the ancestral[family] grave during the equinoctial week[the week of the equinox]. 彼岸中に寺院への参詣または先祖の墓参りをすること.

【彼岸会】 Buddhist services performed during the equinoctial week. It is a 7-day Buddhist memorial services performed during the week of the equinox[around the day of vernal or autumnal equinox]. 彼岸の7日間に行う仏事. ⇨墓参り

ひがんざくら【彼岸桜】〔植物〕spring-equinox cherry tree;〈花〉spring-equinox cherry blossoms; a variety of cherry trees that blossom in full bloom around the time of spring equinox. 春の彼岸頃満開に咲く桜の花.「ひとえざくら」ともいう.

ひがんばな【彼岸花・石蒜】〔植物〕 a cluster-amaryllis; a spider lily. ヒガンバナ科の多年草. 鱗茎は有毒だが薬用とされる.「曼珠沙華」ともいう.

ひきこ【挽(き)子】 a rickshaw man; a rickshaw puller. 車引き. 人力車夫. ⇨人力車

ひきこもり【引き籠もり】 a social withdrawal; a withdrawal from society; a social dropout;（若者）a young man who goes into seclusion; youths who stay alone[hole up] in their rooms and refuse to venture out of their homes.

ひきしお【引き潮】 (an) ebb tide; (a) low tide. ⇨上げ潮

ひきちゃ【挽(き)茶】〔茶道〕powdered green tea (used in the tea ceremony). The powdered tea is whipped to a froth in hot water in the tea ceremony. 茶道で用いる緑茶. お湯にかきまぜて泡立たせる. ☆茶うすでひいて粉にした上等な茶.「抹茶」ともいう. ⇨抹茶

ひきでもの【引き出物】 a "thank-you-for-coming" gift; a present given to guests attending a formal banquet[official party] from the host (as a token of thanks).（謝意のしるしに）宴会などの出席客に対する主

人からの贈物. ¶結婚披露宴での引き出物 presents given to guests at a wedding reception[gifts offered to those attending a wedding dinner] (as an expression of cordial thanks[gratitude]).

ひきど【引き戸】 (open[shut]) a sliding door.

ひきにく【挽肉】 minced[ground] meat. 細かくひいた肉. ¶牛［豚］の挽肉 ground beef[pork].

ひきにげじこ［じけん］【轢き逃げ事故［事件］】 a hit-and-run accident[case].

ひきぬき【引き抜き】〔歌舞伎〕stylized action that costumes can be changed in a mere instant (in a kabuki play). 衣装を一瞬にして着替える.

ひきまく【引き幕】〔歌舞伎〕〔文楽〕 a draw curtain (with broad black, green and orange [persimmon] vertical strips). The curtain is drawn open from stage right to stage left accompanied by wooden clappers.（黒・緑・橙［柿色］の幅広い縦縞の）引き幕. 拍子木の音に合わせ右舞台から左舞台へと引いて開閉する. ⇨定式幕

ひきゃく【飛脚】 a courier; an express messenger (in the Edo period). He was employed to convey[deliver] urgent messages[carry letters and packages] to a distant destination on foot before the Meiji era.（江戸時代の）急使. 明治時代まで急報［手紙や小荷物］を遠地に徒歩で届けた使者. ☆1871年「郵便制度」(the postal service)の開始で廃止された.

びく【魚籠】 a creel; a fish basket; a basket used for carrying fish. 釣った魚を入れるかご.

ひぐらし【蜩】〔虫〕a twilight[an evening] cicada; a green-colored cicada; a clear-toned cicada. セミ科の昆虫. 夏から初秋にかけての夕暮れに鳴く. ⇨せみ

ひけし【火消し】〈消防士〉a firefighter;〈消防組織〉a fire brigade[department] organized

ひ

by the Tokugawa shogunate. 江戸時代の消
防組織.「町火消し」ともいう. ¶(町)**火消し
の出初め式** the New Year's demonstration
of acrobatics on ladders performed by fire
brigades. ⇨出初め式

ひごい【緋鯉】〔魚〕a red carp; a golden carp.
鯉の一変種. 観賞用. ⇨こい

ひごのかみ【肥後守】 a small folding knife.
折り込み[折りたたみ]式の小型ナイフ.

ひし【菱】〔植物〕a water chestnut; a water
nut; a water caltrop. アカバナ科の一年草.
浮水性の植物. 刺がある菱形の果実(ひし
の実)は食用.

ひじき【鹿尾菜】〔植物〕*hijiki* seaweed; edible
brown seaweed; brown algae. ホンダワラ
科の褐藻. 棒状の葉をつけ, 若い芽は炒め
煮や油揚げの煮物として食用にする. ☆
algae「藻類」(algaの複数形).
　〔料理〕**ひじきの煮物** simmered *hijiki* seaweeds and vegetables.

ひしもち【菱餅】 a three-colored[red, white
and green] diamond-shaped rice cake.
Lozenge-shaped rice cakes are offered up
on the elaborately-decorated tiered doll-
stand erected[set up] for the Girls' Festival
(March 3). (紅・白・緑の)三色の菱形に切っ
た餅 (rice cakes cut in lozenges). 桃の節句
の雛壇に供える. ⇨雛壇

ひしゃく【柄杓】❶〔茶道〕ⓐ a bamboo ladle
(used for the teakettle in the tearoom). 茶
室での茶釜用の柄杓. ⓑ a wooden ladle
(used for the water basin (*tsukubai*) in the
tea garden). 茶庭での 蹲 用の柄杓. ⇨蹲.
¶**柄杓で水をくむ** scoop up water with a
ladle[dipper].
　❷〔花祭り〕a wooden dipper（平底）[ladle
（丸底）](used for pouring hydrangea tea
over the statue of Buddha). (仏像に甘茶を
注ぐための)木製柄杓. ⇨花祭り / 甘茶

びしゃもんてん【毘沙門天】❶〈七福神の一
人〉one of the seven Deities of Good Luck.

⇨七福神
　❷〈四天王の一人〉one of the four kings of
Heaven[heavenly kings] in Buddhism. ⇨
四天王(多聞天王)

びしょうじょ【美少女】 a pretty[cute] girl.
¶**美少女アニメ** an animated cartoon featuring pretty girls. **美少女キャラ** a pretty
girl cartoon character. **美少女フィギュア**
a three-dimensional figure of a pretty girl
cartoon character.

ひせいしゃいんのしえんたいさく【非正社員
の支援対策】 measure to support non-per-
manent[nonregular] employees [workers].

びぜんやき【備前焼】 Bizen ceramic and
porcelain ware (produced in the Bizen
province, presently Okayama Prefecture).

ひだかひぶせまつり【日高火防祭】 the
Firemen-Float Parade Festival. (4月). ⇨
付記(1)「日本の祭り」

ひたしもの【浸し物】 parboiled greens;
green leafy vegetables slightly boiled in
water. They are seasoned with *shoyu*[soy
sauce] and sprinkled with sesame seeds or
dried bonito shavings (when eating). ゆで
た青菜に醤油で味をつけ, ゴマまたは鰹節
[花鰹]をふりかけたもの. 通称「お浸し」.
　〔料理〕**ホウレンソウのお浸し** parboiled and
pressed spinach (seasoned with *shoyu* and
dried bonito shavings).

ひたたれ【直垂】 ❶〈武家の礼服〉a court
garment[dress at court] (worn by men in
the *samurai* class); a full[formal] costume
dressed on ceremonial occasions (worn
from the Kamakura period). 昔の宮廷衣装
の一種. 鎌倉時代以降は武家の礼服.
　❷〈鎧の下着〉a dress worn under armor[英
armour]. 鎧の下に着る衣服.

ひたちさくらまつり【日立さくらまつり】
the Cherry-Blossom Festival at Hitachi
City. (4月). ⇨付記(1)「日本の祭り」

ひだら【干鱈】 dried codfish sprinkled with

salt. 薄塩をまぶして干した鱈. ⇨たら

ひだりづかい【左遣い】〔文楽〕 the left-arm [left-hand] manipulator (of the puppeteer trio in bunraku). He is a manipulator who operates the left arm[hand] of a single puppet. 文楽人形の左腕［手］を操る人. 人形遣いの三人遣いの中で第2番目の人 (the second man of the bunraku puppeteer trio) である.「主遣い」(the head manipulator)と「足遣い」(the leg[feet] manipulator)と共演する. ⇨足遣い/主［面］遣い

ひちりき【篳篥】〈雅楽〉*hichiriki*; a Japanese double-reed wind musical instrument (similar to *oboe*). It is a musical reed instrument of a flute with nine holes in the bamboo tube (seven in the front and two in the back). This musical instrument with a strong nasal sound is played in gagaku [ceremonial court music and dance] as well as in Shinto rites. (オーボエに似た)和式の複簧管楽器の一種. 9か所の穴のある竹製の笛楽器(表に7つ, 裏に2つの指穴がある). 強い鼻音のする楽器で雅楽や神社の祭礼時に演奏する. ☆reed instrument「リード楽器」(クラリネットやオーボエなどリードを用いる管楽器). ⇨雅楽

ピッキング lock picking; holing up (in one's room). ☆「ピッキングする人」a lock picker

ひつじ【羊】〔動物〕a sheep (単複同形)；a ram (雄羊)；an ewe(雌羊)；a lamb(子羊). ウシ科の哺乳動物. ¶羊の肉 mutton; lamb (子羊の肉).

ひつじ【未】 the Sheep, one[the eighth] of the 12 animals of the Chinese zodiac. 十二支の第八. ⇨十二支. ¶未の方 the direction of the Sheep[south-southwest]. 方角の名. 南南西. 未の刻 the Hour of the Sheep [1-3 p.m.] 午後2時(およびその前後1-3時の間). 未年 the Year of the Sheep. 未年生まれ (be) born in the Year of the Sheep.

ひったくり〔行為〕 a snatch; a bag[purse]-snatching; a snatch-and-run theft;〈人〉a snatcher; a snatch-and-run thief; a bag [purse] -snatcher;

ヒットさく【ヒット作】〈映画などの〉 a box-office hit; a box-office great success.

ヒットしょうひん【ヒット商品】 a hot-selling product; a hot seller; a big hit.

ひでんか【妃殿下】a princess; Her Highness. ⇨殿下. ¶皇太子妃殿下 Her Imperial Highness the Crown Princess. ☆呼びかけの場合は "Your (Imperial) Highness".

ひとえ【単】 an unlined *kimono* (for summer wear); a *kimono* without a lining (worn in warm season). 裏布のない着物.「単物」(a single-layer unlined *kimono*)の略. ⇨袷

ひとえざくら【一重桜】〔植物〕a single-petaled cherry tree;〈花〉single-petaled cherry blossoms. ⇨さくら

ひとにぎりのしお【ひと握りの塩】〔相撲〕a handful of salt (symbolizing an act of purification). ⇨塩まき

ひとりぐらしろうじん【一人暮らし老人】an elderly person living alone[by oneself]; an old man who leads a solitary life.

ひなあられ【雛霰】 red and white rice crackers (decorated on a tiered stand for *hina* dolls on the Girls' Festival). ひな祭りに雛壇に飾る紅白のあられ. ⇨霰

ひなかざり【雛飾り】 a set of *hina* dolls (displayed on a tiered stand carpeted in red for the Girls' Festival); a set of *hina* dolls (depicting a wedding scene in the Heian period). ⇨雛壇. 赤い毛氈を敷いた段の上に飾られた(平安時代の婚礼の様子を表現した)一揃いの人形

ひなぎく【雛菊】〔植物〕a daisy. キク科の多年草.「デージー」.

ひなげし【雛芥子】〔植物〕 a field poppy; a corn poppy; a red poppy. ケシ科の二年草. 別称「美人草」. ⇨けし

ひ

ひなだん【雛壇】 ❶〈雛祭り〉a tiered stand for displaying *hina* dolls (on the Girls' Festival). *Hina-dan* is a stepped stand [platform] arranged on a tier of five or seven stands covered with a bright red cloth[carpet]. A set of *hina-dan* with these ceremonial dolls and paraphernalia is handed down from generation to generation as an heirloom[a family treasure]. 雛祭りで雛人形を飾る壇. 赤い布[じゅうたん]で覆われた5段式または7段の雛壇 (five or seven tiers of shelves; five-[seven-] tier shelves). 人形や用品を含む雛壇一式は家宝として代々伝えられる.

『**最上段**』(on the top row of a tier of shelves). Dolls representing the emperor and empress dressed in gorgeous ancient court costumes are displayed in front of a miniature folding screen, flanked by two white paper-covered lanterns. 昔の宮中衣服を装った「内裏雛」[男雛 (the emperor doll)・女雛 (the empress doll)]が「屏風」の前に置かれ, 側には2台の「雪洞」(paper-covered lampstand)がある. ⇨内裏雛

『**2段目**』(on the second row from the top). Three court ladies in waiting, and toy banquet trays[stands] with a pair of rice cakes are displayed. 「三人官女」(three ladies of the court)と「高坏」がある. ⇨三人官女

『**3段目**』(on the third row from the top). Five court musicians are displayed.「五人囃子」がある. ⇨五人囃子

『**4段目**』(the fourth row from the top). The ministers of the right and the minister of the left are displayed. Between them are placed (three-colored) diamond-shaped lozenge rice cakes in elaborately-decorated miniature boxes.「左大臣」と「右大臣」, その間に「菱餅」がある. ⇨大臣 (右大臣・左大臣) / 菱餅

『**5段目**』(on the fifth row from the top). Three male court officials, a mandarin orange tree and a cherry tree are displayed. 三人の仕丁 (three male court guards [servants]; three courtiers).「橘」そして「桜の木」がある. ⇨桜 / 橘

『**6段目**』(on the sixth row from the

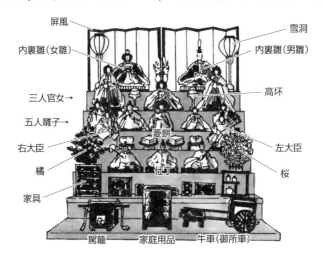

屏風　　　　　　　　　　　　　　雪洞

内裏雛(女雛)　　　　　　　　　　内裏雛(男雛)

三人官女→　　　　　　　　　　　高坏

五人囃子→

菱餅

右大臣　　　　　　　　　　　　　左大臣

橘　　　　　　　　仕丁　　　　　桜

家具

駕籠　　　　家庭用品　　牛車(御所車)

top). Miniature household articles and furnitures, such as a chest of drawers, a dining table set, and a paper-covered floor lampstand (*bonbori*) are on display. 小型の「家庭用品」や「家具」また「雪洞」がある. ⇨ 雪洞

『**7段目**』(on the seventh row from the top); An ox-drawn carriage and a palanquin to carry the dolls are on display. 「牛車[御所車]」と「駕籠」がある.⇨牛車 / 駕籠 ❷〈歌舞伎〉 a tiered platform for musicians (in the kabuki theater). (雛壇のように)囃子の人々が座る, 上下二段の席.

❸〈国会〉 the state ministers' gallery. (雛壇のように)徐々に高くなった大臣席.

ひなにんぎょう【雛人形】 a *hina* doll; (a set of) dolls displayed in a tiered stand on[during] the Girls' Festival (celebrated on Match 3). A set of about 15 dolls represents the emperor and empress, three court ladies, five court musicians, two ministers and three court officials, all attired in ancient court costumes of the Heian period. 雛祭りの雛壇に飾る人形. 15体の人形《「内裏雛(男雛・女雛)」「三人官女」「五人囃子」「二大臣」「三随身」》がある. ⇨雛祭り / 雛壇

ひなまつり【雛祭り】 the Doll Festival; the Girls' Festival[Festival for Girls]; the Peach Blossom Festival (celebrated on March 3). A set of graceful *hina* dolls is displayed[set up] on a tier of five or seven shelves covered with a bright red cloth (*hina-dan*) in families[homes] with daughters to celebrate for the healthy growth of girls in hope of their happy future[marriage]. 子女がいる家庭では幸せな将来[結婚]を願いながら健康な生育を祝って雛壇に優雅な雛人形一式を飾る. 「桃の節句」(桃の花は女性の美徳のシンボル)ともいう. ☆3月4日には娘の婚期

(marriageable age)を逃さぬように, ひな人形を片づける習慣がある. ⇨雛壇 / 雛人形

ひなわじゅう【火縄銃】 a matchlock gun [musket]. ☆1543年ポルトガル人により種子島に伝来.

ビニぼん【ビニ本】 a skin[porno] magazine sold sealed in plastic film.

ひのき【檜】〔植物〕 a *hinoki*; a (Japanese) cypress. ヒノキ科の常緑高木. ☆ cypressは「イトスギ」.⇨檜扇. ☆「人は侍, 木は檜」といわれ, 日本では最良の建築材として使用する. ⇨三方 / 升・枡. ¶ **檜舞台**〔歌舞伎〕〔能楽〕a kabuki (or Noh) stage made of *hinoki*[cypress] boards; a stage boarded with Japanese cypress(檜の板で張った歌舞伎や能楽の舞台). **檜造りの社殿** shrine building made of unpainted cypress wood. 圀伊勢神宮

ひのまる【日の丸】〈旗〉 the Rising Sun; the rising-sun flag; 〈日本の国旗〉Japanese national flag; the national flag of Japan; the flag[colors] of the Rising Sun. 「日章旗」「日の丸の旗」「日の出の旗」などともいう.

【日の丸弁当】〈弁当箱〉 a lunch box containing a red pickled plum in the middle of a white boiled rice.〈ご飯〉(a box lunch of) rice with a red pickled plum in the center. It looks like[resembles] the Japanese flag (a red circle representing a rising sun with a white background). ご飯の中央に赤い梅干を入れた弁当.「日章旗」(日の丸)に似ていることからの呼称. ⇨弁当

ひのみやぐら【火の見櫓】 a fire tower; a fire lookout. 火事を見つけ, その方向を見張る高い建物.

びはくけしょうひん【美白化粧品】 skin whitener; skin-whitening cosmetics; skin-lightening cosmetics.

ひばし【火箸】 (a pair of) fire tongs; (a pair of) metal chopsticks for handling the charcoal fire[burning charcoal] in a brazier. 火鉢の燃える炭火をはさむのに用いる金属製の箸. ⇨火鉢

ひばち【火鉢】 a *hibachi*; a Japanese brazier; a charcoal-burning brazier; a Japanese heating device[appliance] using charcoal as fuel. *Hibachi* is a firebox with the charcoal fire[burning charcoal] on a bed of ashes to warm oneself[one's hands]. 身体[手]を暖めるために灰を入れた上に燃える炭火を置いた火箱. ¶陶器[鉄]製ひばち a ceramic[metal] brazier; a brazier made of ceramic[metal]. 木製ひばち a wooden brazier (with drawers); a brazier made of wood. ⇨長火鉢 / 火箸 / 五徳

ひばり【雲雀】〔鳥〕 a (Japanese) skylark; a lark. ヒバリ科の小鳥.

ひふきだけ【火吹き竹】 a bamboo blower[blowpipe] (used to start a fire). 火をおこすのに用いる竹筒.

ひぶりしんじ【火振り神事】 the Fire-Swinging Festival at Aso Shrine.（3月）. ⇨付記(1)「日本の祭り」

ひぼし【日干し・日乾し】 drying (fish[vegetables]) in the sun.（魚・野菜などを）日光に当てて干すこと. ⇨陰干し / 風干し ¶魚[野菜]を日干しにする dry (fish[vegetables]) in the sun; sun-dry fish[vegetables]. 日干しにした魚[野菜] sun-dried fish[vegetables]; fish[vegetables] dried in the sun.

ひまわり【向日葵】〔植物〕 a sunflower. キク科の一年草. 種子は食用油の材料. 菓子にも用いる. ¶向日葵油 sunflower oil.

ひみこ【卑弥呼】 ⇨邪馬台国の卑弥呼

ひめます【姫鱒】〔魚〕 a kokanee (salmon). サケ科の淡水魚. 食用. ⇨ます

ひもかわうどん【紐皮饂飩】 long, flat wheat noodles; wheat noodles made in long, flat strips. 皮ひものように平たく打ったうどん.「きしめん」(名古屋の名産)ともいう.

⇨きしめん

ひもの【干物・乾物】❶ (salted) dried fish. Big fish are often cut open in half and then dried. 軽く塩をふって干した魚. 大きな魚は半開きにして干す. ⇨あじの干物 ❷ stockfish. 塩引きをしない干し魚. ⇨棒鱈

ひや【冷】❶〈酒〉(a cup of) cold[chilled] *sake*.「冷や酒」の略. ⇔熱燗 ❷〈水〉 (a glass of) cold[chilled] water.「冷や水」の略. ⇨白湯

ひゃくじゅ【百寿】 (celebrate) one's hundredth birthday. 本来は「上寿」といった. 【百寿の祝い】 the celebration of one's hundredth birthday. The Japanese celebrate their 100th birthday. It is the 100th anniversary of one's birth[life], one of the special ages to celebrate one's longevity. 100歳の祝い. ⇨賀

ひゃくしょういっき【百姓一揆】 a peasant riot[uprising]. Peasants rose in a riot when the demands (to reduce their tributes) were refused by the ruler. 農民が(年貢の引き下げを求めて)領主に訴えても受理されない場合, 武装して一揆を起こす反抗運動.

ひゃくにちそう【百日草】〔植物〕 a zinnia. キク科の一年草.

ひゃくにんいっしゅ【百人一首】the Hundred Poems by One Hundred Poets; a collection of one hundred *waka* poems, each by a different poet. 一人一首ずつ100の和歌を集めたもの. ☆藤原定家の撰による. 平安時代初期から鎌倉時代初期までの和歌を選出. 江戸時代以降は「歌ガルタ」として普及する. ⇨小倉百人一首 【百人一首のカルタ】 a pack of traditional Japanese playing cards based on *Hyakunin-isshu*. The cards consist of two decks, 100 cards to be read out (*yomi-fuda*) and 100 cards to be picked up (*tori-fuda*). The game is won when the player picks up the most scattered cards that match the ones read. 百人一首に基づく一組の遊戯カード. カードには「読み札」と「取り札」の2組がある. 読み札に合致するまかれた取り札を最多数とる者が勝つ.「小倉百人一首」「歌がるた」ともいう. ⇨かるた

ひやけサロン【日焼けサロン】 a tanning salon[parlor].

ひやしそうめん【冷やし素麺】 chilled thin [fine] wheat noodles; wheat noodles served cold in a bowl. ⇨素麺

ひやじる【冷や汁】 a simple fare of chilled *miso*-based soup poured over a bowl of steamed rice. 味噌仕立ての冷たい汁をご飯にかける食物. ☆宮崎県の郷土料理.

びゃっこたい【白虎隊】 White Tigers Corps (a group of teenage warriors of the Aizu clan). They committed ritual mass suicide tragically in Mt. Iimori after failing to defend Tsuruga Castle against Imperial troops[the Meiji Government Army] during the Boshin Civil War in 1868. 会津藩の十代の戦士集団. 1868年戊辰の役で官軍に対して鶴ケ城を死守できず, 飯盛山にて悲劇的な集団自決をした.

ひやといはけん【日雇い派遣】 day laborers [workers] dispatched to short-term jobs. ⇨派遣社員. ¶**日雇い派遣制** the day labor dispatch system; the system of dispatching workers hired by the day.

ひやむぎ【冷麦】 cold noodles. 〈氷で冷した麺類〉 thin wheat noodles cooled on ice; thin wheat noodles chilled in icy water; 〈氷で冷して出される麺類〉 thin wheat noodles served cold[served in ice and water]. Slender white noodles are made from wheat flour and served in a bowl of cold water with a few ice cubes. They are eaten by dipping into soy-based broth(*tsuyu*) mixed with some condiments (*yakumi*) of grated ginger and minced green onions. 細

打ちしたうどんで小麦粉から作られ, 角氷を少し浮かべた冷水を入れた器で出される. 卸し生姜やさらしネギの薬味を入れたつゆにつけて食べる. ☆「太さ」の面で「冷麦」(「四角」の切り口)は 1.3〜1.7mm.「素麺」(「丸い」切り口)は 1.3mm. ⇨うどん

ひややっこ【冷奴】 cold *tofu*[bean curd]; *tofu* served cold; chilled *tofu* cut into cubes[blocks]. Cold *tofu* is served with some condiments of grated ginger and minced green onions. 冷水に冷やした豆腐. 卸し生姜やさらしネギなどの薬味といっしょに出される. ⇨奴豆腐

ひょう【豹】〔動物〕 a leopard; a panther. ☆㊧クーガー (cougar). ピューマ (puma).

びょう(う)【廟(宇)】 a mausoleum (enshrining an ancestor's spirit). 祖先の霊をまつる所. ⇨霊廟

ひょうが【氷河】 a glacier. ¶**氷河期** a glacial epoch; an ice age.

ひょうぐし【表具師】 a scroll mounter; a picture framer. 表具(紙または布を張って障子・襖・巻物などに仕立てること(mount))を商業とする人.

ひょうけいほうもん【表敬訪問】 (pay) a courtesy visit to (the president of the company); (pay) a courtesy call on (Mr. Kato).

ひょうざん【氷山】 an iceberg; a floe(氷原). ¶**氷山の一角** the tip of an iceberg.

ひょうしぎ【拍子木】〔歌舞伎・文楽〕(a pair of) hard wooden clappers. A pair of wooden clappers are beaten with both hands in order to announce the opening and closing of the draw curtain (in the kabuki and bunraku theaters). 両手で打ち鳴らす一対の木. 引き幕の開閉を知らせる. ⇨引き幕

ひょうじぎそう【表示偽装】 falsely labeled products.

びょうしょ【廟所】 a mausoleum; a grave; a

ひ

tomb. ⇨霊廟. ¶伊達政宗の廟所（瑞鳳殿）the Mausoleum of Date Masamune.

ひょうたん【瓢箪】❶〔植物〕a gourd; a calabash gourd. ウリ科のつる性植物，またその実. ⇨へちま / 干瓢

❷〈容器〉a bottle gourd; a gourd-shaped bottle (usually filled with *sake* or water). 酒・水を入れるひょうたん形の器.「ひさご」ともいう.

びょうぶ【屏風】 a (portable) folding screen. It is a screen blind made of wooden frame covered with thick Japanese paper. It is often used as a room ornament or room divider. The panels are set up in half folds so that the screen will not fall over. 折りたたみ式の衝立．木枠に厚手の和紙をはって作った衝立 (screen blind made of thick Japanese paper spread on a wooden frame). 部屋の装飾 (room decoration) や仕切り (room partition) にして使う．倒れないように波状に折り曲げて立てる．☆屏風の標準的な高さは5尺［約1.5m］，幅は2尺［約66cm］．⇨枕屏風．¶**四曲屏風** a four-fold[four-panel] screen; a folding screen with four connected panels; a folding fan with four leaves. **絵図入りの金屏風** a gilded[gilt] folding screen with a picture. Gorgeous gold folding screens with pictures are set behind the bride and groom at wedding ceremonies and receptions. (結婚披露宴のときに新郎新婦の背後に立てられる). **屏風絵**〈一幅の絵画〉a painting on a folding screen; 〈絵続き〉a series of paintings on a folding screen; continuous pictures on a folding screen.

びょうぶいわ【屏風岩】 a perpendicular [sheer] cliff.

ひよこ【雛】〔鳥〕a chick; a chicken. ⇨にわとり

ひょっとこ ❶〈人〉a man with a contorted [twisted] face; a clown（道化師）; a jester

（おどけ者）; a funny guy. ゆがんだ［ねじ曲がった］顔つきの人. ☆「火男」の変形した語．火を吹くときのこっけいな顔つき (a funny face)からの呼称．⇨おかめ

❷〈仮面〉a mask of a man with a contorted [twisted] face; a Japanese clownish[clown-like] male mask. ⇨おかめ

ひらがな【平仮名】 *hiragana*; the *hiragana* cursive syllabary. *Hiragana* is one of the two kinds of Japanese *kana* scripts used for Japanese syllabary writing: *katakana* and *hiragana*. *Hiragana* is a cursive form of *kana* script in the Japanese syllabary writing. Japanese children learn how to read and write *hiragana* in the first stage of schooling. 仮名の一種．片仮名と並び，日本語を表記するときに用いる曲線的な形態をなす表音文字．日本の学童は学校教育の初段階で平仮名の読み書きを学ぶ．☆「個々の平仮名」は a *hiragana* character[letter]. ⇨仮名 / 片仮名 / 日本語

ひらぢゃわん【平茶碗】〔茶道〕a flat teabowl (used with a portable brazier (*furo*) in a tea ceremony room). 茶室で風炉といっしょに使う平たい茶碗. ⇨風炉

ひらたけ【平茸】〔植物〕an oyster mushroom; an oyster cap[agaric]. キシメジ科のキノコ．食感がアワビに似ているので「アワビタケ」ともいう．また英語名から「カキキノコ」ともいう．

ひらつかたなばたまつり【平塚七夕まつり】 the Star Festival at Hiratsuka City. (July 7-11). (神奈川県 ; 平塚市)

ひらにわ【平庭】 a flat landscape garden (arranged with balance of trees, rocks or stone lantern on a flat ground). 平地に樹木・岩石・石灯籠がバランスよく配されている風景庭園．圀「桂離宮」(京都府). ⇨築山(庭園)

ひらまく【平幕】〔相撲〕a makuuchi *sumo* wrestler below the rank of *komusubi*; a *maegashira*. 小結以下の幕内力士. 横綱・三役(大関・関脇・小結)でない力士. 「前頭」のこと. ⇨相撲の番付 / 前頭

ひらめ【比目魚・鮃】〔魚〕 a flatfish; a (left-eyed) flounder; a halibut; a sole(舌平目). ヒラメ科の海産硬骨魚. 刺身・すし種として用いる. 特に「縁側」は美味. ☆「左ヒラメ, 右カレイ」(正面から見て両目が左側にあれば「ヒラメ」, 右にあれば「カレイ」). ⇨かれい / 縁側❷

ひろうえん【披露宴】 a reception; a banquet. ¶結婚披露宴 (hold) a wedding reception[banquet]. 襲名披露宴 (hold) a reception to celebrate an actor's succession to a stage name. ⇨襲名

ひろさきねぶた【弘前ねぷた】 the Hirosaki Neputa[Fan-Shaped Float Parade] Festival. (8月). ⇨付記(1)「日本の祭り」

びわ【琵琶】 a *biwa*; a Japanese-style four-stringed[five-stringed] lute with a bent neck. A *biwa* is a wooden lute having four (or five) strings with four (or five) frets. It is played with a triangular plectrum. 曲がった竿を有する日本式の4弦[5弦]楽器. 木製弦楽器で4本(または5本)の弦を張り, フレット(柱)も4本(または5本)あり, 三角形の撥でかき鳴らす. ☆ lute「リュート」14-17世紀頃に使用したギターに似た弦楽器. ¶琵琶法師 a *biwa* Japanese lute player; a *biwa*-playing minstrel.

びわ【枇杷】〔植物〕a loquat(実) ; a loquat tree(木) ; a Japanese medlar[quince]. バラ科の常緑中高木. 果実は食用(ジャムやビワ酒). 葉は薬用.

ひわだぶきやね【檜皮葺き屋根】 a cypress-bark-covered roof; a roof thatched[covered] with layers of Japanese cypress bark. 檜の樹皮で葺いた屋根. ☆神社建築や能舞台などに用いる. ⇨ひのき

びんがた【紅型】*bingata* print (of Okinawa); a hand-woven textile dyed in colorful patterns (of Okinawa). *Bingata* is a fabric [cloth] dyed with bright coloration and attractive motifs developed in Okinawa Prefecture. 沖縄の多彩な模様に染め分けた伝統的な手織り物. ☆鮮やかな発色と魅力的なモチーフで染め上がっている.

びんざさら【編木】a *binzasara* percussion instrument. It is made of 40 to 50 thin wooden slats tied with a string at both ends. To produce a sound, the ends of the slats strung on a cord are held in both hands and manipulated to strike one another. 打楽器の一種. 両端を糸で結んだ40〜50枚の薄いよろい板[木製の小割り板]で作られている. 音を出すには, 紐で結んだ薄板の端を両手で持ち, 相互に打つように操作する. ☆「田楽」(a rice-planting dance)などで用いる. ⇨田楽❶

びんじょうねあげ【便乗値上げ】a follow-up price increase[hike]; an unwarranted price raise; a sneaky price rise; an optimistic increase in price.

ふ

ふ【府】 (urban) prefecture; (Metropolitan) Prefecture. ¶京都府 Kyoto Prefecture. 大阪府 Osaka (Metropolitan) Prefecture. 府庁 the (Metropolitan) Prefectural Office. ⇨県. 府県制 prefectural system. 府民 citizen of Osaka[Kyoto] Prefecture. ⇨県制度

ふ【麩】 *fu*; dried wheat-gluten bread; a dried breadlike food made of wheat gluten (flour). It is used in *sukiyaki*, *nabe-mono*, soup, etc. 小麦粉の中の澱粉質を取り出して加工した食品. すき焼や鍋物, また汁物などに用いる. 「生麩」(京都の名産)「乾麩」「焼き麩」などがある. ⇨すき焼 / 鍋物. ¶てまり麩 a ball-shaped dried wheat-gluten bread.

ふうしょく【風食】 wind erosion; erosion

caused by the wind and waves; weathering. (風化). ⇨海食

ふうじん【風神】 the wind god; the god of the wind(s). ⇨雷神

ふうぞくえいぎょうとりしまりほう【風俗営業取締法】 the Law Regulating Businesses Affecting Public Morals; the Adult Entertainment Establishment Control Law.

ふうぞくさんぎょう【風俗産業】 the sex industry; the sex[flesh] trade.

ふうちちく【風致地区】 a scenic area[zone]; a nature preservation area[district]. 趣のある地域. 自然保護地域. ☆「風致林」 a wood[forest] grown for scenic beauty.

ふうちん【風鎮】 (a pair of) weights for the ends of a hanging scroll. 揺れないように掛け軸の両端に下げる重り(石または玉など).

ふうひょうひがい【風評被害】 financial damage caused by harmful rumors[misinformation].

ふうふべっせい【夫婦別姓】 separate surnames[different family names] of a married couple; separate last names by husband and wife; keeping one's maiden name; keeping one's original surname. 女性が旧姓を守る. 夫婦で異なる姓[名字].

ふうりん【風鈴】 a wind-bell; a windchime; a small hanging glass[porcelain, metal] bell made to tinkle in the wind. Wind bells are often hung from the eaves of the houses in summer to enjoy the cool when they ring in a breeze. ガラス[陶器製・金属製]の小さな釣り鐘形の鈴. 風に揺れて鳴る音で涼を感じるため、夏季に家の軒下に吊るされる.

ふうろ【風炉】 ⇨風炉

ふえ【笛】❶〔能楽〕〈雅楽〉a horizontal flute (used in the Noh play and gagaku). 横笛. ⇨能／雅楽. ¶**笛座** a flute seat (where the flute performers are seated in the Noh stage). (能舞台で笛演奏者が座る座席)

❷〔祭事〕a folk festival flute (used in the festivities of the shrines or temples). 祭事の笛.

ふえばしら【笛柱】〔能楽〕a flute pillar; the rear pillar used by the flute player on the right side of the Noh stage. 能舞台の右側にある笛方の後部の柱. ⇨能「能舞台」

ふか【鱶】〔動物〕a shark; a sea lawyer.「さめ」の別称. ⇨さめ. ¶フカヒレ (dried) shark's fin. フカヒレスープ shark's fin soup. ☆中国料理の高級食品.

ふかあみがさ【深編み笠】 a basket-like straw hat (worn to hide the face). The helmet-like straw hat was often worn by *samurai* warriors and monks to disguise their identity in ancient times. 顔を隠すようにつくられた深い編み笠. 昔，武士や僧侶が身分を隠したりするためよく着用した.

ふかいしすう【不快指数】 the discomfort index[D. I.];〈米 :正式名称〉the temperature-humidity index[T. H. I.]. (温湿指数).

ふかがわめし【深川飯】 (a bowl of) steamed rice topped with boiled *asari* clam meat and minced scallions, flavored with *miso*[bean paste]. 味噌で味付けした浅蜊や刻みネギをのせたご飯. ⇨あさり

ぶがく【舞楽】 *Bugaku*; Japanese traditional court dances with music; ancient court dances performed to the accompaniment of the traditional musical instruments. *Bugaku* features the colorful costumes and the slow and refined motions of the graceful dance as well as the solemn tone of the music. 宮廷舞踊を伴う雅楽. その特徴は厳かな楽の音色と色鮮やかな衣装それに優雅な舞いの緩やかで上品な動きである. ⇨雅楽. ¶**舞楽台** a stage for performing a *bugaku* dance. **舞楽面** a mask worn by a *bugaku* dancer.

ふがくひゃっけい【富岳百景】 one hundred

views of Mt. Fuji. ☆「富岳」は富士山の別称.

ふかざけ【深酒】 heavy drinking; excessive drinking.

ふき【蕗】〔植物〕 a butterbur. キク科の多年草. 日本原産の野菜. 蕗飯や炊き合わせなどにする. ¶**蕗の薹** a butterbur sprout; a sprout[flower-bud] of butterbur; a flower stalk of butterbur; a butterbur flower stalk (早春の若い葉柄と花茎).

〔料理〕 **蕗味噌** miso[bean paste] with chopped butterbur flower stalks. 蕗のとうを混ぜた味噌.

ふきながし【吹流し】 ❶〈旗用〉a streamer; a pennon;〈風見用〉a weather vane; a wind vane.

❷〈鯉のぼり〉a carp-shaped streamer (hoisted in the May wind on the Boys' Festival). 端午の節句に掲げる(鯉)のぼり. ⇨鯉のぼり

ぶぎょう【奉行】 a magistrate; an administrator; a commissioner; the official title given to a high-ranking feudal commissioner working for the shogunate government (during the Edo period). (特に江戸時代の)幕府に仕えた高位武家の職名. ¶**奉行所** a magistrate's[administrator's] office.

①『**寺社奉行**』 a commissioner of temples and shrines; the chief administrator supervising[keeping watch on] the religious affairs of temples and shrines. 寺社関係の行政・訴訟などをつかさどる幕府の役職.

②『**勘定奉行**』 a commissioner of finance; the chief administrator controlling[dealing with] financial affairs of the shogunate government. 老中のもとで, 年貢の徴収や財務および訴訟などをつかさどる幕府の役職.

③『**町奉行**』 a commissioner of judicial problems; the chief administrator overseeing[watching to see] the affairs of judicial problem of towns and townspeople. 町方・町人の訴訟問題を監督する幕府の役職.

ふぐ【河豚】〔魚〕 a fugu; a globefish; a blowfish; a puffer(fish); a swellfish. フグ科の海産硬骨魚. 秋から冬が旬. 内臓に「毒」(deadly poison)がある. 刺身・雑炊・鍋物(てっちり)の定番.「白子」は酢の物や塩焼き,「ひれ」はひれ酒,「皮」は煮こごりなどに使う. ¶**ふぐ中毒** fugu[globefish] poisoning; fugu intoxication. **ふぐ提灯** a globefish-shaped lantern (made from skins filled with air and dried).

〔料理〕**ふぐ刺し** fugu sashimi; thinly sliced raw globefish; thin slices of raw globefish. 関西では「てっさ」ともいう. ⇨薄造りのふぐ. **ふぐ汁** fugu soup; soup cooked with globefish.

【ふぐちり】 fugu stew; globefish stew; a hot-pot meal of globefish and vegetables; a blowfish and vegetables boiled in a hot pot and served with seasoned vinegar. It is eaten by dipping with shoyu and vinegar mixed with ponzu citrus juice. ふぐと野菜で料理したちり鍋. ポン酢醤油に浸して食べる.「ふぐのちり鍋」の略.「てっちり」ともいう. ⇨てっちり(鍋)

ふくごういさん【複合遺産】 Mixed Heritage Site. ⇨ユネスコ世界遺産

ふくごうかざん【複合火山】 a compound [complex] volcano. ⇨火山

ふくさ【袱紗・服紗】❶ a silk wrapping cloth. (贈り物などにかける)絹製の風呂敷. ☆「慶事」(a happy[an auspicious] event)は赤またはエンジ,「弔事」(a funeral event)は紺またはグレー,「慶事・弔事に共通」は紫の配色を用いる.

❷〔茶道〕**【帛紗】** a fukusa; a silk wiping cloth (used in the tea ceremony). A fukusa is a square piece of ceremonial silk cloth for wiping dry tea utensils (the tea scoop, the tea caddy, etc.) and for holding hot utensils (the lid of the hot teakettle, etc.). 茶の湯で，茶器(茶杓，棗など)を拭いたり，熱くなった茶器(茶釜の蓋など)を持つのに用いる絹製の正方形の布．☆小型の帛紗を「古帛紗」(a small square silk cloth used to prevent damage to tea-ceremony objects)という．¶帛紗さばき the handling of a *fukusa* in the tea ceremony.

ふくさずし【袱紗鮨】 ⇨茶巾鮨

ふくしきかざん【複式火山】 a composite volcano. ⇨火山

ふくしずもう【福祉相撲】〔相撲〕a *sumo* wrestling event for charity. 慈善を目的とした相撲．

ふくじゅそう【福寿草】〔植物〕an adonis. キンポウゲ科の多年草．正月の祝い花．「元日草」ともいう．

ふくしょく【副食】 dishes other than the staple food. 主食に添えて食べるもの．別称「おかず」．⇨おかず ⇔主食

ふくじんづけ【福神漬】 small pieces of various sliced vegetables pickled in *shoyu* [soy sauce]; seven kinds of chopped vegetables pickled in *shoyu* (mixed with *mirin*[sweetened *sake*]). (七福神になぞらえて)多種多様な[七種の]野菜を細かく切り，味醂醤油に漬け込んだもの．☆「七種の野菜」とは干し大根・茄子・蓮根・白瓜・生姜・紫蘇の実・ナタ豆．⇨七福神

ふくすけ【福助】 a *fukusuke* doll; a figure of a big-headed dwarf. *Fukusuke* is a doll in the shape of a dwarf[chubby man with a huge head] and a short build. This doll sits on its heels wearing a *kamishimo*[formal dress of a *samurai*] and a topknot hairstyle. It is placed in shops to attract good business because it is believed to bring good luck. 頭でっかちな小人像．小人[頭の大きい小太りな男]で背の低い体格を

した人形．この人形は裃 (sleeveless, wide shouldered ceremonial costume of a *samurai*)を着て，ちょん髷を結い，正座している．福招きの人形として商売繁盛のために店先に置かれている．⇨裃

ふくだま【福玉】 good-luck-bringing ball (made of rice cake). The ball containing some good-luck charms is given by *chaya* to *maiko* in Kyoto on the New Year's Eve. 幸運を呼ぶ玉(餅で作る)．大晦日になると京都では茶屋から舞妓に縁起物が入った玉が贈られる．⇨舞妓 / 茶屋

ふくちゃ【福茶】 a green tea served with a pickled plum in a tiny cup; a green tea made from a pickled plum, or a seaweed tangle, a black soybean, etc. *Fukucha* is drunk on festive[auspicious] occasions or New Year's Day. It is believed to bring drinkers good luck and protect them from illness. 梅干，昆布，黒豆などを加えて煮出した煎茶．祭事[慶事]や正月などに祝って飲む．幸を呼び，無病息災をもたらすといわれる．

ふくとしん【副都心】 a subcenter (of a metropolis[city]). ¶東京新宿副都心 Tokyo subcenter, Shinjuku. 東京臨海副都心 Tokyo waterfront subcenter (at Rainbow Bridge).

ふくのかみ【福の神】 a deity of good luck [fortune]; a god of wealth. ⇨節分

ふくはうち！おにはそと！【福は内！鬼は外！】 Good fortune come in! Demons get out!/ Come in, good luck! Get out, devils!/ In with fortune! Out with the devil! ⇨豆撒き / 節分

ふくぶくろ【福袋】 a lucky[happy] bag; ⊛ a grab bag; ⊕ a lucky dip; a mystery shopping bag (containing commercial goods worth more than the purchase price of the bag). 中身が分からない買い物袋(袋には販売価格以上の価値がある商品が入っ

ている). ¶正月の福袋 a New Year's grab bag[lucky dip] (sold as the first sale of the New Year). 5千円の福袋 a lucky grab bag costing five thousand yen.

ふくまめ【福豆】 parched beans thrown at *Setsubun* (to bring in good fortune and to dispel evil spirits); roasted beans scattered around on the day before the first day of spring. 節分の豆まきに使ういり豆(福は内！鬼は外！). ⇨節分

ふくろう【梟】〔鳥〕an owl; an owlet(梟の子). フクロウ科の猛禽，夜に小動物を捕食する. ☆日本では「不苦労」(苦労知らず)また「福籠」(福がこもる)の縁起物として店先に置く. ⇨みみずく

ふくろうぶたい【ふくろう部隊】 a special night-duty squad (of the police). 特別夜間勤務隊.

ふくろおび【袋帯】a double-woven *obi* [sash] for a *kimono*. 袋織りの帯. 着物用の二重織り[表裏二枚の織物]の帯. 長い袋状に織った厚手の帯. ☆袋帯(長さ約4m,幅約30cm)は正装用(振袖・留袖・訪問着)だが柄は表面 (design on the outside) のみで「丸帯」よりは地味 (restrained[sober] design) である. ⇨丸帯

ふくろくじゅ【福禄寿】⇨七福神

ぶけ【武家】〈武士〉 a *samurai*; a warrior (in the military class); a high-ranking feudal lord (serving the shogunate);〈武門〉the *samurai* class; a warrior[military] family (in feudal times). (公家に対して)武士の家系. 鎌倉時代以後は将軍・大名およびその家臣. ⇨公家

¶武家政権[武家政治] *samurai*[warrior] government. 武家奉公 a service with a *samurai* family as a valet(近侍として武家に仕えること). 武家社会 a *samurai* society. 武家時代 the age of *samurai* rule; the period of warrior; the feudal times. 武家時代の名残 reminders of old feudal times.

【武家諸法度】Laws for the Military Houses [Families]; the Code of the *samurai*. Laws governing *samurai* households were enacted by the Tokugawa shogunate government in 1615 to restrict the feudal lords and their subordinate warriors from building castles and joining in marriage between their families. (revised in 1635). 大名やその家臣を制御するために1615年徳川幕府が発令した法令で，築城また大名同士の結婚などに関する厳しい制限を設けた. ☆参勤交代，領地の保有，武士の衣装などの規定がある.(1635年に改定)

【武家屋敷】a *samurai* residence; a *samurai* mansion. A *samurai* residence area has old houses with earthen walls that belonged to feudal lords and still retain an atmosphere of feudal times. 昔は武家に属し，今は封建時代の名残をとどめる土塀の古い屋敷. ☆「武家造り」(housing for a *samurai* family) が鎌倉時代に生まれる.

ぶげい【武芸】 martial[military] arts; the way of mastering martial[military] arts. 武道に関する技芸. ☆剣術・弓道・馬術などの武芸. ¶武芸者 a master of martial arts. ⇨剣道 / 弓道

ふけそう【普化僧】⇨虚無僧

ふこくきょうへい【富国強兵】wealthy nation and strong army; prosperous country and strong army; policy of increasing nation's wealth and military power[strength];〈スローガン〉Enrich the Country, Strengthen the Military; Rich Nation, Strong Military. 国を富ませ，軍備を強めること.

ふさ【房】〔相撲〕tassels hanging at the four corners of the suspended roof. Four large tassels hang at each corner of the suspended roof above a *sumo* ring. The north tassel is black, the south is red, the east is green and the west is white. The

ふ

four tassels represent the changing of the four seasons and gods who protect the ring from each direction. 4つ房が相撲の土俵上にある吊り屋根の角にぶら下がっている. 北は黒, 南は赤, 東は青, 西は白である. 四季の移り変わりと四方を守護する神を表示する.

ふじ【藤】〔植物〕 a (Japanese) wisteria [wistaria]. マメ科のつる性落葉低木. 観賞用に栽培される. 日本固有の花. ¶**藤棚** a wisteria trellis[arbor]. **藤蔓** a wisteria vine. **藤の花** a wisteria flower.

ぶし【武士】 a *samurai* (封建時代の侍); a (*samurai*) warrior(武人). A *samurai* specializes in military arts and has made fighting his profession. 武芸を修め, 戦闘に従事した者.「侍」ともいう. ¶**武士階級** the *samurai* class; the military class. **武士に二言なし**. A *samurai* never goes back on his word. / A *samurai* never breaks his word.

【武士道】 *Bushido*[bushido]; the *samurai* code; a traditional Japanese chivalry [knighthood]. The traditional military code of ethics and behavior was observed by *samurai* warriors in the feudal society. Emphasis was placed on loyalty to the lord, bravery in battle, and especially the value of honor even above life. 封建社会に生きる武士の武人として遵守すべき倫理と行動の規範. 主君への忠誠, 戦場での武勇, 特に生命に勝る名誉が重視された. ¶**武士道精神** the *samurai* spirit.

ふしかてい【父子家庭】 ⇨片親家族

ふしちょう【不死鳥】 the phoenix[phenix]. 神話にでてくる霊鳥.

ふじばかま【藤袴】〔植物〕 a boneset; a thoroughwort. キク科の多年草.「秋の七草」の一種. ⇨秋の七草

ぶしゃさい【武射祭】 the Archery Festival. (1月). ⇨付記(1)「日本の祭り」

ぶしゅうぎぶくろ【不祝儀袋】 a special envelope for a monetary gift (given) at a funeral[on condolence occasions]. 葬儀用の袋.「香典袋」ともいう. ⇨香典袋

ぶじゅつしなんやく【武術指南役】 a master-instructor in martial arts. 武術・武道の教導者. ⇨武道

ぶしょう【武将】 a military commander; a general of the *samurai* army. 武士(軍団)の大将.

ふじょぼうこう【婦女暴行】 (a) rape; a sexual assault (of[on] a woman).

ふすま【麸】 (wheat) bran. 穀物の殻. ☆小麦を粉にひいたときに出る皮のかす.

ふすま【襖】 a *fusuma*; a (removable papered) sliding door. A *fusuma* is made by pasting thick decorative paper[cloth] on both sides of a wooden frame. It is used as a room-divider in a traditional Japanese house and also as a closet door, running in grooves at the top and bottom. (紙を貼った可動式の)引き戸. 木枠[木製の骨組み]の両面に厚めの装飾的な紙(または布)を貼った建具. 上下の敷居の溝にそって動かし, 和室の仕切り (used as a partition between rooms[used to partition off rooms]) として, また押入れの戸としても用いる.

【襖絵】〈絵が重点〉 a painting[picture] on a *fusuma*[sliding door];〈襖が重点〉 the sliding door with fine painting[picture]. The decorative pictures and designs on the paper of the sliding door create as superb room interior. 襖の紙の上に描かれた美しい絵画や模様は室内装飾としても優れている.

ふせ【布施】 an offering[a monetary offering] to a Buddhist priest[at a Buddhist temple]. 僧[寺]に供物(または献金)を包むこと. 通称「お布施」.

ふせいきょうそうぼうしほう【不正競争防止法】 the Unfair Competition Prevention Law.

ふせき【布石】〈碁〉a strategic arrangement [move] of "*go*" game stones (with the object of completely surrounding the opponent's stones without leaving a vacant point within). 対局の序盤の石の配置. ⇨碁

ふせんしょう【不戦勝】〔相撲〕the default win; the win recorded by default due to the absence of the opponent. 相手の欠場により，戦わずに記録される勝利.

ふせんぱい【不戦敗】〔相撲〕 the default loss; the loss recorded by default due to the absence for a bout. 本人の試合欠場により戦わずに記録される敗北.

ぶた【豚】〔動物〕a pig; ㊍ a hog; a swine (単複同形)；a boar(雄豚)；a sow(雌豚)；a piglet(子豚)；㊍ hog(食肉用). イノシシ科の哺乳動物. 食肉用，皮革用，¶豚肉 pork. 豚のヒレ肉 pork fillet. 豚の挽き肉 ground pork. 豚の脂 pork fat.
〔料理〕豚丼 a pork bowl; (a bowl of) steamed rice topped with thinly slices of stewed pork. 豚の角煮 stewed cubes of pork; cubes of simmered[stewed] tender pork; braised pork belly (cooked in *shoyu* and *mirin*). ⇨角煮. 豚汁 *miso* soup with pork and vegetables. 豚肉の生姜焼き ginger pork sauté; pork sauté(e)d with ginger; ginger-fried pork; pork fried with ginger and *shoyu*[soy sauce].

ふだいた【札板】the wooden boards bearing the pilgrims' names (pasted on the walls or ceilings of temples and shrines). 参詣者の名前を記した木片の板(寺社の壁や天井などに貼り付けてある).

ふだいだいみょう【譜代大名】 ⇨大名

ふたおき【蓋置き】〈台〉a lid[ladle] rest; 〔茶道〕a rest used for placing a lid[ladle] of a hot teakettle (during the tea ceremony). 茶釜の蓋[柄杓]を置く台.

ふだしょ【札所】an amulet-card-distributing temple. It is a temple where a pilgrim receives an amulet card as a token of his/her pilgrimage or offers an amulet card to mark his/ her regular visit. 巡礼者が参詣のしるしに，巡礼の札を受けたり，また納めたりする寺. ☆八十八か所の弘法大師の霊場など. ⇨寺務所

ふだどめ【札止め】〈掲示〉House Full(満席)；Sold Out (完売). ☆「満員」で入場券の発券を中止すること.

ふたもの【蓋物】a lidded dish with delicious food[soup] (in a traditional Japanese meal). (日本料理で)蓋のある椀に入った料理. ☆煮物など汁気の多い食べ物で，蓋を開けると香りや美しい椀が楽しめる.

ふたらさんやよいさい【二荒山弥生祭】 the Spring Festival at Futarasan Shrine. (4月). ⇨付記(1)「日本の祭り」

ぶだんせいじ【武断政治】a military government; a dictatorial government [dictatorship] by the military. 武力による独裁的な政治. ⇦文治政治

ふち【扶持】 salary for *samurai* paid in rice (in the Edo period). ☆江戸時代米で給与された武士のサラリー，「扶持米」(主君が家臣に給付した米)の略. ⇨俸禄

ふちゅうくらやみまつり【府中くらやみまつり】 the Night Parade Festival at Fuchu City. (5月). ⇨付記(1)「日本の祭り」

ふちょう【符丁】 ❶〈符号〉(put) a secret [private] price mark（秘密の値段表，値段を示す店独自の印）.
❷〈暗号〉a code; a password（合言葉）；argots. It is a code language secretly used by traditional trades. 合図の隠語. 仲間同士で使う特別な言葉. ⇨隠語
〔すし屋の符丁〕(a jargon used by *sushi* chefs). 圏「あがり」（お茶: green tea).「おあいそ」（勘定: bill; check).「がり」（生姜: vinegared ginger).「さび」（わさび: horseradish).「しゃり」（すし飯: *sushi* rice).「むらさき」（醤油: soy sauce)など.

ぶつが【仏画】 a Buddhist painting[picture]. 「仏教絵画」ともいう.

ぶっかい【仏界】 the paradise of Buddhist souls. 仏のすむ世界. 浄土のこと.

ぶっかく【仏閣】 a Buddhist temple [cathedral]. 寺の建物. 仏教寺院.

ふつかよい【二日酔い】 (have) a hangover; the morning after. ⇨迎え酒

ぶっきょう【仏教】 Buddhism; (a) religion founded in India by Shakyamuni Buddha. Buddhism teaches that the ultimate goal is to gain enlightenment by overcoming worldly sufferings. Buddhism is roughly divided by two types: Mahayana Buddhism (emphasizing universal salvation) and Hianayana Buddhism (emphasizing individual salvation). Japanese Buddhism emphasizes ancestor worship under the parishioner system.（紀元前5世紀頃）インドで釈迦が説き始めた宗教. 現世の苦悩を克服し, 悟りの世界に至ることを目的とする.「**大乗仏教**」（普遍的な救済）と「**小乗仏教**」（個人的な救済）に大別される. 日本の仏教は檀家制度の下で祖先崇拝を強調する. ⇨釈迦 /大乗仏教 /小乗仏教

¶仏教絵画 Buddhist paintings. 仏教彫刻 Buddhist sculpture. 仏教美術 Buddhist art. 仏教音楽 Buddhist music. 仏教儀式 Buddhist rite[ritual]. 仏教文化 Buddhist [Buddhistic] culture.

ぶっきょうでんらい【仏教伝来】 an introduction of Buddhism to Japan. ☆538年, 一説に552年.

ぶっきょうと【仏教徒】 a Buddhist; a believer in Buddhism.「仏教信者」「仏徒」ともいう.

ぶつぐ【仏具】 Buddhist altar fittings [objects]; articles used on a Buddhist altar. 仏壇に置く器具. 仏事に用いる器具. ¶仏具師 a master of Buddhist altar fittings.

【仏具の三具足】 three articles of a Buddhist altar: a board to place an incense burner, a candlestick and a vase on. 香炉, 燭台, 花瓶を飾った机.

ぶっけ【仏家】 ❶〈寺〉a Buddhist temple. ❷〈僧侶〉a Buddhist priest. ❸〈仏教教団〉a Buddhist order.

ぶっこう【仏工】 an artisan of Buddhist images and utensils. 仏画・仏具をつくる職人. ⇨仏師

ぶつざ【仏座】 the seat of a Buddhist statue. 仏像を安置する台座.

ぶっし【仏師】 a sculptor of the Buddhist statues[images]; a master craftsman of Buddhist statues[images]. 仏像を彫り刻む職人. ☆仏像を制作する彫刻家・画家に与える職業上の肩書き (occupational, formal job title). ⇨仏工

ぶつじ【仏事】 Buddhist service[rites] (for the dead). 仏教に関する行事. 法事, 法要など.

ぶっしき【仏式】 Buddhist rituals[rites] (observed according to Buddhist liturgy). 仏教の儀式. ¶仏式の葬式 Buddhist funerals. ⇨通夜 / 告別式 / 火葬場 / 清めの塩

【関連語】「遺影」portrait of the deceased. 「位牌」wooden mortuary tablet.「一膳飯」a bowl of rice.「献花」floral tribute. 「燭台」candle holder.「経机」desk for Buddhist utensils.「棺」coffin.「香炉」incense burner.「大鈴」large bell.「骨壷」(cinerary) urn.「霊柩車」hearse.「清めの塩」cleansing salt.

ぶっしゃり【仏舎利】 Buddha's relics[remains] (buried under a stupa (or pagoda)). 釈迦の遺体, 遺骨 (Buddha's bones), 遺灰 (Buddha's ashes). 仏舎利搭に埋葬されている.「舎利」ともいう. ⇨舎利 / 舎利殿

【仏舎利塔】 a stupa (ストゥーパ); a pagoda (used for burial of Buddha's relics [remains]). 仏舎利を埋葬するために用いる塔. ⇨七堂伽藍. ☆ pagoda「仏塔」はアジ

ア諸国における仏教やヒンズー教などに見られる多層の仏塔. ⇨五重塔

プッシュホン a push-button telephone; a touch-tone phone.

ぶっしょ【仏書】 Buddhist scriptures. 仏典.

ぶっしん【仏心】 merciful heart of Buddha; Buddha's mercy[love]. 仏の慈悲心.「仏性」.

ぶつぜん【仏前】 ⇨御仏前

ぶつぜんけっこん【仏前結婚】 a Buddhist wedding ceremony; a wedding ceremony performed according to Buddhist rites. 仏の前で挙行する仏式の結婚[式].

ぶっそ【仏祖】 the founder of Buddhism. 仏教の開祖. 釈迦のこと. ⇨仏陀❶

ぶっそう【仏葬】 a Buddhist funeral. ⇨仏式の葬式

ぶつぞう【仏像】 a statue[image] of Buddha; a Buddhist statue[image]. A Buddhist statue[image] is sculpted[painted] as an object of worship in Buddhism. 開眼供養を終えたときに仏像に魂 (the spirit of a Buddhist statue)が吹き込まれ礼拝の対象となりご利益が願える. ☆大別して四種がある. ⇨「如来」「菩薩」「明王」「天部」. ☆ statue「像: 立体の像」. 仏像 (a statue of Buddha). 大仏(a great statue of Buddha). 米国ニューヨークにある有名な「自由の女神像」は the Statue of Libertyという.

ぶっだ【仏陀】 (the) Buddha. ❶〈仏教の創始者〉Gautama Buddha (the founder of Buddhism).「釈迦」または「釈迦牟尼」ともいう. ⇨釈迦

❷〈悟りを開いた人〉the enlightened person; a person who reached the state of spiritual enlightenment and realized the truth. In Buddhism, the path to becoming a Buddha is open to all people. 煩悩を超越し真理を悟った人. 仏になる道はすべての人に開かれている.

ぶつだん【仏壇】 a Buddhist household [family] altar. It is a small Buddhist altar enshrining a Buddhist statue (or picture) in the center, and mortuary tablets with the posthumous names of ancestors in the family at the sides. Flowers, food, and burning incense holder are placed before the altar. 中央には仏像(仏画), 脇に先祖の位牌が安置されている小さな家族の祭壇. 仏壇の前には献花・供物・線香立てなどがある. ⇨神棚(神道)

【関連語】「仏像〈本尊〉」Buddhist image [statue].「位牌」family mortuary tablet.「茶湯器」tea offering cup.「仏飯器」rice offering bowl.「高坏」food offering stand.「経机」lectern for reading sutras.「香炉」incense burner.「線香」incense sticks.「鈴」small bell.「花立て」flower stand.「ローソク立て」candlestick.

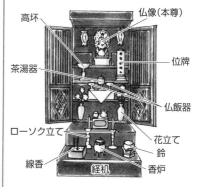

ぶってん【仏典】〈仏書〉Buddhist scriptures [literature] (recording Buddha's teachings); 〈経典〉Buddhist sutras.

ぶつでん【仏殿】 a Buddhist building (enshrining Buddhist images for worship); a Buddhist sanctuary. 仏像を安置する建物. ⇨仏堂

ぶっとう【仏塔】 a stupa; a pagoda. 仏教寺院の塔. ☆仏教やヒンズー教などに見られる. ⇨仏舎利塔

ふ

ぶつどう【仏堂】 a Buddhist hall[sanctuary] (enshrining Buddhist statues for worship). ⇨仏殿

ぶつどう【仏道】 Buddhist doctrines; the teachings of Buddha; Buddhism. 仏の説いた道. ⇨仏教

ぶっぽうそう【仏法僧】❶ Buddha, Buddhist doctrines and Buddhist priest.「仏・法・僧」の三宝.
❷〔鳥〕a (Japanese) scops owl; a (Chinese) broad-billed roller. ブッポウソウ科の鳥. 高山の森林にすむ霊鳥.

ぶつま【仏間】 the room where the family Buddhist altar (containing a Buddhist statue and a mortuary tablet) is placed. (仏像・位牌のある)仏壇を安置する部屋.

ぶつめつ【仏滅】❶ Buddha's death. 仏の入滅. 釈迦の死. **❷** ⇨六曜

ぶつもん【仏門】 becoming a Buddhist priest[monk](僧侶になる); becoming a nun(尼になる); Buddhist priesthood [monk] (仏僧職). ⇨仏道

ふで【筆】〈毛筆〉a writing brush;〈絵筆〉a painting brush. It is made of a tuft of animal hair attached to a pencil-like bamboo stem at one side. It is used for writing Japanese calligraphy and drawing monochrome paintings with India ink. 鉛筆のような竹軸[茎]の片端には動物の毛(馬・狸・羊など)でつくられた房がついている. 墨汁で書を書き, 墨絵[水墨画]などを描くときに用いる. ⇨書道 / 墨. ¶**筆箱[筆入れ]** a brush case. **筆懸け** a writing-brush rack. **筆立て** a brush stand. **筆先** the tip[point] of a writing brush. **筆軸** the stem of a writing brush.

ぶどう【葡萄】〔植物〕(a bunch[cluster] of) grapes(実); a (species of) grape(木); a grapevine (つる). ブドウ科のつる性落葉樹. ブドウ酒やジュースなどの原料. ¶**干しぶどう** raisins. **種無しぶどう** seedless grapes.

ぶどう【武道】❶〈武術〉the martial arts; the military arts. (柔道・剣道・弓道などの)武芸. ⇨武芸
❷〈武士の掟〉the *samurai* code. 武士が遵守すべき道[掟]. ⇨武士道

ふとうこう【不登校】 truancy; school non-attendance; school refusal. ¶**不登校児** a truant; a school dropout.

ふどうみょうおう【不動明王】 the God of Fire; Deity representing the wisdom of the Buddha. His image representing a fierce rage sits cross-legged on a rock with a burning flame on his back. He holds a sword in the right hand to cut away evildoers and a rope in the left hand to tie them up. 大日如来が怒りの相を表したもの. 右手に剣(悪人を切り払う), 左手に縄(悪人を縛る)を持ち, 火炎を背にして座る. ⇨明王

ふどき【風土記】 records of the culture, geography and history of a province [region]; the first topographical and cultural accounts of the provinces in written form. 地方の文化・地理・歴史などが記載されている. ☆奈良時代の地誌. 713年に朝廷が諸国に撰進させた.

ふとまき(ずし)【太巻き(鮨)】 thick rolled *sushi*; *sushi*[vinegared rice] wrapped in a sheet of dried seaweed laver with various ingredients (such as an omelet, mashed fish, vegetables, etc) in the center. 太く巻いたすし. 中央には多様な具(卵・魚・野菜など)を入れ, 海苔で巻いてある.

ふとん【蒲団】 (a set of) *futon*(s); a set of bedding stuffed with cotton; a thick bedquilt and a mattress. 綿を詰めた寝具. 掛け布団と敷き布団. ¶**羽根蒲団** a feather quilt; a quilt filled with feathers. **掛け蒲団** a coverlet; a quilt. **敷蒲団** a mattress; a quilt to be covered with. **わら布団** a straw mattress.

ふな【鮒】〔魚〕a crucian carp. コイ科の淡水硬骨魚. ⇨雀焼

〔料理〕鮒鮨 fermented *sushi* of salted crucian carp (塩漬けのフナでつくる鮨).

鮒の甘露煮 candied[sweetened] crucian carp; crucian carp boiled[simmered] slowly in *mirin*[sweetened *sake*], *shoyu*[soy sauce] and syrup. (とろ火で味醂, 醤油, 糖みつで煮た鮒). ⇨甘露煮

ぶな【橅】〔植物〕 a (Japanese) beech. ブナ科の落葉高木. 材は建築, 器具などに用いる.

¶ブナの原生林 the virgin[primeval] forest of Japanese beech (白神山地〔青森県・秋田県〕: ユネスコ世界自然遺産).

ふなもり【船盛り】 various kinds of *sashimi* [sliced raw fish] served on a boat-shaped platter. 刺身を舟形の容器で(in a container shaped like a boat)盛り付けること. 「姿盛り」ともいう. ☆魚の頭と骨を船に見たて, その中に刺身を盛り付ける.

ふみいし【踏(み)石】 ❶〈庭の〉a stepping-stone (laid in a Japanese garden). 庭園に飛び飛びに置いた石.

❷〈靴脱ぎの所〉a step stone (used for taking off shoes before entering a Japanese house). 家に入る前に靴を脱ぐ所に置く石.

ふみえ【踏(み)絵】〈絵入りの銅版〉a copper tablet[bronze plate] with a picture[an image] of Christ on the cross (or Virgin Mary, Mother of Christ). 十字架上のキリスト(または聖母マリア)の絵[像]がある銅版. ⇨絵踏 / 潜伏キリシタン

ブランドもの【ブランド物】 designer goods; famous-label[famous-maker] goods; brand-name products.

ぶり【鰤】〔魚〕a yellowtail. アジ科の回遊魚. 体長60cm以上, ¶寒鰤 a yellowtail caught in midwinter.

〔出世魚の呼称〕《関東地方》「ワカシ」(1年魚. 15cm以下).「イナダ」(2年魚. 15-40cm). 「ワラサ」(3年魚. 60cm前後)―『ブリ』

(60cm以上).《関西地方》「ツバス」(1年魚. 15cm以下).「ハマチ」(2年魚. 15-40cm). 「メジロ」(3年魚. 60cm前後)

〔料理〕ブリの照り焼き a yellowtail grilled with *mirin*[sweetened *sake*] and *shoyu*[soy sauce]; a slice of yellowtail broiled after being soaked in *mirin* and *shoyu*. (味醂と醤油に浸してから焼いたブリ). ⇨照り焼き.

ブリの大根煮 simmered yellowtail cooked with big *daikon*[white radish] (大根と煮たブリ).

フリーター (和製英語) a job-hopping part-timer[part-time worker]; a free-lancer.

フリーダイヤル a toll-free number[call, service].

ふりかえきゅうじつ【振替休日】 a substitute holiday; a substitute day off; a transferred national holiday; a Monday makeup holiday.

ふりかけ【振り掛け】 seasoned dried condiments[flaked seasonings] for sprinkling over steamed rice. ご飯に振りかけるために香味料を多様に混ぜた食品. ☆胡麻, 海藻, 海苔などの香辛料.

ふりがな【振り仮名】 *furigana*; a Japanese reading aid; *kana* written [printed] beside[above] a *kanji* [Chinese character] to aid in reading. *Furigana* is written next to[above] a *kanji* to show how it is read. 漢字の脇[上]に付ける読み仮名.

プリクラ〈機械〉Print Club; an instant photo-sticker machine; a stick-photo printing machine; an instant photo machine producing tiny sticker fun photos; 〈写真〉a sheet of stickers made from a photo of oneself (and friends).

ふりこめさぎ【振り込め詐欺】 money-transfer fraud; (a group of) swindlers who try to steal money by bank transfer fraud; fraud involving unjustified payment demands; a remittance scam. ⇨オレオレ

詐欺. ¶振り込め詐欺被害者 a victim of billing fraud.

ふりそで【振袖】❶〈長い袖〉long, hanging [pendulous] sleeves (of a *kimono*). 着物の長い袖丈. ⇨留袖. ¶**小振袖** small-sized hanging sleeves (of a *kimono*)〔85cm〕. **中振袖** medium-sized hanging sleeves (of a *kimono*)〔95cm-100cm〕. **大振袖** long-sized hanging sleeves (of a *kimono*)〔約115cm以上〕.
❷〈袖の長い着物〉a long-sleeved *kimono*; the most formal *kimono* with long hanging[pendulous] sleeves. A long-sleeved *kimono* with a colorful pattern is often worn by young unmarried women on such formal[ceremonial] occasions as New Year's Day, Coming-of-Age ceremonies, wedding receptions, commencements, etc. 袖丈の長い着物. 若い未婚者が正月, 成人式, 結婚披露宴や卒業式などの礼服用に着る. ⇨留袖

ブリッ子 a pretentious[priggish] cutie; a cutey girl; a girl who is affectedly cute; a goody-goody. ⊛ a goody-two-shoes.

ふりふりだいこ【振り振り太鼓】 a flat miniature drum with a wooden handle. A short string is hung from each side of a flat frame. A tiny bean is attached to the end of a short string. To make a sound, one holds the handle between both hands and rubs them together. 木製の柄がついた平たい小太鼓. 短い糸(cord)が平たい骨組みの各端にぶら下がっている. 糸の先端には小さな豆粒が付いている. 音を出すには, 両手で柄を握り, 両手をこすり合わせる.

ふるい【篩】a sieve; a sifter(小型); a riddle(目が粗い). 細かい粉と粗い粉をふり分ける道具.

ふるかわまつり【古川祭】 the Float-Parade Festival at Furukawa. (4月). ⇨付記(1)「日本の祭り」

ふるさとそうせい【ふるさと創生】 hometown revival; creation of a good old hometown.

ブルセラショップ a market for underwear and uniforms worn by high-school girls.

ぶれいこう【無礼講】 a social drinking party as equals; a social gathering on intimate terms regardless of rank or seniority. 身分や上下の区別なく礼儀にこだわらずに仲間同士が集まる懇親会.

ふれだいこ【触れ太鼓】〔相撲〕an announcing drum; a drum announcing the next day's *sumo* wrestling tournament. 翌日の相撲興行を知らせる太鼓.

ふろ【風炉】〔茶道〕a portable brazier with a trivet (*gotoku*) (used in the tea ceremony). A brazier (made of iron or pottery) is placed in the *tatami*-mat floor to boil water in the tearoom. An iron teakettle is placed on a trivet over a charcoal fire in the brazier (filled with ashes). 五徳のある可動式の炉〔火鉢〕. 茶室の畳の上に置いて湯を沸かす鉄製・陶製の炉. 火鉢の炭火の上にある五徳に湯沸し器をのせる. ⇨炉 / 火鉢 / 五徳

【風炉釜】〔茶道〕 a small iron teakettle used with a portable brazier (in the tea ceremony). 可動式の風炉といっしょに使用する茶釜. ⇨茶釜

ふろ【風呂】 a bath. The Japanese take a bath not only to clean the body but also to relax themselves. 日本人にとって風呂に入るのは身体を洗うだけでなくつろぐためでもある. ¶**風呂桶** a bathtub. **風呂釜** a bath furnace[heater, boiler]. **風呂屋**(銭湯) a bathhouse; a public bath. **風呂銭**〔代〕a bath fee (for a public bath); a bathhouse charge. **風呂番** a bath attendant. **風呂場** a bathroom. ☆ bathroomは欧米では「個人のトイレ」の意味もある. ⇨五右衛門風呂

ふろしき【風呂敷】 a wrapping cloth (made

of cotton or silk); a square cloth wrapper (used for wrapping and carrying things). It is used to wrap goods[items] in order to make them easier to carry. Some *furoshiki* are decorated with artistic pictures of flowers, and others have the family crest of the owner. （綿または絹製の）ものを包む布．（物を包んで持ち運ぶ）四角［正方形］の布．持ち運びが便利になるように物を包むための布．花などの芸術的な絵で飾られた風呂敷もあれば，所持者の家紋が入っているものもある．☆江戸時代に銭湯に持ち運ぶ衣類［着物］を包むために用いた布を「風呂敷」（'bath' wrapping cloths）と呼んだ．¶**風呂敷包み** a parcel[bundle] wrapped in cloth; a package in a wrapping cloth.

プロバイダー an ISP. Internet Service Providerの頭文字．What is your ISP?「君はどこのプロバイダーですか」

ふろふきだいこん【風呂吹き大根】 softly boiled chunks[rings] of *daikon*[radish] topped with *miso*[bean paste]. 味噌［柚子味噌または胡麻味噌］をのせたやわらかくゆでた厚切り［輪切り］の大根．

ぶんえん【分煙】 separate facilities for smokers and nonsmokers; separation of smoking and nonsmoking areas.

ふんか【噴火】 (volcanic) eruption; volcanic activity（火山活動）．¶富士山最後の噴火 the last eruption of Mt. Fuji (1707年). 噴火山［活火山］an active volcano. ⇨火山 火山噴火 a volcanic eruption. 噴火予知 prediction of a volcanic eruption. 噴火中 (be) in eruption. 噴火口 a crater; a caldera（大きい火口）．⇨火口湖

ぶんかいさん【文化遺産】 Cultural Heritage Site. ⇨ユネスコ世界遺産

ぶんかざい【文化財】 cultural properties [assets]. ¶重要文化財 important cultural properties[assets]. 有形文化財 tangible cultural properties[assets]. 無形文化財 intangible cultural properties[assets]. 重要無形文化財 important intangible cultural properties[assets]. 民俗文化資料 folk cultural properties[assets]. 史跡・名所・天然記念物 historic sites, scenic places and natural monuments. 歴史的建造物 historic buildings and structures. 文化財保護法 the Cultural Properties Protection Law.

【関連語】文化財保護に関する文化庁（Agency for Cultural Affairs）の用語．

①【史跡】Historic Sites. ⇨ 名勝 / 天然記念物．☆「特別史跡」Special Historic Sites. 例「厳島」「五陵郭跡」「金閣寺庭園」など．

②【名勝】Places of Scenic Beauty. ⇨ 史跡 / 天然記念物．☆「特別名勝」Special Places of Scenic Beauty. 例「富士山」「日本三景」「兼六園」など．

③【天燃記念物】 Natural Monuments. ⇨ 名勝 / 史跡．☆「特別記念物」Special Natural Monuments. 例「春日山原生林」「秋吉台・秋芳洞」「西表山猫」「トキ」「コウノトリ」「阿寒湖のマリモ」など．

④【伝統的建造物群】Groups of Traditional Buildings. ①【伝統的建造物群保存地区】Preservation Districts for Groups of Traditional Buildings; Historic Buildings Preservation Districts. 例「小京都」また「小江戸」などの呼称地区に多い．②【重要伝統的建造物群保存地区】 Important Preservation Districts for Groups of Traditional Buildings; Important Historic Buildings Preservation Districts. 例白川郷の「荻町」と五箇山の「相倉」と「菅沼」，また石見銀山地区の「大森」と「温泉津」など．

ぶんかのひ【文化の日】 Culture Day (November 3). The Japanese foster the love of peace and freedom through cultural activities. Various cultural ceremonies are held on this day to express gratitude to people of merit who contributed to cultural progress in Japan. 文化活動をしながら平

和と自由を愛するよう促進する．当日には日本の文化発展に寄与した功労者に謝意を表す文化式典が開催される．

ぶんけ【分家】 a branch family; a cadet family. ⇔本家

ぶんじょうマンション【分譲マンション】 a condominium; a condo; ⑧ a privately-owned flat.

ぶんじんが【文人画】 a painting by a writer-artist[literary artist]; a painting in the literary artist's style. These paintings are developed by the *nanga*-style artists of Japan in the mid-Edo period. 文学的［詩的］な余情を重視する絵画［墨絵］．江戸中期に日本の南画芸術家が発展させた．⇨南画

ぶんちせいじ【文治政治】 a democratic government by laws; democracy by legislation. 法制による民主的な政治．⇔武断政治

ぶんちん【文鎮】〈書道〉a paperweight (made of stone or metal). It is used to hold down plain paper in calligraphy. 単に a weight (used to keep plain papers in place)ともいう．石製または金属製の重し．書道で半紙を押さえるために用いる．⇨書道／半紙

ふんどし【褌】 a loincloth. ❶〈腰布〉a Japanese cotton loincloth worn by men; men's underwear made of a long cloth to be worn around the loins. 男性の木綿腰巻き布．腰回りに締める長い布で作る男性用下着．❷〈相撲〉a traditional silk loincloth worn by *sumo* wrestlers (in the *sumo* ring). ⇨回し

ぶんぶ【文武】 literary and military arts; the sword and the pen. 学問と武芸．¶文武両道 scholarship and the martial arts; a scholar and a soldier. (学問と武芸の両面).

ぶんめいかいか【文明開化】 civilization and enlightenment. People's life style was changed by introducing European cultures after the Meiji Restoration. 明治維新後，欧米の文化が急速に広まり，人々の生活様

式が変わった．

ぶんらく【文楽】 *Bunraku*; the classical puppet theater; the Japanese classical puppet show created through the narrative reciting of the *tayu*[narrator] and *shamisen* accompaniment. Bunraku features large costumed puppets which are manipulated by puppeteers on stage, three puppeteers who manipulate dolls on stage, and a narrator who speaks all the lines to the accompaniment of *shamisen*. 「太夫」の語りと「三味線」の伴奏によって演出される日本古来の「操り人形」芝居．その特徴は衣装をまとった大型の「操り人形」，舞台上での「3人の人形遣い」そして全台詞を語る「太夫」(a chanter who recites the story)の三業の調和である．☆竹本義太夫［1651-1714］によって完成される．「義太夫節」の開祖．⇨義太夫

☆ Bunraku, technically known as ningyo-joruri, was registered as a UNESCO Intangible Cultural Heritage in 2008. 文楽は「人形浄瑠璃」ともいい，2008年(平成20年)にはユネスコ無形文化遺産に登録された．登録名称は『**人形浄瑠璃文楽**』(Ningyo Joruri Bunraku Puppet Theater). ☆人形浄瑠璃は近松門左衛門(1653-1724)が現在の形にした．⇨浄瑠璃

【文楽の戯曲】 a play for the bunraku. Plays for the bunraku can be mainly divided into three plays: Jidai-mono, Sewa-mono and Shinju-mono. ⇨時代物／世話物／心中物

【文楽座】 a bunraku theater. ☆文楽は東京の「国立劇場」(the National Theater)と大阪の「国立文楽劇場」(the National Bunraku Theater)で定期的に公演される．

【文楽舞台】 a bunraku stage. The trio of the puppeteers stand on the lowered parts of the stages (called *honbutai*) and hold the puppets so that their feet are over the boards (called *tesuri*). 三人遣いは「本舞台」

に立ち，人形の足が「手摺」(balustrade)の上にあるように人形を操る．⇨手摺

【文楽人形】 a bunraku puppet. Bunraku puppets have[are made of] carved wooden heads, hands[arms] and feet[legs], a bamboo and cloth framework for the trunk of the body, and a costume that covers the framework. The puppets are from one to one and a half meters tall. 人形は彫刻された木製の「首」，「手足」，身体の胴用の竹製と布製の「骨組」，そしてその骨組みを覆う「衣装」から作られている．大きさは 1～1.5mである．⇨三人遣い(主[面]遣い；左遣い；足遣い)

へ

ペアシート a two-person[double] seat(電車・食堂など); a love seat(劇場・映画など).

へいあんじんぐうたきぎのう 【平安神宮薪能】 the Torchlight Noh Play Performance at Heian Shrine. (6月初旬)．(京都府: 平安神宮)

へいあんちょう【平安朝】〈朝廷〉the Imperial Court during the Heian period;〈時代〉 the Heian period[era]. 平安時代の朝廷．またその時代．

へいか【瓶華】〔華道〕 the thrown-in style of flower arrangement. Flowers are arranged in a cylindrical vase without using needle-point holders. 剣山を用いずに円筒状の花瓶に花を生ける(小原流)．⇨投げ入れ(草月流・池坊流)

へいきんじゅみょう【平均寿命】the average life span; the average span of life. ☆「**平均余命**」は life expectancy.

べいごま【貝独楽】 a small stemless top; a small cast-iron top. It was originally made from a limpet shell (called *bai*) filled with lead (and afterwards only from lead). It is spun with a string on a mat, trying to

knock each other's off. 心棒がない小さなこま．(貝の)貝殻に溶かした鉛を入れたこま(後に鉛のみになる)．ござなどの上でひもを使って回し，相手のこまをはじき出す．☆「貝」は水中にすむ貝殻をもった下等動物．⇨独楽

べいじゅ【米寿】 (celebrate) one's eighty-eighth birthday.

【米寿祝い】 the celebration of one's eighty-eighth birthday. The Japanese celebrate their 88th birthday. It is the 88th anniversary of one's birth[life], one of the special ages to celebrate one's longevity. 88歳の祝い．⇨賀

へいじょうきょう【平城宮】 Heijokyo; the ancient capital of Japan located in Nara basin from 710 to 784. (元明天皇の) 710年から(桓武天皇が長岡に遷都した) 784年まで奈良盆地にあった帝都．奈良の都．☆「平城京跡」はユネスコ世界文化遺産．

べいしょく【米食】rice diet. ¶**米食人種** rice-eating people.

へいしんけい【平真型】〔華道〕the horizontal style of flower arrangement (used in the Sogetsu school). 花を水平に生ける．

へいそく【弊束】 ⇨御幣

へいち【平地】 the level land[ground]; flatlands; flats. 水平な土地．

へいや【平野】 a plain; plains. ¶**関東平野** the Kanto Plains; the plains of Kanto (district). ⇨～ 平

へいわきねんしきてん 【平和記念式典 (広島)】Peace Memorial Ceremony (at Hiroshima). (August 6). ☆「平和祈念式典(長崎)」(August 9).

へいわぼけ【平和ぼけ】complacency[stupor] resulting from a long period of peace.

へきが【壁画】 a mural (painting); a wall painting; a fresco(フレスコ画)．¶**本堂の壁画** mural paintings of the main hall. **壁画古墳** an ancient tomb with a frescoed burial chamber. **壁画家** a mural painter.

へこおび【兵児帯】 a casual waistband; a short[narrow] *kimono* sash (worn by men and children). (男子・子供がつける)短い着物のしごき帯. ⇨三尺帯

へそくり【臍繰り】 secret savings (秘密の貯金); pin money (小銭の貯金); a nest egg (予備の金銭); a small amount of money secretly saved by being frugal means (倹約してこっそり貯めた小額の金銭).

へちま【糸瓜】❶〔植物〕a loofah[luffa]; a sponge gourd[cucumber]; a dishcloth gourd. ウリ科のつる性一年草. 茎からへちま水をとり化粧用 (lotion made from the juice of the dishcloth gourd)とする.
❷〈用具(乾燥繊維)〉a loofah (made from a sponge gourd); a sponge gourd (made from a loofah). It is used for scrubbing one's body[back] in the bath and for scouring dishes[pans] in the kitchen. 浴室で身体[背中]をこするため, また台所で皿[鍋]を磨くために用いる. ⇨たわし

べっきょ【別居】 separation; limited divorce: legal[judicial] separation; living separately [apart] from one's house. ☆「別居妻[夫]」a separated wife[husband]

べっこうざいく【鼈甲細工】 tortoiseshell work. ¶鼈甲縁の眼鏡 glasses with tortoiseshell frames.

べったらづけ【べったら漬け】 lightly pickled *daikon*[radishes]; *daikon* pickled in sweet white *sake*[*ama-zake*]; *daikon* pickled sweetly in rice yeast and a small amount of salt. 大根を麹と薄塩で甘く漬けた漬物. 別称「浅漬」. ⇨甘酒漬け. ☆えびす講の前夜(10月19日)の市場「べったら市」で売られる (a fair selling lightly pickled *daikon*). 東京日本橋の名物. ⇨えびす講

ペットボトル a plastic bottle; a PET bottle. ☆ PET = polyethylene terephtalate(ポリエ

チレンテレフタレート)の頭文字.

べにざけ【紅鮭】〔魚〕a red salmon; a sockeye (salmon).

べにしょうが【紅生姜】 red pickled ginger; pickled ginger tinted with red food dye. 食紅で赤く染めた生姜. ☆「梅酢」(salted *ume*[plum] juice)で漬けるものもある. ⇨生姜

べにばな【紅花】〔植物〕(a) safflower. キク科の二年草. 若芽は食用. 種子は紅花油に(safflower oil). 花からとれる紅色の色素は着色料(coloring agent)として使用する.

へび【蛇】〔爬〕a snake; a serpent (snakeより大). ☆「青大将」a blue-green snake.「錦蛇」a rock snake; an Indian python.「縞蛇」a striped snake.「蝮」a (pit) viper.「波布」a Rukyu poisonous snake.(毒蛇)「がらがら蛇」a rattlesnake.

へびいちご【蛇苺】〔植物〕 an Indian strawberry; a mock-strawberry. バラ科の多年草.

ペリーていとくらいこう【ペリー提督来航】 Commodore (Matthew) Perry's arrival (at Uraga). 1853年マシュー・ペリー(1794-1858)浦賀に投錨.

へん【変】 an incident(事変); a disturbance (動乱). ¶本能寺の変 the Honno-ji Incident; the incident at the Honno-ji Temple (in 1582). 桜田門外の変 the Sakurada-mongai Incident; the Incident outside Sakurada Gate (in 1860).

べんざいてん【弁財天】 ⇨七福神

へんさちきょういく【偏差値教育】 the education giving too much importance on test results[the deviation value] (試験結果[偏差値]重視の教育); the education laying an undue emphasis on students' school records(通信簿を不相応に強調する教育).

ベンチャービジネス a venture business; a high-tech) start-up venture.

べんてん【弁天】 ⇨七福神 / 弁財天

べんとう【弁当】〈昼食: 箱詰め弁当〉 a box

lunch; lunch packed in a box; a packed lunch containing boiled rice and various foods. ☆「弁当箱」は a (*bento*) lunch box. ¶持ち帰り弁当 a take-out lunch. 仕出し弁当 a lunch delivered by a caterer. 弁当代 lunch money. 弁当屋 box lunch shop; a take-out store. 弁当をつくる fix a lunch; prepare a box lunch. ⇨愛妻弁当 / 仕出し弁当 / 幕の内弁当 / 駅弁

べんりや【便利屋】 ⇨万屋

へんれい【返礼】〈贈り物に対して〉 a return present[present in return] (given as an expression of cordial thanks); a return gift[gift in return] (presented as a token of one's gratitude);〈訪問に対して〉a return call[call in return]. 受けた贈物・好意に対して(心からの謝意を表すために)お返しをする. ⇨礼状. ¶返礼する〈贈物に対して〉 make a return present [gift] (to); send a gift back in return;〈訪問に対して〉make a return call (on); 贈り物のお返しに (give something) in return for a gift received.

【返礼の習慣】 the courtesy custom of giving return presents[exchanging gifts]. When one receives a gift of money on such occasions as a wedding or funeral, one customarily returns part of this gift of money. お返しをする儀礼的習慣. 慶事(結婚式)や弔事(葬式)などで金銭を受ける場合には返礼する習慣がある. ⇨半返し

へんろ【遍路】〈巡礼者〉a pilgrim;〈巡礼〉a pilgrimage. *Henro* is the practice of journeying to a series of shrines or temples praying that one's wishes will be granted. 願い事が叶うように祈願をしながら寺社を巡礼する風習. 通称「お遍路(さん)」(a pilgrim (dressed) in white). ☆仏や祖師に関係する寺院を巡り歩いて参拝すること. 弘法大師修行の遺跡である「四国八十八箇所霊場巡り」(the pilgrimage of the eighty-eight Holy Places in Shikoku)は有名. ⇨

巡礼. ¶遍路の旅 (go on) a pilgrimage. 遍路姿 pilgrim costume. 遍路姿の老婆 an old woman dressed as a pilgrim.

ほ

ホイルむし[**やき**]【(魚の)ホイル蒸し[焼き]】 (aluminum) foil-steamed[-broiled] (fish); steamed[broiled] (fish) wrapped in foil. 〔料理〕牡蠣のホイル蒸し foil-steamed [boiled] oyster; steaming[boiling] oyster wrapped in foil. 鮭のホイル焼き foil-broiled salmon; broiling salmon wrapped in foil.【 】

ほうえ【法会】 ❶ a Buddhist memorial service for the repose of the deceased. 故人の追善供養をする. ⇨法要 / 法事
❷ preaching a Buddhist sermon to congregation[people gathered together]. 仏法を会衆に説き聞かすこと.

ほうえ【法衣】 a vestment (worn by a monk or nun); a canonical robe; clerical dress. 僧尼の着る衣服.「僧衣」ともいう.

ほうおう【法皇】 a cloistered emperor; a retired emperor who became a Buddhist priest; a former emperor who abdicated and took Buddhist vows; a former emperor who entered the Buddhist monastery. 仏門に入った上皇. 退位後仏教の誓約をする出家した上皇. ⇨上皇

ほうおう【鳳凰】 a Chinese phoenix. (⑱ phoenixes); a bird in Chinese myth regarded as felicity[an auspicious sign]. It is said to show up when a virtuous monarch appears in the world. 中国の想像上の鳥. めでたいものとされる. 高徳な天子[君主]が世に現れるときに出現するといわれる. ☆「鳳」は雄,「凰」は雌. ¶鳳凰の間 the Phoenix Hall.

【鳳凰像】 a phoenix statue; a statue of a phoenix. The Golden Pavilion is famous

ほ

for its three-story pavilion covered in gold leaf and topped with a bronze statue of a phoenix.「金閣寺」(ユネスコ世界文化遺産)は金箔を装い，赤銅の鳳凰像をのせた三層の楼閣で有名.

【鳳凰堂】 a Phoenix Hall. ¶平等院鳳凰堂(京都府[ユネスコ世界文化遺産]) the Phoenix Hall at Byodoin Temple (designed to represent a phoenix descending to earth). (地上に舞い下りる鳳凰に似せて建立した堂).

ほうがく【邦楽】 traditional Japanese music (for[such as] *shakuhachi*, *koto* and *shamisen*). 日本固有の音楽. 尺八・琴・三味線などで演奏する音楽. ⇨尺八, 琴, 三味線. ☆最近, 和楽器と洋楽器を組み合わせた若手の現代邦楽 (modern Japanese music for [such as] *shakuhachi*, *koto* and *shamisen*) も出現している. ⇦洋楽

ほうかはん(にん)【放火犯(人)】 an arsonist. ☆「放火魔」a firebug; a pyromaniac; an incendiary.「放火殺人」arson homicide.「放火罪」arson.

ぼうかようすい【防火用水】 water reserved for fire fighting; firefighting water. ⇨天水桶

ほうがんびいき【判官贔屓】 ⇨はんがんびいき

ぼうくうずきん【防空頭巾】 an air-raid padded hood; wartime padded headgear. It was worn to protect the head from dangerous objects during World WarⅡ. 空襲時[戦中]にかぶる詰め物の入った防空用頭巾. 第二次世界大戦時に危険物から頭を保護するためにかぶった. ☆現在でも地震時の「防災頭巾」(antidisaster padded hood; padded headgear worn in the time of disaster)として使用する.

ほうけんてきな[ほうけんせいの]【封建的な[封建制の]】 feudal; feudalistic. ☆「封建」とは, 君主がその直轄領以外の土地を大名[諸侯]に分与して統治させ, 主従関係を保つこと. ⇨大名. ¶封建国家 a feudal state. 封建社会 a feudal society. 封建制度 the feudal system; feudalism(封建主義). 封建体制 the feudal government. 封建領主 a feudal lord(大名). 封建時代 feudal times[days]; the age of feudalism

ぼうさいずきん【防災頭巾】 ⇨防空頭巾

ほうさく【豊作】 a good harvest; a bumper crop (of apples); an abundant[a bountiful] harvest (of rice). ⇦凶作

ほうし【法師】 a Buddhist priest[monk]; a bonze. 僧侶のこと, 出家. ⇨僧侶

ほうじ【法事】 a Buddhist memorial service for the repose of the deceased. The Buddhist memorial service is periodically observed at home or at a temple on the anniversary of a person's death. A Buddhist priest will read sutras at this service. 故人の追善供養のために行う仏事. 家または寺にて命日を周期的に記念する. 法事では僧侶が読経をする.「法会」「法要」ともいう. ☆仏教では死後49日は, 今生と来世の生の間にあるとされ,「初七日」の後は「49日」まで7日おきに「法事」を行う.

『**初七日**』the seventh day following[after] a person's death. ⇨初七日. 『**四十九日**』the forty-ninth day following[after] a person's death. 『**百か日**』the one-hundredth day following[after] a person's death.

『**一周忌**』the first anniversary of a person's death.『**三周忌**』the third anniversary of a person's death.『**七回忌**』the seventh anniversary of a person's death.『**十三回忌**』(the thirteenth ~).『**十七回忌**』(the seventeenth ~).『**二十三回忌**』(the twenty-third ~).『**二十七回忌**』(the twenty-seventh ~).『**三十三回忌**』(the thirty-third ~).『**五十回忌**』(the fiftieth ~).

ほうじちゃ【焙茶】 roasted[toasted] green

tea; roasted leaves of *bancha*[coarse tea]. It is brewed in boiling hot water. 茶葉〔番茶〕を火にあぶって作った茶. 熱湯で煎じる. ⇨茶／番茶

ぼうしゅ【芒種】 rice transplanting; the season when rice seedlings are transplanted. 田植えがはじまる季節. ⇨二十四節気

ぼうじゅつ【棒術】 the Japanese martial art of using a stick as a weapon. The contestant keeps the opponent at bay[away] skillfully manipulating the stick and finally overcoming him. 棒を武器として使う武芸. 競技者は棒を操りながら相手を巧みに寄せ付けず, 最後に相手を打ち負かす.

ほうじょう【方丈】 ❶〈人〉a head[chief] priest of a temple; an abbot. 寺の住職. ❷〈部屋〉an abbot's chamber; a living quarters of the head priest. 住職の庵室. 僧侶の居間.

ほうしょうづひきやままつり【放生津曳山祭】the Float-Parade Festival of Hoshozu-Hachiman Shrine. (10月). ⇨付記(1)「日本の祭り」

ほうじょうていえん【方丈庭園】 an abbot's garden; a garden to be viewed from the abbot's quarters (used for meditating [contemplating]). 住職の庵室から眺める庭園(瞑想用). 囲「南禅寺の禅庭園」(京都府)

ぼうず【坊主】 a bonze; a Buddhist monk; a Buddhist priest. ⇨僧侶

ほうせんか【鳳仙花】〔植物〕a (garden) balsam; a touch-me-not. ツリフネソウ科の一年草. 観賞用.

ぼうそうぞく【暴走族】〈個人〉a member of a motorcycle gang; a reckless motorcyclist; 〈集団〉a motorcycle gang[gangster]; a gang of hot-rodders.

ぼうだら【棒鱈】(a bar of) dried cod. ☆タラを背から三枚におろし, 頭・背・腸を除いて干したもの. ⇨たら

ほうちじてんしゃ【放置自転車】 an illegally parked bicycle; a bicycle abandoned by its owner.

ほうちじどうしゃ【放置自動車】 an illegally abandoned automobile. ☆「不法駐車」は an illegally parked car.

ほうとう【宝刀】 a treasured sword. ⇨伝家の宝刀

ぼうねんかい【忘年会】 a forget-the-past-year party; a year-end party (held by colleagues and friends to wind up the past year). ⇨新年会

ほうのうずもう【奉納相撲】〔相撲〕a dedicatory *sumo* wrestling match[exhibition]. It is held in the precincts of Shinto shrine on its festival day to express thanks for a good harvest. 祭礼時に豊作を感謝するために神社の境内で行う相撲.

ぼうはん【防犯】 security; crime prevention. ¶防犯カメラ a security video camera. 防犯ベル[ブザー] a burglar alarm (盗難報知器); a crime prevention buzzer (携帯用ブザー).

ぼうふうりん【防風林】a windbreak (forest); a shelterbelt; plant trees for protection against the wind.

ぼうふら【ぼうふら】 a mosquito larva (履 larvas; larvae); a wriggler. 蚊の幼虫. ⇨蚊

ほうみょう【法名】 ❶〈出家した人の名前〉a name given to a new Buddhist priest; a name given to a person who enters the Buddhist priesthood. 仏門に入る人につける名前. ⇦俗名 ❷〈戒名〉a posthumous Buddhist name. 死者[故人]につける名前. ⇨戒名. ⇦俗名

ほうもつかん【宝物館】 National Treasure House. Treasure house contains many treasures designated as National Treasures or Important Cultural Properties. 国宝や重要文化財などが収蔵されている.

ほうもつでん【宝物殿】 a treasury; the

ほ

treasure repository of a shrine[temple]. 神社仏閣の宝物の収納場所.

ほうもんぎ【訪問着】 a formal visiting *kimono*; a semiformal woman's *kimono*. It is worn by both married and unmarried women on such formal or semiformal occasions as parties and social visits. 女性の正式・略式の礼服. 既婚者または未婚者が会合や儀礼訪問などの正式・非公式な機会に着用する. ☆多種多様な模様が肩 (shoulder) または襟 (collar) から袖 (sleeve) にかけて流れるか, または着物の下半部 (the lower half of the *kimono*) に広がる.

ほうもんはんばい【訪問販売】 call sales; door-to-door sales.

ほうよう【法要】 (hold) a Buddhist memorial service for the repose of the deceased. 故人の追善供養を行う仏法の儀式.「法事」「法会」ともいう. ⇨法事 / 法会

ほうらい【蓬莱】 celebratory offerings piled with seafood and vegetables (on a small square wooden stand (*sanpo*)) used as a New Year decoration. 正月の飾り物として使う(三方の台の上に)魚介類や野菜をのせる祝い物.「蓬莱飾り」の略. ☆三方台の上に米を盛り, 干しアワビ, 昆布, かち栗などを飾った新年の祝い物. ⇨三方

ほうらいしきていえん【蓬莱式庭園】 a landscape garden that has a pond with an islet symbolizing the Land of Eternal Life. 極楽浄土を象徴する島[不老の島]のある池を有する造景庭園. 圀西芳寺(京都).

ぼうりょくキャッチバー【暴力キャッチバー】 a clip joint.

ほうれんそう【ホウレン草】〔植物〕(a bunch of) spinach. アカザ科の一年草・二年草. ゆでて灰汁をとり, 浸し物・和え物などに用いる.

〔料理〕**ホウレン草のお浸し** parboiled and seasoned spinach.

ほうろく【俸禄】 the salary for *samurai*; (a kind of) salary for *samurai* paid in rice during the Edo period. 武士の給料. 江戸時代, 仕える大名から米で与えられた武士の給料.「扶持」ともいう. ⇨扶持

ほおずき【酸漿・鬼灯】〔植物〕 ❶〈植物〉a ground cherry(植物・実のほおずき); a winter cherry; a Chinese-lantern plant(観賞用のほおずき). ナス科の多年草. 種子を取り除き口にふくんで鳴らす玩具となる. ¶**ほおずき提灯** a (small) round red lantern (shaped like a ground cherry). ❷〈酸漿の玩具〉a *hozuki* toy whistle; a balloon-shaped[lantern-shaped] bag of a ground cherry used as a toy whistle. A *hozuki* toy whistle is made by hollowing out the seeds and meat of a ground cherry. By putting it into the mouth and squeezing it against the lips and teeth, it makes a squeaking sound[a squeaky noise]. 風船[提灯]型のほおずき袋(笛玩具用). 種と中身を抜くと玩具の笛になる. 口に入れ, 唇と歯にあてて絞るとちゅうちゅう音を立てる. ¶**ほおずきを鳴らす** make a *hozuki*[ground cherry] toy whistle sound.

【鬼灯市】 a ground-cherry fair; a Chinese lantern plant market. A variety of ground-cherries planted in clay pots are sold at open-air stalls in July. 7月になれば露店では鉢植えのいろいろな「ほおずき」が売られる. ☆東京の浅草寺のほおずき市は有名.

ポーツマスじょうやく【ポーツマス条約】 the Treaty of Portsmouth. 日露戦争の講和条約(1905年). ☆ Portsmouth は米国 New Hampshire 州の海港で日露講和条約の締結地.

ほくが【北画】「北宗画」の略. ❶〈流派〉the Northern school of Chinese paintings. It originated in China and was introduced to Japan in the Kamakura period. 日本画の流派の一つ. 中国から始まり, 鎌倉時代に伝わった. ☆日本の雪舟派, 狩野派などの流

派.⇔南画

❷〈絵画〉 a Hokuga-style painting; a painting in the Hokuga style. A brushwork painting in India ink depicted with refined simplicity. 北画形式の絵画，枯淡な画風の水墨画. ⇨水墨画

ぼくが【墨画】 a monochrome painting in India[Indian] ink. 墨一色で描いた絵.「墨絵」「水墨画」ともいう.

ぼくじゅう【墨汁】❶〈書道〉India[Indian] ink; black liquid ink. It is made by rubbing an ink stick on an inkstone and used for writing calligraphy and drawing monochrome[black-and-white] ink paintings. 棒形の墨を硯の上ですることで作られる. 書道や墨画[墨絵]に用いる. ⇨墨 / 墨画 / 墨絵

❷〈墨の既製品〉 ready-to-use[ready-made] liquid of *sumi*[India ink] (in a bottle). 墨をすった既成の液. ⇨墨

ぼくとう【木刀】〈剣道〉a wooden sword (used in *kendo* practice); a sword-shaped wooden stick. 刀の形に作った木製の棒.「木剣」ともいう.

ぼけ【木瓜】〔植物〕 a Japanese quince; a flowering quince. バラ科の落葉低木. 観賞用.

ほけきょう【法華経】 the Lotus Sutra; Saddharma-Pundarika(正式名).「妙法蓮華経」の略称. 日蓮宗・天台宗の経典. ⇨南無妙法蓮華経

ほこ【鉾・矛】 a halberd; a pike. ☆槍に似て長い柄に両刃の剣のついた昔の攻撃用の武器(arms).

ほこうしゃてんごく【歩行者天国】a vehicle-free promenade; a car-free mall; a pedestrian mall. ☆通称「ホコ天」.

ほこら【祠】 a small shrine 神を祀る小さなやしろ.

ぼさつ【菩薩】 ❶ ⓐ a Bodhisattva(梵語)；ⓑ a Buddhist saint.「菩提薩埵」(悟りを求

める人)の略. ☆主な菩薩に「観音」,「文殊」,「地蔵」,「普賢」などがいる. ⇨観音

❷〈修行者〉a living buddha; a buddha-to-be. He is in pursuit of Buddhahood as a state of spiritual enlightenment. 生きている仏. 仏陀になるために修行する人. 悟りを開いた状態の仏性を追求する. ☆「菩薩」は悟りを開く前の仏.「如来」は悟りを開いた仏. ⇨如来

❸〈仏教になぞらえた神の呼び名〉 the female *Bosatsu* (called *Kannon*[*Kanzeon*] *Bosatsu*). 〔観音(菩薩)〕(女性の菩薩).

ほし(ざかな)【干し(魚)】 dried (fish). ¶干し柿 a dried persimmon. ⇨柿. 干し椎茸 a dried *shiitake* mushroom. ⇨椎茸. 干し大根 a dried *daikon*[radish]. ⇨大根

ぼしかてい【母子家庭】 ⇨片親家族

ほしとりひょう【星取り表】〔相撲〕a score sheet (showing a *sumo* wrestler's number of victories and defeats in a fifteen-day *sumo* tournament); a score card[sheet] (indicating win/loss record in professional *sumo* tournament). A white mark[circle] is used for victory and a black one for defeat. 力士の勝敗数を記入する表. 白印は勝利，黒印は敗北を表示する.

ぼしんせんそう【戊辰戦争】 Boshin Civil War (between the ex-shogunate army[the Tokugawa shogunate] and the new government army[the Meiji Government]). 旧幕府軍と新政府[官軍]との戦い. ☆鳥羽・伏見の戦い(1868年[慶応4年])に始まり, 函館の五稜郭にて旧幕府軍が敗北する(1869年[明治2年]). ⇨付記(2)「日本の歴史年表」

ほそづくり【細造り】 thinly sliced *sashimi* [raw fish]; thin strips of *sashimi*; raw seafood sliced into thin strips. (イカなどを)糸のように細く切った刺身.「糸造り」ともいう. ¶イカの細造り thin slices of raw squid.

ほそまきずし【細巻き鮨】thinly rolled *sushi*.

⇨梅しそ巻き /お新香巻き

ぼだい【菩提】 ❶ Bodhi(梵語); the Supreme Enlightenment(正 覚); Buddhahood as a state of Supreme Enlightenment (transcending worldly desires and evil passions). (煩悩を断ち切って到達した)悟りの境地にある仏性.

❷ the peaceful repose of a departed soul. 死者の冥福. ¶**菩提を弔う** observe religious rites for the peaceful repose of the departed soul(死者の冥福を祈るため法事を行う); pray for the dead (死者のために祈る).

ぼだいじ【菩提寺】 an ancestral temple; a family temple where one's ancestors or family members are buried; a Buddhist temple that houses the graves of one's ancestors or family members. 祖先代々の墓がある寺. 先祖または家族の人の墓がある寺.「檀那寺」ともいう. ¶**伊達家の菩提寺**（瑞巌寺・宮城県） the family temple of the Date clan.

ぼだいじゅ【菩提樹】〔植物〕〈インドの〉 a bo tree; a pipal tree;〈欧州の〉a linden[lime] tree. Sakyamuni Gautama experienced ultimate realization of the supreme truth [became Buddha] under the sacred bo tree. クワ科の常緑高木. インド原産. 釈迦は菩提樹の木の下で悟りを開いた[仏に成った]といわれる. ☆シューベルトの歌曲「菩提樹」の題名は The Linden Tree. ⇨釈迦

ほたてがい【帆立貝】〔貝〕a scallop. イタヤガイ科の海産二枚貝. ☆「貝柱」は the eyes of scallops. ⇨貝柱.「稚貝」is a young scallop.「貝殻」is a scallop shell; a pilgrim shell.

〔料理〕**帆立貝のバター焼き** scallops grilled in butter. **帆立貝のフライ** deep-fried breaded scallops.

ぼたもち【牡丹餅】 a sweet rice ball; a Japanese glutinous rice ball[dumpling] coated[covered] with sweetened *adzuki*

bean paste or yellow soybean flour. 餡子または黄粉でまぶす(もち米)ご飯の団子.「牡丹の花」(春の季節)に似ることから命名された.「お萩」(秋の季節)ともいう. ⇨お萩

ほたる【蛍】〔虫〕a firefly; ⊛ a lightning bug; a glowworm. ホタル科の昆虫. ¶**蛍狩り** firefly hunting[catching]. **蛍籠** a firefly cage; a basket for keeping fireflies. **蛍の光** the glimmer of a firefly.

【蛍火】 the glow of a firefly. The glow of fireflies is believed to be the altered form of the souls of soldiers who had died in war[battle]. 蛍火は戦死した兵士の魂が姿を変えたものと信じられている.

ほたるいか【蛍烏賊】〔魚〕a firefly squid; squid sparkling like fireflies in the dark. *Toyama* squid (found in Toyama Bay) is designated as a special natural monument. ホタルイカモドキ科の軟体動物. 光を発するイカで, 初夏に産卵のために回遊する. 富山湾の蛍烏賊は特別天然記念物に指定されている. 刺身, ゆがいて和え物・みりん干しなどに調理する.

ぼたん【牡丹】❶〔植物〕a (tree) peony. ボタン科の栽培落葉低木. ¶**牡丹園** a peony garden. ⇨しゃくやく

❷ wild boar meat.「いのししの肉」の異称. 〔料理〕**牡丹鍋** wild-boar meat hot pot; a dish[meal] cooked with wild boar meat in a hot pot.

ぼたんインコ【牡丹インコ】〔鳥〕a lovebird. ☆雄雌は仲がよく, 常にいっしょにいる鳥. ☆lovebirds(複数形)は「仲のよい恋人同士」の意. ⇨おしどり夫婦

ぼたんゆき【牡丹雪】 large flakes of snow; heavy snow-flakes.

ぼち【墓地】 a graveyard; a cemetery. ¶**寺の墓地** a graveyard attached to a Buddhist temple.

ポチぶくろ【ポチ袋】 a petit envelope. (お年玉用) a small paper envelope used for giving a New Year's monetary gift. It is customary in Japan for an adult to put money in the envelope and give it to children in the New Year. 正月に大人が子供に金銭を入れて渡す小さな紙袋. ⇨祝儀袋

ほっきがい【北寄貝】〔貝〕a surf clam; a hen clam. バカガイ科の二枚貝. 春から夏が旬. 刺身・すし種・酢の物などに用いる.「姥貝」ともいう.

ほっく【発句】❶ the opening verse;〈連歌〉the first 17 syllables[5-7-5 syllables] of a *renga*[linked verse];〈短歌〉the first 17 syllables[5-7-5 syllables] of a *tanka*[31–syllable poem]. 連歌・短歌で, 最初の五・七・五の句. ⇦挙句

❷ a *haiku* (poem). 俳句のこと. ⇨俳句

ほっくり【木履】 (a pair of) lacquered *geta* [wooden clogs] with rounded soles, worn with a *kimono* by little girls. 丸く底をくりぬいた漆塗りの下駄. 少女が着物を着るときに履く.「ぼくり」の転語.

ポックリびょう【ポックリ病】(a condition resulting in) sudden (painless unexpected) death (at night); sudden unexpected nocturnal death syndrome[SUNDS]. ☆「ぽっくり死ぬ」die suddenly; pop off; drop dead.

ほっけ【鯖】〔魚〕a Atka mackerel (fish). アイナメ科の海産硬骨魚. 焼き物や干物などの食用.

ぼっけん【木剣】⇨木刀

ぼったくりバー a clip joint(法外な金をとるナイトクラブ);㊎ a rip-off bar(法外な金銭を搾取するバー); falling a victim to extortionate demands at a bar (バーの法外な請求の被害にあうこと).

ポツダムせんげん【ポツダム宣言】 the Potsdam Declaration (to demand Japan's unconditional surrender). ☆ドイツ(東北部)のポツダム(ブランデンブルク州の州

都)で米・英・中の首脳が発表した対日共同宣言(日本の無条件降伏を要求する). 1945年受諾.

ほっぽうよんとう(いっかつ)へんかん【北方4島(一括)返還】 the return of all the four northern Japanese islands held by Russia in the Kuril(e) Archipelago (as a package). ☆千島列島の「4島」〈択捉島・国後島・色丹島・歯舞群島〉返還.

ほっぽうりょうどもんだい【北方領土問題】 the Northern Territories issue; the issue of the Russian-held Northern Territories of Japan.

ほてい【布袋】⇨七福神

ほてまつり【帆手まつり】 the Flag-Fluttering Sea Parade Festival. (3月). ⇨付記(1)「日本の祭り」

ほとけ【仏】❶〈仏陀〉(the) Buddha(仏様); Sakyamuni (釈迦). 仏陀, 特に釈迦如来のこと.「仏さま」. ⇨釈迦

❷〈仏像〉 a Buddhist statue[image]; the statue[image] of Buddha. ⇨仏像

❸〈故人〉 the deceased; the dead; a departed soul. 故人, 特に仏式で葬った死者.

❹〈善人〉a merciful person; a saint; a Buddhist who attained the ideal state of spiritual enlightenment. 慈悲深い人. 仏性の人. ☆悟りの境地に達した仏教徒[悟りを開いた人].

ほとけのざ【仏の座】〔植物〕 a henbit; a bee nettle. キク科の二年草.「春の七草」の一種. ⇨春の七草

ほととぎす【杜鵑・時鳥】〔鳥〕a little cuckoo. 形は「カッコウ」に似る小形の鳥.

ポプラ〔植物〕a poplar; a aspen. ヤナギ科の落葉高木. 街路樹にする. ⇨箱柳. ¶**ポプラ並木** a row of poplars. **ポプラ並木の道** a road[an avenue] lined with poplar trees.

ホームヘルパー a home-care aide;㊍ a home help.

ほめごろし【褒め殺し】mock praise (あざ笑

ほ

う賞賛）; mockery by overpraising（褒め過ぎの茶番）; sarcastic praise（皮肉な賞賛）

ほや【海鞘】〔動物〕 a sea squirt; an ascidian. 夏が旬で，「マボヤ」は食用にし，身を酢の物で食す.

ぼら【鯔・鰡】〔魚〕 a mullet; a gray mullet; a black[striped] mullet. ボラ科の近海魚. 卵巣の加工品は「からすみ」. ⇨からすみ 〔出世魚の呼称〕「ハク」（幼少 =3cm以下）. →「オボコ」（小さい頃 =3-18cm）. →「イナ」（淡水に入る［生後1年］頃 =19-30cm）. →「ボラ」（また海に戻って成長する［生後2-4年］頃 =30cm以上）. →「トド」（特に大きく成長した頃，生後5年以上 =50cm以上）.

ほらがい【法螺貝】 ❶〈貝〉a conch (shell); a trumpet shell. フジツガイ科の大形の巻き貝. 食用としては刺身，酢の物，和え物，つぼ焼きなどがある. ☆殻の頭部に穴をあけ，歌口をつけると「陣貝」になる.
❷〈陣貝〉 a conch(-shell) horn; a trumpet(-shell) horn. It was used to be blown as the signal for the charge in a feudal battle. It is now used to be blown by Buddhist ascetics walking in the mountains. 戦国時代の戦時中，軍陣で合図するために「陣貝」として用いた. また今も修験者が山野を歩くときに用いる.

ほり【堀・濠】 a moat(外堀); a ditch(溝); a canal(堀割). ⇨掘割. ¶**外堀** an outer moat. **内堀** an inner moat. **堀に囲まれた皇居** the Imperial Palace surrounded by a moat; a moated Imperial Palace. **堀を巡らした城** a castle surrounded by a moat; a moated castle. **城の周りの堀** the moat around a castle.

ほりごたつ【掘（り）炬燵】 a sunken *kotatsu* [foot warmer] set in a recess in the floor; a *kotatsu* with legroom sunken in the floor; a *kotatsu* with foot space built into the floor. They sit with their legs outstretched in a *kotatsu*. 床板の高さから掘りさげ，脚が伸

ばせる炬燵.「すえ炬燵」ともいう. ☆明治時代に始まる. ⇨炬燵

ポリ袋 a plastic bag. ☆「ポリバケツ」は a plastic bucket.

ほりもの【彫（り）物】 ❶〈彫刻〉(a) carving（木・石の）; (an) engraving（絵などを彫り込んだ）; (a) sculpture（彫刻作品）.「彫り」ともいう. ¶**美しい彫り物で飾った山車** a festival float adorned[decorated] with beautiful carvings[engravings].
❷〈入れ墨〉 a tattoo (⑧ tattoos) ¶**彫り物師** a tattooer[tattooist]; a tattoo artist. ⇨刺青

ほりわり【掘（り）割】 a ditch; a waterway; a canal; a creek. 地面を掘ってつくった浅い水路. ⇨堀. ¶**掘割で泳ぐ錦鯉** colorful carp swimming in the small waterway [creek]. 圏島根県・殿町（江戸時代の武家屋敷通り）

ぼろいち【ぼろ市】 a rag fair; a flea market. A variety of articles are sold at open-air stalls.

ぼん¹【盆】 the Bon Festival; the Lantern Festival; the Buddhist All Souls' Day; the Buddhist observance honoring the spirits of departed ancestors. *Obon* is observed for four days to welcome[console] the souls of departed ancestors who return to visit their families. It takes place from July 13th to 16th on the old lunar calendar. The ancestral spirits are invited to their homes on the evening of the 13th and sent back to the other world on the morning of the 16th. 陰暦7月15日前後［13日から16日まで］の4日の間，死者の霊をまつる仏事. 13日夜には祖先の霊を家庭に迎え，16日朝には彼岸に送る.「盂蘭盆会」の略. 通称「お盆」. ☆太陽暦の現在では8月13-16日をお盆とする所が一般的だが，7月の地域も多い. ⇨迎え火 / 送り火. ☆ All Souls' Day「死者の日」（カトリック用語）11月2日にはすべ

ての死者の霊魂のために祈る. ¶盆市. ⇨
草市. 盆歌 a folk song sung to accompany
a Bon Festival dance. 盆棚 ⇨精霊棚. 盆
供養 a Buddhist memorial service held
for departed ancestors during the Bon
period. 盆提灯 the Bon Festival paper
lantern; a votive paper lantern for the
Festival. 盆灯龍 the Bon Festival lantern; a
dedicatory lantern for the Bon Festival. ⇨
灯籠. 盆休み the Bon holiday period (in
mid-August).

ぼん²【盆】 a tray. ¶茶盆 a tea tray. 食事盆 a
meal tray.

【盆景】 a tray landscape; a miniature
landscape garden arranged[laid out] with
trees and moss on a shallow tray[dish]. 浅
い盆[皿]の上に樹木や苔などを配した小型
の風景庭園. 観賞用. 別称「箱庭」. ⇨盆栽
/箱庭

【盆石】 ① a stone landscape; a miniature
dry landscape garden arranged[laid out]
with stones[rocks] and white sand on a
shallow tray[dish]. 浅い盆[皿]に石[岩]や
白砂などを配した小型の風景庭園. 観賞用.
⇨盆栽

② a tasteful[an elegant] stone arranged on
a tray (used as a decorative stone). 盆の上
にある 趣 のある石(室内観賞用).

ぼんおどり【盆踊り】 a Bon Festival dance
[dancing]; a folk dance performed during
the Bon Festival. The Bon folk dances are
held to welcome the spirits of departed
ancestors back to earth, console and then
send them back to the other world. People
dressed in *yukata* (*kimono*) dance around
the stage to the accompaniment of musical
bands on the evening of the Bon Festival.
盆踊りは祖先の霊を地上に迎えて慰め. そ
の後彼岸の国へと送るために行う. お盆
の夜には浴衣姿の人々が音頭や歌謡の音
楽に合わせて舞台周辺を踊る. ☆8月6日

頃から16日までの間に行われる.「輪踊り」
(dancing in a circle around a raised stage
tower)と「行列踊り」(dancing in a long
line)に大別される.

ポンかん【ポン柑】〔植物〕a *ponkan* orange; a
shaddock. 柑橘類の常緑低木. ☆「ポン」は
原産地インドの地名.

ほんぐう【本宮】 the original Shinto
shrine (from which subordinate shrines
[subshrines] have branched off) ; the
original Shinto shrine (from which a deity
has been franchised to a subshrine) 神霊
を他に分けた元の神社. 圀熊野本宮大社(和
歌山県) (Kumano Hongu Grand Shrine).
☆ユネスコ世界文化遺産. ⇨新宮

ぼんくれ【盆暮】 the Bon Festival and the
year-end. It is customary for the Japanese
to send midsummer and year-end greetings
or gifts. ⇨中元/歳暮

ほんけ【本家】❶〈宗家〉the head[main]
family; the founding family. (分家に対し
て)一門のもとになる家柄. ⇨宗家. ¶生
け花の本家 the head[founding] family of a
school of flower arrangement. ⇨分家
❷〈元祖〉the originator; the original maker
[manufacturer].「本家本元」ともいう.

ぼんけい【盆景】 ⇨盆❷

ぼんさい【盆栽】a *bonsai*; a miniature potted
tree[plant]. *Bonsai* is a miniature potted
tree[plant] dwarfed in a shallow pot by artificial methods of culture, such as pruning
and wiring so that they have a natural appearance. 小型鉢(container)で小さく発育
させた樹木[植物]. 自然の景観を表現する
ように剪定したり, 針金を巻いたりする人
工的な栽培法で, 狭い鉢で小さく植育させ
る小型の樹木[植物]. ⇨盆景/盆石
☆主な「樹形」(*bonsai* style)
①『直幹』formal upright style. The trunk
grows upright[straight up]. 幹が上にまっす
ぐに伸びる.

②『懸崖』 cascading style. The tree grows out of steep cliff far back. 木が崖から乗り出す.

③『斜幹』 slant style. The tree grows obliquely. 木が斜めに伸びる.

④『株立ち』 multiple trunk style. Several trunks grow from a single root. 数本の幹が立ち上がっている.

⑤『模様木』 informal upright style. There is a bend in the trunk, either left or right. 幹が左右に曲がる.

⑥『石付き』 rock planting style. The root of the trees cling to rocks. 石が木の根に絡む.

ほ

直幹　模様木　盆栽
懸崖
斜幹　株立ち　盆石　石付き

ほんざん【本山】 the head temple of a Buddhist sect; a cathedral. 一宗・一派の寺を統括する寺. 圀大本山永平寺(福井県). ⇨総本山／大本山. ☆ cathedral「カテドラル，大聖堂，大寺院」(キリスト教用語)には司教[主教](a bishop)座または大司教(an archbishop)座があり，従ってその司教区[主教区](diocese)を代表する最上位の教会[聖堂]. 正式名「司教座聖堂」.

ほんしゅう【本州】 Honshu; the main island of Japan. ☆東北・関東・中部・近畿・中国の五地方から成る.

ほんしょう【梵鐘】 the Buddhist temple bell; the bell of a Buddhist temple. 寺院のつり鐘. ☆「梵鐘一口」(個数の数え方)

ほんじん【本陣】 ❶〈本営〉the headquarters. 戦時に大将のいる場所.「本営」ともいう.
❷〈大名の宿場〉an officially-appointed[-designated] Japanese-style inn (used as a lodging for a feudal lord or a person of high rank[position] in the Edo period). 江戸時代の宿駅で，大名・貴人が泊まった公的な宿.

ポンず【ポン酢】 bitter-orange juice; tangy citrus juice; juice pressed from a bitter [sour] orange. Bitter orange juice is used to add flavor for a pot cooking. ダイダイ(ユズ・スダチ・カボス・レモンなど)の絞り汁. 鍋料理に風味を添える. ☆オランダ語の「ポンス」(pons：ダイダイの搾り汁)に由来する. ⇨寄せ鍋

〔食品〕**ポン酢醤油** a mixture of vinegar and *shoyu*[soy sauce] with *pons* citrus juice. ポン酢に酢としょうゆを合わせたもの. 味醂・鰹節・昆布などを加えて旨みを出す.

ぼんせき【盆石】 ⇨盆

ほんぜんりょうり【本膳料理】 a formal [regular] setting of dinner; a traditional full-course dinner (served on special occasions). 正式の日本料理の膳立て[配膳]で，本膳，二の膳，三の膳からなる. 単に「本膳」ともいう.「二の膳」「三の膳」に対する「本膳」は the main[principal] course of a dinner.「一の膳」ともいう. 冠婚葬祭(ceremonial functions)などの儀式用の日本料理の原型である. ⇨一の膳. 『一汁三菜』(one soup and three side dishes：ご飯・汁・煮物・膾・焼き物). また『二汁五菜』(two soups and five side dishes)の場合は「二の膳」(extra dishes: 本膳の次に出す膳)が右側につく.

ほんぞん【本尊】 the principal Buddhist statue[image]. *Honzon* is the principal statue[image] of Buddha enshrined as the object of worship venerated as a deity in the main hall[building] of a Buddhist temple. 本堂に祀られたご神体としての中

心的な仏像. ⇨本堂

ぼんち【盆地】 a basin. ¶甲府盆地(山梨県) the Kofu Basin. 海盆 the ocean basin.

ほんでん【本殿】 the Shinto shrine inner sanctuary(最も神聖な場所); the sanctuary of a Shinto shrine (where the object of worship venerated as a deity is enshrined). 神社で神霊のご神体を安置してある至聖所.「中心となる社殿」(the main shrine hall [building])と「奥の社殿」(the inner shrine hall[building]) がある. ⇨拝殿 (oratory)/神体. ☆ sanctuary「至聖所, 内陣, 聖域」はキリスト教の教会などで一番奥にある「最も神聖な祭壇のある場所」.

ほんでんまつり【梵天祭り】 the Bonden Festival of Asahiokayama Shrine in Yokote. (2月). ⇨付記(1)「日本の祭り」

ほんど【本土】 the mainland (国土の中心地); the country proper (本国). ¶日本本土 Japan proper. 中国本土 Mainland China; the Chinese mainland.

ほんとう【本島】 the main island. ¶沖縄本島 Okinawa, the main island of the Okinawa; the Island of Okinawa.

ほんどう【本堂】 the main temple hall[building]. *Hondo* is the main hall[building] of a Buddhist temple where the principal Buddhist statue[image] is enshrined. 寺院で, 本尊を安置してある中心の建物. ⇨本尊

ぼんのう【煩悩】 earthly desires; worldly passions. ☆仏教では煩悩とは人間の心身を悩ます妄念・欲望のこと.「心」の面では evil thoughts,「身」の面で carnal desiresとも表現できよう. ⇨除夜の鐘(108の煩悩)

ほんばしょ【本場所】〔相撲〕a regular[seasonal] *sumo* tournament. A professional *sumo* tournament is held six times a year, each lasting 15 days. The *sekitori* wrestlers in the *juryo* and *makuuchi* divisions wrestle once a day for 15 days. The *sekitori*

wrestler must win 8 of their 15 bouts for a winning record (*kachi-koshi*), which ensures promotions. The *sekikori* wrestler with most wins in the entire tournament captures the championship. 本場所は年6回, 毎回15日間続く. 十両と幕内の関取は15日間1日1回対戦する. 昇格のためには, 関取は15戦中8勝しなくてはいけない. 本場所で最多の勝ち星をあげた関取が優勝する. ⇨相撲の番付 / 関取 / 勝ち越し

ほんぶたい【本舞台】〔歌舞伎〕the main[regular] stage floor (for acting of a kabuki play). (歌舞伎を演ずる)正面中央にある舞台.

ぼんぼり【雪洞】 ❶〈行灯〉a small paper-covered lampstand; a floor lampstand in shape of a hexagon. Wooden[Bamboo] frame of lampstand is covered with a paper lampshade with the top open. 紙で覆われた小型の照明器具. 床に立てて置く六角形の照明器具. 紙で覆われている木製[竹製]の骨組みの上部が開いているランプ笠. ⇨行灯

❷〈手燭〉a paper-covered hand lantern [candlestick]; a hand-carried paper lantern. 紙張りの手に持つあかり.

ほんまぐろ【本鮪】〔魚〕a bluefin tuna. ⇨まぐろ

ほんまる【本丸】 the castle tower[keep]; the main enclosure of a castle; a donjon. 城の主体となる部分. ☆通常, 天守閣があり, 周囲に濠・石垣がある.

ほんめいチョコ【本命チョコ】 a heartfelt gift of chocolate to a man on Valentine's Day.

ぼんりゃくてまえ【盆略点前】〔茶道〕a tray tea ceremony; the most simplified[abbreviated] tea ceremony prepared on a tray. It can be performed anywhere and anytime, using a minimum of tea utensils. 盆の上で茶を点てる簡略化された茶の湯. 最小限の茶器を用いながら, 場所・時間に関係なく行われる. ⇨茶道具

ほ

ほんわり【本割り】〔相撲〕 the regularly scheduled bouts of a *sumo* tournament.（発表された取組表で）予定された相撲試合の正規の取組.

ま

まい【舞】　dancing; a traditional Japanese dance; a refined dance with the stylized form. 日本の伝統的な舞踊；様式化された型をもつ優雅な舞踊. ¶**舞扇**〈舞に用いる扇〉a folding fan for classical Japanese dancing;〈舞人の扇〉a dancer's folding fan; a folding fan used by a dancer.

まいこ【舞子・舞妓】　a *maiko*; an apprentice *geisha*. A *maiko* is a female entertainer who is professionally trained in dancing and singing, and also manners[etiquette] for entertaining guests at Japanese-style banquets. They wear an elaborate traditional coiffure, and a colorful *kimono* with a long *obi* sash hanging from the back. 芸妓見習いの少女. 日本古来の舞踊や音楽，また日本式の宴会などで接客するための作法を専門的に訓練された女性の接客者. 彼女らは凝った伝統的な日本髪を結い，背中から長い帯をたらし，色鮮やかな着物を身に付けている.「半玉」（一人前でない若い芸妓）ともいう. ⇨芸者

まいごふだ【迷子札】　a child's identification tag (in case he/she gets lost). A small wooden plate writing the child's name and address is used as a precaution against getting lost. 迷子になったときの身分証明札. 迷子のときの用心に名前・住所を書き記した札.

まいぞうきん【埋蔵金】　government cash stashed[hidden] in special accounts.

まいぞうぶんかざい【埋蔵文化財】　buried [unexcavated] cultural properties[assets]. ⇨文化財

まいたけ【舞茸】〔植物〕a *maitake* mushroom; a hen of the woods. サルノコシカケ科の食用キノコ.

まいばやし【舞囃子】〔能楽〕a short Noh piece in which a performer dances to the musical accompaniment (hayashi) of the Noh play without wearing the mask and costume. 能楽で演技者が面・装束をつけずに囃子の伴奏に合わせて踊る短い劇.

マイホームしゅぎ【マイホーム主義】a home-oriented[family-oriented] way of life. ¶**マイホーム主義者**　a home-oriented[family-oriented] person; a family man; a homebody.

まえがしら【前頭】〔相撲〕a *maegashira*; the fifth-highest rank of *sumo* wrestlers, and the lowest *makuuchi* rank; the fifth-ranking *sumo* champions in the *makuuchi* division; a *sumo* wrestler in the top division below the rank of *komusubi*. 幕内で第五位の力士.「小結」の下位にある. ☆三役と区別するときは「平幕」と呼ぶ. ⇨相撲の番付. ¶**前頭2枚目** the second-ranked *maegashira*. **前頭筆頭** the top-ranked *maegashira*; the first-ranking *maegashira*.

まえじて【前仕手】〔能楽〕the main[principal] actor in the first part of a Noh play. 能楽第1部での主役. ⇨後仕手 / 仕手

まえずもう【前相撲】〔相撲〕 *sumo* bouts between unranked *sumo* wrestlers. Good results qualify them for entrance into *jonokuchi* division. まだ番付にのらない力士の間で行われる取組. 良い結果を出せば序の口入りの資格を得る.

まえみごろ【前身頃】　the front part of a *kimono*; the (two) front sections[panels] of cloth of a *kimono*. 着物の前部（胴体の前部分をおおうもの）.「まえみ」. ⇦後身頃.

まえみつ【前褌】〔相撲〕the front (part) of a *sumo* wrestler's loincloth. まわしの前（の部分）. ⇨縦褌

まがいぶつ【磨崖仏】Buddha relief sculpture

carved on a rock face. 岩面に刻みつけられた浮き彫りの仏像. 圏大分県・臼杵石仏

まかじき【真旗魚】〔魚〕a spearfish; a (blue) marlin. スズキ目の大型の食用魚. ⇨かじき

まがたま【勾玉】⇨三種の神器

まがりや【曲り屋】⇨南部曲り屋

まきえ【蒔絵】❶〈工芸品〉a gold-silver-inlaid lacquer (work); lacquer ware sprinkled with gold and silver dust in various designs; an artistically-crafted article lacquered with powders of gold and silver in various designs. 金・銀をちりばめた漆の工芸品. 漆で多様な絵模様を描き, 金・銀の粉を蒔き付けてみがいた漆工芸品. ⇨高蒔絵. ¶**金蒔絵の箱** a gold-lacquered box.
❷〈技法〉the Japanese lacquering technique (employing sprinkled powders of gold and silver). 〈金・銀の粉をまき散らしてみがく〉漆工芸の技法.

まきがい【巻き貝】〈貝類〉a conch; a spiral shell; a snail shell. らせん状に巻いている貝類(さざえ, ほら貝など). ⇦二枚貝

まきす【巻き簀】a bamboo rolling mat (used to make a rolled *sushi*). 竹製の巻き上げ式マット(巻き鮨などの形を整えるために用いる).「巻き簀垂れ」の略. ⇨海苔巻き

まきずし【巻き鮨】rolled *sushi* with raw fish or vegetables in the center. *Sushi* rolled[wrapped] up in a sheet of dried laver with slices of raw fish or vegetables (or both) inside. Ingredients are dried *shiitake* mushrooms, dried gourd strips[shavings], omelet, *denbu*[shredded and seasoned fish meat], etc. 焼き海苔で飯を巻き, 魚あるいは野菜(またはその両方)を芯にはさんだ鮨. 具材には干椎茸, 干瓢, 卵焼きや田麩などがある. ⇨鉄火巻き / カッパ巻き

まきもの【巻物】❶〈軸物〉a *makimono*;a hand scroll; a horizontal scroll; a long paper of a continuous picture[picture story] rolled up horizontally in a scroll. 書画[絵つきの物語]を表装した横に長い軸物. ⇨絵巻物. ¶**巻物を巻く** roll up a *makimono*. **巻物を広げる** unroll[unfold] a *makimono*.
❷〈反物〉rolled drapery; rolled (textile) fabrics[cloth]. 軸に巻いた織物.

まくあい【幕間】㊤ an interval[㊅ intermission] between the acts. 一幕から次の幕が開くまでの間. ¶**幕間狂言** an interlude(幕間劇). ⇨幕間狂言

まくうち【幕内】〔相撲〕the *makuuchi*; the highest-ranking division in the professional *sumo* wrestling; the top division of *sumo* wrestlers. 幕内力士. 相撲番付の最上位にいる力士. ☆「横綱」「三役」(「大関」「関脇」「小結」)「前頭」を指す. ⇨相撲の番付

まくした【幕下】〔相撲〕the *makushita*; the third-ranking division[grade] in the professional *sumo* wrestling; below *jūryō* and above *sandanme*.「十両」の下,「三段目」の上. ⇨相撲の番付

まくのうち【幕の内】❶〔相撲〕⇨幕内
❷〈弁当〉. ⇨幕の内弁当

まくのうちべんとう【幕の内弁当】a variety box lunch; a variety of lunch served in a compartmentalized box. A box lunch contains small white rice balls and tidbits[small portions] of various foods packed in a wooden box. 仕切り箱に盛り付けた弁当. 木製の箱には握り飯と多種多様な少量の「おかず」が詰まっている. ☆元来は歌舞伎観劇の幕間[幕の内](between curtains)に食べる弁当 (a box lunch eaten in a theater between acts of a kabuki play)

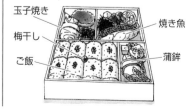

玉子焼き 焼き魚 梅干し ご飯 蒲鉾

のこと.「おかず」(subsidiary dishes)の特色として ①「焼き魚」(grilled[broiled] fish).②「玉子焼き」(sweetened and soy-flavored omelet). ③「蒲鉾」(boiled[steamed] fish paste)など季節によって組み合わせがある.

まくはりメッセ【幕張メッセ】 Makuhari-Messe; a large-scale, four-story exhibition hall with multipurpose meeting facilities. 多目的会合施設のある大規模な4階建ての博覧会場.

まくらえ【枕絵】 an erotic[a pornographic] picture depicting bedroom action. 春画. ⇨ 枕草紙

まくらことば【枕詞】 a poetic[stock] epithet (used in classical *waka*[*tanka*] poem). 和歌・短歌の修辞[形容辞]の一つ.

まくらぞうし【枕草紙】 an erotic picture book. 春画の本. ⇨枕絵

まくらびょうぶ【枕屏風】 a bedside folding screen. 寝床近くにある屏風. ⇨屏風

まぐろ【鮪】〔魚〕a tuna(複 ~(s)); a tunny; a bluefin tuna. サバ科の硬骨魚. ⇨ほんまぐろ
〔料理〕鮪丼 tuna bowl; (a bowl of) rice topped with sliced flesh[meat] of raw tuna. 鮪の卸し和え tuna in grated *daikon* [Japanese radish] seasoned with *shoyu* and vinegar. 鮪の刺し身 slices of raw tuna; sliced raw tuna. マグロのトロ fatty tuna. 《マグロの大トロ heavily marbled fatty tuna. マグロの中トロ moderately fatty tuna. ⇨トロ. 鮪の角煮 stewed cubes of tuna; simmered[stewed] tuna cubes. ⇨角煮. 鮪の漬け丼 seasoned tuna topped on rice.

まくわうり【真桑瓜】〔植物〕a variety of melon; an Oriental melon. ウリ科のつる性一年草. 実は楕円形で食用.

まげ【髷】 ❶〈女性〉a traditional Japanese hairstyle; a chignon (for a woman[*maiko*]). 束髪の髷. ⇨島田(髷) / 丸髷. ¶舞妓の髷を結う do *maiko*'s hair up in a chignon.

❷〈男性・相撲力士〉 a topknot (for a man [*sumo* wrestler]). 髪の束, 丁髷. ⇨丁髷 / 大銀杏. ¶力士の髷を結う tie *sumo* wrestler's hair in a topknot.

まけこし【負け越し】〔相撲〕losing a majority of *sumo* wrestling bouts; *sumo* wrestlers' net losing record; more losses than possible wins for a *sumo* wrestler in a tournament. A losing record generally results in demotion in the ranking. 相撲の勝負で負けた回数が勝った回数より多いこと. 負け越せば番付の降格に影響する. ⇔勝ち越し

まけぼし【負け星】〔相撲〕(receive) a defeat; (rack up) a loss; the black mark indicating a defeat[loss]. ⇔勝ち星

まげもの【髷物】 a *samurai* drama; a period play[story, film]; a genre play[story, film] treating events in the Edo period. (ちょんまげを結っていた)江戸時代を題材とした風俗劇.「時代物」の映画・芝居・小説など.

まげもの【曲げ物】 a round container[receptacle]. It is an oval box made from thin strips of wood shaved from logs, which is bent in a circle and joined at the bottom. 丸い容器. (檜・杉などの)材木から削りとった薄い板片から作る丸い箱で, 円形に曲げて底を取り付ける.

まごのて【孫の手】 a backscratcher; a tool for scratching one's back (with a long wooden handle). Its top is shaped like a baby's hand. (長い木製の柄がある)背中をかく用具. 先端が赤子の手の形をしている.

ましこやき【益子焼】 the Mashiko ceramic and porcelain (produced in Tochigi Prefecture).

ます【升・枡】 ❶〈相撲・寄席などの席〉a box (seat). 相撲・寄席・芝居小屋などでの四角に仕切った見物席.「升席」(a box seat)ともいう. ¶相撲の升(席) a box (seat) where four people can sit to watch *sumo* wrestling.

❷〈計量器〉　a measuring box. It is a small square wooden box[container] used as measuring grain or liquid. It is usually made of Japanese cypress wood without using any nails. 穀物(米など)や液体(酒など)を量る正方形の小箱[容器]．通常は釘を使用せず檜(ひのき)でつくられている．¶**一升枡** a one-*sho*[=1.8 litters] measuring box. **枡酒** *sake* served in a square wooden cup.

ます【鱒】〔魚〕a trout. (単複同形)．サケ科の硬骨魚．¶**虹鱒** a rainbow trout. **川鱒** a brook trout. **銀鱒** a silver trout. **姫鱒** a red trout; a kokanee (salmon). **海鱒** a sea trout.
〔料理〕**鱒鮨** pressed trout *sushi*[vinegared rice]; *sushi* pressed with trout and wrapped in a bamboo leaf. 鱒を並べ(酢飯)を押しながら詰め竹の葉で包んだ鮨．

マスクメロン muskmelon. ☆海外での別名は cantaloupe; honeydew melonなど．

ますせき【升席】　⇨升❶

まぜごはん【混ぜ御飯】　boiled rice mixed with vegetables, meat and other ingredients. 野菜・肉・その他の具を混ぜたご飯．

まち【町】　a town（地方自治体の）; a city（市の）．¶**城下町** a castle town. **門前町** a temple[shrine] town. **宿場町** a post town. **港町** a port town. **由緒ある町** a historic town.

まちあい【待合い】　❶〔茶道〕a waiting room in the tea ceremony. The guests wait in a specified area till they enter the tearoom. 茶室に付属し，客が席入りする前に待ち合わせる所．
❷〔茶屋〕a *machiai*; a high-class *geisha* restaurant; a high-class Japanese-style restaurant to which *geisha* entertainers are called. 客が芸者などを呼んで遊ぶ茶屋．「待合茶屋」の略．⇨芸者

まちぶぎょう【町奉行】　⇨奉行

まちや【町家】　traditional merchant houses on a town street (in Kyoto). ☆通りに面し

た間口は狭く，奥行きが深い庶民の家．

まつ【松】〔植物〕a pine; a pine tree(木)．マツ科の常緑針葉高木．⇨松明．¶**松毬・松笠**(松ぼっくり) a pinecone; a cone. **松の実** a pine nut. (製菓材料に用いる)．**松やに** pine resin; pine-tree gum. **松葉** a pine needle. **松林** a pine wood[grove]; a grove of pine trees. **松原** a pine-covered area (near the seashore).

まつかざり【松飾り】　the New Year's pine decorations (set up on the doorway[gate] of a Japanese house). People simply decorate their doorway[gate] with a straw rope and a white paper on either side of which a New Year's pine branch is attached (instead of *kadomatsu*). (門松の代わりに)松の枝をつけた藁と垂[四手]を戸口[玄関]の両側に飾るだけのこともある．⇨門松 / 垂

まっきガン【末期ガン】　terminal cancer. ☆「末期患者」a terminally-ill patient.

まつたけ【松茸】〔植物〕a ***matsutake*** mushroom; a pine mushroom. *Matsutake* is a fragrant edible mushroom growing at the foot of Japanese red pine trees (*aka-matsu*). キシメジ科のきのこ．赤松などの根に寄生する．美味で食用．⇨きのこ．¶**焼き松茸** *matsutake* mushroom broiled over charcoal fire.
〔料理〕**松茸御飯** rice cooked together with *matsutake* mushrooms and other ingredients. **松茸の土瓶蒸し** *matsutake* mushrooms cooked in an earthenware teapot. ⇨土瓶蒸し

まっちゃ【抹茶】〔茶道〕*matcha*; powdered green tea (used in the tea ceremony); high-quality green tea ground into fine powder. *Matcha* is also called *hikicha*, and has two kinds of consistency: *koicha*[thick, pasty tea] and *usucha*[thin, foamy tea] in the tea ceremony. 茶うすでひいて粉にした高品質の粉末緑茶．抹茶は「挽茶」ともいわれる．

ま

茶道におけるお茶のたて方には「濃茶」と「薄茶」の2種類の濃度がある. ☆「濃茶」は抹茶の量を多くしてたてた茶.「薄茶」は抹茶の量を少なくしてたてた茶. ⇨挽茶 / 濃茶(回し飲み) / 薄茶(各人が飲む)

まつのうち【松の内】 the New Year week; the period between January 1st and 7th; the period from January 1st through 7th; the first seven days of the year. Decorations of pine branches are set up on (both sides of) the entrance to a house during the New Year holidays. 正月の松飾りのある期間. 元旦から7日までの期間をいう. ☆昔は15日までの期間をさした. 正月の松飾りを取り去った頃を「松過ぎ」という. ⇨三が日

まつり【祭り】 a festival; a fete; a celebration. *Matsuri* is essentially native Japanese festival of Shinto origin and observed annually on established dates. ⇨年中行事 ¶祭り囃子 festival music. **日本三大祭** the Three Biggest Festivals in Japan.（祇園祭［京都府］・天神祭［大阪府］・山王祭（または神田祭り）［東京都］）. **京都三大祭** the Three Biggest Festivals in Kyoto.（祇園祭・時代祭・葵祭）. **東北三大祭** the Three Biggest Festivals in Tohoku region.（秋田竿灯・青森ねぶた・仙台七夕）. ⇨付記(1)「日本の祭り」の「三大一覧」(486頁)

【関連語】祭事を行う目的である主要な『祈願』((a) prayer (for)):「家内安全」the safety of one's family; the well-being of one's family; a safe household.「五穀豊穣」a good[rich] harvest (of crops); a bumper crop; an abundant crop.「豊漁」a good [rich] haul; a good catch (of fish).「商売繁盛」prosperity in business; success in one's business.「天下泰平［安泰］」peace of the nation; the peace in the whole country.

まてがい【馬刀貝】〔貝〕a razor clam[shell]. マテガイ科の二枚貝. 春が旬. かみそり貝・イタ貝ともいう. 和え物や塩ゆでなどに用

いる.

まどぎわぞく【窓際族】 dead wood（余剰[むだ]人員）; sidetracked employees（側面におかれた従業員）; surplus workers（過剰人員）; window gazers[window-side workers] who have no real jobs to do in the office (in order to persuade them to retire).（退職勧告のため）事務所では実質上仕事がなく窓越しにいつも外を眺めている勤労者.

まながつお【真魚鰹】〔魚〕a harvest fish; (silver)pomfret. マナガツオ科の海魚. 京漬の味噌漬けまた照り焼きに調理する. ⇨かつお

マナーモード（携帯電話の）the silent[silent-ring] mode (in a cell phone).

まなつび【真夏日】 a tropical day; a day on which the temperature rises[exceeds] above 30℃. 真夏の昼間. 一日の最高気温が摂氏30度以上になった日. ⇔真冬日

まねきねこ【招き猫】 a beckoning cat figure[image]; a small figure[image] of a beckoning cat. It is a porcelain figure [image] of an ornamental cat in a beckoning[an inviting] pose with its left front paw. It is placed on a shelf facing the entrance to a restaurant or shop. It is used as a shopkeeper's charm to attract customers to the restaurant or shop, thus bringing in prosperity[good luck].「左の前足」で人を招いている姿 (an image of a cat with one left front paw in invitation)の陶器製の猫の置物. レストランや商店の店先の棚に置いている. 客を招くという縁起をかつぎ, レストラン[店頭]に飾り, 繁盛[幸運]を祈願する. ☆「右の前足」の招き猫は「金運」(monetary fortune)を願う. また通常は「白色の招き猫」だが「黒色の招き猫」の場合は「厄除け」を願う.

まふゆび【真冬日】 a freezing day; a day on which the temperature stays[drops] below

0℃. 一日の最高気温が摂氏0度未満の日. ⇨真夏日

ままごと【飯事】 playing (at) house; the mimic housekeeping played at by girls, using toy kitchen utensils. 台所の玩具を使いながら少女たちが家事のまねをする遊び.

まむし【蝮】〔爬〕a *mamushi*; a (pit) viper; a copperhead; an asp. クサリヘビ科の毒蛇. ¶**まむし酒** a *mamushi sake*; a *mamushi* liqueur; distilled liquor from a bottle containing a pickled *mamushi*[viper]. ⇨へび

まめ【豆】〔植物〕❶ a bean 楕円形: 大豆・小豆・隠元など「マメ」科植物の総称. ⇨もやし / 五穀. ¶**大豆** a soybean. **そら豆** a broad bean. **小豆** an *adzuki* bean; red bean. **隠元豆** a kidney bean. **豆餅** rice cake pounded with steamed soybeans.
❷ a pea 球形: 豌豆豆・南京豆などの「マメ」. ¶**豌豆豆** a (garden) pea. **南京豆** a peanut; a groundnut. **豆ご飯** rice boiled with green peas.

まめしぼり【豆絞り】 a spotted pattern; a pattern of tiny polka dots. 豆粒ほどの丸い形を一面に絞り染めした布. ¶**豆絞り手ぬぐい** a (hand) towel[㊣ a washcloth] with spotted patterns. **豆絞り浴衣** a *yukata* with spotted patterns. ⇨浴衣

まめたん【豆炭】 an oval[egg-shaped] charcoal briquet(te). ⇨炬燵

まめまき【豆撒き】 the bean-scattering ceremony; the bean-throwing event. This event is observed on the evening of *Setsubun* in falling on February 3 or 4, the day before the first day of spring according to the lunar calendar. People scatter roasted[parched] soybeans inside and outside the home (or at Shinto shrines) to bring in good fortune and drive out evil spirits. It is customary to eat the number of beans equalling one's age to enjoy a year of good health. 節分には「鬼は外, 福は内」と言いながら家の内外に(または神社に)豆を撒く. また一年を健康に過ごすために自分の年の数だけの豆 (the same number of beans as one's age)を食べる習慣がある. ☆「鬼」は病気や自然災害などを擬人化したものである. ⇨節分 / いり豆 / 年男 / 鬼面 / 福は内！鬼は外！

まもりがたな【守り刀】 a sword[dagger] for self-defense; a sword to defend one(self) with. 身の安全を守るために携帯する短刀. 「護身刀」ともいう.

まもりがみ【守り神】 a guardian god[deity]; a tutelary[protecting] god. 身の安全を守る神.「守護神」ともいう.

まもりぶくろ【守り袋】 an amulet case. 守り札を入れる小袋.

まもりふだ【守り札】 a paper charm. ⇨お守り

まやくたんちけん【麻薬探知犬】 drug-sniffing dog; drug detecting dog; a sniffer dog.

まゆだま【繭玉】 a New Year's decoration comprising a bamboo[willow] twig hung with cocoon-shaped rice cakes and good-luck charms, such as a wooden chest for storing gold coins. 竹[柳]の枝などに繭型にまるめた餅や千両箱などの縁起物 (talismans against evils)を吊るした正月の飾り物. ☆元来, 蚕の繭 (silkworm cocoon)の良い生産を願って部屋などに吊るす.

まゆつばもの【眉唾物】a fake (いんちき；虚報)；a fish[fishy] story (ほら話)；a cock-and-bull story (たわいもないでたらめな話)；an unbelievable[incredible] story(信じがたい話). ☆「眉に唾をぬれば狐に騙されない」の俗信に由来.

まよけ【魔除け】an amulet[a charm] (to protect one from evil); a talisman (to ward off evil spirits). 悪事から守る護符.

マリアかんのんぞう【マリア観音像】Maria-Kannon Statue[Image]; the statue[image] combining features of Maria and *Kannon*.

ま

Maria is the mother of Jesus Christ[the (Blessed) Virgin Mary who has the baby Jesus on her breast]. *Kannon* is the Buddhist Deity of Mercy. The statue of *Maria*[the Virgin Mary] was made to look like the *Kannon*[the Deity of Mercy]. When hidden Christians were persecuted during the Tokugawa period, they venerated the *Kannon* disguised as a statue of *Maria* in secret. マリアは「キリストの母」, 観音は「慈悲の神」. マリア像が観音像に似せて(resemble)作られていた. 潜伏キリシタンはキリスト教禁止令 (prohibition of Christianity)で迫害を受けていた徳川幕府時代に「観音像」に偽装させた「マリア像」を密かに崇敬していた.

まりつき【鞠つき】a ball bouncing game. ⇨ 手鞠(手鞠つき)

マリモ【毬藻】〔植物〕a **marimo**; a round green alga; a green ball-shaped moss-weeds (algae); green sponge-like balls of moss-weeds (algae); an aegagropila. A round green *marimo* rises to the surface of the water when the sun shines. シオグサ科の淡水産糸状緑藻.「鮮緑色の球形をなす多数の藻草」. 日が照ると水面に上がる. 英語で moss balls ともいう. ☆ alga(㴑) algae[アルゲ]〔植物〕「藻; 藻類」(seaweed). ¶**特別天然記念物に指定されたマリモ([北海道]阿寒湖)** *marimo*, green ball-shaped moss-weeds, designated as a special natural monument (growing in Lake Akan(ko)). ☆山梨県の山中湖にもある.

まるおび【丸帯】 a formal wide[broad] *obi* [sash] (entirely decorated with a variety of colorful patterns). It is a lavishly decorative *obi* made of a single piece of thick silk cloth, folded in half and sewn. It is worn with a formal *kimono* by women on ceremonial occasions. (全体に多彩な模様を織り込んだ)格式高く幅広い (broad) 飾

り帯. 一枚の絹布地を二つ折りにして縫い合わせた帯. 礼服用の着物の女帯. ☆丸帯 (幅約35cm, 長さ約4m) は振袖や留袖の正装用であるが豪華な帯は花嫁衣装(a bridal costume[*kimono*]) として着用する場合が多い. ⇨振袖(未婚者用) / 留袖(既婚者用)

マルチしょうほう【マルチ商法】 pyramid selling[scheme]; a multilevel marketing system[plan].

マルチにんげん【マルチ人間】 a versatile person (万能の人); a multitalented man [woman] (多才な人).

マルチメディアたいおうじゅうたく【マルチメデイア対応住宅】multimedia compatible house.

まるぼし【丸干し】 fish[vegetables] dried whole. そのままの形で干した魚[野菜]. 〔食品〕**丸干し大根** a *daikon*[radish] dried whole. いわしの丸干し a sardine dried whole.

まるほん【丸本】〔文楽〕a complete text of a bunraku puppet play(*joruri*). 全編を一冊にまとめた浄瑠璃本 [台本].「院本」ともいう. ⇨浄瑠璃

まるまげ【丸髷】 a round[oval] chignon; a hairstyle[hairdo] topped with an elevated oval-shaped, flat chignon on the head. It was formerly worn by married women until the end of the Meiji era. 楕円形の, やや平たい髷の髪型. 昔の既婚女性が結っていた. 江戸時代から明治末期まで流行する.

まわし【回し】〔相撲〕a **mawashi**; a *sumo* wrestler's loincloth; a thick-waisted loincloth worn for *sumo* training and competition. Those of *sekitori*[upper-division wrestlers] are white cotton for training and colored silk for competition. Those of lower division ranks wear dark cotton for both training and competition. 練習や取組で力士が着けるふんどし. 関取の回しは練習用(通称「取り回し」)には白い

木綿製，試合用には多彩な絹製を着ける．幕下以下の力士は練習・試合両用に黒い木綿製を着ける．「締(め)込み」ともいう．⇨化粧回し／土俵入り

まわりどうろう【回り灯籠】 a revolving lantern; a lantern with a revolving inner shade that casts images on the outer shade. 回転するにつれ影絵が回って見える照明器具．「影灯籠」ともいう．

まわりぶたい【回り［廻り］舞台】a revolving [rotating] stage. It is a circular stage that can be revolved[rotated] to permit a second scene to be performed simultaneously with the scene already in progress. It is used for changing scenes rapidly for great dramatic effect on the kabuki stage. すでに進行している場面と次の場面を同時に演じるために回転できる円形の舞台 (platform). 劇的効果をあげるため場面転換を早くする装置 (shifting scenes quickly).

まんが【漫画】(a) *manga*; a cartoon; a comic book;〈風刺漫画〉a caricature;〈4コマ続き漫画〉a comic strip; a strip cartoon;〈米口語〉the comics; the funnies. ⇨アニメ

【漫画カフェ難民】 *manga* café refugee. Without a permanent address, people regularly seek refuge in the Internet and at *manga* cafés. 定住所を持たず，いつもインターネットや漫画喫茶を徘徊する．⇨ネット［ネットカフェ難民］

【漫画喫茶】 a comic book café[coffee shop]; a café with a *manga* [comic book] library. A *manga-kissa* is a combination of a comic book library and a coffee shop where one can get a snack while reading comics. 漫画本と喫茶店の合成語で，そこでは漫画を読みながら軽食 (light meal)がとれる．「マン喫」ともいう．

まんげつ【満月】a full moon. ¶満月の夜(に) (on) the night of the full moon. ⇨月見

まんざい【万歳】 a *manzai* song and dance; a traditional Japanese song and dance to hand-drum accompaniment・performed by a pair of *manzai* traveling entertainers wearing ancient costumes. One entertainer sings cheerful songs of the New Year while the other dance to the accompaniment of his hand-drum during the New Year season. They visit each house wishing families a happy new year in exchange for tips. 古風な(えぼし)姿の2人の芸人による鼓 の伴奏に合わせた歌舞．一人は新年を祝う歌を歌い，もう一人は鼓を打ちながら舞う．心づけを受けた返礼に新年の幸運を願いながら各家庭を訪れる．

まんざい【漫才】 a *manzai* dialog; a comic dialogue (carried on by two comedians as a team); a two-man comedy act; ⊛ a cross talk[crosstalk](掛け合い漫才；当意即妙の応答[やりとり])． *Manzai* is a witty stage dialogue telling humorous stories performed by a pair of comedians who make the audience laugh by their funny verbal exchange[repartee]. 二人の芸人が滑稽な掛け合い話をして観衆 (spectators) を笑わせる演芸．¶漫才師 a comic dialogist; (one of) a comedy duo; a crosstalk comedian．☆「ボケ」(funny man[woman] who plays a fool)と「ツッコミ」(straight man[woman] who berates a funny man).

まんじゅう【饅頭】 a sweetened bean paste bun[dumpling]; a bun[dumpling] stuffed with sweetened bean paste. It is made of[kneaded from] wheat flour (or rice flour) and steamed (or baked) before stuffing[filling] with sweetened *adzuki* red bean paste. A pair of *manju* buns in red and white are often served on auspicious occasions. 小麦粉(または米粉)をこね，中に餡を入れて蒸した(または焼いた)(丸い)パン．紅白一対の饅頭は祝儀用．

まんしゅうこくのけんこく【満州国の建国】

the establishment of the State of Manchuria [Manchukuo]. (1932年)

まんしゅうじへん【満州事変】 the Manchurian Incident (1931年勃発); the military aggression in Manchuria and China.

まんじゅしゃげ【曼珠沙華】 a cluster-amaryllis; a nerine.「彼岸花」の異称. ⇨彼岸花

まんちょう【満潮】 (a) high tide; (a) flood [full] tide. ⇦干潮. ¶満潮時になれば厳島神社は海に浮かんでいるよう見える. At the high tide Miyajima Shrine appears to be floating on the water.

まんどう【万灯】 rows of votive lanterns (used for a Buddhist memorial service). Most lanterns are often hung from a pole in front of a Buddhist statue. (法会で用いる)献灯の列. 仏像の前の竿から吊るされる場合が多い.「まんとう」ともいう.

まんどころ【政所】 ❶ the Administrative Board[office] of the Kamakura shogunate (which dealt with state and financial matters). 鎌倉幕府の政治機関.
❷ a housekeeping office of the Imperial Family (which managed the households in ancient Japan). 皇族・貴人の家政をつかさどった所.
❸ Kampaku's[Sessho's] legal[lawful] wife.「北の政所」の略. 摂政・関白の正妻の尊称. ⇨関白 / 摂政

まんびき【万引】 shoplifting. ¶万引犯(常習犯) a (habitual) shoplifter.

まんぼう【翻車魚】〔魚〕 a sunfish; an ocean sunfish; a headfish; a molebut; a mola. マンボウ科の海産大形硬骨魚. 柔らかい白身は淡白な味.

まんぽけい【万歩計】 a pedometer.「歩数計」(step counter) ともいう. ☆「万歩計」は山佐時計計器株式会社 (YAMASA) の登録商標 (trademark) である.

まんようしゅう【万葉集】 the *Man'yoshu*; the Anthology of Myriad[Ten Thousand] Leaves. The *Man'yoshu* is the oldest extant anthology of Japanese verse[*waka* poem] compiled by Otomo no Yakamochi. It comprises 20 volumes containing some 4,500 poems written by people from various classes at the end of the Nara period. 主として大伴家持の編集による日本最古の現存する歌集. 奈良時代末期(759年)の20巻の編集で, 短歌や長歌など合わせて約4,500首を収録する.

み

み【巳】 the Snake[Serpent], one[the sixth] of the 12 animals of the Chinese zodiac. 十二支の第六. ⇨十二支. ¶巳の方 the direction of the Snake[south-southeast]. 方角の名. 南南東. 巳の刻 the Hour of the Snake [9-11 a.m.] 午前10時(または9-11時頃). 巳年 the Year of the Snake. 巳年生まれ (be) born in the Year of Snake[Serpent].

みあい【見合い】 a marriage interview (arranged by a matchmaker between two potential marriage partners). *Miai* is the first meeting of a single man and woman who are seeking marriage partners through introduction of a go-between in order to get to know each other. 結婚相手を探している独身男女が, 第三者を仲介として相互に知りあうためにはじめて会うこと. ¶見合い写真 an introductory picture[photo] for an arranged marriage (given to one's prospective bride [bridegroom]) (見合い用の自己紹介の写真). 見合いをする meet each other[be formally introduced] with a view to marriage.

【見合結婚】 (an) arranged marriage. Marriage is arranged by matchmaking through a go-between and parents, when the two are attracted each other and decided to marry. 仲人と両親による縁結びで両者が相互に気に入り結婚すること. ⇔恋愛結婚 (love marriage)

みうちびいき【身内びいき】nepotism.

みえ【見得】〔歌舞伎〕(strike) an exaggerated pose of a kabuki actor (which makes his appearance even more impressive) (誇示する姿勢); a flamboyant posture(派手な仕草); a swaggering gesture(威張った姿勢). At the climactic moment, an actor turns towards the audience and remains motionless and strikes an exaggerated pose (*mie*) for a moment to express his emotions vividly. This pose is often emphasized by the sound of clappers. Such a pose is one of the best examples of the stylized beauty of the kabuki play. 歌舞伎役者が見かけをさらに強く印象付けるために行う. 歌舞伎の舞台が最高潮に達したとき, 生き生きした感情を表現するために, 役者が観客に向かってしばらくの間動きを止める. 拍子木の音でさらに強調される. このような見得は歌舞伎の見事な持ち味のひとつである. ⇨荒事 / 屋号

みかづき【三日月】 a new moon(新月); a crescent moon(弦月); a horned[sickle] moon(角状[鎌型]の月). ☆陰暦の三日ごろに出る細い月.

みかど【帝・御門】 a ***mikado***; an emperor (of Japan). A *mikado* is the honorable title used for the emperor of Japan in ancient times. (古代日本の)天皇の尊称. ☆現在は廃止され, 「天皇陛下」を使用する.

みかん【蜜柑】〔植物〕a mandarin (orange); a tangerine (orange); (英) a *satsuma* (orange). ミカン科の常緑樹. ¶**みかんの皮** an orange peel; the rind of an orange. **みかん1房** a segment of a tangerine. **みかん畑** a tangerine orchard. **ミカンで有名な有田**(和歌山県) Arida noted for its tasty mandarin (orange).

みくじ【神籤】 ⇨お神籤

みくだりはん【三行半】 a notice[letter] of divorce; a note declaring one's separation from one's spouse; a note announcing that one wants a divorce. 配偶者から離別を告げる離縁状. ☆昔の離縁状は三行半に書く習慣があったことに由来する.

みくにまつり【三国祭】 the Float-Parade Festival at Mikuni Town. (5月). ⇨付記(1)「日本の祭り」

みけねこ【三毛猫】 a tortoiseshell cat; (米) a calico cat. ⇨ねこ

みこ【巫女・神子】a *miko*; a shrine maiden; a virgin consecrated to a god[deity]. A *miko* is a (unmarried) female attendant served the god of the shrine by offering prayers. She wears a white robe[surplice] (*chihaya*) and a long red pleated skirt-like trousers (*hibakama*). She performs a sacred Shinto dance (*kagura*) to bless worshippers at the shrine. Some shrine maidens sell written oracles and good-luck charms at the shrine. 祈祷をあげながら神社の神に仕える(未婚の)女性. 「白衣」と「緋袴」を着て, 神社で参詣者を祝福するため, 「千早」を羽織って「神楽」を舞う. 巫女によっては神社で御神籤やお守りなどを売る. ⇨市子 /いたこ

みこし【神輿・御輿】 a *mikoshi*; a portable shrine; a sacred palanquin used as a divine vehicle to transport the spirit of a deity. A *mikoshi* bears the emblem of a deity[often a mirror] enshrined in it temporarily during the festival. It is often made of black lacquered wood with gilted decorations and has a carving of a phoenix[sometimes an artificial flower] affixed to the roof. It usually rests on two or four long poles for carrying on the shoulders of *mikoshi* bearers. It is taken out during festivals and paraded through the city streets by the local people[parishioners] wearing *happi* coats and headbands. Whenever the *mikoshi* is carried, the god's purifying power is believed to permeate the area, warding off evil spirits and spreading blessings of gods. 可動型の神社. 神霊を運ぶ神の乗り物としての聖なる輿. その中には祭りが行われている間神の依代[通常は鏡]が一時的に置かれている. 神輿は金箔の装飾をほどこした黒の漆塗りの木材から作られ, 屋根には鳳凰(時には造花)の彫刻がある. 肩に担ぐための2本または4本の梶棒の上に置かれている. 神輿は祭礼時に法被と鉢巻をしめた地元住民[氏子]に担ぎ出される. 御輿が運ばれる時はいつでも神の清めの力がその地域に浸透し, 悪霊を追い払い, 神の恵みが与えられていると信じられている. ☆「み」は接頭語.「こし」(輿)は palanquin.「神輿」は熱田神宮のように「しんよ」と読む神社もある. ☆「わっしょい」は「和し(て)背負え」(みんな仲良く神輿を背負え)の意.

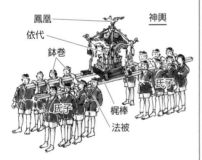

鳳凰　神輿　依代　鉢巻　氏子　氏子　梶棒　法被

みごろ【身頃】 the front[back] part of a *kimono*. 着物の前後をおおう部分. ☆襟・袖・おくみなどを除く. ⇨前身頃 / 後身頃

みこんのはは【未婚の母】 an unwed[unmarried] mother; a single mother.

みさき【岬】 a cape; a promontory; a point (of land). ¶潮岬(和歌山県) Cape Shiono

(misaki). ⇨〜崎

みしまやき【三島焼】 the Mishima ceramic ware (produced in Shizuoka Prefecture).

みす【御簾】 a bamboo blind[screen].「簾」の敬称. ⇨簾

みずあげ【水揚(げ)】〔華道〕treatment for the preservation of cut flowers. There are such ways as burning the ends of cut flowers and cutting the stems in water, to give flowers longer life. 切り花を保存する処置. 生けた花が水を吸い上げるように, 切り花の根を焼き, 水きりをすること. ⇨水切り

みずあめ【水飴】 starch syrup; thick glutinous malt-sugar. でんぷんから作る, 粘り気のある飴.

みずいり【水入り】〔相撲〕a break to let *sumo* wrestlers rest during a prolonged bout; an interrupted *sumo* match. When a *sumo* match is interrupted during a prolonged *sumo* bout, the *sumo* wrestlers take a break before the match resumes. After a short break, they return to the exact[same] position they left off in. The match resumes soon after the referee pats the wrestlers on the belt. 長引く相撲の取組に対する休止. 中断した相撲試合. 相撲の取組が長く勝負がつかないときは, その途中一時引き分けて休止する. その後以前の取組とちょうど同じ位置に戻る. 行司が力士の回しをぱっと打つとすぐに試合が再開する.

みずうみ【湖】a lake. ¶湖の別荘 a villa by the lake[on the lakeside]. ⇨湖

みずおけ【水桶】〈桶〉 a bucket; a (water) pail;〈水槽〉a water tank; a cistern.

みずきり【水切り】〔華道〕cutting the stem [stalk] of a flower in water (to keep it fresh [prolong its life]). 水揚げをよくするために水中で花の茎を切ること. ⇨水揚げ

みずぎわたいさく【水際対策】 a measure to prevent the virus (of new influenza strains) from entering the country[Japan]; a measure to prevent infections by blocking the virus at the country's borders. The government monitors the nation's ports of entry[airports and ports] to prevent a domestic outbreak of the new swine influenza from entering the country [Japan].

みずさし【水指・水差】〔茶道〕a water receptacle (used in a tea ceremony). The container is used to hold water for replenishing the teakettle and for rinsing the tea bowls. (茶道用に)水を入れておく器. 茶釜に補充したり, 茶碗をゆすいだりするために, 水を保管する器.

みずたき【水炊き】boiled chicken and vegetables; chicken and vegetables boiled in a pot of unseasoned hot water at the table. *Mizutaki* is one-pot dish of chunks of chicken boiled plain in broth with vegetables and *tofu*[bean curd]. It is served in a small bowl and eaten by dipping in a citrous-flavored sauce[bitter-orange juice] with condiments. 鶏肉と野菜を味つけしない湯で煮る鍋物. 野菜や豆腐などを出し汁に入れてさっぱりと煮る鍋料理. 小鉢に盛りつけ, 薬味入りのポン酢につけて食べる.

みずちゃや【水茶屋】a tea stall in the Edo period. 江戸時代の茶を飲ませる路上茶屋[休憩所].

みずな【水菜】〔植物〕(a) potherb mustard. 「京菜」ともいう.

みずばしょう【水芭蕉】〔植物〕(a) *mizubasho*; a skunk cabbage (in Oze-ga-hara Marshy Moor). サトイモ科の多年草.

みずひき【水引】a *mizuhiki* (decoration); a decorative paper cord[string]; a gift-tying paper string; a paper string for tying a gift; 〈結ぶひも〉a paper string for binding up the wrapper of a present (for formal occasions); 〈結んだひも〉a paper string tied in a ceremonial knot around the wrapper of a gift (for official occasions). The twisted paper string of *gold and silver* for the wrapper of a gift[gift-wrapping] is used for auspicious occasions (such as weddings), one of *black and white* for mourning occasions (such as funerals) and one of *red and white* for ordinary courtesy gifts. 進物に結ぶ紙製の紐 (a gift-binding string). 慶事(結婚式など)には「金銀」, 弔事(葬儀など)には「黒白」. 通常の儀礼的な進物には「紅白」の水引を用いる. ⇨熨斗 / 結び切り / 花結び

みずほのくに【瑞穂の国】the land of rice; the Land of the Verdant Rice Plants. (みずみずしい稲穂の国); the Land Blessed with Rice Plants; Japan. ☆「日本」の美称.

みずもち【水餅】rice cake soaked[preserved] in water. 水に浸して保存する餅.

みずもの【水物】the dessert that comes after the meal; the dessert served at the end of the traditional Japanese meal. 食後のデザート. 日本料理の最後に出されるデザート. ☆「果物」が主流である. 茶会に出される「和菓子」と区別するために用いる.

みずや【水屋】❶〔茶道〕a pantry[washing place] adjoining to the tearoom (where tea utensils are kept and prepared for a tea ceremony). 茶室のとなりなどにあり, 茶の湯用の茶道具を置く, または用意する所. ❷〈寺社での洗い場〉a washstand for worshippers; a holy cistern located at a shrine or temple where worshippers wash their hands. 参詣者が手を洗うために設けられた寺社にある清めの水槽[洗い台]. 「御手洗」ともいう. ⇨御手洗 ❸〈水屋箪笥〉a kitchen cabinet[cupboard] for tea-things. 「茶箪笥」ともいう.

みずようかん【水羊羹】soft, watery *adzuki*-bean jelly (mixed with agar-agar and sugar). (寒天と砂糖を加えて作った)柔らかくて水分の多い羊羹. ⇨羊羹

み

みそ【味噌】 ***miso***; soybean paste; fermented soybean paste. *Miso* is made by fermenting a mixture of soybeans, malted rice and salt. 大豆に米麹と塩を混ぜて発酵させて作る（調味料）. ☆「カニの味噌」は crab butter.
¶赤味噌 dark *miso*. 白味噌 white *miso*. 甘味噌 lightly salted *miso*. 辛味噌 heavily salted *miso*. 米みそ（信州みそ） *miso* based on rice and soybean. 麦みそ *miso* based on barley. 豆みそ *miso* based on soybean.
〔料理〕味噌和え a salad dressed *miso* and vinegar; a food[fish or vegetables] prepared with *miso* and vinegar（味噌と酢を混ぜたサラダ[食品（魚・野菜）]）. 味噌餡 white sweet bean paste mixed[prepared] with *miso*（味噌を混ぜた餡）. 味噌おでん Japanese hotchpotch cooked in *miso*-flavored sauce（味噌味のソースで調理したおでん）. 味噌粥 rice gruel cooked with *miso*（味噌で調理した粥）. 味噌麹 the mold used to ferment *miso* from rice, barley and soybeans.（米, 大麦, 大豆から味噌を発酵させるために用いるかび）. 味噌煮 food cooked in *miso*（味噌で調理する食品）. ⇨さばの味噌煮

【味噌汁】 ***miso*** soup; soybean paste soup. It is made of *miso*[bean-paste] and various other ingredients, which vary according to the family or region.（いろんな具材を味噌で味付けした汁. 具材は家庭や地域によって異なる）. ¶豆腐とワカメの味噌汁 *miso* soup containing *tofu*[bean curd] and *wakame* seaweed. ⇨汁物

【味噌漬け】 ***miso*** pickles. ¶味噌漬けの魚 fish preserved in *miso*; fish preserved using *miso*. 味噌漬けの野菜 vegetables pickled in *miso*; vegetables pickled using *miso*.

みそか【晦日・三十日】 the last day of the month[EOM; e.o.m.(end of month)]. 月の三十日. 月の最終日. ⇨大晦日. ¶晦日[三十日]そば buckwheat noodles eaten on the last day of the month or year.

【晦日市】 the annual year-end fair (held in the precincts of shrines[temples]). Various types of shuttlecocks and battledores and other New Year's decorations are sold at the open-air fair around the end of December. 寺社の境内で開く年末恒例の市場. 12月中頃には羽子板や門松などが露店市で売られる.

みそぎ【禊】 ***misogi***; (ritual) ablution; a (Shinto) purification ceremony; a purification bath. *Misogi* is a ritual[rite] of cleansing one's mind and body by sprinkling water (of the river or sea). 清めの儀式.（川や海の）水をあびて心身を清める儀式. ⇨浄め. ☆ ablution「沐浴（身体を洗い清めること）」(wash away[remove] both physical and spiritual defilement). ablutions（複数形）「宗教儀式のために身体[顔や手]を洗い清めること」(wash one's body or part of it in a religious rite).

みそさざい【鷦鷯】〔鳥〕a wren; a jenny wren（雌）. ミソサザイ科の小鳥. 美しい鳴き声.

みそのだな【御園棚】〔茶道〕a tea table (used for a garden tea ceremony). It is often placed under a big umbrella set up on the ground. 茶庭に用いる茶卓. 地面に立てた大きな傘の下に置かれている. ⇨野点

みぞれ【霙】sleet. ¶霙の降る日 a sleety day.

みだいどころ【御台所】the wife of a shogun [minister]. 将軍・大臣などの妻の敬称.「御台盤所」の略.

みたましろ【御霊代】 ⇨ 神体

みたまや【御霊屋】 ⇨ 霊廟

みたらし【御手洗】 a holy cistern[place to wash] located at the entrance to a shrine[temple]. Worshippers wash their hands and rinse their mouth with water at a holy cistern before praying to god or Buddha. 寺社の入り口にある清めの水槽[洗い場]. 参詣者は神または仏に祈祷する前に水で手

を洗い，口をすすぐ．⇨水屋❷

みたらしだんご【御手洗団子】 rice-flour dumplings glazed[barbecued] with a soy-and-sugar on sticks[bamboo skewers]. Rice-flour dumplings on sticks[bamboo skewers] are roasted over a charcoal fire after dipping in *shoyu*[soy sauce] and sugar. 米粉で作った団子を棒[竹串]にさし，炭火の上において醤油と砂糖でつけ焼きにする．

みつ【褌】〔相撲〕 a *sumo* wrestler's belt. 力士の回し．⇨前褌／たて褌

みっかぼうず【三日坊主】 a person who quickly gives up; a quitter.

みっきょう【密教】 esoteric Buddhism. ☆仏教の一流派．大日如来の説いた教法．加持・祈祷を重視する．日本では真言宗および台密（天台宗の密教）がある．¶密教美術 esoteric Buddhist art; an art featuring esoteric Buddhism.

ミッドウェーかいせん【ミッドウェー海戦】 the Battle of Midway.（1942年）

みつどもえ【三つ巴】❶ three comma-shaped figures in a circle; three comma-shaped figures that form a circle. 三つの巴（水が渦を巻いて外のほうへ回ろうとする紋様）が輪になったもの．
❷〔紋所の名〕a crest composed of three comma-shaped figures in a circle.

みつどもえのあらそい【三つ巴の争い】〔相撲〕 a three-way battle[three-sided fight, triangular struggle] of *sumo* wrestlers. 相撲の三力士が相互に対戦すること．☆同じような力の三者が二人ずつ争うこと．

みつば【三葉】〔植物〕 *mitsuba*; a Japanese honewort; a stone parsley; a green herb; a wild chervil. It is used in cooking for its aroma. セリ科の多年草．「三葉芹」ともいう．料理の香料に用いる．☆trefoil は「葉が3枚のマメ科のシロツメクサ」のこと．

みつばち【蜜蜂】〔虫〕 a bee; a honey bee.

ミツバチ科の昆虫．一匹の雌ばち（女王蜂：queen bee）を中心に雄ばちと多数の働きばち（worker bee）が集団で生活しながら蜜（honey）を集める．¶蜜蜂の巣 (a) honeycomb; (a) beehive(巣箱)．⇨はち

みつまめ【蜜豆】 *mitsumame*; a sweet snack of agar-agar[*kanten*] cubes in sugar syrup, mixed with boiled beans and fruit. *Mitsumame* is made up of sweet boiled beans and pieces of seasonal fruit, small cubes of gelatin jelly[*kanten*] cubes in sugar syrup and other delicacies with molasses poured over the top. Sometimes a scoop of *adzuki*-bean paste is placed on top. ゆでたえんどう豆と季節の果物，それに賽の目に切った寒天をまぜて糖蜜をかけた食品．時にはひとすくいの餡が上部にのる．⇨餡(餡蜜)

みとめいん【認印】 a signet; an informal [unofficial] personal seal; an unregistered private seal. It is used for such daily informal affairs as mails and packages. 非公式[非登録]の印章．郵便物や小荷物など日常用の略式印章．⇨印鑑 ⇔実印

みどりのおばさん【緑のおばさん】 a traffic patrolwoman; a (school) crossing warden [guard]（交通監視員）；ⓂⒺ a lollipop woman(横断歩道の交通係)．☆「学校交通整理員」の俗称．初期のころ，緑の制服を着用していたことからの名称．☆ lollipop 「横断歩道にある「止まれ」の標識，旗」．

みどりのひ【みどりの日】 Greenery Day.（May 4）. This national holiday was established in 2007 as a day for nature appreciation. This day is celebrated to commune with nature, to be thankful for blessings of nature and to foster an abundant spirit of nature. It was originally designated in 1989 and held annually on April 29, but was moved to May 4. 2007年自然に親しむ日として制定された．自然

に親しみ，その恩恵に感謝し，豊かな心をはぐくむために祝う．元来1989年に制定され4月29日であったが現在は5月4日に移動した．

みどりのまどぐち【緑の窓口】 JR office for the sale of long-distance and express [Shinkansen] train tickets.

みなと【港】 a port（陸地を含む）; a harbor [⊛ harbour].¶港町横浜 the port town of Yokohama. 米の積み出しをする港町（酒田市）a port town for transshipping rice.

みなみまちぶぎょう【南町奉行】a Minami-machi Commissioner[Magistrate] (who has his office in the southern part of Edo). ⇨奉行.¶南町奉行所 the Minamimachi Commissioner's Office. ⇨北町奉行所

みならい【見習い】〈事〉apprenticeship; probation.〈人〉an apprentice（見習い者: 徒弟）; a trainee（訓練生）; a probationer（仮採用者）; a novice（初心者）.¶芸者見習い a *geisha* apprentice. ⇨半玉

みの【蓑】 a straw rain-cape; a sedge[straw] raincoat covering almost the whole body. It is tied at the waist and draped over the lower section. 菅・藁などで編んでつくったマントの雨具で，ほぼ全身を覆う．腰に結び，下部までまとう．⇨菅.¶蓑笠 a straw rain-cape[raincoat] and a sedge-hat.

みのまつり【美濃まつり】the Mino Festival. (4月). ⇨付記(1)「日本の祭り」

みのむし【蓑虫】〔虫〕a bagworm; a basket worm.「ミノガ」の幼虫.

みふねまつり【三船祭】 the Boat Festival on the Oi River. (5月). ⇨付記(1)「日本の祭り」

みみず【蚯蚓】〔虫〕an earthworm; a worm; an angleworm（釣り用）.

みみずく【木菟】〔鳥〕an eared owl; a horned owl. フクロウ科の猛禽. ⇨ふくろう

みや【宮】 ❶〈神社〉a (Shinto) shrine;〈神棚〉a miniature shrine.¶宮大工 a shrine carpenter; a carpenter who makes or

repairs shrines. 宮入り shrine entering; going to worship at the main shrine. ⇨宮参り

❷〈皇族〉an Imperial prince[princess]; a prince[princess] of noble blood. ☆独立して一家を構えた皇族・親王家の尊称.¶三笠宮 Prince Mikasa.

❸〈皇居・御所〉 an Imperial Palace; an Imperial Court.¶宮人 a courtier. 宮仕え serving at the Imperial Court.

みやじまかんげんさい【宮島管弦祭】 the Music Festival of Itsukushima Shrine. (7月). ⇨付記(1)「日本の祭り」

みやつとうろうながし【宮津燈籠流し】 the Lantern-floating Festival at Miyatsu Bay. (8月). ⇨付記(1)「日本の祭り」

みやまいり【宮参り】 ❶〈神社への参詣〉a visit to a Shinto shrine. ⇨参詣 / 七五三.¶伊勢神宮に宮参りする pay a visit to Ise Grand Shrine.

❷〈赤子の宮参り〉a newborn baby's [child's] first visit to a Shinto shrine. Japanese parents take their newborn baby to a Shinto shrine to pray for his/ her good health and growth. The ceremony of purification and blessing is held for a boy on the thirty-second day[for a girl usually on the thirty-third day] after birth. The day for this rite varies according to districts. 日本の親は子供の健やかな成長を祈願して神社に参拝する．出産後男児は32日目［女児は33日目］に清めと祝福の儀式が行われる．日取りは地方(regions)によって異なる．

みょうおう【明王】a Buddhist tutelary deity conquering all evils and leading people to salvation. He is represented with a fierce expression and various kinds of weapons in his hand. He has a halo of flames behind his head. 諸悪を征し，衆生を導く仏教の守護神．獰猛な形相をし，手には多様な武器を持つ．頭の背後には炎の光輪がある．

☆不動明王・愛染明王などがいる.

みょうが【茗荷】〔植物〕*myoga* (ginger); a Japanese ginger;〔食品〕 Japanese ginger. ショウガ科の多年草. 若穂や若芽は薬味, 酢の物, 天ぷら, カツオのたたきなどに用いる. ¶茗荷たけ stalk of young *mioga* ginger.

みょうじん【明神】 a great god; a miracle-working god.「神」の尊称. 奇跡をよぶ神. ⇨大明神

みらいとし【未来都市】 the futuristic city. ¶**未来都市の中のレトロな商店街** a retrospective shopping mall in the futuristic city.(お台場など).

みりん【味醂】 *mirin*; sweetened *sake* (used for seasoning dishes). *Mirin* is sweet *sake* made from glutinous rice, *shochu*[distilled spirits] and yeast. It is used for giving flavor and a sweet taste to Japanese dishes.(調味料用の)甘い酒. 蒸したもち米, 焼酎, 麹などを混ぜて醸造し, 甘くした酒. 料理に風味や甘味 (sweet seasoning)をつけるのに用いる. ☆アルコールはほとんどない(15% 未満). 欧米では mirin の用語を sweet sherry または sugar syrup で代用することもある. ⇨焼酎

〔食品〕味醂干し dried fish seasoned with *mirin*, *shoyu* and sugar.(魚を味醂, 醤油, 砂糖などを混ぜた液に浸してから干[乾燥]したもの). ⇨いわしの味醂干し

みるがい【海松貝・水松貝】〔貝〕 a gaper; a trough shell; a surf[king] clam; a horse clam. バカガイ科の二枚貝. 別名「みるくい」.

みんえいか【民営化】 privatization; denationalization. ⇦ nationalization (国営化)

みんげい【民芸】 folk art; folkcraft(s); folk handicraft(s). ¶**民芸館** a folkcraft museum. **民芸品** a folk piece; an article [object] of folk handicraft. **民芸調の家具** folkish furniture; a folkish piece of furniture.

みんしゅく【民宿】 *minshuku*; a private house[lodging] providing rooms and meals (to transient guests[tourists] at a reasonable price); a Japanese-style tourist home[guesthouse]; 圏 a B & B[Bed & Breakfast]. 短期滞在者に低額で部屋と食事を提供する個人宿泊施設.

みんぞく【民族】 a race; an ethnic group. ¶**アイヌ民族** the Ainu race. ⇨アイヌ. **民族衣装** native costume[dress]; (a) national costume. **民族料理** an ethnic dish[meal, food]. **民族音楽** an ethnic music.

みんぞく【民俗】 folkways; folk customs; ethnic customs. ¶**民俗音楽** folk music. **民俗舞踊** folk dancing; a folk dance. **民俗芸能** folk art[entertainment]. **民俗博物館** folklore museum. **民俗文化財** treasure of popular[tribal] culture; ethnocultural asset. **民俗村** folklore village. ☆飛騨民俗村 Hida open-air Folklore Museum. **民俗文化資料** folk cultural properties[assets]. ⇨文化財

みんみんぜみ【ミンミン蝉】〔虫〕 a robust cicada. セミ科の昆虫. ⇨せみ

みんよう【民謡】 a folk ballad; a folk song (peculiar[unique] to a locality); a folk song (of unknown origin handed down by oral tradition). A folk song is often sung to the accompaniment of *shamisen* and drums.(民衆の中から生まれ伝えられた)民衆の歌謡[郷土民謡].(口頭伝承により起源不明の)民衆の歌謡. 三味線と太鼓の伴奏で歌うことが多い. ¶**民謡「佐渡おけさ」**(佐渡島) folk song and dance called "Sado-Okeasa". **盆踊の民謡** a folk song sung during the Bon Festival dance. **民謡酒場** drinking establishment where customers sing their favorite folk songs.

みんわ【民話】 a folktale; a folk story; a folklore(民俗伝承). ¶**民話劇** folk play [theater]; a play based on a folktale.

み

む

むえんぼち【無縁墓地】 a cemetery for those who have no living relatives; a graveyard for those who left no relatives behind. 弔う縁者のない死者の墓地.

むえんぼとけ【無縁仏】 a person who died leaving no one to tend[take care of] his/her grave. 身元不明の死者.

むかえがね【迎え鐘】 a bell for calling back the dead (suffering in hell). お盆に(地獄で苦しむ)精霊を迎えるために打つ鐘. 圏京都の六道珍皇寺は有名.

むかえざけ【迎え酒】 (have) another drink (in the morning) to cure a hangover. 二日酔いを治すために酒を飲むこと. またその酒. ☆ (have) the hair of the dog (that bit one)の慣用句がある.〈かみついた狂犬の毛をとってつけると傷が治る〉という俗信が由来. したがって He had a hair of the dog (that bit him) as he had a hangover. (二日酔いで迎え酒をやった)といえる.

むかえび【迎え火】 a welcoming bonfire for the returning souls of the dead; a bonfire for welcoming the spirits of the dead (on July 13 or August 13). *Mukae-bi* is the bonfire to welcome back the ancestral spirits safely to this world[their old homes] from the other world[heaven]. A fire is lit to illuminate the way at the gate of a house on the evening of the first day of the Bon Festival. 盂蘭盆の初日[7月13日または8月13日]の夕方, 祖先の霊[精霊](the spirits [souls] of the ancestors)を冥土から現世に迎えるために門前でたく火. ⇨送り火

むかえぼん【迎え盆】 the first day of the Bon Festival when departed souls come back home; the first day of the Bon Festival when people welcome the returning ancestral spirits back home to this world. 祖先の霊を迎えるお盆の初日. ⇨送り盆

むかえみず【迎え水】 sacred water of the Bon Festival. It is offered to welcome the returning ancestral spirits back home safely during the Bon Festival. (祖先の霊を迎えるために捧げる)お盆の清い水.

むかで【百足】〔虫〕 a centipede.¶**百足競争** a centipede's race (between teams of runners with their legs linked together).

むぎ【麦】〔植物〕 barley(大麦); wheat (小麦); oats（燕麦）; rye(ライ麦). イネ科の麦の総称. ⇨五穀. ¶**小麦粉** wheat flour. 麦 麹. malted barely. ⇨麹
〔食品〕**麦焼酎** spirits distilled from barley. **麦茶** a roasted barley tea; a tea made by boiling roasted[parched] barley in water; a tea boiled with roasted[parched] barley. ⇨茶. **麦とろ** grated yam over barley rice; (a bowl of) boiled mixture of rice and barley topped with grated yam. **麦味噌** *miso*[bean paste] with malt; malted barley *miso*. **麦飯** rice cooked[boiled] with barley.

むきみ【剥き身】 stripped[shelled] shellfish: ㋶ shucked shellfish. 殻から取り出した貝の肉. ¶**カキ[ハマグリ]の剥き身** shucked oysters[clams]. ⇨かい/こうかくるい

むくどり【椋鳥】〔鳥〕 a starling; a gray starling. ムクドリ科の小鳥.

むけいぶんかいさん【無形文化遺産】 intangible cultural heritage. ⇨ユネスコ無形文化遺産

むけいぶんかざい【無形文化財】 intangible cultural assets[properties]. ⇨文化財

むこうづけ【向こう付け】 side dishes served [placed] on the opposite[far] side of the main dishes (of rice and soup) from the diner (in the traditional Japanese meal). It is often a dish of *sashimi*[raw sliced fish] or vinegared vegetables arranged in a small ceramic bowl, placed on the diner's individual meal tray. (日本料理で)食事を

する人から主食(飯物と汁物)膳の向こう側
に出される[置く]料理．小鉢に刺身・酢の
物などが配され，各自の食膳盆に盛りつけ
てある．

むし【虫】〔動物〕an insect(昆虫)；a bug(吸
血虫)；a worm(這い虫)；a moth (衣類に
つく虫)．

むしもの【蒸し物】steamed foods; a steamed
dish; foods[vegetables or fish] cooked in
steam and served hot. ⇨茶碗蒸し / 赤飯
〔食品〕蒸しパン steamed bread[bun]. 蒸し羊
羹 steamed (sweetened) *adzuki*-bean paste
[jelly]. ⇨羊羹

むしゃにんぎょう【武者人形】 a Japanese
warrior doll. *Samurai* warrior dolls are
dressed in a suit of armor and helmet
representing feudal generals and other
historic figures. They are displayed on a
tiered stand on the Boys' Festival in May,
praying for the healthy growth of children.
大将や歴史上の人物像を表す鎧・兜一式を
身につけた武者姿の人形．子供の健やかな
成長を願って，五月五日の端午の節句に雛
段に飾る．⇨五月人形

むしゃのこうじせんけ【武者小路千家】 the
Mushanokoji Senke school of the tea ceremony.「三千家」の茶道流派の一つ．⇨千家

むしろ【筵】 a straw[rush] mat (roughly
woven); straw[rush] matting. わらを編んで
つくった敷物．

むすびきり【結び切り】 a square knot[英
reef knot] tied tightly[firmly] in a bow (used
for happy occasions and for wedding gifts).
(水引などを)蝶型に硬く締めたこま結び．
慶事や婚礼の贈り物などに用いる．☆紐の
端を引いてもほどけない．結婚は繰り返す
ものではない (One marries only once.). ⇨
花結び / 水引

むすびのいちばん【結びの一番】〔相撲〕 the
final[last] bout of the day. 当日の最後の取
組．

むちうちしょう【むち打ち症】 (get) a whip-
lash injury[syndrome].

むつ【鯥】〔魚〕a Japanese bluefish. ムツ科の
深海魚．脂ののった白身は高級魚．刺身や
ちり鍋に調理する．

むつごろう【鯥五郎】〔魚〕 a mudskipper; a
mudspringer; a pond skipper. ハゼ科に属
する魚．☆有明海(日本最大の干潟)と八代
海のみに生息する．⇨干潟

むてんかしょくひん【無添加食品】 additive-
free foods; food without additives.

むねあげしき【棟上げ式】 ☆上棟式

むら【村】 a village; a hamlet. ¶村興し(計
画) village revitalization (project). 妙高村
Myoko Village. 清里村 Kiyosato Village.

むらさき【紫】 *shoyu*[soy sauce].「しょうゆ」
のこと．すし屋の用語．⇨符丁

むらさきいがい【紫貽貝】〔貝〕a mussel. 食用
の海産二枚貝．別称「からすがい」．⇨から
すがい

むらめ【紫芽】 young buds of red perilla. 赤
じその芽．白身魚の刺身のツマに使う．

むりしんじゅう【無理心中】 murder-suicide;
forcing one to join a person in suicide. ¶
一家無理心中 a family murder-suicide;
joining a family in suicide.

め

めいじいしん【明治維新】the Meiji Restoration; Restoration of Imperial Rule. Japan's
transformation from an isolated nation into
a modern world power. 江戸幕府が倒れ，
天皇中心とする統一国家体制が成立．鎖国
時代から現代世界の強大国へと移行する日
本の変貌のこと．

めいしゅ【銘酒】high-quality *sake* marketed
under a special name; *sake* of a superior
brand. 有名な銘柄の酒．☆「名酒」(有名な
良質の酒)は famous, top-quality *sake*.

めいしょ【名所】 a famous place; a spot

[place] of scenic interest; sights to see. ¶
名所旧跡 scenic spots[places] of historic interest (in Nara); spots[places] of natural beauty and historical interest (in Kyoto). 名所案内 a guide (book) to famous sights and attractions (of Kyoto).

めいとう【名刀】 a famous Japanese sword; an excellent blade. 名高い刀工が作った刀. ¶正宗の名刀 the noted[celebrated] Masamune sword.

めいとう【銘刀】 a fine sword bearing the name of the swordsmith; a fine Japanese sword with the name of the swordsmith inscribed on it. 名高い刀工の名前が刻んである刀.

メイドカフェ a maid café. It is a kind of cosplay restaurant, originated in Akihabara district (in Tokyo). In the maid café the teenage girls dressed as elegant maids treat the customers as masters and mistresses in a private home rather than merely as café customers. 一種のコスプレ飲食店で, 秋葉原が発祥の地. そこに入れば可愛いメイド服で着飾った十代の少女が, 来店者に対して, 喫茶店というよりは個人の家庭における殿方や奥方に対するように接客する.「メイド喫茶」ともいう.

メイドきっさ【メイド喫茶】 ⇨メイドカフェ

めいにち【命日】 a death anniversary; the anniversary of somebody's death; the day of a person's death. ⇨祥月命日. ¶父の命日 the anniversary of my father's death.

めいわくでんわ【迷惑電話】 a nuisance[an annoying] telephone call（迷惑千万な電話）; a prank call（いたずら電話）

めいわくメール【迷惑メール】 a junk e-mail（広告などのメール）; a spam e-mail（無差別なメール）; a prank[nuisance] e-mail.

めおといわ【夫婦岩】 twin wedded rocks; a pair of large rocks joined by a giant Shinto straw rope.（三重県・二見が浦）

めおとぢゃわん【夫婦茶碗】 a pair of matching teacups[rice bowls] (used by a married couple). *Meoto-chawan* is a pair of husband-and-wife teacups, a large one for the husband and a small one for the wife. 二個一組の大小の夫婦用の茶碗.

めかじき【目梶木・眼旗魚】〔魚〕a swordfish; a broadbill. ⇨かじき

めがのけんかまつり【妻鹿のけんかまつり】 the Mega Fighting Festival. ⇨付記(1)「日本の祭り」(10月)

めキャベツ【芽キャベツ】 Brussels sprouts; ㊇Tom Thumb cabbage（小さいキャベツ）. アブラナ科の一・二年草. キャベツの一変種. 葉のつけ根の茎の部分に小型のキャベツがなり, 甘味がある.

めざし【目刺し】 dried sardines; several salted dried sardines tied in a bundle. Several sardines are fixed together with a straw rope[bamboo skewer] passed through their eyes. They are soaked in salt water overnight and dried in the sun. 数匹連ねて干したイワシ. 目にワラ縄[竹の串]を通して固定している. 一晩塩水で浸してから太陽に干す.

めし【飯】 ❶ ㊇ rice;〈炊いた米〉cooked [boiled] rice. ☆日本語では「米」と「ご飯」は別語であるが, 英語では rice だけで用いる場合が多い. ¶飯粒 a grain of cooked rice. 飯びつ a container for cooked rice; a wooden tub for serving rice. 飯茶碗 a rice bowl.
❷〈食事〉a meal; food. ¶飯の時間 time for a meal. 飯代 meal charge.

メゾネット式アパート ㊇a duplex apartment; ㊇ a maisonette.

めだか【目高】〔魚〕a *medaka*; a (Japanese) killifish（単複同形）. メダカ科の淡水硬骨魚. ¶目高の群 a school of killifish.

メタボリックしょうこうぐん【メタボリック症候群】 metabolic syndrome. ☆「メタボ

腹(太鼓腹)」a potbelly; a paunch.「メタボ診断」diagnosing metabolic syndrome.「メタボ予備軍」metabolic syndrome risk category.

めだましょうひん【目玉商品】〈客の目を引く〉 an eye-catcher; an eye-catching item[article];〈割安〉a loss leader.

めつけ【目付】 a lower superintendent officer (in the feudal times). He ensured the observance of rules, and supervised *gokenin* and *hatamoto*. 江戸幕府の下級監察[監督]役人. 規則が厳守されているかどうかを監督する. また御家人・旗本の監察をつかさどる. ⇨御家人 / 旗本

めつけばしら【目付柱】〔能楽〕the front pillar on the left side of the Noh stage. It is used by the *shite* to find his position on stage. 能舞台の左側にある前方の柱. シテが舞台上で自分の位置を確認するのに用いる. ⇨能「能舞台」

めぬき【目貫】 an ornamental piece attached to the hilt of a Japanese sword. 刀の目釘(刀身の柄に通す飾りの釘).

めばる【眼張】〔魚〕a (black) rockfish; a gopher (rock cod). フサカサゴ科の一種. 煮物, から揚げ, 照り焼きなどに調理する.

めびな【女雛】 the empress doll (displayed as one of the *hina* dolls in the Girls' Festival). ⇨男雛

メール an e-mail[E-mail] (message). ☆ electronic mailの略. ¶メールを送る send an e-mail; to e-mail. メールの添付ファイルを開く open an e-mail attachment. メール配信 an e-mail distribution. 迷惑メール a junk[nuisance] e-mail. 偽メール a fabricated[fudged] e-mail.

メルとも【メル友】 an e-pal; an e-mail pal; an e-mail cyber; a cyber friend; a cyberpal.

メロン〔植物〕a melon. ウリ科の一年草. ☆ muskmelon(マスクメロン), honeydew melon(ハニーデューメロン), netted melon (アミメロン)など. ¶メロンパン a melon-flavored bun.

めん【面】〔剣道〕❶〈用具〉a face guard[mask] (to protect the head); a helmet protector(頭部を覆う防具).〈技〉a *men*; a stroke[blow] to the head. (頭頭を打つこと) ⇨剣道 ❷〔能楽〕a Noh mask. 能に用いる仮面. ¶翁の面 a Noh mask of an old man. ひょっとこの面 a clown's mask.

めん【麺】 noodles; vermicelli; *udon*; *soba*. ¶乾麺 dried noodles. 生麺 uncooked fresh noodles. ゆで麺 boiled noodles. 冷麺 cold noodles. ⇨うどん / そば / そうめん / 汁

【麺汁】 noodle broth; seasoned sauce to dip noodles. ☆関西では「薄味」(light in color and strong in flavor), 関東では「濃味」(dark in color and light in flavor).

めん【綿】 cotton. ¶綿製品 cotton goods [articles]. 綿織物 cotton fabrics[textiles]. 綿布 cotton cloth. 綿糸 cotton thread.

めんたい【明太】〔魚〕 an Alaska pollack; a walleye pollack.「介党鱈」の異名. 朝鮮半島での用語.

めんたいこ【明太子】 ❶ cod roe; ovary of pollack.「介党鱈」の卵巣.「タラコ」. ❷〔食品〕salted cod roe[ovary of pollack] spiced with chili[red] peppers. 明太子[たらこ]を塩漬けにし, 唐辛子を使って熟成させた食品. ⇨辛子明太子

メンチカツ〈和製英語〉a breaded and fried cake of ground[minced] meat; fried cutlet of ground[minced] meat. 挽き肉のカツレツ. ⇨カツ

メンチボール〈和製英語〉 breaded and fried meatball. ☆「メンチ」(挽き肉) minced [ground] meat.

めんるい【麺類】 noodles; vermicelli; noodle dishes; *udon*; *saba*. ⇨麺 / うどん / そば / きしめん

め

も

も【藻】 an alga (®algae:藻類)；seaweed
(海藻)；waterweed(水草)；duckweed(ア
オウキクサ[アヒルの食用])．水中に生え
る植物の総称． ⇨まりも

もうひつ【毛筆】〈書道〉 a brush; a calligrapher's brush (書道用)；a writing brush (書
写用)；a watercolor brush (水彩画用)．¶
毛筆画 a brush-and-ink drawing; a painting
executed with a (writing) brush.

もえ【萌え】 ❶〈若芽〉young buds[leaves];
〈芽生え〉budding into leaves.
❷〈べた惚れ〉(a level of) stylized cuteness
and childlike behavior; attachment;
fascination; crush. ¶**萌えキャラ** a cute
[charming] female character (in the animated cartoon to whom one forms a strong
attachment).

もぎ【裳着】 a ceremony to celebrate a young
woman's Coming-of-Age (in olden times);
an ancient ritual to mark a young woman's
attainment of womanhood. 昔，公家の女
子が成人したことを祝った儀式．☆奈良・
平安時代には12歳頃にはじめて裳を着た
(wear clothes[a *kimono*]). ⇨成人の日／
元服(男子)

もくぎょ【木魚】 a wooden gong[drum] (used
for Buddhist sutra chanting); a fish-shaped
wooden drum; a wooden gong[block]
engraved in the form of fish scales. It is
roughly round in shape and hollow inside.
It is beaten[struck] continuously by a Buddhist priest with a stick (*bai*) while a Buddhist sutra is chanted in a temple. (読経用
の)木製銅鑼．表面を魚鱗状に彫った木製
銅鑼．円形で中空の形をしている．僧侶が
寺で読経する間に「梧」でたたいて鳴らし続
ける．

もぐさ【艾】 ❶〔植〕moxa.「(ニガ)ヨモギ」

(mugwort, wormwood)の異称．
❷〈灸に用いる〉dried and rubbed leaves of
wormwood[mugwort] (used as a cautery).
「ヨモギの葉」を干してもみほぐした綿状の
もの．灸に使用する．⇨蓬／灸

もくせい【木犀】〔植物〕a fragrant olive; a
sweet-scented olive; a sweet osmanthus. モ
クセイ科の常緑小高木．観賞用．「金木犀」
や「銀木犀」などがある．

もくどう【木道】 ® boardwalk (板道)；a
(raised) wooden causeway(木造舗装道路);
a path paved with planks; a log trail[trails
of logs] (laid out as hiking tracks through
the swamp). 厚板張りの小道．(湿原などに
ある)丸太小道．

もくはん【木版】〈版木〉woodblock;〈技術〉
woodblock printing; wood engraving. ⇨版
画．¶**木版刷りの年賀状** blook-printed New
Year's cards.
【木版画】 a woodblock print; a woodcut;
a woodprint; a printing made by means of
engraving woodblocks. ☆絵師 (painter),
彫り師 (woodblock carver), 刷師 (printer)
の三者の技術が結集する．

もぐら【土竜】〔動物〕a mole; a ground hog.
モグラ科の哺乳動物．☆「もぐら叩き」(play)
Wack-A-Mole ¶**モグラ塚** a molehill; a
molecast.

もくれん【木蓮】〔植物〕a (lily) magnolia. モ
クレン科の落葉低木．観賞用．

モザイクがぞう【モザイク画像】 an obscured
[occluded] TV image; a blurred TV image.

もしゅ【喪主】 the chief mourner (representing the family at the funeral). 葬式を行う
家族の代表者．

もず【鴫・百舌】〔鳥〕a shrike; a bullheaded
shrike; a butcher-bird. モズ科の小鳥．

もずく【水雲・海雲・海蘊】〔植物〕a *mozuku*
seaweed; a brown seaweed. 褐藻類モズク
科の海藻．食用(水雲の酢の物など)．
〔食品〕**水雲の酢の物** vinegared *mozuku* sea-

weed; edible *mozuku* seaweed seasoned with vinegar.

もち【餅】 *mochi*; a (sticky) rice cake; (a piece of) rice cake made from steamed glutinous rice with a sticky consistency. *Mochi* is often offered to the gods on New Year's Day and eaten for celebrations because it is considered a symbol of good luck [happiness]. 蒸したもち米から作る. 餅は「幸運の象徴」とみなされているので正月には神への供物にする. そしてお祝いしながら食べる. ⇨お年玉(年魂). ¶餅網 a grid[grill] for toasting rice cake. 餅盆 banquet tray with rice cakes. 餅屋〈店〉a rice-cake shop; 〈人〉a rice-cake dealer. 餅をつく make rice cake; pound steamed rice into cake. ⇨餅つき. 餅を焼く toast [grill] a piece of rice cake (on a grid).

〔食品〕紅白餅 red and white rice cakes. かき餅 sliced and dried rice cakes. 鏡餅 round rice cakes. ⇨鏡餅. 雑煮餅 rice cakes cooked with vegetables on New Year's Day. ⇨雑煮餅. 餅菓子 rice-cake sweets; rice pounded till it is smooth and soft, and stuffed with bean paste(米などを材料にして柔らかくし, 餡子などを入れて作った菓子. 大福餅・柏餅など)

【餅搗き】 rice-cake pounding; rice-cake making; the pounding of steamed glutinous rice to make rice-cake. Steamed glutinous rice is pounded into a paste many times with a wooden pestle in a stone[wooden] mortar till it takes on a sticky consistency[it becomes sticky]. 蒸した糯米を石製[木製]の臼に入れ, 粘り気がでるまで杵でつく.

もちごめ【糯米】 glutinous rice (usually used for making *mochi* or *sekihan*). 餅・赤飯などにする. ⇨米 / 餅 / 赤飯. ⇦うるち米

もちゅう【喪中】 (be) in mourning. ⇨喪服 ¶喪中葉書 mourning-notification postcard.

もつ internal organs[internals]; entrails; guts (内臓); giblets(鳥の).「臓物」の略. ¶もつ焼き barbecued[broiled] giblets. もつ鍋 a stew of giblets. ⇨やきとり

もとカノ【元カノ】 a former[an old] girl-friend; one's ex-girlfriend. ⇦いまカノ (one's current girlfriend)

もとカレ【元カレ】 a former[an old] boy-friend; one's ex-boyfriend; a guy who I used to go out with. ⇦いまカレ (one's current boyfriend)

もとゆい【元結】 a stiff paper string[cord] for tying the hair. 髻(髪の毛をまとめて結んだところ)を結ぶ堅い紙ひも[こより].

もなか【最中】 sweetened bean-paste-filled wafers; two wafers filled with sweetened bean paste; two waferlike cakes (made from glutinous rice) stuffed with sweetened *adzuki*-bean paste. 薄焼きの(もち米で作った)皮を2枚合わせ餡を入れた和菓子. ☆wafer「薄い軽焼き菓子:ウエハース」

ものいい【物言い】〔相撲〕〈反論〉a *sumo* judge's objection against[to] the *sumo* referee's decision;〈抗議〉a *sumo* judges' conference regarding the *sumo* referee's decision. The discussion is held by five judges when the referee's decision for a bout is called into question. They gather in the center of the ring and debate whether the original decision should be upheld or reversed. 取組に関する行司の決定が疑問視される(be doubtful)ときに行う5人の審判員による協議. 土俵の中央に集まり是々非々(是認・否認)を討議する.

もののあわれ【物の哀れ】(feel) the pathos (in things[nature]); (have) compassion (on[for] things[nature]).

もふく【喪服】 (a) mourning dress; (a) *ki-mono* (worn) in mourning[in black]. ☆〈女性〉black formal *kimono* worn at a funeral (usually with family crests on the back and on each sleeve); 〈男性〉 a black Western-style suit with a white shirt and a black tie.

もほうはん【模倣犯】　a copycat criminal [offender](物まねをする犯罪者). ☆「**模倣犯罪**」は a copycat crime.

もみ【樅】〔植物〕a fir (tree). マツ科の常緑針葉高木. 枝や若木はクリスマスツリーに用いる. ¶ **樅の実** a fir cone.

もみがら【籾殻】　chaff; rice husks[hulls](複数形).

もみじ【紅葉】　❶〔植物〕a maple; 〈葉〉maple leaf. カエデ類の異名. ☆「**カエデの葉**」はカナダの象徴で国旗に採用. ⇨かえで
❷〈鹿肉〉 venison. シカ科のシカの肉. ☆日本では冬季に雄の鹿のみ狩猟が可能.

【紅葉狩り】　a traditional pastime of[an excursion for] viewing the changing colors of maple[autumnal] leaves. People enjoy the beautifully-colored leaves of maple trees while hiking or driving in the hills and the mountains. 色づいた紅葉の鑑賞のため山野に出かける遠足.

【紅葉卸(し)】❶ grated *daikon*[radish] colored with red pepper; Japanese *daikon* grated with a small amount of hot red pepper mixed in. It is used as a condiment for *nabemono*, *mizutaki*, etc. 唐辛子を加えて混ぜ合わせて赤く染めた大根卸し. 鍋料理や水炊きの薬味に用いる. ⇨鍋物 / 水炊き
❷ a mixture of grated *daikon*[radish] and grated carrots. 大根と人参を卸して混ぜわせたもの.

もみじマーク【紅葉マーク】　a maple leaf sticker. It is an orange car sticker in the shape of a maple leaf indicating that the driver is over 75 years of age. 75歳以上の運転手を示すオレンジ色の車のステッカー.

もめん【木綿】　cotton; cotton cloth(綿布).
¶ **木綿物** cotton clothes(着物); cotton

goods(タオルなど). **木綿糸** cotton thread; cotton yarn(紡績の). **木綿針** needle for cotton thread.

もめんどうふ【木綿豆腐】　firm[cotton] *tofu*[bean curd]; coarse-grained[coarse-textured] *tofu*. The texture with latticed patterns similar to a cotton cloth is so coarse-grained. It contains less water and appears slightly coarse. 綿布のような格子模様の感触がやや粗い. 水分が少なく, 見た目が少々荒い. ⇨豆腐 / 絹漉し豆腐

もも【桃】〔植物〕 a peach tree(木); a peach (実); a peach blossom(花). バラ科の落葉小高木. 果実は食用. ☆「**水密**」white peach. 「**山桃**」bayberry. ¶ **桃の核**(たね)a peach pit. **桃の皮** a peach peel.

もものせっく【桃の節句】　Peach Blossom Festival; the Doll Festival; the Girls' Festival. (March 3). ☆古来「桃」は邪気を払う霊力(the spiritual power to drive out evil spirits)があるとされてきた(俗信). ⇨ひな祭り

ももひき【股引(き)】〈男性用〉a tight-fitting long underwear[underpants] (worn by men in winter); 〈口語〉long johns; 〈職人用〉close-fitting pants[trousers] (worn by workmen in feudal days). 身体にぴったり合ったスボンのような衣服. (男性の)下着または(昔の職人の)作業着用スボンがある. ¶ **半股引** knee breeches; trunks.

ももわれ【桃割れ】　a hairdo[hairstyle] done up by a young woman (with a chignon tied in a round shape resembling a split peach). This traditional Japanese-style hairstyle was worn by an unmarried woman in the Meiji and Taisho eras. Even today this style of traditional coiffure is worn by a *kimono*-clad woman during the New Year season. 若い娘の日本髪の一種. 桃を二分したように髷を丸く開く結い方をしている. 明治・大正時代に未婚の女性が結って

いた．現在でも正月に着物を着る女性がこの伝統的な髪型を結う．

もやし【萌やし】〈豆〉soybean sprouts (grown in the shade); 〈麦〉barley malt (grown in the shade). 豆・麦の種を水につけ，日陰で芽を出させる．¶**根を取ったもやし** plucked bean sprouts.

もやしっ子 over-protected children（過保護の子供）; spineless children（意気地のない子供）; tall children with little muscular strength[with a feeble constitution]（ひ弱な子供）.

もりあわせのさしみ【盛(り)合わせの刺身】(a plate of) assorted *sashimi*. ⇨刺身

もりじお【盛(り)塩】⇨塩花 / 塩払い

もりそば【盛(り)そば】　***mori-soba***; cool buckwheat noodles topped with no slices of seasoned laver. *Mori-soba* are buckwheat noodles cooled in cold water and served[piled up] on a flat bamboo colander[slatted bamboo tray] placed on a lacquered wooden frame. Buckwheat noodles are not sprinkled with pieces of seasoned laver on top. They are eaten after[by] dipping into a soy-based sauce (*soba-tsuyu*) mixed with *wasabi*[horseradish] and sliced green scallions. 振りかけ海苔のない冷えたそば．茹でたそばを冷水にさらした後，漆塗りの木枠にのせた笊[竹簾を敷いた容器(split-bamboo ware)]に盛りつける．刻んだ焼き海苔を振りかけない．山葵と刻みネギを混ぜたそば汁につけてから食べる．⇨笊そば（振りかけ海苔があるそば）/ そば汁．¶**盛りそば二枚** two bamboo platters[plates] of *mori-soba*; two bamboo platters piled up with *mori-soba*.

もりばな【盛(り)花】〔華道〕Flowers arranged in a flat tray-like vase (*suiban*) with needle point holders (*kenzan*). 水盤 (a wide, shallow tray-like container)などに剣山を用いて多くの花や枝を盛るように生ける．⇨投げ入れ / 天地人

もりぶね【盛り舟】　a boat-shaped container [wooden platter] used for dishing up [serving] assorted *sashimi*[a variety of sliced raw fish]. いろいろな刺身を盛りつける船形の容器[木製の大皿]．

もりやまのひまつり【守山の火まつり】　the Fire Festival in Moriyama City. (1月). ⇨付記(1)「日本の祭り」

モーレツ社員 a workaholic; an eager-beaver employee; a furiously-working employee.

もろきゅう【諸きゅう】　sliced[slices of] cucumber served with unrefined *shoyu*[soy sauce]. きゅうりに諸味醤油を添えたもの．「諸味きゅうり」の略．⇨諸味

もろこ【諸子】〔魚〕a minnow. コイ科の淡水硬骨魚．食用．☆琵琶湖でよく捕れる．

もろみ【諸味・醪】　unrefined *sake*（もろみ酒）; unrefined *shoyu*（もろみ醤油）. 醸造したままで，かすを漉していない酒または醤油．⇨諸きゅう

もん【紋】❶〈家紋〉a (family) crest (usually put on a formal *kimono* or lantern). ⇨家紋 ❷〈紋章〉a coat of arms. かぶとなどについている．

もんごういか【紋甲烏賊】〔魚〕a large-sized cuttlefish. コウイカ科の大形の甲いか．⇨イカ

もんじゃやき【もんじゃ焼き】　a soft savory wheat-flour pancake. It is a thin, Worcestershire sauce pancake containing sliced [shredded] cabbages and meat (or seafood) with various ingredients. It is cooked [baked] on a griddle[hot plate] at the table. 柔らかくて辛味のある小麦粉でつくるパンケーキ状のもの．刻みキャベツや肉(または魚介類)などいろいろな具材を入れ，ウスターソースで味つけた薄いパンケーキ状のもの．食卓の鉄板の上で調理する．

もんしょう【紋章】a crest; a coat of arms.

も

⇨紋. ¶皇室の菊紋章 the chrysanthemum crest of the Imperial family.

もんだいはつげん【問題発言】 a controversial statement.

もんつき【紋付き】 a crested *kimono*(紋のある着物); a *kimono* bearing family crests; a *kimono* marked with family crests.

【紋付き羽織】 a crested *haori*; a short overgarment bearing[embroidered with] family crests. ⇨羽織

【紋付き羽織袴】 long, pleated skirt-like trousers (*hakama*) worn over a short overgarment (*haori*) bearing family crests; costume[garment] consisting of a crested *haori* and *hakama* worn by men on formal occasions. 家紋のついた着物と袴からなる男性用の礼服. ⇨袴

もんどう【問答】 ❶〈討論・教義〉(exchange) questions and answers; (hold) a debate [dialogue]. 一方が問い, 他方が答える. ❷〈禅問答〉the catechism(教義問答); the catechetical method of teaching Zen Buddhism. 教義問答方式で禅宗を教えること. ⇨禅(禅問答)／公案

もんどころ【紋所】 a family crest. 家の定紋. ⇨紋

もんばつせいど【門閥制度】 nepotism; the practice with influence[power] of favoring relatives[friends]. ⇨縁故採用／縁故入学

もんぺ(い) (Japanese-style) pantaloons [baggy work pants] gathered at the ankles. These pants were worn by women during World War II. Even today these pants are worn by women when working in the rural field. 足元のくびれている衣装[和製パンタロン]. 第二次世界大戦中女性が着用したが, 現在でも農家の女性が履いている.

もんめ【匁】 a[one] *momme*. One *momme* equals 3.75 grams. (3.75g). 尺貫法での重さの単位. 一貫の1000分の1. ☆現在も真珠の重さなどに用いる.

や

やえざくら【八重桜】〔植物〕a multi-flowered [double-flowered] cherry tree (木); multipetaled[double-petaled] cherry blossoms (花). 桜の一品種. 花が八重咲き (multi-petaled; double-petaled)の桜. ⇨さくら

やおちょう【八百長】 a fix; a match-fixing; a put-up job; fixing; rigging. ¶八百長相撲 a fixed[rigged] *sumo* match[bout]; a bout fixing. 八百長疑惑(相撲の) suspicion of match-fixing (of a *sumo* bout). 八百長試合 a fixed game; a put-up game

やおよろずのかみ【八百万の神】 myriads[a myriad] of Shinto deities; all the Shinto deities[gods and goddesses]. Shintoism as a polytheistic religion originates with Amaterasu Omikami, the Sun Goddess, and a countless number of mythological deities. 多くの神々. 多神教としての神道の起源は天照大神や無数の神話の神々である. ☆狭義では天照大神をはじめ森羅万象(山・木・水・火など)を神とする. 広義では神格化され, 祀られた人(天皇 ・学者・武士など)も人神とする. ⇨神道

やがすり【矢絣】 cloth with a splashed pattern of arrow-feathers. 矢羽根を図案化した[並べた]文様のかすり. ☆矢は一度射ると戻らないという縁起模様の柄である. ⇨絣 ¶矢絣の着物 a *kimono* with a splashed pattern of arrow-feathers. ☆江戸時代には女性が結婚の際に持たされた. 現在では大学などの卒業式に女性が袴とあわせて着用する.

やかたぶね【屋形船】 a (Japanese-style) house-shaped pleasure boat; a (Japanese-style) roofed pleasure boat with a *tatami* mat and a *shoji* screen. It is used for recreation and sightseeing on the river while enjoying food and drink. 家型の遊覧船. 畳

や障子のある屋根付きの遊覧船．飲食を楽しみながら川の水上で娯楽や観光を満喫する．

やかん【薬缶】㉖ a kettle; ㉕ a teakettle. 湯わかし器．☆元来，薬を煎じるのに用いた．【関連語】「取っ手」handle.「口」spout.「蓋」lid.「底」bottom. ¶薬缶で煮立つお湯 the water boiling in a kettle.

やぎ【山羊】〔動物〕a goat; a he-goat（雄）; a she-goat（雌）; a kid（子山羊）．ウシ科の哺乳動物．肉・毛・乳を利用する．¶山羊ひげ a goatee (beard). 山羊皮 goatskin.

やきあみ【焼(き)網】a gridiron（火に置く焼き網）; a grill（バーベキュー用のこんろ）; a toasting net. ¶焼き網で焼いた魚 fish broiled[㉕ grilled] on a gridiron.

やきいも【焼(き)芋】a baked[roasted] sweet potato; sweet potatoes baked in an iron oven containing heated pebbles. 熱した小石の入った鉄製のオーブンで焼いたサツマイモ．⇨石焼芋

【焼(き)芋屋】a baked sweet-potato vendor[vender]; a vendor pulling a cart with an iron oven containing heated pebbles which bake sweet potatoes. サツマイモを焼くための熱した小石を入れた鉄製オーブンをつんだ車を引く商売人．

やきおにぎり【焼(き)お握り】a toasted[grilled] rice ball; a rice ball toasted with *shoyu*[soy sauce]. The surface of rice ball is covered with *shoyu*[soy sauce] and toasted it until it is golden[light] brown. お握りの表面にしょうゆをつけ，焦げるまで焼く．⇨お握り

やきざかな【焼(き)魚】(a) broiled[grilled] fish. Grilled fish (including sliced salmon, saury, horse mackerel, etc.) are often eaten with *shoyu*[soy sauce], grated radish, sliced lemon and other flavorings. (鮭の切り身，サンマ，アジなどの)焼き魚は醤油や大根おろし，またレモンスライスなどを添えて食べる場合が多い．⇨あじの塩焼き

やきそば【焼(き)蕎麦】crispy fried buckwheat noodles grilled with assorted vegetables and meat. 何種類かの野菜や肉を加えて中華そばの麺をいためたもの．☆「中国風の焼きそば」は chow mein(堅い焼きそば); lo mein(柔らかい焼きそば); fried Chinese noodles. ⇨五目焼きそば

やきだんご【焼(き)団子】a toasted[㉕ grilled] dumpling. ⇨団子

やきどうふ【焼(き)豆腐】broiled[㉕ grilled] *tofu*[bean curd]; *tofu* toasted[scorched] on both sides. 火であぶって両面を焼いた豆腐．⇨豆腐

やきとり【焼(き)鳥】*yakitori*; (Japanese-style) barbecued chicken (on a bamboo skewer); skewered grilled chicken; bite-sized chicken kebab. Chunks of chicken meat and vegetables (such as onions, pimentos, etc.) are arranged on the bamboo skewers and broiled over a charcoal fire. The grilled chicken is either basted with[dipped in] *tare* sauce[sweetened soy-based sauce] or is salted. 日本風のバーベキューのこと．鳥肉と野菜を竹串にさし，炭火の上で焼く (charbroil). その後醤油をベースにした「タレ」または「塩」をつける．☆ kebab[kəbáb]「カバブ」(中近東の肉と野菜の串焼き料理: アラビア語で「あぶり肉」の意). ¶焼き鳥屋 an establishment offering skewered chicken as a specialty.

❶〈串刺しにして<u>焼く鳥</u>〉(pieces of) chicken meat and vegetables <u>arranged</u> on a (bamboo) skewer[stick].

❷〈串刺しにして<u>焼いた鳥</u>〉(bite-sized pieces of) chicken meat and vegetables <u>grilled</u> on a (bamboo) skewer[stick].

《具材 (ingredients)》合鴨 (duck). 鶉の卵 (quail egg). 皮 (skin). 銀杏 (ginkgo nut). 獅子唐 (green chili pepper). 椎茸 (*shiitake* mushroom). 砂肝 (gizzard). 砂ず

り (gizzard). ツクネ (ground chicken ball). ネギマ (chicken and green onion). 手羽先 (winglet). ピーマン (green pepper). 心臓 (heart). 手羽 (wing). ボンジリ (tails). ムネ (breast). モツ (giblets). モモ (thigh; leg). レバー[肝] (liver)など.

やきにく【焼(き)肉】 (marinated) broiled[grilled] meat; thinly sliced meat [beef] broiled on a grill or an iron plate. ¶ 焼肉のたれ sauce for grilled meat. 焼肉定食 a set meal centered on grilled meat. ☆「韓国の焼肉定食」は a Korean-style barbecue set meal centered on grilled meat.

やきのり【焼(き)海苔】 (a sheet of) toasted dried laver. 火であぶった干し海苔. ⇨海苔 / 味付け海苔

やきはまぐり【焼(き)蛤】 grilled[broiled] clams; clams grilled[broiled] on the shell over a charcoal fire. 炭火で殻ごと焼いた蛤.

やきもち【焼(き)餅】 a toasted[roasted] rice cake seasoned[flavored] with *shoyu*[soy sauce]. 火であぶって焼き, しょうゆで味付けした餅. ☆「焼き餅を焼く」(ねたむ・嫉妬する)は (burn with) envy[jealousy].

やきもの【焼(き)物】❶〈陶磁器・土器など〉(a piece of) pottery (陶器); (a piece of) porcelain (磁器); ceramics[ceramic ware] (陶器製品); earthenware (土器); china(ware). ¶焼き物の花びん a porcelain vase; an earthenware vase.
❷〈焼いて作った料理〉broiled dishes; grilled foods.〈魚・肉・野菜など焼いた料理〉broiled[grilled] fish[meat, vegetables]; fish[meat, vegetables] broiled[grilled] over a charcoal fire (or an open gas fire). ⇨塩焼きの魚 / 照り焼き

やぎゅう【野牛】〔動物〕a buffalo (複) buffalo(e)s; buffalo); a wild ox (複) oxen); a bison (単複同形: バイソン). ウシ科の哺乳動物. ☆「水牛」は water buffalo.

やくがいエイズ【薬害エイズ】 AIDS contracted from contaminated blood products; AIDS transmission through[AIDS transmitted by] medical treatment.

やくがいかんえん【薬害肝炎】 drug-caused infections of hepatitis C Virus.

やくしにょらい【薬師如来】 the Buddha of Medicine; the Healing Buddha. He is said to release people from pain and heal their illness by giving them sacred medicine. He usually holds a bottle of medicine in one hand as the symbol of his charitable mission. 衆生の病患を癒す仏. 薬を与えて苦痛を除き, 病気を治す. 慈悲にあふれる使命の象徴として片手には薬瓶を持つ.

やくすぎ【屋久杉】 ⇨杉

やくそう【薬草】 a (medicinal) herb. ¶薬草園 an[英 a] herb garden; medicinal garden.

やくどし【厄年】❶〈不幸な年齢〉an unlucky[a bad] age; a critical age (for a man[woman]).〈災難の転換期〉a climacteric age (for a man[woman]). *Yakudoshi* for men are 25, 42 (great calamity) and 61, and for women are 19, 33 (great calamity), and 37. One's *yakudoshi* is measured by adding one to the actual age. 災害にあいやすい年齢. 数え年で, 男性は25歳, 42歳(大厄), 61歳. 女性は19歳, 33歳(大厄), 37歳である. ☆「42(しに)」は「死」("die"), 「33(さんざん)」は「散々(災難)」("terrible" or "disastrous")の同音異義語 (homophone) として, もっとも不吉な年齢 (the most critical age)とされてきた. 社寺にて「厄払い」(exorcism)をする習慣がある. ⇨厄払い
❷〈不運な年〉an unlucky year; the year of bad luck[calamity]. 災難の多い年.

やくばらい【厄払い】 (pray for an) exorcism (悪魔払い); (hold) a ceremony of exorcism; (observe) a service of driving out evil spirits (悪霊を追い払う). 神仏に祈って災難を取り除く(式). 「厄落とし」と

もいう．☆大晦日や節分の夜など，特に「厄年」に行う．⇨厄年／厄除け．¶**神社で厄払いをしてもらう** hold a service of exorcism[have oneself purified]at a Shinto shrine.

やくみ【薬味】〈香辛料〉condiment(s); spice(s);〈味付け〉a seasoning[flavoring] (to). *Yakumi* is used to add extra flavor to Japanese dishes. 風味を増すように，食べ物に添える香辛料〈唐辛子・山葵・紫蘇または野菜類（ネギ・ショウガなど）〉．「加薬」ともいう．¶**薬味入れ** a cruet; a caster（瓶）. **薬味立て** a cruet stand.

やくようしゅ【薬用酒】 medicinal liquor; medicinal alcoholic beverages; alcoholic beverage for medical use. 薬として用いる酒（「養命酒」など）．「薬酒」や「薬味酒」ともいう．

やくよけ【厄除け】〈お守り〉a protective charm (to ward off mishap); a talisman [an amulet] (to drive out disaster). 災厄を除去すること．¶**厄除けのお札** a protective charm to ward off misfortune. ⇨厄払い

やぐら【櫓】〈小塔〉a turret;〈見張り搭〉a watchtower; a guard tower. ☆戦時には城門や城壁の上に設けられた敵の見張り(lookout)や攻撃(attack)のための高櫓，平時には食料の貯蔵庫(storehouse)として使用する．⇨城．¶**江戸城に現存する櫓** a surviving turret of the old Edo Castle.

やぐらだいこ【櫓太鼓】〔相撲〕the announcing drumbeat for a *sumo* tournament; the drumbeat announcing the start or finish of one of the fifteen days of a *sumo* tournament. 15日間の相撲取組の間（毎日），開場や閉場を知らせるために打ち鳴らす太鼓．

やぐるま【矢車】 a windmill on the top of a pole for carp streamers; the decorative windmill attached to the top of a pole on which carp streamers are raised[put up]. 鯉のぼりの竿の先につける風車．

やぐるまぎく【矢車菊】〔植物〕(a) bluebottle; (a) cornflower. キク科の一年草・二年草. 観賞用．通称「矢車草」．

やご【水蠆】 a dragonfly larva; a larva of a dragonfly. ☆ larva (⑱ larvae)「幼虫」（トンボ）．

やごう【屋号】 ❶〔歌舞伎〕a (kabuki actor's hereditary) stage name; a stage name (of famous kabuki actors according to family lineage). During the exaggerated pose (called *mie*), someone in the audience will often cheer, shouting the actor's stage name (*yago*). 舞台上での役者の呼び名．家系による世襲的な役者の名．「見得」のポーズなどをするとき観客は役者の屋号を叫んで声援することがある．⇨見得 ❷〈店〉the name of a store. 商売上の店の呼び名．

やさい【野菜】 vegetables; greens（菜類の総称）．☆根菜類(roots)，葉菜類(leaves)，果菜類(fruits)がある．¶**野菜サラダ** vegetable salad. **青野菜**[青物] green vegetables. **野菜料理** a vegetable dish. **葉の多い野菜** leafy vegetables. **根菜** root vegetables. **旬の野菜** in-season vegetables. **季節外れの野菜** out-of-season vegetables. **無農薬野菜** pesticide-free vegetables. **繊維の多い野菜** fibrous vegetables. 〔料理〕**野菜炒め** stir-fried vegetables; fried vegetables. **野菜の煮つけ** vegetables simmered in *shoyu*[soy sauce]. **野菜スープ** vegetable soup.

やし【椰子】〔植物〕a palm;〈ココヤシ〉a coconut palm;〈木〉a palm tree. ヤシ科の常緑高木．果実は食用・ヤシ油の原料．☆葉の形が「手のひら」(palm)に似ていることからの呼称．¶**ナツメ椰子** a date palm. **椰子油** palm[coconut] oil; palm[coconut] butter. **ココ椰子**[椰子の実] a coconut.

やし【香具師・野師】 a street stall vendor (at a festival: 商人)；a huckster (at a festival:

呼び売り商人）; a showman (at a festival; 興行師). 祭日［縁日］などに，境内や露店で商品や食べ物を売る商人. または見世物を興行する人.

やじうま【野次馬】〈やじる人〉a heckler.〈見物人〉 spectators; curiosity-seekers; onlookers;〈群集〉a rabble; a mob; onlooking crowd.

やすくにごうし【靖国合祀】 collective enshrinement of the war dead (at Yasukuni Shrine). ¶A級戦犯靖国の合祀 enshrinement of the Class A war criminals at Yasukuni Shrine.

やすくにじんじゃさんけいもんだい【靖国神社参詣問題】 the issue[controversy] of the Prime Minister's[cabinet ministers'] official visit to Yasukuni Shrine.

やすくにじんじゃみたままつり【靖国神社みたま祭】 Memorial Service for the Departed Souls (who died for the country in past wars) at Yasukuni Shrine. (July 13-16).（東京都：靖国神社）

やたい【屋台】❶〈店〉a (portable) stall; ⊛ a (mobile) stand（移動不可：花などを売る）; a (transportable) cart（移動可能：焼き芋などを売る）; a booth (in the shape of a small house used for selling things at festivals)（祭礼時の売店）. *Yatai* is a miniature open-air stall[stand; cart] on wheels with a roof attached (selling cheap dishes). 屋根の付いた小さな車輪付きの売店. 安価な飲食物 (prepared cheap food and drink)を売る. ¶ラーメンの屋台 *ramen*[Chinese-style noodles] stall. 花売り屋台 a flower stand. 焼き芋屋台 sweet potatoes cart. ⇨焼き芋屋
❷〈祭の屋台〉a (festival) float;〈山車〉a wheeled wagon float;〈舞台〉a movable stage (for dancing); a roofed scaffold. ☆「屋台」は中に御神体を祀る移動可能な祭礼の曳き物. また屋根のついた踊りの舞台.

「山車」(festival float (with a stage for dancing or singing))は祭りのとき，飾りものなどをしてひき回す屋台のこと.「山」「檀尻」「鉾」など多数の呼び方がある. ⇨山車

やたて【矢立】❶〈硯箱〉a portable writing set containing a brush-and-ink case. It includes an india-ink stick, a small brush and a flat bowl for making the ink. 硯箱を入れた携帯用の筆記用具. 墨，筆，硯などが入っている.「矢立の硯」の略.
❷〈矢を入れる武具〉a quiver.

やたのかがみ【八咫の鏡】 ⇨三種の神器

やっこだこ【奴凧】 a kite made in the shape of a *samurai*'s manservant[footman] with his arms outspread (of the Edo period).（江戸時代の）両手を広げた武家の下僕の姿に似せて作った凧.

やっこどうふ【奴豆腐】 (a small block of) *tofu*[bean curd] cut into cubes. It is usually served cold, and eaten with *shoyu*[soy sauce] and some condiments. 四角に切った豆腐. 通常は冷やして出され，醤油・薬味をつけて食べる. ⇨冷奴

やつしろみょうけんさい【八代妙見祭】 the Myoken Parade Festival. (11月). ⇨付記(1)「日本の祭り」

やつはし【八つ橋】 a zigzag bridge made of narrow wooden planks (built over the stream). It can be seen in a Japanese garden.（小川などに）幅の狭い木製の厚板で作った稲妻型の橋. 日本庭園によく見られる.

やつはしせんべい【八橋煎餅】a cinnamon-seasoned cracker; a brittle cookie flavored with cinnamon. 肉桂入りの小麦粉を練って焼いたせんべい［和菓子］. 通称「八橋」. 京都名物. ⇨桂皮

やつめうなぎ【八目鰻】〔魚〕 a lamprey (eel); a rock sucker. ヤツメウナギ科の脊椎動物. ☆目の後方にある7対のえら穴と本来の目とを合わせると八目のように見えることか

らの呼称. ⇨うなぎ

やどかり【寄居虫・蝦・宿借り】〔甲〕 a hermit crab; a pagurian. ヤドカリ科の節足動物. 「エビ」と「カニ」の中間の形.

やとわれママ【雇われママ】 the hired head hostess of a drinking establishment.

やないづのはだかまいり【柳津の裸まいり】 the Half-Naked Festival. (1月). ⇨付記(1)「日本の祭り」

やながわなべ【柳川鍋】 loaches casserole; a hotpot of loaches and sliced burdock roots boiled in *shoyu*[soy sauce] and sugar, and covered with beaten eggs. ドジョウの鍋料理. ドジョウとゴボウを砂糖醤油で煮て, 玉子でとじた鍋料理. ☆江戸時代, 日本橋の柳川という料理店が考案したことに由来.

やなぎ【柳】〔植物〕 a willow (tree). ヤナギ科の落葉高木または低木. 種類は多数ある. ¶枝垂れ柳 a drooping willow. 猫柳 a pussy willow. 糸柳 a weeping willow. 赤芽柳 a red-bud willow. 青柳 a green willow. ⇨繭玉

【柳行李】 a wicker clothes box; a wicker suitcase[trunk]. It is woven from[made of] strips of willow twigs. It is used for storing or carrying clothes. 柳の枝を編んでつくった行李. 衣装の保管用・運搬用. ⇨行李

【柳箸】 (a pair of) willow chopsticks. Chopsticks are made from plain unvarnished willow wood and often used on auspicious occasions such as New Year's Day. 柳の白木でつくった箸. 新年の雑煮を食べるときに用いる. ⇨箸

やなぎだる【柳樽】 a cask for celebratory *sake* (used on festive occasions). 祝い事に使う酒樽. ⇨角樽

やなぎば（ぼうちょう）【柳刃（包丁）】 a long thin knife for slicing *sashimi*. 刺身を切るのに用いる長くて細い包丁.

やぶいり【藪入り】 the servants' holiday (given twice a year). Several days of paid vacation were given to young apprentices and servants to return to their parental homes during the Bon season in summer and during the New Year holidays in the old days. Today this custom remains in the form of returning to their parental homes in summer and in winter. 昔盆暮れに奉公人が有給休暇をもらって実家に帰ること. 現代でも夏季・冬季[盆暮れ]に帰省する習慣が残っている.

やぶさめ【流鏑馬】 horseback archery; archery on horseback; the art of shooting arrows from the back of a galloping horse. Archers dressed in colorful hunting costumes use bows to shoot whistling arrows (*kaburaya*) at three diamond-shaped, wooden targets while riding on horseback at full speed. Archers shoot at each target in succession. It was originally practiced as a Shinto rite to pray for abundant harvests, and was later adopted to foster Japanese-style chivalry for *samurai* warriors, who vied with each other in horsemanship and archery. It is now demonstrated as a traditional festive event at Shinto shrines. 色鮮やかな狩り装束の射手が, 馬に乗って疾走しながら弓で「鏑矢」(an arrow that produces sound in flight)を菱形の木製の三つの的に向けて射る. 射手は順次に各的を射る. 元来「流鏑馬」は豊作を祈願する神道の儀式として行われていたが, 後世に至り武士道を養成するために取り入れられ, 武士たちは馬術と弓道を相互に競い合った. 今では神社の伝統的な祭事として行われている. ⇨弓道

やま[-さん][-ざん]【山】 a mountain; a mount. 固有名詞の場合 "Mt." と略す. ⇨～岳 / 峠 / 丘 / 坂 ¶浅間山 Mt. Asama (yama). 富士山 Mt. Fuji (san). 大雪山 Mt. Daisetsu (zan). 日本三名山 the Three Most

Famous Mountains in Japan. ☆富士山［静岡県・山梨県］・白山［石川県・岐阜県］・立山［富山県］.

やまあらし【山荒】〔動物〕 a porcupine; a hedgehog. ヤマアラシ科の哺乳動物.

やまいも【山芋】〔植物〕a yam; a taro root. ヤマイモ科のつる性多年草. 根はすりおろして「とろろ」(grated yam)として食用にする.「山の芋」「大和芋」ともいう. ⇨いも／とろろ／山掛け

やまかけ【山掛け】 (a dish of) sliced raw fish[tuna] topped[dressed] with grated yam. とろろをかけた生魚［鮪］. 〔料理〕山掛けそば (a bowl of) buckwheat noodles in broth topped with grated yam（とろろをかけたつゆそば. 別称「とろろそば」）. 山掛け豆腐 (a dish of) *tofu*[bean curd] topped with grated yam（とろろをかけた豆腐）. 山掛け丼 (a bowl of) rice topped with sliced raw fish[tuna] and grated yam（とろろをかけたご飯に生魚［鮪］をのせる）.

やまがたはながさまつり【山形花笠まつり】 the Yamagata Flower-Sedge-Hat Dance Parade Festival. (8月). ⇨付記(1)「日本の祭り」

やまがとうろうまつり【山鹿灯籠まつり】the Yamaga Lantern Parade Festival. (8月). ⇨付記(1)「日本の祭り」

やまたいこくのひみこ【邪馬台国の卑弥呼】 Himiko, the Queen of Yamatai State; a legendary queen of Yamatai, an ancient country in Japan. ☆邪馬台国は中国の史書「魏志倭人伝」に見える三世紀前半の日本の地方国家.「女王卑弥呼」(Queen Himiko)が統治していた. 場所は大和説・北九州説など諸説がある.

やまだのはるまつり【山田の春祭り】 the Spring Festival at Yamada. (3月). ⇨付記(1)「日本の祭り」

やまと【大和・倭】 ❶ Yamato; an ancient name of Japan. 日本の古称.

❷ the country as ruled by the Yamato Imperial Court in the fourth century (now Nara Prefecture). 4世紀頃に大和朝廷が統治していた旧国名の一つ. 現在の奈良県. ¶大和国家 the Yamato State. 大和魂 the Japanese spirit. 日本人固有の精神. 別称「大和心」. 大和朝廷 the Yamato Imperial Court (the first Imperial government in Japan). 大和民族 the Yamato race; the Japanese race.（日本人を構成する民族. 日本民族）.

【大和絵】 a *Yamato-e* painting. ❶ a painting in the traditional Japanese style. Such paintings of the Japanese scenery expressing native Japanese tastes and sentiments are drawn on sliding doors and folding screens.（唐絵に対して）日本の風物・山水を描いた伝統的な絵画. 襖や屏風などによく描かれる. ⇨唐絵

❷ a traditional Japanese style painting of the late Heian and Kamakura periods. 平安時代・鎌倉時代の大和絵.

【大和言葉】 a native Japanese word; a word of purely Japanese origin; a Japanese word having its pure origin in the time before the introduction of Chinese. 日本固有のことば. 漢語が導入される以前に, その起源をもつ日本のことば,「和語」ともいう. ⇨和歌

【大和［ヤマト］政権】 the Yamato administration[government]; the administration [government] ruled by the Yamato Imperial Court. 4世紀に成立する. 5世紀に大和地方の奈良盆地を拠点に発展する. 氏姓制度が整う.

【大和撫子】the ideal Japanese woman (who has the Japanese graceful feminine ideal); the flower of Japanese womanhood. 理想的な日本女性. 日本女性の美称 (an elegant term for a Japanese woman).

やまといも【大和芋】 a Japanese yam. ナガイモの一品種. 奈良県大和地方の特産. ⇨長芋

やまとに【大和煮】 beef (or whale meat) boiled sweetly in *shoyu*[soy sauce], sugar and ginger. 牛肉（または鯨肉）をしょうゆ, 砂糖, 生姜で甘辛く煮つめた料理.

やまねこ【山猫】〔動物〕 a lynx; a wildcat. ネコ科の哺乳動物. ¶**特別天然記念物であるイリオモテヤマネコの生息地** the natural habitat of the rare Iriomote wildcat, a special natural monument. （西表島に生息）. ⇨ねこ

やまのて【山の手】 the residential districts [hilly sections] (of Tokyo). 都会の高台で, 住宅の多い地域. 東京の旧市内など. ⇨下町. ¶**山の手線** the Yamanote [Tokyo Loop] Line.

やまのひ【山の日】 Mountain Day (August 11). This national holiday was established in 2016 as a day to provide opportunities to get familiar with mountains and be thankful for blessings from mountains. Japan is blessed with an abundance of mountainous regions, and mountain trekking or hiking is a popular activity. この祝日は, 山に親しむ機会を得て, 山の恩恵に感謝する日として2016年（平成28年）に制定された. 日本は山岳地方に多数恵まれ, 山をトレッキングしたり, ハイキングをしたりする活動も人気が高い.

やまびらき【山開き】 an official opening of the mountain-climbing season; the opening of the mountain to climbers (for the year). その年はじめて登山を正式に許可すること.

やまぶき【山吹】〔植物〕 a Japanese rose [globeflower]; a golden kerria. バラ科の落葉低木.

やまぶし【山伏】 ❶〈修験僧〉 an itinerant Buddhist priest[monk]; a Buddhist priest [monk] who leads an ascetic life wandering in the mountains. 山野に寝起きして修行する僧. ❷〈修験者〉 a mountain ascetic; a Buddhist hermit. 仏教の隠者. ⇨山岳(山岳修験者)

やまぼこ【山鉾】 a tall festival float (covered with a roof with a halberd[pole] decorating the top). （頂上に鉾「竿」などを立てた屋根のある）祭りの高い山車. ☆「祇園祭」の山鉾は有名.

やまめ【山女・山女魚】〔魚〕 a *yamame*; a cherry[landlocked] salmon(サケ属の魚); a brook trout (川で一生を終えるマス). ☆関東では「やまべ」, 関西では「はえ」ともいう.

やみカルテル【闇カルテル】 an unauthorized [illegal, unlicensed] cartel.

やみきんゆう【闇金融】 an illegal loan; illegal loaning; illegal money lending;〈口語〉loan shaking; unlawful money-lending; black-market money-lending.

やみサイトはんざい【闇サイト犯罪】 an online [Internet] illegal crime behind the scenes.

やみルート【闇ルート】 (through) illegal channels.

やもり【守宮・家守】〔爬〕 a gecko (復~s, ~es); a house[wall] lizard. ヤモリ科の爬虫類.

やよいしきどき【弥生式土器】 Yayoi pottery[ware].

やらせ【遣らせ】 a staged scene[event](事前に仕組んだ場面[出来事]); a setup (八百長); a faking(まやかし); a rigging (不正操作). ¶**遣らせ場面** a staged[faked] scene; a made-up scene; a prearranged performances. **遣らせ質問** a staged[prearranged] question.

やり【槍】 a spear (武器); a lance (騎兵の); a javelin (槍投げ用). ¶**槍先** a spearhead. **槍持** a spear-bearer.

やりいか【槍烏賊】〔魚〕 a (spear) squid. 刺身は美味. 干したものは「笹するめ」(a dried squid)という.

やりみず【遣り水】 an artificial stream in a garden; an artificial stream running into the pond through a Japanese landscape garden. 日本の造景庭園に水を引き入れて，池に注ぐようにした人工的な小さな流れ. ☆「植木へ遣り水」watering the plants.

ヤンママ〈十代の母親〉 teen mother; a teenaged single mom; a trendy young un-married mother. ☆「ヤングママ」「ヤンキーママ」(和製語)の短縮形.

ゆ

ゆいのう【結納】 engagement[betrothal] gifts exchanging; a ceremonial exchange of engagement[betrothal] gifts. Gifts [presents] are exchanged between the two families of the prospective bride and groom as a confirmation of marriage engagement. Mostly the man gives the woman an engagement ring, a monetary gift and other gifts of good omen (such as sea bream, casks of *sake*, folding fans, etc.). 婚約のしるしに，将来，新郎新婦になる男女の両家が金品などを交わすこと. 婚約指輪・金品・縁起物(鯛, 酒樽, 扇子など)などは男性側が女性側に贈る.

【結納金】 betrothal money (presented by the male[would-be groom] to his fiancée). Money is wrapped in red and white folded paper tied decoratively with gold and silver strings. 男性が女性に贈る婚約金. 金

末広　昆布　するめ　かつお節　酒肴料　熨斗　目録　共白髪

銀の紐(水引)で結んだ紅白の折り畳んだ紙(熨斗)に包む. ☆ would-be groom[groom-to-be]「結婚間近な男性」. ⇨祝儀袋

【結納金半返し】 (custom of) returning half of betrothal money given by the would-be groom. It is customary for the would-be bride to return half of betrothal gift money. 女性が男性から受けた結納金を半分にして返すこと. ☆ would-be bride [bride-to-be]「結婚間近な女性；未来の花嫁」. ⇨半返し

【結納品】 betrothal gifts exchanged between the two families of the couple-to-be. All gifts are offered in odd-number units, as even-numbered offering (which can be divided by two) are avoided. 両家で取り交わす贈物. 品数は偶数(2で割れる)は避け，奇数で贈る. ☆「**目録**」list of engagement of gifts. ⇨熨斗

① 『かつお節』dried bonito symbolizing manliness. 男らしさの象徴.「勝男」.

② 『昆布』dried kelp expressing hope that the couple will be blessed with children. 子宝に恵まれる希望.「子生婦」.

③ 『するめ』dried cuttlefish showing hope that the couple's bond will be long-lasting. 縁を末永く願う.「寿留女」.

④ 『末広』a pair of white folding fans symbolizing hope that the couple will prosper. 繁栄を願う一対の白い扇.「末広がり」.

⑤ 『共白髪』a bundle of hemp string symbolizing hope that the couple will live long lives. 長寿を願う麻紐の束.「白髪交じり」.

⑥ 『酒肴料』food and drink charge. 酒肴に用いる金銭.

ゆうかい【誘拐】 kidnapping; abduction. ¶身代金誘拐 kidnapping for a ransom.

ゆうがお【夕顔】〔植物〕a (white-flowered) gourd; a bottle gourd; a calabash; a moon-flower(よるがお). ウリ科のつる性一年草.

「かんぴょう」に加工される. ⇨かんぴょう

ゆうかく【遊郭】 a red-light district; a licensed quarters.遊女屋が集まる所.「遊里」. ☆1958年に廃止 (abolished in 1958).

ゆうきやさい【有機野菜】 organic vegetables; organically-grown vegetables. ☆「無農薬野菜」は chemical-free vegetables.

ゆうけいぶんかざい【有形文化財】 tangible cultural properties[assets]. ⇨文化財[無形文化財]

ゆうげん【幽玄】〔能楽〕 mysterious and tranquil beauty (on a Noh stage); subtle and profound tranquility (on a Noh stage); quiet beauty and elegant simplicity (in a Noh play).

ゆうしょう【優勝】〔相撲〕 a tournament championship in any division. ¶優勝盃 a championship cup; a trophy.

ゆうせいみんえいか【郵政民営化】 postal service privatization; the privatization of postal services.

ゆうぜん【友禅】 *Yuzen* textiles dyed in elaborate patterns; pictorial silk fabric dyed in the *Yuzen* fashion. *Yuzen* textiles were developed by the painter Miyazaki Yuzensai of Kyoto in the Edo period. *Yuzen* textiles are used as material for *kimono* cloth.「友禅染め」(Yuzen-style dyeing)の略. 絹布に (花鳥風月など) 優雅な模様を染め出したもの. 江戸時代, 京都の画工兼扇絵師宮崎友禅斎 (1654-1736) が創案した. 着物呉服などに使用される. ⇨染物. ¶友禅染法 the *Yuzen* process of dyeing; the *Yuzen* dyeing technique. 友禅の着物 a *Yuzen*-printed *kimono*. 友禅模様 a *Yuzen* pattern.

【友禅五彩】 five bright colors with shadings in a silk fabric dyeing of the Kaga Yuzen fashion. The five colors include vermilion [dark red], indigo, yellow, green, and purple.「蘇芳, 藍, 黄土, 草, 古代紫」. ⇨五彩

ゆうやく【釉薬】 (a) glaze. *Yuyaku* is a powder of glass material applied to the surface of ceramics to give its gloss. 素焼きの陶磁器の表面に光沢を出すのに用いるガラス質の粉末. ⇨上薬. ¶陶磁器にかけた釉薬 *glaze* put on pottery.

ゆか【床】〔文楽〕 *yuka*; an elevated platform projecting from the stage. *Yuka* is a side stage on which the *tayu* narrator and the *shamisen* accompanists sit (facing the audience). 舞台から張り出した高座. (観客に向かいながら) 語りの太夫と三味線の伴奏者が座る演奏用の横舞台.

ゆかた【浴衣】 a *yukata*; a light, unlined *kimono* (for summer wear); an informal [casual] thin cotton *kimono* (for summer wear). *Yukata* is worn for relaxing after taking a bath or in hot weather. People often put on *yukata* when they join the dancing at the Bon festival. 夏着用の木綿のひとえの着物. 入浴後また暑い季節に気楽に着る. 盆踊りなどに参加するときにも着る. ☆「湯帷子」(昔は入浴時に着たひとえの着物. 現在では入浴後に着る) の略. ¶浴衣地 a cotton cloth for a *yukata*.

【浴衣帯】 an *obi*[sash] for a *yukata*. ☆男性用の「角帯」(stiff *obi*[sash] for men) と女性用の「半幅帯」(narrow *obi*[sash] for women) がある. ⇨角帯 / 半幅帯

ゆかん【湯灌】 the washing of a corpse (for burial); washing of the dead body with hot water in a Japanese funeral. 葬儀に備えて遺体を湯で洗い清めること.

ゆき【裄】 sleeve length (of a *kimono*). 袖丈のこと. ☆着物の背縫いから袖口までの長さ.

ゆきづり【雪吊り】〈綱〉 branch-protecting slings[ropes];〈枝を吊り上げること〉 stringing up the branches of trees to prevent damage from the heavy snow. Slings[ropes] are stretched from the tree tops to the lower branches like umbrellas to protect branches from snow damage. 枝を保護する縄. 雪の重みによる被害から保護するために木の枝を吊り上げること. 雪の被害で枝が折れないように, 縄を傘のように木の上方から下枝まで延ばす.

ゆきまつり【雪祭り】 the Snow Festival. ⇨ 付記(1)「日本の祭り」(2月)「札幌雪まつり」

ゆきみざけ【雪見酒】 sipping *sake* while looking out at the snow; drinking *sake* while enjoying a snow scene. 雪景色を見ながら酒を飲むこと.

ゆきみどうろう【雪見燈籠】 a snow-viewing stone lantern with a tripod; a three-legged stone lantern with a broad headpiece[roof]. It is set in a Japanese landscape garden for ornamental purposes. 広い笠のある三脚[四脚]の足がついた石灯籠. 装飾用として日本の風景庭園などに設けてある.

ゆず【柚子・柚】〔植〕 a *yuzu* citron; a small citrus fruit; a Japanese lime. ミカン科の常緑小高木. 果汁はポン酢など果実酢として用いられる. ¶へぎ柚子 the skin of a *yuzu* citron. 針柚子 strips of the *yuzu* citron peel. ⇨柚餅子

〔食品〕柚子胡椒 strips of the dried *yuzu* citron peel and green pepper mixed with salt(針柚子と青唐辛子に塩を混ぜた調味料). 柚子味噌 *yuzu* citron *miso*[bean paste]; *miso* mixed with *yuzu* citron.(柚子の実をすり混ぜた味噌). 柚子酢 *yuzu* citron vinegar.

【柚子湯】 a hot citron bath; a hot bath scented with *yuzu* citrons[limes]. It is believed people can avoid catching cold if they takes a hot bath with some citrus fruits floating in the bathtub. 柚子の実を入れた香のよい風呂. 湯船に柚子を浮かべた熱い風呂に入れば風邪をひかないといわれる. ☆通常は冬至の日 (the day of the winter solstice) に利用する.

ゆすり【強請り】〔行為〕 extortion(強奪); blackmail(恐喝);〈人〉 an extortionist; a blackmailer.

ゆたんぽ【湯たんぽ】 a hot-water bottle [bag]; a foot warmer. It is put in the bedding to keep the feet warm in winter. 足を暖める器具. お湯を入れる容器. 冬季足を暖めるために夜具に入れる.

ゆどうふ【湯豆腐】 boiling *tofu*[bean curd]; boiled *tofu*. Cubes of *tofu* boiled in hot water with a sheet of kelp in an earthenware pot. *Yudofu* is eaten hot with *shoyu*[soy sauce] and some condiments such as dried bonito flakes, minced green onions, grated ginger, etc. 豆腐を土鍋に入れて昆布だしの湯で熱し, 醤油と薬味(カツオ節, ネギ, ショウガなど)をつけ熱いうちに食べる.

ゆとりきょういく【ゆとり教育】 a cram-free education policy(詰め込み教育ではない); an education with latitude(自由範囲のある教育); an education free from pressure(抑圧されない教育).

ユネスコせかいいさん【ユネスコ世界遺産】 UNESCO World Heritage Site.

【関連語】自然遺産 Natural Heritage Site. **文化遺産** Cultural Heritage Site. **複合遺産** Mixed Heritage Site. ☆『日本の世界遺産』は下記のとおりである.

『文化遺産』

(1) 法隆寺地域の仏教建造物 «Buddhist Monuments in the Horyu-ji Area»[1993年12月]

(2) 姫路城 «Himeji-jo»[1993年12月]

(3) 古都京都の文化財 «Historic Monuments of Ancient Kyoto»[1994年12月]

(4) 白川郷・五箇山の合掌造り集落 «Historic Villages of Shirakawa-go and Gokayama»[1995年12月]

(5) 原爆ドーム «Hiroshima Peace Memorial (Genbaku Dome)»[1996年12

(6) 厳島神社 «Itsukushima Shinto Shrine» ［1996年12月］

(7) 古都奈良の文化財 «Historic Monuments of Ancient Nara»［1998年12月］

(8) 日光の寺社 «Shrines and Temples of Nikko»［1999年12月］

(9) 琉球王国のグスク及び関連遺産群 «Gusuku Sites and Related Properties of the Kingdom of Ryukyu»［2000年12月］

(10) 紀伊山地の霊場と参詣道 «Sacred Sites and Pilgrimage Routes in the Kii Mountain Range»［2004年7月］

(11) 石見銀山遺産とその文化的背景 «Iwami Ginzan Silver Mine and its Cultural Landscape»［2007年6月］

(12) 平泉―仏国土（浄土）を表す建築・庭園及び考古学的遺跡群 «Hiraizumi- Temples, Gardens and Archeological Sites Representing Buddhist Pure Land»［2011年6月］

(13) 富士山―信仰の対象と芸術の源泉 «Fujisan, sacred place and source of artistic e inspiration»［2013年6月］

(14) 富岡製糸場と絹産業遺産群 «Tomioka Silk Mill and Related Sites»［2014年6月］

(15) 明治日本の産業革命遺産　製鉄・製鋼, 造船, 石炭産業 «Sites of Japan's Meiji Industrial Revolution: Iron and Steel, Shipbuilding and Coal Mining»［2015年7月］

(16) ル・コルビュジエの建築作品―近代建築運動への顕著な貢献 «The Architectural Work of Le Corbusier, an Outstanding Contribution to the Modern Movements»［2016年7月］

(17)「神宿る島」宗像・沖ノ島と関連遺産 «Sacred Island of Okinoshima and Associated Sites in the Munakata Region»［2017年7月］

(18) 長崎と天草地方の潜伏キリシタン関連遺産 «Hidden Christian Sites in the Nagasaki Region»［2018年6月］

(19) 百舌鳥・古市古墳群-古代日本の墳墓群 «Mozu-Furuichi Kofun Group: Mounded Tombs of Ancient Japan»［20019年7月］

(20) 北海道・北東北の縄文遺跡群 «Jomon Prehistoric Sites in Northern Japan»［2021年7月］

『自然遺産』

(1) 屋久島 «Yakushima»［1993年12月］

(2) 白神山地 «Shirakami-Sanchi»［1993年12月］

(3) 知床 «Shiretoko»［2005年7月］

(4) 小笠原諸島 «Ogasawara Islands»［2011年6月］

(5) 奄美大島, 徳之島, 沖縄島北部及び西表島 «Amami-Oshima Island, Tokunoshima Island, Northern part of Okinawa Island, and Iriomote Island»［2021年7月］

ユネスコむけいぶんかいさん【ユネスコ無形文化遺産】　UNESCO Intangible Cultural Heritage.

［2008年登録］ (1) 能楽. (2) 人形浄瑠璃文楽. (3) 歌舞伎

［2009年登録］ (4) 雅楽. (5) アイヌ古式舞踊(北海道). (6) チャッキラコ(神奈川県). (7) 奥能登のあえのこと(石川県). (8) 小千谷縮・越後上布(新潟県). (9) 早池峰神楽(岩手県). (10) 秋保の田植踊(宮城県). (11) 大日堂舞楽(秋田県). (12) 題目立(奈良県).

［2010年登録］ (13) 組踊(沖縄県). (14) 結城紬(茨城県, 栃木県).

［2011年登録］ (15) 壬生の花田植(広島県). (16) 佐陀神能(島根県).

［2012年登録］ (17) 那智の田楽(和歌山県).

［2013年登録］ (18) 和食(日本人の伝統的な食文化).

［2014年登録］ (19) 和紙：日本の手漉和紙技術(石州半紙・本美濃紙・細川紙).

［2016年登録］ (20) 山・鉾・屋台行事. ☆国

ゆ

の重要無形民俗文化財に指定されてる33件の「山・鉾・屋台行事」より構成されている．京都祇園祭の山鉾行事，日立風流物などを含む．

［2018年登録］(21) 来訪神：仮面・仮装の神々．☆2009年に登録された甑島のトシドンに，男鹿のナマハゲなど9件が追加され拡張登録．

［2020年登録］(22) 伝統建築工匠の技：木造建造物を受け継ぐための伝統技術．

ゆのはな【湯の華［花］】 flowers of sulfur (硫黄の華)；deposits of hot-spring water (温泉の沈殿物)；mineral[salt] encrustations [incrustations] left by hot springs(温泉に残る鉱物質の外被(で覆う物))；sinter (珪華：温泉中に沈殿する温泉華)．The fur of the boiling sulfur-laden water from hot springs (found in the *Yuba*[hot-spring-water field])．湯場にみられる硫黄を帯びた熱い湯垢．別称「湯花」．⇨湯場

ゆば【湯葉・湯波】 (a sheet of) boiled soybean-milk skin[skim]; (a sheet of) dried soybean casein. *Yuba* is made from the skin[skim] forming on the the top of boiled soybean milk. It is used, either raw or dried, as an ingredient in soup and traditional dishes. 豆乳を煮たて，その表面にできたうすい皮［膜］をすくいとって製した食品．生ものと乾燥ものがあり，汁物や伝統料理の食材として用いる．☆栃木県日光市の特産ゆばは「湯波」と書く．製法の異なる中華料理のゆばは「豆腐皮」と書く．「湯皮」「油皮」とも．☆ casein「カゼイン，乾酪素」(牛乳の中のタンパク質；チーズの原料)．

ゆば【湯場】 a hot-spring-water field. The field is full of steam from the boiling sulfur-laden water gushing out of the earth[ground] (in Kusatsu Hot Spring). 地中から湧き出る硫黄を帯びた熱湯の蒸気で満ちた湯畑．圏草津温泉(長野県)．別称「湯畑」．⇨湯の華

ゆびきり【指切り】 a pledge by hooking each other's little finger; a pledge by linking one's little fingers to confirm a promise. Two people[children] extend their little fingers and hook[link] them together as a confirmation of their promise. 約束を守るしるし(as a token of pledge)に，相互に小指をからませながら誓うこと．別称「(指きり)げんまん」．

ゆぶね【湯船・湯槽】 a bathtub; a bath. 別称「浴槽」¶湯船に浸かる soak (oneself) in the bathtub.

ゆべし【柚餅子】 sweet *yuzu* citron-flavored steamed dumplings[rice-cake sweets] (mixed with rice flour, sugar and *miso*[bean paste]). (米粉・砂糖・味噌などを混ぜ)柚子の実の汁を加えて蒸した餅菓子．

ゆみとりしき【弓取式】〔相撲〕the bow-twirling ceremony performed by a *sumo* wrestler (after the final bout of each day). A traditional dance with a bow is performed at the end of each *sumo* tournament by a designated wrestler, the *yumitori*, who is usually from the *makushita* division. (場所中毎日の結びの一番の後に)1人の指名力士(通常は幕下)が弓をとって回転させる儀式．

ゆみはりぢょうちん【弓張り提灯】 a paper lantern with a bow-shaped handle. 弓形の柄［取っ手］がある紙提灯．「屋号」や「火の用心」などの文字を書く円筒形の提灯．

ゆみや【弓矢】 a bow and arrow. ☆「弓」には「弦」(bowstring), 「弓弭」(nock), 「握り」(grip), 「矢」には「矢先」(point), 「篦」(shaft), 「矢羽」(vane)がある．⇨弓道

ゆり【百合】〔植〕a lily. ユリ科の多年草．鑑賞用．根は食用．¶ユリ根 a lily bulb. (「茶碗蒸し」に不可欠)．鬼百合 a tiger lily. 車百合 a wheel lily. 山百合 a golden-band lily. 姫百合 a morning-star lily. 白百合 a white lily.

よ

ようがく【洋楽】　Western music; European music. ⇔邦楽

ようかん【羊羹】*yokan*;〈棒状〉(a bar of) sweet jellied *adzuki*-bean paste;〈小片〉(a slice of) thick jelly of sweet *adzuki*-bean paste. *Yokan* is a confectionery made by kneading (or steaming) a mixture of sweetened *adzuki*-bean paste, sugar and *kanten* gelatin (made from agar-agar). Most *Yokan* comes in a solid bar-like form. 餡子に砂糖・寒天を入れて練り(または蒸し)固めてつくる菓子. 棒状(stick-like)に固めたものが多い. ☆鎌倉・室町時代に中国から伝来する. ⇨水羊羹 (water *yokan*)/ 練り羊羹 (kneaded *yokan*) / 蒸し羊羹 (steamed *yokan*)

ようがん【溶岩】　lava (of volcano). ⇨火口. ¶溶岩流(出) a lava flow[stream]; an overflow[a stream] of lava. 溶岩原 a lava field. 溶岩層 a lava bed. 溶岩台地 a lava plateau. 溶岩湖 a lava lake.

ようきょく【謡曲】〖能楽〗(chant) a Noh song; (intone) a Noh chant. *Yokyoku* is the lyrics delivered in a chanting form in the Noh libretto. The Noh dance is performed to the accompaniment of *Yokyoku*. 能の歌詞を謡の様式で語る叙事詩. またはそれを歌うこと. 謡曲に合わせて能を舞う.「謡」ともいう. ⇨謡

ようじ【楊枝】〈食後に使用〉a toothpick; a pick;〈食べ物を刺す〉a (cocktail) stick. ⇨爪楊枝(食後に使用) / 黒文字

ようじぎゃくたい【幼児虐待】　child abuse; maltreatment[ill-treatment] of children.

ようじごろし【幼児殺し】infanticide.

ようしょく【養殖】　culture; farm; farming; breeding; aquaculture. ¶うなぎの養殖 an eel farm[nursery]. かきの養殖 an oyster farming[culture]. かきの養殖場 an oyster bed[farm]. 養殖魚 hatchery fish. 養殖地 a (fish-)breeding ground. うなぎの養殖地 an eel-breeding ground. (浜名湖など). 養殖真珠 a cultured pearl. ⇔天然真珠 (natural pearl)

ようちゅう【幼虫】a larva (⌷ larvae);〈甲虫〉a grub;〈蝿〉a maggot;〈蛾 や 蜂〉a caterpillar. ⇨ 蝶々

よこがき【横書き】　horizontal writing; the system to write horizontally[across the page] (from left to right[from top to bottom]). ⇔縦書き

よこづな【横綱】　a *yokozuna* (*sumo* wrestler). ❶〈人〉a grand champion *sumo* wrestler; a *sumo* wrestler of the highest rank.
❷〈地位〉the top rank of *sumo* wrestlers; the highest-ranking *sumo* champion in the *makuuchi* division. 幕内の最上位. ⇨相撲の番付

【横綱審議委員会】 the *Yokozuna* Promotion Council. Members of the Japan Sumo Association meet after each tournament (*honbasho*) to decide on the promotion of *sumo* wrestlers to the rank of *yokozuna*. 日本相撲協会の横綱審議委員会の委員が各場所終了後に横綱昇進について審議する.

よこてのぼんでん【横手の梵天】the Bonden Festival in Yokote. (2月). ⇨付記(1)「日本の祭り」

よこはまみなとまつり【横浜港まつり】　the Yokohama Port Festival. (5月). ⇨付記(1)「日本の祭り」

よし【葦】〖植物〗a reed; a ditch reed. イネ科の多年草.「あし」ともいう. ⇨あし ¶葦笛 a reed pipe[flute].
【葦簾】 a reed screen; a reed blind; a screen made of reed stem. 葦の茎で編んだすだれ.
¶葦簾張りの小屋 a hut sheltered with reed screens; a shed walled with reed screens.
【葦戸】 a reed sliding door; a sliding door

made of reed screen. It is often used in summer in place of paper sliding door as it permits the breeze to pass through. 葦簾を張った障子. 風通しがよいので夏にはよく使用される.

よしだのひまつり【吉田の火まつり】 the Fire Festival at Fuji-Yoshida City. (8月). ⇨付記(1)「日本の祭り」

よじょうはんのちゃしつ【四畳半の茶室】〔茶道〕 a four-and-a-half-*tatami* (mat) room in the tea house; a 10-foot-square room in the tea house. *Yojo-han* room is a standard size for a tearoom in a simple, rustic tea ceremony. 侘茶の茶の湯を行う茶室の標準的な大きさ. ⇨茶室 / 侘茶

よせ【寄席】 a *yose*; a traditional Japanese variety theater; ⊛ a vaudeville theater [house]; ⊛ a music hall. ⇨落語 (comic storytelling)/ 講談 (dramatic storytelling)/ 漫才 (comic dialogue). ¶寄席演芸 a variety show entertainment; ⊛ a vaudeville performance; ⊛ a music-hall show. 寄席芸人 a variety show entertainer; ⊛ a vaudevillian; ⊛ a music-hall entertainer.

よせぎざいく【寄せ木細工】 handcrafted [handicraft] mosaic wooden ware; a marquetry (ware). 手作業によるモザイク模様の木製容器.「埋め木細工」ともいう.

よせなべ【寄せ鍋】 a hodge-podge[hotch-potch] of foods; a Japanese style chowder[stew]. *Yosenabe* is a hot pot dish filled with seafood, chicken meat and vegetables, which are cooked at the table in broth made from dried kelp stock. The main ingredients are clams, oysters, fish, chicken meat, prawns, *tofu*[soybean curd], seasonal vegetables, etc. A dipping sauce of either citrus-flavored soy broth or sesame is served when eating. 昆布の出し汁に魚介類・鶏肉・野菜を取り合わせた食卓でつくる鍋料理. 具材は蛤, 牡蠣, 魚, 鶏肉, 海老,

豆腐そして季節の野菜などがある. 食べるときにはポン酢またはゴマだれが出される.

《寄せ鍋の段取り》(具材を入れる順番は「あかさたな」). [あ] (味付けの出し汁を温める). [か] (貝類を入れる). [さ] (魚・鶏肉・海老などを入れる). [た] (大豆からとった豆腐・湯葉などを入れる). [な] (菜っ葉・野菜を入れる)

[あ]味付けの出し汁　[な]菜っ葉・野菜
[た]豆腐・湯葉　[か]貝類　[さ]魚・鶏肉・海老

よなきそば【夜鳴き蕎麦】〈そば〉 *soba*[buck-wheat noodles] sold from a cart by a hawker[vendor] at night. 〈人〉 a vendor selling buckwheat noodles from a cart at night. 夜に屋台で売るそば, また売る人. ⇨屋台

よびだし【呼び出し】〔相撲〕❶〈呼び出すこと〉 an introduction of *sumo* wrestlers by announcing[calling out] their names to the *sumo* ring in a traditional tone and manner before their bouts. 次に取り組む力士の名を古風な口調で呼んで土俵で紹介する. ❷〈呼び出す人〉 a *sumo* ring announcer [caller]; an usher (日本相撲協会用語). He introduces the competing *sumo* wrestlers by announcing [calling out] their names. 控え力士を呼び出す人.「呼び出し奴」の略. ⇨相撲《相撲の取組》

よふかしぞく【夜更かし族】 late-nighters; nighthawks; night owls. ⇦ early-risers[early birds].

よみせ【夜店】〈夜市〉a night fair;〈個々の店〉a night stall[stand, booth]. 夜の露店 ;〈商人〉a night-stall vendor. ⇨屋台

よみふだ【読み札】〈百人一首〉 cards to be read out in the game of *Hyakunin-isshu*; cards containing the first couplets[lines] of a *tanka* poem (which is) read out to players. The first half of a *tanka* poem is printed on a card. 遊戯者に読みあげる短歌の前半部が記された札. 歌カルタでは読むほうの札. ⇨取り札. ⇨百人一首
☆現在の読み札は一首すべて, つまり5・7・5音の上の句と7・7音の下の句の両方が作者名と作者の肖像画とともに美麗に書かれている. 取り札の方は下の句のみで, 文字だけが書かれている.

よめいびり【嫁いびり】 being cruel to the son's wife[daughter-in-law]; to treat[pick on] a son's wife harshly; to ill-treat one's daughter-in-law.

よめしゅうと【嫁姑(間柄)】 the relationship between a wife and her mother-in-law; the relationship between mother-in-law and her daughter-in-law.

よもぎ【蓬】〔植物〕 (a) mugwort; (a) wormwood. キク科の多年草. 若葉は「草餅・草団子」に, また「麩」に入れて香と色が楽しめる. 乾かした繊維から艾をつくる. ⇨艾 / 灸
〔食品〕蓬団子 a rice-flour dumpling mixed and flavored with mugwort leaves; a mugwort-flavor sticky rice-flour dumpling. ⇨草団子. 蓬麩 a dried wheat gluten[bread] cooked with mugwort leaves. ⇨麩. 蓬餅 a rice cake mixed and flavored with mugwort leaves; a mugwort-flavor sticky rice cake. ⇨草餅

よりつき【寄付】〔茶道〕 a waiting room[an arbor] for a tea ceremony. 茶道用の簡単な待合室[休憩所]. ☆通常は3畳の部屋 (a three-mat room)で客が待つ.

よろい【鎧】 (a suit[piece] of) feudal armor [英] armour (fastened together with leather thongs of various colors). 多彩な皮ひもで結ばれている. ¶鎧櫃 an armor chest[case]. 鎧武者 an armor-clad *samurai*[feudal warrior]; a *samurai*[feudal warrior] clad in armor. 鎧直垂 a silk garment[robe] worn by warriors under the armor.

よろずや【万屋】〈何でも屋〉 a Jack-of-all-trades(米) Jacks-of-all-trades); a (general) handyman; an all-rounder.「便利屋」ともいう ;〈店〉a general store.

ら

ライオン[獅子]〔動物〕a lion(雄); a lioness (雌); a lion cub(子). ネコ科の哺乳動物. 別称「しし」

らいごう【来迎】 the descent of Amitabha [Buddha Amida] and Bodhisattvas to welcome a dying person (who is chanting the Buddhist invocation) to the Land of Perfect Bliss. (念仏を唱える)人の臨終の際, 阿弥陀仏や諸菩薩が現れて, 人を極楽浄土に迎えること.「御来迎」ともいう. ¶阿弥陀如来来迎図 a picture depicting the descent of Amitabha. 阿弥陀仏が現れて, 人を極楽浄土に迎える絵図.

らいじん【雷神】 the thunder god; the god of thunder. ⇨風神

らいち【茘枝】〔植物〕 a litchi; a lychee; a litchi(nut)(実).「れいし」ともいう.

らいちょう【雷鳥】〔鳥〕 a (snow) grouse; a rock ptarmigan; a thunderbird. ライチョウ科の鳥. 日本アルプスに生息する. 季節によって羽の色が変化(夏は茶色, 冬は全部白色)する. 日本では特別天然記念物.

らいはい【礼拝】⇨礼拝

ライむぎ【ライ麦】〔植物〕 rye. イネ科の一年草・二年草. 黒パン・ウイスキーの原料. ☆「ライ」(rye)は英語. ¶(ライ麦で作った)黒

パン rye bread.

らくがん【落雁】 *rakugan*; bean flour[rice flour] molded sweets; pressed cake made of bean flour[rice flour] and sugar. *Rakugan* is a hard dry sweet made by mixing bean flour (or rice flour) and starch sugar (or sugared water), and then pressing in a mold and dried. 大豆粉(または米粉)に水飴(または砂糖水)を加えてから，固めて乾燥させた干菓子. ⇨干菓子

らくご【落語】 a *rakugo*; a comic story-telling; a humorous monologue (performed by a professional storyteller). *Rakugo* is a traditional Japanese style comic story ending in a joke[with a punch line] (*ochi*) performed by a single storyteller (*hanashika*) who is seated on a cushion on stage. He tells a comic story by making puns (*dajare*), distinguishing between different roles by facing one way and another. 舞台の座布団に座る「噺家」(a solo storyteller; a professional raconteur)が演じる，最後に「落ち」(a witty surprising ending with unexpected twist in the plot)のある滑稽な話. 噺家はあちこちに顔を向け異なる役柄を演じながら，滑稽な話をする. ⇨古典落語 / 新作落語 / 寄席 / 落ち. ¶**落語家** a professional comic storyteller [raconteur]. 「噺家・咄家」ともいう. ⇨咄家

らくしょく【落飾】 becoming a monk[nun] after cutting off his/ her hair; becoming a monk[nun] after having his/ her head shaved; the shaving of one's hair. (貴人が)髪を剃り落として出家する[僧侶・尼になる]こと.「剃髪」ともいう.

らくだ【駱駝】〔動物〕 a camel ラクダ科の哺乳動物. ¶**らくだのこぶ** camel's hump. ☆アジア産は「ふたこぶらくだ」(背こぶは2個 a Bactrian camel)，アフリカ産は「ひとこぶらくだ」(背こぶは1個 an Arabian camel).

らくのうじょう【酪農場】a dairy farm. ¶

日本最大の私営農場(小岩井農場・岩手県) Koiwai Farm, Japan's largest privately-run dairy (farm). **酪農製品** dairy products.

らくやき【楽焼き】 a hand-made[hand-molded] earthenware[pottery] without using a wheel; an earthenware[pottery] made by hand without using a wheel. A glaze is applied after it is fired at low temperature. (製陶用の)ろくろを使用せず手で形を作る陶器. 低い温度で焼いた後で釉薬をつける. ☆さびれた趣 (rustic quality〈さび〉)があるため茶人 (tea-cult devotee)から愛好されている.

らっかせい【落花生】 a peanut; a groundnut. マメ科の一年草. 別名「南京豆」「ピーナッツ」.

らっかん【落款】 an artist's signature and seal on the painting; a calligrapher's signature and seal on the calligraphy paper. 書画に筆者[半紙に書家]が完成の意味で署名と印を押すこと. ¶**落款入りの絵画** a signed and sealed painting. **落款のない絵画** an unsigned painting.

らっきょう【辣韮】〔植物〕 scallion; shallot bulb. ユリ科の多年草. 欧米にはなく，中国産なので Chinese onion(ネギ)ともいう. 地下茎の鱗形(ユリ根・タマネギなどの球形の茎)は漬物に用いる.「花らっきょう」とは「小粒の酢漬けらっきょう」(vinegared tiny scallion)のこと. ¶**辣韮漬け** a pickled scallion[shallot bulb].

らっこ【猟虎】 (アイヌ語 rakko)〔動物〕 a sea otter; a sea ape. イタチ科の哺乳動物. 毛皮は珍重される.

らっぱずいせん【喇叭水仙】〔植物〕 a daffodil. ⇨すいせん

らでん【螺鈿】 mother-of-pearl. 真珠層(真珠貝などの貝殻の内部の光る部分).

【螺鈿細工】 (a piece of) mother-of-pearl work; a design in mother-of-pearl inlay; an artistically crafted article inlaid with mother-of-pearl or other shells on the lacquer. An iridescent mother-of-pearl is cut into various shapes and set into[pasted] on the lacquered surface of the wood. 貝殻の色つやの美しい真珠層の部分を文様の形に切り, 漆面の木目にはめ込む[はりつける].

らば〔騾馬〕〔動物〕a mule. 雄ロバと雌馬との雑種.

ラベンダー〔植物〕a lavender:〈香料〉lavender. シソ科の植物.

ラムサールじょうやく【ラムサール条約】〈正式名称〉the Ramsar Convention; the Convention on Wetlands of International Importance Especially as Waterfowl Habitat.「国際湿地条約」. ☆特に水鳥の生息地として国際的に重要な湿地に関する条約.

ラムネ soda pop; lemon pop. 清涼飲料水(炭酸水に砂糖と香料を入れた水)の一種. ☆「レモネード」(lemonade)のなまり. ¶ラムネ玉 a glass marble(びんに詰まったガラス玉).

らん【蘭】〔植物〕an orchid. ラン科植物の総称. 観賞用に栽培される.

らん【乱】rebellion(暴動); uprising(叛乱); war(戦乱); riot(反乱); revolt(騒乱). ¶平治の乱 *Heiji* Disturbance[Rebellion]. (1159年. 平氏が朝廷において権力を確立). 応仁の乱 *Onin* War; the War of *Onin*. (1467年~1477年. 京都中心の内乱. 足利家の将軍職の後継ぎ争いをきっかけに天下を二分する. 乱後, 戦国時代に入る). ⇨島原の乱

らんま【欄間】a *ranma*; a (decorative) transom. A *ranma* is made of fine wood[bamboo] with decorative lattices or ornamental openwork screens. It is placed between the ceiling and the lintel beam above the sliding paper doors of a Japanese room. 仕切りの飾り横材[飾り無目]. 飾り格子または飾り透かし彫り[細工]をはめこんだ木製

[竹製]の横木. 和室のふすまの上にある天井と鴨居の間に設けられている.

り

り【里】a *ri*; a league; unit of distance equal to about 4 km. 距離の単位.「一里」は約4キロ(3.92km). 英米では「約3マイル」.

リアスしきかいがん【リアス式海岸】a rias[ria-type] coastline; a deeply indented [sawtoothed] coastline. ☆rias「リアス」奥に行くにつれて次第に浅くなる細長い入り江.「リアス海岸」は陸地が沈んでできた岬と入り江の入り込んだ海岸のこと. 圏 陸中海岸国立公園. riasはスペイン語 ria (深い入り江)の複数形.

りきし【力士】〔相撲〕❶ a *sumo* wrestler (listed in the *makuuchi* and *makushita*). ❷「金剛力士」の略. ⇨仁王

りきゅう【離宮】a detached palace; an Imperial villa. A detached palace[An Imperial villa] is located outside the grounds of the permanent Imperial Palace. 皇居とは別に設けられた宮殿. ¶桂離宮 the Katsura Imperial Villa[Detached Palace].(八条宮智仁親王の別荘. 池や茶室を配した庭園が美しい). 修学院離宮 the Shugakuin Imperial Villa.(後水尾上皇の別荘. 借景庭園を配した山荘で有名).

りす【栗鼠】〔動物〕a squirrel. リス科の哺乳動物. ¶縞栗鼠 a striped squirrel.

りっか【立夏】the beginning of summer (in the lunar calendar); the first calendrical day of summer. 夏に入る日. ⇨二十四節気

りっか【立華・立花】〔華道〕the standing [vertical] form of flowers arranged in a vase. 花瓶に生けた花木を立てる基本様式. ☆書院の床の間の飾り花としてよく用いる. ⇨盛り花／投げ入れ

りっしゅう【立秋】the beginning[first day] of autumn[fall] (in the lunar calendar); the first calendrical day of autumn[fall]. It falls around the August 7 (or 8) in the present calendar. 秋に入る日. ⇨二十四節気

りっしんけい【立真型】〔華道〕 the upright style of a flower arrangement (used in the Sogetsu school). 花木をまっすぐに生ける基本様式(草月流). ⇨直態(池坊流)

りっしゅん【立春】 the beginning of spring (in the lunar calendar); the first calendrical day of spring. It falls on February 4 (or 5) in the present calendar. 春に入る日. ⇨二十四節気

りつぞう【立像】〈仏像〉a standing statue [image] of Buddha; 〈像〉a statue of a standing figure. ⇨座像

りったいテレビ【立体テレビ】 a three-dimensional television[3-D TV]; a stereoscopic television.

りっとう【立冬】 the beginning of winter (in the lunar calendar); the first calendrical day of winter. 冬に入る日. ⇨二十四節気

りつりょう【律令】 the legal codes of the Nara and Heian periods. The legal codes consist of criminal law (*ritsu*) and administrative[civil] law (*ryo*). 奈良時代(710-794)・平安時代(794-1185)の基本法典で、「律」は刑法、「令」は行政法にあたる. ¶律令国家 the State[Nation] governed on the principles of a *Ritsuryo* legal code. 律令制度 a system of centralized government based on the *Ritsuryo* legal codes. Governmental structure is defined by the criminal codes (*Ritsu*) and the administrative[civil] codes (*Ryo*). 律令政治 the government administered[conducted] according to the *Ritsuryo* legal codes. The Emperor and nobles played central roles in the government. (天皇と貴族が中心になって政治を行う).

りつれい【立礼】 a standing bow; a bow of respect made when standing on the floor. 起立して行う礼. ⇨座礼. ⇨お辞儀

りつれいしき【立礼式】〔茶道〕 the upright manner in the tea ceremony. Tea is served at a table with chairs, not on *tatami*-mat floor in the tearoom. 起立しての茶道様式. 茶室の畳の間ではなく椅子付きのテーブルで茶が出される.

リフォームさぎ【リフォーム詐欺】 home repair fraud.

りゅう【竜・龍】 a dragon. ☆想像上の動物. 二本の角と四本の足をもち、巨大な蛇に似ている.

りゅういき【流域】 a river basin[valley]. ¶信濃川流域(長野[千曲川]・新潟・群馬の3県) the Shinano River Basin; the basin of the Shinano River.

りゅうかすいそじさつ【硫化水素自殺】 suicide using poisonous hydrogen sulfide. 有毒ガスの硫化水素を使った自殺. ☆小穴を抜ける気体のため、巻き添え被害(collateral damage)が絶えなかった(2008年).

りゅうきゅう【琉球】 Ryukyu. 形 Ryukyuan. ¶琉球王朝 the Ryukyu Dynasty. 琉球王国 the Ryukyu kingdom. 琉球王 the king of the Ryukyus. 琉球列島[諸島]the Ryukyu Islands; the Ryukyus. 琉球文化 Ryukyuan culture; the culture of the Ryukyu. 琉球貿易 the Ryukyuan trade.

りゅうつうセンター【流通センター】 a distribution center. ¶米の流通センター(鶴岡) a distribution center for the rice harvest.

りゅうは【流派】〔華道〕 a school of flower arrangement. 生け花の流派. ☆The three main schools are Ikenobo (池坊), Ohara-ryu (小原流) and Sogetsuryu (草月流).

りゅうひょう【流氷】 drift ice. ¶流氷原 an ice floe (forming a great ice field in the sea).

りょう【陵】a mausoleum. ⇨陵墓. ¶仁徳天皇陵 the Mausoleum of Emperor Nintoku; the Nintoku Mausoleum, the largest tumulus in Japan.(日本最大の古墳. 世界最大の

墓域面積. 大阪府). ☆ユネスコ世界文化遺産.

りょうしゅ【領主】〈荘園主〉the lord of a manor;〈大名・小名〉a proprietary lord (in the Heian period); the lord of a fief (in the Edo period); a feudal lord (in the Edo period).

りょうてい【料亭】 a high-class Japanese style restaurant. *Ryotei* has private *tatami-mat* guest rooms in traditional Japanese structure, serving formal Japanese cuisine. 高級料亭. 日本の伝統的な建築に畳を敷いた個室があり, 正式な日本料理を出す.

りょうど【領土】a territory; a domain; a possession. 厖 territorial. ¶日本の領土 Japanese territory. 日本の北方領土 the (Russian-held) northern territories of Japan. 領土の争い a territorial conflict[dispute]. 領土権[主権] rights [sovereignty] over territory; territorial rights [sovereignty].

りょうぼ【陵墓】an Imperial mausoleum. 皇族の墓. ☆「陵」は天皇・皇后・太皇太后・皇太后の墓,「墓」はその他の皇族の墓. ⇨霊廟

りょうり【料理】❶ cooking; cookery. 食材を加熱して食す. ¶家庭料理 home cooking. 和食 Japanese cooking. ❷ cuisine. 特定の料理法. ¶中国[フランス]料理 Chinese[French] cuisine. ❸ a dish(一品); dishes. 出来上った[皿に盛った]料理. ¶肉[魚, 野菜]料理 meat[fish, vegetables] dish. ❹ food. 食べ物[食品]. ¶冷凍[缶詰]食品 frozen[canned] food. 飲食物 food and drink (日英語の語順に注意).

りょかん【旅館】a *Ryokan*; a Japanese style inn[hotel]. *Ryokan* usually has *tatami-mat* rooms, sliding doors, and an alcove decorated with a hanging scroll and a flower arrangement in the guest room. 客間は畳部屋で, 襖, 掛け軸や生け花で飾った床の間などがある. ☆通常は「一泊二食付き」(dinner and breakfast charges are included in the room rate)である. ¶旅館の女将[主人] the proprietress[proprietor] of an inn; an innkeeper. 旅館の番頭 an inn manager.

りょくちゃ【緑茶】 green tea(お茶); green tea leaves(茶葉). *Ryokucha* is brewed with non-fermented tea leaves, but processed by steaming and drying. There are mainly three grades of green tea: *gyokuro*, *sencha*, and *bancha*. 茶の若葉を発酵させるのではなく, 蒸してからもみながら乾かして作る.「玉露」「煎茶」「番茶」の三種がある. ⇨玉露 / 煎茶 / 番茶

りんぎせいど【稟議制度】 the system[process] of obtaining sanction for a plan by circulating a draft proposal to reach a consensus. 合意を得るために原案を回覧することによって企画の決済をとる制度. ☆「稟議書」a round-robin.

りんご【林檎】〔植物〕 an apple tree(木); an apple(実); apple blossoms (花). 【関連語】「皮」skin; peel.「種」seed.「芯」core.「果肉」flesh.「柄」stalk. ☆「りんご酒」(apple wine)は⊛ hard cider. ⊛ cider.

りんどう【竜胆】〔植物〕 a gentian; an autumn bellflower. リンドウ科の多年草. 根は苦く, 健胃剤に使用する.

りんね【輪廻】〈仏教用語〉 *samsara*; transmigration of the soul; the cycle of life reincarnation. 霊魂の転生(生まれかわり死にかわること). 生死をくりかえすこと. 別称「流転生死」(the endless cycle of birth and death in the world).

る

ルーズソックス loose-fitting[baggy] white socks (worn by schoolgirls).

446

るすばんでんわ【留守番電話】 (telephone with) an answering machine; a telephone message recorder; an answerphone.

るすろく【留守録】 automatic video[audio] recording; a message left on an answering machine. 自動タイマー録画［録音］記録.

れ

れいえん【霊園】 a cemetery（共同墓地）; a graveyard（墓地）; a memorial park. ¶多磨霊園（東京都）Tama Cemetery (in which are buried some of the nation's great statesmen, generals, admirals and diplomats). 偉大な政治家・陸軍大将・海軍大将・外交官が眠る.

れいきゅうしゃ【霊柩車】a hearse.

れいさい【例祭】 an annual festival; a regular festival. 例年［定例］の祭り. ¶春日大社の例祭（奈良県）the Annual Festival of Kasuga Shrine.

れいざん【霊山】 a holy site[hill]; a sacred [holy] mountain. ¶日本三霊場 the Three Major Holy Sites in Japan. ☆恐山［青森県］・比叡山［京都府・滋賀県］・高野山［和歌山県］.

れいし【茘枝】 ⇨らいち

れいじょう【霊場】 ❶〈聖地〉 a holy[sacred] place; a holy land. ❷〈寺院〉 a Buddhist temple (associated the priest Kobo Daishi). ¶（四国88か所）霊場巡り（をする）(make) a pilgrimage round [circuit] of (eighty-eight) holy Buddhist temples (in Shikoku). ⇨巡礼

れいじょう【礼状】 (send) a "thank-you" letter[note]; a letter[note] of thanks [appreciation]. ☆お中元やお歳暮などの贈り物を受けた時に出す手紙.

れいすいまさつ【冷水摩擦】 (have) a rub-down with a cold wet towel; rubbing oneself with a cold wet towel.

れいぜん【霊前】 ⇨御霊前

れいはい【礼拝】worship. (神をおがむこと). ☆キリスト教では「れいはい」, 仏教では「らいはい」という. ¶礼拝堂 a chapel. 礼拝所 a worship hall; a hall of worship. 礼拝者 a worshipper. ⇨拝礼

れいびょう【霊廟】 a mausoleum (enshrining an ancestor's spirit). 祖先の霊をまつる所. 「廟宇」「廟所」また「御霊屋」などともいう. ¶徳川家康の霊廟 the Mausoleum of Tokugawa Ieyasu (the founder of the Tokugawa shogunate). ☆ mausoleum「壮大な墓」. 複数形は mausolea（ラテン語中性名詞の複数形）または mausoleums（英語式）.

れきしきょうかしょもんだい【歴史教科書問題】the Japanese History Textbook Controversy.

れきしくぶん【歴史区分】 the phase[stage] of the Japanese history. ⇨付記(2)「日本の歴史年表」
【関連語】7時代の区分 (seven major phases) ①『先史時代』(prehistoric period): 〈1〉旧石器時代 (the paleolithic period). 〈2〉縄文時代 (the Jomon period). 〈3〉弥生時代 (the Yayoi period). 〈4〉古墳時代 (the Kofun period).
②『原始時代』(protohistoric period): 飛鳥時代 (the Asuka period): 女帝推古天皇の朝廷, 聖徳太子の摂政, 大化の改新. 律令制の推進など.
③『古代』(ancient period):〈1〉奈良時代 (the Nara period): 710年の平城京の成立, 794年の平安京の成立など. 〈2〉平安時代 (the Heian period):宮廷文化の開花, 藤原氏の朝廷支配, 武士集団の出現など.
④『中世』(medieval period):〈1〉鎌倉時代 (the Kamakura period):鎌倉幕府の成立, 建武の新政, 南北朝時代. 〈2〉室町時代 (the Muromachi period): 日明貿易, 南蛮貿易, 戦国時代.
⑤『近世』(early modern period): 〈1〉安土・

桃山時代 (the Azuchi-Momoyama period): 織田信長・豊臣秀吉・徳川家康の時代. 〈2〉江戸時代 (the Edo period):江戸幕府の成立, 鎖国時代, 大政奉還など.

⑥『近代』(modern period):〈1〉明治時代 (the Meiji era). 〈2〉大正時代 (the Taisho era). 〈3〉昭和時代 (the Showa era):第二次世界大戦の終戦；ポツダム宣言・玉音放送.

⑦『現代』(contemporary period):〈1〉昭和時代 (the Showa era); 終戦後. 〈2〉平成時代 (the Heisei era). 〈3〉令和時代 (the Reiwa era).

れきしてきけんぞうぶつ【歴史的建造物】 historic buildings and structures. ⇨文化財

レジぶくろ【レジ袋】〈ビニール袋〉(supermarket) plastic bags; 〈勘定袋〉(supermarket) checkout bags. ¶レジ袋有料化 charging for plastic bags at retail cash registers. レジ袋消滅運動 a move to reduce checkout counter plastic bags. ☆「レジ」はレジスター (register)の略で,「レジ係」a cashier,「勘定台」checkout counter,「金銭登録器」a cash registerなどの意味がある.

れっとう【列島】 an archipelago(㊰~es,~s); a group[chain] of islands. ¶日本列島 the Japanese Archipelago. 五島列島 the Goto Islands. ⇨島 / 諸島 / 半島

レバー liver(肝臓). ⇨焼き鳥

れんが【連歌】 (a) *renga*; (a) linked verse [poem]. *Renga* is a verse of 5-7-5 syllables alternating with 7-7 syllables, which are composed jointly by more than two persons. The verse of 5-7-5 syllable takes a form of the *haiku* poem. 2人以上の歌人が和歌の上の句(5・7・5)と下の句(7・7)を次々によみ重ねていくもの. 俳句の詩形は連歌の発句部分を指す. ⇨俳句 / 短歌

れんげ【蓮華】 ❶〈蓮の花〉a lotus flower. 仏教では極楽浄土の象徴. ⇨蓮. ¶蓮華座 a lotus plinth[seat, pedestal] (beneath a Buddhist statue[a statue of Buddha]). 蓮の

花の形をした仏像の台座.「蓮台」. ⇨蓮台 ❷〈陶器のさじ〉a porcelain spoon; a china spoon.「散り蓮華」の略.

れんげそう【蓮華草】〔植物〕 (a) Chinese milk vetch. マメ科の二年草.

れんごうぐん【連合軍】 the Allied Forces. ¶連合軍最高司令官総司令部 the General Headquarters[GHQ] of the Allied Forces. 連合国軍総司令官 the Supreme Commander for the Allied Powers[SCAP]. ☆ SCAP Douglas MacArthur arrived at Atsugi Airfield in 1945. 連合国軍総司令官ダグラス・マッカーサーは1945年に厚木飛行場に到着した.

れんこん【蓮根】〔植物〕 a lotus root. スイレン科の多年草. 蓮の地下茎. 蓮の実[種子]は菓子をつくるのに用いる. ⇨蓮. ¶花蓮根 a lotus in the shape of a flower.

れんだい【蓮台】 a lotus plinth[pedestal, platform] on which a Buddhist statue stands. 仏像をのせる, 蓮の花形の台座. ⇨蓮華座

れんたん【練炭】 a coal briquet(te). ⇨炬燵

ろ

ろ【炉】〔茶道〕 an inset hearth; an open hearth sunk in the floor (by removing a corner of the *tatami* mat). It is used to hold an iron teakettle on a tripod in the tea ceremony. はめ込み炉床. (畳の隅を取り除いて)床に埋め込んだ炉床. 茶道で鉄製茶釜を三脚台にのせるのに用いる. ¶炉釜 a big-size iron teakettle for an inset hearth (used in the tea ceremony). 炉畳 a *tatami* mat in which the inset hearth is placed (in the tearoom). 炉縁 a frame board fitted around an inset hearth (of the tearoom).

ろうきょく【浪曲】 narrative singing[story recitation and song] with a single singer on stage accompanied by a *shamisen* player.

三味線を弾き，節をつけて歌いながら物語る．「浪花節」(*naniwabushi* recitation)ともいう．⇨浪花節

ろうし【浪士】 a masterless[lordless] *samurai*; a former retainer[vassal]. ¶赤穂浪士 the forty-seven masterless *samurai* of the Ako domain. 1703年: 赤穂事件. ⇨浪人

ろうじゅう【老中】 a senior councilor in the Tokugawa shogunate; a highest-ranking council member of Elders[State] serving the shogun in the Tokugawa shogunate government (usually chosen from hereditary feudal lord (*fudai-daimyo*)). 徳川幕府の役職名．将軍に直属して政務を総括する最高職．通常譜代大名から選ばれる．⇨大名(譜代)

ろうじょ【老女】 the head maidservant served the wife of the *samurai* family. 武家の奥方に仕えた女中のかしら.

ろうにん【浪人】 ❶〈武士〉a *ronin* (複 *ronin*(s)); a masterless[lordless] wandering *samurai* (in the feudal times). 封建時代に 君主を持たずに放浪する武士［侍］．主家を去り，その禄[給与]を失った武士.「牢人」とも書く．⇨浪士

❷〈高卒者〉 a high-school graduate who failed to enter colleges and decided to prepare for another chance to enter colleges.

❸〈失業者〉a jobless person; a person (who is) out of a job[between jobs].

ローリングぞく【ローリング族】 motorcycle [car] racers who compete on twisty roads.

ろくしゃくふんどし【六尺褌】 a (six-*shaku*-long[six-foot-long]) bleached cotton loincloth worn by men. 男性着用の長さ六尺の晒し木綿のふんどし．⇨尺

ろくまいびょうぶ【六枚屏風】 a six-paneled [six-folded] screen; a folding screen of six panels. ⇨屏風

ろくよう【六曜】 the *rokuyo*; the cyclic six-day divination marked on the folk calendar. Six-day cycle of lucky or unlucky days and times that is incorporated into the Japanese calendar. 民間暦の上で循環する6日の易断[占い]．諸行事の吉凶を占う基準となる六つの星. ☆中国の唐朝 (the Tang Dynasty[618-906]) に登場する陰陽[宇宙の二元力] (the principles of the Yin and Yang ; the positive and negative principles; the Chinese philosophy of cosmic dual forces)から由来し，江戸時代に流行した.

① 『先勝』 early winning day; winning the first game[match]. ☆「午前良し，午後悪し」Lucky in the morning, but unlucky in the afternoon. (何事も早い時間にすれば勝つという日．急用・訴訟などは良い). ⇦先負

② 『友引』 friend-pulling day; one's bad luck (is believed) to affect one's friend. ☆「終日良くもなく悪くもない」Neither lucky nor unlucky all day long. (勝負がつかない．良くも悪くもない日．葬式などをすると続いて友人の誰かが死ぬとういうので避けるとよい．しかし結婚式は差し支えない).

③ 『先負』 early losing day; losing the first game[match]. ☆「朝悪し，午後良し」Unlucky in the morning, but lucky in the afternoon. (物事に対処するには午前は悪いが，午後は吉であるとする日．急用・訴訟などは悪い). ⇦先勝

④ 『仏滅』 Buddha's death (all things' nullification). ☆「最悪．最大の用心が必要」the unluckiest day. Maximum precaution required. (「仏の入滅」であるため万事に凶[不吉] があるとする日．結婚・旅行・移転などに悪い). ⇦大安

⑤ 『大安』 the luckiest day; the greatest safety day. ☆「最良．万事良し」Very lucky. All shall go well. ¶大安吉日 the luckiest day. (万事に吉であるとする日,結婚・旅行・移転などに良い). ⇦仏滅

⑥『赤口』red mouth; better than nothing. ☆「悪し. 午後少し良し」Very unlucky. A little better in the afternoon.（赤舌神が人々を苦しめ, 万事が凶であるとする日）.

ろくろ【轆轤】〈陶工用の〉 a potter's wheel; 〈滑車〉a pulley; 〈旋盤〉a turning lathe.

ろざのだいぶつ【露座の大仏】 an outdoor seated statue of (the) Buddha.

ろじ【露地・路地】 **❶**〔茶道〕〈庭〉a teahouse garden; a garden adjacent[next] to a ceremonial teahouse. Guests[Participants] pass through this garden to enter a teahouse. 茶室の庭. 来客[参加者]は茶室に入るときこの庭を通る. ⇨茶庭 / 外露地 / 内露地 **❷**〔茶道〕〈小道〉a narrow pathway leading to a teahouse in a tea garden. 茶庭にある茶室へ通ずる狭い路地.

ロッキードじけん【ロッキード事件】the Lockheed Scandal.（1976年）

ろてん【露店】 an (open-air) street stall[㊎ booth]. ¶露店商（人）a (open-air) street vendor; a stall keeper.

ろてんぶろ【露天風呂】 an open-air bath; an outdoor bath. ¶露天風呂温泉 an open-air hot-spring bath; a hot-spring bath set in the open[outdoors].

ろば【驢馬】〔動物〕an ass; a donkey. ウマ科の哺乳動物.

ろばたやき【炉端焼き】 a Japanese style barbecue cooked in front of customers in a restaurant. Seafood (or meat) and vegetables are grilled over a charcoal fire on the sunken hearth in the center. 料理店で客の前で焼く日本式バーベキュー. 中央の埋め込み炉床にある炭火で魚介類（または肉）や野菜などを焼く.

わ

わか【和歌】(write) a *waka*[*tanka*]; (compose) a 31-syllable Japanese poem. A *waka* is a form of classical Japanese poem that consists of 31 syllables in the pattern 5-7-5-7-7. 5・7・5・7・7型の31音節からなる定型詩. ⇨短歌 / 俳句

わかおかみ【若女将】a proprietress-to-be (of a Japanese inn). ⇨女将

わかくさやまのやまやき 【若草山の山焼き】 the Grass-Burning-Fire Event on Wakakusa-yama Hill.（1月）. ⇨付記(1)「日本の祭り」

わかさぎ【鰙・公魚・若鷺】〔魚〕 a (Japanese) smelt; a pond smelt; a fresh-water smelt. キュウリウオ科の「淡水魚」(freshwater fish). 晩秋から冬が旬. 茨城県の霞ヶ浦の「わかさぎ」は有名.「ちか」（公魚）と混同されるが, これは「海水魚」(saltwater fish) である. 揚げ物に最適. ¶公魚の天ぷら a deep-fried smelt in batter.

わがし【和菓子】**❶**〈日本固有の菓子〉a Japanese confection[confectionery]; Japanese pastry; Japanese sweets. *Wagashi* is the beautifully crafted pastry expressive of the season. The main ingredients are rice flour (such as *senbei*) and red beans (such as *manju*). 美しく季節感を表現して巧妙にりあげた菓子. 主な成分は米粉（煎餅など）と小豆（饅頭など）などである. ¶和菓子屋 a store selling Japanese style confectionery. 《和菓子の主な種類》「干菓子」dry confection; dry sweets. ⇨らくがん/あられ/せんべい/こんぺいとう.「生菓子」unbaked confection; fresh Japanese sweets. ⇨まんじゅう /ようかん /ねりきり.「餅菓子」rice cake[dumplings] confection. ⇨だんご / だいふく / ぼたもち.「焼き物」baked confection. ⇨栗まんじゅう / どらやき. ☆ confection「菓子, 糖菓」. confectionery「菓子類（菓子の総称）」. ⇔洋菓子 (cake; pastry) **❷**〈茶の湯に出される菓子〉 Japanese sweets[confections] served in the tea ceremony. These sweets are made keeping in mind flavors that will bring out the taste of the tea, and the artistic aspects of color and shape can be appreciated visually as well. 茶の味を引き立てるため風味に気配りし, 色合いや形状の芸術的な面でも鑑賞にたえるように工夫されている. ⇨茶菓子

わかたけに【若竹煮】　bamboo shoots and *wakame* seaweed simmered[cooked] together. 筍と若布の煮物. ⇨筍 / 若布

わかどしより【若年寄】　a second-ranking official in the Tokugawa shogunate government. 徳川幕府の第2位の役人.

わかみず【若水】　the first water drawn from a well on the morning of the New Year's day[the first day of spring]. It is believed that the first water can dispel the evils and bring good health during the coming year. Water is used for offerings to the gods and the family cooking. 元旦(または立春)の早朝, 井戸から汲んで用いる水. また水を汲む行事. 1年の邪気を除き, 人を若返らせるという. 神への供え物また家庭料理に用いる.

わかめ【若布・和布】　*wakame*, soft seaweed; a brown seaweed native to the coasts of Japan. *Wakame* is often used for *miso*[bean paste] soup and also for vinegared food (*su-no-mono*). コンブ目の褐藻. 日本の沿岸各地に見られる茶褐色の海草. 味噌汁や酢の物の定番. ⇨酢の物
〔料理〕若布と豆腐の味噌汁 *miso* soup cooked with *wakame* seaweed and *tofu* [bean curd]. 若布と胡瓜の酢の物 vinegared *wakame* seaweed and cucumber.

ワキ【脇】　〔能楽〕a *waki*; the main supporting[secondary] actor in a Noh play; a deuteragonist in a Noh play. He plays the supporting role[the assistant character] in a Noh drama. He appears without a Noh mask or makeup. He calls the attention of the audience to the leading actor (*shite*: protagonist). 能楽でシテの相手役をつとめる人. 能面や化粧をしないで登場し, 観衆の注目をシテに向けさせる. ⇨シテ(仕手)

【ワキ連】　an assistant accompanying the *waki* in a Noh play.

【ワキ柱】　the *waki* pillar; the front pillar on the right side of the Noh stage. The *waki* [secondary actor] takes his position near the pillar. ⇨能「能舞台」

わきざし【脇差】❶ a short sword (carried along with a long sword). 武士の差した大小両刀のうち, 小刀のこと.
❷ a short sword[dagger] (carried under one's arm or in one's bosom[breast]). 脇または懐に差す刀. ⇨刀

わきじ【脇士】　statues of Buddha flanking a principal statue of Buddha. 本尊の左右に従い立っている仏像. 脇侍, 脇立ともいう. ☆「阿弥陀」の観音・勢至.「釈迦」の文殊・普賢.「薬師」の日光・月光.

わぎゅう【和牛】　〈牛〉a Japanese (breed of) cow;〈和牛肉〉Japanese cattle beef. ⇨牛肉(種類) / 肉(品種). ☆日本三大高級和牛肉 the three top-quality prime beefs in Japan. 神戸牛, 松阪牛, 近江牛(または米沢牛).

わけありしょうひん【訳有り商品】imperfect merchandise; seconds; irregulars.

わけいせいじゃく【和敬清寂】harmony (調和), reverence (尊敬), purity (清浄) and tranquility (静寂) (taught as four basic rules for a tea ceremony). ☆千利休が大成した侘茶の精神[茶道で重んじられる精神]を表現する禅語.「和敬」は茶道における主客相互の心得,「清寂」は茶庭, 茶室, 茶器などに関連する心得.

わけぎ【分葱】〔植物〕a green[Welsh] onion; a cibol. ユリ科の多年草. 酢の物に用いる.
〔料理〕分葱の酢味噌和え a green onion with

vinegared *miso*[bean paste].

わこう【倭寇】(a group of) Japanese pirates. They repeatedly raided[plundered] the coastlines[coastal cities] of East Asia[China and the Korean Peninsula] (from the late Kamakura period to the Muromachi period). (鎌倉末期から室町時代にかけて)東アジアの沿岸を頻繁に襲来した日本の海賊集団. ☆中国や朝鮮がつけた名称. 豊臣秀吉の禁圧により消滅した.

わごと【和事】〔歌舞伎〕a female style of kabuki acting; a love scene in a kabuki play. 歌舞伎で女性的なやわらかいしぐさや演技のこと. ☆濡れ場・世話場などの場面, またはそれをする役. ⇔荒事. ¶和事師 a kabuki actor playing a love scene.

わごん【和琴】(a) *wagon*; (a) 6-stringed zither-like musical instrument. *Wagon* has a board (of paulownia wood) with a flat shallow sound box with six strings (about 180 cm long and 20 cm wide). It is the forerunner of the *koto*（13-stringed musical instrument）and is still used in the gagaku (court music and dance). (桐の)台に6本の弦を張った平らで浅い音響箱(長さ180cm, 幅20cm). 琴の先駆をなし, 現在も雅楽で用いる. ⇨琴 / 雅楽

わこんようさい【和魂洋才】Japanese spirit and Western knowledge; Japanese spirit combined with Western learning. 西洋渡来の学問を融合させた大和魂.

わさび【山葵】(a) *wasabi*; (a) Japanese horseradish. *Wasabi* is a hot aromatic green spice which is made from the root of the *wasabi* plant. アブラナ科の多年草. 日本の特産で, 根茎は和食の代表的な香辛料.「水わさび」(渓流で自生する)と「畑わさび」(山間地で栽培される)がある. ☆山葵は生ものの臭みを消す (odor-removing) ので刺身や寿司を食するときに用いる. ¶卸し山葵 grated *wasabi*. 生山葵 fresh *wasabi*. 粉

山葵 powdered *wasabi*. 山葵入りの鮨 *sushi* seasoned[flavored] with *wasabi*. 山葵卸し（器具）a *wasabi* grater. ☆サビ〔山葵の符丁〕(サビの利いた鮨 / サビ抜きの鮨).〔料理〕山葵醤油 *shoyu*[soy sauce] seasoned with grated *wasabi*. 卸しわさびで味付けた醤油. 山葵漬け sliced *wasabi* stem[root, leaf] pickled with *sake* lees; a *wasabi* stem cut up and preserved in *sake* lees. わさびの茎(根・葉)などを切り刻んで酒かすにつけた食品. 山葵澄まし a clear soup flavored with *wasabi* juice.

わし【和紙】 *washi*. ❶〈手漉きの和紙〉Japanese paper; traditional hand-made Japanese paper; Japanese paper made by hand. *Washi* is made from fibers of the paper mulberry (*kozo*) barks or the paper bush (*mitsumata*) with special care as to the quality of the water. Cut fibers of these plants[*kozo* and *mitsumata*] are immersed in the water (mixed paste) and then pressed into thin sheets. It is used for writing paper of calligraphy. 水質に留意しながらコウゾ（またはミツマタ）の樹皮の繊維からすいた紙. 切った植物繊維は水に浸してから薄紙になるように押して平らにする. 書道の半紙に用いる.
❷〈機械漉きの和紙〉 machine-made Japanese paper; Japanese paper made by machine. *Washi* is made from used paper and wooden pulp. It is used for sliding doors, lampstands and lanterns. 古紙〔故紙〕や材木パルプなどから作る. 障子や襖, 行灯や提灯などに用いる.

わし【鷲】〔鳥〕an eagle; an eaglet(子). ワシタカ科の猛禽. ¶禿鷲 a condor.

わじまぬり【輪島塗り】 Wajima lacquer ware (produced in Ishikawa Prefecture). *Wajima-nuri* is well-known for the refined quality of its finish, the beautiful decoration of gold inlay work, and its

わ

durability. 完成度の高さ，沈金の装飾と持久性でよく知られる．⇨塗り／漆器

わしょく【和食】〈日本風の食べ物〉Japanese food;〈日本料理〉Washoku, traditional Japanese cuisine. ☆2013年ユネスコ無形文化遺産に登録．

わしょっき【和食器】 Japanese serving vessels. ☆「平皿」a flat plate (used mainly for grilled dishes and *sashimi*：焼き物・刺身)．「長角皿」a rectangular plate (used mainly for grilled fish: 焼き魚)．「小鉢」a small bowl (used mainly for vinegared and dressed dishes, and also for marinated greens: 酢の物・和え物・浸し物)．「ご飯茶碗」a rice bowl.「お椀」a soup bowl.⇨碗・椀

わすれなぐさ【勿忘草】 a forget-me-not. ムラサキ科の多年草．

わだいこ【和太鼓】 a Japanese drum. It is used not only in court music and dance but also as stage music and sound effects in kabuki and Noh plays. 和太鼓は雅楽や舞台音楽，また歌舞伎や能の音響効果をあげるために使用する．

わたいれ【綿入れ】 a cotton-quilted *kimono* (綿入れ着物)；a padded[wadded] garment (綿入りの衣類)；a wadded quilt (綿入れの布団)．⇨丹前

わたがし【綿菓子】 cotton candy; ㊧ candy-floss; ㊤ spun sugar. 粗目 (granulated sugar)を溶かして作る綿状の菓子.「綿飴」ともいう．⇨粗目

わだんす【和箪笥】 a Japanese style chest of drawers (used for storing Japanese *kimonos*). 着物を収納する箪笥．

わどうかいちん【和同開珎】 *wado-kaichin* coin[currency] (of the early 8th century). It is the oldest round coin with a square hole in the center. 日本最初の貨幣(708年発行). 中央に四角い穴がある円型の貨幣．

わに【鰐】〔動物〕an alligator (鼻先が広い)；a crocodile(鼻先が細い)． ¶ワニ皮(の鞄)

(a bag made of) alligator[crocodile] skin; a crocodile-skin handbag; an alligator-leather handbag.

わにぐち【鰐口】 a round flat bell with a long rent at the bottom. It is situated over the entrance to a Shinto Shrine or Buddhist temple and rung by worshippers using a pendant hemp rope (hung from the eaves). 円形で平たい中空の音具[鐘]．神殿や仏殿の入り口にあり，参拝者が(軒などに)吊るされた麻縄で打ち鳴らす．

わび【詫び・侘び】 *wabi*; serenity in simplicity; taste for simplicity and quietness; tranquility in the midst of poverty; refinement found in rusticity. 質素で趣があること．⇨さび

わびちゃ【侘茶】 the simple, rustic tea ceremony (developed by Sen no Rikyu [1521-91]). (千利休が大成した)侘れた素朴な茶の湯．☆「和敬清寂」の精神を重視する．⇨和敬清寂

わふうハンバーガー【和風ハンバーガー】 hamburger with Japanese seasoning.

わふく【和服】 (wear) a *kimono*; (have on) Japanese style clothes. ⇨着物

わようせっちゅう【和洋折衷】 semi-Western [semi-European] style; blending[combination] of Japanese and Western elements; a compromise between Japanese and Western systems. 西洋風と日本風の融合. ¶和洋折衷の料理 semi-Western-style dish[cooking, cuisine]; a dish of semi-Western style.

わら【藁】 (rice) straw; the dried stems from the harvested rice plants. 米を収穫した後の稲の干した茎．¶藁馬 a straw(-made) horse (specially used as a charm for a good harvest). (五穀豊穣のお守り用). 草鞋 (a pair of) braided straw *zori*; straws sandals (used for long distance walking). (長距離の歩行用). ⇨草履. 藁人形 a straw(-made)

doll[figure]; a man[woman] of straw (used mainly for religious rites). 藁葺き屋根 a straw-thatched roof. 藁葺き小屋 a straw-thatched cottage.

わらび【蕨】〔植物〕(fern) bracken; (fern) brake; edible fern sprouts. イノモトソウ科の多年性シダ植物．根茎からでんぷん(starch)を採る．

〔食品〕蕨餅 bracken-starch rice cakes [dumplings]; rice cakes[dumplings] made of bracken-root starch.

わらびはだかまつり【和良比はだかまつり】the Half-Naked Festival at Warabi. (2月)．⇨付記(1)「日本の祭り」

わらべうた【童歌】 a traditional children's song; a song created for children ; a song that children sing in their daily lives and that is handed down through their playmates. 子供のために作られた歌．特に生活の中で子供が歌い，遊び仲間を通じて伝承されてきた歌をいう．

わりこみでんわ【割り込み電話】 a call-waiting telephone. ⇨キャッチホン

わりした【割り下】 soy-sauce flavored seasoning; stock[broth] for one-pot dishes; boiled stock[broth] seasoned with *shoyu* [soy sauce], *mirin*[sweetened *sake*] and sugar. It is used as a dip for fried foods and as a seasoning for flavoring *sukiyaki*. しょうゆで味つけした調味料．しょうゆ・みりん・砂糖などを加えて煮立てたつゆ．揚げ物(てんぷらなど)のソースや，すき焼の調味料に用いる．

わりばし【割り箸】 (a pair of) splittable chopsticks (that can be easily split into two sticks); (a pair of) disposable [throwaway] chopsticks (made of plain [unpainted] wood). A pair of half-split chopsticks is usually wrapped in paper. It can be kept in a chopstick holder on each table at cheap restaurants. (白木製の)使い捨て箸．通常

は紙で包まれている．安食堂では各テーブルの箸立てに備えてある．⇨箸

われいたいさい【和霊大祭】 the Summer Festival of Warei Shrine. (7月)．⇨付記(1)「日本の祭り」

わん【碗・椀】 a (small) bowl; a lacquered [wooden] bowl with a lid (for serving food and drink). It is used for soup or other liquid dishes.(飲食物を盛る)小さな陶磁器製(「碗」と書く)〔木製(「椀」と書く)〕の蓋つきの容器．汁椀や茶碗がある．⇨和食器

わん【湾】 a bay(小さい湾)；a gulf(大きい湾：入り海)；an inlet(入り江)；a bight (海岸・川の湾曲部)．¶東京湾 Tokyo Bay; the Bay of Tokyo. 浦賀湾 Uraga Bay (American vessels reached Uraga Bay in 1846). ⇨海 / 内海 / 灘 / 海峡 / 水道

ワンぎり【ワン切り】a *wan-giri* callback scam; a single-ring and-hang-up (solicitation) call; a one-ring hang; a one-ring callback scam.

わんこそば【椀子蕎麦】 buckwheat noodles served in small bowls without stopping. Each mouthful of noodles is served one after another until the diner signals to stop. 間断なく小さな椀で出されるそば．食する者が中止の合図をするまで一口そばが次々に給仕される．☆岩手県の名物.

わ

【付記(1)】
日本の祭り
（名称の「祭，祭り，まつり」は原則として主催団体の表記に準ずる）

1月　January　睦月 むつき

【ゲーター祭り】 1/1

Geta [a Big Wheel]-Tossing-Up Festival. (三重県鳥羽市・八代神社). 県指・重要無形民俗文化財.

Geta is a big, white (2 meters in diameter) wheel made from the branches of a *gumi* tree and covered with paper. *Geta* is made in the image of the sun. During the festival, people push *geta* high into the air using bamboo poles. Then they drop *geta* down with a big shout. The festival is held to pray for a good harvest and a rich haul during the coming year.

ゲーター祭りの白色の大きな輪(アワ, 直径2m)はグミ木の小枝で作り，紙で覆われている．太陽に見立てて作る．この輪を青竹で突きあげ，たたき落とす勇壮な祭り．その年の五穀豊穣・豊漁を祈る．☆「ゲーター」は「迎旦」と書き「正月の初日の出を迎える」の意.

【玉せせり】 1/3

Ball-Catching Festival. (福岡県福岡市・筥崎宮). 正式名「玉取祭」. 500年余の伝統祭事.

There are two teams: the land and the sea. On this day, two teams of half-naked young men wearing loincloths scramble against each other for a lucky wooden ball (*Hoju*) thrown by a Shinto priest. The winner of the land team is believed to have a good harvest that year, while the winner of the sea team is said to have a rich haul during the year.

褌姿の若者による「陽玉(宝珠)」(直径30cm)の争奪戦．陸側が勝てば豊作，浜側が勝てば大漁という年占い.

【武射祭】 1/4

Archery Festival. (栃木県日光市・二荒山神社(ユネスコ世界文化遺産))

On this day shinto priests and parishioners from Futarasan Shrine shoot arrows at Mt. Akagi. Spectators along the lakeside road search for one of the arrows because they are believed to be charms to expel evils.

神主と氏子が二荒山神社から赤城山に向けて矢を射る．湖畔の路上にいる観覧者は放たれた魔除けの矢を探し求める．☆二荒山神と赤城山神が争ったという伝説に由来する.

【花奪祭】 1/6

Flower-Scrambling Festival. (岐阜県郡上市・長滝白山神社). 正式名「六日祭」.「延年の舞」は国指・重要無形民俗文化財で平安時代からの伝承.

Young men scramble against each other for bundles of artificial flowers hung from the ceiling of the shrine. A dance of longevity is performed in the shrine. It is observed to pray for a good harvest and peace of the nation.

神社の天井から吊るした造花の花笠(桜・菊・椿・牡丹・芥子)の男若衆による争奪戦．神社では「長滝の延年」(延年の舞)がある．五穀豊穣と国家安泰を祈願する.

祭

【出初式】 1/6

New Year's Parade of Firemen [New Year's Demonstration of Fire Brigades]. (東京都江東区有明・東京ビッグサイト)

The Tokyo Fire Brigade[㊟ Department] holds a New Year's parade to demonstrate the agility of the Edo-period fire fighters clad in traditional dress (*hikeshi*). Nowadays, new powerful fire engines line up to shoot water high in the air with ultramodern fire-fighting techniques.

江戸の「火消し」の粋を示すため東京の消防士が出そろう新年の行列. 最近では新型の消防車が空中に噴水させる超近代な消防技法を披露する.

【柳津の裸まいり】 1/7

Half-Naked Festival. (福島県河沼郡・柳津円蔵寺). 1,000年余の伝統行事. 別名「七日堂裸詣り」

Hundreds of half-naked men wearing loincloths run up 113 stone stairs of the approach to the temple. In the temple building, they jostle and fight each other to reach the top of the temple rope suspended from the ceiling. The faster they clamber up, the better luck they will have during the year. Afterwards, good-luck charms[talismans] for sound health during the year are given by temple priests to everyone attending the ceremony.

褌姿の若者が寺院参道への113段の石段を駆け上がる. 本堂に吊るされた鰐口の麻綱に群がってよじ登る. 早く登るほどその年の幸運を呼ぶ. 最後に参加者全員はその年の健康増進の護符(牛王宝院の矢)を授かる.

【うそ替え神事】 1/7

Bullfinch Exchanging Rite. (福岡県・太宰府天満宮). 引き続き「鬼すべ神事」(Demon-Chasing Ceremony)が行われる. 200年余の伝統神事.

Uso means a wooden bullfinch figure carved in the shape of the "*uso*" (bullfinch), which is regarded as a symbol of a lucky bird. The bullfinch is believed to be Tenjin-sama's [Sugawara no Michizane's] messenger. People exchange their wooden bullfinch figures with each other in the shrine precincts. On the same night, people hold a demon-chasing ceremony (called *Onisube*) to drive out demons by burning pine torches.

「ウソ」(幸運をよぶ鳥「ウソ」(鷽)の形をした木彫り)は天神様の使者と信じられている. 境内では参詣者が木製のウソを他の人のウソと交換しあう. その夜, 松明を燃やして鬼を追い出し, 厄を払う. ☆「鷽」(ウソ)は「嘘」(うそ[a lie])に通ずることから, 前年度に起こった凶事(the bad luck and disasters of the previous year) などを「嘘」として, 本年は吉事(a wish for the better luck in the year)になることを祈願する.「金製のウソ(6体)」(golden bullfinch figures) はみくじを引く神事で, 引き当てることによって授与される.
⇨鷽人形

【玉垂宮鬼夜】 1/7

Demon-Chasing Rite. (福岡県久留米市・大善寺玉垂宮). 1600年余の伝統祭事. 国指・重要無形民俗文化財.

On this day, 6 huge torches (1 meter in diameter and 12 meters in length) are set afire in the shrine compounds. There is a demon-chasing rite performed by men disguised as demons in front of the burning fires.The rite is observed to drive away the demons and to exorcise evil spirits from the participants.

境内の大松明6基(直径1m. 長さ12m)に点火される. 燃え盛る火の前で鬼に扮した人が追儺行を行う. 邪気を退治し, 参列者の厄除けを行う儀式である.

【守山の火まつり】1月第2土曜日

Fire Festival in Moriyama City. (滋賀県守山市・勝部神社・住吉神社).「**勝部の火まつり・住吉の火まつり**」の総称. 県指・重要無形民俗文化財.

Half-naked young men burn many huge pine torches in the shape of big snakes in the precincts of Katsube and Sumiyoshi shrines. They express thanks to the tutelary deity by offering a portion of the last year's crops at the beginning of the New Year. The festival is observed to pray for good health during the coming year.

褌姿の若衆が大蛇をかたどった多数の大松明に点火し, 新年早々に前年の農作物を氏神に捧げて感謝する. 一年の無病息災を祈願する. ☆勝部神社では大蛇の胴体をかたどった(長さ5~6m, 直径40cm)松明12基に, 住吉神社では頭部をかたどった(長さ5~6m, 直径40cm)松明6基に点火される.

【鳥越神社どんと[どんど]焼き】1/8

Fire Festival of Torikoe Shrine. (東京都台東区・鳥越神社).

New Year's decorations of bamboos and pine trees as well as straw rope festoons are burned in big bonfires as a ceremonial event in the shrine grounds to pray for good health and safety of the families.

正月の飾り物を焼き, 一年の無病息災・家内安全を祈願する.

【十日戎】1/9-11

Ebisu Festival of Imamiya Ebisu Shrine. (大阪府大阪市・今宮戎神社). 起源は四天王寺の建立(593年)の頃.

Ebisu is one of the Seven Gods of Good Luck. The festival is held in honor of *Ebisu*, the god of wealth, in three parts: *Yoi-Ebisu* (the eve of the festival) on the 9th, *Hon-Ebisu* (the main festival day) on the 10th and *Nokori-Fuku* (the last helping of luck) on the 11th. People buy good-luck bamboo branches, praying for prosperity in business.

恵比寿(七福神の一人:商売の神)を祝う日. 9日の「宵戎」, 10日の「本戎」, 11日の「残り福」の3日間. 商売繁盛を願って福笹を買う. ⇨ 七福神(恵比寿)

【中之条鳥追い祭】1/14

Bird-Chasing-Away Festival at Nakano-jo Town. (群馬県吾妻群・伊勢宮). 400年余の伝統祭事. 太鼓(直径130cm)は県指・重要有形民俗文化財.

In this festival, eleven huge drums are beaten by youths while being pulled through the town. It is observed to drive out evil spirits from people and to pray for a good harvest after expelling harmful insects and birds from the crops.

厄除けと農作物の害虫・害鳥を駆除して五穀豊穣を祈願する. 男若衆が大太鼓11台を町中引き回しながら打ち鳴らす.

【どんど焼き】1/14-15

Dondo-Yaki; Fire Festival; Burning Event of New Year's decorations.

This event is held around January 14th or 15th at many places in Japan. This event features a bonfire of the New Year's decorations of pine tree boughs, bamboo branches

祭

and straw festoons as well as the year's first calligraphy.

正月の飾り物(門松・注連縄・書初めなど)を焼く行事．☆「どんと焼き」「とんど焼き」と
もいう．「どんど祭り」「左義長」なども同じ．[例]「大崎八幡どんと祭」(宮城県・大崎八
幡宮)．「大磯左義長」(神奈川県・大磯海岸)．☆この火で焼いた餅には特別な力が宿り，
食するとその年には病気が予防できる(keep away disease for the coming year)といわ
れる(俗信)．正月が終わり，年神を送り出す風習(the custom to see off the deity of the
year to the other world)である．

【四天王寺どやどや】 1/14

Half-Naked Festival. (大阪府大阪市・四天王寺).

Two teams of half-naked young men wearing loincloths and headbands scramble
against each other for a sacred stick with a talisman to ward off evils (called *Goohoin*).
If one team wins against the other in obtaining a talisman to ward off evils, it will get a
good harvest. The ancient court dance with music (called *Shoryoe*) is performed in the
temple grounds.

大勢の褌姿の若者が「牛王宝印」の魔除け札を奪い合う．四天王寺境内で行われる4月22
日の「聖霊会」(聖徳太子の命日にご聖霊を慰めるために行う舞楽法要)は国指・重要無形
民俗文化財．

【野沢の火まつり】 1/15

Fire Festival at Nozawa Spa. (長野県・野沢温泉). 正式名「道祖神火まつり」(**Dosojin
Fire Festival**). 300年余の伝統祭事．国指・重要無形民俗文化財．

A small boat-shaped Shinto shrine (20-meter-high) is made from the beech wood. Two
teams compete against each other for a boat-shaped Shinto shrine. One team tries to set
the shrine on fire and the other team tries to put in out. Finally, a small shrine is set afire
to pray for the sound growth of children as well as a plentiful harvest of crops during
the coming year.

船型の小さな社殿(高さ20m)がブナの木で作られる．火付け役と火消し役相互の攻防戦
が始まる．最後には社殿に点火され，子供の成長と五穀豊穣を祈願する．

【敦賀西町の綱引き(まつり)】 1/15

Tug-of-War Festival. (福井県・敦賀市). 別名「夷子大黒綱引」. 400年余の伝統祭事．
国指・重要無形民俗文化財．

Two teams standing on the east and west sides have a tug-of-war using a long rope (50
m in length and 20 cm in width). One team is called *Ebisu*[the god of commerce] and
the other *Daikoku*[the god of agriculture]. If the Ebisu team wins, they will have a rich
haul. If the Daikoku team wins, they will have a good harvest.

夷子(漁)と大黒(農)の両方東西に分かれ綱(長さ50m, 太さ20cm)を引きあう．夷子が勝
てば豊漁，大黒が勝てば豊作．

【墨塗りまつり】 1/15

Ink-Smearing Festival. (新潟県十日町・松之山温泉薬師堂). 600年余の伝統行事．
300年余の伝統行事．「婿投げ」とあわせて「むこ投げすみ塗り」ともいう．

After burning the New Year's decorations, the ashes are picked up. Snowy mud is added
to the mixture, and participants try to smear it on each other's faces. The rite is observed

祭

to pray for good health during the coming year.

新年の門松や注連飾りを燃やした墨を雪で煉り，それを互いの顔に塗り合い一年の無病息災を祈る。

【三十三間堂大的全国大会】1月中旬

Traditional Archery Contest at Sanjusangendo Hall. (京都府・三十三間堂)

An archery contest is held annually in the outer corridor of the 121-meter-long Sanjusangendo Hall (the world's longest wooden structure) on Sunday closest to January 15th. The contest is observed as part of the Coming-of-Age Day in which new adults participate. Today the contest is performed at the west side of the main hall by the archers who come from all over Japan. The arrows are supposed to hit the target at the end of the hall 60 meters away.

三十三間堂では長さ121mの本堂(世界最長の木造建築物)の軒下で射通す競技を成人の日の一環として行う．現在では全国の弓道愛好家が集まって本堂西側の射程距離60mの遠的で行う．

☆「三十三間堂」(正式名称: 蓮華王院本堂)は1165年創建, 1266年再建．本堂(国宝)の内陣にある支柱の間に33の柱間(33 *ken*[bays] between the pillars[columns])がある．1,001体の観音像(1,001 life-sized statues of the thousand-armed Kannon)が安置されていることで有名．

【若草山の山焼き】1月下旬

Grass-Burning-Fire Event on Wakakusayama Hill. (奈良県・若草山)

This event is held every year around the end of January. The grass on the hill is set afire by priests of Kofuku-ji and Todai-ji temples, and Kasuga Grand Shrine. The entire hill is covered with flames, giving a spectacular sight at night. It is held to get rid of harmful insects.

興福寺・東大寺の僧らと春日大社の神官によって点火される．全山が壮観な火の海になる．害虫駆除のために行う．

祭

2月　February　如月 きさらぎ

【黒川能】2/1-2

Kurokawa Noh Play Performance. (山形県鶴岡市・春日神社). ☆500年の伝統行事. 国指・重要無形民俗文化財．別名「王祇祭」

Noh plays are performed in front of "*Ogi-sama*" (a big 2.4-meter-high fan consisting of three long wooden poles covered with white cloths and wands), which is the object of worship regarded as a deity in the shrine. The play is performed to pray for a good harvest and peace of the nation.

春日神社の依代[ご神体]である「王祇様」(白布をつけた3本の白木を根元で束ねた扇形)の前で能楽を舞う．五穀豊穣と天下泰平を祈る．

【札幌雪まつり】2月初旬

Snow Festival in Sapporo's Odori Park. (北海道札幌市・大通り公園)

Sapporo turns into a snow museum for 7 days, during the second week of February. The festival is one of Japan's largest and most distinctive winter events. It features a contest of large snow statues and ice sculptures in the park, which are made by the soldiers of the Self-Defense Forces and civilian volunteers .

2月第2週目に開幕し，札幌は7日間にわたり雪の博物館に変容する．日本最大の雪の祭典．公園内では自衛隊の隊員や市民の有志によって作られた雪の像(snow statue; the statue made of snow)と氷の彫刻(ice sculpture; the sculpture made of ice)を競う大会もある．☆第二次世界大戦後1950年に札幌観光協会と札幌市の主催によって開催されたことに始まる．

【春日大社節分万燈籠】 2/3

Lantern-Lighting Festival. (奈良県奈良市・春日大社). 800年の伝統行事. ⇨ 春日大社中元万燈籠(8月14-15日)

The festival is well-known for the fantastic scene created by some 3,000 lighted stone and bronze lanterns to welcome the spring season. An ancient court dance with music (*bugaku*) is performed in the shrine precincts at night.

節分を迎え約3,000の灯籠が点火される．境内では舞楽が奉納される．☆「春日大社」(ユネスコ世界文化遺産)は768年藤原家の氏神として藤原永手が創建．参道に並ぶ2,000以上の石灯籠(stone lantern)と回廊に吊るされた1,000以上の金属灯籠(bronze lantern)は壮観である．

【御灯祭】 2/6

Fire Festival. (和歌山県新宮市・神倉神社). 1400年余の伝統行事. 県指・無形民俗文化財.

At night two thousands of people wearing white costumes tied with tough ropes race down the 538 steep stone steps from the top of Mt. Kannokura, holding large burning pine-torches in their hands. The faster they descend[run down] the stone steps, the more luck they will obtain. It is observed to pray for safety of the families during the coming year.

白装束に荒縄を絞めた約2千人の群集が手に燃える松明を持って神社の急な石段(538段)を競って駆け降りる勇壮な祭り．早く石段を降りるほど多福を得る．一年の家内安全を祈願する．☆「かみくら神社」ともいう．熊野速玉大社(ユネスコ世界文化遺産)の摂社.

【黒石寺蘇民祭】 2月中旬

Half-Naked Festival at Kuroishi Temple. (岩手県奥州市・黒石寺[くろいしでら]とも). 1,000以上の伝統行事. 国指・重要無形民俗文化財.

Hundreds of half-naked men wearing loincloths scramble with each other for a *Somin*-bag (containing a good-luck charm[talisman]) in Kuroishi Temple. A winner who manages to get a *Somin*-bag will get a good harvest and good luck.

褌姿の男性数百人が「蘇民袋」(護符が入っている)の争奪戦を演じる．蘇民袋を獲得する勝者が豊作多福を得る．

【大曲の綱引き】 2/15

Tug-of-War Festival. (秋田県大仙市). 290年余の伝統行事. 県指・重要無形民俗文化財.

Two teams engage in a tug-of-war using a long rope (60 cm in diameter and 200 m in length) that is first paraded in the city streets. It is a kind of divination event to pray for a good harvest during the coming year.

2チームによる綱引き(直径60cm，長さ200m)．その年の五穀豊穣を祈願する占い行事．

【かまくら】2/15-16

(Igloo-like) **Snow-Hut Festival**. (秋田県横手市). 400年余の小正月の伝統行事.

Kamakura is an igloo-like round snow hut enshrining the god of water. Children set up *Kamakura* to enjoy indoor parties in them. They build a small altar inside to honor the god of water with offerings of food and flowers. They chat and play sitting around a cozy brazier with a warm charcoal fire. They enjoy themselves by roasting and eating rice cakes inside snow huts.

かまくらは水神を祭る雪の家．子どもたちは室内で遊ぶため，かまくらを作る．また水神に食物や花を捧げるため小さな祭壇を作る．火鉢のそばでだんらんしながら遊ぶ．室内では餅を焼いたり食べたりして楽しむ．

【横手の梵天】2/16-17

Bonden **Festival in Yokote**. (秋田県横手市・旭岡山神社). 300余年の伝統祭事.

Bonden is a 5-meter-long cedar pole[log] affixed with oval-shaped bamboo baskets which are attached to a figure of the animal of the year at the top. Brightly colored cloths and streamers are hung from a long pole[log] adorned with various decorations. Nowadays, the *Bonden* features the decorations reflected by the social aspects of present society. Teams of young men carry dozens of *Bondens* to the local shrine to pray for a bountiful harvest during the coming year.

「ぼんでん」とは5mほどの細長い竿[丸太]の先に円筒形の竹かごをとりつけ，頭上にその年の干支の動物を飾ったもの．飾り立てた長い竿[丸太]から色鮮やかな布や幟が垂れている．最近は現代社会の様相を反映した飾り物がある．若者のチームがその年の豊作を祈願して「ぼんでん」を神社に奉納する．

【八戸えんぶり】2/17-20

Hachinohe *Enburi* **Dance Festival**. (青森県八戸市). 800年の伝統行事．国指・重要無形民俗文化財.

Enburi are the old farming implements to make farmland flat. Teams of dancers dressed in colorful costumes hold *Enburi* in their hands. They perform a variety of simple dances depicting the process of rice-planting through the harvest of crops. It is observed to pray for a rich harvest for the coming year.

華やかな衣装を着た一団が手に「えんぶり」(「朳振」という田畑を耕す農機具)を持ち，種蒔きから収穫までの様子を演じる古式豊かな田植踊を舞う．その年の豊作を願う行事．

祭

【谷汲踊り】2/18

Drum-Beating-Dance Festival. (岐阜県揖斐郡・華厳寺). 別名「豊年踊り」. 県指・重要無形民俗文化財.

Teams of dancers carry a colorful 4-meter-long *shinai* (a framework of split bamboos with colored decorations) on their backs. They dance passionately while beating large drums on their chests. It is held to pray for a good harvest.

舞踊の一団(12名で一組)が色鮮やかな4mの「しない」(多彩に装飾された割竹の骨組み)を背負いながら大太鼓(直径70cm)をかかえ情熱的に踊る．五穀豊穣を祈願する．

【**西大寺会陽**】2月第3土曜日

Half-Naked Men's Competition of Saidaiji Temple.（岡山県岡山市・西大寺）. 別名「**西大寺裸祭り**」. 500年余の伝統祭事. 国指・重要無形文化財.

Thousands of half-naked men wearing loincloths scramble fiercely with each other for a pair of lucky sacred wands[sticks] called *Shingi* (4 cm in diameter and 20 cm in length) thrown in the crowd at midnight by a Buddhist priest. Anybody can compete to be the first to grab lucky amulets of the sacred wands.

深夜に仏僧によって裸の男衆群の中に投下される2本の「宝木」を求めて，数千人の褌姿の裸の若者たちが押し合う争奪戦. だれでも宝木の護符を最初に得ようと競うことが出来る. ☆「会陽」とは修正会結願行事の地域的な名称. ここでは世界最大規模の「裸祭り」のこと.

【**和良比はだか祭り**】2/25

Half-Naked Festival at Warabi.（千葉県四街道市・皇産霊神社）. 別名「**和良比泥んこ祭り**」(**Mud-Splattering Festival**)

Groups of men wearing loincloths jostle each other and wrestle in a muddy rice-field, splattering mud on each other. The festival is held to pray for a good harvest. Children over two years old are also taken to the field to have foreheads smeared with mud to pray for their sound growth.

五穀豊穣を願って田んぼで泥をかけ合う. また子どもの額に泥をつけ成長を願う.

【**北野天満宮梅花祭**】2/25

Plum-Blossom Festival (at Kitano Tenmangu Shrine).（京都市上京区・北野天満宮神社）

Visitors flock to the shrine to enjoy viewing the plum blossoms and participating in an open-air tea ceremony conducted under the plum trees in full blossom.

梅花を観賞し，満開の梅の木の下で野点を楽しむために神社に参集する.

【**国府宮裸まつり**】 2/26

Half-Naked Festival.（愛知県稲沢市・尾張大国霊神社）. 奈良・平安時代からの悪役退散の行事で「儺追神事」(**Demon-Chasing Ceremony**)ともいう.

Thousands of half-naked young men wearing loincloths push and shove each other to reach and touch "*Shin-otoko*" (the festival's designated man of a critical[climacteric] age) in the belief that he can drive out evil spirits. There is a demon-chasing ceremony in which "*Shin-otoko*" has an evil spirit driven out of him by Shinto priests. This festival has been observed to expel evil spirits since the Nara and Heian periods.

数千の裸男が一人の「神男」(厄年の人)に触れて厄を落そうともみあう. 神男の悪疫退治を行う儺追神事が奈良・平安時代より神主によって行われている.

祭

3月　March　弥生 やよい

【**深大寺だるま市**】3/3-4

Daruma-Doll Fair.（東京都調布市・深大寺）. 江戸時代からの伝統行事.

Jindaiji Temple was founded in 733. This fair has been held since the Edo period. Many open-air stalls selling Daruma (papier-mâché figure of Dharma) dolls of all sizes and potted plants are set up inside and outside the temple precincts.

733年創建の深大寺で開かれる達磨市. 植木市も同時に開催. ⇨ だるま(市)

【祭頭祭】3/9

Stick-Clacking Parade Festival. (茨城県・鹿島神宮). 800年余の伝統祭事. 国指・重要無形民俗文化財.

There is a colorful parade of young men dressed in armor and full court costumes of traditional fashion. People individually hold 2-meter-long sticks (*Kashibo*) in their hands. They rhythmically clack their sticks while singing a festive song and crossing their long sticks with each other. This festival is held to pray for a good harvest and peace of the nation.

華やかな装束姿の若者が各自2メートル余の「樫棒」を手に持って練り歩く. 囃子を歌い, 樫棒を相互に交差しながら律動的に樫棒を打ち鳴らす. 五穀豊穣と天下泰平を祈願する.

【帆手まつり】3/10

Flag-Fluttering Sea Parade Festival. (宮城県塩竈市・鹽竈神社). 300年余の伝統祭事.

Sixteen young people carrying the big portable shrines descend[run down] the 202 steps of the shrine. They parade through the city streets with flags fluttering in the wind just as a sail is waving. It is observed to pray for the safety of families and prosperity in business.

荒神輿(重さ約1トン)を担ぐ16名の若者が神社の202階段を下り, 帆を振っているように旗を風に押し立てて町を神幸する. 家内安全・商売繁盛を祈願する.

【高尾山火渡り祭】3月第2日曜日.

Fire-Crossing Rite at Mt. Takao. (東京都八王子市・高尾山薬王院)

In the rite, a big pyre of cedar branches (called *Goma-gi*) is set on fire while Buddhist sutras are chanted. When the flames die down, Buddhist priests, and then lay participants walk barefoot across sacred embers[fire]. It is observed to get protection against disasters and to have good health during the year.

読経の中「護摩木」が燃やされる. 燃えつきた「護摩木」の上を素足で歩く. その年の災害からの保護と健康を祈願する.

祭

【山田の春祭り】3月第2日曜日.

Spring Festival at Yamada. (埼玉県秩父市・恒持神社)

On this day two gorgeous festival floats (preserved since the Edo period) and one festival float (with flower sedge-hat halberd) are paraded through the city streets all day long. It heralds the spring season in the Chichibu area.

豪華な2台の屋台と1台の花笠鉾が終日町中を練り歩く. 秩父地方に春を告げる祭り.

【お水取り】3/1-14

Water-Drawing Ceremony. (奈良県・東大寺二月堂). 別名「二月堂の修二会」. 1,200年余の伝統行事.

Omizutori is held on the night of March 12th with the waving of huge burning torches on the terrace of the Nigatsu-do Hall. This is a part of *Shuni-e* (a religious service known as monks'ascetic training ritual) performed for two weeks (1st through 14th) at the Nigatsu-do Hall of Todai-ji Temple. The Buddhist priests pray for peace of the nation and a rich harvest. They brandish huge burning pine torches on the terrace of the

Nigatsu-do Hall. Worshippers below rush for the showers of burning sparks, because falling sparks are believed to protect against evil spirits. When all the torches have burned out, they draw up fresh water from the holy well (called *Wakasai*) early in the morning of the 13th to offer to Buddha. The ritual signals the advent of a long-awaited spring.

「お水取り」は3月12日の深夜(13日早朝)に二月堂のテラスで大きな燃える松明を振り回す宗教行事(法会).この儀式は修二会の一部である.国家安泰と五穀豊穣を祈る.二月堂の欄干で燃える大松明(長さ6m)を振り回し,参拝者は降り注ぐ火の粉の下に馳せより,厄払いを受ける.その行事を終えると,早朝に井戸(「若狭井」)から水を汲み,仏に捧げる.この法会は春の到来を告げる.

【清涼寺のお松明式】3/15

Torch-Lighting Ceremony at Seiryoji Temple.(京都市右京区嵯峨・清涼寺).

On this day three huge torches made of bamboo, pine and cedar are set up in the temple precincts. At night the sacred torches are set afire to pray for a good harvest of crops during the coming year.

竹・松・杉で作った大松明(早稲・中稲・晩稲に見立てる.高さ6m)3基が境内に立てられる.夜になるとその年の豊作を祈願して松明が点火される.

【近江八幡左義長祭り】3月中旬

Fire Festival of Omihachiman Shrine.(滋賀県近江八幡市):別名「**近江八幡の火祭り**」.国指・重要無形民俗文化財.

Sagicho is a long float with 2-meter-tall pine torch woven from new straw bundles, the top center of which is decorated with the zodiac animal of the year. People dance excitedly around the blazing *Sagicho* floats amid showers of fire sparks. It is believed people will have good health if they can keep themselves warm by the burning fire. This fire festival was started by Oda Nobunaga. People say spring has come with this festival.

燃え盛る「左義長」(わら束で編んだ松明を載せた長い山車で,中心にはその年の干支の動物を飾ってある)の回りに飛ぶ火の粉を浴びながら踊る.燃える火で身体を暖めると健康になると信じられている.織田信長が始めた火祭り.この祭りは春の訪れを告げる.

【火振り神事】3月中旬

Fire-Swinging Festival at Aso Shrine.(熊本県阿蘇市・阿蘇神社).国指・重要無形民俗文化財.「**阿蘇の火まつり**」の中核をなす.

This festival is observed in welcoming the god of the field by making a beautiful circle of fire while swinging large lighted torches (made of a thick rope of grass). It makes a spectacular sight looking like a sea of fire. It is held to pray for a good harvest during the year.

(カヤの綱で作った)大松明に火をつけて田の神を迎える神事.火の海のような光景になる.五穀豊穣を祈願する.

【阿蘇神社泥打祭】3/28

Mud-Throwing Festival.(福岡県朝倉市・阿蘇神社).県指・無形民俗文化財.別名「杷木の泥打」.

祭

On the way to the shrine, children throw mud at the men wearing white costumes and hoods disguised as gods of the rice-paddy field. It is observed to pray for a good harvest during the year.

神社に行く途中，子供(打ち子)が白装束・白頭巾を着た田の神に扮した男(代宮司)に泥を投げつける．豊作を祈願する．

4月　April　卯月 うづき

【御柱祭】4/1~4月中旬

Log-Pillar-Erecting Festival. (長野県諏訪市・諏訪大社)．1200年の伝統行事．国指・重要無形民俗文化財．正式には「式年造営御柱大祭」という．

In the festival, *On-bashira* (literally translated as a huge honored log-pillars) are erected at the four corners in the precincts of Suwa Grand Shrine. The huge logs are drawn by thousands of people with their ropes to the accompaniment of folk songs. The festival has four parts: *Yama-dashi* (the large trees are cut down in the forest and drawn to the town), *Kawa-goshi* (the large logs are carried across the river to be purified), *Sato-biki* (the large logs are paraded through the city streets to the shrine) and *Kan-otoshi* (the huge log-pillars[columns] are erected at one of the corners in the shrine). The festival is held once every six years, in the years of the Tiger and the Monkey in the Chinese zodiac.

山から切り落とした大木(直径約1 m，長さ約17 m，重さ約12tにもなる巨木)を社殿の四隅に立てる行事．祭りは「山出し」，「川越し」(4月)，「里曳き」(5月)，「冠落とし」の４部からなる．6年ごと[7年目]の寅年と申年に行う式年祭．

【日立さくらまつり】4/1-20

Cherry-Blossom Festival at Hitachi City. (茨城県日立市)．ハイライト「日立風流物」(**Gorgeous Float Parade Festival at Hitachi City**. 4月第２土日)「日立ささら」(神峰神社)．国指・重要無形民俗文化財．

The festival features a parade of gorgeous floats (called *Furyumono*) with stages for performing puppet drama. The floats consist of six-story stages, on the top of which classical dramas using puppet dolls are performed.

人形芝居が演じられる「風流物」(6層建ての大きな舞台のある山車：高さ15m，幅3-8m)の行列がある．☆2016年ユネスコ無形文化遺産に登録．

【花祭り】4/8

Flower Festival. ☆正式名称「灌仏会」．

This Buddhist service is observed to celebrate the birthday of (Gautama Sakyamuni) Buddha. It is formally known as *Kanbutsue*, meaning the Buddhist service observed for Buddha's birthday (on April 8). This festival is based on a legend that colorful flowers fell down from the sky when Buddha was born. On this festival, a small statue of Buddha is placed in a small Buddhist chapel decorated with flowers. Worshippers use a ladle to pour sweet tea over the Buddhist statue in celebration of his birthday. (4月8日に行う)釈迦の誕生日を祝う法要．正式名称は「灌仏会」．伝説によれば，釈迦誕生の折，空から多彩な花々が舞い落ちた．祭日には花御堂を設け，参加者は釈迦の誕生を祝い柄

杓で小さな仏像に甘茶をかける．☆「花祭り」の呼称は日本の4月初旬は桜の花が咲く季節であり，仏像を安置する小さな御堂が桜の花で飾られていることに由来．

【一宮けんか祭り】4/10

Rage Festival at Ichinomiya.（新潟県糸魚川市・天津神社）．別名「糸魚川けんか祭り」．

In the morning, two teams of young men living in two districts of the city fight amid violent shoving and pushing to be the first to have their portable shrines consecrated at the shrine. It is held to pray for a good harvest of crops and a rich haul. In the afternoon, there is an elegant performance of ancient court Shinto dance with music (*Hono-bugaku*) which has been designated as a National Important Cultural Property.

午前には2地区（寺町・押上区）の若者のどちらが早く神輿を奉納できるか，2基の神輿で勇壮にぶつけ合いながら先を争う．その年の豊作と豊漁を祈願する．午後には国指定重要民俗文化財である「舞楽」が奉納される．☆春の訪れを告げる雪国に見られる「動」と「静」の壮観な祭事．

【信玄公祭り】4月中旬（金曜日〜土曜日）

Memorial Festival for Takeda Shingen [1521-1573].（山梨県甲府市）

This is a gala procession of over 1,000 armed warrior-lords holding a banner with the motto "*Furinkazan*".

「風林火山」の旗をかざした甲州軍団1000人以上の華やかな鎧武者行列が呼び物．☆「風林火山」Move as swift as a wind, stay as silent as a forest, attack as fierce as fire, and defend as steady as a mountain.

【春の高山祭】4/14-15

Takayama Spring Festival.（岐阜県高山市・日枝神社）．別名「山王祭」．800年余の伝統祭事．国指・重要無形民俗文化財．☆2016年ユネスコ無形文化遺産に登録．⇨ 秋の高山祭（10月9日-10日）

The Festival is held twice a year in spring and autumn at Takayama City. It features a parade of high-wheeled wagon floats with stages on them, some of which are lavishly embellished with gold and decorated with elaborate carvings. Each float has movable marionettes, controlled by rods and wires, which perform amazing feats. There are 12 floats in spring and 11 in autumn, each of which is designated as a National Important Cultural Asset. The gorgeous decorated, high-wheeled floats are so called "Moving Yomei-mon Gates" after the famous gate in Nikko because of their brilliance.

高山祭は高山市において春季(4月)と秋季(10月)の年2回行われる．その特徴は高い舞台付きの屋台行列で，屋台によっては金がふんだんに使われ，豪華絢爛たる彫刻で飾られている．屋台には棒と綱で操られて動くからくり人形(mechanical puppet[doll])があり，珍しい妙技を披露する．春季には12台，秋季には11台の屋台が見られ，いずれも国の重要文化財に指定されている．豪華絢爛たる屋台は，その見事な輝きのため日光の有名な門にちなんで「動く陽明門」とも言われる．

【美濃まつり】4月第2土曜日・日曜日

Mino Festival.（岐阜県美濃市・八幡神社）

The festival features a procession of 30 sacred portable shrines decorated with artificial flowers which are made of special paper produced in Mino district.

祭

美濃特産の京花紙で作った造花を飾る「花神輿」30台の行列が出る.

【長浜曳山まつり】4/14-16

Nagahama Float-Parade Festival. (滋賀県長浜市・長浜八幡宮). 400年余の伝統祭事. 国指・重要無形民俗文化財. ☆2016年ユネスコ無形文化遺産に登録.

The festival features a parade of 13 gorgeous festival floats decorated with gold and silver lacquered work and tapestries (called *Hikiyama*). The floats have beautiful stages for drama, on which local children aged 5 to 12 perform the kabuki play (called *Hikiyama-kyogen*).

祭りの呼び物は絢爛豪華な13基の「曳山」(長さ9m, 高さ7m.)巡行と「曳山狂言」(子供歌舞伎)である. ☆長浜城主豊臣秀吉公に男子が誕生したことにより, 砂金(gold dust)を下賜された町民が山車を作り長浜八幡宮の祭礼に曳き回したのが祭りの起源.

【鎌倉まつり】4月中旬

Kamakura Festival of Tsurugaoka Hachiman-gu Shrine. (神奈川県鎌倉市・鶴岡八幡宮ほか).

The festival features a historic parade of the Feudal Lords and the Horseback Archery performed in the shrine precincts. The "*Shizuka-no-mai*" dance is performed on the ritual dance stage in the shrine.

武者行列と流鏑馬が呼び物. 特に「静の舞」が必見.

【二荒山弥生祭】4/13-17

Spring Festival at Futarasan Shrine. (栃木県日光市・二荒山神社〈ユネスコ世界文化遺産〉). 1200年の伝統行列. 別名「ごた祭り」

The festival features a parade of 13 elegant festival floats colorfully decorated with artificial cherry blossoms which adorn the front and back of the roofs (called *hana-yatai*).

(17日には)屋根の前後に桜の造花を飾る「花屋台」13基(東町8台, 西町5台)が二荒山神社まで巡行する. ☆古くは3月(弥生)に行われたのが呼称の由来. 日光に春を告げる祭り.

【佐渡島のまつり】4/14-27

Sado Island Festival. (新潟県・佐渡島). ☆主要な行事は15・16日に集中.「山王まつり」「徳和まつり」「三川まつり」「おけさ華の乱」「赤泊まつり」などの総称.

There are a variety of events including the parade of the Sado *Okesa* folk song and dance as well as the *Nembutsu* dance. In particular, *Oni-daiko* (demon's drum-beating) is performed by players wearing demon-masks who beat drums violently.

呼び物には「佐渡おけさパレード」や「念仏踊り」, 特に鬼面をかぶり激しく太鼓を打つ「鬼太鼓」がある.

【白久の串人形芝居】4月中旬の日曜日

Puppet Show at Shiroku area. (埼玉県秩父市・豆原区). 県指と国指・重要無形民俗文化財.

A doll is manipulated by two puppeteers: one uses two long bamboo poles (*takegushi*) to manipulate the puppet's hands and the other manipulates the puppet's head. The puppet show has the narrative style of vocal music accompanied by *shamisen* and chanters similar to a Bunraku drama.

祭

2人遣いの人形芝居（1体の人形を2人で操る）．2本の竹串で人形（全長60センチ）の手を操る人［手遣い］と，頭を操る人［主遣い］がいる．文楽同様に三味線と義太夫の語りに合わせて上演する．

【古川祭】4/19-20

Float-Parade Festival at Furukawa. （岐阜県飛騨市古川町・気多若宮神社）．国指・重要無形民俗文化財．☆2016年ユネスコ無形文化遺産に登録．

The festival features a gala parade of 9 elaborate wheeled-wagon floats and the beating performance of a huge drum (an *Okoshi-daiko*) with (90-cm-long) drumsticks beaten by two men on the float. It is held to pray for a good harvest and peace of the nation.

呼び物は豪華絢爛たる7台の「山車巡行」（「静」の部）と「起し太鼓（2人で90cmのばちで背中合わせで太鼓を打つ）行列」（「動」の部）．五穀豊穣と国家安泰を祈願する．

【日高火防祭】4/28-29

Firemen-Floats Parade Festival. （岩手県奥州市水沢区・日高神社）．300年余の祭事．県指・重要無形民俗文化財．

The festival features a parade of 9 huge highly-embellished floats with a doll-stand built in four steeped tiers (called *Hayashi-yatai*). About twenty girls gaily dressed in *kimono* and decorated in their traditional hairstyle are seated on a steeped tier of the floats. They beat small drums and sing folk songs to the accompaniments of *shamisen* and flutes.

祭りの呼び物は4段式のひな壇のある9基の「囃子屋台」の行列．屋台のひな壇には20人ほどの少女が雛人形のように座って並んでいる．太鼓を鳴らし，三味線や笛の音とともに独特の囃子を奏でる．

【上杉まつり】4/29-5/6

Feudal Lord Parade at Uesugi Shrine. （山形県米沢市・上杉神社）

There is a cavalcade of 40 knights and troops of General Uesugi's armed warrior lords along with the passage of the festive portable shrines.

神輿の渡御とともに上杉謙信の甲冑軍団と騎士団の行列がある．

5月　May　皐月 さつき

【府中くらやみまつり】4/30-5/6

Night Parade Festival at Fuchu City. （東京都府中市・大國魂神社）．ハイライトは1,000年の伝統をもつ「競馬式」と「神輿渡御」．

Eight sacred portable shrines are paraded in the evening through the Koshukaido road to the shrine. The portable shrines are carried by a group of youths amid violent pushing and shoving.

（5月3日の神輿渡御）夜中に市内最大の太鼓をのせた神輿8基の旧甲州街道を経由する（本殿から御旅所への）渡御．激しい押し合い圧し合いの中で若者の集団が神輿を担ぐ．

【御車山祭】5/1

Float-Parade Festival in Takaoka City. （富山県高岡市・関野神社）400年余の伝統行事．安土桃山文化の面影を残す優雅な山車は国指定重要無形・有形文化財．☆2016年ユネスコ無形文化遺産に登録．

The Spring Festival of Sekino Shrine has a gala parade of seven gorgeous festival floats (called *Mikurumayama*) which are pulled through the city streets. The festival floats feature intricate metalwork on their huge wheels lacquered with black, gold and silver colors. The stages of the festival floats are decorated with a radiated form of artificial flower sedges and a traditional gorgeous craftwork.

関野神社の春季例祭には「御車山」と呼ばれる７基の曳山(高さ約 8m) の囃子を伴う巡行がある．黒・金・銀の色彩を帯びた漆工の巨大な曳山には入り組んだ金属細工品がほどこされている．曳山のステージは放射状に広げた造花傘や豪華絢爛たる工芸品で飾られている．

【下関先帝祭】5/2-4

Courtesan Festival of Akama Shrine. (山口県下関市・赤間神宮). 国指・重要無形民俗文化財. 正式名「**先帝祭上臈参拝・上臈道中**」

The festival is observed for the repose of Emperor Antoku who committed suicide by drowning at Dannoura in the battle between the Minamoto and Taira clans. After the Heike clan was defeated, many court ladies became war widows. There is a procession of the court ladies accompanied by young girl-attendants for the noble ladies in the parade.

源平合戦で壇ノ浦に入水した安徳天皇(平清盛の孫)を弔う祭り．遊女・官女の衣装をつけた上臈道中がある．

【横浜港まつり】5/3

Yokohama Port Festival. (神奈川県横浜市)

The Festival is held from May 3rd to July 20th. The highlights of this festival are the international Costume Parade and International Fireworks Display.

「みなと祭り」は5月3日から7月20日まで行われる．ハイライトは5月3日の「みなと祭り国際仮装行列」と7月17日の「国際花火大会」．

【博多どんたく】5/3-4

Fancy-Dress Parade Festival in Hakata City. (福岡県福岡市).

The festival features a parade of people dressed in fancy costumes who march through the city streets while clapping wooden rice scoops [utensils for serving rice]. Any visitors are welcome to join in.

自由な仮装でシャモジをたたいて町中を練り歩く福岡市民の祭り．☆「ドンタク」[オランダ語 zondag]は「休日，祝日」(holiday)の意．400以上の「ドンタク隊」の仮装行列で大通りを行列する．約30か所のステージで郷土芸能が行われる．

【浜松まつり】5/3-5

Hamamatsu Festival. (静岡県浜松市・中田島海浜公園). 220年の伝統行事.

The festival includes a big kite-flying contest which features more than 100 large kites flying in the sky over the sand dunes. The kite-fliers try to use string-on-string friction to cut their opponents' kite strings.

呼び物は中田島砂丘で揚げる大凧(一辺3.5m; 麻糸の直径8mm)の糸繰り合戦．摩擦で相手の凧糸を切る．☆「端午の節句」にちなんで開催される．

【興福寺薪能】5/11-12

Torchlight Noh Play Performance at Kofukuji Temple. (奈良県奈良市・興福寺).

1200年の伝統芸能.

In the evening, Noh plays are performed by the light of torch-fires on an open-air stage set up on the lawn of Kofuku-ji Temple.

夜には興福寺の野外舞台で(金春・金剛・観世・宝生の四座の)薪能が演じられる. ☆興福寺は「古都奈良の文化財」の一部としてユネスコ世界文化遺産に登録. 薪能発祥の地.

【青柏祭】 5/3-5

Huge-Float- Parade Festival. (石川県七尾市・大地主神社). 別名「デカ山まつり」. 1,000年余の伝統祭事. 正式名「青柏祭の曳山行事」として国指・重要無形民俗文化財. ☆2016年ユネスコ無形文化遺産に登録.

The festival features a parade of 3 huge 4-wheeled festival floats (called *Dekayama*) of three towns. Each float has a two-story house equipped with stages for life-sized mechanical kabuki dolls. The festival held to pray for a good harvest and peace of the nation.

呼び物は4輪車の「デカ山」(等身大の歌舞伎人形舞台をもつ2階建の曳山) 3基(府中町・魚町・鍛冶町)の行列. 五穀豊穣と天下泰平を祈願する行事. ☆「デカ山」は日本最大級の山車:高さ12m, 上部の開き13m, 車輪の直径2m. 重量20t.

【神田祭】 5月中旬

Kanda Festival (of Kanda Myojin Shrine). (東京都千代田区・神田明神[正式名:神田神社]). 400年余の伝統祭事.

The festival features a parade of a huge portable shrine carried by hundreds of young men, and about over 100 colorfully-decorated portable shrines of all sizes carried by young men with its traditional music and graceful dancing. It is one of Tokyo's three biggest festivals and is also ranked among the top three festivals of Japan.

呼び物は大きな神輿の神幸祭と神田囃子(都指定無形文化財)とともに, 100基以上の大小多様な神輿の宮入. ☆「江戸三大祭り」「日本三大祭り」のひとつ.

【葵祭】 5/15

Hollyhock Festival at Shimogamo and Kamigamo shrines. (京都府・下鴨神社・上賀茂神社).

The festival's name derives from the leaves of *hollyhock*, the sacred crest of the two shrines, which festoon all the participants, ox-drawn carriages and palanquins that take part in the festival parade. The festival features a gay procession of an imperial messenger in an oxcart, his suite of courtiers and court ladies, all elegantly dressed in costumes of the Heian period (794-1185). The gorgeous Imperial procession (which paid homage to the shrines in ancient times) starts from the Kyoto Imperial Palace and ends at Shimogamo and Kamigamo shrines.

葵祭と言われる由来は, 両社の神紋である「葵」の葉と関連し, 祭りの行列に参加する参列者, 牛車それに御輿などのまわりに葵が花づな状に飾られていることから来ている. 祭りの特徴は御所車に乗った勅使と男女従者の一行が全員平安時代の優雅な衣装を身に着けていること. この豪華な朝廷行列(昔神社に参詣した優雅な宮廷行列の再現)は京都御所を出発し, 下鴨・上賀茂の両神社に到着する. ☆「京都三大祭り」のひとつ.

祭

【東照宮春季例大祭】5/17-18

Grand Spring Festival of Toshogu Shrine.（栃木県日光市・東照宮〈ユネスコ世界文化遺産〉）. ☆別名「東照宮千人武者行列」

The *Sennin-Musha-Gyoretsu* (1,000-person procession) is the main event of this festival. It is a gay costumed procession of more than one thousand people masquerading as feudal warriors. The main festival of Tosho-gu Shrine is held on May 17th and 18th, and on October 17th. This procession recalls the large parade held in 1617 when the coffin of Tokugawa Ieyasu was brought from Mt. Kunozan in Shizuoka Prefecture and reburied at Tosho-gu Shrine in Nikko. On the festival day, three sacred portable shrines containing the spirits of Tokugawa Ieyasu, Toyotomi Hideyoshi and Minamotono Yoritomo are carried, accompanied by *samurai* warriors armed with swords, helmets, bows and arrows, and other weapons. The procession led by portable shrines marches from Futarasan Shrine to Tosho-gu Shrine.

「千人武者行列」はこの祭りの主要な行事．武者に仮装した千人以上の人が華やかに行う仮装行列のこと．東照宮大祭は5月17日と18日そして10月17日に行われる．千人武者行列の祭りは徳川家康の棺が1617年に静岡県の久能山から日光の東照宮に改葬された時に行われた大行列を再現したものである．この祭事には，徳川家康，豊臣秀吉，そして源頼朝の御霊を乗せた3基の御輿の行列があり，刀，甲，弓矢その他の武器で武装した大勢の武者が続く．行列は二荒山神社（ユネスコ世界文化遺産）から東照宮まで行進する．☆「流鏑馬」も必見．

【三国祭】5/19-21

Float Parade Festival at Mikuni Town.（福井県坂井市・三国神社）. 300年の伝統祭事. 県指・重要無形民俗文化財.

The festival features a parade of 6 huge (6-meter-high) festival floats which are equipped with huge (3-meter-tall) warrior dolls dressed in armor and helmets. These floats are pulled by the wheeled carts. Men also carry several ship-shaped sacred portable shrines of various sizes.

呼び物は豪華な山車[6m]（大武者人形[3m]が飾られている）6基の行列．山車は荷車で曳かれる．舟形神輿の渡御.

【三社祭】5月第3金曜日〜日曜日

Sanja Festival of Asakusa Shrine.（東京都台東区・浅草神社）. 正式名称「浅草神社例大祭」，1872年に始まる.

Sanja(-sama) are two brothers who found *Kannon*, a small golden statue of deity of mercy, at the Sumida River and their master. They are now deified at Asakusa Shrine. The festival features a gala parade of three huge portable shrines (of *Sanja-sama*) carried on the shoulders of men and women dressed in *happi*-coats.

「三社（さま）」（三社権現とも）は隅田川で黄金の観音を発見した兄弟2人とその師をさす．呼び物は三社さまの大神輿3台の渡御．☆「江戸三大祭り」のひとつ．2日目に行われる「びんざさら舞」（重要無形文化財）も必見．⇨ びんざさら

【三船祭】5月第3日曜日

Boat Festival on the Oi(gawa) River.（京都府・嵐山大堰川・車折神社）. 1,000年余の伝

統祭事.

The festival features a reproduction of the ancient scene of some 20 boats on the Oi(gawa) River flowing through Arashiyama.

平安時代の御船遊びの再現祭り．御座船のほか詩歌，献茶，稚児などを乗せた船20数隻が嵐山の大堰川を上下する．

6月　June　水無月 みなづき

【平安神宮薪能】6/1-2（あるいは5/31-6/1）
Torchlight Noh Play Performance at Heian Shrine. （京都市左京区・平安神宮）

Noh plays are performed in the evening by torchlight on an open-air stage set up in the precincts of Heian Shrine.

【山王祭】6/7-17
Sanno Festival of Hie Shrine. （東京都千代田区・日枝神社）．400年余の伝統祭事.

The festival features a colorful procession of three portable shrines carried by crowds of parishioners wearing ancient costumes. In this parade there are two ox-drawn imperial carriages led by four hundred followers and imperial attendants dressed in costumes of the Heian period.

呼び物は古風な衣装をまとう氏子が運ぶ「神輿の渡御」（3基）と平安朝の衣装を着た従者や官女が伴う「鳳輦の行列」（2基）である．☆「江戸三大祭り」のひとつ.

【加賀百万石まつり】6月第1金曜日〜日曜日
Feudal Lords Parade Festival in Kanazawa City. （石川県金沢市）

The festival commemorates the entry of Lord Maeda Toshiie into Kanazawa Castle in 1583. It includes a long parade of *samurai* warrior lords, demonstrations of fire techniques and a lion's dance troop peculiar to the Kaga district.

前田利家が1583年金沢城に入城した様子を再現．加賀百万石行列，加賀鳶行列，加賀獅子舞などがある.

【チャグチャグ馬コ】6月第2日曜日
Horse Parade Festival. （岩手県盛岡市・鬼越蒼前神社）．250年余の伝統行事．国指・重要無形民俗文化財.「鈴の音」は「後世に残したい日本の音風景百選」のひとつ.

Chagu-chagu refers to the tinkling sound of bells which the horses carry on their backs or tails. The festival features a parade of some 100 colorfully decorated horses carrying children on their backs through the city streets on their way to Morioka Hachiman Shrine from Sozen Shrine (dedicated to the guardian deity of horses).

「チャグチャグ」は馬につけられた鈴の音．蒼前神社から盛岡八幡宮まで子供を乗せた約100頭の馬が行列する（約15キロの行程）.

【鳥越神社の夜祭】6月第2土曜日
Night Festival of Torikoe Shrine. （東京都台東区・鳥越神社）．江戸時代からの祭事.「鳥越祭」，「鳥越夜祭」とも呼ばれる.

The festival features a parade of a huge portable shrine (called *Sengan-mikoshi*, the largest in Tokyo) carried by hundreds of young men. On the top of this huge portable shrine is a big carved phoenix as the divine emblem. A beautiful view of many portable

祭

shrines decorated with 40 lit lanterns can be seen at night.

呼び物は「千貫神輿」(約4トン．長さ6m, 幅4m)の宮入りと灯火の入った40個の弓張提灯をかかげた町神輿の宮入り．

【住吉大社御田植神事】6/14

Rice-Planting Rite at Sumiyoshi Shrine．(大阪市住吉区・住吉大社)．国指・重要無形民俗文化財．

Rice seedlings growing in the nursery are ceremoniously transplanted into the paddy-field by maidens dressed in traditional costumes to the accompaniment of folk songs for rice planting. There are spectacular dance performances and songs in the shrine.

境内の御田での神事．植女は田植え歌に合わせて早苗を植える．神田代舞や風流武者舞などがある．

【竹伐り会】6/20

Bamboo-Cutting Ceremony of Kurama Temple．(京都市左京区・鞍馬寺)．平安時代からの伝統行事．正式名「鞍馬山竹伐り会式」, 別名「蓮華会」．

In this rite with the origin of the Heian period, two groups of four men dressed in monk soldiers compete to cut large bamboo poles representing the snakes (which are the incarnation of evil) into four pieces. It is held to foretell[tell the fortune of] a good harvest.

二組に分かれた4人の法師(西方と東方を代表する4人ずつの合計8名)は弁慶のような装束で大蛇(悪の化身)に見たてた大きな竹を4片に切りつけ,その速さを競う．豊作を占う．

7月　July　文月 ふづき / ふみづき

【博多祇園山笠】7/1-15

Hakata Gion Yamakasa Festival．(福岡市博多区・櫛田神社)．760年余の伝統祭事．国指・重要無形民俗文化財．舁き山の「オイサッ・オイサッ」のかけ声は「後世に残したい日本の音風景百選」のひとつ．☆2016年ユネスコ無形文化遺産に登録．

There are two kinds of festival floats (*Yamakasa*). One is *Kazari-yamakasa* (15-meter-high), a gorgeously decorated festival float which is decked with elaborate dolls and castles. The other is *Kakiyama(kasa)* (6-meter-high), a simply decorated festival float which is made for carrying on the shoulders and used in the *Oiyama* race.

The festival features the exciting race called *Oiyama* climaxing on July 15. Teams of men clad in short *happi*-coats and loincloths dash down the city streets at full speed carrying their own *Kakiyama(kasa)* on their shoulders along a 5-kilometer course.

「山笠」には豪華絢爛たる「飾り山(笠)」(「静」の部分)と簡素な「舁き山(笠)」(「動」の部分)がある．祭りの呼び物は15日のクライマックス「追い山」で, 短い法被に締め込みをつけた1団の男衆(数百人の舁き手)が5キロのコースに沿って「舁き山」を担いで勇壮豪快に町中を走り抜ける．

【祇園祭】7/1-31

Gion Festival．(京都市東山区・八坂神社)．1,000年余の伝統祭事．☆2016年ユネスコ無形文化遺産に登録．

The *Gion Festival* is held on July 1st through 31st in honor of Yasaka Shrine. Its climax is on the 17th day. It originated in 869 when an epidemic raged in Kyoto and killed many people. People erected 66 tall spears (*hoko*) representing the provinces of Japan asking for god's protection. Today the original spears (*hoko*) have been replaced by big festival floats (called "*Hoko*") of the same name. The smaller floats (called "*Yama*") carry big life-size figures of famous historical personages. This festival features the *Yama-boko junko* parade of elaborate festival floats which are carried by many young men through the city to the accompaniment of musicians playing music known as *Gion-bayashi*.

祇園祭は八坂神社に奉納される祭りで7月1日から31日に行われ，そのクライマックスは17日である．その起源は，京都に疫病が流行し大勢の人が死亡した869年にまでさかのぼる．神の御加護を求めて人々は全国の地方を表す66基の大きな槍(鉾)を建てた．今日では昔の槍(鉾)は同じ名前の「大きな山車」(「鉾」)に取り代わる．「小さい山車」(「山」)には有名な歴史上の人物の等身大の人形が飾られる．祭りのハイライトは豪華な山車の「山鉾巡行」で，「祇園囃子」で知られる楽士の音楽に合わせて若者たちが市内を練り歩く．☆山鉾の数は時代によって異なる．現在の山鉾の数は32基(鉾9基・前祭の山14基・後祭の山9基)．その中の29基は国指・重要有形民俗文化財．2009年にユネスコ無形文化遺産に登録．「日本三大祭り」「京都三大祭り」のひとつ．

【あばれ祭】7月第1金曜日・土曜日

Raging-Parade Festival.（石川県能登町・八坂神社）．別名「キリコ祭り」．300年余の伝統祭事．

There is a big rage when the portable shrines are carried on the way to the shrine. Some are thrown into the sea or the river from a bridge. At night there is a parade of 40 big rectangular [oblong] palanquins in the shape of lampstands (called *Kiriko* [6-meter-long ~ 12-meter-long]) covered with lighted paper-lanterns.

輪島塗の豪華な神輿暴れがあり，海中にまたは橋から川中に投げ込んだりして暴れ回る夏祭り．夜になると灯を掲げた「キリコ」(行灯状の長方形の大きな御輿[長さ6m~12mの奉燈])40数本の奉燈行列がある．

【那智の火まつり】7/14

Fire Festival at Kumano-Nachi Shrine.（和歌山県・熊野那智大社〈ユネスコ世界文化遺産〉）．400余年の伝統祭事．正式名称「扇祭」または「扇会式法会」．

The highlight of this festival is the dramatic meeting of the two groups on the stone stairs: one is a group of white-robed Buddhist priests carrying 12 burning torches (in the shape of the bucket[pail]) ascending the stone-stairs and the other is a group of people carrying 12 *Ogi-Mikoshi* [1-meter-wide and 10-meter-long rectangular logs decorated with 32 folding fans] descending from Kumano-Nachi Shrine. It makes a spectacular sight as if it looks like a sea of fire.

ハイライトは石段を上る「大松明」(桶のような輪じめ形)12本を持つ白装束の僧侶の1団と熊野那智大社から下る「扇神輿」(32本の扇を飾り付けた幅1m，高さ10m程の長方形の丸木)12基を担ぐ1団との出会いである．火の海のような壮観な光景を呈する．

【綴子神社大太鼓】7/14-15

Huge-Drum-Beating Parade at Tsuzureko Shrine.（秋田県北秋田市・綴子神社）．750

祭

年の伝統祭事．県指・重要無形民俗文化財．

In the festival there is a parade of 4 large drums (3.8 meters in diameter, 4.52 meters in length and 3.5 ton in weight) in the feudal lord's procession. These drums are usually beaten with long drumsticks by several young men. The festival is held to pray for a good harvest and for a lot of rain.

大太鼓4基を打ち鳴らしながら大名行列とともに行進する．数人（12～16名）の若者が太鼓を長いばちで打ち鳴らす．五穀豊穣と降雨（雨乞い）を祈願する．☆世界最大の太鼓（直径3.8m，胴の長さ4.52m，重さ3.5t）．平成元年にはギネスブックに登録．

【厳島（神社）管弦祭/宮島管弦祭】7月中旬

Music Festival of Itsukushima Shrine.（広島県廿日市市・厳島神社〈ユネスコ世界文化遺産〉）．900年余の伝統神事．

The festival features a colorful sea fleet of gaily-decorated boats sailing on the water to the accompaniment of musical instruments. *Gagaku* [ancient classical court music and dance] is performed on the stage of the barge[boat] bearing a portable shrine (*mikoshi*) as well as musicians and Shinto priests. The barge heads for the shrine in a colorful sea procession with other gaily-decorated boats.

楽器の演奏に合わせて管弦船が海上を渡航する．御座船では雅楽を演奏しながら厳島神社に向かう．☆「雅楽」2009年にユネスコ無形文化遺産に登録．⇨ 管弦

【郡上おどり】from early July to early September   Bon Dance Event at Gujo County.
（岐阜県郡上市）．⇨ 郡上おどり（8月13-16日）

【小倉祇園太鼓】7月第3金曜日～日曜日

Kokura Drum-Beating Gion Festival.（福岡県北九州市・小倉城）．390年余の伝統祭事．県指・無形民俗文化財．映画「無法松の一生」で有名になった勇壮な祭事．別名「小倉祇園祭り」

The festival features more than 100 festival floats carrying large Japanese-style drums (called *Gion-daiko*), which are kept beating all the time during the festival. Drum-beating entertainment takes place at Kokura Castle.

祭り中終始打ち鳴らす「祇園太鼓」をのせた100基以上の山車行列がある．太鼓連打の余興は小倉城で行われる．

【塩竈みなと祭】7月第3月曜日（海の日）

Shiogama Port Festival.（宮城県塩竈市・鹽竈神社・志波彦神社）

There is a sea parade of colorful ships carrying on board 2 sacred portable shrines of Shiogama and Shiwahiko shrines. They make a cruise on Matsushima Bay surrounded by hundreds of gaily-decorated attendant fishing boats.

神社の神輿2基を御座船に奉安させた海上渡御．数百の漁船［供奉船］を伴って松島湾を巡行する．

【津和野の鷺舞】7/20・7/27

Heron Dance at Tsuwano Town.（島根県津和野町・弥栄神社）．460年余の伝統行事．国指・県指・重要無形民俗文化財．

Two dancers dressed as herons (male and female) dance a whirling performance with the musical background of drums, flutes and gongs. There is also a parade of heron dancers performed by many children wearing red and white costumes with heron headdresses placed on top of their heads. The heron dance is performed to pray for the sound health of children.

雌雄二羽の白鷺に扮した２人の舞手が囃子に合わせて旋回しながら舞う．子供による鷺舞の行列もある．鷺舞いは子供の健康を祈願して舞う．

【和霊大祭】7/23-24

Summer Festival of Warei Shrine.（愛媛県宇和島市・和霊神社）．別名「うわじま牛鬼まつり」．300年余の伝統祭事．

The festival features a procession of several monster-shaped floats (called *Ushi-oni*) carried by young men through the town streets. *Ushi-oni* is a 7-meter-long figure of monster which has a horned bovine head with ox-like features, and the body of the demon.

「牛鬼」（頭が牛，胴体が鬼に似る身の丈7mの妖怪人形）の山車行列が町中を練り歩く．
☆和霊神社には日本最大の石造りの大鳥居がある．

【相馬野馬追】7/23-25

Horse-Chasing Festival.（福島県相馬市）．700年余の伝統行事．国指・重要無形民俗文化財．

The festival features horse-racing in which twelve *samurai* horsemen dressed in armor and helmets carrying swords all race over a distance of 1,000 meters in the vast Hibarigahara field. The other feature is a dynamic horse-riding contest in which thousands of horsemen dressed in ancient armor scramble [jostle and fight] for sacred shrine flags (*Shingi*), which are shot up high in the air over the field. On the last day, armed horsemen chase wild horses into an enclosure of the shrine (called *Noma-gake*).

呼び物は雲雀が原における「古式甲冑競馬」と騎馬武者数千騎による「神旗争奪戦」である．最終日には「野馬懸け」（騎馬武者が神社の境内にある竹のかこいの中に野生馬を追い込む行事）がある．

【天神祭】7/24-25

Summer Festival at Tenman-gu Shrine.（大阪市北区・天満宮）．1,000年以上の伝統祭事．別名「天満天神祭」「天満祭」

The *Tenjin Festival* is held on July 24th and 25th at Tenman-gu Shrine, at which Sugawara no Michizane, the god of academics, is enshrined. During the festival, many ancient portable shrines and the festival floats parade the city streets (*riku-togyo*). The climax of this festival is a flotilla of some 100 elaborately decorated ships and other barges[boats] carrying the portable shrines, which sail along the Okawa River (*funa-togyo*). Classical dances and music are performed on the ships, which are illuminated with bright lanterns.

天神祭は学問の神様である菅原道真(845-903)が祭られている天満宮で7月24日と25日に行われる．祭りが行われる間，神輿と山車が多数市内を行列する(陸渡御)．祭りのクライマックスでは豪華に飾り立てた約100隻の御座船や御輿を積んだ神楽船の船団が，大川を巡行する(船渡御)．明るい提灯で照らし出された船上では舞楽などが演じられる．

祭

【戸畑祇園大山笠】7月第4金曜日〜日曜日

Tobata Gion Float Parade Festival. (福岡県北九州市・浅生八幡). 200年余の伝統祭事. 国指・重要無形民俗文化財. ☆2016年ユネスコ無形文化遺産に登録.

The festival features a parade of large, 10-meter-high festival floats festooned with many lanterns (called *Nobori-Yamagasa*). At night these *Nobori-Yamagasa* floats are changed into *Chochin-Yamagasa* [festival floats with a giant 12-tiered pyramid constructed of 309 lighted lanterns].

呼び物は「幟山笠」(約10m)の行列. 夜になると幟山笠から「提灯山笠」(提灯309個をピラミッド形に12段に重ねて飾る山車)に変身する.

【尾張津島天王祭】7月第4土曜日・日曜日

Lantern Festival at Tsushima Shrine. (愛知県・津島神社), 500年余の伝統祭事. 国指・重要無形民俗文化財. ☆2016年ユネスコ無形文化遺産に登録.

The highlight of the festival is a sea parade of 5 boats decorated with thousands of lit lanterns (*Danjiri-bune*) floating down the waters of the Tenno River at night, presenting the beautiful sight to onlookers.

ハイライトは宵祭りで, 数千(約2,750個)の提灯で飾られた5隻の「車楽船」が天王川を渡るところは壮観. ☆1隻に365個(1年を表す)の灯籠がつく.

8月　August　葉月 はづき

【弘前ねぷた】8/1-7

Hirosaki Neputa [Fan-Shaped-Float Parade] Festival. (青森県弘前市). ☆別名「扇ねぷた」(青森の「人形型」に対して弘前の「扇型」). 国指・重要無形民俗文化財.

The festival features a night parade of huge lighted fan-shaped festival floats (*Neputa*). The floats bear their own fantastic designs on lanterns featuring by the beautiful contrast in design of fighting warriors on the front and charming women on the back.

呼び物は「ねぷた」の行列. 山車(約70台)の前部の勇壮な武者と後部の美麗な女性のデザインの対照が壮観である.

【青森ねぶた】8/2-7

Aomori Nebuta [Dummy-Float Parade] Festival. (青森県青森市). 400年余の伝統祭事. 国指・重要無形民俗文化財.

Nebuta are giant dummy floats representing legendary figures and animals which are constructed by frameworks of bamboo and wire, and covered with paper or cloth. They are painted in various colors and illuminated from within by large candles or light bulbs. The festival features a gala parade of the huge *Nebuta* set on festival floats, which are carried through the streets by millions of *kimono*-clad people (*haneto*) to the accompaniment of flutes and drum music with the shouting of "Rassera! Rassera!". The festival is said to have originated from a legend that Sakanoue no Tamuramaro, a local warlord, put down a rebellion by using *Nebuta* successfully in the shape of men and animals to confuse his enemies as the size of his army. It is also believed to dispel sleep in order to go into the Bon season when ancestral spirits are welcomed and entertained.

「ねぶた」とは伝説上の人物や動物を表現した飾り人形の山車のことで, 竹や針金の骨組

みで作られ，紙や布で覆われている．「ねぶた」（高さ約5m，幅約10m）は多様な色彩で描かれ，内部は大きなローソクまたは電球で照明されている．

この祭りの特徴は山車（約30台）に乗せた巨大な「ねぶた」の楽しい行列で，着物姿の数万人の群衆が「ラッセラ！ラッセラ！」と威勢よく叫びながら笛や太鼓の音楽に合わせてねぶたを市中で引き回す．この祭りの起源は，坂上田村麻呂武将が自分の軍隊の大きさを敵軍に錯覚させるために，人物や動物の形をした「ねぶた」を巧みに利用して反乱を鎮圧したという伝説にある．また眠気を払って，先祖の霊を慰めるお盆を迎える祭りだとも言われている．☆「東北三大祭り」のひとつ．

【秋田竿灯まつり】 8/3-6

Akita Kanto Lantern Parade Festival．（秋田県秋田市）．国指・重要無形民俗文化財．

Kanto is a long mast-shaped (10-meter-long) bamboo pole with many lighted paper lanterns hung from nine horizontal crossbeams. It has about 50 lighted lanterns in the form of well-ripened ears of rice, symbolizing an abundant crop of rice. The festival features a parade of stout men skillfully balancing the *Kanto* on their heads, shoulders, chins or hips. Men from many districts compete in showing balancing techniques to the accompaniment of fast-beating drums and high-pitched flutes. The festival is observed not only to drive off the demon of drowsiness that hampers people's work throughout the year but also to pray for a rich harvest.

「竿灯」とは長い帆型の竹竿のこと．その中に9つの水平な横ばりに吊るされた照明の紙提灯がある．「竿灯」には，豊作を象徴する実り豊かな稲穂の形をした照明の提灯が50個ほど吊るされている．祭りの特徴は，たくましい男性が「竿灯」を頭，肩，顎または腰の上で巧みにバランスをとりながら行列するところ．多くの地区から参集した男性はビートの早い太鼓やピッチの高い笛などの伴奏に合わせて絶妙なバランス技術を競って見せ合う．この祭りは，年中作業を妨害する眠気の邪気を追い払うため，また五穀豊穣を祈願するために行われる．☆「東北三大祭り」のひとつ．

【山形花笠まつり】 8/5-7

Yamagata Flower-Sedge-Hat Dance Parade Festival．（山形県山形市）．県指・重要無形民俗文化財．

Hanagasa is a low, round straw hat decorated with brightly-colored artificial flowers (of safflower). The origin of this festival dates back to the Taisho era (1921) when people reclaimed waste land at Lake Tokura(ko) at Obanazawa City. They started to sing the *Hanagasa* folk songs to celebrate the reclamation of waste land. This festival features a gala parade of more than 10,000 dancers wearing *hanagasa* and costumes of the same color and pattern. They dance along the streets to the accompaniment of shamisen and drums, while twirling their *hanagasa* left, right, up and down. The parade is led by gorgeously decorated floats.

「花笠」は明るい色彩の造花（県花の「紅花」）で飾り立てた丸いわら帽子．祭りの起源は大正時代にまでさかのぼり，そのころ尾花沢市の徳良湖で荒れ地を埋め立てた．この開墾工事を祝って花笠音頭を歌ったのが始まり．この祭りの特徴は，花笠をかぶり，色鮮やかな同じ模様の衣装を身につけた1万人以上の踊り子の華やかな行列．上下左右に花笠をくるくる回しながら，三味線と太鼓の音色に包まれて市中を踊る．行列は豪華な山車

祭

に先導される.

【仙台七夕まつり】8/6-8

Star Festival at Sendai City.（宮城県仙台市）. 400年余の伝統祭事. ⇨ 七夕祭り

This festival features the beautiful decorations of bamboo branches decked with long strips of paper of various colors and other glittering materials of fancy designs. People write romantic poems associated with the legend and their wishes on the narrow strips of paper. The Star Festival is usually observed in many countries of Japan on July 7th, but held gorgeously in Sendai City a month later, which started in the time of Date Masamune. This festival is the largest and brightest of its kind in Japan. It is one of the three biggest festivals in Tohoku region along with the Aomori Nebuta Festival and the Akita Kanto Festival.

この祭りの特徴は色とりどりの短冊や派手なデザインをほどこしたきらびやかな飾りを吊るした竹枝の豪華な装飾である. 伝説と関連したロマンチックな詩や願い事などを短冊に書き添える. 七夕祭は, 通常7月7日に日本中で行われるが, 仙台では1か月遅れで豪華に行われる. 伊達正宗(1567-1636)のころに始められた. ☆「東北三大祭り」のひとつ.

【高知よさこいまつり】8/9-12

Yosakoi-Folk-Song Dance Parade Festival.（高知県高知市）. 昭和29年に発足.

Yosakoi means "come in tonight" in the dialect of Kochi City. In this festival, thousands of people dance for three days holding clappers (*naruko*) in their hands. The national competition of *Yosakoi* Dance is held on the last day.

数千の人が両手に「鳴子」(打楽器)をもって3日間踊り続ける. 最終日には全国大会がある.

【阿波おどり】8/12-15

Awa Folk Dance Parade.（徳島県徳島市）. 400年余の伝統祭事.

Awa Odori dates back to 1585 when the people of the castle town danced in the streets in celebration of the completion of Tokushima Castle built by the feudal lord Hachisuka Iemasa. They got drunk and began to dance with an unsteady gait setting formalities aside, when Hachisuka provided Japanese rice wine (*sake*) for them. A variety of *Awa Odori* is held in Tokushima (formerly known as *Awa* province) during the observance of the Bon Festival week from August 12th to 15th. Many large groups of men and women attired in decorative *kimono*-costumes parade through the city streets, singing and dancing enthusiastically in lines to the accompaniment of music played on *shamisen*, flutes and drums.

阿波踊りは1585年にまでさかのぼり, 蜂須賀家政領主が徳島城を完成した時に町人たちはこれを祝って路上で踊ったという. 蜂須賀が町人たちに酒をふるまうと, 町人たちが無礼講で熱狂的に踊りだしたという. 8月12日から15日までのお盆期間中(昔「阿波」で知られる今の)徳島で多種多様な阿波踊りが演じられる. きれいな着物衣装をまとった大勢の男女の大集団が三味線や笛また太鼓などの音楽に合わせ, 列をなして熱狂的に歌い踊りながら町内を練り歩く.

【郡上おどり】8/13-16

Gujo Dance Performance.（岐阜県郡上市八幡町）. 400年余の伝統祭事(盂蘭盆会).

県指・国指・重要無形民俗文化財．

The Gujo Odori (Dance) Festival is held each year from early July to early September. The festival features the dance parade which takes place for four days from August 13th to 16th when people dance all night long from 8 o'clock in the evening to 5 o'clock the next morning.

毎年7月初旬から9月初旬まで踊る．8月13日から16日の4日間の「徹夜踊り」が呼び物．

【春日大社中元万燈籠】8/14-15

Lantern-Lighting Ceremony.（奈良県奈良市・春日大社）．⇨ 春日大社節分万燈籠(2月3日)

The festival is well-kown for its fantastic scene created by some 3,000 stone and bronze lanterns of various sizes which are lit at night on both sides of the approach to Kasuga Grand Shrine.

夜中には春日大社の参道にある三千余の灯籠に点火される．

【山鹿灯籠まつり】8/15-16

Yamaga Lantern Parade Festival.（熊本県山鹿市・大宮神社）．700年の伝統祭事．

The festival features a dance parade of thousands of ladies dressed in *yukata*-kimono, who have pagoda-shaped lighted gold and silver lanterns on their heads. They dance all night long in a very slow tempo. Thousands of lighted lanterns moving slowly and gracefully on the heads gives a fantastic atmosphere to viewers.

数千の浴衣姿の女性が五重塔型の金銀の灯籠を頭にのせて，夜から朝までゆるりと踊る「千人灯籠踊り」が続く．頭の上でゆっくりと優雅にゆらぐ数千の灯火灯籠は幻想的である．

【箱根大文字焼】8/16

Great Bonfire Event at Hakone.（神奈川県箱根町・明星ヶ岳)

A spectacular bonfire in the shape of the Chinese character "dai(大)" meaning "big [large]" is formed by lines of big burning torches on a slope of Mount Myojogatake in Hakone. This event is observed as one of the Bon events to send off the souls of the dead to heaven after their brief return to earth.

明星ヶ岳(924m)の山頂付近で大文字焼きがある．お盆行事の一環として行う．

【大文字五山の送り火】8/16

Great Bonfire Event on Five Mountains in Kyoto.（京都市・如意ヶ嶽[通称：**大文字山**]）

The *Daimonji-Gozan-Okuribi Event* is the spectacular *Daimonji* Bonfire Event held annually on Mount Nyoigatake in Kyoto on the night of August 16th as one of the Bon Festivals. It is observed to send the souls of the ancestors back to heaven after their brief return to earth.

The fire is laid out in the shape of the burning Chinese character "*dai*" which means "large[great]". Other fires are lit separately on four other hills surrounding the city, which are set on fire in the shape of "*hidari-daimonji*" (a smaller "dai"), "*funa-gata*" (a boat), "*myo-ho*" (excellent law [Buddhist teaching]), and a "*torii*" (a Shinto shrine gateway).

祭

大文字五山の送り火は壮大なかがり火の行事のことで，お盆行事の一環として毎年8月16日の夜，京都の如意ヶ嶽(大文字山)で行われる．この行事は現世での短い滞在を終えた祖先の霊を来世に送るために行われる．

かがり火は「大きい」を意味する漢字の「大」(左京区浄土寺・如意ヶ嶽)の形をして燃え広がる．その他の火は町の周辺にある4か所の丘で別々に輝き，「左大文字」(北区大北山・左大文字)，「舟形」(北区西加茂・船山)，「妙・法」(左京区松ヶ崎・西山及び東山)そして「鳥居形」(左京区嵯峨鳥居本・曼荼羅山)の形で点火される．

【宮津燈籠流し】8/16

Lantern-Floating Festival at Miyazu Bay. (京都府宮津市)．400年余の伝統行事.

At night some 10,000 lanterns with lighted candles inside are set afloat in Miyazu Bay to observe as part of the Bon Festival. The bay is aflame with the burning lanterns, presenting a mysterious atmosphere. There are also many straw boats for ancestral spirits to sail in on the sea and thousands of fireworks in the night sky.

お盆の一環として夕方海面に流されるローソクのともる1万余の灯籠で宮津湾一帯は神秘的になる．海上には精霊船，空には数千発の花火が見られる．

【西馬音内盆踊り】8/16-18

Bon Folk Dance at Nishimonai. (秋田県雄勝郡羽後町)．400年余の伝統祭事. 国指・重要無形民俗文化財.

The festival is so unique that the dancers cover their faces with black cloths except their eyes. They parade throughout the city streets till late at night, dancing slowly to the accompaniment of flutes, drums and *shamisen*.

目以外を黒い布で顔を覆った踊り手が，笛・太鼓・三味線に合わせて静かに深夜まで踊る．

【一色大提灯まつり】8/26-27

Big Lantern-Lighting Festival at Isshiki Town. (愛知県幡豆郡一色町・諏訪神社)．450年余の伝統祭事.

The festival features 12 huge brightly-colored lanterns hoisted on the poles of a roof-shaped ceiling. The highest one is 10 meters in height and 6 meters in diameter. This is probably the longest paper lantern of its kind in Japan. At night the huge lanterns (with *yamato-e* paintings) are lighted by Shinto priests, presenting the fantastic scenes.

色鮮やかな大灯籠(高さ10m，直径6m)12張りが吊るされる．この種では日本最大の灯籠. 夜には大きな提灯(「大和絵」が描かれている)が点火されて幻想的な光景が展開する．

【吉田の火祭り】8/26-27

Fire Festival at Fujiyoshida City. (山梨県富士吉田市)．別名「火伏せまつり」「富士浅間神社火祭り」

This festival is held at the closing of the climbing season of Mt. Fuji. In the daytime portable palanquins, modeled in the shape of Mt. Fuji, are paraded from Sengen Shrine through the city streets. At night 70 huge pine torches are set aflame by young people holding big paper lanterns in their hands along the climbing paths onto Mt. Fuji.

富士山の山じまいの祭り．日中は富士山の形をした神輿の渡御．夜には大きな松明(長さ4m，直径1m) 70本に点火される．

祭

9月　September　長月 ながつき

【おわら風の盆】9/1-3

Bon Folk Dance of the Wind. (富山県富山市八尾町). 300年余の伝統芸能.

The streets are decorated with paper lanterns on this day. Long rows of young men in *happi*-coats and close-fitting trousers, and women in *yukata*, whose faces are covered by low-brimmed straw hats, dance to a melancholic music all night long. The folk songs with the unique melancholic melodies (called *Etchu Owara Bushi*) and mysterious dance (*Owara Odori*) are performed to the accompaniment of *shamisen* and *kokyu* [Chinese fiddle: *shamisen*-like string musical instrument played with a bow]. It is held to pray for a good harvest, offering Bon dancing to the god of wind to lull the storms.

市中には灯籠が飾られる. 低いふちとりの麦藁帽(編み笠)で顔を隠した法被と股引き姿の男性と浴衣姿の女性の列が悲しげな旋律にのって一晩中踊りを披露する. ユニークな哀調を帯びた民謡「越中おわら節」と神秘的な「おわら踊り」が三味線や胡弓に合わせて演奏される. 嵐を鎮めるために風の神に盆踊りを奉納しながら五穀豊穣を祈願する.

【岸和田だんじり祭】9月中旬の土曜日・日曜日

Kishiwada Danjiri Festival [Wheeled-Float-Rushing Parade Festival (of Kishiwada City)]. (大阪府・岸和田地区と春木地区). 別名「けんかまつり」. 300年余の伝統祭事.

Danjiri is a large elaborately-decorated wooden festival wheeled float[cart]. The festival features the dramatic "Corner Turning" (*yari-mawashi*) which is a rushing parade of the *danjiri* floats carried by hundreds of men through the city streets. Working both front and rear levers in unison, the team pulling *danjiri* skid [pull and turn] the heavy floats around each street corner as fast and recklessly as possible.

「だんじり」(地車)とは木製の大きな飾り山車[屋台]のこと. 呼び物は勇壮な「やりまわし」で, 数百の曳き手(34チーム)が市中を駆けるだんじりの走りである. 前後のてこを一斉に使い, だんじりの曳き手は出来るだけ早く道路の曲がり角で方向転換させる. ☆「やりまわし」(遣り回し)は岸和田の方言で「走っていって回す;突っ込んでいって回す」の意.「だんじり」の重さ約4t, 高さ4m, 長さ4m, 幅2.5m. 引き縄の長さは100-200m.

【鶴岡八幡宮例大祭】9/14-16

Annual Festival of Tsurugaoka Hachimangu Shrine. (神奈川県鎌倉市・鶴岡八幡宮), 800年余の伝統祭事.

The festival features a parade of sacred portable shrines and high-wheeled floats elaborately decorated with gold and silver. Another attraction is the famous horseback archery or the traditional art of shooting arrows from horseback performed on the last day.

呼び物として「神輿の渡御」と「金銀で飾った山車の行列」そして「流鏑馬」が催される.

【大原はだか祭り】9/23-24

Half-Naked Festival at Ohara Town. (千葉県いすみ市大原・鹿島神社・大原漁港). 400年余の伝統祭事.

Eighteen portable shrines are pushed and shoved into the rough waves of Ohara Beach by many men dressed in loincloths. It is held to pray for a good harvest and a rich haul.

褌姿の男衆が神輿18基とともに大原海岸の荒波を浴びてもみあう. 五穀豊穣と大漁祈

祭

願の行事.

10月　October　神無月 かんなづき

【放生津曳山祭】 10/1-3

Float Parade Festival at Hoshozu-Hachiman Shrine. (富山県射水市・放生津八幡宮).
350年余の伝統祭事.

There is a parade of 13 elaborately-decorated festival floats (8-meter-long) carried throughout the city streets together with the sacred portable shrines. A stage is set up with in the shrine precincts to display life-sized dolls of goddess (*Kijo*) in the center and guards (*Shitenno*) in the four corners of the display. At night, the artificial flowers are replaced by many lighted lanterns on the floats, adding to their beauty and luster.

曳山13台(長さ8m)が神輿といっしょに町を練る. 神社の境内に舞台を設け, 中央には「鬼女」, 四隅には「四天王」の等身大の人形を飾る. 夜になると「提灯山車」(山車にある造花を点火された提灯に取り変える)になり, 壮観である.

【二本松提灯祭り】 10/4-6

Lantern-Float Parade at Nihonmatsu City. (福島県二本松市・二本松神社). 350年余の伝統祭事. 県指・重要無形民俗文化財. 別表記「二本松のちょうちん祭り」

There is a parade of 7 festival floats decorated with hundreds of lanterns and carrying drums (*Taiko-dai*). At night, gorgeously-decorated festival floats carrying hundreds of lit lanterns are paraded to the accompaniment of gongs, flutes and drums (*Gion-bayashi*), presenting a spectacular sight to onlookers.

数百(350個)の灯籠と太鼓を載せて運ぶ7台の「太鼓台」の行列がある. 夜には祇園囃子に合わせながら, かがり火をともした数百の提灯を載せた豪華絢爛たる山車の行列があり, 見る者には壮観に映る.

【長崎くんち】 10/7-9

Nagasaki Kunchi Autumn Festival (at Suwa Shrine). (長崎県長崎市・諏訪神社). 国指・重要無形民俗文化財.「長崎おくんち」ともいう.

Kunchi means the autumn harvest festival in the local dialect spoken in the northern area of Kyushu. This festival originated in the 17th century when the Tokugawa shogunate allowed the Chinese people living in the city to inaugurate this festival in order to draw attention away from Christianity.

The festival features the Chinese-style Dragon/Snake Dance (*Ja-odori*), in which a 20-meter-long dragon/snake with golden eyes is performed in the traditional Chinese fashion. Other interesting features are the boat-shaped floats (*Ja-bune*) and the umbrella-shaped floats (*Kasa-boko*). After the dances, a parade of three sacred portable shrines are carried at a fast pace down the steep seventy-two stone stairs of the shrine. On the last day, they are brought back up to the shrine.

「くんち」の意味は九州北部地方の方言で「秋の収穫祭」のこと. この祭りは17世紀に始まり, 徳川幕府はキリスト教布教への関心をそらすために当時の中国人町民にこの祭りを開始することを許可した.

祭りの特徴は黄金の目をした長さ20mの竜が中国風に舞う中国流の「蛇踊り」. その他興

祭

味深い特徴として，ボート型の山車「蛇船」，笠型の山車「傘鉾」などがある．踊りが終わると，3基の御輿行列が，神社の72段の階段を一気に下へ運ばれる．最終日には神社に戻される．

【那覇大綱挽(おおつなひき)】10月第2日曜日

Naha Tug-of-War Match Festival. （沖縄県那覇市）．400年余の伝統祭事．体育の日（第2月曜）の前日日曜日に行う．17世紀に始まる沖縄最大の伝統行事．

Fifteen thousand people pull and strain a huge rope which is 200 meters long and 2 meters in diameter, accompanied by shouts of encouragement. This event was logged in the Guinness Book of World in 1997 as the largest tug-of-war contest in the world.

15,000の挽き手による全長200m・直径2mの大綱挽．1997年には「世界最大」とギネスブックに認定される．☆2m以上寄った時点で勝負が決定．

【秋の高山祭】10/9-10

Takayama Autumn Festival. （岐阜県高山市・八幡宮）．別名「八幡祭(はちまんまつり)」．800年余の伝統祭事．国指・重要無形民俗文化財．☆2016年ユネスコ無形文化遺産に登録．⇨ 春の高山祭（4月14日-15日）

The festival features a gala procession of 11 lavishly-decorated festival floats, representing the pinnacle of Japan's folk arts. Visitors can see the dexterous movements of wind-up marionettes performing on top of the festival floats. Many lanterns are lit on all the floats, looking more resplendent in the darkness of the night.

豪華な屋台11台の「屋台曳き揃え」がある．屋台の上で演じられる操り人形の巧妙な動きが見物できる．夜になれば屋台の提灯が点火され，暗闇の中で華麗に輝く（宵祭）．☆4台の屋台が市内を巡行するのを「屋台曳き廻し」という．

【川越まつり】10月第3土曜日・日曜日

Kawagoe Festival. （埼玉県川越市）．350年余の伝統祭事．国指・重要無形民俗文化財．☆2016年ユネスコ無形文化遺産に登録．

Kawagoe is called "Little Edo" where there remains many vestiges of the Edo period. The festival features a parade of 20 huge elaborately-decorated festival floats carrying big dolls (masterpieces of the Edo period) and the musical bands (called *Kanda Bayashi*).

「小江戸」の町川越で，大きな人形（江戸時代の傑作）と囃子（神田囃子）を載せた20台の豪華な山車の行列がある．

【妻鹿(めが)のけんかまつり】10/14-15

Mega Fighting Festival. （兵庫県姫路市・松原八幡神社）．☆通称「灘のけんかまつり」，別名「みこし合(あわ)せ」(Portable-Shrine Roughhouse Festival). 県指・重要無形民俗文化財．

The festival features the roughhouse[struggle] of 3 portable shrines shouldered by half-naked youths, who jostle each other amid pushing and shoving in the shrine precincts. They join in the fight, holding bamboo poles in their hands.

3基の神輿「一の丸」(40代の白鉢巻)，「二の丸」(30代の黄鉢巻)，「三の丸」(20代の赤鉢巻)がからみ合う勇壮な祭り．青竹で神輿に立ち向かう．

【西条秋まつり】10/8-17

Saijo Autumn Festival. （愛媛県西条市・伊曽乃神社）　300年余の伝統行事．

The climax of this festival is a lavish procession of about 150 spectacular festival floats

祭

decorated with the roofs and lanterns (*danjiri*) and about 100 sacred portable shrines (*mikoshi-yatai*). The men carrying the portable shrines jostle each other with the festival floats in the Kamo River.

豪華絢爛な屋台形の「だんじり」150台余と「神輿屋台」100台余の豪華な渡御行列がある. 男衆の担ぐ神輿屋台がだんじり屋台と加茂川でもみ合う. ☆ 体育の日前々日の「嘉母神社祭礼」に始まる. ハイライトは15/16日の伊曽乃神社祭礼の「御宮出し」と「川入り」. 最後は17日の「飯積神社祭礼」で太鼓台11台と神輿のかきくらべがある.

【東照宮秋季例大祭】 10/17

Grand Autumn Festival of Nikko Toshogu Shrine. (栃木県日光市・東照宮). 別名「東照宮千人武者行列」 (A Thousand Warriors' Parade at Toshogu Shrine). ⇨ 東照宮春季例大祭(5月17-18日)

The Autumn Festival is conducted on a smaller scale than the Spring Festival. The Autumn Festival features a colorful procession of 1000 people masquerading as feudal lords. There is also a performance of *Yabusame* or horseback archery on the 16th day.

秋季祭は春季祭より規模は小さい. 呼び物は「千人武者行列」と「流鏑馬」である. ⇨流鏑馬(431頁)

【時代祭】 10/22

Festival of the Ages[Eras]. (京都府京都市)

This festival was begun in 1895 when Heian Shrine was built to commemorate the 1,100 anniversary of the transfer of the Imperial Capital to Kyoto in 794. The festival highlight is a procession of people dressed in historical costumes and ancient armor and weapons, each representing various events of Japanese history from the Heian period through to the Meiji era. The parade starts with the 19th century and goes back to the 8th century. The gorgeous historical parade starts from the Kyoto Imperial Palace and ends at Heian Shrine.

この祭りの起源は1895年で, その時794年の京都創建の時代から1100年を祝って平安神宮が建立された. 祭りのハイライトは歴史ゆかりの衣装や昔の武将姿をした人々の行列で, 平安時代から明治時代までの歴史的な時代や出来事を再現している. 行列は19世紀から始まり8世紀にさかのぼる. この豪華な歴史行列は, 京都御所が起点となり, 平安神宮が終着点となっている. ☆〔8つの時代〕明治維新—江戸—安土桃山—室町—吉野—鎌倉—藤原—延暦.「京都三大祭り」のひとつ.

【鞍馬の火まつり】 10/22

Fire Festival at Yuki Shrine in Kurama. (京都市左京区鞍馬・由岐神社). 1,000年余の伝統祭事.

Men wearing only loincloths and short cotton jackets (*hanten*) parade through the streets carrying hundreds of huge lighted torches of all sizes around the portable shrines from 6:00 p.m. to midnight. There is also a procession of children dressed only in loincloths and headbands carrying the small burning torches. They go up to the shrine in the mountain at night. Mt. Kurama is set ablaze with the light of the pine torches, creating the beautiful sight.

午後6時から真夜中にわたり, 褌と袢纏姿の男衆が神輿周辺で数百の燃え盛る大小の松

明を持って市中を練り歩く．燃え盛る松明を持つ褌と鉢巻姿の子どもの行列もある．夜になると，彼らは山中の神社に向かう．鞍馬の山は松明で点火され，幻想的な景観を呈する．

11月　November　霜月 しもつき

【唐津くんち】11/2-4

Karatsu Kunchi Autumn Festival. （佐賀県唐津市・唐津神社）．400年余の伝統祭事，国指・重要無形民俗文化財(唐津くんちの曳山行事)．県指・重要有形民俗文化財(曳山14台：世界にも類をみない漆の工芸品)．☆2016年ユネスコ無形文化遺産に登録．

The festival features a parade of 14 huge colorful festival floats carrying big papier-mâché figures (of famous warriors [such as Minamoto no Yoshitsune] or animals [such as a huge fierce-looking lion]) coated with golden, silver, red and blue lacquer. Each festival float (called *Hikiyama*: 6 meters in height) is drawn through the city streets by teams of bearers selected from 14 families of Karatsu City.

金・銀・赤・青の漆塗りの一閑張りのフィギュア(武者[源義経など]または動物[獅子頭など])を載せた14台の絢爛豪華な曳山の行列がある．各曳山(長さ6m)は唐津市の14町内チームのそれぞれの曳子たちが市中を練り歩く．⇨ 一閑張り(31頁)．☆「くんち」とは「秋の祭日」(the autumn festival in the local dialect)の意．

【箱根大名行列】11/3

Feudal Lord Procession in Hakone. （神奈川県箱根町湯本）．1935年以来の伝統祭事．

It recalls the ceremonious customs in which more than 200 local residents colorfully costumed as a feudal lord and his retainers and vassals parade as the ancient warriors did on the path in the Edo period. They march at a very slow pace from Sounji Temple to Yumoto in the morning and return to Sounji Temple in the afternoon.

この行事は大名と家来の派手な衣装を身につけた住民が，江戸時代に武士が道中に行った行列の風俗を再現したもの．大名行列は午前中早雲寺から湯本の町までとてもゆっくりと練り歩き，午後は早雲寺に戻る．⇨ 大名行列

【八代妙見祭】11/22-23

Myoken Parade Festival. （熊本県八代市・八代神社妙見宮）, 別名「**妙見宮大祭**」350年余の伝統祭事．県指・重要無形民俗文化財．☆2016年ユネスコ無形文化遺産に登録．

Myoken is the name of a deity who is believed to have come to Japan from China in 680, riding on a grotesque animal called a *kida* (a messenger of *Myoken* deity). *Kida* is an imaginary crossbred creature between a turtle and a snake. The festival features a parade of a huge *kida* comprising a long snake's head (2.5 meters in length) and a huge turtle's body (6 meters in height).

妙見とは「亀蛇」(妙見様の使者)と呼ばれる奇妙な動物に乗って，680年に中国から渡来したといわれる神の名前．「亀蛇」は亀と蛇の想像上の雑種動物である．祭りの呼び物は長い蛇の頭と大きな亀の胴体の形をした巨大な亀蛇の行列である．

祭

12月　December　師走 しわす

【秩父夜祭】12/2-3

Chichibu Night Festival.（埼玉県秩父市・秩父神社）. 340年余の伝統祭事. 国指・重要無形民俗文化財.　☆2016年ユネスコ無形文化遺産に登録.

The festival features a parade of 4 gorgeously-decorated festival floats bedecked with lanterns (*yatai*) and 2 huge carts decorated with beautiful carvings (*kasaboko*). The festival floats are pulled through the streets with the musical accompaniment of flutes, drums, gongs and other instruments. The climax of the festival is at night when 4 *dashi* floats and 2 *kasaboko* carts climb the steep slope of the hill (called *Dango-zaka*) in one spurt[without stopping] with a portable shrine. At night, numerous paper lanterns are lit on the festival floats, creating the beautiful sight.

祭りの特色は手の込んだ装飾をほどこした「屋台」4台と豪華な彫刻を刻んだ「笠鉾」2台の行列. 笛, 太鼓, 銅鑼その他の音楽に合わせ市中を練り歩く. クライマックスは山車と笠鉾が神輿とともに一気に急な坂(団子坂)を上るところ. 夜に山車に提灯がともされると幻想の世界になる.

【泉岳寺義士祭】12/13-14

Memorial Service for 47 Loyal Retainers.（東京都港区・泉岳寺）

There is a parade of people masquerading as feudal *samurais* celebrating the memory of the 47 loyal retainers in the Ako Domain who avenged their master by killing his enemy.

討ち入りを果たした赤穂義士47人の武士に扮した行列がある.

【春日若宮おん祭】12/15-18

Grand Festival of Kasuga-Wakamiya Shrine.（奈良県奈良市・春日若宮お旅所）. 870年余の伝統祭事.「神楽・舞楽」は国指・重要無形民俗文化財.

The festival features a splendid procession of people masquerading as courtiers and retainers of ancient times [from the Heian period to the Edo period]. Kagura and Bugaku are also performed in this shrine.

呼び物は春日大社まで練り歩く「時代行列」と「神楽・舞楽」の奉納.　⇨ 神楽/舞楽

【男鹿のなまはげ】12/31

Oga Namahage Festival [Devil Festival in the Oga Peninsula].（秋田県男鹿市・男鹿半島）. 国指・重要無形民俗文化財.　☆2018年ユネスコ無形文化遺産に登録.

Namahage means grotesquely-masked men disguised [dressed up] as fierce devils [demons]. In this festival a group of 2 or 3 *Namahage* people wearing devil's masks and straw raincoats and carrying wooden kitchen knives make door-to-door calls at houses with children to scold lazy children. It is held to encourage children to obey their parents.

鬼の面をつけた若者数人が一組になって, 子供のいる家々を巡回する. 子供が親に従うように鼓舞するために行う.

【おけら詣り】12/31

Sacred Fire Rite (at Yasaka Shrine).（京都市東山区・八坂神社）

At midnight on December 31, *Okera* (medical herb to get rid of poison) is burnt[kindled] at the shrine precincts. Worshippers visit to the shrine to take some of the sacred fire back to their homes. The fire will ward off sickness during the coming year and bring sound health to those who cook their first meal with the sacred fire.

神社で「おけら」(毒を払う薬草)の火を燃やし，それを持ち帰り雑煮をつくると病気にならず健康に過ごせるといわれる．

【大晦日】12/31

New Year's Eve, the last day of the year.　毎月の最後の30日を「晦日」といい，年の最後の12月のみ「大」をつけて「おおみそか」という．　⇨ 紅白歌合戦/ 年越しそば/ 除夜の鐘

祭

三大一覧

1	日本三大祭	祇園祭(京都府) ・ 天神祭(大阪府) ・ 神田祭または山王祭(東京都)
2	日本三大曳山祭り	祇園祭(京都府) ・ 飛騨の高山祭り(岐阜県) ・ 秩父夜祭(埼玉県)または長浜曳山まつり(岐阜県)
3	日本三大山車祭り	祇園祭(京都府) ・ 飛騨の高山祭り(岐阜県) ・ 秩父夜祭(埼玉県)
4	日本三大盆踊り	阿波踊り(徳島県) ・ 郡上踊り(岐阜県) ・ 西馬音内盆踊り(秋田県)
5	日本三大火祭り	鞍馬の火祭り(京都府) ・ 那智の火祭り(和歌山県) ・ 玉垂宮鬼夜(福岡県)
6	日本三大提灯祭り	二本松提灯祭り(福島県) ・ 尾張津島天王祭(愛知県) ・ 秋田竿灯まつり(秋田県)
7	日本三大裸奇祭	四天王寺どやどや(大阪府) ・ 岡山の西大寺会陽(岡山県) ・ 黒石寺蘇民祭(岩手県)[または飛騨古川起し太鼓(岐阜県)]
8	日本三大奇祭	御柱祭(長野県)[または西大寺の会陽(岡山県)] ・ 吉田の火祭り(山梨県) ・ なまはげ(秋田県)
9	日本三大民謡	阿波踊り(徳島県) ・ 郡上八幡踊り(岐阜県) ・ 花笠踊り(秋田県)
10	日本三大川祭り	尾張津島天王祭(愛知県) ・ 厳島神社管弦祭(広島県) ・ 天神祭(大阪府)
11	日本三大くんち	長崎くんち(長崎県) ・ 唐津くんち(佐賀県) ・ 博多くんち(福岡県)
12	日本三大七夕祭り	仙台七夕祭り(宮城県)・湘南平塚七夕祭り(神奈川県)・安城七夕祭り(愛知県)
13	江戸東京三大祭り	三社祭 ・ 山王祭 ・ 神田祭
14	京都三大祭り	祇園祭 ・ 時代祭 ・ 葵祭
15	京都三大火祭り	大文字五山の送り火・鞍馬の火祭り・清涼寺のお松明式
16	関東三大祭り	東照宮千人武者行列(栃木県)・秩父夜祭(埼玉県)・浜降祭(神奈川県)
17	大阪三大祭り	天神祭り・愛染祭り・住吉祭り
18	東北三大祭り	青森ねぶた(青森県)・秋田竿灯まつり(秋田県)・仙台七夕祭(宮城県)
19	北陸三大祭り	青柏祭(香川県)・御車山祭(富山県)・三国祭(福井県)
20	四国三大祭り	阿波踊り(徳島県)・よさこい祭り(高知県)・新居浜太鼓祭(愛媛県)
21	九州三大祭り	福岡の玉せせり ・ 熊本の八代妙見祭 ・ 長崎くんち

祭

【付記(2)】
日本の歴史年表

弥生時代　ca. 300 bc ~ ca. 300　Yayoi period

縄文式土器(Jomon [cord-marked] pottery)と磨製石器(polished stone tools)を中心とする縄文時代(Jomon period)が終わる頃，朝鮮半島から稲作が伝わり，北九州で弥生時代が始まる．弥生式土器(Yayoi earthenware)や青銅器(bronze ware)が製造される．邪馬台国女王の卑弥呼が中国に使者(envoy)を送る．

紀元前4世紀　•弥生時代が始まる．稲作の開始．金属器(青銅器・鉄器)の使用．
The Yayoi period and rice cultivation start. The use of ironware prevails[spreads].

3世紀　•卑弥呼，邪馬台国の女王．☆卑弥呼：中国の史書魏志倭人伝に記されている倭国(ancient Japan)の女王．
Himiko[Pimiko] becomes the shaman Queen of the Yamatai[Yabatai] State of ancient Japan.

ad 239　•卑弥呼，中国(魏)に使者を派遣．
Himiko sends an envoy to China [the Kingdom of Wei].

大和時代　ca. 300 ~ ca. 600　Yamato period

古墳(tomb mounds)が造られ，農業社会で階層分化(stratification)が進む．大陸から仏教と漢字が伝来し，大和朝廷[ヤマト政権]が成立する．この時代の末期を「飛鳥時代」と呼び，日本最初の歴史時代が産声をあげる．

4世紀　•古墳文化の発生．最初の埴輪の作成．
The Tomb Culture is born. The first burial mound figures are found.

•大和朝廷[ヤマト政権]の成立．☆奈良盆地(the Nara basin)を中心とした近畿地方．
The Yamato Court establishes the first unified state in Japan.

•氏姓制度の開始．☆豪族たちが血縁を中心とした氏とよばれる集団を構成．大王から姓とよばれる称号が与えられた．
The family name[surname] system starts.

•漢字の使用開始．☆中国から日本へ伝わる．
The use of Chinese characters[writing] starts.

6世紀頃•儒教の伝来．☆孔子[551-479]を始祖とする思想・信仰の体系．
Confucianism is introduced into Japan.

538　•仏教の伝来．☆一説に552年の伝来．欽明天皇期，百済を経由して伝来する．
Buddhism is introduced into Japan (via Paekche in Korea).

552　•崇仏論争．☆蘇我稲目(崇仏派)と物部尾輿(廃仏派)の宗教論争．
Struggle for the worship of Buddhism.

587　•蘇我馬子(崇仏派)が物部守屋(廃仏派)を滅ぼす．仏教興隆の詔を発す．
Soga no Umako (pro-Buddhism) kills Mononobe no Moriya (anti-Buddhism).
The Imperial Edict for Buddhism Promotion.

588　•蘇我馬子が法興寺(現：飛鳥寺)を建立(元興寺(ユネスコ世界文化遺産)の前身)．
☆日本最古の寺院．

歴史

Houkou-ji Temple is founded by Soga no Umako.

飛鳥時代　ca.600~709　Asuka Period

593~622　•聖徳太子(用明天皇の第二皇子[574-622]．蘇我馬子の娘婿)．第33代推古天皇の摂政となる．天皇中心の政治が開始．

Prince Shotoku becomes regent [acting deputy governor] for Empress Suiko. An Emperor-centered government starts.

593　•四天王寺の建立(大阪)．☆蘇我氏の戦勝を祈願して四天王(the Four Devas)を安置する．

Shitenno-ji Temple is built (by Prince Shotoku).

•厳島神社の創建(広島)．☆平清盛が現在の社殿を造営した(1168年頃)．

Itsukushima Shrine is built (in Hiroshima).

603　•聖徳太子による「冠位十二階」の制定．⇨「冠位十二階」

A Twelve-Cap-Rank System at the Imperial Court is instituted by Prince Shotoku.

604　•聖徳太子による「十七条憲法」の公布[制定]．☆日本最初の憲法．豪族や官僚に対する道徳的な規範．天皇に従い，仏法を敬うことを説く．

A Seventeen-Article Constitution [the Constitution of Seventeen Articles] is promulgated[established] by Prince Shotoku.

607　•遣隋使．☆小野妹子(政治家・男性)を隋に派遣する．中国の記録では600年にも倭国の使者が来たとする．

The Imperial embassy is dispatched (by Prince Shotoku) to China [Sui Dynasty (589-618)]. Ono no Imoko is sent as an envoy to China.

•法隆寺(ユネスコ世界文化遺産)の創建(奈良)．☆世界最古の木造建築．

Horyu-ji Temple is constructed (by Prince Shotoku).

630　•遣唐使．☆犬上御田鍬らを派遣する．☆894年まで10数回派遣する．

The Imperial embassy is dispatched to China [Tang Dynasty (618-907)].

645　•中大兄皇子(後の天智天皇)と中臣鎌足(後の藤原鎌足)が蘇我氏を滅ぼす．大化の改新の開始．

Prince Naka no Oe (later Emperor Tenji) and Nakatomi no Kamatari (later Fujiwara no Kamatari) defeat the Soga clan. The Taika Reform is instituted.

646　•孝徳天皇が大化の改新の詔を発布．☆中央集権的な政治体制(centralized government system)．☆最初の元号(the first era)　⇨元号

Edicts of the Taika Reforms are issued by Emperor Kotoku.

667　•近江大津宮に遷都(capital relocation)．

The capital is moved to Omi (Imperial Palace Otsu no Miya).

668　•天智天皇の即位，近江令を制定．☆古代日本政府による最初の体系的法典(全22巻)．

The Omi Code is issued by Emperor Tenji.

672　•壬申の乱．☆天智天皇の弟大海人皇子(後の天武天皇)が後継をめぐって争い，甥(nephew)の大友皇子を破る．

The Jinshin Disturbance[War].

- 飛鳥[飛鳥浄御原宮]に遷都(capital relocation).　☆天武天皇と持統天皇が営んだ宮.

  The capital is moved to Asuka [Asuka Kiyomihara no Miya].

680　• 薬師寺(ユネスコ世界文化遺産)の建立.　☆天武天皇が皇后(後の持統天皇)の病気回復を祈願して建立.

  Yakushi-ji Temple is founded.

683　• 富本銭の鋳造.　☆日本最古の銅銭.　奈良県明日香村にて出土.

  Minting of copper coins. The first issuance of the oldest copper coins.

684　• 八色の姓の制定.　☆天武天皇が氏に八つの姓(真人, 朝臣, 宿禰, 忌寸, 道師, 臣, 連, 稲置)を授与した制度.　天皇を頂点とするピラミッド型の階層を形成する.

  The establishment of the Eight-Rank[Eight-Cognomen] System. Under this system members of lineage groups (*uji*) are assigned titles of rank, forming a social pyramid with Emperor Tenmu at its apex.

694　• 藤原京に遷都(capital relocation).　☆持統天皇が日本初で最大の中国風都城の藤原京を造営.

  The capital is moved to Fujiwara-kyo. Japan's first Chinese-style town with an orderly grid of streets.

701　• 大宝律令の制定.　☆日本史上最初の「律」(刑罰法令)と「令」(行政法)をそろえて成立した法律.　天皇中心の中央集権国家が政治を行う.　中央には神祇官と太政官が位置する.　⇨ 神祇官 / 太政官

  The compilation of the Taiho Law Code (of penal and administrative laws).

708　• 和同開珎.　☆和銅元年に日本で鋳造・発行された銭貨(銀銭・銅銭).

  Minting of the Wado Kaichin (the issuance of the oldest Japanese coinage).

古代 (Ancient period)
奈良時代　710~794 Nara period

平城京[奈良] (Heijo-kyo[Nara])に都がおかれた時代で, 元明天皇の710年から794年の平安遷都までの時代, 狭義では710年から784年の長岡京遷都までの時代.　律令政治(government based on Ritsuryo [criminal and civil codes])が成熟し, 中国文化が導入された.　仏教が国教(Buddhism gained official recognition as the state religion)に認知され, 日本全土に寺院が創建される.

710　• 平城京に遷都(capital relocation).　☆通称「奈良の都」.　元明天皇の時代.　首都正門の羅城門に始まり, 大内裏正門の朱雀門に終わる.　内裏(天皇が住む宮殿)と大極殿があった.　1952年特別史跡に指定.　1998年「平城京跡」はユネスコ世界文化遺産に登録.

  The capital is moved to Heijo-kyo (now Nara City).

712　• 古事記の撰上.　⇨ 古事記

  The Record of Ancient Matters is compiled.

713　• 風土記の編成.　☆日本最初の地理書の執筆を開始.

  The topography [description of the natural feature of a region] of Japan is compiled.

歴史

720 • 日本書紀の完成． ⇨ 日本書紀
　　　The Chronicles of Japan is compiled.

723 • 三世一身法の制定． ☆三世代または本人一代まで開墾地(reclaimed lands)を非課
　　　税の私有地(ownership of non-taxed private property)として容認された．
　　　The compilation of Sanze Isshin Law [Law of Three Generations or a Lifetime].

741 • 諸国に国分寺・国分尼寺を建立． ☆聖武天皇の命による． 国家安泰(peace of the
　　　nation)と五穀豊穣(abundant harvest of crops)を祈願する． 1説に738年．
　　　The establishments of Provincial Temples for monks[monasteries] and Provincial
　　　Temples for nuns[nunneries] throughout the country.

743 • 聖武天皇が大仏造立の詔を発令． ☆本尊は盧舎那仏，747年鋳造開始，749年完成．
　　　733年に東大寺(ユネスコ世界文化遺産)が創建される(『東大寺要録』)．
　　　The Imperial Edict for Construction of the Great Buddhist Statue is issued by
　　　Emperor Shomu.

752 • 東大寺の大仏の開眼供養(会)． ⇨ 開眼供養
　　　The consecration of the Great Buddhist Statue of Todai-ji Temple.

754 • 鑑真(688-763：唐の僧)の来日． ☆律宗を伝える．
　　　Ganjin, a Chinese Buddhist priest, comes to Japan from China. He introduces the
　　　Ritsu sect of Buddhism.

759 • 鑑真による唐招提寺(ユネスコ世界文化遺産)の創建．
　　　Toshodai-ji Temple is founded by Ganjin.
　　• 万葉集が編集され，783年頃完成する． ☆日本最古の歌集． ⇨ 万葉集
　　　The Anthology of Myriad [Ten Thousand] Leaves is compiled.

784 • 長岡京に遷都(capital relocation)． ☆桓武天皇の命により平城京より長岡京(現在
　　　の京都)に遷都する．
　　　The capital is moved to Nagaoka-kyo.

788 • 最澄による比叡山延暦寺(ユネスコ世界文化遺産)の建立．
　　　Enryaku-ji Temple is founded by Saicho.

平安時代　794~1192　Heian period

　　　桓武天皇が平安京に遷都した794年から鎌倉幕府が成立した1192年までの約400
　　　年間の時代． 日本独自の貴族文化(aristocratic culture)が花開き，武家が登場し，
　　　仮名文字(the Japanese *Kana* syllabary)［平仮名・片仮名］が発展する．

794 • 平安京(現在の京都)に遷都(capital relocation)． 日本の首都と定める． 1868年まで
　　　続く． ☆桓武天皇の政治改革の開始．
　　　The Imperial capital is moved to Heian-kyo (now Kyoto). Capital until 1868.

797 • 坂上田村麻呂，蝦夷を征討． ☆日本史上で最初の征夷大将軍になる． ⇨ 征夷大将
　　　軍❶
　　　Sakanoue no Tamuramaro subjugates Ezo tribes [the aboriginal people] in the
　　　north.

805 • 最澄(767-822：別名「伝教大師」)が天台宗を開く．
　　　The Tendai sect of Buddhism is introduced by Saicho.

806　● 空海(774-835: 別名「弘法大師」)が真言宗を開く. ☆四国八十八箇所巡礼の創始者.
　　　The Shingon sect of Buddhism is introduced by Kukai.

816　● 空海による高野山金剛峰寺(ユネスコ世界文化遺産)の建立.
　　　Kongobu-ji Temple is founded by Kukai on Mt. Koya(san).

858　● 藤原良房, 摂政の職務を行う. ☆皇族以外の臣下として初めて摂政の座につく.
　　　⇨ 摂政
　　　Fujiwara no Yoshifusa becomes the first of the great regents from the Fujiwara clan.

887　● 藤原基経(良房の養子)が日本史上初の関白に就任する. ⇨ 関白
　　　Fujiwara Mototsune becomes the (first) chief adviser to the Emperor (in Japan).

894　● 菅原道真(学者・政治家・右大臣)により遣唐使廃止.
　　　The Mission to China [the dispatching of envoys to Tang Dynasty (China)] is abolished by Sugawara no Michizane.

905　● 古今和歌集の編集. ☆醍醐天皇の勅により紀貫之らが編集. 日本最古の勅撰和歌集.
　　　The completion of the Kokin-Wakashu [A Collection of Old and New Poetries/ A Collection of *tanka* poems in Ancient and Modern Times]. Japan's first poetry anthology (commissioned by Emperor Daigo) is compiled by Ki no Tsurayuki.

935~940　● 平将門の乱. ☆関東で朝廷に反乱を起こす.
　　　The Revolt[Rebellion] of Taira no Masakado.

939~941　● 藤原純友の乱. ☆瀬戸内海で朝廷に反乱を起こす.
　　　The Revolt[Rebellion] of Fujiwara no Sumitomo.

995　● 藤原道長の政権掌握. ☆朝廷支配の黄金時代の開始.
　　　Fujiwara no Michinaga takes power and becomes the head of the Fujiwaras. Golden age of its domination of the imperial court begins.

996　● 清少納言の「枕草子」の完成.
　　　The completion of The Pillow Book (written by Sei Shonagon).

1008　● 紫式部の「源氏物語」の完成.
　　　The completion of The Tale of Genji (written by Murasaki Shikibu).

1016　● 藤原道長, 摂政に就く. ☆摂関政治(体制)で実権を握る. ⇨ 摂関政治
　　　Fujiwara no Michinaga becomes Regent.

1017　● 藤原道長, 太政大臣になる. ⇨ 太政大臣
　　　Fujiwara no Michinaga makes the Grand Minister of State.

1053　● 京都の平等院の鳳凰堂[阿弥陀堂] (ユネスコ世界文化遺産)の建立. ☆998年藤原道長の別荘. 1052年藤原頼通が寺院(平等院)に改める.
　　　The Phoenix Hall [the Amida Hall] in Byodoin Temple is constructed in Kyoto.

1086　● 白河上皇による院政の開始. ⇨ 院政
　　　The System of a Cloister Government is established by the retired Emperor Shirakawa.

1124　● 中尊寺(850年創建)金色堂の建立(藤原清衡).
　　　The Golden Hall in Chuson-ji Temple is constructed by Fujiwara no Kiyohira.

歴史

1156　• 保元の乱. ☆朝廷における平氏と源氏の政権紛争. 武家の時代に入る.
　　　　The Hogen Disturbance [the War of Hogen]. Rivalry between the Taira clan and the Minamoto clan for political power at court begins.

1159　• 平治の乱. ☆平(清盛)氏が源(頼朝)氏を征服し, 朝廷における権力を確立する.
　　　　The Heiji Disturbance [the War of Heiji]. The influence of the Taira clan over the Imperial court establishes after the Taira clan defeated the Minamoto clan.

1167　• 平清盛, 太政大臣になる. ⇨ 太政大臣
　　　　Taira no Kiyomori becomes the Grand Minister of State.

1175　• 法然(1132-1212: 本名「源空」)が浄土宗を開く.
　　　　The Jodo sect of Buddhism is founded by Honen.

1180　• 源平の争乱. ☆平氏政権に対する反乱が起こる. 源頼朝, 平清盛に対して挙兵する.
　　　　Taira-Minamoto War [War between the Tairas and the Minamotos] begins. Minamoto no Yoritomo raises an army against Taira no Kiyomori.

1183　• 平家, 都落ち. ☆源義仲により平家壊滅.
　　　　The Heike clan flees Kyoto.

1185　• 壇ノ浦の戦い. 通称「源平合戦」. ☆源義経による平家の滅亡. ☆壇ノ浦は現在の山口県下関市.
　　　　The Naval Battle of Dannoura[the Gempei Wars]. The Heike clan is defeated[annihi-lated] by Minamoto no Yoshitsune.

中世 (Medieval period)

鎌倉時代　1185 (1192) ~1333　Kamakura period

源頼朝が守護・地頭を設置した1185年, または鎌倉幕府を開いた1192年から北条氏が滅びる1333年までの間の時代. 2度に渡る蒙古襲来(the Mongolian Invasion of Japan)を招く. 前期封建時代.

1185　• 源頼朝, 全国に守護と地頭を置く. ⇨ 守護❷ / 地頭
　　　　Minamoto no Yoritomo appoints Shugo [provincial governor] and Jito [estate steward] in the country.

1189　• 源頼朝, 奥州藤原氏を滅ぼす.
　　　　Minamoto no Yoritomo destroys the Oshu Fujiwara clan.

1191　• 栄西(1141-1215)が臨済宗を開く.
　　　　The Rinzai sect of Buddhism is founded by Eisai.

1192　• 源頼朝, 後鳥羽天皇より征夷大将軍を拝し, 鎌倉幕府を開く. ⇨ 征夷大将軍(241頁)
　　　　Minamoto no Yoritomo is appointed (Seii-tai-) Shogun[Generalissimo] by Emperor Go-Toba. He establishes the Kamakura shogunate government.

1203　• 北条時政が初代執権に就く. ☆源頼朝の死(1199年)後, 北条氏が鎌倉幕府を継ぐ. ⇨ 執権
　　　　Hojo Tokimasa assumes the office of the first regent for the shogun.

1212　• 鴨長明の方丈記の成立.
　　　　An Account of My Hut is written by Kamo no Chomei

1219　• 源実朝の暗殺. 源氏の将軍絶える. ☆北条家の執権支配が続く.

歴史

The Assassination of Minamoto no Sanetomo and the end of the line of Minamoto shoguns. Members of the Hojo clan continue to rule as regents.

1221　• 承久の乱．☆鎌倉幕府を倒し，権力を朝廷にもどすための反乱．敗れた後鳥羽上皇は幕府により隠岐に流罪．

The Jokyu Disturbance. The ex-emperor[abdicated] Go-Toba is sent into exile by the shogunate after he fails his attempt to take back power from the shogunate.

1224　• 親鸞(1173-1263)が浄土真宗(一向宗)を開く．

The Jodo Shinshu sect of Buddhism is founded by Shinran.

1227　• 道元(1200-1253)が禅宗の一派である曹洞宗を開く．永平寺を建立．

The Soto sect of Zen Buddhism is introduced by Dogen. He builds the Eihei-ji Temple.

1232　• 北条泰時，御成敗式目(貞永式目)を制定する．⇨ 御成敗式目

The Codification of the Warrior House Law is promulgated by Hojo Yasutoki.

1252　• 鎌倉・高徳院(浄土宗)の大仏が完成．☆別称「鎌倉大仏」．開基・開山は不祥．

The Great Buddhist Statue[a giant seated statue of the Amida Buddha] is constructed in Kotoku-in Temple at Kamakura.

1253　• 日蓮(1222-1282)が日蓮宗[法華宗]を開く．

The Nichiren sect of Buddhism is founded by Nichiren.

1274　• 文永の役．第1回蒙古襲来．⇨ 元寇

Bun'ei no Eki War. The first Mongolian Invasion of Japan.

1281　• 弘安の役．第2回蒙古襲来．

Koan no Eki War. The second Mongolian Invasion of Japan.

1321　• 後醍醐天皇，院政を廃止して直接政治を行う．☆楠木正成らの武士が活躍．

The Cloister Government is abolished and ruled directly by Emperor Go-Daigo.

1333　• 鎌倉幕府の滅亡．☆新田義貞が鎌倉を攻略する．

The collapse of the Kamakura shogunate government. Nitta Yoshisada captures Kamakura.

室町時代　1336~1573 Muromachi period

足利氏が京都に室町幕府を開いた時代．鎌倉幕府の滅亡から織田信長が足利義昭を将軍に擁立して京都に入り1573年に追放するまでの時代．幕府は「南北朝の動乱」(conflict between the Northern and Southern Courts)に混乱し，「戦国時代」[1467-1573]と呼ばれる内乱(civil strife known as the Sengoku period)が約100年続く．禅宗の影響を受けた水墨画，枯山水，書院造りが広まる．また能・狂言・茶の湯・活け花などが開花する．前期封建時代

1333　• 建武の新政が開始．☆後醍醐天皇の親政(鎌倉幕府を倒し，天皇がみずから行う政治)．⇨ 建武の新政(名称は翌1334年に定められた「建武」の元号に由来する)

Start of the Kenmu Restoration. The direct imperial rule is restored to Emperor Go-Daigo, who reestablished Imperial control by overthrowing the Kamakura shogunate.

1336　• 足利尊氏，建武式目(室町幕府の施政方針を示した要綱)を制定し，政権の骨格を

示す.

Kenmu Shikimoku, the Code of Governmental Principles (describing an administrative policy of the Muromachi; shogunate) is promulgated by Ashikaga Takauji.

南北朝時代　1336~1392　Period of the Northern and Southern Courts.

足利尊氏, 京都にて光明天皇の「北朝」をたてる. 一方, 後醍醐天皇は吉野へ還幸して「南朝(吉野朝廷)」をたてる.

Ashikaga Takauji sets up a new Emperor Komyo on the throne in Kyoto [the Northern Court]. Emperor Go-Daigo moves to Yoshino and establishes the Southern Court to reign at the court at Yoshino.

1338 • 足利尊氏,「北朝」の光明天皇より征夷大将軍に任命され, 京都に室町幕府を開く.

Ashikaga Takauji receives the title of (Seii-Tai-)Shogun from the Northern Court of Emperor Komyo and establishes the Muromachi shogunate government.

1368 • 足利義満が第3代将軍に就く.

Ashikaga Yoshimitsu becomes the third Shogun.

1392 • 南朝と北朝の統一. 別称「明徳の和約」. ☆足利義満により合一する. 南朝の後亀山天皇(南朝最後の第4代天皇)が吉野から京都に帰還して, 北朝の後小松天皇(北朝最後の第6代天皇)に三種の神器を譲って退位して南北朝が合一する.

The Unification[reconciliation] of the Southern and Northern Courts.

1397 • 足利義満, 金閣寺(正式名称「鹿苑寺」. ユネスコ世界文化遺産)を建立. ☆北山文化の開花. 伝統的な公家文化と禅宗の影響を受けた武家文化の融合(茶の湯や活け花また枯山水などの開花).

Kinkaku-ji Temple, the Golden Pavilion, is built by Ashikaga Yoshimitsu in Kyoto.

1401 • 足利義満, 明(中国)に使者を送る.

Ashikaga Yoshimitsu sends envoys to Ming Dynasty [1368-1644] (in China).

1404 • 明との勘合貿易(別称「日明貿易」)の開始. (1551年まで続行). ⇨ 勘合貿易(109頁)

The official tally trade starts with the Ming Dynasty(in China). The Ming-Japanese trade.

戦国時代　1467~1573　The Age of Civil Wars

1467~1477 • 応仁の乱(東軍・細川勝元と西軍・山名持豊の対戦). 室町時代の第8代将軍・足利義政の時代に起こった内乱. 京都の荒廃. 戦国時代に突入. 下克上が始まる. 地方に城下町(戦国大名の居城を中心とする町. 政治・経済・文化の中心地), 門前町, 港町などが栄える. ⇨ 下克上

The Onin Civil War[Rebellion]. Kyoto is laid waste. The war marks the beginning of the Warring States Period. *Gekokujo* starts and castle towns, temple towns and port towns begins to prosper.

1488 • 加賀の一向一揆. ⇨ 一向一揆

The Ikko uprising at Kaga Province.

1489 • 足利義政, 銀閣寺(正式名称「慈照寺」. ユネスコ世界文化遺産)を建立. ☆「東山

歴史

文化」の開花．武家，公家，禅僧らの文化の融合．能楽や庭園に見られる幽玄，わびに通じる美意識の世界が別邸(後の銀閣寺)を造営．

Ginkaku-ji Temple, the Silver Pavilion, is founded by Ashikaga Yoshimitsu in Kyoto.

1543 ● ポルトガル人により種子島に鉄砲[火縄銃]伝来．

The Portuguese introduces the first matchlock guns [matchlock muskets] to Japan on the Tanegashima Island (Southern Kyushu).

1549 ● フランシスコ・ザビエル(イエズス会士)が鹿児島に来航．☆日本最初のキリスト教布教開始．⇨ キリシタン(128頁)

Francis Xavier (Jesuit Catholic priest) introduces Christianity at Kagoshima. Start of the first Christian mission.

1550 ● 南蛮貿易(スペインとポルトガル)の開始．⇨ 南蛮

Nanban trade [Japanese trade with Spain and Portugal] starts.

1553~1564 　● 川中島の戦い(1回～5回)．☆武田信玄と上杉謙信との対戦．北信濃の支配権を巡る．

The Battle of Kawanakajima.

1560 ● 織田信長(2,000の軍勢)，桶狭間にて今川義元(25,000の軍勢)を破る．☆日本史上に残る勇壮な逆転劇．

Oda Nobunaga defeats Imagawa Yoshimoto at the Battle of Okehazama.

1568 ● 織田信長の台頭．☆京都に入り，足利義昭を将軍職につける．

Oda Nobunaga enters Kyoto and appoints Ashikaga Yoshiaki as shogun.

1573 ● 織田信長により室町幕府滅亡．☆第15代足利将軍・足利義昭が京都より放逐される．

The Muromachi shogunate is collapsed by Oda Nobunaga. He ousted Ashikaga Yoshiaki, the 15th Ashikaga Shogun, from Kyoto.

近世 (Early Modern period)

安土・桃山時代　1573~1603　Azuchi-Momoyama period

織田信長・豊臣秀吉が政権を握った時代．信長の安土城，秀吉の桃山城にちなむ名称．天下統一を成就した．ヨーロッパの貿易商や宣教師を通して南蛮文化(Western culture)に触れた．「織豊時代」．

1575 ● 長篠の戦い．☆織田信長(と徳川家康連合軍38,000)は三河国長篠城を巡り武田勝頼(軍15,000)を破る．

The Battle of Nagashino. Oda Nobunaga defeats Takeda Katsuyori.

1576 ● 安土城の築城開始(1579年完成)．☆城址は国指定特別史跡．

Azuchi Castle is built by Nobunaga.

1582 ● 本能寺の変．☆織田信長，家臣明智光秀の襲撃を受け自害．

Honno-ji Incident. Oda Nobunaga is assassinated by his vassal Akechi Mitsuhide at Honno-ji Temple.

● 山崎の戦い．別称「天王山の戦い」．☆羽柴秀吉と明智軍が激突した戦い．

The Battle of Yamazaki.

歴史

- 天正遣欧少年使節.☆九州のキリシタン大名3名(大友宗麟・大村純忠・有馬晴信)が少年施設団(4名:伊東マンショ・千々石ミゲル・中浦ジュリアン・原マルティノ)をローマへ派遣し,ローマ教皇グレゴリウス13世に謁見する.1590年帰国.
  Young envoys are sent[dispatched] by three Christian feudal lords to meet the Pope in Rome.
- 秀吉,太閤検地を開始.☆地検(田畑の測量や収穫量調査)を全国で行う.年貢徴収の効率化.
  Hideyoshi initiates the Taiko Kenchi [national land survey for tax-setting purposes].

1583
- 秀吉,大阪城の築城を開始.☆1588年に完成.
  Osaka Castle is constructed by Hideyoshi.

1585
- 秀吉,関白となる.⇨関白
  Hideyoshi becomes Kampaku [chief adviser to the Emperor].

1586
- 秀吉,太政大臣になり,豊臣に改称.
  Hideyoshi becomes Grand Minister of State and changes his name to Toyotomi.

1587
- 秀吉,バテレン追放令を布告.⇨バテレン追放令
  Hideyoshi issues an edict expelling all Christian missionaries from Japan.

1588
- 秀吉,刀狩令を布告.☆兵農分離政策.⇨刀狩令
  Hideyoshi issues an edict of the Katanagari [confiscation of farmers' swords].

1590
- 小田原攻め.☆秀吉,北条氏を降し,天下を統一する.
  The Siege of Odawara (to eliminate the Hojo clan). Hideyoshi unifies almost all of Japan.

1592~93
- 文禄の役.朝鮮出兵.☆小西行長,加藤清正,小早川隆景ら15万余の大軍.
  The Bunroku Campaign, the first Japanese invasion of Korea.

1597~98
- 慶長の役.朝鮮出兵.☆秀吉の死により撤退.
  The Keicho Campaign, the second Japanese invasion of Korea.

1596
- 長崎にて,26聖人殉教.☆1596年サン・フェリペ号事件(土佐国へスペイン船の漂着事件)がキリスト教迫害のきっかけとなったとの説がある.
  26 Japanese and foreign Christians' martyrdom at Nagasaki.

1598
- 秀吉の死亡.☆石田三成が政権維持のため徳川家康と対立.
  Death of Hideyoshi. Ishida Mitsunari comes to conflict with Tokugawa Ieyasu to maintain the administration.

1600
- 関ヶ原の合戦.☆徳川家康の勝利.全土に覇権を確立.
  Tokugawa Ieyasu wins the Battle of Sekigahara (by defeating the allies of the Toyotomis). He establishes hegemony over Japan.

江戸時代　1603~1868 Edo Period
初期[1603~1716]
◉徳川家康[1542-1616]　初代征夷大将軍・在職期間(1603-1605)

1603
- 徳川家康,征夷大将軍に就任.江戸に徳川幕府を開く.
  Tokugawa Ieyasu receives the title of (Seii-Tai-) Shogun and founds the

Tokugawa shogunate in Edo.

1605　• 日韓和約. ☆朝鮮との国交回復.

The Japan-Korea Peace Agreement

◉徳川秀忠[1579-1632]　第2代征夷大将軍・在職期間(1605-1623)

1609　• 平戸にオランダ商館. オランダ貿易の開始. 朱印船貿易. ⇨ 朱印船/朱印船貿易

The Dutch Factory is established in Hirado. Dutch trade starts. Trade is done by vermilion-sealed ships with a shogunal charter.

　　　• 姫路城(ユネスコ世界文化遺産)の築城. ☆赤松貞範が1346年に築城, 池田輝政が1601年に竣工, 1609年完成・大改修する.

Himeji Castle is constructed by Akamatsu Sadanori and rebuilt by Ikeda Terumasa.

1612~13　• 幕府によるキリスト教の禁教令. 1612年幕府直轄に, 1613年全国に. ☆宗門改(inquisition for suppressing Christianity)の執行

Tokugawa shogunate issues the order banning[edict prohibiting] Christianity.

1614　• 大阪冬の陣. ☆大阪城への攻撃.

The Winter Siege of Osaka Castle.

1615　• 大阪夏の陣. ☆豊臣家の滅亡.

The Summer Siege of Osaka Castle. The Toyotomi clan is destroyed by the Tokugawa shogunate.

　　　• 武家諸法度の発布.(大名・武家を統制する法律). ⇨ 武家諸法度

Enactment of the Buke-Shohatto [Laws for the Military Houses]

◉徳川家光[1604-1651]　第3代征夷大将軍・在職期間(1623-1651)

1633　• 鎖国令を発令(第1次). 海外渡航の禁止. ☆奉書船(将軍が発給した朱印状に加え, 老中の書いた奉書という許可証をもつ船)は除く. ⇨ 朱印状

The National Seclusion Policy. The first edict issues to close Japan to the outside world and ban Japanese from going abroad, with exception of ships carrying messages from the shogun (*Hoshosen*).

1635　• 武家諸法度の改定. 参勤交代の制度化. ⇨ 武家諸法度 / 参勤交代

The Revision of the Buke-Shohatto; formalized system of the Sankin-kotai [mandatory alternating attendance at shogunate's court in Edo].

　　　• 鎖国令(第3次). ☆中国(清)・オランダなど外国船の入港は長崎に限定する.

The Third National Seclusion Policy.

1637~38　• 島原の乱[島原・天草一揆]. ☆16歳の天草四郎をはじめ3万7千人のキリシタンを中心とした農民一揆. ⇨ 島原の乱

The Shimabara Rebellion [an uprising by overtaxed peasants] occurs.

1639　• 鎖国体制の完成. ☆オランダ人を除く全ヨーロッパ人来航を禁止.

The Completion of the National Seclusion Policy. All Westerners except the Dutch are prohibited from entering Japan.

1641　• オランダ東インド会社(Dutch East India Company)の商館を平戸から出島(人工島)に移す.

A Dutch trading firm is moved to Dejima (an artificial island) from Hirado in

歴史

Nagasaki.

◉徳川家綱[1641-1680]　第4代将軍・在職期間(1651-1680)

1657　●明暦の大火，江戸を焼く．☆死者10万以上．江戸城の大部分と350余の寺社を焼失．

　　　The Great Fire of Meireki breaks out in Edo. Death of more than 100,000 victims.

◉徳川綱吉[1646-1709]　第5代将軍・在職期間(1680-1709)

1685　●徳川綱吉(犬公方)，生類憐みの令を発布．☆1709年に廃止．⇨ 生類憐みの令

　　　The Animal Protection Law [the edict on Compassion for Living Creatures] is enacted by Tokugawa Tsunayoshi(Dog Shogun).

1688　●『元禄時代』(1688-1704)の開花：歌舞伎と文楽の黄金時代の到来．

　　　The beginning of the Genroku era. The golden age of Kabuki and Bunraku.

1702　●赤穂事件．☆赤穂藩浪士(四十七士)と大石良雄らが仇敵吉良義央を討つ．(元禄15年12月14日)

　　　The Ako Incident. The Forty-Seven Ronin [masterless *samurai*] Incident. Under the leadership of Oishi Yoshio, the 47 loyal retainers of the Ako domain carry out a vendetta against Kira Yoshihisa.

1707　●富士山の大噴火．

　　　Eruption of Mt. Fuji.

◉徳川家宣[1662-1712]　第6代将軍・在職期間(1709-1712)

◉徳川家継[1709-1716]　第7代将軍・在職期間(1713-1716)

中期[1716-1837]

◉徳川吉宗[1684-1751]　第8代将軍・在職期間(1716-1745)

1716　●徳川吉宗将軍となる．享保の改革[1716-1745](政治は側近ではなく将軍自ら行う政治改革)．財政安定策が開始．☆「江戸三大改革」(寛政の改革[1787]/天保の改革[1841])のひとつ．

　　　Tokugawa Yoshimune becomes shogun. The Kyoho Reforms (aimed at making the shogunate financially solvent) start.

1717　●大岡忠相を南町奉行に登用．☆「大岡越前」(大岡忠相)は吉宗時代の江戸町奉行(Edo City Magistrate, 1717年就任)で，享保の改革の中で小石川養生所(Koishikawa Clinic[Hospital] for the poor people)や町火消(local fire brigade)などを創設した．

　　　Ooka Tadasuke becomes a South Magistrate of Edo (with chief role of police, judge and jury).

1721　●目安箱(施政の参考意見や社会事情の収集のために設けた投書箱)の設置．

　　　The establishment of Suggestion[Complaint] Box.

1732　●享保の大飢饉　☆死者1万2000から97万人．西日本における悪天候と凶作．

　　　Kyoho Famine. Death of 12,000 to 970,000 victims.

◉徳川家重[1711-1761]　第9代将軍・在職期間(1745-1760)

1774　●杉田玄白，前野良沢らの「解体新書」刊行．

　　　The Kaitai Shinsho [A new Book in Dissection]. A translation of the Dutch book,

"New Text on Anatomy" is published by Sugita Genpaku and Maeno Ryotaku.

◉徳川家治[1737-1786]　第10代将軍・在職期間(1760-1786)

1782　•天明の大飢饉[1782～1788]：死者20万人から90万以上．東日本における悪天候と凶作．☆「江戸三大飢饉」(享保の大飢饉[1732] / 天保の大飢饉[1833])のひとつ.
Tenmei Famine. Nationwide death toll ranges from 200,000 to 900,000 victims.

◉徳川家斉　第11代征夷大将軍[1773-1841]・在職期間(1787-1837)

1787　•寛政の改革(1787～1793)．☆(吉宗の孫の)松平定信が老中(senior councilor)になり，幕府の政治を動かす.
Kansei Reforms start. Matsudaira Sadanobu becomes a member of the Shogun's Council of Elders and administers the shogunate government. ☆「鬼平」(長谷川平蔵：江戸時代の旗本．本名長谷川宜以)は火付盗賊改方(inspector of arson and burglary)の長であるが，寛政の改革の一環としてホームレス(無宿人・浮浪人)対策に人足寄場(the shelter for petty criminals to rehabilitate)の建設を立案・設立した.

1800　•伊能忠敬，日本地図作成のため全国測量開始.(1821年完成)
Ino Tadataka starts his cartographic survey of all Japan.

1809　•間宮林蔵がタタール海峡を発見．☆樺太が島であることを確認.
Mamiya Rinzo discovers the Tatar Strait [Mamiya Strait]. He proves that Sakhalin is an island.

1823　•シーボルト(ドイツ人医師)日本(長崎)に到着．☆ヨーロッパの医学・科学を教える.
Philip Franz von Siebold arrives in Japan. He teaches Western medicine and science.

1825　•異国船打払令の発布．☆特にフェートン号事件(1808年長崎港への英国軍艦侵入事件)発生のため.
Shogunate issues an order for the repelling of all foreign vessels[ships].

1833　•天保の大飢饉[1833～1836]．☆死者20万から40万人．全国，特に東北地方における冷害と洪水による被害.
Tempo Famine. Death of 200,000 to 400,000 victims.

1837　•大塩平八郎の乱．☆貧民の救済に無策な幕府に反乱を起こす.
The Rebellion of Oshio Heihachiro.

後期(幕末)[1837～1867]

◉徳川家慶[1793-1853]　第12代将軍・在職期間(1837-1853)

1841　•天保の改革(老中水野忠邦らによる幕府財政や藩政などの刷新)．☆「遠山の金さん」(遠山金四郎)は水野忠邦の下で町奉行(town magistrate)を務めた.
Tempo Reforms start.

◉徳川家定[1824-1858]　第13代将軍・在職期間(1853-1858)

1853　•ペリー総督(東インド艦隊司令長官)率いる軍艦4隻が浦賀に来航．☆「黒船」の到来.
Commodore Matthew Perry (the Commander-in-Chief of the East Indian fleet)

歴史

arrives at Uraga with four warships.

1854　•ペリー提督率いる7隻の艦隊．江戸湾に停泊．日本の開国を強いる．☆下田と箱館(函館)の2港を開く．

Commodore Matthew Perry anchors in Edo Bay with a fleet of seven naval vessels. He compels the opening of Japan to the West.

•神奈川で日米和親条約の締結．☆鎖国の終焉．

The Japan-U.S. Amity Treaty [The Treaty of Peace and Amity between the United States of America and the Empire of Japan] is signed in Kanagawa. Japan's Isolation Policy ends.

1855　•日露和親条約の締結．☆下田，長崎，箱館(函館)を開港する．

The Japan-Russia Amity Treaty is signed.

1856　•アメリカ総領事ハリスが下田に到着．

U.S. Consul General Townsend Harris arrives at Shimoda.

1858　•井伊直弼(大老)が日米修好通商条約を締結．☆「5港開港」神奈川・長崎・箱館(函館)・新潟・兵庫を開港．続いて「安政五カ国条約」でアメリカ・イギリス・ロシア・オランダ・フランスの各国と修好通商条約を結ぶ．

Ii Naosuke (the chief minister of the shogunate) signs the Japan-U.S. Treaty of Amity and Commerce [the Harris Treaty, a trade agreement with U.S.]. The Ansei Commercial Treaties with Five Countries are signed.

◉徳川家茂[1846-1866]　第14代将軍・在職期間(1858-1866)

1858~1859　•安政の大獄．☆井伊直弼が尊王攘夷運動者(吉田松陰，橋本左内等)を弾圧する．⇨尊王攘夷

The Ansei Purge [the Great Political Crackdown of Ansei]. Imperial loyalists are prosecuted by order of Ii Naosuke.

1860　•桜田門外の変．☆(水戸藩士らによる)井伊直弼の暗殺．

The Incident outside Sakurada Gate. The assassination of Ii Naosuke by the *samurais* from the Mito domain.

1862　•生麦事件．☆薩摩藩士が生麦村(現・横浜市鶴見区生麦)にて島津久光の行列の前を横切ったイギリス商人リチャードソンを殺害する．

The Namamugi Incident [Richardson Affairs]. A *samurai* from the Satsuma clan [racial antiforeign domain] kills[assaults] Englishmen at Namamugi (Village), Yokohama.

•公武合体．☆徳川家茂が孝明天皇の妹和宮と結婚する．⇨公武合体

The Union of the Imperial Court and the Shogunate. Princess Kazunomiya Chikako becomes the wife of Tokugawa Iemochi, the 14th Shogun.

1864　•池田屋事件(京都)．☆新撰組は長州藩の尊王攘夷派を襲撃する．⇨新撰組

The Ikedaya Incident. The Shinsengumi (special police force of the Tokugawa shogunate) attacks imperial loyalists from the Choshu clan.

•蛤御門の変[禁門の変]．☆長州藩士が京都御所を襲う．

Hamaguri Rebellion. The rebellion at the Hamaguri Gate of the Imperial Palace in Kyoto.

●徳川慶喜[1837-1913]　第15代将軍・在職期間(1866-1867)
1866　●徳川幕府に対抗し，薩長同盟の成立．☆坂本龍馬が長州藩の木戸孝允と薩摩藩の
　　　西郷隆盛を結びつける．両藩の倒幕 [overthrow the Tokugawa shogunate] 運動が
　　　加速する．
　　　The Satcho [Satsuma-Choshu] Alliance is formed against the Tokugawa
　　　shogunate.
　　　●寺田屋事件．☆坂本龍馬の襲撃．
　　　The Teradaya Incident. The assassination of Sakamoto Ryoma.
1867　●幕府の滅亡．最後の将軍徳川慶喜による大政奉還．☆西郷隆盛，大久保利通，木
　　　戸孝允，岩倉具視らが「王政復古の大号令」(the Decree for the Restoration of
　　　Imperial Rule)を発布する．⇨ 大政奉還
　　　The fall of the Tokugawa shogunate. The Restoration of Imperial Rule is declared.
　　　Formal return of political authority[power] to the Emperor is made by Tokugawa
　　　Yoshinobu, the last Shogun of the Tokugawas.
1868　●戊辰戦争．☆鳥羽伏見の戦い[王政復古後の明治新政府と佐幕派の戦い]．江戸城
　　　の無血開城．
　　　Boshin Civil War begins. The Imperial army defeats the Tokugawas at the Battle
　　　of Toba-Fushimi. Edo Castle falls without bloodshed.

近代 (Modern period)
明治時代　1868～1912　Meiji Era
1868　●明治維新.「明治」と元号改め．
　　　The Meiji Restoration. The new era name, Meiji, is adopted.
　　　●江戸を東京と改称．☆江戸城は「東京城」と改名．
　　　Edo is renamed Tokyo.
　　　●新政府が五箇条の誓文を公布．⇨ 五箇条の誓文
　　　The Five Charter Oaths [Charter Oath of Five Articles] is pledged by the new
　　　Meiji regime.
1869　●東京遷都．☆京都から東京に移る．江戸城は皇居となる．
　　　The capital is moved from Kyoto to Tokyo. Edo Castle becomes the Imperial
　　　Palace.
　　　●版籍奉還．☆諸大名から藩の領有権と人民を明治天皇に返還させる．蝦夷は北海
　　　道に改称される．⇨ 版籍奉還
　　　　The formal return of the *han*[domains] to Emperor Meiji. The feudal lords of
　　　the *han* return their registers of land and people to Emperor Meiji.
　　　●戊辰戦争の終結．☆五稜郭の戦い[箱館戦争]．日本全国を統一する．
　　　The Boshin Civil War ends. The Battle of Hakodate. The whole country is unified
　　　by the new government.
　　　●靖国神社の建立(旧称は「東京招魂社」，1879年に靖国神社と改称)．☆明治維新前
　　　後，戊辰戦争での新政府の戦死者を讃えるために建立．その後日本国のために尽
　　　力した戦没者の英霊を祀る．

歴史

Yasukuni Shrine is founded.   The spirits of the war dead are enshrined.

1871 • 廃藩置県. ⇨ 廃藩置県

Prefectures replace the *han* [feudal domains]. The *han* are abolished[dissolved] and prefectures are established.

• 郵便制度の開始.

The Postal Service is established.

• 岩倉遣外使節団. ☆欧米諸国に派遣された使節団. 約100名(岩倉具視, 伊藤博文, 大久保利通, 木戸孝允等). 1873年帰国.

The Iwakura Mission [Iwakura Embassy]. A Japanese diplomatic delegation goes abroad to study the social systems of the United States and European nations.

1872 • 学制の公布. ☆近代的な学校制度(小・中・大学区)の発足.

The Education Order is issued to establish Japan's first modern school system.

• 四民平等の身分改正. ⇨ 四民平等

Equality of all people.

• 新橋〜横浜間に鉄道開始.

The railroad begins operation between Shimbashi and Yokohama.

1873 • 徴兵令の公布. ☆国民の兵役義務を定める. 1927年兵役法に移行する.

The Conscription Ordinance [Inauguration of universal military service] is enacted.

• 地租改正条例の布告. ☆田畑[農地]の収益を課税物件とする. ⇨地租改正

Land Tax Reform Law is issued.

• キリスト教の解禁. ⇨ 潜伏キリシタン

Ban on Christianity ends.

1874 • 台湾出兵. ☆台湾への軍事出兵.

Taiwan Expedition.

1875 • 樺太・千島交換条約. 別称「サンクトペテルブルク条約」(署名の場所). ☆樺太はロシア, 千島は日本領となる.

The Sakhalin-Kuril Island Exchange Treaty [Treaty of St. Petersburg] gives Sakhalin to Russia and Kuril Islands to Japan.

1877 • 西南戦争. ☆西郷隆盛らの士族による反乱. 西郷隆盛が自害する(commits suicide). The Satsuma Rebellion.

1881 • 国会開設の勅諭.

An Imperial prescript[edict] promises the establishment of a national assembly.

1883 • 鹿鳴館の完成. ☆西洋風社交場になる.

The completion of the Rokumeikan (the site for Western-style social events).

1885 • 内閣制度の発足. ☆初代首相・伊藤博文

Cabinet System is set up. Ito Hirobumi becomes the first prime minister.

1889 • 大日本帝国憲法の発布. ☆宗教の自由(freedom of religion)を公認される.

The promulgation of the Imperial Constitution of Japan [the Constitution of the Empire of Japan].

1890　• 教育勅語を学校に配布. ☆天皇に対する忠君愛国心(loyalty and patriotism)と儒教の道徳(morality of Confucianism)の精神.
The Imperial Prescript on Education is distributed to all schools.
　　　• 第一回帝国議会の開会.
The first session of the Imperial Diet is convened.

1894　• 日清戦争の勃発. (1894-1895). ☆朝鮮半島をめぐる大日本帝国(the Empire of Japan)と大清帝国(Qing Dynasty China)の戦争.
Outbreak of the Sino-Japanese War.

1895　• 下関条約の締結. 別称「日清講和条約」. ☆日清戦争の終結.
The Shimonoseki Treaty is signed. The Sino-Japanese War ends.
　　　• 台湾総督府の設置. ☆台湾支配が始まる.
The Governor-General of Formosa is established.

1902　• 日英同盟の締結. ☆日本とイギリスとの間の軍事同盟.
The Anglo-Japanese Alliance is signed.

1904　• 日露戦争の勃発. (1904-1905)☆大日本帝国とロシア帝国との間での, 朝鮮半島と満州南部を主戦場とする戦争.
Outbreak of the Russo-Japanese War.

1905　• ポーツマス条約の調印. ☆日露戦争の終結.
The Portsmouth Treaty is signed. The Russo-Japanese War ends.

1910　• 日韓併合(条約). ☆大韓帝国は大日本帝国の植民地となる. 朝鮮総督府を置く.
Japanese Annexation (Treaty) of Korea [Japan-Korea Annexation (Treaty)]. Korea becomes a colony of Japan. Government-General of Korea is established.

1912　• 明治天皇の崩御.
Death of Emperor Meiji.

大正時代　1912~1926　Taisho era

1912　• 大正天皇の即位.
The accession of Emperor Taisho.

1914　• 第1次世界大戦に参戦. ☆日本はドイツに宣戦布告.
Entry into World War Ⅰ. Japan declares war on Germany.

1918　• シベリア出兵(1918-1922). ☆連合軍(日・米・英・仏・伊)等がチェコ軍救出の大義名分を掲げてシベリアに出兵する.
Army sent to Siberia.

1919　• ヴェルサイユ条約に調印. ☆第1次世界大戦が終結する.
The Versailles Treaty is signed.

1920　• 国際連盟に加入. ☆日本常任理事国になる.
Japan joins the League of Nations. Japan is granted permanent membership in the Security Council.

1923　• 関東大震災. ☆死者約10万人以上. その余波で憲兵(military police)による社会主義者虐殺(甘粕事件)(the slaughter of the socialists)や朝鮮人大量虐殺(Korean genocide)などが起こり社会不安(social unrest)が拡大する.

歴史

The Great Kanto Earthquake occurs. Death of more than 100,000 victims.

1925 　• 治安維持法の公布.　☆国体[天皇制]や私有財産制を否定する政治活動，また思想・学問を取り締まる.

The Peace Preservation Law [the Maintenance of Public Order Law] is promulgated.

　• 普通選挙法の公布.　☆成人男子のみによる普通選挙を規定する法律.

The Universal Male[Manhood] Suffrage Act is promulgated.

1926 　• 大正天皇の崩御

Death of Emperor Taisho

昭和時代　1926-1989　Showa era
戦 前[1926-1945]

1926 　• 昭和天皇の即位.

Accession of Emperor Showa.

1931 　• 満州事変の勃発(1931~33).　☆柳条湖事件(the Liutiao Lake Incident). 奉天(ほうてん)(Mikden)(現在の瀋陽[Shenyang])郊外の柳条湖で，関東軍(南満州駐留の大日本帝国陸軍; an army group of the Imperial Japanese Army in Southern Manchuria)が南満州鉄道の線路を爆破した事件に端を発す.

Outbreak of the Manchurian Incident.

1932 　• 関東軍が(傀儡)(かいらい)満州国を建国.

The Kwantung[Guandong] Army establishes the (puppet) State of Manchukoku [英Manchukuo].

　• 5・15事件.　☆大日本帝国海軍の青年将校による護憲運動者・犬養毅首相の暗殺.

The May 15th Incident. Prime Minister Inukai Tsuyoshi is assassinated by Imperial Japanese Navy[naval officers].

1933 　• 国際連盟の脱退.　☆日本代表の松岡洋右(ようすけ)が退場(満州国独立は不当とされたので).

Japan withdraws from the League of Nations.

1936 　• 2・26事件.　☆大日本陸軍皇道派(Imperial Way Faction)の青年将校らが1,483名の部隊(1483 troops)を率いたクーデター未遂事件.

The February 26th Incident. An attempted coup d'état fails.

1937 　• 日中戦争[支那事変]勃発(1937-1945).　☆盧溝橋事件(the Marco Polo Bridge Incident:北京の盧溝橋で起きた日本軍と中国国民革命軍との衝突事件)に端を発す.

Outbreak of the Sino-Japanese War.

　• 南京事件(1937-1938)☆南京戦犯裁判では30万人説，東京裁判では20万人説(2010年日中共同研究より).

The Nanjing[Nanking] Massacre.

1940 　• 日独伊三国軍事同盟の締結[調印].

The Tripartite Pact is signed by Japan, Germany and Italy. Japan allies with Germany and Italy.

1941 　• 日ソ中立条約の調印.　☆日ソ間で締結された軍事行動(相互不可侵)に関する中立

条約.

The Japan-Soviet Neutrality Pact is signed.

• 日本軍が真珠湾奇襲，マレー半島，フィリピンへの攻撃.

Japanese attacks on Pearl Harbor (in Hawaii), the Malay Peninsula and the Philippines.

• 太平洋戦争の勃発(1941-1945). 別称「大東亜戦争」. ☆宣戦布告.

Outbreak of the Pacific War. Greater East Asia War breaks out.

1942 • ミッドウェー海戦. ☆日本海軍は主力空母4隻とその戦闘機を一挙に失い大打撃を受ける.

The Naval Battle of (the) Midway (Islands).

1943 • 学徒出陣. ☆20歳以上の男子入隊・出征する. ⇨学徒出陣(84頁)

The mobilization of students to the war.

1945 • 東京大空襲. ☆1944年にも空襲(air raids)を受けるが，特に3月10日B29爆撃機からの焼夷弾(incendiary bomb)による大規模な戦略爆撃.

Bombing of Tokyo in World War II (attacked by the B-29 bomber on March 10).

• 広島(8月6日)・長崎(8月9日)への原爆投下.

Atomic bombs are dropped on Hiroshima and Nagasaki.

• 日本はポツダム宣言を受諾. ☆ポツダム会談での合意に基づいて，米国・英国・中華民国の首脳が大日本帝国への無条件降伏を勧告する13条の宣言.

Japan unconditionally accepts the Potsdam Declaration. Unconditional surrender.

• 玉音放送(8月15日) ☆終戦の詔書. 無条件降伏. ⇨玉音放送(126頁)

The Showa Emperor's speech on radio broadcast. The Emperor announces the termination of the Second World War on August 15. Japan surrenders unconditionally.

• 連合国軍は本土進駐(1945-1952). ☆最高司令官(Supreme commander-in-chief)マッカーサー元帥(General MacArthur)が連合国軍最高司令官総本部(General Head-quarters[GHQ] of the Allied Forces)を設置する.

Occupation of Japan by the Allied Powers.

• 五大改革指令(Five Major Reform Directives). ☆①婦人参政権の承認(approval of women's suffrage)　②労働組合の結成(formation of labor unions)　③教育の民主化(democratic expansion of education)　④農地改革(agrarian [agricultural land] reform)⑤財閥の解体(breakup of the industrial and financial cliques[combines])

• 韓国併合(条約)の終焉

The Japan-Korea Annexation (Treaty) ends.

現代　Contemporary period

戦後 [1946~1988]

1946 • 昭和天皇，人間宣言. ☆1月1日の官報(official gazette)にて発布された.　　⇨現人神

Humanity Declaration; Emperor Showa declares the Emperor as a human being. Emperor Showa renounces his own divinity [denies his own living god].

- 農地改革の施行[開始]. ☆戦後の農地の所有者の変更や法制度など農地を巡る改革運動.

  The Agricultural Land Reforms are implemented[started].

- 日本国憲法の公布. ☆日本国の現在の憲法典. 1947年に施行され, 現在まで改正されていない.

  The Japanese Constitution [The Constitution of Japan] is promulgated.

1947 • 労働基準法の公布

  The Labor Standards Law is promulgated.

- 教育基本法の公布. ☆6・3制義務教育の開始. 男女共学(coeducation)

  The Enactment of the Fundamental Law of Education. The Compulsory Education System consisting of six years of elementary school and three years of junior high school starts.

1949 • 湯川秀樹ノーベル物理学賞を受賞(日本人初).

  Yugawa Hideki is awarded the Nobel Prize for physics. (the first Japanese to receive a Nobel Prize)

1951 • サンフランシスコ平和条約の調印. ☆日本の独立を承認.

  The San Francisco Peace Treaty [the Treaty of Peace with Japan] is signed.

- 日米安全保障条約の締結. 通称「日米安保」. ☆安全保障のため, 日本にアメリカ軍[在日米軍]が駐留することを定める2国間の条約.

  The Japan-US Security Treaty [The Treaty of Mutual Cooperation and Security between the United States of America and Japan] is signed.

1952 • 保安隊の発足

  The National Security Force is formed.

- サンフランシスコ平和条約の発効. ☆日本の国家主権の回復. 米軍の駐在と沖縄の占拠など.

  The San Francisco Peace Treaty takes effect and Japan regains its sovereignty, but the U.S. military is not withdrawn and Okinawa remains occupied.

- 日華平和条約の締結. ☆台湾の中華民国と平和条約を結ぶ.

  The Japan-Taiwan Peace Treaty is concluded.

1953 • NHKテレビ放送の開始.

  NHK television broadcasting starts.

1954 • 自衛隊の発足(保安隊の代用). ☆2007年には防衛省(Ministry of Defense)が成立する.

  The Self-Defense Force is established (in place of the National Security Force).

1955 • 自由民主党[自民党]の結党. ☆鳩山一郎が結成する. 日本社会党(Japan Socialist Party)との2大政党体制を築く.

  The Liberal Democratic Party[LDP] is formed.

1956 • 日ソ共同宣言. ☆ソ連(現ロシア)と国交回復.「北方領土」は返還されず.「北方4島一括返還」(return of all the four northern islands as a package: 〈国後島〉〈色丹島〉〈択捉島〉〈歯舞群島〉)の主張.

  The Japan-Soviet Joint Declaration. Japan reestablishes diplomatic relation with

歴史

Soviet Union. The Soviet Union (currently Russia) refuses to return the Northern Territories to Japan.

- 日本，国際連合に加盟.
  Japan joins the United Nations.

1958　• 東京タワー完成.
　　　　Tokyo Tower is completed.

1959　• 皇太子継宮明仁親王(現天皇)，正田美智子と結婚.
　　　　Marriage of Crown Prince Akihito (current Emperor) and Shoda Michiko.

1960　• 新日米安全保障条約の改定.「日米相互協力及び安全保障条約」(「集団的自衛権」の条項を含む)の成立. ☆米国は日本の防衛義務を負う. 反対する学生による「安保闘争」(the conflict over the Japan-US Security Treaty)が激化する. 岸信介の内閣時代.
　　　　The Revision of the Japan-US Security Treaty. The Japan-US Mutual Cooperation and Security Treaty (including the provision of the right to collective self-defense)

1960年代　• 所得倍増計画の成功. 高度経済成長の実現. ☆池田勇人の内閣時代.
　　　　The Income Doubling Plan and High Economic Growth. The Japanese economy grows rapidly.

1964　• 東京・新大阪間で東海道新幹線の営業開始.
　　　　The Tokaido Shinkansen (Bullet Train) Service starts operation between Tokyo and Shin-Osaka.

- 第18回夏季東京オリンピック大会の開催.
  The Tokyo Summer Olympic Games.

1965　• 日韓基本条約の締結［調印］. ☆日韓国交が回復する. 佐藤栄作内閣と朴正熙内閣.
　　　　The Japan-South-Korea Normalization Treaty. The Treaty on Basic Relations between Japan and the Republic of Korea is signed. Diplomatic relations between Japan and Korea are restored[normalized].

1968　• 小笠原諸島，日本へ返還. ☆英語で the Bonin Islands (無人島)ともいう.
　　　　The Ogasawara Islands are returned.

1970　• 大阪万博［日本万国博覧会］の開催. ☆日本最初の国際博覧会. 名誉総裁は皇太子明仁親王(今上天皇).
　　　　Expo'70 opens in Osaka [the Japan World Exposition, Osaka]

1972　• 沖縄返還協定の調印(1971年)後，復帰する. ☆嘉手納空軍基地(Kadena Air Force Base)などの一部は米軍施設.
　　　　Okinawa is returned to Japan. The Japan-U.S. Agreement on the revision of the Ryukyu Islands and the Daito Islands to Japan.

- 日中共同声明. ☆日中国交が正常化. 田中角栄首相と周恩来首相との間で調印.
  Japan-China Joint Communique is issued. Normalization of diplomatic relations between Japan and the People's Republic of China.

- 札幌冬季オリンピック. ☆日本・アジア最初の冬季オリンピック.
  The Sapporo Winter Games.

歴史

1973 　• 第一次石油ショック[危機]：ガソリン価格の高騰.　☆高度経済成長の終結.
　　　　First Oil Crisis: oil prices spiral.

1975 　• 沖縄海洋博[沖縄国際海洋博覧会]の開催.　☆沖縄県の本土復帰記念事業の一環.
　　　　The Ocean Expo'75 opens in Okinawa. [The 1975 Ocean World Exposition, Okinawa]

　　　• 天皇・皇后初の訪米.
　　　　The Japanese Emperor and Empress make their first visit to the U.S.A.

1976 　• ロッキード事件.　☆「総理の犯罪」の異名で知られる世界的な大規模汚職事件.
　　　　The Lockheed bribery[payoff] scandal.

1978 　• 日米防衛協力指針の協定.　☆「思いやり予算」(budget as host-nation financial support for U.S. forces)が生じる.
　　　　The Guidelines for Japan-U.S. Defense Cooperation.

　　　• 新東京国際空港(成田空港)の開港
　　　　New Tokyo International Airport (Narita Airport) opens.

　　　• 日中平和友好条約の調印.　☆福田赳夫の内閣時代.
　　　　The Japan-China Peace and Friendship Treaty is signed.

　　　• 極東軍事裁判.　☆A級戦犯14人の靖国合祀.　⇨合祀(151頁) /A級戦犯(49頁)
　　　　The International Military Tribunal for the Far East. The war dead of Class-A criminals are collectively enshrined at Yasukuni Shrine.

1980代 • 北朝鮮による日本人拉致疑惑が話題.
　　　　The alleged abduction of Japanese civilians

1982 　• 東北・上越新幹線の開業
　　　　Tohoku and Joetsu Shinkansen Service begins.

1985 　• 国際科学技術博覧会の開催.　☆通称「つくば博」「科学万博」. 筑波研究学園都市のお披露目としての開催.
　　　　The Tsukuba Expo'85 opens. [The International Exposition, Tsukuba, Japan, 1985]

　　　• 男女雇用機会均等法の施行.
　　　　Enactment[Implementation] of the Equal Employment Opportunity Law For Men and Women.

　　　• 日本航空123便墜落事故.　☆群馬県多野郡上野村の御巣鷹の尾根(Osutaka Ridge)に墜落. 乗客524名中520名死亡, 4名生存. 単独機の航空事故としては死者数世界最多. 通称「日航ジャンボ機墜落事故」.
　　　　The plane crash of Japan Airlines Flight 123.

1987 　• 国鉄の民営化.
　　　　Privatization of Japan National Railways.

1988 　• 青函トンネル(2016年まで世界最長[53.85km]の鉄道トンネル)・瀬戸大橋の開通.
　　　　Completion of the Seikan (Railway) Tunnel and the Great Seto Bridge.

　　　• リクルート事件.　☆政治家や官僚が次々と逮捕された未公開株の賄賂の汚職事件.
　　　　Recruit scandal.

1989 　• 昭和天皇の崩御.

歴史

Death of Emperor Showa.

平成時代　1989-2019　Heisei era

1989　• 平成の改元. 皇太子明仁親王の継承.
　　　　Proclamation of new era "Heisei".—Accession of Emperor Akihito.
　　　• 昭和天皇の大喪の礼.
　　　　The funeral of Emperor Showa.
1990　• 明仁天皇即位の礼.
　　　　The Formal Enthronement of Emperor Akihito.
　　　• 国際花と緑の博覧会.　☆通称「花の万博」
　　　　The International Garden and Greenery Exposition, Osaka, Japan, 1990.
1993　•『法隆寺地域の仏教建造物』　☆ユネスコ世界文化遺産に登録.
　　　　Buddhist Monuments in the Horyu-ji Area.
　　　•『姫路城』　☆ユネスコ世界文化遺産に登録.
　　　　Himeji-jo.
　　　•『白神山地』　☆ユネスコ世界自然遺産に登録.
　　　　Sirakami-Sanchi.
　　　•『屋久島』　☆ユネスコ世界自然遺産に登録.
　　　　Yakushima.
　　　• 皇太子徳仁親王と小和田雅子の結婚.
　　　　Marriage of Crown Prince Naruhito and Owada Masako.
1994　•『古都京都の文化財』　☆ユネスコ世界文化遺産に登録.
　　　　Historic Monuments of Ancient Kyoto.
　　　• 関西国際空港の開港
　　　　Kansai International Airport opens.
1995　•『白川郷・五箇山の合掌造り集落』　☆ユネスコ世界文化遺産に登録.
　　　　Historic Villages of Shirakawa-go and Gokayama.
　　　• 阪神・淡路大震災.　☆死者約6,400人以上. 負傷者は約44,000以上.
　　　　The Great Hanshin-Awaji Earthquake.
　　　• 東京地下鉄サリン事件.　☆カルト新興宗教団体のオウム真理教(Aum Shinrikyo, a Japanese new religious cult)が起こした化学兵器(chemical warfare[CW])を使用した世界初の無差別テロ事件. 死者12名, 重軽症者約5,500人以上.
　　　　The Tokyo Subway Sarin[poison] Gas Incident/ The Sarin Gas Attack on the Tokyo subway system.
1996　•『原爆ドーム』　☆ユネスコ世界文化遺産に登録.
　　　　Hiroshima Peace Memorial (Genbaku Dome).
　　　•『厳島神社』　☆ユネスコ世界文化遺産に登録.
　　　　Itsukushima Shinto Shrine.
1997　• 京都議定書の採択.　☆2008年~2012年までの地球温暖化(global warming)の原因となる温室効果ガス(Greenhouse Gas[GHG])削減の協定. 日本はマイナス6％. 正式名称「気候変動に関する国際連合枠組条約の京都議定書」(Kyoto Protocol to

歴史

the United Nations Framework convention on Climate Change).

The Kyoto Protocol is adopted. The International Agreement of Greenhouse Gas Reduction is signed.

1998　•『古都奈良の文化財』　☆ユネスコ世界文化遺産に登録.

Historic Monuments of Ancient Nara.

　　　•(第18回) 長野冬季オリンピック.　☆20世紀最後の冬季オリンピック.

The Nagano Winter Olympic Games.

1999　•『日光の社寺』　☆ユネスコ世界文化遺産に登録.

Shrines and Temple of Nikko.

2000　•『琉球王国のグスク(城跡)及び関連遺産群』　☆ユネスコ世界文化遺産に登録.

Gusuku Sites and Related Properties of the Kingdom of Ryukyu.

　　　•三宅島の雄山噴火.　☆全島民避難.

Mt. Oyama on the Miyakejima Island erupts. All residents evacuate the island.

　　　•九州・沖縄サミット.　正式名称「第26回主要国首脳会議」.　☆日本初の地方開催サミット.　開催記念に「二千円紙幣」(紙面は「守礼門」)が発行される.　⇨ 守礼門(212頁)

The 26th G8 Summit (in Okinawa).

2001　•テロ対策特別措置法の成立.　☆「改正PKO協力法」(the Revised PKO Cooperation Law)の可決.　自衛隊員が国連平和維持軍(Peace-Keeping Forces[PKF])に参加可能.　9月11日「アメリカ同時多発テロ事件」(the September 11 attacks (by Al-Qaeda terrorists))発生.

Anti-Terrorism Special Measures Law is implemented.

2002　•サッカー・ワールド・カップ日韓共催(第17回).

The 2002 FIFA World Cup tournament co-hosted by Japan and the Republic of Korea.

　　　•平壌宣言.　小泉首相の平壌訪問.「日朝首脳会談」.　☆3週間後に拉致被害者5名が帰国.

Pyongyang Declaration. Prime Minister Koizumi visits North Korea. Five Japanese kidnapped and detained [Five abductees] in North Korea return [come back] to Japan.

　　　•住民基本台帳ネットワークシステムの導入.

The Basic Residential Register Network System is implemented.

2003　•自衛隊イラク派遣.　☆イラクの国家再建の支援するための派遣.

The Japanese Iraq Reconstruction and Support Group (by the Japan Self-Defense Forces).

2004　•『紀伊山地の霊場と参詣道』　☆ユネスコ世界文化遺産に登録.

Sacred Sites and Pilgrimage Routes in the Kii Mountain Range.

　　　•新潟県中越地震.　☆M6.8直下型の地震.　死者40名，負傷者約4,500名.

The 2004 Chuetsu Earthquake / Niigata Prefecture Chuetsu Earthquake/ The Mid Niigata Prefecture Earthquake in 2004.

2005　•『知床』　☆ユネスコ世界自然遺産に登録.

歴史

Shiretoko (Peninsula).

- 愛知万博．愛称「愛・地球博」．☆「2005年日本国際博覧会」．21世紀最初の国際博覧会．
  Expo 2005 in Aichi / Love the Earth Expo./ The 2005 World Exposition, Aichi, Japan.

2007
- 第1回東京マラソン．☆30,000人を超える参加者と1万人のボランティア市民．東京都と日本陸上競技連盟の共催．
  The First International Tokyo Marathon with over 30,000 runners and 10,000 volunteers. It is co-sponsored by the Tokyo Metropolitan Government and the Japan Association of Athletics Federations.
- 『石見銀山遺跡とその文化背景』　☆ユネスコ世界文化遺産に登録．
  Iwami Ginzan Silver Mines and its Cultural Landscape.
- 郵政事業の民営化
  privatization of postal services.

2008
- ノーベル賞3人同時受賞．☆小林誠（物理学賞）・益川敏英（物理学賞）・下村脩（化学賞）
  Three scholars are awarded the Nobel Prize for Physics simultaneously.
- 北海道・洞爺湖サミットの開催．正式名称「第34回主要国首脳会議」
  The 34th G8 Summit (In Hokkaido).

2009
- 裁判員制度．
  Introduction of citizen[lay] judge system
- 政権交代．☆自民党から民主党へ交代・政権を握る．
  Regime change; change of government[⊛administration]. The Democratic Party of Japan[DPJ] replaces the Liberal Democratic Party[LDP].

2010
- 平城遷都 1300 年祭．
  Commemorative Events for the 1,300th Anniversary of Nara *Heijo-kyo* Capital.
- 沖縄普天間基地移設問題　☆1439 年琉球王国の成立．1609 年薩摩藩の植民地．1879 年沖縄県の設置．1945 年米国統治下に入る．1972 年日本へ復帰．
  The issue of the relocation of the Futenma Airfield[U.S. Marine Corps Air Station] within Okinawa Prefecture.
- 羽田新国際線ターミナル開業．
  The opening of the New Haneda International Airport.
- ノーベル化学賞2人受賞．☆根岸英一・鈴木章．
  Two scholars are awarded the Nobel Prize for Chemistry simultaneously.
- 東北新幹線青森まで全線開通．☆東京—青森間を結ぶ．
  The opening of the Tohoku Shinkansen Lines.

2011
- 東日本大震災．☆東北地方太平洋沖地震とそれに伴う津波による大規模な地震災害．
  Great Eastern Japan Earthquake.
- 九州新幹線全線開通．☆博多—鹿児島間を結ぶ．
  The opening of the Kyushu Shinkansen Lines.

歴史

- ●『平泉—仏国土(浄土)を表す建築・庭園及び考古学的遺跡群』. ☆ユネスコ世界文化遺産に登録.
  Hiraizumi-Temples. Gardens and Archeological Sites Representing Buddhist Pure Land.
- ●『小笠原諸島』. ☆ユネスコ世界自然遺産に登録.
  Ogasawara Islands.

2012
- ● 東京スカイツリー開業. ☆自立式電波塔として世界最高 (634m).
  The opening of TOKYO SKYTREE (the highest independent transmitter tower in the world).
- ● 尖閣諸島の国有化.
  The nationalization of the Senkaku Islands.
- ● 政権交代. ☆民主党から自民党へ交代・政権を握る.
  Regime Changes; change of government[※ administration].

2013
- ●『富士山—信仰の対象と芸術の源泉』. ☆ユネスコ世界文化遺産に登録.
  Fujisan, sacred place and source of artistic inspiration.
- ●『和食』がユネスコ無形文化遺産に登録される.
  "Washoku" (traditional Japanese cuisine) was registered as a UNESCO Intangible Cultural Heritage.

2014
- ●『富岡製糸場と絹産業遺産群』. ☆ユネスコ世界文化遺産に登録.
  Tomioka Silk Mill and Related Sites.
- ● ノーベル物理学賞を3人受賞. ☆天野浩・赤崎勇・中村修二.
  Three scholars are awarded the Nobel Prize in Physics.
- ● 消費税が8％となる.
  The consumption tax rate was raised (from 5%) to 8%.
- ● 第3次阿部内閣(自由民主党)が誕生する.
  The Third Abe Cabinet (the Liberal Democratic Party) was established.

2015
- ●『明治日本の産業革命遺産　製鉄・製鋼, 造船, 石炭産業』. ☆ユネスコ世界文化遺産に登録.
  Sites of Japan's Meiji Industrial Revolution: Iron and Steel, Shipbuilding and Coal Mining.
- ● ノーベル生理学・医学賞を受賞. ☆大村智.
  Omura Satoshi was awarded the Noble Prize in Physiology or Medicine.
- ● ノーベル物理学賞を受賞. ☆梶田隆章.
  Kajita Takaaki was awarded the Nobel Prize in Physics.
- ● マイナンバー (個人番号)の通知が始まる.
  The notification of My Number (individual Number Card).

2016
- ●『ル・コルビュジエの建築作品—近代建築運動への顕著な貢献』. ☆ユネスコ世界文化遺産に登録.
  The Architectural Work of Le Corbusier, an Outstanding Contribution to the Modern Movements.
- ● ノーベル生理学・医学賞を受賞. ☆大隅良典.

歴史

Osumi Yoshinori was Awarded the Nobel Prize in Physiology or Medicine.

- 熊本地震M6.5. 最大震度7の地震.
  Kumamoto earthquake with a magnitude 6.5. A series of earthquakes with a magnitude 7.0 mainshock.
- G7伊勢志摩サミット開催.
  The G7 Ise-Shia Summit was held.
- アメリカの大統領(バラク・オバマ)がはじめて広島を訪問.
  U.S. President (Barak Obama) made a first visit to Hiroshima.
- 天皇陛下「生前退位」を表明.
  The Emperor expressed his intention to retire while he is well alive [to abdicate before he dies].
- 『山・鉾・屋台行事』. ☆ユネスコ無形文化遺産に登録.
  Japanese yama, hoko and yatai float festivals.

2017 　・『「神宿る島」宗像・沖ノ島と関連遺群』. ☆ユネスコ世界文化遺産に登録.
  Sacred Island of Okinoshima and Associated Sites in the Munakata Region.

2018 　・『長崎と天草地方の潜伏キリシタン関連遺産』. ☆ユネスコ世界文化遺産に登録.
  Hidden Christian Sites in the Nagasaki Region.

- ノーベル生理学・医学賞を受賞. ☆本庶佑.
  Honjo Tasuku was awarded the Nobel Prize in Physiology or Medicine.
- 『来訪神:仮面・仮装の神々』. ☆ユネスコ無形文化遺産に登録.
  Raiho-shin; ritual visits of deities in masks and costumes.

令和時代 2019- Reiwa era

2019 　・令和の改元. ☆「令和」 Beautiful Harmony.
  Proclamation of new era named "Reiwa."
  ☆4月30日の退位後, 明仁天皇は「上皇」, 美智子皇后は「上皇后」なる. 宮内庁による「上皇」(His Majesty the Emperor Emeritus),「上皇后」(Her Majesty the Empress Emerita)の英語表記決定.
  Emperor Akihito became "Emperor Emeritus" and Empress Michiko "Empress Emerita," following his abdication on April 30.
  ☆5月1日皇太子徳仁が「新天皇」として皇位を継承し, その後秋篠宮親王は皇位継承1位となり,「皇嗣」(His Imperial Highness the Crown Prince:宮内庁の英語表記)の称号を受ける.
  After the Crown Prince Naruhito ascended the Chrysanthemum Throne as a "new emperor" on May 1, Prince Akishino, his younger brother, was first in line to the Imperial Throne and called "koshi (the Crown Prince)."
- G-20サミットが大坂にて開催.
  The G-20 Summit was held in Osaka.
- ノーベル化学賞を受賞. ☆吉野彰.
  Yoshino Akira was awarded the Nobel Prize in Chemistry.
- 消費税10%への引き上げ.

歴史

Consumption tax hike to 10% (from 8%).

- •『百舌鳥・古市古墳群-古代日本の墳墓群』．☆ユネスコ世界文化遺産に登録．
  Mozu-Furuichi Kofun Group: Mounded Tombs of Ancient Japan.

2020
- • 4月7日新型コロナウィルスの感染拡大に対応して7都府県を対象に1か月に及ぶ「緊急事態宣言」を発令する（東京都と大阪府ならびに神奈川・千葉・埼玉・兵庫・福岡の各県．4月7日～5月6日）．
  On April 7, the monthlong state of emergency for Tokyo and six other prefectures was declared to curb the spread of the novel [new]coronavirus infections.

- • 5月15日政府は，47県の内39県に関しては新型コロナウイルの発症時に発令した「緊急事態宣言」を解除した．
  On May 15, the government lifted the state of emergency declared over the outbreak of the novel coronavirus in 39 of the country's 47 prefectures.

- • 第32回オリンピック大会東京（『東京オリンピック』『東京パラリンピック』）は，新型コロナウィルスのパンデミックのため2021年に延期される．
  The Games of the XXXII Olympiad in Tokyo was postponed until 2021 due to the new coronavirus pandemic.

2021
- •『北海道・北東北の縄文遺跡群』．☆ユネスコ世界遺産に登録．
  Jomon Prehistoric Sites in Northern Japan.

- •『奄美大島，徳之島，沖縄島北部及び西表島』．☆ユネスコ世界遺産に登録．
  Amami-Oshima Island, Tokunoshima Island, Northern part of Okinawa Island, and Iriomote Island.

- • ノーベル物理学を受賞．☆真鍋淑郎．
  Manabe Syukuro was awarded the Noble Prize in Physics.

- • 東京オリンピック，東京パラリンピックが開催される．☆『東京オリンピック』7月23日から8月8日まで.『東京パラリンピック』8月24日から9月5日まで．
  The Olympic Games was held in 2021 from July 23 to August 8, and the Paralympics from August 24 to September 5.

歴史

【編著者プロフィール】

山口 百々男 (やまぐち ももお)

サレジアン・カレッジ（哲学科・神学科）卒業. ラテン語・イタリア語に精通. 東京大学にて教育学研修後, ハーバード大学留学（英語）. 大阪星光学院中学・高等学校及びサレジオ学院高等学校の元教頭. 旧通訳ガイド養成所（現・日本外国語専門学校及び大阪外語専門学校）の元初代校長兼理事（創業に参画）. 英検1級2次面接の元試験官. 全国語学ビジネス観光教育協会（元理事）付属観光英検センター元顧問. 全専日協（全国専門学校日本語教育協会）元理事.

主な著書：『英語で伝える日本の文化・観光・世界遺産』『英語で伝える江戸の文化・東京の観光』(三修社), 『英語で紹介する観光都市東京』(語研), 『和英日本のことわざ成語辞典』(研究社), 『和英日本文化辞典』(ジャパンタイムズ), 『長崎と天草地方の潜伏キリシタンの関連遺産（ユネスコ世界文化遺産）』(サンパウロ社) など多数.

【英文校閲者プロフィール】

Steven Bates (スティーブン・ベイツ)

Ohio University (BA), American Graduate School of International Management (MBA). 米国にて銀行など金融関係業務に携わる. その後, 教育関係に関心をよせ来日. 元日本外国語専門学校専任教員. 英語による国際関係学科の講義・クラス担任および米国諸大学への留学指導（特にカリフォルニア大学バークレイ校の通信教育）を担当. 在日期間も長く, 日本文化に造詣が深い.

著書に『海外留学に役立つ英会話』『海外留学英語辞典』(ともに山口百々男との共著, 秀文インターナショナル) など.

和英：日本の文化・観光・歴史辞典 [三訂版]

2022 年 5 月 30 日　第 1 刷発行

編著者 ──────── 山口百々男
英文校閲 ──────── Steven Bates

発行者 ──────── 前田俊秀
発行所 ──────── 株式会社 三修社

〒150-0001　東京都渋谷区神宮前 2-2-22
TEL 03-3405-4511　FAX 03-3405-4522
振替 00190-9-72758
https://www.sanshusha.co.jp
編集担当　三井るり子

印刷・製本所 ──────── 萩原印刷株式会社

©M. Yamaguchi 2022 Printed in Japan
ISBN978-4-384-05974-8 C2582

DTP　編集工房 kyonsight
本文イラスト　木村 恵